METHODIST HYMNAL CONCORDANCE

compiled by
Robert F. Klepper

The Scarecrow Press, Inc.
Metuchen, N.J., & London
1987

Library of Congress Cataloging-in-Publication Data

Klepper, Robert F.
   Methodist hymnal concordance.

   Includes index.
   "This volume relates specifically to the
Book of hymns published in 1966 " --CIP preface.
   1. Methodist hymnal--Concordances. 2. Methodist
Church--Hymns--Concordances. 3. Hymns, English--
Concordances. I. Methodist hymnal. 1966.
II. Title.
M2127.M591 1966 Suppl.   783.9'52   86-29811
ISBN 0-8108-1968-6

PREFACE

This <u>Methodist</u> <u>Hymnal</u> <u>Concordance</u> is intended to provide for the text of an entire hymnal all the help that a Bible concordance gives for the text of the Bible. It will help in finding quotations, completing partially remembered phrases, enlarging concepts, suggesting thematic outlines, stimulating idea associations.

This volume relates specifically to <u>The</u> <u>Book</u> <u>of</u> <u>Hymns</u> published in 1966. Edwin E. Voigt was chairman of the Hymnal Committee then and Carlton R. Young was editor. All significant words of the hymnal text are included. There are approximately 40,000 entrees for over 4,000 words.

As aids to using the concordance, I present the following:

A. USAGE SUMMARY

(Hymn no.)	(Hymn phrase)	(Verse location)
:	:	:
78	fairest Lord Jesus, ruler of all nature	(T,1)

(T) = title
(R) = refrain
(1) = number of the verse in which the phrase appears

B. FINDING QUOTATIONS FOR BIBLICAL TEXTS.
     For instance on the theme of "hope" as in 1 Corinthians 13, the following might be suggestive:

<u>The</u> <u>Source</u> <u>of</u> <u>Hope</u>
  64 Star of our hope (2)
  161 Hope of the World (T,1)
  253 Jesus, my strength, my hope (T,1)
<u>Hope</u> <u>as</u> <u>Prayer</u>
  159 Let my soul look up with steadfast hope (2)
  167 let not my star of hope grow dim or disappear (2)
<u>Hope's</u> <u>Enduring</u> <u>Nature</u>
  144 though faith and hope may long be tried (4)
  359 love and joy and hope, like flowers spring (3)
<u>The</u> <u>Courage</u> <u>to</u> <u>Hope</u>
  51 hope and be undismayed (T,1)
  210 hope in him through all thy ways (1)
  333 patient hope and quiet brave endurance (2)
<u>Ethical</u> <u>Fruits</u> <u>of</u> <u>Hope</u>
  306 our fears, our hopes, our aims are one (2)
  542 other hearts in other lands are beating with hopes (1)
  542 with hopes and dreams as true and high as mine (1)

Some of the help this concordance can give may come through reference to the word and its differing forms: "hope", "hopes", "hoping" and even "hopeless". All of these enhance consideration of the basic theme.

C. REMEMBERING.

Suppose you want to find a phrase you remember from a comm "the bread and wine remove; but thou art here." Focus on one of words - "bread" or "wine" or "remove". The others are too commo included in the concordance. Using either major word as a referen will find it is in Hymn No. 326, "Here, O My Lord, I See Thee", ve

D. RELATING THE CONCORDANCE TO HYMNAL INDEXES.

Under the word, "peace", the topical index in the back of the l instructs, "Peace, Inner - see Calmness". Under "calmness" 28 entr given. All are hymn titles, which means general references.

In the concordance there are 112 entrees to "peace" and all ar specific. The comparison between concordance and topical index re the following:

1. Sometimes it is valuable to consider the synonymns and rela words of a subject. The topical index gives some help, a thesaurus suggests more.

2. Generalized references overlook much. Focusing on the exa from the concordance provides a means of selecting the phrases tha meaning to the user or enlarge the user's concepts.

3. It is helpful to survey the phrases of the concordance. Since exact words of the hymn are given, the survey may itself be satisf

4. It can be instructive to turn to the hymn in the hymnal and around the phrase that contains the word.

E. THE NUMERICAL INDEX.

The numerical index in the back of the concordance will enable user of this volume to identify the title of the hymn involved withe turning to the hymnal itself and paging to find the number.

F. WRITE-IN INDEX.

A list of numbers 1 to 552 with blank lines on the side enable user to write in the corresponding numbers from some other hymna this volume can be helpful for hymnals other than the 1964/66 Met Book of Hymns. For example:

_____ 79

write 227 on the line if you use the Pilgrim Hymnal and it tel all the references in this volume to Hymn No. 79 are found in Hyn in the Pilgrim Hymnal.

SOME EXPERIENCES

The patient in the hospital wanted to know if I could identify which hymn included the phrase "kneeling, wait thy word of peace". I could think of other phrases of the hymn, like, "parting hymn of praise" but not the title. The tune of the hymn came to both our minds but not the opening phrase. "I want the exact words and who wrote it", she said.

All through my visit my recall efforts failed, so upon returning home I went to my print-out of my latest Hymnal Concordance (this book). First choice word was "parting". I found it, and turning to the hymn number, discovered the title was the old favorite, "Savior, Again to Thy Dear Name We Raise". Reading the verses, I could see that there was comfort there for the patient.

Without the concordance, would it have been recalled? Likely not when the comfort and assurance were needed. But the volume is a ready reference and will be valuable in many similar situations.

+ + +

My guest paged through my concordance print-out. "What are you looking for?" I asked. "Just checking good and evil," he replied. After the computer work was complete we found that the United Methodist Hymnal has 62 references to "good" and only 18 for "evil".

Most of the "good" references refer to God as good or the Source of good. The references to "evil" cover themes that point to human choices, forgiveness, hostile forces, and God's providential care beyond the power of evil. Some value of the concordance is found in noting the usage of the words and in observing the contrasts between words.

+ + +

I was invited to lead a meditation during Lent of 1986 using slides of crosses of Christ. Some of the artistic presentations were traditional and some different and modern; some from western cultures and some from other cultures. It seemed important to relate to persons of differing views of art. So I used the concordance to find all the references to the "cross". Traditional and unusual artistic paintings were made more meaningful because of the poetry from the hymn writers. The concordance provided the ready reference to find those quotations.

ACKNOWLEDGMENT

I have dedicated this volume to my wife, Dorothy E. Schemske. It is in her home in Arkansas and with her encouragement that I set up my computer equipment and began using the machines for my retirement vocation. This volume is being completed in time for our third Wedding Anniversary. Happy Anniversary, Dorothy!

Robert F. Klepper
Bella Vista, Arkansas
May 1986

able
104 he is able, he is able, he is willing, doubt no more (1)
413 are ye able (T,1,2,3,4)
413 are ye able, said the Master, to be crucified with me (1)
413 are ye able to remember, when a thief lifts up his eyes (2)
413 are ye able when...shadows close around you with the sod (3)

abode
58 eternal arms, their dear abode, we make our habitation (1)
216 the man who once has found abode (T,1)
246 take thee, at thy parting breath, to his divine abode 4)
276 secret of the Lord is theirs ... soul is Christ's abode (1)
293 formed thee for his own abode (1)
294 I love thy kingdom, Lord, the house of thine abode (T,1)
474 forward tends to his abode, to rest in his embrace (2)

abound
5 then let our songs abound and every tear be dry (4)
50 I thank thee, too, that thou hast made joy to abound (2)
125 let the healing streams abound (4)
165 in our hearts and lives abound (2)
203 abound with love and solace for the day (3)
472 blessings abound where'er he reigns (4)
489 make the fruits of grace abound (4)

about
12 art within, a qickening flame, a presence round about (2)
119 though tossed about with many a conflict, many a doubt (3)
230 but God is round about me, and can I be dismayed (1)
244 thou who knowest all about me, stand by me (3)
395 angels sang about his birth; wisemen sought & found him (2)

above
4 sing praise to God who reigns above (T,1)
7 so may we, in lowly station join the choristers above (2)
8 all in heaven above adore thee (1)
8 angel choirs above are singing (2)
15 praise the Lord who reigns above (T,1)
16 though high above all praise, above all blessing high (2)
20 that word above all earthly powers ... abideth (4)
23 saints on earth, with saints above ... voices ... employ (3)
27 thy justice like mountains high soaring above (2)
35 friends on earth and friends above (4)
35 for thy church that evermore lifteth holy hands above (5)
36 Maker of all above, below (1)
38 opening to the sun above (1)
46 guide of all who seek the land above (1)
62 our whole lives one resurrection ... life of life above (4)
63 hope and comfort from above (4)
64 Lord of all life, below, above (4)
86 help thou dost not disdain, help from above (2)
89 thy mighty name salvation ... keeps my happy soul above (2)
90 lo! his star is shining above the stable (1)
90 while birds and flowers and sky above are preaching (3)
93 sung by flaming tongues above (1)
93 seal it for thy courts above (3)
103 flowing forth from the throne of God, pure from above (3)
122 he ever lives above, for me to intercede (2)

130   come quickly from above (5)
143   O bear me safe above, a ransomed soul (4)
149   of unseen things above, of Jesus and his glory (1)
164   above the storms of passion, the murmurs of self-will (3)
167   straight to my home above I travel calmly on (3)
172   O thou who camest from above (T,1)
173   once more to hear thy challenge above our noisy day (5)
180   praise him above, ye heavenly host (4)
183   how happy are the saints above (2)
188   raise my low self above, won by thy deathless love (1)
196   till, gathered to the Church above (5)
201   help us to seek thy kingdom that cometh from above (3)
204   above the noise of selfish strife (1)
204   glorious from thy heaven above shall come the city (6)
205   perfect rest to me is promised in my Father's home above (3)
219   calmness bends serene above, my restlessness to still (3)
224   angels descending, bring from above echoes of mercy (2)
224   watching and waiting, looking above (3)
226   lost in love, in a brighter, brighter world above (3)
227   and have laid up their treasure above (1)
228   for the dear Lamb of God left his glory above (2)
235   O sabbath rest by Galilee! O calm of hills above (3)
242   keeping watch above his own (4)
266   thou soon shall be fitted for service above (4)
273   like the arching of the heavens lift my thoughts above (4)
282   come quickly from above (5)
283   serve thee as thy hosts above (3)
284   that I may sing above to Father, Spirit, and to thee (6)
285   nothing in heaven above (4)
299   died on earth that man might live above (3)
302   come, let us join our friends above (T,1)
302   one family we dwell in him, one Church above, beneath (3)
304   thy bounds are known to God alone,for they are set above (2)
306   the fellowship of kindred minds is like to that above (1)
309   let us then with joy remove to the family above (6)
314   by the call to heaven above us (2)
319   thus anticipate by faith the heavenly feast above (4)
326   yet, passing, points to the glad feast above (5)
328   then only can it closer be, when all are joined above (4)
334   with the Holy Spirit's favor, rest upon them from above (1)
336   still he doth his help afford, and hides our life above (3)
337   firmness with meekness from above to bear thy people (3)
344   give .. wisdom from above, spotless .. peaceable & kind (2)
372   it shineth like a beacon above the darkling world (3)
381   above thy deep & dreamless sleep the silent stars go by (1)
381   for Christ is born of Mary, and gathered all above (2)
386   O sing, all ye citizens of heaven above (2)
390   above its sad & lowly plains they bend on hovering wing (2)
403   his spirit only can bestow, who reigns in light above (1)
404   lo! above the earth rang out the angel chorus (2)
409   all honor and blessing, with angels above (4)
410   message ... that the Lord who reigneth above (3)
413   thy guiding radiance above us shall be a beacon to God (R)
422   pomp .. show, nor lofty pride, nor boast above the least (1)
443   sing we to our God above ... praise eternal as his love (3)
445   He lives, to plead for me above (2)
450   bring us safe through Jordan to thy home above (3)
455   those wounds, yet visible above, in beauty glorified (4)
457   seek the things above (1)

457   hidden life of Christ ... with Christ concealed above (3)
458   joy of all who dwell above, the joy of all below (3)
458   they reign with him above (5)
461   let thy Church on earth become blest as the Church above (3)
464   lo! the promise of a shower drops already from above (4)
465   Eternal, Triune Lord, let all the hosts above (4)
467   thy blessed unction from above is comfort, life & fire (2)
473   O worship the King, all glorious above (T,1)
474   rise, my soul, and haste away to seats prepared above (1)
476   until true wisdom from above . make life's pathway clear (3)
483   when he had purged our stains, he took his seat above (2)
485   calm and courage, faith and hope: O pour them from above (1
489   thus may all our sabbaths prove till we join ... above (4)
489   till we join the Church above (4)
490   my heart's freed from ill, fair blue sky's above (3)
493   praise him above, ye heavenly host (5)
495   spread their white wings above me, watching round my bed (5)
498   shining on our steps from heaven above (1)
499   O Lord, in thy dear love fit us for perfect rest above (4)
502   we lose ourselves in heaven above (6)
505   stars of heaven shine out above (2)
510   while on in Jesus' steps we go to see thy face above (4)
513   all good gifts around us are sent from heaven above (R)
533   rise within the veil and see the saints above (1)
535   they sing the Lamb in hymns above and we in hymns below (2
543   for purple mountain majesties above the fruited plain (1)
547   my heart with rapture thrills, like that above (2)

abreast
242   who would keep abreast of truth (3)

abroad
1   spread thro' all the earth abroad the honors of thy name (2)
5   children of the heavenly King may speak ... joys abroad (2)
24   come, sound his praise abroad, and hymns of glory sing (T,1)
37   spread the flowing seas abroad and built the lofty skies (1)
128   and tell its raptures all abroad (1)
134   come, shed abroad a Savior's love, and... kindle ours (5)
278   Jesus, thine all-victorious love shed in my heart abroad (T)
285   O that it now were shed abroad in this poor stony heart (3)
308   and tempests are abroad (3)
339   convert, and send forth more into thy Church abroad (3)
343   sweet music fills the world abroad with strains of love (1)
344   thy power and love diffused abroad (4)
409   and publish abroad his wonderful name (1)
437   the day of resurrection, earth, tell it out abroad (T,1)
453   spread abroad the victor's fame (3)
471   abroad thy healing influence shower (3)
509   by day, by night, at home, abroad, still we are guarded (2)

absolute
154   hold o'er my being absolute sway (4)

absolve
200   from ease & plenty save us; from pride of place absolve (4)

absolved
127   fully absolved through these I am (2)

abundance
467   the abundance of thy grace (3)

abundant
479   thine abundant life to share (3)
512   God sendeth from his abundant store the waters (1)

abundantly
214   in drought their branches grow abundantly (2)

abuse
258   Our God's bounteous gifts abuse not, Light refuse not (4)
418   how pale thou art with anguish, with sore abuse & scorn (1)

accents
108   O Jesus, thou art pleading in accents meek and low (3)
164   O let me hear thee speaking in accents clear and still (3)
342   until each life's vocation accents thy holy way (3)
437   listening to his accents, may hear, so calm and plain (2)

accept
81   accept the praise I bring (3)
186   accept my hallowed labor now, I do it unto thee (3)
344   Father, accept them in thy Son (4)
345   accept the walls that human hands have raised ...to thee (1)
346   accept the prayers that thousands lift (3)
424   thou didst accept their praises (3)
424   accept the prayers we bring (3)
513   accept the gifts we offer for all thy love imparts (3)

acceptance
2   for thine acceptance proffer all unworthily (4)

accepted
102   this is the Lord's accepted day (5)

acclaim
371   tongues ... acclaim with joy thy wondrous gift to man (4)

acclamation
17   when Christ shall come with shout of acclamation (4)
453   hark, those bursts of acclamation (4)

accomplished
429   accomplished is the sacrifice (1)

accord
5   join in a song with sweet accord (1)
8   fill...heavens with sweet accord: holy, holy, holy Lord (2)
74   let every tongue confess ... one accord ... Jesus Christ (5)
236   with one accord our parting hymn of praise (1)
292   the world to Christ we bring, with one accord (3)
328   tongue can tell our sweet accord ... perfect harmony (1)
449   and sing today with one accord the life laid down (4)
507   all, with one accord, in a perpetual covenant join (1)

according
146   that mind and soul, according well, may make one music (5)
277   according to thy mind & Word, well-pleasing in thy sight (3)

316 according to thy gracious word, in meek humility (T,1)
530 placed according to thy will let us all our work fulfill (3)

account
150 O, thy servant, Lord, prepare, a strict account to give (3)

aching
268 they have left an aching void the world can never fill (3)

across
406 prepare across the earth the King's highway (2)
495 shadows of the evening steal across the sky (1)
543 a thoroughfare for freedom beat across the wilderness (2)
545 in . beauty of the lilies Christ was born across the sea (4)

act
321 every act of brotherhood repeats thy feast again (2)

action
184 it has no spring of action sure, it varies with the wind (2)
186 end of my every action thou, in all things thee I see (3)
273 turn my dreams to noble action, ministries of love (4)

actions
173 thoughts & actions less prone to please the crowd (1)
490 make my conduct good, actions calm and mild (2)

active
139 whose Spirit breathes the active flame (1)
504 active and watchful, stand we all before thee (1)

acts
172 my acts of faith and love repeat (4)
214 their evil acts shall surely come to naught (4)
487 lead and guide our acts of praise (2)

actual
279 give me to feel an idle thought as actual wickedness (2)
280 give me to feel an idle thought as actual wickedness (2)

actuate
530 move and actuate and guide; divers gifts to each divide (3)

addressed
394 angels praising God on high .. thus addressed their song (5)

adds
416 from the cross the radiance streaming adds more luster (3)
416 adds more luster to the day (3)

adoration
17 then I shall bow in humble adoration (4)
55 join me in glad adoration (1)
165 thanks we give & adoration for thy Gospel's joyful sound (2)
264 alone with thee in breathless adoration (2)
400 richer by far is the heart's adoration (4)
524 our hearts we raise in hymns of adoration (1)

adore
8   all in heaven above adore thee (1)
12   enough for me to know thou art, to love thee, and adore (3)
13   where we find thee and adore thee (2)
15   from whom all good proceeds ... earth and heaven adore (1)
16   stand up and bless the Lord; the Lord your God adore (5)
26   holy, holy, holy! all the saints adore thee (2)
27   thine angels adore thee, all veiling their sight (4)
38   joyful, joyful, we adore thee (T,1)
41   rapt in reverence we adore thee (1)
42   praise the Lord! ye heavens adore him (T,1)
49   the one eternal God, whom earth and heaven adore (3)
52   thy goodnesss we adore (3)
55   O let all that is in me adore him (4)
55   gladly forever adore him (4)
66   angels in the height, adore him (4)
77   on heaven's blissful shore his goodness we'll adore (3)
166   I'll ever adore thee in heaven so bright (3)
227   the story repeat, and the lover of sinners adore (3)
332   thine to bless, 'tis only ours to wonder and adore (4)
349   to God the Father, God the Son, and Spirit we adore (4)
357   O ye heights of heaven, adore him (2)
364   yea, Amen! let all adore thee high on thy eternal throne (4)
366   now let all the heavens adore thee (3)
374   come, adore on bended knee Christ the Lord (3)
386   O come, let us adore him, Christ, the Lord (R)
389   with praise our God adore (4)
397   bend the knee before him whom heaven and earth adore (2)
400   angels adore him in slumber reclining (2)
409   then let us adore and give him his right (4)
412   I do adore thee, and will ever pray thee (5)
427   'tis mercy all! let earth adore (2)
452   Him, their true creator, all his works adore (1,4)
454   all the heavenly hosts adore thee (3)
465   Spirit of holiness, let all thy saints adore (3)
465   adore thy sacred energy (3)
470   grant us courage serving thee whom we adore (5)
471   let all thy saving grace adore (1)
476   O God of truth, whom ... reverent souls adore (3)
483   rejoice, the Lord is King, your Lord and King adore (T,1)
492   and nature's God adore (3)
504   thus we adore thee (1)
550   here thy name, O God of love ... children shall adore (4)
550   their children's children shall adore (4)

adored
15   as in heaven on earth adored (3)
54   thy providence protected them who thy great name adored (3)
74   God the Father be by all adored (5)
350   where thou art worshipped and adored (1)
351   by men and heavenly hosts adored (1)
361   his name shall be the Prince of Peace forevermore adored (3)
367   forever be thy name adored for these celestial lines (1)
387   Christ, by highest heaven adored (2)
509   adored through all our changing days (4)
518   be here and everywhere adored (1)

adores
296 from oldest time, on farthest shores ... she adores (2)
296 beneath the pine or palm, one unseen Presence she adores (2)
296 adores with silence, or with psalm (2)

adoring
8 adoring bend the knee while we own the mystery (4)
434 there adoring at this feet mark the miracle of time (3)
459 O Triune God, with heart and voice adoring (5)

adorn
524 bright robes of gold the fields adorn (1)

adorned
363 adorned with prayer and love and joy (2)

adorning
400 Star of the East, the horizon adorning (1,5)

adorns
99 hath he diadem, as monarch, that his brow adorns (3)
458 a royal diadem adorns the mighty victor's brow (1)
550 and spring adorns the earth no more (4)

advent
354 come and cheer our spirits by thine advent here (4)
355 new advent of the love of Christ (3)

afar
32 his voice sublime is heard afar (4)
44 thy glory thou hast spread afar in all the starry frame (1)
64 Lord of all being, throned afar (T,1)
239 they see the triumph from afar (5)
260 no more we seek thee from afar, nor ask thee for a sign (4)
380 and that song from afar has swept over the world (3)
382 brighter visions beam afar (3)
393 glories stream from heaven afar (2)
402 bearing gifts we traverse afar (1)
411 friends in lands afar who battle with the body's ills (2)
419 his blood-red banner streams afar (1)
542 a song of peace for lands afar and mine (1)

affection
62 to him let each affection daily rise and round him move (4)
319 brethren, all, let every heart with kind affection glow (2)
446 comes to glad Jerusalem who with true affection (3)
525 for home, where our affection clings (2)

affections
179 over our wills and affections victorious (3)

affiance
211 his truth be thine affiance, when faint and desolate (2)

afflicted
412 by foes derided, by thine own rejected, O most afflicted (1)

affliction
129 on whom in affliction I call (1)

afford
193 let each his friendly aid afford (2)
265 no tender voice like thine can peace afford (1)
325 not paradise, with all its joys ... such delight afford (1)
334 possess in sweet communion, joys ... earth cannot afford (2)
336 still he doth his help afford, and hides our life above (3)
489 here afford us, Lord, a taste of our everlasting feast (3)

affords
453 O what joy the sight affords (4)
458 highest place ... heaven affords belongs to him by right (2)

affright
373 ye shepherds, shrink not with affright (1)

aflame
11 skies with crimson clouds aflame (2)
352 with hearts aflame (2)
380 every hearth is aflame, and the beautiful sing (3)
407 mighty God, set us aflame to show the glory of thy name (3)
484 in ire and exultation aflame with faith and free (3)

afraid
57 neath sun or moon, by day or night ... not be afraid (3)
141 have faith in God, my heart, trust and be unafraid (T,1)
202 we follow where the Master leads, serene and unafraid (1)
477 bring to our troubled minds, uncertain and afraid (2)

afresh
94 I my Master have denied, I afresh have crucified (2)
326 here taste afresh the calm of sin forgiven (3)

after
70 after death, in distant worlds, the glorious theme renew (4)
85 and seeing think God's thoughts after thee (2)
102 ye restless wanderers after rest (3)
154 mold me and make me after thy will (1)
160 the world forsake, and humbly follow after me (1)
220 till it well-nigh fainted, thirsting after thee (1)
231 a season of clear shining to cheer it after rain (1)
298 hereafter in thy glory evermore with thee to reign (3)
326 feast after feast thus comes and passes by (5)
457 our hearts detached from all below ... after him ascend (1)
475 age after age their tragic empires rise (2)

afterward
96 I sought the Lord, and afterward I knew (T,1)

again
22 he brought us to his fold again (2)
55 let the amen sound from his people again (4)
68 my soul he doth restore again (2)
77 praise yet the Lord again; Alleluia! Amen! (3)
109 sing them over again to me (T,1)
157 and we are whole again (4)
173 again to lead us forward along God's holy way (5)
190 to give and give, and give again (3)

200   as once he spake in Zion, so now he speaks again (1)
204   O tread the city's streets again (5)
212   but then the Holy Spirit revives my soul again (1)
219   I feel thy strong and tender love, and all is well again (1)
231   when comforts are declining, he grants the soul again (1)
236   Savior, again to thy dear name we raise (T,1)
237   when my dust returneth to the dust again (4)
279   drive me to... grace again which makes the wounded whole (4)
280   drive me to...grace again, which makes the wounded whole (4)
306   we shall still be joined in heart and hope to meet again (4)
321   every act of brotherhood repeats thy feast again (2)
329   we turn unfilled to thee again (1)
355   shall we again refuse thee (3)
389   this day again those gates unfold (4)
398   never shall darkness veil thee again from human eyes (1)
398   and helpest them to render light back to thee again (2)
402   gold I bring to crown him again (2)
439   lives again our glorious King, Alleluia (2)
441   love lives again, that with the dead has been (1)
441   thinking that never he would wake again (2)
441   thy touch can call us back to life again (4)
441   love is come again like wheat that springeth green (R)
446   Alleluia yet again to the Spirit raising (5)
472   angels descend with songs again (5)
477   let .. be light again .. set thy judgments in .. earth (5)
481   the tears are wiped from eyes that shall not weep again (1)
483   rejoice, again I say, rejoice (R)
536   and hearts are brave again, and arms are strong (5)
539   God be with you till me meet again (T,R)
540   God be with you till we meet again (T,R)

against
248   ye that are men now serve him against unnumbered foes (2)
305   Christ, the royal Master, leads against the foe (1)
340   thou bidst us go with thee to stand against hell's (2)
340   stand against hell's marshalled powers (2)

age
20   Lord Sabaoth, his name, from age to age the same (2)
21   his truth ... shall from age to age endure (4)
78   laud, honor, might ... glory be ... age to age eternally (4)
130   immense and unconfimed; from age to age it never ends (2)
136   till every age and race and clime shall blend (3)
150   to serve the present age, my calling to fulfill (2)
233   bright youth and snow-crowned age (2)
233   from youth to age, by night and day (4)
269   and age comes on, uncheered by faith or hope (2)
281   which shall from age to age endure (1)
293   never fails from age to age (2)
296   one holy Church of God appears through every age & race (T)
342   from age to age the same (2)
372   a lantern to our footsteps shines on from age to age (1)
452   welcome, happy morning age to age shall say (T,1,4)
460   each from age to age proclaiming God the one (1)
475   age after age their tragic empires rise (2)
490   venerating age, humbly teaching youth (2)

aged
479   to.. child .. youth .. aged love in living deeds to show (4)

ages
28   O God, our help in ages past (T,1,6)
28   a thousand ages in thy sight are like an evening gone (4)
30   his love shall be our strength and stay, while ages roll (3)
63   man decays and ages move; but his mercy waneth never (2)
91   be this the eternal song through all the ages long (4)
120   Rock of Ages, cleft for me, let me hide myself in thee (T,1)
120   Rock of Ages, cleft for me, let me hide myself in thee (3)
205   my song through endless ages: Jesus led me all the way (3)
206   God of the ages, by whose hand (T,1)
221   through eternal ages let his praises ring (1)
288   long as eternal ages roll, thou seest thy Savior's face (2)
288   all in Jesus' presence reign through ages without end (2)
293   on the Rock of Ages founded (1)
298   One in might, and One in glory, while unending ages run (4)
305   this through countless ages men and angels sing (4)
346   through ages long his wisdom and his power display (1)
358   ages are its own; see, it bursts o'er all the earth (2)
371   from days of old, through swiftly rolling ages (2)
380   in the light of that star lie the ages impearled (3)
426   here the King of all the ages throned in light (2)
440   holiest hearts for ages pleading (2)
440   patriarchs from the distant ages (3)
459   O holy Father, who hast led thy children in all the ages (2)
459   led thy children in all the ages with the fire and cloud (2)
467   through ... ages all along this may be our endless song (4)
488   on thee the high and lowly, through ages joined in tune (1)
550   through all ages bear the memory of that holy hour (2)

ago
376   in the bleak midwinter, long ago (1)
532   whose names have perished, lost in the haze of long ago (5)

agree
15   timbrels soft and cymbals loud in his high praise agree (2)
193   let all our hearts agree (4)
309   let us in thy name agree (1)
328   so dear the tie where souls agree in Jesus' dying love (4)
516   Lord, let us in our homes agree .. blessed peace to gain (4)
530   sweetly may we all agree, touched with loving sympathy (4)

ahead
206   new faith to find the paths ahead (1)

aid
21   without our aid he did us make (2)
22   He sovereign power, without our aid made us of clay (2)
48   for I am thy God, and will still give thee aid (2)
57   O whence shall come my aid (1)
106   ever present, truest friend ... near thine aid to lend (2)
118   to thee, lost and undone, for aid I flee (1,5)
193   let each his friendly aid afford (2)
213   Jesus, thy timely aid impart (3)
374   Mary, Joseph, lend your aid (4)
400   dawn on our darkness and lend us thine aid (1,5)

450 life is naught without thee; aid us in our strife (3)
469 light to man's blindness, O be thou our aid (1)
479 counsel, aid, and peace we give (4)
517 that we may bear it meetly ... seek thine aid the more (2)
531 O Love, thy sovereign aid impart to save me (3)

aim
191 men whose aim 'twill be not to defend some ancient creed (1)
253 I want a true regard, a single steady aim (4)
258 when thine aim is good and true (3)

aims
161 who by our own false hopes and aims are spent (1)
260 our dreams, our aims, our work, our lives are prayers (1)
306 our fears, our hopes, our aims are one (2)
520 let all unworthy aims depart, imbue us with thy grace (2)

air
11 with sweet music fill the air (1)
36 thy life is in the quickening air (2)
198 on earth and fire and sea and air (2)
252 prayer ... the Christian's native air (5)
290 their fronded palms in air (5)
376 Cherubim and seraphin thronged the air (3)
379 till the air, everywhere, now with joy is ringing (1)
380 there's a song in the air, there's a star in the sky (T,1)
473 it breathes in the air, it shines in the light (4)
523 the golden sunshine, vernal air, sweet flowers and fruit (2)
541 be with them traversing the air in darkening storms (1)

alabaster
543 thine alabaster cities gleam undimmned by human tears (4)

alarm
160 cross; let not its weight fill thy weak spirit with alarm (2
216 no nightly terrors shall alarm (5)

alarms
184 I sink in life's alarms when by myself I stand (1)
206 forgive ... our wild alarms, our trembling fears (3)
552 from war's alarms, from deadly pestilence (3)

alas
398 long, alas, witholden, now spread from shore to shore (1)
412 alas, my treason, Jesus, hath undone thee (2)

alert
191 men alert and quick his lofty precepts to translate (2)

alien
129 O why should I wander, an alien from thee (3)
476 no alien race, no foreign shore (1)

alight
503 evening lamps alight through all the sky (1)

alike
91   alike at work and prayer to Jesus I repair (1)
236   for dark and light are both alike to thee (3)

alive
336   and are we yet alive and see each other's face (T,1)
527   alive in him, my living Head (4)

allegiance
179   true hearted, whole hearted, fullest allegiance (2)

alleluia
19   supernal anthems echoing, alleluia, alleluia! (3)
19   cry out, dominions, princedoms, powers ... alleluia (1)
19   alleluia, alleluia, alleluia, alleluia, alleluia! (R)
19   alleluia, alleluia (3,4)
60   O praise him, O praise him! Alleluia! Alleluia! Alleluia (R)
60   make music for thy Lord to hear, Alleluia (3)
324   as with ceaseless voice they cry, Alleluia (4)
324   alleluia, alleluia, alleluia, Lord most high (4)
366   come, thou blessed One. God's own beloved son, Alleluia (2)
377   alleluia, alleluia! (R)
393   heavenly hosts sing Alleluia (2)
393   with the angels let us sing Alleluia to our King (4)
402   Alleluia, Alleluia! sounds through the earth and skies (5)
439   raise your joys and triumphs high, Alleluia (1)
439   lives again our glorious King, Alleluia (2)
439   sons of men and angels say, Alleluia (1)
439   once he died, our souls to save, Alleluia (2)
439   where, O death, is now thy sting, Alleluia (2)
439   love's redeeming work is done, Alleluia (3)
439   fought the fight, the battle won, Alleluia (3)
439   death in vain forbids him rise, Alleluia (3)
439   sing, ye heavens, and earth reply, Alleluia (1)
439   soar we now where Christ has led, Alleluia (4)
439   following our exalted Head, Alleluia (4)
439   made like him, like him we rise, Alleluia (4)
439   where's thy victory, boasting grave? Alleluia (2)
439   Christ hath opened paradise, Alleluia (3)
439   ours the cross, the grave, the skies, Alleluia (4)
446   Alleluia now we cry to our King immortal (5)
446   Alleluia yet again to the Spirit raising (5)
446   Alleluia with the Son, God the Father praising (5)
447   the song of triumph has begun: Alleluia (1)
447   all glory to our risen Head! Alleluia (3)
447   that we may live and sing to thee: Alleluia (4)
447   let shouts of holy joy outburst: Alleluia (2)
449   let all mankind rejoice and say: Alleluia (2)
449   and sing with hearts uplifted high: Alleluia (3)
451   o'er death today rose triumphing, Alleluia (1)
451   to seek the tomb where Jesus lay, Alleluia (2)
451   your Lord doth go to Galilee, Alleluia (3)
451   for they eternal life shall win, Alleluia (4)
536   thy name, O Jesus, be forever blest, Alleluia, Alleluia (1)
536   singing to Father, Son, and Holy Ghost, Alleluia (6)

alloy
397   so may we with holy joy, pure and free from sins' alloy (3)

almighty
         3   come, thou almighty King (T, 1)
         3   thou who almighty art, now rule in every heart (3)
         4   what God's almighty power hath made (2)
        26   holy, holy, holy, Lord God almighty (T,1,4)
        27   almighty, victorious, thy great name we praise (1)
        34   how great is God Almighty, who has made all things well (4)
        37   I sing the almighty power of God (T,1)
        43   publishes to every land the work of an almighty hand (1)
        46   while love, almighty love, is near (2)
        55   praise to the Lord, the almighty, the King of creation (T,1)
        55   ponder anew what the Almighty can do (3)
        89   in weakness my almighty power (4)
       194   Almighty Father, who dost give the gift of life to all (3)
       216   with Almighty God abide and in his shadow safely hide (1)
       253   on thee, almighty to create, almighty to renew (1)
       279   Almighty God of truth and love, to me thy power impart (4)
       280   Almighty God of truth and love, to me thy power impart (4)
       283   come, Almighty to deliver, let us all thy life receive (3)
       295   O thou almighty Lord of hosts, who art my God and King (4)
       336   glory and thanks to Jesus give for his almighty grace (1)
       376   sufficed the Lord God Almighty, Jesus Christ (2)
       409   God ruleth on high, almighty to save (2)
       454   by almighty love appointed thou hast full atonement made (2)
       457   by the almighty Spirit led and filled with faith & love (1)
       473   Almighty, thy power hath founded of old (3)
       480   thou, whose almighty Word chaos and darkness heard (T,1)
       493   keep me, King of kings, beneath thine own almighty wings (1)
       513   but it is fed and watered by God's almighty hand (1)
       552   almighty hand leads forth in beauty all the starry band (1)

aloft
       541   aloft in solitudes of space (2)

alone
         4   the Lord is God, and he alone (5)
        22   know that the Lord is God alone (1)
        28   sufficient is thine arm alone (2)
        47   when we are strong, Lord, leave us not alone (3)
        57   my help is from the Lord alone (1)
        57   Lord alone, who heaven and earth has made (1)
        75   thou art the way: to thee alone (T,1)
        75   thy Word alone true wisdom can impart (2)
        78   and things terrestrial, Lord alone (2)
       118   'tis thou alone canst make me whole (2)
       120   thou must save, and thou alone (2)
       125   leave ... leave me not alone, still support & comfort me (2)
       129   or alone in this wilderness rove (2)
       144   though oft I seem to tread alone life's dreary waste (3)
       146   by faith, and faith alone, embrace (1)
       147   when the joys of sense depart, to live by faith alone (4)
       163   not alone the gift of life, but his own self he gave me (2)
       167   since thou on earth has wept and sorrowed oft alone (2)
       173   while we betray so quickly and leave thee there alone (2)
       179   take thy great power and reign there alone (3)
       181   all...we have is thine alone, a trust, O Lord, from thee (1)
       182   and from this moment, live or die to serve my God alone (2)
       183   must Jesus bear the cross alone (T,1)

185   now thee alone I seek, give what is best (2)
188   not for myself alone may my prayer be (3)
202   we bear the strain of earthly care ... bear it not alone (T)
216   because thy trust is God alone (6)
222   dressed in his righteousness alone (4)
242   though the cause of evil prosper...truth alone is strong (4)
248   stand in his strength alone (3)
250   o'ercome through Christ alone, and stand entire at last (2)
257   thou alone to God canst win us (2)
259   thine wholly, thine alone, I'd live (1)
264   alone with thee amid the mystic shadows (2)
264   alone with thee in breathless adoration (2)
266   spend much time in secret with Jesus alone (2)
269   blindly we stumble when we walk alone (3)
282   where Jesus reigns alone (2)
290   assured alone that life and death God's mercy underlies (1)
298   Holy Zion's help forever and her confidence alone (1)
304   thy bounds are known to God alone,for they are set above (2)
319   one fold .. faith .. hope .. Lord, One God alone we know (1)
343   we bid the pealing organ wait to speak alone thy will (3)
346   the Lord our God alone is strong (T,1)
355   by which alone we choose thee (3)
358   will its beams alone gild the spot that gave them birth (2)
360   by thine own eternal spirit rule in all our hearts alone (2)
427   alone thou goest forth, O Lord, in sacrifice to die (T,1)
429   the veil is rent in Christ alone (2)
431   in the garden now the suffering Savior prays alone (1)
438   an empty form alone remains (2)
438   Christ alone our souls will feed (4)
463   by whose mighty power alone all is made & wrought & done (1)
464   Jesus mighty to redeem, he alone the work hath wrought (3)
468   thou in thy everlasting seat remainest God alone (3)
471   in every heart reign thou alone (2)
476   whom love, and love alone can know (2)
479   we, thy servants, bring the worship not of voice alone (1)
479   not of voice alone, but heart (1)
487   through grace alone are we saved (3)
528   sinners alone his grace receive (4)
529   my company before is gone, and I am left alone with thee (1)
531   ah, tear it thence and reign alone (2)
531   reign alone, the Lord of every motion there (2)
535   and saved by grace alone (1)
548   not alone for mighty empire (T,1)
548   not alone for bounteous harvests lift we up our hearts (1)

along
4   all my toilsome way along I sing aloud thy praises (4)
60   ye clouds that sail in heaven along, O praise him (2)
148   to us he gives the keeping of the lights along the shore (1)
148   longing for the lights along the shore (2)
173   again to lead us forward along God's holy way (5)
176   along my pilgrim journey, Savior, let we walk with thee (1)
464   now it spreads along the skies (4)
467   through ... ages all along this may be our endless song (4)
486   whose bones lie white along the trail (2)
526   thy grace along availeth (2)

aloud
- 4   all my toilsome way along I sing aloud thy praises (4)
- 4   all ye who own his power proclaim aloud (5)
- 4   proclaim aloud the wondrous story! (5)
- 409   let all cry aloud and honor the Son (3)

Alpha
- 283   Alpha and Omega be; end of faith as its beginning (2)
- 357   He is Alpha and Omega, He the source, the ending he (1)

already
- 92   through many dangers, toils ... snares I... already come (3)
- 249   forget the steps already trod and onward urge thy way (2)
- 464   lo! the promise of a shower drops already from above (4)
- 481   already in the mind of God that city riseth fair (5)

altar
- 16   O for the living flame from his own altar brought (3)
- 138   my heart an altar, and thy love the flame (5)
- 172   the mean altar of my heart (1)
- 172   kindle a flame of sacred love on ... altar of my heart (1)
- 196   all I have, and all I am, upon his altar lay (3)
- 223   never can prove ... until all on the altar we lay (3)
- 350   in faith we here an altar raise (1)
- 350   altar raise to thy great glory, God of praise (1)
- 382   saints, before the altar bending (4)
- 399   make thee there an altar (2)
- 456   as altar candle sheds its light as surely as a star (2)
- 484   O God of earth and altar, bow down and hear our cry (T,1)
- 486   O God, before whose altar the stars like tapers burn (T,1)
- 524   upon thine altar, Lord, we lay the first fruits (2)
- 545   have builded him an altar in the evening dews and damps (2)

altars
- 64   till all thy living altars claim one holy light (5)
- 295   even thine own altars, where she safe ... may bring (4)
- 332   angels round our altars bow to search it out in vain (3)

altogether
- 309   lowly, meek, in thought & word, altogether like our Lord (3)

alway
- 298   and thy fullest benediction shed within its walls alway (2)

always
- 21   praise, laud, and bless his name always (3)
- 96   always thou lovedst me (3)
- 138   teach me to feel that thou art always nigh (4)
- 154   Christ only, always, living in me (4)
- 187   take my voice ... let me sing always, only, for my King (2)
- 254   what I dream & what I do in my weak days are always two (
- 256   thou mine inheritance, now and always (3)
- 266   abide with him always, and feed on his Word (1)
- 278   I only for his glory burn, and always see his face (3)
- 282   heart that always feels thy blood so freely shed for me (1)
- 283   thee we would be always blessing (3)

321 the bread is always consecrate which men divide with men (2)
459 still imploring thy love and favor, kept to us always (5)
490 always serving thee, sharing thy rich truth (2)

amazing
31 through all his mighty works amazing wisdom shines (3)
92 amazing grace! how sweet the sound (T,1)
415 amazing pity! Grace unknown! and love beyond degree (2)
435 love so amazing, so divine, demands my soul, my life (4)
435 Love so amazing ... demands my soul, my life, my all (4)
527 amazing love! how can it be that thou ... die for me (1)

amber
543 O beautiful for spacious skies, for amber waves of grain (T)

ambition
251 perish every fond ambition, all I've... hoped or known (1)

amen
55 let the amen sound from his people again (4)
472 and earth repeat the loud amen (5)
478 and holiness shall whisper the sweet amen of peace (2)
505 Jubilate! Jubilate! Jubilate! Amen! (R)

America
543 America! America! God shed his grace on thee (1,4)
543 America! America! God mend thine every flaw (2)
543 America! America! May God thy gold refine (3)

amid
20 our helper he amid the flood of mortal ills prevailing (1)
43 no real voice nor sound amid the radiant orbs be found (3)
173 amid our pride and glory to see thy face appear (5)
184 it only stands unbent amid the clashing strife (4)
264 alone with thee amid the mystic shadows (2)
272 amid the encircling gloom, lead thou me on (1)
284 amid the battle's strife (3)
430 till amid the hosts of light, we in thee redeemed (5)
538 and calm amid the storm didst sleep (2)

amidst
347 thy hand unseen amidst us wrought (2)
440 when, amidst earth's closing thunders (4)
446 but today amidst the twelve thou didst stand, bestowing (4)

among
204 among these restless throngs abide (5)
317 O Lord, we pray, come thou among us (3)
442 flowers make glee among the hills (1)

ample
400 vainly we offer each ample oblation (4)

anchor
222 in every high and stormy gale, my anchor holds (2)
222 my anchor holds within the veil (2)
460 'mid the world's despair and turmoil one firm anchor (1)
460 one firm anchor holdeth fast (1)

ancient
3   come, and reign over us, Ancient of Days! (1)
20   still our ancient foe doth seek to work us woe (1)
27   most blessed, most glorious, the Ancient of days (1)
54   in more ancient years (1)
173   O young and fearless prophet of ancient Galilee (T,1)
189   what are ... ancient caste and creed (2)
191   men whose aim 'twill be not to defend some ancient creed (1)
194   and all its ancient deeds of wrong (2)
233   the psalms of ancient days (3)
242   time makes ancient good uncouth (3)
356   remove the veil of ancient words (2)
356   ancient words, their message long obscure (2)
390   peace shall over ... earth its ancient splendors fling (3)
408   in Christ all races meet, their ancient feuds forgetting (2)
408   heal its ancient wrong, come, Prince of Peace, and reign (3)
423   Hosanna in the highest   that ancient song we sing (3)
459   Ancient of Days, who sittest throned in glory (T,1)
470   crown thine ancient Church's story (1)
473   our Shield and Defender, the Ancient of Days (1)
501   thy touch has still its ancient power (6)
505   telling still the ancient story (2)

anew
55   ponder anew what the Almighty can do (3)
133   breathe on me, breath of God, fill me with life anew (T,1)
189   here together, brother men, we pledge the Lord anew (2)
273   God, who touchest earth with beauty, make my heart anew (5)
273   make my heart anew (1)
321   when life anew pours out its wine with rich sufficiency (3)
356   O let thy Word be light anew to every nation's life (3)
407   show us anew in Calvary the wondrous power (1)
497   may we, born anew like morning, to labor rise (2)

angel
2   angel voices, ever singing round thy throne of light (T,1)
2   angel harps forever ringing, rest not day nor night (1)
7   hear the angel voices blending ... praise to God on high (1)
8   angel choirs above are singing (2)
11   join the angel song, all the worlds to him belong (1)
33   clearer sounds the angel hymn,
76   all the angel faces, all the hosts of light (2)
138   no angel visitant, no opening skies (2)
272   and with the morn those angel faces smile (3)
303   and bright with many an angel, and all the martyr throng (2)
357   angel hosts, his praises sing (2)
378   from God our heavenly Father a blessed angel came (3)
383   the first Noel, the angel did say (T,1)
389   the glorious gates of paradise the angel guards no more (4)
394   the angel of the Lord came down, and glory shone around (1)
404   lo! above the earth rang out the angel chorus (2)
404   angel chorus that hailed our Savior's birth (2)
451   an angel clad in white they see (3)
496   angel guards from thee surround us (2)
497   may thine angel guards defend us (1)
527   let angel minds inquire no more (2)

angel's
335 might fill an angel's heart and filled a Savior's hands (2)
373 but hear the angel's warning (1)

angelic
7 with the angelic host we cry (4)
350 here thine angelic spirits send their solemn praise (5)
387 with the angelic host proclaim (1)
454 help, ye bright angelic spirits (4)

angels
19 cry out ... virtues, arch-angels, angels' choirs (1)
27 thine angels adore thee, all veiling their sight (4)
38 stars and angels sing around thee (2)
42 praise him, angels, in the height (1)
66 angels in the height, adore him (4)
71 let angels prostrate fall (1)
79 Jesus shines purer, than all the angels heaven can boast (3)
90 while the angels sing (1)
129 he looks! and ten thousands of angels rejoice (5)
138 teach me to love thee as thine angels love (5)
224 angels descending, bring from above echoes of mercy (2)
227 angels could do nothing more, than to fall at his feet (3)
252 angels in their songs rejoice & cry "Behold he prays" (4)
263 angels to beckon me, nearer, my God, to thee (3)
305 this through countless ages men and angels sing (4)
309 on the wings of angels fly; show how true believers die (6)
312 the Lord of angels came (2)
331 in thy holy incarnation, when the angels sang thy birth (2)
332 angels round our altars bow to search it out in vain (3)
341 angels and men before it fall, and devils fear and fly (1)
366 men and angels sing before thee (3)
366 choir immortal of angels round thy dazzling throne (3)
374 angels we have heard on high (T,1)
374 come to Bethlehem & see him whose birth the angels sing (2)
374 see him in a manger laid whom .. choirs of angels praise (4)
375 love was born at Christmas; star & angels gave the sign (1)
376 angels and archangels may have gathered there (3)
379 as I hear, far and near, sweetest angels voices (1)
381 while mortals sleep, the angels keep their watch (2)
381 angels keep their watch of wondering love (2)
381 we hear the Christmas angels the great glad tidings tell (4)
382 angels, from the realms of glory (T,1)
385 King, whom shepherds guard and angels sing (R)
385 whom angels greet with anthems sweet (1)
386 come and behold him, born the King of angels (1)
386 sing, choirs of angels, sing in exultation (2)
387 hark! the herald angels sing (T,1)
388 hark, the herald angels sing (T,1,R)
390 angels bending near ... earth to touch ... harps of gold (1)
390 world in solemn stillness lay to hear the angels sing (1)
390 and ever o'er its Babel sounds the blessed angels sing (2)
390 whole world give back the song which now the angels sing (3)
393 with the angels let us sing Alleluia to our King (4)
394 angels praising God on high .. thus addressed their song (5)

395 angels sang about his birth; wisemen sought & found him (2)
395 shepherds saw .. wondrous sight, heard .. angels singing (2)
400 angels adore him in slumber reclining (2)
409 the praises of Jesus the angels proclaim (3)
409 all honor and blessing, with angels above (4)
423 the Lord of men and angels rode on in lowly state (2)
424 the company of angels are praising thee on high (2)
431 from heavenly plains is borne the song that angels know (4)
439 sons of men and angels say, Alleluia (1)
450 angels in bright raiment rolled the stone away (1)
453 crown the Savior, angels, crown him (2)
453 saints and angels crowd around him (3)
472 angels descend with songs again (5)
495 through the long night watches may thine angels spread (5)
503 Lord of angels, on our eyes let eternal morning rise (4)
522 give his angels charge at last in the fire the tares (3)
522 give his angels charge at last ... fire .. tares to cast (3)
522 come, with all thine angels, come (4)

angels'
19 cry out dominions, prince-doms, powers...angel's (1)
19 cry out ... virtues, arch-angels, angels' choirs (1)
181 to tend the lone and fatherless is angels' work below (3)

anger
199 love shall tread out the baleful fire of anger (5)
309 free from anger and from pride (5)

angry
148 loud the angry billows roar (2)
538 and bid their angry tumult cease (3)

anguish
95 turn me not away unblest; calm my anguish into rest (3)
103 here bring your wounded hearts, here tell your anguish (1)
259 care, anguish, sorrow, melt away (2)
412 death of anguish and thy bitter passion for my salvation (4)
418 how pale thou art with anguish, with sore abuse & scorn (1)
431 he that in anguish knelt is not forsaken by his God (3)

animating
249 God's all-animating voice that calls thee from on high (3)

announcing
405 to the world its God announcing (2)

annoy
416 hopes deceive and fears annoy (2)

anoint
68 my head thou dost with oil anoint, and my cup overflows (4)
467 anoint and cheer our soiled face with...thy grace (3)

anointed
359 hail to the Lord's anointed, great David's greater Son (T,1)

anointing
467   thou the anointing Spirit art (1)

another
258   now is breaking o'er the earth another day (1)
489   safely through another week (T,1)
500   the dawn leads on another day (3)
510   providence hath brought us through another various year (2)

answer
 96   the whole of love is but my answer, Lord, to thee (3)
 99   saints, apostles, prophets, martyrs answer, Yes (7)
200   we heed, O Lord, thy summons & answer: here are we (3)
200   speak, and, behold! we answer; command, and we obey (4)
238   Christian, answer boldly, "While I breathe I pray" (3)
339   answer ... faith's effectual prayer ... our needs supply (1)
413   and heroic spirits answer now, as then, in Galilee (4)
517   for... children thou hast given we must answer unto thee (1)
545   O be swift, my soul, to answer him; be jubilant, my feet (3)

answered
 18   Word is answered by the Spirit's voice within (3)
 18   thanks to God whose Word is answered (3)
138   teach me the patience of unanswered prayer (4)
413   yea, the sturdy dreamers answered (1)

answers
 13   waits for him who answers prayer (1)
427   till through our pity and our shame love answers (2)
427   love answers love's appeal (2)

antedate
115   and antedate that day (2)

antepast
528   blest with this antepast of heaven (2)

anthem
352   let every anthem rise like incense to the skies (2)
371   myriad tongues, in one great anthem blending (4)
423   through pillared court and temple the lovely anthem rang (1)
455   hark ... heavenly anthem drowns all music but its own (1)

anthems
 19   supernal anthems echoing, alleluia, alleluia! (3)
128   let cheerful anthems fill his house (2)
385   whom angels greet with anthems sweet (1)
424   our praise and prayer and anthems before thee we present (2)
510   we all, with vows and anthems new, before our God appear (2)

anticipate
319   thus anticipate by faith the heavenly feast above (4)

anxious
 53   why should this anxious load press down your weary mind (3)
271   bid my anxious fears subside (3)
275   anxious spirits burn with strong desires for thy return (2)

any
    142   that will not tremble on the brink of any earthly woe (1)
    243   by any lure or guile enticed (2)

anywhere
    153   slaves are we whene'er we share that devotion anywhere (3)
    261   have we trials and temptations ... trouble anywhere (2)

apart
    201   nor seek our own salvation apart from others' need (2)
    363   heart ... make it a temple, set apart (2)
    363   set apart ... from earthly use for heaven's employ (2)

apostles
     84   draw thy protecting net around the catch of... apostles (2)
     99   saints, apostles, prophets, martyrs answer, Yes (7)
    107   as of old the apostles heard it by the Galilean lake (2)
    548   for our prophets and apostles, loyal to the living Word (3)

apostolic
      8   Lo! the apostolic train joins thy sacred name to hallow (3)

appall
    269   and doubts appall, and sorrows still increase (1)

appeal
    427   love answers love's appeal (2)

appear
     92   how precious did that grace appear (2)
    100   and, saved from earth, appear before your Savior's face (4)
    173   amid our pride and glory to see thy face appear (5)
    263   there let the way appear, steps unto heaven (3)
    293   cloud and fire appear for a glory and a covering (3)
    317   lighten our eyes, brightly appear (3)
    325   millions more, still on the way, around the board appear (3)
    337   when the chief Shepherd shall appear (5)
    354   mourns in lonely exile here until the Son of God appear (1)
    382   suddenly the Lord, descending, in... temple shall appear (4)
    401   Day-star, in my heart appear (1)
    454   for saints ... interceding till in glory they appear (3)
    466   O Comforter, draw near, within my heart appear (1)
    468   glory shall ere long appear to dwell within our land (2)
    489   may thy glory meet our eyes while we in thy house appear (3)
    510   we all, with vows and anthems new, before our God appear (2)
    510   Jesus in the clouds appear to saints on earth forgiven (6)
    522   then the full corn shall appear (2)

appeared
    394   spake the seraph and forthwith appeared a shining throng (5)

appearing
    386   Word of the Father, now in flesh appearing (3)

appears
     30   the one eternal God, ere aught that now appears (1)
    122   the bleeding sacrifice in my behalf appears (1)

139   the invisible appears in sight (6)
296   one holy Church of God appears through every age & race (T)
364   Hallelujah! God appears on earth to reign (1)
415   I hide my blushing face while his dear cross appears (4)
478   gladness breaks like morning where'er thy face appears (3)

apple
279   quick as the apple of an eye, O God, my conscience make (3)
280   quick as the apple of an eye, O God, my conscience make (3)
294   dear as the apple of thine eye, and graven on thy hand (2)

applied
114   we...his unknown peace receive & feel his blood applied (3)
226   let thy precious blood applied keep me ... near thy side (1)
420   come, feel with me his blood applied (3)

apply
137   'tis thine the blood to apply and give us eyes to see (1)

appointed
359   hail in the time appointed, his reign on earth begun (1)
454   Paschal Lamb, by God appointed (2)
454   by almighty love appointed thou hast full atonement made (2)
538   bidst the mighty ocean deep its... appointed limits keep (1)

appoints
338   where he appoints we go (2)

approach
21   approach with joy his courts unto (3)
216   nor plague approach thy guarded home (6)
279   help me the first approach to feel of pride (1)
279   first approach to feel of pride or wrong desire (1)
280   help me the first approach to feel of pride or...desire (1)
312   permit them to approach, he cries (2)
527   bold I approach the eternal throne, and claim the crown (4)

approaching
425   to see the approaching sacrifice (3)

approved
53   his goodness stands approved, unchanged from day to day (4)

arch
11   rainbow arch, his covenant sign (2)
64   our rainbow arch thy mercy's sign (3)

archangels
376   angels and archangels may have gathered there (3)

arching
273   like the arching of the heavens lift my thoughts above (4)

ardent
306   before our Father's throne we pour our ardent prayers (2)

ardently
295   thirsty soul longs ardently ... faints thy courts to see (2)

ardor
466   and visit it with thine own ardor glowing (1)

aright
368   Lord, grant us all aright to learn the wisdom it imparts (4)
437   our hearts be pure from evil, that we may see aright (2)

arise
14   let the Creator's praise arise (1)
37   clouds arise, and tempests blow by order from thy throne (3)
90   let us arise, all meaner service scorning (5)
110   quickly arise and away (4)
122   arise, my soul, arise; shake off thy guilty fears (T,1)
246   my soul, be on thy guard, ten thousand foes arise (T,1)
250   soldiers of Christ, arise and put your armor on (T,1)
259   where'er thy healing beams arise (2)
365   great Son of Righteousness, arise (5)
401   Sun of Righteousness, arise (1)
402   glorious now behold him arise, King ... God & sacrifice (5)
464   saw ye not the cloud arise, little as a human hand (4)
481   sobbing human plaint that bids thy walls arise (2)
495   when the morning wakens, then may I arise pure and fresh (6)
502   O may no earth-born cloud arise to hide thee (1)
505   as the darkness deepens o'er us, lo! eternal stars arise (4)
552   our grateful songs before thy throne arise (1)

arm
28   sufficient is thine arm alone (2)
31   strong is his arm, and shall fulfill his great decrees (3)
54   thy right hand thy powerful arm ... succor they implored (3)
70   thine arm, unseen, conveyed me safe (3)
70   thine arm ... led me up to man (3)
75   the rending tomb proclaims thy conquering arm (3)
144   since on thine arm thou bidst me lean (1)
150   arm me with jealous care, as in thy sight to live (3)
160   and brace thy heart and nerve thine arm (2)
220   in thine arm I rest me (2)
248   arm of flesh will fail you, ye dare not trust your own (3)
250   but take, to arm you for the fight, the panoply of God (2)
362   word of our God endureth ... arm of the Lord is strong (3)
534   for the might of thine arm we bless thee (T,1)
534   for the might of thine arm we bless thee, our God (1,2)
538   whose arm hath bound the restless wave (1)
552   be thy strong arm our ever sure defense (3)

armed
20   armed with cruel hate, on earth is not his equal (1)
198   inarmed shall live as comrades free (3)
198   nation with nation, land with land, inarmed shall live (3)
251   armed by faith and winged by prayer (4)
253   a spirit still prepared, and armed with jealous care (3)

armies
239   and all thy armies shine in robes of victory (6)
486   the armies of the living God shall march to victory (4)
548   for the armies of the faithful (3)

armor
246 ne'er think the victory won, nor lay thine armor down (3)
248 put on the gospel armor, each piece put on with prayer (3)
250 soldiers of Christ, arise and put your armor on (T,1)

armored
470 gird our lives that they may be armored (4)
470 armored with all Christ-like graces in the fight (4)

arms
49 who, from our mother's arms hath blessed us on our way (1)
58 eternal arms, their dear abode, we make our habitation (1)
87 when his loving arms receive us (3)
118 open thine arms, and take me in (1,5)
159 but I long to rise in the arms of faith (1)
184 imprison me within thine arms ... strong ... be my hand (1)
261 in his arms he'll take and shield thee (3)
312 and folds them in his arms (1)
341 arms of love that compass me would all mankind embrace (3)
411 as in days of old he takes the wounded to his arms (4)
521 in his mighty arms he bears them (2)
528 he spreads his arms to embrace you all (4)
536 and hearts are brave again, and arms are strong (5)
539 put his arms unfailing round you (3)

army
248 from victory unto victory his army shall he lead (1)
302 one army of the living God, to his command we bow (4)
305 like a mighty army moves the Church of God (2)

arose
444 up from the grave he arose (R)
444 he arose a victor from the dark domain (R)

around
26 casting down their golden crowns around the glassy sea (2)
35 for... love which from our birth over and around us lies (1)
38 stars and angels sing around thee (2)
58 the heavenly shield around them spread (2)
84 draw thy protecting net around the catch of... apostles (2)
91 let all the earth around ring joyous with the sound (3)
143 while life's dark maze I tread & griefs around me spread (3)
164 my foes are ever near me, around me and within (2)
178 around thy steps below (1)
211 though hosts encamp around me, firm in the fight I stand (1)
216 when fearful plagues around prevail (3)
219 around me flows thy quickening life (3)
222 when all around my soul gives way, he... is all my hope (3)
232 they meet around one common mercy seat (3)
238 how the powers of darkness rage thy steps around (1)
249 a cloud of witnesses around holds thee in full survey (2)
289 change and decay in all around I see (2)
304 its heavenly walls unseen around us rise (1)
325 millions more, still on the way, around the board appear (3)
350 here gather us around thy board to keep the feast (3)
394 the angel of the Lord came down, and glory shone around (1)

395   heaven's star shone brightly forth, glory all around him (2)
413   are ye able when . shadows close around you with the sod (3)
433   the bright and morning star shed its beams around me (2)
440   all around the clouds are breaking (1)
453   saints and angels crowd around him (3)
496   though destruction walk around us (2)
499   new mercies, each returning day, hover around us (2)
499   new mercies ... hover around us while we pray (2)
501   the sick, O Lord, around thee lay (1)
505   let our vesper hymn be blending ... holy calm around (1)
513   all good gifts around us are sent from heaven above (R)
534   may the shadow of thy presence around our camp be spread (
549   around us rolls the ceaseless tide of business (2)

arraigned
434   beaten, bound, reviled, arraigned (2)

array
76   all the heavenly orders in their great array (2)
233   still lift your standard high ... march in firm array (5)

arrayed
127   midst flaming worlds, in these arrayed (1)
291   sweet fields arrayed in living green & rivers of delight (1)

arrive
93   I hope, by thy good pleasure, safely to arrive at home (2)

arrows
496   though the arrows past us fly (2)

artist
442   so, as he renews the earth, artist without rival (2)

arts
198   new arts shall bloom of loftier mold (4)

ascend
23   ascend for him our cheerful strain (4)
32   and bid the choral song ascend to celebrate our God (5)
260   our heart's dear guest, to thee our prayers ascend (1)
288   redeemed from earth and pain, Ah! when shall we ascend (2)
294   for her my tears shall fall, for her my prayers ascend (3)
350   may our prayers, when here we bend ...to thee ascend (2)
350   like incense sweet to thee ascend (2)
359   to him shall prayer unceasing and daily vows ascend (4)
457   our hearts detached from all below ... after him ascend (1)
487   hear our prayers as they ascend (1)
503   through ... stars that veil thy face our hearts ascend (3)

ascended
500   to thee our morning hymns ascended (1)

ascending
7   see the morning sun ascending radiant in the eastern sky (T)
474   fire ascending seeks the sun (2)

ascends
358   higher yet that star ascends (2)

ascent
419   they climbed the steep ascent of heaven through peril (3)

ascribe
  54   to thee the glory we ascribe (5)
  71   to him all majesty ascribe, and crown him Lord of all (4)
533   with united breath, ascribe their conquest to the Lamb (1)
533   ascribe ... their triumph to his death (1)

ascribing
409   ascribing salvation to Jesus, our King (2)

ashes
199   and in its ashes plant the tree of peace (5)
200   our strength is dust and ashes, our years a passing hour (3)
303   exult, O dust and ashes; the Lord shall be thy part (3)
466   passions turn to dust and ashes in its heat consuming (2)
532   in peace their sacred ashes rest (6)

aside
143   nor let me ever stray from thee aside (3)
240   cast care aside, lean on thy guide (3)
242   while the coward stands aside (2)
281   my idols all be cast aside (3)
326   here would I lay aside each earthly load (3)
389   he lays aside his majesty and seems as nothing worth (2)
432   that caused the Lord of life to lay aside his crown (2)
432   lay aside his crown for my soul (2)
549   scarcely can we turn aside for one brief hour of prayer (2)

ask
  12   I know thee ... in part, I ask not, Lord, for more (3)
  20   dost ask who that may be? Christ Jesus, it is he (2)
  59   we gather together to ask the Lord's blessing (T,1)
  64   before ... blazing throne we ask no luster of our own (4)
  88   things I would ask him to tell me if he were here (1)
  99   if I ask him to receive me, will he say me nay (6)
124   ask ye what great thing I know (T,1)
138   I ask no dream, no prophet ecstasies (2)
139   and ask the gift unspeaakable (2)
144   I ask not, need not, aught beside (4)
153   grace to ask these gifts of thee (1)
171   show us thy will, we ask (3)
196   I'll take the gifts he hath bestowed, & ... ask for more (1)
196   and humbly ask for more (1)
205   what have I to ask beside (1)
207   nothing you ask will be denied (3)
220   I will ... ask for naught beside thee (1)
234   I dare not ask to fly from thee (4)
260   until we labor for those gifts we ask on bended knee (2)
260   no more we seek thee from afar, nor ask thee for a sign (4)
272   I do not ask to see the distant scene (1)
277   I ask no higher state, indulge me but in this (4)
298   here vouchsafe to all thy servants what they ask of thee (3)
298   what they ask of thee to gain (3)
332   Lord, we ask for nothing more (4)
332   ask the Father's wisdom how...that did the means ordain (3)

384   be near me, Lord Jesus, I ask thee to stay close by me (3)
395   ask the saved of all the race who have found his favor (1)
417   I ask no other sunshine than the sunshine of his face (3)
491   ask that free from peril the hours of dark may be (3)
499   furnish all we ought to ask (3)
529   but who, I ask thee, who art thou (2)
533   I ask them whence their victory came (1)

asks
112   God, the Spirit, asks you why (3)
112   God, your Maker, asks you why (1)
112   fatal cause demands, asks the work of his own hands (1)
112   God, your Savior, asks you why (2)

asleep
384   the little Lord Jesus, asleep on the hay (1)

aspect
32   waves ... with threatening aspect roar (2)

aspire
139   to thee our humble hearts aspire (2)
528   how shall I all to heaven aspire (1)

aspires
464   see how great a flame aspires (T,1)

aspiring
249   his own hand presents the prize to thine aspiring eye (3)

aspirings
430   where our earliest hopes began...our last aspirings end (4)

ass
385   mean estate where ox and ass are feeding (2)
391   ox and ass before him bow and he is in the manger now (1)

assail
207   when dangers fierce your path assail (2)
216   no fatal stroke shall thee assail (3)
220   sin and hell ... with their heaviest storms assail us (2)
221   when the howling storms of doubt and fear assail (2)
244   when the hosts of sin assail ... strength begins to fail (2)
470   scorn thy Christ, assail his ways (2)

assaults
25   guards our way from all the assaults of hell and sin (3)

assembled
310   thou in the midst of us shalt be, assembled in thy name (1)
336   fightings without . fears within since we assembled last (2)

assert
130   assert thy claim, receive thy right (5)

assigned
152   task thy wisdom ... assigned O let me cheerfully fulfill (2)

assist
1   my gracious Master and my God, assist me to proclaim (2)
343   instruments of loftier sound assist his feeble praise (2)

assuage
293   who can faint while such a river ...their thirst assuage (2)

assumes
31   the garments he assumes are light and majesty (1)
389   lo, he assumes our flesh and blood (3)

assurance
224   blessed assurance, Jesus is mine (T,1)
333   O perfect Life, be thou their full assurance (2)
333   assurance of tender charity and steadfast faith (2)
445   what joy the blest assurance gives (1,4)

assured
150   assured, if I my trust betray, I shall forever die (4)
290   assured alone that life and death God's mercy underlies (1)

astray
121   seek us when we go astray (2)
269   without thy guiding hand we go astray (1)
284   nor let me go astray (4)
378   save us all from Satan's power when we were gone astray (1)
517   and be never led astray (3)

asunder
306   when we asunder part, it gives us inward pain (4)

athirst
205   my weary steps may falter, and my soul athirst may be (2)

atone
120   these for sin could not atone (2)

atoned
122   his blood atoned for all our race (2)

atonement
100   Jesus, our great high priest, hath full atonement made (2)
127   for all a full atonement made (4)
412   for man's atonement ... God intercedeth (3)
454   by almighty love appointed thou hast full atonement made (2)

atoning
100   extol the Lamb of God, the all-atoning Lamb (3)
137   O that the world might know the all-atoning Lamb (3)

attained
366   nor eye hath seen, nor ear hath yet attained to hear (3)
366   nor ear hath yet attained to hear what there is ours (3)

attend
3   our prayer attend, come, and thy people bless (2)
24   today attend his voice, nor dare provoke his rod (4)
25   great God, attend, while Zion sings (T,1)

    55   surely his goodness and mercy here daily attend thee (3)
    237 or should pain attend me on my path below (3)
    349 may benedictions here attend the teaching of thy word (3)
    411 where'er they heal ... let love of Christ attend (3)
    461 spirit divine, attend our prayers (T,1,4)
    497 holy dreams and hopes attend us this live-long night (1)

attending
    364 thousand saints attending swell the triumph of his train (1)

attends
    14   eternal truth attends thy word (2)

attentive
    54   O Lord,our fathers oft have told in our attentive ears (T,1)

attraction
    228 has a wondrous attraction for me (2)

attune
    260 attune our lives to thee (2)

aught
    30   the one eternal God, ere aught that now appears (1)
    127 for who aught to my charge shall lay (2)
    144 I ask not, need not, aught beside (4)
    177 nor should I aught with-hold, dear Lord, from thee (1)
    358 doth its beauteous ray aught of joy or hope foretell (1)
    526 for none may boast himself of aught (2)

august
    482 we hail thine august majesty and loud hosanna sing (4)

author
    132 author of the new creation, come with unction (2)
    139 Author of faith, eternal Word (T,1)
    140 Author of faith! to thee I lift my weary, longing eyes (4)
    315 author of life divine, who hast a table spread (T,1)
    452 thou, of life the author, death didst undergo (3)
    547 our fathers' God, to thee, Author of liberty ... we sing (4)

availed
    1   His blood availed for me (4)
    408 the world has waited long, has travailed long in pain (3)

availeth
    526 thy grace along availeth (2)

avowed
    155 his first avowed intent to be a pilgrim (1)

await
    303 I know not, O I know not what joys await us there (1)
    407 await a new creative hour (3)
    440 prophets psalmists seers . sages . await . glory given (3)

awaits
    478 the crown awaits the conquest; lead on, O God of might (3)

awake
105 he calls me still; my heart, awake (4)
180 awake, my soul, and with the sun (T,1)
190 awake, awake to love and work (T,1)
190 awake, awake to love and work, the lark is in the sky (1)
190 worlds awake to cry their blessings on the Lord of life (1)
201 awake in us compassion, O Lord of life divine (3)
249 awake, my soul, stretch every nerve (T,1)
279 awake my soul when sin is nigh, and keep it still awake (3)
280 awake my soul when sin is nigh and keep it still awake (3)
335 let Zion's watchmen all awake (T,1)
366 wake, awake, for night is flying (T,1)
366 awake, Jerusalem, at last (1)
366 the Bridegroom! comes, awake (1)
455 awake, my soul, and sing of him who died for thee (1)
493 to serve my God when I awake (4)
547 let mortal tongues awake; let all that breathe partake (3)

awaken
544 let not thy wrath in its terrors awaken (2)

awakes
353 and life to joy awakes (1)
384 the cattle are lowing, the baby awakes (2)
408 new life, new hope awakes where-e'er men own his sway (1)

awaking
91 when morning gilds the skies, my heart awaking cries (T,1)
264 so does this blessed consciousness, awaking, breathe (3)
440 God's likeness, man awaking, knows the everlasting peace (1)

away
4 the Lord is never far away (3)
17 he bled and died to take away my sin (3)
28 bears all its sons away (5)
38 drive the dark of doubt away (1)
53 I'll drop my burden at his feet, and bear a song away (4)
65 he hath put away our sin (3)
81 and drives away his fear (1)
85 drive sin's night away (1)
95 take my guilt and grief away (1)
95 turn me not away unblest; calm my anguish into rest (3)
99 not till earth and not till heaven pass away (6)
110 roam farther and farther away (1)
110 he will not turn thee away (2)
110 quickly arise and away (4)
137 thou take the veil away and breathe the living Word (2)
138 but take the dimness of my soul away (2)
143 take all my guilt away (1)
143 wipe sorrows tears away (3)
161 lure us away from thee to endless night (3)
228 on a hill far away stood an old rugged cross (T,1)
228 then he'll call me some day to my home far away (4)
229 peace, perfect peace, with loved ones far away (4)
259 care, anguish, sorrow, melt away (2)

band

4   he leads his own, his chosen band (3)
88   into the city I'd follow the children's band (3)
101 come then and join this holy band, and on to glory go (4)
419 a glorious band, the chosen few on whom the Spirit came (3)
552 almighty hand leads forth in beauty all the starry band (1)
552 band of shining worlds in splendor through the skies (1)

bands

394 all meanly wrapped in swathing bands & in a manger laid (4)
438 Christ Jesus lay in death's strong bands (T,1)

bane

416 bane and blessing, pain and pleasure ... are sanctified (4)
416 bane and blessing ... by the cross are sanctified (4)

banish

29   to banish sin from our delight (3)
504 banish our weakness, health and wholeness sending (2)

banished

153 not the first to be banished by our fears from thee (2)

banks

291 on Jordan's stormy banks I stand (T,1)

banner

233 your glorious banner wave on high (1)
248 lift high the royal banner, it must not suffer loss (1)
309 come, and spread thy banner here (2)
331 Jesus spreads his banner o'er us (T,1)
372 it floateth like a banner before God's host unfurled (3)
419 his blood-red banner streams afar (1)
498 spread thy love's broad banner o'er us (3)
539 keep love's banner floating o'er you (4)

banners

305 forward into battle, see his banners go (1)

banquet

318 whose grace unbounded hath this wondrous banquet founded (1)
318 from this banquet let me measure (3)
326 this is the hour of banquet and of song (2)
331 banquet spreads before us of his mystic flesh and blood (1)
331 precious banquet, bread of heaven (1)
457 tasting the celestial powers, we banquet on his love (3)

baptize

534 baptize us with the courage with which thou blessed our (2)

baptizing

342 baptizing in the name of Father, Son, and Spirit (2)

bar

108 O sin that hath no equal, so fast to bar the gate (2)

bare
225 where I may lay me prone, and bare my soul in loneliness (3)
225 of self and sin swept bare (4)
397 as they offered gifts most rare at... manger rude & bare (3)
441 fields of our hearts that dead and bare have been (4)

barren
271 Pilgrim through this barren land (1)

barrier
119 thy love unknown hath broken every barrier down (6)

bars
444 death cannot keep his prey ... He tore the bars away (3)
446 who,triumphant, burst the bars of the tomb's dark portal (5)

base
237 lest by base denial, I depart from thee (1)

based
361 on judgment and on justice based (4)

basely
105 and basely his kind care repay (2)
528 shall I slight my Father's love, or basely fear (3)
528 basely fear his gifts to own (3)

battle
20   he must win the battle (2)
164 I shall not fear the battle if thou art by my side (1)
179 strong in thy strength we will battle for thee (1)
238 gird thee for the battle; watch and pray and fast (2)
238 peace shall follow battle; night shall end in day (3)
243 march on.. soul w. strength ... strong the battle rolls (3)
244 thou who never lost a battle, stand by me (2)
246 O watch and fight and pray; the battle ne'er give o'er (2)
248 this day the noise of battle ... next, the victor's song (4)
305 forward into battle, see his banners go (1)
411 friends in lands afar who battle with the body's ills (2)
411 battle with the body's ills and wage the holy war (2)
439 fought the fight, the battle won, Alleluia (3)
447 the strife is o'er the battle done (T,1)
478 and now, O King eternal, we lift our battle song (1)

battle's
284 amid the battle's strife (3)
288 the battle's fought, the race is won (1)

battlements
308 we mark her goodly battlements & her foundations strong (2)

battleship
548 not for battleship and fortress (2)

beacon
372 it shineth like a beacon above the darkling world (3)
413 thy guiding radiance above us shall be a beacon to God (R)
413 a beacon to God, to love, and loyalty (R)

beam
  29   the Spirit's sanctifying beam (2)
  29   sanctifying beam upon our earthly senses stream (2)
  60   thou burning sun with golden beam (1)
  104 this he give you; 'tis the Spirit's glimmering beam (3)
  382 brighter visions beam afar (3)

beamest
  399 thou beamest forth in truth and light (1)

beaming
  358 see that glory-beaming star (1)
  397 leading onward, beaming bright (1)
  416 when the sun of bliss is beaming light and love (3)

beams
  31   his glories shine with beams so bright (1)
  39   his beams are majesty and light (2)
  148 brightly beams our Father's mercy (T,1)
  257 till thy spirit breaks our night with the beams of truth (2)
  257 beams of truth unclouded (2)
  259 where'er thy healing beams arise (2)
  358 will its beams alone gild the spot that gave them birth (2)
  393 radiant beams from thy holy face (3)
  401 joyless the day's return till thy mercy's beams I see (2)
  433 the bright and morning star shed its beams around me (2)
  488 where Gospel light is glowing with pure & radiant beams (3)
  492 O let thine orient beams the night of sin disperse (2)
  542 and sunlight beams on clover-leaf and pine (2)

bear
  3   come, holy Comforter, thy sacred witness bear (3)
  4   both soul and body bear your part (4)
  10   more than all, the heart must bear the longest part (2)
  29   and give us grace our wrongs to bear (4)
  31   no mortal eye can bear the sight (1)
  53   I'll drop my burden at his feet, and bear a song away (4)
  60   ye who long pain and sorrow bear, praise God (5)
  108 shame on us,Christian brethren, his name & sign who bear (1)
  135 by thee may I strongly live, bravely bear & nobly strive (3)
  138 teach me the struggles of the soul to bear (4)
  143 O bear me safe above, a ransomed soul (4)
  152 give me to bear thy easy yoke (3)
  160 his strength shall bear thy spirit up (2)
  170 help me bear the strain of toil, the fret of care (1)
  176 bear me o'er life's fitful sea (3)
  177 help me the cross to bear, thy wondrous love declare (2)
  183 must Jesus bear the cross alone (T,1)
  183 consecrated cross I'll bear till death shall set me free (3)
  193 each other's cross to bear (2)
  200 who shall I send to shatter the fetters which they bear (2)
  202 we bear the strain of earthly care ... bear it not alone (T)
  209 bear patiently the cross of grief or pain (1)
  210 and bear thee through the evil days (1)
  214 and in their time bear fruit supreme (2)
  220 whate'er we must bear still in thee lies purest pleasure (3)
  223 not a burden we bear, not a sorrow we share (2)

228 to bear it to dark Calvary (2)
228 its shame and reproach gladly bear (4)
231 their wonted fruit should bear (4)
231 it can bring with it nothing but he will bear us through (3)
231 though vine nor fig tree neither ... fruit should bear (4)
239 I'll bear the toil, endure the pain, supported (4)
261 all our sins and griefs to bear (1)
261 O what peace we often forfeit ... needless pain we bear (1)
267 open my mouth, and let me bear gladly the warm truth (3)
267 let me bear gladly the warm truth everywhere (3)
275 thy wings shall my petition bear to him (3)
290 if my heart and flesh are weak to bear an untried pain (2)
292 with us the cross to bear, for Christ our Lord (3)
299 give of thy sons to bear the message glorious (4)
306 we share each other's woes, our mutual burdens bear (3)
309 each the other's burdens bear (4)
337 firmness with meekness from above to bear thy people (3)
337 to bear thy people on their heart (3)
353 not as of old a little child to bear and fight and die (2)
372 to bear before the nations thy true light as of old (4)
406 heralds of Christ, who bear the King's commands (T,1)
414 may not know ... cannot tell, what pains he had to bear (2)
432 caused the Lord of bliss to bear the dreadful curse (1)
432 bear the dreadful curse for my soul (1)
434 learn of Christ to bear the cross (2)
469 his conquering cross no kingdom wills to bear (2)
479 needs and burdens thy compassion bids us bear (3)
482 we bear with thee the scourge and cross (2)
517 that we may bear it meetly ... seek thine aid the more (2)
550 through all ages bear the memory of that holy hour (2)

bearer
19 thou bearer of the eternal Word (2)
85 Heart of God incarnate, Love-bearer to mankind (3)

bearest
317 our human pain still bearest thou with us (2)
427 our sins, not thine, thou bearest, Lord (2)

bearing
17 that on the cross, my burden gladly bearing (3)
377 three wise men bearing gifts of gold (2)
402 bearing gifts we traverse afar (1)
426 very God himself is bearing all the sufferings of time (3)
434 see him meekly bearing all (2)
480 move o'er the waters' face, bearing the lamp of grace (3)

bears
28 bears all its sons away (5)
53 hand which bears all nature up shall guard his children (2)
66 in his hands he gently bears us (3)
122 five bleeding wounds he bears, received on Calvary (3)
160 for only he who bears the cross may hope to wear...crown (4)
168 I'd sing the characters he bears (2)
364 dear tokens of his passion still his dazzling body bears (3)
411 and bears them to the fold (4)
419 patient bears his cross below ... follows in his train (1)
521 in his mighty arms he bears them (2)

beast
422 so lowly doth the Savior ride a paltry borrowed beast (T,1)

beasts
377 but ah! within that stable old the beasts ... behold (2)
377 the beasts a wondrous sight behold (2)
400 low lies his head with the beasts of the stall (2)
506 beneath thy mighty caring the birds & beasts are sharing (2)

beat
151 O how our hearts beat high with joy whene'er we hear (1)
260 not beat with cries on heaven's doors (3)
408 to plow-share beat the sword, to pruning-hook the spear (2)
543 a thoroughfare for freedom beat across the wilderness (2)

beaten
434 beaten, bound, reviled, arraigned (2)

beating
542 but other hearts in other lands are beating with hopes (1)

beauteous
80 how beauteous were the marks divine (T,1)
358 watchman, doth its beauteous ray (1)
358 doth its beauteous ray aught of joy or hope foretell (1)
373 break forth, O beauteous heavenly light (T,1)
492 how beauteous nature now! How dark and sad before (3)
531 I see from far thy beauteous light (1)

beauties
39 his beauties, how divinely bright (2)
367 still new beauties may I see, and still increasing light (3)

beautiful
33 all beautiful the march of days as seasons come and go (T,1)
34 all things bright and beautiful (T,R)
97 beautiful life that has no end (4)
97 beautiful life with such a friend (4)
109 beautiful words, wonderful words,wonderful words of life (R)
187 take my feet ... let them be swift & beautiful for thee (1)
380 the star rains its fire while the beautiful sing (1,2)
380 every hearth is aflame, and the beautiful sing (3)
395 Son of God, of humble birth, beautiful the story (3)
488 O balm of care and sadness, most beautiful, most bright (1)
543 O beautiful for spacious skies, for amber waves of grain (T)
543 O beautiful for pilgrim feet (2)
543 O beautiful for heroes proved in liberating strife (3)
543 O beautiful for patriot dream that sees beyond the years (4)

beauty
6 days of wonder ... beauty ... rapture, filled with light (1)
13 open now thy gates of beauty (1)
33 thou from whose unfathomed law the year in beauty flows (3)
35 for the beauty of the earth (T,1)
35 for the beauty of each hour of the day and of the night (2)
39 the race of men confess the beauty of his holiness (3)
50 so full of splendor and of joy, beauty and light (1)
109 let me more of their beauty see (1)

109	words of life and beauty teach me faith and duty (1)
127	Jesus, thy blood and righteousness my beauty are (T,1)
127	thy blood and...my beauty are, my glorious dress (1)
173	that learns to value beauty, in heart or brain or soul (4)
178	what grace, O Lord, and beauty shone (T,1)
228	a wondrous beauty I see (3)
235	let our ordered lives confess the beauty of thy peace (4)
273	God, who touchest earth with beauty (T,1)
273	God, who touchest earth with beauty, make my heart anew (5)
353	when beauty gilds the eastern hills (1)
353	when Christ our King in beauty comes (4)
353	light and beauty brings (5)
398	Light of the world, thy beauty steals into every heart (2)
402	star with royal beauty bright (R)
442	all the world with beauty fills (1)
442	beauty follows all his ways, as the world he blesses (2)
455	those wounds, yet visible above, in beauty glorified (4)
476	O God of beauty, oft revealed in dreams of human art (4)
477	O day of God, draw nigh in beauty and in power (T,1)
532	peaceful men of skill who builded homes of beauty (4)
545	in . beauty of the lilies Christ was born across the sea (4)
552	almighty hand leads forth in beauty all the starry band (1)

because
119	because thy promise I believe ... I come (5)
149	because I know 'tis true (1)
166	I love thee, because thou hast first loved me (2)
216	because thy trust is God alone (6)
261	all because we do not carry everything to God in prayer (1)
518	but more because of Jesus' blood (3)

beckon
| 263 | angels to beckon me, nearer, my God, to thee (3) |

become
191	until the laws of Christ become the laws and habits (2)
277	old things shall be done away ... all things new become (2)
453	crowns become the victor's brow (1)
461	let thy Church on earth become blest as the Church above (3)
466	for none can guess its grace, till he become the place (3)
520	within .. home let every heart become thy dwelling place (2)

becomes
| 91 | the night becomes as day when from the heart we say (2) |
| 244 | when my life becomes a burden ... nearing chilly Jordan (4) |

bed
384	away in a manger no crib for a bed (T,1)
396	infant holy, infant lowly, for his bed a cattle stall (T,1)
397	as with joyous steps they sped to that lowly manger bed (2)
444	vainly they watch his bed ... vainly they seal the dead (2)
493	dread the grave as little as my bed (3)
495	spread their white wings above me, watching round my bed (5)

beds
| 157 | the healing of his seamless dress is by our beds of pain (4) |
| 239 | must I be carried to the skies on flowery beds of ease (2) |

befall
205   I know whate'er befall me, Jesus doeth all things well (1)
256   Heart of my own heart, whatever befall ... be my vision (4)
497   strong through thee whate'er befall us, O God most wise (2)

before
8   Lord of all, we bow before thee (1)
13   gracious God, I come before thee (2)
21   come ye before him and rejoice (1)
22   before Jehovah's awful throne (T,1)
24   come, worship at this throne; come, bow before the Lord (3)
26   cherubim and seraphim falling down before thee (2)
28   before the hills in order stood (3)
28   before the rising sun (4)
38   hearts unfold like flowers before thee (1)
41   thou whose purpose moves before us toward the goal (4)
41   humbly now we bow before thee (1)
42   sun and moon, rejoice before him (1)
50   a yearning for a deeper peace not known before (4)
55   come now with praises before him (4)
58   the fire divine their steps that led ... before us (2)
58   the fire divine ... still goeth bright before us (2)
64   before ... blazing throne we ask no luster of our own (4)
66   saints triumphant, bow before him (4)
67   thy cross before to guide me (4)
70   before my infant heart could know from whom...comforts (2)
77   let all, with heart and voice, before his throne rejoice (1)
90   haste, let us lay our gifts before the King (1)
90   at eventide before the sun was set (4)
98   and bring all heaven before our eyes (4)
100   and, saved from earth, appear before your Savior's face (4)
122   before the throne my surety stands (1)
140   what did thine only Son endure before I drew my breath (2)
146   may make one music as before (5)
159   pure delight . single hour ... before thy throne I spend (3)
173   while ever on the hill-top before thee loomed the cross (2)
189   human hatreds flee before the radiant eastern skies (1)
196   my vows I will to his great name before his people pay (3)
205   gushing from the rock before me...a spring of joy I see (2)
218   than he went through before (3)
222   faultless to stand before the throne (4)
230   green pastures are before me, which yet I have not seen (3)
240   life with its way before us lies (2)
247   unkown waves before me roll (1)
251   heaven's eternal day's before thee (4)
259   all fear before thy presence flies (2)
266   and run not before him, whatever betide (3)
283   till we cast our crowns before thee (4)
289   hold thou thy cross before my closing eyes (5)
294   I love thy Church, O God! Her walls before thee stand (2)
302   by faith we join our hands with those that went before (5)
303   send hope before to grasp it, till hope be lost in sight (3)
305   with the cross of Jesus going on before (1,R)
306   before our Father's throne we pour our ardent prayers (2)
331   banquet spreads before us of his mystic flesh and blood (1)
333   lowly we kneel in prayer before thy throne (1)
341   angels and men before it fall, and devils fear and fly (1)
341   bold to confess thy glorious name before a world of foes (4)

342   the task looms large before us; we follow without fear (4)
345   in worship bend before thy mercy seat (2)
347   thine own before thy feet we lay (1)
355   we bring our hearts before thy cross (4)
357   powers, dominions, bow before him & extol our God & King (2)
359   before him on the mountains shall peace, the herald, go (3)
366   men and angels sing before thee (3)
372   it floateth like a banner before God's host unfurled (3)
372   to bear before the nations thy true light as of old (4)
382   saints, before the altar bending (4)
391   ox and ass before him bow and he is in the manger now (1)
397   bend the knee before him whom heaven and earth adore (2)
424   the people of the Hebrews with palms before thee went (2)
424   our praise and prayer and anthems before thee we present (2)
424   to thee, before thy passion they sang .. hymns of praise (3)
430   cast our crowns before thy feet (5)
433   near the cross .. Lamb of God bring its scenes before me (3)
440   joy unknown, ... saints shall stand before the throne (4)
468   before him righteousness shall go, his royal harbinger (1)
468   all shall frame to bow them low before thee, Lord (3)
486   O God, before whose altar the stars like tapers burn (T,1)
492   how beauteous nature now! How dark and sad before (3)
496   the perfect day before us breaks in everlasting light (4)
498   thy glory breaks before us through the city's open gate (3)
504   active and watchful, stand we all before thee (1)
509   and peaceful, leave before thy feet (3)
510   we all, with vows and anthems new, before our God appear (2)
517   thou... crowned us with an honor women never knew before (2)
526   I lay my sins before thee (1)
529   my company before is gone, and I am left alone with thee (1)
535   and bow before thy throne (3)
536   who thee by faith before the world confessed (1)
539   smite death's threatening wave before you (4)
545   sifting out the hearts of men before his judgment seat (3)
552   our grateful songs before thy throne arise (1)

beforehand
  96   for thou wert long beforehand with my soul (3)

befriend
  55   if with his love he befriend thee (3)
121   we are thine, do thou befriend us (2)

began
  38   mortals join the happy chorus, which the... stars began (4)
  38   chorus, which the morning stars began (4)
236   with thee began, with thee shall end the day (2)
357   ere the worlds began to be (1)
365   when thy truth began its race, it touched ... every land (3)
430   where our earliest hopes began ..our last aspirings endd (4)
460   spoken by ... Word incarnate, God of God, ere time began (2)
548   strong as when her life began (4)

begin
  14   in every land begin the song (4)
394   good will ... from heaven to men begin and never cease (6)
425   O Christ, thy triumphs now begin o'er captive death (2)
425   triumphs now begin o'er captive death and conqered sin (2)

437   now let the heavens be joyful! Let earth her song begin (3)
498   gather to begin the day with praise (1)
502   now, Lord, the gracious work begin (4)
522   all is safely gathered in ere the winter storms begin (1)
528   where shall my wondering soul begin (T,1)

beginning
59   so from the beginning the fight we were winning (2)
65   as it was without beginning so it lasts without an end (4)
76   who from the beginning was the mighty Word (1)
283   Alpha and Omega be; end of faith as its beginning (2)

begins
244   when the hosts of sin assail ... strength begins to fail (2)

begotten
357   of the Father's love begotten (T,1)

begun
5   the men of grace have found glory begun below (3)
177   some work of love begun, some deed of kindness done (3)
249   blest Savior, introduced by thee have I my race begun (4)
311   bless her works in thee begun (4)
359   hail in the time appointed, his reign on earth begun (1)
447   the song of triumph has begun: Alleluia (1)
464   when he first the work begun, small & feeble was his day (2)
471   and glory ends what grace begun (2)
482   establish thou forevermore the triumph now begun (1)
535   they find their heaven on earth begun (1)

behalf
122   the bleeding sacrifice in my behalf appears (1)

behavior
459   stilling the rude wills of men's wild behavior (3)

beheld
203   but often in some far-off Galilee beheld thee fairer (2)
203   beheld thee fairer yet while serving thee (2)

behest
32   without his high behest ye shall not ... disturb (3)
500   the darkness falls at thy behest (1)

behind
102   ye need not one be left behind (1)
215   behind a frowning providence he hides a smiling face (4)
242   behind the dim unknown, standeth God within the shadow (4)
253   tramples down and casts behind the baits of pleasing ill (2)
507   no more our God forsake, or cast his words behind (3)

behold
1   ye blind, behold your Savior come (6)
36   thee in man's spirit we behold (4)
66   ye behold him face to face (4)
98   there they behold thy mercy seat (1)
117   behold, I freely give the living water (2)
120   and behold thee on thy throne (3)

219 hand in all things I behold ... all things in thy hand (4)
252 angels in their songs rejoice & cry "Behold he prays" (4)
255 O when shall I behold thy face, thou Majesty divine (2)
295 behold, the sparrow findeth out a house wherein to rest (3)
299 behold how many thousands still are lying bound (2)
315 strengthened by thy grace behold without a veil thy face (2)
341 'tis all my business here below to cry "Behold the Lamb" (5)
341 preach him to all & cry in death "...behold the Lamb" (6)
363 behold the King of glory waits (1)
364 every eye shall now behold him robed in dreadful majesty (2)
365 but when our eyes behold thy Word, we read thy name (1)
377 the beasts a wondrous sight behold (2)
386 come and behold him, born the King of angels (1)
387 late in time behold him come (2)
389 behold the wonderful exchange our Lord with us doth make (3)
397 as with gladness men of old did the guiding star behold (T)
402 glorious now behold him arise, King ... God & sacrifice (5)
404 behold throughout the heavens there shone a holy light (1)
420 behold him, all ye that pass by (3)
428 behold the Savior of mankind nailed to the shameful tree (T)
455 crown him the Lord of love; behold his hands and side (4)
549 behold us, Lord, a little space (T,1)

beholding
258 thou with him shalt dwell, beholding Light enfolding (4)

being
9 while life, and thought, and being last (1,4)
64 Lord of all being, throned afar (T,1)
112 God, did your being give, made you with himself to live (1)
154 hold o'er my being absolute sway (4)
318 fount, whence all my being floweth (2)
469 how shall we love thee, holy, hidden Being (4)
498 sure of being safely guided, guarded well from every foe (2)

belief
104 true belief and true repentance (2)
145 kneeling there in deep contrition, help my unbelief (2)
214 not like that go the men of unbelief (3)
214 men of unbelief ... are like chaff the wind doth blow (3)
215 blind unbelief is sure to err and scan his work in vain (5)
401 fill me, Radiancy divine; scatter all my unbelief (3)

believe
1 mournful, broken hearts rejoice; the humble poor believe (5)
94 weep, believe, and sin no more (3)
101 believe in him without delay, and you are fully blest (3)
110 they who believe on his name shall rejoice (4)
111 come, let us, who in Christ believe (T,1)
114 we who in Christ believe that he for us hath died (3)
119 because thy promise I believe ... I come (5)
127 Lord, I believe thy precious blood (3)
127 Lord, I believe were sinners more than sands (4)
175 he will forgive if they only believe (2)
181 and we believe thy word, though dim our faith may be (4)
240 only believe, and thou shalt see that Christ is all (4)
275 believe his Word and trust his grace (3)
413 believe that spirit triumphs .. commend .. soul to God (3)
414 we believe it was for us he hung and suffered there (2)

420 believe the record true (2)
463 we believe in one true   God (T,1)
463 we believe in Jesus Christ, Son of God and Mary's Son (2)

believed
92 the hour I first believed (2)
227 when my heart first believed, what a joy I received (2)

believer's
81 how sweet the name of Jesus sounds in a believer's ear (T,1)

believers
309 show how true believers live (4)
309 on the wings of angels fly; show how true believers die (6)

believes
137 the witness in himself he hath, and consciously believes (4)
139 to him ... in thy name believes eternal life ...is given (4)

believing
146 believing where we cannot prove (1)
282 believing, true, and clean (3)

bells
482 men at last ... ring the bells of brotherhood & peace (3)

belong
11 join the angel song, all the worlds to him belong (1)
14 to every land the strains belong (4)
23 worship and thanks to him belong (1)
23 worship and thanks to him belong who reigns (4)
86 let all the holy throng, who to thy Church belong (4)
153 all our lives belong to thee (3)
218 if life belong, I will be glad that I may long obey (2)
292 inspired with hope and praise, to Christ belong (4)
343 nature's works ... to whom they all belong (1)
440 death and sorrow ... to the former days belong (1)

belongs
218 Lord, it belongs not to my care whether I die or live (T,1)
458 highest place ... heaven affords belongs to him by right (2)
510 all praise to him belongs (1)

beloved
366 come, thou blessed One. God's own beloved son, Alleluia (2)
376 worshiped the beloved with a kiss (3)

below
5 the men of grace have found glory begun below (3)
14 from all the dwell below the skies (T,1)
15 keeps his court below (1)
36 Maker of all above, below (1)
37 not a plant or flower below, but makes thy glories known (3)
64 Lord of all life, below, above (4)
131 sound with...thy saints below, the depth of love divine (4)
134 look how we grovel here below (2)
178 around thy steps below (1)
180 praise him, all creatures here below (4)
181 to tend the lone and fatherless is angels' work below (3)

186   my hands are but engaged below   (5)
193   and spotless here below (3)
209   his voice who ruled them while he dwelt below (2)
226   through .. changing world below lead me gently ..as I go (2)
227   'twas a heaven below my Redeemer to know (3)
237   or should pain attend me on my path below (3)
300   Lord, obediently we'll go, gladly leaving all below (4)
301   if our fellowship below in Jesus be so sweet (5)
338   still in Jesus' footsteps tread & show his praise below (2)
341   'tis all my business here below to cry,"Behold the Lamb" (5)
419   patient bears his cross below ... follows in his train (1)
457   our hearts detached from all below ... after him ascend (1)
458   joy of all who dwell above, the joy of all below (3)
458   they suffer with their Lord below (5)
471   Fountain of light and love below (3)
474   all our sorrows left below .. earth exchanged for heaven (3)
493   praise him, all creatures here below (5)
530   perfecting the saints below (1)
535   they sing the Lamb in hymns above and we in hymns below (2)

bend
   8   adoring bend the knee while we own the mystery (4)
  32   ye nations bend, in reverence bend (5)
  78   at the great name of Jesus, now all knees must bend (2)
 260   we would not bend thy will to ours (3)
 345   meet with those who here in worship bend (2)
 345   in worship bend before thy mercy seat (2)
 350   may our prayers, when here we bend ...to thee ascend (2)
 390   above its sad & lowly plains they bend on hovering wing (2)
 397   bend the knee before him whom heaven and earth adore (2)
 428   and earth's strong pillars bend (2)
 470   bend our pride to thy control (3)
 526   bend down thy gracious ear to me (1)

bended
 185   hear thou the prayer I make on bended knee (1)
 260   until we labor for those gifts we ask on bended knee (2)
 374   come, adore on bended knee Christ the Lord (3)

bending
 382   saints, before the altar bending (4)
 390   angels bending near ... earth to touch ... harps of gold (1)

bends
 219   calmness bends serene above, my restlessness to still (3)

beneath
  15   hallowed be his name beneath (3)
  46   beneath thy shadow we abide (1)
  53   beneath his watchful eye his saints securely dwell (2)
  89   my smile beneath the tyrant's frown (3)
 142   will not murmur nor complain beneath the chastening rod (2)
 207   beneath his wings of love abide (1)
 216   beneath his wings shalt thou confide (4)
 231   beneath the spreading heavens no creature but is fed (3)
 232   'tis found beneath the mercy seat (1)
 264   sweet the repose beneath thy wings o'ershading (4)
 266   each thought and each motive beneath his control (4)

285 nothing in earth beneath desire (4)
296 beneath the pine or palm, one unseen Presence she adores (2)
302 one family we dwell in him, one Church above, beneath (3)
303 beneath the contemplation sink heart and voice oppressed (1)
321 beneath the forms of outward rite (T,1)
417 beneath the cross of Jesus I fain would take my stand (T,1)
421 sinners, plunged beneath that flood (1)
493 keep me, King of kings, beneath thine own almighty wings (1)
503 Lord of life, beneath the dome of the universe thy home (2)
506 beneath thy mighty caring the birds & beasts are sharing (2)
528 groaning beneath your load of sin (5)
531 is there a thing beneath the sun that strives with thee (2)
541 men who fly through lonely ways beneath the sky (2)
550 O God, beneath thy guiding hand (T,1)

benediction
298 and thy fullest benediction shed within its walls alway (2)

bent
184 it only stands unbent amid the clashing strife (4)
283 take away our bent to sinning (2)
459 to thee all knees are bent, all voices pray (1)

beseech
311 we beseech thee, hear us (1,2,3,4,5)

beset
155 who so beset him round with dismal stories (2)
486 who, when fears beset them, stand fast and fight and die (2)

beside
12   beyond the range of sun and star, and yet beside us here (1)
26   only thou art holy; there is none beside thee (3)
59   beside us to guide us, our God with us joining (2)
67   fear no ill, with thee, dear Lord, beside me (4)
118 I give up every plea beside (4)
144 I ask not, need not, aught beside (4)
145 whom have I on earth beside thee...in heaven but thee (4)
161 walk thou beside us lest the tempting by-ways lure us (3)
202 tasks he gives are those he gave beside the restless sea (2)
202 beside us walks our brother Christ (1)
205 what have I to ask beside (1)
214 like trees beside a flowing stream (2)
219 I sink beside the road (2)
220 I will ... ask for naught beside thee (1)
230 my Shepherd is beside me, and nothing can I lack (2)
232 a place than all beside more sweet (2)
235 simple trust like theirs who heard beside the Syrian sea (2)
290 and so beside the silent sea I wait the muffled oar (4)
338 O may we ever walk in him, and nothing know beside (3)
355 nation's pride o'erthrown went down to dust beside thee (2)
369 as thou didst break the loaves beside the sea (1)
544 falsehood and wrong shall not tarry beside thee (3)

best
2   best that thou hast given, earth and heaven render thee (5)
35   for thyself, best Gift Divine! to our race ... given (6)
35   for thyself, best Gift ... to our race so freely given (6)

 50 I thank thee,Lord, that thou hast kept the best in store (4)
107 serve and love thee best of all (5)
149 for those who know it best seem hungering (4)
169 to be the best that I can be for truth ... and thee (4)
185 now thee alone I seek, give what is best (2)
197 by loyal scorn of second best (3)
209 be still my soul: thy best, thy heavenly friend (1)
228 and I love that old cross where the dearest and best (1)
244 when I've done the best I can &... friends misunderstand (3)
256 thou my best thought, by day or by night (1)
260 our best is but thyself in us (3)
269 through joy or sorrow, as thou deemest best (4)
282 thy new, best name of Love (5)
329 from the best bliss that earth imparts (1)
370 all the best we have we owe thee (1)
400 brightest and best of the sons of the morning (T,1)
419 who best can drink his cup of woe, triumphant over pain (1)
423 children sang their praises, the simplest and the best (1)
489 day of all thee week the best, emblem of eternal rest (1)
501 they who fain would serve thee best are conscious most (4)
526 yea, e'en the best life faileth (2)

bestow
101 Jesus shed his precious blood rich blessings to bestow (2)
332 feeble elements bestow a power not theirs to give (2)
403 his spirit only can bestow, who reigns in light above (1)

bestowed
 44 on man thy wisdom ... bestowed a power well-nigh divine (4)
 70 unnumbered comforts to my soul thy tender care bestowed (2)
114 things which freely of his love he hath on us bestowed (4)
196 I'll take the gifts he hath bestowed, & ... ask for more (1)

bestowes
223 for the favor he shows, and the joy he bestowes (3)

bestoweth
 67 thy unction grace bestoweth (5)

bestowing
446 but today amidst the twelve thou didst stand, bestowing (4)
466 and kindle it, thy holy flame bestowing (1)

bestows
223 joy he bestows are for them who will trust and obey (3)
301 gift which he on one bestows, we all delight to prove (2)

Bethel
263 out of my stony griefs Bethel I'll raise (4)

Bethlehem
374 come to Bethlehem & see him whose birth the angels sing (2)
377 in Bethlehem neath starlit skies (T,1)
378 in Bethlehem in Jewry this blessed babe was born (2)
378 how that in Bethlehem was born the Son of God by name (3)
378 went to Bethlehem straightway, the blessed babe to find (4)

380 for the manger of Bethlehem cradles a King (1,2)
381 O Little Town of Bethlehem, how still we see thee lie (T,1)
381 O holy Child of Bethlehem, descend to us, we pray (4)
383 o'er Bethlehem it took its rest (4)
386 O come ye, O come ye to Bethlehem (1)
387 Christ is born in Bethlehem (1)
405 Bethlehem, thou dost all excel (1)

Bethlehem's
123 I know not how that Bethlehem's babe (T,1)
123 how that Bethlehem's babe could in the God-head be (1)
402 born a King on Bethlehem's plain (2)

betide
207 be not dismayed whate'er betide (T,1)
210 he'll give thee strength, whate'er betide thee (1)
266 and run not before him, whatever betide (3)

betray
150 assured, if I my trust betray, I shall forever die (4)
173 while we betray so quickly and leave thee there alone (2)

better
97 I want no better friend; I trust him now (4)
104 if you tarry till you're better, you will never come (4)
162 better lesson cannot be, loving him who first loved me (1)
285 be mine this better part (3)
345 may they who err be guided here to find the better way (3)
469 O give us brother love for better seeing (4)
469 better seeing thy Word made flesh, and in a manger laid (4)
474 thy better portion trace (1)
509 our helper, God, in whom we trust, in better worlds (5)
509 in better worlds our souls shall boast (5)
525 which all our better thought inspires (3)

between
548 memory and hope between (1)

bewildering
459 through seas dry-shod, through weary wastes bewildering (2)

beyond
2 thou who art beyond the farthest mortal eye can scan (2)
12 beyond the range of sun and star, and yet beside us here (1)
30 first ... last: beyond all thought His timeless years! (1)
136 we rise with him to life which soars beyond the grave (4)
206 thou art the thought beyond all thought (2)
206 thou art...the gift beyond our utmost prayer (2)
206 with worlds on worlds beyond our sight (4)
290 I only know I cannot drift beyond his love and care (5)
294 beyond my highest joy I prize her heavenly ways (4)
303 what radiancy of glory, what light beyond compare (1)
368 guide & chart, wherein we read of realms beyond the sky (2)
369 beyond the sacred page I seek thee, Lord (1)
383 in the east, beyond them far (2)
414 there is a green hill far away, beyond the city wall (T,1)
415 amazing pity! Grace unknown! and love beyond degree (2)

419   eagle eye could pierce beyond the grave (2)
433   till my raptured soul shall find rest beyond the river (R)
433   till I reach the golden strand just beyond the river (4)
462   eyes that see, beyond the dark, the dawn and thee (5)
486   O Lord, be ours the glory beyond all earthly fame (4)
543   O beautiful for patriot dream that sees beyond the years (4)

bid

32   and bid the choral song ascend to celebrate our God (5)
138   hast thou not bid me love thee, God and King (3)
143   be thou my guide; bid darkness turn to day (3)
236   then, when thy voice shall bid our conflict cease (4)
262   here...my God, vouchsafe to stay & bid my heart rejoice (3)
271   when I tread the verge of Jordan, bid ... fears subside (3)
271   bid my anxious fears subside (3)
309   bid our strife forever cease (1)
310   bid our inmost souls rejoice in hope of perfect love (5)
343   we bid the pealing organ wait to speak alone thy will (3)
354   bid envy, strife, and quarrels cease (3)
359   to help the poor and needy, and bid the weak be strong (2)
366   halls we see where thou hast bid us sup with thee (2)
538   and bid their angry tumult cease (3)

bidden
102   for God hath bidden all mankind (1)

bidding
162   at thy bidding may I move, prompt to serve & follow thee (2)
423   scorned ... little children should on his bidding wait (2)

bids
1   name ... that bids our sorrows cease (3)
275   and bids me at my Father's throne (1)
275   since he bids me seek his face (3)
300   Jesus Christ, our Father's Son, bids us undismayed go on (3)
301   bids us, each to each restored, together seek his face (1)
301   He bids us build each other up; and, gathered into one (3)
479   making known the needs and burdens thy compassion bids (3)
479   needs and burdens thy compassion bids us bear (3)
481   sobbing human plaint that bids thy walls arise (2)
481   yea, bids us seize the whole of life and build its glory (5)

bidst
119   and that thou bidst me come to thee (1)
144   since on thine arm thou bidst me lean (1)
340   thou bidst us go with thee to stand against hell's (2)
538   bidst the mighty ocean deep its... appointed limits keep (1)

big
215   the clouds ye so much dread are big with mercy (3)

billows
148   loud the angry billows roar (2)

bind
93   let thy goodness, like a fetter, bind my wandering heart (3)
93   let thy goodness ... bind my wandering heart to thee (3)
173   longs to bind God's children into one perfect whole (4)

bind
226   may thy tender love to me bind me closer .. Lord to thee (R)
311   and the broken-hearted bind (3)
354   bind all peoples in one heart and mind (3)
411   bind strong the bond of brotherhood of those who fight (1)
484   bind all our lives together, smite us and save us all (3)

binding
192   his service is the golden cord close binding all mankind (2)
298   binding all the Church in one (1)

binds
38   brother love binds man to man (4)
199   restores the lost, and binds the spirit broken (2)
306   blest be the tie that binds our hearts in Christian love (T)

bird
34   each little bird that sings (1)
38   flashing sea, chanting bird and flowing fountain (2)
84   to bird in flight, controlling wing (1)
264   when the bird waketh, and the shadows flee (1)
521   nesting bird nor star in heaven such a refuge ... given (1)

birds
17   and hear the birds sing sweetly in the trees (2)
45   the birds their carols raise (2)
90   while birds and flowers and sky above are preaching (3)
343   To God the tribes of ocean cry, and birds upon the wing (2)
490   birds pass high in flight, fragrant flowers now bloom (1)
506   beneath thy mighty caring the birds & beasts are sharing (2)
513   the winds and waves obey him, by him the birds are fed (2)

birth
35   for... love which from our birth over and around us lies (1)
41   bringing suns and stars to birth (1)
43   repeats the story of her birth (2)
113   by thy birth and by thy tears (T,1)
297   her charter of salvation, one Lord, one faith, one birth (2)
331   in thy holy incarnation, when the angels sang thy birth (2)
358   will its beams alone gild the spot that gave them birth (2)
359   spring in his path to birth (3)
374   come to Bethlehem & see him whose birth the angels sing (2)
380   there's a tumult of joy o'er the wonderful birth (2)
381   O morning stars, together proclaim the holy birth (2)
382   who sang creation's story now proclaim Messiah's birth (1)
387   born to give them second birth (3)
393   Jesus, Lord, at thy birth (3)
395   angels sang about his birth; wisemen sought & found him (2)
395   Son of God, of humble birth, beautiful the story (3)
404   angel chorus that hailed our Savior's birth (2)
405   the star that told his birth (2)
442   in his grace of glad new birth we must seek revival (2)
477   O day of God, draw nigh as at creation's birth (5)
488   on thee, at the creation, the light first had its birth (2)
549   then let us prove our heavenly birth in all we do & know (5)

bitter
161   to heal earth's wounds and end her bitter strife (2)
317   thy holy face is stained with bitter tears (2)

402 myrrh is mine; its bitter perfume breathes ... gloom (4)
412 death of anguish and thy bitter passion for my salvation (4)
430 here earth's bitter things grow sweet (1)
434 watch with him one bitter hour (1)
446 loosed from Pharaoh's bitter yoke (1)
481 bitter lips in blind despair cry (3)
546 purge this land of bitter things (1)

bitterest
270 stooped to share our sharpest pang, our bitterest tear (1)

bitterness
289 ills have no weight, and tears no bitterness (4)

black
371 o'er fear and doubt, o'er black despair prevailing (1)

blade
441 now the green blade riseth from the buried grain (T,1)
522 first the blade and then the ear (2)

blast
28 our shelter from the stormy blast (1)

blaze
172 let it for thy glory burn with inextinguishable blaze (2)
190 so let the love of Jesus come and set my soul ablaze (2)
191 men with hearts ablaze .. truth to love .. wrong to hate (4)
234 in thy sunshine's blaze its day may brighter, fairer be (2)
464 sets the kingdoms on a blaze (1)

blazing
64 before ... blazing throne we ask no luster of our own (4)

blazoned
203 thy paths of service lead to blazoned heights (1)
203 blazoned heights and slopes of need (1)

bleak
376 in the bleak midwinter, frosty wind made moan (T,1)
376 in the bleak midwinter, long ago (1)
376 in the bleak midwinter a stable place sufficed (2)

bled
17 he bled and died to take away my sin (3)
23 when his creatures sinned, he bled (2)
23 he bled to save us from eternal death (2)
163 he bled, he died to save me (2)
407 the heart that bled and broke to send God's love (1)
426 perfect God on thee has bled (1,4)

bleed
415 alas! and did my Savior bleed (T,1)
428 vast the love that him inclined to bleed & die for thee (1)

bleeding
122 the bleeding sacrifice in my behalf appears (1)
122 five bleeding wounds he bears, received on Calvary (3)

159   nearer, blessed Lord, to thy precious, bleeding side (R)
242   Christ, thy bleeding feet we track (3)
402   sorrowing, sighing, bleeding, dying (4)
420   the bleeding Prince of life and peace (3)
528   his bleeding heart shall make you room (5)

blend
136   till every age and race and clime shall blend (3)
136   shall blend their creeds in one (3)
232   there is a scene where spirits blend (3)
260   but blend our wills to thine (3)
305   blend with ours your voices in the triumph song (4)
340   till earth and heaven together blend their praises (4)
350   their solemn praise with ours to blend (5)
437   all things seen and unseen their notes in gladness blend (3)

blending
7   hear the angel voices blending ... praise to God on high (1)
317   our life with thine forever blending (3)
371   myriad tongues, in one great anthem blending (4)
505   let our vesper hymn be blending ... holy calm around (1)
524   strains of ... holy throng with ours today are blending (3)

bless
2   thousands only live to bless thee (1)
3   our prayer attend, come, and thy people bless (2)
3   come, and thy people bless, and give thy Word success (2)
11   morning, evening, bless his name (2)
16   stand up and bless his glorious name (5)
16   stand up and bless the Lord, ye people of his choice (T,1)
16   stand up and bless the Lord your God (1)
16   stand up and bless the Lord; the Lord your God adore (5)
21   praise, laud, and bless his name always (3)
31   and where his love resolves to bless (2)
39   sing the great Jehovah's praise and bless his holy name (1)
40   bless us with life that has no end (2)
47   with thee to bless, the darkness shines as light (2)
48   for I will be with thee thy troubles to bless (3)
54   in God our shield we will rejoice & ever bless thy name (5)
58   bless the same boundless giver (4)
60   let all things their creator bless (7)
65   O my soul, bless God the Father (T,1)
65   all within me bless his name (1)
65   bless the Father ... forget not ... mercies to proclaim (1)
65   bless the Father, all his creatures (6)
65   all throughout his vast dominion bless the Father (6)
65   bless the Father, o my soul (6)
66   slow to chide and swift to bless (2)
95   heavenly Father, bless me now (T,1)
95   while I rest upon thy word come ... bless me now, O Lord (2)
99   finding, following, keeping, struggling...sure to bless (7)
128   and bless in death a bond so dear (5)
181   to comfort and to bless, to find a balm for woe (3)
199   the holier worship which he deigns to bless restores (2)
236   we stand to bless thee ere our worship cease (1)
257   hear, and bless our prayers and praises (3)
265   O bless me now, my Savior, I come to thee (R)
275   truth and faithfulness engage the waiting soul to bless (3)

289 I fear no foe, with thee at hand to bless (4)
311 bless her works in thee begun (4)
312 for 'twas to bless such souls as these the Lord...came (2)
325 bless the founder's name (4)
332 thine to bless, 'tis only ours to wonder and adore (4)
337 Lord, thine ordained servants bless (1)
347 O Father, deign these walls to bless (3)
349 these walls for thine own sake ... be pleased to bless (2)
349 O Lord, be pleased to bless, we pray (2)
351 bless thou this house that it may be a place most meet (1)
352 source of all strength thou art; thy gospel bless (3)
365 bless the dark world with heavenly light (5)
369 bless thou the truth, dear Lord, to me, to me (2)
369 as thou didst bless the bread by Galilee (2)
384 bless all the dear children in thy tender care (3)
399 toward thee longing doth possess me; turn and bless me (2)
411 O Father, look from heaven and bless ... their works (5)
411 bless ... their works of pure unselfishness (5)
445 He lives, to bless me with his love (2)
449 thy name we bless, O risen Lord (4)
465 bless thine heart-renewing power (3)
487 bless the sermon in this place (4)
502 come near and bless us when we wake (6)
512 to bless the earth, God sendeth (T,1)
512 with the gentle showers doth bless the springing grain (1)
518 thy creatures bless (1)
534 for the might of thine arm we bless thee (T,1)
534 we bless thee, our God, our fathers' God (1,2)
534 for the might of thine arm we bless thee, our God (1,2)
551 with peace our borders bless (2)

blessed
2 Father, Son, and Holy Spirit, blessed Trinity (5)
13 oh, how blessed is this place (1)
26 God in three persons, blessed Trinity! (1,4)
27 most blessed, most glorious, the Ancient of days (1)
49 who, from our mother's arms hath blessed us on our way (1)
49 with ever joyful hearts and blessed peace to cheer us (2)
95 O thou loving, blessed One, rising o'er me like the sun (4)
109 Christ, the blessed one, give to all wonderful words of (2)
115 what a blessed hope is ours while here on earth we stay (2)
116 I am trusting, Lord, in thee, blessed Lamb of Calvary (4)
121 blessed Jesus! thou hast bought us, thine we are (1)
121 blessed Jesus! Hear, O hear us, when we pray (2)
121 blessed Jesus! We will early turn to thee (3)
121 blessed Lord & only Savior, with thy love our bosom fill (4)
121 blessed Jesus! Thou hast loved us, love us still (4)
132 O hear our supplication, Blessed Spirit, God of peace (2)
159 draw me nearer, nearer blessed Lord (R)
159 nearer, blessed Lord, to thy precious, bleeding side (R)
195 until thy blessed face I see (5)
209 all safe and blessed we shall meet at last (3)
217 He leadeth me: O blessed thought (T,1)
218 when grace hath made me meet thy blessed face to see (4)
224 blessed assurance, Jesus is mine (T,1)
245 the Rock's blessed shadow, how sweet (2)
257 blessed Jesus, at thy word (T,1)
264 so does this blessed consciousness, awaking, breathe (3)

265 Most Holy One ... thou blessed Son (5)
265 O make me thine indeed, thou blessed Son (5)
298 what they gain from thee forever ... blessed to retain (3)
303 the pastures of the blessed are decked in glorious sheen (2)
303 O sweet and blessed country, the home of God's elect (4)
303 O sweet and blessed country that eager hearts expect (4)
304 the blessed Church to be (1)
304 O holy kingdom, happy fold, the blessed Church to be (2)
318 let me be a fit partaker of ... blessed food from heaven (2)
321 the blessed cup is only passed true memory of thee (3)
350 how blessed is this place, O Lord (T,1)
366 come, thou blessed One. God's own beloved son, Alleluia (2)
378 in Bethlehem in Jewry this blessed babe was born (2)
378 and laid within a manger upon this blessed morn (2)
378 from God our heavenly Father a blessed angel came (3)
378 went to Bethlehem straightway, the blessed babe to find (4)
390 and ever o'er its Babel sounds the blessed angels sing (2)
391 hath oped the heavenly door ... man is blessed evermore (2)
404 and God sent us salvation that blessed Christmas morn (3)
423 to Jesus, who... blessed them close folded to his breast (1)
424 who in the Lord's name comest, the King and blessed One (1)
459 thy love has blessed the wide world's wondrous story (1)
459 blessed ... with light and life since Eden's dawning day (1)
467 thy blessed unction from above is comfort, life & fire (2)
480 holy and blessed Three, Glorious Trinity, (4)
496 blessed Spirit, brooding o'er us, chase the darkness (4)
498 Father, who hast blessed us all our days (1)
504 all holy Father, Son, and equal Spirit, Trinity blessed (3)
516 Lord, let us in our homes agree .. blessed peace to gain (4)
517 since the day the blessed mother thee ... bore (2)
524 blessed is that land of God where saints abide forever (3)
524 thrice blessed ... harvest song ... never hath an ending (3)
532 they blessed the earth ... blessed of God & man forever (6)
534 baptize us with the courage with which thou blessed our (2)
534 courage with which thou blessed our dead (2)

blessedness
90 preaching the blessedness which simple trust has found (3)
268 where is... blessedness I knew when first I saw the Lord (2)
358 blessedness and light, peace & truth its course portends (2)

blesses
297 one holy name she blesses, partakes one holy food (2)
442 beauty follows all his ways, as the world he blesses (2)

blessest
181 and gladly, as thou blessest us...our first fruits give (2)

blessing
4 our peace and joy and blessing (3)
7 for his mercy ceasing never, for his blessing day by day (3)
7 wisdom, honor, power, blessing ... we cry (4)
16 though high above all praise, above all blessing high (2)
38 thou art giving and forgiving, ever blessing, ever blest (3)
56 to them and their posterity his blessing shall descend (5)
59 we gather together to ask the Lord's blessing (T,1)
88 and I shall fancy his blessing resting on me (2)
93 come, thou fount of every blessing (T,1)

165 Lord, dismiss us with thy blessing (T,1)
266 forgetting in nothing His blessing to seek (1)
276 Lord, we thy presence seek; may ours the blessing be (4)
283 thee we would be always blessing (3)
324 blessing in his hand, Christ our God to earth descendeth (1)
392 he comes to make his blessing flow (3)
399 rich in blessing, rule and might o'er all possessing (1)
409 all honor and blessing, with angels above (4)
416 bane and blessing, pain and pleasure ... are sanctified (4)
454 worship, honor, power, and blessing Christ is worthy (4)
487 thy blessing, Lord, we seek on this thy holy day (3)
489 let us now a blessing seek, waiting in his courts today (1)
495 with thy tenderest blessing may our eyelids close (2)
496 Savior, breathe an evening blessing (T,1)
505 while we kneel confessing, we humbly wait thy blessing (4)
524 we lay the first fruits of thy blessing (2)
529 speak to my heart, in blessing speak (3)
549 on homeliest work thy blessing falls (3)
550 thy blessing came, and still its power shall onward (2)

blessings
   6 blessings ... bounty ... joyful songs to thee we sing (2)
  60 dear mother earth, who day by day unfoldest blessings (4)
  60 unfoldest blessings on our way, O praise him (4)
  97 I go to him for blessings ...He gives them o'er and o'er (2)
 101 Jesus shed his precious blood rich blessings to bestow (2)
 180 praise God, from who all blessings flow (4)
 190 worlds awake to cry their blessings on the Lord of life (1)
 215 and shall break in blessings on your head (3)
 245 if blessings or sorrows prevail (3)
 325 blessings crown the board (1)
 381 God imparts to human hearts the blessings of his heaven (3)
 472 and infant voices shall proclaim their early blessings (3)
 472 their early blessings on his name (3)
 472 blessings abound where'er he reigns (4)
 493 praise God, from whom all blessings flow (5)
 493 for all the blessings of the light (1)
 502 watch by the sick; enrich the poor with blessings (5)
 502 blessings from thy boundless store (5)
 523 for all the blessings earth displays (3)
 525 for all the blessings of the year (T,1)
 530 Christ, from whom all blessings flow (T,1)

blest
  19 ye patriarchs and prophets blest (3)
  25 blest is the man that trusts in thee (4)
  38 thou art giving and forgiving, ever blessing, ever blest (3)
  52 how are thy servants blest, O Lord (T,1)
  56 experience will decide how blest are they (3)
  56 blest are they, and only they, who in his truth confide (3)
  82 sweeter sound than thy blest name, O Savior of mankind (2)
 101 believe in him without delay, and you are fully blest (3)
 110 bring him thy burden and thou shalt be blest (2)
 143 blest Savior, then, in love, fear and distrust remove (4)
 147 blest be the tempest, kind the storm (2)
 168 a blest eternity I'll spend triumphant in his grace (3)
 177 at thy blest mercy seat, pleading for me (2)
 214 the righteous ones shall be forever blest (T,1)

223   not a frown ... cross, but is blest if we trust and obey (2)
224   I in my Savior am happy and blest (3)
227   by my Savior possessed, I was perfectly blest (5)
249   blest Savior, introduced by thee have I my race begun (4)
250   the troubled heart thy comfort blest (4)
255   and none more blest than I (3)
272   so long thy power hath blest me (3)
274   speak! and make me blest indeed (3)
276   blest are the pure in heart for they shall see ... God (T,1)
291   when I shall reach that happy place ... be forever blest (3)
294   the Church our blest Redeemer saved (1)
295   blest are they in thy house that dwell (5)
295   blest is the man whose strength thou art (5)
297   with the vision glorious, her longing eyes are blest (3)
303   Jerusalem the golden, with milk and honey blest (T,1)
303   who art, with God the Father and Spirit, ever blest (4)
306   blest be the tie that binds our hearts in Christian love (T)
329   blest, when our faith can hold thee fast (4)
338   blest be the dear uniting love that will not let us part (T)
352   a joyful sacrifice to thy blest name (2)
365   but the blest volume thou hast writ reveals thy justice (2)
365   till Christ has all the nations blest (4)
445   what joy the blest assurance gives (1,4)
451   how blest are they who have not seen (4)
461   let thy Church on earth become blest as the Church above (3)
463   blest and Holy Trinity, praise forever be to thee (3)
472   and all the sons of want are blest (4)
488   we reach the rest remaining to spirits of the blest (4)
488   Church her voice upraises to thee, blest Three in One (4)
490   may this day be blest, trusting Jesus' love (3)
498   with so blest a friend provided, we upon our way ... go (2)
528   blest with this antepast of heaven (2)
536   thy name, O Jesus, be forever blest, Alleluia, Alleluia (1)
536   O blest communion, fellowship divine (4)

blight
242   God's new Messiah, offering each the bloom or blight (1)

blind
  1   ye blind, behold your Savior come (6)
  9   the Lord pours eyesight on the blind (3)
 92   was blind, but now I see (1)
102   ye poor, and maimed, and halt, and blind (3)
116   I am poor and weak and blind (1)
119   poor, wretched, blind; sight, riches, healing of... mind (4)
125   heal the sick, and lead the blind (3)
136   mists ... of doubt which blind our eyes to thee (2)
215   blind unbelief is sure to err and scan his work in vain (5)
311   may she guide the poor and blind (3)
411   where'er they heal the maimed and blind (3)
462   let us find thy hand when sorrows leave us blind (4)
480   health to the sick in mind, sight to the inly blind (2)
481   bitter lips in blind despair cry (3)

blinded
467   dullness of our blinded sight (2)

blindly
269 blindly we stumble when we walk alone (3)

blindness
344 blindness both of heart and mind (2)
469 light to man's blindness, O be thou our aid (1)

blinds
476 teach us to ban .. ugliness that blinds our eyes to thee (4)

bliss
50 so that earth's bliss may be our guide ... not our chain (3)
63 bliss he wakes and woe he lightens (1)
142 whate'er may come, I'll taste ... the hallowed bliss (4)
142 tastes even now the hallowed bliss of an eternal home (4)
275 the joys I feel, the bliss I share (2)
277 soon or later then translate to my eternal bliss (4)
294 and brighter bliss of heaven (5)
326 the Lamb's great bridal feast of bliss and love (5)
329 from the best bliss that earth imparts (1)
335 souls for whom the Lord did heavenly bliss forego (3)
376 but his mother only, in her maiden bliss, worshiped (3)
391 now ye hear of endless bliss (2)
416 when the sun of bliss is beaming light and love (3)
432 caused the Lord of bliss to bear the dreadful curse (1)
464 all partake the glorious bliss (1)

blissful
77 on heaven's blissful shore his goodness we'll adore (3)
128 fixed on this blissful center, rest (4)
423 and in his blissful presence eternally rejoice (3)

block
309 by thy reconciling love every stumbling block remove (2)

blood
1 his blood can make the foulest clean (4)
1 His blood availed for me (4)
69 is mercy with the Savior; there is healing in his blood (1)
93 to rescue me from danger, interposed his precious blood (2)
100 redemption in his blood throughout the world proclaim (3)
101 Jesus shed his precious blood rich blessings to bestow (2)
106 pleading nought but Jesus' blood, whisper softly (3)
114 we...his unknown peace receive & feel his blood applied (3)
119 but that thy blood was shed for me (1)
119 to thee whose blood can cleanse each spot (2)
120 let the water and the blood (1)
122 his all-redeeming love, his precious blood, to plead (2)
122 his blood atoned for all our race (2)
127 Jesus, thy blood and righteousness my beauty are (T,1)
127 thy blood and...my beauty are, my glorious dress (1)
127 Lord, I believe thy precious blood (3)
127 blood, which at the mercy seat of God...doth...plead (3)
137 make to us the God-head known, & witness with the blood (1)
137 only then, we feel our interest in his blood (2)
137 'tis thine the blood to apply and give us eyes to see (1)
189 for what are sundering strains of blood (2)
198 to spill no drop of blood (2)

208   just to trust his cleansing blood (2)
222   my hope is built on nothing less than Jesus blood and (T,1)
222   nothing less than Jesus' blood and righteousness (1)
222   his oath, his covenant, his blood support me (3)
224   born of his spirit, washed in his blood (1)
226   let thy precious blood applied keep me ... near thy side (1)
227   the favor divine I first found in the blood of the Lamb (2)
227   delight which I felt in the life-giving blood (5)
228   in the old rugged cross, stained with blood so divine (3)
229   the blood of Jesus whispers peace within (1)
282   heart that always feels thy blood so freely shed for me (1)
294   saved with his own precious blood (1)
297   with his own blood he bought her...for her life he died (1)
302   greet the blood redeemed hands on the eternal shore (5)
313   there sup with us in love divine; thy body and thy blood (2)
319   the cup in token of his blood that was for sinners shed (3)
324   in the body and the blood (2)
325   rich blood that Jesus shed to raise our souls to heaven (2)
331   banquet spreads before us of his mystic flesh and blood (1)
332   how the wine transmits his blood (1)
389   lo, he assumes our flesh and blood (3)
414   might go at last to heaven saved by his precious blood (3)
414   trust in his redeeming blood, and try his works to do (5)
420   ye all are bought with Jesus' blood (2)
420   come, feel with me his blood applied (3)
421   there is a fountain filled with blood (T,1)
421   dear dying Lamb, thy precious blood shall never lose (3)
421   thy precious blood shall never lose its power (3)
426   where the blood of Christ was shed (1,4)
431   for others' guilt the Man of Sorrows weeps in blood (3)
435   I sacrifice them to his blood (2)
454   every sin may be forgiven through .. virtue of thy blood (2)
518   but more because of Jesus' blood (3)
527   I ... gain an interest in the Savior's blood (1)

bloody
239   and sailed through bloody seas (2)

bloom
198   new arts shall bloom of loftier mold (4)
214   they gaily bloom and prosper cheerfully (2)
217   sometimes where Eden's bowers bloom (2)
242   God's new Messiah, offering each the bloom or blight (1)
452   bloom in every meadow, leaves on every bough (2)
490   birds pass high in flight, fragrant flowers now bloom (1)

blooming
79   robed in the blooming garb of spring: Jesus is fairer (2)

blossom
27   we blossom and flourish as leaves on the tree (3)
468   truth ... shall bud and blossom then (1)

blossoms
234   from the ground there blossoms red life (4)

blot
119   and waiting not to rid my soul of one dark blot (2)
281   purge me from every evil blot (3)

blow
36 when lightnings flash and storm winds blow (2)
37 clouds arise, and tempests blow by order from thy throne (3)
100 blow ye trumpet, blow! The gladly solemn sound (T,1)
136 blow, wind of God, with wisdom blow (2)
214 men of unbelief ... are like chaff the wind doth blow (3)

blows
232 from every stormy wind that blows (T,1)

blue
43 with all the blue ethereal sky (1)
485 when ever blue the sky shall gleam ... green the sod (2)
490 my heart's freed from ill, fair blue sky's above (3)
495 guard the sailors tossing on the deep, blue sea (3)
542 and skies are everywhere as blue as mine (2)

bluer
542 my country's skies are bluer than the ocean (2)

blush
239 shall I fear to own his cause .. blush to speak his name (1)

blushing
415 I hide my blushing face while his dear cross appears (4)

board
314 our sainted ones in glory seated at our Father's board (3)
325 blessings crown the board (1)
325 millions more, still on the way, around the board appear (3)
350 here gather us around thy board to keep the feast (3)

boast
79 Jesus shines purer, than all the angels heaven can boast (3)
336 then let us make our boast of his redeeming power (4)
422 pomp .. show, nor lofty pride, nor boast above the least (1)
435 forbid it, Lord, that I should boast, save in the death (2)
435 boast, save in the death of Christ, my God (2)
509 in better worlds our souls shall boast (5)
526 for none may boast himself of aught (2)

boasting
439 where's thy victory, boasting grave? Alleluia (2)

bodies
23 His sovereign power our bodies made (2)
338 our bodies may far off remove, we still are one in heart (1)

body
4 both soul and body bear your part (4)
20 the body they may kill: God's truth abideth still (4)
45 kept the folded grave-clothes where the body lay (1)
116 soul and body thine to be wholly thine forevermore (3)
305 we are not divided, all one body we (2)
313 there sup with us in love divine; thy body and thy blood (2)
316 thy body, broken for my sake, my bread from heaven (2)
324 in the body and the blood (2)

342   redeeming soul and body by water and the Word (2)
364   dear tokens of his passion still his dazzling body bears (3)
450   kept the folded grave-clothes where the body lay (1)
530   hear us, who thy nature share, who thy mystic body are (1)
546   cleanse the body of this nation through the glory (2)
546   cleanse the body ... through the glory of the Lord (2)

body's
411   friends in lands afar who battle with the body's ills (2)
411   battle with the body's ills and wage the holy war (2)

boisterious
247   boisterious waves obey thy will (2)

bold
127   bold shall I stand in thy great day (2)
171   give us a conscience bold and good (3)
243   who gainst enthroned wrong stood confident and bold (1)
253   bold to take up, firm to sustain the consecrated cross (2)
341   bold to confess thy glorious name before a world of foes (4)
527   bold I approach the eternal throne, and claim the crown (4)
536   O may thy soldiers, faithful, true, and bold (3)

boldly
238   Christian, answer boldly, "While I breathe I pray" (3)
246   renew it boldly every day, and help divine implore (2)

bond
128   O happy bond, that seals my vows to him (2)
128   and bless in death a bond so dear (5)
193   this is the bond of perfectness, thy spotless charity (6)
411   bind strong the bond of brotherhood of those who fight (1)

bondage
105   shall I give no heed, but still in bondage live (4)
369   then shall all bondage cease, all fetters fall (2)
408   freedom her bondage breaks, and night is turned to day (1)

bonds
89   in bonds my perfect liberty (4)
200   whom shall I send to loosen the bonds of shame and greed (1
213   O burst these bonds and set it free (1)

bones
486   whose bones lie white along the trail (2)

book
131   unseal the sacred book (2)
370   book of books, our people's strength (T,1)

books
370   book of books, our people's strength (T,1)

borders
300   joyful stand on the borders of our land (3)
551   with peace our borders bless (2)

bore
76	faithfully he bore it spotless to the last (3)
80	who like thee so humbly bore the scorn ... scoffs of men (3)
83	he bore the shameful cross ... carried all my grief (2)
420	Father's coeternal Son bore all my sins upon the tree (1)
430	love, which bore the cross for us (2)
458	the cross he bore is life and health (6)
479	whose love ... bore the weight of human need (1)
517	thee, the world's Redeemer bore (2)
517	since the day the blessed mother thee ... bore (2)

born
224	born of his spirit, washed in his blood (1)
264	the solemn hush of nature newly born (2)
264	still, still with thee! as to each new-born morning (3)
270	on thee we cast each earth-born care (1)
284	purge away my sin; from earth-born passions set me free (1)
285	first-born sons of light desire in vain its depths...see (2)
292	new-born souls, whose days, reclaimed from error's ways (4)
324	King of kings, yet born of Mary (3)
343	may earth-born passions die (3)
345	storm of earth-born passion dies (4)
360	born to set thy people free (1)
360	born thy people to deliver, born a child and yet a King (2)
360	born to reign in us forever (2)
361	for unto us a child is born, to us a son is given (2)
374	Christ the Lord, the new-born King (3)
375	love was born at Christmas; star & angels gave the sign (1)
378	in Bethlehem in Jewry this blessed babe was born (2)
378	how that in Bethlehem was born the Son of God by name (3)
378	for Jesus Christ our Savior was born upon this day (1)
379	Christ is born their choirs are singing (1)
381	for Christ is born of Mary, and gathered all above (2)
381	cast out our sin, and enter in, be born in us today (4)
382	come and worship, worship Christ, the new-born King (R)
383	Noel, Noel, Noel, Noel, born is the King of Israel (R)
386	come and behold him, born the King of angels (1)
386	yea, Lord, we greet thee, born this happy morning (3)
387	glory to the new-born King (1)
387	Christ is born in Bethlehem (1)
387	hail the heaven-born Prince of Peace (3)
387	mild he lays his glory by, born that man no more may die (3)
387	born to raise the sons of earth (3)
387	born to give them second birth (3)
388	glory to the new-born King (R)
391	give ye heed to what we say: Jesus Christ is born today (1)
391	Jesus Christ was born for this (2)
391	Christ was born for this (2)
391	Jesus Christ was born to save (3)
391	Christ is born today (1)
391	Christ was born to save (3)
393	Christ the Savior is born (2,4)
394	to you in David's town, this day is born of David's line (3)
396	Christ the babe was born for you (2)
402	born a King on Bethlehem's plain (2)
404	over the hills and everywhere ... Jesus Christ is born (R)
404	down in a lowly manger the humble Christ was born (3)

474　so a soul that's born of　God longs to view his... face (2)
497　may we, born anew like morning, to labor rise (2)
502　O may no earth-born cloud arise to hide thee (1)
527　in vain the first-born seraph tries to sound the depths (2)
545　in...beauty of the lilies Christ was born across the sea(4)

borne
431　from heavenly plains is borne the song that angels know (4)
454　hail ... universal Savior who hast borne our sin & shame (1)

borrow
418　language shall I borrow to thank thee, dearest friend (3)

borrowed
234　my heart restores its borrowed ray (2)
422　so lowly doth the Savior ride a paltry borrowed beast (T,1)

borrows
37　all that borrows life from thee is ever in thy care (3)

bosom
121　blessed Lord & only Savior, with thy love our bosom fill (4)
125　Jesus, lover of my soul,let me to thy bosom fly (T,1)
126　Jesus, lover of my soul,let me to thy bosom fly (T,1)
184　on thy bosom it has leant and found in thee its life (4)
229　on Jesus' bosom naught but calm is found (3)
291　I shall see my Father's face, and in his bosom rest (3)
517　didst deign a child to be cradled on a mother's bosom (1)
521　safely in his bosom gather (1)
545　with a glory in his bosom that transfigures you and me (4)

bough
452　bloom in every meadow, leaves on every bough (2)

bought
62　with that precious life he bought us (2)
121　blessed Jesus! thou hast bought us, thine we are (1)
232　it is the blood-bought mercy seat (2)
297　with his own blood he bought her...for her life he died (1)
420　ye all are bought with Jesus' blood (2)

bound
23　bound every heart with rapturous joy (3)
24　formed the deeps unknown ... gave the seas their bound (2)
100　let all the nations know, to earth's remotest bound (1)
135　be my Lord, and I shall be firmly bound, forever free (4)
163　and thus he bound me to him (1)
221　bound to him eternally by love's strong cord (3)
299　behold how many thousands still are lying bound (2)
299　bound in darksome prison-house of sin (2)
355　upon a cross ... bound thee & mocked thy saving kingship (1)
434　beaten, bound, reviled, arraigned (2)
470　fears and doubts too long have bound us (2)
527　long my imprisoned spirit lay fast bound in sin (3)
527　fast bound in sin and nature's night (3)
538　whose arm hath bound the restless wave (1)

boundaries
173 knows not race nor station as boundaries of the mind (4)

bounding
262 my bounding heart shall own thy sway & echo to thy voice (3)
310 Lord, let every bounding heart the mighty comfort feel (4)

boundless
58 bless the same boundless giver (4)
201 in thy great salvation, show forth thy boundless love (3)
240 His boundless mercy will provide (2)
259 Jesus, thy boundless love to me (T,1)
334 and the Father's boundless love (1)
480 boundless as ocean's tide rolling in fullest pride (4)
502 blessings from thy boundless store (5)

bounds
304 thy bounds are known to God alone,for they are set above (2)
536 from earth's wide bounds, from ocean's farthest coast (6)

bounteous
49 O may this bounteous God though all our life be near us (2)
152 whate'er thy bounteous grace hath given (4)
258 Our God's bounteous gifts abuse not, Light refuse not (4)
511 God ... the source of bounteous yield (1)
515 how wide the bounteous love is spread (3)
524 now, on this... festal day thy bounteous hand confessing (2)
548 not alone for bounteous harvests lift we up our hearts (1)
552 thy bounteous goodness nourish us in peace (3)

bounties
181 may we thy bounties thus as stewards true receive (2)

bountiful
473 thy bountiful care, what tongue can recite (4)

bounty
6 blessings ... bounty ... joyful songs to thee we sing (2)
83 from his bounty I receive such proofs of love divine (4)
104 ye needy, come ... welcome; God's free bounty glorify (2)
486 those who give up life's bounty to serve a race to be (2)
509 by his incessant bounty fed (2)

bow
8 Lord of all, we bow before thee (1)
11 rainbow arch, his covenant sign (2)
17 then I shall bow in humble adoration (4)
22 ye nations, bow with sacred joy (1)
24 come, worship at this throne; come, bow before the Lord (3)
41 humbly now we bow before thee (1)
66 saints triumphant, bow before him (4)
74 given the name to which all knees shall bow (4)
76 at the name of Jesus every knee shall bow (T,1)
78 all hearts must bow; all things celestial thee shall own (2)
95 at the cross of Christ I bow (1)
110 come with thy sins; at his feet lowly bow (3)
116 humbly at thy cross I bow, save me, Jesus, save me now (4)

128   till in life's latest hour I bow (5)
154   as in thy presence humbly I bow (2)
177   in love my soul would bow, my heart fulfill its vow (1)
302   one army of the living God, to his command we bow (4)
332   angels round our altars bow to search it out in vain (3)
357   powers, dominions, bow before him & extol our God & King (
391   ox and ass before him bow and he is in the manger now (1)
425   bow thy meek head to mortal pain (4)
453   every knee to him shall bow (1)
468   all shall frame to bow them low before thee, Lord (3)
484   O God of earth and altar, bow down and hear our cry (T,1)
535   and bow before thy throne (3)

bowed
459   to thee in reverent love our hearts are bowed (2)

bower
468   justice, from her heavenly bower look down on mortal men (1

bowers
217   sometimes where Eden's bowers bloom (2)

bowing
87   at the name of Jesus bowing (4)

bows
428   see ... he bows his sacred head ... bows his head & dies (3)

boy
380   for the virgin's sweet boy is the Lord of the earth (2)

boyhood
171   boyhood faith that shown thy whole life through (1)
171   we thank thee for thy boyhood faith (1)

brace
160   and brace thy heart and nerve thine arm (2)

brain
173   that learns to value beauty, in heart or brain or soul (4)
198   in every heart and brain shall throb the pulse of one (3)

branch
88   waving a branch of a palm tree high in my hand (3)
423   victor palm branch waving, and chanting clear and loud (2)

branches
214   in drought their branches grow abundantly (2)

brand
528   a brand plucked from eternal fire (1)

brave
156   I would be brave, for there is much to dare (1)
198   they shall be gentle, brave, and strong (2)
242   then it is the brave man chooses (2)
333   of patient hope and quiet, brave endurance (2)

532   praise we the wise and brave and strong (2)
532   wise and brave and strong who graced their generation (2)
536   and hearts are brave again, and arms are strong (5)
545   he is wisdom to the mighty, he is honor to the brave (5)

bravely
135   by thee may I strongly live, bravely bear & nobly strive (3)

bread
  47   be thou for us in life our daily bread (3)
  84   give milk...bread or solid food as fits my understanding(3)
103   here see the bread of life; see waters flowing (3)
129   or cry in the desert for bread (3)
161   bringing to hungry souls the bread of life (2)
205   feeds me with the living bread (2)
231   and he who feeds the ravens will give his children bread (3)
271   bread of heaven, feed me till I want no more (1)
296   with bread of life earth's hunger feed (4)
307   giving in Christ the bread eternal (2)
307   as grain ... was in this broken bread made one (4)
313   be known to us in breaking bread, but do not then depart (T)
313   that living bread ... heavenly wine be our immortal food (2)
314   for the bread, which thou hast broken (T.1)
315   furnished with mystic wine and everlasting bread (1)
316   thy body, broken for my sake, my bread from heaven (2)
317   the bread of life, for all men broken (T,1)
318   bread ... for our good, thy glory, given (2)
318   Jesus, bread of life, I pray thee (3)
319   by faith we take the bread of life (3)
319   bread of life with which our souls are fed (3)
320   bread of the world in mercy broken (T,1)
321   the bread is always consecrate which men divide with men (2)
322   bread of the world in mercy broken (T,1)
323   bread of the world in mercy broken (T,1)
326   here would I feed upon the bread of God (3)
326   the bread and wine remove: but thou art here (4)
328   many, and yet but one are we, one undivided bread (2)
328   one with the living bread divine ... now by faith we eat (3)
329   we taste thee, O thou living bread (3)
330   let us break bread together on our knees (T,1)
331   precious banquet, bread of heaven (1)
332   how the bread his flesh imparts (1)
332   who shall say how bread and wine God into man conveys (1)
332   drink herewith divine supplies and eat immortal bread (3)
368   bread of our souls whereon we feed (2)
369   break thou the bread of life, dear Lord, to me (T,1)
369   as thou didst bless the bread by Galilee (2)
438   then let us feast this Easter Day on the true bread (4)
438   feast this Easter Day on the true bread of heaven (4)
479   still the hungry cry for bread (2)
481   from women struggling sore for bread (2)
513   much more, to us his children, he gives our daily bread (2)
515   give us this day our daily bread (1)
515   not e'en the power by which we toil for bread are ours (2)
515   wide as the want of daily bread (3)
515   with which our daily bread we gain (4)

518   give us each day our daily bread (2)
518   the bread of life sent down from heaven (3)
524   who didst give us daily bread, give us the bread eternal (2)

breadth
130   the length,and breadth, and height to prove (1)
130   throughout the world its breadth is known (3)
285   cannot reach the mystery ... length .. breadth .. height (2)
304   the length, the breadth, the height are one (2)

break
215   and shall break in blessings on your head (3)
290   the bruised reed he will not break, but strengthen (2)
330   let us break bread together on our knees (T,1)
356   break forth, O living light of   God (T,1)
356   break forth ... upon the world's dark hour (1)
359   he comes to break oppression, to set the captive free (1)
369   break thou the bread of life, dear Lord, to me (T,1)
369   as thou didst break the loaves beside the sea (1)
373   break forth, O beauteous heavenly light (T,1)
422   thus the great Messiah came to break the tyrant's will (3)
428   but soon he'll break death's envious chain (4)
451   that Easter morn at break of day (2)
529   and wrestle till the break of day (1)
547   let rocks their silence break, the sound prolong (3)

breakers
11   breakers crashing on the shore (3)
247   when at last I near the shore ... fearful breakers roar (3)

breaketh
264   still, still with thee, when purple morning breaketh (T,1)

breaking
258   now is breaking o'er the earth another day (1)
313   be known to us in breaking bread, but do not then depart (T)
373   the power of Satan breaking, our peace eternal making (1)
440   all around the clouds are breaking (1)

breaks
1   He breaks the power of canceled sin (4)
36   and when the morning breaks in power, we hear thy word (3)
189   the day of dawning brotherhood breaks on our eager eyes (1)
257   till thy spirit breaks our night with the beams of truth (2)
289   heaven's morning breaks, and earth's vain shadows flee (5)
353   when morning dawns and light triumphant breaks (1)
408   freedom her bondage breaks, and night is turned to day (1)
428   temple's veil in sunder breaks ... solid marbles rend (2)
478   gladness breaks like morning where'er thy face appears (3)
496   the perfect day before us breaks in everlasting light (4)
498   give us strength to serve and wait till the glory breaks (3)
498   thy glory breaks before us through the city's open gate (3)
529   the morning breaks, the shadows flee (4)

breast
23   burn every breast with Jesus' love (3)
81   and calms the troubled breast (2)

82	thought of thee with sweetness fills the breast (1)
117	weary one, lay down, thy head upon my breast (1)
128	here heavenly pleasures fill my breast (4)
207	lean, weary one, upon his breast (4)
242	who would keep abreast of truth (3)
247	while leaning on thy breast may I hear thee (3)
251	'twill but drive me to thy breast (3)
252	the motion of a hidden fire that trembles in the breast (1)
260	good and ill, deep buried in each breast (2)
268	I hate the sins that ... drove thee from my breast (4)
269	sins that...drove me from my breast (4)
283	O breathe thy loving spirit into every troubled breast (2)
362	and fold the lambs to his breast (3)
423	to Jesus, who... blessed them close folded to his breast (1)
476	O God of love, whose spirit wakes in every human breast (2)
502	rest forever on my Savior's breast (2)
516	and love fills every breast (1)
533	his zeal inspired their breast (2)

breath

9	I'll praise my maker while I've breath (T,1)
9	I'll praise him while he lends me breath (4)
15	praise the Lord in every breath (3)
23	our souls are his immortal breath (2)
51	publish with our latest breath thy love & guardian care (4)
55	all that hath life and breath, come now with praises (4)
60	death, waiting to hush our latest breath (6)
81	proclaim with every fleeting breath (5)
83	to him I owe my life and breath and all the joys I have (3)
120	while I draw this fleeting breath (3)
133	Breathe on me breath of God (T,1,2,3,4)
133	breathe on me, breath of God, fill me with life anew (T,1)
140	what did thine only Son endure before I drew my breath (2)
185	then shall my latest breath whisper thy praise (4)
246	take thee, at thy parting breath, to his divine abode 4)
252	prayer is the Christian's vital breath (5)
291	no chilling winds or poisonous breath can reach (2)
316	while a breath, a pulse remains, will I remember thee (3)
341	happy, if with my latest breath I may but gasp his name (6)
411	will is life and good for all of mortal breath (1)
445	He lives, and grants me daily breath (3)
533	with united breath, ascribe their conquest to the Lamb (1)

breathe

87	if temptations round you gather, breathe that holy name (2)
87	breathe that holy name in prayer (2)
132	come, thou source of joy and gladness, breathe thy life (1)
133	Breathe on me breath of God (T,1,2,3,4)
133	breathe on me, breath of God, fill me with life anew (1)
137	thou take the veil away and breathe the living Word (2)
184	flag can ...be unfurled when thou... breathe from heaven (3)
188	breathe into every wish thy will divine (1)
235	breathe through the pulses of desire thy coolness (5)
238	Christian answer boldly, "While I breathe I pray" (3)
264	so does this blessed consciousness, awaking, breathe (3)
264	breathe each day nearness unto thee and heaven (3)
283	O breathe thy loving spirit into every troubled breast (2)
496	Savior, breathe an evening blessing (T,1)
547	let mortal tongues awake; let all that breathe partake (3)

breathes
139 whose Spirit breathes the active flame (1)
402 myrrh is mine; its bitter perfume breathes ... gloom (4)
402 breathes a life of gathering gloom (4)
473 it breathes in the air, it shines in the light (4)

breathless
264 alone with thee in breathless adoration (2)
434 tomb where they laid his breathless clay (4)

breeze
17 and hear the brook and feel the gentle breeze (2)
184 it wants the needed fire to glow ... the breeze to nerve (3)
343 there is a voice in every star, in every breeze a song (1)
547 let music swell the breeze (3)

breezes
513 the breezes and the sunshine, and soft, refreshing rain (1)

brethren
108 shame on us,Christian brethren, his name & sign who bear (1)
178 one with thyself, may every eye in us, thy brethren see (4)
300 fear not, brethren; joyful stand (3)
319 brethren, all, let every heart with kind affection glow (2)
379 brethren, come, from all that grieves you, you are freed (2)
528 come, O my guilty brethren, come (5)
538 O Trinity of love and power, our brethren shield (4)
538 our brethren shield in danger's hour (4)

bridal
326 the Lamb's great bridal feast of bliss and love (5)

bride
297 from heaven he came and sought her to be his holy bride (1)

Bridegroom
366 the Bridegroom comes, awake (1)

bridle
84 to untamed colt, the bridle, (1)

brief
346 his hands built not for one brief day (1)
549 scarcely can we turn aside for one brief hour of prayer (2)

bright
19 bright seraphs, cherubim and thrones (1)
29 o splendor of God's glory bright (T,1)
31 his glories shine with beams so bright (1)
34 all things bright and beautiful (T,R)
39 his beauties, how divinely bright (2)
50 my God, I thank thee,who hast made the earth so bright (T,1)
58 the fire divine ... still goeth bright before us (2)
60 thou fire so masterful and bright (3)
80 who like thee so mild, so bright ... did ever go (2)

117   look unto me, thy morn shall rise ... thy day be bright (3)
142   faith that shines more bright & clear when tempests rage (3)
166   I'll ever adore thee in heaven so bright (3)
186   thy bright example I pursue, to thee in all things rise (4)
209   all now mysterious shall be bright at last (2)
215   he treasures up his bright designs (2)
230   bright skies will soon be o'er me, where darkest clouds (3)
233   bright youth and snow-crowned age (2)
251   show thy face, and all is bright (2)
256   may I reach heaven's joys, O bright heaven's Sun (4)
263   then, with my waking thoughts bright with thy praise (4)
264   so shall it be the last, in that bright morning (5)
303   and bright with many an angel, and all the martyr throng (2)
329   make all our moments calm and bright (5)
379   hail the star, that from far bright with hope is burning (3)
393   all is calm, all is bright (1)
397   leading onward, beaming bright (1)
399   O morning star, how fair and bright (T,1)
402   star with royal beauty bright (R)
403   thine shall be a path, though thorny, bright (4)
408   the Day-star clear and bright of every man and nation (1)
410   and the dawning to noon-day bright (R)
418   how does that visage languish .. once was bright as morn (1)
433   the bright and morning star shed its beams around me (2)
440   O to enter that bright portal (4)
446   the queen of seasons, bright with the day of splendor (3)
450   angels in bright raiment rolled the stone away (1)
454   help, ye bright angelic spirits (4)
456   and have the bright immensities received our risen Lord (T)
488   O balm of care and sadness, most beautiful, most bright (1)
495   grant to little children visions bright of thee (3)
513   we thank thee...O Father, for all things bright & good (3)
524   bright robes of gold the fields adorn (1)
533   how great their joys, how bright their glories be (1)
547   long may our land be bright with freedom's holy light (4)

brighten
318   sun, who all my life dost brighten (2)

brightens
34   the sunset, and the morning that brightens up the sky (2)
63   God is love; his mercy brightens (T,1)
63   his mercy brightens all the path in which we rove (1)
333   grant them the joy which brightens earthly sorrow (3)

brighter
33   splendors ... burn brighter through the cold (2)
79   and all the twinkling starry host: Jesus shines brighter (3)
194   to brighter hopes and kindlier things (1)
226   lost in love, in a brighter, brighter world above (3)
234   in thy sunshine's blaze its day may brighter, fairer be (2)
294   and brighter bliss of heaven (5)
299   O Zion, haste to bring the brighter day (4)
353   brighter than the rising morn when he, victorious, rose (3)
353   brighter than the glorious morn ... this fair morning be (4)
382   brighter visions beam afar (3)
498   every day will be the brighter when ... thy face we see (3)

brightest
    50   that shadows fall on brightest hours, that thorns remain (3)
  294   Zion ... be given the brightest glories earth can yield (5)
  400   brightest and best of the sons of the morning (T,1)

brightly
  148   brightly beams our Father's mercy (T,1)
  317   lighten our eyes, brightly appear (3)
  395   heaven's star shone brightly forth, glory all around him (2)
  498   praise for light so brightly shining on our steps (1)

brightness
    63   through the gloom his brightness streameth (3)
  284   when this life is past, I may the eternal brightness see (5)
  460   Christ the ... brightness of the Father's glory (2)

bring
    14   your lofty themes, ye mortals, bring (3)
    15   all the powers of music bring, the music of the heart (2)
    54   as thou didst to them, to us deliverance bring (4)
    58   we bring thee, Lord, the praise they brought (1)
    58   their joy unto their Lord we bring (3)
    66   to his feet thy tribute bring (1)
    71   bring forth the royal diadem and crown him Lord of all (1)
    79   freely and joyously now would we bring (2)
    81   accept the praise I bring (3)
    86   hither our children bring to shout thy praise (1)
    98   such ever bring thee where they come (2)
    98   and bring all heaven before our eyes (4)
  103   here bring your wounded hearts, here tell your anguish (1)
  110   bring him thy burden and thou shalt be blest (2)
  120   in my hand no price I bring; simply to thy cross I cling (2)
  125   my trust on thee is stayed ... help from thee I bring (2)
  129   and let the sweet tokens of pardoning grace bring joy (4)
  129   bring joy to my desolate heart (4)
  157   we may not climb ... to bring the Lord Christ down (2)
  168   when my dear Lord will bring me home (3)
  174   bring ... day of brotherhood ... end the night of wrong (2)
  177   some offering bring thee now, something for thee (1)
  179   freely and joyously now would we bring (2)
  224   angels descending, bring from above echoes of mercy (2)
  231   let the unknown tomorrow bring with it what it may (2)
  231   it can bring with it nothing but he will bear us through (3)
  237   bring to my remembrance sad Gethsemane (2)
  239   by faith they bring it night (5)
  242   ere her cause bring fame and profit (2)
  246   fight on, my soul, till death...bring thee to thy God (4)
  251   heaven will bring me sweeter rest (3)
  276   the Lord, who left the throne our life & peace to bring (2)
  277   bring the glorious liberty from sorrow, fear and sin (1)
  292   the world to Christ we bring, with loving zeal (1)
  292   the world to Christ we bring, with fervent prayer (2)
  292   the world to Christ we bring, with one accord (3)
  292   the world to Christ we bring, with joyful song (4)
  295   even thine own altars, where she safe ... may bring (4)

299   O Zion, haste to bring the brighter day (4)
303   Jesus, in mercy bring us to that dear land of rest (4)
312   we bring them, Lord, in thankful hands (3)
342   in heaven & earth thy power ... bring God's kingdom here (4)
343   to God the powers that dwell on high ... tribute bring (2)
343   their tuneful tribute bring (2)
344   discipline ... to train and bring them up for heaven (1)
352   glad songs to thee we sing; glad hearts to thee we bring (4)
355   doomed to death, must bring to doom the power (2)
355   O love that triumphs over loss we bring our hearts (4)
355   we bring our hearts before thy cross (4)
360   now thy gracious kingdom bring (2)
376   if I were a shepherd, I would bring a lamb (4)
377   to you the joyous news we bring (3)
380   Ay! we shout to the lovely evangel they bring (4)
385   so bring him incense, gold, and myrrh (3)
385   haste to bring him laud, the babe, the son of Mary (R)
394   glad tidings of great joy I bring to you and all mankind (2)
397   all our costliest treasures bring, Christ to thee (3)
397   treasures bring, Christ, to thee, our heavenly King (3)
397   bring our ransomed souls at last where they need no star (4)
402   gold I bring to crown him again (2)
406   pass on and carry swift the news ye bring (1)
420   crucified for me and you to bring us rebels near to God (2)
424   accept the prayers we bring (3)
427   that, as we share this hour, thy cross may bring ... joy (4)
427   thy cross may bring us to thy joy and resurrection power (4)
433   near the cross .. Lamb of God bring its scenes before me (3)
445   He lives, to bring me safely there (3)
449   to all the world glad news we bring (1)
449   bring flowers of song to strew his way (2)
450   bring us safe through Jordan to thy home above (3)
454   thou didst free salvation bring (1)
454   bring your sweetest, noblest lays (4)
454   who died, eternal life to bring (2)
464   to bring fire on earth he came (1)
470   bring her bud to glorious flower (1)
472   let every creature rise and bring his grateful honors (5)
477   bring to our troubled minds, uncertain and afraid (2)
477   bring justice to our land, that all may dwell secure (3)
477   bring to our world of strife thy sovereign word of peace (4)
479   we, thy servants, bring the worship not of voice alone (1)
480   thou who didst come to bring ... healing and sight (2)
480   didst come to bring on thy redeeming wing (2)
489   bring relief for all complaints (4)
504   bring us to heaven, where thy saints united joy (2)
510   bring the grand sabbatic year, the jubilee of heaven (6)
511   so we today first fruits would bring (1)
522   even so,Lord, quickly come, bring thy final harvest home (4)
524   bring sacrifice of praise ... shouts of exultation (1)

bringest
29   o thou that bringest light from light (1)
85   God's light to earth thou bringest to drive sin's night (1)
85   God's thought to earth thou bringest (2)
85   God's love to earth thou bringest in living deeds (3)
85   God's will to earth thou bringest that all ... may learn (4)
362   O Zion, that bringest good tidings, get thee up (2)

bringing
41   bringing suns and stars to birth (1)
132   bringing down the richest treasure man can wish (1)
161   bringing to hungry souls the bread of life (2)
370   bringing freedom, spreading truth (1)

brings
89   comfort it brings and power and peace (2)
104   every grace that brings you nigh (2)
197   the chance of life that each day brings (1)
353   light and beauty brings (5)
358   traveler, yes; it brings the day, promised day of Israel (1)
385   the King of kings salvation brings (3)
387   light and life to all he brings (3)
438   and brings us life from heaven (1)
442   brothers, praise him, for he brings all to resurrection (3)
453   rich the trophies Jesus brings (2)
505   brings the night its peace profound (1)
525   common things which every day and hour brings (2)

brink
142   that will not tremble on the brink of any earthly woe (1)

broad
304   deep in loving human hearts its broad foundations rise (1)
498   spread thy love's broad banner o'er us (3)
524   where golden fields spread fair and broad (3)

broadening
170   far down the future's broadening way (4)

broader
69   love of God is broader than the measure of man's mind (2)

broke
407   the heart that bled and broke to send God's love (1)

broken
1   mournful, broken hearts rejoice; the humble poor believe (5)
42   laws which never shall be broken (1)
89   the healing of my broken heart (3)
119   thy love unknown hath broken every barrier down (6)
145   heal my wounded, broken spirit, save me by thy grace (3)
146   they are but broken lights of thee (4)
175   chords that were broken will vibrate once more (3)
199   restores the lost, and binds the spirit broken (2)
293   he, whose word cannot be broken formed thee (1)
307   as grain ... was in this broken bread made one (4)
314   for the bread, which thou hast broken (T.1)
316   thy body, broken for my sake, my bread from heaven (2)
317   the bread of life, for all men broken (T,1)
320   bread of the world in mercy broken (T,1)
320   look on the heart by sorrow broken (2)
322   bread of the world in mercy broken (T,1)
323   bread of the world in mercy broken (T,1)
429   middle wall is broken down and all mankind may enter in (2)

brood
- 131   brood o'er our nature's night (3)
- 538   O Holy Spirit, who didst brood upon the waters (3)
- 538   who didst brood upon the waters dark and rude (3)

brooding
- 407   thy Spirit's ceaseless, brooding power (3)
- 496   blessed Spirit, brooding o'er us, chase the darkness (4)

broods
- 189   one tender comfort broods upon the struggling human soul (3)

brook
- 17   and hear the brook and feel the gentle breeze (2)
- 368   brook by the traveler's way (1)

brother
- 35   for the joy of human love, brother, sister, parent,child (4)
- 38   brother love binds man to man (4)
- 38   thou our Father, Christ our brother (3)
- 168   then with my Savior, brother, friend (3)
- 189   here together, brother men, we pledge the Lord anew (2)
- 199   O brother man, fold to thy heart thy brother (T,1)
- 202   beside us walks our brother Christ (1)
- 202   our brother Christ ... makes our task his own (1)
- 202   brotherhood still rests in him, the brother of us all (2)
- 469   O give us brother love for better seeing (4)
- 482   O Christ, Redeemer, Brother, Friend, ride on, ride on (4)

brother's
- 193   and feel his brother's care (2)

brotherhood
- 136   earth ... form one brotherhood by whom thy will is done (3)
- 173   who would unite the nations in brotherhood for all (3)
- 174   bring ... day of brotherhood ... end the night of wrong (2)
- 189   the day of dawning brotherhood breaks on our eager eyes (1)
- 189   to this clear call of brotherhood our hearts...ring (3)
- 189   call of brotherhood our hearts responsive ring (3)
- 194   visions of a larger good & holier dreams of brotherhood (1)
- 202   brotherhood still rests in him, the brother of us all (2)
- 321   every act of brotherhood repeats thy feast again (2)
- 378   with true love & brotherhood each other now embrace (4)
- 411   bind strong the bond of brotherhood of those who fight (1)
- 481   city...whose laws are love, whose ways are brotherhood (4)
- 482   men at last shall ring the bells of brotherhood (3)
- 482   ring the bells of brotherhood and peace (3)
- 532   rich in art, made richer still the brotherhood of duty (4)
- 543   crown thy good with brotherhood...sea to shining sea (1,4)
- 548   find its full fruition in the brotherhood of man (4)

brothers
- 174   as brothers of the Son of man, rise up, O men of God (4)
- 192   join hands...brothers of the faith whate'er your race (3)
- 305   brothers, we are treading where the saints have trod (2)
- 442   brothers, praise him, for he brings all to resurrection (3)

brought
16   O for the living flame from his own altar brought (3)
22   he brought us to his fold again (2)
58   we bring thee, Lord, the praise they brought (1)
67   and home, rejoicing, brought me (3)
76   brought it back victorious when from death he passed (3)
92   'tis grace hath brought me safe thus far (3)
123   I only know...matchless love...brought God's love (2)
123   only know...manger child has brought God's life to me (1)
336   yet out of all the Lord hath brought us by his love (3)
362   valleys shall be exalted, the lofty hills brought low (1)
378   unto certain shepherds brought tidings of the same (3)
412   who was the guilty? who brought this upon thee (2)
437   our Christ hath brought us over with hymns of victory (1)
446   God hath brought his Israel into joy from sadness (1)
489   God has brought us on our way (1)
499   through sleep and darkness safely brought, restored (1)
510   providence hath brought us through another various year (2)
511   as men of old their first fruits brought (T,1)
511   brought ... to God, the giver of all good (1)
511   first fruits brought of orchard, flock and field (1)

brow
83   majestic sweetness sits enghroned upon the Savior's brow(T)
99   hath he diadem, as monarch, that his brow adorns (3)
108   thorns thy brow encircle, & tears thy face have marred (2)
166   I love thee for wearing the thorns on thy brow (2)
166   I'll sing with the glittering crown on my brow (3)
355   new thorns to pierce that steady brow (1)
431   'tis midnight, and on Olive's brow (T,1)
453   crowns become the victor's brow (1)
458   a royal diadem adorns the mighty victor's brow (1)

bruised
104   come,ye weary, heavy laden bruised & mangled by the fall (4)
290   the bruised reed he will not break, but strengthen (2)

buckler
216   his faithfulness shall ever be a shield and buckler (4)

bud
468   truth from the earth, like to a flower, shall bud (1)
468   truth ... shall bud and blossom then (1)
470   bring her bud to glorious flower (1)

build
171   build us a tower of Christ-like height (2)
222   my hope is build on nothing less than Jesus blood and (T,1)
301   He bids us build each other up; and, gathered into one (3)
355   O wounded hands of Jesus, build in us thy new creation (4)
406   build ye the road, and falter not, nor stay (2)
406   Lord, give us faith and strength the road to build (3)
477   finely build for days to come foundations that endure (3)
481   give us, O God, the strength to build the city (4)
481   yea, bids us seize the whole of life and build its glory (5)

482   we go with thee to claim and build a city unto God (2)
520   build thou a hallowed dwelling (4)
520   build ... dwelling where true joy and peace endure (4)

builded
532   peaceful men of skill who builded homes of beauty (4)
545   have builded him an altar in the evening dews and damps (2)

Builder
171   O Carpenter of Nazareth, Builder of life divine (2)

builder's
347   thy will was in the builder's thought (2)

builders
348   by wise master builders squared, here be living stones (4)

building
469   building proud towers which shall not reach to heaven (3)

builds
210   who trust in God's unchanging love builds on the rock (1)
210   builds on the rock that naught can move (1)

built
31   the Lord Jehovah reigns, his throne is built on high (T,1)
37   spread the flowing seas abroad and built the lofty skies (1)
39   he framed the globe; he built the sky (2)
345   temple stands, built over earth and sea (1)
346   his hands built not for one brief day (1)
475   built while they dream, and in that dreaming weep (2)

bulwark
20   a bulwark never failing (1)

bulwarks
191   the patriots nations need ... the bulwarks of the state (4)

burden
17   that on the cross, my burden gladly bearing (3)
53   I'll drop my burden at his feet, and bear a song away (4)
110   bring him thy burden and thou shalt be blest (2)
223   not a burden we bear, not a sorrow we share (2)
244   when my life becomes a burden ... nearing chilly Jordan (4)
252   prayer is the burden of a sigh, the falling of a tear (2)
279   the burden of my soul remove, the hardness from my heart (4)
280   burden from my soul remove, the hardness from my heart (4)
417   burning of the noon-tide heat and the burden of the day (1)
498   every burden will be lighter when ... it comes from thee (3)
517   when all the work is over and we lay the burden down (5)

burdened
157   last low whispers of our dead are burdened with his name (5)
201   the hopeless and the burdened, the crippled and the weak (1)
204   from woman's grief, man's burdened toil (3)

burdening
270   on thee we fling our burdening woe (4)

burdens
53   come, cast your burdens on the Lord (1)
203   neath the burdens there, thy sovereignty has held (3)
306   we share each other's woes, our mutual burdens bear (3)
309   each the other's burdens bear (4)
479   making known the needs and burdens thy compassion bids (3)
479   needs and burdens thy compassion bids us bear (3)
505   now, our wants and burdens leaving to his care (3)
505   at his touch our burdens fall (3)

buried
175   feelings lie buried that grace can restore (3)
260   good and ill, deep buried in each breast (2)
441   now the green blade riseth from the buried grain (T,1)
452   'tis thine own third morning, rise, O buried Lord (3)

burn
23   burn every breast with Jesus' love (3)
33   splendors ... burn brighter through the cold (2)
43   all the stars that round her burn ... confirm (2)
64   kindling hearts that burn for thee (5)
136   burn, winged fire! inspire our lips with flaming love (2)
172   let it for thy glory burn with inextinguishable blaze (2)
275   anxious spirits burn with strong desires for thy return (2)
278   I only for his glory burn, and always see his face (3)
466   O let it freely burn, till earthly passions turn to dust (2)
486   O God, before whose altar the stars like tapers burn (T,1)

burning
60   thou burning sun with golden beam (1)
148   let the lower lights be burning (R)
153   grant us in this burning hour grace (1)
242   by the light of burning martyrs (3)
258   ready burning be the incense of thy powers (2)
370   light of knowledge, ever burning, shed on us (3)
379   hail the star, that from far bright with hope is burning (3)
417   burning of the noon-tide heat and the burden of the day (1)

burns
141   Have faith in God, my mind ... oft thy light burns low (2)

burst
213   O burst these bonds and set it free (1)
224   visions of rapture now burst on my sight (2)
446   Christ hath burst his prison (2)
446   who, triumphant, burst the bars of the tomb's dark portal (5)

bursts
358   ages are its own; see, it bursts o'er all the earth (2)
453   hark, those bursts of acclamation (4)

business
341   my business here below to cry, "Behold the Lamb" (5)
549   around us rolls the ceaseless tide of business (2)
549   ceaseless tide of business, toil, and care (2)

busy
 63 chance and change are busy ever (2)

buy
 104 without money, come to Jesus Christ and buy (2)

calendar
 514 all our labor ... watching, all our calendar of care (3)

call
 38 call us to rejoice in thee (2)
 48 when through the deep waters I call thee to go (3)
 76 'tis the Father's pleasure we should call him Lord (1)
 78 O Christ, thou Savior of us all ... hear us when we call (1)
 78 we pray thee, hear us when we call (1)
 84 know thee ... and call thee heavenly Father (3)
 93 streams of mercy never ceasing call for songs (1)
 93 call for songs of loudest praise (1)
 102 sent by my Lord, on you I call (2)
 102 come thou, this moment, at his call (5)
 104 not the righteous; sinners Jesus came to call (4)
 107 by thy mercies, Savior, may we hear thy call (5)
 109 sinner, list to the loving call (2)
 109 sweetly echo the gospel call (3)
 129 on whom in affliction I call (1)
 137 saves whoe'er on Jesus call, and perfects them in love (4)
 157 we own thy sway, we hear thy call (6)
 163 naught ... I have my own I call ... hold it for the giver (2
 173 O grant that love of country may help us hear his call (3)
 189 to this clear call of brotherhood our hearts ... ring (3)
 196 offer the sacrifice of praise, and call upon his name (4)
 197 in duty's call, thy call we hear to fuller life (2)
 202 centuries still we hear the Master's winsome call (2)
 221 listening every moment to the Spirit's call (4)
 228 then he'll call me some day to my home far away (4)
 236 call us, O Lord, to thine eternal peace (4)
 248 the trumpet call obey (2)
 298 to this temple, where we call thee, come, O Lord (2)
 314 by the call to heaven above us (2)
 329 thou savest those that on thee call (2)
 335 and heed the call they give (1)
 342 we hear the call, O Lord, that comes from thee (1)
 342 we call each new disciple to follow thee, O Lord (2)
 362 a call from the ways untrod (1,4)
 441 thy touch can call us back to life again (4)
 477 the quiet of a steadfast faith, calm of a call obeyed (2)
 491 call on thee that sinless the hours of dark may be (2)
 491 Lover of men, O hear our call, and guard and save us (4)
 528 outcasts of men, to you I call (4)
 530 still for more on thee we call ...who fillest all in all (2)
 531 my heart that lowly waits thy call (4)
 545 trumpet that shall never call retreat (3)

called
 18 his the voice that called a nation (1)
 56 when in distress to him I called, he to my rescue came (2)
 153 thou hast called us for this hour (R)

236 that in this house have called upon thy name (2)
419 who saw his Master in the sky, and called on him to save (2)
479 called from worship unto service, forth ... we go (4)
528 I, a child of wrath & hell ... be called a child of God (2)
529 thyself hast called me by my name (2)
534 thou hast called us to the journey (1)

callest
262 thou callest me to seek thy face,'tis all I wish to seek (4)

calleth
90 still as of old he calleth, "Follow me" (5)

calling
105 God calling yet! shall I not hear (T,1)
105 God is calling yet! (1,2,3,4,5)
110 Jesus is tenderly calling thee home (T,1)
110 calling today, calling today (1,2)
110 calling today, Jesus is tenderly calling today (R)
110 Jesus is calling the weary to rest (2)
145 while on others thou art calling, do not pass me by (1,R)
150 to serve the present age, my calling to fulfill (2)
200 the voice of God is calling its summons unto men (T,1)
235 the gracious calling of the Lord (2)
517 may we keep our holy calling stainless in... fair renown (5)

calling's
301 our high calling's glorious hope ... hand in hand go on (3)

calls
86 while in our mortal pain none calls on thee in vain (2)
105 he calls me still; can I delay (2)
105 he calls me still; my heart, awake (4)
107 Jesus calls us o'er the tumult (T,1)
107 Jesus calls us from the worship of the vain (3)
107 still he calls, in cares and pleasures (4)
107 Jesus calls us! (5)
248 where duty calls or danger, be never wanting there (3)
249 God's all-animating voice that calls thee from on high (3)
275 that calls me from a world of care (1)
312 hark, how he calls the tender lambs (1)
391 calls you one and calls you all (3)
391 calls you all to gain his everlasting hall (3)
488 to holy convocations the silver trumpet calls (3)
497 gird us for the task that calls us (2)
528 he calls you now, invites you home (5)

calm
36 we feel thy calm at evening's hour (3)
89 thou hidden source of calm repose (T,1)
95 turn me not away unblest; calm my anguish into rest (3)
144 safe ... calm ... satisfied the soul that clings to thee (4)
229 on Jesus' bosom naught but calm is found (3)
232 there is a calm, a sure retreat (1)
235 O sabbath rest by Galilee! O calm of hills above (3)
235 O still, small voice of calm (5)
264 in the calm dew and freshness of the morn (2)
266 take time to be holy, be calm in thy soul (4)

268 a calm and heavenly frame (1)
268 calm and serene my frame (6)
326 here taste afresh the calm of sin forgiven (3)
329 make all our moments calm and bright (5)
393 all is calm, all is bright (1)
437 listening to his accents, may hear, so calm and plain (2)
437 hear, so calm and plain his own "All hail" (2)
477 the quiet of a steadfast faith, calm of a call obeyed (2)
485 all pity, care, and love, all calm and courage...pour (1)
485 calm and courage, faith and hope: O pour them from above (1)
490 make my conduct good, actions calm and mild (2)
495 Jesus, give the weary calm and sweet repose (2)
505 let our vesper hymn be blending ... holy calm around (1)
538 and calm amid the storm didst sleep (2)

calming
459 and calming passion's fierce and stormy gales (3)

calmly
147 if on a quiet sea, toward heaven we calmly sail (T,1)
167 straight to my home above I travel calmly on (3)

calmness
219 calmness bends serene above, my restlessness to still (3)

calms
81 and calms the troubled breast (2)
333 grant them the peace which calms all earthly strife (3)

Calvaries
242 toiling up new Calvaries ever (3)

Calvary
74 humbling thyself to death on Calvary (3)
116 I am trusting, Lord, in thee, blessed Lamb of Calvary (4)
122 five bleeding wounds he bears, received on Calvary (3)
143 my faith looks up to thee, thou Lamb of Calvary (T,1)
228 to bear it to dark Calvary (2)
237 or, in darker semblance, cross-crowned Calvary (2)
407 show us anew in Calvary the wondrous power (1)

Calvary's
123 know not how that Calvary's cross a world ... could free (2)
123 Calvary's cross a world from sin could free (2)
166 and purchased my pardon on Calvary's tree (2)
433 healing stream flows from Calvary's mountain (1)
434 Calvary's mournful mountain climb (3)

cam'st
355 Lord Christ, when first thou cam'st to men (T,1)

came
54 thee ... from whom salvation came (5)
56 when in distress to him I called, he to my rescue came (2)
76 from the lips of sinners unto whom he came (3)
104 not the righteous; sinners Jesus came to call (4)
117 I came to Jesus as I was, weary and worn and sad (1)
117 I came to Jesus, and I drank of that life-giving stream (2)

136 so ... we know ... power of him who came mankind to save (4)
247 chart and compass came from thee (1)
297 from heaven he came and sought her to be his holy bride (1)
308 kings and empires ... of old that went and came (1)
312 for 'twas to bless such souls as these the Lord...came (2)
312 the Lord of angels came (2)
332 explains the wondrous way how through these virtues came (2)
370 till they came, who told the story of the   Word (2)
375 love came down at Christmas (T,1)
378 from God our heavenly Father a blessed angel came (3)
383 and by the light of that same star three wise men came (3)
383 three wise men came from country far (3)
390 it came upon the midnight clear (T,1)
394 the angel of the Lord came down, and glory shone around (1)
405 out of thee the Lord from heaven came to rule his Israel (1)
419 a glorious band, the chosen few on whom the Spirit came (3)
422 thus the great Messiah came to break the tyrant's will (3)
441 forth he came at Easter, like the risen grain (3)
455 rose victorious in the strife for those he came to save (2)
464 to bring fire on earth he came (1)
528 he came the lost to seek and save (4)
533 I ask them whence their victory came (1)
550 thy blessing came, and still its power shall onward (2)
550 laws, freedom, truth, and faith in God came (3)
550 faith in God came with those exiles o'er the waves (3)

camest
74 thou camest to us in lowliness of thought (2)
172 O thou who camest from above (T,1)

camp
211 though hosts encamp around me, firm in the fight I stand (1)
534 may the shadow of thy presence around our camp be spread (2)

camps
545 I have seen him in the watchfires of a hundred ... camps (2)
545 watchfires of a hundred circling camps (2)

can
1 his blood can make the foulest clean (4)
2 thou who art beyond the farthest mortal eye can scan (2)
2 can we feel that thou art near ... hear ...? yea, we can (2)
2 can it be that thou regardest songs of sinful man? (2)
2 can we feel that thou art near us and wilt hear us? (2)
10 church with psalms must shout, no door can keep them out (2)
12 what heart can comprehend thy name (2)
17 sent him to die, I scarce can take it in (3)
20 his rage we can endure, for lo, his doom is sure (3)
22 he can create, and he destroy (1)
31 no mortal eye can bear the sight (1)
37 everwhere that man can be, thou, God, art present there (3)
48 what more can he say than to you he hath said (1)
55 ponder anew what the Almighty can do (3)
71 sinners, whose love can ne'er forget the wormwood and (3)
75 thy Word alone true wisdom can impart (2)
79 Jesus shines purer, than all the angels heaven can boast (3)
82 nor voice can sing, nor heart can frame (2)
82 nor can the memory find a sweeter sound than thy... name (2)

82 ah, this nor tongue nor pen can show (4)
94 depth of mercy! can there be mercy still reserved for me (1)
94 can my God his wrath forbear (1)
97 when I am sad, to him I go, no other one can cheer me so (1)
103 earth has no sorrow but heaven can remove (3)
105 shall I not rise? Can I his loving voice despise (2)
105 he calls me still; can I delay (2)
114 how can a sinner know his sins on earth forgiven? (T,1)
114 can my gracious Savior show my name inscribed in heaven (1)
119 to thee whose blood can cleanse each spot (2)
122 he owns me for his child; I can no longer fear (4)
132 bringing down the richest treasure man can wish (1)
132 richest treasure man can wish or God can send (1)
137 no man can truly say that Jesus is the Lord unless (2)
141 life nor death can pluck his children from his hands (3)
149 it satisfies my longings as nothing else can do (1)
157 for him no depths can drown (2)
163 those ties which naught can sever (1)
163 what power my soul can sever (3)
169 to be the best that I can be for truth ... and thee (4)
175 feelings lie buried that grace can restore (3)
184 flag can ...be unfurled when thou... breathe from heaven (3)
185 when they can sing with me, more love, O Christ, to thee (3)
205 can I doubt his tender mercy (1)
210 builds on the rock that naught can move (1)
211 what terror can confound me, with God at my right hand (1)
223 but we never can prove the delights of his love until (3)
223 never can prove ... until all on the altar we lay (3)
226 trusting thee I cannot stray .. can never .. lose my way (2)
227 tongue can never express the sweet comfort and peace (1)
230 but God is round about me, and can I be dismayed (1)
230 my Shepherd is beside me, and nothing can I lack (2)
231 set free from present sorrow we cheerfully can say (2)
231 it can bring with it nothing but he will bear us through (3)
244 when I've done the best I can &... friends misunderstand (3)
252 speech that infant lips can try (3)
253 give me on thee to wait till I can all things do (1)
258 see thou render all thy feeble strength can pay (1)
259 no thought can reach, no tongue declare (1)
261 can we find a friend so faithful (2)
265 no tender voice like thine can peace afford (1)
268 they have left an aching void the world can never fill (3)
282 life nor death can part from him that dwells within (3)
289 what but thy grace can foil the tempter's power (3)
289 who, like thyself, my guide and stay can be (3)
290 no harm from him can come to me on ocean or on shore (4)
291 no chilling winds or poisonous breath can reach (2)
291 can reach that healthful shore (2)
293 what can shake thy sure repose (1)
293 who can faint while such a river ...their thirst assuage (2)
294 Zion ... be given the brightest glories earth can yield (5)
305 gates of hell can never gainst that Church prevail (3)
328 tongue can tell our sweet accord ... perfect harmony (1)
328 then only can it closer be, when all are joined above (4)
329 blest, when our faith can hold thee fast (4)
332 how can heavenly spirits rise by earthly matter fed (3)
336 saves us to the uttermost till we can sin no more (4)
338 joy .. grief .. time .. place .. life nor death can part (4)

370 shedding light that none can measure (1)
376 what can I give him, poor as I am (4)
376 yet what can I give him: give my heart (4)
395 such a babe in such a place, can he be the Savior (1)
403 his spirit only can bestow, who reigns in light above (1)
415 drops of grief can ne'er repay the debt of love I owe (5)
415 here, Lord, I give myself away; 'tis all that I can do (5)
417 upon that cross of Jesus mine eye at times can see (2)
419 who best can drink his cup of woe, triumphant over pain (1)
430 pressing onward as we can ..to this our hearts must tend (4)
441 thy touch can call us back to life again (4)
466 for none can guess its grace, till he become the place (3)
467 where thou art guide, no ill can come (3)
469 sharing not our griefs, no joy can share (2)
473 thy bountiful care, what tongue can recite (4)
476 whom love, and love alone can know (2)
501 thy kind but searching glance can scan the very wounds (5)
501 no word from thee can fruitless fall (6)
523 what can to thee, O Lord, be given, who givest all (4)
527 and can it be that I should gain (T, 1)
527 amazing love! how can it be that thou ... die for me (1)
527 how can it be that thou, my Lord, shouldst die for me (1)
527 who can explore his strange design (2)
531 my heart is pained, nor can it be at rest (1)
531 nor can it be at rest till it finds rest in thee (1)
545 I can read his righteous sentence by the dim ... lamps (2)
549 scarcely can we turn aside for one brief hour of prayer (2)

can't
212 if you can't preach like Peter ... can't pray like Paul (2)

Canaan
281 enter ... promised rest ... Canaan of thy perfect love (5)

Canaan's
271 land me safe on Canaan's side (3)
291 cast a wishful eye to Canaan's fair and happy land (1)

canceled
1 He breaks the power of canceled sin (4)

candle
456 as altar candle sheds its light as surely as a star (2)

cannot
103 earth has no sorrow that heaven cannot heal (1)
105 I cannot stay; my heart I yield without delay (5)
118 I own it cannot be that I should fit myself for thee (3)
146 believing where we cannot prove (1)
159 there are depths of love that I cannot know till (4)
162 better lesson cannot be, loving him who first loved me (1)
184 it cannot freely move till thou hast wrought its chain (2)
184 it cannot drive the world until itself be driven (3)
220 foes who would molest me cannot reach me here (2)
221 standing on the promises that cannot fail (2)
221 standing on the promises I cannot fail (4)
226 trusting thee I cannot stray .. can never .. lose my way (2)
230 my hope I cannot measure, my path to life is free (3)

231 for while in him confiding, I cannot but rejoice (4)
234 I cannot close my heart to thee (3)
285 cannot reach the mystery ... length .. breadth .. height (2)
290 I only know I cannot drift beyond his love and care (5)
293 he, whose word cannot be broken formed thee (1)
305 we have Christ's own promise, and that cannot fail (3)
334 possess in sweet communion, joys ... earth cannot afford (2)
376 our God, heaven cannot hold him, nor earth sustain (2)
399 ever joined to thee in love that cannot falter (2)
412 therefore, kind Jesus, since I cannot pay thee (5)
414 may not know ... cannot tell, what pains he had to bear (2)
444 death cannot keep his prey ... He tore the bars away (3)
449 that love, that life which cannot die (3)
468 his footsteps cannot err (1)
483 His kingdom cannot fail, he rules o'er earth and heaven (3)
496 darkness cannot hide from thee (3)
501 what if thy form we cannot see (2)
502 for without thee I cannot live (3)
529 Traveler unkown, whom still I hold, but cannot see (1)
122 he cannot turn away the presence of his Son (4)

canopy
473 whose robe is the light, whose canopy space (2)

canst
 75 thou only canst inform the mind and purify the heart (2)
118 'tis thou alone canst make me whole (2)
140 surely thou canst not let me die (3)
141 God's mercy holds a wiser plan than thou canst fully know (2
170 in peace that only thou canst give (4)
200 but thou canst use our weakness to magnify thy power (3)
247 mother stills ... child ... canst hush ... ocean wild (1)
257 thou alone to God canst win us (2)
496 thou canst save, and thou canst heal (1)

canticle
 91 be this while life is mine my canticle divine (4)

canyon
 11 towering mountain, canyon deep (3)

captain
 46 captain of Israel's host (T,1)
 76 crown him as your captain in temptation's hour (4)
408 its captain of salvation (1)
536 thou, Lord, their captain in the well-fought fight (2)

captive
 62 earth and hell hath captive led (3)
141 I rest, heart, mind, and soul the captive of thy grace (4)
184 make me a captive, Lord, and then I shall be free (T,1)
354 o come, o come, Emmanuel, and ransom captive Israel (T,1)
359 he comes to break oppression, to set the captive free (1)
425 O Christ, thy triumphs now begin o'er captive death (2)
425 triumphs now begin o'er captive death and conqered sin (2)

captives
479 still the captives long for freedom (2)

capture
    84   life, thy gift to those whom thou dost capture (2)

car
    32   he yokes the whirlwind to his car (4)

care
    37   all that borrows life from thee is ever in thy care (3)
    51   publish with our latest breath thy love & guardian care (4)
    53   trust his constant care (1)
    56   your wants shall be his care (4)
    57   watchful and unslumbering care his own he safely keeps (2)
    60   praise God and on him cast your care (5)
    70   unnumbered comforts to my soul thy tender care bestowed (2)
    98   prayer to strengthen faith and sweeten care (4)
   105   and basely his kind care repay (2)
   121   much we need thy tender care (1)
   150   arm me with jealous care, as in thy sight to live (3)
   156   I would be pure,for there are those who care (1)
   170   help me bear the strain of toil, the fret of care (1)
   175   rescue the perishing, care for the dying (T,1,R)
   193   and feel his brother's care (2)
   202   we bear the strain of earthly care ... bear it not alone (T)
   207   through every day, o'er all the way He will take care (R)
   207   God will take care of you (1,2,3,4,R)
   216   he shall with all-protecting care preserve thee (3)
   218   Lord, it belongs not to my care whether I die or live (T,1)
   237   grant that I may ever cast my care on thee (3)
   240   cast care aside, lean on thy guide (3)
   253   Jesus, my strength, my hope, on thee I cast my care (T,1)
   253   a spirit still prepared, and armed with jealous care (3)
   258   God hath tended with his care thy helpless hours (2)
   259   care, anguish, sorrow, melt away (2)
   261   are we weak & heavy laden, cumbered with a load of care (3)
   262   with thee conversing, we forget all time & toil and care (2)
   270   on thee we cast each earth-born care (1)
   275   that calls me from a world of care (1)
   275   I'll cast on him my every care and wait for thee (3)
   284   with care and woe oppressed (2)
   290   I only know I cannot drift beyond his love and care (5)
   309   let us for each other care (4)
   335   not a cause of small import the pastor's care demands (2)
   384   bless all the dear children in thy tender care (3)
   485   all pity, care, and love, all calm and courage...pour (1)
   488   O balm of care and sadness, most beautiful, most bright (1)
   494   free from care, from labor free (1)
   505   now, our wants and burdens leaving to his care (3)
   505   leaving to his care who cares for all (3)
   509   the future ... we to thy guardian care commit (3)
   510   Father, thy mercies past we own, and thy continued care (3)
   514   all our labor ... watching, all our calendar of care (3)
   519   ne'er forget God's daily care (T,1)
   530   kindly for each other care; every member feel its share (4)
   531   to save me from low-thoughted care (3)
   549   ceaseless tide of business, toil, and care (2)

careless
   186   careless through outward cares I go (5)

cares
  63 he with earthly cares entwineth hope and comfort (4)
 107 still he calls, in cares and pleasures (4)
 186 careless through outward cares I go (5)
 294 to her my cares and toils be given (3)
 294 till cares and toils shall endd (3)
 306 are one, our comforts and our cares (2)
 489 from our worldly cares set free (2)
 505 leaving to his care who cares for all (3)

caring
 506 beneath thy mighty caring the birds & beasts are sharing (2)

carols
  45 the birds their carols raise (2)
 377 our sweetest carols gayly ring to welcome Christ (3)

carpenter
 171 O Carpenter of Nazareth, Builder of life divine (2)
 186 Son of the carpenter, receive this humble work of mine (2)

carried
  83 he bore the shameful cross ... carried all my grief (2)
 239 must I be carried to the skies on flowery beds of ease (2)

carry
 261 what a privilege to carry everything to God in prayer (1)
 261 all because we do not carry everything to God in prayer (1)
 406 pass on and carry swift the news ye bring (1)

casket
 372 it is the sacred casket where gems of truth are stored (2)

cast
   4 cast each false idol from his throne (5)
  53 come, cast your burdens on the Lord (1)
  60 praise God and on him cast your care (5)
 237 grant that I may ever cast my care on thee (3)
 240 cast care aside, lean on thy guide (3)
 243 who, thrust in prison or cast to flame (1)
 253 Jesus, my strength, my hope, on thee I cast my care (T,1)
 255 why restless, why cast down, my soul (4)
 270 on thee we cast each earth-born care (1)
 275 I'll cast on him my every care and wait for thee (3)
 281 my idols all be cast aside (3)
 283 till we cast our crowns before thee (4)
 291 cast a wishful eye to Canaan's fair and happy land (1)
 329 where'er our changeful lot is cast (4)
 381 cast out our sin, and enter in, be born in us today (4)
 408 cast out our pride & shame that hinder to enthrone thee (3)
 430 cast our crowns before thy feet (5)
 473 and round it hath cast, like a mantle, the sea (3)
 507 no more our God forsake, or cast his words behind (3)
 522 give his angels charge at last ... fire .. tares to cast (3)
 552 in this free land by thee our lot is cast (2)

caste
 189 what are ... ancient caste and creed (2)

casting
  26   casting down their golden crowns around the glassy sea (2)

casts
  253   tramples down and casts behind the baits of pleasing ill (2)
  528   outcasts of men, to you I call (4)

catch
  84   draw thy protecting net around the catch of... apostles (2)
  204   we catch the vision of thy tears (2)
  279   catch .. wandering of my will .. quench .. kindling fire (1)
  280   to catch the wandering of my will (1)
  464   O that all might catch the flame (1)

cattle
  384   the cattle are lowing, the baby awakes (2)
  396   infant holy, infant lowly, for his bed a cattle stall (T,1)

cause
  48   I'll strengthen thee,help thee, and cause thee to stand (2)
  112   fatal cause demands, asks the work of his own hands (1)
  239   shall I fear to own his cause .. blush to speak his name (1)
  242   some great cause, God's new Messiah (1)
  242   ere her cause bring fame and profit (2)
  242   though the cause of evil prosper . truth alone is strong (4)
  335   not a cause of small import the pastor's care demands (2)
  354   and cause us in her ways to go (2)
  364   cause of endless exultation to his ransomed worshipers (3)
  457   maintainer of our cause (2)

caused
  432   caused the Lord of bliss to bear the dreadful curse (1)
  432   that caused the Lord of life to lay aside his crown (2)
  527   died he for me, who caused his pain (1)

causes
  436   Oh! sometimes it causes me to tremble, tremble, tremble (R)

cease
    1   name ... that bids our sorrows cease (3)
   22   when rolling years shall cease to move (4)
   59   the wicked oppressing now cease from distressing (1)
   92   and mortal life shall cease (5)
  106   when our days of toil shall cease (3)
  136   and sin and sorrow cease (1)
  146   they have their day and cease to be (4)
  173   justice conquers violence and wars at last shall cease (3)
  199   wild war music o'er the earth shall cease (5)
  208   just from sin and self to cease (3)
  235   till all our strivings cease (4)
  236   we stand to bless thee ere our worship cease (1)
  236   then, when thy voice shall bid our conflict cease (4)
  243   not long the conflict, soon the holy war shall cease (4)
  259   and when the storms of life shall cease (3)
  309   bid our strife forever cease (1)
  354   bid envy, strife, and quarrels cease (3)
  358   let thy wandering cease; hie thee to thy quiet home (3)

369 then shall all bondage cease, all fetters fall (2)
394 good will ... from heaven to men begin and never cease (6)
406 when war shall be no more and strife shall cease (3)
440 soon the storms of time shall cease (1)
455 scepter sways from pole to pole, that wars may cease (3)
474 cease, ye pilgrims, cease to mourn (3)
476 help us to spread thy gracious reign till greed .. cease (2)
476 till greed and hate shall cease (2)
477 that war may haunt .. earth no more and desolation cease (4)
478 lead on, O King eternal, till sin's fierce war ... cease (2)
485 hasten, Lord ... perfect day when pain & death ... cease (2)
505 cease we fearing, cease we grieving (3)
538 and bid their angry tumult cease (3)

ceaseless
187 let them flow in ceaseless praise (1)
324 as with ceaseless voice they cry, Alleluia (4)
407 thy Spirit's ceaseless, brooding power (3)
531 make me thy duteous child, that I ceaseless may...cry (3)
531 that I ceaseless may, Abba, Father, cry (3)
549 around us rolls the ceaseless tide of business (2)
549 ceaseless tide of business, toil, and care (2)

ceasing
7 for his mercy ceasing never, for his blessing day by day (3)
8 cherubim and seraphim, in unceasing chorus praising (2)
93 streams of mercy never ceasing call for songs (1)
283 pray and praise thee without ceasing (3)
359 to him shall prayer unceasing and daily vows ascend (4)
402 King forever, ceasing never over us all to reign (2)
409 and thanks never ceasing, and infinite love (4)
454 loudest praises, without ceasing (4)

celebrate
15 celebrate the eternal God with harp and psaltery (2)
32 and bid the choral song ascend to celebrate our God (5)

celestial
5 celestial fruit on earthly ground (3)
8 hark, the glad celestial hymn (2)
67 with food celestial feedeth (2)
78 all hearts must bow; all things celestial thee shall own (2)
101 dwell in that celestial land, where joys immortal flow (4)
131 expand thy wings, celestial Dove (3)
172 the pure celestial fire to impart (1)
302 on the eagle wings of love to joys celestial rise (1)
367 forever be thy name adored for these celestial lines (1)
457 tasting the celestial powers, we banquet on his love (3)
467 lighten with celestial fire (1)

center
38 center of unbroken praise (2)
64 center and soul of every sphere (1)
128 fixed on this blissful center, rest (4)

centuries
202 centuries still we hear the Master's winsome call (2)

certain
111 in sure and certain hope rejoice (3)
378 and unto certain shepherds brought tidings of the same (3)
383 was to certain poor shepherhds in fields as they lay (1)
477 bring to our troubled minds, uncertain and afraid (2)

chaff
214 not like that are the men of unbelief but are like chaff (3)
214 men of unbelief are like chaff that the wind doth blow (3)

chain
50 so that earth's bliss may be our guide ... not our chain (3)
58 unbroken be the golden chain, keep on the song forever (4)
184 it cannot freely move till thou hast wrought its chain (2)
428 but soon he'll break death's envious chain (4)

chains
32 the Lord uplifts his awful hand and chains you (2)
32 and chains you to the shore (2)
407 we hear the throb of surging life, the clank of chains (2)
472 the prisoner leaps to loose his chains (4)
527 my chains fell off, my heart was free (3)

chalice
67 what transport of delight from thy pure chalice floweth (5)

challenge
173 once more to hear thy challenge above our noisy day (5)
197 the challenge of our tasks to face (3)

challenges
481 how its splendor challenges the souls that greatly dare (5)

chance
63 chance and change are busy ever (2)
197 the chance of life that each day brings (1)

change
63 chance and change are busy ever (2)
209 in every change he faithful will remain (1)
209 when change and tears are past (3)
230 in heavenly love abiding no change my heart shall fear (T,1)
251 hope shall change to glad fruition (4)
289 change and decay in all around I see (2)
492 with joy we view the pleasing change (3)

changed
53 his goodness stands approved, unchanged from day to day (4)
270 and trembling faith is changed to fear (3)
283 changed from glory into glory (4)
296 unchanged by changing place (1)
329 thy truth unchanged hath ever stood (2)
372 O Truth unchanged, unchanging, O Light of our dark sky (1)

changeful
329 where'er our changeful lot is cast (4)

changeless
- 30 established is his law, and changeless it shall stand (2)
- 63 will his changeless goodness prove (3)
- 143 pure, warm, and changeless be, a living fire (2)
- 473 hath stablished it fast by a changeless decree (3)
- 505 their Creator's changeless love (2)

changes
- 47 faith's fair vision changes into sight (2)
- 230 and safe is such confiding, for nothing changes here (1)

changest
- 289 O thou who changest not, abide with me (2)

changeth
- 27 and wither and perish, but naught changeth thee (3)
- 240 He changeth not, and thou art dear (4)

changing
- 33 in ever-changing words of light, the wonder of thy name (3)
- 56 through all the changing scenes of life (T,1)
- 144 help me, throughout life's changing scene, by faith (1)
- 167 each changing future scene I gladly trust with thee (3)
- 210 who trust in God's unchanging love builds on the rock (1)
- 222 I rest on his unchanging grace (2)
- 226 through .. changing world below lead me gently ..as I go (2)
- 296 unchanged by changing place (91)
- 365 the rolling sun, the changing light ...thy power confess (2)
- 372 O Truth unchanged, unchanging, O Light of our dark sky (1)
- 460 God hath ... spoken his unchanging Word (1)
- 460 God abides, his Word unchanging (3)
- 509 adored through all our changing days (4)

chant
- 91 powers of darkness fear when this sweet chant they hear (2)
- 357 hymn & chant & high thanksgiving & unwearied praises be (3)
- 454 help to chant Emmanuel's praise (4)

chanting
- 38 flashing sea, chanting bird and flowing fountain (2)
- 233 on through life's long path still chanting as ye go (4)
- 423 victor palm branch waving, and chanting clear & loud (2)

chaos
- 480 thou, whose almighty Word chaos and darkness heard (T,1)
- 480 chaos and darkness heard and took their flight (1)

characters
- 168 I'd sing the chartacters he bears (2)

charge
- 127 for who aught to my charge shall lay (2)
- 150 a charge to keep I have, a God to glorify (T,1)
- 335 let them from the mouth of God...solemn charge receive (1)
- 337 in humble hope their charge resign (5)
- 522 give his angels charge at last...fire...tares to cast (3)

chariots
473   his chariots of wrath the deep thunderclouds form (2)

charity
193   this is the bond of perfectness, thy spotless charity (6)
305   one in hope and doctrine, one in charity (2)
333   assurance of tender charity and steadfast faith (2)

charm
237   with forbidden pleasures would this vain world charm (2)
251   not in joy to charm me were that joy unmixed with thee (3)
435   all the vain things that charm me most, I sacrifice them (2)

charmed
128   charmed to confess the voice divine (3)

charms
1   Jesus! the name that charms our fears (3)
312   shepherd stand with all engaging charms (1)
411   for still his love works wondrous charms (4)

chart
247   chart and compass came from thee (1)
368   guide & chart, wherein we read of realms beyond the sky (2)
372   it is the chart and compass that o'er life's surging sea (3)

charter
297   her charter of salvation, one Lord, one faith, one birth (2)

chase
224   heir of salvation, purchase of God (1)
255   when heated in the chase (1)
329   chase the dark night of sin away (5)
496   blessed Spirit, brooding o'er us, chase the darkness (4)
496   chase the darkness of our night (4)
531   chase this self-will from all my heart (3)

chastening
142   will not murmur nor complain beneath the chastening rod (2)

chastens
59   he chastens and hastens his will to make known (1)

cheap
481   hark, how from men whose lives are held more cheap (2)
481   lives are held more cheap than merchandise (2)

cheer
49   with ever joyful hearts and blessed peace to cheer us (2)
97   when I am sad, to him I go, no other one can cheer me so (1)
125   raise the fallen, cheer the faint (3)
213   and raise my head, and cheer my heart (3)
231   a season of clear shining to cheer it after rain (1)
337   to warn the sinner, cheer the saint (4)
354   come and cheer our spirits by thine advent here (4)
367   springs of consolation rise to cheer the fainting mind (2)
401   inward light impart, cheer my eyes and warm my heart (2)
467   anoint and cheer our soiled face with...thy grace (3)

cheereth
274 longing for thy voice that cheereth (1)

cheerful
14 in cheerful sounds all voices raise (4)
21 sing to the Lord with cheerful voice (1)
23 ascend for him our cheerful strain (4)
128 let cheerful anthems fill his house (2)
210 only be still, and wait his leisure in cheerful hope (2)

cheerfully
152 task thy wisdom ... assigned O let me cheerfully fulfill (2)
214 they gaily bloom and prosper cheerfully (2)
231 set free from present sorrow we cheerfully can say (2)

cheering
129 thy soul-cheering comfort impart (4)
259 O Love, how cheering is thy ray (2)

cheerless
401 dark and cheerless is the morn unaccompanied by thee (2)

cheers
64 star of our hope, thy softened light cheers (2)
64 cheers the long watches of the night (2)
205 cheers each winding path I tread (2)
331 cheers our famished souls with food (1)
492 sun itself is but thy shade, yet cheers both earth & sky (1)

cherish
79 O thou of God and man the son, thee will I cherish (1)
228 so I'll cherish the old rugged cross (R)

cherished
532 in silent love be cherished (5)

cherubim
8 cherubim and seraphim, in unceasing chorus praising (2)
19 bright seraphs, cherubim and thrones (1)
19 higher than ... cherubim more glorious than ... seraphim (2)
26 cherubim and seraphim falling down before thee (2)
324 Cherubim, with sleepless eye, veil their faces (4)
376 Cherubim and seraphin thronged the air (3)

chide
66 slow to chide and swift to bless (2)

chief
94 me, the chief of sinners, spare (1)
337 when the chief Shepherd shall appear (5)
349 O living Christ, chief cornerstone (T,1)

child
35 for the joy of human love, brother, sister, parent,child (4)
41 child of earth, yet full of yearning (2)
60 thou leadest home the child of God (6)
84 O Guide to every child of thine (T,1)

84	thank we all the mighty Child through whom we know thee (3
84	Child through whom we know thee, God of peace (3)
87	child of sorrow and of woe (1)
115	how happy every child of grace (T,1)
122	he owns me for his child; I can no longer fear (4)
123	only know ... manger child has brought God's life to me (1)
175	waiting the penitent child to receive (2)
247	mother stills ... child ... canst hush ... ocean wild (1)
353	not as of old a little child to bear and fight and die (2)
360	born thy people to deliver, born a child and yet a King (2)
361	for unto us a child is born, to us a son is given (2)
373	this child ... our confidence and joy shall be (1)
373	this child, now weak in infancy (1)
381	O holy Child of Bethlehem, descend to us, we pray (4)
385	child ... who, laid to rest, on Mary's lap is sleeping (1)
385	what child is this (T,1)
393	round yon virgin mother and child (1)
395	gentle Mary laid her child lowly in a manger (T,1,3)
440	child of God, lift up thy head (3)
475	yet thou, her child, whose head is crowned with flame (1)
476	no child unsought, unknown (1)
479	forth in thy dear name we go to the child, the youth (4)
479	to.. child .. youth .. aged love in living deeds to show (4)
490	Father, I implore, safely keep this child (2)
502	if some poor wandering child of thine have spurned (4)
517	didst deign a child to be cradled on a mother's bosom (1)
528	I, a child of wrath & hell ... be called a child of God (2)
531	make me thy duteous child, that I ceaseless may...cry (3)

child's
162   with a child's glad heart of love (2)

childhood
157   our lips of childhood frame (5)

childhood's
204   from tender childhood's helplessness (3)

childlike
368   to its heavenly teaching turn with ... childlike hearts (4)

children

5	children of the heavenly King may speak ... joys abroad (2)
11	men and children everywhere (T,1)
53	hand which bears all nature up shall guard his children (2)
53	that hand .... shall guard his children well (2)
65	to their children's children ...his righteousness extend (4)
86	hither our children bring to shout thy praise (1)
88	first let me hear how the children stood round his knee (2)
108	I died for you, my children, and will ye treat me so (3)
136	holiness which makes thy children whole (4)
141	life nor death can pluck his children from his hands (3)
173	longs to bind God's children into one perfect whole (4)
195	as thou hast sought, so let me seek ... erring children (1)
195	erring children lost and lone (1)
201	these, Father, are thy children thou sendest us to find (2)
231	and he who feeds the ravens will give his children bread (3)
236	from harm and danger keep thy children free (3)

266 make friends of God's children, help those who are weak (1)
267 open my heart and let me prepare love with thy children (3)
267 love with thy children thus to share (3)
300 children of the heavenly King (T,1)
344 Father ... to whom we for our children cry (1)
384 bless all the dear children in thy tender care (3)
423 Hosanna, loud hosanna the little children sang (T,1)
423 children sang their praises, the simplest and the best (1)
423 scorned ... little children should on his bidding wait (2)
424 to whom the lips of children made sweet hosannas ring (1)
459 O holy Father, who hast led thy children in all the ages (2)
459 led thy children in all the ages with the fire and cloud (2)
473 frail children of dust, and feeble as frail (5)
479 still the children wander homeless (2)
479 that thy children, Lord, in freedom may thy mercy know (4)
479 that thy children ... may thy mercy know, and live (4)
495 grant to little children visions bright of thee (3)
506 O Father, while we sleep, thy children keep (R)
513 much more, to us his children, he gives our daily bread (2)
515 thy children live by daily food (1)
516 children early lisp his fame and parents hold him dear (2)
517 for... children thou hast given we must answer unto thee (1)
517 children thou hast given still may be our joy and crown (5)
521 children of the heavenly Father (T,1)
521 nor ... ever from the Lord his children sever (3)
521 God his children ne'er forsaketh (4)
550 here thy name, O God of love ... children shall adore (4)
550 their children's children shall adore (4)

children's
 65 to their children's children ...his righteousness extend (4)
 88 into the city I'd follow the children's band (3)
470 cure thy children's warring madness (3)
481 from little children's cries (2)
515 as large as is thy children's need (3)
550 their children's children shall adore (4)

chilling
291 no chilling winds or poisonous breath can reach (2)

chilly
244 when my life becomes a burden ... nearing chilly Jordan (4)

choice
 16 stand up and bless the Lord, ye people of his choice (T,1)
 77 praise is his gracious choice: Alleluia! Amen! (1)
128 O happy day, that fixed my choice (T,1)
128 fixed my choice on thee, my Savior and my God (1)
242 choice goes by forever twixt that darkness & that light (1)
531 to taste thy love, be all my choice (4)

choicest
  2 heart and minds ... hands and voices ... choicest melody (4)
510 inspires our choicest songs (1)

choir
366 where we are with the choir immortal (3)
366 choir immortal of angels round thy dazzling throne (3)

choirs
8   angel choirs above are singing (2)
19   cry out ... virtues, arch-angels, angels' choirs (1)
374   see him in a manger laid whom .. choirs of angels praise (4)
379   Christ is born   their choirs are singing (1)
386   sing, choirs of angels, sing in exultation (2)

choose
51   leave to his sovereign sway to choose and to command (3)
187   take my intellect ... use every power as thou ... choose (2)
272   I loved to choose and see my path (2)
355   by which alone we choose thee (3)

chooses
242   then it is the brave man chooses (2)

choosing
20   the man of God's own choosing (2)

choral
32   and bid the choral song ascend to celebrate our God (5)

chords
175   chords that were broken will vibrate once more (3)
453   hark, those loud triumphant chords (4)

choristers
7   so may we, in lowly station join the choristers above (2)

chorus
8   cherubim and seraphim, in unceasing chorus praising (2)
38   mortals join the happy chorus, which the... stars began (4)
38   chorus, which the morning stars began (4)
189   the chorus clearer grows that shepherds heard of old (1)
343   with them loud chorus raise (2)
404   lo! above the earth rang out the angel chorus (2)
404   angel chorus that hailed our Savior's birth (2)
544   singing in chorus from ocean to ocean (4)

chose
210   known to him who chose us for his own (2)

chosen
4   he leads his own, his chosen band (3)
71   chosen seed of Israel's race, ye ransomed from the fall (2)
98   great Shepherd of thy chosen few (3)
298   chosen of the Lord and precious (1)
419   a glorious band, the chosen few on whom the Spirit came (3)
552   thy Word our law, thy paths our chosen way (2)

Christ
16   then be his love in Christ proclaimed (4)
17   when Christ shall come with shout of acclamation (4)
20   dost ask who that may be? Christ Jesus, it is he (2)
23   raise to Christ our joyful strain (1)
38   thou our Father, Christ our brother (3)
60   Christ our Lord the way hath trod (6)
62   praise to Christ our gracious head (3)

62   Christ, the risen Christ, victorious (3)
74   let every tongue confess ... one accord ... Jesus Christ (5)
74   confess ...in heaven and earth that Jesus Christ is Lord (5)
77   loud praise to Christ our King; Alleluia! Amen! (1)
78   O Christ, thou Savior of us all ... hear us when we call (1)
84   praise in all simplicity the guiding Christ,our shepherd (1)
86   Christ our triumphant King, we come thy name to sing (1)
86   Jesus, thou Christ of God, by thy perennial Word lead (3)
86   unite to swell the song to Christ our King (4)
90   the Christ of God, the life, the truth, the way (2)
91   may Jesus Christ be praised! (R)
95   at the cross of Christ I bow (1)
102   all things in Christ are ready now (2)
102   in Christ a hearty welcome find (3)
102   ye all may come to Christ and live (4)
104   without money, come to Jesus Christ and buy (2)
109   Christ,the blessed one, give to all wonderful words of (2)
111   come, let us, who in   Christ believe (T,1)
114   we who in Christ believe that he for us hath died (3)
115   our life in Christ concealed (2)
123   I only know a living Christ, our immortality (3)
124   Jesus Christ, the crucified (1,2,3,4)
125   thou, O Christ, art all I want (3)
136   till Christ shall dwell in human hearts (1)
154   fill with thy spirit till all shall see Christ ...in me (4)
154   Christ only, always, living in me (4)
157   we may not climb ... to bring the Lord Christ down (2)
160   take up thy cross and follow Christ (4)
161   thou Christ of great compassion (1)
161   O Christ, o'er death victorious (5)
169   to consecrate myself to thee, O Jesus   Christ, I come (1)
174   lift high the cross of   Christ (4)
185   more love to thee, O Christ, more love to thee (T,1)
185   this is my earnest plea: more love, O Christ, to thee (1)
185   more love, O Christ, to thee ... more love to thee (R)
185   this all my prayer shall be: more love O Christ, to thee (2)
185   when they can sing with me, more love, O Christ, to thee (3)
185   this still its prayer shall be: more love, O Christ (4)
188   draw thou my soul, O Christ, closer to thine (T,1)
188   lead forth my soul, O Christ, one with thine own (2)
188   lift thou thy world, O Christ, closer to thee (3)
188   ever, O Christ, through mine let thy life shine (1)
191   live out the laws of Christ in ... thought & word & deed (1)
191   until the laws of Christ become the laws and habits (2)
192   in Christ there is no east or west (T,1)
192   in Christ now meet both east and west (4)
202   beside us walks our brother Christ (1)
202   our brother Christ ... makes our task his own (1)
218   enough that Christ knows all, and I shall be with him (5)
218   Christ leads me through no darker rooms than he went (3)
221   standing on the promises of Christ my King (1)
221   standing on the promises of Christ the Lord (3)
222   on Christ, the solid rock, I stand (R)
233   the cross of Christ your King (1)
240   Christ is the path, and Christ the prize (2)
240   Christ is thy strength, and Christ thy right (1)
240   Christ is its life, and Christ its love (3)
240   trust ... trusting soul shall prove Christ is its life (3)

240   Christ is all-in-all to thee (4)
240   only believe, and thou shalt see that Christ is all (4)
242   Christ, thy bleeding feet we track (3)
243   heroic warriors, ne'er from Christ ... enticed (2)
248   till every foe is vanquished, and Christ is Lord indeed (1)
250   soldiers of Christ, arise and put your armor on (T,1)
250   o'ercome through Christ alone, and stand entire at last (2)
250   till Christ the Lord descends from high (3)
250   till Christ descends ... and takes the conquerors home (3)
269   lead us through Christ, the true and living Way (1)
278   Christ is all the world to me, and all my heart is love (4)
281   the mind which was in Christ impart (4)
282   where only Christ is heard to speak (2)
285   the love of Christ to me (1)
292   the world to Christ we bring, with loving zeal (1)
292   Christ for the world we sing! (T,1,2,3,4)
292   with us the cross to bear, for Christ our Lord (3)
292   sinsick and sorrow-worn, whom Christ doth heal (1)
292   the world to Christ we bring, with fervent prayer (2)
292   the world to Christ we bring, with one accord (3)
292   the world to Christ we bring, with joyful song (4)
292   inspired with hope and praise, to Christ belong (4)
297   the Church's one foundation is Jesus Christ her Lord (T,1)
298   Christ is made the sure foundation (T,1)
298   Christ the head and cornerstone (1)
300   Jesus Christ, our Father's Son, bids us undismayed go on (3)
301   Christ, the true, the only light (1)
305   Christ, the royal Master, leads against the foe (1)
305   glory, laud, and honor unto Christ the King (4)
307   giving in Christ the bread eternal (2)
324   blessing in his hand, Christ our God to earth descendeth (1)
334   may the grace of Christ our Savior (T,1)
348   Jesus Christ, its cornerstone (4)
349   O living Christ, chief cornerstone (T,1)
349   Christ, with love's persuasive power (3)
353   when Christ our King in beauty comes (4)
353   hail, Christ the Lord! (5)
355   Lord Christ, when first thou cam'st to men (T,1)
355   new advent of the love of Christ (3)
357   Christ, to thee with God the Father (3)
365   till Christ has all the nations blest (4)
372   still guides, O Christ, to thee (3)
374   come, adore on bended knee Christ the Lord (3)
374   Christ the Lord, the new-born King (3)
376   sufficed the Lord God Almighty, Jesus Christ (2)
377   our sweetest carols gayly ring to welcome Christ (3)
377   welcome Christ, the infant King (3)
378   for Jesus Christ our Savior was born upon this day (1)
379   Christ is born   their choirs are singing (1)
381   for Christ is born of Mary, and gathered all above (2)
381   where meek souls will receive him... dear Christ enters (3)
382   come and worship, worship Christ, the new-born King (R)
385   this, this is Christ the King (R)
386   O come, let us adore him, Christ, the Lord (R)
387   Christ is born in Bethlehem (1)
387   Christ, by highest heaven adored (2)
387   Christ, the everlasting Lord (2)
391   give ye heed to what we say: Jesus Christ is born today (1)

463   we believe in Jesus Christ, Son of God and Mary's Son (2)
470   lo! the hosts of evil round us scorn thy Christ (2)
470   scorn thy Christ, assail his ways (2)
476   O God of righteousness & grace, seen in Christ, thy Son (5)
476   Christ is formed in all mankind and every land is thine (5)
481   holy city ... where Christ, the Lamb, doth reign (1)
481   cry   Christ hath died in vain   (3)
482   O thou eternal Christ of God, ride on (T,1)
482   O Christ, Redeemer, Brother, Friend, ride on, ride on (4)
487   let the mind of Christ abide in us on this thy holy day (3)
488   for our salvation Christ rose from depths of earth (2)
501   O Savior Christ, our woes dispel (3)
501   O Savior Christ, thou too art man (5)
507   join ourselves to Christ the Lord (1)
511   all life in Christ made new (2)
511   the Church of Christ is stirring us to make the dream (2)
527   claim the crown, through Christ my own (4)
530   Christ, from whom all blessings flow (T,1)
530   names and sects and parties fall: thou, O Christ art all (5)
530   thou, O Christ, art all-in-all (5)
538   O Christ, whose voice the waters heard (2)
542   let Christ be lifted up till all men serve him (3)
545   in . beauty of the lilies Christ was born across the sea (4)

Christ's
    4   o ye who name Christ's holy name (5)
276   secret of the Lord is theirs ... soul is Christ's abode (1)
305   we have Christ's own promise, and that cannot fail (3)
410   and Christ's great kingdom shall come on earth (R)

Christian
107   saying, Christian, follow me (1)
107   saying, Christian, love me more (3)
107   Christian, love me more than these (4)
108   shame on us,Christian brethren, his name & sign who bear (1)
231   sometimes a light surprises the Christian while he sings (T)
238   Christian, answer boldly, "while I breathe I pray" (3)
238   Christian, up and smite them, counting gain but loss (1)
238   Christian, dost thou see them on the holy ground (T,1)
238   Christian, never tremble, never be downcast (2)
238   Christian, dost thou feel them, how they work within (2)
238   Christian, dost thou hear them, how they speak thee fair (3)
286   Lord, I want to be a Christian in my heart (T,1)
305   onward, Christian soldiers! marching as to war (T,1,R)
306   blest be the tie that binds our hearts in Christian love (T)
385   good Christian, fear (2)
391   good Christian men, rejoice (T,1,2,3)
449   good Christian men, rejoice and sing (T,1)

Christian's
106   ever near the Christian's side (1)
252   prayer is the Christian's vital breath (5)
252   prayer ... the Christian's native air (5)

Christians
    77   come, Christians, join to sing Alleluia! Amen! (T,1)

Christly
192   all Christly souls are one in him (4)

churches
337 thy servants in the churches be (2)

circling
47 through all the circling years, we trust in thee (1)
50 so many gentle thoughts and deeds circling us round (2)
272 amid the encircling gloom, lead thou me on (1)
390 when with the ever circling years shall come the time (3)
545 watchfires of a hundred circling camps (2)

cities
543 thine alabaster cities gleam undimmned by human tears (4)
551 our cities with prosperity ... fields with plenteousness (2)

citizens
386 O sing, all ye citizens of heaven above (2)

city
41 soaring spire and ruined city, these our hopes ... show (3)
41 spire and ruined city, these our hopes and failures show (3)
84 praise in all simplicity the guiding Christ,our shepherd (1)
88 into the city I'd follow the children's band (3)
200 no field or mart is silent, no city street is dumb (2)
204 glorious from thy heaven above shall come the city (6)
204 shall come the city of our   God (6)
293 Zion, city of our God (1,3)
300 lift your eyes ... sons of light Zion's city is in sight (4)
405 earth has many a noble city (T,1)
414 there is a green hill far away, beyond the city wall (T,1)
481 O holy city, seen of John (T,1)
481 holy city ... where Christ, the Lamb, doth reign (1)
481 give us, O God, the strength to build the city (4)
481 city that hath stood too long a dream (4)
481 city ... whose laws are love, whose ways are brotherhood (4)
481 already in the mind of God that city riseth fair (5)
482 we go with thee to claim and build a city unto God (2)

city's
204 O tread the city's streets again (5)
498 thy glory breaks before us through the city's open gate (3)

clad
451 an angel clad in white they see (3)

claim
8 all on earth thy scepter claim (1)
8 though in essence only One; undivided God we claim thee (4)
64 till all thy living altars claim one holy light (5)
130 assert thy claim, receive thy right (5)
189 one claim unites all men in God to serve each human need (2
310 Jesus, we look to thee, thy promised presence claim (T,1)
364 claim the kingdom for thine own (4)
453 mocking thus the Savior's claim (3)
482 we go with thee to claim and build a city unto God (2)
527 bold I approach the eternal throne, and claim the crown (4)
527 claim the crown, through Christ my own (4)
549 claim the kingdom of the earth for thee, and not thy foe (5)

claims
   533   our glorious leader claims our praise (2)

clan
   204   where sound the cries of race and clan (1)
   371   to every land, to every race and clan (4)

clangor
   199   stormy clangor of wild war music o'er the earth (5)

clank
   407   we hear the throb of surging life, the clank of chains (2)

clarion
   544   thunder thy clarion, the lightning thy sword (1)

clash
   548   save the people from the clash of race and creed (4)

clashing
   184   it only stands unbent amid the clashing strife (4)
   478   not with swords loud clashing nor roll of stirring drums (2)

class
   548   from the strife of class & faction make our nation free (4)

clay
   22   He sovereign power, without our aid made us of clay (2)
   22   made us of clay and formed us men (2)
   138   no sudden rending of the veil of clay (2)
   154   thou art the potter; I am the clay (1)
   434   tomb where they laid his breathless clay (4)

clean
   1   his blood can make the foulest clean (4)
   282   believing, true, and clean (3)

cleanse
   116   I will cleanse you from all sin (2)
   119   to thee whose blood can cleanse each spot (2)
   119   wilt welcome, pardon, cleanse, relieve (5)
   121   grace to cleanse and power to free (3)
   188   cleanse it from guilt & wrong; teach it salvation's song (3)
   260   O cleanse our prayers from human dross (2)
   281   cleanse me from every sinful thought (3)
   365   Lord, cleanse my sins, my soul renew (6)
   487   save us and cleanse our hearts (2)
   546   cleanse the body of this nation through the glory (2)
   546   cleanse the body ... through the glory of the Lord (2)

cleansed
   307   unite it, cleansed and conformed into thy will (3)

cleansing
   208   just to trust his cleansing blood (2)
   208   plunge me neath the healing, cleansing flood (2)
   226   every day, every hour, let me feel thy cleansing power (R)

clear
   36   but higher far, and far more clear (4)
   60   thou flowing water, pure and clear (3)
  135   wake my spirit, clear my sight (1)
  136   when love speaks loud and clear (3)
  142   faith that shines more bright & clear when tempests rage (3)
  153   heaven's trumpets ringing clear (2)
  164   O let me hear thee speaking in accents clear and still (3)
  170   by some clear, winning word of love (2)
  189   to this clear call of brotherhood our hearts ... ring (3)
  191   with vision clear and mind equipped His will to learn (3)
  231   a season of clear shining to cheer it after rain (1)
  254   let thy clear light forever shine (1)
  267   voices of truth thou sendest clear (2)
  311   may her voice be ever clear, warning of a judgment near (2)
  390   it came upon the midnight clear (T,1)
  408   the Day-star clear and bright of every man and nation (1)
  423   victor palm branch waving, and chanting clear and loud (2)
  476   until true wisdom from above . make life's pathway clear (3)

clearer
   33   clearer sounds the angel hymn, "Good will to men" (2)
  189   the chorus clearer grows that shepherds heard of old (1)

clearest
  366   with harp and cymbal's clearest tone (3)

clears
   51   he gently clears thy way; wait thou his time (2)
  324   powers of hell may vanish as the darkness clears away (3)

cleave
  193   to thee, inseparably joined, let all our spirits cleave (5)
  281   and let my spirit cleave to thee (4)
  546   cleave our darkness with thy sword (2)

cleaving
  263   or if, on joyful wing cleaving the sky (5)

cleft
  120   Rock of Ages, cleft for me, let me hide myself in thee (T,1)
  120   Rock of Ages, cleft for me, let me hide myself in thee (3)

climb
  157   we may not climb the heavenly steeps (2)
  157   we may not climb ... to bring the Lord Christ down (2)
  434   Calvary's mournful mountain climb (3)
  462   when weary feet refuse to climb, give us thy vision (5)

climbed
  419   they climbed the steep ascent of heaven through peril (3)

climbing
  245   or climbing the mountain way steep (3)
  287   climbing Jacob's ladder ... soldiers of the cross (T,1)
  287   we are climbing higher, higher ... soldiers of the cross (5)

clime
- 136 till every age and race and clime shall blend (3)
- 476 who lightest every earnest mind of every clime and shore (3)
- 482 until in every land and clime thine ends of love are won (4)
- 551 of every clime and coast, O hear us for our native land (1)

cling
- 120 in my hand no price I bring; simply to thy cross I cling (2)
- 138 I see thy cross; there teach my heart to cling (3)
- 144 with patient uncomplaining love, still ... cling to thee (2)
- 144 by faith to cling to thee (1) ..."Cling to me" (3)
- 228 I will cling to the old rugged cross (R)

clinging
- 226 I am clinging, clinging close to thee (1)

clings
- 144 safe ... calm ... satisfied the soul that clings to thee (4)
- 525 for home, where our affection clings (2)

close
- 120 when my eyes shall close in death (3)
- 192 his service is the golden cord close binding all mankind (2)
- 226 I am clinging, clinging close to thee (1)
- 234 I cannot close my heart to thee (3)
- 251 soon shall close thy earthly mission (4)
- 268 so shall my walk be close with God (6)
- 289 swift to its close ebbs out life's little day (2)
- 290 forgive me if too close I lean my human heart on thee (3)
- 384 be near me, Lord Jesus, I ask thee to stay close by me (3)
- 384 close by me forever, and love me, I pray (3)
- 413 are ye able when...shadows close around you with the sod (3)
- 423 to Jesus, who... blessed them close folded to his breast (1)
- 493 with sweet sleep my eyelids close (4)
- 495 with thy tenderest blessing may our eyelids close (2)
- 509 that mercy crowns it till it close (1)

closed
- 108 O Jesus, thou art standing outside the fast-closed door (T)

closely
- 99 if I still hold closely to him, what hath he at last (5)
- 152 and closely walk with thee to heaven (4)
- 163 and round my heart still closely twine those ties (1)

closer
- 105 shall he knock, and I my heart the closer lock (3)
- 159 and be closer drawn to thee (1)
- 170 still with thee in closer, dearer company (2)
- 188 draw thou my soul, O Christ, closer to thine (T,1)
- 188 lift thou thy world, O Christ, closer to thee (3)
- 226 may thy tender love to me bind me closer .. Lord to thee (R)
- 268 O for a closer walk with God (T,1)
- 328 then only can it closer be, when all are joined above (4)

closing
- 264 its closing eyes look up to thee in prayer (4)
- 289 hold thou thy cross before my closing eyes (5)
- 440 when, amidst earth's closing thunders (4)

clothe
231 who gives the lilies clothing will clothe his people,too (3)
235 reclothe us in our rightful mind (1)
337 and clothe them with thy righteousness (1)
466 and clothe me round the while my path illuming (2)

clothed
32 the Lord our God is clothed with might (T,1)
32 clothed with might, the winds obey his will (1)
205 when my spirit, clothed immortal, wings its flight (3)
527 clothed in righteousness divine (4)

clothes
450 kept the folded grave-clothes where the body lay (1)
519 health and food and clothes to wear (1)

clothing
231 who gives the lilies clothing will clothe his people,too (3)
452 earth with joy confesses, clothing her for spring (2)

cloud
46 the cloud of thy protecting love (1)
249 a cloud of witnesses around holds thee in full survey (2)
289 through cloud and sunshine, Lord, abide with me (3)
293 cloud and fire appear for a glory and a covering (3)
293 round each habitation hovering, see the cloud and fire (3)
459 led thy children in all the ages with the fire and cloud (2)
464 saw ye not the cloud arise, little as a human hand (4)
502 O may no earth-born cloud arise to hide thee (1)
533 the long cloud of witnesses show the same path to heaven (2)

cloudless
403 who dwells in cloudless light enshrined (2)

clouds
11 skies with crimson clouds aflame (2)
27 thy clouds which are fountains of goodness and love (2)
37 clouds arise, and tempests blow by order from thy throne (3)
38 melt the clouds of sin and sadness (1)
51 through waves and clouds and storms (2)
60 ye clouds that sail in heaven along, O praise him (2)
64 all, save the clouds of sin, are thine (3)
132 pierce the clouds of nature's night (1)
139 the clouds disperse, the shadows fly (6)
215 the clouds ye so much dread are big with mercy (3)
230 where darkest clouds have been (3)
230 bright skies will soon be o'er me, where darkest clouds (3)
354 disperse the gloomy clouds of night (4)
364 lo, he comes with clouds descending (T,1)
372 till, clouds & darkness ended ... see thee face to face (4)
397 need no star to guide, where no clouds thy glory hide (4)
440 all around the clouds are breaking (1)
473 his chariots of wrath the deep thunderclouds form (2)
510 Jesus in the clouds appear to saints on earth forgiven (6)

cloudy
271   let the fire and cloudy pillar lead me all my journey (2)

cloven
390   still through the cloven skies they come (2)

clover
542   but other lands have sunlight too, and clover (2)

coast
536   from earth's wide bounds, from ocean's farthest coast (6)
551   of every clime and coast, O hear us for our native land (1)

coat
490   glad for cotton coat, plain food satisfies (3)

coeternal
420   Father's coeternal Son bore all my sins upon the tree (1)

cold
33   splendors ... burn brighter through the cold (2)
34   the cold wind in the winter, the pleasant summer sun (3)
81   and cold my warmest thought (4)
134   kindle a flame of sacred love in...cold hearts of ours (1)
134   our love so faint, so cold to thee & thine to us so great (4)
143   when death's cold, sullen stream shall o'er me roll (4)
217   e'en death's cold wave I will not flee (4)
350   descend to kindle spirits cold (2)
383   on a cold winter's night that was so deep (1)
400   cold on his cradle the dew-drops are shining (2)
402   sealed in a stone-cold tomb (4)

colors
34   he made their glowing colors (1)

colt
84   to untamed colt, the bridle (1)

combine
2   art...music's measure for thy pleasure all combine (3)
32   ye winds of night, your force combine (3)
520   O Lord, may church and home combine (T,1)
520   church and home combine to teach thy perfect way (1)

combined
344   learning and holiness combined (1)

come
1   ye blind, behold your Savior come (6)
3   come, thou almighty King (T,1)
3   come, and thy people bless, and give thy Word success (2)
3   come, holy Comforter, thy sacred witness bear (3)
3   come, and reign over us, Ancient of Days! (1)
3   come, thou incarnate Word, gird on thy mighty sword (2)
5   come, ye who love the Lord, and let your joys be known (T,1)
11   nations, come, your voices raise to the Lord in hymns (1)
13   gracious God, I come before thee (2)
13   come thou also unto me (2)

17	when Christ shall come with shout of acclamation (4)
21	come ye before him and rejoice (1)
23	come, let us tune our loftiest song (T,1)
24	come, worship at this throne; come, bow before the Lord (3)
24	come, sound his praise abroad, and hymns of glory sing (T,1)
24	come ... people of his choice...own your gracious God (4)
28	our hope for years to come (1,6)
33	all beautiful the march of days as seasons come and go (T,1)
39	come, the great day, the glorious hour (3)
40	come unto us and dwell with us (2)
53	come, cast your burdens on the Lord (1)
55	all that hath life and breath, come now with praises (4)
55	come now with praises before him (4)
57	O whence shall come my aid (1)
58	we come unto our Fathers' God (T,1)
58	ye saints to come, take up the strain (4)
77	come, Christians, join to sing Alleluia! Amen! (T,1)
77	come, lift your hearts on high; Alleluia! Amen! (2)
78	come in thy holy might, we pray (3)
86	Christ our triumphant King, we come thy name to sing (1)
92	through many dangers, toils ... snares I... already come (3)
93	come, thou fount of every blessing (T,1)
93	here I raise mine Ebenezer, hither to thy help I'm come (2)
95	while I rest upon thy word come ... bless me now, O Lord (2)
98	such ever bring thee where they come (2)
99	"Come to me...and coming be at rest " (1)
101	come, every soul by sin oppressed (T,1)
101	come then and join this holy band, and on to glory go (4)
102	come, sinners, to the gospel feast (T,1)
102	come, all the world! come, sinner, thou! (2)
102	come, all ye souls by sin oppressed (3)
102	ye all may come to Christ and live (4)
102	come thou, this moment, at his call (5)
103	come, ye disconsolate, where'er ye languish (T,1)
103	come to the mercy seat, fervently kneel (1)
103	come to the feast of love; come, ever knowing (3)
104	come, ye sinners, poor and needy (T,1)
104	come ... weak and wounded, sick and sore (1)
104	ye needy, come ... welcome; God's free bounty glorify (2)
104	without money, come to Jesus Christ and buy (2)
104	come,ye weary, heavy laden bruised & mangled by the fall (4)
104	if you tarry till you're better, you will never come (4)
106	wanderer, come, Follow me, I'll guide thee home (R)
110	Jesus is waiting, O come to him now (3)
110	come with thy sins; at his feet lowly bow (3)
110	come, and no longer delay (3)
111	come, let us, who in Christ believe (T,1)
111	come quickly in ... nor ever hence remove (4)
111	come quickly in, thou heavenly guest (4)
117	come unto me and rest (1)
119	and that thou bidst me come to thee (1)
119	O Lamb of God, I come, I come! (R)
119	because thy promise I believe ... I come (5)
119	now, to be thine, yea, thine alone...I come (6)
130	come quickly ... my Lord, & take possession of thine own (4)
130	come quickly from above (5)
131	come, Holy Ghost, our hearts inspire (T,1)
131	come, Holy Ghost, for moved by thee the prophets wrote (2)

132 come, thou source of joy and gladness, breathe thy life (1)
132 author of the new creation, come with unction (2)
132 come with unction and with power (2)
134 come, Holy Spirit, heavenly Dove (T,1,5)
134 come, shed abroad a Savior's love, and... kindle ours (5)
137 Spirit of faith, come down, reveal the things of God (T,1)
142 whate'er may come, I'll taste ... the hallowed bliss (4)
147 but should the surges rise and rest delay to come (2)
168 well, the delightful day will come (3)
169 to consecrate myself to thee, O Jesus Christ, I come (1)
169 with no reserve and no delay, with all my heart, I come (2)
169 I would serve thee with all my might ... to thee I come (3)
169 Lord of my life, I come (4)
185 let sorrow do its work, come grief or pain (3)
190 come, let thy voice be one with theirs (2)
190 so let the love of Jesus come and set my soul ablaze (2)
197 thy kingdom come on earth, O Lord (4)
197 we pray in deed and word, thy kingdom come on earth (4)
204 glorious from thy heaven above shall come the city (6)
204 shall come the city of our God (6)
214 their evil acts shall surely come to naught (4)
214 past deeds shall come and them ensnare (4)
216 no evil shall upon thee come (6)
218 come, Lord, when grace hath made me meet (4)
222 when he shall come with trumpet sound (4)
225 make in my heart a quiet place ... come & dwell therein (1)
250 o'ercome through Christ alone, and stand entire at last (2)
250 still let the Spirit cry, in all his soldiers "Come" (3)
252 O Thou by whom we come to God ... Life ... Truth ... Way (6)
258 come, my soul, thou must be waking (T ,1)
258 come to him who made this splendor (1)
265 O bless me now, my Savior, I come to thee (R)
265 come quickly and abide or life is vain (3)
277 O come, and dwell with me, spirit of power within (T,1)
282 come quickly from above (5)
283 joy of heaven, to earth come down (1)
283 come, Almighty to deliver, let us all thy life receive (3)
290 no harm from him can come to me on ocean or on shore (4)
298 to this temple, where we call thee, come, O Lord (2)
298 come, O Lord of hosts, today (2)
302 come, let us join our friends above (T,1)
304 Thy kingdom come (1)
309 come, and spread thy banner here (2)
310 ' thy name salvation is, which here we come to prove (2)
314 world where thou... send us let thy kingdom come, O Lord (4)
316 when thou shalt in thy kingdom come ... Lord remember me (4)
317 O Lord, we pray, come thou among us (3)
318 come into the daylight's splendor (1)
325 all things are ready, come away (4)
325 come to your places at the feast (4)
344 come, Father, Son, and Holy Ghost (T,1)
352 come, O thou God of grace (T,1)
353 the King shall come (T,1)
353 the King shall come when morning dawns (5)
353 thy people pray, come quickly, King of kings (5)
354 o come, o come, Emmanuel, and ransom captive Israel (T,1)
354 rejoice! rejoice! Emmanuel shall come to thee, O Israel (R)
354 O come, thou Wisdom from on high (2)
354 O come, Desire of nations (3)

354   O come, thou Day-spring (4)
354   come and cheer our spirits by thine advent here (4)
358   lo, the Prince of Peace, lo, the Son of God is come (3)
359   he shall come down like showers upon the fruitful earth (3)
360   come, thou long expected Jesus (T,1)
363   Redeemer, come, with us abide (3)
364   Hallelujah! everlasting God, come down (4)
366   come forth, ye virgins, night is past (1)
366   her Star is risen; her Light is come (2)
366   come, thou blessed One. God's own beloved son, Alleluia (2)
374   come to Bethlehem & see him whose birth the angels sing (2)
374   come, adore on bended knee Christ the Lord (3)
379   brethren, come, from all that grieves you, you are freed (2)
379   come, then, let us hasten yonder (3)
381   O come to us, abide with us, our Lord Emmanuel (4)
382   come and worship, worship Christ, the new-born King (R)
385   come, peasant, King, to own him (3)
386   O come, all ye faithful, joyful and triumphant (T,1)
386   come and behold him, born the King of angels (1)
386   O come ye, O come ye to Bethlehem (1)
386   O come, let us adore him, Christ, the Lord (R)
387   late in time behold him come (2)
390   still through the cloven skies they come (2)
390   shall come the time foretold (3)
390   when with the ever circling years shall come the time (3)
392   joy to the world, the Lord is come (T,1)
408   heal its ancient wrong, come, Prince of Peace, and reign (3)
410   and Christ's great kingdom shall come on earth (R)
410   that all of the world's great peoples might come (4)
410   might come to the truth of God (4)
420   come, sinners, see your Savior die (3)
420   come, feel with me his blood applied (3)
440   there on high our welcome waits (2)
441   love is come again like wheat that springeth green (R)
446   come, ye faithful, raise the strain (T,1)
448   come, ye faithful, raise the strain (T,1) (see 446)
452   come then, true and faithful, now fulfill thy word (3)
457   come, let us rise with Christ our Head (T,1)
461   O come, great Spirit, come (1,4)
461   come as the fire, and purge our hearts (2)
461   come as the dove & spread thy wings ... of peaceful love (3)
466   come down, O Love divine, seek thou this soul of mine (T,1)
467   come, Holy Ghost, our souls inspire (T,1)
467   where thou art guide, no ill can come (3)
468   the Lord will come and not be slow (T,1)
468   the nations all whom thou hast made shall come (3)
469   thy kingdom come, O Lord, thy will be done (1,2,3,4)
477   come with thy timeless judgment . match our present hour (1)
477   finely build for days to come foundations that endure (3)
478   lead on, O King eternal, the day of march has come (T,1)
480   thou who didst come to bring ... healing and sight (2)
480   didst come to bring on thy redeeming wing (2)
481   within whose four-square walls shall come no night (1)
483   rejoice in glorious hope! Our Lord the judge shall come (4)
489   here we come thy name to praise (3)
496   sin and want we come confessing (1)
502   come near and bless us when we wake (6)
507   come, let us use the grace divine (T,1)

507 if thou art well pleased to hear, come down (4)
507 come down and meet us now (4)
508 come, let us use the grace divine (T,1) (same as 507)
511 to make the dream come true (2)
522 come, ye thankful people come (T,1)
522 come to God's own temple, come (1)
522 God shall come, and shall take his harvest home (3)
522 even so,Lord, quickly come, bring thy final harvest home (4)
522 come, with all thine angels, come (4)
522 for the Lord our God shall come (3)
528 come, O my guilty brethren, come (5)
529 come, O thou traveler unknown (T,1)
542 thy kingdom come; on earth thy will be done (3)

comely
490 warrior-like and strong, comely as a groom (1)

comes
 91 the night becomes as day when from the heart we say (2)
151 through the truth that comes from God (2)
218 he that into God's kingdom comes must enter by this door (3)
232 and heaven comes down our souls to greet (4)
242 once to every man and nation comes the moment to decide (T)
244 when my life becomes a burden ... nearing chilly Jordan (4)
269 and age comes on, uncheered by faith or hope (2)
326 feast after feast thus comes and passes by (5)
342 we hear the call, O Lord, that comes from thee (1)
353 when Christ our King in beauty comes (4)
359 he comes to break oppression, to set the captive free (1)
359 he comes with succor speedy to those who suffer wrong (2)
364 lo, he comes with clouds descending (T,1)
366 the Bridegrooml comes, awake (1)
366 for her Lord comes down all-glorious (2)
370 wisdom comes to those who know thee (1)
376 heaven and earth shall flee away when he comes to reign (2)
380 comes down through the night from the heavenly throng (4)
392 he comes to make his blessing flow (3)
446 with the royal feast of feasts, comes its joy to render (3)
446 comes to glad Jerusalem who with true affection (3)
478 with deeds of love and mercy, the heavenly kingdom comes (2)
498 every burden will be lighter when ... it comes from thee (3)
498 when we know it comes from thee (3)
506 long our day of testing, now comes the hour of resting (3)

comest
424 who in the Lord's name comest, the King and blessed One (1)

cometh
201 help us to seek thy kingdom that cometh from above (3)
237 when my last hour cometh, fraught with strife and pain (4)
238 in the strength that cometh by the holy cross (1)

comfort
 63 he with earthly cares entwineth hope and comfort (4)
 63 hope and comfort from above (4)
 67 thy rod and staff my comfort still (4)
 68 thy rod and staff me comfort still (3)
 87 it will joy and comfort give you (1)

89 comfort it brings and power and peace (2)
125 leave ... leave me not alone, still support & comfort me (2)
129 my comfort by day and my song in the night (1)
129 thy soul-cheering comfort impart (4)
145 thou the spring of all my comfort, more than life for me (4)
181 to comfort and to bless, to find a balm for woe (3)
189 one tender comfort broods upon the struggling human soul (3)
205 heavenly peace, divinest comfort (1)
217 O words with heavenly comfort fraught (1)
227 sweet comfort and peace of a soul in its earliest love (1)
227 tongue can never express the sweet comfort and peace (1)
227 that sweet comfort was mine (2)
250 the troubled heart thy comfort blest (4)
310 Lord, let every bounding heart the mighty comfort feel (4)
378 O tidings of comfort and joy, comfort and joy (R)
467 thy blessed unction from above is comfort, life & fire (2)
467 comfort, life and fire of love (2)
479 hope and health, good will and comfort (4)
484 from all the easy speeches that comfort cruel men (2)
489 may thy Gospel's joyful sound conquer sinners, comfort (4)
489 conquer sinners, comfort saints (4)
495 comfort every sufferer watching late in pain (4)
526 he is merciful and just, here is my comfort and my trust (3)

comforter
3 come, holy Comforter, thy sacred witness bear (3)
103 here speaks the Comforter, tenderly saying (2)
345 let the comforter and friend, thy Holy Spirit, meet (2)
466 O Comforter, draw near, within my heart appear (1)

comforts
70 unnumbered comforts to my soul thy tender care bestowed (2)
70 before my infant heart could know from whom...comforts (2)
70 from whom those comforts flowed (2)
231 when comforts are declining, he grants the soul again (1)
289 when other helpers fail and comforts flee (1)
306 are one, our comforts and our cares (2)
463 who upholds and comforts us in all trials, fears & needs (3)

coming
47 God of the coming years ... we follow thee (3)
57 thy going out, thy coming in, forever he will guide (4)
99 "Come to me...and coming be at rest" (1)
116 I am coming to the cross (T,1)
236 grant us thy peace, Lord, through the coming night (3)
362 proclaim to a desolate people the coming of their King (2)
381 no ear may hear his coming, but in this world of sin (3)
444 waiting the coming day (1)
491 guard us through the coming night (1,2,3)
545 mine eyes have seen the glory of the coming of the Lord (T)
545 he is coming like the glory of the morning on the wave (5)

command
22 wide as the world is thy command (4)
37 moon shines full at his command, and all the stars obey (1)
51 leave to his sovereign sway to choose and to command (3)
200 speak, and, behold! we answer; command, and we obey (4)
302 one army of the living God, to his command we bow (4)
342 we welcome thy command (4)

commanding
   61   he, with all-commanding might, filled the new-made world (2)
   139   with strong commanding evidence their... origin display (5)

commandments
   65   unto those who still remember his commandments, and obey (5)

commands
   406   heralds of Christ, who bear the King's commands (T,1)

commend
   413   believe that spirit triumphs .. commend .. soul to God (3)
   551   Lord of the nations, thus to thee our country we commend (4)

commit
   509   the future ... we to thy guardian care commit (3)

common
   111   our common Savior praise (1)
   189   one common faith unites us all, we seek one common goal (3)
   197   the sacredness of common things (1)
   202   the common hopes that make us men were his in Galilee (2)
   232   they meet around one common mercy seat (3)
   301   we all partake the joy of one; the common peace we feel (4)
   482   in mart & court and parliament the common good increase (3)
   499   the trvial round, the common task will furnish all (3)
   525   for life and health, those common things (2)
   525   common things which every day and hour brings (2)

commonweal
   136   God's glorious commonweal (2)

commune
   159   with thee, my God, I commune as friend with friend (3)
   494   Lord, we would commune with thee (1)

communion
   40   grant unto us communion with thee (2)
   192   in him shall true hearts everywhere ... communion find (2)
   192   their high communion find (2)
   294   her sweet communion, solemn vows (4)
   297   and mystic sweet communion with those whose rest is won (4)
   334   possess in sweet communion, joys ... earth cannot afford (2)
   536   O blest communion, fellowship divine (4)

company
   170   still with thee in closer, dearer company (2)
   424   the company of angels are praising thee on high (2)
   529   my company before is gone, and I am left alone with thee (1)

compare
   303   what radiancy of glory, what light beyond compare (1)

compass
   247   chart and compass came from thee (1)
   341   arms of love that compass me would all mankind embrace (3)
   372   it is the chart and compass that o'er life's surging sea (3)

compassion
    65   like the pity of a father hath... Lord's compassion been (3)
   161   thou Christ of great compassion (1)
   201   awake in us compassion, O Lord of life divine (3)
   204   the sweet compassion of thy face (4)
   283   Jesus, thou art all compassion (1)
   371   see thy compassion in the Savior's face (3)
   427   give us compassion for thee, Lord (4)
   479   as, O Lord, thy deep compassion healed the sick (2)
   479   making known the needs and burdens thy compassion bids (3)
   479   needs and burdens thy compassion bids us bear (3)

complain
   142   will not murmur nor complain beneath the chastening rod (2)

complaints
   489   bring relief for all complaints (4)

complete
    87   when our journey is complete (4)
   172   and make my sacrifice complete (4)
   408   whole round world complete, from sunrise to its setting (2)
   430   we in thee redeemed, complete (5)
   434   God's own sacrifice complete (3)

completing
   370   many diverse scrolls completing (2)

compose
   435   or thorns compose so rich a crown (3)

comprehend
    12   what heart can comprehend thy name (2)

comrades
   198   inarmed shall live as comrades free (3)

concealed
   115   our life in Christ concealed (2)
   457   life of Christ is ours with Christ concealed above (3)
   457   hidden life of Christ ... with Christ concealed above (3)

conceived
   440   never that full joy conceived (2)

concert
   357   every voice in concert ring evermore and evermore (2)

concern
   253   a jealous, just concern for thine, immortal praise (4)

concord
    91   ye nations of mankind, in this your concord find (3)

condemnation
   527   no condemnation now I dread (4)

condemned
359 souls, condemned and dying, are precious in his sight (2)

condescend
31 and will this sovereign King of glory condescend (4)
77 he is our guide and friend; to us he'll condescend (2)

condescending
426 O mysterious condescending! O abandonment sublime! (3)

condition
251 how rich is my condition: God & heaven are still my own (1)

conduct
167 through sorrow or through joy, conduct me as thine own (1)
266 thy friends in thy conduct his likeness shall see (2)
490 make my conduct good, actions calm and mild (2)

cover
125 cover my defenseless head with the shadow of thy wing (2)
125 grace to cover all my sin (4)

covered
512 with corn the vales are covered (2)

covering
293 cloud and fire appear for a glory and a covering (3)
469 through the thick darkness covering every nation (1)

coward
242 while the coward stands aside (2)

cradle
380 and we greet in his cradle our Savior and King (4)
384 and stay by my cradle till morning is nigh (2)
400 cold on his cradle the dew-drops are shining (2)
405 Eastern sages at his cradle make oblations rich and rare (3)

cradled
517 didst deign a child to be cradled on a mother's bosom (1)

cradles
380 for the manger of Bethlehem cradles a King (1,2)

craft
20 his craft and power are great (1)

craftman's
2 craftman's art and music's measure for thy pleasure (3)

crag
272 o'er crag and torrent, till the night is gone (3)

crashing
11 breakers crashing on the shore (3)

craved
185 once earthly joy I craved, sought peace and rest (2)

create
22   he can create, and he destroy (1)
173 create in us... splendor that dawns when hearts are kind (4)
201 create in us a yearning for those whom thou dost seek (1)
201 create in us thy spirit; give us a love like thine (3)
253 on thee, almighty to create, almighty to renew (1)
273 with thy spirit recreate me, pure and strong and true (1)

created
424 and mortal men and all things created make reply (2)

creed
189 what are sundering strains of blood...and creed (2)
189 what are ... ancient caste and creed (2)
191 men whose aim 'twill be not to defend some ancient creed (1)
407 the futile cries of superstition's cruel creed (2)
548 save the people from the clash of race and creed (4)

creeds
136 shall blend their creeds in one (3)

crib
384 away in a manger no crib for a bed (T,1)

cried
227 "He hath loved me," I cried, "He hath suffered and died (4)

cries
91 when morning gilds the skies, my heart awaking cries (T,1)
113 by thy cross and dying cries, by thy one great sacrifice (2)
115 this earth, he cries, is not my place (1)
204 where sound the cries of race and clan (1)
260 not beat with cries on heaven's doors (3)
312 permit them to approach, he cries (2)
407 the futile cries of superstition's cruel creed (2)
428 receive my soul, he cries (3)
481 from little children's cries (2)

crimes
415 for crimes that I have done he groaned upon the tree (2)

crimson
11 skies with crimson clouds aflame (2)
101 crimson flood that washes white as snow (2)
101 plunge now into the crimson flood (2)

crippled
201 the hopeless and the burdened, the crippled and the weak (1)

crooked
362 make straight all the crooked places (1,4)

crops
514 take the finest of our harvest, crops we grow (1)
514 in these crops of your creation, take, O God: (3)
514 these crops ... they are our prayer (3)
514 crops we grow that men may live (1)

cross

17	that on the cross, my burden gladly bearing (3)
67	thy cross before to guide me (4)
83	he bore the shameful cross ... carried all my grief (2)
95	at the cross of Christ I bow (1)
112	thankless creatures, why will you cross his love and die (1)
113	by thy cross and dying cries, by thy one great sacrifice (2)
116	I am coming to(4)
120	in my hand no price I bring; simply to thy cross I cling (2)
123	know not how that Calvary's cross a world ... could free (2)
123	Calvary's cross a world from sin could free (2)
138	I see thy cross; there teach my heart to cling (3)
141	have faith in God, my soul, His cross forever stands (3)
159	nearer ... to the cross where thou hast died (R)
159	till I cross the narrow sea (4)
160	take up thy cross (1,2,3,4)
160	cross-let not its weight fill thy weak spirit with alarm(2)
160	take up thy cross, nor heed the shame (3)
160	take up thy cross,the Savior said (T,1)
160	thy Lord for thee the cross endured (3)
160	cross endured to save thy soul from death and hell (3)
160	take up thy cross and follow Christ (4)
160	for only he who bears the cross may hope to wear...crown (4)
161	by thy cross didst save us from death and dark despair (4)
173	while ever on the hill-top before thee loomed the cross (2)
174	lift high the cross of Christ (4)
177	help me the cross to bear, thy wondrous love declare (2)
183	must Jesus bear the cross alone (T,1)
183	there's a cross for everyone ... there's a cross for me (1)
183	consecrated cross I'll bear till death shall set me free (3)
193	each other's cross to bear (2)
204	where cross the crowded ways of life (T,1)
209	bear patiently the cross of grief or pain (1)
223	not a grief nor a loss, not a frown or a cross (2)
223	not a frown ... cross, but is blest if we trust and obey (3)
228	in the old rugged cross, stained with blood so divine (3)
228	so I'll cherish the old rugged cross (R)
228	on a hill 'far away stood an old rugged cross (T,1)
228	and I love that old cross where the dearest and best (1)
228	O that old rugged cross, so despised by the world (2)
228	I will cling to the old rugged cross (R)
228	to the old rugged cross I will ever be true (4)
228	for 'twas on that old cross Jesus suffered and died (3)
233	the cross of Christ your King (1)
234	O Cross that liftest up my head (4)
238	in the strength that cometh by the holy cross (1)
239	am I a soldier of the cross, a follower of the Lamb (T,1)
242	with the cross that turns not back (3)
248	ye soldiers of the cross (1)
251	Jesus, I my cross have taken (T,1)
253	bold to take up, firm to sustain the consecrated cross (2)
263	e'en though it be a cross that raiseth me (1)
287	if you love him, why not serve him... soldiers ... cross (4)
287	every round goes higher ... soldiers of the cross (2)
287	climbing Jacob's ladder ... soldiers of the cross (T,1)
287	sinner, do you love my Jesus ... soldiers of the cross (3)
287	we are climbing higher, higher ... soldiers of the cross (5)

289 hold thou thy cross before my closing eyes (5)
292 with us the cross to bear, for Christ our Lord (3)
305 with the cross of Jesus going on before (1,R)
336 let us take up the cross till we the crown obtain (5)
355 upon a cross ... bound thee & mocked thy saving kingship (1)
355 we bring our hearts before thy cross (4)
415 I hide my blushing face while his dear cross appears (4)
416 in the cross of Christ I glory (T,1,5)
416 never shall the cross forsake me (2)
416 from the cross the radiance streaming adds more luster (3)
416 by the cross are sanctified (4)
417 beneath the cross of Jesus I fain would take my stand (T,1)
417 upon that cross of Jesus mine eye at times can see (2)
417 I take, O cross, thy shadow for my abiding place (3)
417 my sinful self my only shame, my glory all the cross (3)
419 patient bears his cross below, he follows in his train (1)
419 and mocked the cross and flame (3)
426 cross of Jesus, cross of sorrow (T,1,4)
427 that, as we share this hour, thy cross may bring ... joy (4)
427 thy cross may bring us to thy joy and resurrection power (4)
430 never further than thy cross, never higher than thy feet (T)
430 sin, which laid the cross on thee (2)
430 love, which bore the cross for us (2)
430 through thy cross made pure and white (5)
433 Jesus, keep me hear the cross (T,1)
433 in the cross, in the cross, be my glory ever (R)
433 near the cross, a trembling soul, love & mercy found me (2)
433 near the cross... Lamb of God bring its scenes before me (3)
433 near the cross I'll watch & wait, hoping, trusting ever (4)
434 learn of Christ to bear the cross (2)
435 when I survey the wondrous cross (T,1)
435 cross on which the Prince of Glory died (1)
439 ours the cross, the grave, the skies, Alleluia (4)
443 didst once, upon the cross, Alleluia (1)
443 didst once, upon the cross ... suffer to redeem our loss (1)
443 endured the cross and grave, Alleluia (2)
443 endured the cross & grave ... sinners to redeem and save (2)
457 every vanquished foe submits to his victorious cross (2)
458 to them the cross with all its shame (4)
458 cross ... with all its grace, is given (4)
458 the cross he bore is life and health (6)
463 by whose cross & death are we rescued from sin's misery (2)
469 his conquering cross no kingdom wills to bear (2)
478 thy cross is lifted o'er us, we journey in its light (3)
479 on the cross, forsaken, work thy mercy's perfect deed (1)
482 we bear with thee the scourge and cross (2)
498 Jesus, for thy love most tender on the cross ... shown (2)
498 on the cross for sinners shown (2)
506 Savior's cross is winning forgiveness for the sinning (4)
528 shall I, the hallowed cross to shun (3)

crossed
302 part of his host have crossed the flood (4)
550 our exiled fathers crossed the sea (1)

crossing
302 part are crossing now (4)

crowd
  22 we'll crowd thy gates with thankful songs (3)
 173 thoughts & actions less prone to please the crowd (1)
 351 who honor truth, nor fear the crowd (3)
 423 from Olivet they followed mid an exultant crowd (2)
 440 life eternal! O what wonders crowd on faith (4)
 453 saints and angels crowd around him (3)

crowded
 204 where cross the crowded ways of life (T,1)

crown
  71 bring forth the royal diadem and crown him Lord of all (1)
  71 and crown him Lord of all (1,2,3,4,5)
  71 to him all majesty ascribe, and crown him Lord of all (4)
  76 crown him as your captain in temptation's hour (4)
  79 thee will I honor, thou, my soul's glory, joy and crown (1)
  87 King of kings in heaven we'll crown him (4)
  89 in shame my glory and my crown (3)
  99 yea, a crown, in very surety, but of thorns (3)
 160 for only he who bears the cross may hope to wear...crown (4)
 160 may hope to wear the glorious crown (4)
 166 I'll sing with the glittering crown on my brow (3)
 183 go home my crown to wear, for there's a crown for me (3)
 184 it must its crown resign (4)
 228 and exchange it some day for a crown (R)
 240 lay hold on life ..it shall be thy joy & crown eternally (1)
 243 look up! the victor's crown at length! (4)
 246 work of faith will not be done till thou obtain .. crown (3)
 248 to him that overcometh a crown of life shall be (4)
 249 a heavenly race demands thy zeal and an immortal crown (1)
 270 and sorrow crown each lingering year (2)
 283 all thy faithful mercies crown (1)
 325 blessings crown the board (1)
 336 let us take up the cross till we the crown obtain (5)
 402 gold I bring to crown him again (2)
 418 now scornfully surrounded with thorns, thine only crown (1)
 419 the Son of God goes forth to war, a kingly crown to gain (1)
 432 that caused the Lord of life to lay aside his crown (2)
 432 lay aside his crown for my soul (2)
 435 or thorns compose so rich a crown (3)
 453 crown him, crown him, crown him, crown him (1,2,3,4)
 453 crown the Savior, angels, crown him (2)
 453 crown the Savior King of kings (2)
 455 crown him with many crowns, the Lamb upon his throne (T,1)
 455 crown him the Lord of life, who triumphed o'er the grave (2)
 455 crown him the Lord of peace, whose power a scepter sways (3)
 455 crown him the Lord of love; behold his hands and side (4)
 459 praise we the goodness that doth crown our days (5)
 470 crown thine ancient Church's story (1)
 472 and endless praises crown his head (2)
 478 the crown awaits the conquest; lead on, O God of might (3)
 517 children thou hast given still may be our joy and crown (5)
 527 bold I approach the eternal throne, and claim the crown (4)
 527 claim the crown, through Christ my own (4)
 536 and win with them the victor's crown of gold (3)
 543 crown thy good with brotherhood ... sea to shining sea (1,4)
 546 crown, O God, thine own endeavor (2)

crowned
44   with honor thou hast crowned his head (4)
83   his head with radiant glories crowned (1)
233   bright youth and snow-crowned age (2)
237   or, in darker semblance, cross-crowned Calvary (2)
249   crowned with victory at thy feet I'll lay .. honors down (4)
288   and thou art crowned at last (1)
346   true wisdom is with reverence crowned (4)
353   crowned with glory like the sun . lights the morning sky (2)
355   mocked ... by thorns with which they crowned thee (1)
453   sinners in derision crowned him (3)
458   the head that once was crowned with thorns (T,1)
458   is crowned with glory now (1)
475   yet thou, her child, whose head is crowned with flame (1)
517   thou... crowned us with an honor women never knew before (2)

crownest
512   the year with good he crownest ... earth his mercy fills (2)

crowns
26   casting down their golden crowns around the glassy sea (2)
232   and glory crowns the mercy seat (4)
283   till we cast our crowns before thee (4)
305   crowns and thrones may perish, kingdoms rise and wane (3)
430   cast our crowns before thy feet (5)
453   crowns become the victor's brow (1)
455   crown him with many crowns, the Lamb upon his throne (T,1)
509   that mercy crowns it till it close (1)

crucified
94   I my Master have denied, I afresh have crucified (2)
124   Jesus Christ, the crucified (1,2,3,4)
338   nothing desire, nothing esteem, but Jesus crucified (3)
355   the power which crucified thee (2)
412   'twas I, Lord Jesus, I ... denied thee; I crucified thee (2)
413   are ye able, said the Master, to be crucified with me (1)
414   where the dear Lord was crucified .. died to save us all (1)
420   my Lord, my Love, is crucified (1,2,3)
420   crucified for me and you to bring us rebels near to God (2)
426   robed in mortal flesh is dying crucified by sin for me (2)
436   were you there when they crucified my Lord (1)
462   Spirit redeeming, give us grace when crucified (3)
462   give us grace when crucified to seek thy face (3)

Crucify
112   will you let him die in vain? Crucify your Lord again? (2)

cruel
20   armed with cruel hate, on earth is not his equal (1)
407   the futile cries of superstition's cruel creed (2)
484   from all the easy speeches that comfort cruel men (2)

crusade
189   join the glorious new crusade of our great Lord and King (3)

crushed
175   down in the human heart, crushed by the tempter (3)

crust
242   when we share her wretched crust (2)

cry
7   wisdom, honor, power, blessing ... we cry (4)
7   with the angelic host we cry (4)
19   cry out, dominions, princedoms, powers ... alleluia (1)
19   cry out ... virtues, arch-angels, angels' choirs (1)
44   oh, what is man! I cry (2)
122   forgive him, O forgive, they cry (3)
122   and Father, Abba, Father, cry (5)
129   or cry in the desert for bread (3)
137   cry, with joy unspeakable, "...my Lord, my God!" (2)
145   pass me not, O gentle Savior, hear my humble cry (T,1)
145   Savior, Savior, hear my humble cry (R)
185   this be the parting cry my heart shall raise (4)
190   worlds awake to cry their blessings on the Lord of life (1)
250   still let the Spirit cry, in all his soldiers, "Come" (3)
252   angels in their songs rejoice and cry,"Behold he prays" (4)
257   hear the cry thy people raises (3)
288   and still to God salvation cry, salvation to the Lamb (1)
295   my very heart and flesh cry out, O Loving God, for thee (2)
318   at thy feet I cry, my Maker (2)
324   as with ceaseless voice they cry, Alleluia (4)
339   Lord of the harvest, hear the needy servants' cry (T,1)
341   'tis all my business here below to cry,"Behold the Lamb" (5)
341   preach him to all and cry in death,"...behold the Lamb" (6)
343   To God the tribes of ocean cry, and birds upon the wing (2)
344   Father ... to whom we for our children cry (1)
366   at the thrilling cry rejoices (1)
380   there's a mother's deep prayer and a baby's low cry (1)
409   let all cry aloud and honor the Son (3)
425   hark! all the tribes hosanna cry (1)
434   It is finished, hear him cry (3)
446   Alleluia now we cry to our King immortal (5)
475   peals forth in joy man's old undaunted cry (3)
479   still the hungry cry for bread (2)
481   bitter lips in blind despair cry (3)
481   cry Christ hath died in vain (3)
484   O God of earth and altar, bow down and hear our cry (T,1)
526   out of the depths I cry to thee (T,1)
531   make me thy duteous child, that I ceaseless may...cry (3)
531   that I ceaseless may, Abba, Father, cry (3)
538   hear us when we cry to thee for those in peril on... sea (R)

crying
200   I hear my people crying in cot and mine and slum (2)
362   there's a voice in the wilderness crying (T,1,4)
366   the watchmen on the heights are crying (1)
384   but little Lord Jesus, no crying he makes (2)

crystal
33   the hand that shaped the rose hath wrought the crystal (1)
33   the crystal of the snow (1)
33   thyself the vision passing by in crystal and in rose (3)
271   open now the crystal fountain (2)
273   like the springs and running waters make me crystal pure (2)
524   where flows the crystal river (3)

cultivate
342   we cultivate the nature God plants in every heart (3)

cumbered
261   are we weak & heavy laden, cumbered with a load of care (3)

cup
  68   my head thou dost with oil anoint, and my cup overflows (4)
196   sacred cup of saving grace I will with thanks receive (2)
204   the cup of water given for thee still holds ...thy grace (4)
316   thy testamental cup I take, and thus remember thee (2)
317   he drank the cup on Golgatha. His grace we trust (1)
319   the cup in token of his blood that was for sinners shed (3)
321   the blessed cup is only passed true memory of thee (3)
419   who best can drink his cup of woe, triumphant over pain (1)

cure
103   earth has no sorrow that heaven cannot cure (2)
120   be of sin the double cure (1)
470   cure thy children's warring madness (3)

curse
392   far as the curse is found (3)
407   the curse of greed, the moan of pain (2)
432   caused the Lord of bliss to bear the dreadful curse (1)
432   bear the dreadful curse for my soul (1)

cut
429   cut off for sins, but not his own (1)

cymbal's
366   with harp and cymbal's clearest tone (3)

cymbals
  15   timbrels soft and cymbals loud in his high praise agree (2)

daily
  47   be thou for us in life our daily bread (3)
  55   surely his goodness and mercy here daily attend thee (3)
  62   to him let each affection daily rise and round him move (4)
  93   to grace how great a debtor daily I'm constrained to be (3)
128   that vow renewed shall daily hear (5)
152   my daily labor to pursue (1)
180   thy daily stage of duty run (1)
197   O Workman true, may we fulfill in daily life (2)
197   fulfill in daily life thy Father's will (2)
221   overcoming daily with the Spirit's sword (3)
321   in our daily life may flame the passion of thy heart (4)
335   watch thou daily o'er their souls (4)
342   and let our daily living reveal thee everywhere (1)
359   to him shall prayer unceasing and daily vows ascend (4)
445   He lives, and grants me daily breath (3)
498   praise for mercies daily twining round us golden cords (1)
499   if on our daily course our mind be set to hallow (3)
513   much more, to us his children, he gives our daily bread (2)
515   thy children live by daily food (1)
515   and daily must the prayer be said (1)

515 give us this day our daily bread (1)
515 wide as the want of daily bread (3)
515 with which our daily bread we gain (4)
518 give us each day our daily bread (2)
519 ne'er forget God's daily care (T,1)
524 who didst give us daily bread, give us the bread eternal (2)
539 daily manna still provide you (2)
549 from daily tasks set free (1)

dale
203 o'er hill and dale in saffron flame and red (4)

damnation
484 from sleep and from damnation, deliver us, good Lord (2)

damps
545 have builded him an altar in the evening dews and damps (2)

dancing
273 like thy dancing waves in sunlight make me glad and free (3)
442 and set the meadows dancing (1)

danger
46 as far from danger as from fear (2)
93 to rescue me from danger, interposed his precious blood (2)
142 when in danger knows no fear, in darkness feels no doubt (3)
236 from harm and danger keep thy children free (3)
248 courage rise with danger & strength to strength oppose (2)
248 where duty calls or danger, be never wanting there (3)
379 voice from yonder manger...Flee...danger (2)
379 voice...doth entreat: Flee from woe and danger (2)

danger's
538 our brethren shield in danger's hour (4)

dangers
52 in midst of dangers, fears, and death (3)
92 through many dangers, toils ... snares I... already come (3)
207 when dangers fierce your path assail (2)

dare
24 today attend his voice, nor dare provoke his rod (4)
105 and shall I dare his spirit grieve (3)
156 I would be brave, for there is much to dare (1)
198 spill no drop of blood but dare all (2)
198 dare all that may plant man's lordship firm on earth (2)
222 I dare not trust the sweetest frame (1)
234 I dare not ask to fly from thee (4)
248 arm of flesh will fail you, ye dare not trust your own (3)
292 with us the work to share, with us reproach to dare (3)
351 and dare to trust the living God (3)
481 how its splendor challenges the souls that greatly dare (5)
502 for without thee I dare not die (3)

daring
153 daring hearts and spirits free (1)

dark
- 31 subdues the powers of hell, confounds their dark designs (3)
- 38 drive the dark of doubt away (1)
- 43 solemn silence ... move round the dark terrestrial ball (3)
- 67 in death's dark vale I fear no ill (4)
- 68 yea, though I walk in death's dark vale (3)
- 117 I am this dark world's light (3)
- 119 and waiting not to rid my soul of one dark blot (2)
- 143 while life's dark maze I tread & griefs around me spread (3)
- 148 dark the night of sin has settled (2)
- 161 by thy cross didst save us from death and dark despair (4)
- 204 on shadowed thresholds dark with fears (2)
- 206 though there be dark, unchartered space (4)
- 228 to bear it to dark Calvary (2)
- 229 peace, perfect peace, in this dark world of sin (T,1)
- 236 for dark and light are both alike to thee (3)
- 272 the night is dark, & I am far from home, lead thou me on (1)
- 292 redeemed at countless cost, from dark despair (2)
- 329 chase the dark night of sin away (5)
- 354 and death's dark shadows put to flight (4)
- 356 break forth ... upon the world's dark hour (1)
- 365 bless the dark world with heavenly light (5)
- 372 O Truth unchanged, unchanging, O Light of our dark sky (1)
- 381 yet in thy dark streets shineth the everlasting light (1)
- 401 dark and cheerless is the morn unaccompanied by thee (2)
- 406 through desert ways, dark fen, and deep morass (2)
- 434 go to dark Gethsemane (T,1)
- 440 death and sorrow, earth's dark story (1)
- 441 wheat that in dark earth many days has lain (1)
- 444 he arose a victor from the dark domain (R)
- 446 all the winter of our sins, long and dark, is flying (2)
- 446 neither might the gates of death ... tomb's dark portal (4)
- 446 who, triumphant, burst the bars of the tomb's dark portal (5)
- 462 eyes that see, beyond the dark, the dawn and thee (5)
- 473 and dark is his path on the wings of the storm (2)
- 491 we pray thee that offenseless the hours of dark may be (1)
- 491 call on thee that sinless the hours of dark may be (2)
- 491 ask that free from peril the hours of dark may be (3)
- 492 how beauteous nature now! How dark and sad before (3)
- 496 though the night be dark and dreary (3)
- 538 who didst brood upon the waters dark and rude (3)

darkened
- 74 that in our darkened hearts thy grace might shine (1)
- 203 we've felt thy touch in sorrow's darkened way (3)
- 398 Light of the world, Illumine ... darkened earth of thine (3)

darkening
- 340 see the thronged and darkening way (1)
- 541 be with them traversing the air in darkening storms (1)
- 541 in darkening storms or sunshine fair (1)

darker
- 218 Christ leads me through no darker rooms than he went (3)
- 237 or, in darker semblance, cross-crowned Calvary (2)

darkest
12 that makes the darkest way I go an open path to thee (4)
50 that in the darkest spot of earth some love is found (2)
63 the hour that darkest seemeth will his... goodness prove (3)
89 my light in Satan's darkest hour (4)
230 where darkest clouds have been (3)
230 bright skies will soon be o'er me, where darkest clouds (3)
427 this is the earth's darkest hour (3)
480 and in earth's darkest place, let there be light (3)

darkling
372 it shineth like a beacon above the darkling world (3)

darkness
20 the Prince of Darkness grim, we tremble not for him (3)
26 holy, holy, holy! though the darkness hide thee (3)
47 with thee to bless, the darkness shines as light (2)
78 redeem us for eternal day from every power of darkness (3)
85 thru thy life so radiant, earth's darkness turns to day (1)
91 powers of darkness fear, when this sweet chant they hear (2)
106 groping on in darkness drear (2)
142 when in danger knows no fear, in darkness feels no doubt (3)
143 be thou my guide; bid darkness turn to day (3)
148 in the darkness may be lost (3)
200 I see my people falling in darkness and despair (2)
211 in darkness and temptation, my light, my help is near (1)
213 the darkness shineth as the light (1)
222 when darkness veils his lovely face (2)
233 as warriors through the darkness toil (5)
236 turn thou for us its darkness into light (3)
238 how the powers of darkness rage thy steps around (1)
242 choice goes by forever twixt that darkness & that light (1)
250 tread all the powers of darkness down (3)
257 our knowledge, sense and sight lie in deepest darkness (2)
257 lie in deepest darkness shrouded (2)
263 darkness be over me, my rest a stone (2)
270 no path we shun, no darkness dread (2)
284 through darkness & perplexity point ...the heavenly way (4)
289 the darkness deepens; Lord, with me abide (1)
324 powers of hell may vanish as the darkness clears away (3)
358 darkness takes its flight; doubt & terror are withdrawn (3)
359 give them songs for sighing ... darkness turn to light (2)
361 the people that in darkness sat (T,1)
371 Word ... shines through the darkness of our earthly way (1)
372 till, clouds & darkness ended ... see thee face to face (4)
398 never shall darkness veil thee again from human eyes (1)
400 dawn on our darkness and lend us thine aid (1,5)
403 in whom no darkness is (2)
403 thou shalt own thy darkness passed away (3)
410 for the darkness shall turn to dawning (R)
415 well might .. sun in darkness hide . shut his glories in (3)
452 tread the path of darkness, saving strength to show (3)
469 through the thick darkness covering every nation (1)
480 thou, whose almighty Word chaos and darkness heard (T,1)
480 chaos and darkness heard and took their flight (1)
486 face the darkness undismayed and turn their loss to gain (3)

491 O Jesus, make their darkness light (2)
496 darkness cannot hide from thee (3)
496 blessed Spirit, brooding o'er us, chase the darkness (4)
496 chase the darkness of our night (4)
497 God, that madest earth and heaven, darkness and light (T,1)
499 through sleep and darkness safely brought, restored (1)
500 the darkness falls at thy behest (1)
505 as the darkness deepens o'er us, lo! eternal stars arise (4)
520 reveal thy face where darkness else might be (3)
536 thou, in the darkness drear, their one true light (2)
546 cleave our darkness with thy sword (2)

darksome
213 if in this darksome wild I stray (2)
269 involved in shadows of a darksome night (3)
299 bound in darksome prison-house of sin (2)

daughters
293 well supply thy sons and daughters (2)
446 Jacob's sons and daughters (1)
451 O sons and daughters, let us sing (T,1)
517 sons and daughters look on life with eager eyes (4)
517 when our growing sons and daughters took on life (4)

dauntless
213 dauntless, intired, I follow thee (4)

David's
359 hail to the Lord's anointed, great David's greater Son (T,1)
394 to you in David's town, this day is born of David's line (3)
399 Root of Jesse, David's Son, my Lord and Master (1)
424 thou art the King of Israel, thou David's royal Son (1)

dawn
64 our noontide is thy gracious dawn (3)
135 Holy Spirit, Truth divine, dawn upon this soul of mine (T,1)
358 for the morning seems to dawn (3)
393 with the dawn of redeeming grace (3)
400 dawn on our darkness and lend us thine aid (1,5)
462 spirit of life, in this new dawn (T,1)
462 eyes that see, beyond the dark, the dawn and thee (5)
500 as o'er each continent and island the dawn leads on (3)
500 the dawn leads on another day (3)

dawning
189 day of dawning brotherhood breaks on our eager eyes (1)
264 O in that hour, fairer than daylight dawning shall rise (5)
410 for the darkness shall turn to dawning (R)
410 and the dawning to noon-day bright (R)
459 blessed...with light & life since Eden's dawning day (1)
dawns
173 create in us...splendor that dawns when hearts are kind (4)
189 at length there dawns the glorious day (T,1)
233 toil till dawns the golden day (5)
264 dawns the sweet consciousness, I am with thee (1)
333 morrow that dawns upon eternal love and life (3)
353 when morning dawns and light triumphant breaks (1)

353   the King shall come when morning dawns (5)
479   till thy love's revealing light ... dawns (3)
479   light in its height and depth and greatness dawns (3)
479   dawns upon our quickened sight (3)

day

2   angel harps forever ringing, rest not day nor night (1)
7   for his mercy ceasing never, for his blessing day by day (3)
25   to spend one day with thee on earth exceeds a thousand (1)
25   one day with thee ... exceeds a thousand days of mirth (1)
25   God is our sun, he makes our day (3)
28   they fly, forgotten, as a dream dies at the opening day (5)
29   o day, all days illumining (1)
33   day unto day utter speech ... night to night proclaim (3)
35   for the beauty of each hour of the day and of the night (2)
37   I sing the wisdom that ordained the sun to rule the day (1)
38   fill us with the light of day (1)
39   come, the great day, the glorious hour (3)
43   the unwearied sun, from day to day
47   with each new day, when morning lifts the veil (1)
51   so shall this night soon endd in joyous day (2)
53   his goodness stands approved, unchanged from day to day (4)
57   neath sun or moon, by day or night ... not be afraid (3)
60   dear mother earth, who day by day unfoldest blessings (4)
62   language, glad and golden, speaking to us day and night (1)
64   sheds on our path the glow of day (2)
78   redeem us for eternal day from every power of darkness (3)
85   thru thy life so radiant, earth's darkness turns to day (1)
90   Light of the village life from day to day (4)
91   the night becomes as day when from the heart we say (2)
97   my life .. joy .. all; he is my strength ... day to day (1)
97   he watches o'er me day and night (3)
97   following him by day and night, He's my friend (3)
102   this is the Lord's accepted day (5)
107   day by day his sweet voice soundeth (1)
115   and antedate that day (2)
117   look unto me, thy morn shall rise ... thy day be bright (3)
127   bold shall I stand in thy great day (2)
128   O happy day, that fixed my choice (T,1)
129   my comfort by day and my song in the night (1)
143   be thou my guide; bid darkness turn to day (3)
143   O let me from this day be wholly thine (1)
146   they have their day and cease to be (4)
146   our little systems have their day (4)
152   hasten to thy glorious day (3)
155   I'll labor night and day to be a pilgrim (3)
162   Savior, teach me, day by day, thine own lesson to obey (T,1)
168   well, the delightful day will come (3)
169   in the glad morning of my day (2)
173   once more to hear thy challenge above our noisy day (5)
174   bring ... day of brotherhood ... end the night of wrong (2)
177   that each departing day henceforth may see (3)
180   direct, control, suggest this day (3)
189   at length there dawns the glorious day (T,1)
189   glorious day by prophets long foretold (1)
189   the day of dawning brotherhood breaks on our eager eyes (1)
197   the chance of life that each day brings (1)

203 abound with love and solace for the day (3)
205 my spirit ... wings its flight to realms of day (3)
207 through every day, o'er all the way He will take care (R)
216 no deadly shaft by day shall harm (5)
216 nor plagues that waste in noonday light (5)
218 if short, yet why should I be sad to soar to endless day (2)
224 praising my Savior all the day long (R)
226 every day, every hour, let me feel thy cleansing power (R)
227 Jesus all the day long was my joy and my song (4)
228 and exchange it some day for a crown (R)
228 then he'll call me some day to my home far away (4)
233 toil till dawns the golden day (5)
233 from youth to age, by night and day (4)
234 in thy sunshine's blaze its day may brighter, fairer be (2)
236 with thee began, with thee shall endd the day (2)
238 but that toil shall make thee some day all mine own (4)
238 peace shall follow battle; night shall endd in day (3)
239 when that illustrious day shall rise (6)
245 O sometimes how long seems the day (2)
246 renew it boldly every day, and help divine implore (2)
248 forth to the mighty conquest in this his glorious day (2)
248 this day the noise of battle ... next, the victor's song (4)
250 and win the well-fought day (3)
256 thou my best thought, by day or by night (1)
258 now is breaking o'er the earth another day (1)
258 Light enfolding all things in unclouded day (4)
264 breathe each day nearness unto thee and heaven (3)
272 I loved the garish day (2)
277 hasten the joyful day which shall my sins consume (2)
289 swift to its close ebbs out life's little day (2)
291 o'er ... wide-extended plains shines one eternal day (2)
291 lives out its earthly day (3)
299 O Zion, haste to bring the brighter day (4)
324 Light of light descendeth from the realms of endless day (3)
333 and to life's day the glorious unknown morrow (3)
337 by day and night strict guard to keep (4)
346 his hands built not for one brief day (1)
358 traveler, yes; it brings the day, promised day of Israel (1)
371 guiding our steps to thine eternal day (1)
378 for Jesus Christ our Savior was born upon this day (1)
383 and so it continued both day and night (2)
389 this day again those gates unfold (4)
394 to you in David's town, this day is born of David's line (3)
397 Holy Jesus, every day keep us in the narrow way (4)
401 more & more thyself display, shining to the perfect day (3)
403 that light hath on thee shone in which is perfect day (3)
406 to see the promise of the day fulfilled (3)
408 freedom her bondage breaks, and night is turned to day (1)
416 adds more luster to the day (3)
417 burning of the noon-tide heat and the burden of the day (1)
421 the dying thief rejoiced to see that fountain in his day (2)
422 while men of low degree exalt and usher in the day (4)
422 the day of peace we long to see (4)
433 help me walk from day to day with its shadow o'er me (3)
437 the day of resurrection, earth, tell it out abroad (T,1)
438 then let us feast this Easter Day on the true bread (4)
438 feast this Easter Day on the true bread of heaven (4)
442 day is fast reviving (1)

443 our triumphant holy day (1)
444 waiting the coming day (1)
446 the queen of seasons, bright with the day of splendor (3)
451 that Easter morn at break of day (2)
451 on this most holy day of days, our hearts ... we raise (5)
459 blessed ... with light and life since Eden's dawning day (1)
464 when he first the work begun, small & feeble was his day (2)
477 O day of God, draw nigh in beauty and in power (T,1)
477 O day of God, draw nigh as at creation's birth (5)
478 lead on, O King eternal, the day of march has come (T,1)
480 where the Gospel's day sheds not its glorious day (1)
485 hasten, Lord ... perfect day when pain & death ... cease (2)
487 Jesus, we want to meet on this thy holy day (T,1)
487 we gather round thy throne on this thy holy day (1)
487 look into our hearts & minds today ... this thy holy day (1)
487 we kneel in awe and fear on this thy holy day (2)
487 pray God to teach us here on this thy holy day (2)
487 our faith from seed to flower raise on this thy holy day (2)
487 thy blessing, Lord, we seek on this thy holy day (3)
487 give joy of thy victory on this thy holy day (3)
487 let the mind of Christ abide in us on this thy holy day (3)
487 our minds we dedicate on this thy holy day (4)
487 heart and soul consecrate on this thy holy day (4)
488 O day of rest and gladness (T,1)
488 O day of joy and light (1)
488 new graces ever gaining from this our day of rest (4)
489 day of all thee week the best, emblem of eternal rest (1)
489 may we rest this day in thee (2)
490 may this day be blest, trusting Jesus' love (3)
491 the day is past and over; all thanks, O Lord, to thee (T,1)
491 the joys of day are over; we lift our hearts to thee (2)
491 the toils of day are over; we raise our hymn to thee (3)
492 live this short, revolving day as if it were our last (4)
493 the ill that I this day have done (2)
493 rise glorious at the Judgment Day (3)
494 softly now the light of day fades upon our sight away (T,1)
494 soon from us the light of day shall forever pass away (3)
495 now the day is over, night is drawing nigh (T,1)
496 the perfect day before us breaks in everlasting light (4)
497 who the day for toil hast given, for rest the night (1)
498 gather to begin the day with praise (1)
498 every day will be the brighter when ... thy face we see (3)
499 new mercies, each returning day, hover around us (2)
499 help us, this & every day to live more nearly as we pray (4)
500 the day thou gavest, Lord, is ended (T,1)
500 the dawn leads on another day (3)
500 and rests not now by day or night (2)
503 day is dying in the west (T,1)
503 when forever from our sight pass the stars, the day (4)
503 pass the stars, the day, the night (4)
506 the day is slowly wending toward its silent ending (T,1)
506 long our day of testing, now comes the hour of resting (3)
509 by day, by night, at home, abroad, still we are guarded (2)
515 give us this day our daily bread (1)
515 since every day by thee we live, may grateful hearts (4)
517 since the day the blessed mother thee ... bore (2)
518 give us each day our daily bread (2)
522 from his field shall in that day all offenses purge away (3)

524 now, on this... festal day thy bounteous hand confessing (2)
525 common things which every day and hour brings (2)
529 and wrestle till the break of day (1)
545 his day is marching on (2)
552 lead us from night to never-ending day (4)

day's
251 heaven's eternal day's before thee (4)
401 joyless the day's return till thy mercy's beams I see (2)
532 fulfilled their day's endeavor (6)

daylight
264 fairer than morning, lovelier than daylight (1)
264 O in that hour, fairer than daylight dawning shall rise (5)

daylight's
318 come into the daylight's splendor (1)

days
6 days of wonder ... beauty ... rapture, filled with light (1)
9 days of praise shall ne'er be past while life ... last (1,4)
25 one day with thee ... exceeds a thousand days of mirth (1)
27 most blessed, most glorious, the Ancient of days (1)
29 o day, all days illumining (1)
33 all beautiful the march of days as seasons come and go (T,1)
54 thy wonders in their days performed (1)
62 let all our future days tell this story (2)
67 so through all the length of days (6)
97 I'll trust him when life's fleeting days shall end (4)
106 when our days of toil shall cease (3)
107 days of toil and hours of ease (4)
117 till traveling days are done (3)
168 I would to everlasting days make all his glories known (2)
182 myself, my residue of days, I consecrate to thee (1)
187 take my moments and my days (1)
190 Great Lord of years and days (2)
207 through days of toil when heart doth fail (2)
210 and bear thee through the evil days (1)
211 mercy thy days shall lengthen (2)
227 now my remnant of days would I speak of his praise (6)
233 the psalms of ancient days (3)
251 swift shall pass thy pilgrim days (4)
254 what I dream & what I do in my weak days are always two ▸
255 I sigh to think of happier days, when thou...wast nigh (3)
292 new-born souls, whose days, reclaimed from error's ways (4)
307 didst give man food for all his days (2)
365 nights and days thy power confess (2)
371 from days of old, through swiftly rolling ages (2)
390 lo! the days are hastening on, by prophet seen of old (3)
411 as in days of old he takes the wounded to his arms (4)
440 death and sorrow ... to the former days belong (1)
441 wheat that in dark earth many days has lain (1)
441 he that for three days in the grave had lain (3)
442 through each wonder of fair days God himself expresses (2)
447 the three sad days have quickly sped (3)
451 on this most holy day of days, our hearts ... we raise (5)
459 Ancient of Days, who sittest throned in glory (T,1)
459 praise we the goodness that doth crown our days (5)

470   grant us courage for the living of these days (2)
473   our Shield and Defender, the Ancient of Days (1)
475   old now is earth and none may count her days (1)
477   finely build for days to come foundations that endure (3)
478   through days of preparation thy grace has made us strong (1)
498   Father, who hast blessed us all our days (1)
509   adored through all our changing days (4)
510   who kindly lengthens out our days (1)
510   residue of days or hours thine, wholly thine, shall be (5)
523   for peaceful homes and healthful days (3)

days'
446   and from three days' sleep in death as a sun hath risen (2)

dazzle
164   I see the sights that dazzle, the tempting sounds I hear (2)

dazzling
364   dear tokens of his passion still his dazzling body bears (3)
366   choir immortal of angels round thy dazzling throne (3)

dead
1   new life the dead receive (5)
62   welcome story! love lives on, and death is dead (3)
157   last low whispers of our dead are burdened with his name (5)
234   I lay in dust life's glory dead (4)
320   and in whose death our sins are dead (1)
440   Jesus lives who once was dead (3)
441   love lives again, that with the dead has been (1)
441   quick from the dead my risen Lord is seen (3)
441   fields of our hearts that dead and bare have been (4)
444   vainly they watch his bed ... vainly they seal the dead (2)
445   he lives, he lives, who once was dead (1)
447   He rises glorious from the dead (3)
452   lo! the dead is living, God forevermore (1,4)
457   dead to sin, his members live the life of righteousness (3)
479   still in grief men mourn their dead (2)
534   courage with which thou blessed our dead (2)

deadly
216   no deadly shaft by day shall harm (5)
418   mine was the transgression, but thine the deadly pain (2)
552   from war's alarms, from deadly pestilence (3)

deaf
1   hear him, ye deaf; his praise, ye dumb (6)

deals
65   who with thee so kindly deals (2)

dear
58   eternal arms, their dear abode, we make our habitation (1)
58   safe in the same dear dwelling place (4)
60   dear mother earth, who day by day unfoldest blessings (4)
67   fear no ill, with thee, dear Lord, beside me (4)
96   as thou, dear Lord, on me (2)
105   earth's pleasures shall I still hold dear (1)
108   dear Savior, enter, enter, and leave us nevermore (3)

128 and bless in death a bond so dear (5)
129 where dost thou, dear Shepherd, resort with thy sheep (2)
129 restore, my dear Savior, the light of thy face (4)
168 when my dear Lord will bring me home (3)
177 nor should I aught with-hold, dear Lord, from thee (1)
177 in joy, in grief, through life, dear Lord, for thee (4)
219 embosomed deep in thy dear love (4)
228 for the dear Lamb of God left his glory above (2)
235 dear Lord and Father of mankind (T,1)
236 Savior, again to thy dear name we raise (T,1)
240 He changeth not, and thou art dear (4)
254 dear Master, in whose life I see (T,1)
260 our heart's dear guest, to thee our prayers ascend (1)
270 O Love divine, forever dear (4)
294 dear as the apple of thine eye, and graven on thy hand (2)
303 Jesus, in mercy bring us to that dear land of rest (4)
309 each to each unite, endear (2)
310 we meet on earth for thy dear sake (3)
311 telling of a Savior dear (2)
321 Master ... symbols shared thine own dear self impart (4)
328 so dear the tie where souls agree in Jesus' dying love (4)
338 blest be the dear uniting love that will not let us part (T)
341 Jesus! the name to sinners dear (2)
341 name to sinners dear, the name to sinners given (2)
350 keep the feast with thee, dear Lord (3)
360 dear desire of every nation, joy of every longing heart (1)
364 dear tokens of his passion still his dazzling body bears (3)
367 O may these heavenly pages be my ever dear delight (3)
369 break thou the bread of life, dear Lord, to me (T,1)
369 bless thou the truth, dear Lord, to me, to me (2)
372 O make thy Church, dear Savior, a lamp of purest gold (4)
381 where meek souls will receive him... dear Christ enters (3)
384 bless all the dear children in thy tender care (3)
414 where the dear Lord was crucified .. died to save us all (1)
415 I hide my blushing face while his dear cross appears (4)
421 dear dying Lamb, thy precious blood shall never lose (3)
479 forth in thy dear name we go to the child, the youth (4)
489 pray ... through the dear Redeemer's name (2)
493 forgive me, Lord, for thy dear Son, the ill (2)
499 O Lord, in thy dear love fit us for perfect rest above (4)
502 sun of my soul, thou Savior dear (T,1)
516 children early lisp his fame and parents hold him dear (2)
525 for all the friends we hold so dear (1)
122 the Father hears him pray, His dear anointed One (4)

dearer
12 dearer than all things I know is child-like faith to me (4)
170 still with thee in closer, dearer company (2)
400 dearer to God are the prayers of the poor (4)

dearest
228 and I love that old cross where the dearest and best (1)
268 the dearest idol I have known, whate'er that idol be ((5)
418 language shall I borrow to thank thee, dearest friend (3)

dearly
414 O dearly, dearly has he loved, and we must love him, too (5)

death

9	when my voice is lost in death (1,4)
18	life redeemed from death and sin (3)
18	deeds and words and death and rising tell the grace (2)
18	death and rising tell the grace in heaven's plan (2)
23	he bled to save us from eternal death (2)
42	sin and death shall not prevail (2)
51	let us in life, in death, thy steadfast truth declare (4)
52	in midst of dangers, fears, and death (3)
52	death ... shall join our souls to thee (4)
52	death, when death shall be our lot (4)
60	thou, most kind and gentle death (6)
60	death, waiting to hush our latest breath (6)
62	welcome story! love lives on, and death is dead (3)
70	after death, in distant worlds, the glorious theme renew (4)
74	by thy death was God's salvation wrought (2)
74	humbling thyself to death on Calvary (3)
75	from sin and death we flee (1)
75	who put their trust in thee... death nor hell shall harm (3)
76	brought it back victorious when from death he passed (3)
81	may the music of thy name refresh my soul in death (5)
83	he makes me triumph over death (3)
89	my life in death, my heaven in hell (4)
120	when my eyes shall close in death (3)
124	who is life in life to me ... the death of death will be (3)
128	and bless in death a bond so dear (5)
129	say, why in the valley of death should I weep (2)
140	what pain ... labor to secure my soul from endless death (2)
141	life nor death can pluck his children from his hands (3)
151	we will be true to thee till death (R)
160	cross endured to save thy soul from death and hell (3)
160	nor think till death to lay it down (4)
161	by thy cross didst save us from death and dark despair (4)
161	O Christ, o'er death victorious (5)
163	shall life or death, or earth or hell (3)
167	sing in life or death, "My Lord, thy will be done" (3)
172	till death thy endless mercies seal (4)
178	patient love was seen in all thy life and death of woe (1)
183	consecrated cross I'll bear till death shall set me free (3)
252	his watchword at the gates of death (5)
259	O Jesus, in that solemn hour, in death as life (3)
271	death of death and hell's destruction (3)
282	life nor death can part from him that dwells within (3)
285	stronger his love than death or hell (2)
289	in life, in death, O Lord, abide with me (5)
290	assured alone that life and death God's mercy underlies (1)
291	sickness and sorrow, pain and death are felt ... no more (2)
302	though now divided by...the narrow stream of death (3)
310	O might thy quickening voice the death of sin remove (5)
320	and in whose death our sins are dead (1)
333	with child-like trust that fears nor pain nor death (2)
338	joy .. grief .. time .. place .. life nor death can part (4)
341	preach him to all & cry in death, "...behold the Lamb (6)
353	left .. lonesome place of death, despite .. rage of foes (3)
355	doomed to death, must bring to doom the power (2)
361	shined on them who long in shades of death have been (1)
411	those who fight with death (1)
412	death of anguish and thy bitter passion for my salvation (4)

413   yea ... to the death we follow thee (1)
425   O Christ, thy triumphs now begin o'er captive death (2)
425   triumphs now begin o'er captive death and conqered sin (2)
429   the reign of sin and death is o'er (3)
435   forbid it, Lord, that I should boast, save in the death (2)
435   boast, save in the death of Christ, my God (2)
437   from death to life eternal, from earth unto the sky (1)
438   the reign of death was ended (2)
438   when life and death contended (2)
439   where, O death, is now thy sting, Alleluia (2)
439   death in vain forbids him rise, Alleluia (3)
440   death and sorrow, earth's dark story (1)
440   death and sorrow ... to the former days belong (1)
444   death cannot keep his prey ... He tore the bars away (3)
445   He lives, and I shall conquer death (3)
446   and from three days' sleep in death as a sun hath risen (2)
446   neither might the gates of death ... tomb's dark portal (4)
447   the powers of death have done their worst (2)
450   endless is the victory thou o'er death hast won (1,R)
450   for her Lord now liveth; death hath lost its sting (2)
451   o'er death today rose triumphing, Alleluia (1)
452   thou, of life the author, death didst undergo (3)
455   lives that death may die (2)
458   though shame and death to him (6)
463   by whose cross & death are we rescued from sin's misery (2)
476   whose life and death reveal thy face (5)
483   the keys of death and hell are to our Jesus given (3)
485   hasten, Lord ... perfect day when pain & death ... cease (2)
509   when death shall interrupt our songs and seal in silence (5)
521   neither life nor death shall ever from the Lord .. sever (3)
527   for me, who him to death pursued (1)
528   a slave redeemed from death and sin (1)
530   love, like death, hath all destroyed (5)
533   ascribe ... their triumph to his death (1)

death's
67   in death's dark vale I fear no ill (4)
68   yea, though I walk in death's dark vale (3)
123   Joseph's tomb could solve death's mystery (3)
123   I know not how that Joseph's tomb could solve death's (3)
143   when death's cold, sullen stream shall o'er me roll (4)
217   e'en death's cold wave I will not flee (4)
289   where is death's sting, where, grave, thy victory (4)
354   and death's dark shadows put to flight (4)
428   but soon he'll break death's envious chain (4)
438   Christ Jesus lay in death's strong bands (T,1)
447   from death's dread sting thy servants free (4)
539   smite death's threatening wave before you (4)

deathless
184   deathless it shall reign (2)
188   raise my low self above, won by thy deathless love (1)
370   light of knowledge ... shed on us thy deathless learning (3)
440   join, O man, the deathless voices (3)
450   make us more than conquerors through thy deathless love (3)
548   the glory that illumines patriot lives of deathless fame (3)

debt
415   drops of grief can ne'er repay the debt of love I owe (5)

debtor
93   to grace how great a debtor daily I'm constrained to be (3)

decay
289   change and decay in all around I see (2)
362   the works of men decay (2)
474   sun and moon and stars decay (1)

decays
63   man decays and ages move; but his mercy waneth never (2)

deceitful
144   what though the world deceitful prove (2)

deceive
251   human hearts and looks deceive me (2)
416   hopes deceive and fears annoy (2)

decide
56   O make but trial of his love; experience will decide (3)
56   experience will decide how blest are they (3)
242   once to every man and nation comes the moment to decide (T)
242   decide in the strife of truth with falsehood (1)

deck
318   deck thyself, my soul, with gladness (T,1)

decked
303   the pastures of the blessed are decked in glorious sheen (2)

declare
45   morning light, the lily white declare (2)
45   lily white declare their maker's praise (2)
51   let us in life, in death, thy steadfast truth declare (4)
177   help me the cross to bear, thy wondrous love declare (2)
233   God's wondrous praise declare (2)
259   no thought can reach, no tongue declare (1)
343   all nature's works his praise declare (T,1)
365   the heavens declare thy glory, Lord (T,1)
523   sweet flowers and fruit thy love declare (2)
529   I need not tell thee who I am, my sin and misery declare (2)

declining
231   when comforts are declining, he grants the soul again (1)
506   but mid the light declining the evening star is shining (1)

decree
473   hath stablished it fast by a changeless decree (3)
486   at whose inscrutable decree the planets wheel and turn (1)

decrees
31   strong is his arm, and shall fulfill his great decrees (3)
31   his great decrees and sovereign will (3)

dedicate
487   our minds we dedicate on this thy holy day (4)

deed
18	Word was spoken in the deed that made the earth (1)
177	some work of love begun, some deed of kindness done (3)
191	live out the laws of Christ in ... thought & word & deed (1)
197	we pray in deed and word, thy kingdom come on earth (4)
199	each smile a hymn, each kindly deed a prayer (1)
479	on the cross, forsaken, work thy mercy's perfect deed (1)
485	rise like incense, each to thee, in noble thought & deed (1)

deeds
15	praise him for his noble deeds (1)
18	deeds and words and death and rising tell the grace (2)
50	so many gentle thoughts and deeds circling us round (2)
85	God's love to earth thou bringest in living deeds (3)
85	living deeds that prove how sweet to serve all others (3)
88	words full of kindness, deeds full of grace (2)
194	and all its ancient deeds of wrong (2)
201	help us by deeds of mercy to show that thou art kind (2)
214	past deeds shall come and them ensnare (4)
254	O thou, whose deeds and dreams were one (2)
478	with deeds of love and mercy, the heavenly kingdom comes (2)
479	to.. child .. youth .. aged love in living deeds to show (4)
517	that in all we do or say little ones our deeds may copy (3)

deemest
269	through joy or sorrow, as thou deemest best (4)

deep
11	towering mountain, canyon deep (3)
30	deep writ upon the human heart, on sea or land (2)
40	deep seas obey thy voice (1)
48	when through the deep waters I call thee to go (3)
83	he saw me plunged in deep distress (2)
90	divine and human, in his deep revealing of God and man (4)
106	wading deep the dismal flood (3)
145	kneeling there in deep contrition, help my unbelief (2)
215	deep in unfathomable mines of never-failing skill (2)
219	embosomed deep in thy dear love (4)
245	O sometimes the shadows are deep (T,1)
260	good and ill, deep buried in each breast (2)
304	deep in loving human hearts its broad foundations rise (1)
318	let me measure, Lord, how vast and deep its treasure (3)
380	there's a mother's deep prayer and a baby's low cry (1)
381	above thy deep & dreamless sleep the silent* stars go by (1)
383	on a cold winter's night that was so deep (1)
399	O deep within my heart now shine (2)
405	see them give, in deep devotion, gold and frankincense (3)
406	through desert ways, dark fen, and deep morass (2)
473	his chariots of wrath the deep thunderclouds form (2)
479	as, O Lord, thy deep compassion healed the sick (2)
495	guard the sailors tossing on the deep, blue sea (3)
538	bidst the mighty ocean deep its... appointed limits keep (1)
538	who walkedst on the foaming deep (2)
548	Lord, we would with deep thanksgiving praise thee (1)

deepening
503	while the deepening shadows fall (3)

deepens
33   love deepens round the hearth (2)
289   the darkness deepens; Lord, with me abide (1)
505   as the darkness deepens o'er us, lo! eternal stars arise (4)

deeper
50   a yearning for a deeper peace not known before (4)
235   in deeper reverence, praise (1)
517   grant us then a deeper insight & new powers of sacrifice (4)

deepest
48   and sanctify to thee thy deepest distress (3)
217   sometimes mid scenes of deepest gloom (2)
257   our knowledge, sense and sight lie in deepest darkness (2)
257   lie in deepest darkness shrouded (2)

deeply
364   deeply wailing, shall the true Messiah see (2)

deeps
24   formed the deeps unknown ... gave the seas their bound (2)
157   in vain we search the lowest deeps (2)

deface
378   this holy tide of Christmas all other doth deface (4)
485   man's rude work deface no more the paradise of God (2)

defeats
124   defeats my fiercest foes ... consoles my saddest woes (2)

defend
55   Lord, who doth prosper thy work and defend thee (3)
121   keep thy flock, from sin defend us (2)
155   since, Lord, thou dost defend us with thy spirit (3)
191   men whose aim 'twill be not to defend some ancient creed (1)
314   in thy service, Lord, defend us (4)
497   may thine angel guards defend us (1)

defender
59   and pray that thou still our defender wilt be (3)
163   so mighty a defender (3)
473   our Shield and Defender, the Ancient of Days (1)
473   our Maker, Defender, Redeemer, and Friend (5)

defense
28   and our defense is sure (2)
52   how sure is their defense (1)
552   be thy strong arm our ever sure defense (3)

defenseless
125   cover my defenseless head with the shadow of thy wing (2)

defied
544   God the all-righteous One! man hath defied thee (3)

degree
415   amazing pity! Grace unknown! and love beyond degree (2)
422   while men of low degree exalt and usher in the day (4)

deign
   347   O Father, deign these walls to bless (3)
   517   didst deign a child to be cradled on a mother's bosom (1)

deigneth
   318   yet to dwell with thee he deigneth (1)

deigns
   199   the holier worship which he deigns to bless restores (2)

Deity
   387   hail the incarnate Deity (2)
   402   frankincense to offer have I, incense owns a Deity nigh (3)
   465   incarnate Deity, let ... ransomed race render in thanks (2)

delay
   101   believe in him without delay, and you are fully blest (3)
   102   this is the time; no more delay (5)
   105   he calls me still; can I delay (2)
   105   I cannot stay; my heart I yield without delay (5)
   110   come, and no longer delay (3)
   147   but should the surges rise and rest delay to come (2)
   169   with no reserve and no delay, with all my heart, I come (2)

delight
    29   to banish sin from our delight (3)
    35   for the heart and mind's delight (3)
    56   make you his service your delight (4)
    67   what transport of delight from thy pure chalice floweth (5)
   115   by faith I see the land of rest, the saints' delight (1)
   129   O thou, in whose presence my soul takes delight (T,1)
   159   O the pure delight of a single hour (3)
   159   delight of a single hour that before thy throne I spend (3)
   166   in mansions of glory and endless delight (3)
   224   perfect submission, perfect delight (2)
   227   O the rapturous height of that holy delight (5)
   227   delight which I felt in the life-giving blood (5)
   291   filled with delight my raptured soul lives (3)
   291   sweet fields arrayed in living green & rivers of delight (1)
   301   gift which he on one bestows, we all delight to prove (2)
   325   not paradise, with all its joys ... such delight afford (1)
   367   O may these heavenly pages be my ever dear delight (3)

delightest
   424   who in all good delightest, thou good and gracious King (3)

delightful
   168   well, the delightful day will come (3)

delightfully
   152   for thee delightfully employ whate'er ... hath given (4)

delights
   124   that delights and stirs me so (1)
   124   this is that great thing I know ... delights & stirs me (4)
   223   but we never can prove the delights of his love until (3)

deliver
   283   come, Almighty to deliver, let us all thy life receive (3)
   360   born thy people to deliver, born a child and yet a King (2)
   484   from sleep and from damnation, deliver us, good Lord (2)

deliverance
    54   as thou didst to them, to us deliverance bring (4)

deliverer
   271   strong deliverer, be thou still my strength and shield (2)

deliverer's
   528   or sing my great deliverer's praise (1)

demand
   324   our full homage to demand (1)

demands
   112   fatal cause demands, asks the work of his own hands (1)
   175   rescue the perishing, duty demands it (4)
   249   a heavenly race demands thy zeal and an immortal crown (1)
   335   not a cause of small import the pastor's care demands (2)
   435   love so amazing, so divine, demands my soul, my life (4)
   435   Love so amazing ... demands my soul, my life, my all (4)

denial
   237   lest by base denial, I depart from thee (1)

denied
    94   I my Master have denied, I afresh have crucified (2)
   207   nothing you ask will be denied (3)
   242   the multitude make virtue of the faith they had denied (2)
   355   awful love, which found no room in life where sin denied (2)
   412   'twas I, Lord Jesus, I ... denied thee; I crucified thee (2)

denies
   517   love that nothing good denies (4)

deny
    97   how could I this friend deny, when he's so true to me (3)
   160   if thou wouldst my disciple be; deny thyself (1)
   430   here we learn to serve and give, &, rejoicing, self deny (3)

Deo
   374   gloria in excelsis Deo, gloria in excelsis Deo (R)

depart
     3   ne'er from us depart, Spirit of power! (3)
   111   worst need keep him out no more or force him to depart (2)
   147   when the joys of sense depart, to live by faith alone (4)
   237   lest by base denial, I depart from thee (1)
   274   though least and lowest, let me not unheard depart (3)
   313   be known to us in breaking bread, but do not then depart (T)
   520   let all unworthy aims depart, imbue us with thy grace (2)

departing
   177   that each departing day henceforth may see (3)

depend
    56   God preserves the souls of those who on his truth depend (5)

deplore
    94   now my foul revolt deplore (3)
  470   save us from weak resignation to the evils we deplore (5)

depressed
  509   in scenes exalted or depressed thou art our joy ... rest (4)

depth
    38   ocean depth of happy rest (3)
    94   depth of mercy (T,1)
    94   depth of mercy! can there be mercy still reserved for me (1)
  130   and depth of sovereign grace (1)
  130   the depth of humble love (5)
  131   sound with...thy saints below, the depth of love divine (4)
  332   O the depth of love divine, the unfathomable grace (T,1)
  479   light in its height and depth and greatness dawns (3)
  531   whose height, whose depth unfathomed no man knows (1)

depths
  157   for him no depths can drown (2)
  159   there are depths of love that I cannot know till (4)
  195   wing my words, that they may reach the hidden depths (3)
  195   the hidden depths of many a heart (3)
  234   in thine ocean depths its flow may richer, fuller be (1)
  309   all the depths of love express (5)
  488   for our salvation Christ rose from depths of earth (2)
  526   out of the depths I cry to thee (T,1)
  527   in vain the first-born seraph tries to sound the depths (2)
  527   seraph tries to sound the depths of love divine (2)

derided
  412   by foes derided, by thine own rejected, O most afflicted (1)
  469   by wars and tumults love is mocked, derided (2)

derision
  453   sinners in derision crowned him (3)

derive
  523   to thee, from whom we all derive our life our gifts (5)

descend
    56   to them and their posterity his blessing shall descend (5)
  132   as a gracious shower descend (1)
  136   descend upon thy Church once more & make it truly thine (1)
  137   Spirit of faith, descend and show the virtue of his name (3)
  138   Spirit of God, descend upon my heart (T,1)
  350   here let thy sacred fire of old descend (2)
  350   descend to kindle spirits cold (2)
  352   dwell in this holy place, e'en now descend (1)
  381   O holy Child of Bethlehem, descend to us, we pray (4)
  461   descend with all thy gracious powers (1,4)
  472   angels descend with songs again (5)

descended
  138   the kindling of the heaven descended Dove (5)
  463   who descended from his throne and for us salvation won (2)

descendeth
  58 their song to us descendeth (3)
  324 blessing in his hand, Christ our God to earth descendeth (1)
  324 Light of light descendeth from the realms of endless day (3)

descending
  224 angels descending, bring from above echoes of mercy (2)
  364 lo, he comes with clouds descending (T,1)
  382 suddenly the Lord, descending, in... temple shall appear (4)
  460 Light of Light, to earth descending (2)
  505 now, on land and sea descending (T,1)

descends
  250 till Christ the Lord descends from high (3)
  250 till Christ descends ... and takes the conquerors home (3)
  473 it streams from the hills, it descends to the plain (4)

desert
  46 we shall not in the desert stray (2)
  48 I will not, I will not desert to his foes (5)
  106 gently lead us by the hand, pilgrims in a desert land (1)
  129 or cry in the desert for bread (3)
  362 prepare in the desert a highway ... for our God (1,4)
  406 through desert ways, dark fen, and deep morass (2)

deserve
  418 lo, here I fall, my Savior! 'Tis I deserve thy place (2)

deserving
  210 and all deserving love hath sent (2)
  412 think on thy pity ... love unswerving, not my deserving (5)

design
  2 thou ... ears and hands and voices for thy praise design (3)
  48 the flame shall not hurt thee, I only design (4)
  171 shapest man to God's own law, thyself the fair design (2)
  180 all I design or do or say (3)
  527 who can explore his strange design (2)

designs
  31 subdues the powers of hell, confounds their dark designs (3)
  215 he treasures up his bright designs (2)

desire
  135 kindle every high desire; perish self in thy pure fire (2)
  172 Jesus, confirm my heart's desire to work ... for thee (3)
  200 purge us of low desire; lift us to high resolve (4)
  235 breathe through the pulses of desire thy coolness (5)
  252 prayer is the soul's sincere desire (T,1)
  253 a pure desire that all may learn and glorify thy grace (4)
  259 O Jesus, nothing may I see ... desire, or seek but thee (2)
  279 first approach to feel of pride or wrong desire (1)
  280 help me the first approach to feel of pride or...desire (1)
  280 of pride or wrong desire (1)
  285 first-born sons of light desire in vain its depths...see (2)

285   nothing in earth beneath desire (4)
338   nothing desire, nothing esteem, but Jesus crucified (3)
354   O come, Desire of nations (3)
360   dear desire of every nation, joy of every longing heart (1)
382   seek the great Desire of nations (3)

desired
344   good desired and wanted most ...thy richest grace supply (1)

desires
55   hast thou not seen how thy desires ... hath been granted (2)
55   desires ... granted in what he ordaineth (2)
98   to teach our faint desires to rise (4)
275   anxious spirits burn with strong desires for thy return (2)

desirest
513   and what thou most desirest, our humble, thankful hearts (3)

desolate
103   joy of the desolate, light of the straying (2)
129   bring joy to my desolate heart (4)
211   his truth be thine affiance, when faint and desolate (2)
362   proclaim to a desolate people the coming of their King (2)

desolation
477   that war may haunt .. earth no more and desolation cease (4)

despair
161   by thy cross didst save us from death and dark despair (4)
200   I see my people falling in darkness and despair (2)
292   redeemed at countless cost, from dark despair (2)
371   o'er fear and doubt, o'er black despair prevailing (1)
377   no one to lighten their despair (1)
460   'mid the world's despair and turmoil one firm anchor (1)
481   bitter lips in blind despair cry (3)
486   like those to conquer for thy sake despair ... doubt (4)
486   conquer for thy sake despair and doubt and shame (4)
529   weak, but confident in self-despair (3)

despise
105   shall I not rise? Can I his loving voice despise (2)
178   thy foes might hate, despise, revile (2)
251   let the world despise and leave me (2)
261   do thy friends despise, forsake thee (3)

despised
228   O that old rugged cross, so despised by the world (2)
251   destitute, despised, forsaken (1)
454   hail, thou once despised Jesus (T,1)

despite
353   left the lonesome place of death, despite the rage (3)
353   left the lonesome place...despite the rage of foes (3)

destitute
251   destitute, despised, forsaken (1)

destroy
  22 he can create, and he destroy (1)

destroyed
  530 love, like death, hath all destroyed (5)

destruction
  65 who redeems thee from destruction (2)
  271 death of death and hell's destruction (3)
  496 though destruction walk around us (2)

detached
  457 filled with faith and love, our hearts detached (1)
  457 our hearts detached from all below ... after him ascend (1)

determined
  214 obey the laws of God in their determined quest (1)
  214 their determined quest to follow in the saints' pathway (1)

devils
  20 though this world, with devils filled should threaten (3)
  25 devils at thy presence flee (4)
  341 angels and men before it fall, and devils fear and fly (1)

devious
  86 guiding in love and truth through devious ways (1)

devote
  415 would he devote that sacred head for sinners such as I (1)

devoted
  227 may they all be devoted to him (6)

devotion
  134 hosannas languish on our tongues and our devotion dies (3)
  153 slaves are we whene'er we share that devotion anywhere (3)
  345 and pure devotion rise (4)
  400 say, shall we yield him, in costly devotion (3)
  405 see them give, in deep devotion, gold and frankincense (3)
  544 so shall thy people, with thankful devotion praise him (4)

dew
  180 disperse my sins as morning dew (2)
  190 the fields are wet with diamond dew (1)
  264 in the calm dew and freshness of the morn (2)
  473 and sweetly distills in the dew and the rain (4)

dews
  235 drop thy still dews of quietness (4)
  502 when the soft dews of kindly sleep (2)
  545 have builded him an altar in the evening dews and damps (2)

diadem
  71 bring forth the royal diadem and crown him Lord of all (1)
  99 hath he diadem, as monarch, that his brow adorns (3)
  458 a royal diadem adorns the mighty victor's brow (1)

diamond
190   the fields are wet with diamond dew (1)

die
  17   sent him to die, I scarce can take it in (3)
  86   so now, and till we die sound we thy praises high (4)
102   nor suffer him to die in vain (4)
112   sinners, turn, why will you die (T,1,2,3)
112   thankless creatures, why will you cross his love and die (1)
112   will you let him die in vain? Crucify your Lord again? (2)
112   ransomed sinners, why will you slight his grace, and die (2)
112   long-sought sinners, why will you grieve ... God and die (3)
113   Savior, look with pitying eye; Savior, help me, or I die (R)
122   nor let that ramsomed sinner die (3)
133   so shall I never die (4)
137   who did for every sinner die hath surely died for me (1)
140   surely thou canst not let me die (3)
146   he thinks he was not made to die (2)
150   assured, if I my trust betray, I shall forever die (4)
182   and from this moment, live or die to serve my God alone (2)
218   Lord, it belongs not to my care whether I die or live (T,1)
239   shall conquer though they die (5)
285   I thirst, I faint, I die to prove ... love (1)
309   on the wings of angels fly; show how true believers die (6)
343   may earth-born passions die (3)
344   thine, wholly thine, to die and live (3)
353   not as of old a little child to bear and fight and die (2)
387   mild he lays his glory by, born that man no more may die (3)
415   and did my Sovereign die (1)
420   come, sinners, see your Savior die (3)
421   redeeming love has been my theme, & shall be till I die (4)
425   in lowly pomp ride on to die (2,4)
427   alone thou goest forth, O Lord, in sacrifice to die (T,1)
428   vast the love that him inclined to bleed & die for thee (1)
430   here we gather love to live; here we gather faith to die (3)
434   learn of Jesus Christ to die (3)
449   that love, that life which cannot die (3)
455   lives that death may die (2)
484   our earthly rulers falter, our people drift and die (1)
486   who, when fears beset them, stand fast and fight and die (2)
493   teach me to die, that so I may rise glorious (3)
500   nor die the strains of praise away (3)
502   for without thee I dare not die (3)
507   promise, in this sacred hour, for God to live and die (2)
527   amazing love! how can it be that thou ... die for me (1)
527   how can it be that thou, my Lord, shouldst die for me (1)
545   as he died to make men holy, let us die to make man free (4

died
  17   he bled and died to take away my sin (3)
102   and live for him who died for all (5)
108   I died for you, my children, and will ye treat me so (3)
112   God ... died himself, that you might live (2)
114   we who in Christ believe that he for us hath died (3)
118   Lord, I am lost, but thou hast died (4)
124   faith in him who died to save (4)

137	who did for every sinner die hath surely died for me (1)
143	as thou hast died for me, O may my love to thee (2)
163	he bled, he died to save me (2)
175	tell the poor wanderer a Savior has died (4)
212	just tell the love of Jesus, and say he died for all (2)
227	"He hath loved me," I cried, "He hath suffered and died (4)
227	suffered and died to redeem a poor rebel like me (4)
227	who hath died my poor soul to redeem (6)
228	for 'twas on that old cross Jesus suffered and died (3)
259	be thou my guide, and save me, who for me hast died (3)
297	with his own blood he bought her...for her life he died (1)
299	or of the life he died for them to win (2)
299	died on earth that man might live above (3)
414	where the dear Lord was crucified .. died to save us all (1)
414	died that we might be forgiven ... died to make us good (3)
415	God, the mighty maker, died for man the creature's sin (3)
420	the incarnate God hath died for me (1)
420	the Son of God for me hath died (1)
435	cross on which the Prince of Glory died (1)
439	once he died, our souls to save, Alleluia (2)
454	who died, eternal life to bring (2)
455	awake, my soul, and sing of him who died for thee (1)
455	his glories now we sing who died, and rose on high (2)
455	all hail, Redeemer, hail! for thou hast died for me (4)
481	cry Christ hath died in vain (3)
527	died he for me, who caused his pain (1)
545	as he died to make men holy, let us die to make man free (4)
547	land where my fathers died, land of the pilgrims' pride (1)

diedst
529	'tis Love! thou diedst for me! (4)

dies
28	they fly, forgotten, as a dream dies at the opening day (5)
32	in distant peals it dies (4)
134	hosannas languish on our tongues and our devotion dies (3)
140	O let me now receive that gift! my soul without it dies (4)
345	storm of earth-born passion dies (4)
345	round these hallowed walls the storm of... passion dies (4)
428	see ... he bows his sacred head ... bows his head & dies (3)
429	'tis finished The Messiah dies (T,1)
505	soon as dies the sunset glory, stars of heaven shine (2)

diffused
344	thy power and love diffused abroad (4)
527	thine eye diffused a quickening ray (3)

dim
167	let not my star of hope grow dim or disappear (2)
181	and we believe thy word, though dim our faith may be (4)
218	the eye of faith is dim (5)
230	His wisdom ever waketh, his sight is never dim (2)
242	behind the dim unknown, standeth God within the shadow (4)
289	earth's joys grow dim; its glories pass away (2)
545	I can read his righteous sentence by the dim ... lamps (2)
545	dim and flaring lamps (2)

dimmed
371 undimmed by time, the Word is still revealing (3)
431 the star is dimmed that lately shone (1)

dimness
138 but take the dimness of my soul away (2)

dims
269 while passion stains, and folly dims our youth (2)

din
202 through din of market, whirl of wheels (1)

direct
180 direct, control, suggest this day (3)

direction
46 we shall not full direction need (2)

directs
370 inspired those whose wisdom still directs us (3)

disappear
167 let not my star of hope grow dim or disappear (2)
267 everything false will disappear (2)
326 too soon we rise: the symbols disappear (4)

disappointment
209 when disappointment, grief, and fear are gone (3)

disaster
155 he who would valiant be 'gainst all disaster (T,1)

discern
350 may we discern thy presence here (3)

discerning
253 I want a godly fear, a quick discerning eye (3)

disciple
160 if thou wouldst my disciple be; deny thyself (1)
342 we call each new disciple to follow thee, O Lord (2)
431 e'n the disciple that he loved heeds not (2)

disciples
201 we would be thy disciples, and all the hungry feed (2)
342 go, make of all disciples (T,1,2,3,4)

discipline
344 the sacred discipline be given (1)
344 discipline ... to train and bring them up for heaven (1)

disclose
405 incense doth their God disclose (4)

disconsolate
103 come, ye disconsolate, where'er ye languish (T,1)

discouraged
212   sometimes I feel discouraged and think my work's in vain (1)
219   discouraged in... work of life, disheartened by its load (2)
261   we...never be discouraged, take it to the Lord in prayer (2)

discouragement
155   there's no discouragement shall make him once relent (1)

disdain
86   help thou dost not disdain, help from above (2)
186   thy majesty did not disdain to be employed for us (1)

diseases
65   thy diseases all who heals (2)

disheartened
219   discouraged in... work of life, disheartened by its load (2)

disjoined
344   unite the pair . long disjoined, knowledge & vital piety (3)

dismal
106   wading deep the dismal flood (3)
155   who so beset him round with dismal stories (2)

dismay
378   God rest you merry, Gentlemen, let nothing you dismay (T,1)

dismayed
48   fear not, I am with thee; O be not dismayed (2)
51   give to the winds thy fears; hope and be undismayed (T,1)
207   be not dismayed whate'er betide (T,1)
230   but God is round about me, and can I be dismayed (1)
300   Jesus Christ, our Father's Son, bids us undismayed go on (3)
486   face the darkness undismayed and turn their loss to gain (3)

dismiss
165   Lord, dismiss us with thy blessing (T,1)

disordered
131   on our disordered spirits move ... let ... now be light (3)

dispel
132   Holy Ghost, dispel our sadness (T,1)
476   dispel the gloom of error's night, of ignorance & fear (3)
501   O Savior Christ, our woes dispel (3)

dispels
220   God dispels our fear (2)

display
43   does his Creator's power display (1)
139   with strong commanding evidence their...origin display (5)
139   their heavenly origin display (5)
346   through ages long his wisdom and his power display (1)
346   his wondrous works...his wisdom and his power display (1)
401   more thyself display, shining to the perfect day (3)
471   the triumphs of thy love display (2)

displayed
17   thy power throughout the universe displayed (1)
37   Lord, how thy wonders are displayed (2)
41   when we see thy lights of heaven ...thy power displayed (2)
41   moon and stars, thy power displayed (2)
394   to human view displayed (4)

displays
523   for all the blessings earth displays (3)

dissolve
415   dissolve my heart in thankfulness (4)

distant
32   in distant peals it dies (4)
65   far as east from west is distant (3)
70   after death, in distant worlds, the glorious theme renew (4)
272   I do not ask to see the distant scene (1)
440   patriarchs from the distant ages (3)
536   steals on the ear the distant triumph song (5)

distills
473   and sweetly distills in the dew and the rain (4)

distinctions
530   love ... rendered all distinctions void (5)
530   distinctions void; names and sects and parties fall (5)

distraction
186   from all distraction free (5)

distress
9   he helps the stranger in distress (3)
48   and sanctify to thee thy deepest distress (3)
56   when in distress to him I called, he to my rescue came (2)
66   grace and favor to our fathers in distress (2)
83   he saw me plunged in deep distress (2)
251   man may trouble and distress me (3)
275   in seasons of distress and grief (1)
279   and mourn for the minutest fault in exquisite distress (2)
280   and mourn for the minutest fault in exquisite distress (2)

distressed
99   art thou sore distressed (1)
317   our hearts distressed by people's grief (2)

distressing
4   through all grief distressing (3)
59   the wicked oppressing now cease from distressing (1)

distrust
143   blest Savior, then, in love, fear and distrust remove (4)

disturb
32   without his high behest ye shall not ... disturb (3)
32   shall not, in the mountain pine, disturb a sparrows nest (3)

divers
501   O in what divers pains they met (1)
530   move and actuate and guide; divers gifts to each divide (3)

diverse
370   many diverse scrolls completing (2)

divide
321   the bread is always consecrate which men divide with men (2)
484   the walls of gold entomb us, the swords of scorn divide (1)
530   move and actuate and guide; divers gifts to each divide (3)

divided
8   though in essence only One; undivided God we claim thee (4)
128   now rest, my long-divided heart (4)
302   though now divided by...the narrow stream of death (3)
305   we are not divided, all one body we (2)
328   many, and yet but one are we, one undivided bread (2)
469   races and peoples, lo, we stand divided (2)

divine
38   lift us to the joy divine (3)
43   the hand that made us is divine (3)
44   on man thy wisdom ... bestowed a power well-nigh divine (4)
58   the fire divine their steps that led ... before us (2)
58   the fire divine ... still goeth bright before us (2)
59   ordaining, maintaining his kingdom divine (2)
74   all praise to thee, for thou, O King divine (T,1)
80   how beauteous were the marks divine (T,1)
80   marks divine, that in thy meekness used to shine (1)
80   marks divine ... that lit the lonely pathway (1)
83   from his bounty I receive such proofs of love divine (4)
85   O Son of God incarnate, O Son of man divine (T,1)
85   O Will of God incarnate, so human, so divine (4)
89   thou all sufficient love divine (1)
90   divine and human, in his deep revealing of God and man (4)
91   be this while life is mine my canticle divine (4)
128   charmed to confess the voice divine (3)
131   sound with...thy saints below, the depth of love divine (4)
133   this earthly part of me glows with thy fire divine (3)
135   Holy Spirit, Truth divine, dawn upon this soul of mine (T,1)
135   Holy Spirit, Love divine, glow within this heart of mine (2)
135   Holy Spirit, Power divine (3)
135   Holy Spirit, Right divine (4)
136   O Spirit of the living God, thou light and fire divine (T,1)
146   thou seemest human and divine (3)
154   touch me and heal me, Savior divine (3)
159   by the power of grace divine (2)
171   O Carpenter of Nazareth, Builder of life divine (2)
188   breathe into every wish thy will divine (1)
201   awake in us compassion, O Lord of life divine (3)
224   O what a foretaste of glory divine (1)
227   the favor divine I first found in the blood of the Lamb (2)
228   in the old rugged cross, stained with blood so divine (3)
246   renew it boldly every day, and help divine implore (2)
246   take thee, at thy parting breath, to his divine abode 4)
255   O when shall I behold thy face, thou Majesty divine (2)
260   thy gifts divine implore (1)

260   but live thy life divine (3)
267   open my eyes, illumine me, Spirit divine (R)
270   O Love Divine, that stooped to share (T,1)
270   O Love divine, forever dear (4)
282   a heart in every thought renewed and full of love divine (4)
283   love divine, all loves excelling (T,1)
285   O love divine, how sweet thou art (T,1)
295   for thee I long, for love divine (3)
313   there sup with us in love divine; thy body & thy blood (2)
315   author of life divine, who hast a table spread (T,1)
328   one with the living bread divine ... now by faith we eat (3)
332   O the depth of love divine, the unfathomable grace (T,1)
332   drink herewith divine supplies and eat immortal bread (3)
367   Divine instructor, gracious Lord, be thou forever near (4)
372   Church from thee, her Master, received the gift divine (2)
375   love all lovely, Love divine (1)
375   worship we the God-head, Love incarnate, Love divine (2)
398   till everything that's human be filled with the divine (3)
400   odors of Edom and offerings divine (3)
401   fill me, Radiancy divine; scatter all my unbelief (3)
413   remold them, make us, like thee, divine (R)
420   O Love divine, what hast thou done (T,1)
435   love so amazing, so divine, demands my soul, my life (4)
456   where his loving people meet to share the gift divine (2)
461   spirit divine, attend our prayers (T,1,4)
461   Spirit divine ... make this world thy home (4)
461   spirit divine attend our prayers (4)
466   come down, O Love divine, seek thou this soul of mine (T,1)
476   inspire thy heralds of good news to live thy life divine (5)
502   spurned today the voice divine (4)
508   come, let us use the grace divine (T,1) (same as 507)
515   suns glow, rains fall, by power divine (2)
520   shine, Light Divine, reveal thy face (3)
520   grant, Love Divine, in every place glad fellowship (3)
527   seraph tries to sound the depths of love divine (2)
527   clothed in righteousness divine (4)
536   O blest communion, fellowship divine (4)
543   till all success be nobleness and every gain divine (3)
552   thy love divine hath led us in the past (2)
552   fill all our lives with love and grace divine (4)

divinely
14   in songs of praise divinely sing (3)
39   his beauties, how divinely bright (2)
344   store with thoughts divinely true (2)

divinest
205   heavenly peace, divinest comfort (1)

doctrine
305   one in hope and doctrine, one in charity (2)

doing
199   him whose holy work was doing good (3)

domain
8   infinite thy vast domain, everlasting is thy reign (1)
11   through his far domain, love is king where he doth reign (2)
444   he arose a victor from the dark domain (R)

dome
503 Lord of life, beneath the dome of the universe thy home (2)

dominations
76 thrones and dominations, stars upon their way (2)

dominion
41 hast given man dominion o'er the wonders of thy hand (3)
65 all throughout his vast dominion bless the Father (6)
357 honor, glory, & dominion, and eternal victory, evermore (3)
398 till every tongue and nation, from sin's dominion free (3)
546 solace .. its wide dominion .. the healing of thy wings (1)

dominions
19 cry out, dominions, princedoms, powers ... alleluia (1)
357 powers, dominions, bow before him & extol our God & King (2)

done
49 wondrous things hath done, in whom his world rejoices (1)
117 till traveling days are done (3)
128 'tis done: the great transaction's done (3)
136 earth ... form one brotherhood by whom thy will is done (3)
167 My Lord, thy will be done (1,2,3)
174 rise up, O men of God! Have done with lesser things (T,1)
177 some work of love begun, some deed of kindness done (3)
217 when my task on earth is done (4)
244 when I've done the best I can &... friends misunderstand (3)
246 work of faith will not be done till thou obtain .. crown (3)
250 having all things done, and all your conflicts passed (2)
277 old things shall be done away ... all things new become (2)
415 for crimes that I have done he groaned upon the tree (2)
420 O Love divine, what hast thou done (T,1)
429 the great redeeming work is done (1)
439 love's redeeming work is done, Alleluia (3)
447 the strife is o'er the battle done (T,1)
447 the powers of death have done their worst (2)
463 by whose mighty power alone all is made & wrought & done (1)
468 and wonders great by thy strong hand are done (3)
469 thy kingdom come, O Lord, thy will be done (1,2,3,4)
475 nor till that hour shall God's whole will be done (3)
476 by whom thy will was done (5)
482 if so thy will is done (2)
493 the ill that I this day have done (2)
542 thy kingdom come; on earth thy will be done (3)
542 myself I give thee; let thy will be done (3)
549 as thou wouldst have it done (6)

doom
20 his rage we can endure, for lo, his doom is sure (3)
355 doomed to death, must bring to doom the power (2)

doomed
355 doomed to death, must bring to doom the power (2)

door
10 church with psalms must shout, no door can keep them out (2)
25 nor ... should tempt my feet to leave thy door (2)

108   O Jesus, thou art standing outside the fast-closed door (T)
108   O Lord, with shame and sorrow we open now the door (3)
111   stands knocking at the door of every sinner's heart (2)
218   he that into God's kingdom comes must enter by this door (3)
347   let their door a gateway be to lead us...to thee (3)
348   open wide, O God, thy door for the outcast and the poor (3)
391   hath oped the heavenly door ... man is blessed evermore (2)
464   He the door hath opened wide (3)
548   for the open door to manhood in the land the people rule (2)

doors
260   not beat with cries on heaven's doors (3)

double
120   be of sin the double cure (1)

doubt
 38   drive the dark of doubt away (1)
104   he is able, he is able, he is willing; doubt no more (1)
106   leave us not to doubt and fear (2)
119   though tossed about with many a conflict, many a doubt (3)
136   mists ... of doubt which blind our eyes to thee (2)
138   to check the rising doubt,the rebel sigh (4)
142   when in danger knows no fear, in darkness feels no doubt (3)
205   can I doubt his tender mercy (1)
210   nor doubt our inmost wants are known to him (2)
221   when the howling storms of doubt and fear assail (2)
281   from doubt and fear and sorrow free (4)
358   darkness takes its flight; doubt & terror are withdrawn (3)
371   o'er fear and doubt, o'er black despair prevailing (1)
450   no more we doubt thee, glorious Prince of life (3)
486   like those to conquer for thy sake despair ... doubt (4)
486   conquer for thy sake despair and doubt and shame (4)

doubts
147   soon shall our doubts and fears all yield to thy control (3)
269   and doubts appall, and sorrows still increase (1)
470   fears and doubts too long have bound us (2)

dove
131   expand thy wings, celestial Dove (3)
134   come, Holy Spirit, heavenly Dove (T,1,5)
138   the kindling of the heaven descended Dove (5)
268   return, O holy Dove, return, sweet messenger of rest (4)
461   come as the dove & spread thy wings ... of peaceful love (3)
480   Spirit of truth and love, life-giving, holy Dove (3)

down
 17   when I look down from lofty mountain grandeur (2)
 26   casting down their golden crowns around the glassy sea (2)
 26   cherubim and seraphim falling down before thee (2)
 53   why should this anxious load press down your weary mind (3)
 68   he makes me down to lie in pastures green (1)
117   weary one, lay down, thy head upon my breast (1)
117   thirsty one, stoop down and drink and live (2)
119   thy love unknown hath broken every barrier down (6)
132   bringing down the richest treasure man can wish (1)
137   Spirit of faith, come down, reveal the things of God (T,1)

122 with confidence I now draw nigh (4)
140 if thou withdraw thyself from me, ah! whither shall I go (1)
159 draw me nearer, nearer blessed Lord (R)
164 but, Jesus, draw thou nearer, & shield my soul from sin (2)
188 draw thou my soul, O Christ, closer to thine (T,1)
246 hosts of sin . pressing hard to draw thee from the skies (1)
350 when in faith our souls draw near (3)
466 O Comforter, draw near, within my heart appear (1)
477 O day of God, draw nigh in beauty and in power (T,1)
477 O day of God, draw nigh as at creation's birth (5)
501 we, oppressed with various ills, draw near (2)
531 each moment draw from earth away my heart (4)

drawing
363 the King of kings is drawing near (1)
495 now the day is over, night is drawing nigh (T,1)

drawn
159 and be closer drawn to thee (1)
257 drawn from earth to love thee solely (1)
372 it is the heaven-drawn picture of thee, the living Word (2)
421 drawn from Emmanuel's veins (1)

dread
215 the clouds ye so much dread are big with mercy (3)
270 no path we shun, no darkness dread (2)
394 fear not, said he, for mighty dread had seized (2)
394 mighty dread had seized their troubled mind (2)
447 from death's dread sting thy servants free (4)
493 teach me to live, that I may dread the grave as little (3)
493 dread the grave as little as my bed (3)
527 no condemnation now I dread (4)

dreadful
364 every eye shall now behold him robed in dreadful majesty (2)
432 caused the Lord of bliss to bear the dreadful curse (1)
432 bear the dreadful curse for my soul (1)
438 It was a stranger and dreadful strife (2)

dream
  28 they fly, forgotten, as a dream dies at the opening day (5)
104 nor of fitness fondly dream (3)
138 I ask no dream, no prophet ecstasies (2)
143 when ends life's transient dream (4)
254 what I dream & what I do in my weak days are always two (2)
362 power and pomp of nations shall pass like a dream away (2)
462 letting thine all-pervading power fulfill the dream (1)
462 fulfill the dream of this high hour (1)
475 built while they dream, and in that dreaming weep (2)
481 city that hath stood too long a dream (4)
511 to make the dream come true (2)
511 the Church of Christ is stirring us to make the dream (2)
543 O beautiful for patriot dream that sees beyond the years (4)

dreamers
413 yea, the sturdy dreamers answered (1)

dreaming
475 built while they dream, and in that dreaming weep (2)

dreamless
381   above thy deep & dreamless sleep the silent stars go by (1)

dreams
149   all the golden fancies of all our golden dreams (2)
194   visions of a larger good & holier dreams of brotherhood (1)
254   O thou, whose deeds and dreams were one (2)
260   our dreams, our aims, our work, our lives are prayers (1)
263   yet in my dreams I'd be nearer, my God, to thee (2)
273   turn my dreams to noble action, ministries of love (4)
476   O God of beauty, oft revealed in dreams of human art (4)
482   O thou whose dreams enthrall the heart, ride on (3)
497   holy dreams and hopes attend us this live-long night (1)
542   here are my hopes, my dreams, my holy shrine (1)
542   with hopes and dreams as true and high as mine (1)

drear
106   groping on in darkness drear (2)
536   thou, in the darkness drear, their one true light (2)

dreary
144   though oft I seem to tread alone life's dreary waste (3)
144   life's dreary waste with thorns o'er-grown (3)
496   though the night be dark and dreary (3)

dress
127   thy blood and...my beauty are, my glorious dress (1)
157   the healing of his seamless dress is by our beds of pain (4)

dressed
222   dressed in his righteousness alone (4)

drew
128   He drew me and I followed on (3)
140   what did thine only Son endure before I drew my breath (2)
163   he drew me with the cords of love (1)
383   this star drew nigh to the northwest (4)

drift
290   I only know I cannot drift beyond his love and care (5)
484   our earthly rulers falter, our people drift and die (1)

drink
18   here we drink of joy unmeasured (3)
117   thirsty one, stoop down and drink and live (2)
326   here drink with thee the royal wine of heaven (3)
329   we drink of thee, the fountain-head (3)
330   Let us drink wine together on our knees (2)
332   drink herewith divine supplies and eat immortal bread (3)
419   who best can drink his cup of woe, triumphant over pain (1)
438   He is our meat and drink indeed (4)

drive
38   drive the dark of doubt away (1)
85   God's light to earth thou bringest to drive sin's night (1)
85   drive sin's night away (1)
184   it cannot drive the world until itself be driven (3)

drive

251 'twill but drive me to thy breast (3)
279 drive me to... grace again which makes the wounded whole (4)
280 drive me to...grace again, which makes the wounded whole (4)

driven
184 it cannot drive the world until itself be driven (3)

drives
81 and drives away his fear (1)
147 kind the storm which drives us nearer home (2)

driving
202 and thrust of driving trade (1)

drooping
270 when drooping pleasure turns to grief (3)

drop
53 I'll drop my burden at his feet, and bear a song away (4)
198 to spill no drop of blood (2)
235 drop thy still dews of quietness (4)

drops
400 cold on his cradle the dew-drops are shining (2)
415 drops of grief can ne'er repay the debt of love I owe (5)
464 lo! the promise of a shower drops already from above (4)

dross
48 thy dross to consume, and thy gold to refine (4)
116 I am counting all but dross (1)
260 O cleanse our prayers from human dross (2)
430 here earth's precious things seem dross (1)

drought
214 in drought their branches grow abundantly (2)

drove
268 made thee mourn and drove thee from my breast (4)
268 I hate the sins that ... drove thee from my breast (4)

drown
157 for him no depths can drown (2)

drowns
455 hark ... heavenly anthem drowns all music but its own (1)

drums
478 not with swords loud clashing nor roll of stirring drums (2)

dry
5 then let our songs abound and every tear be dry (4)

due
227 whether many or few, all my years are his due (6)

dull
180 shake off dull sloth (1)

dullness
- 467 enable with perpetual light the dullness of... sight (2)
- 467 dullness of our blinded sight (2)

dumb
- 1 hear him, ye deaf; his praise, ye dumb (6)
- 200 no field or mart is silent, no city street is dumb (2)
- 235 let sense be dumb, let flesh retire (5)
- 316 when these failing lips grow dumb ... mind & memory flee (4)

dungeon
- 151 living still, in spite of dungeon, fire and sword (1)
- 527 I woke, the dungeon flamed with light (3)

dust
- 146 thou wilt not leave us in the dust (2)
- 200 our strength is dust and ashes, our years a passing hour (3)
- 234 I lay in dust life's glory dead (4)
- 237 when my dust returneth to the dust again (4)
- 303 exult, O dust and ashes; the Lord shall be thy part (3)
- 351 when time in lowly dust has laid these stored walls (4)
- 355 nation's pride o'erthrown went down to dust beside thee (2)
- 355 our pride is dust; our vaunt is stilled (4)
- 462 touch thou our dust with spirit-hand (2)
- 466 O let it freely burn, till earthly passions turn to dust (2)
- 466 passions turn to dust and ashes in its heat consuming (2)
- 473 frail children of dust, and feeble as frail (5)

duteous
- 531 make me thy duteous child, that I ceaseless may...cry (3)

duties
- 229 peace, perfect peace, by thronging duties pressed (2)
- 242 new occasions teach new duties (3)

duty
- 13 where my soul in joyful duty waits (1)
- 85 all who would obey thee may learn from thee their duty (4)
- 85 learn from thee their duty, the truth, the life, the way (4)
- 109 words of life and beauty teach me faith and duty (1)
- 173 thy steadfast face set forward where love and duty shone (2)
- 175 rescue the perishing, duty demands it (4)
- 180 thy daily stage of duty run (1)
- 248 where duty calls or danger, be never wanting there (3)
- 398 and glorifies with duty life's poorest, humblest part (2)
- 532 rich in art, made richer still the brotherhood of duty (4)

duty's
- 197 in duty's call, thy call we hear to fuller life (2)

dwell
- 14 from all the dwell below the skies (T,1)
- 21 all people that on earth do dwell (T,1)
- 28 still may we dwell secure (2)
- 40 come unto us and dwell with us (2)
- 53 beneath his watchful eye his saints securely dwell (2)
- 98 thou ... dost dwell with those of humble mind (2)
- 101 dwell in that celestial land, where joys immortal flow (4)

136   till Christ shall dwell in human hearts (1)
146   but more of reverence in us dwell (5)
205   here by faith in him to dwell (1)
225   make in my heart a quiet place ... come & dwell therein (1)
258   thou with him shalt dwell, beholding Light enfolding (4)
276   to dwell in lowliness with men, their pattern &... King (2)
277   O come, and dwell with me, spirit of power within (T,1)
295   blest are they in thy house that dwell (5)
297   like them, the meek & lowly, on high may dwell with thee (4
302   one family we dwell in him, one Church above, beneath (3)
318   yet to dwell with thee he deigneth (1)
343   to God the powers that dwell on high ... tribute bring (2)
352   dwell in this holy place, e'en now descend (1)
387   pleased as man with men to dwell, Jesus our Emmanuel (2)
403   for God, by grace, shall dwell in thee (4)
458   joy of all who dwell above, the joy of all below (3)
465   let all the sons of men record and dwell upon thy love (4)
468   glory shall ere long appear to dwell within our land (2)
472   people and realms of every tongue dwell (3)
472   dwell on his love with sweetest song (3)
476   kindness dwell in human hearts and... earth find peace (2)
477   bring justice to our land, that all may dwell secure (3)
494   from sin & sorrow free, take us Lord, to dwell with thee (3)

dwelleth
85   in whom God's glory dwelleth,in whom man's virtues shine (1)

dwelling
36   the indwelling God, proclaimed of old (4)
39   his dwelling place, how fair (2)
58   safe in the same dear dwelling place (4)
68   in God's house forevermore my dwelling place shall be (5)
216   thy dwelling place the Highest One (6)
256   thou in me dwelling, and I with thee one (2)
276   for his dwelling & his throne selects the pure in heart (3)
283   fix in us thy humble dwelling (1)
295   how lovely is thy dwelling place, O Lord of hosts (T,1)
466   the place wherein the Holy Spirit makes his dwelling (3)
506   all evil thoughts expelling, now make in us thy dwelling (5)
520   within .. home let every heart become thy dwelling place (2)
520   build thou a hallowed dwelling where ... joy & peace (4)
520   hallowed dwelling where true joy and peace endure (4)

dwells
199   where pity dwells, the peace of God is there (1)
282   life nor death can part from him that dwells within (3)
403   who dwells in cloudless light enshrined (2)

dwelt
209   his voice who ruled them while he dwelt below (2)

dying
113   by thy cross and dying cries, by thy one great sacrifice (2)
134   and shall we then forever live at this poor dying rate (4)
150   a never-dying soul to save, and fit it for the sky (1)
175   rescue the perishing, care for the dying (T,1,R)
177   Savior, thy dying love thou gavest me (T,1)
237   Jesus, take me, dying, to eternal life (4)

270 living or dying, thou art near (4)
299 with none to tell them of the Savior's dying (2)
316 this will I do, my dying Lord, I will remember thee (1)
325 pardon and peace to dying men and endless life are given (2)
328 so dear the tie where souls agree in Jesus' dying love (4)
359 souls, condemned and dying, are precious in his sight (2)
402 sorrowing, sighing, bleeding, dying (4)
417 the very dying form of One who suffered there for me (2)
418 for this thy dying sorrow, thy pity without end (3)
421 the dying thief rejoiced to see that fountain in his day (2)
421 dear dying Lamb, thy precious blood shall never lose (3)
426 robed in mortal flesh is dying crucified by sin for me (2)
503 day is dying in the west (T,1)

eager
  86 shepherd of eager youth (T,1)
 148 eager eyes are watching, longing for the lights (2)
 189 the day of dawning brotherhood breaks on our eager eyes (1)
 303 O sweet and blessed country that eager hearts expect (4)
 517 sons and daughters look on life with eager eyes (4)

eagle
  41 made him fly with eagle pinion (3)
 232 ah! there on eagle wings we soar (4)
 302 on the eagle wings of love to joys celestial rise (1)
 419 the martyr first, whose eagle eye could pierce (2)
 419 eagle eye could pierce beyond the grave (2)

ear
  35 for the joy of ear and eye (3)
  43 in reason's ear they all rejoice and utter forth (3)
  81 how sweet the name of Jesus sounds in a believer's ear (T,1)
 267 and while the wave-notes fall on my ear (2)
 366 nor ear hath yet attained to hear what there is ours (3)
 381 no ear may hear his coming, but in this world of sin (3)
 516 happy the home where Jesus' name is sweet to every ear (2)
 522 first the blade and then the ear (2)
 526 bend down thy gracious ear to me (1)
 536 steals on the ear the distant triumph song (5)

earliest
 227 sweet comfort and peace of a soul in its earliest love (1)
 430 where our earliest hopes began ..our last aspirings endd (4)

early
  26 early in the morning our song shall rise to thee (1)
  90 we would see Jesus in the early morning (5)
 121 blessed Jesus! We will early turn to thee (3)
 121 early let us seek thy favor, early let us do thy will (4)
 171 who with the eyes of early youth eternal things did see (1)
 434 early hasten to the tomb (4)
 472 and infant voices shall proclaim their early blessings (3)
 472 their early blessings on his name (3)
 516 children early lisp his fame and parents hold him dear (2)

earnest
 185 this is my earnest plea: more love, O Christ, to thee (1)
 342 inspire our ways of learning ... earnest, fervent prayer (1)

476 who lightest every earnest mind of every clime and shore (3)
520 steadfast faith & earnest prayer keep sacred vows secure (4)

earnestly
175 plead with them earnestly, plead with them gently (2)

ears
1 music in the sinner's ears ... life and health and peace (3)
2 thou ... ears and hands and voices for thy praise design (3)
45 and to my listening ears all nature sings (1)
54 O Lord, our fathers oft have told in our attentive ears (T,1)
257 open thou our ears and heart (3)
522 but the fruitful ears to store in his garner evermore (3)

earth
1 spread thro' all the earth abroad the honors of thy name (2)
2 best that thou hast given, earth and heaven render thee (5)
8 all on earth thy scepter claim (1)
9 he made the sky and earth and seas, with all their train (2)
10 the earth is not too low, his praises there may grow (1)
13 there a heaven on earth must be (2)
15 as in heaven on earth adored (3)
15 from whom all good proceeds ... earth and heaven adore (1)
18 Word was spoken in the deed that made the earth (1)
20 armed with cruel hate, on earth is not his equal (1)
21 all people that on earth do dwell (T,1)
22 earth, with her ten thousand tongues, shall fill (3)
23 saints on earth, with saints above ... voices ... employ (3)
25 to spend one day with thee on earth exceeds a thousand (1)
26 all thy works ... praise thy name in earth & sky & sea (4)
28 or earth received her frame (3)
33 sounds the angel hymn, "Good will to men on earth" (2)
35 for the beauty of the earth (T,1)
35 friends on earth and friends above (4)
35 peace on earth, and joy in heaven (6)
36 God of earth, the sky, the sea (T,1)
37 goodness of the Lord, that filled the earth with food (2)
38 earth and heaven reflect thy rays (2)
39 let all on earth their voices raise (T,1)
39 hour, when earth shall feel his saving power (3)
40 maker of earth and sky (1)
41 full of wonder is thy name o'er all the earth (1)
41 child of earth, yet full of yearning (2)
42 heaven, and earth, and all creation, laud and magnify (2)
43 nightly, to the listening earth repeats the story (2)
44 O Lord, our Lord, in all the earth (T,1)
44 Lord, our Lord, in all the earth how excellent thy name (5)
45 let the heavens ring! God reigns: let the earth be glad (3)
49 the one eternal God, whom earth and heaven adore (3)
50 my God, I thank thee, who hast made the earth so bright (T,1)
50 that in the darkest spot of earth some love is found (2)
57 Lord alone, who heaven and earth has made (1)
60 dear mother earth, who day by day unfoldest blessings (4)
62 earth and hell hath captive led (3)
74 confess ...in heaven and earth that Jesus Christ is Lord (5)
85 God's light to earth thou bringest to drive sin's night (1)
85 God's thought to earth thou bringest (2)
85 God's love to earth thou bringest in living deeds (3)
85 God's will to earth thou bringest that all ... may learn (4)

87 Hope of earth and joy of heaven (R)
91 let all the earth around ring joyous with the sound (3)
99 not till earth and not till heaven pass away (6)
100 and, saved from earth, appear before your Savior's face (4)
103 earth has no sorrow that heaven cannot cure (2)
103 earth has no sorrow that heaven cannot heal (1)
103 earth has no sorrow but heaven can remove (3)
114 how can a sinner know his sins on earth forgiven? (T,1)
115 this earth, he cries, is not my place (1)
115 what a blessed hope is ours while here on earth we stay (2)
118 weary of earth, myself, and sin (1,5)
136 earth ... form one brotherhood by whom thy will is done (3)
136 and earth shall win true holiness (4)
138 wean it from earth, through all its pulses move (1)
145 whom have I on earth beside thee...in heaven but thee (4)
163 shall life or death, or earth or hell (3)
167 since thou on earth has wept and sorrowed oft alone (2)
188 till earth, as heaven, fulfill God's holy will (3)
192 fellowship of love throughout the whole wide earth (1)
192 one in him throughout the whole wide earth (4)
197 thy kingdom come on earth, O Lord (4)
197 we pray in deed and word, thy kingdom come on earth (4)
198 on earth and fire and sea and air (2)
198 dare all that may plant man's lordship firm on earth (2)
198 every life shall be a song when all... earth is paradise (4)
199 so shall the wide earth seem our Father's temple (3)
199 wild war music o'er the earth shall cease (5)
199 stormy clangor of wild war music o'er the earth (5)
217 when my task on earth is done (4)
218 if thy work on earth be sweet, what will thy glory be (4)
220 though the earth be shaking, every heart be quaking (2)
257 drawn from earth to love thee solely (1)
258 now is breaking o'er the earth another day (1)
262 thyself reveal, while here o'er earth we rove (1)
273 God, who touchest earth with beauty (T,1)
273 God, who touchest earth with beauty, make my heart anew (5)
281 whose word, when heaven and earth shall pass, remains (1)
283 joy of heaven, to earth come down (1)
285 nothing in earth beneath desire (4)
285 let earth and heaven and all things go (4)
288 redeemed from earth and pain, Ah! when shall we ascend (2)
294 Zion ... be given the brightest glories earth can yield (5)
297 elect from every nation, yet one o'er all the earth (2)
297 yet she on earth hath union with God the Three in One (4)
299 died on earth that man might live above (3)
302 saints on earth unite to sing with those to glory gone (2)
302 all the servants of our King, in earth & heaven are one (2)
308 a mountain that shall fill the earth (4)
310 we meet on earth for thy dear sake (3)
311 while on earth her faith is tried (1)
324 blessing in his hand, Christ our God to earth descendeth (1)
324 of old on earth he stood, Lord of lords in human vesture (2)
329 from the best bliss that earth imparts (1)
331 in thy fasting and temptation ...thy labors on the earth (2)
334 possess in sweet communion, joys ... earth cannot afford (2)
340 till earth and heaven together blend their praises (4)
341 though earth and hell oppose (4)
341 Jesus! the name high over all, in hell or earth or sky (T,1)

342 in heaven & earth thy power ... bring God's kingdom here (4)
344 till all our earth is filled with God (4)
345 temple stands, built over earth and sea (1)
357 let no tongue on earth be silent (2)
358 ages are its own; see, it bursts o'er all the earth (2)
359 hail in the time appointed, his reign on earth begun (1)
359 he shall come down like showers upon the fruitful earth (3)
360 hope of all the earth thou art (1)
361 on his shoulder ever rests all power on earth and heaven (2)
364 Hallelujah! God appears on earth to reign (1)
365 sun, moon ... stars convey thy praise round the... earth (3)
365 convey thy praise round the whole earth and never stand (3)
368 without thee how could earth be trod (3)
372 still that light she lifteth o'er all the earth to shine (2)
376 our God, heaven cannot hold him, nor earth sustain (2)
376 heaven and earth shall flee away when he comes to reign (2)
376 earth stood hard as iron, water like a stone (1)
380 for the virgin's sweet boy is the Lord of the earth (2)
380 every hearth is aflame, and the beautiful sing (3)
381 praises sing to God the King, and peace to men on earth (2)
382 wing your flight o'er all the earth (1)
383 and to the earth it gave great light (2)
387 peace on earth and mercy mild (1)
387 born to raise the sons of earth (3)
389 takes ...a servant's form who made the heaven and earth (2)
390 angels bending near ... earth to touch ... harps of gold (1)
390 peace on the earth, good will to me (1)
390 peace shall over ... earth its ancient splendors fling (3)
392 let earth receive her King (1)
394 all glory be to God on high, and to the earth be peace (6)
395 praise his name in all the earth; Hail the King of glory (3)
397 bend the knee before him whom heaven and earth adore (2)
398 Light of the world, Illumine ... darkened earth of thine (3)
398 thy light, so glad & golden, shall set on earth no more (1)
402 Alleluia, Alleluia! sounds through the earth and skies (5)
404 lo! above the earth rang out the angel chorus (2)
405 earth has many a noble city (T,1)
405 seen in fleshly form on earth (2)
406 prepare across the earth the King's highway (2)
410 and Christ's great kingdom shall come on earth (R)
427 'tis mercy all! let earth adore (2)
437 the day of resurrection, earth, tell it out abroad (T,1)
437 from death to life eternal, from earth unto the sky (1)
437 now let the heavens be joyful! Let earth her song begin (3)
439 sing, ye heavens, and earth reply, Alleluia (1)
441 wheat that in dark earth many days has lain (1)
441 laid in the earth like grain that sleeps unseen (2)
442 so, as he renews the earth, artist without rival (2)
452 earth with joy confesses, clothing her for spring (2)
460 Light of Light, to earth descending (2)
461 let thy Church on earth become blest as the Church above (3
464 to bring fire on earth he came (1)
468 truth from the earth, like to a flower, shall bud (1)
468 rise, God, judge thou the earth in might (2)
468 this wicked earth redress (2)
471 not heaven's hosts shall swifter move than we on earth (4)
471 not ... swifter ... than we on earth, to do thy will (4)

472 and earth repeat the loud amen (5)
473 the earth with its store of wonders untold (3)
474 time shall soon this earth remove (1)
474 all our sorrows left below .. earth exchanged for heaven (3)
475 old now is earth and none may count her days (1)
475 earth might be fair and all men glad and wise (2)
475 earth shall be fair, and all her people one (3)
475 now, even now, once more from earth to sky peals forth (3)
476 kindness dwell in human hearts and... earth find peace (2)
477 that war may haunt .. earth no more and desolation cease (4)
477 let .. be light again .. set thy judgments in .. earth (5)
483 His kingdom cannot fail, he rules o'er earth and heaven (3)
484 O God of earth and altar, bow down and hear our cry (T,1)
485 just rule ... fill ... earth with health & light & peace (2)
486 though earth and sea and heaven unite thy praise to sing (1)
488 for our salvation Christ rose from depths of earth (2)
492 sun itself is but thy shade, yet cheers both earth & sky (1)
497 God, that madest earth and heaven, darkness and light (T,1)
500 unsleeping while earth rolls onward into light (2)
503 heaven is touching earth with rest (1)
503 Heaven and earth are full of thee (R)
503 Heaven and earth are praising thee, O Lord most high (R)
510 Jesus in the clouds appear to saints on earth forgiven (6)
512 to bless the earth, God sendeth (T,1)
512 the year with good he crownest ... earth his mercy fills (2)
515 the life of earth and seed is thine (2)
523 O Lord of heaven and earth and sea (T,1)
523 for all the blessings earth displays (3)
525 for peace on earth, both far and near, we thank thee (1)
531 then shall my heart from earth be free (2)
531 each moment draw from earth away my heart (4)
532 they blessed the earth ... blessed of God & man forever (6)
535 walking in all his ways, they find their heaven on earth (9)
535 they find their heaven on earth begun (1)
542 thy kingdom come; on earth thy will be done (3)
544 earth hath forsaken meekness & mercy . slighted thy word (2)
549 claim the kingdom of the earth for thee, and not thy foe (5)
550 and spring adorns the earth no more (4)

earth's

50 so that earth's bliss may be our guide ... not our chain (3)
85 thru thy life so radiant, earth's darkness turns to day (1)
100 let all the nations know, to earth's remotest bound (1)
105 earth's pleasures shall I still hold dear (1)
161 to heal earth's wounds and end her bitter strife (2)
194 look down on all earth's sin and strife (3)
289 earth's joys grow dim; its glories pass away (2)
289 heaven's morning breaks, and earth's vain shadows flee (5)
296 with bread of life earth's hunger feed (4)
407 send God's love to earth's remotest part (1)
427 this is the earth's darkest hour (3)
428 and earth's strong pillars bend (2)
430 here earth's precious things seem dross (1)
430 here earth's bitter things grow sweet (1)
440 death and sorrow, earth's dark story (1)
440 when, amidst earth's closing thunders (4)
471 let all earth's sons thy mercy prove (1)

480   and in earth's darkest place, let there be light (3)
500   thy throne shall never, like earth's proud empires, pass (4)
536   from earth's wide bounds, from ocean's farthest coast (6)
542   this is my prayer, O Lord of all earth's kingdoms (3)

earthly
   5   celestial fruit on earthly ground (3)
   7   for his lovingkindness ever shed upon our earthly way (3)
  20   that word above all earthly powers ... abideth (4)
  29   sanctifying beam upon our earthly senses stream (2)
  63   he with earthly cares entwineth hope and comfort (4)
116   friends and time and earthly store (3)
133   this earthly part of me glows with thy fire divine (3)
134   fond of these earthly toys (2)
142   that will not tremble on the brink of any earthly woe (1)
144   and earthly friends and hopes remove (2)
185   once earthly joy I craved, sought peace and rest (2)
202   we bear the strain of earthly care ... bear it not alone (T)
236   grant us thy peace throughout our earthly life (4)
251   soon shall close thy earthly mission (4)
291   lives out its earthly day (3)
324   ponder nothing earthly minded (1)
326   here would I lay aside each earthly load (3)
332   how can heavenly spirits rise by earthly matter fed (3)
333   grant them the joy which brightens earthly sorrow (3)
333   grant them the peace which calms all earthly strife (3)
363   set apart ... from earthly use for heaven's employ (2)
371   Word ... shines through the darkness of our earthly way (1)
397   and, when earthly things are past (4)
466   O let it freely burn, till earthly passions turn to dust (2)
484   our earthly rulers falter, our people drift and die (1)
486   O Lord, be ours the glory beyond all earthly fame (4)

ease
  25   tents of ease nor thrones of power should tempt my feet (2)
  89   my rest in toil, my ease in pain (3)
107   days of toil and hours of ease (4)
176   not for ease or worldly pleasure (2)
200   from ease & plenty save us; from pride of place absolve (4)
239   must I be carried to the skies on flowery beds of ease (2)
497   let not ease and self enthrall us (2)

east
  65   far as east from west is distant (3)
192   in Christ there is no east or west (T,1)
192   in Christ now meet both east and west (4)
383   they looked up and saw a star shining in the east (2)
383   in the east, beyond them far (2)
400   Star of the East, the horizon adorning (1,5)

Easter
438   then let us feast this Easter Day on the true bread (4)
438   feast this Easter Day on the true bread of heaven (4)
441   forth he came at Easter, like the risen grain (3)
451   that Easter morn at break of day (2)

eastern
7   see the morning sun ascending radiant in the eastern sky (T)
189   human hatreds flee before the radiant eastern skies (1)
353   when beauty gilds the eastern hills (1)
398   flooding the eastern skies (1)
405   Eastern sages at his cradle make oblations rich and rare (3)

easy
152   give me to bear thy easy yoke (3)
484   from all the easy speeches that comfort cruel men (2)

eat
328   one with the living bread divine ... now by faith we eat (3)
332   drink herewith divine supplies and eat immortal bread (3)

ebbing
157   forever shared, forever whole, a never-ebbing sea (1)

ebbs
289   swift to its close ebbs out life's little day (2)

Ebenezer
93   here I raise mine Ebenezer, hither to thy help I'm come (2)

echo
109   sweetly echo the gospel call (3)
262   my bounding heart shall own thy sway & echo to thy voice (3)
380   we rejoice in the light, and we echo the song (4)

echoes
129   reechoes the praise of the Lord (5)
195   that I may speak in living echoes of thy tone (1)
224   angels descending, bring from above echoes of mercy (2)
224   echoes of mercy, whispers of love (2)

echoing
19   supernal anthems echoing, alleluia, alleluia! (3)
374   and the mountains in reply echoing their joyous strains (1)

ecstacies
288   O happy, happy soul! in ecstacies of praise (2)

ecstasies
138   I ask no dream, no prophet ecstasies (2)

Eden's
217   sometimes where Eden's bowers bloom (2)
459   blessed ... with light and life since Eden's dawning day (1)

Edom
400   odors of Edom and offerings divine (3)

effect
197   in work that gives effect to prayer (4)

effectual
122   they pour effectual prayers; they strongly plead for me (3)
339   answer ... faith's effectual prayer ... our needs supply (1)

effort
   81   weak is the effort of my heart (4)
  197   by effort true to meet each test (3)

elect
  297   elect from every nation, yet one o'er all the earth (2)
  303   O sweet and blessed country, the home of God's elect (4)

elements
  332   feeble elements bestow a power not theirs to give (2)

eloquent
  486   silent courage pleads to heaven more eloquent than song (3)

else
   56   fear him, ye saints, and ... have nothing else to fear (4)
   56   fear him...and you will then have nothing else to fear (3)
  149   it satisfies my longings as nothing else can do (1)
  256   naught be all else to me, save that thou art (1)
  520   reveal thy face where darkness else might be (3)

emblem
  228   the emblem of suffering and shame (1)
  489   day of all thee week the best, emblem of eternal rest (1)

embosomed
  219   embosomed deep in thy dear love (4)

embrace
  112   wooed you to embrace his love (3)
  146   by faith, and faith alone, embrace (1)
  196   all his promises embrace, and to his glory live (2)
  341   arms of love that compass me would all mankind embrace (3)
  378   with true love and brotherhood each other now embrace (4)
  474   forward tends to his abode, to rest in his embrace (2)
  503   gather us who seek thy face to the fold of thy embrace (2)
  528   he spreads his arms to embrace you all (4)

Emmanuel
  354   o come, o come, Emmanuel, and ransom captive Israel (T,1)
  354   rejoice! rejoice! Emmanuel shall come to thee, O Israel (R)
  381   O come to us, abide with us, our Lord Emmanuel (4)
  387   pleased as man with men to dwell, Jesus our Emmanuel (2)

Emmanuel's
    5   we're marching thro' Emmanuel's ground (4)
  421   drawn from Emmanuel's veins (1)
  454   help to chant Emmanuel's praise (4)

empire
  113   by the empire all thine own (3)
  548   not alone for mighty empire (T,1)
  548   mighty empire, stretching far o'er land and sea (1)

empires
  308   kings and empires ... of old that went and came (1)

308   O where are kings and empires now (T,1)
475   age after age their tragic empires rise (2)
500   thy throne shall never, like earth's proud empires, pass (4)

employ
  1   your loosened tongues employ (6)
  9   praise shall employ my nobler powers (1,4)
 23   saints on earth, with saints above ... voices ... employ (3)
 23   your voices in his praise employ (3)
 56   praises of my God shall still my heart and tongue employ (1)
 87   his songs our tongues employ (3)
152   for thee delightfully employ whate'er ... hath given (4)
262   let this my every hour employ, till I thy glory see (5)
363   set apart ... from earthly use for heaven's employ (2)
392   let men their songs employ (2)

employed
186   thy majesty did not disdain to be employed for us (1)

empower
411   empower the hands and hearts and wills of friends (2)

emptiness
347   fill with thy love their emptiness (3)

empty
256   riches I heed not, nor man's empty praise (3)
438   an empty form alone remains (2)

enable
467   enable with perpetual light the dullness of... sight (2)

encamp
211   though hosts encamp around me, firm in the fight I stand (1)

encircle
108   thorns thy brow encircle, & tears thy face have marred (2)

encircling
272   amid the encircling gloom, lead thou me on (1)

encompass
203   they reach thy throne, encompass land and sea (1)

end
 40   bless us with life that has no end (2)
 46   our end, the glory of the Lord (1)
 51   so shall this night soon end in joyous day (2)
 65   as it was without beginning so it lasts without an end (4)
 77   life shall not end the strain; Aalleluia! Amen! (3)
 81   Jesus...my Lord, my life, my way, my end (3)
 97   I'll trust him when life's fleeting days shall end (4)
 97   beautiful life that has no end (4)
155   we know we at the end shall life inherit (3)
161   to heal earth's wounds and end her bitter strife (2)
164   O Jesus, I have promised to serve thee to the end (T,1)
164   Jesus, I have promised to serve thee to the end (4)

174   bring ... day of brotherhood ... end the night of wrong (2)
186   end of my every action thou, in all things thee I see (3)
208   I know that thou art with me, wilt be with me to the end (4)
209   through thorny ways leads to a joyful end (1)
236   with thee began, with thee shall end the day (2)
238   peace shall follow battle; night shall end in day (3)
238   and the end of sorrow shall be near my throne (4)
283   Alpha and Omega be; end of faith as its beginning (2)
288   all in Jesus' presence reign through ages without end (2)
294   till cares and toils shall end (3)
352   filled with thy majesty, till time shall end (1)
356   unite us in thy will, O Lord, & end all sinful strife (2)
359   his kingdom still increasing, a kingdom without end (4)
361   his reign shall have no end (4)
418   for this thy dying sorrow, thy pity without end (3)
430   where our earliest hopes began...our last aspirings end (4)
437   for Christ the Lord hath risen, our joy that hath no end (3)
455   his reign shall know no end (3)
473   thy mercies how tender, how firm to the end (5)
503   and shadows end (4)

endear
309   each to each unite, endear (2)

endeared
193   Jesus, united by grace, and each to each endeared (T,1)

endeavor
48   that soul, though all hell should endeavor to shake (5)
58   the same sweet theme endeavor (4)
179   valiant endeavor and loving obedience (2)
258   pray that he may prosper ever each endeavor (3)
532   fulfilled their day's endeavor (6)
546   crown, O God, thine own endeavor (2)

ended
99   sorrow vanquished, labor ended, Jordan passed (5)
243   faith's warfare ended, won the home of endless peace (4)
258   for the night is safely ended (2)
372   till, clouds & darkness ended ... see thee face to face (4)
438   the reign of death was ended (2)
452   speak his sorrows ended; hail his triumph now (2)
500   the day thou gavest, Lord, is ended (T,1)

endeth
58   we send it on, the song that never endeth (3)

ending
298   One in might, and One in glory, while unending ages run (4)
308   we hear within the solemn voice of her unending song (2)
317   Immanuel, heaven's joy unending (3)
333   that theirs may be the love which knows no ending (1)
357   He is Alpha and Omega, He the source, the ending he (1)
504   saints united joy without ending (2)
506   the day is slowly wending toward its silent ending (T,1)
524   thrice blessed ... harvest song ... never hath an ending (3)
552   lead us from night to never-ending day (4)

endless
  19 respond, ye souls in endless rest (3)
  28 to endless years the same (3)
 140 what pain ... labor to secure my soul from endless death (2)
 161 lure us away from thee to endless night (3)
 166 in mansions of glory and endless delight (3)
 172 till death thy endless mercies seal (4)
 205 my song through endless ages: Jesus led me all the way (3)
 218 if short, yet why should I be sad to soar to endless day (2)
 234 life that shall endless be (4)
 243 faith's warfare ended, won the home of endless peace (4)
 300 there... endless home shall be... Lord we soon shall see (4)
 324 Light of light descendeth from the realms of endless day (3)
 325 pardon and peace to dying men and endless life are given (2)
 364 cause of endless exultation to his ransomed worshipers (3)
 367 Father of mercies, in thy Word what endless glory shines (T)
 391 now ye hear of endless bliss (2)
 450 endless is the victory thou o'er death hast won (1,R)
 467 through ... ages all along this may be our endless song (4)
 472 to him shall endless prayer be made (2)
 472 and endless praises crown his head (2)

ends
  28 short as the watch that ends the night (4)
 130 immense and unconfined; from age to age it never ends (2)
 143 when ends life's transient dream (4)
 471 and glory ends what grace begun (2)
 482 until in every land and clime thine ends of love are won (4)

endued
 250 stand ...in his great might ... all his strength endued (2)
 297 and to one hope she presses, with every grace endued (2)

endurance
 333 of patient hope and quiet, brave endurance (2)

endure
  20 his rage we can endure, for lo, his doom is sure (3)
  21 his truth ... shall from age to age endure (4)
  61 for his mercies shall endure, ever faithful, ever sure (R)
 133 will one will, to do and to endure (2)
 140 what did thine only Son endure before I drew my breath (2)
 239 I'll bear the toil, endure the pain, supported (4)
 281 which shall from age to age endure (1)
 477 finely build for days to come foundations that endure (3)
 520 hallowed dwelling where true joy and peace endure (4)

endured
 160 thy Lord for thee the cross endured (3)
 160 cross endured to save thy soul from death and hell (3)
 443 endured the cross & grave ... sinners to redeem and save (2)

endures
   9 while ... immortality endures (1,4)
  92 he will my shield and portion be as long as life endures (4)

endureth
 362 word of our God endureth ... arm of the Lord is strong (3)

energy
465   adore thy sacred energy (3)

enfold
76   let his will enfold you in its light and power (4)
96   thou didst reach forth thy hand and mine enfold (2)

enfolding
258   thou with him shalt dwell, beholding Light enfolding (4)
258   Light enfolding all things in unclouded day (4)
503   heart of love enfolding all (3)

engage
150   O may it all my powers engage to do my Master's will (2)
275   truth and faithfulness engage the waiting soul to bless (3)

engaged
186   my hands are but engaged below   (5)

engaging
312   shepherd stand with all engaging charms (1)

enhancing
442   gold the green enhancing (1)

enjoy
25   might I enjoy the meanest place within thy house (2)

enjoyed
268   what peaceful hours I once enjoyed! (3)

enlighten
318   light, who dost my soul enlighten (2)

enough
12   enough for me to know thou art, to love thee, and adore (3)
50   we have enough, yet not too much, to long for more (4)
218   eye of faith grows dim...enough that Christ knows all (5)
218   enough that Christ knows all, and I shall be with him (5)
272   one step enough for me (1)
414   there was no other good enough to pay the price of sin (4)

enrich
502   watch by the sick; enrich the poor with blessings (5)

enriching
512   waters of the spring-time, enriching it once more (1)

enshrined
85   O Mind of God incarnate, O Thought in flesh enshrined (2)
403   who dwells in cloudless light enshrined (2)

enslave
184   enslave it with thy matchless love (2)

ensnare
214   past deeds shall come and them ensnare (4)

enter
13	Zion, let me enter there (1)
13	to my heart O enter thou, let it be thy temple now (2)
21	o enter then his gates with praise (3)
108	dear Savior, enter, enter, and leave us nevermore (3)
111	rejoice that thou wilt enter in (3)
176	the gate of life eternal may I enter, Lord, with thee (3)
218	he that into God's kingdom comes must enter by this door (3)
262	enter into my Master's joy, and find my heaven in thee (4)
281	enter ... promised rest ... Canaan of thy perfect love (5)
283	visit us with thy salvation; enter every trembling heart (1)
381	cast out our sin, and enter in, be born in us today (4)
429	middle wall is broken down and all mankind may enter in (2)
440	O to enter that bright portal (4)

entered
383	then entered in those wise men three (5)

enters
220	the Lord of gladness, Jesus, enters in (3)
252	he enters heaven with prayer (5)
381	where meek souls will receive him... dear Christ enters (3)

enthrall
482	O thou whose dreams enthrall the heart, ride on (3)
497	let not ease and self enthrall us (2)

enthralled
203	our hearts enthralled while serving thee (3)

enthrone
76	in your hearts enthrone him (4)
385	let loving hearts enthrone him (3)
408	cast out our pride & shame that hinder to enthrone thee (3)
453	in the seat of power enthrone him (2)

enthroned
83	majestic sweetness sits enthroned upon the Savior's brow (T)
243	who gainst enthroned wrong stood confident and bold (1)
288	with saints enthroned on high thou...thy Lord proclaim (1)
454	Jesus, hail! enthroned in glory, there forever to abide (3)
457	enthroned at God's right hand he sits (2)

enticed
243	heroic warriors, ne'er from Christ ... enticed (2)
243	by any lure or guile enticed (2)

entire
250	o'ercome through Christ alone, and stand entire at last (2)

entirely
259	myself to thee entirely give (1)

entomb
484	the walls of gold entomb us, the swords of scorn divide (1)

entrance
474	yet a season, and you know happy entrance will be given (3)

entreat
    379   voice...doth entreat: Flee from woe and danger (2)

entwineth
     63   he with earthly cares entwineth hope and comfort (4)

envious
    428   but soon he'll break death's envious chain (4)
    469   envious of heart, blind-eyed, with tongues confounded (3)

envy
     29   with love all envy to subdue (4)
    354   bid envy, strife, and quarrels cease (3)

epiphany
    405   Jesus, whom the Gentiles worshiped at thy glad epiphany (5)

equal
     20   armed with cruel hate, on earth is not his equal (1)
    108   O sin that hath no equal, so fast to bar the gate (2)
    174   Church ... her strength unequal to her task (3)
    504   all holy Father, Son, and equal Spirit, Trinity blessed (3)
    528   how shall I equal triumphs raise (1)

equipped
    191   with vision clear and mind equipped His will to learn (3)

equity
    359   to take away transgression, and rule in equity (1)

err
    215   blind unbelief is sure to err and scan his work in vain (5)
    345   may they who err be guided here to find the better way (3)
    468   his footsteps cannot err (1)

errand
    200   send us upon thine errand, let us thy servants be (3)
    296   O living Church, thine errand speed (4)

errands
    296   feet on mercy's errands swift do make her pilgrimage (3)

erring
     46   by thine unerring spirit led (2)
    175   weep o'er the erring one, lift up the fallen (1)
    195   as thou hast sought, so let me seek ... erring children (1)
    195   erring children lost and lone (1)
    509   by his unerring counsel led (2)

error
    136   until our minds are free from mists of error (2)
    344   error and ignorance remove (2)
    492   the mists of error and of vice which shade the universe (2)

error's
    269   unhelped by thee, in error's maze we grope (2)
    292   new-born souls, whose days, reclaimed from error's ways (4)
    476   dispel the gloom of error's night, of ignorance & fear (3)

errors
  492 may we this life improve, to mourn for errors past (4)

escape
  59 let thy congregation escape tribulation (3)

escaped
  275 oft escaped the tempter's snare by thy return ... prayer (1)

escapes
  494 thou, whose all-pervading eye naught escapes (2)
  494 eye naught escapes without, within (2)

essence
  8 though in essence only One; undivided God we claim thee (4)

establish
  482 establish thou forevermore the triumph now begun (1)

established
  30 established is his law, and changeless it shall stand (2)

estate
  385 why lies he in such mean estate (2)
  385 mean estate where ox and ass are feeding (2)

esteem
  338 nothing desire, nothing esteem, but Jesus crucified (3)

eternal
  3 eternal praise be, hence, evermore (4)
  3 to thee, great One in Three eternal praises be (4)
  14 eternal are thy mercies, Lord (2)
  14 eternal truth attends thy word (2)
  15 celebrate the eternal God with harp and psaltery (2)
  19 thou bearer of the eternal Word (2)
  23 he bled to save us from eternal death (2)
  28 and our eternal home (1)
  28 be ...our guard while troubles last and our eternal home (6)
  30 the one eternal God, ere aught that now appears (1)
  30 he hath eternal life implanted in the soul (3)
  40 eternal life with thee (2)
  49 the one eternal God, whom earth and heaven adore (3)
  52 eternal wisdom is their guide, their help omnipotence (1)
  58 eternal arms, their dear abode, we make our habitation (1)
  58 rich with the same eternal grace (4)
  69 the heart of the Eternal is most wonderfully kind (2)
  74 wherefore, by God's eternal purpose thou art exalted (4)
  75 that life to win, whose joys eternal flow (4)
  78 redeem us for eternal day from every power of darkness (3)
  91 be this the eternal song through all the ages long (4)
  97 eternal life, eternal joy, he's my friend (4)
  134 our souls, how heavily they go to reach eternal joys (2)
  139 Author of faith, eternal Word (T,1)
  139 to him ... in thy name believes eternal life ...is given (4)
  139 eternal life with thee is given (4)
  142 tastes even now the hallowed bliss of an eternal home (4)

152   still to things eternal look (3)
171   who with the eyes of early youth eternal things did see (1)
176   the gate of life eternal may I enter, Lord, with thee (3)
221   through eternal ages let his praises ring (1)
236   call us, O Lord, to thine eternal peace (4)
237   Jesus, take me, dying, to eternal life (4)
250   God supplies through his eternal Son (1)
251   heaven's eternal day's before thee (4)
277   soon or later then translate to my eternal bliss (4)
284   when this life is past, I may the eternal brightness see (5)
288   long as eternal ages roll, thou seest thy Savior's face (2)
291   o'er ... wide-extended plains shines one eternal day (2)
293   streams of living waters, springing from eternal love (2)
302   greet the blood redeemed hands on the eternal shore (5)
307   giving in Christ the bread eternal (2)
308   unshaken as eternal hills, immovable she stands (4)
326   here grasp with firmer hand eternal grace (1)
333   morrow that dawns upon eternal love and life (3)
342   thee, our Father, in thy eternal Word (1)
347   thy wise eternal purpose ran (2)
351   eternal God and sovereign Lord (T,1)
352   speak, O eternal Lord, out of thy living Word (3)
357   honor, glory, & dominion, and eternal victory, evermore (3)
360   by thine own eternal spirit rule in all our hearts alone (2)
364   yea, Amen! let all adore thee high on thy eternal throne (4)
371   guiding our steps to thine eternal day (1)
373   the power of Satan breaking, our peace eternal making (1)
420   Father's coeternal Son bore all my sins upon the tree (1)
437   from death to life eternal, from earth unto the sky (1)
437   the Lord in rays eternal of resurrection light (2)
438   his grace ... doth impart eternal sunshine to the heart (3)
440   Christ has passed the eternal gates (2)
443   sing we to our God above ... praise eternal as his love (3)
451   for they eternal life shall win, Alleluia (4)
454   who died, eternal life to bring (2)
458   King of kings, & Lord of lords, & heaven's eternal light (2)
460   God is King, his throne eternal (1)
465   Eternal, Triune Lord, let all the hosts above (4)
467   praise to thy eternal merit, Father, Son and Holy Spirit (R)
469   Father eternal, ruler of creation (T,1)
471   eternal Son, eternal Love (T,1)
472   the weary find eternal rest (4)
476   Eternal God, whose power upholds (T,1)
478   lead on, O King eternal, the day of march has come (T,1)
478   and now, O King eternal, we lift our battle song (1)
478   lead on, O King eternal, till sin's fierce war ... cease (2)
478   lead on, O King eternal, we follow, not with fears (3)
482   O thou eternal Christ of God, ride on (T,1)
483   and take his servants up to their eternal home (4)
489   day of all thee week the best, emblem of eternal rest (1)
503   Lord of angels, on our eyes let eternal morning rise (4)
505   as the darkness deepens o'er us, lo! eternal stars arise (4)
524   who didst give us daily bread, give us the bread eternal (2)
527   bold I approach the eternal throne, and claim the crown (4)
528   a brand plucked from eternal fire (1)
538   eternal Father, strong to save (T,1)
546   Judge eternal, throned in splendor (T,1)
550   till these eternal hills remove (4)

eternally
78 laud, honor, might ... glory be ... age to age eternally (4)
206 in thy strong hand eternally rests the ... years (3)
221 bound to him eternally by love's strong cord (3)
240 lay hold on life ..it shall be thy joy & crown eternally (1)
248 he with the King of glory shall reign eternally (4)
366 we rejoice, and sing to thee our hymn of joy eternally (3)
423 and in his blissful presence eternally rejoice (3)

eternity
3 to eternity love and adore! (4)
22 vast as eternity thy love (4)
82 Jesus, be thou our glory now and through eternity (5)
125 rise to all eternity (4)
129 he speaks! and eternity, filled with his voice (5)
133 but live with thee the perfect life of thine eternity (4)
168 a blest eternity I'll spend triumphant in his grace (3)
177 through all eternity, something for thee (4)
235 silence of eternity, interpreted by love (3)
413 are ye able? Still the Master whispers down eternity (4)
455 and hail him as thy matchless King through all eternity (1)
455 thy praise and glory shall not fail throughout eternity (4)
544 yet to eternity standeth thy Word (3)

ethereal
43 with all the blue ethereal sky (1)

evangel
380 Ay! we shout to the lovely evangel they bring (4)

eve
502 abide with me from morn till eve (3)

even
142 tastes even now the hallowed bliss of an eternal home (4)
152 run my course with even joy (4)
157 warm, sweet, tender, even yet a present help is he (3)
195 O use me, Lord, use even me, just as thou wilt and when (5)
295 even thine own altars, where she safe ... may bring (4)
475 now, even now, once more from earth to sky peals forth (3)
501 at even, ere the sun was set (T,1)
522 even so,Lord, quickly come, bring thy final harvest home (4)

evening
4 by morning glow or evening shade his watchful eye ne'er (2)
11 morning, evening, bless his name (2)
28 a thousand ages in thy sight are like an evening gone (4)
43 soon as the evening shades prevail (2)
60 ye lights of evening, find a voice (2)
462 Spirit of love, at evening time when weary (5)
495 shadows of the evening steal across the sky (1)
496 Savior, breathe an evening blessing   (T,1)
501 hear, in this solemn evening hour (6)
503 wait and worship while the night sets her evening lamps (1)
503 evening lamps alight through all the sky (1)
506 but mid the light declining the evening star is shining (1)
513 he paints the wayside flower, he lights the evening star (2)
545 have builded him an altar in the evening dews and damps (2)

evening's
36   we feel thy calm at evening's hour (3)

eventide
90   at eventide before the sun was set (4)
289   abide with me, fast falls the eventide (T,1)
501   once more 'tis eventide, and we, oppressed (2)

ever
2   angel voices, ever singing round thy throne of light (T,1)
2   honor, glory, might, and merit thine shall ever be (5)
4   an ever present help and stay (3)
7   for his lovingkindness ever shed upon our earthly way (3)
28   time, like an ever rolling stream (5)
37   all that borrows life from thee is ever in thy care (3)
38   thou art giving and forgiving, ever blessing, ever blest (3)
38   ever singing, march we onward (4)
49   with ever joyful hearts and blessed peace to cheer us (2)
54   in God our shield we will rejoice & ever bless thy name (5)
59   thy name be ever praised! O Lord, make us free (3)
61   for his mercies shall endure, ever faithful, ever sure (R)
63   chance and change are busy ever (2)
65   ever under his control (6)
80   who like thee so mild, so bright ... did ever go (2)
86   ever be thou our guide (3)
87   take the name of Jesus ever as a shield from every snare (2)
98   such ever bring thee where they come (2)
103   come to the feast of love; come, ever knowing (3)
106   ever near the Christian's side (1)
106   ever present, truest friend ... near thine aid to lend (2)
111   come quickly in ... nor ever hence remove (4)
122   he ever lives above, for me to intercede (2)
143   nor let me ever stray from thee aside (3)
164   O let me feel thee near me, the world is ever near (2)
164   my foes are ever near me, around me and within (2)
165   ever faithful ... to the truth may we be found (2)
166   I'll ever adore thee in heaven so bright (3)
166   if ever I loved thee, Lord Jesus,'tis now (R)
169   I would live ever in the light (3)
169   I would work ever for the right (3)
173   while ever on the hill-top before thee loomed the cross (2)
187   take myself, and I will be ever, only, all for thee (3)
188   ever, O Christ, through mine let thy life shine (1)
193   ever toward each other move, and ever move toward thee (4)
216   his faithfulness shall ever be a shield and buckler (4)
217   nor ever murmur nor repine; content whatever lot I see (3)
228   to the old rugged cross I will ever be true (4)
230   His wisdom ever waketh, his sight is never dim (2)
231   the theme of God's salvation, and find it ever new (2)
237   grant that I may ever cast my care on thee (3)
242   toiling up new Calvaries ever (3)
256   I ever with thee and thou with me, Lord (2)
258   pray that he may prosper ever each endeavor (3)
258   but that he may ever thwart thee and convert thee (3)
271   songs of praises I will ever give to thee (3)
272   I was not ever thus (2)
273   keep me ever, by thy spirit, pure and strong and true (5)

295   they ever give thee praise (5)
298   ever Three and ever One (4)
303   the Prince is ever in them; the day-light is serene (2)
303   who art, with God the Father and Spirit, ever blest (4)
311   may her voice be ever clear, warning of a judgment near (2)
326   thou art here, nearer than ever, still my shield and sun (4)
329   thy truth unchanged hath ever stood (2)

329   O Jesus, ever with us stay (5)
338   O may we ever walk in him, and nothing know beside (3)
344   and ever by thy Spirit guide (4)
348   ever, Lord, thy name be known (1)
352   this temple, reared to thee, O may it ever be filled (1)
361   on his shoulder ever rests all power on earth and heaven (2)
367   O may these heavenly pages be my ever dear delight (3)
370   light of knowledge, ever burning, shed on us (3)
390   and ever o'er its Babel sounds the blessed angels sing (2)
390   when with the ever circling years shall come the time (3)
397   so may we with willing feet ever seek thy mercy seat (2)
399   ever joined to thee in love that cannot falter (2)
412   I do adore thee, and will ever pray thee (5)
420   and say, was ever grief like his (3)
423   O may we ever praise him with heart and life and voice (3)
428   O Lamb of God, was ever pain, was ever love, like thine (4)
433   in the cross, in the cross, be my glory ever (R)
433   near the cross I'll watch & wait, hoping, trusting ever (4)
455   flowers of paradise extend their fragrance ever sweet (3)
460   with the Father ever one (2)
463   ever present help in need (1)
464   more & more it spreads and grows ever mighty to prevail (2)
466   and let thy glorious light shine ever on my sight (2)
485   when ever blue the sky shall gleam ... green the sod (2)
488   new graces ever gaining from this our day of rest (4)
507   the covenant we this moment make be ever kept in mind (3)
520   love like thine, that none shall ever stray (1)
521   neither life nor death shall ever from the Lord .. sever (3)
521   nor ... ever from the Lord his children sever (3)
523   O may we ever with thee live, who givest all (5)
552   and glory, laud, and praise be ever thine (4)
552   be thy strong arm our ever sure defense (3)

everlasting
  8   infinite thy vast domain, everlasting is thy reign (1)
 28   from everlasting thou art God (3)
 66   praise the everlasting King (1)
468   thou in thy everlasting seat remainest God alone (3)
489   here afford us, Lord, a taste of our everlasting feast (3)
496   the perfect day before us breaks in everlasting light (4)
551   be thou her refuge and her trust, her everlasting friend (4)

evermore
  3   eternal praise be, hence, evermore (4)
 26   which wert, and art, and evermore shalt be (2)
 29   Father of glory evermore ... Father of all grace & might (3)
 35   for thy church that evermore lifteth holy hands above (5)
 49   for thus it was, is now, and shall be evermore (3)
 66   evermore his praises sing, Alleluia! Alleluia! (1)
148   from his lighthouse evermore (1)

349   all praise and honor, glory, power be now and evermore (4)
357   that future years shall see, evermore and evermore (1)
357   every voice in conceret ring evermore and evermore (2)
357   honor, glory, & dominion, and eternal victory, evermore (3)
391   hath oped the heavenly door ... man is blessed evermore (2)
397   so, most gracious Lord, may we evermore be led to thee (1)
427   then let all praise be given thee who livest evermore (3)
446   that thy peace which evermore passeth human knowing (4)
470   let the search for thy salvation be our glory evermore (5)
482   ride on till tyranny and greed are evermore undone (3)
483   rejoice, give thanks, and sing, and triumph evermore (1)
487   as we go, lead us, Lord; we shall be thine evermore (4)
522   but the fruitful ears to store in his garner evermore (3)
538   thus evermore shall rise to thee glad hymns of praise (4)

everwhere
37   everwhere that man can be, thou, God, art present there (3)

every
3   thou who almighty art, now rule in every heart (3)
4   every faithless murmur stills (1)
5   then let our songs abound and every tear be dry (4)
6   we, thy people , praise thee, God of every nation! (T,1,2)
10   let all the world in every corner sing (T,1,2)
14   to every land the strains belong (4)
14   sung through every land by every tongue (1)
14   in every land begin the song (4)
15   praise the Lord in every breath (3)
15   praise him every tuneful string: (2)
15   him, in whom they move and live, let every creature sing (3)
23   bound every heart with rapturous joy (3)
23   burn every breast with Jesus' love (3)
33   life mounts in every throbbing vein (2)
35   offering up on every shore her pure sacrifice of love (5)
41   o how wondrous, o how glorious is thy name in every land (4)
43   publishes to every land the work of an almighty hand (1)
58   seek thee as thy saints ... sought in every generation (1)
64   center and soul of every sphere (1)
66   saints triumphant ... gathered in from every race (4)
70   through every period of my life thy goodness I'll pursue (4)
71   let every kindred, every tribe on this terrestrial ball (4)
74   let every tongue confess ... one accord ... Jesus Christ (5)
76   at the name of Jesus every knee shall bow (T,1)
76   every tongue confess him King of glory now (1)
78   redeem us for eternal day from every power of darkness (3)
81   proclaim with every fleeting breath (5)
82   O Hope of every contrite heart, O Joy of all the meek (3)
84   O Guide to every child of thine (T,1)
87   take the name of Jesus ever as a shield from every snare (2)
90   shining revealed through every task most lowly (2)
93   come, thou fount of every blessing (T,1)
95   Light and life art thou within: Savior ...from every sin (4)
98   and every place is hallowed ground (1)
101   come, every soul by sin oppressed (T,1)
102   let every soul be Jesus' guest (1)
104   every grace that brings you nigh (2)
111   stands knocking at the door of every sinner's heart (2)

115   how happy every child of grace (T,1)
116   I am every whit made whole; glory, glory to the Lamb! (5)
118   I give up every plea beside (4)
119   thy love unknown hath broken every barrier down (6)
135   kindle every high desire; perish self in thy pure fire (2)
136   till every age and race and clime shall blend (3)
137   who did for every sinner die hath surely died for me (1)
137   testify to all mankind, and speak in every heart (3)
141   God will fulfill in every part each promise he has made (1)
142   though pressed by every foe (1)
147   teach us, in every state,to make thy will our own (4)
152   and every moment watch and pray (3)
178   one with thyself, may every eye in us, thy brethren see (4)
186   end of my every action thou, in all things thee I see (3)
187   take my intellect ... use every power as thou ... choose (2)
188   breathe into every wish thy will divine (1)
198   in every heart and brain shall throb the pulse of one (3)
198   every life shall be a song when all... earth is paradise (4)
201   who lovest all thy lost ones on every mountain steep (1)
205   gives me grace for every trial (2)
207   through every day, o'er all the way He will take care (R)
209   in every change he faithful will remain (1)
219   I look to thee in every need and never look in vain (T,1)
220   though the earth be shaking, every heart be quaking (2)
221   listening every moment to the Spirit's call (4)
222   in every high and stormy gale, my anchor holds (2)
226   every day, every hour, let me feel thy cleansing power (R)
232   from every stormy wind that blows (T,1)
232   from every swelling tide of woes (1)
242   once to every man and nation comes the moment to decide (T)
246   renew it boldly every day, and help divine implore (2)
248   till every foe is vanquished, and Christ is Lord indeed (1)
249   awake, my soul, stretch every nerve (T,1)
251   perish every fond ambition, all I've... hoped or known (1)
255   when every heart was tuned to praise (3)
261   Jesus knows our every weakness (2)
262   let this my every hour employ, till I thy glory see (5)
265   I need thee every hour (T,1,2,3,4,5)
265   I need thee, O I need thee, every hour I need thee (R)
274   with obedience glad & steady still to follow every word (4)
275   I'll cast on him my every care and wait for thee (3)
278   scatter .. life through every part .. sanctify the whole (2)
281   purge me from every evil blot (3)
281   cleanse me from every sinful thought (3)
282   a heart in every thought renewed and full of love divine (4)
283   visit us with thy salvation; enter every trembling heart (1)
283   O breathe thy loving spirit into every troubled breast (2)
287   every round goes higher ... soldiers of the cross (2)
289   I need thy presence every passing hour (3)
296   one holy Church of God appears through every age & race (T)
297   elect from every nation, yet one o'er all the earth (2)
297   and to one hope she presses, with every grace endued (2)
299   proclaim to every people, tongue, and nation (3)
301   grace through every vessel flows in purest streams (2)
309   by thy reconciling love every stumbling block remove (2)
310   Lord, let every bounding heart the mighty comfort feel (4)
319   every humble, contrite heart is made a welcome guest (1)

319	brethren, all, let every heart with kind affection glow (2)
321	thy supper, Lord, is spread in every quiet upper room (1)
321	every act of brotherhood repeats thy feast again (2)
342	we cultivate the nature God plants in every heart (3)
343	there is a voice in every star, in every breeze a song (1)
352	let every anthem rise like incense to the skies (2)
356	O let thy Word be light anew to every nation's life (3)
357	every voice in conceret ring evermore and evermore (2)
360	dear desire of every nation, joy of every longing heart (1)
364	every eye shall now behold him robed in dreadful majesty (2)
365	in every star thy wisdom shines (1)
365	when thy truth began its race, it touched ... every land (3)
365	thy truth ... touched and glanced on every land (3)
371	to every land, to every race and clan (4)
380	every hearth is aflame, and the beautiful sing (3)
392	let every heart prepare him room (1)
397	Holy Jesus, every day keep us in the narrow way (4)
398	Light of the world, thy beauty steals into every heart (2)
398	till every tongue and nation, from sin's dominion free (3)
408	the Day-star clear and bright of every man and nation (1)
440	every humble spirit shares it (2)
452	bloom in every meadow, leaves on every bough (2)
453	every knee to him shall bow (1)
454	every sin may be forgiven through .. virtue of thy blood (2)
457	every vanquished foe submits to his victorious cross (2)
469	through the thick darkness covering every nation (1)
471	in every heart reign thou alone (2)
472	rise with every morning sacrifice (2)
472	people and realms of every tongue dwell (3)
472	let every creature rise and bring his grateful honors (5)
476	O God of love, whose spirit wakes in every human breast (2)
476	who lightest every earnest mind of every clime and shore (3)
476	Christ is formed in all mankind and every land is thine (5)
479	consecrating to thy purpose every gift thou dost impart (1)
482	until in every land and clime thine ends of love are won (4)
495	comfort every sufferer watching late in pain (4)
498	sure of being safely guided, guarded well from every foe (2)
498	every day will be the brighter when ... thy face we see (3)
498	every burden will be lighter when ... it comes from thee (3)
499	new every morning is the love (T,1)
499	help us, this & every day to live more nearly as we pray (4)
502	be every mourner's sleep tonight like infant's slumbers (5)
515	since every day by thee we live, may grateful hearts (4)
516	and love fills every breast (1)
516	happy the home where Jesus' name is sweet to every ear (2)
518	for life and health and every good (2)
520	within .. home let every heart become thy dwelling place (2)
520	grant, Love Divine, in every place glad fellowship (3)
525	common things which every day and hour brings (2)
530	kindly for each other care; every member feel its share (4)
531	reign alone, the Lord of every motion there (2)
543	America! America! God mend thine every flaw (2)
543	till all success be nobleness and every gain divine (3)
547	from every mountain side let freedom ring (1)
551	of every clime and coast, O hear us for our native land (1)
551	O guard our shores from every foe (2)

everyone
   34   the ripe fruits in the garden: He made them everyone (3)
  183   there's a cross for everyone ... there's a cross for me (1)
everything
  261   what a privilege to carry everything to God in prayer (1)
  261   all because we do not carry everything to God in prayer (1)
  267   everything false will disappear (2)
  398   till everything that's human be filled with the divine (3)

everywhere
   11   men and children everywhere (T,1)
   45   he speaks to me everywhere (2)
   63   everywhere his glory shineth (4)
  192   in him shall true hearts everywhere ... communion find (2)
  267   let me bear gladly the warm truth everywhere (3)
  342   and let our daily living reveal thee everywhere (1)
  379   till the air, everywhere, now with joy is ringing (1)
  404   over the hills and everywhere ... Jesus Christ is born (R)
  518   be here and everywhere adored (1)
  542   and skies are everywhere as blue as mine (2)

evidence
  139   with strong commanding evidence their... origin display (5)

evil
   57   from evil he will keep thee safe (4)
  116   long has evil reigned within (2)
  210   and bear thee through the evil days (1)
  214   therefore the evil shall receive but grief (3)
  214   their evil acts shall surely come to naught (4)
  216   no evil shall upon thee come (6)
  242   for the good or evil side (1)
  242   though the cause of evil prosper . truth alone is strong (4)
  258   when thou evil wouldst pursue (3)
  281   purge me from every evil blot (3)
  296   redeem the evil time (4)
  307   save it from evil, guard it still (3)
  410   song that shall conquer evil & shatter the spear & sword (2)
  437   our hearts be pure from evil, that we may see aright (2)
  470   lo! the hosts of evil round us scorn thy Christ (2)
  495   those who plan some evil, from their sins restrain (4)
  506   all evil thoughts expelling, now make in us thy dwelling (5)
  521   from all evil things he spares them (2)

evils
  470   save us from weak resignation to the evils we deplore (5)

exalt
   56   O magnify the Lord with me, with me exalt his name (2)
  422   while men of low degree exalt and usher in the day (4)

exalted
   74   wherefore, by God's eternal purpose thou art exalted (4)
   74   thou art exalted o'er all creatures now (4)
  168   the forms of love he wears, exalted on his throne (2)
  179   under the standard exalted and royal (1)
  362   valleys shall be exalted, the lofty hills brought low (1,4)

424   to thee, now high exalted, our melody we raise (3)
439   following our exalted Head, Alleluia (4)
457   worthy to be exalted thus, the Lamb for sinner slain (2)
482   O Thou who art the Life and Light, Exalted Lord and King (4)
509   in scenes exalted or depressed thou art our joy ... rest (4)

example
186   thy bright example I pursue, to thee in all things rise (4)
199   follow with reverent steps the great example of him (3)

exceeding
440   O what glory, far exceeding all... eye has yet preceived (2)

exceeds
25   to spend one day with thee on earth exceeds a thousand (1)
25   one day with thee ... exceeds a thousand days of mirth (1)

excel
405   Bethlehem, thou dost all excel (1)

excellent
44   how excellent thy name (1)
44   Lord, our Lord, in all the earth how excellent thy name (5)
48   laid for your faith in his excellent Word (1)

excelling
283   love divine, all loves excelling (T,1)

excelsis
374   gloria in excelsis Deo, gloria in excelsis Deo (R)

exchange
228   and exchange it some day for a crown (R)
389   behold the wonderful exchange our Lord with us doth make (3)

exchanged
474   all our sorrows left below .. earth exchanged for heaven (3)

excuses
325   nor weak excuses frame (4)

exile
354   mourns in lonely exile here until the Son of God appear (1)

exiled
550   our exiled fathers crossed the sea (1)

exiles
550   faith in God came with those exiles o'er the waves (3)

expand
131   expand thy wings, celestial Dove (3)

expanses
33   o'er white expanses sparkling pure (2)

expect
303   O sweet and blessed country that eager hearts expect (4)

expected
360   come, thou long expected Jesus (T,1)

expelling
506   all evil thoughts expelling, now make in us thy dwelling (5)

experience
 56   O make but trial of his love; experience will decide (3)
 56   experience will decide how blest are they (3)

explains
332   explains the wondrous way how through these virtues came (2)

explore
527   who can explore his strange design (2)

expounding
460   age-long Word expounding God's own message now as then (3)

express
227   tongue can never express the sweet comfort and peace (1)
309   all the depths of love express (5)

expressed
252   prayer ... unuttered or expressed (1)
260   secret thought .. hidden plan, wrought ..or unexpressed (2)

expresses
442   through each wonder of fair days God himself expresses (2)

exquisite
279   and mourn for the minutest fault in exquisite distress (2)
280   and mourn for the minutest fault in exquisite distress (2)

extend
 65   to their children's children ...his righteousness extend (4)
361   his righteous government and power shall over all extend (4)
455   round his pierced feet fair flowers of paradise extend (3)
455   flowers of paradise extend their fragrance ever sweet (3)

extended
291   o'er ... wide-extended plains shines one eternal day (2)

extends
130   thy sovereign grace to all extends (2)

extol
 23   extol the Lamb with loftiest song (4)
 59   we all do extol thee, thou leader triumphant (3)
100   extol the Lamb of God, the all-atoning Lamb (3)
357   powers, dominions, bow before him & extol our God & King (2)
409   that name all-victorious of Jesus extol (1)

exult
 303 exult, O dust and ashes; the Lord shall be thy part (3)

exultant
 423 from Olivet they followed mid an exultant crowd (2)

exultation
 364 cause of endless exultation to his ransomed worshipers (3)
 386 sing, choirs of angels, sing in exultation (2)
 484 in ire and exultation aflame with faith and free (3)
 524 bring sacrifice of praise ... shouts of exultation (1)

exulting
 233 raise high your free, exulting song (2)

eye
 2 thou who art beyond the farthest mortal eye can scan (2)
 4 by morning glow or evening shade his watchful eye ne'er (2)
 4 his watchful eye ne'er sleepeth (2)
 26 though the eye of sinful man thy glory may not see (3)
 31 no mortal eye can bear the sight (1)
 35 for the joy of ear and eye (3)
 37 where'er I turn my eye (2)
 53 beneath his watchful eye his saints securely dwell (2)
 113 Savior, look with pitying eye; Savior, help me, or I die (R)
 139 and God is seen by mortal eye (6)
 178 one with thyself, may every eye in us, thy brethren see (4)
 218 the eye of faith is dim (5)
 249 his own hand presents the prize to thine aspiring eye (3)
 252 the upward glancing of an eye, when none but God is near (2)
 253 I want a godly fear, a quick discerning eye (3)
 279 quick as the apple of an eye, O God, my conscience make (3)
 280 quick as the apple of an eye, O God, my conscience make (3)
 291 cast a wishful eye to Canaan's fair and happy land (1)
 294 dear as the apple of thine eye, and graven on thy hand (2)
 324 Cherubim, with sleepless eye, veil their faces (4)
 364 every eye shall now behold him robed in dreadful majesty (2)
 366 nor eye hath seen, nor ear hath yet attained to hear (3)
 399 here in sadness eye and heart long for thy gladness (2)
 417 upon that cross of Jesus mine eye at times can see (2)
 419 the martyr first, whose eagle eye could pierce (2)
 419 eagle eye could pierce beyond the grave (2)
 440 O what glory, far exceeding all... eye has yet preceived (2)
 494 thou, whose all-pervading eye naught escapes (2)
 494 eye naught escapes without, within (2)
 527 thine eye diffused a quickening ray (3)

eyed
 469 envious of heart, blind-eyed, with tongues confounded (3)
eyelids
 495 with thy tenderest blessing may our eyelids close (2)
 502 my wearied eyelids gently steep (2)

eyes
 27 in light inaccessible hid from our eyes (1)
 34 he gave us eyes to see them, and lips that we might tell (4)

57   unto the hills I lift mine eyes (T,1)
98   and bring all heaven before our eyes (4)
120   when my eyes shall close in death (3)
136   mists ... of doubt which blind our eyes to thee (2)
137   'tis thine the blood to apply and give us eyes to see (1)
140   Author of faith! to thee I lift my weary, longing eyes (4)
148   eager eyes are watching, longing for the lights (2)
171   who with the eyes of early youth eternal things did see (1)
189   the day of dawning brotherhood breaks on our eager eyes (1)
198   and light of knowledge in their eyes (1)
203   but in the eyes of men, redeemed and free, a splendor (4)
240   lift up thine eyes, and seek his face (2)
264   its closing eyes look up to thee in prayer (4)
267   open my eyes that I may see (T,1)
267   open my eyes, that I may hear voices of truth (2)
267   open my eyes, illumine me, Spirit divine (R)
289   hold thou thy cross before my closing eyes (5)
297   with the vision glorious, her longing eyes are blest (3)
300   lift your eyes ... sons of light Zion's city is in sight (4)
317   lighten our eyes, brightly appear (3)
365   but when our eyes behold thy Word, we read thy name (1)
398   never shall darkness veil thee again from human eyes (1)
401   inward light impart, cheer my eyes and warm my heart (2)
413   are ye able to remember, when a thief lifts up his eyes (2)
415   and melt mine eyes to tears (4)
425   look down with sad and wondering eyes to see (3)
434   Christ is risen! He meets our eyes (4)
462   to read forgiveness in thine eyes (3)
462   eyes that see, beyond the dark, the dawn and thee (5)
476   teach us to ban .. ugliness that blinds our eyes to thee (4)
481   the tears are wiped from eyes that shall not weep again (1)
489   may thy glory meet our eyes while we in thy house appear (3)
495   pure and fresh and sinless in thy holy eyes (6)
497   when the constant sun returning unseals our eyes (2)
502   to hide thee from thy servant's eyes (1)
503   Lord of angels, on our eyes let eternal morning rise (4)
517   sons and daughters look on life with eager eyes (4)
545   mine eyes have seen the glory of the coming of the Lord (T)

eyesight
    9   the Lord pours eyesight on the blind (3)

face
    66   ye behold him face to face (4)
    82   sweeter far thy face to see and in thy presence rest (1)
    88   all in the love-light of Jesus' face (2)
   100   and, saved from earth, appear before your Savior's face (4)
   108   thorns thy brow encircle, and tears thy face have marred (2)
   129   restore, my dear Savior, the light of thy face (4)
   145   trusting only in thy merit would I seek thy face (3)
   146   whom we, that have not seen thy face (1)
   162   singing, till thy face I see, of his love (4)
   168   and I shall see his face (3)
   173   thy steadfast face set forward where love and duty shone (2)
   173   amid our pride and glory to see thy face appear (5)
   177   and when thy face I see, my ransomed soul shall be (4)

324 veil their faces to the presence (4)
409 fall down on their faces and worship the Lamb (3)

facing
470 grant us courage for the facing of this hour (1)

faction
548 from the strife of class & faction make our nation free (4)

fadeless
103 hope of the penitent, fadeless and pure (2)

fades
494 softly now the light of day fades upon our sight away (T,1)

fail
42 never shall his promise fail (2)
47 we own thy mercies, Lord, which never fail (1)
92 yea, when this flesh and heart shall fail (5)
207 through days of toil when heart doth fail (2)
220 Jesus will not fail us (2)
221 standing on the promises that cannot fail (2)
221 standing on the promises I cannot fail (4)
237 grant that I may never fail thy hand to see (3)
244 when the hosts of sin assail ... strength begins to fail (2)
248 arm of flesh will fail you, ye dare not trust your own (3)
254 I see all that I would, but fail to be (1)
289 when other helpers fail and comforts flee (1)
305 we have Christ's own promise, and that cannot fail (3)
455 thy praise and glory shall not fail throughout eternity (4)
470 grant us courage that we fail not man nor thee (4)
473 in Thee do we trust, nor find Thee to fail (5)
483 His kingdom cannot fail, he rules o'er earth and heaven (3)

faileth
67 Shepherd ... whose goodness faileth never (1)
67 thy goodness faileth never (6)
526 yea, e'en the best life faileth (2)

failing
20 a bulwark never failing (1)
215 deep in unfathomable mines of never-failing skill (2)
316 when these failing lips grow dumb ... mind & memory flee (4)
316 when these failing lips grow dumb...Lord, remember me (4)
371 O God of light, thy Word, a lamp unfailing (T,1)
539 put his arms unfailing round you (3)

fails
293 never fails from age to age (2)
293 grace, which like the Lord, the giver, never fails (2)

failures
41 spire and ruined city, these our hopes and failures show (3)
219 shamed by its failures or its fears, I sink (2)
244 in the midst of faults and failures, stand by me (3)

fain
417   beneath the cross of Jesus I fain would take my stand (T,1)
501   they who fain would serve thee best are conscious most (4)

faint
98   to teach our faint desires to rise (4)
106   hearts grow faint, and hopes give o'er, whisper softly (2)
125   raise the fallen, cheer the faint (3)
134   our love so faint,so cold to thee & thine to us so great (4)
184   my power is faint and low till I have learned to serve (3)
211   his truth be thine affiance, when faint and desolate (2)
240   faint not nor fear, for he is near (4)
285   I thirst, I faint, I die to prove ... love (1)
292   the poor, and them that mourn, the faint and overborne (1)
293   who can faint while such a river ...their thirst assuage (2)
337   to watch and pray, and never faint (4)
546   feed thy faint and hungry peoples with...thy Word (2)

fainted
220   till it well-nigh fainted, thirsting after thee (1)

fainting
9   the Lord supports the fainting mind (3)
124   revives my fainting heart, healing all it hidden smart (2)
143   may thy rich grace impart strength to my fainting heart (2)
148   some poor fainting, struggling seaman you may rescue (R)
321   upper room where fainting souls are fed (1)
367   springs of consolation rise to cheer the fainting mind (2)
418   O make me thine forever, and should I fainting be (3)

faints
295   thirsty soul longs ardently ... faints thy courts to see (2)

fair
29   to make ill-fortune turn to fair (4)
39   his dwelling place, how fair (2)
45   he shines in all that's fair (2)
47   faith's fair vision changes into sight (2)
79   fair are the meadows, fairer still the woodlands (2)
79   fair is the sunshine, fairer still the moonlight (3)
171   shapest man to   God's own law, thyself the fair design (2)
233   strong men and maidens fair (2)
238   Christian, dost thou hear them, how they speak thee fair (3)
291   cast a wishful eye to Canaan's fair and happy land (1)
348   let thy church rise, strong and fair (1)
353   brighter than the glorious morn ... this fair morning be (4)
377   no room ... for Joseph or Madonna fair (1)
399   O morning star, how fair and bright (T,1)
399   thou art holy, fair and glorious, all victorious (1)
442   through each wonder of fair days God himself expresses (2)
455   round his pierced feet fair flowers of paradise extend (3)
475   earth might be fair and all men glad and wise (2)
475   earth shall be fair, and all her people one (3)
476   till ... know the loveliness of lives made fair and free (4)
481   already in the mind of God that city riseth fair (5)
490   my heart's freed from ill, fair blue sky's above (3)

517   may we keep our holy calling stainless in... fair renown (5)
524   where golden fields spread fair and broad (3)
541   in darkening storms or sunshine fair (1)

fairer
  5   marching ... to fairer worlds on high (4)
 79   fair are the meadows, fairer still the woodlands (2)
 79   robed in the blooming garb of spring: Jesus is fairer (2)
 79   fair is the sunshine, fairer still the moonlight (3)
203   but often in some far-off Galilee beheld thee fairer (2)
203   beheld thee fairer yet while serving thee (2)
234   in thy sunshine's blaze its day may brighter, fairer be (2)
264   fairer than morning, lovelier than daylight (1)
264   O in that hour, fairer than daylight dawning shall rise (5)
365   we read thy name in fairer lines (1)
405   fairer than the sun at morning was the star (2)

fairest
 79   fairest Lord Jesus, ruler of all nature (T,1)

faith
  5   fruit ... from faith and hope may grow (3)
 12   dearer than all things I know is child-like faith to me (4)
 47   lead us by faith to hope's true promised land (2)
 48   laid for your faith in his excellent Word (1)
 86   lead us to where thou hast trod, our faith make strong (3)
 98   prayer to strengthen faith and sweeten care (4)
109   words of life and beauty teach me faith and duty (1)
115   by faith I see the land of rest, the saints' delight (1)
124   faith in him who died to save (4)
137   Spirit of faith, come down, reveal the things of God (T,1)
137   Spirit of faith, descend and show the virtue of his name (3)
137   inspire the living faith, which whosoe'er receives (4)
137   that faith that conquers all, and doth the mountain move (4)
139   Author of faith, eternal Word (T,1)
139   faith like its finisher and Lord today as yesterday (1)
139   by faith we know thee strong to save (3)
139   whate'er we hope, by faith we have (3)
139   faith lends its realizing light (6)
139   increase in us the kindled fire...work of faith fulfill (2)
141   have faith in God, my heart, trust and be unafraid (T,1)
141   Have faith in God, my mind ... oft thy light burns low (2)
141   have faith in God, my soul, His cross forever stands (3)
142   O for a faith that will not shrink (T,1)
142   Lord, give me such a faith as this (4)
142   faith that shines more bright & clear when tempests rage (3)
143   my faith looks up to thee, thou Lamb of Calvary (T,1)
144   help me, throughout life's changing scene, by faith (1)
144   though faith and hope may long be tried (4)
144   by faith to cling to thee (1)
146   by faith, and faith alone, embrace (1)
147   when the joys of sense depart, to live by faith alone (4)
151   faith of our fathers, holy faith   (R)
151   faith of our fathers (T,1,2,3)
157   faith has still its Olivet, and love its Galilee (3)
159   but I long to rise in the arms of faith (1)

170   in work that keeps faith sweet and strong (3)
171   boyhood faith that shown thy whole life through (1)
171   we thank thee for thy boyhood faith (1)
172   my acts of faith and lover repeat (4)
177   my feeble faith looks up, Jesus, to thee (2)
181   and we believe thy word, though dim our faith may be (4)
189   our loyal love, our stalwart faith (2)
189   one common faith unites us all, we seek one common goal (3)
192   join hands ... brothers of the faith whate'er your race (3)
205   here by faith in him to dwell (1)
206   new faith to find the paths ahead (1)
208   in simple faith to plunge me neath the healing ... flood (2)
218   the eye of faith is dim (5)
232   though sundered far, by faith they meet (3)
239   by faith they bring it night (5)
242   the multitude make virtue of the faith they had denied (2)
243   the sons of fathers we by whom our faith is taught (2)
246   work of faith will not be done till thou obtain .. crown (3)
251   armed by faith and winged by prayer (4)
251   faith to sight and, prayer to praise (4)
269   and age comes on, uncheered by faith or hope (2)
270   and trembling faith is changed to fear (3)
283   Alpha and Omega be; end of faith as its beginning (2)
297   her charter of salvation, one Lord, one faith, one birth (2)
302   by faith we join our hands with those that went before (5)
307   knowledge and faith and life immortal Jesus ... imparts (1)
311   while on earth her faith is tried (1)
319   one fold .. faith .. hope .. Lord, One God alone we know (1)
319   by faith we take the bread of life (3)
319   in faith and memory thus we sing the wonders of his love (4)
319   thus anticipate by faith the heavenly feast above (4)
328   one with the living bread divine ... now by faith we eat (3)
329   blest, when our faith can hold thee fast (4)
333   assurance of tender charity and steadfast faith (2)
337   wisdom and zeal and faith impart (3)
345   may faith grow firm, and love grow warm (4)
346   science walks ... to seek the God that faith hath found (4)
350   in faith we here an altar raise (1)
350   when in faith our souls draw near (3)
356   may one Lord .. faith .. Word, one Spirit lead us still (4)
406   Lord, give us faith and strength the road to build (3)
421   by faith, I saw the stream thy flowing wounds supply (4)
430   here we gather love to live; here we gather faith to die (3)
438   faith lives upon no other! Alleluia! (4)
440   life eternal! O what wonders crowd on faith (4)
451   and yet whose faith hath constant been (4)
457   by the almighty Spirit led and filled with faith & love (1)
459   from thee have flowed, as from a mighty river ... faith (4)
459   from thee...our faith and hope, our fellowship and peace (4)
460   one sure faith yet standing fast (4)
462   give us the faith that follows on (1)
471   in us the work of faith fulfill (4)
477   the quiet of a steadfast faith, calm of a call obeyed (2)
484   in ire and exultation aflame with faith and free (3)
485   calm and courage, faith and hope: O pour them from above (1)
487   our faith from seed to flower raise on this thy holy day (2)

505   hope and faith and love rise glorious (4)
517   hope to trust them, faith to guide them (4)
520   steadfast faith & earnest prayer keep sacred vows secure (4)
533   give me the wings of faith to rise within the veil (T,1)
536   who thee by faith before the world confessed (1)
548   keep her faith in simple manhood (4)
550   laws, freedom, truth, and faith in God came (3)
550   faith in God came with those exiles o'er the waves (3)

faith's
  47   faith's fair vision changes into sight (2)
243   faith's warfare ended, won the home of endless peace (4)
339   answer ... faith's effectual prayer ... our needs supply (1)

faithful
  57   thy faithful keeper is the Lord (3)
  61   for his mercies shall endure, ever faithful, ever sure (R)
106   Holy Spirit, faithful guide (T,1)
161   we would be faithful to thy gospel glorious (5)
165   ever faithful ... to the truth may we be found (2)
177   give me a faithful heart, likeness to thee (3)
179   truehearted, wholehearted, faithful and loyal (T,1)
209   in every change he faithful will remain (1)
214   their joyful, faithful hearts obey the laws of God (1)
217   His faithful follower I would be (R)
261   can we find a friend so faithful (2)
283   all thy faithful mercies crown (1)
324   he will give to all.. faithful .. self for heavenly food (2)
332   fills .. faithful people's hearts with...the life of God (1)
386   O come, all ye faithful, joyful and triumphant (T,1)
446   come, ye faithful, raise the strain (T,1)
448   come, ye faithful, raise the strain (T,1) (see 446)
451   the faithful women went their way to seek the tomb (2)
452   come then, true and faithful, now fulfill thy word (3)
526   I rest upon his faithful word to them of contrite spirit (3)
536   O may thy soldiers, faithful, true, and bold (3)
548   for the armies of the faithful (3)

faithfully
  76   faithfully he bore it spotless to the last (3)
210   so do thine own part faithfully, and trust his word (3)

faithfulness
  66   Alleluia! Alleluia! glorious in his faithfulness (2)
216   his faithfulness shall ever be a shield and buckler (4)
275   truth and faithfulness engage the waiting soul to bless (3)

faithless
  4   every faithless murmur stills (1)
534   journey which faithless feet ne'er trod (1)

fall
  29   o thou true Sun, on us thy glance let fall (2)
  29   on us thy glance let fall in royal radiance (2)
  50   that shadows fall on brightest hours, that thorns remain (3)
  71   let angels prostrate fall (1)

71	chosen seed of Israel's race, ye ransomed from the fall (2)
71	O that with yonder sacred throng we at his feet may fall (5)
82	to those who fall, how kind thou art (3)
97	without him I would fall (1)
104	come,ye weary, heavy laden bruised & mangled by the fall (4)
199	then shall all shackles fall (4)
227	angels could do nothing more, than to fall at his feet (3)
237	nor for fear or favor suffer me to fall (1)
267	and while the wave-notes fall on my ear (2)
294	for her my tears shall fall, for her my prayers ascend (3)
330	when I fall on my knees with my face to the rising sun (R)
341	angels and men before it fall, and devils fear and fly (1)
369	then shall all bondage cease, all fetters fall (2)
409	fall down on their faces and worship the Lamb (3)
418	lo, here I fall, my Savior! 'Tis I deserve thy place (2)
460	through the rise and fall of nations (3)
501	no word from thee can fruitless fall (6)
503	while the deepening shadows fall (3)
505	at his touch our burdens fall (3)
515	suns glow, rains fall, by power divine (2)
530	names & sects & parties fall: thou, O Christ art all (5)

fallen

118	fallen, till in me thine image shine (2)
125	raise the fallen, cheer the faint (3)
175	weep o'er the erring one, lift up the fallen (1)
376	snow had fallen, snow on snow (1)

falling

26	cherubim and seraphim falling down before thee (2)
87	falling prostrate at his feet (4)
200	I see my people falling in darkness and despair (2)
252	prayer is the burden of a sigh, the falling of a tear (2)
278	my steadfast soul, from falling free ... no longer move (4)

falls

11	waterfalls that never sleep (3)
289	abide with me, fast falls the eventide (T,1)
289	fast falls the eventide; the darkness deepens (1)
488	today on weary nations the heavenly manna falls (3)
500	the darkness falls at thy behest (1)
549	on homeliest work thy blessing falls (3)

false

4	cast each false idol from his throne (5)
125	false and full of sin I am (3)
161	who by our own false hopes and aims are spent (1)
267	everything false will disappear (2)

falsehood

242	in the strife of truth with falsehood (1)
544	falsehood and wrong shall not tarry beside thee (3)

falsely

194	of tarnished honor, falsely strong (2)

falter
205   my weary steps may falter, and my soul athirst may be (2)
399   ever joined to thee in love that cannot falter (2)
406   build ye the road, and falter not, nor stay (2)
484   our earthly rulers falter, our people drift and die (1)

faltering
219   to nerve my faltering will (3)

fame
176   nor for fame my prayer shall be (2)
242   ere her cause bring fame and profit (2)
453   spread abroad the victor's fame (3)
486   O Lord, be ours the glory beyond all earthly fame (4)
516   children early lisp his fame and parents hold him dear (2)
548   the glory that illumines patriot lives of deathless fame (3)

family
302   one family we dwell in him, one Church above, beneath (3)
309   let us then with joy remove to the family above (6)

famished
204   from famished souls, from sorrow's stress (3)
331   cheers our famished souls with food (1)

famous
532   now praise we great and famous men (T,1)

fancies
149   all the golden fancies of all our golden dreams (2)
149   more wonderful it seems than all the golden fancies (2)
155   than fancies flee away! I'll fear not what men say (3)

fancy
88   and I shall fancy his blessing resting on me (2)

far
4   the Lord is never far away (3)
11   through his far domain, love is king where he doth reign (2)
12   O thou in all thy might so far (T,1)
36   but higher far, and far more clear (4)
46   as far from danger as from fear (2)
64   Lord of all being, throned afar (T,1)
65   far as east from west is distant (3)
82   sweeter far thy face to see and in thy presence rest (1)
92   'tis grace hath brought me safe thus far (3)
115   a country far from mortal sight (1)
170   in hope that sends a shining ray far down the future's (4)
170   far down the future's broadening way (4)
178   far more for others' sins than... wrongs that we receive (3)
228   on a hill far away stood an old rugged cross (T,1)
228   then he'll call me some day to my home far away (4)
229   peace, perfect peace, with loved ones far away (4)
232   though sundered far, by faith they meet (3)
272   the night is dark, & I am far from home, lead thou me on (1)
338   our bodies may far off remove, we still are one in heart (1)
340   who wander far shall seek and find and serve thee well (3)

354 and order all things far and nigh (2)
379 hail the star, that from far bright with hope is burning (3)
379 as I hear, far and near, sweetest angels voices (1)
383 in the east, beyond them far (2)
383 three wise men came from country far (3)
392 far as the curse is found (3)
400 richer by far is the heart's adoration (4)
414 there is a green hill far away, beyond the city wall (T,1)
435 that were an offering far too small (4)
440 O what glory, far exceeding all... eye has yet preceived (2)
456 heaven ... knows neither near nor far (2)
466 shall far outpass the power of human telling (3)
467 keep far our foes; give peace at home (3)
476 no time, no near nor far (1)
480 through the world far and wide, let there be light (4)
513 he only is the Maker of all things near and far (2)
525 for peace on earth, both far and near, we thank thee (1)
531 I see from far thy beauteous light (1)
548 mighty empire, stretching far o'er land and sea (1)

farewell
105 vain world, farewell, from thee I part (5)

farm
511 farm .. market, shop .. home, of mind and heart and hand (1)
514 God, whose farm is all creation (T,1)

farther
110 roam farther and farther away (1)

farthest
2 thou who art beyond the farthest mortal eye can scan (2)
206 no farthest reach where thou art not (2)
296 from oldest time, on farthest shores ... she adores (2)
536 from earth's wide bounds, from ocean's farthest coast (6)

fashioned
442 He who skies & meadows paints fashioned all your virtue (3)

fast
108 O sin that hath no equal, so fast to bar the gate (2)
238 gird thee for the battle; watch and pray and fast (2)
289 abide with me, fast falls the eventide (T,1)
329 blest, when our faith can hold thee fast (4)
442 day is fast reviving (1)
460 one firm anchor holdeth fast (1)
460 one sure faith yet standing fast (3)
473 hath stablished it fast by a changeless decree (3)
486 who, when fears beset them, stand fast and fight and die (2)
527 long my imprisoned spirit lay fast bound in sin (3)
527 fast bound in sin and nature's night (3)

faster
274 speak, that I may follow faster (2)

fasting
331 in thy fasting and temptation ...thy labors on the earth (2)

fatal
  112   fatal cause demands, asks the work of his own hands (1)
  216   no fatal stroke shall thee assail (3)

fateful
  545   he hath loosed the fateful lightning of his ... sword (1)

father
  2   Father, Son, and Holy Spirit, blessed Trinity (5)
  3   Father all glorious, o'er all victorious (1)
  8   holy Father, holy Son, holy Spirit: three we name thee (4)
  19   God ... Father, ... Son, ... Spirit, Three in One (4)
  27   great Father of glory, pure Father of light (4)
  29   the Father, too, our prayers implore (3)
  29   Father of glory evermore ... Father of all grace & might (3)
  31   and will he write his name, my Father and my friend? (4)
  38   thou our Father, Christ our brother (3)
  38   father love is reigning o'er us (4)
  49   all praise and thanks to God the Father now be given (3)
  60   praise, praise the Father, praise the Son (7)
  65   O my soul, bless God the Father (T,1)
  65   bless the Father ... forget not ... mercies to proclaim (1)
  65   like the pity of a father hath... Lord's compassion been (3)
  65   bless the Father, all his creatures (6)
  65   all throughout his vast dominion bless the Father (6)
  65   bless the Father, o my soul (6)
  74   God the Father be by all adored (5)
  75   he who would the Father seek, must seek him...by thee (1)
  78   to God the Father ... Son ... Spirit ... Three in One (4)
  84   know thee ... and call thee heavenly Father (3)
  95   heavenly Father, bless me now (T,1)
  122   and Father, Abba, Father, cry (5)
  140   Father, I stretch my hands to thee (T,1)
  180   praise Father, Son, and Holy Ghost (4)
  192   who serves my Father as a son is surely kin to me (3)
  194   Almighty Father, who dost give the gift of life to all (3)
  201   these, Father, are thy children thou sendest us to find (2)
  220   who love the Father ... still have peace (3)
  235   dear Lord and Father of mankind (T,1)
  256   thou my great Father, and I thy true son (2)
  260   O gracious Father of mankind (T,1)
  269   lead us, O Father, in the paths of peace (T,1)
  269   lead us, O Father, in the paths of truth (2)
  269   lead us, O Father, in the paths of right (3)
  269   lead us, O Father, to thy heavenly rest (4)
  284   that I may sing above to Father, Spirit, and to thee (6)
  298   laud and honor to the Father ...to the Son ...the Spirit (4)
  303   who art, with God the Father and Spirit, ever blest (4)
  307   Father, we thank thee who hast planted (T,1)
  342   thee, our Father, in thy eternal Word (1)
  342   baptizing in the name of Father, Son, and Spirit (2)
  344   Father ... to whom we for our children cry (1)
  344   Father, accept them in thy Son (4)
  344   come, Father, Son, and Holy Ghost (T,1)
  347   O Father, deign these walls to bless (3)
  349   to God the Father, God the Son, and Spirit we adore (4)

357   Christ, to thee with God the Father (3)
367   Father of mercies, in thy Word what endless glory shines (T)
378   from God our heavenly Father a blessed angel came (3)
386   Word of the Father, now in flesh appearing (3)
405   unto thee, with God the Father and the Spirit, glory be (5)
411   O Father, look from heaven and bless ... their works (5)
443   Father, Son, and Holy Ghost (3)
446   Alleluia with the Son, God the Father praising (5)
459   O holy Father, who hast led thy children in all the ages (2)
460   with the Father ever one (2)
463   Father, Son, and Holy Ghost (1)
465   Father, in whom we live, in whom we are, and move (T,1)
467   praise to thy eternal merit, Father, Son and Holy Spirit (R)
467   teach us to know the Father, Son, and Thee (4)
469   Father eternal, ruler of creation (T,1)
488   to Holy Ghost be praises, to Father, and to Son (4)
490   Father, I implore, safely keep this child (2)
492   to God the Father, Son, and Spirit, One in Three (5)
493   praise Father, Son, and Holy Ghost (5)
498   Father, who hast blessed us all our days (1)
498   at thy feet, our God and Father (T,1)
504   Father, we praise thee, now the night is over (T,1)
504   all holy Father, Son, and equal Spirit, Trinity blessed (3)
506   O Father, while we sleep, thy children keep (R)
510   Father, thy mercies past we own, and thy continued care (3)
513   we thank thee...O Father, for all things bright & good (3)
521   children of the heavenly Father (T,1)
528   O how shall I the goodness tell, Father (2)
531   that I ceaseless may, Abba, Father, cry (3)
536   singing to Father, Son, and Holy Ghost, Alleluia (6)
538   eternal Father, strong to save (T,1)
122   the Father hears him pray, His dear anointed One (4)

fatherless
9   widow and the fatherless (3)
181   to tend the lone and fatherless is angels' work below (3)
199   and feeds the widow and the fatherless (2)

fathers
54   O Lord,our fathers oft have told in our attentive ears (T,1)
54   as ... God our fathers owned, so thou art still our King (4)
66   praise him for his grace and favor to our fathers (2)
66   grace and favor to our fathers in distress (2)
151   faith of our fathers, holy faith (R)
151   faith of our fathers (T,1,2,3)
233   send forth the hymns our fathers loved (3)
243   the sons of fathers we by whom our faith is taught (2)
300   we are traveling home to God in the way our fathers trod (2)
532   the fathers named in story (1)
547   land where my fathers died, land of the pilgrims' pride (1)
550   our exiled fathers crossed the sea (1)
552   God of our fathers (T,1)

fathers'
58   we come unto our Fathers' God (T,1)
534   we bless thee, our God, our fathers' God (1,2)
547   our fathers' God, to thee, Author of liberty ... we sing (4)

fault
279 and mourn for the minutest fault in exquisite distress (2)
280 and mourn for the minutest fault in exquisite distress (2)
494 pardon each infirmity, open fault, and secret sin (2)

faultless
222 faultless to stand before the throne (4)

faults
244 in the midst of faults and failures, stand by me (3)

favor
66 praise him for his grace and favor to our fathers (2)
66 grace and favor to our fathers in distress (2)
121 early let us seek thy favor, early let us do thy will (4)
223 for the favor he shows, and the joy he bestowes (3)
227 the favor divine I first found in the blood of the Lamb (2)
237 nor for fear or favor suffer me to fall (1)
334 with the Holy Spirit's favor, rest upon them from above (1)
395 ask the saved of all the race who have found his favor (1)
400 vainly with gifts would his favor secure (4)
418 look on me with thy favor, vouchsafe to me thy grace (2)
454 by thy merits we find favor (1)
459 still imploring thy love and favor, kept to us always (5)

favored
364 once for favored sinners slain (1)

favoring
147 we'll own the favoring gale (1)

favors
528 unmindful of his favors prove (3)

fear
16 who would not fear his holy name and laud and magnify (2)
20 we will not fear (3)
39 all nations fear his name (3)
46 as far from danger as from fear (2)
48 fear not, I am with thee; O be not dismayed (2)
56 fear him, ye saints, and ... have nothing else to fear (4)
56 fear him...and you will then have nothing else to fear (3)
67 in death's dark vale I fear no ill (4)
67 fear no ill, with thee, dear Lord, beside me (4)
68 yet will I fear no ill for thou art with me (3)
81 and drives away his fear (1)
91 powers of darkness fear, when this sweet chant they hear (2)
92 'twas grace that taught my heart to fear (2)
106 leave us not to doubt and fear (2)
122 he owns me for his child; I can no longer fear (4)
127 from sin and fear, from guilt and shame (2)
142 when in danger knows no fear, in darkness feels no doubt (3)
143 blest Savior, then, in love, fear and distrust remove (4)
155 than fancies flee away! I'll fear not what men say (3)
164 I shall not fear the battle if thou art by my side (1)
209 when disappointment, grief, and fear are gone (3)

211 God is my strong salvation; what foe have I to fear (T,1)
213 no foes, no violence I fear (2)
220 God dispels our fear (2)
221 when the howling storms of doubt and fear assail (2)
223 never fear, only trust and obey (4)
230 in heavenly love abiding no change my heart shall fear (T,1)
237 nor for fear or favor suffer me to fall (1)
239 shall I fear to own his cause .. blush to speak his name (1)
240 faint not nor fear, for he is near (4)
243 to fear no ill, to fight the holy fight they fought (2)
247 hear thee say to me, "Fear not, I will pilot thee" (3)
253 I want a godly fear, a quick discerning eye (3)
257 now to seek and love and fear thee (1)
259 all fear before thy presence flies (2)
270 and trembling faith is changed to fear (3)
277 bring the glorious liberty from sorrow, fear and sin (1)
279 I want a principle within of watchful, godly fear (T,1)
280 I want a principle within of watchful, godly fear (T,1)
281 from doubt and fear and sorrow free (4)
289 I fear no foe, with thee at hand to bless (4)
293 and all fear of want remove (2)
300 fear not, brethren; joyful stand (3)
317 with godly fear, we seek thy presence (2)
324 and with fear and trembling stand (1)
341 angels and men before it fall, and devils fear and fly (1)
341 scatters all ... guilty fear .. turns .. hell to heaven (2)
342 the task looms large before us; we follow without fear (4)
345 who mourn ...they who fear, be strengthened as they pray (3)
351 who honor truth, nor fear the crowd (3)
371 o'er fear and doubt, o'er black despair prevailing (1)
382 watching long in hope and fear (4)
385 good Christian, fear (2)
391 now ye need not fear the grave (3)
394 fear not, said he, for mighty dread had seized (2)
408 Christ is throned as Lord, men ... forsake their fear (2)
450 lovingly he greets thee, scatters fear and gloom (2)
468 surely to such as do him fear salvation is at hand (2)
469 in wrath and fear, by jealousies surrounded (3)
476 dispel the gloom of error's night, of ignorance & fear (3)
487 we kneel in awe and fear on this thy holy day (2)
507 never will throw off his fear who hears our solemn vow (4)
528 shall I slight my Father's love, or basely fear (3)
528 basely fear his gifts to own (3)

feared
291 felt and feared no more (2)
404 the shepherds feared and trembled (2)

fearful
113 by thy fearful conflict there (2)
161 speak to our fearful hearts by conflict rent (1)
215 ye fearful saints, fresh courage take (3)
216 when fearful plagues around prevail (3)
247 when at last I near the shore ... fearful breakers roar (3)

fearing
505 cease we fearing, cease we grieving (3)

fearless
173   O young and fearless prophet of ancient Galilee (T,1)
173   O young and fearless prophet, we need thy presence here (5)
291   though Jordan waves may roll, I'll fearless launch away (3)

fears
1   Jesus! the name that charms our fears (3)
47   through all our hopes and fears, thy hand we see (1)
51   give to the winds thy fears; hope & be undismayed (T,1)
52   from all our griefs and fears, O Lord (2)
52   in midst of dangers, fears, and death (3)
92   and grace my fears relieved (2)
113   by thy human griefs and fears (1)
119   fightings and fears within, without (3)
122   arise, my soul, arise; shake off thy guilty fears (T,1)
147   soon shall our doubts and fears all yield to thy control (3)
153   not the first to be banished by our fears from thee (2)
204   on shadowed thresholds dark with fears (2)
206   forgive ... our wild alarms, our trembling fears (3)
219   shamed by its failures or its fears, I sink (2)
271   when I tread the verge of Jordan, bid ... fears subside (3)
271   bid my anxious fears subside (3)
272   and spite of fears, pride ruled my will (2)
306   our fears, our hopes, our aims are one (2)
333   with child-like trust that fears nor pain nor death (2)
336   fightings without . fears within since we assembled last (2)
360   from our fears and sins release us (1)
381   hopes and fears of all the years are met in thee tonight (1)
416   hopes deceive and fears annoy (2)
431   from all removed, the Savior wrestles lone with fears (2)
463   who upholds and comforts us in all trials, fears & needs (3)
470   fears and doubts too long have bound us (2)
478   lead on, O King eternal, we follow, not with fears (3)
486   who, when fears beset them, stand fast and fight and die (2)
514   take our ... hopes and fears of sun and rain (2)

feast
86   thou hast prepared the feast of heavenly love (2)
102   come, sinners, to the gospel feast (T,1)
103   come to the feast of love; come, ever knowing (3)
111   sup with us, and let the feast be everlasting love (4)
317   spread with reverence this holy feast ... remember thee (1)
319   thus anticipate by faith the heavenly feast above (4)
319   in memory of the Savior's love, we keep the sacred feast (T)
320   be thy feast to us the token (2)
321   every act of brotherhood repeats thy feast again (2)
325   come to your places at the feast (4)
326   here let me feast, and feasting, still prolong the hour (2)
326   the feast, though not the love, is past and gone (4)
326   feast after feast thus comes and passes by (5)
326   yet, passing, points to the glad feast above (5)
326   the Lamb's great bridal feast of bliss and love (5)
329   and long to feast upon thee still (3)
350   here gather us around thy board to keep the feast (3)
350   keep the feast with thee, dear Lord (3)
366   for his marriage feast prepare (1)
438   then let us feast this Easter Day on the true bread (4)

438   feast this Easter Day on the true bread of heaven (4)
446   with the royal feast of feasts, comes its joy to render (3)
489   here afford us, Lord, a taste of our everlasting feast (3)
518   and grant that we may feast in paradise with thee (1)

feasted
325   millions of souls, in glory now ... fed and feasted here (3)

feasting
326   here let me feast, and feasting, still prolong the hour (2)

feasts
446   with the royal feast of feasts, comes its joy to render (3)

fed
231   beneath the spreading heavens no creature but is fed (3)
319   bread of life with which our souls are fed (3)
320   the token that by thy grace our souls are fed (2)
321   upper room where fainting souls are fed (1)
325   millions of souls, in glory now ... fed and feasted here (3)
328   who thy mysterious supper share, here at thy table fed (2)
332   how can heavenly spirits rise by earthly matter fed (3)
509   by his incessant bounty fed (2)
513   the winds and waves obey him, by him the birds are fed (2)
513   but it is fed and watered by God's almighty hand (1)
518   by thine own hand may we be fed (2)
524   by thee the souls of men are fed with gifts of grace (2)
524   souls of men are fed with gifts of grace supernal (2)

feeble
66   well our feeble frame he knows (3)
139   the things unknown to feeble sense (5)
148   trim your feeble lamp, my brother! (3)
177   my feeble faith looks up, Jesus, to thee (2)
215   judge not the Lord by feeble sense (4)
244   when I'm growing old and feeble, stand by me (4)
258   see thou render all thy feeble strength can pay (1)
332   feeble elements bestow a power not theirs to give (2)
343   instruments of loftier sound assist his feeble praise (2)
464   when he first the work begun, small & feeble was his day (2)
473   frail children of dust, and feeble as frail (5)

feebly
536   we feebly struggle, they in glory shine (4)

feed
21   we are his flock, he doth us feed (2)
61   all things living he doth feed (3)
121   in thy pleasant pastures feed us (1)
129   to feed them in pastures of love (2)
201   we would be thy disciples, and all the hungry feed (2)
266   abide with him always, and feed on his Word (1)
271   bread of heaven, feed me till I want no more (1)
296   with bread of life earth's hunger feed (4)
315   and feed and train us up for heaven (1)
326   here would I feed upon the bread of   God (3)
337   nourish the lambs and feed thy sheep (4)
362   he shall feed his flock like a shepherd (3)

368　bread of our souls whereon we feed (2)
438　Christ alone our souls will feed (4)
445　He lives, my hungry soul to feed (2)
546　feed thy faint and hungry peoples with...thy Word (2)
546　feed ... with the richness of thy Word (2)

feedeth
67　with food celestial feedeth (2)

feeding
378　left their flocks a feeding in tempest, storm, and wind (4)
385　mean estate where ox and ass are feeding (2)

feeds
9　he saves the oppressed, he feeds the poor (2)
199　and feeds the widow and the fatherless (2)
205　feeds me with the living bread (2)
231　and he who feeds the ravens will give his children bread (3)

feel
2　can we feel that thou art near ... hear ...? yea, we can (2)
2　can we feel that thou art near us and wilt hear us? (2)
17　and hear the brook and feel the gentle breeze (2)
36　we feel thy calm at evening's hour (3)
39　hour, when earth shall feel his saving power (3)
93　prone to wander, Lord, I feel it (3)
94　God is love! I know,I feel, Jesus weeps & loves me still (4)
104　all the fitness he requireth is to feel your need of him (3)
114　we...his unknown peace receive & feel his blood applied (3)
115　we feel the resurrection near (2)
137　only then, we feel our interest in his blood (2)
138　teach me to feel that thou art always nigh (4)
162　thus may I rejoice to show that I feel the love I owe (4)
164　O let me feel thee near me, the world is ever near (2)
193　and feel his brother's care (2)
212　sometimes I feel discouraged and think my work's in vain (1)
219　I feel thy strong and tender love, and all is well again (1)
226　every day, every hour, let me feel thy cleansing power (R)
234　feel the promise is not vain that morn shall tearless be (3)
238　Christian, dost thou feel them, how they work within (2)
262　speak to our hearts . let us feel . kindling of thy love (1)
275　the joys I feel, the bliss I share (2)
279　a sensibility of sin, a pain to feel it near (1)
279　help me the first approach to feel of pride (1)
279　first approach to feel of pride or wrong desire (1)
279　give me to feel an idle thought as actual wickedness (2)
280　a sensibility of sin, a pain to feel it near (1)
280　help me the first approach to feel of pride or...desire (1)
280　give me to feel an idle thought as actual wickedness (2)
301　we all partake the joy of one; the common peace we feel (4)
310　Lord, let every bounding heart the mighty comfort feel (4)
363　let us thy inner presence feel (3)
365　nations ...that see the light or feel the sun (4)
420　come, feel with me his blood applied (3)
427　make us thy sorrow feel (2)
434　ye that feel the tempter's power (1)
489　may we feel thy presence near (3)
501　we know and feel that thou art here (2)

528   know ... feel my sins forgiven (2)
530   kindly for each other care; every member feel its share (4)
531   to feel thy power, to hear thy voice, to taste thy love (4)

feelings
175   feelings lie buried that grace can restore (3)

feels
142   when in danger knows no fear, in darkness feels no doubt (3)
282   heart that always feels thy blood so freely shed for me (1)

feet
25   tents of ease nor thrones of power should tempt my feet (2)
25   nor ... should tempt my feet to leave thy door (2)
53   I'll drop my burden at his feet, and bear a song away (4)
66   to his feet thy tribute bring (1)
71   go spread your trophies at his feet (3)
71   O that with yonder sacred throng we at his feet may fall (5)
87   falling prostrate at his feet (4)
99   in his feet and hands are wound-prints, and his side (2)
110   come with thy sins; at his feet lowly bow (3)
170   teach me the wayward feet to stay (2)
174   tread where his feet have trod (4)
187   take my feet ... let them be swift & beautiful for thee (1)
187   my love ... I pour at thy feet its treasure-store (3)
204   and follow where thy feet have trod (6)
223   then in fellowship sweet we will sit at his feet (4)
227   angels could do nothing more, than to fall at his feet (3)
242   Christ, thy bleeding feet we track (3)
245   and sometimes how weary my feet (2)
249   crowned with victory at thy feet I'll lay .. honors down (4)
272   keep thou my feet (1)
278   then shall my feet no longer rove rooted .. fixed in God (1)
296   feet on mercy's errands swift do make her pilgrimage (3)
318   at thy feet I cry, my Maker (2)
324   at his feet the six-winged seraph (4)
342   we at thy feet would stay (3)
346   and science walks with humble feet (4)
347   thine own before thy feet we lay (1)
350   the sinner pardon at thy feet (4)
368   Lamp of our feet (T,1)
397   so may we with willing feet ever seek thy mercy seat (2)
430   never further than thy cross, never higher than thy feet (T)
430   cast our crowns before thy feet (5)
434   there adoring at this feet mark the miracle of time (3)
435   see, from his head, his hands, his feet, sorrow and love (3)
455   round his pierced feet fair flowers of paradise extend (3)
456   there stands he with unhurrying feet (2)
462   when weary feet refuse to climb, give us thy vision (5)
470   set out feet on lofty places (4)
498   at thy feet, our God and Father (T,1)
509   and peaceful, leave before thy feet (3)
517   little feet our steps may follow in a safe & narrow way (3)
534   journey which faithless feet ne'er trod (1)
534   O keep us in the pathway their saintly feet have trod (2)
543   O beautiful for pilgrim feet (2)
543   pilgrim feet, whose stern, impassioned stress (2)
545   O be swift, my soul, to answer him; be jubilant, my feet (3)
550   where their pilgrim feet have trod ... God ... guards (3)

fell
- 20   one little word shall fell him (3)
- 220   sin and hell in conflict fell (2)
- 527   my chains fell off, my heart was free (3)

fellowship
- 192   fellowship of love throughout the whole wide earth (1)
- 192   one great fellowship of love (1)
- 223   then in fellowship sweet we will sit at his feet (4)
- 232   where friend holds fellowship with friend (3)
- 301   if our fellowship below in Jesus be so sweet (5)
- 306   the fellowship of kindred minds is like to that above (1)
- 326   prolong the hour of fellowship with thee (2)
- 403   so shalt thou know that fellowship of love (1)
- 459   from thee have flowed...our fellowship and peace (4)
- 459   from thee...our faith and hope, our fellowship and peace (4)
- 520   grant, Love Divine, in every place glad fellowship (3)
- 520   glad fellowship with thee (3)
- 536   O blest communion, fellowship divine (4)

felt
- 114   what we have felt and seen with confidence we tell (2)
- 203   we've felt thy touch in sorrow's darkened way (3)
- 227   delight which I felt in the life-giving blood (5)
- 291   sickness and sorrow, pain and death are felt ... no more (2)
- 291   felt and feared no more (2)

fen
- 272   sure it still will lead me on o'er moor and fen (3)
- 406   through desert ways, dark fen, and deep morass (2)

fervent
- 172   in humble prayer and fervent praise (2)
- 292   the world to Christ we bring, with fervent prayer (2)
- 342   inspire our ways of learning ... earnest, fervent prayer (1)

fervently
- 103   come to the mercy seat, fervently kneel (1)

festal
- 326   giving sweet foretaste of the festal joy (5)
- 524   on this our festal day thy bounteous hand confessing (2)

festival
- 438   so let us keep the festival where-to the Lord invites us (3)

fetter
- 93   let thy goodness, like a fetter, bind my wandering heart (3)

fetters
- 200   who shall I send to shatter the fetters which they bear (2)
- 369   then shall all bondage cease, all fetters fall (2)

feuds
- 408   in Christ all races meet, their ancient feuds forgetting (2)

few
<pre>
 98   great Shepherd of thy chosen few (3)
227   whether many or few, all my years are his due (6)
339   the harvest truly, Lord, is great; the laborers are few (2)
419   a glorious band, the chosen few on whom the Spirit came (3)
</pre>

field
<pre>
 33   laid a silent loveliness on hill and wood and field (1)
 38   field and forest, vale and mountain, flowery meadow (2)
200   no field or mart is silent, no city street is dumb (2)
231   all the field should wither .. flocks nor herds be there (4)
362   like the flowers of the field they perish (2)
382   shepherds in the field abiding (2)
402   field and fountain, moor and mountain (1)
511   first fruits brought of orchard, flock and field (1)
522   all the world is God's own field (2)
522   from his field shall in that day all offenses purge away (3)
</pre>

fields
<pre>
190   the fields are wet with diamond dew (1)
291   sweet fields arrayed in living green & rivers of delight (1)
311   judge her not for fields unwon (4)
383   in fields where they lay keeping their sheep (1)
383   was telds and floods, rocks, hills and plains repeat (2)
441   fields of our hearts that dead and bare have been (4)
478   henceforth in fields of conquest thy tents ... our home (1)
513   plow the fields and scatter the good seed on the land (1)
513   we plow the fields (T,1)
524   bright robes of gold the fields adorn (1)
524   where golden fields spread fair and broad (3)
551   our cities with prosperity ... fields with plenteousness (2)
</pre>

fierce
<pre>
207   when dangers fierce your path assail (2)
459   and calming passion's fierce and stormy gales (3)
478   lead on, O King eternal, till sin's fierce war ... cease (2)
536   and when the strife is fierce, the warfare long (5)
</pre>

fiercest
<pre>
124   defeats my fiercest foes ... consoles my saddest woes (2)
</pre>

fiery
<pre>
 48   when through fiery trials thy pathways shall lie (4)
</pre>

fig
<pre>
231   though vine nor fig tree neither ... fruit should bear (4)
</pre>

fight
<pre>
 59   so from the beginning the fight we were winning (2)
155   no foes shall stay his might, though he with giants fight (2
211   though hosts encamp around me, firm in the fight I stand (1)
239   sure I must fight, if I would reign (4)
240   fight the good fight with all thy might (T,1)
241   fight the good fight (T,1) (words identical to 240)
243   to fear no ill, to fight the holy fight they fought (2)
246   O watch and fight and pray; the battle ne'er give o'er (2)
</pre>

246 fight on, my soul, till death...bring thee to thy God (4)
250 but take, to arm you for the fight, the panoply of God (2)
250 wrestle and fight and pray (3)
353 not as of old a little child to bear and fight and die (2)
411 bind strong the bond of brotherhood of those who fight (1)
411 those who fight with death (1)
439 fought the fight, the battle won, Alleluia (3)
453 from the fight returned victorious (1)
470 armored with all Christ-like graces in the fight (4)
470 in the fight to set men free (4)
486 who, when fears beset them, stand fast and fight and die (2)
536 thou, Lord, their captain in the well-fought fight (2)
536 fight as the saints who nobly fought of old (3)

fightings
119 fightings and fears within, without (3)
336 fightings without . fears within since we assembled last (2)

filial
279 grant me the filial awe I pray .. tender conscience give (3)
280 grant me the filial awe, I pray, the tender conscience (3)

filled
  6 days of wonder ... beauty ... rapture, filled with light (1)
 13 filled with solace, light and grace! (1)
 20 though this world, with devils filled should threaten (3)
 37 goodness of the Lord, that filled the earth with food (2)
 61 he, with all-commanding might, filled the new-made world (2)
 61 filled the new-made world with light (2)
129 he speaks! and eternity, filled with his voice (5)
187 take my lips ... let them be filled with messages from (2)
224 filled with his goodness, lost in his love (3)
227 as if filled with the fulness of God (5)
291 filled with delight my raptured soul lives (3)
329 we turn unfilled to thee again (1)
335 might fill an angel's heart and filled a Savior's hands (2)
344 till all our earth is filled with God (4)
352 this temple, reared to thee, O may it ever be filled (1)
352 filled with thy majesty, till time shall endd (1)
398 till everything that's human be filled with the divine (3)
421 there is a fountain filled with blood (T,1)
457 by the almighty Spirit led and filled with faith & love (1)

fillest
530 still for more on thee we call ...who fillest all in all (2)

filling
138 one holy passion filling all my frame (5)
299 O Zion, haste, thy mission high fulfilling (T,1)

fills
  4 with healing balm my soul he fills (1)
 82 thought of thee with sweetness fills the breast (1)
116 Jesus comes! He fills my soul! Perfected in him I am (5)
219 thy presence fills my solitude (3)
332 fills .. faithful people's hearts with...the life of God (1)
343 sweet music fills the world abroad with strains of love (1)

401   Christ, whose glory fills the skies (T,1)
442   all the world with beauty fills (1)
512   the year with good he crownest ... earth his mercy fills (2)
516   and love fills every breast (1)

filth
281   from all the filth of self and pride (3)

final
153   thou our final loyalty (3)
522   even so,Lord, quickly come, bring thy final harvest home (4)

find
    9   none shall find his promise vain (2)
  12   or searching find thee out (2)
  13   where we find thee and adore thee (2)
  53   sweet refreshment find (3)
  60   ye lights of evening, find a voice (2)
  82   nor can the memory find a sweeter sound than thy... name (2)
  85   in thee love's ways we find (3)
  91   ye nations of mankind, in this your concord find (3)
  96   I find, I walk, I love, but oh, the whole of love (3)
  99   if I find him, if I follow, what his guerdon here (4)
102   in Christ a hearty welcome find (3)
116   I shall full salvation find (1)
119   yea, all I need, in thee to find (4)
125   more than all in thee I find (3)
137   the grace which all may find, the saving power, impart (3)
138   O let me seek thee, and O let me find (3)
145   let me at thy throne of mercy find a sweet relief (2)
152   in all my works thy presence find (2)
181   to comfort and to bless, to find a balm for woe (3)
184   my heart is weak and poor until it master find (2)
192   in him shall true hearts everywhere ... communion find (2)
192   their high communion find (2)
201   these, Father, are thy children thou sendest us to find (2)
206   no height but we may find thee there (2)
206   new faith to find the paths ahead (1)
210   though undeserving; thou yet shalt find it true for thee (3)
225   where thou ... all my soul possess and I may find myself (2)
231   the theme of God's salvation, and find it ever new (2)
235   in purer lives thy service find (1)
261   can we find a friend so faithful (2)
261   thou wilt find a solace there (3)
262   enter into my Master's joy, and find my heaven in thee (4)
264   but sweeter still, to wake and find thee there (4)
283   let us all in thee inherit, let us find that second rest (2)
285   when shall I find my willing heart all taken up by thee (1)
304   with love and longing turn to find their rest in thee (1)
304   our hearts in love and worship turn to find themselves (2)
304   hearts ... turn to find themselves in thee (2)
304   hearts with love & longing ... find their rest in thee (1)
311   seek the lost until she find (3)
329   to them that find thee, all in all (2)
340   who wander far shall seek and find and serve thee well (3)
345   may they who err be guided here to find the better way (3)
350   here let the weary one find rest (4)

360 let us find our rest in thee (1)
367 thirsty souls receive supplies .. sweet refreshment find (2)
367 teach me to love thy sacred Word ... find my Savior (4)
369 and I shall find my peace, my all-in-all (2)
378 went to Bethlehem straightway, the blessed babe to find (4)
394 the heavenly babe you there shall find (4)
403 thou shalt find thy heart made truly his (2)
433 till my raptured soul shall find rest beyond the river (R)
454 by thy merits we find favor (1)
462 Spirit consoling, let us find thy hand (4)
462 let us find thy hand when sorrows leave us blind (4)
472 the weary find eternal rest (4)
473 in Thee do we trust, nor find Thee to fail (5)
476 in whom all hearts find rest (2)
476 kindness dwell in human hearts and... earth find peace (2)
499 mind be set to hallow all we find (3)
535 walking in all his ways, they find their heaven on earth (9)
535 they find their heaven on earth begun (1)
548 till it find its full fruition in the brotherhood of man (4)

findeth
295 behold, the sparrow findeth out a house wherein to rest (3)

finding
99 finding, following, keeping, struggling...sure to bless (7)

finds
531 nor can it be at rest till it finds rest in thee (1)

finely
477 finely build for days to come foundations that endure (3)

finest
514 take the finest of our harvest, crops we grow (1)

fingers
40 thy fingers spread the mountains and plains (1)

finish
283 finish ...thy new creation, pure and spotless let us be (4)
355 to finish thy salvation (4)

finished
337 when their work is finished here (5)
429 'tis finished The Messiah dies (T,1)
434 It is finished, hear him cry (3)

finisher
139 faith like its finisher and Lord today as yesterday (1)

fire
58 the fire divine their steps that led ... before us (2)
58 the fire divine ... still goeth bright before us (2)
60 thou fire so masterful and bright (3)
131 source of... old prophetic fire, fountain of life & love (1)
133 this earthly part of me glows with thy fire divine (3)

135   kindle every high desire; perish self in thy pure fire (2)
136   O Spirit of the living God, thou light and fire divine (T,1)
143   pure, warm, and changeless be, a living fire (2)
151   living still, in spite of dungeon, fire and sword (1)
172   the pure celestial fire to impart (1)
172   still let me guard the holy fire (3)
184   it wants the needed fire to glow ... the breeze to nerve (3)
198   on earth and fire and sea and air (2)
199   love shall tread out the baleful fire of anger (5)
235   speak through the earth-quake, wind and fire (5)
252   the motion of a hidden fire that trembles in the breast (1)
271   let the fire and cloudy pillar lead me all my journey (2)
278   refining fire, go through my heart; illuminate my soul (2)
279   catch .. wandering of my will .. quench .. kindling fire (1)
280   and quench the kindling fire (1)
293   cloud and fire appear for a glory and a covering (3)
293   round each habitation hovering, see the cloud and fire (3)
350   here let thy sacred fire of old descend (2)
380   the star rains its fire while the beautiful sing (1,2)
459   led thy children in all the ages with the fire and cloud (2)
461   come as the fire, and purge our hearts (2)
464   to bring fire on earth he came (1)
467   lighten with celestial fire (1)
467   thy blessed unction from above is comfort, life & fire (2)
467   comfort, life and fire of love (2)
474   fire ascending seeks the sun (2)
522   give his angels charge at last ... fire .. tares to cast (3)
528   a brand plucked from eternal fire (1)
538   from rock and tempest, fire and foe protect them (4)
546   with thy living fire of judgment purge this land (1)

fires
18   his the fires that tried her worth (1)
464   Jesus' love the nations fires (1)
525   and warms our lives with heavenly fires (3)
545   I have seen him in the watchfires of a hundred ... camps (2)
545   watchfires of a hundred circling camps (2)

firm
22   firm as a rock thy truth must stand (4)
48   how firm a foundation, ye saints of the Lord (T,1)
195   that I may stand firm on the rock, and strong in thee (2)
198   dare all that may plant man's lordship firm on earth (2)
211   though hosts encamp around me, firm in the fight I stand (1)
233   still lift your standard high ... march in firm array (5)
253   bold to take up, firm to sustain the consecrated cross (2)
274   with a step more firm and free (2)
345   may faith grow firm, and love grow warm (4)
460   'mid the world's despair and turmoil one firm anchor (1)
460   one firm anchor holdeth fast (1)
473   thy mercies how tender, how firm to the end (5)

firmament
43   the spacious firmament on high (T,1)
440   see that glowing firmament (4)

firmer
326 here grasp with firmer hand eternal grace (1)

firmly
 21 his truth at all times firmly stood (4)
135 be my Lord, and I shall be firmly bound, forever free (4)

firmness
337 firmness with meekness from above to bear thy people (3)

first
 30 first ... last: beyond all thought His timeless years! (1)
 88 first let me hear how the children stood round his knee (2)
 92 the hour I first believed (2)
153 not the first to be banished by our fears from thee (2)
155 his first avowed intent to be a pilgrim (1)
157 through him the first fond prayers are said (5)
162 better lesson cannot be, loving him who first loved me (1)
162 singing ... of his love who first loved me (4)
162 loving him who first loved me (1,2,3)
166 I love thee, because thou hast first loved me (2)
180 guard my first springs of thought and will (2)
181 and gladly, as thou blessest us...our first fruits give (2)
227 the favor divine I first found in the blood of the Lamb (2)
227 when my heart first believed, what a joy I received (2)
256 thou and thou only, first in my heart (3)
268 where is... blessedness I knew when first I saw the Lord (2)
279 help me the first approach to feel of pride (1)
279 first approach to feel of pride or wrong desire (1)
280 help me the first approach to feel of pride or...desire (1)
355 Lord Christ, when first thou cam'st to men (T,1)
383 the first Noel, the angel did say (T,1)
419 the martyr first, whose eagle eye could pierce (2)
460 God the first and God the last (1,3)
464 when he first the work begun, small & feeble was his day (2)
488 on thee, at the creation, the light first had its birth (2)
511 as men of old their first fruits brought (T,1)
511 so we today first fruits would bring (1)
511 first fruits brought of orchard, flock and field (1)
522 first the blade and then the ear (2)
524 we lay the first fruits of thy blessing (2)
524 upon thine altar, Lord, we lay the first fruits (2)

Fisherman
 84 thou man-pursuing Fisherman, who harmest not but savest (2)

fit
118 I own it cannot be that I should fit myself for thee (3)
150 a never-dying soul to save, and fit it for the sky (1)
318 let me be a fit partaker of ... blessed food from heaven (2)
384 and fit us for heaven to live with thee there (3)
499 O Lord, in thy dear love fit us for perfect rest above (4)
504 Monarch of all things, fit us for thy mansions (2)

fitful
176 bear me o'er life's fitful sea (3)

fitness
104 all the fitness he requireth is to feel your need of him (3)
104 nor of fitness fondly dream (3)

fits
84 give milk or bread or solid food as fits (3)
84 milk or bread or solid food as fits my understanding (3)

fitted
266 thou soon shall be fitted for service above (4)

five
122 five bleeding wounds he bears, received on Calvary (3)

fix
283 fix in us thy humble dwelling (1)

fixed
93 praise the mount! I'm fixed upon it (1)
128 O happy day, that fixed my choice (T,1)
128 fixed my choice on thee, my Savior and my God (1)
128 fixed on this blissful center, rest (4)
278 then shall my feet no longer rove rooted .. fixed in God (1)

flag
184 flag can ...be unfurled when thou... breathe from heaven (3)

flame
11 skies with crimson clouds aflame (2)
12 art within, a qickening flame, a presence round about (2)
16 O for the living flame from his own altar brought (3)
48 the flame shall not hurt thee, I only design (4)
64 one holy light, one heavenly flame (5)
134 with all thy quickening powers kindle a flame (1,5)
134 kindle a flame of sacred love in ... cold hearts of ours (1)
138 my heart an altar, and thy love the flame (5)
139 whose Spirit breathes the active flame (1)
172 kindle a flame of sacred love on ... altar of my heart (1)
198 with flame of freedom in their souls (1)
203 o'er hill and dale in saffron flame and red (4)
243 who, thrust in prison or cast to flame (1)
321 in our daily life may flame the passion of thy heart (4)
419 and mocked the cross and flame (3)
461 purge our hearts like sacrificial flame (2)
464 see how great a flame aspires (T,1)
464 O that all might catch the flame (1)
466 and kindle it, thy holy flame bestowing (1)
475 yet thou, her child, whose head is crowned with flame (1)

flamed
527 I woke, the dungeon flamed with light (3)

flames
64 thy glory flames from sun and star (1)

flaming
- 93 sung by flaming tongues above (1)
- 127 midst flaming worlds, in these arrayed (1)
- 136 burn, winged fire! inspire our lips with flaming love (2)
- 136 inspire our lips with flaming love and zeal to preach (2)
- 351 from hence send forth a race of men of flaming heart (3)
- 351 race of men of flaming heart and stalwart mind (3)
- 456 do flaming suns his footsteps trace (1)
- 476 whose power upholds both flower and flaming star (1)

flaring
- 545 dim and flaring lamps (2)

flash
- 36 when lightnings flash and storm winds blow (2)

flashing
- 38 flashing sea, chanting bird and flowing fountain (2)

flaw
- 543 America! America! God mend thine every flaw (2)

fled
- 48 to you who for refuge to Jesus have fled (1)
- 290 and so beside the silent sea I wait the muffled oar (4)

flee
- 25 devils at thy presence flee (4)
- 75 from sin and death we flee (1)
- 118 to thee, lost and undone, for aid I flee (1,5)
- 155 than fancies flee away! I'll fear not what men say (3)
- 189 human hatreds flee before the radiant eastern skies (1)
- 216 to him for safety I will flee (2)
- 217 e'en death's cold wave I will not flee (4)
- 264 when the bird waketh, and the shadows flee (1)
- 264 when the soul waketh, and life's shadows flee (5)
- 289 when other helpers fail and comforts flee (1)
- 289 heaven's morning breaks, and earth's vain shadows flee (5)
- 316 when these failing lips grow dumb ... mind & memory flee (4)
- 376 heaven and earth shall flee away when he comes to reign (2)
- 379 voice...doth entreat: Flee from woe and danger (2)
- 529 the morning breaks, the shadows flee (4)

fleeting
- 81 proclaim with every fleeting breath (5)
- 97 I'll trust him when life's fleeting days shall endd (4)
- 120 while I draw this fleeting breath (3)
- 226 till this fleeting, fleeting life is o'er (3)

flesh
- 18 Word incarnate glorified the flesh of man (2)
- 85 O Mind of God incarnate, O Thought in flesh enshrined (2)
- 92 yea, when this flesh and heart shall fail (5)
- 235 let sense be dumb, let flesh retire (5)
- 248 arm of flesh will fail you, ye dare not trust your own (3)
- 290 if my heart and flesh are weak to bear an untried pain (2)

295   my very heart and flesh cry out, O Loving God, for thee (2)
324   let all mortal flesh keep silence (T,1)
331   banquet spreads before us of his mystic flesh and blood (1)
332   how the bread his flesh imparts (1)
370   praise him for the Word made flesh (3)
386   Word of the Father, now in flesh appearing (3)
387   veiled in flesh the   God-head see (2)
389   lo, he assumes our flesh and blood (3)
426   robed in mortal flesh is dying crucified by sin for me (2)
469   better seeing thy Word made flesh, and in a manger laid (4)

fleshly
405   seen in fleshly form on earth (2)

flew
  83   he flew to my relief (2)

flickering
234   I yield my flickering torch to thee (2)

flies
259   all fear before thy presence flies (2)

flight
  84   to bird in flight, controlling wing (1)
205   when my spirit, clothed immortal, wings its flight (3)
205   my spirit ... wings its flight to realms of day (3)
354   and death's dark shadows put to flight (4)
358   darkness takes its flight; doubt & terror are withdrawn (3)
382   wing your flight o'er all the earth (1)
480   chaos and darkness heard and took their flight (1)
480   speed forth thy flight (3)
490   birds pass high in flight, fragrant flowers now bloom (91)

fling
270   on thee we fling our burdening woe (4)
363   fling wide the portals of your heart (2)
390   peace shall over ... earth its ancient splendors fling (3)

floateth
372   it floateth like a banner before God's host unfurled (3)

floating
539   keep love's banner floating o'er you (4)

floats
343   Lord, while the music round us floats (3)
390   still ... heavenly music floats o'er all the weary world (2)

flock
  21   we are his flock, he doth us feed (2)
  84   we'll follow thee, a King's own flock (1)
121   keep thy flock, from sin defend us (2)
274   where the Shepherd leads the flock (2)
362   he shall feed his flock like a shepherd (3)
487   in thy flock may we be found (3)
511   first fruits brought of orchard, flock and field (1)

flocks
231   all the field should wither .. flocks nor herds be there (4)
231   flocks nor herds be there; yet God the same abiding (4)
378   left their flocks a feeding in tempest, storm, and wind (4)
382   watching o'er your flocks by night (2)
394   while shepherds watched their flocks by night (T,1)
396   flocks were sleeping (2)
404   while shepherds kept their watching o'er silent flocks (1)
404   o'er silent flocks by night (1)
512   the flocks in pastures graze (2)

flood
11   storm and flood and ocean's roar (3)
20   our helper he amid the flood of mortal ills prevailing (1)
101   crimson flood that washes white as snow (2)
101   plunge now into the crimson flood (2)
106   wading deep the dismal flood (3)
208   in simple faith to plunge me neath the healing ... flood (2)
208   plunge me neath the healing, cleansing flood (2)
222   support me in the whelming flood (3)
239   must I not stem the flood (3)
260   thy power flows in like flood tides from the sea (4)
302   part of his host have crossed the flood (4)
421   sinners, plunged beneath that flood (1)

flooding
398   flooding the eastern skies (1)

floods
213   when rising floods my soul o'erflow (3)
392   while fields and floods, rocks, hills and plains repeat (2)

flourish
27   we blossom and flourish as leaves on the tree (3)
521   in his holy courts they flourish (2)

flow
36   thy present life through all doth flow (1)
48   the rivers of woe shall not thee overflow (3)
67   where streams of living water flow (2)
75   that life to win, whose joys eternal flow (4)
83   his lips with grace o'erflow (1)
101   dwell in that celestial land, where joys immortal flow (4)
120   could my tears forever flow (2)
180   praise God, from who all blessings flow (4)
187   let them flow in ceaseless praise (1)
195   o'erflow in kindling thought and glowing word (4)
195   until my very heart o'erflow in kindling thought (4)
213   when rising floods my soul o'erflow (3)
234   in thine ocean depths its flow may richer, fuller be (1)
271   whence the healing stream doth flow (2)
359   righteousness, in fountains, from hill to valley flow (3)
392   he comes to make his blessing flow (3)
435   sorrow and love flow mingled down (3)
471   o'er all the nations let it flow (3)

485   from thee all skill and science flow (T,1)
493   praise God, from whom all blessings flow (5)
530   Christ, from whom all blessings flow (T,1)

flowed
70   from whom those comforts flowed (2)
120   from thy wounded side which flowed (1)
459   from thee have flowed, as from a mighty river ... faith (4)

flower
34   each little flower that opens (1)
35   hill and vale, and tree and flower (2)
37   not a plant or flower below, but makes thy glories known (3)
468   truth from the earth, like to a flower, shall bud (1)
470   bring her bud to glorious flower (1)
476   whose power upholds both flower and flaming star (1)
487   our faith from seed to flower raise on this thy holy day (2)
513   he paints the wayside flower, he lights the evening star (2)
      hill and vale, and tree and flower (2)

flowers
38   hearts unfold like flowers before thee (1)
60   the flowers and fruits that in thee grow (4)
90   while birds and flowers and sky above are preaching (3)
359   love, joy and hope, like flowers, spring in his path (3)
362   like the flowers of the field they perish (2)
442   spring has now unwrapped the flowers (T,1)
442   flowers make glee among the hills (1)
449   bring flowers of song to strew his way (2)
455   round his pierced feet fair flowers of paradise extend (3)
455   flowers of paradise extend their fragrance ever sweet (3)
490   birds pass high in flight, fragrant flowers now bloom (91)
506   sharing ... the hand that gives the flowers (2)
523   the golden sunshine, vernal air, sweet flowers and fruit (2)
523   sweet flowers and fruit thy love declare (2)

flowery
38   field and forest, vale and mountain, flowery meadow (2)
239   must I be carried to the skies on flowery beds of ease (2)

floweth
30   his spirit floweth free, high surging where it will (2)
67   what transport of delight from thy pure chalice floweth (5)
318   fount, whence all my being floweth (2)

flowing
33   sent the hoary frost of heaven,the flowing waters sealed (1)
37   spread the flowing seas abroad and built the lofty skies (1)
38   flashing sea, chanting bird and flowing fountain (2)
60   thou flowing water, pure and clear (3)
103   here see the bread of life; see waters flowing (3)
103   flowing forth from the throne of God, pure from above (3)
157   immortal love, forever full, forever flowing free (T,1)
158   immortal love, forever full, forever flowing free (T,1)
214   like trees beside a flowing stream (2)
331   wine of gladness, flowing free (1)

421 by faith, I saw the stream thy flowing wounds supply (4)
488 living water flowing with soul-refreshing streams (3)

flows

33 thou from whose unfathomed law the year in beauty flows (3)
66 Alleluia! Alleluia! widely yet his mercy flows (3)
68 my head thou dost with oil anoint, and my cup overflows (4)
219 around me flows thy quickening life (3)
260 through open gates thy power flows in (4)
260 thy power flows in like flood tides from the sea (4)
301 grace through every vessel flows in purest streams (2)
306 and often for each other flows the sympathizing tear (3)
420 pardon for all flows from his side (2)
433 healing stream flows from calvary's mountain (1)
476 in speech that flows to melody, in holiness of heart (4)
524 where flows the crystal river (3)

fly

10 the heavens are not too high, his praise may thither fly (1)
28 they fly, forgotten, as a dream dies at the opening day (5)
41 made him fly with eagle pinion (3)
105 shall life's swift passing years all fly (1)
125 Jesus, lover of my soul, let me to thy bosom fly (T,1)
126 Jesus, love of my soul, let me to thy bosom fly (T,1)
139 the clouds disperse, the shadows fly (6)
234 I dare not ask to fly from thee (4)
245 O then to the Rock let me fly ... Rock ... higher than I (R)
253 and sees the tempter fly (3)
263 sun, moon, and stars forgot, upward I fly (5)
309 on the wings of angels fly; show how true believers die (6)
341 angels and men before it fall, and devils fear and fly (1)
496 though the arrows past us fly (2)
541 Lord, guard and guide the men who fly (T,1)
541 men who fly through the great spaces of the sky (1)
541 O God, protect the men who fly through lonely ways (2)
541 men who fly through lonely ways beneath the sky (2)

flying

366 wake, awake, for night is flying (T,1)
446 all the winter of our sins, long and dark, is flying (2)

foaming

538 who walkedst on the foaming deep (2)

foe

20 still our ancient foe doth seek to work us woe (1)
142 though pressed by every foe (1)
151 we will love both friend and foe in all our strife (3)
156 I would be friend of all, the foe, the friendless (2)
211 God is my strong salvation; what foe have I to fear (T,1)
248 till every foe is vanquished, and Christ is Lord indeed (1)
289 I fear no foe, with thee at hand to bless (4)
305 Christ, the royal Master, leads against the foe (1)
457 every vanquished foe submits to his victorious cross (2)
498 sure of being safely guided, guarded well from every foe (2)

538   from rock and tempest, fire and foe protect them (4)
549   claim the kingdom of the earth for thee, and not thy foe (5)
551   O guard our shores from every foe (2)

foes
  25   guards ... from foes without and foes within (3)
  48   I will not, I will not desert to his foes (5)
  66   rescues us from all our foes (3)
  68   my table thou hast furnished in presence of my foes (4)
  89   my help and refuge from my foes (1)
124   defeats my fiercest foes ... consoles my saddest woes (2)
129   thy foes will rejoice when my sorrows they see (3)
155   no foes shall stay his might, though he with giants fight (2
164   my foes are ever near me, around me and within (2)
178   thy foes might hate, despise, revile (2)
213   no foes, no violence I fear (2)
220   foes who would molest me cannot reach me here (2)
239   are there no foes for me to face (3)
246   my soul, be on thy guard, ten thousand foes arise (T,1)
248   ye that are men now serve him against unnumbered foes (2)
251   foes may hate, and friends may shun me (2)
293   thou mayest smile at all thy foes (1)
341   bold to confess thy glorious name before a world of foes (4)
353   left .. lonesome place of death, despite .. rage of foes (3)
412   by foes derided, by thine own rejected, O most afflicted (1)
444   with a mighty triumph o'er his foes (R)
467   keep far our foes; give peace at home (3)
471   till all thy foes confess thy sway (2)

foil
289   what but thy grace can foil the tempter's power (3)

fold
  22   he brought us to his fold again (2)
  93   wandering from the fold of God (2)
199   O brother man, fold to thy heart thy brother (T,1)
304   O shepherd of the nameless fold (T,1)
304   O holy kingdom, happy fold, the blessed Church to be (2)
319   one fold .. faith .. hope .. Lord, One God alone we know (1)
362   and fold the lambs to his breast (3)
411   and bears them to the fold (4)
467   who dost thy seven-fold gifts impart (1)
503   gather us who seek thy face to the fold of thy embrace (2)
539   with his sheep securely fold you (1)

folded
  45   kept the folded grave-clothes where the body lay (1)
423   to Jesus, who... blessed them close folded to his breast (1)
450   kept the folded grave-clothes where the body lay (1)

folds
121   for our use thy folds prepare (1)
312   and folds them in his arms (1)

folk
532   and made our folk a nation (2)

follies
166   for thee all the follies of sin I resign (1)

follow
    8   and the white robed martyrs follow (3)
   47   God of the coming years ... we follow thee (3)
   47   through paths unknown we follow thee (3)
   68   goodness and mercy all my life shall surely follow me (5)
   84   we'll follow thee, a King's own flock (1)
   88   into the city I'd follow the children's band (3)
   90   still as of old he calleth "Follow me" (5)
   99   if I find him, if I follow, what his guerdon here (4)
  106   wanderer, come, Follow me, I'll guide thee home (R)
  107   saying, Christian, follow me (1)
  155   let him with constancy follow the Master (1)
  160   the world forsake, and humbly follow after me (1)
  160   take up thy cross and follow Christ (4)
  162   at thy bidding may I move, prompt to serve & follow thee (2)
  162   strong to follow in thy grace (3)
  164   O Jesus, thou hast promised to all who follow thee (4)
  164   O give me grace to follow My Master and my Friend (4)
  188   joyful to follow thee through paths unknown (2)
  199   follow with reverent steps the great example of him (3)
  202   we follow where the Master leads, serene and unafraid (1)
  204   and follow where thy feet have trod (6)
  213   dauntless, untired, I follow thee (4)
  214   their determined quest to follow in the saints' pathway (1)
  235   let us, like them, without a word rise up & follow thee (2)
  238   peace shall follow battle; night shall endd in day (3)
  251   all to leave and follow thee (1)
  266   in joy or in sorrow, still follow the Lord (3)
  274   speak, that I may follow faster (2)
  274   with obedience glad & steady still to follow every word (4)
  300   only thou our leader be, and we still will follow thee (4)
  342   we call each new disciple to follow thee, O Lord (2)
  342   the task looms large before us; we follow without fear (4)
  366   we follow till the halls we see where ... sup with thee (2)
  366   we follow ... we see where thou hast bid us sup (2)
  383   and to follow the star wherever it went (3)
  413   yea ... to the death we follow thee (1)
  413   the sturdy dreamers answered ... we follow thee (1)
  419   O God, to us may grace be given to follow in their train (3)
  478   lead on, O King eternal, we follow, not with fears (3)
  517   little feet our steps may follow in a safe & narrow way (3)

followed
  128   He drew me and I followed on (3)
  423   from Olivet they followed mid an exultant crowd (2)
  527   I rose, went forth, and followed thee (3)

follower
  217   His faithful follower I would be (R)
  239   am I a soldier of the cross, a follower of the Lamb (T,1)

followest
  234   O Light that followest all my way (2)

following
- 97   following him I know I'm right (3)
- 97   following him by day and night, He's my friend (3)
- 99   finding, following, keeping, struggling...sure to bless (7)
- 402   following yonder star (1)
- 439   following our exalted Head, Alleluia (4)
- 533   following ... incarnate God ... gained the promised rest (2)

follows
- 419   who follows in his train (1,2)
- 419   patient bears his cross below ... follows in his train (1)
- 442   beauty follows all his ways, as the world he blesses (2)
- 462   give us the faith that follows on (1)

folly
- 269   while passion stains, and folly dims our youth (2)

fond
- 134   fond of these earthly toys (2)
- 157   through him the first fond prayers are said (5)
- 251   perish every fond ambition, all I've... hoped or known (1)

fondly
- 104   nor of fitness fondly dream (3)

food
- 37   goodness of the Lord, that filled the earth with food (2)
- 67   with food celestial feedeth (2)
- 84   give milk . bread or solid food as fits my understanding (3)
- 297   one holy name she blesses, partakes one holy food (2)
- 307   didst give man food for all his days (2)
- 313   that living bread ... heavenly wine be our immortal food (2)
- 318   let me be a fit partaker of ... blessed food from heaven (2)
- 324   he will give to all.. faithful .. self for heavenly food (2)
- 331   cheers our famished souls with food (1)
- 490   glad for cotton coat, plain food satisfies (3)
- 513   seed-time & the harvest, our life, our health, our food (3)
- 515   thy children live by daily food (1)
- 518   we thank thee, Lord, for this our food (2,3)
- 519   health and food and clothes to wear (1)

foolish
- 67   perverse and foolish oft I strayed (3)
- 160   nor let thy foolish pride rebel (3)
- 235   forgive our foolish ways (1)
- 475   turn back, O man, forswear thy foolish ways (T,1)

foot
- 57   he will not let thy foot be moved (2)
- 161   a-foot on dusty highways (3)
- 446   led them with unmoistened foot through... Red Sea waters (1)

footsteps
- 215   he plants his footsteps in the sea (1)
- 338   still in Jesus' footsteps tread & show his praise below (2)
- 372   a lantern to our footsteps shines on from age to age (1)

456 do flaming suns his footsteps trace (1)
468 his footsteps cannot err (1)
533 they marked the footsteps that he trod (2)

footstool
545 so the world shall be his footstool (5)

forbear
94 can my God his wrath forbear (1)

forbid
435 forbid it, Lord, that I should boast, save in the death (2)

forbidden
237 with forbidden pleasures would this vain world charm (2)

forbids
439 death in vain forbids him rise, Alleluia (3)

force
32 ye winds of night, your force combine (3)
111 worst need keep him out no more or force him to depart (2)
184 force me to render up my sword and I shall conqueror be (1)

fore'er
106 weary souls fore'er rejoice (1)
463 Holy Ghost, who from both fore'er proceeds (3)

forego
335 souls for whom the Lord did heavenly bliss forego (3)

foreign
476 no alien race, no foreign shore (1)

foreshows
405 myrrh his sepulcher foreshows (4)

forest
17 when through the woods and forest glades I wander (2)
38 field and forest, vale and mountain, flowery meadow (2)
400 myrrh from the forest and gold from the mine (3)

foretaste
224 O what a foretaste of glory divine (1)
326 giving sweet foretaste of the festal joy (5)

foretell
358 doth its beauteous ray aught of joy or hope foretell (1)

foretold
189 glorious day by prophets long foretold (1)
390 shall come the time foretold (3)

forever
2 angel harps forever ringing, rest not day nor night (1)
9 his truth forever stands secure (2)

```
 20   His kingdom is forever (4)
 21   his mercy is forever sure (4)
 23   who reigns, and shall forever reign (1,4)
 43   forever singing as they shine (3)
 55   gladly forever adore him (4)
 57   thy going out, thy coming in, forever he will guide (4)
 58   unbroken be the golden chain, keep on the song forever (4)
 66   praise him, still the same forever (2)
 67   I nothing lack if I am his and he is mine forever (1)
 67   sing thy praise within thy house forever (6)
 77   singing forever more Alleluia! Amen! (3)
109   Jesus, only Savior, sanctify forever (3)
120   could my tears forever flow (2)
127   forever doth for sinners plead (3)
134   and shall we then forever live at this poor dying rate (4)
135   be my Lord, and I shall be firmly bound, forever free (4)
141   have faith in God, my soul, His cross forever stands (3)
150   assured, if I my trust betray, I shall forever die (4)
157   forever shared, forever whole, a never-ebbing sea (1)
157   immortal love, forever full, forever flowing free (T,1)
158   immortal love, forever full, forever flowing free (T,1)
161   thou art our Lord! Thou dost forever reign! (5)
163   for I am his, and he is mine, forever and forever (1)
163   all are his and his forever (2)
163   no, I am his forever (3)
164   be thou forever near me, my Master and my Friend (1)
209   hour ... when we shall be forever with the Lord (3)
214   the righteous ones shall be forever blest (T,1)
228   where his glory forever I'll share (4)
242   choice goes by forever twixt that darkness & that light (1)
253   forever standing on its guard and watching unto prayer (3)
254   let thy clear light forever shine (1)
270   O Love divine, forever dear (4)
281   remains and stands forever sure (1)
291   there God the Son forever reigns and scatters night away (2)
291   when I shall reach that happy place ... be forever blest (3)
298   Holy Zion's help forever and her confidence alone (1)
298   what they gain from thee forever ... blessed to retain (3)
303   His only, his forever thou shalt be, and thou art (3)
309   bid our strife forever cease (1)
317   our life with thine forever blending (3)
335   souls that must forever live in rapture or in woe (3)
359   his name shall stand forever ... name to us is love (4)
360   born to reign in us forever (2)
367   forever be thy name adored for these celestial lines (1)
367   Divine instructor, gracious Lord, be thou forever near (4)
384   close by me forever, and love me, I pray (3)
402   King forever, ceasing never over us all to reign (2)
418   O make me thine forever, and should I fainting be (3)
444   and he lives forever with his saints to reign (R)
454   Jesus, hail! enthroned in glory, there forever to abide (3)
457   Lord our King, who reigns for us...shall forever reign (2)
463   blest and Holy Trinity, praise forever be to thee (3)
492   be glory, as it was, is now, and shall forever be (5)
494   soon from us the light of day shall forever pass away (3)
500   thy kingdom stands, and grows forever, till all ... own (4)
```

502 rest forever on my Savior's breast (2)
503 when forever from our sight pass the stars, the day (4)
522 there, forever purified, in thy presence to abide (4)
524 blessed is that land of God where saints abide forever (3)
532 they blessed the earth ... blessed of God & man forever (6)
536 thy name, O Jesus, be forever blest, Alleluia, Alleluia (1)

forevermore
16 henceforth forevermore (5)
68 in God's house forevermore my dwelling place shall be (5)
116 soul and body thine to be wholly thine forevermore (3)
297 she waits the consumation of peace forevermore (3)
333 whom thou forevermore dost join in one (1)
361 his name shall be the Prince of Peace forevermore adored (3)
452 lo! the dead is living, God forevermore (1,4)
482 establish thou forevermore the triumph now begun (1)

forfeit
261 O what peace we often forfeit ... needless pain we bear (1)

forge
549 thine is the loom, the forge, the mart (4)

forget
45 ne'er forget that though the wrong seems oft so strong (3)
65 bless the Father ... forget not ... mercies to proclaim (1)
71 sinners, whose love can ne'er forget the wormwood and (3)
71 ne'er forget the wormwood and the gall (3)
156 I would be giving, and forget the gift (2)
249 forget the steps already trod and onward urge thy way (2)
262 with thee conversing, we forget all time & toil and care (2)
519 ne'er forget God's daily care (T,1)

forgets
59 sing praises to his name: he forgets not his own (1)

forgetting
266 forgetting in nothing His blessing to seek (1)
408 in Christ all races meet, their ancient feuds forgetting (2)

forgive
122 forgive him, O forgive, they cry (3)
175 he will forgive if they only believe (2)
206 forgive our wavering trust in thee (3)
206 forgive...our wild alarms, our trembling fears (3)
235 forgive our foolish ways (1)
290 forgive me if too close I lean my human heart on thee (3)
493 forgive me, Lord, for thy dear Son, the ill (2)

forgiven
66 ransomed, healed, restored, forgiven (1)
115 happy ... who knows his sins forgiven (1)
196 who hath my sins forgiven (5)
326 here taste afresh the calm of sin forgiven (3)
365 noblest wonders...in souls renewed, & sins forgiven (6)
414 died that we might be forgiven...died to make us good (3)

forgiven (continued)

forgiveness

forgiveth

forgiving

forgot

forgotten

form

formal

formed

former

forms

forsake
48   I'll never, no, never, no, never forsake (5)
105   I wait, but he does not forsake (4)
160   the world forsake, and humbly follow after me (1)
261   do thy friends despise, forsake thee (3)
408   Christ is throned as Lord, men ... forsake their fear (2)
416   never shall the cross forsake me (2)
507   no more our God forsake, or cast his words behind (3)

forsaken
251   destitute, despised, forsaken (1)
431   he that in anguish knelt is not forsaken by his God (3)
479   on the cross, forsaken, work thy mercy's perfect deed (1)
544   earth hath forsaken meekness & mercy . slighted thy word (2)

forsaketh
521   though he giveth or he taketh, God ... ne'er forsaketh (4)
521   God his children ne'er forsaketh (4)

forsook
210   God never yet forsook at need the soul that trusted him (3)

forswear
475   turn back, O man, forswear thy foolish ways (T,1)

forth
11   tell ye forth his might, Lord of life ... truth & right (3)
21   Him serve with mirth, his praise forth tell (1)
43   in reason's ear they all rejoice and utter forth (3)
43   utter forth a glorious voice (3)
71   bring forth the royal diadem and crown him Lord of all (1)
94   Savior stands, holding forth his wounded hands (4)
96   thou didst reach forth thy hand and mine enfold (2)
103   flowing forth from the throne of God, pure from above (3)
152   forth in thy name, O Lord, I go (T,1)
168   could I sound the glories forth which in my Savior shine (1)
188   lead forth my soul, O Christ, one with thine own (2)
201   in thy great salvation, show forth thy boundless love (3)
233   send forth the hymns our fathers loved (3)
248   forth to the mighty conquest in this his glorious day (2)
295   her young ones forth may bring (4)
339   convert, and send forth more into thy Church abroad (3)
351   from hence send forth a race of men of flaming heart (3)
356   break forth, O living light of God (T,1)
356   break forth ... upon the world's dark hour (1)
356   one great Church go forth in might to work God's .. will (4)
366   come forth, ye virgins, night is past (1)
373   break forth, O beauteous heavenly light (T,1)
395   heaven's star shone brightly forth, glory all around him (2)
399   thou beamest forth in truth and light (1)
419   the Son of God goes forth to war (T,1)
419   the Son of God goes forth to war, a kingly crown to gain (1)
427   alone thou goest forth, O Lord, in sacrifice to die (T,1)
441   forth he came at Easter, like the risen grain (3)
475   now, even now, once more from earth to sky peals forth (3)
475   peals forth in joy man's old undaunted cry (3)
476   O send us forth, thy prophets true (1)

476   send us forth ... to make all lands thine own ((1)
479   called from worship unto service, forth ... we go (4)
479   forth in thy dear name we go to the child, the youth (4)
480   speed forth thy flight (3)
527   I rose, went forth, and followed thee (3)
544   show forth thy pity on high where thou reignest (1)
545   he has sounded forth the trumpet (3)
552   almighty hand leads forth in beauty all the starry band (1)

forthwith
394   spake the seraph and forthwith appeared a shining throng (5)

fortress
20   a mighty fortress is our God (T,1)
536   thou wast their rock, their fortress, and their might (2)
548   not for battleship and fortress (2)

fortune
29   to make ill-fortune turn to fair (4)

forward
173   thy steadfast face set forward where love and duty shone (2)
173   again to lead us forward along God's holy way (5)
305   forward into battle, see his banners go (1)
474   forward tends to his abode, to rest in his embrace (2)

fought
239   while others fought to win the prize (2)
243   to fear no ill, to fight the holy fight they fought (2)
250   and win the well-fought day (3)
288   the battle's fought, the race is won (1)
439   fought the fight, the battle won, Alleluia (3)
532   who helped the right, and fought the wrong (2)
536   thou, Lord, their captain in the well-fought fight (2)
536   fight as the saints who nobly fought of old (3)

foul
94   now my foul revolt deplore (3)

foulest
1   his blood can make the foulest clean (4)

found
5   the men of grace have found glory begun below (3)
40   with thee are found the gifts of life (2)
43   no real voice nor sound amid the radiant orbs be found (3)
50   that in the darkest spot of earth some love is found (2)
90   preaching the blessedness which simple trust has found (3)
92   I once was lost, but now am found (1)
96   it was not I that found, O Savior true (1)
96   No, I was found of thee (1)
98   where'er they seek thee thou art found (1)
117   I looked to Jesus, and I found in him my star, my sun (3)
117   I found in him a resting place, and he has made me glad (1)
125   plenteous grace with thee is found (4)
128   here have I found a nobler part (4)
155   do but themselves confound, His strength the more is (2)

163   I've found a Friend, O such a Friend (T,1,2,3)
165   ever faithful ... to the truth may we be found (2)
184   on thy bosom it has leant and found in thee its life (4)
203   we've sought and found thee in the secret place (2)
216   the man who once has found abode (T,1)
222   O may I then in him be found (4)
227   the favor divine I first found in the blood of the Lamb (2)
229   on Jesus' bosom naught but calm is found (3)
232   'tis found beneath the mercy seat (1)
275   my soul has often found relief (1)
346   science walks ... to seek the God that faith hath found (4)
355   awful love, which found no room in life where sin denied (2)
392   far as the curse is found (3)
395   ask the saved of all the race who have found his favor (1)
395   angels sang about his birth; wisemen sought & found him (2)
433   near the cross, a trembling soul, love & mercy found me (2)
487   in thy flock may we be found (3)
531   my heart ... be free, when it hath found repose in thee (2)

foundation
48   how firm a foundation, ye saints of the Lord (T,1)
297   the Church's one foundation is Jesus Christ her Lord (T,1)
298   Christ is made the sure foundation (T,1)
349   in grateful service ... now their strong foundation lay (2)

foundations
304   deep in loving human hearts its broad foundations rise (1)
308   we mark her goodly battlements & her foundations strong (2)
477   finely build for days to come foundations that endure (3)

founded
293   on the Rock of Ages founded (1)
318   whose grace unbounded hath this wondrous banquet founded (1)
473   Almighty, thy power hath founded of old (3)

founder's
325   bless the founder's name (4)

fount
93   come, thou fount of every blessing (T,1)
318   fount, whence all my being floweth (2)
329   thou fount of life! thou light of men (1)
368   stream from the fount of heavenly grace (1)

fountain
38   flashing sea, chanting bird and flowing fountain (2)
125   thou of life the fountain art (4)
131   source of... old prophetic fire, fountain of life & love (1)
271   open now the crystal fountain (2)
402   field and fountain, moor and mountain (1)
421   there is a fountain filled with blood (T,1)
421   the dying thief rejoiced to see that fountain in his day (2)
433   there a precious fountain, free to all, a healing stream (1)
471   Fountain of light and love below (3)

fountains
27   thy clouds which are fountains of goodness and love (2)
266   thus led by his spirit to fountains of love (4)
359   righteousness, in fountains, from hill to valley flow (3)

four
481 within whose four-square walls shall come no night (1)

fowler's
216 preserve thee from the fowler's snare (3)

fragrance
455 flowers of paradise extend their fragrance ever sweet (3)

fragrant
490 birds pass high in flight, fragrant flowers now bloom (1)

frail
473 frail children of dust, and feeble as frail (5)

frame
28 or earth received her frame (3)
43 spangled heavens, a shining frame (1)
44 thy glory thou hast spread afar in all the starry frame (1)
66 well our feeble frame he knows (3)
82 nor voice can sing, nor heart can frame (2)
138 one holy passion filling all my frame (5)
157 our lips of childhood frame (5)
222 I dare not trust the sweetest frame (1)
268 a calm and heavenly frame (1)
268 calm and serene my frame (6)
325 nor weak excuses frame (4)
456 where light-years frame the Pleiades (1)
468 all shall frame to bow them low before thee, Lord (3)

framed
39 he framed the globe; he built the sky (2)

frankincense
383 gold and myrrh and frankincense (5)
402 frankincense to offer have I, incense owns a Deity nigh (3)
405 see them give, in deep devotion, gold and frankincense (3)
405 gold and frankincense and myrrh (3)

fraternity
198 pulse of one fraternity (3)

fraud
213 no fraud, while thou, my God, art near (2)

fraught
217 O words with heavenly comfort fraught (1)
237 when my last hour cometh, fraught with strife and pain (4)

free
1 He sets the prisoner free (4)
30 his spirit floweth free, high surging where it will (2)
49 and free us from all ills in this world and the next (2)
52 thy mercy sets us free (2)
59 thy name be ever praised! O Lord, make us free (3)
64 grant us thy truth to make us free (5)
74 who wast a servant that we might be free (3)

85	free wills ... thou givest, that we may make them thine (4)
104	ye needy, come ... welcome; God's free bounty glorify (2)
121	grace to cleanse and power to free (3)
123	know not how that Calvary's cross a world ... could free (2)
123	Calvary's cross a world from sin could free (2)
135	be my Lord, and I shall be firmly bound, forever free (4)
136	until our minds are free from mists of error (2)
151	mankind shall then be truly free (2)
153	daring hearts and spirits free (1)
153	keeping free our spirits still (4)
157	immortal love, forever full, forever flowing free (T,1)
158	immortal love, forever full, forever flowing free (T,1)
169	just as I am, young, strong and free (4)
170	in lowly paths of service free (1)
177	all that I am and have, thy gifts so free (4)
179	song of our spirits, rejoicing and free (R)
182	with a glad heart and free (1)
183	must ... all the world go free (1)
183	consecrated cross I'll bear till death shall set me free (3)
184	make me a captive, Lord, and then I shall be free (T,1)
186	from all distraction free (5)
193	till thou hast made us free indeed (3)
198	inarmed shall live as comrades free (3)
203	but in the eyes of men, redeemed and free, a splendor (4)
213	O burst these bonds and set it free (1)
230	my hope I cannot measure, my path to life is free (3)
231	set free from present sorrow we cheerfully can say (2)
233	raise high your free, exulting song (2)
236	from harm and danger keep thy children free (3)
267	wonderful key that shall unclasp and set me free (1)
273	like thy dancing waves in sunlight make me glad and free (3)
274	with a step more firm and free (2)
278	my steadfast soul, from falling free ... no longer move (4)
281	from doubt and fear and sorrow free (4)
282	a heart from sin set free (1)
284	purge away my sin; from earth-born passions set me free (1)
309	free from anger and from pride (5)
331	wine of gladness, flowing free (1)
359	he comes to break oppression, to set the captive free (1)
360	born to set thy people free (1)
396	thus rejoicing, free from sorrow (2)
397	so may we with holy joy, pure and free from sins' alloy (3)
398	till every tongue and nation, from sin's dominion free (3)
407	wondrous power that makes men free (1)
429	and all may live from sin set free (3)
433	there a precious fountain, free to all, a healing stream (1)
447	from death's dread sting thy servants free (4)
454	thou didst free salvation bring (1)
470	free our hearts to work and praise (2)
470	in the fight to set men free (4)
476	till ... know the loveliness of lives made fair and free (4)
484	in ire and exultation aflame with faith and free (3)
486	through lands from sin set free ... God shall march (4)
489	from our worldly cares set free (2)
491	ask that free from peril the hours of dark may be (3)
494	free from care, from labor free (1)
494	from sin & sorrow free, take us Lord, to dwell with thee (3)

501   for none are wholly free from sin (4)
522   gather thou thy people in, free from sorrow ... from sin (4)
527   my chains fell off, my heart was free (3)
531   then shall my heart from earth be free (2)
531   my heart ... be free, when it hath found repose in thee (2)
545   as he died to make men holy, let us die to make man free (4
547   my native country, thee, Land of the noble free (2)
548   from the strife of class & faction make our nation free (4)
548   make our nation free indeed (4)
549   from daily tasks set free (1)
552   in this free land by thee our lot is cast (2)
         a heart from sin set free (1)

freed
379   brethren, come, from all that grieves you, you are freed (2)
479   healed the sick and freed the soul (2)
490   my heart's freed from ill, fair blue sky's above (3)

freedom
198   with flame of freedom in their souls (1)
370   bringing freedom, spreading truth (1)
408   freedom her bondage breaks, and night is turned to day (1)
479   still the captives long for freedom (2)
479   that thy children, Lord, in freedom may thy mercy know (4)
543   a thoroughfare for freedom beat across the wilderness (2)
547   from every mountain side let freedom ring (1)
548   for the priceless gift of freedom (2)
550   laws, freedom, truth, and faith in God came (3)

freedom's
547   and ring from all the trees sweet freedom's song (3)
547   long may our land be bright with freedom's holy light (4)

freely
 35   for thyself, best Gift ... to our race so freely given (6)
 79   freely and joyously now would we bring (2)
109   all so freely given, wooing us to heaven (2)
114   things which freely of his love he hath on us bestowed (4)
117   behold, I freely give the living water (2)
125   freely let me take of thee (4)
179   freely surrendered and wholly thine own (3)
179   freely and joyously now would we bring (2)
184   it cannot freely move till thou hast wrought its chain (2)
282   heart that always feels thy blood so freely shed for me (1)
310   we meet, the grace to take which thou hast freely given (3)
466   O let it freely burn, till earthly passions turn to dust (2)
519   freely we these gifts receive (1)

fresh
215   ye fearful saints, fresh courage take (3)
264   a fresh and solemn splendor still is given (3)
315   our needy souls sustain with fresh supplies of love (2)
495   when the morning wakens, then may I arise pure and fresh (6)
495   pure and fresh and sinless in thy holy eyes (6)

freshness
204   the freshness of thy grace (4)
264   in the calm dew and freshness of the morn (2)

fret
170 help me bear the strain of toil, the fret of care (1)

friend
 55 if with his love he befriend thee (3)
 77 he is our guide and friend; to us he'll condescend (2)
 81 Jesus, my Savior, shepherd, friend (3)
 97 when I am sad, he makes me glad, He's my friend (1)
 97 my friend in trials sore (2)
 97 sunshine and rain, harvest of grain, He's my friend (2)
 97 how could I this friend deny, when he's so true to me (3)
 97 following him by day and night, He's my friend (3)
 97 I want no better friend; I trust him now (4)
 97 beautiful life with such a friend (4)
 97 eternal life, eternal joy, he's my friend (4)
106 ever present, truest friend ... near thine aid to lend (2)
118 Jesus, the sinner's friend, to thee (T,1,5)
121 we are thine, do thou befriend us (2)
144 O Holy Savior, friend unseen (T,1)
151 we will love both friend and foe in all our strife (3)
156 I would be friend of all, the foe, the friendless (2)
159 with thee, my God, I commune as friend with friend (3)
163 I've found a Friend, O such a Friend (T,1,2,3)
164 be thou forever near me, my Master and my Friend (1)
164 O give me grace to follow My Master and my Friend (4)
168 then with my Savior, brother, friend (3)
169 Friend of the young, who lovest me (1)
176 more than friend or life to me (1)
208 precious Jesus, Savior, friend (4)
209 be still my soul: thy best, thy heavenly friend (1)
220 truest friend to me, long my heart hath panted (1)
232 where friend holds fellowship with friend (3)
239 is this vile world a friend to grace to help me...to God (3)
260 our spirits' unseen friend, high heaven's Lord (1)
261 what a friend we have in Jesus (T,1)
261 can we find a friend so faithful (2)
345 let the comforter and friend, thy Holy Spirit, meet (2)
411 and prove the Savior friend (3)
418 language shall I borrow to thank thee, dearest friend (3)
457 and only wish the joy to know of our triumphant friend (1)
473 our Maker, Defender, Redeemer, and Friend (5)
482 O Christ, Redeemer, Brother, Friend, ride on, ride on (4)
487 thou art our heavenly Friend (1)
498 with so blest a friend provided, we upon our way ... go (2)
551 be thou her refuge and her trust, her everlasting friend (4)

friendless
156 I would be friend of all, the foe, the friendless (2)

friendly
193 let each his friendly aid afford (2)

friends
 19 O friends, in gladness let us sing (4)
 35 friends on earth and friends above (4)
116 friends and time and earthly store (3)
144 and earthly friends and hopes remove (2)

66 saints triumphant ... gathered in from every race (4)
67 what transport of delight from thy pure chalice floweth (5)
70 before my infant heart could know from whom...comforts (2)
70 from whom those comforts flowed (2)
71 chosen seed of Israel's race, ye ransomed from the fall (2)
75 from sin and death we flee (1)
76 who from the beginning was the mighty Word (1)
76 from the lips of sinners unto whom he came (3)
76 brought it back victorious when from death he passed (3)
78 redeem us for eternal day from every power of darkness (3)
83 he saves me from the grave (3)
83 from his bounty I receive such proofs of love divine (4)
84 from sordid waves of worldly sea preserve us, Lord (2)
85 from thee we learn what love is (3)
85 all who would obey thee may learn from thee their duty (4)
85 learn from thee their duty, the truth, the life, the way (4)
86 help thou dost not disdain, help from above (2)
87 take the name of Jesus ever as a shield from every snare (2)
89 my help and refuge from my foes (1)
89 from sin ... grief & shame, I hide me, Jesus in thy name (1)
90 Light of the village life from day to day (2)
91 the night becomes as day when from the heart we say (2)
93 wandering from the fold of God (2)
93 to rescue me from danger, interposed his precious blood (2)
95 Light and life art thou within: Savior ...from every sin (4)
100 and, saved from earth, appear before your Savior's face (4)
102 my message as from God receive (4)
103 flowing forth from the throne of God, pure from above (3)
105 vain world, farewell, from thee I part (5)
107 turned from home and toil and kindred (2)
107 Jesus calls us from the worship of the vain (3)
107 from each idol that would keep us (3)
110 why from the sunshine of love wilt thou roam (1)
111 yield to be saved from sin (3)
115 a country far from mortal sight (1)
116 I will cleanse you from all sin (2)
120 from thy wounded side which flowed (1)
120 save from wrath and make me pure (1)
121 keep thy flock, from sin defend us (2)
123 Calvary's cross a world from sin could free (2)
125 my trust on thee is stayed ... help from thee I bring (2)
127 from sin and fear, from guilt and shame (2)
129 O why should I wander, an alien from thee (3)
130 immense and unconfimed; from age to age it never ends (2)
130 come quickly from above (5)
132 spread thy light from the height which knows no measure (1)
136 until our minds are free from mists of error (2)
138 wean it from earth, through all its pulses move (1)
140 if thou withdraw thyself from me, ah! whither shall I go (1)
140 what pain ... labor to secure my soul from endless death (2)
141 life nor death can pluck his children from his hands (3)
143 nor let me ever stray from thee aside (3)
143 O let me from this day be wholly thine (1)
146 let knowledge grow from more to more (5)
148 from his lighthouse evermore (1)
149 message of salvation from God's own holy Word (3)
151 through the truth that comes from God (2)

153   not the first to be banished by our fears from thee (2)
160   cross endured to save thy soul from death and hell (3)
161   save us, thy people, from consuming passion (1)
161   God's gift from highest heaven (2)
161   lure us away from thee to endless night (3)
161   by thy cross didst save us from death and dark despair (4)
161   didst save us...from sin and guilt (4)
162   learning how to love from thee (3)
163   from him who loves me now so well, what power ... sever (3)
164   no wander from the pathway if thou wilt be my guide (1)
164   but, Jesus, draw thou nearer, & shield my soul from sin (2)
172   O thou who camest from above (T,1)
175   snatch them in pity from sin and the grave (1)
177   nor should I aught with-hold, dear Lord, from thee (1)
178   gentleness and grace...spring from union,Lord, with thee (4)
180   praise God, from who all blessings flow (4)
181   all...we have is thine alone, a trust, O Lord, from thee (1)
182   and from this moment, live or die to serve my God alone (2)
184   flag can ...be unfurled when thou... breathe from heaven (3)
186   from all distraction free (5)
187   take my lips ... let them be filled with messages from (2)
188   cleanse it from guilt & wrong; teach it salvation's song (3)
200   from ease & plenty save us; from pride of place absolve (4)
201   nor seek our own salvation apart from others' need (2)
201   help us to seek thy kingdom that cometh from above (3)
204   from tender childhood's helplessness (3)
204   O Master, from the mountainside, make haste to heal (5)
204   from paths where hide the lures of greed (2)
204   from woman's grief, man's burdened toil (3)
204   from famished souls, from sorrow's stress (3)
204   glorious from thy heaven above shall come the city (6)
205   gushing from the rock before me...a spring of joy I see (2)
208   just from Jesus simply taking life & rest & joy & peace (3)
208   just from sin and self to cease (3)
216   preserve thee from the fowler's snare (3)
224   angels descending, bring from above echoes of mercy (2)
225   a little shelter from life's stress (3)
231   set free from present sorrow we cheerfully can say (2)
232   from every stormy wind that blows (T,1)
232   from every swelling tide of woes (1)
233   from youth to age, by night and day (4)
234   from the ground there blossoms red life (4)
234   I dare not ask to fly from thee (4)
235   take from our souls the strain and stress (4)
236   from harm and danger keep thy children free (3)
236   guard thou the lips from sin, the hearts from shame (2)
237   lest by base denial, I depart from thee (1)
239   they see the triumph from afar (5)
243   heroic warriors, ne'er from Christ ... enticed (2)
246   hosts of sin . pressing hard to draw thee from the skies (1)
247   chart and compass came from thee (1)
248   from victory unto victory his army shall he lead (1)
249   God's all-animating voice that calls thee from on high (3)
250   from strength to strength go on (3)
250   till Christ the Lord descends from high (3)
251   thou, from hence, my all shalt be (1)
251   haste thee on from grace to glory (4)

355 from old unfaith our souls release (3)
359 righteousness, in fountains, from hill to valley flow (3)
360 from our fears and sins release us (1)
362 a call from the ways untrod (1,4)
363 set apart ... from earthly use for heaven's employ (2)
366 she wakes, she rises from her gloom (2)
368 stream from the fount of heavenly grace (1)
368 true manna from on high (2)
370 each his word from God repeating (2)
371 from days of old, through swiftly rolling ages (2)
372 O Word of God incarnate, O Wisdom from on high (T,1)
372 praise thee for the radiance ... from the hallowed page (1)
372 a lantern to our footsteps shines on from age to age (1)
372 Church from thee, her Master, received the gift divine (2)
378 save us all from Satan's power when we were gone astray (1)
378 from God our heavenly Father a blessed angel came (3)
379 hark! a voice from yonder manger, soft and sweet (2)
379 voice...doth entreat: Flee from woe and danger (2)
379 brethren, come, from all that grieves you, you are freed (2)
379 hail the star, that from far bright with hope is burning (3)
380 and that song from afar has swept over the world (3)
380 comes down through the night from the heavenly throng (4)
382 angels, from the realms of glory (T,1)
383 three wise men came from country far (3)
384 I love thee, Lord Jesus, look down from the sky (2)
390 from heaven's all-gracious King (1)
393 glories stream from heaven afar (2)
393 radiant beams from thy holy face (3)
394 good will ... from heaven to men begin and never cease (6)
396 thus rejoicing, free from sorrow (2)
397 so may we with holy joy, pure and free from sins' alloy (3)
398 never shall darkness veil thee again from human eyes (1)
398 long, alas, witholden, now spread from shore to shore (1)
398 till every tongue and nation, from sin's dominion free (3)
398 rise in... new creation which springs from love and thee (3)
400 myrrh from the forest and gold from the mine (3)
401 Day-spring from on high, be near (1)
405 out of thee the Lord from heaven came to rule his Israel (1)
408 whole round world complete, from sunrise to its setting (2)
411 O Father, look from heaven and bless ... their works (5)
416 from the cross the radiance streaming adds more luster (3)
417 from my stricken heart with tears two wonders I confess (2)
420 pardon for all flows from his side (2)
421 drawn from Emmanuel's veins (1)
423 from Olivet they followed mid an exultant crowd (2)
429 and all may live from sin set free (3)
431 from all removed, the Savior wrestles lone with fears (2)
431 from heavenly plains is borne the song that angels know (4)
433 healing stream flows from calvary's mountain (1)
433 help me walk from day to day with its shadow o'er me (3)
434 turn not from his griefs away (1)
435 see, from his head, his hands, his feet, sorrow and love (3)
437 from death to life eternal, from earth unto the sky (1)
437 our hearts be pure from evil, that we may see aright (2)
438 and brings us life from heaven (1)
440 patriarchs from the distant ages (3)
441 now the green blade riseth from the buried grain (T,1)

441   quick from the dead my risen Lord is seen (3)
444   up from the grave he arose (R)
444   he arose a victor from the dark domain (R)
446   loosed from Pharaoh's bitter yoke (1)
446   God hath brought his Israel into joy from sadness (1)
446   and from three days' sleep in death as a sun hath risen (2)
446   from his light, to whom we give laud and praise undying (2)
447   He rises glorious from the dead (3)
447   from death's dread sting thy servants free (4)
450   Lo! Jesus meets thee, risen from the tomb (2)
453   from the fight returned victorious (1)
455   scepter sways from pole to pole, that wars may cease (3)
456   the heaven that hides him from our sight knows (2)
457   our hearts detached from all below ... after him ascend (1)
459   from thee have flowed, as from a mighty river ... faith (4)
459   from thee...our faith and hope, our fellowship and peace (4)
460   each from age to age proclaiming God the one (1)
463   who descended from his throne and for us salvation won (2)
463   by whose cross & death are we rescued from sin's misery (2)
463   Holy Ghost, who from both fore'er proceeds (3)
464   worthy ... work of him...who spake a world from naught (3)
464   lo! the promise of a shower drops already from above (4)
467   thy blessed unction from above is comfort, life & fire (2)
468   truth from the earth, like to a flower, shall bud (1)
468   justice, from her heavenly bower look down on mortal men (1)
470   save us from weak resignation to the evils we deplore (5)
472   his kingdom spread from shore to shore (1)
473   it streams from the hills, it descends to the plain (4)
474   rise from transitory things toward heaven (1)
475   would man but wake from out his haunted sleep (2)
475   now, even now, once more from earth to sky peals forth (3)
476   until true wisdom from above . make life's pathway clear (3)
479   called from worship unto service, forth ... we go (4)
481   the tears are wiped from eyes that shall not weep again (1)
481   hark, how from men whose lives are held more cheap (2)
481   from women struggling sore for bread (2)
481   from little children's cries (2)
481   wring gold from human pain (3)
484   take not thy thunder from us, but take away our pride (1)
484   from all ... terror teaches, from lies of tongue and pen (2)
484   from all the easy speeches that comfort cruel men (2)
484   from sale and profanation of honor and the sword (2)
484   from sleep and from damnation, deliver us, good Lord (2)
485   from thee all skill and science flow (T,1)
485   calm and courage, faith and hope: O pour them from above (1)
486   through lands from sin set free ... God shall march (4)
487   our faith from seed to flower raise on this thy holy day (2)
488   for our salvation Christ rose from depths of earth (2)
488   on thee our Lord victorious the Spirit sent from heaven (2)
488   new graces ever gaining from this our day of rest (4)
489   from our worldly cares set free (2)
490   my heart's freed from ill, fair blue sky's above (3)
491   ask that free from peril the hours of dark may be (3)
491   guard and save us from them all (4)
492   we lift our hearts to thee, O Day-star from on high (T,1)
493   praise God, from whom all blessings flow (5)

494   free from care, from labor free (1)
494   from sin & sorrow free, take us Lord, to dwell with thee (3)
494   soon from us the light of day shall forever pass away (3)
495   those who plan some evil, from their sins restrain (4)
496   angel guards from thee surround us (2)
496   darkness cannot hide from thee (3)
498   shining on our steps from heaven above (1)
498   sure of being safely guided, guarded well from every foe (2)
498   every burden will be lighter when ... it comes from thee (3)
498   when we know it comes from thee (3)
501   for none are wholly free from sin (4)
501   no word from thee can fruitless fall (6)
502   to hide thee from thy servant's eyes (1)
502   abide with me from morn till eve (3)
502   blessings from thy boundless store (5)
503   when forever from our sight pass the stars, the day (4)
512   God sendeth from his abundant store the waters (1)
513   all good gifts around us are sent from heaven above (R)
515   may the hands be pure from stain with which...we gain (4)
518   the bread of life sent down from heaven (3)
521   from all evil things he spares them (2)
521   neither life nor death shall ever from the Lord .. sever (3)
521   nor ... ever from the Lord his children sever (3)
522   from his field shall in that day all offenses purge away (3)
522   gather thou thy people in, free from sorrow ... from sin (4)
523   to thee, from whom we all derive our life our gifts (5)
528   a slave redeemed from death and sin (1)
528   a brand plucked from eternal fire (1)
530   Christ, from whom all blessings flow (T,1)
531   I see from far thy beauteous light (1)
531   then shall my heart from earth be free (2)
531   to save me from low-thoughted care (3)
531   chase this self-will from all my heart (3)
531   from all its hidden mazes there (3)
531   each moment draw from earth away my heart (4)
536   for all the saints, who from their labors rest (T,1)
536   from earth's wide bounds, from ocean's farthest coast (6)
537   for all the saints, who from their labors rest (T,1)
538   from rock and tempest, fire and foe protect them (4)
538   glad hymns of praise from land and sea (4)
544   praise him who saved them from peril and sword (4)
544   singing in chorus from ocean to ocean (4)
547   from every mountain side let freedom ring (1)
547   and ring from all the trees sweet freedom's song (3)
548   save the people from the clash of race and creed (4)
548   from the strife of class & faction make our nation free (4)
549   from daily tasks set free (1)
551   O guard our shores from every foe (2)
552   lead us from night to never-ending day (4)
552   from war's alarms, from deadly pestilence (3)
        a heart from sin set free (1)

fronded
290   I know not where his islands lift their fronded palms (5)
290   their fronded palms in air (5)

frost
    33   sent the hoary frost of heaven,the flowing waters sealed (1)

frosty
    376   in the bleak midwinter, frosty wind made moan (T,1)

frown
    89   my smile beneath the tyrant's frown (3)
    223   not a grief nor a loss, not a frown or a cross (2)
    223   not a frown ... cross, but is blest if we trust and obey (2)

frowning
    215   behind a frowning providence he hides a smiling face (4)

fruit
    5   fruit ... from faith and hope may grow (3)
    5   celestial fruit on earthly ground (3)
    214   and in their time bear fruit supreme (2)
    231   their wonted fruit should bear (4)
    231   though vine nor fig tree neither ... fruit should bear (4)
    514   ripened in this fruit and grain (2)
    522   fruit unto his praise to yield (2)
    523   the golden sunshine, vernal air, sweet flowers and fruit (2)
    523   sweet flowers and fruit thy love declare (2)

fruited
    543   for purple mountain majesties above the fruited plain (1)

fruitful
    359   he shall come down like showers upon the fruitful earth (3)
    512   the wilderness is fruitful, and joyful are the hills (2)
    522   but the fruitful ears to store in his garner evermore (3)

fruition
    251   hope shall change to glad fruition (4)
    548   till it find its full fruition in the brotherhood of man (4)

fruitless
    194   of selfish greed and fruitless gain (2)
    501   no word from thee can fruitless fall (6)

fruits
    34   the ripe fruits in the garden: He made them everyone (3)
    60   the flowers and fruits that in thee grow (4)
    165   may the fruits of thy salvation in our hearts and lives (2)
    181   and gladly, as thou blessest us...our first fruits give (2)
    489   make the fruits of grace abound (4)
    511   as men of old their first fruits brought (T,1)
    511   so we today first fruits would bring (1)
    511   first fruits brought of orchard, flock and field (1)
    524   we lay the first fruits of thy blessing (2)
    524   upon thine altar, Lord, we lay the first fruits (2)

fulfill
    31   strong is his arm, and shall fulfill his great decrees (3)
    139   increase in us the kindled fire...work of faith fulfill (2)

141   God will fulfill in every part each promise he has made (1)
150   to serve the present age, my calling to fulfill (2)
152   task thy wisdom ... assigned O let me cheerfully fulfill (2)
177   in love my soul would bow, my heart fulfill its vow (1)
188   till earth, as heaven, fulfill God's holy will (3)
197   O Workman true, may we fulfill in daily life (2)
197   fulfill in daily life thy Father's will (2)
265   and thy rich promises in me fulfill (4)
296   fulfill thy task sublime (4)
452   come then, true and faithful, now fulfill thy word (3)
462   letting thine all-pervading power fulfill the dream (1)
462   fulfill the dream of this high hour (1)
471   in us the work of faith fulfill (4)
530   placed according to thy will let us all our work fulfill (3)

fulfilled
406   to see the promise of the day fulfilled (3)
532   fulfilled their day's endeavor (6)

fulfilling
299   O Zion, haste, thy mission high fulfilling (T,1)

fulfillment
214   sought to gain fulfillment of their prayer (4)

full
37   moon shines full at his command, and all the stars obey (1)
41   o how glorious, full of wonder (T,1)
41   full of wonder is thy name o'er all the earth (1)
41   child of earth, yet full of yearning (2)
46   we shall not full direction need (2)
50   so full of splendor and of joy, beauty and light (1)
61   his full hand supplies their need (3)
88   words full of kindness, deeds full of grace (2)
100   Jesus, our great high priest, hath full atonement made (2)
104   full of pity, love, and power (1)
116   I shall full salvation find (1)
125   false and full of sin I am (3)
125   thou art full of truth and grace (3)
127   for all a full atonement made (4)
157   immortal love, forever full, forever flowing free (T,1)
158   immortal love, forever full, forever flowing free (T,1)
233   with voice as full and strong as ocean's surging praise (3)
249   a cloud of witnesses around holds thee in full survey (2)
282   a heart in every thought renewed and full of love divine (4)
324   our full homage to demand (1)
333   O perfect Life, be thou their full assurance (2)
383   full reverently upon the knee (5)
428   and in full glory shine (4)
440   never that full joy conceived (2)
454   by almighty love appointed thou hast full atonement made (2)
503   Heaven and earth are full of thee (R)
522   then the full corn shall appear (2)
548   till it find its full fruition in the brotherhood of man (4)

fuller
 197 to fuller life, through work sincere (2)
 197 in duty's call, thy call we hear to fuller life (2)
 234 in thine ocean depths its flow may richer, fuller be (1)

fullest
 179 true hearted, whole hearted, fullest allegiance (2)
 298 and thy fullest benediction shed within its walls alway (2)
 480 boundless as ocean's tide rolling in fullest pride (4)

fully
 101 believe in him without delay, and you are fully blest (3)
 127 fully absolved through these I am (2)
 141 God's mercy holds a wiser plan than thou canst fully know (2
 339 O let them spread thy name, their mission fully prove (4)
 351 in larger worlds more fully prove the wonders of... love (4)
 351 more fully prove the wonders of redeeming love (4)
 418 now scornfully surrounded with thorns, thine only crown (1)
 438 let us joyful be and sing to God right thankfully (1)
 473 O gratefully sing his power and his love (1)

fulness
 132 rest upon this congregation ...the fulness of thy grace (2)
 195 O fill me with thy fulness, Lord (4)
 205 O the fulness of his love (3)
 227 as if filled with the fulness of God (5)
 313 till all thy life we gain, and all thy fulness prove (2)

furnish
 499 the trivial round, the common task will furnish all (3)
 499 furnish all we ought to ask (3)

furnished
  68 my table thou hast furnished in presence of my foes (4)
 315 furnished with mystic wine and everlasting bread (1)

further
 430 never further than thy cross (T)
 430 never further than thy cross, never higher than thy feet (1)

futile
 407 we hear the futile cries (2)
 407 the futile cries of superstition's cruel creed (2)

future
  62 let all our future days tell this story (2)
 139 future and past subsisting now (3)
 167 each changing future scene I gladly trust with thee (3)
 209 God doth undertake to guide the future (2)
 209 guide the future as He has the past (2)
 229 peace, perfect peace, our future all unknown (5)
 242 yet that scaffold sways the future (4)
 290 I know not what the future hath of marvel or surprise (T,1)
 357 that future years shall see, evermore and evermore (1)
 509 the future, all to us unknown (3)
 509 the future ... we to thy guardian care commit (3)

future's
170 in hope that sends a shining ray far down the future's (4)
170 far down the future's broadening way (4)

gaily
214 they gaily bloom and prosper cheerfully (2)

gain
89 in war my peace, in loss my gain (3)
194 of selfish greed and fruitless gain (2)
214 sought to gain fulfillment of their prayer (4)
298 what they ask of thee to gain (3)
298 what they gain from thee forever ... blessed to retain (3)
303 strive, man, to win that glory, toil ..to gain .. light (3)
313 till all thy life we gain, and all thy fulness prove (2)
336 gladly reckon all things loss so we may Jesus gain (5)
391 calls you all to gain his everlasting hall (3)
417 content to let the world go by, to know no gain nor loss (3)
418 what ...my Lord, hast suffered was all for sinner's gain (2)
419 the Son of God goes forth to war, a kingly crown to gain (1)
435 my richest gain I count but loss (1)
481 lust and greed for gain in street and shop and tenement (3)
486 face the darkness undismayed and turn their loss to gain (3)
515 may the hands be pure from stain with which...we gain (4)
515 with which our daily bread we gain (4)
516 Lord, let us in our homes agree .. blessed peace to gain (4)
527 I ... gain an interest in the Savior's blood (1)
527 and can it be that I should gain (T,1)
543 till all success be nobleness and every gain divine (3)

gained
533 following ... incarnate God ... gained the promised rest (2)

gaining
488 new graces ever gaining from this our day of rest (4)

gainst
155 he who would valiant be 'gainst all disaster (T,1)
243 who gainst enthroned wrong stood confident and bold (1)
243 gainst lies & lusts & wrongs let courage rule our souls (3)
248 ye that are men now serve him against unnumbered foes (2)
305 Christ, the royal Master, leads against the foe (1)
305 gates of hell can never gainst that Church prevail (3)
340 thou bidst us go with thee to stand against hell's (2)
340 stand against hell's marshalled powers (2)

gale
147 we'll own the favoring gale (1)
222 in every high and stormy gale, my anchor holds (2)

gales
459 and calming passion's fierce and stormy gales (3)

Galilean
107 as of old the apostles heard it by the Galilean lake (2)
454 hail, thou Galilean King (1)

Galilee
  157 faith has still its Olivet, and love its Galilee (3)
  171 O Master Workman of the race, thou man of Galilee (T,1)
  173 O young and fearless prophet of ancient Galilee (T,1)
  202 the common hopes that make us men were his in Galilee (2)
  203 but often in some far-off Galilee beheld thee fairer (2)
  369 as thou didst bless the bread by Galilee (2)
  413 and heroic spirits answer now, as then, in Galilee (4)
  451 your Lord doth go to Galilee, Alleluia (3)

gall
  71 ne'er forget the wormwood and the gall (3)

garb
  79 robed in the blooming garb of spring: Jesus is fairer (2)

garden
  34 the ripe fruits in the garden: He made them everyone (3)
  431 in the garden now the suffering Savior prays alone (1)

garish
  272 I loved the garish day (2)

garments
  31 the garments he assumes are light and majesty (1)
  425 road with palms and scattered garments strowed (1)

garner
  522 but the fruitful ears to store in his garner evermore (3)

gasp
  341 happy, if with my latest breath I may but gasp his name (6)

gate
  108 O sin that hath no equal, so fast to bar the gate (2)
  176 the gate of life eternal may I enter, Lord, with thee (3)
  350 this thy house, the gate of heaven (5)
  414 he only could unlock the gate of heaven and let us in (4)
  454 opened is the gate of heaven (2)
  498 thy glory breaks before us through the city's open gate (3)

gates
  13 open now thy gates of beauty (1)
  21 o enter then his gates with praise (3)
  22 we'll crowd thy gates with thankful songs (3)
  252 his watchword at the gates of death (5)
  260 through open gates thy power flows in (4)
  305 gates of hell can never gainst that Church prevail (3)
  363 lift up your heads, ye mighty gates (T,1)
  389 the glorious gates of paradise the angel guards no more (4)
  389 this day again those gates unfold (4)
  440 Christ has passed the eternal gates (2)
  446 neither might the gates of death ... tomb's dark portal (4)
  464 shakes the trembling gates of hell (2)
  536 through gates of pearl streams in the countless host (6)

gateway
347 let their door a gateway be to lead us...to thee (3)

gather
59 we gather together to ask the Lord's blessing (T,1)
87 if temptations round you gather, breathe that holy name (2)
220 though the storms may gather, still have peace within (3)
311 gather all the nations in (5)
350 here gather us around thy board to keep the feast (3)
351 thy sons, O God, who gather here (2)
430 here we gather love to live; here we gather faith to die (3)
487 we gather round thy throne on this thy holy day (1)
498 gather to begin the day with praise (1)
498 we with grateful hearts would gather (1)
503 gather us who seek thy face to the fold of thy embrace (2)
521 safely in his bosom gather (1)
522 gather thou thy people in, free from sorrow ... from sin (4)

gathered
66 saints triumphant ... gathered in from every race (4)
66 gathered in from every race. Alleluia (4)
90 with all the listening people gathered round (3)
196 till, gathered to the Church above (5)
257 we are gathered all to hear thee (1)
301 He bids us build each other up; and, gathered into one (3)
307 so from all lands thy Church be gathered (4)
307 gathered into the kingdom by thy Son (4)
376 angels and archangels may have gathered there (3)
381 for Christ is born of Mary, and gathered all above (2)
522 all is safely gathered in ere the winter storms begin (1)

gathering
402 breathes a life of gathering gloom (4)

gathers
416 light of sacred story gathers round its head sublime (1,5)

gave
24 formed the deeps unknown ... gave the seas their bound (2)
34 he gave us eyes to see them, and lips that we might tell (4)
54 not their courage nor their sword ... salvation gave (2)
161 we render back the love thy mercy gave us (4)
163 not alone the gift of life, but his own self he gave me (2)
190 to serve right gloriously the God who gave all worlds (3)
202 tasks he gives are those he gave beside the restless sea (2)
358 will its beams alone gild the spot that gave them birth (2)
375 love was born at Christmas; star & angels gave the sign (1)
383 and to the earth it gave great light (2)

gavest
177 Savior, thy dying love thou gavest me (T,1)
500 the day thou gavest, Lord, is ended (T,1)

gayly
377 our sweetest carols gayly ring to welcome Christ (3)

gaze
  37 if I survey the ground I tread, or gaze upon the sky (2)
  364 with what rapture gaze we on those glorious scars (3)

gazing
  430 learn thy love while gazing thus (2)

gems
  372 it is the sacred casket where gems of truth are stored (2)
  400 gems of the mountain and pearls of the ocean (3)

generation
  58 seek thee as thy saints ... sought in every generation (1)
  532 wise and brave and strong who graced their generation (2)

Gentiles
  405 Jesus, whom the Gentiles worshiped at thy glad epiphany (5)

gentle
  17 and hear the brook and feel the gentle breeze (2)
  35 for all gentle thoughts and mild (4)
  50 so many gentle thoughts and deeds circling us round (2)
  53 how gentle God's commands! how kind his precepts are! (T,1)
  60 thou, most kind and gentle death (6)
  145 pass me not, O gentle Savior, hear my humble cry (T,1)
  198 they shall be gentle, brave, and strong (2)
  312 see Israel's Gentle Shepherd stand (T,1)
  395 gentle Mary laid her child lowly in a manger (T,1,3)
  512 with the gentle showers doth bless the springing grain (1)

Gentlemen
  378 God rest you merry, Gentlemen, let nothing you dismay (T,1)

gentleness
  178 gentleness and grace...spring from union,Lord, with thee (4)
  520 with gentleness and love like thine (1)

gentlest
  144 thy voice of love, in gentlest tone, still whispers (3)

gently
  51 he gently clears thy way; wait thou his time (2)
  55 shieldeth thee under his wings ... so gently sustaineth (2)
  66 in his hands he gently bears us (3)
  67 on his shoulder gently laid (3)
  106 gently lead us by the hand, pilgrims in a desert land (1)
  175 plead with them earnestly, plead with them gently (2)
  226 through .. changing world below lead me gently ..as I go (2)
  502 my wearied eyelids gently steep (2)

get
  362 O Zion, that bringest good tidings, get thee up (2)
  362 get thee up to the heights and sing (2)

Gethsemane
  237 bring to my remembrance sad Gethsemane (2)
  434 go to dark Gethsemane (T,1)

Ghost
131   come, Holy Ghost, our hearts inspire (T,1)
131   come, Holy Ghost, for moved by thee the prophets wrote (2)
132   Holy Ghost, dispel our sadness (T,1)
180   praise Father, Son, and Holy Ghost (4)
344   come, Father, Son, and Holy Ghost (T,1)
357   and, O Holy Ghost, to thee (3)
443   Father, Son, and Holy Ghost (3)
459   O Holy Ghost, the Lord and the Life-giver (4)
463   Father, Son, and Holy Ghost (1)
463   we confess the Holy Ghost (3)
463   Holy Ghost, who from both fore'er proceeds (3)
467   come, Holy Ghost, our souls inspire (T,1)
488   to Holy Ghost be praises, to Father, and to Son (4)
493   praise Father, Son, and Holy Ghost (5)
536   singing to Father, Son, and Holy Ghost, Alleluia (6)

giant
190   see how the giant sun soars up (2)

giants
155   no foes shall stay his might, though he with giants fight (2

gift
35   for thyself, best Gift Divine! to our race ... given (6)
35   for thyself, best Gift ... to our race so freely given (6)
84   life, thy gift to those whom thou dost capture (2)
139   and ask the gift unspeaakable (2)
156   I would be giving, and forget the gift (2)
161   God's gift from highest heaven (2)
163   not alone the gift of life, but his own self he gave me (2)
172   and still stir up thy gift in me (3)
181   we give thee but thine own, whate'er the gift may be (T,1)
194   Almighty Father, who dost give the gift of life to all (3)
194   gift of life to all who live (3)
206   thou art...the gift beyond our utmost prayer (2)
296   truth is her prophetic gift, the soul, her sacred page (3)
301   gift which he on one bestows, we all delight to prove (2)
314   by thy gift of peace restored (2)
346   sovereign God, receive . gift thy willing servants offer (3)
347   no gift have we, Lord of all gifts, to offer thee (1)
371   tongues ... acclaim with joy thy wondrous gift to man (4)
372   Church from thee, her Master, received the gift divine (2)
374   love to God and all men, love for plea and gift and sign (3)
381   how silently, how silently the wondrous gift is given (3)
456   where his loving people meet to share the gift divine (2)
479   consecrating to thy purpose every gift thou dost impart (1)
548   for the priceless gift of freedom (2)

gifted
532   praise we ... the singers sweetly gifted (3)

gifts
20   the Spirit and the gifts are ours through Him (4)
40   with thee are found the gifts of life (2)
49   with countless gifts of love, and still is ours today (1)

90	haste, let us lay our gifts before the King (1)
153	grace to ask these gifts of thee (1)
177	all that I am and have, thy gifts so free (4)
196	I'll take the gifts he hath bestowed, & ... ask for more (1)
258	Our God's bounteous gifts abuse not, Light refuse not (4)
260	thy gifts divine implore (1)
260	dost not wait till human speech thy gifts ... implore (1)
260	until we labor for those gifts we ask on bended knee (2)
318	through the gifts thou here dost give me (3)
337	graces and gifts to each supply (1)
347	no gift have we, Lord of all gifts, to offer thee (1)
377	three wise men bearing gifts of gold (2)
397	as they offered gifts most rare at... manger rude & bare (3)
400	vainly with gifts would his favor secure (4)
402	bearing gifts we traverse afar (1)
405	sacred gifts of mystic meaning (4)
452	all good gifts returned with her returning King (2)
467	who dost thy seven-fold gifts impart (1)
513	all good gifts around us are sent from heaven above (R)
513	accept the gifts we offer for all thy love imparts (3)
515	may grateful hearts thy gifts receive (4)
519	freely we these gifts receive (1)
523	to thee, from whom we all derive our life our gifts (5)
523	our life, our gifts, our power to give (5)
524	by thee the souls of men are fed with gifts of grace (2)
524	souls of men are fed with gifts of grace supernal (2)
528	basely fear his gifts to own (3)
530	move and actuate and guide; divers gifts to each divide (3)

gild
| 358 | will its beams alone gild the spot that gave them birth (2) |

gilds
| 91 | when morning gilds the skies, my heart awaking cries (T,1) |
| 353 | when beauty gilds the eastern hills (1) |

Gilead
| 212 | there is a balm in Gilead, to make the wounded whole (T,R) |
| 212 | there is a balm in Gilead, to heal the sinsick soul (R) |

gird
3	come, thou incarnate Word, gird on thy mighty sword (2)
238	gird thee for the battle; watch and pray and fast (2)
470	gird our lives that they may be armored (4)
497	gird us for the task that calls us (2)

girded
| 473 | pavilioned in splendor, and girded with praise (1) |

girt
| 442 | He with glory girt you (3) |

give
3	come, and thy people bless, & give thy Word success (2)
4	give God all praise and glory (5)
15	glory to their Maker give, and homage to their King (3)
29	give us grace our wrongs to bear (4)

48   for I am thy God, and will still give thee aid (2)
51   give to the winds thy fears; hope and be undismayed (T,1)
83   had I a thousand hearts to give, Lord ... all be thine (4)
84   give milk . bread or solid food as fits my understanding (3)
87   it will joy and comfort give you (1)
90   Lord, we are thine, we give ourselves to thee (5)
101   he will surely give you rest, by trusting in his word (1)
104   this he give you; 'tis the Spirit's glimmering beam (3)
105   shall I give no heed, but still in bondage live (4)
106   hearts grow faint, and hopes give o'er, whisper softly (2)
107   give our hearts to thine obedience (5)
109   Christ,the blessed one, give to all wonderful words of (2)
111   to him with joyful voices give the glory of his grace (1)
112   God, did your being give, made you with himself to live (1)
116   here I give my all to thee (3)
117   behold, I freely give the living water (2)
118   I give up every plea beside (4)
137   'tis thine the blood to apply and give us eyes to see (1)
140   and here I will unwearied lie, till thou thy Spirit give (3)
142   Lord, give me such a faith as this (4)
150   O, thy servant, Lord, prepare, a strict account to give (3)
152   give me to bear thy easy yoke (3)
153   give us courage, let us hear heaven's trumpets ringing (2)
164   O give me grace to follow My Master and my Friend (4)
165   thanks we give & adoration for thy Gospel's joyful sound (2)
169   my life to give, my vows to pay (2)
170   in peace that only thou cast give (4)
171   give us a conscience bold and good (3)
171   give us a purpose true (3)
174   give heart and mind and soul and strength to serve (1)
177   give me a faithful heart, likeness to thee (3)
178   O give us hearts to love like thee (3)
181   we give thee but thine own, whate'er the gift may be (T,1)
181   and gladly, as thou blessest us...our first fruits give (2)
185   now thee alone I seek, give what is best (2)
186   worth to my meanest labor give by joining it to thine (2)
188   in thee my strength renew; give me my work to do (2)
190   to give and give, and give again (3)
194   Almighty Father, who dost give the gift of life to all (3)
201   create in us thy spirit; give us a love like thine (3)
206   give us courage now to stand (1)
210   he'll give thee strength, whate'er betide thee (1)
211   the Lord will give thee peace (2)
218   and this thy grace must give (1)
231   and he who feeds the ravens will give his children bread (3)
233   rejoice, give thanks and sing (1)
233   rejoice, rejoice, rejoice, give thanks and sing (R)
234   I give thee back the life I owe (1)
246   O watch and fight and pray; the battle ne'er give o'er (2)
253   give me on thee to wait till I can all things do (1)
259   myself to thee entirely give (1)
271   songs of praises I will ever give to thee (3)
276   O give the pure and lowly heart, a temple meet for thee (4)
279   give me to feel an idle thought as actual wickedness (2)
279   grant me the filial awe I pray .. tender conscience give (3)
280   the tender conscience give (3)
280   give me to feel an idle thought as actual wickedness (2)

281   give me a new, a perfect heart (4)
285   give me thy only love (4)
285   give me thy only love to know (4)
295   they ever give thee praise (5)
297   O happy ones and holy! Lord, give us grace that we (4)
299   give of thy sons to bear the message glorious (4)
299   give of thy wealth to speed them on their way (4)
307   didst give man food for all his days (2)
309   to thy Church the pattern give (4)
314   now we give thee thanks, O Lord (1)
318   through the gifts thou here dost give me (3)
324   he will give to all.. faithful .. self for heavenly food (2)
332   feeble elements bestow a power not theirs to give (2)
335   and heed the call they give (1)
336   glory and thanks to Jesus give for his almighty grace (1)
344   give .. wisdom from above, spotless .. peaceable & kind (2)
344   in these, whom up to thee we give (3)
348   may thy spirit here give rest (2)
352   O give success! (3)
359   give them songs for sighing ... darkness turn to light (2)
362   and give to the weary rest (3)
376   what can I give him, poor as I am (4)
376   yet what can I give him: give my heart (4)
379   all you need I will surely give you (2)
387   born to give them second birth (3)
390   whole world give back the song which now the angels sing (3)
391   give ye heed to what we say: Jesus Christ is born today (1)
405   see them give, in deep devotion, gold and frankincense (3)
406   Lord, give us faith and strength the road to build (3)
409   then let us adore and give him his right (4)
410   we've a message to give to the nations (3)
415   here, Lord, I give myself away; 'tis all that I can do (5)
427   give us compassion for thee, Lord (4)
430   here we learn to serve and give, &, rejoicing, self deny (3)
446   from his light, to whom we give laud and praise undying (2)
454   loudest praises ... meet it is for us to give (4)
457   to him our willing hearts we give (3)
462   give us the faith that follows on (1)
462   Spirit creative, give us light (2)
462   Spirit redeeming, give us grace when crucified (3)
462   give us grace when crucified to seek thy face (3)
462   when weary feet refuse to climb, give us thy vision (5)
467   keep far our foes; give peace at home (3)
469   O give us brother love for better seeing (4)
479   counsel, aid, and peace we give (4)
481   give us, O God, the strength to build the city (4)
483   rejoice, give thanks, and sing, and triumph evermore (1)
486   man in his weakness yet may give a worthier offering (1)
486   those who give up life's bounty to serve a race to be (2)
487   give joy of thy victory on this thy holy day (3)
495   Jesus, give the weary calm and sweet repose (2)
498   give us strength to serve and wait till the glory breaks (3)
507   give up ourselves, through Jesus' power (2)
511   a world in need now summons us to labor,love and give (2)
514   God ... take the gratitude we give (1)
515   give us this day our daily bread (1)
518   give us each day our daily bread (2)

522 give his angels charge at last ... fire .. tares to cast (3)
523 our life, our gifts, our power to give (5)
524 who didst give us daily bread, give us the bread eternal (2)
533 give me the wings of faith to rise within the veil (T,1)
538 and give, for wild confusion, peace (3)
542 myself I give thee; let thy will be done (3)
544 give to us peace in our time, O Lord (1,2,3)
548 but for conquests of the spirit give we thanks to thee (2)
548 give we thanks to thee, O Lord (2)
548 for all heroes of the spirit, give we thanks ... O Lord (3)

given
  2 best that thou hast given, earth and heaven render thee (5)
 35 for thyself, best Gift Divine! to our race ... given (6)
 35 for thyself, best Gift ... to our race so freely given (6)
 41 hast given man dominion o'er the wonders of thy hand (3)
 49 all praise and thanks to God the Father now be given (3)
 74 given the name to which all knees shall bow (4)
 89 to me, with thy great name, are given pardon (2)
 89 to me ... are given pardon and holiness and heaven (2)
109 all so freely given, wooing us to heaven (2)
139 to him ... in thy name believes eternal life ...is given (4)
139 eternal life with thee is given (4)
152 whate'er thy bounteous grace hath given (4)
152 for thee delightfully employ whate'er ... hath given (4)
161 still let thy spirit unto us be given (2)
190 what God hath given thee (3)
204 the cup of water given for thee still holds ...thy grace (4)
263 all that thou sendest me, in mercy given (3)
264 a fresh and solemn splendor still is given (3)
294 to her my cares and toils be given (3)
294 Zion ... be given the brightest glories earth can yield (5)
310 we meet, the grace to take which thou hast freely given (3)
315 preserve the life thyself hast given (1)
318 bread ... for our good, thy glory, given (2)
325 pardon and peace to dying men and endless life are given (2)
331 taste it, kindly given, in remembrance, Lord, of thee (1)
341 Jesus ... name to sinners dear ... name to sinners given (2)
344 the sacred discipline be given (1)
350 grant the vision inly given of this thy house (5)
352 glory and praises be in love now given (4)
361 for unto us a child is born, to us a son is given (2)
381 how silently, how silently the wondrous gift is given (3)
386 Jesus, to thee be all glory given (3)
419 O God, to us may grace be given to follow in their train (3)
427 then let all praise be given thee who livest evermore (3)
438 for our offences given (1)
440 prophets psalmists seers . sages . await . glory given (3)
454 life is given through thy name (1)
458 cross ... with all its grace, is given (4)
464 he hath given the word of grace (3)
474 yet a season, and you know happy entrance will be given (3)
483 the keys of death and hell are to our Jesus given (3)
488 thus on thee most glorious a triple light was given (2)
497 who the day for toil hast given, for rest the night (1)
517 for... children thou hast given we must answer unto thee (1)
517 children thou hast given still may be our joy and crown (5)

518   let manna to our souls be given (3)
521   nesting bird nor star in heaven such a refuge ... given (1)
523   what can to thee, O Lord, be given, who givest all (4)
533   for his own pattern given (2)

giver

38   giver of immortal gladness (1)
58   bless the same boundless giver (4)
163   that I have ... I hold it for the giver (2)
163   naught...I have my own I call...hold it for the giver (2)
293   grace, which like the Lord, the giver, never fails (2)
459   O Holy Ghost, the Lord and the Life-giver (4)
511   men of old their first fruits brought...to God the giver (1)
511   brought ... to God, the giver of all good (1)
515   O God, thou giver of all good (T,1)

gives

97   I go to him for blessings ...He gives them o'er and o'er (2)
148   to us he gives the keeping of the lights along the shore (1)
197   in work that gives effect to prayer (4)
202   tasks he gives are those he gave beside the restless sea (2)
205   gives me grace for every trial (2)
222   when all around my soul gives way, he... is all my hope (3)
231   who gives the lilies clothing will clothe his people,too (3)
306   when we asunder part, it gives us inward pain (4)
389   for he uncloses heaven today and gives to us his Son (1)
445   what joy the blest assurance gives (1,4)
457   who gives us power and peace (3)
459   thine is the quickening power that gives increase (4)
506   sharing ... the hand that gives the flowers (2)
513   much more, to us his children, he gives our daily bread (2)

givest

27   to all, life thou givest, to both great and small (3)
60   thou givest man both warmth and light (3)
84   thou givest us that good unseen the world knows not (3)
85   free wills ... thou givest, that we may make them thine (4)
171   O Thou who dost the vision send and givest each his task (3)
523   when harvests ripen, thou art there, who givest all (2)
523   how shall we show our love to thee, who givest all (1)
523   we owe thee thankfulness and praise, who givest all (3)
523   what can to thee, O Lord, be given, who givest all (4)
523   O may we ever with thee live, who givest all (5)

giveth

65   who forgiveth thy transgressions (2)
521   though he giveth or he taketh, God ... ne'er forsaketh (4)

giving

38   thou art giving and forgiving, ever blessing, ever blest (3)
117   I came to Jesus, and I drank of that life-giving stream (2)
156   I would be giving, and forget the gift (2)
227   delight which I felt in the life-giving blood (5)
307   giving in Christ the bread eternal (2)
326   giving sweet foretaste of the festal joy (5)
480   Spirit of truth and love, life-giving, holy Dove (3)

glad
       3   in this glad hour (3)
       8   prophets swell the glad refrain (3)
       8   hark, the glad celestial hymn (2)
      19   raise the glad strain, alleluia! (1)
      45   let the heavens ring! God reigns: let the earth be glad (3)
      55   join me in glad adoration (1)
      62   language, glad and golden, speaking to us day and night (1)
      62   their glad story, God is life, and God is love (4)
      97   when I am sad, he makes me glad, He's my friend (1)
     100   ye weary spirits, rest; ye mournful souls, be glad (2)
     117   I found in him a resting place, and he has made me glad (1)
     162   with a child's glad heart of love (2)
     169   in the glad morning of my day (2)
     182   with a glad heart and free (1)
     208   I'm so glad I learned to trust thee, precious Jesus (4)
     218   if life belong, I will be glad that I may long obey (2)
     251   hope shall change to glad fruition (4)
     273   like thy dancing waves in sunlight make me glad and free (3)
     274   with obedience glad & steady still to follow every word (4)
     299   publish glad tidings, tidings of peace (R)
     326   yet, passing, points to the glad feast above (5)
     329   glad, when thy gracious smile we see (4)
     352   glad songs to thee we sing; glad hearts to thee we bring (4)
     377   to you we sing this glad Noel (3)
     381   we hear the Christmas angels the great glad tidings tell (4)
     394   glad tidings of great joy I bring to you and all mankind (2)
     398   thy light, so glad & golden, shall set on earth no more (1)
     405   Jesus, whom the Gentiles worshiped at thy glad epiphany (5)
     442   in his grace of glad new birth we must seek revival (2)
     446   comes to glad Jerusalem who with true affection (3)
     449   to all the world glad news we bring (1)
     475   earth might be fair and all men glad and wise (2)
     490   glad for cotton coat, plain food satisfies (3)
     520   grant, Love Divine, in every place glad fellowship (3)
     520   glad fellowship with thee (3)
     538   thus evermore shall rise to thee glad hymns of praise (4)
     538   glad hymns of praise from land and sea (4)

glades
      17   when through the woods and forest glades I wander (2)

gladly
      17   that on the cross, my burden gladly bearing (3)
      55   gladly forever adore him (4)
     100   blow ye trumpet, blow! The gladly solemn sound (T,1)
     167   each changing future scene I gladly trust with thee (3)
     176   gladly will I toil & suffer, only let me walk with thee (2)
     181   and gladly, as thou blessest us...our first fruits give (2)
     228   its shame and reproach gladly bear (4)
     258   gladly hail the sun returning (2)
     267   open my mouth, and let me bear gladly the warm truth (3)
     267   let me bear gladly the warm truth everywhere (3)
     275   gladly take my station there and wait for thee (2)
     300   Lord, obediently we'll go, gladly leaving all below (4)
     318   let me gladly here obey thee (3)
     336   gladly reckon all things loss so we may Jesus gain (5)
     510   our lips & lives ... gladly show the wonders of thy love (4)

gladness
   19   O friends, in gladness let us sing (4)
   38   giver of immortal gladness (1)
   132 come, thou source of joy and gladness, breathe thy life (1)
   220 the Lord of gladness, Jesus, enters in (3)
   232 place where Jesus sheds the oil of gladness on our heads (2)
   233 in gladness and in woe (4)
   318 deck thyself, my soul, with gladness (T,1)
   331 wine of gladness, flowing free (1)
   366 your lamps with gladness take; Alleluia! (1)
   397 as with gladness men of old did the guiding star behold (T)
   399 here in sadness eye and heart long for thy gladness (2)
   437 the passover of gladness, the passover of God (1)
   437 all things seen and unseen their notes in gladness blend (3)
   446 raise the strain of triumphant gladness (1)
   450 let his church with gladness hymns of triumph sing (2)
   470 shame our wanton, selfish gladness (3)
   478 gladness breaks like morning where'er thy face appears (3)
   488 O day of rest and gladness (T,1)
   506 may weariness and sadness be lulled to peace & gladness (3)

gladsome
   61   let us with a gladsome mind (T,1)
   61   let us then with gladsome mind praise the Lord (4)
   62   gladsome is the theme and glorious (3)
   374 gladsome tidings be which inspire your heavenly song (2)

glance
   29   O thou true Sun, on us thy glance let fall (2)
   29   on us thy glance let fall in royal radiance (2)
   501 thy kind but searching glance can scan the very wounds (5)

glanced
   365 thy truth ... touched and glanced on every land (3)

glancing
   252 the upward glancing of an eye, when none but God is near (2)

glassy
   26   casting down their golden crowns around the glassy sea (2)

gleam
   60   thou silver moon with softer gleam (1)
   148 send a gleam across the wave (R)
   485 when ever blue the sky shall gleam ... green the sod (2)
   543 thine alabaster cities gleam undimmned by human tears (4)

gleaming
   504 thine is the glory, gleaming and resounding (3)
   504 glory, gleaming and resounding through all creation (3)

glee
   442 flowers make glee among the hills (1)

glimmering
   104 this he give you; 'tis the Spirit's glimmering beam (3)
   139 unseen by reason's glimmering ray (5)

glimpses
  267 that I may see glimpses of truth thou hast for me (1)

glittering
  166 I'll sing with the glittering crown on my brow (3)

globe
  39 he framed the globe; he built the sky (2)

gloom
  63 through the gloom his brightness streameth (3)
  217 sometimes mid scenes of deepest gloom (2)
  272 amid the encircling gloom, lead thou me on (1)
  289 shine through the gloom and point me to the skies (5)
  366 she wakes, she rises from her gloom (2)
  401 pierce the gloom of sin and grief (3)
  402 myrrh is mine; its bitter perfume breathes ... gloom (4)
  402 breathes a life of gathering gloom (4)
  434 all is solitude and gloom; who hath taken him away (4)
  450 lovingly he greets thee, scatters fear and gloom (2)
  476 dispel the gloom of error's night, of ignorance & fear (3)

gloomy
  318 leave the gloomy haunts of sadness (1)
  354 disperse the gloomy clouds of night (4)

gloria
  374 gloria in excelsis Deo, gloria in excelsis Deo (R)

glories
    1 glories of my God and King, the triumphs of his grace (1)
  31 his glories shine with beams so bright (1)
  37 not a plant or flower below, but makes thy glories known (3)
  83 his head with radiant glories crowned (1)
  168 could I sound the glories forth which in my Savior shine (1)
  168 I would to everlasting days make all his glories known (2)
  289 earth's joys grow dim; its glories pass away (2)
  294 Zion ... be given the brightest glories earth can yield (5)
  294 glories earth can yield and brighter bliss of heaven (5)
  392 makes the nations prove the glories of his righeeousness (4)
  393 glories stream from heaven afar (2)
  415 well might .. sun in darkness hide . shut his glories in (3)
  455 his glories now we sing who died, and rose on high (2)
  533 how great their joys, how bright their glories be (1)

glorified
  18 Word incarnate glorified the flesh of man (2)
  344 thy name confessed and glorified (4)
  455 those wounds, yet visible above, in beauty glorified (4)
  464 Jesus' word is glorified (3)

glorifies
  398 and glorifies with duty life's poorest, humblest part (2)

glorify
  104 ye needy, come ... welcome; God's free bounty glorify (2)
  150 a charge to keep I have, a God to glorify (T,1)

253   a pure desire that all may learn and glorify thy grace (4)
468   and glorify thy name. For great thou art (3)
507   His name to glorify (2)

glorious
    3   Father all glorious, o'er all victorious (1)
    6   tell thy goodness ... thy mercies ... thy glorious might (1)
   16   stand up and bless his glorious name (5)
   19   higher than ... cherubim more glorious than ... seraphim (2)
   25   the glorious hosts of heaven obey (4)
   27   most blessed, most glorious, the Ancient of days (1)
   39   come, the great day, the glorious hour (3)
   41   o how glorious, full of wonder (T,1)
   41   o how wondrous, o how glorious is thy name in every land (4)
   42   praise the Lord! for he is glorious (2)
   43   utter forth a glorious voice (3)
   50   so many glorious things are here, noble and right (1)
   62   by him upholden hang the glorious orbs of light (1)
   62   gladsome is the theme and glorious (3)
   66   Alleluia! Alleluia! glorious in his faithfulness (2)
   70   after death, in distant worlds, the glorious theme renew (4)
   80   so meek, so lowly, yet so high, so glorious in humility (3)
  115   with his glorious presence here his life in us revealed (2)
  127   thy blood and...my beauty are, my glorious dress (1)
  136   God's glorious commonweal (2)
  136   prefected by thee, we reach creation's glorious goal (4)
  151   whene'er we hear that glorious word (1)
  152   hasten to thy glorious day (3)
  160   may hope to wear the glorious crown (4)
  161   we would be faithful to thy gospel glorious (5)
  168   I'd sing his glorious righteousness (1)
  179   yielding henceforth to our glorious King (2)
  179   true-hearted, whole-hearted, Savior all-glorious (3)
  189   at length there dawns the glorious day (T,1)
  189   glorious day by prophets long foretold (1)
  189   join the glorious new crusade of our great Lord and King (3)
  204   glorious from thy heaven above shall come the city (6)
  233   your glorious banner wave on high (1)
  239   thy saints in all this glorious war shall conquer (5)
  248   forth to the mighty conquest in this his glorious day (2)
  257   glorious Lord, thy self impart (3)
  264   shall rise the glorious thought, I am with thee (5)
  277   bring the glorious liberty from sorrow, fear and sin (1)
  281   hallow thy great and glorious name (2)
  288   servant of God, well done! thy glorious warfare's past (T)
  293   glorious things of thee are spoken (T,1,3)
  297   with the vision glorious, her longing eyes are blest (3)
  299   give of thy sons to bear the message glorious (4)
  300   glorious in his works and ways (1)
  301   our high calling's glorious hope ... hand in hand go on (3)
  303   the pastures of the blessed are decked in glorious sheen (2)
  331   in thy glorious resurrection ... we, Lord, remember thee (2)
  333   and to life's day the glorious unknown morrow (3)
  341   bold to confess thy glorious name before a world of foes (4)
  353   brighter than the glorious morn ... this fair morning be (4)
  360   raise us to thy glorious throne (2)
  361   a glorious light have seen (1)

364 with what rapture gaze we on those glorious scars (3)
366 for her Lord comes down all-glorious (2)
368 will of his glorious Son (3)
389 the glorious gates of paradise the angel guards no more (4)
390 that glorious song of old (1)
399 thou art holy, fair and glorious, all victorious (1)
402 glorious now behold him arise, King ... God & sacrifice (5)
409 his kingdom is glorious and rules over all (1)
419 a glorious band, the chosen few on whom the Spirit came (3)
439 lives again our glorious King, Alleluia (2)
447 He rises glorious from the dead (3)
450 no more we doubt thee, glorious Prince of life (3)
451 the King of heaven, the glorious King (1)
453 look, ye saints! the sight is glorious (T,1)
464 all partake the glorious bliss (1)
466 and let thy glorious light shine ever on my sight (2)
470 bring her bud to glorious flower (1)
473 O worship the King, all glorious above (T,1)
474 longs to view his glorious face (92)
480 where the Gospel's day sheds not its glorious day (1)
480 holy and blessed Three, Glorious Trinity, (4)
480 Glorious Trinity, Grace, Love and Might (4)
483 rejoice in glorious hope! Our Lord the judge shall come (4)
488 thus on thee most glorious a triple light was given (2)
493 teach me to die, that so I may rise glorious (3)
493 rise glorious at the Judgment Day (3)
505 hope and faith and love rise glorious (4)
522 raise the glorious harvest home (4)
532 praise we the glorious names we know (5)
533 our glorious leader claims our praise (2)
535 thee in thy glorious realm they praise (3)

gloriously
190 to serve right gloriously the God who gave all worlds (3)

glory
2 honor, glory, might, and merit thine shall ever be (5)
3 thy sovereign majesty may we in glory see (4)
4 to God all praise and glory (R)
4 give God all praise and glory (5)
5 the men of grace have found glory begun below (3)
6 songs of glory, songs of triumph to our God and King (2)
7 alleluia! alleluia! glory be to God on high (1,2)
7 alleluia! alleluia! glory be to God above! (2)
7 alleluia! alleluia! glory be to God alway! (3)
11 holy, holy, to our God all glory be! (R)
15 glory to their Maker give, and homage to their King (3)
24 come, sound his praise abroad, and hymns of glory sing (T,1)
26 though the eye of sinful man thy glory may not see (3)
27 great Father of glory, pure Father of light (4)
29 o splendor of God's glory bright (T,1)
29 Father of glory evermore ... Father of all grace & might (3)
31 and will this sovereign King of glory condescend (4)
35 for the glory of the skies (1)
38 God of glory, Lord of love (1)
39 his glory let the people know (1)
39 and reigns in glory there (2)

44	thy glory thou hast spread afar in all the starry frame (1)
44	with glory like to thine (4)
44	thy glory, Lord, proclaim (5)
44	mighty works and wondrous grace thy glory ... proclaim (5)
46	our end, the glory of the Lord (1)
54	to thee the glory we ascribe (5)
59	thou, Lord, wast at our side, all glory be thine (2)
60	let them his glory also show (4)
63	everywhere his glory shineth (4)
64	thy glory flames from sun and star (1)
74	didst yield the glory that of right was thine (1)
76	every tongue confess him King of glory now (1)
78	laud, honor, might ... glory be ... age to age eternally (4)
79	thee will I honor, thou, my soul's glory, joy and crown (1)
82	Jesus, be thou our glory now and through eternity (5)
85	in whom God's glory dwelleth, in whom man's virtues shine (1)
89	in shame my glory and my crown (3)
101	come then and join this holy band, and on to glory go (4)
111	to him with joyful voices give the glory of his grace (1)
116	I am every whit made whole; glory, glory to the Lamb! (5)
124	what the high reward I win, whose the name I glory in (1)
149	of unseen things above, of Jesus and his glory (1)
149	'twill be my theme in glory (R)
149	when in scenes of glory I sing the new, new song (4)
164	that where thou art in glory there shall thy servant be (4)
166	in mansions of glory and endless delight (3)
172	let it for thy glory burn with inextinguishable blaze (2)
173	amid our pride and glory to see thy face appear (5)
180	in thy sole glory may unite (3)
195	thy rest, thy joy, thy glory share (5)
196	all his promises embrace, and to his glory live (2)
203	we've seen thy glory like a mantle spread o'er hill and (4)
218	if thy work on earth be sweet, what will thy glory be (4)
221	glory in the highest, I will shout and sing (1)
223	what a glory he sheds on our way (1)
224	O what a foretaste of glory divine (1)
228	for the dear Lamb of God left his glory above (2)
228	where his glory forever I'll share (4)
232	and glory crowns the mercy seat (4)
234	I lay in dust life's glory dead (4)
239	the glory shall be thine (6)
243	still made their glory in thy name (1)
248	he with the King of glory shall reign eternally (4)
251	haste thee on from grace to glory (4)
262	let this my every hour employ, till I thy glory see (5)
278	I only for his glory burn, and always see his face (3)
283	changed from glory into glory (4)
283	glory in thy perfect love (3)
293	cloud and fire appear for a glory and a covering (3)
298	hereafter in thy glory evermore with thee to reign (3)
298	One in might, and One in glory, while unending ages run (4)
302	saints on earth unite to sing with those to glory gone (2)
303	what radiancy of glory, what light beyond compare (1)
303	strive, man, to win that glory, toil ..to gain .. light (3)
305	glory, laud, and honor unto Christ the King (4)
314	our sainted ones in glory seated at our Father's board (3)
318	bread ... for our good, thy glory, given (2)
325	millions of souls, in glory now ... fed and feasted here (3)

336   glory and thanks to Jesus give for his almighty grace (1)
349   all praise and honor, glory, power be now and evermore (4)
350   altar raise to thy great glory, God of praise (1)
352   glory and praises be in love now given (4)
353   crowned with glory like the sun . lights the morning sky (2)
357   honor, glory, & dominion, and eternal victory, evermore (3)
363   behold the King of glory waits (1)
364   Savior, take the power and glory (4)
365   the heavens declare thy glory, Lord (T,1)
367   Father of mercies, in thy Word what endless glory shines (T)
370   told the story of the Word, and showed his glory (2)
382   angels, from the realms of glory (T,1)
386   glory to God, all glory in the highest (2)
386   Jesus, to thee be all glory given (3)
387   glory to the new-born King (1)
387   mild he lays his glory by, born that man no more may die (3)
388   glory to the new-born King (R)
394   the angel of the Lord came down, and glory shone around (1)
394   all glory be to God on high, and to the earth be peace (6)
395   heaven's star shone brightly forth, glory all around him (2)
395   praise his name in all the earth; Hail the King of glory (3)
396   saw the glory, heard the story, tidings of a Gospel true (2)
397   need no star to guide, where no clouds thy glory hide (4)
401   Christ, whose glory fills the skies (T,1)
405   unto thee, with God the Father and the Spirit, glory be (5)
407   mighty God, set us aflame to show the glory of thy name (3)
409   all glory and power, all wisdom and might (4)
416   in the cross of Christ I glory (T,1,5)
417   my sinful self my only shame, my glory all the cross (3)
424   all glory, laud, and honor, to thee, Redeemer, King (T,1)
428   and in full glory shine (4)
433   in the cross, in the cross, be my glory ever (R)
435   cross on which the Prince of Glory died (1)
440   sing with all the sons of glory (T,1)
440   O what glory, far exceeding all... eye has yet preceived (2)
440   prophets psalmists seers . sages . await . glory given (3)
442   He with glory girt you (3)
445   He lives, all glory to his name (4)
447   all glory to our risen Head! Alleluia (3)
450   thine is the glory, risen, conquering Son (T,1,R)
454   Jesus, hail! enthroned in glory, there forever to abide (3)
454   for saints ... interceding till in glory they appear (3)
455   thy praise and glory shall not fail throughout eternity (4)
458   is crowned with glory now (1)
459   Ancient of Days, who sittest throned in glory (T,1)
460   Christ the ... brightness of the Father's glory (2)
465   glory, power, and praise receive for thy creating love (1)
468   glory shall ere long appear to dwell within our land (2)
470   God of Grace and God of glory (T,1)
470   let the search for thy salvation be our glory evermore (5)
471   and glory ends what grace begun (2)
481   yea, bids us seize the whole of life and build its glory (5)
486   O Lord, be ours the glory beyond all earthly fame (4)
489   may thy glory meet our eyes while we in thy house appear (:
492   be glory, as it was, is now, and shall forever be (5)
498   give us strength to serve and wait till the glory breaks (3)
498   thy glory breaks before us through the city's open gate (3)
503   through the glory and the grace of the stars (3)

504   thine is the glory, gleaming and resounding (3)
504   glory, gleaming and resounding through all creation (3)
505   soon as dies the sunset glory, stars of heaven shine (2)
517   Lord of life and King of glory (T,1)
523   to thee all praise and glory be (1)
532   praise the Lord who now as then reveals in man his glory (1)
536   we feebly struggle, they in glory shine (4)
545   mine eyes have seen the glory of the coming of the Lord (T)
545   with a glory in his bosom that transfigures you and me (4)
545   he is coming like the glory of the morning on the wave (5)
546   cleanse the body of this nation through the glory (2)
546   cleanse the body ... through the glory of the Lord (2)
548   the glory that illumines patriot lives of deathless fame (3)
552   and glory, laud, and praise be ever thine (4)

glow

4   by morning glow or evening shade his watchful eye ne'er (2)
36   thy love is in the sunshine's glow (2)
64   sheds on our path the glow of day (2)
135   Holy Spirit, Love divine, glow within this heart of mine (2)
184   it wants the needed fire to glow ... the breeze to nerve (3)
319   brethren, all, let every heart with kind affection glow (2)
515   suns glow, rains fall, by power divine (2)

glowing

34   he made their glowing colors (1)
128   well may this glowing heart rejoice (1)
195   o'erflow in kindling thought and glowing word (4)
440   see that glowing firmament (4)
466   and visit it with thine own ardor glowing (1)
488   where Gospel light is glowing with pure & radiant beams (3)

glows

133   this earthly part of me glows with thy fire divine (3)
416   lo! it glows with peace and joy (2)

go

12   that makes the darkest way I go an open path to thee (4)
20   let goods and kindred go, this mortal life also (4)
33   all beautiful the march of days as seasons come & go (T,1)
48   when through the deep waters I call thee to go (3)
71   go spread your trophies at his feet (3)
80   who like thee so mild, so bright ... did ever go (2)
80   who like thee ... go so patient through a world of woe (2)
87   take it, then, where'er you go (1)
97   when I am sad, to him I go, no other one can cheer me so (1)
97   I go to him for blessings ...He gives them o'er and o'er (2)
101   come then and join this holy band, and on to glory go (4)
121   seek us when we go astray (2)
134   our souls, how heavily they go to reach eternal joys (2)
140   if thou withdraw thyself from me, ah! whither shall I go (1)
152   forth in thy name, O Lord, I go (T,1)
183   must ... all the world go free (1)
183   go home my crown to wear, for there's a crown for me (3)
186   careless through outward cares I go (5)
214   not like that go the men of unbelief (3)
223   what he says we will do, where he sends we will go (4)

226 through .. changing world below lead me gently ..as I go (2)
233 yes, on through life's long path still chanting as ye go (4)
234 O Love that wilt not let me go (T,1)
250 from strength to strength go on (3)
269 without thy guiding hand we go astray (1)
278 refining fire, go through my heart; illuminate my soul (2)
284 nor let me go astray (4)
285 let earth and heaven and all things go (4)
300 Jesus Christ, our Father's Son, bids us undismayed go on (3)
300 Lord, obediently we'll go, gladly leaving all below (4)
301 our high calling's glorious hope ... hand in hand go on (3)
305 forward into battle, see his banners go (1)
338 where he appoints we go (2)
340 we go to win the lost to thee; O Help us, Lord, we pray (1)
340 thou bidst us go with thee to stand against hell's (2)
342 go, make of all disciples (T,1,2,3,4)
354 and cause us in her ways to go (2)
356 one great Church go forth in might to work God's...will (4)
359 before him on the mountains shall peace, the herald, go (3)
362 where the Lord our God may go (1,4)
366 for ye must go to meet him there (1)
381 above thy deep & dreamless sleep the silent stars go by (1)
404 go, tell it on the mountain (T,R)
414 might go at last to heaven saved by his precious blood (3)
417 content to let the world go by, to know no gain nor loss (3)
434 go to dark Gethsemane (T,1)
451 your Lord doth go to Galilee, Alleluia (3)
468 before him righteousness shall go, his royal harbinger (1)
479 called from worship unto service, forth ... we go (4)
479 forth in thy dear name we go to the child, the youth (4)
482 we go with thee to claim and build a city unto God (2)
486 their unconsidered lives go up like incense to the sky (2)
487 as we go, lead us, Lord; we shall be thine evermore (4)
491 how many are the perils through which we have to go (4)
498 with so blest a friend provided, we upon our way ... go (2)
510 while on in Jesus' steps we go to see thy face above (4)
538 protect them wheresoe'er they go (4)

goading
238 striving, tempting, luring, goading into sin (2)

goal
41 thou whose purpose moves before us toward the goal (4)
41 toward the goal that thou hast planned (4)
136 prefected by thee, we reach creation's glorious goal (4)
189 one common faith unites us all, we seek one common goal (3)
245 and rough seems the path to the goal (1)
470 grant us courage lest we miss thy kingdom's goal (3)

God
1 glories of my God and King, the triumphs of his grace (1)
1 my gracious Master and my God, assist me to proclaim (2)
2 here, great God, today we offer of thine own to thee (4)
4 the God of power, the God of love (1)
4 the God of all creation (1)
4 sing praise to God who reigns above (T,1)
4 to God all praise and glory (R)

4	the God of our salvation (1)
4	give God all praise and glory (5)
4	the Lord is God, and he alone (5)
5	let those refuse to sing who never knew our God (2)
6	we, thy people , praise thee, God of every nation! (T,1,2)
6	songs of glory, songs of triumph to our God and King (2)
7	alleluia! alleluia! glory be to God on high (1,2)
7	hear the angel voices blending ... praise to God on high (1)
7	praising God for his great love (2)
7	alleluia! alleluia! glory be to God above! (2)
7	alleluia! alleluia! glory be to God alway! (3)
8	holy God, we praise thy name (T,1)
8	though in essence only One; undivided God we claim thee (4)
9	happy the man whose hopes rely on Israel's God (2)
10	sing: my God and King! (1,2)
11	holy, holy, to our God all glory be! (R)
13	gracious God, I come before thee (2)
15	praise the holy God of love, and all his greatness show (1)
15	celebrate the eternal God with harp and psaltery (2)
16	stand up and bless the Lord your God (1)
16	God is our strength and song, and his salvation ours (4)
16	stand up and bless the Lord; the Lord your God adore (5)
17	O Lord my God, when I in awesome wonder (1)
17	then sings my soul, my Savior God to thee (R)
17	and when I think that God, his Son not sparing (3)
17	and there proclaim, my God, how great thou art (4)
18	God is speaking; praise him for his open Word (3)
18	thanks to God whose word was spoken (T,1)
18	God has spoken; praise him for his open Word (1,2)
18	thanks to God whose Word incarnate (2)
18	thanks to God whose Word is answered (3)
19	God ... Father, ... Son, ... Spirit, Three in One (4)
20	God hath willed His truth to triumph through us (3)
20	a mighty fortress is our God (T,1)
21	know that the Lord is God indeed (2)
21	for why! the Lord our God is good (4)
22	know that the Lord is God alone (1)
24	Jehovah is the sovereign God, the universal King (1)
24	come ... people of his choice...own your gracious God (4)
25	O God, our King, whose sovereign sway (4)
25	great God, attend, while Zion sings (T,1)
25	O God of grace (2)
25	God is our sun, he makes our day (3)
25	God is our shield, he guards our way (3)
26	holy, holy, holy, Lord God almighty (T,1,4)
26	God in three persons, blessed Trinity! (1,4)
27	immortal, invisible, God only wise (T,1)
28	O God, our help in ages past (T,1,6)
28	from everlasting thou art God (3)
30	the one eternal God, ere aught that now appears (1)
32	the Lord our God is clothed with might (T,1)
32	and bid the choral song ascend to celebrate our God (5)
34	all things wise and wonderful: .. Lord God made them all (R)
34	how great is God Almighty, who has made all things well (4)
36	God of earth, the sky, the sea (T,1)
36	the indwelling God, proclaimed of old (4)
37	I sing the almighty power of God (T,1)

37 everwhere that man can be, thou, God, art present there (3)
38 God of glory, Lord of love (1)
40 many and great, O God, are thy things (T,1)
41 Spirit in our spirit speaking, make us sons of God (4)
42 God hath made his saints victorious (2)
42 praise the God of our salvation (2)
45 God is the ruler yet (3)
45 let the heavens ring! God reigns: let the earth be glad (3)
47 God of our life ... we trust in thee (T,1)
47 God of the past ... with us abide (2)
47 God of the past, our times are in thy hand (2)
47 God of the coming years ... we follow thee (3)
48 for I am thy God, and will still give thee aid (2)
49 all praise and thanks to God the Father now be given (3)
49 now thank we all our God with heart and hands and voices (T
49 O may this bounteous God though all our life be near us (2)
49 the one eternal God, whom earth and heaven adore (3)
50 my God, I thank thee,who hast made the earth so bright (T,1)
51 God hears thy sighs and counts thy tears (1)
51 God shall lift up thy head (1)
54 as ... God our fathers owned, so thou art still our King (4)
54 in God our shield we will rejoice & ever bless thy name (5)
56 praises of my God shall still my heart and tongue employ (1)
56 God preserves the souls of those who on his truth depend (5)
58 we come unto our Fathers' God (T,1)
59 beside us to guide us, our God with us joining (2)
60 all creatures of our God and King (T,1)
60 ye who long pain and sorrow bear, praise God (5)
60 praise God and on him cast your care (5)
60 thou leadest home the child of God (6)
62 God is love, by him upholden (T,1)
62 their great story, God is love, and God is light (1)
62 their glad story, God is life, and God is love (4)
63 God is love; his mercy brightens (T,1)
63 God is wisdom, God is love (R)
65 O my soul, bless God the Father (T,1)
66 Alleluia! Alleluia! praise with us the God of grace (4)
69 love of God is broader than the measure of man's mind (2)
70 when all thy mercies, O my God, my rising soul surveys (T,1)
74 God the Father be by all adored (5)
78 to God the Father ... Son ... Spirit ... Three in One (4)
79 O thou of God and man the son, thee will I cherish (1)
80 pathway, trod in wondrous love, O Son of God (1)
84 Child through whom we know thee, God of peace (3)
85 O Son of God incarnate, O Son of man divine (T,1)
85 O Mind of God incarnate, O Thought in flesh enshrined (2)
85 that men in thee may see what God is like (2)
85 Heart of God incarnate, Love-bearer to mankind (3)
85 O Will of God incarnate, so human, so divine (4)
86 Jesus, thou Christ of God, by thy perennial Word lead (3)
90 the Christ of God, the life, the truth, the way (2)
90 divine and human, in his deep revealing of God and man (4)
90 God and man in loving service met (4)
93 wandering from the fold of God (2)
93 prone to leave the God I love (3)
94 can my God his wrath forbear (1)
94 God is love! I know,I feel, Jesus weeps & loves me still (4)

100	extol the Lamb of God, the all-atoning Lamb (3)
102	for God hath bidden all mankind (1)
102	my message as from God receive (4)
103	flowing forth from the throne of God, pure from above (3)
105	God calling yet! shall I not hear (T,1)
105	God is calling yet! (1,2,3,4,5)
105	the voice of God hath reached my heart (5)
112	God, the Spirit, asks you why (3)
112	God, your Maker, asks you why (1)
112	God, did your being give, made you with himself to live (1)
112	God, your Savior, asks you why (2)
112	God, who did your souls retrieve (2)
112	God ... died himself, that you might live (2)
112	long-sought sinners, why will you grieve ... God and die (3)
114	we by his Spirit prove and know the things of God (4)
119	O Lamb of God, I come, I come! (R)
122	my God is reconciled; his pardoning voice I hear (4)
128	fixed my choice on thee, my Savior and my God (1)
130	what shall I do my God to love (T,1)
130	my loving God to praise (1)
131	God, through himself, we then shall know (4)
132	richest treasure man can wish or God can send (1)
132	O hear our supplication, Blessed Spirit, God of peace (2)
133	Breathe on me breath of God (T,1,2,3,4)
133	breathe on me, breath of God, fill me with life anew (T,1)
135	Word of God and inward light (1)
136	O Spirit of the living God, thou light and fire divine (T,1)
136	blow, wind of God, with wisdom blow (2)
137	Spirit of faith, come down, reveal the things of God (T,1)
137	cry with joy unspeakable "...my Lord, my God" (2)
138	Spirit of God, descend upon my heart (T,1)
138	hast thou not bid me love thee, God and King (3)
139	and God is seen by mortal eye (6)
141	have faith in God, my heart, trust and be unafraid (T,1)
141	Have faith in God, my mind ... oft thy light burns low (2)
141	have faith in God, my soul, His cross forever stands (3)
141	God will fulfill in every part each promise he has made (1)
142	in the hour of grief or pain will lean upon its God (2)
146	strong Son of God, immortal love (T,1)
147	with grateful hearts, O God, to thee (1)
150	a charge to keep I have, a God to glorify (T,1)
151	through the truth that comes from God (2)
153	God of love and God of power (T,1)
153	God of love and God of power (R)
153	God of love ... God of power make us worthy of this hour (4)
159	when I kneel in prayer, and with thee, my God (3)
159	with thee, my God, I commune as friend with friend (3)
174	as brothers of the Son of man, rise up, O men of God (4)
174	rise up, o men of God, his kingdom tarries long (2)
180	praise God, from who all blessings flow (4)
182	and from this moment, live or die to serve my God alone (2)
189	one claim unites all men in God to serve each human need (2)
190	what God hath given thee (3)
190	to serve right gloriously the God who gave all worlds (3)
191	God send us men (T,1,2,3,4)
196	render to my God for all his mercy's store (1)
196	what shall I render to my God (T,1)
196	the God of all-redeeming grace my God I will proclaim (4)

196   praise him, ye saints, the God of love (5)
199   where pity dwells, the peace of God is there (1)
200   the voice of God is calling its summons unto men (T,1)
204   shall come the city of our   God (6)
206   God of the ages, by whose hand (T,1)
207   God will take care of you (1,2,3,4,R)
209   leave to thy God to order and provide (1)
209   God doth undertake to guide ... future as ... the past (2)
210   if thou but suffer God to guide thee (T,1)
210   God never yet forsook at need the soul that trusted him (3)
211   God is my strong salvation; what foe have I to fear (T,1)
211   what terror can confound me, with God at my right hand (1)
213   no fraud, while thou, my God, art near (2)
214   obey the laws of   God in their determined quest (1)
214   their joyful, faithful hearts obey the laws of God (1)
214   when God shall judge, their lot be woe (3)
215   God moves in a mysterious way his wonders to perform (T,1)
215   God is his own interpreter, and he will make it plain (5)
216   within the secret place of   God (1)
216   with Almighty God abide and in his shadow safely hide (1)
216   I of the Lord my God will say, "He is my refuge ... (2)
216   my God, in him my trust shall be (2)
216   because thy trust is God alone (6)
217   since God through Jordan leadeth me (4)
220   God dispels our fear (2)
221   standing on the promises of God (1,2,3,4,R)
221   standing on the promises of God my Savior (R)
221   by the living Word of God I shall prevail (2)
224   heir of salvation, purchase of God (1)
227   as if filled with the fulness of God (5)
228   for the dear Lamb of God left his glory above (2)
230   but God is round about me, and can I be dismayed (1)
231   yet God the same abiding, his praise shall tune my voice (4)
239   is this vile world a friend to grace to help me...to God (3)
242   behind the dim unknown, standeth God within the shadow (4)
246   fight on, my soul, till death...bring thee to thy God (4)
250   God supplies through his eternal Son (1)
250   strong in the strength which God supplies (1)
250   but take, to arm you for the fight, the panoply of God (2)
251   God of wisdom, love, and might (2)
251   how rich is my condition: God & heaven are still my own (1)
252   the upward glancing of an eye, when none but God is near (2)
252   O Thou by whom we come to God ... Life ... Truth ... Way (6)
255   so longs my soul, O God, for thee & thy refreshing grace (1)
255   for thee my God .. living God, my thirsty soul doth pine (2)
255   praise of him who is thy God, thy Savior, and thy King (4)
257   thou alone to God canst win us (2)
257   Light of light, from God proceeding (3)
258   God hath tended with his care thy helpless hours (2)
261   what a privilege to carry everything to God in prayer (1)
261   all because we do not carry everything to God in prayer (1)
262   here...my God, vouchsafe to stay & bid my heart rejoice (3)
262   labor is rest .. pain is sweet if thou, my God, art here (2)
263   nearer, my God, to thee, nearer to thee (T,1,R)
263   still all my song shall be, nearer, my God, to thee (1)
263   yet in my dreams I'd be nearer, my God, to thee (2)
263   angels to beckon me, nearer, my God, to thee (3)

263 so by my woes to be nearer, my God, to thee (4)
263 still all my song shall be, nearer, my God, to thee (5)
267 ready, my God thy will to see (R)
267 silently now I wait for thee, ready my God (R)
268 O for a closer walk with God (T,1)
268 so shall my walk be close with God (6)
273 God, who touchest earth with beauty (T,1)
273 God, who touchest earth with beauty, make my heart anew (5)
275 I hasten to the place where God my Savior shows his face (2)
276 blest are the pure in heart for they shall see ... God (T,1)
278 then shall my feet no longer rove rooted .. fixed in God (1)
279 quick as the apple of an eye, O God, my conscience make (3)
279 Almighty God of truth and love, to me thy power impart (4)
280 Almighty God of truth and love, to me thy power impart (4)
280 quick as the apple of an eye, O God, my conscience make (3)
281 God of all power and truth and grace (T,1)
282 O for a heart to praise my God (T,1)
285 God only knows the love of God (3)
288 servant of God, well done! thy glorious warfare's past (T)
288 and still to God salvation cry, salvation to the Lamb (1)
291 there God the Son forever reigns and scatters night away (2)
293 Zion, city of our God (1,3)
295 O thou almighty Lord of hosts, who art my God and King (4)
295 my very heart and flesh cry out, O Loving God, for thee (2)
296 one holy Church of God appears through every age & race (T)
297 yet she on earth hath union with God the Three in One (4)
299 mission ... to tell to all the world that God is Light (1)
299 God, in whom they live and move, is Love (3)
300 we are traveling home to God in the way our fathers trod (2)
302 one army of the living God, to his command we bow (4)
303 who art, with God the Father and Spirit, ever blest (4)
304 thy bounds are known to God alone,for they are set above (2)
305 like a mighty army moves the Church of God (2)
308 not like kingdoms of the world thy holy Church, O God (3)
309 let us thus in God abide (5)
319 one fold .. faith .. hope .. Lord, One God alone we know (1)
324 blessing in his hand, Christ our God to earth descendeth (1)
326 here would I feed upon the bread of God (3)
330 let us praise God together on our knees (3)
332 who shall say how bread and wine God into man conveys (1)
332 fills .. faithful people's hearts with...the life of God (1)
335 let them from the mouth of God ... solemn charge receive (1)
337 O God, may they and we be thine (5)
339 as workers with their God (3)
342 we cultivate the nature God plants in every heart (3)
343 stormy sea sings praise to God ... thunder & the shower (1)
343 To God the tribes of ocean cry, and birds upon the wing (2)
343 to God the powers that dwell on high ... tribute bring (2)
343 Great God, to thee we consecrate our voices & our skill (3)
344 till all our earth is filled with God (4)
345 hands have raised, O God, to thee (1)
346 the Lord our God alone is strong (T,1)
346 sovereign God, receive . gift thy willing servants offer (3)
346 science walks ... to seek the God that faith hath found (4)
348 open wide, O God, thy door for the outcast and the poor (3)
349 to God the Father, God the Son, and Spirit we adore (4)
350 altar raise to thy great glory, God of praise (1)

351   eternal God and sovereign Lord (T,1)
351   thy sons, O God, who gather here (2)
351   and dare to trust the living God (3)
352   come, O thou God of grace (T,1)
352   till we our God and King shall praise in heaven (4)
354   mourns in lonely exile here until the Son of God appear (1)
356   break forth, O living light of God (T,1)
356   restore to us thy truth, O God, & make its meaning sure (2)
357   powers, dominions, bow before him & extol our God & King (2
357   Christ, to thee with God the Father (3)
358   lo, the Prince of Peace, lo, the Son of God is come (3)
362   prepare in the desert a highway ... for our God (1,4)
362   where the Lord our God may go (1,4)
362   word of our God endureth ... arm of the Lord is strong (3)
364   Hallelujah! God appears on earth to reign (1)
364   Hallelujah! everlasting God, come down (4)
368   Word of the ever-living God (3)
370   each his word from God repeating (2)
370   praise we God, who hath inspired those (3)
371   O God of light, thy Word, a lamp unfailing (T,1)
372   O Word of God incarnate, O Wisdom from on high (T,1)
374   love to God and all men, love for plea and gift and sign (3)
376   our God, heaven cannot hold him, nor earth sustain (2)
376   sufficed the Lord God Almighty, Jesus Christ (2)
378   God rest you merry, Gentlemen, let nothing you dismay (T,1)
378   from God our heavenly Father a blessed angel came (3)
378   how that in Bethlehem was born the Son of God by name (3)
381   praises sing to God the King, and peace to men on earth (2)
381   God imparts to human hearts the blessings of his heaven (3)
382   God with men is now residing (2)
386   glory to God, all glory in the highest (2)
387   God and sinners reconciled (1)
389   let all together praise our God upon his lofty throne (T,1)
389   with praise our God adore (4)
393   Son of God, love's pure light (3)
394   angels praising God on high .. thus addressed their song (5)
394   all glory be to God on high, and to the earth be peace (6)
395   Son of God, of humble birth, beautiful the story (3)
400   dearer to God are the prayers of the poor (4)
402   worship him, God on high (3)
402   glorious now behold him arise, King ... God & sacrifice (5)
403   for God, by grace, shall dwell in thee (4)
403   God himself is light (4)
404   and God sent us salvation that blessed Christmas morn (3)
405   to the world its God announcing (2)
405   incense doth their God disclose (4)
405   unto thee, with God the Father and the Spirit, glory be (5)
407   mighty God, set us aflame to show the glory of thy name (3)
409   ye servants of God, your Master proclaim (T,1)
409   God ruleth on high, almighty to save (2)
409   Salvation to God, who sits on the throne (3)
410   and show us that God is love (3)
410   might come to the truth of God (4)
411   O God, whose will is life and good (T,1)
412   for man's atonement ... God intercedeth (3)
412   while he nothing heedeth, God intercedeth (3)
413   thy guiding radiance above us shall be a beacon to God (R)

413   a beacon to   God, to love, and loyalty (R)
413   believe that spirit triumphs .. commend .. soul to   God (3)
415   God, the mighty maker, died for man the creature's sin (3)
419   the Son of God goes forth to war (T,1)
419   the Son of God goes forth to war, a kingly crown to gain (1)
419   O God, to us may grace be given to follow in their train (3)
420   the incarnate God hath died for me (1)
420   the Son of God for me hath died (1)
420   crucified for me and you to bring us rebels near to God (2)
421   till all the ransomed Church of God be saved (3)
425   then take, O God, thy power, and reign (4)
426   perfect God on thee has bled (1,4)
426   very God himself is bearing all the sufferings of time (3)
428   O Lamb of God, was ever pain, was ever love, like thine (4)
431   he that in anguish knelt is not forsaken by his God (3)
433   near the cross .. Lamb of God bring its scenes before me (3)
435   boast, save in the death of Christ, my God (2)
437   the passover of gladnesss, the passover of God (1)
438   let us joyful be and sing to God right thankfully (1)
440   God has promised, Christ prepares it (2)
440   child of God, lift up thy head (3)
440   know with thee, O God immortal, Jesus Christ (4)
442   through each wonder of fair days God himself expresses (2)
443   sing we to our God above ... praise eternal as his love (3)
446   God hath brought his Israel into joy from sadness (1)
446   Alleluia   with the Son, God the Father praising (5)
452   lo! the dead is living, God forevermore (1,4)
454   Paschal Lamb, by God appointed (2)
454   peace is made twixt man and God (2)
459   O Triune God, with heart and voice adoring (5)
460   God hath spoken by his prophets (T,1)
460   God hath ... spoken his unchanging Word (1)
460   each from age to age proclaiming God the one (1)
460   God the one, the righteous Lord (1)
460   God is King, his throne eternal (1)
460   God the first and God the last (1,3)
460   God hath spoken by Christ Jesus (2)
460   spoken by ... Word incarnate, God of God, ere time began (2)
460   Man, revealing God to man (2)
460   God yet speaketh by his Spirit (3)
460   God abides, his Word unchanging (3)
463   we believe in one true   God (T,1)
463   we believe in Jesus Christ, Son of God and Mary's Son (2)
464   sons of God your Savior praise (3)
468   rise, God, judge thou the earth in might (2)
468   thou in thy everlasting seat remainest God alone (3)
470   God of Grace and God of glory (T,1)
474   so a soul that's born of   God longs to view his... face (2)
475   still wilt not hear thine inner God proclaim (1)
476   Eternal God, whose power upholds (T,1)
476   O God of love, whose spirit wakes in every human breast (2)
476   O God of truth, whom science seeks (3)
476   O God of truth, whom ... reverent souls adore (3)
476   O God of beauty, oft revealed in dreams of human art (4)
476   O God of righteousness & grace, seen in Christ, thy Son (5)
477   O day of God, draw nigh in beauty and in power (T,1)
477   O day of God, draw nigh as at creation's birth (5)

478 the crown awaits the conquest; lead on, O God of might (3)
481 give us, O God, the strength to build the city (4)
481 already in the mind of God that city riseth fair (5)
482 O thou eternal Christ of God, ride on (T,1)
482 we go with thee to claim and build a city unto God (2)
483 Jesus, the Savior, reigns, the God of truth and love (2)
484 O God of earth and altar, bow down and hear our cry (T,1)
485 man's rude work deface no more the paradise of God (2)
486 O God, before whose altar the stars like tapers burn (T,1)
486 till through world made noble ... God shall march (4)
486 through lands from sin set free ... God shall march (4)
486 the armies of the living God shall march to victory (4)
487 pray God to teach us here on this thy holy day (2)
488 sing holy, holy, holy, to the great God Triune (1)
489 God has brought us on our way (1)
491 be thou our souls' perserver, O God, for thou dost know (4)
492 and nature's God adore (3)
492 to God the Father, Son, and Spirit, One in Three (5)
493 all praise to thee, my God, this night (T,1)
493 sleep that may me more vigorous make to serve my God (4)
493 to serve my God when I awake (4)
493 praise God, from whom all blessings flow (5)
497 God, that madest earth and heaven, darkness and light (T,1)
497 strong through thee whate'er befall us, O God most wise (2)
498 at thy feet, our God and Father (T,1)
499 new thoughts of God, new hopes of heaven (2)
503 holy, holy, holy, Lord God of Hosts (R)
507 promise, in this sacred hour, for God to live and die (2)
507 no more our God forsake, or cast his words behind (3)
509 Great God, we sing that mighty hand (T,1)
509 we are guarded by our God (2)
509 our helper, God, in whom we trust, in better worlds (5)
510 we all, with vows and anthems new, before our God appear (2)
511 brought ... to God, the giver of all good (1)
511 God ... the source of bounteous yield (1)
511 to make our life an offering to God, that man may live (2)
512 God sendeth from his abundant store the waters (1)
512 to bless the earth, God sendeth (T,1)
514 God, whose farm is all creation (T,1)
514 God ... take the gratitude we give (1)
514 in these crops of your creation, take, O God (3)
515 O God, thou giver of all good (T,1)
516 happy the home when God is there (T,1)
521 God his own doth tend and nourish (2)
521 though he giveth or he taketh, God ... ne'er forsaketh (4)
521 God his children ne'er forsaketh (4)
522 God, our Maker, doth provide ...our wants to be supplied (1)
522 God shall come, and shall take his harvest home (3)
522 for the Lord our God shall come (3)
524 blessed is that land of God where saints abide forever (3)
528 I, a child of wrath & hell ... be called a child of God (2)
531 thou hidden love of God, whose height (T,1)
531 I am thy Love, thy God, thy all (4)
532 they blessed the earth ... blessed of God & man forever (6)
533 following ... incarnate God ... gained the promised rest (2)
534 we bless thee, our God, our fathers' God (1,2)
534 for the might of thine arm we bless thee, our God (1,2)

217   still 'tis God's hand that leadeth me (1)
218   he that into God's kingdom comes must enter by this door (3)
231   the theme of God's salvation, and find it ever new (2)
233   God's wondrous praise declare (2)
240   run the straight race through God's good grace (2)
242   some great cause, God's new Messiah (1)
242   God's new Messiah, offering each the bloom or blight (1)
249   God's all-animating voice that calls thee from on high (3)
251   God's own hand shall guide thee there (4)
258   Our God's bounteous gifts abuse not, Light refuse not (4)
266   make friends of God's children, help those who are weak (1)
290   assured alone that life and death God's mercy underlies (1)
303   O sweet and blessed country, the home of God's elect (4)
342   in heaven & earth thy power ... bring God's kingdom here (4)
349   of God's great temple thou (1)
356   one great Church go forth in might to work God's .. will (4)
356   work God's perfect will (4)
366   come, thou blessed One. God's own beloved son, Alleluia (2)
372   it floateth like a banner before God's host unfurled (3)
407   the heart that bled and broke to send God's love (1)
407   send God's love to earth's remotest part (1)
434   God's own sacrifice complete (3)
438   but now at God's right hand he stands (1)
440   God's likeness, man awaking, knows the everlasting peace (1)
457   enthroned at God's right hand he sits (2)
460   age-long Word expounding God's own message now as then (3)
475   nor till that hour shall God's whole will be done (3)
481   where the sun that shineth is God's grace for human good (4)
513   but it is fed and watered by God's almighty hand (1)
519   ne'er forget God's daily care (T,1)
522   come to God's own temple, come (1)
522   all the world is God's own field (2)

godly
253   I want a godly fear, a quick discerning eye (3)
279   I want a principle within of watchful, godly fear (T,1)
280   I want a principle within of watchful, godly fear (T,1)
317   with godly fear, we seek thy presence (2)

goes
8   morn to set of sun, through the church the song goes on (3)
190   as he goes meekly by (1)
242   choice goes by forever twixt that darkness & that light (1)
287   every round goes higher ... soldiers of the cross (2)
419   the Son of God goes forth to war (T,1)
419   the Son of God goes forth to war, a kingly crown to gain (1)
469   nation by nation still goes unforgiven (3)

goest
427   alone thou goest forth, O Lord, in sacrifice to die (T,1)

goeth
58   the fire divine ... still goeth bright before us (2)

going
57   thy going out, thy coming in, forever he will guide (4)
98   and, going, take thee to their home (2)
305   with the cross of Jesus going on before (1,R)

gold
48   thy dross to consume, and thy gold to refine (4)
187   take my silver and my gold (2)
372   O make thy Church, dear Savior, a lamp of purest gold (4)
377   three wise men bearing gifts of gold (2)
383   and offered there, in his presence, their gold and myrrh (5)
383   gold and myrrh and frankincense (5)
385   so bring him incense, gold, and myrrh (3)
390   angels bending near ... earth to touch ... harps of gold (1)
400   myrrh from the forest and gold from the mine (3)
402   gold I bring to crown him again (2)
405   see them give, in deep devotion, gold and frankincense (3)
405   gold and frankincense and myrrh (3)
405   gold the King of kings proclaimeth (4)
442   gold the green enhancing (1)
481   wring gold from human pain (3)
484   the walls of gold entomb us, the swords of scorn divide (1)
524   bright robes of gold the fields adorn (1)
536   and win with them the victor's crown of gold (3)
543   America! America! may God thy gold refine (3)

golden
26   casting down their golden crowns around the glassy sea (2)
58   unbroken be the golden chain, keep on the song forever (4)
60   thou burning sun with golden beam (1)
62   language, glad and golden, speaking to us day and night (1)
97   he sends the harvest's golden grain (2)
107   the vain world's golden store (3)
149   all the golden fancies of all our golden dreams (2)
149   more wonderful it seems than all the golden fancies (2)
192   his service is the golden cord close binding all mankind (2)
233   toil till dawns the golden day (5)
303   Jerusalem the golden, with milk and honey blest (T,1)
398   thy light, so glad & golden, shall set on earth no more (1)
433   till I reach the golden strand just beyond the river (4)
498   praise for mercies daily twining round us golden cords (1)
498   twining round us golden cords of love (1)
523   the golden sunshine, vernal air, sweet flowers and fruit (2)
524   where golden fields spread fair and broad (3)

Golgatha
317   he drank the cup on Golgatha. His grace we trust (1)

gone
28   a thousand ages in thy sight are like an evening gone (4)
209   when disappointment, grief, and fear are gone (3)
263   though like a wanderer, the sun gone down (2)
272   o'er crag and torrent, till the night is gone (3)
302   saints on earth unite to sing with those to glory gone (2)
326   the feast, though not the love, is past and gone (4)
378   save us all from Satan's power when we were gone astray (1)
529   my company before is gone, and I am left alone with thee (1)

good
15   from whom all good proceeds ... earth and heaven adore (1)
21   for why! the Lord our God is good (4)
33   Good will to men on earth (2)
37   and then pronounced them good (2)

```
 41  mixture strange of good and ill (2)
 67  Good Shepherd, may I sing thy praise within thy house (6)
 69  welcome for the sinner and more graces for the good (1)
 82  how good to those who seek (3)
 84  thou givest us that good unseen the world knows not (3)
 92  the Lord has promised good to me (4)
 93  I hope, by thy good pleasure, safely to arrive at home (2)
136  preach to all thy great good news (2)
152  and prove thy good and perfect will (2)
155  he will make good his right to be a pilgrim (2)
171  give us a conscience bold and good (3)
194  visions of a larger good & holier dreams of brotherhood (1)
199  him whose holy work was doing good (3)
219  thy providence turns all to good (3)
223  while we do his good will he abides with us still (1)
240  fight the good fight with all thy might (T,1)
240  run the straight race through God's good grace (2)
241  fight the good fight (T,1) (words identical to 240)
242  for the good or evil side (1)
242  time makes ancient good uncouth (3)
257  thou must work all good within us (2)
258  when thine aim is good and true (3)
260  good and ill, deep buried in each breast (2)
260  thou hearest these, the good and ill (2)
282  perfect & right & pure & good, a copy, Lord, of thine (4)
318  bread ... for our good, thy glory, given (2)
329  to them that seek thee, thou art good (2)
344  good desired and wanted most ...thy richest grace supply (1)
362  O Zion, that bringest good tidings, get thee up (2)
377  and so, good friends, we wish you well (3)
385  good Christian, fear (2)
390  peace on the earth, good will to me (1)
391  good Christian men, rejoice (T,1,2,3)
394  good will ... from heaven to men begin and never cease (6)
411  O God, whose will is life and good (T,1)
411  will is life and good for all of mortal breath (1)
411  proclaim the good Physician's mind (3)
412  lo, the Good Shepherd for the sheep is offered (3)
414  died that we might be forgiven ... died to make us good (3)
414  there was no other good enough to pay the price of sin (4)
424  who in all good delightest, thou good and gracious King (3)
449  good Christian men, rejoice and sing (T,1)
452  all good gifts returned with her returning King (2)
476  inspire thy heralds of good news to live thy life divine (5)
479  hope and health, good will and comfort (4)
481  where the sun that shineth is God's grace for human good (4)
482  in mart & court and parliament the common good increase (3)
484  from sleep and from damnation, deliver us, good Lord (2)
490  make my conduct good, actions calm and mild (2)
511  brought ... to God, the giver of all good (1)
511  the wealth of this good land (1)
512  the year with good he crownest ... earth his mercy fills (2)
513  plow the fields and scatter the good seed on the land (1)
513  all good gifts around us are sent from heaven above (R)
513  we thank thee...O Father, for all things bright & good (3)
515  O God, thou giver of all good (T,1)
517  love that nothing good denies (4)
```

518   for life and health and every good (2)
543   crown thy good with brotherhood ... sea to shining sea (1,4)

goodly
308   we mark her goodly battlements & her foundations strong (2)

goodness
6   tell thy goodness ... thy mercies ... thy glorious might (1)
27   thy clouds which are fountains of goodness and love (2)
37   I sing the goodness of the Lord (2)
37   goodness of the Lord, that filled the earth with food (2)
52   thy goodness we adore (3)
53   his goodness stands approved, unchanged from day to day (4)
55   surely his goodness and mercy here daily attend thee (3)
63   the hour that darkest seemeth will his... goodness prove (3)
63   will his changeless goodness prove (3)
67   Shepherd ... whose goodness faileth never (1)
67   thy goodness faileth never (6)
68   goodness and mercy all my life shall surely follow me (5)
70   through every period of my life thy goodness I'll pursue (4)
77   on heaven's blissful shore his goodness we'll adore (3)
93   let thy goodness, like a fetter, bind my wandering heart (3)
93   let thy goodness ... bind my wandering heart to thee (3)
224   filled with his goodness, lost in his love (3)
279   no more thy goodness grieve (3)
280   no more thy goodness grieve (3)
340   and make thy goodness known (4)
459   praise we the goodness that doth crown our days (5)
509   thy goodness all our hopes shall raise (4)
528   O how shall I the goodness tell, Father (2)
528   how ... goodness tell ... which thou to me hast showed (2)
552   thy bounteous goodness nourish us in peace (3)

goods
20   let goods and kindred go, this mortal life also (4)

gospel
100   the gospel trumpet hear, the news of heavenly grace (4)
102   come, sinners, to the gospel feast (T,1)
109   sweetly echo the gospel call (3)
161   we would be faithful to thy gospel glorious (5)
248   put on the gospel armor, each piece put on with prayer (3)
352   source of all strength thou art; thy gospel bless (3)
365   nor ... spreading Gospel rest till through the world (4)
365   thy Gospel makes the simple wise (5)
396   saw the glory, heard the story, tidings of a Gospel true (2)
488   where Gospel light is glowing with pure & radiant beams (3)

Gospel's
165   thanks we give & adoration for thy Gospel's joyful sound (2)
480   where the Gospel's day sheds not its glorious day (1)
489   may thy Gospel's joyful sound conquer sinners, comfort (4)

government
361   his righteous government and power shall over all extend (4)

grace

1	glories of my God and King, the triumphs of his grace (1)
5	the men of grace have found glory begun below (3)
18	deeds and words and death and rising tell the grace (2)
18	death and rising tell the grace in heaven's plan (2)
25	O God of grace (2)
29	Father of glory evermore ... Father of all grace & might (3)
29	and give us grace our wrongs to bear (4)
31	his truth confirms and seals the grace (2)
39	his saving grace proclaim (1)
39	his saving grace proclaim (3)
44	what the son of man, that thou dost visit him in grace (3)
44	mighty works and wondrous grace thy glory ... proclaim (5)
46	our strength, thy grace; our rule, thy word (1)
48	my grace, all-sufficient, shall be thy supply (4)
49	and keep us in his grace, and guide us when perplexed (2)
58	the grace those sinners that subdued (2)
58	grace ... doth vanquish, doth restore us (2)
58	rich with the same eternal grace (4)
66	praise him for his grace and favor to our fathers (2)
66	grace and favor to our fathers in distress (2)
66	Alleluia! Alleluia! praise with us the God of grace (4)
67	thy unction grace bestoweth (5)
71	hail him who saves you by his grace (2)
74	that in our darkened hearts thy grace might shine (1)
83	his lips with grace o'erflow (1)
88	words full of kindness, deeds full of grace (2)
92	'twas grace that taught my heart to fear (2)
92	and grace my fears relieved (2)
92	how precious did that grace appear (2)
92	'tis grace hath brought me safe thus far (3)
92	and grace will lead me home (3)
93	tune my heart to sing thy grace (1)
93	to grace how great a debtor daily I'm constrained to be (3)
95	now, O Lord, this very hour, send thy grace (2)
95	send thy grace and show thy power (2)
100	the gospel trumpet hear, the news of heavenly grace (4)
104	every grace that brings you nigh (2)
111	to him with joyful voices give the glory of his grace (1)
111	thro' grace we harken to thy voice (3)
112	ransomed sinners, why will you slight his grace, and die (2)
112	will you not his grace receive ... still refuse to live (3)
115	how happy every child of grace (T,1)
118	what shall I say thy grace to move (4)
121	grace to cleanse and power to free (3)
122	and sprinkles now the throne of grace (2)
125	thou art full of truth and grace (3)
125	plenteous grace with thee is found (4)
125	grace to cover all my sin (4)
129	and let the sweet tokens of pardoning grace bring joy (4)
130	thy sovereign grace to all extends (2)
130	grace ... it reaches all mankind (2)
130	and depth of sovereign grace (1)
130	grace ... wide as infinity ... it never passed by one (3)
132	rest upon this congregation ...the fulness of thy grace (2)
137	the grace which all may find, the saving power, impart (3)
141	I rest, heart, mind, and soul the captive of thy grace (4)

143   may thy rich grace impart strength to my fainting heart (2)
145   heal my wounded, broken spirit, save me by thy grace (3)
152   whate'er thy bounteous grace hath given (4)
153   grant us in this burning hour grace (1)
153   grace to ask these gifts of thee (1)
159   by the power of grace divine (2)
162   strong to follow in thy grace (3)
164   O give me grace to follow My Master and my Friend (4)
165   triumph in redeeming grace (1)
168   and magnify the wondrous grace which made salvation mine (1)
168   a blest eternity I'll spend triumphant in his grace (3)
175   feelings lie buried that grace can restore (3)
178   what grace, O Lord, and beauty shone (T,1)
179   King of our lives, by thy grace we will be (1)
179   King of our lives, by thy grace we will be (R)
182   Lord, in the strength of grace (T,1)
193   Jesus, united by grace, and each to each endeared (T,1)
196   sacred cup of saving grace I will with thanks receive (2)
196   the God of all-redeeming grace my God I will proclaim (4)
197   thou Master Workman, grant us grace (3)
204   the cup of water given for thee still holds ...thy grace (4)
204   the freshness of thy grace (4)
205   gives me grace for every trial (2)
206   still may we trust thy love and grace (4)
208   Jesus, precious Jesus! O for grace to trust him more (R)
215   but trust him for his grace (4)
217   when by thy grace the victory's won (4)
218   and this thy grace must give (1)
218   when grace hath made me meet thy blessed face to see (4)
218   come, Lord, when grace hath made me meet (4)
222   I rest on his unchanging grace (2)
225   a little place of mystic grace (4)
239   is this vile world a friend to grace to help me...to God (3)
240   run the straight race through God's good grace (2)
251   haste thee on from grace to glory (4)
253   a pure desire that all may learn and glorify thy grace (4)
255   so longs my soul, O God, for thee & thy refreshing grace (1)
262   to hear the whispers of thy grace & hear thee inly speak (4)
275   believe his Word and trust his grace (3)
278   no longer ... my heart shall mourn ... purified by grace (3)
279   drive me to... grace again which makes the wounded whole (4)
280   drive me to...grace again, which makes the wounded whole (4)
281   God of all power and truth and grace (T,1)
289   what but thy grace can foil the tempter's power (3)
293   grace, which like the Lord, the giver, never fails (2)
295   the tabernacles of thy grace how pleasant, Lord, they be (1)
297   and to one hope she presses, with every grace endued (2)
297   O happy ones and holy! Lord, give us grace that we (4)
301   Lord, who joins us by his grace (1)
301   grace through every vessel flows in purest streams (2)
310   we meet, the grace to take which thou hast freely given (3)
315   strengthened by thy grace behold without a veil thy face (2)
317   he drank the cup on Golgatha. His grace we trust (1)
318   whose grace unbounded hath this wondrous banquet founded (1)
320   the token that by thy grace our souls are fed (2)
326   here grasp with firmer hand eternal grace (1)
332   O the depth of love divine, the unfathomable grace (T,1)

332	sure and real is the grace, the manner be unknown (4)
332	let the wisest mortal show how we the grace receive (2)
334	may the grace of Christ our Savior (T,1)
336	glory and thanks to Jesus give for his almighty grace (1)
338	partakers of the Savior's grace ... same in mind & heart (4)
339	thy universal grace proclaim, thine all-redeeming love (4)
341	that the world might taste & see the riches of his grace (3)
341	his only righteousness I show, his saving grace proclaim (5)
344	good desired and wanted most ...thy richest grace supply (1)
351	make known to them thy saving grace (2)
352	come, O thou God of grace (T,1)
363	thy grace and love in us reveal (3)
365	volume thou hast writ reveals thy justice and thy grace (2)
366	the strong in grace, in truth victorious (2)
368	stream from the fount of heavenly grace (1)
371	revealing to sinful men thy justice and thy grace (3)
392	he rules the world with truth and grace (4)
393	with the dawn of redeeming grace (3)
403	for God, by grace, shall dwell in thee (4)
415	amazing pity! Grace unknown! and love beyond degree (2)
418	look on me with thy favor, vouchsafe to me thy grace (2)
419	O God, to us may grace be given to follow in their train (3)
422	his scepter is his kindliness, his grandeur is his grace (2)
438	his grace ... doth impart eternal sunshine to the heart (3)
438	Word of grace hath purged away the old and wicked leaven (4)
442	in his grace of glad new birth we must seek revival (2)
458	cross ... with all its grace, is given (4)
462	Spirit redeeming, give us grace when crucified (3)
462	give us grace when crucified to seek thy face (3)
464	kindled by a spark of grace (1)
464	he hath given the word of grace (3)
465	render ... their lives to thee for thy redeeming grace (2)
466	for none can guess its grace, till he become the place (3)
467	anoint and cheer our soiled face with...thy grace (3)
467	the abundance of thy grace (3)
470	God of Grace and God of glory (T,1)
471	let all thy saving grace adore (1)
471	and glory ends what grace begun (2)
471	Spirit of grace and health and power (3)
473	O tell of his might, O sing of his grace (2)
476	O God of righteousness & grace, seen in Christ, thy Son (5)
478	through days of preparation thy grace has made us strong (1)
480	move o'er the waters' face, bearing the lamp of grace (3)
480	Glorious Trinity, Grace, Love and Might (4)
481	where the sun that shineth is God's grace for human good (4)
487	through grace alone are we saved (3)
489	while we pray for pardoning grace (2)
489	make the fruits of grace abound (4)
503	through the glory and the grace of the stars (3)
507	come, let us use the grace divine (T,1)
508	come, let us use the grace divine (T,1) (same as 507)
520	let all unworthy aims depart, imbue us with thy grace (2)
521	unto them his grace he showeth (3)
523	for means of grace and hopes of heaven (4)
524	by thee the souls of men are fed with gifts of grace (2)
524	souls of men are fed with gifts of grace supernal (2)
526	thy grace along availeth (2)

526   thy grace hath wrought whate'er in him is worthy (2)
526   but must confess thy grace hath wrought (2)
528   sinners alone his grace receive (4)
535   and saved by grace alone (1)
535   we in the kingdom of thy grace: The kingdoms are but one (3)
541   uphold them with thy saving grace (2)
543   America! America! God shed his grace on thee (1)
543   America! America! God shed his grace on thee (4)
552   fill all our lives with love and grace divine (4)

graced
532   wise and brave and strong who graced their generation (2)

graces
69   welcome for the sinner and more graces for the good (1)
132   on our souls thy graces shower (2)
337   graces and gifts to each supply (1)
470   armored with all Christ-like graces in the fight (4)
488   new graces ever gaining from this our day of rest (4)

gracious
1   my gracious Master and my God, assist me to proclaim (2)
4   his gracious mercy keepeth (2)
13   gracious God, I come before thee (2)
19   most gracious, magnify the Lord (2)
24   come ... people of his choice...own your gracious God (4)
62   praise to Christ our gracious head (3)
64   our noontide is thy gracious dawn (3)
77   praise is his gracious choice: Alleluia! Amen! (1)
114   can my gracious Savior show my name inscribed in heaven (1)
132   as a gracious shower descend (1)
166   my gracious Redeemer, my Savior art thou (1)
235   the gracious calling of the Lord (2)
260   O gracious Father of mankind (T,1)
265   most gracious Lord (1)
274   waiting for thy gracious word (1)
282   thy nature, gracious Lord, impart (5)
316   according to thy gracious word, in meek humility (T,1)
329   glad, when thy gracious smile we see (4)
360   now thy gracious kingdom bring (2)
367   Divine instructor, gracious Lord, be thou forever near (4)
390   from heaven's all-gracious King (1)
397   so, most gracious Lord, may we evermore be led to thee (1)
424   who in all good delightest, thou good and gracious King (3)
461   descend with all thy gracious powers (1,4)
461   descend with all thy gracious powers (4)
476   help us to spread thy gracious reign till greed .. cease (2)
490   with the gracious light I my toil resume (1)
498   when thy gracious face we see (3)
502   now, Lord, the gracious work begin (4)
526   bend down thy gracious ear to me (1)

grain
97   he sends the harvest's golden grain (2)
97   sunshine and rain, harvest of grain, He's my friend (2)
307   as grain, once scattered on the hillsides (4)
307   as grain ... was in this broken bread made one (4)

441 now the green blade riseth from the buried grain (T,1)
441 laid in the earth like grain that sleeps unseen (2)
441 forth he came at Easter, like the risen grain (3)
512 with the gentle showers doth bless the springing grain (1)
513 sends the snow in winter ... warmth to swell the grain (1)
514 ripened in this fruit and grain (2)
522 Lord of harvest, grant that we wholesome grain ... be (2)
522 grant that we wholesome grain and pure may be (2)
543 O beautiful for spacious skies, for amber waves of grain (T)

grand
510 bring the grand sabbatic year, the jubilee of heaven (6)

grandeur
17 when I look down from lofty mountain grandeur (2)
36 thy grandeur in the march of night (3)
273 like .. rocks of towering grandeur make me strong & sure (2)
422 his scepter is his kindliness, his grandeur is his grace (2)

grant
40 grant unto us communion with thee (2)
64 grant us thy truth to make us free (5)
75 grant us that way to know, that truth to keep (4)
141 Lord Jesus, make me whole; grant me no resting place (4)
153 grant us in this burning hour grace (1)
173 O grant that love of country may help us hear his call (3)
197 thou Master Workman, grant us grace (3)
236 grant us thy peace upon our homeward way (2)
236 grant us thy peace, Lord, through the coming night (3)
236 grant us thy peace throughout our earthly life (4)
237 grant that I may never fail thy hand to see (3)
237 grant that I may ever cast my care on thee (3)
279 grant me the filial awe I pray .. tender conscience give (3)
280 grant me the filial awe, I pray, the tender conscience (3)
333 grant them the joy which brightens earthly sorrow (3)
333 grant them the peace which calms all earthly strife (3)
343 O grant its rich and swelling notes may lift our souls (3)
350 grant the vision inly given of this thy house (5)
368 Lord, grant us all aright to learn the wisdom it imparts (4)
470 grant us wisdom, grant us courage (R)
470 grant us courage for the facing of this hour (1)
470 grant us courage for the living of these days (2)
470 grant us courage lest we miss thy kingdom's goal (3)
470 grant us courage that we fail not man nor thee (4)
470 grant us courage serving thee whom we adore (5)
479 as we worship, grant us vision (3)
490 birds pass high in flight, fragrant flowers now bloom (1)
495 grant to little children visions bright of thee (3)
517 grant us, then, pure hearts and patient (3)
517 grant us then a deeper insight & new powers of sacrifice (4)
518 and grant that we may feast in paradise with thee (1)
520 grant, Love Divine, in every place glad fellowship (3)
522 Lord of harvest, grant that we wholesome grain ... be (2)
522 grant that we wholesome grain and pure may be (2)

granted
55 hast thou not seen how thy desires ... hath been granted (2)
55 desires ... granted in what he ordaineth (2)

grantest
 526 thou grantest pardon through thy love (2)

grants
  9 grants the prisoner sweet release (3)
 231 when comforts are declining, he grants the soul again (1)
 445 He lives, and grants me daily breath (3)
 458 to whom he manifests his love & grants his name to know (3)

grapes
 545 he is trampling out the vintage where the grapes (1)
 545 where the grapes of wrath are stored (1)

grasp
 303 send hope before to grasp it, till hope be lost in sight (3)
 326 here grasp with firmer hand eternal grace (1)

grass
  45 in the rustling grass I hear him pass (2)

grateful
  4 that men may hear the grateful song (4)
  35 Lord of all, to thee we raise this our hymn of grateful (R)
  35 this our hymn of grateful praise (R)
 147 with grateful hearts, O God, to thee (1)
 347 hence with grateful hearts today (1)
 349 in grateful service ... now their strong foundation lay (2)
 472 let every creature rise and bring his grateful honors (5)
 472 his grateful honors to our King (5)
 498 we with grateful hearts would gather (1)
 509 with grateful hearts the past we own (3)
 515 since every day by thee we live, may grateful hearts (4)
 515 may grateful hearts thy gifts receive (4)
 552 our grateful songs before thy throne arise (1)

gratefully
 473 O gratefully sing his power and his love (1)

gratitude
 199 each loving life a psalm of gratitude (3)
 514 God ... take the gratitude we give (1)

grave
  83 he saves me from the grave (3)
 113 by thy triumph o'er the grave (3)
 124 him who triumphed o'er the grave (4)
 136 we rise with him to life which soars beyond the grave (4)
 175 snatch them in pity from sin and the grave (1)
 289 where is death's sting, where, grave, thy victory (4)
 391 now ye need not fear the grave (3)
 419 eagle eye could pierce beyond the grave (2)
 421 tongue lies silent in the grave (5)
 439 ours the cross, the grave, the skies, Alleluia (4)
 441 in the grave they laid him, Love whom men had slain (2)
 441 he that for three days in the grave had lain (3)
 443 who endured the cross and grave, Alleluia (2)
 443 endured the cross & grave ... sinners to redeem and save (2)

444   up from the grave he arose (R)
444   low in the grave he lay (T,1)
455   crown him the Lord of life, who triumphed o'er the grave (2)
493   teach me to live, that I may dread the grave as little (3)
493   dread the grave as little as my bed (3)

graven
294   dear as the apple of thine eye, and graven on thy hand (2)

graves
550   the God they trusted guards their graves (3)

gray
462   in the gray valley let us hear thy silent voice (4)

graze
512   the flocks in pastures graze (2)

great
1   my great Redeemer's praise (1)
2   here, great God, today we offer of thine own to thee (4)
3   to thee, great One in Three eternal praises be (4)
7   praising God for his great love (2)
14   the great salvation loud proclaim (3)
17   how great thou art (T,R)
17   and there proclaim, my God, how great thou art (4)
20   his craft and power are great (1)
25   great God, attend, while Zion sings (T,1)
27   almighty, victorious, thy great name we praise (1)
27   to all, life thou givest, to both great and small (3)
27   great Father of glory, pure Father of light (4)
31   strong is his arm, and shall fulfill his great decrees (3)
31   his great decrees and sovereign will (3)
34   all creatures great and small (R)
34   how great is God Almighty, who has made all things well (4)
35   for that great, great love of thine (4)
39   sing the great Jehovah's praise and bless his holy name (1)
39   come, the great day, the glorious hour (3)
40   many and great, O God, are thy things (T,1)
43   their great Original proclaim (1)
54   thy providence protected them who thy great name adored (3)
62   their great story, God is love, and God is light (1)
76   all the heavenly orders in their great array (2)
78   at the great name of Jesus, now all knees must bend (2)
86   thou art the great high priest (2)
89   to me, with thy great name, are given pardon (2)
93   to grace how great a debtor daily I'm constrained to be (3)
98   great Shepherd of thy chosen few (3)
100   Jesus, our great high priest, hath full atonement made (2)
113   by thy cross and dying cries, by thy one great sacrifice (2)
124   ask ye what great thing I know (T,1)
124   this is that great thing I know ... delights & stirs me (4)
127   bold shall I stand in thy great day (2)
128   'tis done: the great transaction's done (3)
134   our love so faint,so cold to thee & thine to us so great (4)
136   preach to all thy great good news (2)
161   thou Christ of great compassion (1)

174 rise up, and make her great (3)
179 take thy great power and reign there alone (3)
186 all I think or speak or do is one great sacrifice (4)
189 join the glorious new crusade of our great Lord and King (3)
190 Great Lord of years and days (2)
192 one great fellowship of love (1)
196 my vows I will to his great name before his people pay (3)
199 follow with reverent steps the great example of him (3)
201 in thy great salvation, show forth thy boundless love (3)
242 some great cause, God's new Messiah (1)
250 stand ...in his great might ... all his strength endued (2)
253 to thee and thy great name (4)
256 thou my great Father, and I thy true son (2)
271 guide me, O thou great Jehovah (T,1)
281 hallow thy great and glorious name (2)
282 my great Redeemer's throne (2)
283 let us see thy great salvation perfectly restored (4)
297 the great Church victorious shall be the Church at rest (3)
326 the Lamb's great bridal feast of bliss and love (5)
339 the harvest truly, Lord, is great; the laborers are few (2)
340 of thy great love to tell (3)
343 Great God, to thee we consecrate our voices & our skill (3)
349 of God's great temple thou (1)
350 altar raise to thy great glory, God of praise (1)
352 to the great One in Three (4)
356 one great Church go forth in might to work God's .. will (4)
359 hail to the Lord's anointed, great David's greater Son (T,1)
361 the Wonderful, the Counselor, the great and mighty Lord (3)
365 great Son of Righteousness, arise (5)
371 myriad tongues, in one great anthem blending (4)
379 here let all, great and small kneel in awe and wonder (3)
381 we hear the Christmas angels the great glad tidings tell (4)
382 seek the great Desire of nations (3)
383 and to the earth it gave great light (2)
394 glad tidings of great joy I bring to you and all mankind (2)
408 One Lord, in one great name united us all who own thee (3)
409 the great congregation his triumph shall sing (2)
410 and Christ's great kingdom shall come on earth (R)
410 that all of the world's great peoples might come (4)
422 thus the great Messiah came to break the tyrant's will (3)
429 the great redeeming work is done (1)
461 O come, great Spirit, come (1,4)
464 see how great a flame aspires (T,1)
468 and glorify thy name. For great thou art (3)
468 and wonders great by thy strong hand are done (3)
488 sing holy, holy, holy, to the great God Triune (1)
509 Great God, we sing that mighty hand (T,1)
510 sing to the Great Jehovah's praise (T,1)
528 or sing my great deliverer's praise (1)
532 now praise we great and famous men (T,1)
532 praise we the great of heart and mind (3)
533 how great their joys, how bright their glories be (1)
541 men who fly through the great spaces of the sky (1)
547 protect us by thy might, Great God, our King (4)

greater
203 a splendor greater yet while serving thee (4)
359 hail to the Lord's anointed, great David's greater Son (T,1)

greatly
481   how its splendor challenges the souls that greatly dare (5)

greatness
15   praise the holy God of love, and all his greatness show (1)
285   the greatness of redeeming love (1)
479   light in its height and depth and greatness dawns (3)

greed
194   of selfish greed and fruitless gain (2)
200   whom shall I send to loosen the bonds of shame and greed (1)
204   from paths where hide the lures of greed (2)
407   the curse of greed, the moan of pain (2)
476   help us to spread thy gracious reign till greed .. cease (2)
476   till greed and hate shall cease (2)
481   O shame to us who rest content while lust and greed (3)
481   lust and greed for gain in street and shop and tenement (3)
482   ride on till tyranny and greed are evermore undone (3)

green
68   he makes me down to lie in pastures green (1)
230   green pastures are before me, which yet I have not seen (3)
291   sweet fields arrayed in living green & rivers of delight (1)
414   there is a green hill far away, beyond the city wall (T,1)
441   now the green blade riseth from the buried grain (T,1)
441   love is come again like wheat that springeth green (R)
442   gold the green enhancing (1)
485   when ever blue the sky shall gleam ... green the sod (2)

greet
232   and heaven comes down our souls to greet (4)
302   greet the blood redeemed hands on the eternal shore (5)
380   and we greet in his cradle our Savior and King (4)
385   whom angels greet with anthems sweet (1)
386   yea, Lord, we greet thee, born this happy morning (3)
396   praises voicing greet the morrow (2)
490   rise to greet the sun, reddening the sky (T,1)

greets
450   lovingly he greets thee, scatters fear and gloom (2)

grief
4   through all grief distressing (3)
83   he bore the shameful cross ... carried all my grief (2)
89   from sin ... grief & shame, I hide me, Jesus in thy name (1)
89   in grief my joy unspeakable (4)
95   take my guilt and grief away (1)
142   in the hour of grief or pain will lean upon its   God (2)
161   who by this sign didst conquer grief and pain (5)
177   in joy, in grief, through life, dear Lord, for thee (4)
185   let sorrow do its work, come grief or pain (3)
204   from woman's grief, man's burdened toil (3)
209   bear patiently the cross of grief or pain (1)
209   when disappointment, grief, and fear are gone (3)
214   therefore the evil shall receive but grief (3)
223   not a grief nor a loss, not a frown or a cross (2)

251 not in grief to harm ... while thy love is left to me (3)
253 a soul inured to pain, to hardship, grief and loss (2)
270 when drooping pleasure turns to grief (3)
275 in seasons of distress and grief (1)
317 our hearts distressed by people's grief (2)
338 joy .. grief .. time .. place .. life nor death can part (4)
401 pierce the gloom of sin and grief (3)
415 drops of grief can ne'er repay the debt of love I owe (5)
418 O sacred Head ... with grief and shame weighed down (1)
420 and say, was ever grief like his (3)
431 heeds not his Master's grief and tears (2)
479 still in grief men mourn their dead (2)

griefs
52 from all our griefs and fears, O Lord (2)
113 by thy human griefs and fears (1)
143 while life's dark maze I tread & griefs around me spread (3)
261 all our sins and griefs to bear (1)
263 out of my stony griefs Bethel I'll raise (4)
434 turn not from his griefs away (1)
469 sharing not our griefs, no joy can share (2)

grieve
105 and shall I dare his spirit grieve (3)
112 long-sought sinners, why will you grieve ... God and die (3)
178 like thee, O Lord, to grieve (3)
279 no more thy goodness grieve (3)
280 no more thy goodness grieve (3)
519 may we not his spirit grieve (1)

grieved
279 let me weep my life away for having grieved thy love (2)
280 let me weep my life away for having grieved thy love (2)

grieves
379 brethren, come, from all that grieves you, you are freed (2)

grieving
441 when our hearts are wintry, grieving, or in pain (4)
505 cease we fearing, cease we grieving (3)

grim
20 the Prince of Darkness grim, we tremble not for him (3)

groaned
415 for crimes that I have done he groaned upon the tree (2)

groaning
528 groaning beneath your load of sin (5)

groans
428 hark, how he groans, while nature shakes (2)

groom
490 warrior-like and strong, comely as a groom (1)

grope
269 unhelped by thee, in error's maze we grope (2)

groping
106   groping on in darkness drear (2)

ground
   5   we're marching thro' Emmanuel's ground (4)
   5   celestial fruit on earthly ground (3)
  24   watery worlds are all his own, and all the solid ground (2)
  37   if I survey the ground I tread, or gaze upon the sky (2)
  98   and every place is hallowed ground (1)
222   all other ground is sinking sand (R)
234   from the ground there blossoms red life (4)
238   Christian, dost thou see them on the holy ground (T,1)
392   nor thorns infest the ground (3)
394   all seated on the ground (1)

grovel
134   look how we grovel here below (2)

grow
   5   fruit ... from faith and hope may grow (3)
  10   the earth is not too low, his praises there may grow (1)
  41   teach us more of human pity that we in thine image grow (3)
  60   the flowers and fruits that in thee grow (4)
  67   where the verdant pastures grow (2)
106   hearts grow faint, and hopes give o'er, whisper softly (2)
146   let knowledge grow from more to more (5)
167   let not my star of hope grow dim or disappear (2)
193   up unto thee, our living Head let us in all things grow (3)
214   in drought their branches grow abundantly (2)
289   earth's joys grow dim; its glories pass away (2)
316   when these failing lips grow dumb ... mind & memory flee (4)
345   may faith grow firm, and love grow warm (4)
392   no more let sins and sorrows grow (3)
430   here earth's bitter things grow sweet (1)
514   take the finest of our harvest, crops we grow (1)
514   crops we grow that men may live (1)

growing
244   when I'm growing old and feeble, stand by me (4)
442   life in all.. growing powers toward .. light is striving (1)
517   when our growing sons and daughters look on life (4)

grown
144   life's dreary waste with thorns o'er-grown (3)
522   unto joy or sorrow grown (2)

grows
189   the chorus clearer grows that shepherds heard of old (1)
464   more & more it spreads and grows ever mighty to prevail (2)
500   thy kingdom stands, and grows forever, till all ... own (4)

guard
  28   be ...our guard while troubles last and our eternal home (6)
  31   his wrath and justice stand to guard his holy law (2)
  53   hand which bears all nature up shall guard his children (2)

53   that hand .... shall guard his children well (2)
172   still let me guard the holy fire (3)
180   guard my first springs of thought and will (2)
236   guard thou the lips from sin, the hearts from shame (2)
246   my soul, be on thy guard, ten thousand foes arise (T,1)
253   forever standing on its guard and watching unto prayer (3)
307   save it from evil, guard it still (3)
337   by day and night strict guard to keep (4)
385   King, whom shepherds guard and angels sing (R)
491   guard us through the coming night (1,2,3)
491   Lover of men, O hear our call, and guard and save us (4)
491   guard and save us from them all (4)
495   guard the sailors tossing on the deep, blue sea (3)
541   Lord, guard and guide the men who fly (T,1)
551   O guard our shores from every foe (2)

guarded
216   nor plague approach thy guarded home (6)
498   sure of being safely guided, guarded well from every foe (2)
509   by day, by night, at home, abroad, still we are guarded (2)
509   we are guarded by our   God (2)

guardian
51   publish with our latest breath thy love & guardian care (4)
57   thy guardian never sleeps (2)
121   be the guardian of our way (2)
164   O speak, and make me listen, thou guardian of my soul (3)
509   the future ... we to thy guardian care commit (3)
552   be thou our ruler, guardian, guide and stay (2)

guards
25   guards our way from all the assaults of hell and sin (3)
25   guards ... from foes without and foes within (3)
25   God is our shield, he guards our way (3)
389   the glorious gates of paradise the angel guards no more (4)
496   angel guards from thee surround us (2)
497   may thine angel guards defend us (1)
550   where their pilgrim feet have trod ... God ... guards (3)
550   the God they trusted guards their graves (3)

guerdon
99   if I find him, if I follow, what his guerdon here (4)

guess
466   for none can guess its grace, till he become the place (3)

guest
102   let every soul be Jesus' guest (1)
111   come quickly in, thou heavenly guest (4)
260   our heart's dear guest, to thee our prayers ascend (1)
318   as thy guest in heaven receive me (3)
319   every humble, contrite heart is made a welcome guest (1)

guidance
42   laws ... for our guidance hath he made (1)

guide

29	to guide whate'er we nobly do (4)
46	guide of all who seek the land above (1)
47	be thou our guide (2)
49	and keep us in his grace, and guide us when perplexed (2)
50	so that earth's bliss may be our guide ... not our chain (3)
52	eternal wisdom is their guide, their help omnipotence (1)
57	thy going out, thy coming in, forever he will guide (4)
59	beside us to guide us, our God with us joining (2)
67	thy cross before to guide me (4)
77	he is our guide and friend; to us he'll condescend (2)
84	O Guide to every child of thine (T,1)
86	ever be thou our guide (3)
99	hath he marks to lead me to him if he be my guide (2)
106	Holy Spirit, faithful guide (T,1)
106	wanderer, come, Follow me, I'll guide thee home (R)
125	safe into the haven guide; O receive my soul at last (1)
143	be thou my guide; bid darkness turn to day (3)
163	so kind and true and tender, so wise a counselor & guide (3)
164	no wander from the pathway if thou wilt be my guide (1)
170	and guide them in the homeward way (2)
205	who through life has been my guide (1)
209	God doth undertake to guide ... future as ... the past (2)
210	if thou but suffer God to guide thee (T,1)
230	wherever he may guide me, no want shall turn me back (2)
240	cast care aside, lean on thy guide (3)
251	God's own hand shall guide thee there (4)
254	shine to shame and guide this life of mine (1)
259	be thou my guide, and save me, who for me hast died (3)
266	take time to be holy, let him be thy guide (3)
271	guide me, O thou great Jehovah (T,1)
289	who, like thyself, my guide and stay can be (3)
311	be her Savior, Lord, and guide (1)
311	may she guide the poor and blind (3)
344	and ever by thy Spirit guide (4)
351	be pleased to guide, each lengthening year, thy sons (2)
365	and make thy Word my guide to heaven (6)
368	guide & chart, wherein we read of realms beyond the sky (2)
397	need no star to guide, where no clouds thy glory hide (4)
400	guide where our infant Redeemer is laid (1,5)
402	guide us to thy perfect light (R)
467	where thou art guide, no ill can come (3)
487	lead and guide our acts of praise (2)
517	hope to trust them, faith to guide them (4)
530	move and actuate and guide; divers gifts to each divide (3)
539	by his counsels guide, uphold you (1)
541	Lord, guard and guide the men who fly (T,1)
552	be thou our ruler, guardian, guide and stay (2)

guided

345	may they who err be guided here to find the better way (3)
498	sure of being safely guided, guarded well from every foe (2)

guides

372	mid mists & rocks & quick-sands, still guides ...to thee (3)
372	still guides, O Christ, to thee (3)

guiding
84 praise in all simplicity the guiding Christ,our shepherd (1)
86 guiding in love and truth through devious ways (1)
269 without thy guiding hand we go astray (1)
342 lo, I am with you alway. We take thy guiding hand (4)
371 guiding our steps to thine eternal day (1)
397 as with gladness men of old did the guiding star behold (T)
413 thy guiding radiance above us shall be a beacon to God (R)
550 O God, beneath thy guiding hand (T,1)

guile
243 by any lure or guile enticed (2)

guilt
95 take my guilt and grief away (1)
127 from sin and fear, from guilt and shame (2)
143 take all my guilt away (1)
161 didst save us...from sin and guilt (4)
188 cleanse it from guilt & wrong; teach it salvation's song (3)
431 for others' guilt the Man of Sorrows weeps in blood (3)
526 our works could ne'er our guilt remove (2)

guilty
122 arise, my soul, arise; shake off thy guilty fears (T,1)
341 scatters all ... guilty fear .. turns .. hell to heaven (2)
350 the guilty soul a sure retreat (4)
421 lose all their guilty stains (1)
528 come, O my guilty brethren, come (5)

gushing
205 gushing from the rock before me...a spring of joy I see (2)

habitation
58 eternal arms, their dear abode, we make our habitation (1)
132 make our hearts thy habitation (2)
293 round each habitation hovering, see the cloud and fire (3)

habits
191 until the laws of Christ become the laws and habits (2)
191 laws and habits of the state (2)

hail
71 all hail the power of Jesus' name (T,1) (also 72,73)
71 hail him who saves you by his grace (2)
258 gladly hail the sun returning (2)
353 hail, Christ the Lord! (5)
359 hail to the Lord's anointed, great David's greater Son (T,1)
359 hail in the time appointed, his reign on earth begun (1)
379 hail the star, that from far bright with hope is burning (3)
387 hail the heaven-born Prince of Peace (3)
387 hail the Sun of Righteousness (3)
387 hail the incarnate Deity (2)
395 praise his name in all the earth; Hail the King of glory (3)
398 light of the world, we hail thee (T,1)
437 hear, so calm and plain, his own "All hail" (2)
452 speak his sorrows ended; hail his triumph now (2)
454 hail, thou once despised Jesus (T,1)
454 hail, thou Galilean King (1)

454 hail ... universal Savior who hast borne our sin & shame (1)
455 and hail him as thy matchless King through all eternity (1)
455 all hail, Redeemer, hail! for thou hast died for me (4)
482 we hail thine august majesty and loud hosanna sing (4)

hailed
397 as with joy they hailed its light (1)
404 angel chorus that hailed our Savior's birth (2)

hall
391 calls you all to gain his everlasting hall (3)
434 see him at the judgment hall (2)

Hallelujah
545 Glory! glory! Hallelujah ... His truth is marching on (R)

hallow
8 Lo! the apostolic train joins thy sacred name to hallow (3)
281 hallow thy great and glorious name (2)
314 hallow all our lives, O Lord (2)
499 if on our daily course our mind be set to hallow (3)
499 mind be set to hallow all we find (3)
500 thy praise shall hallow now our rest (1)

hallowed
15 hallowed be his name beneath (3)
94 oft profaned his hallowed name (2)
98 and every place is hallowed ground (1)
142 whate'er may come, I'll taste ... the hallowed bliss (4)
142 tastes even now the hallowed bliss of an eternal home (4)
186 accept my hallowed labor now, I do it unto thee (3)
345 round these hallowed walls the storm of... passion dies (4)
372 praise thee for the radiance ... from the hallowed page (1)
520 build thou a hallowed dwelling where ... joy & peace (4)
520 hallowed dwelling where true joy and peace endure (4)
528 shall I, the hallowed cross to shun (3)

halls
303 they stand, those halls of Zion, all jubilant with song (2)
346 and let these halls thy temple be (3)
366 we follow till the halls we see where ... sup with thee (2)
366 halls we see where thou hast bid us sup with thee (2)

halt
102 ye poor, and maimed, and halt, and blind (3)

hand
4 as with a mother's tender hand (3)
31 the thunders of his hand keep the wide world in awe (2)
32 the Lord uplifts his awful hand and chains you (2)
33 the hand that shaped the rose hath wrought the crystal (1)
41 man ... creature that thy hand hath made (2)
41 hast given man dominion o'er the wonders of thy hand (3)
43 publishes to every land the work of an almighty hand (1)
43 the hand that made us is divine (3)
45 of skies and seas; his hand the wonders wrought (1)
47 in all the past ... thy hand we see (1)
47 through all our hopes and fears, thy hand we see (1)

47   God of the past, our times are in thy hand (2)
48   upheld by my righteous, omnipotent hand (2)
51   how wise, how strong his hand (3)
53   hand which bears all nature up shall guard his children (2)
53   that hand .... shall guard his children well (2)
54   thy right hand thy powerful arm ..1 his full hand supplies their need (3)
88   waving a branch of a palm tree high in my hand (3)
96   thou didst reach forth thy hand and mine enfold (2)
106 gently lead us by the hand, pilgrims in a desert land (1)
108 O Jesus, thou art knocking, and lo, that hand is scarred (2)
120 in my hand no price I bring; simply to thy cross I cling (2)
167 into thy hand of love I would my all resign (1)
184 imprison me within thine arms ... strong ... be my hand (1)
195 I may stretch out a loving hand to wrestlers (2)
206 God of the ages, by whose hand (T,1)
206 by whose hand through years long past our lives were led (1)
206 in thy strong hand eternally rests the ... years (3)
211 what terror can confound me, with God at my right hand (1)
213 O let thy hand support me still (4)
217 for by his hand he leadeth me (R)
217 still 'tis God's hand that leadeth me (1)
217 He leadeth me, by his own hand he leadeth me (R)
217 still 'tis his hand that leadeth me (2)
217 by waters still, o'er troubled sea ... hand ... leadeth (2)
217 Lord, I would place my hand in thine (3)
219 hand in all things I behold ... all things in thy hand (4)
237 grant that I may never fail thy hand to see (3)
243 upheld and strengthened by thy hand (3)
249 his own hand presents the prize to thine aspiring eye (3)
251 God's own hand shall guide thee there (4)
269 without thy guiding hand we go astray (1)
271 hold me with thy powerful hand (1)
289 I fear no foe, with thee at hand to bless (4)
294 dear as the apple of thine eye, and graven on thy hand (2)
301 our high calling's glorious hope ... hand in hand go on (3)
324 blessing in his hand, Christ our God to earth descendeth (1)
326 here grasp with firmer hand eternal grace (1)
337 Savior, like stars in thy right hand thy servants ... be (2)
340 heart to heart, & hand to hand ... make thine honor ours (2)
342 lo, I am with you alway. We take thy guiding hand (4)
346 ocean ... sleeps in the hollow of his hand (2)
347 thy hand unseen amidst us wrought (2)
438 but now at God's right hand he stands (1)
457 enthroned at God's right hand he sits (2)
462 touch thou our dust with spirit-hand (2)
462 Spirit consoling, let us find thy hand (4)
462 let us find thy hand when sorrows leave us blind (4)
464 saw ye not the cloud arise, little as a human hand (4)
468 surely to such as do him fear salvation is at hand (2)
468 and wonders great by thy strong hand are done (3)
490 all my countless needs thy kind hand supplies (3)
506 sharing ... the hand that gives the flowers (2)
509 mighty hand by which supported still we stand (1)
509 Great God, we sing that mighty hand (T,1)
511 farm .. market, shop .. home, of mind and heart and hand (1)
513 but it is fed and watered by God's almighty hand (1)
518 by thine own hand may we be fed (2)
524 now, on this... festal day thy bounteous hand confessing (2)

550   O God, beneath thy guiding hand (T,1)
552   almighty hand leads forth in beauty all the starry band (1)

handiwork
44   when I regard the wondrous heavens,thy handiwork on high (2)

handle
326   here would I touch and handle things unseen (1)

hands
2   thou ... ears and hands and voices for thy praise design (3)
2   heart and minds ... hands and voices ... choicest melody (4)
17   consider all the worlds thy hands have made (1)
35   for thy church that evermore lifteth holy hands above (5)
40   thy hands have set the heavens with stars (1)
49   now thank we all our God with heart and hands and voices (T
66   in his hands he gently bears us (3)
94   Savior stands, holding forth his wounded hands (4)
99   in his feet and hands are wound-prints, and his side (2)
112   fatal cause demands, asks the work of his own hands (1)
122   my name is written on his hands (1)
140   Father, I stretch my hands to thee (T,1)
141   life nor death can pluck his children from his hands (3)
186   my hands are but engaged below   (5)
187   take my hands ... let them move ... impulse of thy love (1)
192   join hands ... brothers of the faith whate'er your race (3)
267   place in my hands the wonderful key (1)
302   by faith we join our hands with those that went before (5)
302   greet the blood redeemed hands on the eternal shore (5)
308   a house not made with hands (4)
312   we bring them, Lord, in thankful hands (3)
335   might fill an angel's heart and filled a Savior's hands (2)
345   accept the walls that human hands have raised ...to thee (1)
345   hands have raised, O God, to thee (1)
346   his hands built not for one brief day (1)
351   these storied walls our hands have made (4)
355   O wounded hands of Jesus, build in us thy new creation (4)
406   immortal tidings in your mortal hands (1)
411   empower the hands and hearts and wills of friends (2)
435   see, from his head, his hands, his feet, sorrow and love (3)
455   crown him the Lord of love; behold his hands and side (4)
515   may the hands be pure from stain with which...we gain (4)
529   look on thy hands, and read it there (2)

hang
62   by him upholden hang the glorious orbs of light (1)

hangs
125   other refuge have I none; hangs my helpless soul on thee (2)
464   hangs o'er all the thirsty land (4)

happier
255   I sigh to think of happier days, when thou...wast nigh (3)

happiness
300   they are happy now ... we soon their happiness shall see (2)

happy
9   happy the man whose hopes rely on Israel's God (2)
38   ocean depth of happy rest (3)
38   mortals join the happy chorus, which the... stars began (4)
89   thy mighty name salvation ... keeps my happy soul above (2)
115   how happy every child of grace (T,1)
115   happy ... who knows his sins forgiven (1)
128   O happy day, that fixed my choice (T,1)
128   O happy bond, that seals my vows to him (2)
183   how happy are the saints above (2)
223   trust and obey, for there's no other way to be happy (R)
223   no other way to be happy in Jesus, but to trust and obey (R)
224   I in my Savior am happy and blest (3)
227   O how happy are they who the Savior obey (T,1)
288   O happy, happy soul! in ecstacies of praise (2)
291   cast a wishful eye to Canaan's fair and happy land (1)
291   when I shall reach that happy place ... be forever blest (3)
297   O happy ones and holy! Lord, give us grace that we (4)
300   they are happy now ... we soon their happiness shall see (2)
304   O holy kingdom, happy fold, the blessed Church to be (2)
305   onward, then, ye people, join our happy throng (4)
328   how happy are thy servants, Lord, who thus remember thee (T)
341   happy, if with my latest breath I may but gasp his name (6)
386   yea, Lord, we greet thee, born this happy morning (3)
452   welcome, happy morning   age to age shall say (T,1,4)
474   yet a season, and you know happy entrance will be given (3)
516   happy the home where Jesus' name is sweet to every ear (2)
516   happy the home where prayer is heard (3)
516   happy the home where ... praise is wont to rise (3)
516   happy the home when God is there (T,1)
535   happy the souls to Jesus joined (T,1)

harbinger
468   before him righteousness shall go, his royal harbinger (1)

harbor
148   trying now to make the harbor (3)

hard
246   hosts of sin . pressing hard to draw thee from the skies (1)
251   life with trials hard may press me (3)
376   earth stood hard as iron, water like a stone (1)

hardness
279   the burden of my soul remove, the hardness from my heart (4)
280   burden from my soul remove, the hardness from my heart (4)

hardship
253   a soul inured to pain, to hardship, grief and loss (2)

hark
8   hark, the glad celestial hymn (2)
312   hark, how he calls the tender lambs (1)
388   hark, the herald angels sing (T,1,R)
428   hark, how he groans, while nature shakes (2)
453   hark, those bursts of acclamation (4)

453 hark, those loud triumphant chords (4)
455 hark ... heavenly anthem drowns all music but its own (1)
481 hark, how from men whose lives are held more cheap (2)

harken
111 thro' grace we harken to thy voice (3)

harlots
528 harlots and publicans and thieves (4)

harm
 75 who put their trust in thee... death nor hell shall harm (3)
216 no deadly shaft by day shall harm (5)
236 from harm and danger keep thy children free (3)
237 or its sordid treasures spread to work me harm (2)
251 not in grief to harm ... while thy love is left to me (3)
290 no harm from him can come to me on ocean or on shore (4)

harmest
 84 thou man-pursuing Fisherman, who harmest not but savest (2)

harmony
 35 for the mystic harmony liking sense to sound and sight (3)
328 tongue can tell our sweet accord ... perfect harmony (1)

harp
 15 celebrate the eternal God with harp and psaltery (2)
366 with harp and cymbal's clearest tone (3)

harps
  2 angel harps forever ringing, rest not day nor night (1)
390 angels bending near ... earth to touch ... harps of gold (1)

hart
255 as pants the hart for cooling streams (T,1)

harvest
 97 sunshine and rain, harvest of grain, He's my friend (2)
339 Lord of the harvest, hear the needy servants' cry (T,1)
339 the harvest truly, Lord, is great; the laborers are few (2)
513 seed-time & the harvest, our life, our health, our food (3)
514 take the finest of our harvest, crops we grow (1)
522 raise the song of harvest home (1)
522 Lord of harvest, grant that we wholesome grain ... be (2)
522 God shall come, and shall take his harvest home (3)
522 even so,Lord, quickly come, bring thy final harvest home (4)
522 raise the glorious harvest home (4)
524 thrice blessed ... harvest song ... never hath an ending (3)

harvest's
 97 he sends the harvest's golden grain (2)

harvests
523 when harvests ripen, thou art there, who givest all (2)
548 not alone for bounteous harvests lift we up our hearts (1)

haste
- 53 haste to your heavenly Father's throne (3)
- 90 haste, let us lay our gifts before the King (1)
- 204 O Master, from the mountainside, make haste to heal (5)
- 204 make haste to heal these hearts of pain (5)
- 251 haste thee on from grace to glory (4)
- 299 O Zion, haste, thy mission high fulfilling (T,1)
- 299 O Zion, haste to bring the brighter day (4)
- 385 haste to bring him laud, the babe, the son of Mary (R)
- 474 rise, my soul, and haste away to seats prepared above (1)

hasten
- 152 hasten to thy glorious day (3)
- 164 O speak to reassure me, to hasten or control (3)
- 275 I hasten to the place where God my Savior shows his face (2)
- 277 hasten the joyful day which shall my sins consume (2)
- 379 come, then, let us hasten yonder (3)
- 434 early hasten to the tomb (4)
- 485 hasten, Lord ... perfect day when pain & death ... cease (2)
- 485 hasten, Lord...thy just rule (2)

hastening
- 142 will not murmur nor complain beneath the chastening rod (2)
- 209 the hour is hastening on (3)
- 390 lo! the days are hastening on, by prophet seen of old (3)

hastens
- 59 he chastens and hastens his will to make known (1)

hate
- 20 armed with cruel hate, on earth is not his equal (1)
- 178 thy foes might hate, despise, revile (2)
- 191 men with hearts ablaze .. truth to love .. wrong to hate (4)
- 191 wrong to hate; these are the patriots nations need (4)
- 251 foes may hate, and friends may shun me (2)
- 268 I hate the sins that ... drove thee from my breast (4)
- 268 I hate the sins that made thee mourn (4)
- 355 in the night of hate and war we perish as we lose thee (3)
- 412 that man to judge thee hath in hate pretended (1)
- 476 till greed and hate shall cease (2)

hatreds
- 189 human hatreds flee before the radiant eastern skies (1)

haunt
- 477 that war may haunt .. earth no more and desolation cease (4)

haunted
- 475 would man but wake from out his haunted sleep (2)

haunts
- 204 in haunts of wretchedness and need (2)
- 318 leave the gloomy haunts of sadness (1)

haven
- 125 safe into the haven guide; O receive my soul at last (1)

hay
90 there in a manger on the hay reclining (1)
384 the little Lord Jesus, asleep on the hay (1)

haze
532 names have perished, lost in the haze of long ago (5)

head
44 with honor thou hast crowned his head (4)
51 God shall lift up thy head (1)
62 praise to Christ our gracious head (3)
68 my head thou dost with oil anoint, and my cup overflows (4)
83 his head with radiant glories crowned (1)
117 weary one, lay down, thy head upon my breast (1)
123 how that Bethlehem's babe could in the God-head be (1)
125 cover my defenseless head with the shadow of thy wing (2)
127 with joy shall I lift up my head (1)
137 make to us the God-head known, & witness with the blood (1)
193 up unto thee, our living Head let us in all things grow (3)
206 new faith to find the paths ahead (1)
213 and raise my head, and cheer my heart (3)
215 and shall break in blessings on your head (3)
234 O Cross that liftest up my head (4)
298 Christ the head and cornerstone (1)
329 we drink of thee, the fountain-head (3)
338 joined in one spirit to our Head (2)
375 worship we the God-head, Love incarnate, Love divine (2)
384 the little Lord Jesus laid down his sweet head (1)
387 veiled in flesh the   God-head see (2)
400 low lies his head with the beasts of the stall (2)
415 would he devote that sacred head for sinners such as I (1)
416 light of sacred story gathers round its head sublime (1,5)
418 O sacred head, now wounded (T,1)
418 O sacred Head ... with grief and shame weighed down (1)
425 bow thy meek head to mortal pain (4)
428 see ... he bows his sacred head ... bows his head & dies (3)
435 see, from his head, his hands, his feet, sorrow and love (3)
439 following our exalted Head, Alleluia (4)
440 child of God, lift up thy head (3)
445 he lives, my everlasting Head (1)
457 come, let us rise with Christ our Head (T,1)
458 the head that once was crowned with thorns (T,1)
472 and endless praises crown his head (2)
475 yet thou, her child, whose head is crowned with flame (1)
527 alive in him, my living Head (4)

headed
34 the purple-headed mountain, the river running by (2)

heads
232 place where Jesus sheds the oil of gladness on our heads (2)
363 lift up your heads, ye mighty gates (T,1)

heal
95 hear and heal me now, I pray (1)
103 earth has no sorrow that heaven cannot heal (1)

118 pity and heal my sin-sick soul (2)
125 heal the sick, and lead the blind (3)
145 heal my wounded, broken spirit, save me by thy grace (3)
154 touch me and heal me, Savior divine (3)
161 to heal earth's wounds and endd her bitter strife (2)
204 O Master, from the mountainside, make haste to heal (5)
204 make haste to heal these hearts of pain (5)
212 there is a balm in Gilead, to heal the sinsick soul (R)
292 sinsick and sorrow-worn, whom Christ doth heal (1)
408 heal its ancient wrong, come, Prince of Peace, and reign (3)
411 where'er they heal the maimed and blind (3)
411 where'er they heal ... let love of Christ attend (3)
422 to heal the people of their shame, and nobleness instill (3)
496 thou canst save, and thou canst heal (1)
501 and in thy mercy heal us all (6)

healed
66 ransomed, healed, restored, forgiven (1)
479 as, O Lord, thy deep compassion healed the sick (2)
479 healed the sick and freed the soul (2)

healing
4 with healing balm my soul he fills (1)
69 is mercy with the Savior; there is healing in his blood (1)
89 the healing of my broken heart (3)
90 we would see Jesus in his work of healing (4)
119 poor, wretched, blind; sight, riches, healing of... mind (4)
124 revives my fainting heart, healing all it hidden smart (2)
125 let the healing streams abound (4)
157 the healing of his seamless dress is by our beds of pain (4)
208 in simple faith to plunge me neath the healing ... flood (2)
208 plunge me neath the healing, cleansing flood (2)
231 it is the Lord, who rises with healing in his wings (1)
259 where'er thy healing beams arise (2)
271 whence the healing stream doth flow (2)
371 questing hearts that long for peace and healing see (3)
387 risen with healing in his wings (3)
433 there a precious fountain, free to all, a healing stream (1)
433 healing stream flows from calvary's mountain (1)
471 abroad thy healing influence shower (3)
480 thou who didst come to bring ... healing and sight (2)
546 solace .. its wide dominion .. the healing of thy wings (1)

heals
65 thy diseases all who heals (2)
81 it soothes his sorrows, heals his wounds (1)

health
1 music in the sinner's ears ... life and health and peace (3)
55 O my soul, praise him, for he is thy health & salvation (1)
284 in all my pain and misery be thou my health and life (3)
458 the cross he bore is life and health (6)
471 Spirit of grace and health and power (3)
479 hope and health, good will and comfort (4)
480 health to the sick in mind, sight to the inly blind (2)
485 just rule ... fill ... earth with health & light & peace (2)
504 banish our weakness, health and wholeness sending (2)
513 seed-time & the harvest, our life, our health, our food (3)

518   for life and health and every good (2)
519   health and food and clothes to wear (1)
525   for life and health, those common things (2)

healthful
291   can reach that healthful shore (2)
523   for peaceful homes and healthful days (3)

hear
1   hear him, ye deaf; his praise, ye dumb (6)
2   can we feel that thou art near ... hear ...? yea, we can (2)
2   can we feel that thou art near us and wilt hear us? (2)
4   that men may hear the grateful song (4)
7   hear the angel voices blending ... praise to God on high (1)
17   I see the stars, I hear the rolling thunder (1)
17   and hear the birds sing sweetly in the trees (2)
17   and hear the brook and feel the gentle breeze (2)
36   and when the morning breaks in power, we hear thy word (3)
36   we hear thy word, "Let there be light" (3)
45   in the rustling grass I hear him pass (2)
55   all ye who hear,now to his temple draw near (1)
60   make music for thy Lord to hear, Alleluia (3)
78   O Christ, thou Savior of us all ... hear us when we call (1)
78   we pray thee, hear us when we call (1)
88   tell me the stories of Jesus I love to hear (T,1)
88   first let me hear how the children stood round his knee (2)
91   powers of darkness fear, when this sweet chant they hear (2)
95   hear and heal me now, I pray (1)
100   the gospel trumpet hear, the news of heavenly grace (4)
105   God calling yet! shall I not hear (T,1)
106   while they hear that sweetest voice (1)
106   while they hear that sweetest voice whispering softly (1)
107   by thy mercies, Savior, may we hear thy call (5)
110   hear him today, hear him today (4)
121   blessed Jesus! Hear, O hear us, when we pray (2)
122   my God is reconciled; his pardoning voice I hear (4)
128   that vow renewed shall daily hear (5)
132   O hear our supplication, Blessed Spirit, God of peace (2)
136   truth which all may hear (3)
143   Savior divine! now hear me while I pray (1)
145   pass me not, O gentle Savior, hear my humble cry (T,1)
145   Savior, Savior, hear my humble cry (R)
149   hungering and thirsting to hear it like the rest (4)
151   O how our hearts beat high with joy whene'er we hear (1)
151   whene'er we hear that glorious word (1)
153   give us courage, let us hear heaven's trumpets ringing (2)
157   we own thy sway, we hear thy call (6)
164   I see the sights that dazzle, the tempting sounds I hear (2)
164   O let me hear thee speaking in accents clear and still (3)
173   O grant that love of country may help us hear his call (3)
173   once more to hear thy challenge above our noisy day (5)
185   hear thou the prayer I make on bended knee (1)
197   in duty's call, thy call we hear to fuller life (2)
200   I hear my people crying in cot and mine and slum (2)
202   centuries still we hear the Master's winsome call (2)
204   we hear thy voice, O Son of man (1)
238   Christian, dost thou hear them, how they speak thee fair (3)

247   while leaning on thy breast may I hear thee (3)
247   hear thee say to me, "Fear not, I will pilot thee" (3)
257   we are gathered all to hear thee (1)
257   hear the cry thy people raises (3)
257   hear, and bless our prayers and praises (3)
260   to hear thy voice we need but love ... listen & be still (3)
262   to hear the whispers of thy grace & hear thee inly speak (4)
267   open my eyes, that I may hear voices of truth (2)
298   with thy wonted loving-kindness hear thy people (2)
298   hear thy people when they pray (2)
308   we hear within the solemn voice of her unending song (2)
311   we beseech thee, hear us (1,2,3,4,5)
339   Lord of the harvest, hear the needy servants' cry (T,1)
342   we hear the call, O Lord, that comes from thee (1)
366   nor eye hath seen, nor ear hath yet attained to hear (3)
366   nor ear hath yet attained to hear what there is ours (3)
373   but hear the angel's warning (1)
379   all my hear this night rejoices (T,1)
379   as I hear, far and near, sweetest angels voices (1)
381   no ear may hear his coming, but in this world of sin (3)
381   we hear the Christmas angels the great glad tidings tell (4)
390   world in solemn stillness lay to hear the angels sing (1)
391   now ye hear of endless bliss (2)
407   we hear the throb of surging life, the clank of chains (2)
433   Jesus, keep me hear the cross (T,1)
434   It is finished, hear him cry (3)
437   listening to his accents, may hear, so calm and plain (2)
437   hear, so calm and plain his own "All hail!" (2)
459   pray we that thou wilt hear us, still imploring (5)
462   in the gray valley let us hear thy silent voice (4)
462   let us hear thy silent voice: "Lo, I am near" (4)
475   still wilt not hear thine inner God proclaim (1)
480   hear us, we humbly pray (1)
484   O God of earth and altar, bow down and hear our cry (T,1)
487   hear our prayers as they ascend (1)
491   Lover of men, O hear our call, and guard and save us (4)
501   hear, in this solemn evening hour (6)
507   if thou art well pleased to hear, come down (4)
526   Lord, hear me, I implore thee (1)
529   I hear thy whisper in my heart (4)
530   hear us, who thy nature share, who thy mystic body are (1)
531   to feel thy power, to hear thy voice, to taste thy love (4)
538   hear us when we cry to thee for those in peril on... sea (R)
542   O hear my song, thou God of all the nations (2)
542   O hear my prayer, thou God of all the nations (3)
551   of every clime and coast, O hear us for our native land (1)

heard
32   his voice sublime is heard afar (4)
107   as of old the apostles heard it by the Galilean lake (2)
117   I heard the voice of Jesus say (T,1,2,3)
128   high heavens, that heard the solemn vow (5)
149   some have never heard the message of salvation (3)
159   I have heard thy voice, and it told thy love to me (1)
159   I am thine, O Lord, I have heard thy voice (T,1)
189   the chorus clearer grows that shepherds heard of old (1)
193   and know our prayer is heard (1)

235   simple trust like theirs who heard beside the Syrian sea (2)
274   Master, let it now be heard (1)
274   though least and lowest, let me not unheard depart (3)
274   make me ready when thy voice is truly heard (4)
282   where only Christ is heard to speak (2)
349   here make his message heard (3)
374   angels we have heard on high (T,1)
395   shepherds saw .. wondrous sight, heard .. angels singing (2)
396   saw the glory, heard the story, tidings of a Gospel true (2)
431   unheard by mortals are the strains that sweetly soothe (4)
480   thou, whose almighty Word chaos and darkness heard (T,1)
480   chaos and darkness heard and took their flight (1)
516   happy the home where prayer is heard (3)
538   O Christ, whose voice the waters heard (2)
538   waters heard and hushed their raging at thy word (2)

heard'st
550   thou heard'st well pleased, the song, the prayer (2)

hearest
253   know thou hearest my prayer (1)
253   with humble confidence look up and know thou hearest (1)
260   thou hearest these, the good and ill (2)

heareth
274   Master, speak! thy servant heareth (T,1)

hearing
437   and, hearing, may raise the victory strain (2)

hears
51   God hears thy sighs and counts thy tears (1)
366   midnight hears the welcome voices (1)
366   Zion hears the watchmen singing (2)
507   never will throw off his fear who hears our solemn vow (4)
122   the Father hears him pray, His dear anointed One (4)

heart
2   heart and minds ... hands and voices ... choicest melody (4)
3   thou who almighty art, now rule in every heart (3)
4   be joyful in the Lord, my heart (4)
10   more than all, the heart must bear the longest part (2)
12   what heart can comprehend thy name (2)
13   to my heart O enter thou, let it be thy temple now (2)
15   all the powers of music bring, the music of the heart (2)
16   with heart and soul and voice (1)
23   bound every heart with rapturous joy (3)
30   deep writ upon the human heart, on sea or land (2)
35   for the heart and mind's delight (3)
45   why should my heart be sad? The Lord is King (3)
49   now thank we all our God with heart and hands and voices (T)
56   praises of my God shall still my heart and tongue employ (1)
60   ye men of tender heart, forgiving others, take your part (5)
64   yet to each loving heart how near (1)
69   the heart of the Eternal is most wonderfully kind (2)
70   before my infant heart could know from whom...comforts (2)
75   thou only canst inform the mind and purify the heart (2)

77	let all, with heart and voice, before his throne rejoice (1)
79	Jesus is purer, who makes the woeful heart to sing (2)
81	weak is the effort of my heart (4)
82	nor voice can sing, nor heart can frame (2)
82	O Hope of every contrite heart, O Joy of all the meek (3)
85	Heart of God incarnate, Love-bearer to mankind (3)
89	the healing of my broken heart (3)
91	when morning gilds the skies, my heart awaking cries (T,1)
91	the night becomes as day when from the heart we say (2)
92	'twas grace that taught my heart to fear (2)
92	yea, when this flesh and heart shall fail (5)
93	tune my heart to sing thy grace (1)
93	let thy goodness, like a fetter, bind my wandering heart (3)
93	let thy goodness ... bind my wandering heart to thee (3)
93	here's my heart, O take and seal it (3)
105	shall he knock, and I my heart the closer lock (3)
105	he calls me still; my heart, awake (4)
105	I cannot stay; my heart I yield without delay (5)
105	the voice of God hath reached my heart (5)
111	stands knocking at the door of every sinner's heart (2)
116	long my heart has sighed for thee (2)
124	revives my fainting heart, healing all it hidden smart (2)
125	spring thou up within my heart (4)
128	well may this glowing heart rejoice (1)
128	now rest, my long-divided heart (4)
129	bring joy to my desolate heart (4)
130	my longing heart vouchsafe to make thine ... throne (4)
133	until my heart is pure, until with thee I will one will (2)
135	Holy Spirit, Love divine, glow within this heart of mine (2)
137	testify to all mankind, and speak in every heart (3)
138	Spirit of God, descend upon my heart (T,1)
138	all, all thine own, soul, heart and strength and mind (3)
138	my heart an altar, and thy love the flame (5)
138	I see thy cross; there teach my heart to cling (3)
141	have faith in God, my heart, trust and be unafraid (T,1)
141	I rest, heart, mind, and soul the captive of thy grace (4)
143	may thy rich grace impart strength to my fainting heart (2)
160	and brace thy heart and nerve thine arm (2)
162	with a child's glad heart of love (2)
163	and round my heart still closely twine those ties (1)
163	my heart, my strength, my life, my all are his (2)
169	with no reserve and no delay, with all my heart, I come (2)
170	help me the slow of heart to move (2)
172	the mean altar of my heart (1)
172	kindle a flame of sacred love on ... altar of my heart (1)
173	that learns to value beauty, in heart or brain or soul (4)
174	give heart and mind and soul and strength to serve (1)
175	down in the human heart, crushed by the tempter (3)
175	touched by a loving heart, wakened by kindness (3)
177	in love my soul would bow, my heart fulfill its vow (1)
177	give me a faithful heart, likeness to thee (3)
178	unwearied ... forgiveness still, thy heart ... only love (2)
182	with a glad heart and free (1)
184	my heart is weak and poor until it master find (2)
185	this be the parting cry my heart shall raise (4)
186	my heart is still with thee (5)
187	take my heart, it is thine own (3)

187   my heart ... it shall be thy royal throne (3)
195   the hidden depths of many a heart (3)
195   until my very heart o'erflow in kindling thought (4)
198   in every heart and brain shall throb the pulse of one (3)
199   O brother man, fold to thy heart thy brother (T,1)
204   thy heart has never known recoil (3)
207   through days of toil when heart doth fail (2)
210   heart content to take whate'er thy Father's pleasure (2)
211   his might thy heart shall strengthen (2)
213   search, prove my heart, it yearns for thee (1)
213   when sinks my heart in waves of woe (3)
213   and raise my head, and cheer my heart (3)
219   let me ... think of thee ... new heart springs up in me (2)
220   truest friend to me, long my heart hath panted (1)
220   though the earth be shaking, every heart be quaking (2)
225   make in my heart a quiet place ... come & dwell therein (1)
227   when my heart first believed, what a joy I received (2)
230   the storm may roar without me, my heart may low be laid (1)
230   in heavenly love abiding no change my heart shall fear (T,1)
233   rejoice, ye pure in heart (T,1)
234   my heart restores its borrowed ray (2)
234   I cannot close my heart to thee (3)
250   the troubled heart thy comfort blest (4)
255   when every heart was tuned to praise (3)
256   be thou my vision, O Lord of my heart (T,1)
256   thou and thou only, first in my heart (3)
256   Heart of my own heart, whatever befall ... be my vision (4)
257   open thou our ears and heart (3)
259   O knit my thankful heart to thee (1)
262   here...my God, vouchsafe to stay & bid my heart rejoice (3)
262   my bounding heart shall own thy sway & echo to thy voice (3)
267   open my heart and let me prepare love with thy children (3)
273   God, who touchest earth with beauty, make my heart anew (5)
273   make my heart anew (1)
274   Master speak ...thou knowest ..the yearning of my heart (3)
276   blest are the pure in heart for they shall see ... God (T,1)
276   for his dwelling & his throne selects the pure in heart (3)
276   O give the pure and lowly heart, a temple meet for thee (4)
278   Jesus, thine all-victorious love shed in my heart abroad (T)
278   refining fire, go through my heart; illuminate my soul (2)
278   no longer ... my heart shall mourn ... purified by grace (3)
278   Christ is all the world to me, and all my heart is love (4)
279   the burden of my soul remove, the hardness from my heart (4)
280   burden from my soul remove, the hardness from my heart (4)
281   give me a new, a perfect heart (4)
282   O for a heart to praise my God (T,1)
282   heart that always feels thy blood so freely shed for me (1)
282   a heart resigned, submissive, meek (2)
282   a humble, lowly, contrite heart (3)
282   a heart in every thought renewed and full of love divine (4)
282   a heart from sin set free (1)
282   write thy new name upon my heart (5)
283   visit us with thy salvation; enter every trembling heart (1)
285   when shall I find my willing heart all taken up by thee (1)
285   O that it now were shed abroad in this poor stony heart (3)
286   Lord I want to be like Jesus in my heart (4)
286   Lord, I want to be more loving in my heart (2)

286   Lord, I want to be a Christian in my heart (T,1)
286   Lord, I want to be more holy in my heart (3)
290   if my heart and flesh are weak to bear an untried pain (2)
290   forgive me if too close I lean my human heart on thee (3)
295   my very heart and flesh cry out, O Loving God, for thee (2)
295   in whose heart are thy ways (5)
303   beneath the contemplation sink heart and voice oppressed (1)
306   we shall still be joined in heart and hope to meet again (4)
309   make us of one heart and mind, courteous, pitiful & kind (3)
310   Lord, let every bounding heart the mighty comfort feel (4)
313   Savior, abide with us, and spread thy table in our heart (1)
319   every humble, contrite heart is made a welcome guest (1)
319   brethren, all, let every heart with kind affection glow (2)
320   look on the heart by sorrow broken (2)
321   in our daily life may flame the passion of thy heart (4)
335   might fill an angel's heart and filled a Savior's hands (2)
337   to bear thy people on their heart (3)
338   our bodies may far off remove, we still are one in heart (1)
338   partakers of the Savior's grace ... same in mind & heart (4)
340   heart to heart, & hand to hand ... make thine honor ours (2)
342   we cultivate the nature God plants in every heart (3)
344   blindness both of heart and mind (2)
348   rest to the heart by sin oppressed (2)
351   from hence send forth a race of men of flaming heart (3)
351   race of men of flaming heart and stalwart mind (3)
352   do thou the truth impart unto each waiting heart (3)
354   bind all peoples in one heart and mind (3)
360   dear desire of every nation, joy of every longing heart (1)
363   fling wide the portals of your heart (2)
363   heart ... make it a temple, set apart (2)
366   all her heart with joy is springing (2)
376   yet what can I give him: give my heart (4)
391   with heart and soul and voice (1,2,3)
392   let every heart prepare him room (1)
398   Light of the world, thy beauty steals into every heart (2)
399   thou hast won my heart to serve thee solely (1)
399   O deep within my heart now shine (2)
399   here in sadness eye and heart long for thy gladness (2)
401   inward light impart, cheer my eyes and warm my heart (2)
401   Day-star, in my heart appear (1)
403   thou shalt find thy heart made truly his (2)
407   who hast the nations in thy heart (1)
407   the heart that bled and broke to send God's love (1)
415   dissolve my heart in thankfulness (4)
417   from my stricken heart with tears two wonders I confess (2)
423   O may we ever praise him with heart and life and voice (3)
438   his grace ... doth impart eternal sunshine to the heart (3)
459   O Triune God, with heart and voice adoring (5)
466   O Comforter, draw near, within my heart appear (1)
469   envious of heart, blind-eyed, with tongues confounded (3)
471   in every heart reign thou alone (2)
476   in speech that flows to melody, in holiness of heart (4)
479   not of voice alone, but heart (1)
482   O thou whose dreams enthrall the heart, ride on (3)
483   lift up your heart, lift up your voice (R)
487   heart and soul consecrate on this thy holy day (4)
503   heart of love enfolding all (3)

511   farm .. market, shop .. home, of mind and heart and hand (1)
520   within .. home let every heart become thy dwelling place (2)
527   my chains fell off, my heart was free (3)
528   refuse ... to impart by hiding it within my heart (3)
528   his bleeding heart shall make you room (5)
529   speak to my heart, in blessing speak (3)
529   I hear thy whisper in my heart (4)
531   my heart is pained, nor can it be at rest (1)
531   that strives with thee my heart to share (2)
531   then shall my heart from earth be free (2)
531   my heart ... be free, when it hath found repose in thee (2)
531   chase this self-will from all my heart (3)
531   each moment draw from earth away my heart (4)
531   my heart that lowly waits thy call (4)
532   praise we the great of heart and mind (3)
542   this is my home, the country where my heart is (1)
547   my heart with rapture thrills, like that above (2)
       a heart from sin set free (1)

heart's
47   our heart's true home when all our years have sped (3)
172   Jesus, confirm my heart's desire to work ... for thee (3)
260   our heart's dear guest, to thee our prayers ascend (1)
400   richer by far is the heart's adoration (4)
490   my heart's freed from ill, fair blue sky's above (3)

hearted
179   truehearted, wholehearted, faithful and loyal (T,1)
179   true hearted, whole hearted, fullest allegiance (2)
179   true-hearted, whole-hearted, Savior all-glorious (3)
311   and the broken-hearted bind (3)

hearth
33   love deepens round the hearth (2)
380   every hearth is aflame, and the beautiful sing (3)

hearts
1   mournful, broken hearts rejoice; the humble poor believe (5)
38   hearts unfold like flowers before thee (1)
41   lifting up our hearts in praise (1)
41   'tis thy will our hearts are seeking (4)
49   with ever joyful hearts and blessed peace to cheer us (2)
52   in the confidence of prayer our hearts take hold on thee (2)
64   kindling hearts that burn for thee (5)
74   that in our darkened hearts thy grace might shine (1)
76   in your hearts enthrone him (4)
77   come, lift your hearts on high; Alleluia! Amen! (2)
78   all hearts must bow; all things celestial thee shall own (2)
83   had I a thousand hearts to give, Lord ... all be thine (4)
98   here, to our waiting hearts, proclaim the sweetness (3)
102   O let his love your hearts constrain (4)
103   here bring your wounded hearts, here tell your anguish (1)
106   hearts grow faint, and hopes give o'er, whisper softly (2)
107   give our hearts to thine obedience (5)
131   come, Holy Ghost, our hearts inspire (T,1)
132   make our hearts thy habitation (2)
134   kindle a flame of sacred love in ... cold hearts of ours (1)

136 till Christ shall dwell in human hearts (1)
139 to thee our humble hearts aspire (2)
147 with grateful hearts, O God, to thee (1)
151 O how our hearts beat high with joy whene'er we hear (1)
153 daring hearts and spirits free (1)
161 speak to our fearful hearts by conflict rent (1)
165 fill our hearts with joy and peace (1)
165 may the fruits of thy salvation in our hearts and lives (2)
165 in our hearts and lives abound (2)
173 stand with humble courage for truth with hearts uncowed (1)
173 create in us... splendor that dawns when hearts are kind (4)
178 O give us hearts to love like thee (3)
189 to this clear call of brotherhood our hearts ... ring (3)
189 our hearts responsive ring (3)
191 men with hearts ablaze .. truth to love .. wrong to hate (4)
192 in him shall true hearts everywhere ... communion find (2)
193 let all our hearts agree (4)
194 lift up our hearts, O King of kings (T,1)
203 our hearts enthralled while serving thee (3)
204 make haste to heal these hearts of pain (5)
214 their joyful, faithful hearts obey the laws of God (1)
236 guard thou the lips from sin, the hearts from shame (2)
251 human hearts and looks deceive me (2)
257 let our hearts and souls be stirred (1)
262 speak to our hearts . let us feel . kindling of thy love (1)
270 our hearts still whispering, "Thou art near!" (2)
283 set our hearts at liberty (2)
303 O sweet and blessed country that eager hearts expect (4)
304 deep in loving human hearts its broad foundations rise (1)
304 our hearts in love and worship turn to find themselves (2)
304 hearts ... turn to find themselves in thee (2)
304 hearts with love & longing ... find their rest in thee (1)
306 blest be the tie that binds our hearts in Christian love (T)
307 planted thy holy name within our hearts (1)
314 in our hearts keep watch and ward (4)
317 our hearts distressed by people's grief (2)
328 hearts and minds and spirits join, and all in Jesus meet (3)
329 Jesus, thou joy of loving hearts (T,1)
332 fills .. faithful people's hearts with...the life of God (1)
347 hence with grateful hearts today (1)
352 with hearts aflame (2)
352 glad songs to thee we sing; glad hearts to thee we bring (4)
355 O love that triumphs over loss we bring our hearts (4)
355 we bring our hearts before thy cross (4)
360 by thine own eternal spirit rule in all our hearts alone (2)
363 our hearts to thee we open wide (3)
368 to its heavenly teaching turn with ... childlike hearts (4)
368 simple, child-like hearts (4)
371 questing hearts that long for peace and healing see (3)
374 while our hearts in love we raise (4)
381 God imparts to human hearts the blessings of his heaven (3)
385 let loving hearts enthrone him (3)
410 that shall turn their hearts to the right (1)
410 song ... that shall lift their hearts to the Lord (2)
411 empower the hands and hearts and wills of friends (2)
430 pressing onward as we can ..to this our hearts must tend (4)
437 our hearts be pure from evil, that we may see aright (2)

440 holiest hearts for ages pleading (2)
441 when our hearts are wintry, grieving, or in pain (4)
441 fields of our hearts that dead and bare have been (4)
449 and sing with hearts uplifted high: Alleluia (3)
451 on this most holy day of days, our hearts ... we raise (5)
451 our hearts and voices, Lord, we raise to thee (5)
457 our hearts detached from all below ... after him ascend (1)
457 to him our willing hearts we give (3)
459 to thee in reverent love our hearts are bowed (2)
460 speaketh to the hearts of men (3)
461 come as the fire, and purge our hearts (2)
461 purge our hearts like sacrificial flame (2)
464 kindled in some hearts it is (1)
470 free our hearts to work and praise (2)
471 inflame our hearts with perfect love (4)
476 in whom all hearts find rest (2)
476 kindness dwell in human hearts and... earth find peace (2)
487 look into our hearts & minds today ... this thy holy day (1)
487 save us and cleanse our hearts (2)
491 the joys of day are over; we lift our hearts to thee (2)
492 we lift our hearts to thee, O Day-star from on high (T,1)
498 we would praise thee and surrender all our hearts (2)
498 surrender all our hearts to be thine own (2)
498 we with grateful hearts would gather (1)
503 through ... stars that veil thy face our hearts ascend (3)
506 O Spirit, pure and holy, possess these hearts so lowly (5)
509 with grateful hearts the past we own (3)
513 and what thou most desirest, our humble, thankful hearts (3)
515 since every day by thee we live, may grateful hearts (4)
515 may grateful hearts thy gifts receive (4)
516 unite our hearts in love to thee (4)
517 grant us, then, pure hearts and patient (3)
524 to thee, O Lord, our hearts we raise (T,1)
524 our hearts we raise in hymns of adoration (1)
536 and hearts are brave again, and arms are strong (5)
542 but other hearts in other lands are beating with hopes (1)
542 and hearts united learn to live as one (3)
545 sifting out the hearts of men before his judgment seat (3)
548 not alone for bounteous harvests lift we up our hearts (1)
548 lift we up our hearts to thee (1)
552 thy true religion in our hearts increase (3)

hearty
102 in Christ a hearty welcome find (3)

heat
417 burning of the noon-tide heat and the burden of the day (1)
466 passions turn to dust and ashes in its heat consuming (2)

heated
255 when heated in the chase (1)

heaven
2 best that thou hast given, earth and heaven render thee (5)
8 all in heaven above adore thee (1)
13 there a heaven on earth must be (2)
15 as in heaven on earth adored (3)

15   from whom all good proceeds ... earth and heaven adore (1)
16   and wing to heaven our thought! (3)
25   the glorious hosts of heaven obey (4)
33   sent the hoary frost of heaven,the flowing waters sealed (1)
35   peace on earth, and joy in heaven (6)
38   earth and heaven reflect thy rays (2)
41   when we see thy lights of heaven ...thy power displayed (2)
42   heaven, and earth, and all creation, laud and magnify (2)
49   the one eternal God, whom earth and heaven adore (3)
57   Lord alone, who heaven and earth has made (1)
60   ye clouds that sail in heaven along, O praise him (2)
66   praise, my soul, the King of heaven (T,1)
74   confess ...in heaven and earth that Jesus Christ is Lord (5)
79   Jesus shines purer, than all the angels heaven can boast (3)
87   Hope of earth and joy of heaven (R)
87   King of kings in heaven we'll crown him (4)
89   to me ... are given pardon and holiness and heaven (2)
89   my life in death, my heaven in hell (4)
98   and bring all heaven before our eyes (4)
99   not till earth and not till heaven pass away (6)
103   earth has no sorrow that heaven cannot cure (2)
103   earth has no sorrow that heaven cannot heal (1)
103   earth has no sorrow but heaven can remove (3)
106   nothing left but heaven and prayer (1)
109   all so freely given, wooing us to heaven (2)
114   can my gracious Savior show my name inscribed in heaven (1)
115   I seek my place in heaven (1)
115   the heaven prepared for me (1)
138   the kindling of the heaven descended Dove (5)
139   pardon and holiness and heaven (4)
145   whom have I on earth beside thee...in heaven but thee (4)
147   if on a quiet sea, toward heaven we calmly sail (T,1)
152   and closely walk with thee to heaven (4)
161   God's gift from highest heaven (2)
166   I'll ever adore thee in heaven so bright (3)
184   flag can ...be unfurled when thou... breathe from heaven (3)
188   till earth, as heaven, fulfill God's holy will (3)
196   we sing the songs of heaven (5)
204   glorious from thy heaven above shall come the city (6)
227   what a heaven in Jesus's name (2)
227   'twas a heaven below my Redeemer to know (3)
232   and heaven comes down our souls to greet (4)
251   how rich is my condition: God & heaven are still my own (1)
251   heaven will bring me sweeter rest (3)
252   he enters heaven with prayer (5)
256   High King of heaven, my treasure thou art (3)
256   High King of heaven, my victory won (4)
262   enter into my Master's joy, and find my heaven in thee (4)
263   there let the way appear, steps unto heaven (3)
264   breathe each day nearness unto thee and heaven (3)
271   bread of heaven, feed me till I want no more (1)
281   whose word, when heaven and earth shall pass, remains (1)
283   joy of heaven, to earth come down (1)
283   till in heaven we take our place (4)
285   let earth and heaven and all things go (4)
285   nothing in heaven above (4)
294   and brighter bliss of heaven (5)

297 from heaven he came and sought her to be his holy bride (1)
302 all the servants of our King, in earth & heaven are one (2)
310 that we may meet in heaven (3)
314 by the call to heaven above us (2)
315 and feed and train us up for heaven (1)
316 thy body, broken for my sake, my bread from heaven (2)
318 let me be a fit partaker of ... blessed food from heaven (2)
318 as thy guest in heaven receive me (3)
324 rank on rank the host of heaven spreads its vanguard (3)
325 the King of heaven his table spreads (T,1)
325 rich blood that Jesus shed to raise our souls to heaven (2)
326 here drink with thee the royal wine of heaven (3)
331 precious banquet, bread of heaven (1)
340 till earth and heaven together blend their praises (4)
341 scatters all ... guilty fear .. turns .. hell to heaven (2)
342 in heaven & earth thy power ... bring God's kingdom here (4)
344 discipline ... to train and bring them up for heaven (1)
350 this thy house, the gate of heaven (5)
352 till we our God and King shall praise in heaven (4)
357 O ye heights of heaven, adore him (2)
361 on his shoulder ever rests all power on earth and heaven (2)
365 and make thy Word my guide to heaven (6)
368 with thee how could ... heaven itself be won (3)
376 our God, heaven cannot hold him, nor earth sustain (2)
376 heaven and earth shall flee away when he comes to reign (2)
381 God imparts to human hearts the blessings of his heaven (3)
384 and fit us for heaven to live with thee there (3)
386 O sing, all ye citizens of heaven above (2)
387 Christ, by highest heaven adored (2)
389 for he uncloses heaven today and gives to us his Son (1)
389 takes ...a servant's form who made the heaven and earth (2)
389 and we of heaven partake (3)
392 and heaven and nature sing (1)
393 glories stream from heaven afar (2)
394 good will ... from heaven to men begin and never cease (6)
397 bend the knee before him whom heaven and earth adore (2)
405 out of thee the Lord from heaven came to rule his Israel (1)
411 O Father, look from heaven and bless ... their works (5)
414 might go at last to heaven saved by his precious blood (3)
414 he only could unlock the gate of heaven and let us in (4)
419 they climbed the steep ascent of heaven through peril (3)
423 for Christ is our Redeemer, the Lord of heaven our King (3)
429 the living way to heaven is seen (2)
438 feast this Easter Day on the true bread of heaven (4)
438 and brings us life from heaven (1)
440 Life eternal! heaven rejoices (3)
440 saints all longing for their heaven (3)
451 the King of heaven, the glorious King (1)
452 hell today is vanquished, heaven is won today (1,4)
453 while the vault of heaven rings (2)
454 opened is the gate of heaven (2)
456 the heaven that hides him from our sight knows (2)
456 heaven ... knows neither near nor far (2)
458 highest place ... heaven affords belongs to him by right (2)
458 name an everlasting name; their joy the joy of heaven (4)
469 building proud towers which shall not reach to heaven (3)

474   rise from transitory things toward heaven (1)
474   rise ... toward heaven, thy native place (1)
474   all our sorrows left below .. earth exchanged for heaven (3)
483   His kingdom cannot fail, he rules o'er earth and heaven (3)
486   though earth and sea and heaven unite thy praise to sing (1)
486   silent courage pleads to heaven more eloquent than song (3)
488   on thee our Lord victorious the Spirit sent from heaven (2)
497   God, that madest earth and heaven, darkness and light (T,1)
498   shining on our steps from heaven above (1)
499   new thoughts of God, new hopes of heaven (2)
502   in the ocean of thy love we lose ourselves in heaven (6)
502   we lose ourselves in heaven above (6)
503   heaven is touching earth with rest (1)
503   Heaven and earth are full of thee (R)
503   Heaven and earth are praising thee, O Lord most high (R)
504   bring us to heaven, where thy saints united joy (2)
505   soon as dies the sunset glory, stars of heaven shine (2)
505   stars of heaven shine out above (2)
510   bring the grand sabbatic year, the jubilee of heaven (6)
513   all good gifts around us are sent from heaven above (R)
518   the bread of life sent down from heaven (3)
521   nesting bird nor star in heaven such a refuge ... given (1)
523   O Lord of heaven and earth and sea (T,1)
523   for means of grace and hopes of heaven (4)
528   how shall I all to heaven aspire (1)
528   blest with this antepast of heaven (2)
533   the long cloud of witnesses show the same path to heaven (2)
535   walking in all his ways, they find their heaven on earth (9)
535   they find their heaven on earth begun (1)

heaven's
18   death and rising tell the grace in heaven's plan (2)
77   on heaven's blissful shore his goodness we'll adore (3)
153   give us courage, let us hear heaven's trumpets ringing (2)
153   heaven's trumpets ringing clear (2)
251   heaven's eternal day's before thee (4)
256   may I reach heaven's joys, O bright heaven's Sun (4)
260   our spirits' unseen friend, high heaven's Lord (1)
260   not beat with cries on heaven's doors (3)
289   heaven's morning breaks, and earth's vain shadows flee (5)
317   Immanuel, heaven's joy unending (3)
354   fill the whole world with heaven's peace (3)
363   set apart ... from earthly use for heaven's employ (2)
390   from heaven's all-gracious King (1)
395   heaven's star shone brightly forth, glory all around him (2)
458   King of kings, & Lord of lords, & heaven's eternal light (2)
471   not heaven's hosts shall swifter move than we on earth (4)

heavenly
5   children of the heavenly King may speak ... joys abroad (2)
15   all the reach of heavenly art (2)
32   he speaks, and in his heavenly height (1)
53   haste to your heavenly Father's throne (3)
58   the heavenly shield around them spread (2)
58   the heavenly shield ... is still high holden o'er us (2)
64   one holy light, one heavenly flame (5)

76	all the heavenly orders in their great array (2)
84	know thee ... and call thee heavenly Father (3)
86	thou hast prepared the feast of heavenly love (2)
95	heavenly Father, bless me now (T,1)
100	the gospel trumpet hear, the news of heavenly grace (4)
111	come quickly in, thou heavenly guest (4)
115	we more than taste the heavenly powers (2)
128	here heavenly pleasures fill my breast (4)
134	come, Holy Spirit, heavenly Dove (T,1,5)
139	their heavenly origin display (5)
157	we may not climb the heavenly steeps (2)
180	praise him above, ye heavenly host (4)
205	heavenly peace, divinest comfort (1)
209	be still my soul: thy best, thy heavenly friend (1)
217	O words with heavenly comfort fraught (1)
230	in heavenly love abiding no change my heart shall fear (T,1)
249	a heavenly race demands thy zeal and an immortal crown (1)
268	a calm and heavenly frame (1)
269	lead us, O Father, to thy heavenly rest (4)
284	through darkness & perplexity point ...the heavenly way (4)
294	beyond my highest joy I prize her heavenly ways (4)
300	children of the heavenly King (T,1)
304	its heavenly walls unseen around us rise (1)
313	that living bread ... heavenly wine be our immortal food (2)
319	thus anticipate by faith the heavenly feast above (4)
324	he will give to all.. faithful .. self for heavenly food (2)
326	this is the heavenly table spread for me (2)
332	how can heavenly spirits rise by earthly matter fed (3)
332	let us taste the heavenly powers (4)
335	souls for whom the Lord did heavenly bliss forego (3)
351	by men and heavenly hosts adored (1)
351	and secret of thy heavenly peace (2)
365	bless the dark world with heavenly light (5)
367	O may these heavenly pages be my ever dear delight (3)
368	stream from the fount of heavenly grace (1)
368	to its heavenly teaching turn with ... childlike hearts (4)
373	break forth, O beauteous heavenly light (T,1)
374	gladsome tidings be which inspire your heavenly song (2)
378	from God our heavenly Father a blessed angel came (3)
380	comes down through the night from the heavenly throng (4)
390	still ... heavenly music floats o'er all the weary world (2)
391	hath oped the heavenly door ... man is blessed evermore (2)
393	heavenly hosts sing Alleluia (2)
393	holy infant so tender and mild sleep in heavenly peace (1)
394	the heavenly babe you there shall find (4)
397	treasures bring, Christ, to thee, our heavenly King (3)
399	thou heavenly Brightness! Light divine! (2)
431	from heavenly plains is borne the song that angels know (4)
443	unto Christ, our heavenly King (2)
443	praise him, all ye heavenly host (3)
454	all the heavenly hosts adore thee (3)
455	hark ... heavenly anthem drowns all music but its own (1)
456	there heavenly splendors shine (2)
463	praised by all the heavenly host (1)
468	justice, from her heavenly bower look down on mortal men (1)
478	with deeds of love and mercy, the heavenly kingdom comes (2)

487   thou art our heavenly Friend (1)
488   today on weary nations the heavenly manna falls (3)
493   praise him above, ye heavenly host (5)
516   and one their heavenly rest (1)
521   children of the heavenly Father (T,1)
525   and warms our lives with heavenly fires (3)
549   then let us prove our heavenly birth in all we do & know (5)

heavens
  8   fill .. heavens with sweet accord: holy, holy, holy Lord (2)
 10   the heavens are not too high, his praise may thither fly (1)
 22   high as the heavens our voices raise (3)
 40   thy hands have set the heavens with stars (1)
 42   praise the Lord! ye heavens adore him (T,1)
 43   spangled heavens, a shining frame (1)
 44   when I regard the wondrous heavens,thy handiwork on high (2)
 45   let the heavens ring! God reigns: let the earth be glad (3)
128   high heavens, that heard the solemn vow (5)
231   beneath the spreading heavens no creature but is fed (3)
273   like the arching of the heavens lift my thoughts above (4)
318   high o'er all the heavens he reigneth (1)
365   the heavens declare thy glory, Lord (T,1)
366   now let all the heavens adore thee (3)
404   behold throughout the heavens there shone a holy light (1)
437   now let the heavens be joyful! Let earth her song begin (3)
439   sing, ye heavens, and earth reply, Alleluia (1)

heaviest
220   sin and hell ... with their heaviest storms assail us (2)

heavily
134   our souls, how heavily they go to reach eternal joys (2)

heavy
104   come,ye weary, heavy laden bruised & mangled by the fall (4)
261   are we weak & heavy laden, cumbered with a load of care (3)

Hebrews
424   the people of the Hebrews with palms before thee went (2)

heed
105   shall I give no heed, but still in bondage live (4)
160   take up thy cross, nor heed the shame (3)
200   we heed, O Lord, thy summons, and answer: here are we (3)
256   riches I heed not, nor man's empty praise (3)
335   and heed the call they give (1)
391   give ye heed to what we say: Jesus Christ is born today (1)

heedeth
412   while he nothing heedeth, God intercedeth (3)

heedless
 70   with heedless steps I ran (3)

heeds
431   e'n the disciple that he loved heeds not (2)
431   heeds not his Master's grief and tears (2)

height
32	he speaks, and in his heavenly height (1)
42	praise him, angels, in the height (1)
66	angels in the height, adore him (4)
130	the length,and breadth, and height to prove (1)
130	and sink me to perfection's height (5)
132	spread thy light from the height which knows no measure (1)
171	build us a tower of Christ-like height (2)
206	no height but we may find thee there (2)
227	O the rapturous height of that holy delight (5)
285	cannot reach the mystery ... length .. breadth .. height (2)
301	what height of rapture shall we know when...we meet (5)
304	the length, the breadth, the height are one (2)
358	traveler, o'er yon mountain's height see (1)
479	light in its height and depth and greatness dawns (3)
531	thou hidden love of God, whose height (T,1)
531	whose height, whose depth unfathomed no man knows (1)

heights
159	there are heights of joy that I may not reach till (4)
203	thy paths of service lead to blazoned heights (1)
203	blazoned heights and slopes of need (1)
309	all the heights of holiness (5)
357	O ye heights of heaven, adore him (2)
362	get thee up to the heights and sing (2)
366	the watchmen on the heights are crying (1)

heir
224	heir of salvation, purchase of God (1)

held
173	we marvel at the purpose that held thee to thy course (2)
203	neath the burdens there, thy sovereignty has held (3)
219	held in thy law, I stand (4)
481	hark, how from men whose lives are held more cheap (2)
481	lives are held more cheap than merchandise (2)

hell
25	guards our way from all the assaults of hell and sin (3)
31	subdues the powers of hell, confounds their dark designs (3)
48	that soul, though all hell should endeavor to shake (5)
62	earth and hell hath captive led (3)
75	who put their trust in thee... death nor hell shall harm (3)
89	my life in death, my heaven in hell (4)
160	cross endured to save thy soul from death and hell (3)
163	shall life or death, or earth or hell (3)
220	sin and hell in conflict fell (2)
220	sin and hell ... with their heaviest storms assail us (2)
285	stronger his love than death or hell (2)
305	gates of hell can never gainst that Church prevail (3)
324	powers of hell may vanish as the darkness clears away (3)
341	scatters all ... guilty fear .. turns .. hell to heaven (2)
341	though earth and hell oppose (4)
341	Jesus! the name high over all, in hell or earth or sky (T,1)
452	hell today is vanquished, heaven is won today (1,4)

464   shakes the trembling gates of hell (2)
483   the keys of death and hell are to our Jesus given (3)
528   I, a child of wrath & hell ... be called a child of God (2)

hell's
271   death of death and hell's destruction (3)
340   thou bidst us go with thee to stand against hell's (2)
340   stand against hell's marshalled powers (2)

help
3   help us thy name to sing, help us to praise! (1)
4   an ever present help and stay (3)
27   all praise we would render: O help us to see (4)
28   O God, our help in ages past (T,1,6)
48   I'll strengthen thee,help thee, and cause thee to stand (2)
52   eternal wisdom is their guide, their help omnipotence (1)
57   my help is from the Lord alone (1)
86   help thou dost not disdain, help from above (2)
89   my help and refuge from my foes (1)
93   here I raise mine Ebenezer, hither to thy help I'm come (2)
113   Savior,look with pitying eye; Savior, help me, or I die (R)
125   my trust on thee is stayed ... help from thee I bring (2)
140   no other help I know (1)
144   help me, throughout life's changing scene, by faith (1)
145   kneeling there in deep contrition, help my unbelief (2)
150   help me to watch and pray and on thyself rely (4)
154   wounded and weary, help me, I pray (3)
157   warm, sweet, tender, even yet a present help is he (3)
167   help me still to say, "My Lord, thy will be done" (1)
170   help me bear the strain of toil, the fret of care (1)
170   help me the slow of heart to move (2)
173   O help us walk unflinching in paths that lead to peace (3)
173   O grant that love of country may help us hear his call (3)
177   help me the cross to bear, thy wondrous love declare (2)
193   help us to help each other, Lord (2)
201   help us by deeds of mercy to show that thou art kind (2)
201   help us to seek thy kingdom that cometh from above (3)
211   in darkness and temptation, my light, my help is near (1)
239   is this vile world a friend to grace to help me...to God (3)
246   renew it boldly every day, and help divine implore (2)
254   help me, oppressed by things undone (2)
257   help us by thy spirit's pleading (3)
266   make friends of God's children, help those who are weak (1)
268   help me to tear it from thy throne and worship only thee (5)
279   help me the first approach to feel of pride (1)
280   help me the first approach to feel of pride or...desire (1)
289   help of the helpless, O abide with me (1)
298   Holy Zion's help forever and her confidence alone (1)
336   still he doth his help afford, and hides our life above (3)
340   we go to win the lost to thee; O Help us, Lord, we pray (1)
359   to help the poor and needy, and bid the weak be strong (2)
433   help me walk from day to day with its shadow o'er me (3)
445   He lives, to help in time of need (2)
454   help, ye bright angelic spirits (4)
454   help to sing of Jesus' merits (4)
454   help to chant Emmanuel's praise (4)

463 ever present help in need (1)
476 help us to spread thy gracious reign till greed .. cease (2)
499 help us, this & every day to live more nearly as we pray (4)
526 his help I wait with patience (3)

helped
269 unhelped by thee, in error's maze we grope (2)
532 who helped the right, and fought the wrong (2)

helper
20 our helper he amid the flood of mortal ills prevailing (1)
509 our helper, God, in whom we trust, in better worlds (5)

helpers
289 when other helpers fail and comforts flee (1)

helpest
398 and helpest them to render light back to thee again (2)

helpless
125 other refuge have I none; hangs my helpless soul on thee (2)
258 God hath tended with his care thy helpless hours (2)
289 help of the helpless, O abide with me (1)

helplessness
204 from tender childhood's helplessness (3)

helps
9 he helps the stranger in distress (3)

hence
3 eternal praise be, hence, evermore (4)
111 come quickly in ... nor ever hence remove (4)
220 hence, all thoughts of sadness! (3)
251 thou, from hence, my all shalt be (1)
347 hence with grateful hearts today (3)
351 from hence send forth a race of men of flaming heart (3)
529 speak, or thou never hence shalt move (3)

henceforth
16 henceforth forevermore (5)
177 that each departing day henceforth may see (3)
179 yielding henceforth to our glorious King (2)
478 henceforth in fields of conquest thy tents ... our home (1)

herald
359 before him on the mountains shall peace, the herald, go (3)
387 hark! the herald angels sing (T,1)
388 hark! the herald angels sing (T,1,R)

heralds
88 one of his heralds...I would sing loudest hosannas (3)
406 heralds of Christ, who bear the King's commands (T,1)
442 praise him, seers, heroes, kings, heralds of perfection (3)
476 inspire thy heralds of good news to live thy life divine (5)

herds
231 all the field should wither...flocks nor herds be there (4)

hereafter
298 hereafter in thy glory evermore with thee to reign (3)

herewith
332 drink herewith divine supplies and eat immortal bread (3)

hero's
370 statesmen's, teacher's, hero's treasure (1)

heroes
442 praise him, seers, heroes, kings, Heralds of perfection (3)
543 O beautiful for heroes proved in liberating strife (3)
548 for all heroes of the spirit, give we thanks ... O Lord (3)

heroic
243 heroic warriors, ne'er from Christ ... enticed (2)
413 and heroic spirits answer now, as then, in Galilee (4)

herself
295 the swallow also for herself provided hath a nest (3)

hid
27 in light inaccessible hid from our eyes (1)

hidden
89 thou hidden source of calm repose (T,1)
124 revives my fainting heart, healing all it hidden smart (2)
195 wing my words, that they may reach the hidden depths (3)
195 the hidden depths of many a heart (3)
252 the motion of a hidden fire that trembles in the breast (1)
260 secret thought .. hidden plan, wrought ..or unexpressed (2)
457 hidden life of Christ ... with Christ concealed above (3)
469 how shall we love thee, holy, hidden Being (4)
531 thou hidden love of God, whose height (T,1)
531 from all its hidden mazes there (3)

hide
26 holy, holy, holy! though the darkness hide thee (3)
89 from sin and grief and shame, I hide me, Jesus (1)
89 I hide me, Jesus, in thy name (1)
120 Rock of Ages, cleft for me, let me hide myself in thee (T,1)
120 Rock of Ages, cleft for me, let me hide myself in thee (3)
125 hide me, O my Savior hide (1)
204 from paths where hide the lures of greed (2)
216 with Almighty God abide and in his shadow safely hide (1)
216 his outspread pinions shall thee hide (4)
220 I will suffer naught to hide thee (1)
397 need no star to guide, where no clouds thy glory hide (4)
407 in lands, where shadows hide the light (3)
415 well might .. sun in darkness hide . shut his glories in (3)
415 I hide my blushing face while his dear cross appears (4)
496 darkness cannot hide from thee (3)
501 the very wounds that shame would hide (5)
502 O may no earth-born cloud arise to hide thee (1)
502 to hide thee from thy servant's eyes (1)
539 neath his wings securely hide you (2)

hides
215 behind a frowning providence he hides a smiling face (4)
336 still he doth his help afford, and hides our life above (3)
456 the heaven that hides him from our sight knows (2)

hideth
27 'tis only the splendor of light hideth thee (4)

hiding
247 hiding rock and treacherous shoal (1)
528 refuse ... to impart by hiding it within my heart (3)

hie
358 let thy wandering cease; hie thee to thy quiet home (3)

high
5 marching ... to fairer worlds on high (4)
7 alleluia! alleluia! glory be to God on high (1,2)
7 hear the angel voices blending ... praise to God on high (1)
10 the heavens are not too high, his praise may thither fly (1)
15 timbrels soft and cymbals loud in his high praise agree (2)
16 though high above all praise, above all blessing high (2)
22 high as the heavens our voices raise (3)
27 thy justice like mountains high soaring above (2)
30 his spirit floweth free, high surging where it will (2)
31 the Lord Jehovah reigns, his throne is built on high (T,1)
32 without his high behest ye shall not ... disturb (3)
39 he made the shining worlds on high (2)
42 hosts on high, his power proclaim (2)
43 the spacious firmament on high (T,1)
44 when I regard the wondrous heavens,thy handiwork on high (2)
58 the heavenly shield ... is still high holden o'er us (2)
58 we raise it high, we send it on, the song (3)
77 come, lift your hearts on high; Alleluia! Amen (2)
80 so meek, so lowly, yet so high, so glorious in humility (3)
86 thou art the great high priest (2)
86 so now, and till we die sound we thy praises high (4)
88 waving a branch of a palm tree high in my hand (3)
100 Jesus, our great high priest, hath full atonement made (2)
113 by thy high, majestic throne (3)
124 what the high reward I win, whose the name I glory in (1)
125 while the tempest still is high (1)
128 high heavens, that heard the solemn vow (5)
135 kindle every high desire; perish self in thy pure fire (2)
151 O how our hearts beat high with joy whene'er we hear (1)
174 lift high the cross of Christ (4)
192 their high communion find (2)
200 purge us of low desire; lift us to high resolve (4)
222 in every high and stormy gale, my anchor holds (2)
233 your glorious banner wave on high (1)
233 raise high your free, exulting song (2)
233 still lift your standard high ... march in firm array (5)
248 lift high the royal banner, it must not suffer loss (1)
249 God's all-animating voice that calls thee from on high (3)
250 till Christ the Lord descends from high (3)
252 prayer .. sublimest strains .. reach the Majesty on high (3)
256 High King of heaven, my treasure thou art (3)
256 High King of heaven, my victory won (4)

260 our spirits' unseen friend, high heaven's Lord (1)
288 with saints enthroned on high thou...thy Lord proclaim (1)
297 like them, the meek & lowly, on high may dwell with thee (4)
299 O Zion, haste, thy mission high fulfilling (T,1)
301 our high calling's glorious hope ... hand in hand go on (3)
318 high o'er all the heavens he reigneth (1)
324 alleluia, alleluia, alleluia, Lord most high (4)
337 pour out thy spirit from on high (T,1)
341 Jesus! the name high over all, in hell or earth or sky (T,1)
343 to God the powers that dwell on high ... tribute bring (2)
343 lift our souls on high (3)
354 O come, thou Wisdom from on high (2)
357 hymn & chant & high thanksgiving & unwearied praises be (3)
364 yea, Amen! let all adore thee high on thy eternal throne (4)
368 true manna from on high (2)
372 O Word of God incarnate, O Wisdom from on high (T,1)
374 angels we have heard on high (T,1)
394 angels praising God on high .. thus addressed their song (5)
394 all glory be to God on high, and to the earth be peace (6)
401 Day-spring from on high, be near (1)
402 worship him, God on high (3)
409 God ruleth on high, almighty to save (2)
424 the company of angels are praising thee on high (2)
424 to thee, now high exalted, our melody we raise (3)
439 raise your joys and triumphs high, Alleluia (1)
440 there on high our welcome waits (2)
449 and sing with hearts uplifted high: Alleluia (3)
455 his glories now we sing who died, and rose on high (2)
462 fulfill the dream of this high hour (1)
488 on thee the high and lowly, through ages joined in tune (1)
490 birds pass high in flight, fragrant flowers now bloom (91)
492 we lift our hearts to thee, O Day-star from on high (T,1)
503 Heaven and earth are praising thee, O Lord most high (R)
542 with hopes and dreams as true and high as mine (1)
544 show forth thy pity on high where thou reignest (1)

higher
19 higher than ... cherubim more glorious than ... seraphim (2)
36 but higher far, and far more clear (4)
245 O then to the Rock let me fly ... Rock ... higher than I (R)
277 I ask no higher state, indulge me but in this (4)
287 every round goes higher ... soldiers of the cross (2)
287 we are climbing higher, higher ... soldiers of the cross (5)
358 higher yet that star ascends (2)
430 never further than thy cross, never higher than thy feet (T)

highest
49 the Son, and him who reigns with them in highest heaven (3)
146 the highest, holiest manhood, thou (3)
161 God's gift from highest heaven (2)
171 that it may be our highest joy, our Father's work to do (3)
216 thy dwelling place the Highest One (6)
221 glory in the highest, I will shout and sing (1)
260 our highest thought thy will (3)
294 beyond my highest joy I prize her heavenly ways (4)
386 glory to God, all glory in the highest (2)
387 Christ, by highest heaven adored (2)
423 Hosanna in the highest that ancient song we sing (3)

453 Jesus takes the highest station (4)
458 highest place ... heaven affords belongs to him by right (2)

highway
362 prepare in the desert a highway ... for our God (1,4)
406 make straight, make straight the highway of the King (1)
406 prepare across the earth the King's highway (2)
406 upon the highway of the Prince of Peace (3)

highways
161 a-foot on dusty highways (3)

hill
33 laid a silent loveliness on hill and wood and field (1)
35 hill and vale, and tree and flower (2)
203 we've seen thy glory like a mantle spread o'er hill and (4)
203 o'er hill and dale in saffron flame and red (4)
213 and lead me to thy holy hill (4)
228 on a hill far away stood an old rugged cross (T,1)
359 righteousness, in fountains, from hill to valley flow (3)
414 there is a green hill far away, beyond the city wall (T,1)
482 be the road uphill or down, unbroken or well trod (2)
512 the seed by him provided is sown o'er hill and plain (1)

hills
28 before the hills in order stood (3)
57 unto the hills I lift mine eyes (T,1)
235 O sabbath rest by Galilee! O calm of hills above (3)
308 unshaken as eternal hills, immovable she stands (4)
353 when beauty gilds the eastern hills (1)
362 valleys shall be exalted, the lofty hills brought low (1,4)
392 while fields and floods, rocks, hills and plains repeat (2)
395 all the hills were ringing (2)
404 over the hills and everywhere ... Jesus Christ is born (R)
442 flowers make glee among the hills (1)
473 it streams from the hills, it descends to the plain (4)
512 the wilderness is fruitful, and joyful are the hills (2)
524 the hills with joy are ringing (1)
547 I love thy rocks and rills, thy woods and templed hills (2)
550 till these eternal hills remove (4)
551 let our hills and valleys shout the songs of liberty (3)

hillsides
307 as grain, once scattered on the hillsides (4)

hinder
408 cast out our pride & shame that hinder to enthrone thee (3)

hither
86 hither our children bring to shout thy praise (1)
93 here I raise mine Ebenezer, hither to thy help I'm come (2)

hoary
33 sent the hoary frost of heaven, the flowing waters sealed (1)

hold
44 oh, what is man, in thy regard to hold so large a place (3)
52 in the confidence of prayer our hearts take hold on thee (2)

96   'twas not so much that I on thee took hold (2)
99   if I still hold closely to him, what hath he at last (5)
105 earth's pleasures shall I still hold dear (1)
154 hold o'er my being absolute sway (4)
163 naught ... I have my own I call ... hold it for the giver (2
240 lay hold on life ..it shall be thy joy & crown eternally (1)
271 hold me with thy powerful hand (1)
289 hold thou thy cross before my closing eyes (5)
329 blest, when our faith can hold thee fast (4)
376 our God, heaven cannot hold him, nor earth sustain (2)
446 nor the watchers, nor the seal hold thee as a mortal (4)
516 children early lisp his fame and parents hold him dear (2)
525 for all the friends we hold so dear (1)
529 Traveler unkown, whom still I hold, but cannot see (1)

holden
58   the heavenly shield ... is still high holden o'er us (2)

holdeth
460 one firm anchor holdeth fast (1)

holding
94   Savior stands, holding forth his wounded hands (4)
258 thou with him shalt dwell, beholding Light enfolding (4)

holds
141 God's mercy holds a wiser plan than thou canst fully know (2
204 the cup of water given for thee still holds ...thy grace (4)
222 in every high and stormy gale, my anchor holds (2)
222 my anchor holds within the veil (2)
232 where friend holds fellowship with friend (3)
249 a cloud of witnesses around holds thee in full survey (2)

holier
194 visions of a larger good & holier dreams of brotherhood (1)
199 the holier worship which he deigns to bless restores (2)

holiest
146 the highest, holiest manhood, thou (3)
440 holiest hearts for ages pleading (2)

holiness
3   Spirit of holiness, on us descend! (2)
39   the race of men confess the beauty of his holiness (3)
89   to me ... are given pardon and holiness and heaven (2)
136 and earth shall win true holiness (4)
136 holiness which makes thy children whole (4)
139 pardon and holiness and heaven (4)
281 and perfect holiness in me (2)
309 all the heights of holiness (5)
344 learning and holiness combined (3)
422 his royalty is holiness, and love is in his face (2)
465 Spirit of holiness, let all thy saints adore (3)
476 in speech that flows to melody, in holiness of heart (4)
478 and holiness shall whisper the sweet amen of peace (2)

hollow
346 ocean ... sleeps in the hollow of his hand (2)

holy

2	Father, Son, and Holy Spirit, blessed Trinity (5)
3	come, holy Comforter, thy sacred witness bear (3)
4	o ye who name Christ's holy name (5)
8	holy God, we praise thy name (T,1)
8	fill .. heavens with sweet accord: holy, holy, holy Lord (2)
8	holy Father, holy Son, holy Spirit: three we name thee (4)
11	holy, holy, to our God all glory be! (R)
15	praise the holy God of love, and all his greatness show (1)
16	who would not fear his holy name and laud and magnify (2)
19	ye watchers and ye holy ones (T,1)
19	ye holy twelve, ye martyrs strong (3)
26	holy, holy, holy, Lord God almighty (T,1,4)
26	holy,holy, holy! merciful and mighty (1,4)
26	holy, holy, holy! all the saints adore thee (2)
26	holy, holy, holy! though the darkness hide thee (3)
26	only thou art holy; there is none beside thee (3)
31	his wrath and justice stand to guard his holy law (2)
35	for thy church that evermore lifteth holy hands above (5)
39	sing the great Jehovah's praise and bless his holy name (1)
62	wandering from his holy ways (2)
64	till all thy living altars claim one holy light (5)
64	one holy light, one heavenly flame (5)
76	there let him subdue all that is not holy (4)
78	come in thy holy might, we pray (3)
86	let all the holy throng, who to thy Church belong (4)
87	if temptations round you gather, breathe that holy name (2)
87	breathe that holy name in prayer (2)
90	Mary's son most holy, Light of the village life (2)
101	come then and join this holy band, and on to glory go (4)
106	Holy Spirit, faithful guide (T,1)
125	just and holy is thy name; I am all unrighteousness (3)
131	come, Holy Ghost, our hearts inspire (T,1)
131	come, Holy Ghost, for moved by thee the prophets wrote (2)
132	Holy Ghost, dispel our sadness (T,1)
134	come, Holy Spirit, heavenly Dove (T,1,5)
135	Holy Spirit, Truth divine, dawn upon this soul of mine (T,1)
135	Holy Spirit, Love divine, glow within this heart of mine (2)
135	Holy Spirit, Power divine (3)
135	Holy Spirit, Right divine (4)
138	one holy passion filling all my frame (5)
144	O Holy Savior, friend unseen (T,1)
149	message of salvation from God's own holy Word (3)
151	faith of our fathers, holy faith (R)
172	still let me guard the holy fire (3)
173	again to lead us forward along God's holy way (5)
180	praise Father, Son, and Holy Ghost (4)
188	till earth, as heaven, fulfill God's holy will (3)
199	him whose holy work was doing good (3)
200	take us, and make us holy; teach us thy will and way (4)
212	but then the Holy Spirit revives my soul again (1)
213	and lead me to thy holy hill (4)
227	O the rapturous height of that holy delight (5)
231	in holy contemplation we sweetly then pursue the theme (2)
238	Christian, dost thou see them on the holy ground (T,1)
238	in the strength that cometh by the holy cross (1)
243	not long the conflict, soon the holy war shall cease (4)
243	to fear no ill, to fight the holy fight they fought (2)

257 by thy teachings sweet and holy (1)
265 Most Holy One ... thou blessed Son (5)
266 take time to be holy, speak oft with thy Lord (T,1)
266 take time to be holy, the world rushes on (2)
266 take time to be holy, let him be thy guide (3)
266 take time to be holy, be calm in thy soul (4)
268 return, O holy Dove, return, sweet messenger of rest (4)
286 Lord, I want to be more holy in my heart (3)
296 one holy Church of God appears through every age & race (T)
297 from heaven he came and sought her to be his holy bride (1)
297 one holy name she blesses, partakes one holy food (2)
298 Holy Zion's help forever and her confidence alone (1)
304 O holy kingdom, happy fold, the blessed Church to be (2)
307 planted thy holy name within our hearts (1)
308 not like kingdoms of the world thy holy Church, O God (3)
311 may she holy triumphs win, overthrow the hosts of sin (4)
317 spread with reverence this holy feast ... remember thee (1)
317 thy holy face is stained with bitter tears (2)
329 shed o'er the world thy holy light (5)
331 in thy holy incarnation, when the angels sang thy birth (2)
334 with the Holy Spirit's favor, rest upon them from above (1)
342 until each life's vocation accents thy holy way (3)
344 come, Father, Son, and Holy Ghost (T,1)
345 let the comforter and friend, thy Holy Spirit, meet (2)
352 dwell in this holy place, e'en now descend (1)
357 and, O Holy Ghost, to thee (3)
378 this holy tide of Christmas all other doth deface (4)
381 O holy Child of Bethlehem, descend to us, we pray (4)
381 O morning stars, together proclaim the holy birth (2)
393 silent night, holy night (T,1,2,3,4)
393 holy infant so tender and mild sleep in heavenly peace (1)
393 radiant beams from thy holy face (3)
396 infant holy, infant lowly, for his bed a cattle stall (T,1)
397 so may we with holy joy, pure and free from sins' alloy (3)
397 Holy Jesus, every day keep us in the narrow way (4)
399 thou art holy, fair and glorious, all victorious (1)
404 behold throughout the heavens there shone a holy light (1)
411 battle with the body's ills and wage the holy war (2)
412 ah, holy Jesus, how hast thou offended (T,1)
443 Father, Son, and Holy Ghost (3)
443 our triumphant holy day (1)
447 let shouts of holy joy outburst: Alleluia (2)
451 on this most holy day of days, our hearts ... we raise (5)
459 O holy Father, who hast led thy children in all the ages (2)
459 O holy Jesus, Prince of Peace and Savior (3)
459 O Holy Ghost, the Lord and the Life-giver (4)
463 Father, Son, and Holy Ghost (1)
463 we confess the Holy Ghost (3)
463 Holy Ghost, who from both fore'er proceeds (3)
463 blest and Holy Trinity, praise forever be to thee (3)
466 and kindle it, thy holy flame bestowing (1)
466 the place wherein the Holy Spirit makes his dwelling (3)
467 come, Holy Ghost, our souls inspire (T,1)
467 praise to thy eternal merit, Father, Son and Holy Spirit (R)
469 how shall we love thee, holy, hidden Being (4)
480 Spirit of truth and love, life-giving, holy Dove (3)
480 holy and blessed Three, Glorious Trinity, (4)

481   O holy city, seen of John (T,1)
481   holy city ... where Christ, the Lamb, doth reign (1)
482   O Holy Savior of mankind, ride on (2)
487   Jesus, we want to meet on this thy holy day (T,1)
487   we gather round thy throne on this thy holy day (1)
487   look into our hearts & minds today ... this thy holy day (1)
487   we kneel in awe and fear on this thy holy day (2)
487   pray God to teach us here on this thy holy day (2)
487   our faith from seed to flower raise on this thy holy day (2)
487   thy blessing, Lord, we seek on this thy holy day (3)
487   give joy of thy victory on this thy holy day (3)
487   let the mind of Christ abide in us on this thy holy day (3)
487   our minds we dedicate on this thy holy day (4)
487   heart and soul consecrate on this thy holy day (4)
487   Holy Spirit, make us whole (4)
488   sing holy, holy, holy, to the great God Triune (1)
488   to holy convocations the silver trumpet calls (3)
488   to Holy Ghost be praises, to Father, and to Son (4)
493   praise Father, Son, and Holy Ghost (5)
495   pure and fresh and sinless in thy holy eyes (6)
497   holy dreams and hopes attend us this live-long night (1)
503   holy, holy, holy, Lord God of Hosts (R)
504   all holy Father, Son, and equal Spirit, Trinity blessed (3)
505   let our vesper hymn be blending ... holy calm around (1)
506   O Spirit, pure and holy, possess these hearts so lowly (5)
517   may we keep our holy calling stainless in... fair renown (5)
521   in his holy courts they flourish (2)
521   to preserve them pure and holy (4)
524   strains of ... holy throng with ours today are blending (3)
536   singing to Father, Son, and Holy Ghost, Alleluia (6)
538   O Holy Spirit, who didst brood upon the waters (3)
542   here are my hopes, my dreams, my holy shrine (1)
545   as he died to make men holy, let us die to make man free (4
547   long may our land be bright with freedom's holy light (4)
549   and met within thy holy place to rest awhile with thee (1)
550   through all ages bear the memory of that holy hour (2)

homage
15   glory to their Maker give, and homage to their King (3)
324   our full homage to demand (1)

home
17   and take me home, what joy shall fill my heart! (4)
28   and our eternal home (1)
28   be ...our guard while troubles last and our eternal home (6)
47   our heart's true home when all our years have sped (3)
60   thou leadest home the child of God (6)
67   and home, rejoicing, brought me (3)
92   and grace will lead me home (3)
93   I hope, by thy good pleasure, safely to arrive at home (2)
98   and, going, take thee to their home (2)
100   return, ye ransomed sinners, home (R)
106   wanderer, come, Follow me, I'll guide thee home (R)
107   turned from home and toil and kindred (2)
110   Jesus is tenderly calling thee home (T,1)
142   tastes even now the hallowed bliss of an eternal home (4)
147   kind the storm which drives us nearer home (2)

167   straight to my home above I travel calmly on (3)
168   when my dear Lord will bring me home (3)
183   go home my crown to wear, for there's a crown for me (3)
197   through quiet work in shop and home (1)
205   perfect rest to me is promised in my Father's home above (3)
216   nor plague approach thy guarded home (6)
228   then he'll call me some day to my home far away (4)
243   faith's warfare ended, won the home of endless peace (4)
250   till Christ descends ... and takes the conquerors home (3)
272   the night is dark, & I am far from home, lead thou me on (1)
300   there... endless home shall be... Lord we soon shall see (4)
300   we are traveling home to God in the way our fathers trod (2)
303   O sweet and blessed country, the home of God's elect (4)
358   let thy wandering cease; hie thee to thy quiet home (3)
417   a home within the wilderness, a rest upon the way (1)
450   bring us safe through Jordan to thy home above (3)
461   make this house thy home (1)
461   Spirit divine ... make this world thy home (4)
467   keep far our foes; give peace at home (3)
478   henceforth in fields of conquest thy tents ... our home (1)
483   and take his servants up to their eternal home (4)
503   Lord of life, beneath the dome of the universe thy home (2)
509   by day, by night, at home, abroad, still we are guarded (2)
511   first fruits would bring...of... shop and home (1)
511   wealth of this good land ... shop and home (1)
516   happy the home where Jesus' name is sweet to every ear (2)
516   happy the home where prayer is heard (3)
516   happy the home where ... praise is wont to rise (3)
516   happy the home when God is there (T,1)
520   O Lord, may church and home combine (T,1)
520   within .. home let every heart become thy dwelling place (2)
520   may church and home combine to teach thy perfect way (1)
522   raise the song of harvest home (1)
522   God shall come, and shall take his harvest home (3)
522   even so,Lord, quickly come, bring thy final harvest home (4)
522   raise the glorious harvest home (4)
525   for home, where our affection clings (2)
528   he calls you now, invites you home (5)
542   this is my home, the country where my heart is (1)
548   for the home, the church, the school (2)

homeless
479   still the children wander homeless (2)

homeliest
549   on homeliest work thy blessing falls (3)

homes
380   in the homes of the nations that Jesus is King (3)
516   Lord, let us in our homes agree .. blessed peace to gain (4)
523   for peaceful homes and healthful days (3)
532   peaceful men of skill who builded homes of beauty (4)

homeward
170   and guide them in the homeward way (2)
236   grant us thy peace upon our homeward way (2)

honey
303   Jerusalem the golden, with milk and honey blest (T,1)

honor
2   honor, glory, might, and merit thine shall ever be (5)
7   wisdom, honor, power, blessing ... we cry (4)
44   with honor thou hast crowned his head (4)
78   laud, honor, might ... glory be ... age to age eternally (4)
79   thee will I honor, thou, my soul's glory, joy and crown (1)
194   of tarnished honor, falsely strong (2)
298   laud and honor to the Father ...to the Son ...the Spirit (4)
305   glory, laud, and honor unto Christ the King (4)
340   heart to heart, & hand to hand ... make thine honor ours (2)
349   all praise and honor, power be now and evermore (4)
351   who honor truth, nor fear the crowd (3)
357   honor, glory, & dominion, and eternal victory, evermore (3)
409   let all cry aloud and honor the Son (3)
409   all honor and blessing, with angels above (4)
424   all glory, laud, and honor, to thee, Redeemer, King (T,1)
454   worship, honor, power, and blessing Christ is worthy (4)
484   from sale and profanation of honor and the sword (2)
517   thou... crowned us with an honor women never knew before (2
545   he is wisdom to the mighty, he is honor to the brave (5)

honors
1   spread thro' all the earth abroad the honors of thy name (2)
249   crowned with victory at thy feet I'll lay .. honors down (4)
472   let every creature rise and bring his grateful honors (5)
472   his grateful honors to our King (5)

hook
408   to plow-share beat the sword, to pruning-hook the spear (2)

hope
5   fruit ... from faith and hope may grow (3)
28   our hope for years to come (1,6)
51   give to the winds thy fears; hope and be undismayed (T,1)
52   praise thee for thy mercies past, & humbly hope for more (3)
63   he with earthly cares entwineth hope and comfort (4)
63   hope and comfort from above (4)
64   star of our hope, thy softened light cheers (2)
82   O Hope of every contrite heart, O Joy of all the meek (3)
87   Hope of earth and joy of heaven (R)
92   his word my hope secures (4)
93   I hope, by thy good pleasure, safely to arrive at home (2)
103   hope of the penitent, fadeless and pure (2)
111   in sure and certain hope rejoice (3)
115   what a blessed hope is ours while here on earth we stay (2)
129   my hope, my salvation, my all (1)
139   whate'er we hope, by faith we have (3)
144   though faith and hope may long be tried (4)
159   Let my soul look up with a steadfast hope (2)
160   for only he who bears the cross may hope to wear...crown (4)
160   may hope to wear the glorious crown (4)
161   hope of the world T,1,2,3,4,5)
167   let not my star of hope grow dim or disappear (2)
170   in hope that sends a shining ray far down the future's (4)

209 thy hope, thy confidence let nothing shake (2)
210 and hope in him through all thy ways (1)
210 only be still, and wait his leisure in cheerful hope (2)
222 when all around my soul gives way, he... is all my hope (3)
222 my hope is build on nothing less than Jesus blood and (T,1)
222 he then is all my hope and stay (3)
230 my hope I cannot measure, my path to life is free (3)
251 hope shall change to glad fruition (4)
253 Jesus, my strength, my hope, on thee I cast my care (T,1)
255 hope still, and thou shalt sing the praise of him (4)
269 and age comes on, uncheered by faith or hope (2)
292 inspired with hope and praise, to Christ belong (4)
297 and to one hope she presses, with every grace endued (2)
301 our high calling's glorious hope ... hand in hand go on (3)
303 send hope before to grasp it, till hope be lost in sight (3)
305 one in hope and doctrine, one in charity (2)
306 we shall still be joined in heart and hope to meet again (4)
310 bid our inmost souls rejoice in hope of perfect love (5)
319 one fold .. faith .. hope .. Lord, One God alone we know (1)
333 of patient hope and quiet, brave endurance (2)
337 in humble hope their charge resign (5)
358 doth its beauteous ray aught of joy or hope foretell (1)
359 love, joy and hope, like flowers, spring in his path (3)
360 hope of all the earth thou art (1)
379 hail the star, that from far bright with hope is burning (3)
382 watching long in hope and fear (4)
408 new life, new hope awakes where-e'er men own his sway (1)
419 twelve valiant saints, their hope they knew (3)
458 his people's hope ... their everlasting theme (6)
459 from thee...our faith and hope, our fellowship and peace (4)
479 hope and health, good will and comfort (4)
485 calm and courage, faith and hope: O pour them from above (1)
505 hope and faith and love rise glorious (4)
517 hope to trust them, faith to guide them (4)
526 and thus my hope is in the Lord and not in my own merit (3)
548 memory and hope between (1)

hope's
  47 lead us by faith to hope's true promised land (2)

hoped
  251 perish every fond ambition, all I've... hoped or known (1)
  251 all I've sought or hoped or known (1)

hopeless
  201 the hopeless and the burdened, the crippled and the weak (1)

hopes
    9 happy the man whose hopes rely on Israel's God (2)
   41 soaring spire and ruined city, these our hopes ... show (3)
   41 spire and ruined city, these our hopes and failures show (3)
   47 through all our hopes and fears, thy hand we see (1)
  106 hearts grow faint, and hopes give o'er, whisper softly (2)
  144 and earthly friends and hopes remove (2)
  161 who by our own false hopes and aims are spent (1)
  194 to brighter hopes and kindlier things (1)
  202 the common hopes that make us men were his in Galilee (2)
  306 our fears, our hopes, our aims are one (2)

381   hopes and fears of all the years are met in thee tonight (1)
416   hopes deceive and fears annoy (2)
430   where our earliest hopes began ..our last aspirings endd (4)
497   holy dreams and hopes attend us this live-long night (1)
499   new thoughts of God, new hopes of heaven (2)
509   thy goodness all our hopes shall raise (4)
514   take our ... hopes and fears of sun and rain (2)
523   for means of grace and hopes of heaven (4)
542   here are my hopes, my dreams, my holy shrine (1)
542   but other hearts in other lands are beating with hopes (1)
542   with hopes and dreams true and high as mine (1)

hoping
433   near the cross I'll watch & wait, hoping, trusting ever (4)

horizon
400   Star of the East, the horizon adorning (1,5)

hosanna
423   Hosanna, loud hosanna the little children sang (T,1)
423   Hosanna in the highest   that ancient song we sing (3)
425   hark! all the tribes hosanna cry (1)
482   we hail thine august majesty and loud hosanna sing (4)

hosannas
88   one of his heralds, yes, I would sing loudest hosannas (3)
134   hosannas languish on our tongues and our devotion dies (3)
424   to whom the lips of children made sweet hosannas ring (1)

host
7   with the angelic host we cry (4)
46   captain of Israel's host (T,1)
79   all the twinking starry host: Jesus shines brighter (3)
180   praise him above, ye heavenly host (4)
302   part of his host have crossed the flood (4)
324   rank on rank the host of heaven spreads its vanguard (3)
372   it floateth like a banner before God's host unfurled (3)
387   with the angelic host proclaim (1)
443   praise him, all ye heavenly host (3)
463   praised by all the heavenly host (1)
482   mighty host, by thee redeemed, is marching in thy train (1)
493   praise him above, ye heavenly host (5)
536   through gates of pearl streams in the countless host (6)

hostel
377   no room inside the hostel there for Joseph (1)
377   the hostel rang with song and shout (2)

hosts
6   we, thy people, praise thee, Lord of hosts eternal! (1,2)
25   the glorious hosts of heaven obey (4)
42   hosts on high, his power proclaim (2)
76   all the angel faces, all the hosts of light (2)
124   with the countless hosts of light (3)
211   though hosts encamp around me, firm in the fight I stand (1)
244   when the hosts of sin assail ... strength begins to fail (2)
246   hosts of sin . pressing hard to draw thee from the skies (1)
250   strong in the Lord of hosts, and in his mighty power (1)

283 serve thee as thy hosts above (3)
295 O thou almighty Lord of hosts, who art my God and King (4)
295 how lovely is thy dwelling place, O Lord of hosts (T,1)
298 come, O Lord of hosts, today (2)
311 may she holy triumphs win, overthrow the hosts of sin (4)
351 by men and heavenly hosts adored (1)
357 angel hosts, his praises sing (2)
393 heavenly hosts sing Alleluia (2)
430 till amid the hosts of light, we in thee redeemed (5)
454 all the heavenly hosts adore thee (3)
465 Eternal, Triune Lord, let all the hosts above (4)
470 lo! the hosts of evil round us scorn thy Christ (2)
471 not heaven's hosts shall swifter move than we on earth (4)
503 holy, holy, holy, Lord God of Hosts (R)

hour
3 in this glad hour (3)
35 for the beauty of each hour of the day and of the night (2)
36 we feel thy calm at evening's hour (3)
39 come, the great day, the glorious hour (3)
39 hour, when earth shall feel his saving power (3)
63 the hour that darkest seemeth will his... goodness prove (3)
76 crown him as your captain in temptation's hour (4)
89 my light in Satan's darkest hour (4)
92 the hour I first believed (2)
95 mercy now, O Lord, I plead in this hour of utter need (3)
95 now, O Lord, this very hour, send thy grace (2)
113 by thy conflict in... hour of the subtle tempter's power (1)
113 by thy lonely hour of prayer (2)
128 till in life's latest hour I bow (5)
142 in the hour of grief or pain will lean upon its   God (2)
153 grant us in this burning hour grace (1)
153 thou hast called us for this hour (R)
153 God of love ... God of power make us worthy of this hour (4)
159 pure delight . single hour ... before thy throne I spend (3)
200 our strength is dust and ashes, our years a passing hour (3)
209 the hour is hastening on (3)
209 hour ... when we shall be forever with the Lord (3)
226 every day, every hour, let me feel thy cleansing power (R)
237 in the hour of trial, Jesus, plead for me (T,1)
237 when my last hour cometh, fraught with strife and pain (4)
259 O Jesus, in that solemn hour, in death as life (3)
262 let this my every hour employ, till I thy glory see (5)
264 O in that hour, fairer than daylight dawning shall rise (5)
265 I need thee every hour (T,1,2,3,4,5)
265 I need thee, O I need thee, every hour I need thee (R)
275 sweet hour of prayer (T,1,2,3)
289 I need thy presence every passing hour (3)
326 this is the hour of banquet and of song (2)
326 here let me feast, and feasting, still prolong the hour (2)
326 prolong the hour of fellowship with thee (2)
356 break forth ... upon the world's dark hour (1)
407 await a new creative hour (3)
427 this is the earth's darkest hour (3)
427 that, as we share this hour, thy cross may bring ... joy (4)
434 watch with him one bitter hour (1)
462 fulfill the dream of this high hour (1)
470 grant us courage for the facing of this hour (1)

475 nor till that hour shall God's whole will be done (3)
477 come with thy timeless judgment . match our present hour (1)
501 hear, in this solemn evening hour (6)
506 long our day of testing, now comes the hour of resting (3)
507 promise, in this sacred hour, for God to live and die (2)
525 common things which every day and hour brings (2)
538 our brethren shield in danger's hour (4)
549 scarcely can we turn aside for one brief hour of prayer (2)
550 through all ages bear the memory of that holy hour (2)

hours
50 that shadows fall on brightest hours, that thorns remain (3)
107 days of toil and hours of ease (4)
258 God hath tended with his care thy helpless hours (2)
268 what peaceful hours I once enjoyed! (3)
491 we pray thee that offenseless the hours of dark may be (1)
491 call on thee that sinless the hours of dark may be (2)
491 ask that free from peril the hours of dark may be (3)
510 residue of days or hours thine, wholly thine, shall be (5)

house
25 might I enjoy the meanest place within thy house (2)
67 Good Shepherd, may I sing thy praise within thy house (6)
67 sing thy praise within thy house forever (6)
68 in God's house forevermore my dwelling place shall be (5)
128 let cheerful anthems fill his house (2)
148 from his lighthouse evermore (1)
236 that in this house have called upon thy name (2)
294 I love thy kingdom, Lord, the house of thine abode (T,1)
295 behold, the sparrow findeth out a house wherein to rest (3)
295 blest are they in thy house that dwell (5)
299 bound in darksome prison-house of sin (2)
308 a house not made with hands (4)
348 may they know this house their own (3)
350 grant the vision inly given of this thy house (5)
350 this thy house, the gate of heaven (5)
351 bless thou this house that it may be a place most meet (1)
461 make this house thy home (1)
489 may thy glory meet our eyes while we in thy house appear (3)

hover
499 new mercies, each returning day, hover around us (2)
499 new mercies ... hover around us while we pray (2)

hovering
293 round each habitation hovering, see the cloud and fire (3)
390 above its sad & lowly plains they bend on hovering wing (2)

how
13 oh, how blessed is this place (1)
17 how great thou art (T,R)
17 and there proclaim, my God, how great thou art (4)
34 how great is God Almighty, who has made all things well (4)
37 Lord, how thy wonders are displayed (2)
38 teach us how to love each other (3)
39 his beauties, how divinely bright (2)
39 his dwelling place, how fair (2)
41 o how glorious, full of wonder (T,1)

41 o how wondrous, o how glorious is thy name in every land (4)
44 how excellent thy name (1)
44 Lord, our Lord, in all the earth how excellent thy name (5)
48 how firm a foundation, ye saints of the Lord (T,1)
51 how wise, how strong his hand (3)
52 how are thy servants blest, O Lord (T,1)
52 how sure is their defense (1)
53 how gentle God's commands! how kind his precepts are! (T,1)
55 hast thou not seen how thy desires ... hath been granted (2)
56 experience will decide how blest are they (3)
64 yet to each loving heart how near (1)
80 how beauteous were the marks divine (T,1)
81 how sweet the name of Jesus sounds in a believer's ear (T,1)
82 to those who fall, how kind thou art (3)
82 how good to those who seek (3)
82 ah, this nor tongue nor pen can show (4)
85 living deeds that prove how sweet to serve all others (3)
85 how sweet to serve all others, when we all others love (3)
87 precious name, O how sweet! (R)
87 name of Jesus! How it thrills our souls with joy (3)
88 first let me hear how the children stood round his knee (2)
92 amazing grace! how sweet the sound (T,1)
92 how precious did that grace appear (2)
93 to grace how great a debtor daily I'm constrained to be (3)
95 send thy grace and show thy power (2)
97 how could I this friend deny, when he's so true to me (3)
114 how can a sinner know his sins on earth forgiven? (T,1)
114 can my gracious Savior show my name inscribed in heaven (1)
115 how happy every child of grace (T,1)
123 how that Bethlehem's babe could in the God-head be (1)
123 I know not how that Bethlehem's babe (T,1)
123 know not how that Calvary's cross a world ... could free (2)
123 I know not how that Joseph's tomb could solve death's (3)
134 look how we grovel here below (2)
134 our souls, how heavily they go to reach eternal joys (2)
137 Spirit of faith, descend and show the virtue of his name (3)
146 our wills are ours, we know not how (3)
151 and preach thee, too, as love knows how (3)
151 O how our hearts beat high with joy whene'er we hear (1)
162 learning how to love from thee (3)
162 thus may I rejoice to show that I feel the love I owe (4)
171 show us thy will, we ask (3)
183 how happy are the saints above (2)
190 see how the giant sun soars up (2)
195 thy love to tell, thy praise to show (4)
201 help us by deeds of mercy to show that thou art kind (2)
201 in thy great salvation, show forth thy boundless love (3)
208 how I've proved him o'er and o'er (R)
208 Jesus, Jesus, how I trust him (R)
227 O how happy are they who the Savior obey (T,1)
238 how the powers of darkness rage thy steps around (1)
238 Christian, dost thou feel them, how they work within (2)
238 Christian, dost thou hear them, how they speak thee fair (3)
245 sorrows, sometimes how they sweep like tempests (1)
245 O sometimes how long seems the day (2)
245 and sometimes how weary my feet (2)
245 the Rock's blessed shadow, how sweet (2)
251 how rich is my condition: God & heaven are still my own (1)

252 Lord, teach us how to pray (6)
259 O Love, how cheering is thy ray (2)
268 How sweet their memories still (3)
285 O love divine, how sweet thou art (T,1)
295 how lovely is thy dwelling place, O Lord of hosts (T,1)
295 the tabernacles of thy grace how pleasant, Lord, they be (1)
299 behold how many thousands still are lying bound (2)
299 tell how he stooped to save his lost creation (3)
312 hark, how he calls the tender lambs (1)
318 let me measure, Lord, how vast and deep its treasure (3)
328 how happy are thy servants, Lord, who thus remember thee (T
332 how the bread his flesh imparts (1)
332 who shall say how bread and wine God into man conveys (1)
332 how can heavenly spirits rise by earthly matter fed (3)
332 how the wine transmits his blood (1)
332 explains the wondrous way how through these virtues came (2)
350 how blessed is this place, O Lord (T,1)
368 without thee how could earth be trod (3)
368 with thee how could ... heaven itself be won (3)
378 how that in Bethlehem was born the Son of God by name (3)
381 O little town of Bethlehem, how still we see thee lie (T,1)
381 how silently, how silently the wondrous gift is given (3)
399 O morning star, how fair and bright (T,1)
412 ah, holy Jesus, how hast thou offended (T,1)
418 how pale thou art with anguish, with sore abuse & scorn (1)
418 how does that visage languish .. once was bright as morn (1)
428 hark, how he groans, while nature shakes (2)
451 how blest are they who have not seen (4)
464 see how great a flame aspires (T,1)
469 how shall we love thee, holy, hidden Being (4)
473 thy mercies how tender, how firm to the endd (5)
481 hark, how from men whose lives are held more cheap (2)
481 how its splendor challenges the souls that greatly dare (5)
491 how many are the perils through which we have to go (4)
492 how beauteous nature now! How dark and sad before (3)
502 be my last thought, how sweet to rest (2)
515 how wide the bounteous love is spread (3)
523 how shall we show our love to thee, who givest all (1)
527 amazing love! how can it be that thou ... die for me (1)
527 how can it be that thou, my Lord, shouldst die for me (1)
528 how shall I all to heaven aspire (1)
528 how shall I equal triumphs raise (1)
528 O how shall I the goodness tell, Father (2)
528 how ... goodness tell ... which thou to me hast showed (2)
533 how great their joys, how bright their glories be (1)

however
269 however rough and steep the path may be (4)

howling
32 and sweeps the howling skies (4)
221 when the howling storms of doubt and fear assail (2)

human
30 deep writ upon the human heart, on sea or land (2)
35 for the joy of human love, brother, sister, parent,child (4)
41 teach us more of human pity that we in thine image grow (3)
41 conscious of our human need (4)

85	in human form thou speakest to men the Father's mind (2)
85	O Will of God incarnate, so human, so divine (4)
90	divine and human, in his deep revealing of God and man (4)
113	by thy human griefs and fears (1)
136	till Christ shall dwell in human hearts (1)
146	thou seemest human and divine (3)
175	down in the human heart, crushed by the tempter (3)
189	human hatreds flee before the radiant eastern skies (1)
189	one tender comfort broods upon the struggling human soul (3)
189	one claim unites all men in God to serve each human need (2)
251	human hearts and looks deceive me (2)
260	dost not wait till human speech thy gifts ... implore (1)
260	O cleanse our prayers from human dross (2)
290	forgive me if too close I lean my human heart on thee (3)
304	deep in loving human hearts its broad foundations rise (1)
317	our human pain still bearest thou with us (2)
324	of old on earth he stood, Lord of lords in human vesture (2)
333	O perfect Love, all human thought transcending (T,1)
345	accept the walls that human hands have raised ...to thee (1)
381	God imparts to human hearts the blessings of his heaven (3)
394	to human view displayed (4)
398	never shall darkness veil thee again from human eyes (1)
398	till everything that's human be filled with the divine (3)
446	that thy peace which evermore passeth human knowing (4)
464	saw ye not the cloud arise, little as a human hand (4)
466	shall far outpass the power of human telling (3)
476	O God of love, whose spirit wakes in every human breast (2)
476	kindness dwell in human hearts and... earth find peace (2)
476	O God of beauty, oft revealed in dreams of human art (4)
479	whose love ... bore the weight of human need (1)
481	there swells the sobbing human plaint (2)
481	sobbing human plaint that bids thy walls arise (2)
481	wring gold from human pain (3)
481	where the sun that shineth is God's grace for human good (4)
543	thine alabaster cities gleam undimmned by human tears (4)

humanity
173	thy life is still a summons to serve humanity (1)

humble
1	mournful, broken hearts rejoice; the humble poor believe (5)
17	then I shall bow in humble adoration (4)
98	thou ... dost dwell with those of humble mind (2)
130	the depth of humble love (5)
139	to thee our humble hearts aspire (2)
145	pass me not, O gentle Savior, hear my humble cry (T,1)
145	Savior, Savior, hear my humble cry (R)
156	I would be humble, for I know my weakness (2)
172	in humble prayer and fervent praise (2)
173	stand with humble courage for truth with hearts uncowed (1)
186	Son of the carpenter, receive this humble work of mine (2)
253	with humble confidence look up and know thou hearest (1)
282	a humble, lowly, contrite heart (3)
283	fix in us thy humble dwelling (1)
312	nor scorn their humble name (2)
319	every humble, contrite heart is made a welcome guest (1)
337	in humble hope their charge resign (5)
339	on thee we humble wait, our wants are in thy view (2)

346   and science walks with humble feet (4)
395   Son of God, of humble birth, beautiful the story (3)
404   down in a lowly manger the humble Christ was born (3)
440   every humble spirit shares it (2)
479   Lord, whose love through humble service (T,1)
513   and what thou most desirest, our humble, thankful hearts (3)

humbled
76   humbled for a season, to receive a name (3)

humbleness
60   worship him in humbleness, O praise him! Alleluia! (7)

humblest
398   and glorifies with duty life's poorest, humblest part (2)

humbling
74   humbling thyself to death on Calvary (3)

humbly
41   humbly now we bow before thee (1)
52   praise thee for thy mercies past, & humbly hope for more (3)
80   who like thee so humbly bore the scorn ... scoffs of men (3)
116   humbly at thy cross I bow, save me, Jesus, save me now (4)
154   as in thy presence humbly I bow (2)
160   the world forsake, and humbly follow after me (1)
196   and humbly ask for more (1)
480   hear us, we humbly pray (1)
490   venerating age, humbly teaching youth (2)
505   while we kneel confessing, we humbly wait thy blessing (4)

humility
80   so meek, so lowly, yet so high, so glorious in humility (3)
316   according to thy gracious word, in meek humility (T,1)

hundred
545   I have seen him in the watchfires of a hundred ... camps (2)
545   watchfires of a hundred circling camps (2)

hung
414   we believe it was for us he hung and suffered there (2)

hunger
296   with bread of life earth's hunger feed (4)
407   the peoples hunger for thee, Lord (2)

hungering
149   hungering and thirsting to hear it like the rest (4)
149   for those who know it best seem hungering (4)

hungry
81   'tis manna to the hungry soul and to the weary, rest (2)
161   bringing to hungry souls the bread of life (2)
201   we would be thy disciples, and all the hungry feed (2)
445   He lives, my hungry soul to feed (2)
479   still the hungry cry for bread (2)
546   feed thy faint and hungry peoples with...thy Word (2)

hurt
48 the flame shall not hurt thee, I only design (4)
318 never to my hurt invited, be thy love with love requited (3)

hush
60 death, waiting to hush our latest breath (6)
247 as a mother stills her child thou canst hush (1)
247 thou canst hush the ocean wild (1)
264 the solemn hush of nature newly born (2)

hushed
538 waters heard and hushed their raging at thy word (2)

hymn
8 hark, the glad celestial hymn (2)
33 clearer sounds the angel hymn,
35 Lord of all, to thee we raise this our hymn of grateful (R)
35 this our hymn of grateful praise (R)
199 each smile a hymn, each kindly deed a prayer (1)
236 with one accord our parting hymn of praise (1)
357 hymn & chant & high thanksgiving & unwearied praises be (3)
366 we rejoice, and sing to thee our hymn of joy eternally (3)
491 the toils of day are over; we raise our hymn to thee (3)
505 let our vesper hymn be blending ... holy calm around (1)

hymns
11 voices raise to the Lord in hymns of praise (1)
11 nations, come, your voices raise to the Lord in hymns (1)
24 come, sound his praise abroad, and hymns of glory sing (T,1)
233 send forth the hymns our fathers loved (3)
294 her hymns of love and praise (4)
424 to thee, before thy passion they sang .. hymns of praise (3)
437 our Christ hath brought us over with hymns of victory (1)
443 hymns of praise then let us sing (2)
450 let his church with gladness hymns of triumph sing (2)
500 to thee our morning hymns ascended (1)
524 our hearts we raise in hymns of adoration (1)
535 they sing the Lamb in hymns above and we in hymns below (2)
538 thus evermore shall rise to thee glad hymns of praise (4)
538 glad hymns of praise from land and sea (4)

identical
241 fight the good fight (T,1) (words identical to 240)

idle
84 to untamed colt, the bridle, (1)
279 give me to feel an idle thought as actual wickedness (2)
280 give me to feel an idle thought as actual wickedness (2)

idol
4 cast each false idol from his throne (5)
107 from each idol that would keep us (3)
268 the dearest idol I have known, whate'er that idol be ((5)

idols
281 my idols all be cast aside (3)

if

507   if thou art well pleased to hear, come down (4)
526   if each should have its rightful meed (1)
526   if thou rememberest each misdeed (1)
529   and tell me if thy name be Love (3)
549   work shall be prayer, if all be wrought as thou wouldst (6)

ignorance
  344   error and ignorance remove (2)
  476   dispel the gloom of error's night, of ignorance & fear (3)

ill
   41   mixture strange of good and ill (2)
   67   in death's dark vale I fear no ill (4)
   67   fear no ill, with thee, dear Lord, beside me (4)
   68   yet will I fear no ill for thou art with me (3)
  243   to fear no ill, to fight the holy fight they fought (2)
  253   tramples down and casts behind the baits of pleasing ill (2)
  260   good and ill, deep buried in each breast (2)
  260   thou hearest these, the good and ill (2)
  467   where thou art guide, no ill can come (3)
  490   my heart's freed from ill, fair blue sky's above (3)
  493   forgive me, Lord, for thy dear Son, the ill (2)
  493   the ill that I this day have done (2)

ills
   20   our helper he amid the flood of mortal ills prevailing (1)
   49   and free us from all ills in this world and the next (2)
  289   ills have no weight, and tears no bitterness (4)
  411   friends in lands afar who battle with the body's ills (2)
  411   battle with the body's ills and wage the holy war (2)
  501   we, oppressed with various ills, draw near (2)

illume
  147   thy tender mercies shall illume the midnight of the soul (3)

illuminate
  278   refining fire, go through my heart; illuminate my soul (2)

Illumine
  267   open my eyes, illumine me, Spirit divine (R)
  398   Light of the world, Illumine ... darkened earth of thine (3)

illumine
  267   open my eyes, illumine me, Spirit divine (R)
  398   Light of the world, Illumine ... darkened earth of thine (3)

illumines
  548   the glory that illumines patriot lives of deathless fame (3)

illuming
  466   and clothe me round the while my path illuming (2)

illumining
   29   o day, all days illumining (1)

illustrious
  239   when that illustrious day shall rise (6)

image
36   man's spirit ... thine image and thyself are there (4)
41   teach us more of human pity that we in thine image grow (3)
118   fallen, till in me thine image shine (2)

imbue
520 let all unworthy aims depart, imbue us with thy grace (2)

Immanuel
317 Immanuel, heaven's joy unending (3)

immense
130 immense and unconfimed; from age to age it never ends (2)

immensities
456 and have the bright immensities received our risen Lord (T)

immortal
23   our souls are his immortal breath (2)
27   immortal, invisible, God only wise (T,1)
38   giver of immortal gladness (1)
101 dwell in that celestial land, where joys immortal flow (4)
146 strong Son of God, immortal love (T,1)
157 immortal love, forever full, forever flowing free (T,1)
158 immortal love, forever full, forever flowing free (T,1)
205 when my spirit, clothed immortal, wings its flight (3)
249 a heavenly race demands thy zeal and an immortal crown (1)
253 a jealous, just concern for thine, immortal praise (4)
307 knowledge and faith and life immortal Jesus ... imparts (1)
313 that living bread ... heavenly wine be our immortal food (2)
332 drink herewith divine supplies and eat immortal bread (3)
366 where we are with the choir immortal (3)
366 choir immortal of angels round thy dazzling throne (3)
371 sages, who wrote the message with immortal pen (2)
406 immortal tidings in your mortal hands (1)
440 know with thee, O God immortal, Jesus Christ (4)
446 Alleluia now we cry to our King immortal (5)
527 'tis mystery all! the Immortal dies! (2)

immortality
9   while ... immortality endures (1,4)
123 I only know a living Christ, our immortality (3)

immovable
308 unshaken as eternal hills, immovable she stands (4)

impart
75   thy Word alone true wisdom can impart (2)
129 thy soul-cheering comfort impart (4)
137 the grace which all may find, the saving power, impart (3)
143 may thy rich grace impart strength to my fainting heart (2)
172 the pure celestial fire to impart (1)
195 teach the precious things thou dost impart (3)
213 Jesus, thy timely aid impart (3)
257 glorious Lord, thy self impart (3)
276 still to the lowly soul he doth himself impart (3)

279 Almighty God of truth and love, to me thy power impart (4)
280 Almighty God of truth and love, to me thy power impart (4)
281 the mind which was in Christ impart (4)
282 thy nature, gracious Lord, impart (5)
321 Master ... symbols shared thine own dear self impart (4)
337 wisdom and zeal and faith impart (3)
352 do thou the truth impart unto each waiting heart (3)
401 inward light impart, cheer my eyes and warm my heart (2)
438 his grace ... doth impart eternal sunshine to the heart (3)
467 who dost thy seven-fold gifts impart (1)
479 consecrating to thy purpose every gift thou dost impart (1)
528 refuse his righteousness to impart (3)
528 refuse ... to impart by hiding it within my heart (3)
531 O Love, thy sovereign aid impart to save me (3)

imparts
307 knowledge and faith and life immortal Jesus ... imparts (1)
307 Jesus thy Son to us imparts (1)
329 from the best bliss that earth imparts (1)
332 how the bread his flesh imparts (1)
368 Lord, grant us all aright to learn the wisdom it imparts (4)
381 God imparts to human hearts the blessings of his heaven (3)
513 accept the gifts we offer for all thy love imparts (3)

impassioned
543 pilgrim feet, whose stern, impassioned stress (2)

impearled
380 in the light of that star lie the ages impearled (3)

implanted
30 he hath eternal life implanted in the soul (3)

implore
29 the Father, too, our prayers implore (3)
246 renew it boldly every day, and help divine implore (2)
260 thy gifts divine implore (1)
260 dost not wait till human speech thy gifts ... implore (1)
490 Father, I implore, safely keep this child (2)
526 Lord, hear me, I implore thee (1)

implored
54 thy right hand thy powerful arm ... succor they implored (3)

imploring
459 pray we that thou wilt hear us, still imploring (5)
459 still imploring thy love and favor, kept to us always (5)

import
335 not a cause of small import the pastor's care demands (2)

imprison
184 imprison me within thine arms ... strong ... be my hand (1)

imprisoned
527 long my imprisoned spirit lay fast bound in sin (3)

improve
492 may we this life improve, to mourn for errors past (4)

impulse
187 take my hands ... let them move ... impulse of thy love (1)

inaccessible
27 in light inaccessible hid from our eyes (1)

inarmed
198 inarmed shall live as comrades free (3)
198 nation with nation, land with land, inarmed shall live (3)

incarnate
3 come, thou incarnate Word, gird on thy mighty sword (2)
18 Word incarnate glorified the flesh of man (2)
18 thanks to God whose Word incarnate (2)
85 O Son of God incarnate, O Son of man divine (T,1)
85 O Mind of God incarnate, O Thought in flesh enshrined (2)
85 Heart of God incarnate, Love-bearer to mankind (3)
85 O Will of God incarnate, so human, so divine (4)
372 O Word of God incarnate, O Wisdom from on high (T,1)
375 worship we the God-head, Love incarnate, Love divine (2)
387 hail the incarnate Deity (2)
420 the incarnate God hath died for me (1)
460 God hath spoken by...the Word incarnate (2)
460 the Word incarnate, God of God, ere time began (2)
465 incarnate Deity, let ... ransomed race render in thanks (2)
533 following ... incarnate God ... gained the promised rest (2)

incarnation
331 in thy holy incarnation, when the angels sang thy birth (2)
412 for me, kind Jesus, was thy incarnation (4)

incense
258 ready burning be the incense of thy powers (2)
350 like incense sweet to thee ascend (2)
352 let every anthem rise like incense to the skies (2)
383 gold and myrrh and frankincense (5)
385 so bring him incense, gold, and myrrh (3)
402 frankincense to offer have I, incense owns a Deity nigh (3)
405 see them give, in deep devotion, gold and frankincense (3)
405 gold and frankincense and myrrh (3)
405 incense doth their God disclose (4)
485 rise like incense, each to thee, in noble thought & deed (1)
486 their unconsidered lives go up like incense to the sky (2)

incessant
509 by his incessant bounty fed (2)

incline
94 now incline me to repent; let me now my sins lament (3)

inclined
428 vast the love that him inclined to bleed & die for thee (1)

increase
139 increase in us the kindled fire...work of faith fulfill (2)
211 his love thy joy increase (2)
239 increase my courage, Lord (4)
269 and doubts appall, and sorrows still increase (1)
459 thine is the quickening power that gives increase (4)
482 in mart & court and parliament the common good increase (3)
552 thy true religion in our hearts increase (3)

increasing
359 his kingdom still increasing, a kingdom without endd (4)
367 still new beauties may I see, and still increasing light (3)

indeed
21 know that the Lord is God indeed (2)
193 till thou hast made us free indeed (3)
210 the soul that trusted him indeed (3)
248 till every foe is vanquished, and Christ is Lord indeed (1)
265 O make me thine indeed, thou blessed Son (5)
274 speak! and make me blest indeed (3)
438 He is our meat and drink indeed (4)
548 make our nation free indeed (4)

indulge
277 I ask no higher state, indulge me but in this (4)

indwelling
36 the indwelling God, proclaimed of old (4)

inextinguishable
172 let it for thy glory burn with inextinguishable blaze (2)

infallible
114 and publish to the sons of men the signs infallible (2)

infancy
373 this child, now weak in infancy (1)

infant
70 tender care bestowed before my infant heart could know (2)
70 before my infant heart could know from whom...comforts (2)
252 speech that infant lips can try (3)
377 welcome Christ, the infant King (3)
382 yonder shines the infant light (2)
393 holy infant so tender and mild sleep in heavenly peace (1)
396 infant holy, infant lowly, for his bed a cattle stall (T,1)
400 guide where our infant Redeemer is laid (1,5)
472 and infant voices shall proclaim their early blessings (3)

infant's
502 be every mourner's sleep tonight like infant's slumbers (5)
502 like infant's slumbers pure and light (5)

infest
392 nor thorns infest the ground (3)

infinite
8   infinite thy vast domain, everlasting is thy reign (1)
409   and thanks never ceasing, and infinite love (4)

infinity
130   grace ... wide as infinity ... it never passed by one (3)

infirmity
494   pardon each infirmity, open fault, and secret sin (2)

inflame
471   inflame our hearts with perfect love (4)

influence
131   let us thine influence prove (1)
471   abroad thy healing influence shower (3)

inform
75   thou only canst inform the mind and purify the heart (2)

inherit
155   we know we at the end shall life inherit (3)
283   let us all in thee inherit, let us find that second rest (2)

inheritance
256   thou mine inheritance, now and always (3)

inly
262   to hear the whispers of thy grace & hear thee inly speak (4)
350   grant the vision inly given of this thy house (5)
480   health to the sick in mind, sight to the inly blind (2)
531   and inly sigh for thy repose (1)

inmost
210   nor doubt our inmost wants are known to him (2)
310   bid our inmost souls rejoice in hope of perfect love (5)
531   speak to my inmost soul and say,

inner
363   let us thy inner presence feel (3)
475   still wilt not hear thine inner God proclaim (1)

inquire
527   let angel minds inquire no more (2)

inscribed
114   can my gracious Savior show my name inscribed in heaven (1)

inscrutable
486   at whose inscrutable decree the planets wheel and turn (1)

inseparably
193   to thee, inseparably joined, let all our spirits cleave (5)

inside
377   no room inside the hostel there for Joseph (1)

insight
517 grant us then a deeper insight & new powers of sacrifice (4)

inspire
16   to touch our lips, our minds inspire (3)
131 come, Holy Ghost, our hearts inspire (T,1)
136 burn, winged fire! inspire our lips with flaming love (2)
136 inspire our lips with flaming love and zeal to preach (2)
137 inspire the living faith, which whosoe'er receives (4)
143 my zeal inspire (2)
342 inspire our ways of learning ... earnest, fervent prayer (1)
374 gladsome tidings be which inspire your heavenly song (2)
467 come, Holy Ghost, our souls inspire (T,1)
476 inspire thy heralds of good news to live thy life divine (5)

inspired
292 inspired with hope and praise, to Christ belong (4)
370 praise we God, who hath inspired those (3)
370 inspired those whose wisdom still directs us (3)
533 his zeal inspired their breast (2)
549 prayer, by thee inspired and taught ... with work be one (6)

inspires
214 but righteousness inspires those who have sought (4)
510 inspires our choicest songs (1)
525 which all our better thought inspires (3)

instant
529 be conquered by my instant prayer (3)

instill
422 to heal the people of their shame, and nobleness instill (3)

instructor
367 Divine instructor, gracious Lord, be thou forever near (4)

instruments
343 instruments of loftier sound assist his feeble praise (2)

intellect
187 take my intellect ... use every power as thou ... choose (2)

intent
155 his first avowed intent to be a pilgrim (1)
383 to seek for a king was their intent (3)

intercede
122 he ever lives above, for me to intercede (2)

intercedeth
412 for man's atonement ... God intercedeth (3)
412 while he nothing heedeth, God intercedeth (3)

interceding
454 for saints ... interceding till in glory they appear (3)

interest
    137   only then, we feel our interest in his blood (2)
    527   I ... gain an interest in the Savior's blood (1)

interposed
     93   to rescue me from danger, interposed his precious blood (2)

interpreted
    235   silence of eternity, interpreted by love (3)

interpreter
    215   God is his own interpreter, and he will make it plain (5)

interrupt
    509   when death shall interrupt our songs and seal in silence (5)

interstellar
    456   the Lord of interstellar space and conqueror of time (1)

introduced
    249   blest Savior, introduced by thee have I my race begun (4)

inured
    253   a soul inured to pain, to hardship, grief and loss (2)

invisible
     27   immortal, invisible, God only wise (T,1)
    139   the invisible appears in sight (6)

invitation
    102   the invitation is to all (2)

invited
    318   never to my hurt invited, be thy love with love requited (3)

invites
    438   so let us keep the festival where-to the Lord invites us (3)
    528   he calls you now, invites you home (5)

involved
    269   involved in shadows of a darksome night (3)

inward
    135   Word of God and inward light (1)
    306   when we asunder part, it gives us inward pain (4)
    401   inward light impart, cheer my eyes and warm my heart (2)

ire
    484   in ire and exultation aflame with faith and free (3)

iron
    376   earth stood hard as iron, water like a stone (1)

island
    500   as o'er each continent and island the dawn leads on (3)

islands
    290   I know not where his islands lift their fronded palms (5)

Israel
    354 O come, O come, Emmanuel, & ransom captive Israel (T,1)
    354 rejoice!...Emmanuel shall come to thee, O Israel (R)
    358 traveler, yes; it brings the...promised day of Israel (1)
    383 Noel, Noel, Noel, Noel, born is the King of Israel (R)
    405 out of thee the Lord from heaven came to rule his Israel (1)
    424 thou art the King of Israel, thou David's royal Son (1)
    446 God hath brought his Israel into joy from sadness (1)

Israel's
      9 happy the man whose hopes rely on Israel's God (2)
     46 captain of Israel's host (T,1)
     71 chosen seed of Israel's race, ye ransomed from the fall (2)
    312 see Israel's Gentle Shepherd stand (T,1)
    360 Israel's strength and consolation (1)

Jacob's
    287 climbing Jacob's ladder ... soldiers of the cross (T,1)
    446 Jacob's sons and daughters (1)

jealous
    150 arm me with jealous care, as in thy sight to live (3)
    253 a spirit still prepared, and armed with jealous care (3)
    253 a jealous, just concern for thine, immortal praise (4)

jealousies
    469 in wrath and fear, by jealousies surrounded (3)

Jehovah
     24 Jehovah is the sovereign God, the universal King (1)
     31 the Lord Jehovah reigns, his throne is built on high (T,1)
    271 guide me, O thou great Jehovah (T,1)

Jehovah's
     22 before Jehovah's awful throne (T,1)
     39 sing the great Jehovah's praise and bless his holy name (1)
    510 sing to the Great Jehovah's praise (T,1)

Jerusalem
    303 Jerusalem the golden, with milk and honey blest (T,1)
    366 awake, Jerusalem, at last (1)
    446 comes to glad Jerusalem who with true affection (3)

Jesse
    399 Root of Jesse, David's Son, my Lord and Master (1)

Jesus
     20 dost ask who that may be? Christ Jesus, it is he (2)
     48 to you who for refuge to Jesus have fled (1)
     48 the soul that on Jesus still leans for repose (5)
     74 let every tongue confess ... one accord ... Jesus Christ (5)
     74 confess ...in heaven and earth that Jesus Christ is Lord (5)
     76 at the name of Jesus every knee shall bow (T,1)
     78 at the great name of Jesus, now all knees must bend (2)
     79 fairest Lord Jesus, ruler of all nature (T,1)
     79 robed in the blooming garb of spring: Jesus is fairer (2)
     79 Jesus is purer, who makes the woeful heart to sing (2)

79	and all the twinkling starry host: Jesus shines brighter (3)
79	Jesus shines purer, than all the angels heaven can boast (3)
81	how sweet the name of Jesus sounds in a believer's ear (T,1)
81	Jesus, my Savior, shepherd, friend (3)
81	Jesus ... my prophet, priest, and king (3)
81	Jesus ... my Lord, my life, my way, my end (3)
82	Jesus, the very thought of thee (T,1)
82	love of Jesus, what it is none but his loved ones know (4)
82	Jesus, our only joy be thou, as thou our prize wilt be (5)
82	Jesus, be thou our glory now and through eternity (5)
86	Jesus, thou Christ of God, by thy perennial Word lead (3)
87	take the name of Jesus with you (T,1)
87	take the name of Jesus ever as a shield from every snare (2)
87	at the name of Jesus bowing (4)
88	tell me the stories of Jesus I love to hear (T,1)
88	stories of Jesus, tell them to me (1)
88	Jesus is King (3)
89	from sin ... grief & shame, I hide me, Jesus in thy name (1)
89	Jesus, my all-in-all thou art (3)
90	we would see Jesus (T,1,2,3,4,5)
90	we would see Jesus on the mountain teaching (3)
90	we would see Jesus in his work of healing (4)
90	we would see Jesus in the early morning (5)
91	may Jesus Christ be praised! (R)
91	alike at work and prayer to Jesus I repair (1)
93	Jesus sought me when a stranger (2)
94	God is love! I know, I feel, Jesus weeps & loves me still (4)
97	Jesus is all the world to me (T,1,2,3,4)
98	Jesus, where'er thy people meet (T,1)
100	Jesus, our great high priest, hath full atonement made (2)
101	Jesus shed his precious blood rich blessings to bestow (2)
101	Jesus is the truth, the way that leads you into rest (3)
104	Jesus ready stands to save you (1)
104	without money, come to Jesus Christ and buy (2)
104	not the righteous; sinners Jesus came to call (4)
107	Jesus calls us o'er the tumult (T,1)
107	Jesus calls us from the worship of the vain (3)
107	Jesus calls us! (5)
108	O Jesus, thou art standing outside the fast-closed door (T)
108	O Jesus, thou art knocking, and lo, that hand is scarred (2)
108	O Jesus, thou art pleading in accents meek and low (3)
109	Jesus, only Savior, sanctify forever (3)
110	Jesus is tenderly calling thee home (T,1)
110	calling today, Jesus is tenderly calling today (R)
110	Jesus is calling the weary to rest (2)
110	Jesus is waiting, O come to him now (3)
110	Jesus is pleading; O list to his voice (4)
116	Jesus sweetly speaks to me (2)
116	Jesus comes! He fills my soul! Perfected in him I am (5)
116	humbly at thy cross I bow, save me, Jesus, save me now (4)
117	I looked to Jesus, and I found in him my star, my sun (3)
117	I heard the voice of Jesus say (T,1,2,3)
117	I came to Jesus as I was, weary and worn and sad (1)
117	I came to Jesus, and I drank of that life-giving stream (2)
118	Jesus, the sinner's friend, to thee (T,1,5)
124	Jesus Christ, the crucified (1,2,3,4)
125	Jesus, lover of my soul, let me to thy bosom fly (T,1)

250 who ... strength of Jesus trusts is more than conqueror (1)
251 Jesus, I my cross have taken (T,1)
253 Jesus, my strength, my hope, on thee I cast my care (T,1)
257 blessed Jesus, at thy word (T,1)
259 Jesus, thy boundless love to me (T,1)
259 O Jesus, nothing may I see ... desire, or seek but thee (2)
259 O Jesus, in that solemn hour, in death as life (3)
261 what a friend we have in Jesus (T,1)
261 Jesus knows our every weakness (2)
266 spend much time in secret with Jesus alone (2)
266 by looking to Jesus, like him thou shalt be (2)
266 and, looking to Jesus, still trust in his Word (3)
268 where is the soul-refreshing view of Jesus and his word (2)
278 Jesus, thine all-victorious love shed in my heart abroad (T)
282 where Jesus reigns alone (2)
283 Jesus, thou art all compassion (1)
284 Lord Jesus, think on me (T,1,2,3,4,5,6)
286 Lord I want to be like Jesus in my heart (4)
287 sinner, do you love my Jésus ... soldiers of the cross (3)
297 the Church's one foundation is Jesus Christ her Lord (T,1)
299 tidings of Jesus, redemption and release   (R)
300 Jesus Christ, our Father's Son, bids us undismayed go on (3)
301 if our fellowship below in Jesus be so sweet (5)
303 Jesus, in mercy bring us to that dear land of rest (4)
305 with the cross of Jesus going on before (1,R)
305 but the Church of Jesus constant will remain (3)
307 knowledge and faith and life immortal Jesus ... imparts (1)
307 Jesus thy Son to us imparts (1)
309 Jesus, Lord, we look to thee (T,1)
310 Jesus, we look to thee, thy promised presence claim (T,1)
311 Jesus, with thy Church abide (T,1)
318 Jesus, bread of life, I pray thee (3)
325 rich blood that Jesus shed to raise our souls to heaven (2)
328 hearts and minds and spirits join, and all in Jesus meet (3)
329 Jesus, thou joy of loving hearts (T,1)
329 O Jesus, ever with us stay (5)
331 Jesus spreads his banner o'er us (T,1)
335 may they in Jesus ...they preach, their own Redeemer see (4)
336 glory and thanks to Jesus give for his almighty grace (1)
336 gladly reckon all things loss so we may Jesus gain (5)
338 nothing desire, nothing esteem, but Jesus crucified (3)
341 Jesus ... name to sinners dear ... name to sinners given (2)
348 Jesus Christ, its cornerstone (4)
355 O wounded hands of Jesus, build in us thy new creation (4)
360 come, thou long expected Jesus (T,1)
375 worship we our Jesus, but where-with for sacred sign (2)
376 sufficed the Lord God Almighty, Jesus Christ (2)
378 for Jesus Christ our Savior was born upon this day (1)
380 in the homes of the nations that Jesus is King (3)
383 right over the place where Jesus lay (4)
384 the little Lord Jesus laid down his sweet head (1)
384 the little Lord Jesus, asleep on the hay (1)
384 but little Lord Jesus, no crying he makes (2)
384 I love thee, Lord Jesus, look down from the sky (2)
384 be near me, Lord Jesus, I ask thee to stay close by me (3)
386 Jesus, to thee be all glory given (3)
387 pleased as man with men to dwell, Jesus our Emmanuel (2)

102   let every soul be Jesus' guest (1)
106   pleading nought but Jesus' blood, whisper softly (3)
107   leaving all for Jesus' sake (2)
222   nothing less than Jesus' blood and righteousness (1)
222   but wholly lean on Jesus' name (1)
229   to do the will of Jesus: this is rest (2)
229   on Jesus' bosom naught but calm is found (3)
229   in Jesus' keeping we are safe, and they (4)
288   all in Jesus' presence reign through ages without end (2)
328   so dear the tie where souls agree in Jesus' dying love (4)
338   still in Jesus' footsteps tread & show his praise below (2)
420   ye all are bought with Jesus' blood (2)
446   welcomes in unwearied strains Jesus' resurrection (3)
454   help to sing of Jesus' merits (4)
464   Jesus' love the nations fires (1)
464   Jesus' word is glorified (3)
490   may this day be blest, trusting Jesus' love (3)
507   give up ourselves, through Jesus' power (2)
510   while on in Jesus' steps we go to see thy face above (4)
516   happy the home where Jesus' name is sweet to every ear (2)
518   but more because of Jesus' blood (3)

Jesus's
227   what a heaven in Jesus's name (2)

Jewry
378   in Bethlehem in Jewry this blessed babe was born (2)

John
481   O holy city, seen of John (T,1)

join
5   join in a song with sweet accord (1)
7   so may we, in lowly station join the choristers above (2)
11   join the angel song, all the worlds to him belong (1)
31   join all my powers to praise the Lord! (4)
38   mortals join the happy chorus, which the... stars began (4)
52   death ... shall join our souls to thee (4)
55   join me in glad adoration (1)
71   we'll join the everlasting song (5)
77   come, Christians, join to sing Alleluia! Amen! (T,1)
101   come then and join this holy band, and on to glory go (4)
189   join the glorious new crusade of our great Lord and King (3)
192   join hands ... brothers of the faith whate'er your race (3)
302   come, let us join our friends above (T,1)
302   by faith we join our hands with those that went before (5)
305   onward, then, ye people, join our happy throng (4)
328   hearts and minds and spirits join, and all in Jesus meet (3)
333   whom thou forevermore dost join in one (1)
387   join the triumph of the skies (1)
440   join, O man, the deathless voices (3)
489   thus may all our sabbaths prove till we join ... above (4)
489   till we join the Church above (4)
507   all, with one accord, in a perpetual covenant join (1)
507   join ourselves to Christ the Lord (1)
530   join us, in one spirit ... let us still receive of thine (2)

joined
193 to thee, inseparably joined, let all our spirits cleave (5)
306 we shall still be joined in heart and hope to meet again (4)
328 then only can it closer be, when all are joined above (4)
338 joined in one spirit to our Head (2)
344 unite the pair . long disjoined, knowledge & vital piety (3)
399 ever joined to thee in love that cannot falter (2)
488 on thee the high and lowly, through ages joined in tune (1)
535 happy the souls to Jesus joined (T,1)

joining
59 beside us to guide us, our God with us joining (2)
186 worth to my meanest labor give by joining it to thine (2)

joins
8 Lo! the apostolic train joins thy sacred name to hallow (3)
301 Lord, who joins us by his grace (1)
512 all nature joins in singing a joyful song of praise (2)

Jordan
99 sorrow vanquished, labor ended, Jordan passed (5)
217 since God through Jordan leadeth me (4)
244 when my life becomes a burden ... nearing chilly Jordan (4)
271 when I tread the verge of Jordan, bid ... fears subside (3)
291 though Jordan waves may roll, I'll fearless launch away (3)
450 bring us safe through Jordan to thy home above (3)

Jordan's
291 on Jordan's stormy banks I stand (T,1)

Joseph
374 Mary, Joseph, lend your aid (4)
377 no room inside the hostel there for Joseph (1)
377 no room ... for Joseph or Madonna fair (1)

Joseph's
123 Joseph's tomb could solve death's mystery. (3)
123 I know not how that Joseph's tomb could solve death's (3)

journey
80 and like thee, all my journey run (4)
87 when our journey is complete (4)
176 along my pilgrim journey, Savior, let we walk with thee (1)
269 only with thee we journey safely on (3)
271 let the fire and cloudy pillar lead me all my journey (2)
300 as we journey let us sing (1)
478 thy cross is lifted o'er us, we journey in its light (3)
534 thou hast called us to the journey (1)
534 journey which faithless feet ne'er trod (1)

journeys
203 he who journeys in them walks with thee (1)
472 where'er the sun does his successive journeys run (1)

joy
1 leap, ye lame, for joy (6)
4 our peace and joy and blessing (3)

```
 14   shout for joy and Savior's name (3)
 17   and take me home, what joy shall fill my heart! (4)
 18   here we drink of joy unmeasured (3)
 21   approach with joy his courts unto (3)
 22   ye nations, bow with sacred joy (1)
 23   bound every heart with rapturous joy (3)
 25   the joy that from thy presence springs (1)
 25   might I enjoy the meanest place within thy house (2)
 35   for the joy of ear and eye (3)
 35   for the joy of human love, brother, sister, parent,child (4)
 35   peace on earth, and joy in heaven (6)
 38   all thy works with joy surround thee (2)
 38   well-spring of the joy of living (3)
 38   lift us to the joy divine (3)
 50   so full of splendor and of joy, beauty and light (1)
 50   I thank thee, too, that thou hast made joy to abound (2)
 50   I thank thee more that all our joy is touched with pain (3)
 56   in trouble and in joy (1)
 58   their joy unto their Lord we bring (3)
 79   thee will I honor, thou, my soul's glory, joy and crown (1)
 82   O Hope of every contrite heart, O Joy of all the meek (3)
 82   Jesus, our only joy be thou, as thou our prize wilt be (5)
 87   it will joy and comfort give you (1)
 87   Hope of earth and joy of heaven (R)
 87   name of Jesus! How it thrills our souls with joy (3)
 89   joy and everlasting love (2)
 89   in grief my joy unspeakable (4)
 92   I shall possess, within the veil ... life of joy & peace (5)
 97   my life .. joy .. all; he is my strength ... day to day (1)
 97   eternal life, eternal joy, he's my friend (4)
103   joy of the desolate, light of the straying (2)
127   with joy shall I lift up my head (1)
129   and let the sweet tokens of pardoning grace bring joy (4)
129   bring joy to my desolate heart (4)
132   come, thou source of joy and gladness, breathe thy life (1)
136   fill it with love and joy and power (1)
137   cry, with joy unspeakable, "...my Lord, my God" (2)
151   O how our hearts beat high with joy whene'er we hear (1)
152   run my course with even joy (4)
159   there are heights of joy that I may not reach till (4)
165   fill our hearts with joy and peace (1)
167   through sorrow or through joy, conduct me as thine own (1)
171   that it may be our highest joy, our Father's work to do (3)
177   in joy, in grief, through life, dear Lord, for thee (4)
183   now they taste unmingled love, and joy without a tear (2)
185   once earthly joy I craved, sought peace and rest (2)
195   thy rest, thy joy, thy glory share (5)
205   gushing from the rock before me...a spring of joy I see (2)
208   just from Jesus simply taking life & rest & joy & peace (3)
211   his love thy joy increase (2)
223   for the favor he shows, and the joy he bestowes (3)
223   joy he bestows are for them who will trust and obey (3)
227   Jesus all the day long was my joy and my song (4)
227   when my heart first believed, what a joy I received (2)
234   O Joy that seekest me through pain (3)
240   lay hold on life ..it shall be thy joy & crown eternally (1)
251   not in joy to charm me were that joy unmixed with thee (3)
```

262 enter into my Master's joy, and find my heaven in thee (4)
265 in joy or in pain (3)
266 in joy or in sorrow, still follow the Lord (3)
269 through joy or sorrow, as thou deemest best (4)
283 joy of heaven, to earth come down (1)
284 and share thy joy at last (5)
294 beyond my highest joy I prize her heavenly ways (4)
301 we all partake the joy of one; the common peace we feel (4)
301 a peace to sensual minds unknown, a joy unspeakable (4)
309 let us then with joy remove to the family above (6)
310 thy name is life and joy and peace and everlasting love (2)
317 Immanuel, heaven's joy unending (3)
318 there with joy thy praises render unto him (1)
318 joy, the sweetest man e'er knoweth (2)
326 giving sweet foretaste of the festal joy (5)
329 Jesus, thou joy of loving hearts (T,1)
333 grant them the joy which brightens earthly sorrow (3)
338 joy .. grief .. time .. place .. life nor death can part (4)
349 as here with joy this stone we lay (1)
353 and life to joy awakes (1)
358 doth its beauteous ray aught of joy or hope foretell (1)
359 love, joy and hope, like flowers, spring in his path (3)
360 dear desire of every nation, joy of every longing heart (1)
363 adorned with prayer and love and joy (2)
366 all her heart with joy is springing (2)
366 we rejoice, and sing to thee our hymn of joy eternally (3)
371 tongues ... acclaim with joy thy wondrous gift to man (4)
373 this child ... our confidence and joy shall be (1)
378 O tidings of comfort and joy, comfort and joy (R)
379 till the air, everywhere, now with joy is ringing (1)
380 there's a tumult of joy o'er the wonderful birth (2)
392 joy to the world, the Lord is come (T,1)
392 joy to the world! the Savior reigns (2)
392 repeat the sounding joy (2)
394 glad tidings of great joy I bring to you and all mankind (2)
397 as with joy they hailed its light (1)
397 so may we with holy joy, pure and free from sins' alloy (3)
399 fill me with joy and strength to be thy member (2)
416 lo! it glows with peace and joy (2)
427 that, as we share this hour, thy cross may bring ... joy (4)
427 thy cross may bring us to thy joy and resurrection power (4)
437 Christ the Lord hath risen, our joy that hath no endd (3)
438 Christ is himself the joy of all (3)
440 never that full joy conceived (2)
440 joy unknown, ... saints shall stand before the throne (4)
445 what joy the blest assurance gives (1,4)
446 God hath brought his Israel into joy from sadness (1)
446 with the royal feast of feasts, comes its joy to render (3)
447 let shouts of holy joy outburst: Alleluia (2)
452 earth with joy confesses, clothing her for spring (2)
453 O what joy the sight affords (4)
457 and only wish the joy to know of our triumphant friend (1)
458 joy of all who dwell above, the joy of all below (3)
458 name an everlasting name; their joy the joy of heaven (4)
458 their profit & their joy to know the mystery of his love (5)
469 sharing not our griefs, no joy can share (2)
475 peals forth in joy man's old undaunted cry (3)

487   give joy of thy victory on this thy holy day (3)
488   O day of joy and light (1)
492   with joy we view the pleasing change (3)
501   O with what joy they went away (1)
504   bring us to heaven, where thy saints united joy (2)
504   saints united joy without ending (2)
509   in scenes exalted or depressed thou art our joy ... rest (4)
517   children thou hast given still may be our joy and crown (5)
520   build thou a hallowed dwelling where ... joy & peace (4)
520   hallowed dwelling where true joy and peace endure (4)
522   unto joy or sorrow grown (2)
524   the hills with joy are ringing (1)

joyful
  4   be joyful in the Lord, my heart (4)
  6   blessings ... bounty ... joyful songs to thee we sing (2)
  6   joyful songs we sing to thee, songs of glory (2)
 13   where my soul in joyful duty waits (1)
 23   raise to Christ our joyful strain (1)
 38   joyful, joyful, we adore thee (T,1)
 38   joyful music leads us sunward (4)
 49   with ever joyful hearts and blessed peace to cheer us (2)
 86   and joyful sing (4)
111   to him with joyful voices give the glory of his grace (1)
165   thanks we give & adoration for thy Gospel's joyful sound (2)
180   joyful rise to pay thy morning sacrifice (1)
188   joyful to follow thee through paths unknown (2)
209   through thorny ways leads to a joyful end (1)
214   their joyful, faithful hearts obey the laws of God (1)
263   or if, on joyful wing cleaving the sky (5)
277   hasten the joyful day which shall my sins consume (2)
292   the world to Christ we bring, with joyful song (4)
300   fear not, brethren; joyful stand (3)
300   joyful stand on the borders of our land (3)
312   joyful that we ourselves are thine ... offspring (3)
352   a joyful sacrifice to thy blest name (2)
386   O come, all ye faithful, joyful and triumphant (T,1)
387   joyful, all ye nations rise (1)
438   let us joyful be and sing to God right thankfully (1)
489   may thy Gospel's joyful sound conquer sinners, comfort (4)
512   the wilderness is fruitful, and joyful are the hills (2)
512   all nature joins in singing a joyful song of praise (2)

joyless
401   joyless the day's return till thy mercy's beams I see (2)

joyous
 51   so shall this night soon end in joyous day (2)
 91   let all the earth around ring joyous with the sound (3)
374   and the mountains in reply echoing their joyous strains (1)
374   why your joyous strain prolong (2)
377   to you the joyous news we bring (3)
397   as with joyous steps they sped to that lowly manger bed (2)

joyously
179   freely and joyously now would we bring (2)

joys
    5   come, ye who love the Lord, and let your joys be known (T,1)
    5   children of the heavenly King may speak ... joys abroad (2)
  75   that life to win, whose joys eternal flow (4)
  83   to him I owe my life and breath and all the joys I have (3)
 101   dwell in that celestial land, where joys immortal flow (4)
 107   in our joys and in our sorrows   (4)
 134   our souls, how heavily they go to reach eternal joys (2)
 147   when the joys of sense depart, to live by faith alone (4)
 209   sorrow forgot, love's purest joys restored (3)
 256   may I reach heaven's joys, O bright heaven's Sun (4)
 275   the joys I feel, the bliss I share (2)
 289   earth's joys grow dim; its glories pass away (2)
 302   on the eagle wings of love to joys celestial rise (1)
 303   I know not, O I know not what joys await us there (1)
 325   not paradise, with all its joys ... such delight afford (1)
 334   possess in sweet communion, joys ... earth cannot afford (2)
 416   joys that through all time abide (4)
 439   raise your joys and triumphs high, Alleluia (1)
 491   the joys of day are over; we lift our hearts to thee (2)
 533   how great their joys, how bright their glories be (1)
 535   Church triumphant in thy love, their mighty joys we know (2)

jubilant
 303   they stand, those halls of Zion, all jubilant with song (2)
 545   O be swift, my soul, to answer him; be jubilant, my feet (3)

Jubilate
 505   Jubilate! Jubilate! Jubilate! Amen! (R)

jubilee
 100   the year of jubilee is come! (R)
 374   shepherds, why this jubilee (2)
 451   voices, Lord, we raise to thee, in jubilee and praise (5)
 510   bring the grand sabbatic year, the jubilee of heaven (6)

judge
 214   when God shall judge, their lot be woe (3)
 215   judge not the Lord by feeble sense (4)
 311   judge her not for work undone (4)
 311   judge her not for fields unwon (4)
 412   that man to judge thee hath in hate pretended (1)
 468   rise, God, judge thou the earth in might (2)
 483   rejoice in glorious hope! Our Lord the judge shall come (4)
 546   Judge eternal, throned in splendor (T,1)

judgest
  78   redeem us...when thou judgest all the sons of men (3)

judgment
 311   may her voice be ever clear, warning of a judgment near (2)
 361   on judgment and on justice based (4)
 434   see him at the judgment hall (2)
 477   come with thy timeless judgment . match our present hour (1)
 493   rise glorious at the Judgment Day (3)
 545   sifting out the hearts of men before his judgment seat (3)
 546   with thy living fire of judgment purge this land (1)

judgments
365   thy laws are pure, thy judgments right (5)
477   let .. be light again .. set thy judgments in .. earth (5)

jungles
406   through jungles, sluggish seas, and mountain pass (2)

just
4   lo! all is just and all is right (2)
119   just as I am, without one plea (T,1)
119   Just as I am (1,2,3,4,5,6)
119   just as I am thou wilt receive (5)
125   just and holy is thy name; I am all unrighteousness (3)
146   and thou hast made him: thou art just (2)
149   that is just the reason I tell it now to thee (2)
154   whiter than snow,Lord, wash me just now (2)
169   just as I am, thine own to be (T,1)
169   just as I am, young, strong and free (4)
195   O use me, Lord, use even me, just as thou wilt and when (5)
195   just as thou wilt, and when, and where (5)
208   just from Jesus simply taking life & rest & joy & peace (3)
208   just to rest upon his promise (1)
208   just to trust his cleansing blood (2)
208   just from sin and self to cease (3)
212   just tell the love of Jesus, and say he died for all (2)
242   and 'tis prosperous to be just (2)
253   a jealous, just concern for thine, immortal praise (4)
433   till I reach the golden strand just beyond the river (4)
485   just rule ... fill ... earth with health & light & peace (2)
526   he is merciful and just, here is my comfort and my trust (3)

justice
27   thy justice like mountains high soaring above (2)
31   his wrath and justice stand to guard his holy law (2)
69   a kindness in his justice which is more than liberty (1)
173   justice conquers violence and wars at last shall cease (3)
361   on judgment and on justice based (4)
365   but the blest volume thou hast writ reveals thy justice (2)
365   volume thou hast writ reveals thy justice and thy grace (2)
371   revealing to sinful men thy justice and thy grace (3)
468   justice, from her heavenly bower look down on mortal men (1,
477   bring justice to our land, that all may dwell secure (3)
548   God of justice, save the people (4)

keenest
243   in keenest strife, Lord, may we stand (3)

keep
10   church with psalms must shout, no door can keep them out (2
31   the thunders of his hand keep the wide world in awe (2)
49   and keep us in his grace, and guide us when perplexed (2)
57   from evil he will keep thee safe (4)
58   unbroken be the golden chain, keep on the song forever (4)
65   unto such as keep his covenant ... steadfast in his way (5)
75   grant us that way to know, that truth to keep (4)
107   from each idol that would keep us (3)
108   O shame,thrice shame upon us, to keep his standing there (1)

111   worst need keep him out no more or force him to depart (2)
121   keep thy flock, from sin defend us (2)
125   make and keep me pure within (4)
150   a charge to keep I have, a God to glorify (T,1)
210   sing, pray,and keep his ways unswerving (3)
226   let thy precious blood applied keep me ... near thy side (1)
236   from harm and danger keep thy children free (3)
242   they must upward still & onward who would keep ... truth (3)
242   who would keep abreast of truth (3)
245   O near to the Rock let me keep (3)
272   keep thou my feet (1)
273   keep me ever, by thy spirit, pure and strong and true (5)
279   awake my soul when sin is nigh, and keep it still awake (3)
280   awake my soul when sin is nigh and keep it still awake (3)
314   may the Church that waiteth for thee keep love's tie (3)
314   keep love's tie unbroken, Lord (3)
314   in our hearts keep watch and ward (4)
319   in memory of the Savior's love, we keep the sacred feast (T)
324   let all mortal flesh keep silence (T,1)
337   by day and night strict guard to keep (4)
350   here gather us around thy board to keep the feast (3)
350   keep the feast with thee, dear Lord (3)
381   while mortals sleep, the angels keep their watch (2)
381   angels keep their watch of wondering love (2)
397   Holy Jesus, every day keep us in the narrow way (4)
433   Jesus, keep me hear the cross (T,1)
437   Let the round world keep triumph, & all that is therein (3)
438   so let us keep the festival where-to the Lord invites us (3)
444   death cannot keep his prey ... He tore the bars away (3)
467   keep far our foes; give peace at home (3)
490   Father, I implore, safely keep this child (2)
491   O Jesus, keep us in thy sight (1,3)
493   keep me, King of kings, beneath thine own almighty wings (1)
506   O Father, while we sleep, thy children keep (R)
517   may we keep our holy calling stainless in... fair renown (5)
520   steadfast faith & earnest prayer keep sacred vows secure (4)
534   O keep us in the pathway their saintly feet have trod (2)
538   bidst the mighty ocean deep its... appointed limits keep (1)
539   keep love's banner floating o'er you (4)
548   keep her faith in simple manhood (4)

keeper
57   thy faithful keeper is the Lord (3)

keepeth
4   his gracious mercy keepeth (2)

keeping
99   finding, following, keeping, struggling...sure to bless (7)
148   to us he gives the keeping of the lights along the shore (1)
153   keeping free our spirits still (4)
229   in Jesus' keeping we are safe, and they (4)
242   keeping watch above his own (4)
383   in fields where they lay keeping their sheep (1)
385   while shepherds watch are keeping (1)
396   shepherds keeping vigil till the morning new (2)
500   through all the world her watch is keeping (2)

keeps
- 15   keeps his court below (1)
- 57   watchful and unslumbering care his own he safely keeps (2)
- 89   thy mighty name salvation ... keeps my happy soul above (2)
- 170   in work that keeps faith sweet and strong (3)

kept
- 45   kept the folded grave-clothes where the body lay (1)
- 50   I thank thee,Lord, that thou hast kept the best in store (4)
- 404   while shepherds kept their watching o'er silent flocks (1)
- 450   kept the folded grave-clothes where the body lay (1)
- 459   still imploring thy love and favor, kept to us always (5)
- 507   the covenant we this moment make be ever kept in mind (3)
- 534   thou hast kept thy pilgrim people (1)
- 534   kept ... people by the strength of thy staff and rod (1)

key
- 131   unlock the truth, thyself the key (2)
- 267   wonderful key that shall unclasp and set me free (1)
- 267   place in my hands the wonderful key (1)

keys
- 483   the keys of death and hell are to our Jesus given (3)

kill
- 20   the body they may kill: God's truth abideth still (4)

kin
- 192   who serves my Father as a son is surely kin to me (3)

kind
- 53   how gentle God's commands! how kind his precepts are! (T,1)
- 60   thou, most kind and gentle death (6)
- 61   praise the Lord, for he is kind (1,4)
- 69   the heart of the Eternal is most wonderfully kind (2)
- 82   to those who fall, how kind thou art (3)
- 105   and basely his kind care repay (2)
- 147   blest be the tempest, kind the storm (2)
- 147   kind the storm which drives us nearer home (2)
- 163   so kind and true and tender, so wise a counselor & guide (3)
- 173   create in us... splendor that dawns when hearts are kind (4)
- 201   help us by deeds of mercy to show that thou art kind (2)
- 309   make us of one heart and mind, courteous, pitiful & kind (3)
- 319   brethren, all, let every heart with kind affection glow (2)
- 344   give .. wisdom from above, spotless .. peaceable & kind (2)
- 412   for me, kind Jesus, was thy incarnation (4)
- 412   therefore, kind Jesus, since I cannot pay thee (5)
- 490   all my countless needs thy kind hand supplies (3)
- 501   thy kind but searching glance can scan the very wounds (5)

kindle
- 134   with all thy quickening powers kindle a flame (1,5)
- 134   kindle a flame of sacred love in ... cold hearts of ours (1)
- 134   come, shed abroad a Savior's love, and... kindle ours (5)
- 135   kindle every high desire; perish self in thy pure fire (2)
- 172   kindle a flame of sacred love on ... altar of my heart (1)

350 descend to kindle spirits cold (2)
466 and kindle it, thy holy flame bestowing (1)

kindled
139 increase in us the kindled fire...work of faith fulfill (2)
464 kindled by a spark of grace (1)
464 kindled in some hearts it is (1)

kindles
479 use the love thy spirit kindles still to save (2)

kindlier
194 to brighter hopes and kindlier things (1)

kindliness
422 his scepter is his kindliness, his grandeur is his grace (2)

kindling
64 kindling hearts that burn for thee (5)
138 the kindling of the heaven descended Dove (5)
195 o'erflow in kindling thought and glowing word (4)
195 until my very heart o'erflow in kindling thought (4)
262 speak to our hearts . let us feel . kindling of thy love (1)
279 catch .. wandering of my will .. quench .. kindling fire (1)
280 and quench the kindling fire (1)

kindly
65 who with thee so kindly deals (2)
151 by kindly words and virtuous life (3)
199 each smile a hymn, each kindly deed a prayer (1)
272 lead kindly Light (T,1)
331 taste it, kindly given, in remembrance, Lord, of thee (1)
502 when the soft dews of kindly sleep (2)
510 who kindly lengthens out our days (1)
530 kindly for each other care; every member feel its share (4)

kindness
7 for his lovingkindness ever shed upon our earthly way (3)
69 a kindness in his justice which is more than liberty (1)
88 words full of kindness, deeds full of grace (2)
175 touched by a loving heart, wakened by kindness (3)
177 some work of love begun, some deed of kindness done (3)
298 with thy wonted loving-kindness hear thy people (2)
476 kindness dwell in human hearts and... earth find peace (2)

kindred
20 let goods and kindred go, this mortal life also (4)
71 let every kindred, every tribe on this terrestrial ball (4)
107 turned from home and toil and kindred (2)
306 the fellowship of kindred minds is like to that above (1)

king
1 glories of my God and King, the triumphs of his grace (1)
3 come, thou almighty King (T, 1)
5 children of the heavenly King may speak ... joys abroad (2)
6 songs of glory, songs of triumph to our God and King (2)

11	through his far domain, love is king where he doth reign (2)
15	glory to their Maker give, and homage to their King (3)
24	Jehovah is the sovereign God, the universal King (1)
25	O God, our King, whose sovereign sway (4)
31	and will this sovereign King of glory condescend (4)
45	why should my heart be sad? The Lord is King (3)
54	as ... God our fathers owned, so thou art still our King (4)
55	praise to the Lord, the almighty, the King of creation (T,1)
60	all creatures of our God and King (T,1)
66	praise, my soul, the King of heaven (T,1)
66	praise the everlasting King (1)
67	the King of love my Shepherd is (T,1)
74	all praise to thee, for thou, O King divine (T,1)
76	every tongue confess him King of glory now (1)
77	loud praise to Christ our King; Alleluia! Amen! (1)
81	Jesus ... my prophet, priest, and king (3)
86	Christ our triumphant King, we come thy name to sing (1)
86	unite to swell the song to Christ our King (4)
87	King of kings in heaven we'll crown him (4)
88	Jesus is King (3)
90	haste, let us lay our gifts before the King (1)
135	King within my conscience reign (4)
138	hast thou not bid me love thee, God and King (3)
174	to serve the King of kings (1)
179	King of our lives, by thy grace we will be (1)
179	King of our lives, by thy grace we will be (R)
179	yielding henceforth to our glorious King (2)
187	take my voice ... let me sing always, only, for my King (2)
189	join the glorious new crusade of our great Lord and King (3)
194	lift up our hearts, O King of kings (T,1)
221	standing on the promises of Christ my King (1)
233	the cross of Christ your King (1)
248	he with the King of glory shall reign eternally (4)
255	praise of him who is thy God, thy Savior, and thy King (4)
256	High King of heaven, my treasure thou art (3)
256	High King of heaven, my victory won (4)
276	to dwell in lowliness with men, their pattern &... King (2)
295	O thou almighty Lord of hosts, who art my God and King (4)
300	children of the heavenly King (T,1)
302	all the servants of our King, in earth & heaven are one (2)
305	glory, laud, and honor unto Christ the King (4)
324	King of kings, yet born of Mary (2)
325	the King of heaven his table spreads (T,1)
352	till we our God and King shall praise in heaven (4)
353	the King shall come (T,1)
353	when Christ our King in beauty comes (4)
353	the King shall come when morning dawns (5)
353	thy people pray, come quickly, King of kings (5)
357	powers, dominions, bow before him & extol our God & King
360	born thy people to deliver, born a child and yet a King (2)
362	proclaim to a desolate people the coming of their King (2)
363	behold the King of glory waits (1)
363	the King of kings is drawing near (1)
374	Christ the Lord, the new-born King (3)
377	welcome Christ, the infant King (3)
380	in the homes of the nations that Jesus is King (3)

380   and we greet in his cradle our Savior and King (4)
381   praises sing to God the King, and peace to men on earth (2)
382   come and worship, worship Christ, the new-born King (R)
383   Noel, Noel, Noel, Noel, born is the King of Israel (R)
383   to seek for a king was their intent (3)
385   this, this is Christ the King (R)
385   King, whom shepherds guard and angels sing (R)
385   come, peasant, King, to own him (3)
385   the King of kings salvation brings (3)
386   come and behold him, born the King of angels (1)
387   glory to the new-born King (1)
388   glory to the new-born King (R)
390   from heaven's all-gracious King (1)
392   let earth receive her King (1)
393   with the angels let us sing Alleluia to our King (4)
395   praise his name in all the earth; Hail the King of glory (3)
397   treasures bring, Christ, to thee, our heavenly King (3)
402   born a King on Bethlehem's plain (2)
402   King forever, ceasing never over us all to reign (2)
402   glorious now behold him arise, King ... God & sacrifice (5)
405   gold the King of kings proclaimeth (4)
406   make straight, make straight the highway of the King (1)
409   ascribing salvation to Jesus, our King (2)
422   ride on, O King, ride on your way (4)
423   for Christ is our Redeemer, the Lord of heaven our King (3)
424   all glory, laud, and honor, to thee, Redeemer, King (T,1)
424   thou art the King of Israel, thou David's royal Son (1)
424   who in the Lord's name comest, the King and blessed One (1)
424   who in all good delightest, thou good and gracious King (3)
426   here the King of all the ages throned in light (2)
439   lives again our glorious King, Alleluia (2)
443   unto Christ, our heavenly King (2)
446   Alleluia now we cry to our King immortal (5)
449   now is the triumph of our King (1)
451   the King of heaven, the glorious King (1)
452   all good gifts returned with her returning King (2)
453   crown the Savior King of kings (2)
453   King of kings, and Lord of lords (4)
454   hail, thou Galilean King (1)
455   and hail him as thy matchless King through all eternity (1)
457   Lord our King, who reigns for us...shall forever reign (2)
458   King of kings, & Lord of lords, & heaven's eternal light (2)
460   God is King, his throne eternal (1)
472   his grateful honors to our King (5)
473   O worship the King, all glorious above (T,1)
478   lead on, O King eternal, the day of march has come (T,1)
478   and now, O King eternal, we lift our battle song (1)
478   lead on, O King eternal, till sin's fierce war ... cease (2)
478   lead on, O King eternal, we follow, not with fears (3)
482   O Thou who art the Life and Light, Exalted Lord and King (4)
483   rejoice, the Lord is King, your Lord and King adore (T,1)
493   keep me, King of kings, beneath thine own almighty wings (1)
517   Lord of life and King of glory (T,1)
544   God the omnipotent! King who ordainest (T,1)
546   Lord of lords and King of kings (1)
547   protect us by thy might, Great God, our King (4)

King's
    84 we'll follow thee, a King's own flock (1)
    406 heralds of Christ, who bear the King's commands (T,1)
    406 prepare across the earth the King's highway (2)

kingdom
    4 within the kingdom of his might (2)
    20 His kingdom is forever (4)
    59 ordaining, maintaining his kingdom divine (2)
    174 rise up, o men of God, his kingdom tarries long (2)
    197 thy kingdom come on earth, O Lord (4)
    197 we pray in deed and word, thy kingdom come on earth (4)
    201 help us to seek thy kingdom that cometh from above (3)
    218 he that into God's kingdom comes must enter by this door (3)
    294 I love thy kingdom, Lord, the house of thine abode (T,1)
    304 Thy kingdom come (1)
    304 O holy kingdom, happy fold, the blessed Church to be (2)
    307 gathered into the kingdom by thy Son (4)
    314 world where thou... send us let thy kingdom come, O Lord (4)
    316 when thou shalt in thy kingdom come ... Lord remember me (
    342 in heaven & earth thy power ... bring God's kingdom here (4)
    355 to seek the kingdom of thy peace (3)
    359 his kingdom still increasing, a kingdom without endd (4)
    360 now thy gracious kingdom bring (2)
    364 claim the kingdom for thine own (4)
    409 his kingdom is glorious and rules over all (1)
    410 and Christ's great kingdom shall come on earth (R)
    410 the kingdom of love and light (R)
    469 thy kingdom come, O Lord, thy will be done (1,2,3,4)
    469 his conquering cross no kingdom wills to bear (2)
    472 his kingdom spread from shore to shore (1)
    478 with deeds of love and mercy, the heavenly kingdom comes (2
    482 thine is the kingdom and the power (1)
    483 His kingdom cannot fail, he rules o'er earth and heaven (3)
    500 thy kingdom stands, and grows forever, till all ... own (4)
    535 we in the kingdom of thy grace: The kingdoms are but one (3
    542 thy kingdom come; on earth thy will be done (3)
    549 claim the kingdom of the earth for thee, and not thy foe (5)

kingdom's
    470 grant us courage lest we miss thy kingdom's goal (3)

kingdoms
    305 crowns and thrones may perish, kingdoms rise and wane (3)
    308 not like kingdoms of the world thy holy Church, O God (3)
    464 sets the kingdoms on a blaze (1)
    535 we in the kingdom of thy grace: The kingdoms are but one (3
    542 this is my prayer, O Lord of all earth's kingdoms (3)

kingly
    419 the Son of God goes forth to war, a kingly crown to gain (1)

kings
    87 King of kings in heaven we'll crown him (4)
    174 to serve the King of kings (1)
    194 lift up our hearts, O King of kings (T,1)

308   kings and empires ... of old that went and came (1)
308   O where are kings and empires now (T,1)
324   King of kings, yet born of Mary (2)
353   thy people pray, come quickly, King of kings (5)
363   the King of kings is drawing near (1)
371   speaking to saints, to prophets, kings, and sages (2)
385   the King of kings salvation brings (3)
402   we three kings of Orient are (T,1)
405   gold the King of kings proclaimeth (4)
442   praise him, seers, heroes, kings, Heralds of perfection (3)
453   crown the Savior King of kings (2)
453   King of kings, and Lord of lords (4)
458   King of kings, & Lord of lords, & heaven's eternal light (2)
493   keep me, King of kings, beneath thine own almighty wings (1)
546   Lord of lords and King of kings (1)

kingship
355   upon a cross ... bound thee & mocked thy saving kingship (1)

kiss
376   worshiped the beloved with a kiss (3)

knee
8   adoring bend the knee while we own the mystery (4)
76   at the name of Jesus every knee shall bow (T,1)
88   first let me hear how the children stood round his knee (2)
185   hear thou the prayer I make on bended knee (1)
260   until we labor for those gifts we ask on bended knee (2)
374   come, adore on bended knee Christ the Lord (3)
383   full reverently upon the knee (5)
397   bend the knee before him whom heaven and earth adore (2)
453   every knee to him shall bow (1)
517   throned upon a mother's knee (1)

kneel
103   come to the mercy seat, fervently kneel (1)
159   when I kneel in prayer, and with thee, my God (3)
333   lowly we kneel in prayer before thy throne (1)
379   here let all, great and small kneel in awe and wonder (3)
487   we kneel in awe and fear on this thy holy day (2)
505   while we kneel confessing, we humbly wait thy blessing (4)

kneeling
145   kneeling there in deep contrition, help my unbelief (2)
236   then, lowly kneeling, wait thy word of peace (1)

knees
74   given the name to which all knees shall bow (4)
78   at the great name of Jesus, now all knees must bend (2)
330   when I fall on my knees with my face to the rising sun (R)
330   let us break bread together on our knees (T,1)
330   Let us drink wine together on our knees (2)
330   let us praise God together on our knees (3)
459   to thee all knees are bent, all voices pray (1)

knelt
235 where Jesus knelt to share with thee the silence (3)
431 he that in anguish knelt is not forsaken by his God (3)

knew
5 let those refuse to sing who never knew our God (2)
96 I sought the Lord, and afterward I knew (T,1)
163 he loved me ere I knew him (1)
268 where is... blessedness I knew when first I saw the Lord (2)
419 twelve valiant saints, their hope they knew (3)
517 thou... crowned us with an honor women never knew before (2

knit
259 O knit my thankful heart to thee (1)

knock
105 shall he knock, and I my heart the closer lock (3)

knocking
108 O Jesus, thou art knocking, and lo, that hand is scarred (2)
111 stands knocking at the door of every sinner's heart (2)

know
2 we know that thou rejoicest o'er each work of thine (3)
12 enough for me to know thou art, to love thee, and adore (3)
12 dearer than all things I know is child-like faith to me (4)
12 I know thee ... in part, I ask not, Lord, for more (3)
21 know that the Lord is God indeed (2)
22 know that the Lord is God alone (1)
39 his glory let the people know (1)
70 before my infant heart could know from whom...comforts (2)
75 grant us that way to know, that truth to keep (4)
82 love of Jesus, what it is none but his loved ones know (4)
84 thank we all the mighty Child through whom we know thee (3
84 Child through whom we know thee, God of peace (3)
84 know thee ... and call thee heavenly Father (3)
94 God is love! I know,I feel, Jesus weeps & loves me still (4)
97 following him I know I'm right (3)
100 let all the nations know, to earth's remotest bound (1)
114 how can a sinner know his sins on earth forgiven? (T,1)
114 we by his Spirit prove and know the things of God (4)
120 could my zeal no languor know (2)
123 I know not how that Bethlehem's babe (T,1)
123 know not how that Calvary's cross a world ... could free (2)
123 I only know ... matchless love ... brought God's love (2)
123 only know ... manger child has brought God's life to me (1)
123 I only know a living Christ, our immortality (3)
123 I know not how that Joseph's tomb could solve death's (3)
124 ask ye what great thing I know (T,1)
124 this is that great thing I know ... delights & stirs me (4)
131 God, through himself, we then shall know (4)
136 so ... we know ... power of him who came mankind to save (4
137 O that the world might know the all-atoning Lamb (3)
139 by faith we know thee strong to save (3)
140 no other help I know (1)
141 God's mercy holds a wiser plan than thou canst fully know (2

146 our wills are ours, we know not how (3)
149 because I know 'tis true (1)
149 for those who know it best seem hungering (4)
152 thee, only thee, resolved to know in all I think (1)
152 only thee...to know in all I think or speak or do (1)
155 we know we at the end shall life inherit (3)
156 I would be humble, for I know my weakness (2)
159 there are depths of love that I cannot know till (4)
166 Lord Jesus, I love thee, I know thou art mine (T,1)
171 did ye not know it is my work My Father's work to do (1)
193 and know our prayer is heard (1)
205 I know whate'er befall me, Jesus doeth all things well (1)
208 and to know, "Thus saith the Lord" (1)
208 I know ... thou art with me, wilt be with me to the end (4)
209 the waves and winds still know his voice who ruled them (2)
225 and know as I am known (3)
227 'twas a heaven below my Redeemer to know (3)
229 Jesus we know, and he is on the throne (5)
238 well I know thy trouble, O my servant true (4)
253 know thou hearest my prayer (1)
253 with humble confidence look up and know thou hearest (1)
270 content to suffer while we know ... thou art near (4)
274 speak to me by name, O Master, let me know it is to me (2)
285 give me thy only love to know (4)
290 I know not where his islands lift their fronded palms (5)
290 I know not what the future hath of marvel or surprise (T,1)
290 I only know I cannot drift beyond his love and care (5)
301 what height of rapture shall we know when...we meet (5)
303 I know not, O I know not what joys await us there (1)
310 present we know thou art, but O thyself reveal (4)
319 one fold .. faith .. hope .. Lord, One God alone we know (1)
338 O may we ever walk in him, and nothing know beside (3)
348 may they know this house their own (3)
370 wisdom comes to those who know thee (1)
403 so shalt thou know that fellowship of love (1)
414 may not know ... cannot tell, what pains he had to bear (2)
417 content to let the world go by, to know no gain nor loss (3)
431 from heavenly plains is borne the song that angels know (4)
440 know with thee, O God immortal, Jesus Christ (4)
440 know ... Jesus Christ whom thou hast sent (4)
445 I know that my Redeemer lives (T,1,4)
455 his reign shall know no endd (3)
457 and only wish the joy to know of our triumphant friend (1)
458 to whom he manifests his love & grants his name to know (3)
458 their profit & their joy to know the mystery of his love (5)
467 teach us to know the Father, Son, and Thee (4)
474 yet a season, and you know happy entrance will be given (3)
476 whom love, and love alone can know (2)
476 till ... know the loveliness of lives made fair and free (4)
479 that thy children, Lord, in freedom may thy mercy know (4)
479 that thy children ... may thy mercy know, and live (4)
491 be thou our souls' perserver, O God, for thou dost know (4)
498 when we know it comes from thee (3)
501 we know and feel that thou art here (2)
528 know ... feel my sins forgiven (2)
532 praise we the glorious names we know (5)

535 Church triumphant in thy love, their mighty joys we know (2)
549 then let us prove our heavenly birth in all we do & know (5)

knowest
244 thou who knowest all about me, stand by me (3)
274 Master speak ...thou knowest ..the yearning of my heart (3)
274 knowest all its truest need (3)

knoweth
318 joy, the sweetest man e'er knoweth (2)
521 and their sorrows all he knoweth (3)

knowing
103 come to the feast of love; come, ever knowing (3)
396 oxen lowing, little knowing Christ the babe is Lord (2)
446 that thy peace which evermore passeth human knowing (4)

knowledge
108 O love that passeth knowledge, so patiently to wait (2)
146 let knowledge grow from more to more (5)
198 and light of knowledge in their eyes (1)
218 my knowledge of that life is small (5)
257 our knowledge, sense and sight lie in deepest darkness (2)
307 knowledge and faith and life immortal Jesus ... imparts (1)
344 in knowledge pure their mind renew (2)
344 unite the pair . long disjoined, knowledge & vital piety (3)
354 to us the path of knowledge show (2)
370 light of knowledge, ever burning, shed on us (3)
370 light of knowledge ... shed on us thy deathless learning (3)
551 unite us in the sacred love of knowledge, truth & thee (3)

known
5 come, ye who love the Lord, and let your joys be known (T,1)
37 not a plant or flower below, but makes thy glories known (3)
50 a yearning for a deeper peace not known before (4)
59 he chastens and hastens his will to make known (1)
75 make all my wants and wishes known (1)
130 throughout the world its breadth is known (3)
137 make to us the God-head known, & witness with the blood (1)
168 I would to everlasting days make all his glories known (2)
188 through me thy truth be shown, thy love made known (2)
197 O Son of Man, who madest known (T,1)
198 a loftier race than e'er the world hath known shall rise (1)
204 thy heart has never known recoil (3)
210 known to him who chose us for his own (2)
210 nor doubt our inmost wants are known to him (2)
225 and know as I am known (3)
251 perish every fond ambition, all I've... hoped or known (1)
251 all I've sought or hoped or known (1)
268 the dearest idol I have known, whate'er that idol be ((5)
275 make all my wants and wishes known (1)
304 thy bounds are known to God alone,for they are set above (2)
313 be known to us in breaking bread, but do not then depart (T)
340 and make thy goodness known (4)
348 ever, Lord, thy name be known (1)
351 make known to them thy saving grace (2)
479 making known the needs and burdens thy compassion bids (3)

knows
66   well our feeble frame he knows (3)
84   thou givest us that good unseen the world knows not (3)
84   the world knows not nor treasures (3)
115 happy ... who knows his sins forgiven (1)
132 spread thy light from the height which knows no measure (1)
142 when in danger knows no fear, in darkness feels no doubt (3)
146 thou madest man, he knows not why (2)
151 and preach thee, too, as love knows how (3)
173 knows not race nor station as boundaries of the mind (4)
218 enough that Christ knows all, and I shall be with him (5)
230 He knows the way he taketh, and I will walk with him (2)
261 Jesus knows our every weakness (2)
285 God only knows the love of God (3)
333 that theirs may be the love which knows no ending (1)
416 peace is there, that knows no measure (4)
440 God's likeness, man awaking, knows the everlasting peace (1)
456 the heaven that hides him from our sight knows (2)
456 heaven ... knows neither near nor far (2)
531 whose height, whose depth unfathomed no man knows (1)

labor
99   many a sorrow, many a labor, many a tear (4)
99   sorrow vanquished, labor ended, Jordan passed (5)
140 what path...labor to secure my soul from endless death (2)
152 my daily labor to pursue (1)
155 I'll labor night and day to be a pilgrim (3)
175 strength for thy labor the Lord will provide (4)
186 worth to my meanest labor give by joining it to thine (2)
186 accept my hallowed labor now, I do it unto thee (3)
260 until we labor for those gifts we ask on bended knee (2)
262 labor is rest...pain is sweet if thou, my God, art here (2)
494 free from care, from labor free (1)
497 may we, born anew like morning, to labor rise (2)
511 a world in need now summons us to labor, love & give (2)
514 all our labor ... watching, all our calendar of care (3)
514 all our labor...watching...they are our prayer (3)

laborers
339 harvest truly, Lord, is great; the laborers are few (2)

laboring
9   he sends the laboring conscience peace (3)

labors
331 in thy fasting & temptation...thy labors on the earth (2)
536 for all the saints, who from their labors rest (T,1)
537 for all the saints, who from their labors rest (T,1)

lack
67   I nothing lack if I am his and he is mine forever (1)
230 my Shepherd is beside me, and nothing can I lack (2)

ladder
287 climbing Jacob's ladder ... soldikers of the cross (T,1)

laden
- 104   come,ye weary, heavy laden bruised & mangled by the fall (4)
- 261   are we weak & heavy laden, cumbered with a load of care (3)

laid
- 33   laid a silent loveliness on hill and wood and field (1)
- 48   laid for your faith in his excellent Word (1)
- 67   on his shoulder gently laid (3)
- 227   and have laid up their treasure above (1)
- 230   the storm may roar without me, my heart may low be laid (1)
- 348   on this stone now laid with prayer (T,1)
- 351   when time in lowly dust has laid these stored walls (4)
- 374   see him in a manger laid whom .. choirs of angels praise (4)
- 378   and laid within a manger upon this blessed morn (2)
- 384   the little Lord Jesus laid down his sweet head (1)
- 385   child ... who, laid to rest, on Mary's lap is sleeping (1)
- 394   all meanly wrapped in swathing bands & in a manger laid (4)
- 395   gentle Mary laid her child lowly in a manger (T,1,3)
- 400   guide where our infant Redeemer is laid (1,5)
- 430   sin, which laid the cross on thee (2)
- 434   tomb where they laid his breathless clay (4)
- 436   were you there when they laid him in the tomb (3)
- 441   in the grave they laid him, Love whom men had slain (2)
- 441   laid in the earth like grain that sleeps unseen (2)
- 449   and sing today with one accord the life laid down (4)
- 449   the life laid down, the life restored (4)
- 454   all our sins on thee were laid (2)
- 469   better seeing thy Word made flesh, and in a manger laid (4)

lain
- 441   wheat that in dark earth many days has lain (1)
- 441   he that for three days in the grave had lain (3)

lake
- 107   as of old the apostles heard it by the Galilean lake (2)

lamb
- 23   extol the Lamb with loftiest song (4)
- 100   extol the Lamb of God, the all-atoning Lamb (3)
- 116   I am trusting, Lord, in thee, blessed Lamb of Calvary (4)
- 119   O Lamb of God, I come, I come! (R)
- 137   O that the world might know the all-atoning Lamb (3)
- 143   my faith looks up to thee, thou Lamb of Calvary (T,1)
- 220   thine I am, O spotless Lamb (1)
- 227   the favor divine I first found in the blood of the Lamb (2)
- 228   for the dear Lamb of God left his glory above (2)
- 239   am I a soldier of the cross, a follower of the Lamb (T,1)
- 268   a light to shine upon the road that leads me to the Lamb (1)
- 268   purer light shall mark .. road that leads me to the Lamb (6)
- 288   and still to God salvation cry, salvation to the Lamb (1)
- 341   'tis all my business here...to cry "Behold the Lamb" (5)
- 341   preach him to all & cry in death "...behold the Lamb" (6)
- 376   if I were a shepherd, I would bring a lamb (4)
- 409   fall down on their faces and worship the Lamb (3)
- 421   dear dying Lamb, thy precious blood shall never lose (3)
- 428   O Lamb of God, was ever pain, was ever love, like thine (4)
- 433   near the cross .. Lamb of God bring its scenes before me (3)

454 Paschal Lamb, by God appointed (2)
455 crown him with many crowns, the Lamb upon his throne (T,1)
457 worthy to be exalted thus, the Lamb for sinner slain (2)
481 holy city ... where Christ, the Lamb, doth reign (1)
533 with united breath, ascribe their conquest to the Lamb (1)
535 they sing the Lamb in hymns above and we in hymns below (2)

Lamb's
326 the Lamb's great bridal feast of bliss and love (5)

lambs
312 hark, how he calls the tender lambs (1)
337 nourish the lambs and feed thy sheep (4)
362 and fold the lambs to his breast (3)

lame
1 leap, ye lame, for joy (6)

lament
94 now incline me to repent; let me now my sins lament (3)

lamp
148 trim your feeble lamp, my brother! (3)
368 Lamp of our feet (T,1)
368 Lamp ... whereby we trace our path when wont to stray (1)
371 O God of light, thy Word, a lamp unfailing (T,1)
372 O make thy Church, dear Savior, a lamp of purest gold (4)
480 move o'er the waters' face, bearing the lamp of grace (3)

lamps
366 your lamps with gladness take; Alleluia! (1)
503 wait and worship while the night sets her evening lamps (1)
503 evening lamps alight through all the sky (1)
545 I can read his righteous sentence by the dim ... lamps (2)
545 dim and flaring lamps (2)

land
14 to every land the strains belong (4)
14 sung through every land by every tongue (1)
14 in every land begin the song (4)
30 deep writ upon the human heart, on sea or land (2)
32 rebel, ye waves, and o'er the land ... roar (2)
41 master over sea and land (3)
41 o how wondrous, o how glorious is thy name in every land (4)
43 publishes to every land the work of an almighty hand (1)
46 guide of all who seek the land above (1)
47 lead us by faith to hope's true promised land (2)
101 dwell in that celestial land, where joys immortal flow (4)
106 gently lead us by the hand, pilgrims in a desert land (1)
115 by faith I see the land of rest, the saints' delight (1)
171 that we the land may view (2)
198 nation with nation, land with land, inarmed shall live (3)
203 they reach thy throne, encompass land and sea (1)
271 land me safe on Canaan's side (3)
271 Pilgrim through this barren land (1)
291 cast a wishful eye to Canaan's fair and happy land (1)
300 joyful stand on the borders of our land (3)

303 Jesus, in mercy bring us to that dear land of rest (4)
346 mountains ... watch in silence o'er the land (2)
365 when thy truth began its race, it touched ... every land (3)
365 thy truth ... touched and glanced on every land (3)
371 to every land, to every race and clan (4)
417 the shadow of a mighty rock within a weary land (1)
464 hangs o'er all the thirsty land (4)
468 glory shall ere long appear to dwell within our land (2)
476 Christ is formed in all mankind and every land is thine (5)
477 bring justice to our land, that all may dwell secure (3)
482 until in every land and clime thine ends of love are won (4)
505 now, on land and sea descending (T,1)
511 the wealth of this good land (1)
513 plow the fields and scatter the good seed on the land (1)
524 blessed is that land of God where saints abide forever (3)
538 glad hymns of praise from land and sea (4)
542 a song of peace for their land and for mine (2)
546 with thy living fire of judgment purge this land (1)
546 purge this land of bitter things (1)
547 my country, 'tis of thee, sweet land of liberty (T,1)
547 sweet land of liberty, of thee I sing (1)
547 land where my fathers died, land of the pilgrims' pride (1)
547 my native country, thee, Land of the noble free (2)
547 long may our land be bright with freedom's holy light (4)
548 mighty empire, stretching far o'er land and sea (1)
548 for the open door to manhood in the land the people rule (2)
549 thine ... the wealth of land and sea (4)
551 of every clime and coast, O hear us for our native land (1)
551 the land we love the most (1)
552 in this free land by thee our lot is cast (2)

lands
79 fair are the meadows, fairer still the woodlands (2)
307 so from all lands thy Church be gathered (4)
407 in lands, where shadows hide the light (3)
411 friends in lands afar who battle with the body's ills (2)
476 send us forth ... to make all lands thine own ((1)
486 through lands from sin set free ... God shall march (4)
542 a song of peace for lands afar and mine (1)
542 but other hearts in other lands are beating with hopes (1)
542 but other lands have sunlight too, and clover (2)

language
62 language, glad and golden, speaking to us day and night (1)
136 the language all men understand (3)
418 language shall I borrow to thank thee, dearest friend (3)

languid
99 art thou weary, art thou languid (T,1)

languish
103 come, ye disconsolate, where'er ye languish (T,1)
134 hosannas languish on our tongues and our devotion dies (3)
418 how does that visage languish .. once was bright as morn (1)

languor
120 could my zeal no languor know (2)

lantern
372 a lantern to our footsteps shines on from age to age (1)

lap
385 child ... who, laid to rest, on Mary's lap is sleeping (1)

lapse
296 unwasted by the lapse of years (1)

large
44 oh, what is man, in thy regard to hold so large a place (3)
342 the task looms large before us; we follow without fear (4)
515 as large as is thy children's need (3)
515 what large provision thou hast made (3)

larger
194 visions of a larger good & holier dreams of brotherhood (1)
351 in larger worlds more fully prove the wonders of... love (4)

lark
190 awake, awake to love and work, the lark is in the sky (T,1)

last
9 praise shall ne'er be past while life & thought...last (1,4)
28 be ...our guard while troubles last and our eternal home (6)
30 first ... last: beyond all thought His timeless years (1)
76 faithfully he bore it spotless to the last (3)
99 if I still hold closely to him, what hath he at last (5)
125 safe into the haven guide; O receive my soul at last (1)
157 last low whispers of our dead are burdened with his name (5)
173 justice conquers violence and wars at last shall cease (3)
209 all now mysterious shall be bright at last (2)
209 all safe and blessed we shall meet at last (3)
228 till my trophies at last I lay down (R)
237 when my last hour cometh, fraught with strife and pain (4)
247 when at last I near the shore ... fearful breakers roar (3)
250 o'ercome through Christ alone, and stand entire at last (2)
264 so shall it be the last, in that bright morning (5)
284 and share thy joy at last (5)
288 and thou art crowned at last (1)
294 sure as thy truth shall last (5)
336 fightings without . fears within since we assembled last (2)
366 awake, Jerusalem, at last (1)
397 bring our ransomed souls at last where they need no star (4)
414 might go at last to heaven saved by his precious blood (3)
430 where our earliest hopes began ..our last aspirings endd (4)
460 God the first and God the last (1,3)
482 men at last ... ring the bells of brotherhood & peace (3)
486 who with love and meekness outlast the years of wrong (3)
492 live this short, revolving day as if it were our last (4)
502 be my last thought, how sweet to rest (2)
522 give his angels charge at last ... fire .. tares to cast (3)

lasts
65 as it was without beginning so it lasts without an end (4)

late
387 late in time behold him come (2)
495 comfort every sufferer watching late in pain (4)

lately
    431   the star is dimmed that lately shone (1)

later
    277   soon or later then translate to my eternal bliss (4)

latest
    51   publish with our latest breath thy love & guardian care (4)
    60   death, waiting to hush our latest breath (6)
    128   till in life's latest hour I bow (5)
    185   then shall my latest breath whisper thy praise (4)
    341   happy, if with my latest breath I may but gasp his name (6)

laud
    16   who would not fear his holy name and laud and magnify (2)
    21   praise, laud, and bless his name always (3)
    42   laud and magnify his name (2)
    42   heaven, and earth, and all creation, laud and magnify (2)
    78   laud, honor, might ... glory be ... age to age eternally (4)
    298   laud and honor to the Father ...to the Son ...the Spirit (4)
    305   glory, laud, and honor unto Christ the King (4)
    385   haste to bring him laud, the babe, the son of Mary (R)
    424   all glory, laud, and honor, to thee, Redeemer, King (T,1)
    446   from his light, to whom we give laud and praise undying (2)
    552   and glory, laud, and praise be ever thine (4)

laugh
    156   I would look up, and laugh and love and lift (2)

launch
    291   though Jordan waves may roll, I'll fearless launch away (3)

law
    30   established is his law, and changeless it shall stand (2)
    31   his wrath and justice stand to guard his holy law (2)
    33   thou from whose unfathomed law the year in beauty flows (3)
    36   there is thy power; thy law is there (2)
    171   shapest man to God's own law, thyself the fair design (2)
    219   held in thy law, I stand (4)
    543   confirm thy soul in self-control, thy liberty in law (2)
    552   thy Word our law, thy paths our chosen way (2)

laws
    42   laws which never shall be broken (1)
    42   laws ... for our guidance hath he made (1)
    191   live out the laws of Christ in ... thought & word & deed (1)
    191   until the laws of Christ become the laws and habits (2)
    191   laws and habits of the state (2)
    214   obey the laws of God in their determined quest (1)
    214   their joyful, faithful hearts obey the laws of God (1)
    365   thy laws are pure, thy judgments right (5)
    481   city ... whose laws are love, whose ways are brotherhood (4)
    550   laws, freedom, truth, and faith in God came (3)

lay
    45   kept the folded grave-clothes where the body lay (1)
    90   haste, let us lay our gifts before the King (1)
    117   weary one, lay down, thy head upon my breast (1)

127	for who aught to my charge shall lay (2)
160	nor think till death to lay it down (4)
196	all I have, and all I am, upon his altar lay (3)
223	never can prove ... until all on the altar we lay (3)
225	where I may lay me prone, and bare my soul in loneliness (3)
228	till my trophies at last I lay down (R)
234	I lay in dust life's glory dead (4)
240	lay hold on life ..it shall be thy joy & crown eternally (1)
246	ne'er think the victory won, nor lay thine armor down (3)
249	crowned with victory at thy feet I'll lay .. honors down (4)
326	here would I lay aside each earthly load (3)
347	thine own before thy feet we lay (1)
348	seeds of truth be sown where we lay this cornerstone (2)
348	where we lay this cornerstone (1,2,3)
349	as here with joy this stone we lay (1)
349	in grateful service ... now their strong foundation lay (2)
383	in fields where they lay keeping their sheep (1)
383	was to certain poor shepherds in fields as they lay (1)
383	right over the place where Jesus lay (4)
384	the stars in the sky looked down where he lay (1)
390	world in solemn stillness lay to hear the angels sing (1)
395	there he lay, the undefiled, to the world a stranger (1)
432	that caused the Lord of life to lay aside his crown (2)
432	lay aside his crown for my soul (2)
438	Christ Jesus lay in death's strong bands (T,1)
444	low in the grave he lay (T,1)
450	kept the folded grave-clothes where the body lay (1)
451	to seek the tomb where Jesus lay, Alleluia (2)
501	the sick, O Lord, around thee lay (1)
517	when all the work is over and we lay the burden down (5)
524	we lay the first fruits of thy blessing (2)
524	upon thine altar, Lord, we lay the first fruits (2)
526	I lay my sins before thee (1)
527	long my imprisoned spirit lay fast bound in sin (3)

lays
387	mild he lays his glory by, born that man no more may die (3)
389	he lays aside his majesty and seems as nothing worth (2)
454	bring your sweetest, noblest lays (4)

lead
19	lead their praises, alleluia! (2)
47	lead us by faith to hope's true promised land (2)
86	Jesus, thou Christ of God, by thy perennial Word lead (3)
86	lead us to where thou hast trod, our faith make strong (3)
92	and grace will lead me home (3)
99	hath he marks to lead me to him if he be my guide (2)
106	gently lead us by the hand, pilgrims in a desert land (1)
121	Savior, like a shepherd lead us (T,1)
125	heal the sick, and lead the blind (3)
173	O help us walk unflinching in paths that lead to peace (3)
173	again to lead us forward along God's holy way (5)
176	lead me through the vale of shadows (3)
188	lead forth my soul, O Christ, one with thine own (2)
203	thy paths of service lead to blazoned heights (1)
213	and lead me to thy holy hill (4)
226	through .. changing world below lead me gently ..as I go (2)
248	from victory unto victory his army shall he lead (1)
269	lead us, O Father, in the paths of peace (T,1)

269 lead us through Christ, the true and living Way (1)
269 lead us, O Father, in the paths of truth (2)
269 lead us, O Father, in the paths of right (3)
269 lead us, O Father, to thy heavenly rest (4)
271 let the fire and cloudy pillar lead me all my journey (2)
272 lead kindly Light (T,1)
272 the night is dark, & I am far from home, lead thou me on (1)
272 amid the encircling gloom, lead thou me on (1)
272 nor prayed that thou shouldst lead me on (2)
272 but now lead thou me on (2)
272 sure it still will lead me on o'er moor and fen (3)
347 let their door a gateway be to lead us...to thee (3)
347 lead us from ourselves to thee (3)
356 may one Lord .. faith .. Word, one Spirit lead us still (4)
362 in pastures of peace he'll lead them (3)
478 lead on, O King eternal, the day of march has come (T,1)
478 lead on, O King eternal, till sin's fierce war ... cease (2)
478 lead on, O King eternal, we follow, not with fears (3)
478 the crown awaits the conquest; lead on, O God of might (3)
487 lead and guide our acts of praise (2)
487 as we go, lead us, Lord; we shall be thine evermore (4)
552 lead us from night to never-ending day (4)

leader
59 we all do extol thee, thou leader triumphant (3)
300 only thou our leader be, and we still will follow thee (4)
533 our glorious leader claims our praise (2)

leadest
60 thou leadest home the child of God (6)
219 thou leadest me by unsought ways (4)

leadeth
67 my ransomed soul he leadeth (2)
68 he leadeth me the quiet waters by (1)
217 for by his hand he leadeth me (R)
217 He leadeth me: O blessed thought (T,1)
217 still 'tis God's hand that leadeth me (1)
217 He leadeth me, by his own hand he leadeth me (R)
217 still 'tis his hand that leadeth me (2)
217 by waters still, o'er troubled sea ... hand ... leadeth (2)
217 since God through Jordan leadeth me (4)

leading
397 leading onward, beaming bright (1)
402 westward leading, still proceeding (R)

leads
4 he leads his own, his chosen band (3)
38 joyful music leads us sunward (4)
101 Jesus is the truth, the way that leads you into rest (3)
202 we follow where the Master leads, serene and unafraid (1)
205 all the way my Savior leads me (T,1,2,3)
209 through thorny ways leads to a joyful end (1)
218 Christ leads me through no darker rooms than he went (3)
268 a light to shine upon the road that leads me to the Lamb (1)
268 purer light shall mark .. road that leads me to the Lamb (6)
274 where the Shepherd leads the flock (2)
305 Christ, the royal Master, leads against the foe (1)

486   trail which leads the world to thee (2)
500   as o'er each continent and island the dawn leads on (3)
500   the dawn leads on another day (3)
552   almighty hand leads forth in beauty all the starry band (1)

leaf
270   the murmuring wind, the quivering leaf ... tell us (3)
270   quivering leaf shall softly tell us thou art near (3)
542   and sunlight beams on clover-leaf and pine (2)

lean
142   in the hour of grief or pain will lean upon its   God (2)
144   since on thine arm thou bidst me lean (1)
207   lean, weary one, upon his breast (4)
222   but wholly lean on Jesus' name (1)
240   cast care aside, lean on thy guide (3)
290   forgive me if too close I lean my human heart on thee (3)
326   and all my weariness upon thee lean (1)

leaning
247   while leaning on thy breast may I hear thee (3)

leans
48   the soul that on Jesus still leans for repose (5)

leant
184   on thy bosom it has leant and found in thee its life (4)

leap
1   leap, ye lame, for joy (6)

leaps
472   the prisoner leaps to loose his chains (4)

learn
80   learn of thee, the lowly one (4)
85   from thee we learn what love is (3)
85   God's will to earth thou bringest that all ... may learn (4)
85   all who would obey thee may learn from thee their duty (4)
85   learn from thee their duty, the truth, the life, the way (4)
191   His will to learn, his work to do (3)
191   with vision clear and mind equipped His will to learn (3)
204   till sons of men shall learn thy love (6)
253   a pure desire that all may learn and glorify thy grace (4)
346   let those learn, who here shall meet (4)
351   a place most meet to learn of thee (1)
368   Lord, grant us all aright to learn the wisdom it imparts (4)
430   learn thy love while gazing thus (2)
430   here we learn to serve and give, &, rejoicing, self deny (3)
434   learn of Jesus Christ to pray (1)
434   learn of Christ to bear the cross (2)
434   learn of Jesus Christ to die (3)
542   and hearts united learn to live as one (3)

learned
184   my power is faint and low till I have learned to serve (3)
208   I'm so glad I learned to trust thee, precious Jesus (4)

learning
162   learning how to love from thee (3)
342   inspire our ways of learning ... earnest, fervent prayer (1)
344   learning and holiness combined (3)
370   light of knowledge ... shed on us thy deathless learning (3)

learns
173   that learns to value beauty, in heart or brain or soul (4)

least
274   though least and lowest, let me not unheard depart (3)
279   O may the least omissions pain my reawakened soul (4)
280   O may the least omission pain my reawakened soul (4)
422   pomp .. show, nor lofty pride, nor boast above the least (1)

leave
25   nor ... should tempt my feet to leave thy door (2)
47   when we are strong, Lord, leave us not alone (3)
51   leave to his sovereign sway to choose and to command (3)
93   prone to leave the God I love (3)
106   leave us not to doubt and fear (2)
108   dear Savior, enter, enter, and leave us nevermore (3)
125   leave ... leave me not alone, still support & comfort me (2)
146   thou wilt not leave us in the dust (2)
173   while we betray so quickly and leave thee there alone (2)
209   leave to thy God to order and provide (1)
251   all to leave and follow thee (1)
251   let the world despise and leave me (2)
283   suddenly return and never, nevermore thy temples leave (3)
318   leave the gloomy haunts of sadness (1)
382   sages, leave your contemplations (3)
462   let us find thy hand when sorrows leave us blind (4)
509   and peaceful, leave before thy feet (3)

leaven
438   Word of grace hath purged away the old and wicked leaven (4)

leaves
27   we blossom and flourish as leaves on the tree (3)
452   bloom in every meadow, leaves on every bough (2)

leaving
107   leaving all for Jesus' sake (2)
300   Lord, obediently we'll go, gladly leaving all below (4)
505   nng to his care who cares for all (3)

led
46   by thine unerring spirit led (2)
58   the fire divine their steps that led ... before us (2)
62   earth and hell hath captive led (3)
70   thine arm ... led me up to man (3)
205   my song through endless ages: Jesus led me all the way (3)
206   by whose hand through years long past our lives were led (1)
266   thus led by his spirit to fountains of love (4)
397   so, most gracious Lord, may we evermore be led to thee (1)
439   soar we now where Christ has led, Alleluia (4)

446 led them with unmoistened foot through... Red Sea waters (1)
457 by the almighty Spirit led and filled with faith & love (1)
459 O holy Father, who hast led thy children in all the ages (2)
459 led thy children in all the ages with the fire and cloud (2)
509 by his unerring counsel led (2)
517 and be never led astray (3)
552 thy love divine hath led us in the past (2)

left
102 ye need not one be left behind (1)
106 nothing left but heaven and prayer (3)
228 for the dear Lamb of God left his glory above (2)
251 they have left my Savior, too (2)
251 not in grief to harm ... while thy love is left to me (3)
268 they have left an aching void the world can never fill (3)
276 the Lord, who left the throne our life & peace to bring (2)
279 if to the right or left I stray (2)
280 if to the right or left I stray (2)
353 left .. lonesome place of death, despite .. rage of foes (3)
355 till not a stone was left on stone (2)
378 left their flocks a feeding in tempest, storm, and wind (4)
474 all our sorrows left below .. earth exchanged for heaven (3)
529 my company before is gone, and I am left alone with thee (1)
548 souls that passed and left no name (3)

legions
447 but Christ their legions hath dispersed (2)

leisure
210 only be still, and wait his leisure in cheerful hope (2)

lend
106 ever present, truest friend ... near thine aid to lend (2)
374 Mary, Joseph, lend your aid (4)
393 wondrous star, lend thy light (4)
400 dawn on our darkness and lend us thine aid (1,5)

lendeth
58 the Spirit who in them did sing to us his music lendeth (3)

lends
9 I'll praise him while he lends me breath (4)
139 faith lends its realizing light (6)

length
67 so through all the length of days (6)
130 the length,and breadth, and height to prove (1)
189 at length there dawns the glorious day (T,1)
285 cannot reach the mystery ... length .. breadth .. height (2)
304 the length, the breadth, the height are one (2)

lengthen
211 mercy thy days shall lengthen (2)

lengthening
351 be pleased to guide, each lengthening year, thy sons (2)

lengthens
510   who kindly lengthens out our days (1)

less
173   thoughts & actions less prone to please the crowd (1)
222   my hope is build on nothing less than Jesus blood and (T,1)
222   nothing less than Jesus' blood and righteousness (1)

lesser
174   rise up, O men of God! Have done with lesser things (T,1)

lesson
162   better lesson cannot be, loving him who first loved me (1)
162   Savior, teach me, day by day, thine own lesson to obey (T,1)

lest
161   walk thou beside us lest the tempting by-ways lure us (3)
237   lest by base denial, I depart from thee (1)
470   grant us courage lest we miss thy kingdom's goal (3)

let
5   come, ye who love the Lord, and let your joys be known (T,1)
5   let those refuse to sing who never knew our God (2)
5   then let our songs abound and every tear be dry (4)
10   let all the world in every corner sing (T,1,2)
13   Zion, let me enter there (1)
13   to my heart O enter thou, let it be thy temple now (2)
14   let the Creator's praise arise (1)
14   let the Redeemer's name be sung (1)
15   let all things praise the Lord (3)
19   O friends, in gladness let us sing (4)
20   let goods and kindred go, this mortal life also (4)
23   come, let us tune our loftiest song (T,1)
29   o thou true Sun, on us thy glance let fall (2)
29   on us thy glance let fall in royal radiance (2)
36   we hear thy word, "Let there be light" (3)
39   let all on earth their voices raise (T,1)
39   his glory let the people know (1)
45   let the heavens ring! God reigns: let the earth be glad (3)
51   let us in life, in death, thy steadfast truth declare (4)
55   O let all that is in me adore him (4)
55   let the amen sound from his people again (4)
57   he will not let thy foot be moved (2)
59   let thy congregation escape tribulation (3)
60   let them his glory also show (4)
60   let all things their creator bless (7)
61   let us with a gladsome mind (T,1)
61   let us then with gladsome mind praise the Lord (4)
62   let all our future days tell this story (2)
62   to him let each affection daily rise and round him move (4)
71   let angels prostrate fall (1)
71   let every kindred, every tribe on this terrestrial ball (4)
74   let this mind be in us which was in thee (3)
74   let every tongue confess ... one accord ... Jesus Christ (5)
76   there let him subdue all that is not holy (4)
76   there let him subdue ... all that is not true (4)
76   let his will enfold you in its light and power (4)

77   let all, with heart and voice, before his throne rejoice (1)
77   let praises fill the sky; Alleluia! Amen! (2)
86   let all the holy throng, who to thy Church belong (4)
88   first let me hear how the children stood round his knee (2)
90   haste, let us lay our gifts before the King (1)
90   let us arise, all meaner service scorning (5)
91   let all the earth around ring joyous with the sound (3)
93   let thy goodness, like a fetter, bind my wandering heart (3)
93   let thy goodness ... bind my wandering heart to thee (3)
94   now incline me to repent; let me now my sins lament (3)
100   let all the nations know, to earth's remotest bound (1)
102   let every soul be Jesus' guest (1)
102   O let his love your hearts constrain (4)
104   let not conscience make you linger (3)
109   let me more of their beauty see (1)
111   come, let us, who in   Christ believe (T,1)
111   sup with us, and let the feast be everlasting love (4)
112   will you let him die in vain? Crucify your Lord again? (2)
120   Rock of Ages, cleft for me, let me hide myself in thee (T,1)
120   let the water and the blood (1)
120   Rock of Ages, cleft for me, let me hide myself in thee (3)
121   early let us seek thy favor, early let us do thy will (4)
122   nor let that ramsomed sinner die (3)
125   Jesus, lover of my soul,let me to thy bosom fly (T,1)
125   let the healing streams abound (4)
125   freely let me take of thee (4)
126   Jesus, love of my soul,let me to thy bosom fly (T,1)
128   let cheerful anthems fill his house (2)
129   and let the sweet tokens of pardoning grace bring joy (4)
131   let us thine influence prove (1)
131   on our disordered spirits move ... let ... now be light (3)
138   O let me seek thee, and O let me find (3)
140   surely thou canst not let me die (3)
140   O let me now receive that gift! my soul without it dies (4)
143   nor let me ever stray from thee aside (3)
143   O let me from this day be wholly thine (1)
145   let me at thy throne of mercy find a sweet relief (2)
146   let knowledge grow from more to more (5)
148   let the lower lights be burning (R)
152   task thy wisdom ... assigned O let me cheerfully fulfill (2)
153   give us courage, let us hear heaven's trumpets ringing (2)
155   let him with constancy follow the Master (1)
159   Let my soul look up with a steadfast hope (2)
160   cross; let not its weight fill thy weak spirit with alarm (2
160   nor let thy foolish pride rebel (3)
161   still let thy spirit unto us be given (2)
164   O let me feel thee near me, the world is ever near (2)
164   O let me hear thee speaking in accents clear and still (3)
165   let us each, thy love possessing, triumph (1)
167   let not my star of hope grow dim or disappear (2)
170   O Master, let me walk with thee (T,1)
170   with thee, O Master, let me live (4)
172   let it for thy glory burn with inextinguishable blaze (2)
172   still let me guard the holy fire (3)
176   along my pilgrim journey, Savior, let we walk with thee (1)
176   gladly will I toil & suffer, only let me walk with thee (2)
185   let sorrow do its work, come grief or pain (3)

187   take my life, and let it be consecrated, Lord, to thee (T,1)
187   let them flow in ceaseless praise (1)
187   take my feet ... let them be swift & beautiful for thee (1)
187   take my voice ... let me sing always, only, for my King (2)
187   take my lips ... let them be filled with messages from (2)
187   take my hands ... let them move ... impulse of thy love (1)
188   ever, O Christ, through mine let thy life shine (1)
190   come, let thy voice be one with theirs (2)
190   so let the love of Jesus come and set my soul ablaze (2)
193   let each his friendly aid afford (2)
193   up unto thee, our living Head let us in all things grow (3)
193   let all our hearts agree (4)
193   let us, still we pray, possess the mind that was in thee (6)
193   to thee, inseparably joined, let all our spirits cleave (5)
195   as thou hast sought, so let me seek ... erring children (1)
200   send us upon thine errand, let us thy servants be (3)
206   and wait thy word, let there be light (4)
209   thy hope, thy confidence let nothing shake (2)
213   O let thy hand support me still (4)
219   let me ... think of thee ... new heart springs up in me (2)
221   through eternal ages let his praises ring (1)
226   let thy precious blood applied keep me ... near thy side (1)
226   every day, every hour, let me feel thy cleansing power (R)
226   let me love thee more and more (3)
231   let the unknown tomorrow bring with it what it may (2)
234   O Love that wilt not let me go (T,1)
235   let our ordered lives confess the beauty of thy peace (4)
235   let us, like them, without a word rise up & follow thee (2)
235   let sense be dumb, let flesh retire (5)
243   gainst lies & lusts & wrongs let courage rule our souls (3)
245   O then to the Rock let me fly ... Rock ... higher than I (R)
245   O near to the Rock let me keep (3)
250   still let the Spirit cry, in all his soldiers, "Come" (3)
251   let the world despise and leave me (2)
254   let thy clear light forever shine (1)
257   let our hearts and souls be stirred (1)
262   speak to our hearts . let us feel . kindling of thy love (1)
262   let this my every hour employ, till I thy glory see (5)
263   there let the way appear, steps unto heaven (3)
266   take time to be holy, let him be thy guide (3)
267   open my mouth, and let me bear gladly the warm truth (3)
267   let me bear gladly the warm truth everywhere (3)
267   open my heart and let me prepare love with thy children (3)
271   let the fire and cloudy pillar lead me all my journey (2)
273   like .. straightness of the pine trees let me upright be (3)
274   Master, let it now be heard (1)
274   though least and lowest, let me not unheard depart (3)
274   speak to me by name, O Master, let me know it is to me (2)
279   let me weep my life away for having grieved thy love (2)
280   let me weep my life away for having grieved thy love (2)
281   and let my spirit cleave to thee (4)
283   let us all in thee inherit, let us find that second rest (2)
283   come, Almighty to deliver, let us all thy life receive (3)
283   finish ...thy new creation, pure and spotless let us be (4)
283   let us see thy great salvation perfectly restored (4)
284   let me thy loving servant be ... taste thy promised rest (2)
284   nor let me go astray (4)

285 let earth and heaven and all things go (4)
300 as we journey let us sing (1)
302 come, let us join our friends above (T,1)
309 let us in thy name agree (1)
309 let us for each other care (4)
309 let us thus in God abide (5)
309 let us then with joy remove to the family above (6)
310 Lord, let every bounding heart the mighty comfort feel (4)
314 world where thou... send us let thy kingdom come, O Lord (4)
318 let me be a fit partaker of ... blessed food from heaven (2)
318 let me gladly here obey thee (3)
318 from this banquet let me measure (3)
318 let me measure, Lord, how vast and deep its treasure (3)
319 brethren, all, let every heart with kind affection glow (2)
324 let all mortal flesh keep silence (T,1)
326 here let me feast, and feasting, still prolong the hour (2)
330 let us break bread together on our knees (T,1)
330 Let us drink wine together on our knees (2)
330 let us praise God together on our knees (3)
332 let us taste the heavenly powers (4)
332 let the wisest mortal show how we the grace receive (2)
335 let them from the mouth of God ... solemn charge receive (1)
335 let Zion's watchmen all awake (T,1)
336 then let us make our boast of his redeeming power (4)
336 let us take up the cross till we the crown obtain (5)
338 blest be the dear uniting love that will not let us part (T)
339 let them speak thy Word of power (3)
339 O let them spread thy name, their mission fully prove (4)
342 and let our daily living reveal thee everywhere (1)
343 like them, let man the throne surround (2)
344 truth and love let all men see (3)
345 let the comforter and friend, thy Holy Spirit, meet (2)
346 and let these halls thy temple be (3)
346 let those learn, who here shall meet (4)
347 let their door a gateway be to lead us...to thee (3)
348 let thy church rise, strong and fair (1)
350 here let thy sacred fire of old descend (2)
350 here let the weary one find rest (4)
352 let every anthem rise like incense to the skies (2)
356 O let thy Word be light anew to every nation's life (3)
357 let no tongue on earth be silent (2)
358 let thy wandering cease; hie thee to thy quiet home (3)
360 let us find our rest in thee (1)
363 let us thy inner presence feel (3)
364 yea, Amen! let all adore thee high on thy eternal throne (4)
366 now let all the heavens adore thee (3)
378 God rest you merry, Gentlemen, let nothing you dismay (T,1)
379 come, then, let us hasten yonder (3)
379 here let all, great and small kneel in awe and wonder (3)
385 let loving hearts enthrone him (3)
386 O come, let us adore him, Christ, the Lord (R)
389 let all together praise our God upon his lofty throne (T,1)
392 let earth receive her King (1)
392 let men their songs employ (2)
392 let every heart prepare him room (1)
392 no more let sins and sorrows grow (3)
393 with the angels let us sing Alleluia to our King (4)

409	let all cry aloud and honor the Son (3)
409	then let us adore and give him his right (4)
411	where'er they heal ... let love of Christ attend (3)
414	he only could unlock the gate of heaven and let us in (4)
417	content to let the world go by, to know no gain nor loss (3)
418	Lord, let me never, never outlive my love to thee (3)
427	then let all praise be given thee who livest evermore (3)
427	'tis mercy all! let earth adore (2)
437	now let the heavens be joyful! Let earth her song begin (3)
437	Let the round world keep triumph, & all that is therein (3)
438	let us joyful be and sing to God right thankfully (1)
438	so let us keep the festival where-to the Lord invites us (3)
438	then let us feast this Easter Day on the true bread (4)
443	hymns of praise then let us sing (2)
447	let shouts of holy joy outburst: Alleluia (2)
449	let all mankind rejoice and say: Alleluia (2)
450	let his church with gladness hymns of triumph sing (2)
451	O sons and daughters, let us sing (T,1)
457	come, let us rise with Christ our Head (T,1)
461	let our whole soul an offering be to our Redeemer's name (2)
461	let thy Church on earth become blest as the Church above (3)
462	Spirit consoling, let us find thy hand (4)
462	let us find thy hand when sorrows leave us blind (4)
462	in the gray valley let us hear thy silent voice (4)
462	let us hear thy silent voice: "Lo, I am near" (4)
465	incarnate Deity, let ... ransomed race render in thanks (2)
465	Spirit of holiness, let all thy saints adore (3)
465	Eternal, Triune Lord, let all the hosts above (4)
465	let all the sons of men record and dwell upon thy love (4)
466	O let it freely burn, till earthly passions turn to dust (2)
466	and let thy glorious light shine ever on my sight (2)
470	let the search for thy salvation be our glory evermore (5)
471	let all earth's sons thy mercy prove (1)
471	let all thy saving grace adore (1)
471	o'er all the nations let it flow (3)
472	let every creature rise and bring his grateful honors (5)
477	let .. be light again .. set thy judgments in .. earth (5)
480	let there be light (1,2,3,4)
480	O now, to all mankind, let there be light (2)
480	and in earth's darkest place, let there be light (3)
480	through the world far and wide, let there be light (4)
487	let the mind of Christ abide in us on this thy holy day (3)
489	let us now a blessing seek, waiting in his courts today (1)
492	O let thine orient beams the night of sin disperse (2)
497	let not ease and self enthrall us (2)
502	let him no more lie down in sin (4)
503	Lord of angels, on our eyes let eternal morning rise (4)
505	let our vesper hymn be blending ... holy calm around (1)
507	come, let us use the grace divine (T,1)
508	come, let us use the grace divine (T,1) (same as 507)
516	Lord, let us in our homes agree .. blessed peace to gain (4)
518	let manna to our souls be given (3)
520	let all unworthy aims depart, imbue us with thy grace (2)
520	within .. home let every heart become thy dwelling place (2)
527	let angel minds inquire no more (2)

530 join us, in one spirit...let us still receive of thine (2)
530 placed according to thy will let us all our work fulfill (3)
542 let Christ be lifted up till all men serve him (3)
542 myself I give thee; let thy will be done (3)
544 let not thy wrath in its terrors awaken (2)
545 as he died to make men holy, let us die to make man free (4)
547 from every mountain side let freedom ring (1)
547 let music swell the breeze (3)
547 let mortal tongues awake; let all that breathe partake (3)
547 let rocks their silence break, the sound prolong (3)
549 then let us prove our heavenly birth in all we do & know (5)
551 let our hills and valleys shout the songs of liberty (3)

letting
462 letting thine all-pervading power fulfill the dream (1)

liberating
543 O beautiful for heroes proved in liberating strife (3)

liberty
69 a kindness in his justice which is more than liberty (1)
89 in bonds my perfect liberty (4)
277 bring the glorious liberty from sorrow, fear and sin (1)
283 set our hearts at liberty (2)
543 confirm thy soul in self-control, thy liberty in law (2)
547 my country, 'tis of thee, sweet land of liberty (T,1)
547 sweet land of liberty, of thee I sing (1)
547 our fathers' God, to thee, Author of liberty ... we sing (4)
551 let our hills and valleys shout the songs of liberty (3)

lie
48 when through fiery trials thy pathways shall lie (4)
68 he makes me down to lie in pastures green (1)
105 and still my soul in slumber lie (1)
140 and here I will unwearied lie, till thou thy Spirit give (3)
175 feelings lie buried that grace can restore (3)
257 our knowledge, sense and sight lie in deepest darkness (2)
257 lie in deepest darkness shrouded (2)
291 where my possessions lie (1)
380 in the light of that star lie the ages impearled (3)
381 O little town of Bethlehem, how still we see thee lie (T,1)
486 whose bones lie white along the trail (2)
502 let him no more lie down in sin (4)

lies
35 for... love which from our birth over and around us lies (1)
220 whate'er we must bear still in thee lies purest pleasure (3)
240 life with its way before us lies (2)
243 gainst lies & lusts & wrongs let courage rule our souls (3)
377 a babe within a manger lies (1)
385 why lies he in such mean estate (2)
400 low lies his head with the beasts of the stall (2)
421 when this poor lisping, stammering tongue lies silent (5)
421 tongue lies silent in the grave (5)
484 from all ... terror teaches, from lies of tongue and pen (2)

life

1	music in the sinner's ears ... life and health and peace (3)
1	new life the dead receive (5)
9	days of praise shall ne'er be past while life ... last (1,4)
9	while life, and thought, and being last (1,4)
11	tell ye forth his might, Lord of life ... truth & right (3)
18	life redeemed from death and sin (3)
20	let goods and kindred go, this mortal life also (4)
27	to all, life thou givest, to both great and small (3)
27	in all life thou livest, the true life of all (3)
30	he hath eternal life implanted in the soul (3)
33	life mounts in every throbbing vein (2)
36	thy present life through all doth flow (1)
36	thy life is in the quickening air (2)
37	all that borrows life from thee is ever in thy care (3)
38	in the triumph song of life (4)
40	eternal life with thee (2)
40	with thee are found the gifts of life (2)
40	bless us with life that has no end (2)
47	God of our life ... we trust in thee (T,1)
47	be thou for us in life our daily bread (3)
49	O may this bounteous God though all our life be near us (2)
51	let us in life, in death, thy steadfast truth declare (4)
52	life, while thou preservest life, a sacrifice shall be (4)
55	all that hath life and breath, come now with praises (4)
56	through all the changing scenes of life (T,1)
62	with that precious life he bought us (2)
62	Love is life, our lives be praise (2)
62	our whole lives one resurrection ... life of life above (4)
62	their glad story, God is life, and God is love (4)
64	sun of our life, thy quickening ray sheds on our path (2)
64	Lord of all life, below, above (4)
68	goodness and mercy all my life shall surely follow me (5)
70	through every period of my life thy goodness I'll pursue (4)
75	thou art the Life (3)
75	thou art the Way, the Truth, the Life (4)
75	that life to win, whose joys eternal flow (4)
77	life shall not endd the strain; Alleluia! Amen! (3)
81	Jesus ... my Lord, my life, my way, my end (3)
83	to him I owe my life and breath and all the joys I have (3)
84	life, thy gift to those whom thou dost capture (2)
85	thru thy life so radiant, earth's darkness turns to day (1)
85	learn from thee their duty, the truth, the life, the way (4)
89	my life in death, my heaven in hell (4)
90	Mary's son most holy, Light of the village life (2)
90	Light of the village life from day to day (2)
90	the Christ of God, the life, the truth, the way (2)
91	be this while life is mine my canticle divine (4)
92	he will my shield and portion be as long as life endures (4)
92	and mortal life shall cease (5)
92	I shall possess, within the veil ... life of joy & peace (5)
95	Light and life art thou within: Savior ...from every sin (4)
97	my life .. joy .. all; he is my strength ... day to day (1)
97	beautiful life that has no endd (4)
97	beautiful life with such a friend (4)
97	eternal life, eternal joy, he's my friend (4)
103	here we see the bread of life; see waters flowing (3)

353 and life to joy awakes (1)
355 awful love, which found no room in life where sin denied (2)
356 O let thy Word be light anew to every nation's life (3)
369 break thou the bread of life, dear Lord, to me (T,1)
387 light and life to all he brings (3)
402 breathes a life of gathering gloom (4)
407 we hear the throb of surging life, the clank of chains (2)
408 new life, new hope awakes where-e'er men own his sway (1)
411 O God, whose will is life and good (T,1)
411 will is life and good for all of mortal breath (1)
416 when the woes of life o'ertake me (2)
420 the bleeding Prince of life and peace (3)
423 O may we ever praise him with heart and life and voice (3)
427 but thou dost light and life restore (3)
432 that caused the Lord of life to lay aside his crown (2)
435 love so amazing, so divine, demands my soul, my life (4)
435 Love so amazing ... demands my soul, my life, my all (4)
437 from death to life eternal, from earth unto the sky (1)
438 the victory remained with life (2)
438 when life and death contended (2) ·
438 and brings us life from heaven (1)
440 Life eternal! heaven rejoices (3)
440 life eternal! O what wonders crowd on faith (4)
441 thy touch can call us back to life again (4)
442 life in all.. growing powers toward .. light is striving (1)
447 the victory of life is won (1)
449 the Lord of life is risen for aye (2)
449 praise we in songs of victory that love, that life (3)
449 that love, that life which cannot die (3)
449 and sing today with one accord the life laid down (4)
449 the life laid down, the life restored (4)
450 no more we doubt thee, glorious Prince of life (3)
450 life is naught without thee; aid us in our strife (3)
451 for they eternal life shall win, Alleluia (4)
452 thou, of life the author, death didst undergo (3)
454 life is given through thy name (1)
454 who died, eternal life to bring (2)
455 crown him the Lord of life, who triumphed o'er the grave (2)
457 dead to sin, his members live the life of righteousness (3)
457 hidden life of Christ ... with Christ concealed above (3)
458 the cross he bore is life and health (6)
459 blessed ... with light and life since Eden's dawning day (1)
462 spirit of life, in this new dawn (T,1)
467 thy blessed unction from above is comfort, life & fire (2)
467 comfort, life and fire of love (2)
469 Spirit of life, which moved ere form was made (1)
476 whose life and death reveal thy face (5)
476 inspire thy heralds of good news to live thy life divine (5)
479 thine abundant life to share (3)
481 yea, bids us seize the whole of life and build its glory (5)
482 O Thou who art the Life and Light, Exalted Lord and King (4)
492 may we this life improve, to mourn for errors past (4)
499 restored to life and power and thought (1)
503 Lord of life, beneath the dome of the universe thy home (2)
511 to make our life an offering to God, that man may live (2)
511 all life in Christ made new (2)
513 seed-time & the harvest, our life, our health, our food (3)

515   the life of earth and seed is thine (2)
517   Lord of life and King of glory (T,1)
517   sons and daughters look on life with eager eyes (4)
517   when our growing sons and daughters look on life (4)
518   for life and health and every good (2)
518   the bread of life sent down from heaven (3)
521   neither life nor death shall ever from the Lord .. sever (3)
523   to thee, from whom we all derive our life our gifts (5)
523   our life, our gifts, our power to give (5)
525   for life and health, those common things (2)
526   yea, e'en the best life faileth (2)
543   and mercy more than life (3)
548   strong as when her life began (4)

life's
  97   I'll trust him when life's fleeting days shall end (4)
105   shall life's swift passing years all fly (1)
107   tumult of our life's wild, restless sea (1)
128   till in life's latest hour I bow (5)
143   while life's dark maze I tread & griefs around me spread (3)
143   when ends life's transient dream (4)
144   help me, throughout life's changing scene, by faith (1)
144   though oft I seem to tread alone life's dreary waste (3)
144   life's dreary waste with thorns o'er-grown (3)
157   we touch him in life's throng and press (4)
176   bear me o'er life's fitful sea (3)
184   I sink in life's alarms when by myself I stand (1)
225   a little shelter from life's stress (3)
233   yes, on through life's long path still chanting as ye go (4)
234   I lay in dust life's glory dead (4)
245   but toiling in life's dusty way (2)
247   Jesus, Savior, pilot me over life's tempestuous sea (T,1)
264   when the soul waketh, and life's shadows flee (5)
289   swift to its close ebbs out life's little day (2)
333   and to life's day the glorious unknown morrow (3)
342   until each life's vocation accents thy holy way (3)
372   it is the chart and compass that o'er life's surging sea (3)
398   and glorifies with duty life's poorest, humblest part (2)
412   for me ... thy mortal sorrow, and thy life's oblation (4)
476   until true wisdom from above . make life's pathway clear (3)
486   those who give up life's bounty to serve a race to be (2)
539   when life's perils thick confound you (3)

lift
  38   lift us to the joy divine (3)
  51   God shall lift up thy head (1)
  57   unto the hills I lift mine eyes (T,1)
  60   lift up your voice and with us sing Alleluia! Alleluia! (1)
  77   come, lift your hearts on high; Alleluia! Amen! (2)
127   with joy shall I lift up my head (1)
140   Author of faith! to thee I lift my weary, longing eyes (4)
156   I would look up, and laugh and love and lift (2)
174   lift high the cross of Christ (4)
175   weep o'er the erring one, lift up the fallen (1)
188   lift thou thy world, O Christ, closer to thee (3)
194   lift up our hearts, O King of kings (T,1)
194   and lift us to a nobler life (3)

38	fill us with the light of day (1)
39	his beams are majesty and light (2)
42	praise him, all ye stars of light (1)
45	morning light ... lily white declare ... maker's praise (2)
47	with thee to bless, the darkness shines as light (2)
50	so full of splendor and of joy, beauty and light (1)
60	thou givest man both warmth and light (3)
61	filled the new-made world with light (2)
62	by him upholden hang the glorious orbs of light (1)
62	their great story, God is love, and God is light (1)
64	star of our hope, thy softened light cheers (2)
64	Lord ... whose light is truth, whose warmth is love (4)
64	till all thy living altars claim one holy light (5)
64	one holy light, one heavenly flame (5)
76	all the angel faces, all the hosts of light (2)
76	let his will enfold you in its light and power (4)
78	thy people's everlasting light (1)
80	thou Son of man, thou Light of light (2)
85	God's light to earth thou bringest to drive sin's night (1)
88	all in the love-light of Jesus' face (2)
89	my light in Satan's darkest hour (4)
90	Mary's son most holy, Light of the village life (2)
90	Light of the village life from day to day (2)
95	Light and life art thou within: Savior ...from every sin (4)
103	joy of the desolate, light of the straying (2)
117	I am this dark world's light (3)
117	and in that light of life I'll walk (3)
124	with the countless hosts of light (3)
129	restore, my dear Savior, the light of thy face (4)
131	on our disordered spirits move ... let ... now be light (3)
132	spread thy light from the height which knows no measure (1)
135	Word of God and inward light (1)
136	O Spirit of the living God, thou light and fire divine (T,1)
139	faith lends its realizing light (6)
141	Have faith in God, my mind ... oft thy light burns low (2)
161	showing to wandering souls the path of light (3)
169	I would live ever in the light (3)
198	and light of knowledge in their eyes (1)
206	and wait thy word, let there be light (4)
211	in darkness and temptation, my light, my help is near (1)
213	the darkness shineth as the light (1)
213	be thou my light, be thou my way (2)
216	nor plagues that waste in noonday light (5)
223	when we walk with the Lord in the light of his Word (T,1)
224	perfect submission, perfect delight (2)
227	O the rapturous height of that holy delight (5)
227	delight which I felt in the life-giving blood (5)
231	sometimes a light surprises the Christian while he sings (T)
234	O Light that followest all my way (2)
236	turn thou for us its darkness into light (3)
236	for dark and light are both alike to thee (3)
242	God's new Messiah, offering each the bloom or blight (1)
242	choice goes by forever twixt that darkness & that light (1)
242	by the light of burning martyrs (3)
254	let thy clear light forever shine (1)
256	waking or sleeping, thy presence my light (1)
257	Light of light, from God proceeding (3)
258	Our God's bounteous gifts abuse not, Light refuse not (4)

258	thou with him shalt dwell, beholding Light enfolding (4)
258	Light enfolding all things in unclouded day (4)
268	a light to shine upon the road that leads me to the Lamb (1)
268	purer light shall mark .. road that leads me to the Lamb (6)
272	lead kindly Light (T,1)
285	first-born sons of light desire in vain its depths...see (2)
299	mission ... to tell to all the world that God is Light (1)
300	lift your eyes ... sons of light Zion's city is in sight (4)
301	Christ, the true, the only light (1)
303	the Prince is ever in them; the day-light is serene (2)
303	what radiancy of glory, what light beyond compare (1)
303	strive, man, to win that glory, toil ..to gain .. light (3)
318	light, who dost my soul enlighten (2)
324	Light of light descendeth from the realms of endless day (3)
325	not paradise, with all its joys ... such delight afford (1)
329	thou fount of life! thou light of men (1)
329	shed o'er the world thy holy light (5)
353	when morning dawns and light triumphant breaks (1)
353	light and beauty brings (5)
356	break forth, O living light of God (T,1)
356	O let thy Word be light anew to every nation's life (3)
358	blessedness and light, peace & truth its course portends (2)
359	give them songs for sighing ... darkness turn to light (2)
361	a glorious light have seen (1)
361	the light has shined on them (1)
365	the rolling sun, the changing light ...thy power confess (2)
365	nations ...that see the light or feel the sun (4)
365	bless the dark world with heavenly light (5)
366	her Star is risen; her Light is come (2)
367	still new beauties may I see, and still increasing light (3)
370	shedding light that none can measure (1)
370	light of knowledge, ever burning, shed on us (3)
370	light of knowledge ... shed on us thy deathless learning (3)
371	O God of light, thy Word, a lamp unfailing (T,1)
372	O Truth unchanged, unchanging, O Light of our dark sky (1)
372	still that light she lifteth o'er all the earth to shine (2)
372	to bear before the nations thy true light as of old (4)
373	break forth, O beauteous heavenly light (T,1)
380	in the light of that star lie the ages impearled (3)
380	we rejoice in the light, and we echo the song (4)
381	yet in thy dark streets shineth the everlasting light (1)
382	yonder shines the infant light (2)
383	and by the light of that same star three wise men came (3)
383	and to the earth it gave great light (2)
387	light and life to all he brings (3)
393	Son of God, love's pure light (3)
393	wondrous star, lend thy light (4)
397	as with joy they hailed its light (1)
398	light of the world, we hail thee (T,1)
398	Light of the world, thy beauty steals into every heart (2)
398	and helpest them to render light back to thee again (2)
398	Light of the world, Illumine ... darkened earth of thine (3)
398	thy light, so glad & golden, shall set on earth no more (1)
399	thou beamest forth in truth and light (1)
399	thou heavenly Brightness! Light divine! (2)
401	inward light impart, cheer my eyes and warm my heart (2)
401	Christ, the true, the only light (1)
402	guide us to thy perfect light (R)

403　who dwells in cloudless light enshrined (2)
403　his spirit only can bestow, who reigns in light above (1)
403　that light hath on thee shone in which is perfect day (3)
403　God himself is light (4)
404　behold throughout the heavens there shone a holy light (1)
407　in lands, where shadows hide the light (3)
408　Christ is the world's true light (T,1)
410　a story of truth and mercy, a story of peace and light (1)
410　the kingdom of love and light (R)
416　light of sacred story gathers round its head sublime (1,5)
416　when the sun of bliss is beaming light and love (3)
416　light and love upon my way (3)
426　here the King of all the ages throned in light (2)
426　throned in light ere worlds could be (2)
427　but thou dost light and life restore (3)
430　till amid the hosts of light, we in thee redeemed (5)
437　the Lord in rays eternal of resurrection light (2)
442　life in all.. growing powers toward .. light is striving (1)
446　from his light, to whom we give laud and praise undying (2)
456　as altar candle sheds its light as surely as a star (2)
458　King of kings, & Lord of lords, & heaven's eternal light (2)
459　blessed ... with light and life since Eden's dawning day (1)
460　Light of Light, to earth descending (2)
462　Spirit creative, give us light (2)
466　and let thy glorious light shine ever on my sight (2)
467　enable with perpetual light the dullness of... sight (2)
469　light to man's blindness, O be thou our aid (1)
471　Fountain of light and love below (3)
473　whose robe is the light, whose canopy space (2)
473　it breathes in the air, it shines in the light (4)
477　let .. be light again .. set thy judgments in .. earth (5)
478　thy cross is lifted o'er us, we journey in its light (3)
479　till thy love's revealing light ... dawns (3)
479　light in its height and depth and greatness dawns (3)
480　let there be light (1,2,3,4)
480　and in earth's darkest place, let there be light (3)
480　through the world far and wide, let there be light (4)
482　O Thou who art the Life and Light, Exalted Lord and King (4
485　just rule ... fill ... earth with health & light & peace (2)
488　O day of joy and light (1)
488　on thee, at the creation, the light first had its birth (2)
488　thus on thee most glorious a triple light was given (2)
488　where Gospel light is glowing with pure & radiant beams (3)
490　with the gracious light I my toil resume (1)
491　O Jesus, make their darkness light (2)
493　for all the blessings of the light (1)
494　softly now the light of day fades upon our sight away (T,1)
494　soon from us the light of day shall forever pass away (3)
496　the perfect day before us breaks in everlasting light (4)
497　God, that madest earth and heaven, darkness and light (T,1)
498　ppraise for light so brightly shining on our steps (1)
500　unsleeping while earth rolls onward into light (2)
502　like infant's slumbers pure and light (5)
506　but mid the light declining the evening star is shining (1)
520　shine, Light Divine, reveal thy face (3)
527　I woke, the dungeon flamed with light (3)
531　I see from far thy beauteous light (1)

536 thou, in the darkness drear, their one true light (2)
547 long may our land be bright with freedom's holy light (4)
light's
29 o Light of light, light's living spring (1)
318 come into the daylight's splendor (1)

lighten
317 lighten our eyes, brightly appear (3)
318 light, who dost my soul enlighten (2)
377 no one to lighten their despair (1)
467 lighten with celestial fire (1)

lightens
63 bliss he wakes and woe he lightens (1)

lighter
498 every burden will be lighter when ... it comes from thee (3)

lightest
476 who lightest every earnest mind of every clime and shore (3)
lighthouse
148 from his lighthouse evermore (1)

lightning
544 thunder thy clarion, the lightning thy sword (1)
545 he hath loosed the fateful lightning of his ... sword (1)
545 lightning of his terrible swift sword (1)

lightnings
36 when lightnings flash and storm winds blow (2)

lights
41 when we see thy lights of heaven ...thy power displayed (2)
60 ye lights of evening, find a voice (2)
146 they are but broken lights of thee (4)
148 let the lower lights be burning (R)
148 to us he gives the keeping of the lights along the shore (1)
148 eager eyes are watching, longing for the lights (2)
148 longing for the lights along the shore (2)
353 crowned with glory like the sun...lights the morning sky (2)
438 Christ is...the Sun that warms and lights us (3)
513 he paints the wayside flower, he lights the evening star (2)

like
12 dearer than all things I know is child-like faith to me (4)
22 when like wandering sheep we strayed (2)
27 thy justice like mountains high soaring above (2)
28 a thousand ages in thy sight are like an evening gone (4)
28 time, like an ever rolling stream (5)
38 hearts unfold like flowers before thee (1)
44 with glory like to thine (4)
65 like the pity of a father hath... Lord's compassion been (3)
66 father-like he tends and spares us (3)
69 wideness in God's mercy like the wideness of the sea (1)
80 who like thee so mild, so bright ... did ever go (2)
80 who like thee ... go so patient through a world of woe (2)
80 who like thee so humbly bore the scorn ... scoffs of men (3)
80 and like thee, all my journey run (4)

85	that men in thee may see what God is like (2)
92	that saved a wretch like me (1)
93	let thy goodness, like a fetter, bind my wandering heart (3)
95	O thou loving, blessed One, rising o'er me like the sun (4)
121	Savior, like a shepherd lead us (T,1)
139	faith like its finisher and Lord today as yesterday (1)
149	hungering and thirsting to hear it like the rest (4)
171	build us a tower of Christ-like height (2)
171	see, like thee, our noblest work our Father's work to do (2)
178	like thee, O Lord, to grieve (3)
178	O give us hearts to love like thee (3)
201	create in us thy spirit; give us a love like thine (3)
203	we've seen thy glory like a mantle spread o'er hill and (4)
212	if you can't preach like Peter ... can't pray like Paul (2)
214	like trees beside a flowing stream (2)
214	not like that go the men of unbelief (3)
214	men of unbelief ... are like chaff the wind doth blow (3)
227	suffered and died to redeem a poor rebel like me (4)
235	simple trust like theirs who heard beside the Syrian sea (2)
235	let us, like them, without a word rise up & follow thee (2)
236	for dark and light are both alike to thee (3)
243	like those strong men of old (1)
244	when the world is tossing me like ship upon the sea (1)
245	sorrows, sometimes how they sweep like tempests (1)
245	like tempests over the soul (1)
251	thou art not, like man, untrue (2)
260	thy power flows in like flood tides from the sea (4)
263	though like a wanderer, the sun gone down (2)
265	no tender voice like thine can peace afford (1)
266	by looking to Jesus, like him thou shalt be (2)
273	like the springs and running waters make me crystal pure (2)
273	like .. rocks of towering grandeur make me strong & sure (2)
273	like thy dancing waves in sunlight make me glad and free (3)
273	like .. straightness of the pine trees let me upright be (3)
273	like the arching of the heavens lift my thoughts above (4)
286	Lord I want to be like Jesus in my heart (4)
289	who, like thyself, my guide and stay can be (3)
293	grace, which like the Lord, the giver, never fails (2)
297	like them, the meek & lowly, on high may dwell with thee (4)
305	like a mighty army moves the Church of God (2)
306	the fellowship of kindred minds is like to that above (1)
308	not like kingdoms of the world thy holy Church, O God (3)
309	lowly, meek, in thought & word, altogether like our Lord (3)
333	with child-like trust that fears nor pain nor death (2)
337	Savior, like stars in thy right hand thy servants ... be (2)
343	like them, let man the throne surround (2)
350	like incense sweet to thee ascend (2)
352	let every anthem rise like incense to the skies (2)
353	crowned with glory like the sun...lights the morning sky (2)
359	he shall come down like showers upon the fruitful earth (3)
359	love, joy and hope, like flowers, spring in his path (3)
362	like the flowers of the field they perish (2)
362	power and pomp of nations shall pass like a dream away (2)
362	he shall feed his flock like a shepherd (3)
372	it floateth like a banner before God's host unfurled (3)
372	it shineth like a beacon above the darkling world (3)
376	earth stood hard as iron, water like a stone (1)
413	remold them, make us, like thee, divine (R)

419   like him... pardon on his tongue in midst of mortal pain (2)
420   and say, was ever grief like his (3)
428   O Lamb of God, was ever pain, was ever love, like thine (4)
439   made like him, like him we rise, Alleluia (4)
441   laid in the earth like grain that sleeps unseen (2)
441   forth he came at Easter, like the risen grain (3)
441   love is come again like wheat that springeth green (R)
461   purge our hearts like sacrificial flame (2)
468   truth from the earth, like to a flower, shall bud (1)
470   armored with all Christ-like graces in the fight (4)
472   his name like sweet perfume shall rise (2)
473   and round it hath cast, like a mantle, the sea (3)
478   gladness breaks like morning where'er thy face appears (3)
485   rise like incense, each to thee, in noble thought & deed (1)
486   O God, before whose altar the stars like tapers burn (T,1)
486   their unconsidered lives go up like incense to the sky (2)
486   like those to conquer for thy sake despair ... doubt (4)
497   may we, born anew like morning, to labor rise (2)
500   thy throne shall never, like earth's proud empires, pass (4)
502   be every mourner's sleep tonight like infant's slumbers (5)
502   like infant's slumbers pure and light (5)
511   a world redeemed by Christ-like love (2)
520   with gentleness and love like thine (1)
520   love like thine, that none shall ever stray (1)
530   love, like death, hath all destroyed (5)
532   whose music like a mighty wind the souls of men uplifted (3)
545   he is coming like the glory of the morning on the wave (5)
547   my heart with rapture thrills, like that above (2)

likeness
177   give me a faithful heart, likeness to thee (3)
266   thy friends in thy conduct his likeness shall see (2)
440   God's likeness, man awaking, knows the everlasting peace (1)

lilies
231   who gives the lilies clothing will clothe his people, too (3)
545   in . beauty of the lilies Christ was born across the sea (4)

lily
45   morning light ... lily white declare ... maker's praise (2)
244   O thou Lily of the   Valley, stand by me (4)

limits
538   bidst the mighty ocean deep its... appointed limits keep (1)

line
394   to you in David's town, this day is born of David's line (3)

lines
365   we read thy name in fairer lines (1)
367   forever be thy name adored for these celestial lines (1)

linger
104   let not conscience make you linger (3)

lingering
270   and sorrow crown each lingering year (2)

lips
16	to touch our lips, our minds inspire (3)
34	he gave us eyes to see them, and lips that we might tell (4)
76	from the lips of sinners unto whom he came (3)
83	his lips with grace o'erflow (1)
136	burn, winged fire! inspire our lips with flaming love (2)
136	inspire our lips with flaming love and zeal to preach (2)
157	our lips of childhood frame (5)
187	take my lips ... let them be filled with messages from (2)
236	guard thou the lips from sin, the hearts from shame (2)
252	speech that infant lips can try (3)
316	when these failing lips grow dumb ... mind & memory flee (4)
340	teach thou our lips of thee to speak (3)
424	to whom the lips of children made sweet hosannas ring (1)
481	bitter lips in blind despair cry (3)
510	our lips & lives ... gladly show the wonders of thy love (4)

lisp
516	children early lisp his fame and parents hold him dear (2)

lisping
421	when this poor lisping, stammering tongue lies silent (5)

list
109	sinner, list to the loving call (2)
110	Jesus is pleading; O list to his voice (4)

listen
164	O speak, and make me listen, thou guardian of my soul (3)
260	to hear thy voice we need but love ... listen & be still (3)

listening
1	He speaks, and listening to his voice (5)
43	nightly, to the listening earth repeats the story (2)
45	and to my listening ears all nature sings (1)
90	with all the listening people gathered round (3)
221	listening every moment to the Spirit's call (4)
274	I am listening, Lord, for thee (1,4)
437	listening to his accents, may hear, so calm and plain (2)

lit
80	marks divine ... that lit the lonely pathway (1)
377	in Bethlehem neath starlit skies (T,1)
395	all the plains were lit that night (2)

little
20	one little word shall fell him (3)
34	each little flower that opens (1)
34	each little bird that sings (1)
146	our little systems have their day (4)
225	a little shrine of quietness, all sacred to itself (2)
225	a little shelter from life's stress (3)
225	a little place of mystic grace (4)
289	swift to its close ebbs out life's little day (2)
353	not as of old a little child to bear and fight and die (2)
381	O little town of Bethlehem, how still we see thee lie (T,1)
384	the little Lord Jesus laid down his sweet head (1)

384   the little Lord Jesus, asleep on the hay (1)
384   but little Lord Jesus, no crying he makes (2)
396   oxen lowing, little knowing Christ the babe is Lord (2)
423   Hosanna, loud hosanna the little children sang (T,1)
423   scorned ... little children should on his bidding wait (2)
464   saw ye not the cloud arise, little as a human hand (4)
481   from little children's cries (2)
493   teach me to live, that I may dread the grave as little (3)
493   dread the grave as little as my bed (3)
495   grant to little children visions bright of thee (3)
517   that in all we do or say little ones our deeds may copy (3)
517   little feet our steps may follow in a safe & narrow way (3)
549   behold us, Lord, a little space (T,1)

live

  2   thousands only live to bless thee (1)
 15   him, in whom they move and live, let every creature sing (3)
 38   all who live in love are thine (3)
102   and live for him who died for all (5)
102   ye all may come to Christ and live (4)
105   shall I give no heed, but still in bondage live (4)
112   God, did your being give, made you with himself to live (1)
112   God ... died himself, that you might live (2)
112   will you not his grace receive ... still refuse to live (3)
117   thirsty one, stoop down and drink and live (2)
117   and now I live in him (2)
133   but live with thee the perfect life of thine eternity (4)
134   and shall we then forever live at this poor dying rate (4)
135   by thee may I strongly live, bravely bear & nobly strive (3)
140   O speak, and I shall live (3)
147   when the joys of sense depart, to live by faith alone (4)
150   arm me with jealous care, as in thy sight to live (3)
169   I would live ever in the light (3)
170   with thee, O Master, let me live (4)
182   and from this moment, live or die to serve my God alone (2)
191   live out the laws of Christ in ... thought & word & deed (1)
194   gift of life to all who live (3)
196   all his promises embrace, and to his glory live (2)
198   inarmed shall live as comrades free (3)
198   nation with nation, land with land, inarmed shall live (3)
218   Lord, it belongs not to my care whether I die or live (T,1)
259   thine wholly, thine alone, I'd live (1)
260   but live thy life divine (3)
299   God, in whom they live and move, is Love (3)
299   died on earth that man might live above (3)
309   show how true believers live (4)
335   souls that must forever live in rapture or in woe (3)
336   and are we yet alive and see each other's face (T,1)
344   thine, wholly thine, to die and live (3)
384   and fit us for heaven to live with thee there (3)
418   Lord, let me never, never outlive my love to thee (3)
429   and all may live from sin set free (3)
430   here we gather love to live; here we gather faith to die (3)
447   that we may live and sing to thee: Alleluia (4)
457   dead to sin, his members live the life of righteousness (3)
465   Father, in whom we live, in whom we are, and move (T,1)

476   inspire thy heralds of good news to live thy life divine (5)
479   that thy children ... may thy mercy know, and live (4)
492   live this short, revolving day as if it were our last (4)
493   teach me to live, that I may dread the grave as little (3)
499   help us, this & every day to live more nearly as we pray (4)
502   for without thee I cannot live (3)
507   promise, in this sacred hour, for God to live and die (2)
511   to make our life an offering to God, that man may live (2)
514   crops we grow that men may live (1)
515   thy children live by daily food (1)
515   since every day by thee we live, may grateful hearts (4)
523   O may we ever with thee live, who givest all (5)
527   alive in him, my living Head (4)
542   and hearts united learn to live as one (3)

lives
36   creation lives and moves in thee (1)
62   Love is life, our lives be praise (2)
62   welcome story! love lives on, and death is dead (3)
62   our whole lives one resurrection ... life of life above (4)
69   lives would be all sunshine in the sweetness of our Lord (2)
112   He,' who all your lives hath strove (3)
122   he ever lives above, for me to intercede (2)
153   all our lives belong to thee (3)
153   offering lives if it's thy will (4)
157   we test our lives by thine (6)
161   take thou our lives, and use them as thou wilt (4)
165   may the fruits of thy salvation in our hearts and lives (2)
165   in our hearts and lives abound (2)
179   King of our lives, by thy grace we will be (1,R)
206   by whose hand through years long past our lives were led (1)
235   let our ordered lives confess the beauty of thy peace (4)
235   in purer lives thy service find (1)
260   our dreams, our aims, our work, our lives are prayers (1)
260   our lives are prayers thou lovest more (1)
260   attune our lives to thee (2)
269   until our lives are perfected in thee (4)
291   filled with delight my raptured soul lives (3)
291   lives out its earthly day (3)
314   hallow all our lives, O Lord (2)
344   thy wisdom in their lives be shown (4)
438   faith lives upon no other! Alleluia! (4)
439   lives again our glorious King, Alleluia (2)
440   Jesus lives who once was dead (3)
441   love lives again, that with the dead has been (1)
444   and he lives forever with his saints to reign (R)
445   he lives, my everlasting Head (1)
445   I know that my Redeemer lives (T,1,4)
445   He lives, to plead for me above (2)
445   He lives, to bless me with his love (2)
445   He lives, to help in time of need (2)
445   He lives, and grants me daily breath (3)
445   He lives, and I shall conquer death (3)
445   He lives, my mansion to prepare (3)
445   He lives, to bring me safely there (3)
445   He lives, all glory to his name (4)
445   He lives, my Savior, still the same (4)

445 He lives, my hungry soul to feed (2)
445 he lives, he lives, who once was dead (1)
455 lives that death may die (2)
465 render ... their lives to thee for thy redeeming grace (2)
470 gird our lives that they may be armored (4)
476 till ... know the loveliness of lives made fair and free (4)
481 hark, how from men whose lives are held more cheap (2)
481 lives are held more cheap than merchandise (2)
484 bind all our lives together, smite us and save us all (3)
486 their unconsidered lives go up like incense to the sky (2)
510 our lips & lives ... gladly show the wonders of thy love (4)
525 and warms our lives with heavenly fires (3)
548 the glory that illumines patriot lives of deathless fame (3)
552 fill all our lives with love and grace divine (4)

livest
27 in all life thou livest, the true life of all (3)
427 then let all praise be given thee who livest evermore (3)

liveth
450 for her Lord now liveth; death hath lost its sting (2)

living
16 O for the living flame from his own altar brought (3)
29 o Light of light, light's living spring (1)
30 praise to the living God! all praised be his name (T,1,3)
38 well-spring of the joy of living (3)
61 all things living he doth feed (3)
64 till all thy living altars claim one holy light (5)
67 where streams of living water flow (2)
85 God's love to earth thou bringest in living deeds (3)
85 living deeds that prove how sweet to serve all others (3)
117 behold, I freely give the living water (2)
123 I only know a living Christ, our immortality (3)
136 O Spirit of the living God, thou light and fire divine (T,1)
136 teach us to utter living words of truth (3)
137 thou take the veil away and breathe the living Word (2)
137 inspire the living faith, which whosoe'er receives (4)
143 pure, warm, and changeless be, a living fire (2)
151 living still, in spite of dungeon, fire and sword (1)
154 Christ only, always, living in me (4)
193 up unto thee, our living Head let us in all things grow (3)
195 that I may speak in living echoes of thy tone (1)
205 feeds me with the living bread (2)
221 by the living Word of God I shall prevail (2)
255 for thee my God .. living God, my thirsty soul doth pine (2)
269 lead us through Christ, the true and living Way (1)
270 living or dying, thou art near (4)
291 sweet fields arrayed in living green & rivers of delight (1)
293 see, the streams of living waters (2)
293 streams of living waters, springing from eternal love (2)
296 O living Church, thine errand speed (4)
302 one army of the living God, to his command we bow (4)
313 that living bread ... heavenly wine be our immortal food (2)
328 one with the living bread divine ... now by faith we eat (3)
329 we taste thee, O thou living bread (3)
342 and let our daily living reveal thee everywhere (1)

348   by wise master builders squared, here be living stones (4)
348   living stones prepared for the temple near thy throne (4)
349   O living Christ, chief cornerstone (T,1)
351   and dare to trust the living God (3)
352   speak, O eternal Lord, out of thy living Word (3)
356   break forth, O living light of God (T,1)
368   Word of the ever-living God (3)
369   my spirit pants for thee, O living word (1)
372   it is the heaven-drawn picture of thee, the living Word (2)
429   the living way to heaven is seen (2)
452   lo! the dead is living, God forevermore (1,4)
470   grant us courage for the living of these days (2)
479   to.. child .. youth .. aged love in living deeds to show (4)
484   tie in a living tether the prince and priest and thrall (3)
484   lift up a living nation, a single sword to thee (3)
486   the armies of the living God shall march to victory (4)
488   living water flowing with soul-refreshing streams (3)
527   alive in him, my living Head (4)
546   with thy living fire of judgment purge this land (1)
548   standing in the living present (1)
548   for our prophets and apostles, loyal to the living Word (3)

lo

8   Lo! the apostolic...joins thy sacred name to hallow (3)
20   his rage we can endure, for lo, his doom is sure (3)
40   lo, at thy word the waters were formed (1)
108   O Jesus, thou art knocking, and lo, that hand is scarred (2)
342   lo, I am with you alway. We take thy guiding hand (4)
358   lo, the Prince of Peace, lo, the Son of God is come (3)
364   lo, he comes with clouds descending (T,1)
389   lo, he assumes our flesh and blood (3)
412   lo, the Good Shepherd for the sheep is offered (3)
418   lo, here I fall, my Savior! 'Tis I deserve thy place (2)
450   Lo! Jesus meets thee risen from the tomb (2)
462   let us hear thy silent voice: "Lo, I am near" (4)
469   races and peoples, lo, we stand divided (2)

load

53   why should this anxious load press down your weary mind (3)
219   discouraged in... work of life, disheartened by its load (2)
261   are we weak & heavy laden, cumbered with a load of care (3)
326   here would I lay aside each earthly load (3)
528   groaning beneath your load of sin (5)

loaves

369   as thou didst break the loaves beside the sea (1)

lock

105   shall he knock, and I my heart the closer lock (3)

lodestone

193   touched by the lodestone of thy love (3)

loftier

198   a loftier race than e'er the world hath known shall rise (1)
198   new arts shall bloom of loftier mold (4)
343   instruments of loftier sound assist his feeble praise (2)

245 O sometimes how long seems the day (2)
248 the strife will not be long (4)
270 though long the weary way we tread (2)
272 so long thy power hath blest me (3)
272 faces...which I have loved long since and lost awhile (3)
288 long as eternal ages roll, thou seest thy Savior's face (2)
295 for thee I long, for love divine (3)
329 and long to feast upon thee still (3)
344 unite the pair...long disjoined, knowledge & vital piety (3)
346 through ages long his wisdom and his power display (1)
356 ancient words, their message long obscure (2)
360 come, thou long expected Jesus (T,1)
361 shined on them who long in shades of death have been (1)
371 questing hearts that long for peace and healing see (3)
376 in the bleak midwinter, long ago (1)
382 watching long in hope and fear (4)
398 long, alas, witholden, now spread from shore to shore (1)
399 here in sadness eye and heart long for thy gladness (2)
408 the world has waited long, has travailed long in pain (3)
422 the day of peace we long to see (4)
446 all the winter of our sins, long and dark, is flying (2)
460 age-long Word expounding God's own message now as then (3)
466 so the yearning strong, with which the soul will long (3)
468 glory shall ere long appear to dwell within our land (2)
470 fears and doubts too long have bound us (2)
479 still the captives long for freedom (2)
481 city that hath stood too long a dream (4)
486 those oppressed or lonely ... long at strife with pain (3)
495 through the long night watches may thine angels spread (5)
497 holy dreams and hopes attend us this live-long night (1)
506 long our day of testing, now comes the hour of resting (3)
527 long my imprisoned spirit lay fast bound in sin (3)
532 whose names have perished, lost in the haze of long ago (5)
533 the long cloud of witnesses show the same path to heaven (2)
536 and when the strife is fierce, the warfare long (5)
547 long may our land be bright with freedom's holy light (4)

longer
110 come, and no longer delay (3)
122 he owns me for his child; I can no longer fear (4)
187 take my will & make it thine; it shall be no longer mine (3)
278 then shall my feet no longer rove rooted .. fixed in God (1)
278 no longer ... my heart shall mourn ... purified by grace (3)
278 my steadfast soul, from falling free ... no longer move (4)

longest
10 more than all, the heart must bear the longest part (2)

longing
130 my longing heart vouchsafe to make thine ... throne (4)
140 Author of faith! to thee I lift my weary, longing eyes (4)
148 eager eyes are watching, longing for the lights (2)
148 longing for the lights along the shore (2)
274 longing for thy voice that cheereth (1)
297 with the vision glorious, her longing eyes are blest (3)
304 with love and longing turn to find their rest in thee (1)
304 hearts with love & longing ... find their rest in thee (1)

360 dear desire of every nation, joy of every longing heart (1)
399 toward thee longing doth possess me; turn and bless me (2)
440 saints all longing for their heaven (3)

longings
149 it satisfies my longings as nothing else can do (1)

longs
173 longs to bind God's children into one perfect whole (4)
255 so longs my soul, O God, for thee & thy refreshing grace (1)
295 thirsty soul longs ardently ... faints thy courts to see (2)
474 so a soul that's born of God longs to view his... face (2)
474 longs to view his glorious face (2)

look
17 when I look down from lofty mountain grandeur (2)
113 Savior,look with pitying eye; Savior, help me, or I die (R)
117 look unto me, thy morn shall rise ... thy day be bright (3)
134 look how we grovel here below (2)
152 still to things eternal look (3)
156 I would look up, and laugh and love and lift (2)
159 Let my soul look up with a steadfast hope (2)
194 look down on all earth's sin and strife (3)
219 I look to thee in every need and never look in vain (T,1)
225 where I may look upon thy face (4)
237 when thou seest me waver, with a look recall (1)
243 look up! the victor's crown at length! (4)
253 with humble confidence look up and know thou hearest (1)
264 its closing eyes look up to thee in prayer (4)
309 Jesus, Lord, we look to thee (T,1)
310 Jesus, we look to thee, thy promised presence claim (T,1)
320 look on the heart by sorrow broken (2)
320 look on the tears by sinners shed (2)
384 I love thee, Lord Jesus, look down from the sky (2)
411 O Father, look from heaven and bless ... their works (5)
418 look on me with thy favor, vouchsafe to me thy grace (2)
425 the winged squadrons of the sky look down (3)
425 look down with sad and wondering eyes to see (3)
453 look, ye saints! the sight is glorious (T,1)
468 justice, from her heavenly bower look down on mortal men (1)
487 look into our hearts and minds today (1)
487 look into our hearts...on this thy holy day (1)
517 sons and daughters look on life with eager eyes (4)
517 when our growing sons and daughters look on life (4)
529 look on thy hands, and read it there (2)

looked
117 I looked to Jesus, and I found in him my star, my sun (3)
377 yet none there were who looked without (2)
383 they looked up and saw a star shining in the east (2)
384 the stars in the sky looked down where he lay (1)

looking
224 watching and waiting, looking above (3)
266 by looking to Jesus, like him thou shalt be (2)
266 and, looking to Jesus, still trust in his Word (3)

looks
- 143 my faith looks up to thee, thou Lamb of Calvary (T,1)
- 177 my feeble faith looks up, Jesus, to thee (2)
- 251 human hearts and looks deceive me (2)
- 253 that looks to thee when sin is near (3)

loom
- 549 thine is the loom, the forge, the mart (4)

loomed
- 173 while ever on the hill-top before thee loomed the cross (2)

looms
- 342 the task looms large before us; we follow without fear (4)

loose
- 472 the prisoner leaps to loose his chains (4)

loosed
- 446 loosed from Pharaoh's bitter yoke (1)
- 545 he hath loosed the fateful lightning of his ... sword (1)

loosen
- 200 whom shall I send to loosen the bonds of shame and greed (1)

loosened
- 1 your loosened tongues employ (6)

Lord
- 2 confess thee Lord of might (1)
- 4 the Lord is never far away (3)
- 4 be joyful in the Lord, my heart (4)
- 4 the Lord is God, and he alone (5)
- 5 come, ye who love the Lord, and let your joys be known (T,1)
- 6 we, thy people, praise thee, Lord of hosts eternal! (1,2)
- 7 Lord, we would to thee draw nigh (4)
- 8 Lord of all, we bow before thee (1)
- 8 fill .. heavens with sweet accord: holy, holy, holy Lord (2)
- 9 the Lord pours eyesight on the blind (3)
- 9 the Lord supports the fainting mind (3)
- 11 voices raise to the Lord in hymns of praise (1)
- 11 nations, come, your voices raise to the Lord in hymns (1)
- 11 tell ye forth his might, Lord of life ... truth & right (3)
- 12 I know thee ... in part, I ask not, Lord, for more (3)
- 14 eternal are thy mercies, Lord (2)
- 15 praise the Lord in every breath (3)
- 15 praise the Lord who reigns above (T,1)
- 15 let all things praise the Lord (3)
- 16 stand up and bless the Lord, ye people of his choice (T,1)
- 16 stand up and bless the Lord your God (1)
- 16 stand up and bless the Lord; the Lord your God adore (5)
- 17 O Lord my God, when I in awesome wonder (1)
- 19 most gracious, magnify the Lord (2)
- 20 Lord Sabaoth, his name, from age to age the same (2)
- 21 sing to the Lord with cheerful voice (1)
- 21 know that the Lord is God indeed (2)
- 21 for why! the Lord our God is good (4)

22   know that the Lord is God alone (1)
24   come, worship at this throne; come, bow before the Lord (3)
26   holy, holy, holy, Lord God almighty (T,1,4)
31   the Lord Jehovah reigns, his throne is built on high (T,1)
32   the Lord our God is clothed with might (T,1)
32   the Lord uplifts his awful hand and chains you (2)
34   all things wise and wonderful: .. Lord God made them all (R)
35   Lord of all, to thee we raise this our hymn of grateful (R)
37   Lord, how thy wonders are displayed (2)
37   I sing the goodness of the Lord (2)
37   goodness of the Lord, that filled the earth with food (2)
38   God of glory, Lord of love (1)
44   O Lord, our Lord, in all the earth (T,1)
44   thy glory, Lord, proclaim (5)
44   Lord, our Lord, in all the earth how excellent thy name (5)
45   why should my heart be sad? The Lord is King (3)
46   our end, the glory of the Lord (1)
47   when we are strong, Lord, leave us not alone (3)
47   we own thy mercies, Lord, which never fail (1)
47   Lord ... our refuge be (3)
47   Lord, by the stripes which wounded thee (4)
48   how firm a foundation, ye saints of the Lord (T,1)
50   I thank thee,Lord, that thou hast kept the best in store (4)
52   how are thy servants blest, O Lord (T,1)
52   from all our griefs and fears, O Lord (2)
53   come, cast your burdens on the Lord (1)
54   O Lord,our fathers oft have told in our attentive ears (T,1)
55   praise to the Lord, the almighty, the King of creation (T,1)
55   praise to the Lord (1,2,3,4)
55   Lord, who o'er all things so wondrously reigneth (2)
55   Lord, who doth prosper thy work and defend thee (3)
56   O magnify the Lord with me, with me exalt his name (2)
57   my help is from the Lord alone (1)
57   Lord alone, who heaven and earth has made (1)
57   thy faithful keeper is the Lord (3)
58   we bring thee,Lord, the praise they brought (1)
58   their joy unto their Lord we bring (3)
59   thou, Lord, wast at our side, all glory be thine (2)
59   thy name be ever praised! O Lord, make us free (3)
60   make music for thy Lord to hear, Alleluia (3)
60   Christ our Lord the way hath trod (6)
61   praise the Lord, for he is kind (1,4)
61   let us then with gladsome mind praise the Lord (4)
64   Lord of all being,throned afar (T,1)
64   Lord of all life, below, above (4)
64   Lord ... whose light is truth, whose warmth is love (4)
67   fear no ill, with thee, dear Lord, beside me (4)
69   lives would be all sunshine in the sweetness of our Lord (2)
71   bring forth the royal diadem and crown him Lord of all (1)
71   and crown him Lord of all (1,2,3,4,5)
71   to him all majesty ascribe, and crown him Lord of all (4)
74   confess ...in heaven and earth that Jesus Christ is Lord (5)
75   must seek him, Lord, by thee (1)
76   'tis the Father's pleasure we should call him Lord (1)
77   praise yet the Lord again; Alleluia! Amen! (3)
78   and things terrestrial, Lord alone (2)
79   fairest Lord Jesus, ruler of all nature (T,1)

80	wondrous Lord, my soul would be ... conformed to thee (4)
81	Jesus ... my Lord, my life, my way, my endd (3)
83	had I a thousand hearts to give, Lord ... all be thine (4)
84	from sordid waves of worldly sea preserve us, Lord (2)
90	Lord, we are thine, we give ourselves to thee (5)
92	the Lord has promised good to me (4)
93	prone to wander, Lord, I feel it (3)
95	mercy now, O Lord, I plead in this hour of utter need (3)
95	now, O Lord, this very hour, send thy grace (2)
95	while I rest upon thy word come ... bless me now, O Lord (2)
96	I sought the Lord, and afterward I knew (T,1)
96	as thou, dear Lord, on me (2)
96	the whole of love is but my answer, Lord, to thee (3)
101	there's mercy with the Lord (1)
102	sent by my Lord, on you I call (2)
108	O Lord, with shame and sorrow we open now the door (3)
112	will you let him die in vain? Crucify your Lord again? (2)
116	I am trusting, Lord, in thee, blessed Lamb of Calvary (4)
118	Lord, I am sin, but thou art love (4)
118	Lord, I am lost, but thou hast died (4)
121	blessed Lord & only Savior, with thy love our bosom fill (4)
127	Lord, I believe thy precious blood (3)
127	Lord, I believe were sinners more than sands (4)
129	reechoes the praise of the Lord (5)
130	come quickly ... my Lord, & take possession of thine own (4)
135	be my Lord, and I shall be firmly bound, forever free (4)
137	no man can truly say that Jesus is the Lord unless (2)
137	cry with joy unspeakable, "...my Lord, my God" (2)
139	faith like its finisher and Lord today as yesterday (1)
141	Lord Jesus, make me whole; grant me no resting place (4)
142	Lord, give me such a faith as this (4)
146	and thou, O Lord, art more than they (4)
150	O, thy servant, Lord, prepare, a strict account to give (3)
152	forth in thy name, O Lord, I go (T,1)
154	have thine own way, Lord, have thine own way (T,1,2,3,4)
154	whiter than snow, Lord, wash me just now (2)
155	since, Lord, thou dost defend us with thy spirit (3)
157	we may not climb ... to bring the Lord Christ down (2)
157	O Lord and Master of us all; whate'er our name or sign (6)
159	I am thine, O Lord, I have heard thy voice (T,1)
159	draw me nearer, nearer blessed Lord (R)
159	nearer, blessed Lord, to thy precious, bleeding side (R)
159	consecrate me now to thy service, Lord (2)
160	thy Lord for thee the cross endured (3)
165	Lord, dismiss us with thy blessing (T,1)
166	Lord Jesus, I love thee, I know thou art mine (T,1)
166	if ever I loved thee, Lord Jesus,'tis now (R)
167	My Lord, thy will be done (1,2,3)
168	when my dear Lord will bring me home (3)
169	Lord of my life, I come (4)
175	strength for thy labor the Lord will provide (4)
176	the gate of life eternal may I enter, Lord, with thee (3)
177	nor should I aught with-hold, dear Lord, from thee (1)
177	in joy, in grief, through life, dear Lord, for thee (4)
178	what grace, O Lord, and beauty shone (T,1)
178	like thee, O Lord, to grieve (3)
178	gentleness and grace...spring from union,Lord, with thee (4)
180	Lord, I my vows to thee renew (2)

181   all...we have is thine alone, a trust, O Lord, from thee (1)
181   whate'er for thine we do, O Lord, we do it unto thee (4)
182   Lord, in the strength of grace (T,1)
184   make me a captive, Lord,and then I shall be free (T,1)
186   thou didst not, Lord, refuse (1)
187   take my life, and let it be consecrated, Lord, to thee (T,1)
187   take my love, my Lord   (3)
189   here together, brother men, we pledge the Lord anew (2)
189   join the glorious new crusade of our great Lord and King (3)
190   worlds awake to cry their blessings on the Lord of life (1)
190   Great Lord of years and days (2)
193   help us to help each other, Lord (2)
195   Lord, speak to me (T,1)
195   O fill me with thy fullness, Lord (4)
195   O use me, Lord, use even me, just as thou wilt and when (5)
195   O teach me, Lord, that I may teach (3)
197   thy kingdom come on earth, O Lord (4)
200   we heed, O Lord, thy summons, and answer: here are we (3)
201   awake in us compassion, O Lord of life divine (3)
203   we thank thee, Lord (T,1)
208   and to know "Thus saith the Lord" (1)
209   be still my soul; the Lord is on thy side (1)
209   hour ... when we shall be forever with the Lord (3)
211   place on the Lord reliance; my soul, with courage wait (2)
211   the Lord will give thee peace (2)
215   judge not the Lord by feeble sense (4)
216   I of the Lord my God will say, "He is my refuge ... (2)
217   Lord, I would place my hand in thine (3)
218   Lord, it belongs not to my care whether I die or live (T,1)
218   come, Lord, when grace hath made me meet (4)
220   the Lord of gladness, Jesus, enters in (3)
221   standing on the promises of Christ the Lord (3)
223   when we walk with the Lord in the light of his Word (T,1)
226   may thy tender love to me bind me closer .. Lord to thee (R)
231   it is the Lord, who rises with healing in his wings (1)
235   the gracious calling of the Lord (2)
235   dear Lord and Father of mankind (T,1)
236   grant us thy peace, Lord, through the coming night (3)
236   call us, O Lord, to thine eternal peace (4)
239   increase my courage, Lord (4)
243   in keenest strife, Lord, may we stand (3)
248   till every foe is vanquished, and Christ is Lord indeed (1)
250   strong in the Lord of hosts, and in his mighty power (1)
250   till Christ the Lord descends from high (3)
252   Lord, teach us how to pray (6)
255   when thou, O Lord, wast nigh (3)
256   be thou my vision, O Lord of my heart (T,1)
256   I ever with thee and thou with me, Lord (2)
257   glorious Lord, thy self impart (3)
260   our spirits' unseen friend, high heaven's Lord (1)
261   we...never be discouraged, take it to the Lord in prayer (2)
261   take it to the Lord in prayer (2,3)
262   talk with us, Lord (T,1)
265   most gracious Lord (1)
266   take time to be holy, speak oft with thy Lord (T,1)
266   in joy or in sorrow, still follow the Lord (3)
268   where is... blessedness I knew when first I saw the Lord (2)
274   I am listening, Lord, for thee (1,4)

324	alleluia, alleluia, alleluia, Lord most high (4)
326	here, O My Lord, I see thee face to face (T,1)
327	here, O my Lord, I see thee face to face (T,1)
328	how happy are thy servants, Lord, who thus remember thee (T)
330	O Lord, have mercy on me (R)
331	taste it, kindly given, in remembrance, Lord, of thee (1)
331	in thy glorious resurrection ... we, Lord, remember thee (2)
332	Lord, we ask for nothing more (4)
334	may they abide in union with each other and the Lord (2)
335	souls for whom the Lord did heavenly bliss forego (3)
336	yet out of all the Lord hath brought us by his love (3)
337	Lord, thine ordained servants bless (1)
339	Lord of the harvest, hear the needy servants' cry (T,1)
339	the harvest truly, Lord, is great; the laborers are few (2)
340	we go to win the lost to thee; O Help us, Lord, we pray (1)
342	we hear the call, O Lord, that comes from thee (1)
342	we call each new disciple to follow thee, O Lord (2)
343	Lord, while the music round us floats (3)
346	the Lord our God alone is strong (T,1)
347	no gift have we, Lord of all gifts, to offer thee (1)
348	ever, Lord, thy name be known (1)
349	O Lord, be pleased to bless, we pray (2)
350	how blessed is this place, O Lord (T,1)
350	keep the feast with thee, dear Lord (3)
351	eternal God and sovereign Lord (T,1)
352	speak, O eternal Lord, out of thy living Word (3)
355	Lord Christ, when first thou cam'st to men (T,1)
356	unite us in thy will, O Lord, and endd all sinful strife (2)
356	may one Lord .. faith .. Word, one Spirit lead us still (4)
361	the Wonderful, the Counselor, the great and mighty Lord (3)
362	where the Lord our God may go (1,4)
362	word of our God endureth ... arm of the Lord is strong (3)
365	the heavens declare thy glory, Lord (T,1)
365	Lord, cleanse my sins, my soul renew (6)
366	for her Lord comes down all-glorious (2)
367	Divine instructor, gracious Lord, be thou forever near (4)
368	Lord, grant us all aright to learn the wisdom it imparts (4)
369	break thou the bread of life, dear Lord, to me (T,1)
369	beyond the sacred page I seek thee, Lord (1)
369	bless thou the truth, dear Lord, to me, to me (2)
374	come, adore on bended knee Christ the Lord (3)
374	Christ the Lord, the new-born King (3)
376	sufficed the Lord God Almighty, Jesus Christ (2)
378	now to the Lord sing praises, all you within this place (5)
380	for the virgin's sweet boy is the Lord of the earth (2)
381	O come to us, abide with us, our Lord Emmanuel (4)
382	suddenly the Lord, descending, in... temple shall appear (4)
384	the little Lord Jesus laid down his sweet head (1)
384	the little Lord Jesus, asleep on the hay (1)
384	but little Lord Jesus, no crying he makes (2)
384	I love thee, Lord Jesus, look down from the sky (2)
384	be near me, Lord Jesus, I ask thee to stay close by me (3)
386	O come, let us adore him, Christ, the Lord (R)
386	yea, Lord, we greet thee, born this happy morning (3)
387	Christ, the everlasting Lord (2)
389	behold the wonderful exchange our Lord with us doth make (3)
392	joy to the world, the Lord is come (T,1)

393 Jesus, Lord, at thy birth (3)
394 the angel of the Lord came down, and glory shone around (1)
394 the Savior, who is Christ the Lord (3)
396 oxen lowing, little knowing Christ the babe is Lord (2)
396 Christ the babe is Lord of all (1)
397 so, most gracious Lord, may we evermore be led to thee (1)
399 Root of Jesse, David's Son, my Lord and Master (1)
405 out of thee the Lord from heaven came to rule his Israel (1)
406 Lord, give us faith and strength the road to build (3)
407 the peoples hunger for thee, Lord (2)
408 Christ is throned as Lord, men ... forsake their fear (2)
408 One Lord, in one great name united us all who own thee (3)
410 song ... that shall lift their hearts to the Lord (2)
410 message ... that the Lord who reigneth above (3)
412 'twas I, Lord Jesus, I ... denied thee; I crucified thee (2)
413 Lord, we are able. Our spirits are thine (R)
414 where the dear Lord was crucified .. died to save us all (1)
415 here, Lord, I give myself away; 'tis all that I can do (5)
418 what ...my Lord, hast suffered was all for sinner's gain (2)
418 Lord, let me never, never outlive my love to thee (3)
420 my Lord, my Love, is crucified (1,2,3)
423 the Lord of men and angels rode on in lowly state (2)
423 for Christ is our Redeemer, the Lord of heaven our King (3)
427 alone thou goest forth, O Lord, in sacrifice to die (T,1)
427 our sins, not thine, thou bearest, Lord (2)
427 give us compassion for thee, Lord (4)
432 caused the Lord of bliss to bear the dreadful curse (1)
432 that caused the Lord of life to lay aside his crown (2)
435 forbid it, Lord, that I should boast, save in the death (2)
436 were you there when they crucified my Lord (1)
437 the Lord in rays eternal of resurrection light (2)
437 Christ the Lord hath risen, our joy that hath no endd (3)
438 so let us keep the festival where-to the Lord invites us (3)
439 Christ the Lord is risen today, Alleluia! (T,1)
441 quick from the dead my risen Lord is seen (3)
444 Jesus my Savior ... Jesus my Lord (1,2,3)
447 Lord, by the stripes that wounded thee (4)
449 the Lord of life is risen for aye (2)
449 thy name we bless. O risen Lord (2)
450 for her Lord now liveth; death hath lost its sting (2)
451 your Lord doth go to Galilee, Alleluia (3)
451 our hearts and voices, Lord, we raise to thee (5)
451 voices, Lord, we raise to thee, in jubilee and praise (5)
452 'tis thine own third morning, rise, O buried Lord (3)
453 King of kings, and Lord of lords (4)
455 crown him the Lord of life, who triumphed o'er the grave (2)
455 crown him the Lord of peace, whose power a scepter sways (3)
455 crown him the Lord of love; behold his hands and side (4)
456 and have the bright immensities received our risen Lord (T)
456 the Lord of interstellar space and conqueror of time (1)
457 Lord our King, who reigns for us...shall forever reign (2)
458 King of kings, & Lord of lords, & heaven's eternal light (2)
458 they suffer with their Lord below (5)
459 O Holy Ghost, the Lord and the Life-giver (4)
460 God the one, the righteous Lord (1)
464 the Lord will shortly pour all the spirit of his love (4)
465 Eternal, Triune Lord, let all the hosts above (4)

468   the Lord will come and not be slow (T,1)
468   all shall frame to bow them low before thee, Lord (3)
469   thy kingdom come, O Lord, thy will be done (1,2,3,4)
479   Lord, whose love through humble service (T,1)
479   as, O Lord, thy deep compassion healed the sick (2)
479   that thy children, Lord, in freedom may thy mercy know (4)
482   O Thou who art the Life and Light, Exalted Lord and King (4)
483   rejoice, the Lord is King, your Lord and King adore (T,1)
483   rejoice in glorious hope! Our Lord the judge shall come (4)
484   from sleep and from damnation, deliver us, good Lord (2)
485   part them, Lord, to each and all, as each & all ... need (1)
485   hasten, Lord ... perfect day when pain & death ... cease (2)
486   O Lord, be ours the glory beyond all earthly fame (4)
487   thy blessing, Lord, we seek on this thy holy day (3)
487   as we go, lead us, Lord; we shall be thine evermore (4)
488   on thee our Lord victorious the Spirit sent from heaven (2)
489   here afford us, Lord, a taste of our everlasting feast (3)
491   the day is past and over; all thanks, O Lord, to thee (T,1)
493   forgive me, Lord, for thy dear Son, the ill (2)
494   free from care, from labor free, Lord we would commune (1)
494   Lord, we would commune with thee (1)
494   from sin & sorrow free, take us Lord, to dwell with thee (3)
499   O Lord, in thy dear love fit us for perfect rest above (4)
500   the day thou gavest, Lord, is ended (T,1)
500   so be it, Lord; thy throne shall never...pass away (4)
501   the sick, O Lord, around thee lay (1)
501   and none, O Lord, have perfect rest (4)
502   now, Lord, the gracious work begin (4)
503   holy, holy, holy, Lord God of Hosts (R)
503   Heaven and earth are praising thee, O Lord most high (R)
503   Lord of life, beneath the dome of the universe thy home (2)
503   Lord of angels, on our eyes let eternal morning rise (4)
507   join ourselves to Christ the Lord (1)
513   then thank the Lord, O thank the Lord for all his love (R)
516   Lord, let us in our homes agree .. blessed peace to gain (4)
517   Lord of life and King of glory (T,1)
518   we thank thee, Lord, for this our food (2,3)
518   be present at our table, Lord (T,1)
520   O Lord, may church and home combine (T,1)
521   neither life nor death shall ever from the Lord .. sever (3)
521   nor ... ever from the Lord his children sever (3)
522   Lord of harvest, grant that we wholesome grain ... be (2)
522   even so,Lord, quickly come, bring thy final harvest home (4)
522   for the Lord our God shall come (3)
523   O Lord of heaven and earth and sea (T,1)
523   what can to thee, O Lord, be given, who givest all (4)
524   to thee, O Lord, our hearts we raise (T,1)
524   upon thine altar, Lord, we lay the first fruits (2)
525   we thank thee, O Lord (1,2,3)
526   Lord, hear me, I implore thee (1)
526   and thus my hope is in the Lord and not in my own merit (3)
527   how can it be that thou, my Lord, shouldst die for me (1)
531   reign alone, the Lord of every motion there (2)
532   praise the Lord who now as then reveals in man his glory (1)
536   thou, Lord, their captain in the well-fought fight (2)
541   Lord, guard and guide the men who fly (T,1)

542   this is my prayer, O Lord of all earth's kingdoms (3)
544   give to us peace in our time, O Lord (1,2,3)
544   peace to the nations, and praise to the Lord (4)
545   mine eyes have seen the glory of the coming of the Lord (T)
546   Lord of lords and King of kings (1)
546   cleanse the body ... through the glory of the Lord (2)
548   Lord, we would with deep thanksgiving praise thee (1)
548   give we thanks to thee, O Lord (2)
548   for all heroes of the spirit, give we thanks ... O Lord (3)
549   behold us, Lord, a little space (T,1)
551   Lord, while for all mankind we pray (T,1)
551   Lord of the nations, thus to thee our country we commend (4)

Lord's

59   we gather together to ask the Lord's blessing (T,1)
65   like the pity of a father hath... Lord's compassion been (3)
68   the Lord's my Shepherd, I'll not want (T,1)
102   this is the Lord's accepted day (5)
128   I am my Lord's and he is mine (3)
359   hail to the Lord's anointed, great David's greater Son (T,1)
424   who in the Lord's name comest, the King and blessed One (1)

lords

324   of old on earth he stood, Lord of lords in human vesture (2)
453   King of kings, and Lord of lords (4)
458   King of kings, & Lord of lords, & heaven's eternal light (2)
546   Lord of lords and King of kings (1)

lordship

198   dare all that may plant man's lordship firm on earth (2)

lose

226   trusting thee I cannot stray .. can never .. lose my way (2)
265   temptations lose their power when thou art nigh (2)
355   in the night of hate and war we perish as we lose thee (3)
421   lose all their guilty stains (1)
421   dear dying Lamb, thy precious blood shall never lose (3)
421   thy precious blood shall never lose its power (3)
502   in the ocean of thy love we lose ourselves in heaven (6)
502   we lose ourselves in heaven above (6)

losing

20   our striving would be losing (2)

loss

89   in war my peace, in loss my gain (3)
223   not a grief nor a loss, not a frown or a cross (2)
238   Christian, up and smite them, counting gain but loss (1)
248   lift high the royal banner, it must not suffer loss (1)
253   a soul inured to pain, to hardship, grief and loss (2)
336   gladly reckon all things loss so we may Jesus gain (5)
355   O love that triumphs over loss we bring our hearts (4)
417   content to let the world go by, to know no gain nor loss (3)
434   shun not suffering, shame, or loss (2)
435   my richest gain I count but loss (1)
443   didst once, upon the cross ... suffer to redeem our loss (1)
486   face the darkness undismayed and turn their loss to gain (3)

lost

9	when my voice is lost in death (1,4)
70	transported with the view, I'm lost in wonder, love, and (1)
70	lost in wonder, love, and praise (1)
92	I once was lost, but now am found (1)
113	by thy power the lost to save (3)
118	to thee, lost and undone, for aid I flee (1,5)
118	and lost, I am, till thou art mine (2)
118	Lord, I am lost, but thou hast died (4)
148	in the darkness may be lost (3)
159	and my will be lost in thine (2)
195	erring children lost and lone (1)
199	restores the lost, and binds the spirit broken (2)
201	who lovest all thy lost ones on every mountain steep (1)
224	filled with his goodness, lost in his love (3)
226	lost in love, in a brighter, brighter world above (3)
226	till my soul is lost in love (3)
228	for a world of lost sinners was slain (1)
244	thou who never lost a battle, stand by me (2)
272	faces...which I have loved long since and lost awhile (3)
283	lost in wonder, love and praise (4)
292	the wayward and the lost, by restless passions tossed (2)
299	one soul should perish lost in shades of night (1)
299	tell how he stooped to save his lost creation (3)
303	send hope before to grasp it, till hope be lost in sight (3)
311	seek the lost until she find (3)
340	we go to win the lost to thee; O Help us, Lord, we pray (1)
429	Satan hath lost his mortal power (3)
438	his sting is lost forever! Alleluia! (2)
450	for her Lord now liveth; death hath lost its sting (2)
501	and some have lost the love they had (3)
528	he came the lost to seek and save (4)
532	whose names have perished, lost in the haze of long ago (5)

lot

52	death, when death shall be our lot (4)
214	when God shall judge, their lot be woe (3)
217	nor ever murmur nor repine; content whatever lot I see (3)
329	where'er our changeful lot is cast (4)
552	in this free land by thee our lot is cast (2)

loud

14	the great salvation loud proclaim (3)
15	timbrels soft and cymbals loud in his high praise agree (2)
77	loud praise to Christ our King; Alleluia! Amen! (1)
136	when love speaks loud and clear (3)
148	loud the angry billows roar (2)
343	with them loud chorus raise (2)
423	Hosanna, loud hosanna the little children sang (T,1)
423	victor palm branch waving, and chanting clear and loud (2)
438	loud songs of Alleluia! Alleluia! (1)
453	hark, those loud triumphant chords (4)
472	and earth repeat the loud amen (5)
478	not with swords loud clashing nor roll of stirring drums (2)
482	we hail thine august majesty and loud hosanna sing (4)

loudest
  14 fill the world with loudest praise (4)
  88 one of his heralds, yes, I would sing loudest hosannas (3)
  93 call for songs of loudest praise (1)
 454 loudest praises, without ceasing (4)
 454 loudest praises ... meet it is for us to give (4)

love
   3 to eternity love and adore! (4)
   4 the God of power, the God of love (1)
   5 come, ye who love the Lord, and let your joys be known (T,1)
   7 praising God for his great love (2)
  11 through his far domain, love is king where he doth reign (2)
  12 in all thy love so near (1)
  12 enough for me to know thou art, to love thee, and adore (3)
  15 praise the holy God of love, and all his greatness show (1)
  16 then be his love in Christ proclaimed (4)
  22 vast as eternity thy love (4)
  23 burn every breast with Jesus' love (3)
  26 perfect in power, in love, and purity (3)
  27 thy clouds which are fountains of goodness and love (2)
  29 with love all envy to subdue (4)
  30 his love shall be our strength and stay, while ages roll (3)
  31 and where his love resolves to bless (2)
  31 I love his name, I love his word (4)
  33 love deepens round the hearth (2)
  35 for... love which from our birth over and around us lies (1)
  35 for the joy of human love, brother, sister, parent,child (4)
  35 offering up on every shore her pure sacrifice of love (5)
  35 for that great, great love of thine (6)
  36 thy love is in the sunshine's glow (2)
  38 God of glory, Lord of love (1)
  38 brother love binds man to man (4)
  38 all who live in love are thine (3)
  38 teach us how to love each other (3)
  38 father love is reigning o'er us (4)
  41 what is man that thou shouldst love him (2)
  41 yet thy love doth seek him still (2)
  46 the cloud of thy protecting love (1)
  46 while love, almighty love, is near (2)
  49 with countless gifts of love, and still is ours today (1)
  50 that in the darkest spot of earth some love is found (2)
  51 publish with our latest breath thy love & guardian care (4)
  55 if with his love he befriend thee (3)
  56 O make but trial of his love; experience will decide (3)
  62 God is love, by him upholden (T,1)
  62 their great story, God is love, and God is light (1)
  62 through that precious love he sought us (2)
  62 Love is life, our lives be praise (2)
  62 welcome story! love lives on, and death is dead (3)
  62 their glad story, God is life, and God is love (4)
  63 God is love; his mercy brightens (T,1)
  63 God is wisdom, God is love (R)
  64 Lord ... whose light is truth, whose warmth is love (4)
  67 the King of love my Shepherd is (T,1)
  67 but yet in love he sought me (3)
  69 love of God is broader than the measure of man's mind (2)

69	if our love were but more simple, we should take him at (2)
70	transported with the view, I'm lost in wonder, love, and (1)
70	lost in wonder, love, and praise (1)
71	sinners, whose love can ne'er forget the wormwood and (3)
77	his love shall never end: Alleluia! Amen! (2)
80	pathway, trod in wondrous love, O Son of God (1)
81	till then I would thy love proclaim (5)
82	love of Jesus, what it is none but his loved ones know (4)
83	from his bounty I receive such proofs of love divine (4)
85	from thee we learn what love is (3)
85	God's love to earth thou bringest in living deeds (3)
85	how sweet to serve all others, when we all others love (3)
86	guiding in love and truth through devious ways (1)
86	thou hast prepared the feast of heavenly love (2)
88	tell me the stories of Jesus I love to hear (T,1)
89	thou all sufficient love divine (1)
89	joy and everlasting love (2)
93	mount of thy redeeming love (1)
93	prone to leave the God I love (3)
96	I find, I walk, I love, but oh, the whole of love (3)
96	the whole of love is but my answer, Lord, to thee (3)
102	O let his love your hearts constrain (4)
103	come to the feast of love; come, ever knowing (3)
104	full of pity, love, and power (1)
107	saying, Christian, love me more (3)
107	Christian, love me more than these (4)
107	serve and love thee best of all (5)
108	O love that passeth knowledge, so patiently to wait (2)
110	why from the sunshine of love wilt thou roam (1)
111	sup with us, and let the feast be everlasting love (4)
112	thankless creatures, why will you cross his love and die (1)
112	wooed you to embrace his love (3)
114	things which freely of his love he hath on us bestowed (4)
118	Lord, I am sin, but thou art love (4)
119	thy love unknown hath broken every barrier down (6)
121	blessed Lord & only Savior, with thy love our bosom fill (4)
121	blessed Jesus! Thou hast loved us, love us still (4)
122	his all-redeeming love, his precious blood, to plead (2)
123	I only know ... matchless love ... brought God's love (2)
126	Jesus, love of my soul,let me to thy bosom fly (T,1)
128	to him who merits all my love (2)
129	to feed them in pastures of love (2)
130	what shall I do my God to love (T,1)
130	the depth of humble love (5)
131	source of... old prophetic fire, fountain of life & love (1)
131	sound with...thy saints below, the depth of love divine (4)
133	that I may love what thou dost love (1)
134	kindle a flame of sacred love in ... cold hearts of ours (1)
134	come, shed abroad a Savior's love, and... kindle ours (5)
134	our love so faint,so cold to thee & thine to us so great (4)
135	Holy Spirit, Love divine, glow within this heart of mine (2)
136	fill it with love and joy and power (1)
136	burn, winged fire! inspire our lips with flaming love (2)
136	inspire our lips with flaming love and zeal to preach (2)
136	when love speaks loud and clear (3)
137	saves whoe'er on Jesus call, and perfects them in love (4)
138	and make me love thee as I ought to love (1)

138　hast thou not bid me love thee, God and King (3)
138　teach me to love thee as thine angels love (5)
138　my heart an altar, and thy love the flame (5)
143　as thou hast died for me, O may my love to thee (2)
143　blest Savior, then, in love, fear and distrust remove (4)
144　with patient uncomplaining love, still...cling to thee (2)
144　thy voice of love, in gentlest tone, still whispers (3)
146　strong Son of God, immortal love (T,1)
149　I love to tell the story (T,1,2,3,4,R)
149　of Jesus and his love (1)
149　to tell the old, old story of Jesus and his love (R)
151　we will love both friend and foe in all our strife (3)
151　and preach thee, too, as love knows how (3)
153　God of love and　God of power (T,1)
153　God of love and God of power (R)
153　God of love ... God of power make us worthy of this hour (4)
156　I would look up, and laugh and love and lift (2)
157　immortal love, forever full, forever flowing free (T,1)
157　faith has still its Olivet, and love its Galilee (3)
158　immortal love, forever full, forever flowing free (T,1)
159　I have heard thy voice, and it told thy love to me (1)
159　there are depths of love that I cannot know till (4)
161　we render back the love thy mercy gave us (4)
162　with a child's glad heart of love (2)
162　learning how to love from thee (3)
162　thus may I rejoice to show that I feel the love I owe (4)
162　singing, till thy face I see, of his love (4)
162　singing ... of his love who first loved me (4)
163　he drew me with the cords of love (1)
165　let us each, thy love possessing, triumph (1)
166　Lord Jesus, I love thee, I know thou art mine (T,1)
166　I love thee, because thou hast first loved me (2)
166　I love thee for wearing the thorns on thy brow (2)
167　into thy hand of love I would my all resign (1)
168　the forms of love he wears, exalted on his throne (2)
170　by some clear, winning word of love (2)
172　kindle a flame of sacred love on ... altar of my heart (1)
173　thy steadfast face set forward where love and duty shone (2)
173　O grant that love of country may help us hear his call (3)
177　Savior, thy dying love thou gavest me (T,1)
177　in love my soul would bow, my heart fulfill its vow (1)
177　some work of love begun, some deed of kindness done (3)
177　help me the cross to bear, thy wondrous love declare (2)
178　unwearied ... forgiveness still, thy heart ... only love (2)
178　patient love was seen in all thy life and death of woe (1)
178　O give us hearts to love like thee (3)
183　now they taste unmingled love, and joy without a tear (2)
184　enslave it with thy matchless love (2)
185　more love to thee, O Christ, more love to thee (T,1)
185　this is my earnest plea: more love, O Christ, to thee (1)
185　more love, O Christ, to thee ... more love to thee (R)
185　this all my prayer shall be: more love O Christ, to thee (2)
185　when they can sing with me, more love, O Christ, to thee (3)
185　this still its prayer shall be: more love, O Christ (4)
187　take my love, my Lord　(3)
187　my love ... I pour at thy feet its treasure-store (3)
187　take my hands ... let them move ... impulse of thy love (1)

270 O Love divine, forever dear (4)
273 turn my dreams to noble action, ministries of love (4)
278 Jesus, thine all-victorious love shed in my heart abroad (T)
278 Christ is all the world to me, and all my heart is love (4)
279 let me weep my life away for having grieved thy love (2)
279 Almighty God of truth and love, to me thy power impart (4)
280 Almighty God of truth and love, to me thy power impart (4)
280 let me weep my life away for having grieved thy love (2)
281 enter ... promised rest ... Canaan of thy perfect love (5)
282 a heart in every thought renewed and full of love divine (4)
282 thy new, best name of Love (5)
283 love divine, all loves excelling (T,1)
283 pure, unbounded love thou art (1)
283 glory in thy perfect love (3)
283 lost in wonder, love and praise (4)
284 the strains of praise and love (6)
285 the greatness of redeeming love (1)
285 O love divine, how sweet thou art (T,1)
285 I thirst, I faint, I die to prove ... love (1)
285 give me thy only love (4)
285 the love of Christ to me (1)
285 stronger his love than death or hell (2)
285 God only knows the love of God (3)
285 thy only love do I require (4)
285 give me thy only love to know (4)
287 if you love him, why not serve him... soldiers ... cross (4)
287 sinner, do you love my Jesus ... soldiers of the cross (3)
290 I only know I cannot drift beyond his love and care (5)
293 streams of living waters, springing from eternal love (2)
294 I love thy kingdom, Lord, the house of thine abode (T,1)
294 her hymns of love and praise (4)
294 I love thy Church, O God! Her walls before thee stand (2)
295 for thee I long, for love divine (3)
299 God, in whom they live and move, is Love (3)
301 in purest streams of love (2)
302 on the eagle wings of love to joys celestial rise (1)
304 with love and longing turn to find their rest in thee (1)
304 our hearts in love and worship turn to find themselves (2)
304 hearts with love & longing ... find their rest in thee (1)
304 measured by his love (2)
306 blest be the tie that binds our hearts in Christian love (T)
307 Church ... perfect it in thy love (3)
309 by thy reconciling love every stumbling block remove (2)
309 all the depths of love express (5)
310 thy name is life and joy and peace and everlasting love (2)
310 bid our inmost souls rejoice in hope of perfect love (5)
313 there sup with us in love divine; thy body and thy blood (2)
314 by this pledge that thou dost love us (2)
315 our needy souls sustain with fresh supplies of love (2)
316 remember thee, and all thy pains, and all thy love to me (3)
318 never to my hurt invited, be thy love with love requited (3)
319 in faith and memory thus we sing the wonders of his love (4)
319 in memory of the Savior's love, we keep the sacred feast (T)
326 the feast, though not the love, is past and gone (4)
326 the Lamb's great bridal feast of bliss and love (5)
328 so dear the tie where souls agree in Jesus' dying love (4)
332 O the depth of love divine, the unfathomable grace (T,1)

416	light and love upon my way (3)
417	the wonders of redeeming love and my unworthiness (2)
418	Lord, let me never, never outlive my love to thee (3)
420	O Love divine, what hast thou done (T,1)
420	my Lord, my Love, is crucified (1,2,3)
421	redeeming love has been my theme, & shall be till I die (4)
422	his royalty is holiness, and love is in his face (2)
427	till through our pity and our shame love answers (2)
427	love answers love's appeal (2)
428	vast the love that him inclined to bleed & die for thee (1)
428	O Lamb of God, was ever pain, was ever love, like thine (4)
430	learn thy love while gazing thus (2)
430	love, which bore the cross for us (2)
430	here we gather love to live; here we gather faith to die (3)
432	what wondrous love is this, O my soul (T,1,2)
433	near the cross, a trembling soul, love & mercy found me (2)
434	love to man his soul sustained (2)
435	see, from his head, his hands, his feet, sorrow and love (3)
435	sorrow and love flow mingled down (3)
435	did e'er such love and sorrow meet (3)
435	love so amazing, so divine, demands my soul, my life (4)
435	Love so amazing ... demands my soul, my life, my all (4)
441	love lives again, that with the dead has been (1)
441	in the grave they laid him, Love whom men had slain (2)
441	love is come again like wheat that springeth green (R)
443	sing we to our God above ... praise eternal as his love (3)
445	He lives, to bless me with his love (2)
449	praise we in songs of victory that love, that life (3)
449	that love, that life which cannot die (3)
450	make us more than conquerors through thy deathless love (3)
454	by almighty love appointed thou hast full atonement made (2)
457	by the almighty Spirit led and filled with faith & love (1)
457	tasting the celestial powers, we banquet on his love (3)
458	to whom he manifests his love & grants his name to know (3)
458	their profit & their joy to know the mystery of his love (5)
459	thy love has blessed the wide world's wondrous story (1)
459	to thee in reverent love our hearts are bowed (2)
459	still imploring thy love and favor, kept to us always (5)
461	come as the dove & spread thy wings ... of peaceful love (3)
462	Spirit of love, at evening time when weary (5)
464	Jesus' love the nations fires (1)
464	the Lord will shortly pour all the spirit of his love (4)
465	glory, power, and praise receive for thy creating love (1)
465	let all the sons of men record and dwell upon thy love (4)
466	come down, O Love divine, seek thou this soul of mine (T,1)
467	comfort, life and fire of love (2)
469	by wars and tumults love is mocked, derided (2)
469	how shall we love thee, holy, hidden Being (4)
469	if we love not the world which thou hast made (4)
469	O give us brother love for better seeing (4)
471	eternal Son, eternal Love (T,1)
471	the triumphs of thy love display (2)
471	Fountain of light and love below (3)
471	inflame our hearts with perfect love (4)
472	dwell on his love with sweetest song (3)
473	O gratefully sing his power and his love (1)
476	O God of love, whose spirit wakes in every human breast (2)

476 whom love, and love alone can know (2)
478 with deeds of love and mercy, the heavenly kingdom comes (2)
479 Lord, whose love through humble service (T,1)
479 whose love ... bore the weight of human need (1)
479 use the love thy spirit kindles still to save (2)
479 to.. child .. youth .. aged love in living deeds to show (4)
480 Spirit of truth and love, life-giving, holy Dove (3)
480 Glorious Trinity, Grace, Love and Might (4)
481 city ... whose laws are love, whose ways are brotherhood (4)
482 and thou in love shalt reign (1)
482 until in every land and clime thine ends of love are won (4)
483 Jesus, the Savior, reigns, the God of truth and love (2)
485 all pity, care, and love, all calm and courage...pour (1)
486 who with love and meekness outlast the years of wrong (3)
490 may this day be blest, trusting Jesus' love (3)
498 twining round us golden cords of love (1)
498 Jesus, for thy love most tender on the cross ... shown (2)
499 new every morning is the love (T,1)
499 new ... the love our wakening and uprising prove (1)
499 O Lord, in thy dear love fit us for perfect rest above (4)
501 and some have lost the love they had (3)
502 in the ocean of thy love we lose ourselves in heaven (6)
503 heart of love enfolding all (3)
505 their Creator's changeless love (2)
505 hope and faith and love rise glorious (4)
506 sharing ... the love that sends the showers (2)
510 our lips & lives ... gladly show the wonders of thy love (4)
511 a world in need now summons us to labor,love and give (2)
511 a world redeemed by Christ-like love (2)
513 then thank the Lord, O thank the Lord for all his love (R)
513 accept the gifts we offer for all thy love imparts (3)
515 how wide the bounteous love is spread (3)
516 and love fills every breast (1)
516 unite our hearts in love to thee (4)
516 unite ... in love to thee, and love to all will reign (4)
516 parents love the sacred Word and all its wisdom prize (3)
517 love that nothing good denies (4)
520 with gentleness and love like thine (1)
520 love like thine, that none shall ever stray (1)
520 grant, Love Divine, in every place glad fellowship (3)
523 sweet flowers and fruit thy love declare (2)
523 how shall we show our love to thee, who givest all (1)
525 for love of thine, which never tires (3)
526 thou grantest pardon through thy love (2)
527 seraph tries to sound the depths of love divine (2)
528 shall I slight my Father's love, or basely fear (3)
529 and tell me if thy name be Love (3)
529 pure, universal love thou art (4)
529 thy nature and thy name is Love (4)
530 love, like death, hath all destroyed (5)
530 love ... rendered all distinctions void (5)
531 thou hidden love of God, whose height (T,1)
531 O Love, thy sovereign aid impart to save me (3)
531 I am thy Love, thy God, thy all (4)
531 to feel thy power, to hear thy voice, to taste thy love (4)
531 to taste thy love, be all my choice (4)
532 in silent love be cherished (5)

lovely
  222 when darkness veils his lovely face (2)
  295 how lovely is thy dwelling place, O Lord of hosts (T,1)
  375 love all lovely, Love divine (1)
  380 Ay! we shout to the lovely evangel they bring (4)
  423 through pillared court & temple the lovely anthem rang (1)

lover
  125 Jesus, lover of my soul, let me to thy bosom fly (T,1)
  227 the story repeat, and the lover of sinners adore (3)
  491 Lover of men, O hear our call, and guard and save us (4)
loves
   94 God is love! I know...feel, Jesus weeps & loves me still (4)
  163 from him who loves me now so well, what power...sever (3)
  283 love divine, all loves excelling (T,1)

lovest
  169 Friend of the young, who lovest me (1)
  201 who lovest all thy lost ones on every mountain steep (1)
  260 our lives are prayers thou lovest\more (1)

loving
   64 yet to each loving heart how near (1)
   90 God and man in loving service met (4)
   95 O thou loving, blessed One, rising o'er me like the sun (4)
  105 shall I not rise? Can I his loving voice despise (2)
  109 sinner, list to the loving call (2)
  130 my loving God to praise (1)
  162 better lesson cannot be, loving him who first loved me (1)
  162 loving him who first loved me (1,2,3)
  175 touched by a loving heart, wakened by kindness (3)
  179 valiant endeavor and loving obedience (2)
  193 O may we all the loving mind that was in thee receive (5)
  195 I may stretch out a loving hand to wrestlers (2)
  199 each loving life a psalm of gratitude (3)
  283 O breathe thy loving spirit into every troubled breast (2)
  284 let me thy loving servant be ... taste thy promised rest (2)
  286 Lord, I want to be more loving in my heart (2)
  292 the world to Christ we bring, with loving zeal (1)
  295 my very heart and flesh cry out, O Loving God, for thee (2)
  304 deep in loving human hearts its broad foundations rise (1)
  329 Jesus, thou joy of loving hearts (T,1)
  385 let loving hearts enthrone him (3)
  456 where his loving people meet to share the gift divine (2)
  521 his the loving purpose solely to preserve them (4)
  530 sweetly may we all agree, touched with loving sympathy (4)

lovingkindness
    7 for his lovingkindness ever shed upon our earthly way (3)

lovingly
  450 lovingly he greets thee, scatters fear and gloom (2)

low
   10 the earth is not too low, his praises there may grow (1)
  108 O Jesus, thou art pleading in accents meek and low (3)
  141 Have faith in God, my mind ... oft thy light burns low (2)

157 last low whispers of our dead are burdened with his name (5)
184 my power is faint and low till I have learned to serve (3)
188 raise my low self above, won by thy deathless love (1)
200 purge us of low desire; lift us to high resolve (4)
230 the storm may roar without me, my heart may low be laid (1
362 valleys shall be exalted, the lofty hills brought low (1,4)
380 there's a mother's deep prayer and a baby's low cry (1)
400 low lies his head with the beasts of the stall (2)
422 while men of low degree exalt and usher in the day (4)
444 low in the grave he lay (T,1)
468 all shall frame to bow them low before thee, Lord (3)

lower
148 let the lower lights be burning (R)

lowest
157 in vain we search the lowest deeps (2)
274 though least and lowest, let me not unheard depart (3)

lowing
384 the cattle are lowing, the baby awakes (2)
396 oxen lowing, little knowing Christ the babe is Lord (2)

lowliness
74 thou camest to us in lowliness of thought (2)
276 to dwell in lowliness with men, their pattern &... King (2)

lowly
7 so may we, in lowly station join the choristers above (2)
80 so meek, so lowly, yet so high, so glorious in humility (3)
80 learn of thee, the lowly one (4)
90 shining revealed through every task most lowly (2)
108 in lowly patience waiting to pass the threshold o'er (1)
110 come with thy sins; at his feet lowly bow (3)
170 in lowly paths of service free (1)
236 then, lowly kneeling, wait thy word of peace (1)
276 still to the lowly soul he doth himself impart (3)
276 O give the pure and lowly heart, a temple meet for thee (4)
282 a humble, lowly, contrite heart (3)
297 like them, the meek & lowly, on high may dwell with thee (4
309 lowly, meek, in thought & word, altogether like our Lord (3)
333 lowly we kneel in prayer before thy throne (1)
351 when time in lowly dust has laid these stored walls (4)
390 above its sad & lowly plains they bend on hovering wing (2)
395 gentle Mary laid her child lowly in a manger (T,1,3)
396 infant holy, infant lowly, for his bed a cattle stall (T,1)
397 as with joyous steps they sped to that lowly manger bed (2)
404 down in a lowly manger the humble Christ was born (3)
422 so lowly doth the Savior ride a paltry borrowed beast (T,1)
423 the Lord of men and angels rode on in lowly state (2)
425 in lowly pomp ride on to die (2,4)
488 on thee the high and lowly, through ages joined in tune (1)
506 O Spirit, pure and holy, possess these hearts so lowly (5)
531 my heart that lowly waits thy call (4)

loyal
179 truehearted, wholehearted, faithful and loyal (T,1)
179 peal out the watchward! Loyal forever! (R)
189 our loyal love, our stalwart faith (2)
197 by loyal scorn of second best (3)
548 for our prophets and apostles, loyal to the living Word (3)

loyalty
153 thou our final loyalty (3)
413 a beacon to   God, to love, and loyalty (R)

lulled
506 may weariness and sadness be lulled to peace & gladness (3)

lure
161 walk thou beside us lest the tempting by-ways lure us (3)
161 lure us away from thee to endless night (3)
243 by any lure or guile enticed (2)

lures
204 from paths where hide the lures of greed (2)

luring
238 striving, tempting, luring, goading into sin (2)

lust
481 O shame to us who rest content while lust and greed (3)
481 lust and greed for gain in street and shop and tenement (3)

luster
64 before ... blazing throne we ask no luster of our own (4)
416 from the cross the radiance streaming adds more luster (3)
416 adds more luster to the day (3)

lusts
243 gainst lies & lusts & wrongs let courage rule our souls (3)

lying
299 behold how many thousands still are lying bound (2)

made
4 what God's almighty power hath made (2)
9 he made the sky and earth and seas, with all their train (2)
17 consider all the worlds thy hands have made (1)
18 Word was spoken in the deed that made the earth (1)
22 He sovereign power, without our aid made us of clay (2)
22 made us of clay and formed us men (2)
23 His sovereign power our bodies made (2)
34 all things wise and wonderful: .. Lord God made them all (R)
34 he made their glowing colors (1)
34 he made their tiny wings (1)
34 the ripe fruits in the garden: He made them everyone (3)
34 how great is God Almighty, who has made all things well (4)
37 that made the mountains rise (1)
39 he made the shining worlds on high (2)
41 man ... creature that thy hand hath made (2)
41 made him fly with eagle pinion (3)

42   laws ... for our guidance hath he made (1)
42   God hath made his saints victorious (2)
43   the hand that made us is divine (3)
50   my God, I thank thee, who hast made the earth so bright (T,1)
50   I thank thee, too, that thou hast made joy to abound (2)
57   Lord alone, who heaven and earth has made (1)
61   he, with all-commanding might, filled the new-made world (2)
61   filled the new-made world with light (2)
100   Jesus, our great high priest, hath full atonement made (2)
112   God, did your being give, made you with himself to live (1)
116   I am every whit made whole; glory, glory to the Lamb! (5)
117   I found in him a resting place, and he has made me glad (1)
127   for all a full atonement made (4)
141   God will fulfill in every part each promise he has made (1)
146   he thinks he was not made to die (2)
146   and thou hast made him: thou art just (2)
168   and magnify the wondrous grace which made salvation mine (1
184   my will is not my own till thou hast made it thine (4)
188   through me thy truth be shown, thy love made known (2)
193   till thou hast made us free indeed (3)
218   when grace hath made me meet thy blessed face to see (4)
218   come, Lord, when grace hath made me meet (4)
243   still made their glory in thy name (1)
258   come to him who made this splendor (1)
268   I hate the sins that made thee mourn (4)
298   Christ is made the sure foundation (T,1)
299   he who made all nations is not willing one ... perish (1)
307   as grain ... was in this broken bread made one (4)
308   a house not made with hands (4)
319   every humble, contrite heart is made a welcome guest (1)
351   these storied walls our hands have made (4)
370   praise him for the Word made flesh (3)
376   in the bleak midwinter, frosty wind made moan (T,1)
389   takes ...a servant's form who made the heaven and earth (2)
403   thou shalt find thy heart made truly his (2)
411   unselfishness made consecrate to thee (5)
424   to whom the lips of children made sweet hosannas ring (1)
430   through thy cross made pure and white (5)
439   made like him, like him we rise, Alleluia (4)
454   by almighty love appointed thou hast full atonement made (2)
454   peace is made twixt man and God (2)
463   by whose mighty power alone all is made & wrought & done (
468   the nations all whom thou hast made shall come (3)
469   Spirit of life, which moved ere form was made (1)
469   if we love not the world which thou hast made (4)
469   better seeing thy Word made flesh, and in a manger laid (4)
472   to him shall endless prayer be made (2)
476   till ... know the loveliness of lives made fair and free (4)
478   through days of preparation thy grace has made us strong (1)
486   till through world made noble ... God shall march (4)
511   all life in Christ made new (2)
515   what large provision thou hast made (3)
532   and made our folk a nation (2)
532   rich in art, made richer still the brotherhood of duty (4)

madest
146   thou madest man, he knows not why (2)
197   O Son of Man, who madest known (T,1)
497   God, that madest earth and heaven, darkness and light (T,1)

madness
470   cure thy children's warring madness (3)

Madonna
377   no room ... for Joseph or Madonna fair (1)

magnify
16   who would not fear his holy name and laud and magnify (2)
19   most gracious, magnify the Lord (2)
42   laud and magnify his name (2)
42   heaven, and earth, and all creation, laud and magnify (2)
56   O magnify the Lord with me, with me exalt his name (2)
168   and magnify the wondrous grace which made salvation mine (1)
200   but thou canst use our weakness to magnify thy power (3)

maiden
376   but his mother only, in her maiden bliss, worshiped (3)

maidens
233   strong men and maidens fair (2)

maimed
102   ye poor, and maimed, and halt, and blind (3)
411   where'er they heal the maimed and blind (3)

maintainer
457   maintainer of our cause (2)

maintaining
59   ordaining, maintaining his kingdom divine (2)

majestic
83   majestic sweetness sits enthroned upon the Savior's brow (T)
113   by thy high, majestic throne (3)

majesties
543   for purple mountain majesties above the fruited plain (1)

majesty
3   thy sovereign majesty may we in glory see (4)
31   the garments he assumes are light and majesty (1)
39   his beams are majesty and light (2)
71   to him all majesty ascribe, and crown him Lord of all (4)
186   thy majesty did not disdain to be employed for us (1)
252   prayer .. sublimest strains .. reach the Majesty on high (3)
255   O when shall I behold thy face, thou Majesty divine (2)
352   filled with thy majesty, till time shall end (1)
364   every eye shall now behold him robed in dreadful majesty (2)
389   he lays aside his majesty and seems as nothing worth (2)
425   ride on, ride on in majesty (T,1,2,3,4)
482   we hail thine august majesty and loud hosanna sing (4)

make
1   his blood can make the foulest clean (4)
21   without our aid he did us make (2)
29   to make ill-fortune turn to fair (4)
41   Spirit in our spirit speaking, make us sons of God (4)

56 O make but trial of his love; experience will decide (3)
56 make you his service your delight (4)
58 eternal arms, their dear abode, we make our habitation (1)
59 he chastens and hastens his will to make known (1)
59 thy name be ever praised! O Lord, make us free (3)
60 make music for thy Lord to hear, Alleluia (3)
64 grant us thy truth to make us free (5)
68 me to walk doth make within the paths of righteousness (2)
75 make all my wants and wishes known (1)
85 free wills ... thou givest, that we may make them thine (4)
86 lead us to where thou hast trod, our faith make strong (3)
104 let not conscience make you linger (3)
118 'tis thou alone canst make me whole (2)
120 save from wrath and make me pure (1)
125 make and keep me pure within (4)
130 my longing heart vouchsafe to make thine ... throne (4)
132 make our hearts thy habitation (2)
136 descend upon thy Church once more & make it truly thine (1)
137 make to us the God-head known, & witness with the blood (1)
138 and make me love thee as I ought to love (1)
141 Lord Jesus, make me whole; grant me no resting place (4)
146 our wills are ours, to make them thine (3)
146 that mind and soul, according well, may make one music (5)
146 may make one music as before (5)
147 teach us, in every state,to make thy will our own (4)
148 trying now to make the harbor (3)
153 God of love ... God of power make us worthy of this hour (4)
154 mold me and make me after thy will (1)
155 there's no discouragement shall make him once relent (1)
155 he will make good his right to be a pilgrim (2)
164 O speak, and make me listen, thou guardian of my soul (3)
168 I would to everlasting days make all his glories known (2)
172 and make my sacrifice complete (4)
174 rise up, and make her great (3)
184 make me a captive, Lord,and then I shall be free (T,1)
185 hear thou the prayer I make on bended knee (1)
187 take my will & make it thine; it shall be no longer mine (3)
200 take us, and make us holy; teach us thy will and way (4)
202 the common hopes that make us men were his in Galilee (2)
204 O Master, from the mountainside, make haste to heal (5)
204 make haste to heal these hearts of pain (5)
212 there is a balm in Gilead, to make the wounded whole (T,R)
215 God is his own interpreter, and he will make it plain (5)
225 make in my heart a quiet place ... come & dwell therein (1)
238 but that toil shall make thee some day all mine own (4)
242 the multitude make virtue of the faith they had denied (2)
265 O make me thine indeed, thou blessed Son (5)
266 make friends of God's children, help those who are weak (1)
273 like the springs and running waters make me crystal pure (2)
273 like .. rocks of towering grandeur make me strong & sure (2)
273 like thy dancing waves in sunlight make me glad and free (3)
273 God, who touchest earth with beauty, make my heart anew (5)
273 make my heart anew (1)
274 speak! and make me blest indeed (3)
274 make me ready when thy voice is truly heard (4)
275 make all my wants and wishes known (1)
279 quick as the apple of an eye, O God, my conscience make (3)

280 quick as the apple of an eye, O God, my conscience make (3)
284 and make me pure within (1)
296 feet on mercy's errands swift do make her pilgrimage (3)
307 thou, Lord, didst make all for thy pleasure (2)
309 make us of one heart and mind, courteous, pitiful & kind (3)
329 make all our moments calm and bright (5)
336 then let us make our boast of his redeeming power (4)
340 and make thy goodness known (4)
340 heart to heart, & hand to hand ... make thine honor ours (2)
342 go, make of all disciples (T,1,2,3,4)
349 here make his message heard (3)
351 make known to them thy saving grace (2)
356 restore to us thy truth, O God, & make its meaning sure (2)
362 make straight all the crooked places (1,4)
363 heart ... make it a temple, set apart (2)
365 and make thy Word my guide to heaven (6)
372 O make thy Church, dear Savior, a lamp of purest gold (4)
389 behold the wonderful exchange our Lord with us doth make (3)
392 he comes to make his blessing flow (3)
399 make thee there an altar (2)
405 Eastern sages at his cradle make oblations rich and rare (3)
406 make straight, make straight the highway of the King (1)
413 remold them, make us, like thee, divine (R)
414 died that we might be forgiven ... died to make us good (3)
418 O make me thine forever, and should I fainting be (3)
424 and mortal men and all things created make reply (2)
427 make us thy sorrow feel (2)
442 flowers make glee among the hills (1)
450 make us more than conquerors through thy deathless love (3)
461 make this house thy home (1)
461 Spirit divine ... make this world thy home (4)
462 make us souls that understand (2)
476 send us forth ... to make all lands thine own ((1)
476 until true wisdom from above...make life's pathway clear (3)
479 to save and make men whole (2)
487 Holy Spirit, make us whole (4)
489 make the fruits of grace abound (4)
490 make my conduct good, actions calm and mild (2)
491 O Jesus, make their darkness light (2)
493 sleep that may me more vigorous make to serve my God (4)
506 all evil thoughts expelling, now make in us thy dwelling (5)
507 the covenant we this moment make be ever kept in mind (3)
511 to make our life an offering to God, that man may live (2)
511 to make the dream come true (2)
511 the Church of Christ is stirring us to make the dream (2)
528 his bleeding heart shall make you room (5)
531 make me thy duteous child, that I ceaseless may...cry (3)
545 as he died to make men holy, let us die to make man free (4)
548 from the strife of class & faction make our nation free (4)
548 make our nation free indeed (4)

maker
9 I'll praise my maker while I've breath (T,1)
15 glory to their Maker give, and homage to their King (3)
36 Maker of all above, below (1)
40 maker of earth and sky (1)
112 God, your Maker, asks you why (1)

318   at thy feet I cry, my Maker (2)
400   Maker and Monarch and Savior of all (2)
415   God, the mighty maker, died for man the creature's sin (3)
442   Praise the Maker, all ye saints (3)
473   our Maker, Defender, Redeemer, and Friend (5)
513   he only is the Maker of all things near and far (2)
522   God, our Maker, doth provide ...our wants to be supplied (1)

maker's
45   morning light ... lily white declare ... maker's praise (2)

makes
12   that makes the darkest way I go an open path to thee (4)
25   God is our sun, he makes our day (3)
37   not a plant or flower below, but makes thy glories known (3)
68   he makes me down to lie in pastures green (1)
79   Jesus is purer, who makes the woeful heart to sing (2)
81   it makes the wounded spirit whole (2)
83   he makes me triumph over death (3)
97   when I am sad, he makes me glad, He's my friend (1)
136   holiness which makes thy children whole (4)
202   our brother Christ ... makes our task his own (1)
242   time makes ancient good uncouth (3)
279   drive me to... grace again which makes the wounded whole (4)
280   drive me to...grace again, which makes the wounded whole (4)
365   thy Gospel makes the simple wise (5)
384   but little Lord Jesus, no crying he makes (2)
392   makes the nations prove the glories of his righeeousness (4)
407   wondrous power that makes men free (1)
466   the place wherein the Holy Spirit makes his dwelling (3)

making
373   the power of Satan breaking, our peace eternal making (1)
479   making known the needs and burdens thy compassion bids (3)

man
9   happy the man whose hopes rely on Israel's God (2)
18   Word incarnate glorified the flesh of man (2)
20   were not the right man on our side (2)
20   the man of God's own choosing (2)
25   blest is the man that trusts in thee (4)
26   though the eye of sinful man thy glory may not see (3)
37   everwhere that man can be, thou, God, art present there (3)
38   brother love binds man to man (4)
41   what is man that thou shouldst love him (2)
41   man ... creature that thy hand hath made (2)
41   hast given man dominion o'er the wonders of thy hand (3)
44   oh, what is man, in thy regard to hold so large a place (3)
44   what the son of man, that thou dost visit him in grace (3)
44   on man thy wisdom ... bestowed a power well-nigh divine (4)
60   thou givest man both warmth and light (2)
63   man decays and ages move; but his mercy waneth never (2)
70   thine arm ... led me up to man (3)
79   O thou of God and man the son, thee will I cherish (1)
80   thou Son of man, thou Light of light (2)
84   thou man-pursuing Fisherman, who harmest not but savest (2)
85   O Son of God incarnate, O Son of man divine (T,1)

90	divine and human, in his deep revealing of God and man (4)
90	God and man in loving service met (4)
132	bringing down the richest treasure man can wish (1)
132	richest treasure man can wish or God can send (1)
137	no man can truly say that Jesus is the Lord unless (2)
146	thou madest man, he knows not why (2)
171	O Master Workman of the race, thou man of Galilee (T,1)
171	shapest man to God's own law, thyself the fair design (2)
174	as brothers of the Son of man, rise up, O men of God (4)
186	servant of all, to toil for man (T,1)
197	O Son of Man, who madest known (T,1)
199	O brother man, fold to thy heart thy brother (T,1)
204	we hear thy voice, O Son of man (1)
216	the man who once has found abode (T,1)
242	once to every man and nation comes the moment to decide (T)
242	then it is the brave man chooses (2)
251	thou art not, like man, untrue (2)
251	man may trouble and distress me (3)
295	blest is the man whose strength thou art (5)
299	died on earth that man might live above (3)
303	strive, man, to win that glory, toil ..to gain .. light (3)
307	didst give man food for all his days (2)
318	joy, the sweetest man e'er knoweth (2)
332	who shall say how bread and wine God into man conveys (1)
343	like them, let man the throne surround (2)
371	tongues ... acclaim with joy thy wondrous gift to man (4)
376	if I were a wise man, I would do my part (4)
387	pleased as man with men to dwell, Jesus our Emmanuel (2)
387	mild he lays his glory by, born that man no more may die (3)
391	hath oped the heavenly door ... man is blessed evermore (2)
408	the Day-star clear and bright of every man and nation (1)
412	that man to judge thee hath in hate pretended (1)
415	God, the mighty maker, died for man the creature's sin (3)
426	perfect man on thee did suffer (1,4)
431	for others' guilt the Man of Sorrows weeps in blood (3)
434	love to man his soul sustained (2)
440	God's likeness, man awaking, knows the everlasting peace (1)
440	join, O man, the deathless voices (3)
453	see the Man of Sorrows now (1)
454	peace is made twixt man and God (2)
460	Man, revealing God to man (2)
470	grant us courage that we fail not man nor thee (4)
475	turn back, O man, forswear thy foolish ways (T,1)
475	would man but wake from out his haunted sleep (2)
486	man in his weakness yet may give a worthier offering (1)
501	O Savior Christ, thou too art man (5)
511	to make our life an offering to God, that man may live (2)
531	whose height, whose depth unfathomed no man knows (1)
532	praise the Lord who now as then reveals in man his glory (1)
532	they blessed the earth ... blessed of God & man forever (6)
544	God the all-righteous One! man hath defied thee (3)
545	as he died to make men holy, let us die to make man free (4)
548	till it find its full fruition in the brotherhood of man (4)

man's

2	craftman's art and music's measure for thy pleasure (3)
36	thee in man's spirit we behold (4)

476 Christ is formed in all mankind and every land is thine (5)
480 O now, to all mankind, let there be light (2)
482 O Holy Savior of mankind, ride on (2)
551 Lord, while for all mankind we pray (T,1)

manna
81 'tis manna to the hungry soul and to the weary, rest (2)
368 true manna from on high (2)
488 today on weary nations the heavenly manna falls (3)
518 let manna to our souls be given (3)
539 daily manna still provide you (2)

manner
332 sure and real is the grace, the manner be unknown (4)

mansion
445 he lives, my mansion to prepare (3)

mansions
166 in mansions of glory and endless delight (3)
504 Monarch of all things, fit us for thy mansions (2)

mantle
203 we've seen thy glory like a mantle spread o'er hill and (4)
473 and round it hath cast, like a mantle, the sea (3)

many
40 many and great, O God, are thy things (T,1)
50 so many gentle thoughts and deeds circling us round (2)
50 so many glorious things are here, noble and right (1)
92 through many dangers, toils ... snares I... already come (3)
99 many a sorrow, many a labor, many a tear (4)
119 though tossed about with many a conflict, many a doubt (3)
167 My Jesus, as thou wilt! Though seen through many a tear (2)
195 the hidden depths of many a heart (3)
227 whether many or few, all my years are his due (6)
299 behold how many thousands still are lying bound (2)
303 and bright with many an angel, and all the martyr throng (2)
328 many, and yet but one are we, one undivided bread (2)
370 many diverse scrolls completing (2)
405 earth has many a noble city (T,1)
441 wheat that in dark earth many days has lain (1)
455 crown him with many crowns, the Lamb upon his throne (T,1)
491 how many are the perils through which we have to go (4)

marbles
428 temple's veil in sunder breaks ... solid marbles rend (2)

march
33 all beautiful the march of days as seasons come and go (T,1)
36 thy grandeur in the march of night (3)
38 ever singing, march we onward (4)
233 still lift your standard high ... march in firm array (5)
243 march on, o soul, with strength (T,1)
243 march on.. soul w. strength ... strong the battle rolls (3)
243 march on, O soul, march on, with strength (4)
478 lead on, O King eternal, the day of march has come (T,1)

486   till through world made noble ... God shall march (4)
486   through lands from sin set free ... God shall march (4)
486   the armies of the living God shall march to victory (4)

marching
5   we're marching thro' Emmanuel's ground (4)
5   marching ... to fairer worlds on high (4)
305   onward, Christian soldiers! marching as to war (T,1,R)
482   mighty host, by thee redeemed, is marching in thy train (1)
545   his truth is marching on (1)
545   his day is marching on (2)
545   our God is marching on (3,5)
545   while God is marching on (4)
545   Glory! glory! Hallelujah ... His truth is marching on (R)

mark
268   purer light shall mark .. road that leads me to the Lamb (6)
308   we mark her goodly battlements & her foundations strong (2)
434   there adoring at this feet mark the miracle of time (3)

marked
533   they marked the footsteps that he trod (2)

market
202   through din of market, whirl of wheels (1)
511   farm .. market, shop .. home, of mind and heart and hand (1)

marks
80   how beauteous were the marks divine (T,1)
80   marks divine, that in thy meekness used to shine (1)
80   marks divine ... that lit the lonely pathway (1)
99   hath he marks to lead me to him if he be my guide (2)

marred
108   thorns thy brow encircle, and tears thy face have marred (2)

marriage
366   for his marriage feast prepare (1)

marshalled
340   stand against hell's marshalled powers (2)

mart
200   no field or mart is silent, no city street is dumb (2)
482   in mart & court and parliament the common good increase (3)
549   thine is the loom, the forge, the mart (4)

martyr
303   and bright with many an angel, and all the martyr throng (2)
419   the martyr first, whose eagle eye could pierce (2)

martyrs
8   and the white robed martyrs follow (3)
19   ye holy twelve, ye martyrs strong (3)
99   saints, apostles, prophets, martyrs answer, Yes (7)
242   by the light of burning martyrs (3)

marvel
173 we marvel at the purpose that held thee to thy course (2)
290 I know not what the future hath of marvel or surprise (T,1)

marveled
203 and marveled at the radiance of thy face (2)

marveling
41 marveling at thy mystic ways (1)

Mary
324 King of kings, yet born of Mary (2)
374 Mary, Joseph, lend your aid (4)
378 the which his mother Mary did nothing take in scorn (2)
381 for Christ is born of Mary, and gathered all above (2)
385 haste to bring him laud, the babe, the son of Mary (R)
395 gentle Mary laid her child lowly in a manger (T,1,3)

Mary's
90 Mary's son most holy, Light of the village life (2)
385 child ... who, laid to rest, on Mary's lap is sleeping (1)
463 we believe in Jesus Christ, Son of God and Mary's Son (2)

master
1 my gracious Master and my God, assist me to proclaim (2)
41 master over sea and land (3)
94 I my Master have denied, I afresh have crucified (2)
154 search me and try me, Master, today (2)
155 let him with constancy follow the Master (1)
157 O Lord and Master of us all; whate'er our name or sign (6)
164 be thou forever near me, my Master and my Friend (1)
164 O give me grace to follow My Master and my Friend (4)
170 O Master, let me walk with thee (T,1)
170 with thee, O Master, let me live (4)
171 O Master Workman of the race, thou man of Galilee (T,1)
184 my heart is weak and poor until it master find (2)
197 thou Master Workman, grant us grace (3)
202 we follow where the Master leads, serene and unafraid (1)
204 O Master, from the mountainside, make haste to heal (5)
254 dear Master, in whose life I see (T,1)
274 Master, speak! thy servant heareth (T,1)
274 Master, let it now be heard (1)
274 Master, speak! (T,1,3,4)
274 Master speak ...thou knowest ..the yearning of my heart (3)
274 Master, speak! O, speak to me (4)
274 speak to me by name, O Master, let me know it is to me (2)
305 Christ, the royal Master, leads against the foe (1)
321 Master ... symbols shared thine own dear self impart (4)
342 revealing in our witness the master teacher's art (3)
348 by wise master builders squared, here be living stones (4)
356 show us the way the Master trod; reveal his saving power (1)
372 Church from thee, her Master, received the gift divine (2)
399 Root of Jesse, David's Son, my Lord and Master (1)
407 O Master of the waking world (T,1)
409 ye servants of God, your Master proclaim (T,1)
413 are ye able, said the Master, to be crucified with me (1)
413 are ye able? Still the Master whispers down eternity (4)
419 who saw his Master in the sky, and called on him to save (2)

Master's
150   O may it all my powers engage to do my Master's will (2)
202   centuries still we hear the Master's winsome call (2)
262   enter into my Master's joy, and find my heaven in thee (4)
431   heeds not his Master's grief and tears (2)

masterful
60   thou fire so masterful and bright (3)

match
477   come with thy timeless judgment . match our present hour (1)

matchless
15   praise him for his matchless power (1)
123   I only know ... matchless love ... brought God's love (2)
168   O could I speak the matchless worth (T,1)
184   enslave it with thy matchless love (2)
455   and hail him as thy matchless King through all eternity (1)

matter
207   no matter what may be the test (4)
332   how can heavenly spirits rise by earthly matter fed (3)

may
3   thy sovereign majesty may we in glory see (4)
4   that men may hear the grateful song (4)
5   children of the heavenly King may speak ... joys abroad (2)
5   fruit ... from faith and hope may grow (3)
7   so may we, in lowly station join the choristers above (2)
10   the heavens are not too high, his praise may thither fly (1)
10   the earth is not too low, his praises there may grow (1)
20   the body they may kill: God's truth abideth still (4)
20   dost ask who that may be? Christ Jesus, it is he (2)
26   though the eye of sinful man thy glory may not see (3)
28   still may we dwell secure (2)
49   O may this bounteous God though all our life be near us (2)
50   so that earth's bliss may be our guide ... not our chain (3)
67   Good Shepherd, may I sing thy praise within thy house (6)
71   O that with yonder sacred throng we at his feet may fall (5)
81   may the music of thy name refresh my soul in death (5)
85   that men in thee may see what God is like (2)
85   free wills ... thou givest, that we may make them thine (4)
85   God's will to earth thou bringest that all ... may learn (4)
85   all who would obey thee may learn from thee their duty (4)
91   may Jesus Christ be praised! (R)
98   here may we prove the power of prayer (4)
102   ye all may come to Christ and live (4)
107   by thy mercies, Savior, may we hear thy call (5)
128   well may this glowing heart rejoice (1)
133   that I may love what thou dost love (1)
135   by thee may I strongly live, bravely bear & nobly strive (3)
136   truth which all may hear (3)
137   the grace which all may find, the saving power, impart (3)
142   whate'er may come, I'll taste ... the hallowed bliss (4)
143   may thy rich grace impart strength to my fainting heart (2)
143   as thou hast died for me, O may my love to thee (2)

144 though faith and hope may long be tried (4)
146 that mind and soul, according well, may make one music (5)
146 may make one music as before (5)
148 some poor fainting, struggling seaman you may rescue (R)
148 you may rescue, you may save (R)
148 in the darkness may be lost (3)
150 O may it all my powers engage to do my Master's will (2)
157 we may not climb the heavenly steeps (2)
157 we may not climb ... to bring the Lord Christ down (2)
159 there are heights of joy that I may not reach till (4)
160 for only he who bears the cross may hope to wear...crown (4)
160 may hope to wear the glorious crown (4).
162 at thy bidding may I move, prompt to serve & follow thee (2)
162 thus may I rejoice to show that I feel the love I owe (4)
165 may the fruits of thy salvation in our hearts and lives (2)
165 ever faithful ... to the truth may we be found (2)
167 my Jesus, as thou wilt! O may thy will be mine (T,1)
171 that we the land may view (2)
171 that it may be our highest joy, our Father's work to do (3)
173 O grant that love of country may help us hear his call (3)
176 the gate of life eternal may I enter, Lord, with thee (3)
177 that each departing day henceforth may see (3)
178 one with thyself, may every eye in us, thy brethren see (4)
180 in thy sole glory may unite (3)
181 we give thee but thine own, whate'er the gift may be (T,1)
181 may we thy bounties thus as stewards true receive (2)
181 and we believe thy word, though dim our faith may be (4)
188 not for myself alone may my prayer be (3)
193 O may we all the loving mind that was in thee receive (5)
195 that I may speak in living echoes of thy tone (1)
195 wing my words, that they may reach the hidden depths (3)
195 that I may stand firm on the rock, and strong in thee (2)
195 I may stretch out a loving hand to wrestlers (2)
195 O teach me, Lord, that I may teach (3)
197 O Workman true, may we fulfill in daily life (2)
198 dare all that may plant man's lordship firm on earth (2)
205 my weary steps may falter, and my soul athirst may be (2)
206 no height but we may find thee there (2)
206 still may we trust thy love and grace (4)
207 all you may need he will provide (3)
207 no matter what may be the test (4)
218 if life belong, I will be glad that I may long obey (2)
220 though the storms may gather, still have peace within (3)
222 O may I then in him be found (4)
225 where I may look upon thy face (4)
225 where I may lay me prone, and bare my soul in loneliness (3)
225 where thou ... all my soul possess and I may find myself (2)
226 may thy tender love to me bind me closer .. Lord to thee (R)
227 may they all be devoted to him (6)
230 the storm may roar without me, my heart may low be laid (1)
230 wherever he may guide me, no want shall turn me back (2)
231 let the unknown tomorrow bring with it what it may (2)
234 in thy sunshine's blaze its day may brighter, fairer be (2)
234 in thine ocean depths its flow may richer, fuller be (1)
237 grant that I may never fail thy hand to see (3)
237 grant that I may ever cast my care on thee (3)

243   in keenest strife, Lord, may we stand (3)
247   while leaning on thy breast may I hear thee (3)
247   may I hear thee say to me,
251   foes may hate, and friends may shun me (2)
251   man may trouble and distress me (3)
251   life with trials hard may press me (3)
253   a pure desire that all may learn and glorify thy grace (4)
256   may I reach heaven's joys, O bright heaven's Sun (4)
258   pray that he may prosper ever each endeavor (3)
258   but that he may ever thwart thee and convert thee (3)
259   O Jesus, nothing may I see ... desire, or seek but thee (2)
267   open my eyes that I may see (T,1)
267   that I may see glimpses of truth thou hast for me (1)
267   open my eyes, that I may hear voices of truth (2)
269   however rough and steep the path may be (4)
274   speak, that I may follow faster (2)
276   Lord, we thy presence seek; may ours the blessing be (4)
279   from thee that I no more may stray (3)
279   O may the least omissions pain my reawakened soul (4)
280   O may the least omission pain my reawakened soul (4)
280   from thee that I no more may stray (3)
281   that I thy mercy may proclaim (2)
281   that all mankind thy truth may see (2)
281   thy word may to the utmost prove (5)
284   when this life is past, I may the eternal brightness see (5)
284   that I may sing above to Father, Spirit, and to thee (6)
291   though Jordan waves may roll, I'll fearless launch away (3)
295   even thine own altars, where she safe ... may bring (4)
295   her young ones forth may bring (4)
297   like them, the meek & lowly, on high may dwell with thee (4)
305   crowns and thrones may perish, kingdoms rise and wane (3)
310   that we may meet in heaven (3)
311   may her voice be ever clear, warning of a judgment near (2)
311   may she guide the poor and blind (3)
311   may she holy triumphs win, overthrow the hosts of sin (4)
314   may the Church that waiteth for thee keep love's tie (3)
321   in our daily life may flame the passion of thy heart (4)
324   powers of hell may vanish as the darkness clears away (3)
333   that theirs may be the love which knows no ending (1)
334   may the grace of Christ our Savior (T,1)
334   may they abide in union with each other and the Lord (2)
335   that they may watch for thee (4)
335   may they in Jesus ...they preach, their own Redeemer see (4)
336   gladly reckon all things loss so we may Jesus gain (5)
337   O God, may they and we be thine (5)
338   our bodies may far off remove, we still are one in heart (1)
338   O may we ever walk in him, and nothing know beside (3)
341   happy, if with my latest breath I may but gasp his name (6)
343   may earth-born passions die (3)
343   O grant its rich and swelling notes may lift our souls (3)
345   may they who err be guided here to find the better way (3)
345   may faith grow firm, and love grow warm (4)
348   may thy spirit here give rest (2)
348   may they know this house their own (3)
349   may benedictions here attend the teaching of thy word (3)
350   may our prayers, when here we bend ...to thee ascend (2)

350   may we discern thy presence here (3)
351   bless thou this house that it may be a place most meet (1)
352   this temple, reared to thee, O may it ever be filled (1)
355   still our wrongs may weave thee now new thorns (1)
356   may one Lord .. faith .. Word, one Spirit lead us still (4)
362   where the Lord our God may go (1,4)
367   O may these heavenly pages be my ever dear delight (3)
367   still new beauties may I see, and still increasing light (3)
376   angels and archangels may have gathered there (3)
381   no ear may hear his coming, but in this world of sin (3)
387   mild he lays his glory by, born that man no more may die (3)
397   so may we with willing feet ever seek thy mercy seat (2)
397   so may we with holy joy, pure and free from sins' alloy (3)
397   so, most gracious Lord, may we evermore be led to thee (1)
414   may not know ... cannot tell, what pains he had to bear (2)
419   O God, to us may grace be given to follow in their train (3)
421   there may I, though vile as he, wash all my sins away (2)
423   O may we ever praise him with heart and life and voice (3)
427   that, as we share this hour, thy cross may bring ... joy (4)
427   thy cross may bring us to thy joy and resurrection power (4)
429   middle wall is broken down and all mankind may enter in (2)
429   and all may live from sin set free (3)
437   our hearts be pure from evil, that we may see aright (2)
437   listening to his accents, may hear, so calm and plain (2)
437   and, hearing, may raise the victory strain (2)
447   that we may live and sing to thee: Alleluia (4)
454   every sin may be forgiven through .. virtue of thy blood (2)
455   lives that death may die (2)
455   scepter sways from pole to pole, that wars may cease (3)
467   through ... ages all along this may be our endless song (4)
470   gird our lives that they may be armored (4)
475   old now is earth and none may count her days (1)
477   bring justice to our land, that all may dwell secure (3)
477   that war may haunt .. earth no more and desolation cease (4)
479   that thy children, Lord, in freedom may thy mercy know (4)
479   that thy children ... may thy mercy know, and live (4)
486   man in his weakness yet may give a worthier offering (1)
487   in thy flock may we be found (3)
489   may we rest this day in thee (2)
489   may we feel thy presence near (3)
489   may thy glory meet our eyes while we in thy house appear (3)
489   may thy Gospel's joyful sound conquer sinners, comfort (4)
489   thus may all our sabbaths prove till we join ... above (4)
490   may this day be blest, trusting Jesus' love (3)
491   we pray thee that offenseless the hours of dark may be (1)
491   call on thee that sinless the hours of dark may be (2)
491   ask that free from peril the hours of dark may be (3)
492   may we this life improve, to mourn for errors past (4)
493   that with the world, myself, and thee...at peace may be (2)
493   I, ere I sleep, at peace may be (2)
493   teach me to live, that I may dread the grave as little (3)
493   teach me to die, that so I may rise glorious (3)
493   O may my soul on thee repose and with sweet sleep (4)
493   sleep that may me more vigorous make to serve my God (4)
495   with thy tenderest blessing may our eyelids close (2)
495   through the long night watches may thine angels spread (5)
495   when the morning wakens, then may I arise pure and fresh (6)

497   may thine angel guards defend us (1)
497   may we, born anew like morning, to labor rise (2)
502   O may no earth-born cloud arise to hide thee (1)
506   may weariness and sadness be lulled to peace & gladness (3)
511   to make our life an offering to God, that man may live (2)
514   crops we grow that men may live (1)
515   since every day by thee we live, may grateful hearts (4)
515   may grateful hearts thy gifts receive (4)
515   may the hands be pure from stain with which...we gain (4)
517   that we may bear it meetly ... seek thine aid the more (2)
517   that in all we do or say little ones our deeds may copy (3)
517   little feet our steps may follow in a safe & narrow way (3)
517   may we keep our holy calling stainless in... fair renown (5)
517   children thou hast given still may be our joy and crown (5)
518   and grant that we may feast in paradise with thee (1)
518   by thine own hand may we be fed (2)
519   may we not his spirit grieve (1)
520   O Lord, may church and home combine (T,1)
520   may church and home combine to teach thy perfect way (1)
522   grant that we wholesome grain and pure may be (2)
523   O may we ever with thee live, who givest all (5)
526   who may abide thy presence (1)
526   for none may boast himself of aught (2)
530   sweetly may we all agree, touched with loving sympathy (4)
531   that I ceaseless may, Abba, Father, cry (3)
534   may the shadow of thy presence around our camp be spread (2
536   O may thy soldiers, faithful, true, and bold (3)
543   America! America! may God thy gold refine (3)
547   long may our land be bright with freedom's holy light (4)

mayest
293   thou mayest smile at all thy foes (1)

mayst
549   these .. not the only walls wherein thou mayst be sought (3)

maze
143   while life's dark maze I tread & griefs around me spread (3)
269   unhelped by thee, in error's maze we grope (2)

mazes
531   from all its hidden mazes there (3)

meadow
38   field and forest, vale & mountain, flowery meadow (2)
452   bloom in every meadow, leaves on every bough (2)

meadows
79   fair are the meadows, fairer still the woodlands (2)
442   He who skies & meadows paints fashioned all your virtue (3)
442   and set the meadows dancing (1)

mean
172   the mean altar of my heart (1)
385   why lies he in such mean estate (2)
385   mean estate where ox and ass are feeding (2)
529   with thee all night I mean to stay (1)

meaner
  90   let us arise, all meaner service scorning (5)

meanest
  25   might I enjoy the meanest place within thy house (2)
  186   worth to my meanest labor give by joining it to thine (2)
meaning
  356   restore to us thy truth, O God, & make its meaning sure (2)
  405   sacred gifts of mystic meaning (4)

meanly
  394   all meanly wrapped in swathing bands & in a manger laid (4)

means
  332   ask the Father's wisdom how...that did the means ordain (3)
  523   for means of grace and hopes of heaven (4)

measure
  2   craftman's art and music's measure for thy pleasure (3)
  2   art...music's measure for thy pleasure all combine (3)
  69   love of God is broader than the measure of man's mind (2)
  132 spread thy light from the height which knows no measure (1)
  230 my hope I cannot measure, my path to life is free (3)
  318 from this banquet let me measure (3)
  318 let me measure, Lord, how vast and deep its treasure (3)
  370 shedding light that none can measure (1)
  416 peace is there, that knows no measure (4)

measured
  18   here we drink of joy unmeasured (3)
  304 measured by his love (2)
  345 thou, whose unmeasured temple stands (T,1)

meat
  438 He is our meat and drink indeed (4)

meditation
  504 singing, we offer prayer and meditation (1)

meed
  526 if each should have its rightful meed (1)

meek
  80   so meek, so lowly, yet so high, so glorious in humility (93)
  82   O Hope of every contrite heart, O Joy of all the meek (3)
  108 O Jesus, thou art pleading in accents meek and low (3)
  282 a heart resigned, submissive, meek (2)
  297 like them, the meek & lowly, on high may dwell with thee (4)
  309 lowly, meek, in thought & word, altogether like our Lord (3)
  316 according to thy gracious word, in meek humility (T,1)
  381 where meek souls will receive him...dear Christ enters (3)
  399 O Sovereign meek and lowly! (1)
  425 O Savior meek, pursue thy road with palms (1)
  425 bow thy meek head to mortal pain (4)

meekly
190 as he goes meekly by (1)
434 see him meekly bearing all (2)

meekness
80 marks divine, that in thy meekness used to shine (1)
337 firmness with meekness from above to bear thy people (3)
486 who with love and meekness outlast the years of wrong (3)
544 earth hath forsaken meekness & mercy...slighted thy word (2)

meet
98 Jesus, where'er thy people meet (T,1)
192 in Christ now meet both east and west (4)
192 in him meet south and north (4)
197 by effort true to meet each test (3)
209 all safe and blessed we shall meet at last (3)
218 when grace hath made me meet thy blessed face to see (4)
218 come, Lord, when grace hath made me meet (4)
232 they meet around one common mercy seat (3)
232 though sundered far, by faith they meet (3)
276 O give the pure & lowly heart, a temple meet for thee (4)
301 what height of rapture shall we know when...we meet (5)
301 when round his throne we meet (5)
306 we shall still be joined in heart & hope to meet again (4)
310 we meet, the grace to take which thou hast freeely given(3)
310 that we may meet in heaven (3)
310 we meet on earth for thy dear sake (3)
328 hearts & minds & spirits join, and all in Jesus meet (3)
332 only meet us in thy ways and perfect us in one (4)
345 let the comforter and friend, thy Holy Spirit, meet (2)
345 meet with those who here in worship bend (2)
346 let those learn, who here shall meet (4)
351 bless thou this house that it may be a place most meet (1)
351 a place most meet to learn of thee (1)
366 for ye must go to meet him there (1)
408 in Christ all races meet, their ancient feuds forgetting (2)
435 did e'er such love and sorrow meet (3)
454 loudest praises...meet it is for us to give (4)
456 where his loving people meet to share the gift divine (2)
487 Jesus, we want to meet on this thy holy day (T,1)
489 may thy glory meet our eyes while we in thy house appear (3)
507 come down and meet us now (4)
539 God be with you till we meet again (T,R) (also 540)

meetly
517 that we may bear it meetly...seek thine aid the more (2)

meets
434 Christ is risen! He meets our eyes (4)
450 Lo! Jesus meets thee, risen from the tomb (2)

melodious
93 teach me some melodious sonnet (1)

melody
2 heart and minds...hands and voices...choicest melody (4)
424 to thee, now high exalted, our melody we raise (3)
476 in speech that flows to melody, in holiness of heart (4)

melt
- 38 melt the clouds of sin and sadness (1)
- 259 care, anguish, sorrow, melt away (2)
- 415 and melt mine eyes to tears (4)

member
- 399 fill me with joy and strength to be thy member (2)
- 530 kindly for each other care; every member feel its share (4)

members
- 457 dead to sin, his members live the life of righteousness (3)

memories
- 268 How sweet their memories still (3)

memory
- 82 nor can the memory find a sweeter sound than thy... name (2)
- 316 when these failing lips grow dumb ... mind & memory flee (4)
- 319 in faith and memory thus we sing the wonders of his love (4)
- 319 in memory of the Savior's love, we keep the sacred feast (T)
- 321 the blessed cup is only passed true memory of thee (3)
- 548 memory and hope between (1)
- 550 through all ages bear the memory of that holy hour (2)

men
- 4 that men may hear the grateful song (4)
- 5 the men of grace have found glory begun below (3)
- 11 men and children everywhere (T,1)
- 22 made us of clay and formed us men (2)
- 33 good will to men on earth (2)
- 39 the race of men confess the beauty of his holiness (3)
- 60 ye men of tender heart, forgiving others, take your part (5)
- 78 redeem us...when thou judgest all the sons of men (3)
- 80 who like thee so humbly bore the scorn ... scoffs of men (3)
- 85 in human form thou speakest to men the Father's mind (2)
- 85 that men in thee may see what God is like (2)
- 114 and publish to the sons of men the signs infallible (2)
- 136 the language all men understand (3)
- 155 than fancies flee away! I'll fear not what men say (3)
- 174 rise up, O men of God! Have done with lesser things (T,1)
- 174 rise up, O men of God! the Church for you doth wait (3)
- 174 as brothers of the Son of man, rise up, O men of God (4)
- 174 rise up, o men of God, his kingdom tarries long (2)
- 189 here together, brother men, we pledge the Lord anew (2)
- 189 one claim unites all men in God to serve each human need (2)
- 191 God send us men (T,1,2,3,4)
- 191 men alert and quick his lofty precepts to translate (2)
- 191 men whose aim 'twill be not to defend some ancient creed (1)
- 191 men with hearts ablaze .. truth to love .. wrong to hate (4)
- 200 the voice of God is calling its summons unto men (T,1)
- 202 the common hopes that make us men were his in Galilee (2)
- 203 but in the eyes of men, redeemed and free, a splendor (4)
- 204 till sons of men shall learn thy love (6)
- 214 not like that go the men of unbelief (3)
- 214 men of unbelief ... are like chaff the wind doth blow (3)
- 233 strong men and maidens fair (2)
- 243 like those strong men of old (1)
- 248 ye that are men now serve him against unnumbered foes (2)

276 to dwell in lowliness with men, their pattern &... King (2)
305 this through countless ages men and angels sing (4)
317 the bread of life, for all men broken (T,1)
321 the bread is always consecrate which men divide with men (2)
325 pardon and peace to dying men and endless life are given (2)
329 thou fount of life! thou light of men (1)
341 angels and men before it fall, and devils fear and fly (1)
344 truth and love let all men see (3)
351 by men and heavenly hosts adored (1)
351 from hence send forth a race of men of flaming heart (3)
351 race of men of flaming heart and stalwart mind (3)
355 Lord Christ, when first thou cam'st to men (T,1)
362 the works of men decay (2)
366 men and angels sing before thee (3)
371 thou hast revealed thy will to mortal men (2)
371 revealing to sinful men thy justice and thy grace (3)
374 love to God and all men, love for plea and gift and sign (3)
377 three wise men bearing gifts of gold (2)
381 praises sing to God the King, and peace to men on earth (2)
382 God with men is now residing (2)
383 and by the light of that same star three wise men came (3)
383 three wise men came from country far (3)
383 then entered in those wise men three (5)
387 pleased as man with men to dwell, Jesus our Emmanuel (2)
391 good Christian men, rejoice (T,1,2,3)
392 let men their songs employ (2)
394 good will ... from heaven to men begin and never cease (6)
397 as with gladness men of old did the guiding star behold (T)
398 thou robest in thy splendor the simplest ways of men (2)
402 prayer and praising all men raising (3)
407 wondrous power that makes men free (1)
407 thy witness in the souls of men (3)
408 new life, new hope awakes where-e'er men own his sway (1)
408 Christ is throned as Lord, men ... forsake their fear (2)
422 while men of low degree exalt and usher in the day (4)
423 the Lord of men and angels rode on in lowly state (2)
424 and mortal men and all things created make reply (2)
439 sons of men and angels say, Alleluia (1)
441 in the grave they laid him, Love whom men had slain (2)
449 good Christian men, rejoice and sing (T,1)
460 speaketh to the hearts of men (3)
465 let all the sons of men record and dwell upon thy love (4)
468 justice, from her heavenly bower look down on mortal men (1)
470 in the fight to set men free (4)
475 earth might be fair and all men glad and wise (2)
479 still in grief men mourn their dead (2)
479 to save and make men whole (2)
481 hark, how from men whose lives are held more cheap (2)
482 men at last ... ring the bells of brotherhood & peace (3)
484 from all the easy speeches that comfort cruel men (2)
491 Lover of men, O hear our call, and guard and save us (4)
511 as men of old their first fruits brought (T,1)
514 crops we grow that men may live (1)
524 by thee the souls of men are fed with gifts of grace (2)
524 souls of men are fed with gifts of grace supernal (2)
528 outcasts of men, to you I call (4)
532 now praise we great and famous men (T,1)

532 whose music like a mighty wind the souls of men uplifted (3)
532 praise we the peaceful men of skill (4)
532 peaceful men of skill who builded homes of beauty (4)
541 Lord, guard and guide the men who fly (T,1)
541 men who fly through the great spaces of the sky (1)
541 O God, protect the men who fly through lonely ways (2)
541 men who fly through lonely ways beneath the sky (2)
542 let Christ be lifted up till all men serve him (3)
545 sifting out the hearts of men before his judgment seat (3)
545 as he died to make men holy, let us die to make man free (4)

men's
370 statesmen's, teacher's, hero's treasure (1)
459 stilling the rude wills of men's wild behavior (3)

mend
543 America! America! God mend thine every flaw (2)

merchandise
481 lives are held more cheap than merchandise (2)

mercies
6 tell thy goodness ... thy mercies ... thy glorious might (1)
14 eternal are thy mercies, Lord (2)
47 we own thy mercies, Lord, which never fail (1)
52 praise thee for thy mercies past, & humbly hope for more (3)
61 for his mercies shall endure, ever faithful, ever sure (R)
65 bless the Father ... forget not ... mercies to proclaim (1)
70 when all thy mercies, O my God, my rising soul surveys (T,1)
98 thy former mercies here renew (3)
107 by thy mercies, Savior, may we hear thy call (5)
147 thy tender mercies shall illume the midnight of the soul (3)
172 till death thy endless mercies seal (4)
283 all thy faithful mercies crown (1)
367 Father of mercies, in thy Word what endless glory shines (T)
473 thy mercies how tender, how firm to the endd (5)
498 praise for mercies daily twining round us golden cords (1)
499 new mercies, each returning day, hover around us (2)
499 new mercies ... hover around us while we pray (2)
510 Father, thy mercies past we own, and thy continued care (3)
529 to me, to all, thy mercies move (4)

merciful
26 holy,holy, holy! merciful and mighty (1,4)
175 Jesus is merciful, Jesus will save (R)
526 he is merciful and just, here is my comfort and my trust (3)

mercy
4 his gracious mercy keepeth (2)
7 for his mercy ceasing never, for his blessing day by day (3)
21 his mercy is forever sure (4)
52 thy mercy sets us free (2)
55 surely his goodness and mercy here daily attend thee (3)
63 God is love; his mercy brightens (T,1)
63 his mercy brightens all the path in which we rove (1)
63 man decays and ages move; but his mercy waneth never (2)
66 Alleluia! Alleluia! widely yet his mercy flows (3)

68	goodness and mercy all my life shall surely follow me (5)
69	there's a wideness in God's mercy (T,1)
69	wideness in God's mercy like the wideness of the sea (1)
69	is mercy with the Savior; there is healing in his blood (1)
93	streams of mercy never ceasing call for songs (1)
94	depth of mercy (T,1)
94	depth of mercy! can there be mercy still reserved for me (1)
95	mercy now, O Lord, I plead in this hour of utter need (3)
98	there they behold thy mercy seat (1)
101	there's mercy with the Lord (1)
103	come to the mercy seat, fervently kneel (1)
121	thou hast mercy to relieve us (3)
127	blood, which at the mercy seat of God...doth...plead (3)
141	God's mercy holds a wiser plan than thou canst fully know (2
145	let me at thy throne of mercy find a sweet relief (2)
148	brightly beams our Father's mercy (T,1)
161	we render back the love thy mercy gave us (4)
177	at thy blest mercy seat, pleading for me (2)
201	help us by deeds of mercy to show that thou art kind (2)
205	can I doubt his tender mercy (1)
211	mercy thy days shall lengthen (2)
215	the clouds ye so much dread are big with mercy (3)
224	angels descending, bring from above echoes of mercy (2)
224	echoes of mercy, whispers of love (2)
232	'tis found beneath the mercy seat (1)
232	it is the blood-bought mercy seat (2)
232	they meet around one common mercy seat (3)
232	and glory crowns the mercy seat (4)
237	should thy mercy send me sorrow, toil, and woe (3)
240	His boundless mercy will provide (2)
263	all that thou sendest me, in mercy given (3)
281	that I thy mercy may proclaim (2)
290	assured alone that life and death God's mercy underlies (1)
303	Jesus, in mercy bring us to that dear land of rest (4)
307	watch o'er thy Church, O Lord, in mercy (3)
320	bread of the world in mercy broken (T,1)
320	wine of the soul in mercy shed (1)
322	bread of the world in mercy broken (T,1)
323	bread of the world in mercy broken (T,1)
330	O Lord, have mercy on me (R)
345	in worship bend before thy mercy seat (2)
387	peace on earth and mercy mild (1)
397	so may we with willing feet ever seek thy mercy seat (2)
410	a story of truth and mercy, a story of peace and light (1)
427	'tis mercy all! let earth adore (2)
433	near the cross, a trembling soul, love & mercy found me (2)
471	let all earth's sons thy mercy prove (1)
478	with deeds of love and mercy, the heavenly kingdom comes (2)
479	that thy children, Lord, in freedom may thy mercy know (4)
479	that thy children ... may thy mercy know, and live (4)
497	slumber sweet thy mercy send us (1)
501	and in thy mercy heal us all (6)
509	that mercy crowns it till it close (1)
509	the opening year thy mercy shows (1)
512	the year with good he crownest ... earth his mercy fills (2)
543	and mercy more than life (3)
544	earth hath forsaken meekness & mercy...slighted thy word (2)

mid
- 217   sometimes mid scenes of deepest gloom (2)
- 225   mid all the traffic of the ways (T,1)
- 297   mid toil and tribulation, and tumult of her war (3)
- 372   mid mists & rocks & quick-sands, still guides ...to thee (3)
- 423   from Olivet they followed mid an exultant crowd (2)
- 460   'mid the world's despair and turmoil one firm anchor (1)
- 506   but mid the light declining the evening star is shining (1)

middle
- 429   middle wall is broken down and all mankind may enter in (2)

midnight
- 64   our midnight is thy smile withdrawn (3)
- 147   thy tender mercies shall illume the midnight of the soul (3)
- 366   midnight hears the welcome voices (1)
- 390   it came upon the midnight clear (T,1)
- 431   'tis midnight, and on Olive's brow (T,1)
- 431   'tis midnight (1,2,3,4)

midst
- 38   victors in the midst of strife (4)
- 52   in midst of dangers, fears, and death (3)
- 127   midst flaming worlds, in these arrayed (1)
- 244   in the midst of tribulation, stand by me (2)
- 244   in the midst of faults and failures, stand by me (3)
- 310   thou in the midst of us shalt be, assembled in thy name (1)
- 362   he stands in the midst of nations (3)
- 419   like him... pardon on his tongue in midst of mortal pain (2)

midwinter
- 376   in the bleak midwinter, frosty wind made moan (T,1)
- 376   in the bleak midwinter, long ago (1)
- 376   in the bleak midwinter a stable place sufficed (2)

might
- 2   confess thee Lord of might (1)
- 2   honor, glory, might, and merit thine shall ever be (5)
- 4   within the kingdom of his might (2)
- 6   tell thy goodness ... thy mercies ... thy glorious might (1)
- 11   tell ye forth his might, Lord of life ... truth & right (3)
- 12   O thou in all thy might so far (T,1)
- 25   might I enjoy the meanest place within thy house (2)
- 27   nor wanting, nor wasting, thou rulest in might (2)
- 29   Father of glory evermore ... Father of all grace & might (3)
- 32   the Lord our God is clothed with might (T,1)
- 34   he gave us eyes to see them, and lips that we might tell (4)
- 61   he, with all-commanding might, filled the new-made world (2)
- 74   that in our darkened hearts thy grace might shine (1)
- 74   who wast a servant that we might be free (3)
- 78   come in thy holy might, we pray (3)
- 78   laud, honor, might ... glory be ... age to age eternally (4)
- 112   God ... died himself, that you might live (2)
- 137   O that the world might know the all-atoning Lamb (3)
- 138   stoop to my weakness, might as thou art (1)
- 155   no foes shall stay his might, though he with giants fight (2
- 169   I would serve thee with all my might ... to thee I come (3)

178 thy foes might hate, despise, revile (2)
180 that all my powers, with all their might ((3)
211 his might thy heart shall strengthen (2)
227 O that all his salvation might see (4)
240 fight the good fight with all thy might (T,1)
250 stand ...in his great might ... all his strength endued (2)
251 God of wisdom, love, and might (2)
298 One in might, and One in glory, while unending ages run (4)
299 died on earth that man might live above (3)
310 O might thy quickening voice the death of sin remove (5)
335 might fill an angel's heart and filled a Savior's hands (2)
341 that the world might taste & see the riches of his grace (3)
356 one great Church go forth in might to work God's .. will (4)
399 rich in blessing, rule and might o'er all possessing (1)
409 all glory and power, all wisdom and might (4)
410 that all of the world's great peoples might come (4)
410 might come to the truth of God (4)
414 died that we might be forgiven ... died to make us good (3)
414 might go at last to heaven saved by his precious blood (3)
415 well might .. sun in darkness hide . shut his glories in (3)
446 neither might the gates of death ... tomb's dark portal (4)
464 O that all might catch the flame (1)
468 rise, God, judge thou the earth in might (2)
473 O tell of his might, O sing of his grace (2)
475 earth might be fair and all men glad and wise (2)
478 the crown awaits the conquest; lead on, O God of might (3)
480 Glorious Trinity, Grace, Love and Might (4)
520 reveal thy face where darkness else might be (3)
534 for the might of thine arm we bless thee (T,1)
534 for the might of thine arm we bless thee, our God (1,2)
536 thou wast their rock, their fortress, and their might (2)
547 protect us by thy might, Great God, our King (4)

mightier
198 and mightier music thrill the skies (4)
219 thought of thee is mightier than sin & pain & sorrow are (1)

mighty
  3 come, thou incarnate Word, gird on thy mighty sword (2)
 20 a mighty fortress is our God (T,1)
 26 holy,holy, holy! merciful and mighty (1,4)
 31 through all his mighty works amazing wisdom shines (3)
 42 worlds his mighty voice obeyed (1)
 44 mighty works and wondrous grace thy glory ... proclaim (5)
 76 who from the beginning was the mighty Word (1)
 84 thank we all the mighty Child through whom we know thee (3)
 89 thy mighty name salvation ... keeps my happy soul above (2)
163 so mighty a defender (3)
175 tell them of Jesus the mighty to save (1)
248 forth to the mighty conquest in this his glorious day (2)
250 strong in the Lord of hosts, and in his mighty power (1)
271 I am weak, but thou art mighty (1)
305 like a mighty army moves the Church of God (2)
310 Lord, let every bounding heart the mighty comfort feel (4)
336 what troubles have see seen, what mighty conflicts past (2)
361 the Wonderful, the Counselor, the great and mighty Lord (3)
363 lift up your heads, ye mighty gates (T,1)

394　fear not, said he, for mighty dread had seized (2)
394　mighty dread had seized their troubled mind (2)
407　mighty God, set us aflame to show the glory of thy name (3)
415　God, the mighty maker, died for man the creature's sin (3)
417　the shadow of a mighty rock within a weary land (1)
444　with a mighty triumph o'er his foes (R)
458　a royal diadem adorns the mighty victor's brow (1)
459　from thee have flowed, as from a mighty river ... faith (4)
463　by whose mighty power alone all is made & wrought & done (1
464　more & more it spreads and grows ever mighty to prevail (2)
464　Jesus mighty to redeem, he alone the work hath wrought (3)
471　take to thyself thy mighty power (1)
482　mighty host, by thee redeemed, is marching in thy train (1)
506　beneath thy mighty caring the birds & beasts are sharing (2)
509　mighty hand by which supported still we stand (1)
509　Great God, we sing that mighty hand (T,1)
521　in his mighty arms he bears them (2)
532　whose music like a mighty wind the souls of men uplifted (3)
535　Church triumphant in thy love, their mighty joys we know (2)
538　bidst the mighty ocean deep its... appointed limits keep (1)
545　he is wisdom to the mighty, he is honor to the brave (5)
548　not alone for mighty empire (T,1)
548　mighty empire, stretching far o'er land and sea (1)

mild
　35　for all gentle thoughts and mild (4)
　80　who like thee so mild, so bright ... did ever go (2)
387　peace on earth and mercy mild (1)
387　mild he lays his glory by, born that man no more may die (3)
393　holy infant so tender and mild sleep in heavenly peace (1)
490　make my conduct good, actions calm and mild (2)

milk
　84　give milk . bread or solid food as fits my understanding (3)
303　Jerusalem the golden, with milk and honey blest (T,1)

millions
325　millions of souls, in glory now ... fed and feasted here (3)
325　millions more, still on the way, around the board appear (3)

mind
　　9　the Lord supports the fainting mind (3)
　53　why should this anxious load press down your weary mind (3)
　61　let us with a gladsome mind (T,1)
　61　let us then with gladsome mind praise the Lord (4)
　69　love of God is broader than the measure of man's mind (2)
　74　let this mind be in us which was in thee (3)
　75　thou only canst inform the mind and purify the heart (2)
　85　O Mind of God incarnate, O Thought in flesh enshrined (2)
　85　in human form thou speakest to men the Father's mind (2)
　98　thou ... dost dwell with those of humble mind (2)
119　poor, wretched, blind; sight, riches, healing of... mind (4)
138　all, all thine own, soul, heart and strength and mind (3)
141　Have faith in God, my mind ... oft thy light burns low (2)
141　I rest, heart, mind, and soul the captive of thy grace (4)
146　that mind and soul, according well, may make one music (5)
173　knows not race nor station as boundaries of the mind (4)

174 give heart and mind and soul and strength to serve (1)
191 with vision clear and mind equipped His will to learn (3)
193 O may we all the loving mind that was in thee receive (5)
193 let us, still we pray, possess the mind that was in thee (6)
235 reclothe us in our rightful mind (1)
253 I want a sober mind, a self-renouncing will (2)
277 according to thy mind & Word, well-pleasing in thy sight (3)
281 the mind which was in Christ impart (4)
309 make us of one heart and mind, courteous, pitiful & kind (3)
316 when these failing lips grow dumb ... mind & memory flee (4)
338 partakers of the Savior's grace ... same in mind & heart (4)
344 blindness both of heart and mind (2)
344 in knowledge pure their mind renew (2)
351 race of men of flaming heart and stalwart mind (3)
354 bind all peoples in one heart and mind (3)
367 springs of consolation rise to cheer the fainting mind (2)
378 the shepherds at those tidings rejoiced much in mind (4)
394 mighty dread had seized their troubled mind (2)
411 proclaim the good Physician's mind (3)
476 who lightest every earnest mind of every clime and shore (3)
480 health to the sick in mind, sight to the inly blind (2)
481 already in the mind of God that city riseth fair (5)
487 let the mind of Christ abide in us on this thy holy day (3)
499 if on our daily course our mind be set to hallow (3)
499 mind be set to hallow all we find (3)
507 the covenant we this moment make be ever kept in mind (3)
511 farm... market, shop... home, of mind and heart and hand (1)
532 praise we the great of heart and mind (3)

mind's
35 for the heart and mind's delight (3)

minded
324 ponder nothing earthly minded (1)

minds
2 heart and minds ... hands and voices ... choicest melody (4)
16 to touch our lips, our minds inspire (3)
136 until our minds are free from mists of error (2)
260 more than our minds seek thee (4)
301 a peace to sensual minds unknown, a joy unspeakable (4)
306 the fellowship of kindred minds is like to that above (1)
328 hearts and minds and spirits join, and all in Jesus meet (3)
477 bring to our troubled minds, uncertain and afraid (2)
487 look into our hearts & minds today ... this thy holy day (1)
487 our minds we dedicate on this thy holy day (4)
527 let angel minds inquire no more (2)

mine
57 unto the hills I lift mine eyes (T,1)
67 I nothing lack if I am his and he is mine forever (1)
89 secure I am if thou art mine (1)
91 be this while life is mine my canticle divine (4)
93 here I raise mine Ebenezer, hither to thy help I'm come (2)
96 thou didst reach forth thy hand and mine enfold (2)
118 and lost, I am, till thou art mine (2)
128 I am my Lord's and he is mine (3)

135 Holy Spirit, Truth divine, dawn upon this soul of mine (T,1)
135 Holy Spirit, Love divine, glow within this heart of mine (2)
135 fill and nerve this will of mine (3)
163 for I am his, and he is mine, forever and forever (1)
166 Lord Jesus, I love thee, I know thou art mine (T,1)
167 my Jesus, as thou wilt! O may thy will be mine (T,1)
168 and magnify the wondrous grace which made salvation mine (
186 Son of the carpenter, receive this humble work of mine (2)
187 take my will & make it thine; it shall be no longer mine (3)
188 ever, O Christ, through mine let thy life shine (1)
200 I hear my people crying in cot and mine and slum (2)
224 blessed assurance, Jesus is mine (T,1)
227 that sweet comfort was mine (2)
238 but that toil shall make thee some day all mine own (4)
254 shine to shame and guide this life of mine (1)
256 thou mine inheritance, now and always (3)
285 this only portion, Lord, be mine (3)
285 be mine this better part (3)
375 love shall be our token; love be yours and love be mine (3)
400 myrrh from the forest and gold from the mine (3)
401 visit, then, this soul of mine (3)
402 myrrh is mine; its bitter perfume breathes...gloom (4)
415 and melt mine eyes to tears (4)
417 upon that cross of Jesus mine eye at times can see (2)
418 mine was the transgression, but thine the deadly pain (2)
435 were the whole realm of nature mine (4)
466 come down, O Love divine, seek thou this soul of mine (T,1)
527 Jesus, and all in him, is mine (4)
542 a song of peace for lands afar and mine (1)
542 with hopes and dreams as true and high as mine (1)
542 and skies are everywhere as blue as mine (2)
542 a song of peace for their land and for mine (2)
545 mine eyes have seen the glory of the coming of the Lord (T)

mines
215 deep in unfathomable mines of never-failing skill (2)
548 the glory that illumines patriot lives of deathless fame (3)

mingled
435 sorrow and love flow mingled down (3)

ministries
273 turn my dreams to noble action, ministries of love (4)

minutest
279 and mourn for the minutest fault in exquisite distress (2)
280 and mourn for the minutest fault in exquisite distress (2)

miracle
434 there adoring at this feet mark the miracle of time (3)

mirth
21 Him serve with mirth, his praise forth tell (1)
25 one day with thee ... exceeds a thousand days of mirth (1)

misdeed
526 if thou rememberest each misdeed (1)

misery
284 in all my pain and misery be thou my health and life (3)
463 by whose cross & death are we rescued from sin's misery (2)
529 I need not tell thee who I am, my sin and misery declare (2)

miss
46 nor miss our providential way (2)
470 grant us courage lest we miss thy kingdom's goal (3)

mission
251 soon shall close thy earthly mission (4)
299 O Zion, haste, thy mission high fulfilling (T,1)
299 mission ... to tell to all the world that God is Light (1)
339 O let them spread thy name, their mission fully prove (4)

mists
136 until our minds are free from mists of error (2)
136 mists ... of doubt which blind our eyes to thee (2)
372 mid mists & rocks & quick-sands, still guides ...to thee (3)
462 lifting the raveled mists of night (2)
492 the mists of error and of vice which shade the universe (2)

misunderstand
244 when I've done the best I can &... friends misunderstand (3)

mite
187 not a mite would I withhold (2)

mixture
41 mixture strange of good and ill (2)

moan
376 in the bleak midwinter, frosty wind made moan (T,1)
407 the curse of greed, the moan of pain (2)

mocked
355 upon a cross ... bound thee & mocked thy saving kingship (1)
355 mocked ... by thorns with which they crowned thee (1)
419 and mocked the cross and flame (3)
469 by wars and tumults love is mocked, derided (2)

mocking
453 mocking thus the Savior's claim (3)

mold
154 mold me and make me after thy will (1)
198 new arts shall bloom of loftier mold (4)

molest
220 foes who would molest me cannot reach me here (2)
232 where sin and sense molest no more (4)

moment
102 come thou, this moment, at his call (5)
152 and every moment watch and pray (3)
182 and from this moment, live or die to serve my God alone (2)
221 listening every moment to the Spirit's call (4)

242 once to every man and nation comes the moment to decide (
279 that moment, Lord, reprove (2)
280 that moment, Lord, reprove (2)
507 the covenant we this moment make be ever kept in mind (3)
531 each moment draw from earth away my heart (4)

moments
187 take my moments and my days (1)
329 make all our moments calm and bright (5)

monarch
99 hath he diadem, as monarch, that his brow adorns (3)
400 Maker and Monarch and Savior of all (2)
504 Monarch of all things, fit us for thy mansions (2)

monarch's
184 if it would reach a monarch's throne (4)

monarchs
32 ye monarchs, wait his nod (5)

money
104 without money, come to Jesus Christ and buy (2)

moon
35 sun and moon, and stars of light (2)
37 moon shines full at his command, and all the stars obey (1)
41 moon and stars, thy power displayed (2)
42 sun and moon, rejoice before him (1)
43 the moon takes up the wondrous tale (2)
44 the moon and stars ordained by thee (2)
57 neath sun or moon, by day or night ... not be afraid (3)
60 thou silver moon with softer gleam (1)
263 sun, moon, and stars forgot, upward I fly (5)
365 sun, moon ... stars convey thy praise round the... earth (3)
474 sun and moon and stars decay (1)

moonlight
79 fair is the sunshine, fairer still the moonlight (3)

moons
472 till moons shall wax and wane no more (1)

moor
272 sure it still will lead me on o'er moor and fen (3)
402 field and fountain, moor and mountain (1)

morass
406 through desert ways, dark fen, and deep morass (2)

more
10 more than all, the heart must bear the longest part (2)
12 I know thee ... in part, I ask not, Lord, for more (3)
14 till suns shall rise and set no more (2)
19 higher than ... cherubim more glorious than ... seraphim (2)
36 but higher far, and far more clear (4)
41 teach us more of human pity that we in thine image grow (3

48	what more can he say than to you he hath said (1)
50	I thank thee more that all our joy is touched with pain (3)
50	we have enough, yet not too much, to long for more (4)
52	praise thee for thy mercies past, & humbly hope for more (3)
54	in more ancient years (1)
69	a kindness in his justice which is more than liberty (1)
69	welcome for the sinner and more graces for the good (1)
69	if our love were but more simple, we should take him at (2)
80	my soul would be still more and more conformed to thee (4)
94	weep, believe, and sin no more (3)
102	this is the time; no more delay (5)
104	he is able, he is able, he is willing; doubt no more (1)
107	saying, Christian, love me more (3)
107	Christian, love me more than these (4)
109	let me more of their beauty see (1)
111	worst need keep him out no more or force him to depart (2)
115	we more than taste the heavenly powers (2)
125	more than all in thee I find (3)
127	Lord, I believe were sinners more than sands (4)
127	sinners more than sands upon the ocean shore (4)
136	descend upon thy Church once more & make it truly thine (1)
142	faith that shines more bright & clear when tempests rage (3)
145	thou the spring of all my comfort, more than life for me (4)
146	and thou, O Lord, art more than they (4)
146	let knowledge grow from more to more (5)
146	but more of reverence in us dwell (5)
149	what seems, each time I tell it, more wonderfully sweet (3)
149	more wonderful it seems than all the golden fancies (2)
155	do but themselves confound, His strength the more is (2)
173	once more to hear thy challenge above our noisy day (5)
175	chords that were broken will vibrate once more (3)
176	more than friend or life to me (1)
178	far more for others' sins than... wrongs that we receive (3)
185	more love to thee, O Christ, more love to thee (T,1)
185	this is my earnest plea: more love, O Christ, to thee (1)
185	more love, O Christ, to thee ... more love to thee (R)
185	this all my prayer shall be: more love O Christ, to thee (2)
185	when they can sing with me, more love, O Christ, to thee (3)
185	this still its prayer shall be: more love, O Christ (4)
196	I'll take the gifts he hath bestowed, & ... ask for more (1)
196	and humbly ask for more (1)
208	Jesus, precious Jesus! O for grace to trust him more (R)
226	Savior, more than life to me (T,1)
226	let me love thee more and more (3)
227	angels could do nothing more, than to fall at his feet (3)
232	where sin and sense molest no more (4)
232	a place than all beside more sweet (2)
250	who ... strength of Jesus trusts is more than conqueror (1)
255	and none more blest than I (3)
260	our lives are prayers thou lovest more (1)
260	more than our minds seek thee (4)
260	no more we seek thee from afar, nor ask thee for a sign (4)
271	bread of heaven, feed me till I want no more (1)
274	with a step more firm and free (2)
279	from thee that I no more may stray (3)
279	no more thy goodness grieve (3)
280	from thee that I no more may stray (3)

404 and God sent us salvation that blessed Christmas morn (3)
418 how does that visage languish .. once was bright as morn (1)
451 that Easter morn at break of day (2)
502 abide with me from morn till eve (3)

morning
  4 by morning glow or evening shade his watchful eye ne'er (2)
  7 see the morning sun ascending radiant in the eastern sky (T)
 11 morning, evening, bless his name (2)
 26 early in the morning our song shall rise to thee (1)
 34 the sunset, and the morning that brightens up the sky (2)
 36 and when the morning breaks in power, we hear thy word (3)
 38 chorus, which the morning stars began (4)
 45 morning light ... lily white declare ... maker's praise (2)
 47 with each new day, when morning lifts the veil (1)
 90 we would see Jesus in the early morning (5)
 91 when morning gilds che skies, my heart awaking cries (T,1)
169 in the glad morning of my day (2)
180 joyful rise to pay thy morning sacrifice (1)
180 disperse my sins as morning dew (2)
264 still, still with thee, when purple morning breaketh (T,1)
264 still, still with thee! as to each new-born morning (3)
264 so shall it be the last, in that bright morning (5)
264 in that bright morning when the soul waketh (5)
264 fairer than morning, lovelier than daylight (1)
289 heaven's morning breaks, and earth's vain shadows flee (5)
353 when morning dawns and light triumphant breaks (1)
353 crowned with glory like the sun...lights the morning sky (2)
353 brighter than the glorious morn ... this fair morning be (4)
353 fair morning be when Christ oiur King in beauty comes (4)
353 the King shall come when morning dawns (5)
358 for the morning seems to dawn (3)
373 and usher in the morning (1)
381 O morning stars, together proclaim the holy birth (2)
384 and stay by my cradle till morning is nigh (2)
386 yea, Lord, we greet thee, born this happy morning (3)
396 shepherds keeping vigil till the morning new (2)
399 O morning star, how fair and bright (T,1)
400 brightest and best of the sons of the morning (T,1)
405 fairer than the sun at morning was the star (2)
433 the bright and morning star shed its beams around me (2)
452 welcome, happy morning age to age shall say (T,1,4)
452 'tis thine own third morning, rise, O buried Lord (3)
472 rise with every morning sacrifice (2)
478 gladness breaks like morning where'er thy face appears (3)
495 when the morning wakens, then may I arise pure and fresh (6)
497 may we, born anew like morning, to labor rise (2)
499 new every morning is the love (T,1)
499 new every morning is the love our wakening...prove (1)
500 to thee our morning hymns ascended (1)
503 Lord of angels, on our eyes let eternal morning rise (4)
529 the morning breaks, the shadows flee (4)
545 he is coming like the glory of the morning on the wave (5)

morns
 33 the radiant morns unfold (2)

morrow
333   and to life's day the glorious unknown morrow (3)
333   morrow that dawns upon eternal love and life (3)
396   praises voicing greet the morrow (2)

mortal
2   thou who art beyond the farthest mortal eye can scan (2)
20   let goods and kindred go, this mortal life also (4)
20   our helper he amid the flood of mortal ills prevailing (1)
31   no mortal eye can bear the sight (1)
86   while in our mortal pain none calls on thee in vain (2)
92   and mortal life shall cease (5)
115   a country far from mortal sight (1)
139   and God is seen by mortal eye (6)
237   on thy truth relying, through that mortal strife (4)
324   let all mortal flesh keep silence (T,1)
332   let the wisest mortal show how we the grace receive (2)
347   through mortal motive, scheme .. plan thy... purpose ran (2)
371   thou hast revealed thy will to mortal men (2)
411   will is life and good for all of mortal breath (1)
412   for me, kind Jesus, was...thy mortal sorrow (4)
412   for me ... thy mortal sorrow, and thy life's oblation (4)
419   like him... pardon on his tongue in midst of mortal pain (2)
424   and mortal men and all things created make reply (2)
425   bow thy meek head to mortal pain (4)
426   robed in mortal flesh is dying crucified by sin for me (2)
429   Satan hath lost his mortal power (3)
446   nor the watchers, nor the seal hold thee as a mortal (4)
468   justice, from her heavenly bower look down on mortal men (1)
509   seal in silence mortal tongues (5)
547   let mortal tongues awake; let all that breathe partake (3)

mortals
14   your lofty themes, ye mortals, bring (3)
38   mortals join the happy chorus, which the... stars began (4)
381   while mortals sleep, the angels keep their watch (2)
431   unheard by mortals are the strains that sweetly soothe (4)

most
19   most gracious, magnify the Lord (2)
27   most blessed, most glorious, the Ancient of days (1)
60   thou, most kind and gentle death (6)
69   the heart of the Eternal is most wonderfully kind (2)
90   Mary's son most holy, Light of the village life (2)
90   shining revealed through every task most lowly (2)
265   most gracious Lord (1)
265   Most Holy One ... thou blessed Son (5)
324   alleluia, alleluia, alleluia, Lord most high (4)
344   good desired and wanted most ...thy richest grace supply (1)
351   bless thou this house that it may be a place most meet (1)
351   a place most meet to learn of thee (1)
397   as they offered gifts most rare at... manger rude & bare (3)
397   so, most gracious Lord, may we evermore be led to thee (1)
412   by foes derided, by thine own rejected, O most afflicted (1)
435   all the vain things that charm me most, I sacrifice them (2)
451   on this most holy day of days, our hearts ... we raise (5)

488 O balm of care and sadness, most beautiful, most bright (1)
488 thus on thee most glorious a triple light was given (2)
497 strong through thee whate'er befall us, O God most wise (2)
498 Jesus, for thy love most tender on the cross ... shown (2)
501 they who fain would serve thee best are conscious most (4)
501 conscious most of wrong within (4)
503 Heaven and earth are praising thee, O Lord most high (R)
513 and what thou most desirest, our humble, thankful hearts (3)
548 praise thee most for things unseen (1)
551 the land we love the most (1)

mother
60 dear mother earth, who day by day unfoldest blessings (4)
247 mother stills ... child ... canst hush ... ocean wild (1)
376 but his mother only, in her maiden bliss, worshiped (3)
378 the which his mother Mary did nothing take in scorn (2)
393 round yon virgin mother and child (1)
517 since the day the blessed mother thee ... bore (2)

mother's
4 as with a mother's tender hand (3)
49 who, from our mother's arms hath blessed us on our way (1)
380 there's a mother's deep prayer and a baby's low cry (1)
517 didst deign a child to be cradled on a mother's bosom (1)
517 throned upon a mother's knee (1)

motion
252 the motion of a hidden fire that trembles in the breast (1)
531 reign alone, the Lord of every motion there (2)

motive
266 each thought and each motive beneath his control (4)
347 through mortal motive, scheme .. plan thy... purpose ran (2)

mount
93 mount of thy redeeming love (1)

mountain
11 towering mountain, canyon deep (3)
17 when I look down from lofty mountain grandeur (2)
32 shall not, in the mountain pine, disturb a sparrows nest (3)
34 the purple-headed mountain, the river running by (2)
38 field and forest, vale and mountain, flowery meadow (2)
90 we would see Jesus on the mountain teaching (3)
137 that faith that conquers all, and doth the mountain move (4)
201 who lovest all thy lost ones on every mountain steep (1)
245 or climbing the mountain way steep (3)
308 a mountain that shall fill the earth (4)
400 gems of the mountain and pearls of the ocean (3)
402 field and fountain, moor and mountain (1)
404 go, tell it on the mountain (T,R)
406 through jungles, sluggish seas, and mountain pass (2)
433 healing stream flows from calvary's mountain (1)
434 Calvary's mournful mountain climb (3)
543 for purple mountain majesties above the fruited plain (1)
547 from every mountain side let freedom ring (1)

mountain's
358 traveler, o'er yon mountain's height see (1)

mountains
27   thy justice like mountains high soaring above (2)
37   that made the mountains rise (1)
40   thy fingers spread the mountains and plains (1)
346   mountains lift their solemn forms to watch in silence (2)
346   mountains ... watch in silence o'er the land (2)
359   before him on the mountains shall peace, the herald, go (3)
374   and the mountains in reply echoing their joyous strains (1)

mountainside
204   O Master, from the mountainside, make haste to heal (5)

mounts
33   life mounts in every throbbing vein (2)

mourn
268   I hate the sins that made thee mourn (4)
278   no longer ... my heart shall mourn ... purified by grace (3)
279   and mourn for the minutest fault in exquisite distress (2)
280   and mourn for the minutest fault in exquisite distress (2)
292   the poor, and them that mourn, the faint and overborne (1)
345   who mourn ...they who fear, be strengthened as they pray (3)
474   cease, ye pilgrims, cease to mourn (3)
479   still in grief men mourn their dead (2)
492   may we this life improve, to mourn for errors past (4)

mourner's
502   be every mourner's sleep tonight like infant's slumbers (5)

mournful
1   mournful, broken hearts rejoice; the humble poor believe (5)
100   ye weary spirits, rest; ye mournful souls, be glad (2)
434   Calvary's mournful mountain climb (3)

mourning
219   and turnest my mourning into praise (4)

mourns
354   mourns in lonely exile here until the Son of God appear (1)

mouth
267   open my mouth, and let me bear gladly the warm truth (3)
335   let them from the mouth of God ... solemn charge receive (1)

move
15   him, in whom they move and live, let every creature sing (3)
22   when rolling years shall cease to move (4)
43   solemn silence ... move round the dark terrestrial ball (3)
62   to him let each affection daily rise and round him move (4)
63   man decays and ages move; but his mercy waneth never (2)
118   what shall I say thy grace to move (4)
128   while to that sacred shrine I move (2)
131   on our disordered spirits move ... let ... now be light (3)
137   that faith that conquers all, and doth the mountain move (4)
138   wean it from earth, through all its pulses move (1)
162   at thy bidding may I move, prompt to serve & follow thee (2)
170   help me the slow of heart to move (2)

184 it cannot freely move till thou hast wrought its chain (2)
187 take my hands ... let them move ... impulse of thy love (1)
193 ever toward each other move, and ever move toward thee (4)
210 builds on the rock that naught can move (1)
278 my steadfast soul, from falling free ... no longer move (4)
299 God, in whom they live and move, is Love (3)
465 Father, in whom we live, in whom we are, and move (T,1)
471 not heaven's hosts shall swifter move than we on earth (4)
480 move o'er the waters' face, bearing the lamp of grace (3)
529 speak, or thou never hence shalt move (3)
529 to me, to all, thy mercies move (4)
530 move and actuate and guide; divers gifts to each divide (3)

moved
57 he will not let thy foot be moved (2)
96 he moved my soul to seek him, seeking me (1)
131 come, Holy Ghost, for moved by thee the prophets wrote (2)
131 moved by thee, the prophets wrote and spoke (2)
469 Spirit of life, which moved ere form was made (1)

moves
36 creation lives and moves in thee (1)
41 thou whose purpose moves before us toward the goal (4)
215 God moves in a mysterious way his wonders to perform (T,1)
305 like a mighty army moves the Church of God (2)

much
50 we have enough, yet not too much, to long for more (4)
96 'twas not so much that I on thee took hold (2)
121 much we need thy tender care (1)
149 it did so much for me (2)
156 I would be strong, for there is much to suffer (1)
156 I would be brave, for there is much to dare (1)
215 the clouds ye so much dread are big with mercy (3)
266 spend much time in secret with Jesus alone (2)
378 the shepherds at those tidings rejoiced much in mind (4)
513 much more, to us his children, he gives our daily bread (2)

muffled
290 and so beside the silent sea I wait the muffled oar (4)

multitude
242 the multitude make virtue of the faith they had denied (2)

multitudes
204 yet long these multitudes to see ... thy face (4)

murmur
4 every faithless murmur stills (1)
142 will not murmur nor complain beneath the chastening rod (2)
217 nor ever murmur nor repine; content whatever lot I see (3)

murmuring
270 the murmuring wind, the quivering leaf ... tell us (3)

murmurs
164 above the storms of passion, the murmurs of self-will (3)

music
1	music in the sinner's ears ... life and health and peace (3)
11	with sweet music fill the air (1)
15	all the powers of music bring, the music of the heart (2)
38	joyful music leads us sunward (4)
45	round me rings the music of the spheres (1)
58	the Spirit who in them did sing to us his music lendeth (3)
60	make music for thy Lord to hear, Alleluia (3)
81	may the music of thy name refresh my soul in death (5)
146	that mind and soul, according well, may make one music (5)
146	may make one music as before (5)
198	and mightier music thrill the skies (4)
199	wild war music o'er the earth shall cease (5)
199	stormy clangor of wild war music o'er the earth (5)
343	sweet music fills the world abroad with strains of love (1)
343	Lord, while the music round us floats (3)
390	still ... heavenly music floats o'er all the weary world (2)
455	hark ... heavenly anthem drowns all music but its own (1)
532	whose music like a mighty wind the souls of men uplifted (3)
547	let music swell the breeze (3)

music's
2	craftman's art and music's measure for thy pleasure (3)
2	art ... music's measure for thy pleasure all combine (3)

must
10	more than all, the heart must bear the longest part (2)
10	church with psalms must shout, no door can keep them out (2)
13	there a heaven on earth must be (2)
20	he must win the battle (2)
22	firm as a rock thy truth must stand (4)
75	he who would the Father seek, must seek him...by thee (1)
75	must seek him, Lord, by thee (1)
78	at the great name of Jesus, now all knees must bend (2)
78	all hearts must bow; all things celestial thee shall own (2)
120	thou must save, and thou alone (2)
167	if I must weep with thee, "My Lord, thy will be done" (2)
183	must Jesus bear the cross alone (T,1)
183	must ... all the world go free (1)
184	it must its crown resign (4)
218	and this thy grace must give (1)
218	he that into God's kingdom comes must enter by this door (3)
220	whate'er we must bear still in thee lies purest pleasure (3)
239	must I be carried to the skies on flowery beds of ease (2)
239	must I not stem the flood (3)
239	sure I must fight, if I would reign (4)
242	they must upward still & onward who would keep ... truth (3)
248	lift high the royal banner, it must not suffer loss (1)
257	thou must work all good within us (2)
258	come, my soul, thou must be waking (T ,1)
335	souls that must forever live in rapture or in woe (3)
355	doomed to death, must bring to doom the power (2)
366	for ye must go to meet him there (1)
414	O dearly, dearly has he loved, and we must love him, too (5)
430	pressing onward as we can ..to this our hearts must tend (4)
442	in his grace of glad new birth we must seek revival (2)
515	and daily must the prayer be said (1)
517	for... children thou hast given we must answer unto thee (1)
526	but must confess thy grace hath wrought (2)

mutual
306   we share each other's woes, our mutual burdens bear (3)

myriad
371   myriad tongues, in one great anthem blending (4)

myriads
129   and myriads wait for his word (5)

myrrh
383   and offered there, in his presence, their gold and myrrh (5)
383   gold and myrrh and frankincense (5)
385   so bring him incense, gold, and myrrh (3)
400   myrrh from the forest and gold from the mine (3)
402   myrrh is mine; its bitter perfume breathes ... gloom (4)
405   gold and frankincense and myrrh (3)
405   myrrh his sepulcher foreshows (4)

myself
118   weary of earth, myself, and sin (1,5)
118   I own it cannot be that I should fit myself for thee (3)
120   Rock of Ages, cleft for me, let me hide myself in thee (T,1)
120   Rock of Ages, cleft for me, let me hide myself in thee (3)
169   to consecrate myself to thee, O Jesus Christ, I come (1)
182   myself, my residue of days, I consecrate to thee (1)
184   I sink in life's alarms when by myself I stand (1)
187   take myself, and I will be ever, only, all for thee (3)
188   not for myself alone may my prayer be (3)
225   where thou ... all my soul possess and I may find myself (2)
259   myself to thee entirely give (1)
415   here, Lord, I give myself away; 'tis all that I can do (5)
493   that with the world, myself, and thee...at peace may be (2)
542   myself I give thee; let thy will be done (3)

mysterious
209   all now mysterious shall be bright at last (2)
215   God moves in a mysterious way his wonders to perform (T,1)
328   who thy mysterious supper share, here at thy table fed (2)
426   O mysterious condescending! O abandonment sublime! (3)

mystery
8   adoring bend the knee while we own the mystery (4)
123   Joseph's tomb could solve death's mystery (3)
285   cannot reach the mystery ... length .. breadth .. height (2)
458   their profit & their joy to know the mystery of his love (5)
527   'tis mystery all! the Immortal dies! (2)

mystic
35   for the mystic harmony linking sense to sound and sight (3)
41   marveling at thy mystic ways (1)
225   a little place of mystic grace (4)
264   alone with thee amid the mystic shadows (2)
297   and mystic sweet communion with those whose rest is won (4)
315   furnished with mystic wine and everlasting bread (1)
331   banquet spreads before us of his mystic flesh and blood (1)
405   sacred gifts of mystic meaning (4)
530   hear us, who thy nature share, who thy mystic body are (1)

nailed
- 364 pierced and nailed him to the tree (2)
- 428 behold the Savior of mankind nailed to the shameful tree (T)
- 436 were you there when they nailed him to the tree (2)

name
- 1 spread thro' all the earth abroad the honors of thy name (2)
- 1 Jesus! the name that charms our fears (3)
- 1 name ... that bids our sorrows cease (3)
- 3 help us thy name to sing, help us to praise! (1)
- 4 o ye who name Christ's holy name (5)
- 7 round thy throne, thy name confessing, (4)
- 8 holy God, we praise thy name (T,1)
- 8 Lo! the apostolic train joins thy sacred name to hallow (3)
- 8 holy Father, holy Son, holy Spirit: three we name thee (4)
- 11 morning, evening, bless his name (2)
- 12 what heart can comprehend thy name (2)
- 14 let the Redeemer's name be sung (1)
- 14 shout for joy and Savior's name (3)
- 15 hallowed be his name beneath (3)
- 16 stand up and bless his glorious name (5)
- 16 who would not fear his holy name and laud and magnify (2)
- 20 Lord Sabaoth, his name, from age to age the same (2)
- 21 praise, laud, and bless his name always (3)
- 26 all thy works ... praise thy name in earth & sky & sea (4)
- 27 almighty, victorious, thy great name we praise (1)
- 30 praise to the living God! all praised be his name (T,1,3)
- 31 and will he write his name, my Father and my friend? (4)
- 31 I love his name, I love his word (4)
- 33 in ever-changing words of light, the wonder of thy name (3)
- 39 sing the great Jehovah's praise and bless his holy name (1)
- 39 all nations fear his name (3)
- 41 full of wonder is thy name o'er all the earth (1)
- 41 o how wondrous, o how glorious is thy name in every land (4)
- 42 laud and magnify his name (2)
- 44 how excellent thy name (1)
- 44 Lord, our Lord, in all the earth how excellent thy name (5)
- 54 thy providence protected them who thy great name adored (3)
- 54 in God our shield we will rejoice & ever bless thy name (5)
- 56 O magnify the Lord with me, with me exalt his name (2)
- 47 sing praises to his name: he forgets not his own (1)
- 59 thy name be ever praised! O Lord, make us free (3)
- 71 all hail the power of Jesus' name (T,1)
- 72 all hail the power of Jesus' name (T,1)
- 73 all hail the power of Jesus' name (T,1)
- 74 given the name to which all knees shall bow (4)
- 76 at the name of Jesus every knee shall bow (T,1)
- 76 humbled for a season, to receive a name (3)
- 78 at the great name of Jesus, now all knees must bend (2)
- 81 how sweet the name of Jesus sounds in a believer's ear (T,1)
- 81 may the music of thy name refresh my soul in death (5)
- 82 nor can the memory find a sweeter sound than thy... name (2)
- 82 sweeter sound than thy blest name, O Savior of mankind (2)
- 86 Christ our triumphant King, we come thy name to sing (1)
- 87 take the name of Jesus with you (T,1)
- 87 precious name, O how sweet! (R)

87	take the name of Jesus ever as a shield from every snare (2)
87	if temptations round you gather, breathe that holy name (2)
87	breathe that holy name in prayer (2)
87	O the precious name of Jesus! (3)
87	name of Jesus! How it thrills our souls with joy (3)
87	at the name of Jesus bowing (4)
89	from sin ... grief & shame, I hide me, Jesus in thy name (1)
89	thy mighty name salvation ... keeps my happy soul above (2)
89	to me, with thy great name, are given pardon (2)
94	oft profaned his hallowed name (2)
98	the sweetness of thy saving name (3)
108	shame on us,Christian brethren, his name & sign who bear (1)
110	they who believe on his name shall rejoice (4)
114	can my gracious Savior show my name inscribed in heaven (1)
122	my name is written on his hands (1)
124	what the high reward I win, whose the name I glory in (1)
125	just & holy is thy name; I am all unrighteousness (3)
137	Spirit of faith, descend and show the virtue of his name (3)
139	to him ... in thy name believes eternal life ...is given (4)
152	forth in thy name, O Lord, I go (T,1)
157	last low whispers of our dead are burdened with his name (5)
157	O Lord and Master of us all; whate'er our name or sign (6)
196	offer the sacrifice of praise, and call upon his name (4)
196	my vows I will to his great name before his people pay (3)
222	but wholly lean on Jesus' name (1)
227	what a heaven in Jesus's name (2)
236	Savior, again to thy dear name we raise (T,1)
236	that in this house have called upon thy name (2)
239	shall I fear to own his cause .. blush to speak his name (1)
243	still made their glory in thy name (1)
253	to thee and thy great name (4)
274	speak to me by name, O Master, let me know it is to me (2)
281	hallow thy great and glorious name (2)
282	write thy new name upon my heart (5)
282	thy new, best name of Love (5)
297	one holy name she blesses, partakes one holy food (2)
307	planted thy holy name within our hearts (1)
309	let us in thy name agree (1)
310	thy name salvation is, which here we come to prove (2)
310	thy name is life and joy and peace and everlasting love (2)
310	thou in the midst of us shalt be, assembled in thy name (1)
312	nor scorn their humble name (2)
325	bless the founder's name (4)
339	O let them spread thy name, their mission fully prove (4)
341	Jesus ... name to sinners dear ... name to sinners given (2)
341	bold to confess thy glorious name before a world of foes (4)
341	happy, if with my latest breath I may but gasp his name (6)
341	Jesus! the name high over all, in hell or earth or sky (T,1)
342	baptizing in the name of Father, Son, and Spirit (2)
344	thy name confessed and glorified (4)
348	ever, Lord, thy name be known (1)
352	a joyful sacrifice to thy blest name (2)
359	his name shall stand forever; that name to us is love (4)
361	his name shall be the Prince of Peace forevermore adored (3)
365	but when our eyes behold thy Word, we read thy name (1)
365	we read thy name in fairer lines (1)
367	forever be thy name adored for these celestial lines (1)

378 how that in Bethlehem was born the Son of God by name (3)
395 praise his name in all the earth; Hail the King of glory (3)
407 mighty God, set us aflame to show the glory of thy name (3)
408 One Lord, in one great name united us all who own thee (3)
409 and publish abroad his wonderful name (1)
409 that name all-victorious of Jesus extol (1)
424 who in the Lord's name comest, the King and blessed One (1)
445 He lives, all glory to his name (4)
449 thy name we bless, O risen Lord (4)
453 own his title, praise his name (3)
454 life is given through thy name (1)
458 to whom he manifests his love & grants his name to know (3)
458 name an everlasting name; their joy the joy of heaven (4)
461 let our whole soul an offering be to our Redeemer's name (2)
472 his name like sweet perfume shall rise (2)
472 their early blessings on his name (3)
479 forth in thy dear name we go to the child, the youth (4)
489 pray ... through the dear Redeemer's name (2)
489 here we come thy name to praise (3)
507 His name to glorify (2)
516 happy the home where Jesus' name is sweet to every ear (2)
529 thyself hast called me by my name (2)
529 tell me thy name and tell me now (2)
529 and tell me if thy name be Love (3)
529 thy nature and thy name is Love (4)
536 thy name, O Jesus, be forever blest, Alleluia, Alleluia (1)
547 thy name I love (2)
548 souls that passed and left no name (3)
550 here thy name, O God of love ... children shall adore (4)

name's
68 e'en for his own name's sake (2)

named
532 the fathers named in story (1)

nameless
304 O shepherd of the nameless fold (T,1)

names
106 wondering if our names were there (3)
530 names and sects and parties fall: thou, O Christ art all (5)
532 praise we the glorious names we know (5)
532 whose names have perished, lost in the haze of long ago (5)

narrow
159 till I cross the narrow sea (4)
175 back to the narrow way patiently win them (4)
302 though now divided by...the narrow stream of death (3)
397 Holy Jesus, every day keep us in the narrow way (4)
517 little feet our steps may follow in a safe & narrow way (3)

natal
382 ye have seen his natal star (3)

nation
18 his the voice that called a nation (1)
198 nation with nation, land with land, inarmed shall live (3)

242   once to every man and nation comes the moment to decide (T)
297   elect from every nation, yet one o'er all the earth (2)
299   proclaim to every people, tongue, and nation (3)
360   dear desire of every nation, joy of every longing heart (1)
398   till every tongue and nation, from sin's dominion free (3)
408   the Day-star clear and bright of every man and nation (1)
469   through the thick darkness covering every nation (1)
469   nation by nation still goes unforgiven (3)
484   lift up a living nation, a single sword to thee (3)
532   and made our folk a nation (2)
546   cleanse the body of this nation through the glory (2)
548   from the strife of class & faction make our nation free (4)
548   make our nation free indeed (4)

nation's
355   nation's pride o'erthrown went down to dust beside thee (2)
356   O let thy Word be light anew to every nation's life (3)

nations
11   nations, come, your voices raise to the Lord in hymns (1)
22   ye nations, bow with sacred joy (1)
32   ye nations bend, in reverence bend (5)
39   his wonders to the nations show (1)
39   all nations fear his name (3)
91   ye nations of mankind, in this your concord find (3)
100   let all the nations know, to earth's remotest bound (1)
151   we will strive to win all nations unto thee (2)
173   who would unite the nations in brotherhood for all (3)
191   the patriots nations need ... the bulwarks of the state (4)
299   he who made all nations is not willing one ... perish (1)
311   gather all the nations in (5)
354   O come, Desire of nations (3)
362   power and pomp of nations shall pass like a dream away (2)
362   he stands in the midst of nations (3)
365   till Christ has all the nations blest (4)
365   nations ...that see the light or feel the sun (4)
372   to bear before the nations thy true light as of old (4)
380   in the homes of the nations that Jesus is King (3)
382   seek the great Desire of nations (3)
387   joyful, all ye nations rise (1)
392   makes the nations prove the glories of his righeeousness (4)
407   who hast the nations in thy heart (1)
410   we've a story to tell to the nations (T,1)
410   we've a song to be sung to the nations (2)
410   we've a message to give to the nations (3)
410   we've a Savior to show to the nations (4)
460   through the rise and fall of nations (3)
464   Jesus' love the nations fires (1)
468   thou art he who shall by right the nations all possess (2)
468   the nations all whom thou hast made shall come (3)
471   o'er all the nations let it flow (3)
488   today on weary nations the heavenly manna falls (3)
542   this is my song, O God of all the nations (T,1)
542   O hear my song, thou God of all the nations (2)
542   O hear my prayer, thou God of all the nations (3)
544   peace to the nations, and praise to the Lord (4)
551   Lord of the nations, thus to thee our country we commend (4)

native
- 252   prayer ... the Christian's native air (5)
- 474   rise ... toward heaven, thy native place (1)
- 547   my native country, thee, Land of the noble free (2)
- 551   of every clime and coast, O hear us for our native land (1)

nature
- 45   and to my listening ears all nature sings (1)
- 53   hand which bears all nature up shall guard his children (2)
- 79   fairest Lord Jesus, ruler of all nature (T,1)
- 264   the solemn hush of nature newly born (2)
- 282   thy nature, gracious Lord, impart (5)
- 342   we cultivate the nature God plants in every heart (3)
- 392   and heaven and nature sing (1)
- 428   hark, how he groans, while nature shakes (2)
- 435   were the whole realm of nature mine (4)
- 492   how beauteous nature now! How dark and sad before (3)
- 512   all nature joins in singing a joyful song of praise (2)
- 529   thy nature and thy name is Love (4)
- 530   hear us, who thy nature share, who thy mystic body are (1)

nature's
- 131   brood o'er our nature's night (3)
- 132   pierce the clouds of nature's night (1)
- 343   nature's works ... to whom they all belong (1)
- 343   all nature's works his praise declare (T,1)
- 492   and nature's God adore (3)
- 527   fast bound in sin and nature's night (3)

naught
- 27   and wither and perish, but naught changeth thee (3)
- 163   those ties which naught can sever (1)
- 163   naught ... I have my own I call ... hold it for the giver (2
- 210   builds on the rock that naught can move (1)
- 214   their evil acts shall surely come to naught (4)
- 220   I will suffer naught to hide thee (1)
- 220   I will ... ask for naught beside thee (1)
- 229   on Jesus' bosom naught but calm is found (3)
- 256   naught be all else to me, save that thou art (1)
- 364   those who set at naught and sold him (2)
- 427   is this thy sorrow naught to us who pass unheeding by (1)
- 450   life is naught without thee; aid us in our strife (3)
- 464   worthy ... work of him...who spake a world from naught (3)
- 494   thou, whose all-pervading eye naught escapes (2)
- 494   eye naught escapes without, within (2)

nay
- 99   if I ask him to receive me, will he say me nay (6)

Nazareth
- 171   O Carpenter of Nazareth, Builder of life divine (2)

ne'er
- 3   ne'er from us depart, Spirit of power! (3)
- 4   by morning glow or evening shade his watchful eye ne'er (2)
- 4   his watchful eye ne'er sleepeth (2)
- 9   days of praise shall ne'er be past while life ... last (1,4)
- 45   ne'er forget that though the wrong seems oft so strong (3)
- 71   sinners, whose love can ne'er forget the wormwood (3)

243   heroic warriors, ne'er from Christ ... enticed (2)
246   O watch and fight and pray; the battle ne'er give o'er (2)
246   ne'er think the victory won, nor lay thine armor down (3)
415   drops of grief can ne'er repay the debt of love I owe (5)
519   ne'er forget God's daily care (T,1)
521   though he giveth or he taketh, God ... ne'er forsaketh (4)
521   God his children ne'er forsaketh (4)
526   our works could ne'er our guilt remove (2)
534   journey which faithless feet ne'er trod (1)

near
  2   can we feel that thou art near ... hear ...? yea, we can (2)
  2   can we feel that thou art near us and wilt hear us? (2)
 12   in all thy love so near (1)
 46   while love, almighty love, is near (2)
 49   O may this bounteous God though all our life be near us (2)
 55   all ye who hear,now to his temple draw near (1)
 64   yet to each loving heart how near (1)
106   ever near the Christian's side (1)
106   ever present, truest friend ... near thine aid to lend (2)
115   we feel the resurrection near (2)
164   be thou forever near me, my Master and my Friend (1)
164   O let me feel thee near me, the world is ever near (2)
164   my foes are ever near me, around me and within (2)
211   in darkness and temptation, my light, my help is near (1)
213   no fraud, while thou, my God, art near (2)
226   let thy precious blood applied keep me ... near thy side (1)
238   and the endd of sorrow shall be near my throne (4)
240   faint not nor fear, for he is near (4)
245   O near to the Rock let me keep (3)
247   when at last I near the shore ... fearful breakers roar (3)
252   the upward glancing of an eye, when none but God is near (2)
253   that looks to thee when sin is near (3)
265   stay thou near by (2)
270   we smile at pain when thou art near (1)
270   our hearts still whispering, "Thou art near" (2)
270   quivering leaf shall softly tell us thou art near (3)
270   content to suffer while we know ... thou art near (4)
270   living or dying, thou art near (4)
279   a sensibility of sin, a pain to feel it near (1)
280   a sensibility of sin, a pain to feel it near (1)
293   showing that the Lord is near (3)
311   may her voice be ever clear, warning of a judgment near (2)
348   living stones prepared for the temple near thy throne (4)
350   when in faith our souls draw near (3)
363   the King of kings is drawing near (1)
367   Divine instructor, gracious Lord, be thou forever near (4)
379   as I hear, far and near, sweetest angels voices (1)
384   be near me, Lord Jesus, I ask thee to stay close by me (3)
390   angels bending near ... earth to touch ... harps of gold (1)
401   Day-spring from on high, be near (1)
420   crucified for me and you to bring us rebels near to God (2)
433   near the cross, a trembling soul, love & mercy found me (2)
433   near the cross .. Lamb of God bring its scenes before me (3)
433   near the cross I'll watch & wait, hoping, trusting ever (4)
456   heaven ... knows neither near nor far (2)
462   let us hear thy silent voice: "Lo, I am near" (4)
466   O Comforter, draw near, within my heart appear (1)

476   no time, no near nor far (1)
489   may we feel thy presence near (3)
501   we, oppressed with various ills, draw near (2)
502   it is not night if thou be near (1)
502   come near and bless us when we wake (6)
513   he only is the Maker of all things near and far (2)
525   for peace on earth, both far and near, we thank thee (1)

nearer
125   while the nearer waters roll (1)
147   kind the storm which drives us nearer home (2)
159   draw me nearer, nearer blessed Lord (R)
159   nearer ... to the cross where thou hast died (R)
159   nearer, blessed Lord, to thy precious, bleeding side (R)
164   but, Jesus, draw thou nearer, & shield my soul from sin (2)
263   nearer, my God, to thee, nearer to thee (T,1,R)
263   still all my song shall be, nearer, my God, to thee (1)
263   yet in my dreams I'd be nearer, my God, to thee (2)
263   angels to beckon me, nearer, my God, to thee (3)
263   so by my woes to be nearer, my God, to thee (4)
263   still all my song shall be, nearer, my God, to thee (5)
326   thou art here, nearer than ever, still my shield and sun (4)

nearing
244   when my life becomes a burden ... nearing chilly Jordan (4)

nearly
499   help us, this & every day to live more nearly as we pray (4)

nearness
264   breathe each day nearness unto thee and heaven (3)

neath
57   neath sun or moon, by day or night ... not be afraid (3)
203   neath the burdens there, thy sovereignty has held (3)
208   in simple faith to plunge me neath the healing ... flood (2)
208   plunge me neath the healing, cleansing flood (2)
377   in Bethlehem neath starlit skies (T,1)
539   neath his wings securely hide you (2)

need
41   conscious of our human need (4)
46   we shall not full direction need (2)
61   his full hand supplies their need (3)
95   mercy now, O Lord, I plead in this hour of utter need (3)
102   ye need not one be left behind (1)
104   all the fitness he requireth is to feel your need of him (3)
111   worst need keep him out no more or force him to depart (2)
119   yea, all I need, in thee to find (4)
121   much we need thy tender care (1)
144   I ask not, need not, aught beside (4)
173   O young and fearless prophet, we need thy presence here (5)
189   one claim unites all men in God to serve each human need (2)
191   the patriots nations need ... the bulwarks of the state (4)
200   whom shall I send to succor my people in their need (1)
201   nor seek our own salvation apart from others' need (2)
203   blazoned heights and slopes of need (1)
204   in haunts of wretchedness and need (2)

207 all you may need he will provide (3)
210 God never yet forsook at need the soul that trusted him (3)
219 I look to thee in every need and never look in vain (T,1)
260 to hear thy voice we need but love ... listen & be still (3)
265 I need thee every hour (T,1,2,3,4,5)
265 I need thee, O I need thee, every hour I need thee (R)
274 knowest all its truest need (3)
289 I need thy presence every passing hour (3)
379 all you need I will surely give you (2)
391 now ye need not fear the grave (3)
397 bring our ransomed souls at last where they need no star (4)
397 need no star to guide, where no clouds thy glory hide (4)
445 He lives, to help in time of need (2)
463 ever present help in need (1)
479 whose love ... bore the weight of human need (1)
481 no night, nor need, nor pain (1)
485 part them, Lord, to each and all, as each & all ... need (1)
511 a world in need now summons us to labor,love and give (2)
515 as large as is thy children's need (3)
528 no need of him the righteous have (4)
529 I need not tell thee who I am, my sin and misery declare (2)

needed
184 it wants the needed fire to glow ... the breeze to nerve (3)

needless
261 O what peace we often forfeit ... needless pain we bear (1)

needs
339 answer ... faith's effectual prayer ... our needs supply (1)
463 who upholds and comforts us in all trials, fears & needs (3)
479 making known the needs and burdens thy compassion bids (3)
479 needs and burdens thy compassion bids us bear (3)
490 all my countless needs thy kind hand supplies (3)

needy
104 come, ye sinners, poor and needy (T,1)
104 ye needy, come ... welcome; God's free bounty glorify (2)
315 our needy souls sustain with fresh supplies of love (2)
339 Lord of the harvest, hear the needy servants' cry (T,1)
359 to help the poor and needy, and bid the weak be strong (2)

neither
231 though vine nor fig tree neither ... fruit should bear (4)
446 neither might the gates of death ... tomb's dark portal (4)
456 heaven ... knows neither near nor far (2)
521 neither life nor death shall ever from the Lord .. sever (3)

nerve
135 fill and nerve this will of mine (3)
160 and brace thy heart and nerve thine arm (2)
184 it wants the needed fire to glow ... the breeze to nerve (3)
219 to nerve my faltering will (3)
249 awake, my soul, stretch every nerve (T,1)

nest
32 shall not, in the mountain pine, disturb a sparrows nest (3)
295 the swallow also for herself provided hath a nest (3)

nesting
521   nesting bird nor star in heaven such a refuge ... given (1)

net
84   draw thy protecting net around the catch of... apostles (2)

never
4   the Lord is never far away (3)
5   let those refuse to sing who never knew our God (2)
7   for his mercy ceasing never, for his blessing day by day (3)
11   waterfalls that never sleep (3)
20   a bulwark never failing (1)
42   laws which never shall be broken (1)
42   never shall his promise fail (2)
47   we own thy mercies, Lord, which never fail (1)
48   I'll never, no, never, no, never forsake (5)
57   thy guardian never sleeps (2)
58   we send it on, the song that never endeth (3)
63   man decays and ages move; but his mercy waneth never (2)
67   Shepherd ... whose goodness faileth never (1)
67   thy goodness faileth never (6)
77   his love shall never end: Alleluia! Amen! (2)
93   streams of mercy never ceasing call for songs (1)
104   if you tarry till you're better, you will never come (4)
130   immense and unconfined; from age to age it never ends (2)
130   grace ... wide as infinity ... it never passed by one (3)
133   so shall I never die (4)
149   some have never heard the message of salvation (3)
204   thy heart has never known recoil (3)
210   God never yet forsook at need the soul that trusted him (3)
219   I look to thee in every need and never look in vain (T,1)
223   but we never can prove the delights of his love until (3)
223   never can prove ... until all on the altar we lay (3)
223   never fear, only trust and obey (4)
226   trusting thee I cannot stray .. can never .. lose my way (2)
227   tongue can never express the sweet comfort and peace (1)
230   His wisdom ever waketh, his sight is never dim (2)
237   grant that I may never fail thy hand to see (3)
238   Christian, never tremble, never be downcast (2)
244   thou who never lost a battle, stand by me (2)
248   where duty calls or danger, be never wanting there (3)
261   we...never be discouraged, take it to the Lord in prayer (2)
268   they have left an aching void the world can never fill (3)
283   suddenly return and never, nevermore thy temples leave (3)
293   never fails from age to age (2)
293   grace, which like the Lord, the giver, never fails (2)
305   gates of hell can never gainst that Church prevail (3)
318   never to my hurt invited, be thy love with love requited (3)
337   to watch and pray, and never faint (4)
359   the tide of time shall never his covenant remove (4)
365   convey thy praise round the whole earth and never stand (3)
394   good will ... from heaven to men begin and never cease (6)
398   never shall darkness veil thee again from human eyes (1)
402   King forever, ceasing never over us all to reign (2)
409   and thanks never ceasing, and infinite love (4)
416   never shall the cross forsake me (2)
418   Lord, let me never, never outlive my love to thee (3)
421   dear dying Lamb, thy precious blood shalal never lose (3)

421 thy precious blood shall never lose its power (3)
430 never further than thy cross, never higher than thy feet (T)
440 never that full joy conceived (2)
441 thinking that never he would wake again (2)
496 thou art he... never weary, watchest where thy people be (3)
500 the voice of prayer is never silent (3)
500 so be it, Lord; thy throne shall never ... pass away (4)
500 thy throne shall never, like earth's proud empires, pass (4)
501 and some have never loved thee well (3)
507 never will throw off his fear who hears our solemn vow (4)
517 thou... crowned us with an honor women never knew before (2)
517 and be never led astray (3)
524 thrice blessed ... harvest song ... never hath an ending (3)
525 for love of thine, which never tires (3)
529 speak, or thou never hence shalt move (3)
545 trumpet that shall never call retreat (3)

nevermore
108 dear Savior, enter, enter, and leave us nevermore (3)
283 suddenly return and never, nevermore thy temples leave (3)

new
1 new life the dead receive (5)
47 with each new day, when morning lifts the veil (1)
132 author of the new creation, come with unction (2)
149 when in scenes of glory I sing the new, new song (4)
189 join the glorious new crusade of our great Lord and King (3)
198 new arts shall bloom of loftier mold (4)
206 new faith to find the paths ahead (1)
219 let me ... think of thee ... new heart springs up in me (2)
231 the theme of God's salvation, and find it ever new (2)
242 some great cause, God's new Messiah (1)
242 God's new Messiah, offering each the bloom or blight (1)
242 toiling up new Calvaries ever (3)
242 new occasions teach new duties (3)
277 old things shall be done away ... all things new become (2)
281 give me a new, a perfect heart (4)
282 write thy new name upon my heart (5)
282 thy new, best name of Love (5)
283 finish ...thy new creation, pure and spotless let us be (4)
297 she is his new creation by water and the word (1)
342 we call each new disciple to follow thee, O Lord (2)
355 still our wrongs may weave thee now new thorns (1)
355 new thorns to pierce that steady brow (1)
355 new advent of the love of Christ (3)
355 O wounded hands of Jesus, build in us thy new creation (4)
367 still new beauties may I see, and still increasing light (3)
396 shepherds keeping vigil till the morning new (2)
398 rise in... new creation which springs from love and thee (3)
407 await a new creative hour (3)
408 new life, new hope awakes where-e'er men own his sway (1)
442 in his grace of glad new birth we must seek revival (2)
462 spirit of life, in this new dawn (T,1)
488 new graces ever gaining from this our day of rest (4)
499 new every morning is the love (T,1)
499 new mercies, each returning day, hover around us (2)
499 new ... the love our wakening and uprising prove (1)

499 new perils past, new sins forgiven (2)
499 new thoughts of God, new hopes of heaven (2)
499 new mercies ... hover around us while we pray (2)
510 we all, with vows and anthems new, before our God appear (2)
511 all life in Christ made new (2)
517 grant us then a deeper insight & new powers of sacrifice (4)

newly
264 the solemn hush of nature newly born (2)

news
100 the gospel trumpet hear, the news of heavenly grace (4)
136 preach to all thy great good news (2)
377 to you the joyous news we bring (3)
406 pass on and carry swift the news ye bring (1)
449 to all the world glad news we bring (1)
476 inspire thy heralds of good news to live thy life divine (5)

next
49 and free us from all ills in this world and the next (2)
248 this day the noise of battle ... next, the victor's song (4)

nigh
7 Lord, we would to thee draw nigh (4)
44 on man thy wisdom ... bestowed a power well-nigh divine (4)
104 every grace that brings you nigh (2)
122 with confidence I now draw nigh (4)
138 teach me to feel that thou art always nigh (4)
220 till it well-nigh fainted, thirsting after thee (1)
255 when thou, O Lord, wast nigh (3)
255 I sigh to think of happier days, when thou...wast nigh (3)
265 temptations lose their power when thou art nigh (2)
279 awake my soul when sin is nigh, and keep it still awake (3)
280 awake my soul when sin is nigh and keep it still awake (3)
354 and order all things far and nigh (2)
383 this star drew nigh to the northwest (4)
384 and stay by my cradle till morning is nigh (2)
402 frankincense to offer have I, incense owns a Deity nigh (3)
409 and still he is nigh, his presence we have (2)
477 O day of God, draw nigh in beauty and in power (T,1)
477 O day of God, draw nigh as at creation's birth (5)
495 now the day is over, night is drawing nigh (T,1)
496 we are safe, if thou art nigh (2)
502 abide with me when night is nigh (3)
503 for thou art nigh (2)

night
2 angel harps forever ringing, rest not day nor night (1)
11 countless stars by night that shine (2)
28 short as the watch that ends the night (4)
32 ye winds of night, your force combine (3)
33 the solemn splendors of the night (2)
33 day unto day utter speech ... night to night proclaim (3)
35 for the beauty of each hour of the day and of the night (2)
36 thy grandeur in the march of night (3)
51 so shall this night soon end in joyous day (2)
57 neath sun or moon, by day or night ... not be afraid (3)
62 language, glad and golden, speaking to us day and night (1)

64 cheers the long watches of the night (2)
85 God's light to earth thou bringest to drive sin's night (1)
85 drive sin's night away (1)
91 the night becomes as day when from the heart we say (2)
97 he watches o'er me day and night (3)
97 following him by day and night, He's my friend (3)
129 my comfort by day and my song in the night (1)
131 brood o'er our nature's night (3)
132 pierce the clouds of nature's night (1)
148 dark the night of sin has settled (2)
155 I'll labor night and day to be a pilgrim (3)
161 lure us away from thee to endless night (3)
174 bring ... day of brotherhood ... end the night of wrong (2)
216 nor pestilence that walks by night (5)
233 from youth to age, by night and day (4)
236 grant us thy peace, Lord, through the coming night (3)
238 peace shall follow battle; night shall end in day (3)
239 by faith they bring it night (5)
256 thou my best thought, by day or by night (1)
257 till thy spirit breaks our night with the beams of truth (2)
258 for the night is safely ended (2)
269 involved in shadows of a darksome night (3)
272 the night is dark, & I am far from home, lead thou me on (1)
272 o'er crag and torrent, till the night is gone (3)
291 there God the Son forever reigns and scatters night away (2)
299 one soul should perish lost in shades of night (1)
329 chase the dark night of sin away (5)
337 by day and night strict guard to keep (4)
354 disperse the gloomy clouds of night (4)
355 in the night of hate and war we perish as we lose thee (3)
358 watchman, tell us of the night (T,1,2,3)
366 wake, awake, for night is flying (T,1)
366 come forth, ye virgins, night is past (1)
379 all my hear this night rejoices (T,1)
380 comes down through the night from the heavenly throng (4)
382 watching o'er your flocks by night (2)
383 on a cold winter's night that was so deep (1)
383 and so it continued both day and night (2)
393 silent night, holy night (T,1,2,3,4)
394 while shepherds watched their flocks by night (T,1)
395 all the plains were lit that night (2)
401 triumph o'er the shades of night (1)
402 O star of wonder, star of night (R)
404 o'er silent flocks by night (1)
408 freedom her bondage breaks, and night is turned to day (1)
431 'tis midnight, and on Olive's brow (T,1)
431 'tis midnight (1,2,3,4)
438 the night of sin is ended! Alleluia! (3)
462 lifting the raveled mists of night (2)
476 dispel the gloom of error's night, of ignorance & fear (3)
481 within whose four-square walls shall come no night (1)
481 no night, nor need, nor pain (1)
491 guard us through the coming night (1,2,3)
492 O let thine orient beams the night of sin disperse (2)
493 all praise to thee, my God, this night (T,1)
495 now the day is over, night is drawing nigh (T,1)
495 through the long night watches may thine angels spread (5)
496 though the night be dark and dreary (3)

496 chase the darkness of our night (4)
497 who the day for toil hast given, for rest the night (1)
497 holy dreams and hopes attend us this live-long night (1)
500 and rests not now by day or night (2)
502 it is not night if thou be near (1)
502 abide with me when night is nigh (3)
503 wait and worship while the night sets her evening lamps (1)
503 pass the stars, the day, the night (4)
504 Father, we praise thee, now the night is over (T,1)
505 brings the night its peace profound (1)
509 by day, by night, at home, abroad, still we are guarded (2)
527 fast bound in sin and nature's night (3)
529 with thee all night I mean to stay (1)
552 lead us from night to never-ending day (4)

nightly
43 nightly, to the listening earth repeats the story (2)
216 no nightly terrors shall alarm (5)

nights
365 nights and days thy power confess (2)

noble
15 praise him for his noble deeds (1)
50 so many glorious things are here, noble and right (1)
242 then to side with truth is noble (2)
273 turn my dreams to noble action, ministries of love (4)
405 earth has many a noble city (T,1)
485 rise like incense, each to thee, in noble thought & deed (1)
486 till through world made noble ... God shall march (4)
547 my native country, thee, Land of the noble free (2)

nobleness
422 to heal the people of their shame, and nobleness instill (3)
543 till all success be nobleness and every gain divine (3)

nobler
9 praise shall employ my nobler powers (1,4)
128 here have I found a nobler part (4)
194 and lift us to a nobler life (3)
421 in a nobler, sweeter song, I'll sing thy power to save (5)

noblest
171 see, like thee, our noblest work our Father's work to do (2)
365 thy noblest wonders here we view in souls renewed (6)
365 noblest wonders ... in souls renewed, and sins forgiven (6)
454 bring your sweetest, noblest lays (4)

nobly
29 to guide whate'er we nobly do (4)
135 by thee may I strongly live, bravely bear & nobly strive (3)
536 fight as the saints who nobly fought of old (3)

nod
32 ye monarchs, wait his nod (5)

Noel
377 to you we sing this glad Noel (3)

383   the first Noel, the angel did say (T,1)
383   Noel, Noel, Noel, Noel, born is the King of Israel (R)

noise
204   above the noise of selfish strife (1)
248   this day the noise of battle ... next, the victor's song (4)

noisy
173   once more to hear thy challenge above our noisy day (5)

none
9   none shall find his promise vain (2)
26   only thou art holy; there is none beside thee (3)
82   love of Jesus, what it is none but his loved ones know (4)
86   while in our mortal pain none calls on thee in vain (2)
125   other refuge have I none; hangs my helpless soul on thee (2)
252   the upward glancing of an eye, when none but God is near (2)
255   and none more blest than I (3)
299   with none to tell them of the Savior's dying (2)
370   shedding light that none can measure (1)
377   yet none there were who looked without (2)
466   for none can guess its grace, till he become the place (3)
475   old now is earth and none may count her days (1)
501   and none, O Lord, have perfect rest (4)
501   for none are wholly free from sin (4)
520   love like thine, that none shall ever stray (1)
526   for none may boast himself of aught (2)

noonday
216   nor plagues that waste in noonday light (5)

noontide
64   our noontide is thy gracious dawn (3)
417   burning of the noon-tide heat and the burden (1)

north
192   in him no south or north (1)
192   in him meet south and north (4)

northwest
383   this star drew nigh to the northwest (4)

not
2   angel harps forever ringing, rest not day nor night (1)
10   the heavens are not too high, his praise may thither fly (1)
10   the earth is not too low, his praises there may grow (1)
12   I know thee ... in part, I ask not, Lord, for more (3)
16   who would not fear his holy name and laud and magnify (2)
17   and when I think that God, his Son not sparing (3)
20   the Prince of Darkness grim, we tremble not for him (3)
20   armed with cruel hate, on earth is not his equal (1)
20   we will not fear (3)
20   were not the right man on our side (2)
26   though the eye of sinful man thy glory may not see (3)
32   without his high behest ye shall not ... disturb (3)
32   shall not, in the mountain pine, disturb a sparrows nest (3)
37   not a plant or flower below, but makes thy glories known (3)

42   sin and death shall not prevail (2)
46   we shall not in the desert stray (2)
46   we shall not full direction need (2)
47   when we are strong, Lord, leave us not alone (3)
48   fear not, I am with thee; O be not dismayed (2)
48   the rivers of woe shall not thee overflow (3)
48   the flame shall not hurt thee, I only design (4)
48   I will not, I will not desert to his foes (5)
50   so that earth's bliss may be our guide ... not our chain (3)
50   we have enough, yet not too much, to long for more (4)
50   a yearning for a deeper peace not known before (4)
54   not their courage nor their sword ... salvation gave (2)
54   not their number nor ... strength ...their country save (2)
55   hast thou not seen how thy desires ... hath been granted (2)
57   he will not let thy foot be moved (2)
57   neath sun or moon, by day or night ... not be afraid (3)
59   sing praises to his name: he forgets not his own (1)
65   bless the Father ... forget not ... mercies to proclaim (1)
68   the Lord's my Shepherd, I'll not want (T,1)
76   there let him subdue all that is not holy (4)
76   there let him subdue ... all that is not true (4)
77   life shall not end the strain; Alleluia! Amen! (3)
84   thou man-pursuing Fisherman, who harmest not but savest (2)
84   thou givest us that good unseen the world knows not (3)
84   the world knows not nor treasures (3)
86   help thou dost not disdain, help from above (2)
95   turn me not away unblest; calm my anguish into rest (3)
96   it was not I that found, O Savior true (1)
96   I walked and sank not on the storm-vexed sea (2)
96   'twas not so much that I on thee took hold (2)
99   not till earth and not till heaven pass away (6)
102   ye need not one be left behind (1)
104   let not conscience make you linger (3)
104   not the righteous; sinners Jesus came to call (4)
105   God calling yet! shall I not hear (T,1)
105   shall I not rise? Can I his loving voice despise (2)
105   I wait, but he does not forsake (4)
106   leave us not to doubt and fear (2)
110   he will not turn thee away (2)
112   will you not his grace receive ... still refuse to live (3)
115   this earth, he cries, is not my place (1)
119   and waiting not to rid my soul of one dark blot (2)
120   these for sin could not atone (2)
123   I know not how that Bethlehem's babe (T,1)
123   know not how that Calvary's cross a world ... could free (2)
123   I know not how that Joseph's tomb could solve death's (3)
125   leave ... leave me not alone, still support & comfort me (2)
138   hast thou not bid me love thee, God and King (3)
140   surely thou canst not let me die (3)
142   O for a faith that will not shrink (T,1)
142   that will not tremble on the brink of any earthly woe (1)
142   will not murmur nor complain beneath the chastening rod (2)
144   I ask not, need not, aught beside (4)
145   pass me not, O gentle Savior, hear my humble cry (T,1)
145   while on others thou art calling, do not pass me by (1,R)
146   whom we, that have not seen thy face (1)
146   thou madest man, he knows not why (2)

146   he thinks he was not made to die (2)
146   our wills are ours, we know not how (3)
146   thou wilt not leave us in the dust (2)
153   not the first to be banished by our fears from thee (2)
155   than fancies flee away! I'll fear not what men say (3)
157   we may not climb the heavenly steeps (2)
157   we may not climb ... to bring the Lord Christ down (2)
159   there are heights of joy that I may not reach till (4)
160   cross; let not its weight fill thy weak spirit with alarm (2
163   not alone the gift of life, but his own self he gave me (2)
164   I shall not fear the battle if thou art by my side (1)
167   let not my star of hope grow dim or disappear (2)
171   did ye not know it is my work My Father's work to do (1)
173   knows not race nor station as boundaries of the mind (4)
176   not for ease or worldly pleasure (2)
184   my will is not my own till thou hast made it thine (4)
186   thou didst not, Lord, refuse (1)
186   thy majesty did not disdain to be employed for us (1)
187   not a mite would I withhold (2)
188   not for myself alone may my prayer be (3)
191   men whose aim 'twill be not to defend some ancient creed (1)
202   we bear the strain of earthly care ... bear it not alone (T)
206   no farthest reach where thou art not (2)
207   be not dismayed whate'er betide (T,1)
214   not like that go the men of unbelief (3)
215   judge not the Lord by feeble sense (4)
217   e'en death's cold wave I will not flee (4)
218   Lord, it belongs not to my care whether I die or live (T,1)
220   Jesus will not fail us (2)
222   I dare not trust the sweetest frame (1)
223   not a burden we bear, not a sorrow we share (2)
223   not a grief nor a loss, not a frown or a cross (2)
223   not a frown ... cross, but is blest if we trust and obey (2)
230   green pastures are before me, which yet I have not seen (3)
234   O Love that wilt not let me go (T,1)
234   feel the promise is not vain that morn shall tearless be (3)
234   I dare not ask to fly from thee (4)
239   must I not stem the flood (3)
240   He changeth not, and thou art dear (4)
240   faint not nor fear, for he is near (4)
242   with the cross that turns not back (3)
243   not long the conflict, soon the holy war shall cease (4)
246   work of faith will not be done till thou obtain .. crown (3)
248   lift high the royal banner, it must not suffer loss (1)
248   arm of flesh will fail you, ye dare not trust your own (3)
248   the strife will not be long (4)
251   thou art not, like man, untrue (2)
251   not in grief to harm ... while thy love is left to me (3)
251   not in joy to charm me were that joy unmixed with thee (3)
256   riches I heed not, nor man's empty praise (3)
258   Our God's bounteous gifts abuse not, Light refuse not (4)
260   dost not wait till human speech thy gifts ... implore (1)
260   we would not bend thy will to ours (3)
260   not beat with cries on heaven's doors (3)
261   all because we do not carry everything to God in prayer (1)
266   and run not before him, whatever betide (3)
272   I do not ask to see the distant scene (1)

272 I was not ever thus (2)
272 remember not past years (2)
274 though least and lowest, let me not unheard depart (3)
287 if you love him, why not serve him... soldiers ... cross (4)
289 O thou who changest not, abide with me (2)
290 I know not where his islands lift their fronded palms (5)
290 I know not what the future hath of marvel or surprise (T,1)
290 the bruised reed he will not break, but strengthen (2)
299 he who made all nations is not willing one ... perish (1)
300 fear not, brethren; joyful stand (3)
303 I know not, O I know not what joys await us there (1)
305 we are not divided, all one body we (2)
308 not like kingdoms of the world thy holy Church, O God (3)
308 a house not made with hands (4)
311 judge her not for work undone (4)
311 judge her not for fields unwon (4)
313 be known to us in breaking bread, but do not then depart (T)
325 not paradise, with all its joys ... such delight afford (1)
326 the feast, though not the love, is past and gone (4)
332 feeble elements bestow a power not theirs to give (2)
335 not a cause of small import the pastor's care demands (2)
338 blest be the dear uniting love that will not let us part (T)
346 his hands built not for one brief day (1)
353 not as of old a little child to bear and fight and die (2)
355 till not a stone was left on stone (2)
373 ye shepherds, shrink not with affright (1)
391 now ye need not fear the grave (3)
394 fear not, said he, for mighty dread had seized (2)
406 build ye the road, and falter not, nor stay (2)
412 think on thy pity ... love unswerving, not my deserving (5)
414 may not know ... cannot tell, what pains he had to bear (2)
427 our sins, not thine, thou bearest, Lord (2)
429 cut off for sins, but not his own (1)
431 e'n the disciple that he loved heeds not (2)
431 heeds not his Master's grief and tears (2)
431 he that in anguish knelt is not forsaken by his God (3)
434 turn not from his griefs away (1)
434 shun not suffering, shame, or loss (2)
451 how blest are they who have not seen (4)
455 thy praise and glory shall not fail throughout eternity (4)
464 saw ye not the cloud arise, little as a human hand (4)
468 the Lord will come and not be slow (T,1)
469 sharing not our griefs, no joy can share (2)
469 building proud towers which shall not reach to heaven (3)
469 if we love not the world which thou hast made (4)
470 grant us courage that we fail not man nor thee (4)
471 not heaven's hosts shall swifter move than we on earth (4)
471 not ... swifter ... than we on earth, to do thy will (4)
475 still wilt not hear thine inner God proclaim (1)
478 not with swords loud clashing nor roll of stirring drums (2)
478 lead on, O King eternal, we follow, not with fears (3)
479 we, thy servants, bring the worship not of voice alone (1)
479 not of voice alone, but heart (1)
480 where the Gospel's day sheds not its glorious day (1)
481 the tears are wiped from eyes that shall not weep again (1)
484 take not thy thunder from us, but take away our pride (1)
497 let not ease and self enthrall us (2)

500   and rests not now by day or night (2)
502   it is not night if thou be near (1)
502   for without thee I dare not die (3)
515   thou art in all; not e'en the powers by which we toil (2)
515   not e'en the power by which we toil for bread are ours (2)
519   may we not his spirit grieve (1)
526   and thus my hope is in the Lord and not in my own merit (3)
529   I need not tell thee who I am, my sin and misery declare (2)
544   let not thy wrath in its terrors awaken (2)
544   falsehood and wrong shall not tarry beside thee (3)
548   not alone for mighty empire (T,1)
548   not alone for bounteous harvests lift we up our hearts (1)
548   not for battleship and fortress (2)
548   not for conquests of the sword (2)
549   these .. not the only walls wherein thou mayst be sought (3)
549   claim the kingdom of the earth for thee, and not thy foe (5)

notes
267   and while the wave-notes fall on my ear (2)
343   O grant its rich and swelling notes may lift our souls (3)
437   all things seen and unseen their notes in gladness blend (3)

nothing
56   fear him, ye saints, and ... have nothing else to fear (4)
56   fear him...and you will then have nothing else to fear (3)
67   I nothing lack if I am his and he is mine forever (1)
106   nothing left but heaven and prayer (3)
149   it satisfies my longings as nothing else can do (1)
207   nothing you ask will be denied (3)
209   thy hope, thy confidence let nothing shake (2)
222   my hope is build on nothing less than Jesus blood and (T,1)
222   nothing less than Jesus' blood and righteousness (1)
227   angels could do nothing more, than to fall at his feet (3)
230   and safe is such confiding, for nothing changes here (1)
230   my Shepherd is beside me, and nothing can I lack (2)
231   it can bring with it nothing but he will bear us through (3)
259   O Jesus, nothing may I see ... desire, or seek but thee (2)
266   forgetting in nothing His blessing to seek (1)
285   nothing in earth beneath desire (4)
285   nothing in heaven above (4)
324   ponder nothing earthly minded (1)
332   Lord, we ask for nothing more (4)
338   O may we ever walk in him, and nothing know beside (3)
338   nothing desire, nothing esteem, but Jesus crucified (3)
378   God rest you merry, Gentlemen, let nothing you dismay (T,1)
378   the which his mother Mary did nothing take in scorn (2)
389   he lays aside his majesty and seems as nothing worth (2)
412   while he nothing heedeth, God intercedeth (3)
517   love that nothing good denies (4)

nought
106   pleading nought but Jesus' blood, whisper softly (3)

nourish
337   nourish the lambs and feed thy sheep (4)
521   God his own doth tend and nourish (2)
552   thy bounteous goodness nourish us in peace (3)

now

3	thou who almighty art, now rule in every heart (3)
13	open now thy gates of beauty (1)
13	to my heart O enter thou, let it be thy temple now (2)
30	the one eternal God, ere aught that now appears (1)
41	humbly now we bow before thee (1)
49	all praise and thanks to God the Father now be given (3)
49	now thank we all our God with heart and hands and voices (T)
49	for thus it was, is now, and shall be evermore (3)
55	all ye who hear,now to his temple draw near (1)
55	all that hath life and breath, come now with praises (4)
55	come now with praises before him (4)
59	the wicked oppressing now cease from distressing (1)
74	thou art exalted o'er all creatures now (4)
76	every tongue confess him King of glory now (1)
78	at the great name of Jesus, now all knees must bend (2)
79	freely and joyously now would we bring (2)
82	Jesus, be thou our glory now and through eternity (5)
86	so now, and till we die sound we thy praises high (4)
92	I once was lost, but now am found (1)
92	was blind, but now I see (1)
94	now incline me to repent; let me now my sins lament (3)
94	now my foul revolt deplore (3)
95	heavenly Father, bless me now (T,1)
95	hear and heal me now, I pray (1)
95	mercy now, O Lord, I plead in this hour of utter need (3)
95	now, O Lord, this very hour, send thy grace (2)
95	while I rest upon thy word come ... bless me now, O Lord (2)
97	I want no better friend; I trust him now (4)
101	only trust him, only trust him, only trust him now (R)
101	he will save you, he will save you, he will save you now (R)
101	plunge now into the crimson flood (2)
102	all things in Christ are ready now (2)
108	O Lord, with shame and sorrow we open now the door (3)
110	Jesus is waiting, O come to him now (3)
116	humbly at thy cross I bow, save me, Jesus, save me now (4)
117	and now I live in him (2)
119	now, to be thine, yea, thine alone...I come (6)
122	and sprinkles now the throne of grace (2)
122	with confidence I now draw nigh (4)
128	now rest, my long-divided heart (4)
131	on our disordered spirits move ... let ... now be light (3)
139	future and past subsisting now (3)
140	O let me now receive that gift! my soul without it dies (4)
142	tastes even now the hallowed bliss of an eternal home (4)
143	Savior divine! now hear me while I pray (1)
148	trying now to make the harbor (3)
149	that is just the reason I tell it now to thee (2)
159	consecrate me now to thy service, Lord (2)
163	from him who loves me now so well, what power ... sever (3)
166	if ever I loved thee, Lord Jesus,'tis now (R)
177	some offering bring thee now, something for thee (1)
179	freely and joyously now would we bring (2)
183	now they taste unmingled love, and joy without a tear (2)
185	now thee alone I seek, give what is best (2)
186	accept my hallowed labor now, I do it unto thee (3)
192	in Christ now meet both east and west (4)

200 as once he spake in Zion, so now he speaks again (1)
206 give us courage now to stand (1)
209 all now mysterious shall be bright at last (2)
224 visions of rapture now burst on my sight (2)
227 now my remnant of days would I speak of his praise (6)
248 ye that are men now serve him against unnumbered foes (2)
256 thou mine inheritance, now and always (3)
257 now to seek and love and fear thee (1)
258 now is breaking o'er the earth another day (1)
265 O bless me now, my Savior, I come to thee (R)
267 silently now I wait for thee, ready my God (R)
271 open now the crystal fountain (2)
272 but now lead thou me on (2)
274 Master, let it now be heard (1)
281 O that I now, from sin released (5)
285 O that it now were shed abroad in this poor stony heart (3)
300 they are happy now ... we soon their happiness shall see (2)
302 though now divided by...the narrow stream of death (3)
302 part are crossing now (4)
308 O where are kings and empires now (T,1)
314 now we give thee thanks, O Lord (1)
325 millions of souls, in glory now ... fed and feasted here (3)
328 one with the living bread divine ... now by faith we eat (3)
348 on this stone now laid with prayer (T,1)
349 vouchsafe thy presence now (1)
349 all praise and honor, glory, power be now and evermore (4)
349 in grateful service ... now their strong foundation lay (2)
352 dwell in this holy place, e'en now descend (1)
352 glory and praises be in love now given (4)
355 still our wrongs may weave thee now new thorns (1)
360 now thy gracious kingdom bring (2)
364 every eye shall now behold him robed in dreadful majesty (2)
366 now let all the heavens adore thee (3)
373 this child, now weak in infancy (1)
378 now to the Lord sing praises, all you within this place (5)
378 with true love and brotherhood each other now embrace (4)
379 till the air, everywhere, now with joy is ringing (1)
382 who sang creation's story now proclaim Messiah's birth (1)
382 God with men is now residing (2)
386 Word of the Father, now in flesh appearing (3)
390 whole world give back the song which now the angels sing (3)
391 ox and ass before him bow and he is in the manger now (1)
391 now ye hear of endless bliss (2)
391 now ye need not fear the grave (3)
398 long, alas, witholden, now spread from shore to shore (1)
399 O deep within my heart now shine (2)
402 glorious now behold him arise, King ... God & sacrifice (5)
413 and heroic spirits answer now, as then, in Galilee (4)
418 O sacred head, now wounded (T,1)
418 now scornfully surrounded with thorns, thine only crown (1)
424 to thee, now high exalted, our melody we raise (3)
425 O Christ, thy triumphs now begin o'er captive death (2)
425 triumphs now begin o'er captive death and conqered sin (2)
431 in the garden now the suffering Savior prays alone (1)
437 now let the heavens be joyful! Let earth her song begin (3)
438 but now at God's right hand he stands (1)
439 where, O death, is now thy sting, Alleluia (2)

439 soar we now where Christ has led, Alleluia (4)
441 now the green blade riseth from the buried grain (T,1)
442 spring has now unwrapped the flowers (T,1)
446 Alleluia now we cry to our King immortal (5)
449 now is the triumph of our King (1)
450 for her Lord now liveth; death hath lost its sting (2)
452 speak his sorrows ended; hail his triumph now (2)
452 come then, true and faithful, now fulfill thy word (3)
453 see the Man of Sorrows now (1)
455 his glories now we sing who died, and rose on high (2)
458 is crowned with glory now (1)
460 age-long Word expounding God's own message now as then (3)
464 now the Word doth swiftly run (2)
464 now it wins its widening way (2)
464 sin's strongholds it now o'erthrows (2)
464 now it spreads along the skies (4)
475 old now is earth and none may count her days (1)
475 now, even now, once more from earth to sky peals forth (3)
478 and now, O King eternal, we lift our battle song (1)
480 O now, to all mankind, let there be light (2)
482 establish thou forevermore the triumph now begun (1)
489 let us now a blessing seek, waiting in his courts today (1)
490 birds pass high in flight, fragrant flowers now bloom (91)
492 be glory, as it was, is now, and shall forever be (5)
494 softly now the light of day fades upon our sight away (T,1)
495 now the day is over, night is drawing nigh (T,1)
500 thy praise shall hallow now our rest (1)
500 and rests not now by day or night (2)
502 now, Lord, the gracious work begin (4)
504 Father, we praise thee, now the night is over (T,1)
505 now, on land and sea descending (T,1)
505 now, our wants and burdens leaving to his care (3)
506 long our day of testing, now comes the hour of resting (3)
506 all evil thoughts expelling, now make in us thy dwelling (5)
507 come down and meet us now (4)
511 a world in need now summons us to labor,love and give (2)
524 now, on this... festal day thy bounteous hand confessing (2)
527 no condemnation now I dread (4)
528 he calls you now, invites you home (5)
529 tell me thy name and tell me now (2)
529 yield to me now, for I am weak (3)
532 now praise we great and famous men (T,1)
532 praise the Lord who now as then reveals in man his glory (1)

number
54 'twas not their number nor their strength (2)
54 not...nor their strength that did their country save (2)

o'ercome
250 o'ercome through Christ alone, and stand entire at last (2)

o'erflow
83 his lips with grace o'erflow (1)
195 o'erflow in kindling thought and glowing word (4)
195 until my very heart o'erflow in kindling thought (4)
213 when rising floods my soul o'erflow (3)

o'ershading
    264   sweet the repose beneath thy wings o'ershading (4)

o'ertake
    416   when the woes of life o'ertake me (2)

o'erthrown
    355   nation's pride o'erthrown went down to dust beside thee (2)

o'erthrows
    464   sin's strongholds it now o'erthrows (2)

oar
    290   and so beside the silent sea I wait the muffled oar (4)

oath
    222   his oath, his covenant, his blood support me (3)

obedience
    107   give our hearts to thine obedience (5)
    179   valiant endeavor and loving obedience (2)
    274   with obedience glad & steady still to follow every word (4)

obediently
    300   Lord, obediently we'll go, gladly leaving all below (4)

obey
     25   the glorious hosts of heaven obey (4)
     32   the winds obey his will (1)
     37   moon shines full at his command, and all the stars obey (1)
     40   deep seas obey thy voice (1)
     65   unto those who still remember his commandments, and obey (5)
     85   all who would obey thee may learn from thee their duty (4)
    162   Savior, teach me, day by day, thine own lesson to obey (T,1)
    200   speak, and, behold! we answer; command, and we obey (4)
    214   obey the laws of God in their determined quest (1)
    214   their joyful, faithful hearts obey the laws of God (1)
    218   if life belong, I will be glad that I may long obey (2)
    223   abides with us still & with all who will trust and obey (1)
    223   trust and obey, for there's no other way to be happy (R)
    223   no other way to be happy in Jesus, but to trust and obey (R)
    223   not a frown ... cross, but is blest if we trust and obey (2)
    223   joy he bestows are for them who will trust and obey (3)
    223   never fear, only trust and obey (4)
    227   O how happy are they who the Savior obey (T,1)
    247   boisterious waves obey thy will (2)
    248   the trumpet call obey (2)
    258   but his Spirit's voice obey (4)
    318   let me gladly here obey thee (3)
    513   the winds and waves obey him, by him the birds are fed (2)

obeyed
     42   worlds his mighty voice obeyed (1)
    477   the quiet of a steadfast faith, calm of a call obeyed (2)

oblation
    400   vainly we offer each ample oblation (4)
    412   for me ... thy mortal sorrow, and thy life's oblation (4)

oblations
405 Eastern sages at his cradle make oblations rich and rare (3)

obscure
356 ancient words, their message long obscure (2)

obtain
246 work of faith will not be done till thou obtain .. crown (3)
336 let us take up the cross till we the crown obtain (5)

obtained
301 who have obtained the prize (1)

occasions
242 new occasions teach new duties (3)

ocean
38 ocean depth of happy rest (3)
127 sinners more than sands upon the ocean shore (4)
234 in thine ocean depths its flow may richer, fuller be (1)
247 as a mother stills her child thou canst hush the ocean (1)
247 thou canst hush the ocean wild (1)
290 no harm from him can come to me on ocean or on shore (4)
343 To God the tribes of ocean cry, and birds upon the wing (2)
346 ocean ... sleeps in the hollow of his hand (2)
346 the rolling ocean, rocked with storms, sleeps (2)
400 gems of the mountain and pearls of the ocean (3)
474 rivers to the ocean run, nor stay in all their course (2)
502 in the ocean of thy love we lose ourselves in heaven (6)
538 bidst the mighty ocean deep its... limits keep (1)
538 mighty ocean deep its own appointed limits keep (1)
542 my country's skies are bluer than the ocean (2)
544 singing in chorus from ocean to ocean (4)

ocean's
11 storm and flood and ocean's roar (3)
233 with voice as full and strong as ocean's surging praise (3)
480 boundless as ocean's tide rolling in fullest pride (4)
536 from earth's wide bounds, from ocean's farthest coast (6)

odors
400 odors of Edom and offerings divine (3)

offences
438 for our offences given (1)

offended
412 ah, holy Jesus, how hast thou offended (T,1)

offenseless
491 we pray thee that offenseless the hours of dark may be (1)

offenses
522 from his field shall in that day all offenses purge away (3)

offer
2   here, great God, today we offer of thine own to thee (4)
109   offer pardon and peace to all (3)
196   offer the sacrifice of praise, and call upon his name (4)
346   sovereign God, receive . gift thy willing servants offer (3)
347   no gift have we, Lord of all gifts, to offer thee (1)
400   vainly we offer each ample oblation (4)
402   frankincense to offer have I, incense owns a Deity nigh (3)
504   singing, we offer prayer and meditation (1)
513   accept the gifts we offer for all thy love imparts (3)

offered
383   and offered there, in his presence, their gold and myrrh (5)
397   as they offered gifts most rare at... manger rude & bare (3)
412   lo, the Good Shepherd for the sheep is offered (3)

offering
35   offering up on every shore her pure sacrifice of love (5)
153   offering lives if it's thy will (4)
177   some offering bring thee now, something for thee (1)
242   God's new Messiah, offering each the bloom or blight (1)
435   that were an offering far too small (4)
461   let our whole soul an offering be to our Redeemer's name (2)
486   man in his weakness yet may give a worthier offering (1)
511   to make our life an offering to God, that man may live (2)

offerings
400   odors of Edom and offerings divine (3)

offspring
312   joyful that we ourselves are thine ... offspring (3)
387   offspring of the virgin's womb (2)

oft
45   ne'er forget that though the wrong seems oft so strong (3)
54   O Lord,our fathers oft have told in our attentive ears (T,1)
67   perverse and foolish oft I strayed (3)
94   oft profaned his hallowed name (2)
141   Have faith in God, my mind ... oft thy light burns low (2)
144   though oft I seem to tread alone life's dreary waste (3)
167   since thou on earth has wept and sorrowed oft alone (2)
266   take time to be holy, speak oft with thy Lord (T,1)
275   oft escaped the tempter's snare by thy return ... prayer (1)
476   O God of beauty, oft revealed in dreams of human art (4)

often
41   from thy ways so often turning (2)
203   but often in some far-off Galilee beheld thee fairer (2)
261   O what peace we often forfeit ... needless pain we bear (1)
275   my soul has often found relief (1)
306   and often for each other flows the sympathizing tear (3)

oil
68   my head thou dost with oil anoint, and my cup overflows (4)
232   place where Jesus sheds the oil of gladness on our heads (2)

old
30	in prophet's word he spoke of old; he speaketh still (2)
36	the indwelling God, proclaimed of old (4)
90	still as of old he calleth, "Follow me" (5)
107	as of old the apostles heard it by the Galilean lake (2)
131	source of... old prophetic fire, fountain of life & love (1)
149	to tell the old, old story of Jesus and his love (R)
149	'twill be the old, old story that I have loved so long (4)
189	the chorus clearer grows that shepherds heard of old (1)
228	in the old rugged cross, stained with blood so divine (3)
228	so I'll cherish the old rugged cross (R)
228	on a hill far away stood an old rugged cross (T,1)
228	and I love that old cross where the dearest and best (1)
228	O that old rugged cross, so despised by the world (2)
228	I will cling to the old rugged cross (R)
228	to the old rugged cross I will ever be true (4)
228	for 'twas on that old cross Jesus suffered and died (3)
243	like those strong men of old (1)
244	when I'm growing old and feeble, stand by me (4)
277	old things shall be done away ... all things new become (2)
308	kings and empires ... of old that went and came (1)
324	of old on earth he stood, Lord of lords in human vesture (2)
350	here let thy sacred fire of old descend (2)
353	not as of old a little child to bear and fight and die (2)
355	from old unfaith our souls release (3)
371	from days of old, through swiftly rolling ages (2)
372	to bear before the nations thy true light as of old (4)
390	that glorious song of old (1)
390	lo! the days are hastening on, by prophet seen of old (3)
397	as with gladness men of old did the guiding star behold (T)
411	as in days of old he takes the wounded to his arms (4)
438	Word of grace hath purged away the old and wicked leaven (
473	Almighty, thy power hath founded of old (3)
475	old now is earth and none may count her days (1)
475	peals forth in joy man's old undaunted cry (3)
511	as men of old their first fruits brought (T,1)
536	fight as the saints who nobly fought of old (3)

oldest
296	from oldest time, on farthest shores ... she adores (2)

Olive's
431	'tis midnight, and on Olive's brow (T,1)

Olivet
157	faith has still its Olivet, and love its Galilee (3)
423	from Olivet they followed mid an exultant crowd (2)

Omega
283	Alpha and Omega be; endd of faith as its beginning (2)
357	He is Alpha and Omega, He the source, the ending he (1)

omission
280	O may the least omission pain my reawakened soul (4)

omissions
279	O may the least omissions pain my reawakened soul (4)

omnipotence
52   eternal wisdom is their guide, their help omnipotence (1)

omnipotent
48   upheld by my righteous, omnipotent hand (2)

once
76   at his voice creation sprang at once to sight (2)
92   I once was lost, but now am found (1)
136   descend upon thy Church once more & make it truly thine (1)
155   there's no discouragement shall make him once relent (1)
173   once more to hear thy challenge above our noisy day (5)
175   chords that were broken will vibrate once more (3)
183   who once went sorrowing here (2)
185   once earthly joy I craved, sought peace and rest (2)
200   as once he spake in Zion, so now he speaks again (1)
216   the man who once has found abode (T,1)
242   once to every man and nation comes the moment to decide (T)
268   what peaceful hours I once enjoyed! (3)
307   as grain, once scattered on the hillsides (4)
364   once for favored sinners slain (1)
418   how does that visage languish .. once was bright as morn (1)
439   once he died, our souls to save, Alleluia (2)
440   Jesus lives who once was dead (3)
443   didst once, upon the cross ... suffer to redeem our loss (1)
445   he lives, he lives, who once was dead (1)
454   hail, thou once despised Jesus (T,1)
458   the head that once was crowned with thorns (T,1)
475   now, even now, once more from earth to sky peals forth (3)
501   once more 'tis eventide, and we, oppressed (2)
512   waters of the spring-time, enriching it once more (1)

one
3   to thee, great One in Three eternal praises be (4)
8   in essence only One; undivided God we claim thee (4)
19   God ... Father, ... Son, ... Spirit, Three in One (4)
20   one little word shall fell him (3)
25   to spend one day with thee on earth exceeds a thousand (1)
25   one day with thee ... exceeds a thousand days of mirth (1)
30   the one eternal God, ere aught that now appears (1)
40   thou star-abiding one (2)
49   the one eternal God, whom earth and heaven adore (3)
58   his song in them, in us, is one (3)
60   praise the Spirit, Three in One (7)
62   our whole lives one resurrection ... life of life above (4)
64   till all thy living altars claim one holy light (5)
64   one holy light, one heavenly flame (5)
74   let every tongue confess ... one accord ... Jesus Christ (5)
78   to God the Father ... Son ... Spirit ... Three in One (4)
80   learn of thee, the lowly one (4)
88   one of his heralds, yes, I would sing loudest hosannas (3)
95   O thou loving, blessed One, rising o'er me like the sun (4)
97   when I am sad, to him I go, no other one can cheer me so (1)
102   ye need not one be left behind (1)
109   Christ,the blessed one, give to all wonderful words of (2)
113   by thy cross and dying cries, by thy one great sacrifice (2)
117   weary one, lay down, thy head upon my breast (1)
117   thirsty one, stoop down and drink and live (2)

119   just as I am, without one plea (T,1)
119   and waiting not to rid my soul of one dark blot (2)
122   the Father hears him pray, his dear anointed one (4)
130   grace ... wide as infinity ... it never passed by one (3)
133   will one will, to do and to endure (2)
133   until my heart is pure, until with thee I will one will (2)
136   shall blend their creeds in one (3)
138   one·holy passion filling all my frame (5)
146   that mind and soul, according well, may make one music (5)
146   may make one music as before (5)
173   longs to bind God's children into one perfect whole (4)
175   weep o'er the erring one, lift up the fallen (1)
178   one with thyself, may every eye in us, thy brethren see (4)
186   all I think or speak or do is one great sacrifice (4)
188   lead forth my soul, O Christ, one with thine own (2)
189   one common faith unites us all, we seek one common goal (3)
189   one tender comfort broods upon the struggling human soul (3)
189   one claim unites all men in God to serve each human need (2
190   come, let thy voice be one with theirs (2)
192   all Christly souls are one in him (4)
192   one great fellowship of love (1)
192   one in him throughout the whole wide earth (4)
198   pulse of one fraternity (3)
198   in every heart and brain shall throb the pulse of one (3)
207   lean, weary one, upon his breast (4)
216   thy dwelling place the Highest One (6)
232   they meet around one common mercy seat (3)
236   with one accord our parting hymn of praise (1)
254   O thou, whose deeds and dreams were one (2)
256   thou in me dwelling, and I with thee one (2)
265   Most Holy One ... thou blessed Son (5)
272   one step enough for me (1)
291   o'er ... wide-extended plains shines one eternal day (2)
292   the world to Christ we bring, with one accord (3)
296   one holy Church of God appears through every age & race (T)
296   beneath the pine or palm, one unseen Presence she adores (2)
297   the Church's one foundation is Jesus Christ her Lord (T,1)
297   elect from every nation, yet one o'er all the earth (2)
297   her charter of salvation, one Lord, one faith, one birth (2)
297   one holy name she blesses, partakes one holy food (2)
297   and to one hope she presses, with every grace endued (2)
297   yet she on earth hath union with God the Three in One (4)
298   ever Three and ever One (4)
298   binding all the Church in one (1)
298   One in might, and One in glory, while unending ages run (4)
299   he who made all nations is not willing one ... perish (1)
299   one soul should perish lost in shades of night (1)
301   gift which he on one bestows, we all delight to prove (2)
301   He bids us build each other up; and, gathered into one (3)
301   we all partake the joy of one...common peace we feel (4)
302   all the servants of our King, in earth & heaven are one (2)
302   one family we dwell in him, one Church above, beneath (3)
302   one army of the living God, to his command we bow (4)
304   the length, the breadth, the height are one (2)
305   we are not divided, all one body we (2)
305   one in hope and doctrine, one in charity (2)
306   our fears, our hopes, our aims are one (2)
306   are one, our comforts and our cares (2)

307 as grain ... was in this broken bread made one (4)
309 make us of one heart and mind, courteous, pitiful & kind (3)
319 one fold .. faith .. hope .. Lord, One God alone we know (1)
328 many, and yet but one are we, one undivided bread (2)
328 one with the living bread divine ... now by faith we eat (3)
332 only meet us in thy ways and perfect us in one (4)
333 whom thou forevermore dost join in one (1)
338 joined in one spirit to our Head (2)
338 our bodies may far off remove, we still are one in heart (1)
346 his hands built not for one brief day (1)
350 here let the weary one find rest (4)
352 to the great One in Three (4)
354 bind all peoples in one heart and mind (3)
356 may one Lord .. faith .. Word, one Spirit lead us still (4)
356 one great Church go forth in might to work God's .. will (4)
366 of one pearl each shining portal (3)
371 myriad tongues, in one great anthem blending (4)
377 no one to lighten their despair (1)
391 calls you one and calls you all (3)
408 One Lord, in one great name united us all who own thee (3)
417 the very dying form of One who suffered there for me (2)
424 who in the Lord's name comest, the King and blessed One (1)
434 watch with him one bitter hour (1)
449 and sing today with one accord the life laid down (4)
460 each from age to age proclaiming God the one (1)
460 God the one, the righteous Lord (1)
460 'mid the world's despair and turmoil one firm anchor (1)
460 one firm anchor holdeth fast (1)
460 with the Father ever one (2)
460 one sure faith yet standing fast (3)
463 we believe in one true God (T,1)
467 Thee, of both, to be but One (4)
475 earth shall be fair, and all her people one (3)
488 Church her voice upraises to thee, blest Three in One (4)
492 to God the Father, Son, and Spirit, One in Three (5)
507 all, with one accord, in a perpetual covenant join (1)
516 when one their wish, and one their prayer (1)
516 and one their heavenly rest (1)
530 join us, in one spirit ... let us still receive of thine (2)
535 we in the kingdom of thy grace: The kingdoms are but one (3)
536 thou, in the darkness drear, their one true light (2)
536 yet all are one in thee, for all are thine (4)
542 and hearts united learn to live as one (3)
549 scarcely can we turn aside for one brief hour of prayer (2)
549 prayer, by thee inspired and taught ... with work be one (6)

ones
19 ye watchers and ye holy ones (T,1)
82 love of Jesus, what it is none but his loved ones know (4)
201 who lovest all thy lost ones on every mountain steep (1)
214 the righteous ones shall be forever blest (T,1)
229 peace, perfect peace, with loved ones far away (4)
295 her young ones forth may bring (4)
297 O happy ones and holy! Lord, give us grace that we (4)
314 our sainted ones in glory seated at our Father's board (3)
517 that in all we do or say little ones our deeds may copy (3)

only

2	thousands only live to bless thee (1)
8	though in essence only One; undivided God we claim thee (4)
26	only thou art holy; there is none beside thee (3)
27	'tis only the splendor of light hideth thee (4)
27	immortal, invisible, God only wise (T,1)
48	the flame shall not hurt thee, I only design (4)
56	blest are they, and only they, who in his truth confide (3)
75	thou only canst inform the mind and purify the heart (2)
82	Jesus, our only joy be thou, as thou our prize wilt be (5)
101	only trust him, only trust him, only trust him now (R)
109	Jesus, only Savior, sanctify forever (3)
118	to thee I all resign; thine is the work and only thine (3)
121	blessed Lord & only Savior, with thy love our bosom fill (4)
123	I only know ... matchless love ... brought God's love (2)
123	only know ... manger child has brought God's life to me (1)
123	I only know a living Christ, our immortality (3)
137	only then, we feel our interest in his blood (2)
140	what did thine only Son endure before I drew my breath (2)
145	trusting only in thy merit would I seek thy face (3)
152	thee, only thee, resolved to know in all I think (1)
152	only thee...to know in all I think or speak or do (1)
154	Christ only, always, living in me (4)
160	for only he who bears the cross may hope to wear...crown (4)
170	in peace that only thou canst give (4)
175	he will forgive if they only believe (2)
176	gladly will I toil & suffer, only let me walk with thee (2)
178	unwearied ... forgiveness still, thy heart ... only love (2)
184	it only stands unbent amid the clashing strife (4)
187	take my voice ... let me sing always, only, for my King (2)
187	take myself, and I will be ever, only, all for thee (3)
210	only be still, and wait his leisure in cheerful hope (2)
223	never fear, only trust and obey (4)
240	only believe, and thou shalt see that Christ is all (4)
256	thou and only, first in my heart (3)
268	help me to tear it from thy throne and worship only thee (5)
269	only with thee we journey safely on (3)
278	I only for his glory burn, and always see his face (3)
282	where only Christ is heard to speak (2)
285	give me thy only love (4)
285	God only knows the love of God (3)
285	this only portion, Lord, be mine (3)
285	thy only love do I require (4)
285	give me thy only love to know (4)
290	I only know I cannot drift beyond his love and care (5)
300	only thou our leader be, and we still will follow thee (4)
301	Christ, the true, the only light (1)
303	His only, his forever thou shalt be, and thou art (3)
321	the blessed cup is only passed true memory of thee (3)
328	then only can it closer be, when all are joined above (4)
332	only meet us in thy ways and perfect us in one (4)
332	thine to bless, 'tis only ours to wonder and adore (4)
341	his only righteousness I show, his saving grace proclaim (5)
376	but his mother only, in her maiden bliss, worshiped (3)
401	Christ, the true, the only light (1)
403	his spirit only can bestow, who reigns in light above (1)
414	he only could unlock the gate of heaven and let us in (4)
417	my sinful self my only shame, my glory all the cross (3)

418 now scornfully surrounded with thorns, thine only crown (1)
457 and only wish the joy to know of our triumphant friend (1)
513 he only is the Maker of all things near and far (2)
549 these .. not the only walls wherein thou mayst be sought (3)

onward
38 ever singing, march we onward (4)
242 they must upward still & onward who would keep ... truth (3)
249 forget the steps already trod and onward urge thy way (2)
305 onward, Christian soldiers! marching as to war (T,1,R)
305 onward, then, ye people, join our happy throng (4)
397 leading onward, beaming bright (1)
430 pressing onward as we can ..to this our hearts must tend (4)
474 press onward to the prize (3)
500 unsleeping while earth rolls onward into light (2)
550 thy blessing came, and still its power shall onward (2)

oped
391 hath oped the heavenly door ... man is blessed evermore (2)

open
12 that makes the darkest way I go an open path to thee (4)
13 open now thy gates of beauty (1)
18 God is speaking; praise him for his open Word (3)
18 God has spoken; praise him for his open Word (1,2)
94 put him to an open shame (2)
108 O Lord, with shame and sorrow we open now the door (3)
118 open thine arms, and take me in (1,5)
257 open thou our ears and heart (3)
260 through open gates thy power flows in (4)
267 open my eyes that I may see (T,1)
267 open my mouth, and let me bear gladly the warm truth (3)
267 open my heart and let me prepare love with thy children (3)
267 open my eyes, that I may hear voices of truth (2)
267 open my eyes, illumine me, Spirit divine (R)
271 open now the crystal fountain (2)
348 open wide, O God, thy door for the outcast and the poor (3)
363 our hearts to thee we open wide (3)
494 pardon each infirmity, open fault, and secret sin (2)
498 thy glory breaks before us through the city's open gate (3)
528 his open side shall take you in (5)
548 for the open door to manhood in the land the people rule (2)

opened
439 Christ hath opened paradise, Alleluia (3)
454 opened is the gate of heaven (2)
464 He the door hath opened wide (3)

opening
28 they fly, forgotten, as a dream dies at the opening day (5)
38 opening to the sun above (1)
138 no angel visitant, no opening skies (2)
509 the opening year thy mercy shows (1)

opens
34 each little flower that opens (1)

oppose
248   courage rise with danger & strength to strength oppose (2)
341   though earth and hell oppose (4)

oppressed
9   he saves the oppressed, he feeds the poor (2)
101   come, every soul by sin oppressed (T,1)
102   come, all ye souls by sin oppressed (3)
254   help me, oppressed by things undone (2)
284   with care and woe oppressed (2)
303   beneath the contemplation sink heart and voice oppressed (1)
348   rest to the heart by sin oppressed (2)
486   those oppressed or lonely ... long at strife with pain (3)
501   once more 'tis eventide, and we, oppressed (2)
501   we, oppressed with various ills, draw near (2)

oppressing
59   the wicked oppressing now cease from distressing (1)

oppression
359   he comes to break oppression, to set the captive free (1)

orbs
43   no real voice nor sound amid the radiant orbs be found (3)
62   by him upholden hang the glorious orbs of light (1)

orchard
511   first fruits brought of orchard, flock and field (1)

ordain
332   ask the Father's wisdom how...that did the means ordain (3)

ordained
37   I sing the wisdom that ordained the sun to rule the day (1)
44   the moon and stars ordained by thee (2)
337   Lord, thine ordained servants bless (1)

ordainest
544   God the omnipotent! King who ordainest (T,1)

ordaineth
55   desires ... granted in what he ordaineth (2)

ordaining
59   ordaining, maintaining his kingdom divine (2)

order
28   before the hills in order stood (3)
37   clouds arise, and tempests blow by order from thy throne (3)
209   leave to thy God to order and provide (1)
354   and order all things far and nigh (2)

ordered
131   on our disordered spirits move ... let ... now be light (3)
235   let our ordered lives confess the beauty of thy peace (4)

orders
76   all the heavenly orders in their great array (2)

organ
  343   we bid the pealing organ wait to speak alone thy will (3)

orient
  402   we three kings of Orient are (T,1)
  492   O let thine orient beams the night of sin disperse (2)

origin
  139   with strong commanding evidence their... origin display (5)
  139   their heavenly origin display (5)

Original
    43   their great Original proclaim (1)

Orion's
  456   and point Orion's sword (1)

other
    38   teach us how to love each other (3)
    97   when I am sad, to him I go, no other one can cheer me so (1)
  125   other refuge have I none; hangs my helpless soul on thee (2)
  140   no other help I know (1)
  193   help us to help each other, Lord (2)
  193   ever toward each other move, and ever move toward thee (4)
  199   to worship rightly is to love each other (1)
  222   all other ground is sinking sand (R)
  223   trust and obey, for there's no other way to be happy (R)
  223   no other way to be happy in Jesus, but to trust and obey (R)
  289   when other helpers fail and comforts flee (1)
  301   He bids us build each other up; and, gathered into one (3)
  306   and often for each other flows the sympathizing tear (3)
  309   let us for each other care (4)
  334   may they abide in union with each other and the Lord (2)
  378   with true love and brotherhood each other now embrace (4)
  378   this holy tide of Christmas all other doth deface (4)
  414   there was no other good enough to pay the price of sin (4)
  417   I ask no other sunshine than the sunshine of his face (3)
  530   kindly for each other care; every member feel its share (4)
  542   but other hearts in other lands are beating with hopes (1)
  542   but other lands have sunlight too, and clover (2)

other's
  193   each other's cross to bear (2)
  306   we share each other's woes, our mutual burdens bear (3)
  309   each the other's burdens bear (4)
  336   and are we yet alive and see each other's face (T,1)

others
    60   ye men of tender heart, forgiving others, take your part (5)
    85   living deeds that prove how sweet to serve all others (3)
    85   how sweet to serve all others, when we all others love (3)
  145   while on others thou art calling, do not pass me by (1,R)
  239   while others fought to win the prize (2)

others'
  178   far more for others' sins than... wrongs that we receive (3)
  201   nor seek our own salvation apart from others' need (2)
  431   for others' guilt the Man of Sorrows weeps in blood (3)

ought
    81   when I see thee as thou art, I'll praise thee as I ought (4)
  138   and make me love thee as I ought to love (1)
  499   furnish all we ought to ask (3)

ourselves
    90   Lord, we are thine, we give ourselves to thee (5)
  312   joyful that we ourselves are thine ... offspring (3)
  347   lead us from ourselves to thee (3)
  502   in the ocean of thy love we lose ourselves in heaven (6)
  502   we lose ourselves in heaven above (6)
  507   give up ourselves, through Jesus' power (2)
  507   join ourselves to Christ the Lord (1)

out
    12   or searching find thee out (2)
    19   cry out, dominions, princedoms, powers ... alleluia (1)
    19   cry out ... virtues, arch-angels, angels' choirs (1)
    57   thy going out, thy coming in, forever he will guide (4)
  111   worst need keep him out no more or force him to depart (2)
  179   peal out the watchward! Loyal forever! (R)
  195   I may stretch out a loving hand to wrestlers (2)
  199   love shall tread out the baleful fire of anger (5)
  263   out of my stony griefs Bethel I'll raise (4)
  289   swift to its close ebbs out life's little day (2)
  291   lives out its earthly day (3)
  295   my very heart and flesh cry out, O Loving God, for thee (2)
  295   behold, the sparrow findeth out a house wherein to rest (3)
  299   pour out thy soul for them in prayer victorious (4)
  321   when life anew pours out its wine with rich sufficiency (3)
  332   angels round our altars bow to search it out in vain (3)
  336   yet out of all the Lord hath brought us by his love (3)
  337   pour out thy spirit from on high (T,1)
  352   speak, O eternal Lord, out of thy living Word (3)
  381   cast out our sin, and enter in, be born in us today (4)
  404   lo! above the earth rang out the angel chorus (2)
  405   out of thee the Lord from heaven came to rule his Israel (1)
  408   cast out our pride & shame that hinder to enthrone thee (3)
  437   the day of resurrection, earth, tell it out abroad (T,1)
  470   set out feet on lofty places (4)
  475   would man but wake from out his haunted sleep (2)
  505   stars of heaven shine out above (2)
  510   who kindly lengthens out our days (1)
  526   out of the depths I cry to thee (T,1)
  545   he is trampling out the vintage where the grapes (1)
  545   sifting out the hearts of men before his judgment seat (3)

outburst
  447   let shouts of holy joy outburst: Alleluia (2)

outcast
    74   by thee the outcast and the poor were sought (2)
  348   open wide, O God, thy door for the outcast and the poor (3)

outcasts
  528   outcasts of men, to you I call (4)

outlast
486 who with love and meekness outlast the years of wrong (3)

outlive
418 Lord, let me never, never outlive my love to thee (3)

outpass
466 shall far outpass the power of human telling (3)

outside
108 O Jesus, thou art standing outside the fast-closed door (T)

outspread
216 his outspread pinions shall thee hide (4)

outward
186 careless through outward cares I go (5)
321 beneath the forms of outward rite (T,1)

over
  3 come, and reign over us, Ancient of Days! (1)
 35 for... love which from our birth over and around us lies (1)
 41 master over sea and land (3)
 83 he makes me triumph over death (3)
109 sing them over again to me (T,1)
170 in trust that triumphs over wrong (3)
179 over our wills and affections victorious (3)
245 like tempests over the soul (1)
247 Jesus, Savior, pilot me over life's tempestuous sea (T,1)
263 darkness be over me, my rest a stone (2)
341 Jesus! the name high over all, in hell or earth or sky (T,1)
345 temple stands, built over earth and sea (1)
355 O love that triumphs over loss we bring our hearts (4)
361 his righteous government and power shall over all extend (4)
380 and that song from afar has swept over the world (3)
383 right over the place where Jesus lay (4)
390 peace shall over ... earth its ancient splendors fling (3)
402 King forever, ceasing never over us all to reign (2)
404 over the hills and everywhere ... Jesus Christ is born (R)
409 his kingdom is glorious and rules over all (1)
419 who best can drink his cup of woe, triumphant over pain (1)
437 our Christ hath brought us over with hymns of victory (1)
491 day is past & over; all thanks, O Lord, to thee (T,1)
491 joys of day are over; we lift our hearts to thee (2)
491 toils of day are over; we raise our hymn to thee (3)
495 now the day is over, night is drawing nigh (T,1)
504 Father, we praise thee, now the night is over (T,1)
517 when all the work is over and we lay the burden down (5)

overborne
292 the poor, and them that mourn, the faint and overborne (1)

overcometh
248 to him that overcometh a crown of life shall be (4)

overcoming
221 overcoming daily with the Spirit's sword (3)

overflow
48 the rivers of woe shall not thee overflow (3)

overflows
68 my head thou dost with oil anoint, and my cup overflows (4)

overthrow
311 may she holy triumphs win, overthrow the hosts of sin (4)

owe
83 to him I owe my life and breath and all the joys I have (3)
162 thus may I rejoice to show that I feel the love I owe (4)
234 I give thee back the life I owe (1)
370 all the best we have we owe thee (1)
415 drops of grief can ne'er repay the debt of love I owe (5)
459 to thee we owe the peace that still prevails (3)
523 we owe thee thankfulness and praise, who givest all (3)

own
2 here, great God, today we offer of thine own to thee (4)
4 he leads his own, his chosen band (3)
4 all ye who own his power proclaim aloud (5)
8 adoring bend the knee while we own the mystery (4)
16 O for the living flame from his own altar brought (3)
20 did we in our own strength confide (2)
20 the man of God's own choosing (2)
24 watery worlds are all his own, and all the solid ground (2)
24 come ... people of his choice...own your gracious God (4)
47 we own thy mercies, Lord, which never fail (1)
51 so shall thou, wondering, own his way (3)
57 watchful and unslumbering care his own he safely keeps (2)
59 sing praises to his name: he forgets not his own (1)
64 before ... blazing throne we ask no luster of our own (4)
68 e'en for his own name's sake (2)
78 all hearts must bow; all things celestial thee shall own (2)
84 we'll follow thee, a King's own flock (1)
112 fatal cause demands, asks the work of his own hands (1)
113 by the empire all thine own (3)
118 I own it cannot be that I should fit myself for thee (3)
130 come quickly ... my Lord, & take possession of thine own (4)
138 all, all thine own, soul, heart and strength and mind (3)
147 we'll own the favoring gale (1)
147 teach us, in every state,to make thy will our own (4)
149 message of salvation from God's own holy Word (3)
154 have thine own way, Lord, have thine own way (T,1,2,3,4)
157 we own thy sway, we hear thy call (6)
161 who by our own false hopes and aims are spent (1)
162 Savior, teach me, day by day, thine own lesson to obey (T,1)
163 not alone the gift of life, but his own self he gave me (2)
163 naught ... I have my own I call ... hold it for the giver (2
167 through sorrow or through joy, conduct me as thine own (1)
169 just as I am, thine own to be (T,1)
171 shapest man to God's own law, thyself the fair design (2)
179 freely surrendered and wholly thine own (3)
181 we give thee but thine own, whate'er the gift may be (T,1)
182 thy ransomed servant, I restore to thee thine own (2)
184 my will is not my own till thou hast made it thine (4)
187 take my heart, it is thine own (3)

188   lead forth my soul, O Christ, one with thine own (2)
201   nor seek our own salvation apart from others' need (2)
202   our brother Christ ... makes our task his own (1)
210   so do thine own part faithfully, and trust his word (3)
215   God is his own interpreter, and he will make it plain (5)
217   He leadeth me, by his own hand he leadeth me (R)
238   but that toil shall make thee some day all mine own (4)
239   shall I fear to own his cause .. blush to speak his name (1)
242   keeping watch above his own (4)
248   arm of flesh will fail you, ye dare not trust your own (3)
249   his own hand presents the prize to thine aspiring eye (3)
251   how rich is my condition: God & heaven are still my own (1)
251   God's own hand shall guide thee there (4)
256   Heart of my own heart, whatever befall ... be my vision (4)
262   my bounding heart shall own thy sway & echo to thy voice (3)
293   formed thee for his own abode (1)
294   saved with his own precious blood (1)
295   even thine own altars, where she safe ... may bring (4)
297   with his own blood he bought her...for her life he died (1)
305   we have Christ's own promise, and that cannot fail (3)
321   Master ... symbols shared thine own dear self impart (4)
335   may they in Jesus ...they preach, their own Redeemer see (4)
340   with thine own pity, Savior (T,1)
347   thine own before thy feet we lay (1)
348   may they know this house their own (3)
349   these walls for thine own sake ... be pleased to bless (2)
358   ages are its own; see, it bursts o'er all the earth (2)
360   by thine own eternal spirit rule in all our hearts alone (2)
364   claim the kingdom for thine own (4)
366   come, thou blessed One. God's own beloved son, Alleluia (2)
385   come, peasant, King, to own him (3)
403   thou shalt own thy darkness passed away (3)
408   new life, new hope awakes where-e'er men own his sway (1)
408   One Lord, in one great name united us all who own thee (3)
412   by foes derided, by thine own rejected, O most afflicted (1)
429   cut off for sins, but not his own (1)
434   God's own sacrifice complete (3)
437   hear, so calm and plain his own "All hail" (2)
452   'tis thine own third morning, rise, O buried Lord (3)
453   own his title, praise his name (3)
455   hark ... heavenly anthem drowns all music but its own (1)
460   age-long Word expounding God's own message now as then (3)
466   and visit it with thine own ardor glowing (1)
476   send us forth ... to make all lands thine own ((1)
493   keep me, King of kings, beneath thine own almighty wings (1)
498   surrender all our hearts to be thine own (2)
500   thy kingdom stands, and grows forever, till all ... own (4)
500   till all thy creatures own thy sway (4)
509   with grateful hearts the past we own (3)
510   Father, thy mercies past we own, and thy continued care (3)
518   by thine own hand may we be fed (2)
521   God his own doth tend and nourish (2)
522   come to God's own temple, come (1)
522   all the world is God's own field (2)
526   and thus my hope is in the Lord and not in my own merit (3)
527   claim the crown, through Christ my own (4)
528   basely fear his gifts to own (3)
533   for his own pattern given (2)

owned
    54   as ... God our fathers owned, so thou art still our King (4)

owns
  122   he owns me for his child; I can no longer fear (4)
  402   frankincense to offer have I, incense owns a Deity nigh (3)

ox
  385   mean estate where ox and ass are feeding (2)
  391   ox and ass before him bow and he is in the manger now (1)

oxen
  396   oxen lowing, little knowing Christ the babe is Lord (2)

page
  296   truth is her prophetic gift, the soul, her sacred page (3)
  369   beyond the sacred page I seek thee, Lord (1)
  372   praise thee for the radiance ... from the hallowed page (1)

pages
  367   O may these heavenly pages be my ever dear delight (3)

paid
  127   thou hast for all a ranson paid (4)

pain
   50   I thank thee more that all our joy is touched with pain (3)
   60   ye who long pain and sorrow bear, praise God (5)
   86   while in our mortal pain none calls on thee in vain (2)
   89   my rest in toil, my ease in pain (3)
  140   what pain ... labor to secure my soul from endless death (2)
  142   in the hour of grief or pain will lean upon its God (2)
  157   the healing of his seamless dress is by our beds of pain (4)
  161   who by this sign didst conquer grief and pain (5)
  185   let sorrow do its work, come grief or pain (3)
  194   thy world is weary of its pain (2)
  204   make haste to heal these hearts of pain (5)
  209   bear patiently the cross of grief or pain (1)
  219   thought of thee is mightier than sin & pain & sorrow are (1)
  234   O Joy that seekest me through pain (3)
  237   or should pain attend me on my path below (3)
  237   when my last hour cometh, fraught with strife and pain (4)
  239   I'll bear the toil, endure the pain, supported (4)
  253   a soul inured to pain, to hardship, grief and loss (2)
  261   O what peace we often forfeit ... needless pain we bear (1)
  262   labor is rest .. pain is sweet if thou, my God, art here (2)
  265   in joy or in pain (3)
  270   we smile at pain when thou art near (1)
  279   a sensibility of sin, a pain to feel it near (1)
  279   O may the least omissions pain my reawakened soul (4)
  280   O may the least omission pain my reawakened soul (4)
  280   a sensibility of sin, a pain to feel it near (1)
  284   in all my pain and misery be thou my health and life (3)
  288   redeemed from earth and pain, Ah! when shall we ascend (2)
  290   if my heart and flesh are weak to bear an untried pain (2)
  291   sickness and sorrow, pain and death are felt ... no more (2)
  306   when we asunder part, it gives us inward pain (4)
  317   our human pain still bearest thou with us (2)

333 with child-like trust that fears nor pain nor death (2)
407 the curse of greed, the moan of pain (2)
408 the world has waited long, has travailed long in pain (3)
416 bane and blessing, pain and pleasure ... are sanctified (4)
418 mine was the transgression, but thine the deadly pain (2)
419 who best can drink his cup of woe, triumphant over pain (1)
419 like him... pardon on his tongue in midst of mortal pain (2)
419 through peril, toil, and pain (3)
425 bow thy meek head to mortal pain (4)
428 O Lamb of God, was ever pain, was ever love, like thine (4)
441 when our hearts are wintry, grieving, or in pain (4)
481 no night, nor need, nor pain (1)
481 wring gold from human pain (3)
485 hasten, Lord ... perfect day when pain & death ... cease (2)
486 those oppressed or lonely ... long at strife with pain (3)
495 comfort every sufferer watching late in pain (4)
527 died he for me, who caused his pain (1)

pained
531 my heart is pained, nor can it be at rest (1)

pains
316 remember thee, and all thy pains, and all thy love to me (3)
414 may not know ... cannot tell, what pains he had to bear (2)
501 O in what divers pains they met (1)

paints
442 He who skies & meadows paints fashioned all your virtue (3)
513 he paints the wayside flower, he lights the evening star (2)

pair
344 unite the pair . long disjoined, knowledge & vital piety (3)

pale
418 how pale thou art with anguish, with sore abuse & scorn (1)

palm
88 waving a branch of a palm tree high in my hand (3)
296 beneath the pine or palm, one unseen Presence she adores (2)
423 victor palm branch waving, and chanting clear and loud (2)

palms
290 I know not where his islands lift their fronded palms (5)
290 their fronded palms in air (5)
424 the people of the Hebrews with palms before thee went (2)
425 O Savior meek, pursue thy road with palms (1)
425 road with palms and scattered garments strowed (1)

paltry
422 so lowly doth the Savior ride a paltry borrowed beast (T,1)

pang
270 stooped to share our sharpest pang, our bitterest tear (1)

panoply
250 but take, to arm you for the fight, the panoply of God (2)

panted
220   truest friend to me, long my heart hath panted (1)

pants
255   as pants the hart for cooling streams (T,1)
369   my spirit pants for thee, O living word (1)

paradise
198   every life shall be a song when all... earth is paradise (4)
325   not paradise, with all its joys ... such delight afford (1)
389   the glorious gates of paradise the angel guards no more (4)
413   that his pardoned soul is worthy of a place in paradise (2)
439   Christ hath opened paradise, Alleluia (3)
455   round his pierced feet fair flowers of paradise extend (3)
455   flowers of paradise extend their fragrance ever sweet (3)
462   today with thee in paradise (3)
485   man's rude work deface no more the paradise of God (2)
518   and grant that we may feast in paradise with thee (1)

pardon
89   to me, with thy great name, are given pardon (2)
89   to me ... are given pardon and holiness and heaven (2)
109   offer pardon and peace to all (3)
119   wilt welcome, pardon, cleanse, relieve (5)
139   into himself he all receives, pardon and holiness (4)
139   pardon and holiness and heaven (4)
166   and purchased my pardon on Calvary's tree (2)
228   to pardon and sanctify me (3)
325   pardon and peace to dying men and endless life are given (2)
350   the sinner pardon at thy feet (4)
419   like him... pardon on his tongue in midst of mortal pain (2)
420   pardon for all flows from his side (2)
494   pardon each infirmity, open fault, and secret sin (2)
526   thou grantest pardon through thy love (2)

pardoned
413   that his pardoned soul is worthy of a place in paradise (2)

pardoning
122   my God is reconciled; his pardoning voice I hear (4)
129   and let the sweet tokens of pardoning grace bring joy (4)
489   while we pray for pardoning grace (2)

parent
35   for the joy of human love, brother, sister, parent,child (4)

parents
516   children early lisp his fame and parents hold him dear (2)
516   parents love the sacred Word and all its wisdom prize (3)

parliament
482   in mart & court and parliament the common good increase (3)

part
4   both soul and body bear your part (4)
10   more than all, the heart must bear the longest part (2)
12   I know thee ... in part, I ask not, Lord, for more (3)

60	ye men of tender heart, forgiving others, take your part (5)
105	vain world, farewell, from thee I part (5)
128	here have I found a nobler part (4)
133	this earthly part of me glows with thy fire divine (3)
141	God will fulfill in every part each promise he has made (1)
210	so do thine own part faithfully, and trust his word (3)
278	scatter .. life through every part .. sanctify the whole (2)
282	life nor death can part from him that dwells within (3)
285	be mine this better part (3)
302	part of his host have crossed the flood (4)
302	part are crossing now (4)
303	exult, O dust and ashes; the Lord shall be thy part (3)
306	when we asunder part, it gives us inward pain (4)
338	blest be the dear uniting love that will not let us part (T)
338	joy .. grief .. time .. place .. life nor death can part (4)
376	if I were a wise man, I would do my part (4)
398	and glorifies with duty life's poorest, humblest part (2)
407	send God's love to earth's remotest part (1)
485	part them, Lord, to each and all, as each & all ... need (1)

partake
301	we all partake the joy of one; the common peace we feel (4)
389	and we of heaven partake (3)
464	all partake the glorious bliss (1)
547	let mortal tongues awake; let all that breathe partake (3)

partaker
| 318 | let me be a fit partaker of ... blessed food from heaven (2) |

partakers
| 338 | partakers of the Savior's grace ... same in mind & heart (4) |

partakes
| 297 | one holy name she blesses, partakes one holy food (2) |

parties
| 530 | names and sects and parties fall: thou, O Christ art all (5) |

parting
185	this be the parting cry my heart shall raise (4)
236	with one accord our parting hymn of praise (1)
246	take thee, at thy parting breath, to his divine abode 4)

Paschal
| 454 | Paschal Lamb, by God appointed (2) |

pass
45	in the rustling grass I hear him pass (2)
99	not till earth and not till heaven pass away (6)
108	in lowly patience waiting to pass the threshold o'er (1)
145	pass me not, O gentle Savior, hear my humble cry (T,1)
145	while on others thou art calling, do not pass me by (1,R)
251	swift shall pass thy pilgrim days (4)
281	whose word, when heaven and earth shall pass, remains (1)
289	earth's joys grow dim; its glories pass away (2)
362	power and pomp of nations shall pass like a dream away (2)
406	pass on and carry swift the news ye bring (1)

406 through jungles, sluggish seas, and mountain pass (2)
420 behold him, all ye that pass by (3)
427 is this thy sorrow naught to us who pass unheeding by (1)
490 birds pass high in flight, fragrant flowers now bloom (91)
494 soon from us the light of day shall forever pass away (3)
500 so be it, Lord; thy throne shall never ... pass away (4)
500 thy throne shall never, like earth's proud empires, pass (4)
503 when forever from our sight pass the stars, the day (4)
503 pass the stars, the day, the night (4)

passed
76 brought it back victorious when from death he passed (3)
99 sorrow vanquished, labor ended, Jordan passed (5)
130 grace ... wide as infinity ... it never passed by one (3)
130 or it had passed by me (3)
250 having all things done, and all your conflicts passed (2)
321 the blessed cup is only passed true memory of thee (3)
403 thou shalt own thy darkness passed away (3)
440 Christ has passed the eternal gates (2)
548 souls that passed and left no name (3)

passes
326 feast after feast thus comes and passes by (5)

passeth
108 O love that passeth knowledge, so patiently to wait (2)
446 that thy peace which evermore passeth human knowing (4)

passing
33 thyself the vision passing by in crystal and in rose (3)
105 shall life's swift passing years all fly (1)
200 our strength is dust and ashes, our years a passing hour (3)
289 I need thy presence every passing hour (3)
326 yet, passing, points to the glad feast above (5)

passion
138 one holy passion filling all my frame (5)
161 save us, thy people, from consuming passion (1)
164 above the storms of passion, the murmurs of self-will (3)
269 while passion stains, and folly dims our youth (2)
321 in our daily life may flame the passion of thy heart (4)
345 storm of earth-born passion dies (4)
345 round these hallowed walls the storm of... passion dies (4)
364 dear tokens of his passion still his dazzling body bears (3)
412 death of anguish and thy bitter passion for my salvation (4)
424 to thee, before thy passion they sang .. hymns of praise (3)

passion's
459 and calming passion's fierce and stormy gales (3)

passions
284 purge away my sin; from earth-born passions set me free (1)
292 the wayward and the lost, by restless passions tossed (2)
343 may earth-born passions die (3)
466 O let it freely burn, till earthly passions turn to dust (2)
466 passions turn to dust and ashes in its heat consuming (2)

passover
437   the passover of gladnesss, the passover of God (1)

past
    9   days of praise shall ne'er be past while life ... last (1,4)
   28   O God, our help in ages past (T,1,6)
   47   in all the past ... thy hand we see (1)
   47   God of the past ... with us abide (2)
   47   God of the past, our times are in thy hand (2)
   52   praise thee for thy mercies past, & humbly hope for more (3)
  125   till the storm of life is past (1)
  139   future and past subsisting now (3)
  206   by whose hand through years long past our lives were led (1)
  209   God doth undertake to guide ... future as ... the past (2)
  209   when change and tears are past (3)
  214   past deeds shall come and them ensnare (4)
  272   remember not past years (2)
  284   when this life is past, I may the eternal brightness see (5)
  288   servant of God, well done! thy glorious warfare's past (T)
  326   the feast, though not the love, is past and gone (4)
  336   what troubles have see seen, what mighty conflicts past (2)
  366   come forth, ye virgins, night is past (1)
  397   and, when earthly things are past (4)
  491   the day is past and over; all thanks, O Lord, to thee (T,1)
  492   may we this life improve, to mourn for errors past (4)
  496   though the arrows past us fly (2)
  499   new perils past, new sins forgiven (2)
  509   with grateful hearts the past we own (3)
  510   Father, thy mercies past we own, and thy continued care (3)
  552   thy love divine hath led us in the past (2)

pastor's
  335   not a cause of small import the pastor's care demands (2)

pastures
   67   where the verdant pastures grow (2)
   68   he makes me down to lie in pastures green (1)
  121   in thy pleasant pastures feed us (1)
  129   to feed them in pastures of love (2)
  230   green pastures are before me, which yet I have not seen (3)
  303   the pastures of the blessed are decked in glorious sheen (2)
  362   in pastures of peace he'll lead them (3)
  512   the flocks in pastures graze (2)

path
   12   that makes the darkest way I go an open path to thee (4)
   63   his mercy brightens all the path in which we rove (1)
   64   sun of our life, thy quickening ray sheds on our path (2)
   64   sheds on our path the glow of day (2)
  161   showing to wandering souls the path of light (3)
  205   cheers each winding path I tread (2)
  207   when dangers fierce your path assail (2)
  230   my hope I cannot measure, my path to life is free (3)
  233   yes, on through life's long path still chanting as ye go (4)
  237   or should pain attend me on my path below (3)
  240   Christ is the path, and Christ the prize (2)
  245   and rough seems the path to the goal (1)

252   the path of prayer thyself hast trod (6)
269   however rough and steep the path may be (4)
270   no path we shun, no darkness dread (2)
272   I loved to choose and see my path (2)
354   to us the path of knowledge show (2)
359   love, joy and hope, like flowers, spring in his path (3)
359   spring in his path to birth (3)
368   Lamp ... whereby we trace our path when wont to stray (1)
372   teach thy wandering pilgrims by this their path to trace (4)
403   thine shall be a path, though thorny, bright (4)
410   Savior ... who the path of sorrow hath trod (4)
452   tread the path of darkness, saving strength to show (3)
466   and clothe me round the while my path illuming (2)
473   and dark is his path on the wings of the storm (2)
533   the long cloud of witnesses show the same path to heaven (2)

paths

47   through paths unknown we follow thee (3)
68   me to walk doth make within the paths of righteousness (2)
70   when in the slippery paths of youth (3)
170   in lowly paths of service free (1)
173   O help us walk unflinching in paths that lead to peace (3)
188   joyful to follow thee through paths unknown (2)
203   thy paths of service lead to blazoned heights (1)
204   from paths where hide the lures of greed (2)
206   new faith to find the paths ahead (1)
269   lead us, O Father, in the paths of peace (T,1)
269   lead us, O Father, in the paths of truth (2)
269   lead us, O Father, in the paths of right (3)
552   thy Word our law, thy paths our chosen way (2)

pathway

80   marks divine ... that lit the lonely pathway (1)
80   pathway, trod in wondrous love, O Son of God (1)
164   no wander from the pathway if thou wilt be my guide (1)
214   their determined quest to follow in the saints' pathway (1)
476   until true wisdom from above . make life's pathway clear (3)
534   O keep us in the pathway their saintly feet have trod (2)

pathways

48   when through fiery trials thy pathways shall lie (4)

patience

108   in lowly patience waiting to pass the threshold o'er (1)
138   teach me the patience of unanswered prayer (4)
170   teach me thy patience (3)
526   his help I wait with patience (3)
549   in truth and patience wrought (3)

patient

80   who like thee ... go so patient through a world of woe (2)
144   with patient uncomplaining love, still ... cling to thee (2)
178   patient love was seen in all thy life and death of woe (1)
191   of steadfast will, patient, courageous, strong and true (3)
333   of patient hope and quiet, brave endurance (2)
419   patient bears his cross below ... follows in his train (1)
517   grant us, then, pure hearts and patient (3)

patiently
   108 O love that passeth knowledge, so patiently to wait (2)
   175 back to the narrow way patiently win them (4)
   209 bear patiently the cross of grief or pain (1)

patriarchs
   19   ye patriarchs and prophets blest (3)
   440 patriarchs from the distant ages (3)

patriot
   543 O beautiful for patriot dream that sees beyond the years (4)
   548 the glory that illumines patriot lives of deathless fame (3)

patriots
   191 the patriots nations need ... the bulwarks of the state (4)

pattern
   276 to dwell in lowliness with men, their pattern &... King (2)
   309 to thy Church the pattern give (4)
   533 for his own pattern given (2)

Paul
   212 if you can't preach like Peter ... can't pray like Paul (2)

pavilioned
   473 pavilioned in splendor, and girded with praise (1)

pay
   169 my life to give, my vows to pay (2)
   180 joyful rise to pay thy morning sacrifice (1)
   196 my vows I will to his great name before his people pay (3)
   258 see thou render all thy feeble strength can pay (1)
   412 therefore, kind Jesus, since I cannot pay thee (5)
   414 there was no other good enough to pay the price of sin (4)

peace
     1 music in the sinner's ears...life & health & peace (3)
     4 our peace and joy and blessing (3)
     9 he sends the laboring conscience peace (3)
    35 peace on earth, and joy in heaven (6)
    49 with ever joyful hearts & blessed peace to cheer us (2)
    50 a yearning for a deeper peace not known before (4)
    84 Child through whom we know thee, God of peace (3)
    89 comfort it brings and power and peace (2)
    89 in war my peace, in loss my gain (3)
    92 I shall possess, within the veil...life of joy & peace (5)
   109 offer pardon and peace to all (3)
   114 we...his unknown peace receive & feel his blood applied (3)
   132 O hear our supplication, Blessed Spirit, God of peace (2)
   136 fill it...with righteousness and peace (1)
   159 till I rest in peace with thee (4)
   165 fill our hearts with joy and peace (1)
   170 in peace that only thou canst give (4)
   173 O help us walk unflinshing in paths that lead to peace (3)
   185 once earthly joy I craved, sought peace and rest (2)
   199 and in its ashes plant the tree of peace (5)
   199 where pity dwells, the peace of God is there (1)
   205 heavenly peace, divinest comfort (1)

208   just from Jesus simply taking life & rest & joy & peace (3)
211   the Lord will give thee peace (2)
220   though the storms may gather, still have peace within (3)
220   who love the Father ... still have peace (3)
227   sweet comfort and peace of a soul in its earliest love (1)
227   tongue can never express the sweet comfort and peace (1)
229   peace, perfect peace, our future all unknown (5)
229   peace, perfect peace, in this dark world of sin (T,1)
229   peace, perfect peace, with sorrows surging round (3)
229   the blood of Jesus whispers peace within (1)
229   peace, perfect peace, by thronging duties pressed (2)
229   peace, perfect peace, with loved ones far away (4)
235   let our ordered lives confess the beauty of thy peace (4)
236   then, lowly kneeling, wait thy word of peace (1)
236   grant us thy peace upon our homeward way (2)
236   grant us thy peace, Lord, through the coming night (3)
236   grant us thy peace throughout our earthly life (4)
236   call us, O Lord, to thine eternal peace (4)
238   peace shall follow battle; night shall end in day (3)
243   faith's warfare ended, won the home of endless peace (4)
259   in suffering be thy love my peace (3)
261   O what peace we often forfeit ... needless pain we bear (1)
265   no tender voice like thine can peace afford (1)
269   lead us, O Father, in the paths of peace (T,1)
276   the Lord, who left the throne our life & peace to bring (2)
297   she waits the consumation of peace forevermore (3)
299   publish glad tidings, tidings of peace (R)
301   we all partake the joy of one; the common peace we feel (4)
301   a peace to sensual minds unknown, a joy unspeakable (4)
309   show thyself the Prince of Peace (1)
310   thy name is life and joy and peace and everlasting love (2)
314   by thy gift of peace restored (2)
325   pardon and peace to dying men and endless life are given (2)
333   grant them the peace which calms all earthly strife (3)
351   and secret of thy heavenly peace (2)
354   fill the whole world with heaven's peace (3)
355   to seek the kingdom of thy peace (3)
358   blessedness and light, peace & truth its course portends (2)
358   lo, the Prince of Peace, lo, the Son of God is come (3)
359   before him on the mountains shall peace, the herald, go (3)
361   his name shall be the Prince of Peace forevermore adored (3)
362   in pastures of peace he'll lead them (3)
369   and I shall find my peace, my all-in-all (2)
371   questing hearts that long for peace and healing see (3)
373   the power of Satan breaking, our peace eternal making (1)
381   praises sing to God the King, and peace to men on earth (2)
387   peace on earth and mercy mild (1)
387   hail the heaven-born Prince of Peace (3)
390   peace on the earth, good will to me (1)
390   peace shall over ... earth its ancient splendors fling (3)
393   holy infant so tender and mild sleep in heavenly peace (1)
394   all glory be to God on high, and to the earth be peace (6)
406   upon the highway of the Prince of Peace (3)
408   heal its ancient wrong, come, Prince of Peace, and reign (3)
410   a story of truth and mercy, a story of peace and light (1)
416   lo! it glows with peace and joy (2)
416   peace is there, that knows no measure (4)

420 the bleeding Prince of life and peace (3)
422 the day of peace we long to see (4)
440 God's likeness, man awaking, knows the everlasting peace (1)
446 that thy peace which evermore passeth human knowing (4)
454 peace is made twixt man and God (2)
455 crown him the Lord of peace, whose power a scepter sways (3)
457 who gives us power and peace (3)
459 O holy Jesus, Prince of Peace and Savior (3)
459 to thee we owe the peace that still prevails (3)
459 from thee...our faith and hope, our fellowship and peace (4)
467 keep far our foes; give peace at home (3)
476 kindness dwell in human hearts and... earth find peace (2)
477 bring to our world of strife thy sovereign word of peace (4)
478 and holiness shall whisper the sweet amen of peace (2)
479 counsel, aid, and peace we give (4)
482 men at last ... ring the bells of brotherhood & peace (3)
485 just rule ... fill ... earth with health & light & peace (2)
493 that with the world, myself, and thee...at peace may be (2)
493 I, ere I sleep, at peace may be (2)
505 brings the night its peace profound (1)
506 may weariness and sadness be lulled to peace & gladness (3)
516 Lord, let us in our homes agree .. blessed peace to gain (4)
520 build thou a hallowed dwelling where ... joy & peace (4)
520 hallowed dwelling where true joy and peace endure (4)
525 for peace on earth, both far and near, we thank thee (1)
532 in peace their sacred ashes rest (6)
538 and give, for wild confusion, peace (3)
542 a song of peace for lands afar and mine (1)
542 a song of peace for their land and for mine (2)
544 give to us peace in our time, O Lord (1,2,3)
544 peace to the nations, and praise to the Lord (4)
551 with peace our borders bless (2)
552 thy bounteous goodness nourish us in peace (3)

peaceable
344 give .. wisdom from above, spotless .. peaceable & kind (2)

peaceful
247 'twixt me and the peaceful rest (3)
268 what peaceful hours I once enjoyed! (3)
390 with peaceful wings unfurled (2)
461 come as the dove & spread thy wings ... of peaceful love (3)
509 and peaceful, leave before thy feet (3)
523 for peaceful homes and healthful days (3)
532 praise we the peaceful men of skill (4)
532 peaceful men of skill who builded homes of beauty (4)

peal
179 peal our the watchword! silence it never! (R)
179 peal out the watchward! Loyal forever! (R)

pealing
343 we bid the pealing organ wait to speak alone thy will (3)

peals
32 in distant peals it dies (4)
475 now, even now, once more from earth to sky peals forth (3)
475 peals forth in joy man's old undaunted cry (3)

pearl
    366 of one pearl each shining portal (3)
    536 through gates of pearl streams in the countless host (6)

pearls
    400 gems of the mountain and pearls of the ocean (3)

peasant
    385 come, peasant, King, to own him (3)

pen
    82   ah, this nor tongue nor pen can show (4)
    371 sages, who wrote the message with immortal pen (2)
    484 from all ... terror teaches, from lies of tongue and pen (2)

penitent
    103 hope of the penitent, fadeless and pure (2)
    175 waiting the penitent child to receive (2)

people
    3   our prayer attend, come, and thy people bless (2)
    3   come, and thy people bless, and give thy Word success (2)
    6   we, thy people , praise thee, God of every nation! (T,1,2)
    6   we, thy people, praise thee, Lord of hosts eternal! (1,2)
    6   we, thy people praise thee ... praise thee evermore! (1,2)
    16   stand up and bless the Lord, ye people of his choice (T,1)
    21   all people that on earth do dwell (T,1)
    24   come ... people of his choice...own your gracious God (4)
    39   his glory let the people know (1)
    55   let the amen sound from his people again (4)
    90   with all the listening people gathered round (3)
    98   Jesus, where'er thy people meet (T,1)
    161 save us, thy people, from consuming passion (1)
    196 my vows I will to his great name before his people pay (3)
    200 whom shall I send to succor my people in their need (1)
    200 I hear my people crying in cot and mine and slum (2)
    200 I see my people falling in darkness and despair (2)
    231 who gives the lilies clothing will clothe his people,too (3)
    257 hear the cry thy people raises (3)
    298 with thy wonted loving-kindness hear thy people (2)
    298 hear thy people when they pray (2)
    299 proclaim to every people, tongue, and nation (3)
    305 onward, then, ye people, join our happy throng (4)
    337 firmness with meekness from above to bear thy people (3)
    337 to bear thy people on their heart (3)
    352 be in each song of praise which here thy people raise (2)
    353 thy people pray, come quickly, King of kings (5)
    360 born to set thy people free (1)
    360 born thy people to deliver, born a child and yet a King (2)
    361 the people that in darkness sat (T,1)
    362 proclaim to a desolate people the coming of their King (2)
    422 to heal the people of their shame, and nobleness instill (3)
    424 the people of the Hebrews with palms before thee went (2)
    456 where his loving people meet to share the gift divine (2)
    470 on thy people pour thy power (1)
    472 people and realms of every tongue dwell (3)
    475 earth shall be fair, and all her people one (3)

333 O perfect Love, all human thought transcending (T,1)
333 O perfect Life, be thou their full assurance (2)
356 work God's perfect will (4)
401 more & more thyself display, shining to the perfect day (3)
402 guide us to thy perfect light (R)
403 that light hath on thee shone in which is perfect day (3)
426 perfect man on thee did suffer (1,4)
426 perfect God on thee has bled (1,4)
471 inflame our hearts with perfect love (4)
479 on the cross, forsaken, work thy mercy's perfect deed (1)
485 hasten, Lord ... perfect day when pain & death ... cease (2)
496 the perfect day before us breaks in everlasting light (4)
499 Q Lord, in thy dear love fit us for perfect rest above (4)
501 and none, O Lord, have perfect rest (4)
520 may church and home combine to teach thy perfect way (1)

perfected
116 Jesus comes! He fills my soul! Perfected in him I am (5)
269 until our lives are perfected in thee (4)

perfecting
530 perfecting the saints below (1)

perfection
442 praise him, seers, heroes, kings, Heralds of perfection (3)

perfection's
130 and sink me to perfection's height

perfectly
227 by my Savior possessed, I was perfectly blest (5)
283 let us see thy great salvation perfectly restored (4)

perfectness
193 this is the bond of perfectness, thy spotless charity (6)

perfects
137 saves whoe'er on Jesus call, and perfects them in love (4)

perform
215 God moves in a mysterious way his wonders to perform (T,1)

performed
54 thy wonders in their days performed (1)

perfume
402 myrrh is mine; its bitter perfume breathes ... gloom (4)
472 his name like sweet perfume shall rise (2)

peril
419 they climbed the steep ascent of heaven through peril (3)
419 through peril, toil, and pain (3)
491 ask that free from peril the hours of dark may be (3)
538 hear us when we cry to thee for those in peril on... sea (R)
544 praise him who saved them from peril and sword (4)

periled
84 to periled sailor, rudder (1)

perils
491 how many are the perils through which we have to go (4)
499 new perils past, new sins forgiven (2)
539 when life's perils thick confound you (3)

period
70 through every period of my life thy goodness I'll pursue (4)

perish
27 and wither and perish, but naught changeth thee (3)
135 kindle every high desire; perish self in thy pure fire (2)
251 perish every fond ambition, all I've... hoped or known (1)
299 he who made all nations is not willing one ... perish (1)
299 one soul should perish lost in shades of night (1)
305 crowns and thrones may perish, kingdoms rise and wane (3)
355 in the night of hate and war we perish as we lose thee (3)
362 like the flowers of the field they perish (2)

perished
532 whose names have perished, lost in the haze of long ago (5)

perishing
175 rescue the perishing, duty demands it (4)
175 rescue the perishing, care for the dying (T,1,R)

permit
312 permit them to approach, he cries (2)

perpetual
467 enable with perpetual light the dullness of... sight (2)
507 all, with one accord, in a perpetual covenant join (1)

perplexed
49 and keep us in his grace, and guide us when perplexed (2)

perplexity
284 through darkness & perplexity point ...the heavenly way (4)

perserver
491 be thou our souls' perserver, O God, for thou dost know (4)

persons
26 God in three persons, blessed Trinity! (1,4)

persuasive
349 Christ, with love's persuasive power (3)

pervading
462 letting thine all-pervading power fulfill the dream (1)
494 thou, whose all-pervading eye naught escapes (2)

perverse
67 perverse and foolish oft I strayed (3)

pestilence
216 nor pestilence that walks by night (5)
552 from war's alarms, from deadly pestilence (3)

Peter
212 if you can't preach like Peter ... can't pray like Paul (2)

petition
275 thy wings shall my petition bear to him (3)

Pharaoh's
446 loosed from Pharaoh's bitter yoke (1)

Physician's
411 proclaim the good Physician's mind (3)

picture
372 it is the heaven-drawn picture of thee, the living Word (2)

piece
248 put on the gospel armor, each piece put on with prayer (3)

pierce
132 pierce the clouds of nature's night (1)
355 new thorns to pierce that steady brow (1)
401 pierce the gloom of sin and grief (3)
419 the martyr first, whose eagle eye could pierce (2)
419 eagle eye could pierce beyond the grave (2)

pierced
364 pierced and nailed him to the tree (2)
455 round his pierced feet fair flowers of paradise extend (3)

piety
344 unite the pair...long disjoined, knowledge & vital piety (3)

pilgrim
155 his first avowed intent to be a pilgrim (1)
155 he will make good his right to be a pilgrim (2)
155 I'll labor night and day to be a pilgrim (3)
176 along my pilgrim journey, Savior, let we walk with thee (1)
251 swift shall pass thy pilgrim days (4)
271 Pilgrim through this barren land (1)
534 thou hast kept thy pilgrim people (1)
543 O beautiful for pilgrim feet (2)
543 pilgrim feet, whose stern, impassioned stress (2)
550 where their pilgrim feet have trod ... God ... guards (3)

pilgrimage
296 feet on mercy's errands swift do make her pilgrimage (3)

pilgrims
106 gently lead us by the hand, pilgrims in a desert land (1)
372 teach thy wandering pilgrims by this their path to trace (4)
474 cease, ye pilgrims, cease to mourn (3)

pilgrims'
547 land where my fathers died, land of the pilgrims' pride (1)

pillar
271 let the fire and cloudy pillar lead me all my journey (2)

pillared
423 through pillared court and temple the lovely anthem rang (1)

pillars
428 and earth's strong pillars bend (2)

pilot
247 Jesus, Savior, pilot me over life's tempestuous sea (T,1)
247 wondrous sovereign of the sea, Jesus Savior, pilot me (2)
247 Jesus, Savior, Pilot me (T,1,2)

pine
32 shall not, in the mountain pine, disturb a sparrows nest (3)
255 for thee my God .. living God, my thirsty soul doth pine (2)
273 like .. straightness of the pine trees let me upright be (3)
296 beneath the pine or palm, one unseen Presence she adores (2)
542 and sunlight beams on clover-leaf and pine (2)

pinion
41 made him fly with eagle pinion (3)

pinions
216 his outspread pinions shall thee hide (4)

pitiful
309 make us of one heart and mind, courteous, pitiful & kind (3)

pity
41 teach us more of human pity that we in thine image grow (3)
65 like the pity of a father hath... Lord's compassion been (3)
104 full of pity, love, and power (1)
118 pity and heal my sin-sick soul (2)
175 snatch them in pity from sin and the grave (1)
199 where pity dwells, the peace of God is there (1)
340 with thine own pity, Savior (T,1)
412 think on thy pity ... love unswerving, not my deserving (5)
418 for this thy dying sorrow, thy pity without end (3)
427 till through our pity and our shame love answers (2)
485 all pity, care, and love, all calm and courage...pour (1)
544 show forth thy pity on high where thou reignest (1)

pitying
113 Savior,look with pitying eye; Savior, help me, or I die (R)

place
13 oh, how blessed is this place (1)
25 might I enjoy the meanest place within thy house (2)
39 his dwelling place, how fair (2)
44 oh, what is man, in thy regard to hold so large a place (3)
58 safe in the same dear dwelling place (4)
68 in God's house forevermore my dwelling place shall be (5)
98 and every place is hallowed ground (1)
115 this earth, he cries, is not my place (1)
115 I seek my place in heaven (1)
117 I found in him a resting place, and he has made me glad (1)
124 who will place me on his right (3)
141 Lord Jesus, make me whole; grant me no resting place (4)

200   from ease & plenty save us; from pride of place absolve (4)
203   we've sought and found thee in the secret place (2)
211   place on the Lord reliance; my soul, with courage wait (2)
216   within the secret place of   God (1)
216   thy dwelling place the Highest One (6)
217   Lord, I would place my hand in thine (3)
225   make in my heart a quiet place ... come & dwell therein (1)
225   a little place of mystic grace (4)
232   place where Jesus sheds the oil of gladness on our heads (2)
232   a place than all beside more sweet (2)
267   place in my hands the wonderful key (1)
275   I hasten to the place where God my Savior shows his face (2)
283   till in heaven we take our place (4)
291   when I shall reach that happy place ... be forever blest (3)
295   how lovely is thy dwelling place, O Lord of hosts (T,1)
296   unchanged by changing place (91)
338   joy .. grief .. time .. place .. life nor death can part (4)
350   how blessed is this place, O Lord (T,1)
351   bless thou this house that it may be a place most meet (1)
351   a place most meet to learn of thee (1)
352   dwell in this holy place, e'en now descend (1)
353   left .. lonesome place of death, despite .. rage of foes (3)
376   in the bleak midwinter a stable place sufficed (2)
378   now to the Lord sing praises, all you within this place (5)
383   right over the place where Jesus lay (4)
395   such a babe in such a place, can he be the Savior (1)
413   that his pardoned soul is worthy of a place in paradise (2)
417   I take, O cross, thy shadow for my abiding place (3)
418   lo, here I fall, my Savior! 'Tis I deserve thy place (2)
454   there thou dost our place prepare (3)
458   highest place ... heaven affords belongs to him by right (2)
466   for none can guess its grace, till he become the place (3)
466   the place wherein the Holy Spirit makes his dwelling (3)
474   rise ... toward heaven, thy native place (1)
480   and in earth's darkest place, let there be light (3)
487   bless the sermon in this place (4)
520   within ...home let every heart become thy dwelling place (2)
520   grant, Love Divine, in every place glad fellowship (3)
549   and met within thy holy place to rest awhile with thee (1)

placed
530   placed according to thy will let us all our work fulfill (3)

places
325   come to your places at the feast (4)
362   make straight all the crooked places (1,4)
470   set out feet on lofty places (4)

plague
216   nor plague approach thy guarded home (6)

plagues
216   when fearful plagues around prevail (3)
216   nor plagues that waste in noonday light (5)

plain
215   God is his own interpreter, and he will make it plain (5)

402 born a King on Bethlehem's plain (2)
437 listening to his accents, may hear, so calm and plain (2)
437 hear, so calm and plain his own, "All hail" (2)
473 it streams from the hills, it descends to the plain (4)
490 glad for cotton coat, plain food satisfies (3)
512 the seed by him provided is sown o'er hill and plain (1)
543 for purple mountain majesties above the fruited plain (1)

plains
40 thy fingers spread the mountains and plains (1)
291 o'er ... wide-extended plains shines one eternal day (2)
374 sweetly singing o'er the plains (1)
390 above its sad & lowly plains they bend on hovering wing (2)
392 while fields and floods, rocks, hills and plains repeat (2)
395 all the plains were lit that night (2)
431 from heavenly plains is borne the song that angels know (4)

plaint
481 there swells the sobbing human plaint (2)
481 sobbing human plaint that bids thy walls arise (2)

plan
18 death and rising tell the grace in heaven's plan (2)
141 God's mercy holds a wiser plan than thou canst fully know (2
260 secret thought... hidden plan, wrought...or unexpressed (2)
347 through mortal motive, scheme... plan thy... purpose ran (2)
495 those who plan some evil, from their sins restrain (4)

planets
43 all the planets in their turn confirm the tidings (2)
486 at whose inscrutable decree the planets wheel and turn (1)

planned
41 toward the goal that thou hast planned (4)

planning
514 all our thinking, planning, waiting (2)

plant
37 not a plant or flower below, but makes thy glories known (3)
198 dare all that may plant man's lordship firm on earth (2)
199 and in its ashes plant the tree of peace (5)

planted
307 planted thy holy name within our hearts (1)
307 Father, we thank thee who hast planted (T,1)

plants
215 he plants his footsteps in the sea (1)
342 we cultivate the nature God plants in every heart (3)

plea
118 I give up every plea beside (4)
119 just as I am, without one plea (T,1)
185 this is my earnest plea: more love, O Christ, to thee (1)
374 love to God and all men, love for plea and gift and sign (3)

plead
95   mercy now, O Lord, I plead in this hour of utter need (3)
122   his all-redeeming love, his precious blood, to plead (2)
122   they pour effectual prayers; they strongly plead for me (3)
127   blood, which at the mercy seat of God...doth...plead (3)
127   forever doth for sinners plead (3)
175   plead with them earnestly, plead with them gently (2)
237   in the hour of trial, Jesus, plead for me (T,1)
445   He lives, to plead for me above (2)

pleading
106   pleading nought but Jesus' blood, whisper softly (3)
108   O Jesus, thou art pleading in accents meek and low (3)
110   Jesus is pleading; O list to his voice (4)
177   at thy blest mercy seat, pleading for me (2)
257   help us by thy spirit's pleading (3)
385   for sinners here the silent Word is pleading (2)
440   holiest hearts for ages pleading (2)
454   there for sinners thou art pleading (3)

pleads
486   silent courage pleads to heaven more eloquent than song (3)

pleasant
34   the cold wind in the winter, the pleasant summer sun (3)
121   in thy pleasant pastures feed us (1)
149   'tis pleasant to repeat (3)
295   the tabernacles of thy grace how pleasant, Lord, they be (1)

please
173   thoughts & actions less prone to please the crowd (1)

pleased
349   these walls for thine own sake ... be pleased to bless (2)
349   O Lord, be pleased to bless, we pray (2)
351   be pleased to guide, each lengthening year, thy sons (2)
387   pleased as man with men to dwell, Jesus our Emmanuel (2)
507   if thou art well pleased to hear, come down (4)
550   thou heard'st well pleased, the song, the prayer (2)

pleasing
253   tramples down and casts behind the baits of pleasing ill (2)
277   according to thy mind & Word, well-pleasing in thy sight (3)
492   with joy we view the pleasing change (3)

pleasure
2   craftman's art and music's measure for thy pleasure (3)
2   art ... music's measure for thy pleasure all combine (3)
76   'tis the Father's pleasure we should call him Lord (1)
93   I hope, by thy good pleasure, safely to arrive at home (2)
176   not for ease or worldly pleasure (2)
210   heart content to take whate'er thy Father's pleasure (2)
220   Jesus, priceless treasure, source of purest pleasure (T,1)
220   whate'er we must bear still in thee lies purest pleasure (3)
270   when drooping pleasure turns to grief (3)
307   thou, Lord, didst make all for thy pleasure (2)
416   bane and blessing, pain and pleasure ... are sanctified (4)

pleasures
   105   earth's pleasures shall I still hold dear (1)
   107   still he calls, in cares and pleasures (4)
   128   here heavenly pleasures fill my breast (4)
   237   with forbidden pleasures would this vain world charm (2)

pledge
   189   here together, brother men, we pledge the Lord anew (2)
   314   by this pledge that thou dost love us (2)

Pleiades
   456   where light-years frame the Pleiades (1)

plenteous
   125   plenteous grace with thee is found (4)

plenteousness
   551   our cities with prosperity ... fields with plenteousness (2)

plentiful
   89   in want my plentiful supply (4)

plenty
   200   from ease & plenty save us; from pride of place absolve (4)

plow
   513   plow the fields and scatter the good seed on the land (1)
   513   we plow the fields (T,1)

plowing
   514   take our plowing, seeding, reaping (2)

pluck
   141   life nor death can pluck his children from his hands (3)

plucked
   528   a brand plucked from eternal fire (1)

plunge
   101   plunge now into the crimson flood (2)
   208   in simple faith to plunge me neath the healing ... flood (2)
   208   plunge me neath the healing, cleansing flood (2)

plunged
   83   he saw me plunged in deep distress (2)
   421   sinners, plunged beneath that flood (1)

poets
   370   poets, prophets, scholars, saints (2)

point
   284   through darkness & perplexity point ...the heavenly way (4)
   289   shine through the gloom and point me to the skies (5)
   456   and point Orion's sword (1)

points
   326   yet, passing, points to the glad feast above (5)

poisonous
291 no chilling winds or poisonous breath can reach (2)

pole
43 spread the truth from pole to pole (2)
455 scepter sways from pole to pole, that wars may cease (3)

pomp
362 power and pomp of nations shall pass like a dream away (2)
422 pomp... show, nor lofty pride, nor boast above the least (1)
425 in lowly pomp ride on to die (2,4)

ponder
55 ponder anew what the Almighty can do (3)
324 ponder nothing earthly minded (1)

poor
1 mournful, broken hearts rejoice; the humble poor believe (5)
9 he saves the oppressed, he feeds the poor (2)
74 by thee the outcast and the poor were sought (2)
102 ye poor, and maimed, and halt, and blind (3)
104 come, ye sinners, poor and needy (T,1)
116 I am poor and weak and blind (1)
119 poor, wretched, blind; sight, riches, healing of... mind (4)
121 poor and sinful though we be (3)
134 and shall we then forever live at this poor dying rate (4)
148 some poor fainting, struggling seaman you may rescue (R)
148 some poor seaman, tempest-tossed (3)
175 tell the poor wanderer a Savior has died (4)
184 my heart is weak and poor until it master find (2)
227 suffered and died to redeem a poor rebel like me (4)
227 who hath died my poor soul to redeem (6)
285 O that it now were shed abroad in this poor stony heart (3)
292 the poor, and them that mourn, the faint and overborne (1)
311 may she guide the poor and blind (3)
348 open wide, O God, thy door for the outcast and the poor (3)
359 to help the poor and needy, and bid the weak be strong (2)
376 what can I give him, poor as I am (4)
383 was to certain poor shepherds in fields as they lay (1)
400 dearer to God are the prayers of the poor (4)
421 when this poor lisping, stammering tongue lies silent (5)
470 rich in things and poor in soul (3)
502 if some poor wandering child of thine have spurned (4)
502 watch by the sick; enrich the poor with blessings (5)

poorest
398 and glorifies with duty life's poorest, humblest part (2)

portal
366 of one pearl each shining portal (3)
440 O to enter that bright portal (4)
446 neither might the gates of death ... tomb's dark portal (4)
446 who, triumphant, burst the bars of the tomb's dark portal (5)

portals
363 fling wide the portals of your heart (2)

portends
358   blessedness and light, peace & truth its course portends (2)

portion
  92   he will my shield and portion be as long as life endures (4)
176   thou my everlasting portion (T,1)
242   though her portion be the scaffold (4)
285   this only portion, Lord, be mine (3)
474   thy better portion trace (1)

possess
  92   I shall possess, within the veil ... life of joy & peace (5)
193   let us, still we pray, possess the mind that was in thee (6)
225   where thou ... all my soul possess and I may find myself (2)
334   possess in sweet communion, joys ... earth cannot afford (2)
399   toward thee longing doth possess me; turn and bless me (2)
468   thou art he who shall by right the nations all possess (2)
506   O Spirit, pure and holy, possess these hearts so lowly (5)

possessed
227   by my Savior possessed, I was perfectly blest (5)

possessing
165   let us each, thy love possessing, triumph (1)
399   rich in blessing, rule and might o'er all possessing (1)

possession
130   come quickly ... my Lord, & take possession of thine own (4)

possessions
291   where my possessions lie (1)

posterity
  56   to them and their posterity his blessing shall descend (5)

potter
154   thou art the potter; I am the clay (1)

pour
122   they pour effectual prayers; they strongly plead for me (3)
187   my love ... I pour at thy feet its treasure-store (3)
299   pour out thy soul for them in prayer victorious (4)
306   before our Father's throne we pour our ardent prayers (2)
337   pour out thy spirit from on high (T,1)
435   and pour contempt on all my pride (1)
464   the Lord will shortly pour all the spirit of his love (4)
470   on thy people pour thy power (1)
485   all pity, care, and love, all calm and courage...pour (1)
485   calm and courage, faith and hope: O pour them from above (1)

poured
314   for the wine, which thou hast poured (91)

pours
   9   the Lord pours eyesight on the blind (3)
321   when life anew pours out its wine with rich sufficiency (3)

power

1	He breaks the power of canceled sin (4)
4	the God of power, the God of love (1)
4	what God's almighty power hath made (2)
4	all ye who own his power proclaim aloud (5)
7	wisdom, honor, power, blessing ... we cry (4)
15	praise him for his matchless power (1)
17	thy power throughout the universe displayed (1)
20	his craft and power are great (1)
22	He sovereign power, without our aid made us of clay (2)
23	His sovereign power our bodies made (2)
25	tents of ease nor thrones of power should tempt my feet (2)
26	perfect in power, in love, and purity (3)
36	there is thy power; thy law is there (2)
36	and when the morning breaks in power, we hear thy word (3)
37	I sing the almighty power of God (T,1)
39	hour, when earth shall feel his saving power (3)
41	when we see thy lights of heaven ...thy power displayed (2)
41	moon and stars, thy power displayed (2)
42	hosts on high, his power proclaim (2)
43	does his creator's power display (1)
44	on man thy wisdom ... bestowed a power well-nigh divine (4)
71	all hail the power of Jesus' name (T,1)
72	all hail the power of Jesus' name (T,1)
73	all hail the power of Jesus' name (T,1)
76	let his will enfold you in its light and power (4)
78	redeem us for eternal day from every power of darkness (3)
89	comfort it brings and power and peace (2)
89	in weakness my almighty power (4)
95	send thy grace and show thy power (2)
98	here may we prove the power of prayer (4)
104	full of pity, love, and power (1)
113	by thy conflict in... hour of the subtle tempter's power (1)
113	by thy power the lost to save (3)
121	grace to cleanse and power to free (3)
132	come with unction and with power (2)
135	Holy Spirit, Power divine (3)
136	fill it with love and joy and power (1)
136	so ... we know ... power of him who came mankind to save (4
137	the grace which all may find, the saving power, impart (3)
153	God of love and God of power (T,1)
153	God of love and God of power (R)
153	God of love ... God of power make us worthy of this hour (4)
154	power, all power, surely is thine (3)
159	by the power of grace divine (2)
163	from him who loves me now so well, what power ... sever (3)
163	what power my soul can sever (3)
179	take thy great power and reign there alone (3)
184	my power is faint and low till I have learned to serve (3)
187	take my intellect ... use every power as thou ... choose (2)
200	but thou canst use our weakness to magnify thy power (3)
226	every day, every hour, let me feel thy cleansing power (R)
250	strong in the Lord of hosts, and in his mighty power (1)
259	in weakness be thy love my power (3)
260	through open gates thy power flows in (4)
260	thy power flows in like flood tides from the sea (4)
265	temptations lose their power when thou art nigh (2)

272   so long thy power hath blest me (3)
277   O come, and dwell with me, spirit of power within (T,1)
279   Almighty God of truth and love, to me thy power impart (4)
280   Almighty God of truth and love, to me thy power impart (4)
281   God of all power and truth and grace (T,1)
289   what but thy grace can foil the tempter's power (3)
307   thine is the power, be thine the praise (2)
332   feeble elements bestow a power not theirs to give (2)
336   then let us make our boast of his redeeming power (4)
339   let them speak thy Word of power (3)
342   in heaven & earth thy power ... bring God's kingdom here (4)
343   strains of love and power (1)
344   thy power and love diffused abroad (4)
346   through ages long his wisdom and his power display (1)
346   his wondrous works ... his wisdom and his power display (1)
349   Christ, with love's persuasive power (3)
349   all praise and honor, glory, power be now and evermore (4)
355   doomed to death, must bring to doom the power (2)
355   the power which crucified thee (2)
356   show us the way the Master trod; reveal his saving power (1)
361   on his shoulder ever rests all power on earth and heaven (2)
361   his righteous government and power shall over all extend (4)
362   power and pomp of nations shall pass like a dream away (2)
364   Savior, take the power and glory (4)
365   the rolling sun, the changing light ...thy power confess (2)
365   nights and days thy power confess (2)
373   the power of Satan breaking, our peace eternal making (1)
378   save us all from Satan's power when we were gone astray (1)
407   show us anew in Calvary the wondrous power (1)
407   wondrous power that makes men free (1)
407   thy Spirit's ceaseless, brooding power (3)
409   all glory and power, all wisdom and might (4)
421   thy precious blood shall never lose its power (3)
421   in a nobler, sweeter song, I'll sing thy power to save (5)
425   then take, O God, thy power, and reign (4)
427   thy cross may bring us to thy joy and resurrection power (4)
429   Satan hath lost his mortal power (3)
434   ye that feel the tempter's power (1)
438   stripped of power, no more he reigns (2)
453   in the seat of power enthrone him (2)
454   worship, honor, power, and blessing Christ is worthy (4)
455   crown him the Lord of peace, whose power a scepter sways (3)
457   who gives us power and peace (3)
459   thine is the quickening power that gives increase (4)
462   letting thine all-pervading power fulfill the dream (1)
463   by whose mighty power alone all is made & wrought & done (1)
465   glory, power, and praise receive for thy creating love (1)
465   bless thine heart-renewing power (3)
466   shall far outpass the power of human telling (3)
470   on thy people pour thy power (1)
471   take to thyself thy mighty power (1)
471   Spirit of grace and health and power (3)
473   O gratefully sing his power and his love (1)
473   Almighty, thy power hath founded of old (3)
476   Eternal God, whose power upholds (T,1)
476   whose power upholds both flower and flaming star (1)
477   O day of God, draw nigh in beauty and in power (T,1)

482 thine is the kingdom and the power (1)
499 restored to life and power and thought (1)
501 thy touch has still its ancient power (6)
507 give up ourselves, through Jesus' power (2)
515 suns glow, rains fall, by power divine (2)
515 not e'en the power by which we toil for bread are ours (2)
523 our life, our gifts, our power to give (5)
531 to feel thy power, to hear thy voice, to taste thy love (4)
538 O Trinity of love and power, our brethren shield (4)
550 thy blessing came, and still its power shall onward (2)

powerful
54 thy right hand thy powerful arm ... succor they implored (3)
271 hold me with thy powerful hand (1)

powers
9 praise shall employ my nobler powers (1,4)
15 all the powers of music bring, the music of the heart (2)
16 with all our ransomed powers (4)
19 cry out, dominions, princedoms, powers ... alleluia (1)
20 that word above all earthly powers ... abideth (4)
31 subdues the powers of hell, confounds their dark designs (3)
31 join all my powers to praise the Lord! (4)
91 powers of darkness fear, when this sweet chant they hear (2)
115 we more than taste the heavenly powers (2)
134 with all thy quickening powers kindle a flame (1,5)
150 O may it all my powers engage to do my Master's will (2)
180 that all my powers, with all their might ((3)
238 how the powers of darkness rage thy steps around (1)
250 tread all the powers of darkness down (3)
258 ready burning be the incense of thy powers (2)
324 powers of hell may vanish as the darkness clears away (3)
332 let us taste the heavenly powers (4)
340 stand against hell's marshalled powers (2)
343 to God the powers that dwell on high ... tribute bring (2)
357 powers, dominions, bow before him & extol our God & King
442 life in all...growing powers toward... light is striving (1)
447 the powers of death have done their worst (2)
457 tasting the celestial powers, we banquet on his love (3)
461 descend with all thy gracious powers (1,4)
510 all our consecrated powers a sacrifice to thee (5)
515 thou art in all; not e'en the powers by which we toil (2)
517 grant us then a deeper insight & new powers of sacrifice (4)

praise
1 hear him, ye deaf; his praise, ye dumb (6)
1 my great Redeemer's praise (1)
2 thou ... ears and hands and voices for thy praise design (3)
3 eternal praise be, hence, evermore (4)
4 sing praise to God who reigns above (T,1)
4 to God all praise and glory (R)
4 give God all praise and glory (5)
6 we, thy people , praise thee, God of every nation! (T,1,2)
6 we, thy people, praise thee, Lord of hosts eternal! (1,2)
6 we,thy people praise thee ... praise thee evermore! (1,2)
7 hear the angel voices blending ... praise to God on high (1)
8 holy God, we praise thy name (T,1)

```
 9   I'll praise my maker while I've breath (T,1)
 9   days of praise shall ne'er be past while life ... last (1,4)
 9   praise shall employ my nobler powers (1,4)
 9   I'll praise him while he lends me breath (4)
10   the heavens are not too high, his praise may thither fly (1)
11   voices raise to the Lord in hymns of praise (1)
14   fill the world with loudest praise (4)
14   let the Creator's praise arise (1)
14   thy praise shall sound from shore to shore (2)
14   in songs of praise divinely sing (3)
15   praise the Lord in every breath (3)
15   praise the Lord who reigns above (T,1)
15   praise the holy God of love, and all his greatness show (1)
15   praise him for his noble deeds (1)
15   praise him for his matchless power (1)
15   timbrels soft and cymbals loud in his high praise agree (2)
15   praise him every tuneful string: (2)
15   let all things praise the Lord (3)
16   though high above all praise, above all blessing high (2)
18   God is speaking; praise him for his open Word (3)
18   God has spoken; praise him for his open Word (1,2)
21   Him serve with mirth, his praise forth tell (1)
21   praise, laud, and bless his name always (3)
21   o enter then his gates with praise (3)
22   shall fill thy courts with sounding praise (3)
23   your voices in his praise employ (3)
24   come, sound his praise abroad, and hymns of glory sing (T,1)
26   all thy works ... praise thy name in earth & sky & sea (4)
27   all praise we would render: O help us to see (4)
27   almighty, victorious, thy great name we praise (1)
30   praise to the living God! all praised be his name (T,1,3)
31   join all my powers to praise the Lord! (4)
35   this our hymn of grateful praise (R)
38   center of unbroken praise (2)
39   sing the great Jehovah's praise and bless his holy name (1)
41   lifting up our hearts in praise (1)
42   praise the Lord! ye heavens adore him (T,1)
42   praise him, angels, in the height (1)
42   praise him, all ye stars of light (1)
42   praise the Lord! for he hath spoken (1)
42   praise the Lord! for he is glorious (2)
42   praise the God of our salvation (2)
45   morning light ... lily white declare ... maker's praise (2)
49   all praise and thanks to God the Father now be given (3)
52   praise thee for thy mercies past, & humbly hope for more (3)
55   praise to the Lord, the almighty, the King of creation (T,1)
55   O my soul, praise him, for he is thy health & salvation (1)
55   praise to the Lord (1,2,3,4)
58   we bring thee,Lord, the praise they brought (1)
60   O praise him, O praise him! Alleluia! Alleluia! Alleluia (R)
60   ye clouds that sail in heaven along, O praise him (2)
60   thou rising morn, in praise rejoice (2)
60   unfoldest blessings on our way, O praise him (4)
60   ye who long pain and sorrow bear, praise God (5)
60   praise God and on him cast your care (5)
60   worship him in humbleness, O praise him! Alleluia! (7)
60   praise, praise the Father, praise the Son (7)
```

60   praise the Spirit, Three in One (7)
61   praise the Lord, for he is kind (1,4)
61   let us then with gladsome mind praise the Lord (4)
62   Love is life, our lives be praise (2)
62   praise to Christ our gracious head (3)
66   praise, my soul, the King of heaven (T,1)
66   praise the everlasting King (1)
66   praise him for his grace and favor to our fathers (2)
66   praise him, still the same forever (2)
66   Alleluia! Alleluia! praise with us the God of grace (4)
67   Good Shepherd, may I sing thy praise within thy house (6)
67   sing thy praise within thy house forever (6)
70   lost in wonder, love, and praise (1)
74   all praise to thee, for thou, O King divine (T,1)
77   loud praise to Christ our King; Alleluia! Amen! (1)
77   praise is his gracious choice: Alleluia! Amen! (1)
77   praise yet the Lord again; Alleluia! Amen! (3)
81   accept the praise I bring (3)
81   when I see thee as thou art, I'll praise thee as I ought (4)
84   praise in all simplicity the guiding Christ,our shepherd (1)
86   hither our children bring to shout thy praise (1)
93   call for songs of loudest praise (1)
93   praise the mount! I'm fixed upon it (1)
111 our common Savior praise (1)
129 reechoes the praise of the Lord (5)
130 my loving God to praise (1)
168 in Loftiest songs of sweetest praise (2)
172 in humble prayer and fervent praise (2)
180 praise God, from who all blessings flow (4)
180 praise him, all creatures here below (4)
180 praise him above, ye heavenly host (4)
180 praise Father, Son, and Holy Ghost (4)
185 then shall my latest breath whisper thy praise (4)
187 let them flow in ceaseless praise (1)
190 shout with their shout of praise (2)
195 thy love to tell, thy praise to show (4)
196 offer the sacrifice of praise, and call upon his name (4)
196 praise him, ye saints, the God of love (5)
219 and turnest my mourning into praise (4)
227 now my remnant of days would I speak of his praise (6)
231 yet God the same abiding, his praise shall tune my voice (4)
233 with voice as full and strong as ocean's surging praise (3)
233 God's wondrous praise declare (2)
235 in deeper reverence, praise (1)
236 with one accord our parting hymn of praise (1)
251 faith to sight and, prayer to praise (4)
253 a jealous, just concern for thine, immortal praise (4)
255 when every heart was tuned to praise (3)
255 hope still, and thou shalt sing the praise of him (4)
255 praise of him who is thy God, thy Savior, and thy King (4)
256 riches I heed not, nor man's empty praise (3)
263 then, with my waking thoughts bright with thy praise (4)
282 O for a heart to praise my God (T,1)
283 pray and praise thee without ceasing (3)
283 lost in wonder, love and praise (4)
284 the strains of praise and love (6)
288 O happy, happy soul! in ecstacies of praise (2)

292 inspired with hope and praise, to Christ belong (4)
294 her hymns of love and praise (4)
295 they ever give thee praise (5)
300 sing our Savior's worthy praise (1)
301 all praise to our redeeming Lord (T,1)
307 thine is the power, be thine the praise (2)
330 let us praise God together on our knees (3)
338 still in Jesus' footsteps tread & show his praise below (2)
343 all nature's works his praise declare (T,1)
343 stormy sea sings praise to God ... thunder & the shower (1)
343 instruments of loftier sound assist his feeble praise (2)
349 all praise and honor, glory, power be now and evermore (4)
350 altar raise to thy great glory, God of praise (1)
350 here thine angelic spirits send their solemn praise (5)
350 their solemn praise with ours to blend (5)
352 be in each song of praise which here thy people raise (2)
352 till we our God and King shall praise in heaven (4)
365 sun, moon ... stars convey thy praise round the... earth (3)
365 convey thy praise round the whole earth and never stand (3)
370 praise we God, who hath inspired those (3)
370 praise him for the Word made flesh (3)
370 praise him...for the Spirit which protects us (3)
372 praise thee for the radiance ... from the hallowed page (1)
374 see him in a manger laid whom .. choirs of angels praise (4)
389 let all together praise our God upon his lofty throne (T,1)
389 with praise our God adore (4)
395 praise his name in all the earth; Hail the King of glory (3)
423 O may we ever praise him with heart and life and voice (3)
424 our praise and prayer and anthems before thee we present (2)
424 to thee, before thy passion they sang .. hymns of praise (3)
427 then let all praise be given thee who livest evermore (3)
442 Praise the Maker, all ye saints (3)
442 praise him, seers, heroes, kings, Heralds of perfection (3)
442 brothers, praise him, for he brings all to resurrection (3)
443 hymns of praise then let us sing (2)
443 sing we to our God above ... praise eternal as his love (3)
443 praise him, all ye heavenly host (3)
446 from his light, to whom we give laud and praise undying (2)
449 praise we in songs of victory that love, that life (3)
451 voices, Lord, we raise to thee, in jubilee and praise (5)
453 own his title, praise his name (3)
454 help to chant Emmanuel's praise (4)
455 and all be prayer and praise (3)
455 thy praise and glory shall not fail throughout eternity (4)
459 praise we the goodness that doth crown our days (5)
463 blest and Holy Trinity, praise forever be to thee (3)
464 sons of God your Savior praise (3)
465 glory, power, and praise receive for thy creating love (1)
467 praise to thy eternal merit, Father, Son and Holy Spirit (R)
470 free our hearts to work and praise (2)
473 pavilioned in splendor, and girded with praise (1)
486 though earth and sea and heaven unite thy praise to sing (1)
487 lead and guide our acts of praise (2)
489 here we come thy name to praise (3)
493 all praise to thee, my God, this night (T,1)
493 praise God, from whom all blessings flow (5)
493 praise him, all creatures here below (5)

493   praise Father, Son, and Holy Ghost (5)
493   praise him above, ye heavenly host (5)
498   gather to begin the day with praise (1)
498   ppraise for light so brightly shining on our steps (1)
498   praise for mercies daily twining round us golden cords (1)
498   we would praise thee and surrender all our hearts (2)
500   thy praise shall hallow now our rest (1)
500   nor die the strains of praise away (3)
504   Father, we praise thee, now the night is over (T,1)
510   sing to the Great Jehovah's praise (T,1)
510   all praise to him belongs (1)
512   all nature joins in singing a joyful song of praise (2)
516   happy the home where ... praise is wont to rise (3)
522   fruit unto his praise to yield (2)
523   to thee all praise and glory be (1)
523   we owe thee thankfulness and praise, who givest all (3)
524   bring sacrifice of praise ... shouts of exultation (1)
528   or sing my great deliverer's praise (1)
532   now praise we great and famous men (T,1)
532   praise the Lord who now as then reveals in man his glory (1)
532   praise we the wise and brave and strong (2)
532   praise we the great of heart and mind (3)
532   praise we ... the singers sweetly gifted (3)
532   praise we the peaceful men of skill (4)
532   praise we the glorious names we know (5)
533   our glorious leader claims our praise (2)
535   thee in thy glorious realm they praise (3)
538   thus evermore shall rise to thee glad hymns of praise (4)
538   glad hymns of praise from land and sea (4)
544   so shall thy people, with thankful devotion praise him (4)
544   praise him who saved them from peril and sword (4)
544   peace to the nations, and praise to the Lord (4)
548   Lord, we would with deep thanksgiving praise thee (1)
548   praise thee most for things unseen (1)
552   and glory, laud, and praise be ever thine (4)

praised
30   praise to the living God! all praised be his name (T,1,3)
463   praised by all the heavenly host (1)

praises
3   to thee, great One in Three eternal praises be (4)
4   all my toilsome way along I sing aloud thy praises (4)
10   the earth is not too low, his praises there may grow (1)
19   lead their praises, alleluia! (2)
55   all that hath life and breath, come now with praises (4)
55   come now with praises before him (4)
56   praises of my God shall still my heart and tongue employ (1)
59   sing praises to his name: he forgets not his own (1)
66   evermore his praises sing, Alleluia! Alleluia! (1)
77   let praises fill the sky; Alleluia! Amen! (2)
86   so now, and till we die sound we thy praises high (4)
221   through eternal ages let his praises ring (1)
257   hear, and bless our prayers and praises (3)
271   songs of praises I will ever give to thee (3)
318   there with joy thy praises render unto him (1)
340   till earth and heaven together blend their praises (4)

340   their praises at thy throne (4)
352   glory and praises be in love now given (4)
357   angel hosts, his praises sing (2)
357   hymn & chant & high thanksgiving & unwearied praises be (3)
378   now to the Lord sing praises, all you within this place (5)
381   praises sing to God the King, and peace to men on earth (2)
396   praises voicing greet the morrow (2)
409   the praises of Jesus the angels proclaim (3)
423   children sang their praises, the simplest and the best (1)
424   thou didst accept their praises (3)
454   loudest praises, without ceasing (4)
454   loudest praises ... meet it is for us to give (4)
472   and endless praises crown his head (2)
488   to Holy Ghost be praises, to Father, and to Son (4)
488   Church her voice upraises to thee, blest Three in One (4)

praising

7   praising God for his great love (2)
8   cherubim and seraphim, in unceasing chorus praising (2)
224   this is my story, this is my song, praising my Savior (R)
224   praising my Savior all the day long (R)
394   angels praising God on high... thus addressed their song (5)
402   prayer and praising all men raising (3)
424   the company of angels are praising thee on high (2)
446   Alleluia with the Son, God the Father praising (5)
503   Heaven and earth are praising thee, O Lord most high (R)

pray

59   pray that thou still our defender wilt be (3)
78   we pray thee, hear us when we call (1)
78   come in thy holy might, we pray (3)
95   hear and heal me now, I pray (1)
121   blessed Jesus! Hear, O hear us, when we pray (2)
143   Savior divine! now hear me while I pray (1)
150   help me to watch and pray and on thyself rely (4)
152   every moment watch and pray (3)
154   wounded and weary, help me, I pray (3)
193   let us...we pray, possess the mind that was in thee (6)
197   we pray in deed and word, thy kingdom come on earth (4)
210   sing, pray, and keep his ways unswerving (3)
212   if you can't preach like Peter...can't pray like Paul (2)
238   gird thee for the battle; watch and pray and fast (2)
238   Christian answer boldly, "While I breathe, I pray" (3)
246   O watch & fight & pray; the battle ne'er give o'er (2)
250   wrestle and fight and pray (3)
252   Lord, teach us how to pray (6)
258   pray that he may prosper ever each endeavor (3)
260   content to pray, in life and love, and toil (4)
279   grant me the filial awe I pray...tender conscience give (3)
280   grant me the filial awe, I pray, the tender conscience (3)
283   pray and praise thee without ceasing (3)
298   hear thy people when they pray (2)
317   O Lord, we pray, come thou among us (3)
318   Jesus, bread of life, I pray thee (3)
337   to watch and pray, and never faint (4)
340   we go to win the lost to thee; O help us, Lord, we pray (1)
345   who mourn...they who fear, be strengthened as they pray (3)

349   O Lord, be pleased to bless, we pray (2)
353   thy people pray, come quickly, King of kings (5)
381   O holy Child of Bethlehem, descend to us, we pray (4)
384   close by me forever, and love me, I pray (3)
412   I do adore thee, and will ever pray thee (5)
434   learn of Jesus Christ to pray (1)
459   to thee all knees are bent, all voices pray (1)
459   pray we that thou wilt hear us, still imploring (5)
480   hear us, we humbly pray (1)
487   pray God to teach us here on this thy holy day (2)
489   while we pray for pardoning grace (2)
489   pray ... through the dear Redeemer's name (2)
491   we pray thee that offenseless the hours of dark may be (1)
499   new mercies ... hover around us while we pray (2)
499   help us, this & every day to live more nearly as we pray (4)
551   Lord, while for all mankind we pray (T,1)
122   the Father hears him pray, His dear anointed One (4)

prayed
272   nor prayed that thou shouldst lead me on (2)
419   he prayed for them that did the wrong (2)

prayer
3   our prayer attend, come, and thy people bless (2)
13   waits for him who answers prayer (1)
52   in the confidence of prayer our hearts take hold on thee (2)
87   breathe that holy name in prayer (2)
91   alike at work and prayer to Jesus I repair (1)
98   here may we prove the power of prayer (4)
98   prayer to strengthen faith and sweeten care (4)
106   nothing left but heaven and prayer (3)
113   by thy lonely hour of prayer (2)
138   teach me the patience of unanswered prayer (4)
159   when I kneel in prayer, and with thee, my God (3)
172   in humble prayer and fervent praise (2)
176   nor for fame my prayer shall be (2)
177   some song to raise, or prayer, something for thee (2)
185   hear thou the prayer I make on bended knee (1)
185   this all my prayer shall be: more love O Christ, to thee (2)
185   this still its prayer shall be: more love, O Christ (4)
188   not for myself alone may my prayer be (3)
193   and know our prayer is heard (1)
197   in work that gives effect to prayer (4)
199   each smile a hymn, each kindly deed a prayer (1)
206   thou art...the gift beyond our utmost prayer (2)
214   sought to gain fulfillment of their prayer (4)
225   and talk with thee in prayer (4)
248   put on the gospel armor, each piece put on with prayer (3)
251   armed by faith and winged by prayer (4)
251   faith to sight and, prayer to praise (4)
252   prayer is the soul's sincere desire (T,1)
252   prayer is the burden of a sigh, the falling of a tear (2)
252   prayer is the simplest form of speech (3)
252   prayer .. sublimest strains .. reach the Majesty on high (3)
252   prayer is the contrite sinner's voice (4)
252   prayer is the Christian's vital breath (5)
252   prayer ... the Christian's native air (5)

252   he enters heaven with prayer (5)
252   the path of prayer thyself hast trod (6)
252   prayer ... unuttered or expressed (1)
253   know thou hearest my prayer (1)
253   forever standing on its guard and watching unto prayer (3
261   what a privilege to carry everything to God in prayer (1)
261   we...never be discouraged, take it to the Lord in prayer (2)
261   take it to the Lord in prayer (2,3)
261   all because we do not carry everything to God in prayer (1)
264   its closing eyes look up to thee in prayer (4)
275   sweet hour of prayer (T,1,2,3)
275   oft escaped the tempter's snare by thy return ... prayer (1)
292   the world to Christ we bring, with fervent prayer (2)
299   pour out thy soul for them in prayer victorious (4)
333   lowly we kneel in prayer before thy throne (1)
339   answer ... faith's effectual prayer ... our needs supply (1)
342   inspire our ways of learning ... earnest, fervent prayer (1)
348   on this stone now laid with prayer (T,1)
359   to him shall prayer unceasing and daily vows ascend (4)
363   adorned with prayer and love and joy (2)
380   there's a mother's deep prayer and a baby's low cry (1)
402   prayer and praising all men raising (3)
424   our praise and prayer and anthems before thee we present (2)
455   and all be prayer and praise (3)
472   to him shall endless prayer be made (2)
500   the voice of prayer is never silent (3)
504   singing, we offer prayer and meditation (1)
514   these crops ... they are our prayer (3)
515   and daily must the prayer be said (1)
516   when one their wish, and one their prayer (1)
516   happy the home where prayer is heard (3)
520   steadfast faith & earnest prayer keep sacred vows secure (4)
529   be conquered by my instant prayer (3)
542   this is my prayer, O Lord of all earth's kingdoms (3)
542   O hear my prayer, thou God of all the nations (3)
549   scarcely can we turn aside for one brief hour of prayer (2)
549   work shall be prayer, if all be wrought as thou wouldst (6)
549   prayer, by thee inspired and taught ... with work be one (6)
550   with prayer and psalm they worshiped thee (1)
550   thou heard'st well pleased, the song, the prayer (2)

prayers
  29   the Father, too, our prayers implore (3)
 122   pour effectual prayers; they strongly plead for me (3)
 157   through him the first fond prayers are said (5)
 257   hear, and bless our prayers and praises (3)
 260   our heart's dear guest, to thee our prayers ascend (1)
 260   our dreams, our aims, our work, our lives are prayers (1)
 260   our lives are prayers thou lovest more (1)
 260   O cleanse our prayers from human dross (2)
 294   for her my tears shall fall, for her my prayers ascend (3)
 306   before our Father's throne we pour our ardent prayers (2)
 346   accept the prayers that thousands lift (3)
 350   may our prayers, when here we bend ...to thee ascend (2)
 400   dearer to God are the prayers of the poor (4)
 424   accept the prayers we bring (3)
 461   spirit divine, attend our prayers (T,1,4)
 487   hear our prayers as they ascend (1)

praying
308 but, Lord, thy Church is praying yet (1)
308 Church is praying yet, a thousand years the same (1)

prays
252 angels in their songs rejoice & cry,"Behold he prays" (4)
431 in the garden now the suffering Savior prays alone (1)

preach
136 inspire our lips with flaming love and zeal to preach (2)
136 preach to all thy great good news (2)
151 and preach thee, too, as love knows how (3)
212 if you can't preach like Peter ... can't pray like Paul (2)
335 may they in Jesus ...they preach, their own Redeemer see (4)
341 I may but grasp his name; preach him to all and cry (6)
341 preach him to all and cry in death,"...Behold the Lamb" (6)

preaching
90 while birds and flowers and sky above are preaching (3)
90 preaching the blessedness which simple trust has found (3)

precepts
53 how gentle God's commands! how kind his precepts are! (T,1)
191 men alert and quick his lofty precepts to translate (2)

precious
62 through that precious love he sought us (2)
62 with that precious life he bought us (2)
87 precious name, O how sweet! (R)
87 O the precious name of Jesus! (3)
92 how precious did that grace appear (2)
93 to rescue me from danger, interposed his precious blood (2)
101 Jesus shed his precious blood rich blessings to bestow (2)
122 his all-redeeming love, his precious blood, to plead (2)
127 Lord, I believe thy precious blood (3)
159 nearer, blessed Lord, to thy precious, bleeding side (R)
195 teach the precious things thou dost impart (3)
208 Jesus, precious Jesus! O for grace to trust him more (R)
208 precious Jesus, Savior, friend (4)
208 I'm so glad I learned to trust thee, precious Jesus (4)
226 let thy precious blood applied keep me ... near thy side (1)
261 precious Savior, still our refuge (3)
294 saved with his own precious blood (1)
298 chosen of the Lord and precious (1)
331 he the banquet spreads before us...precious banquet (1)
331 precious banquet, bread of heaven (1)
359 souls, condemned and dying, are precious in his sight (2)
414 might go at last to heaven saved by his precious blood (3)
421 dear dying Lamb, thy precious blood shalal never lose (3)
421 thy precious blood shall never lose its power (3)
428 'Tis done! the precious ransom's paid! (3)
430 here earth's precious things seem dross (1)
433 there a precious fountain, free to all, a healing stream (1)

preparation
478 through days of preparation thy grace has made us strong (1)

prepare
121 for our use thy folds prepare (1)
150 O, thy servant, Lord, prepare, a strict account to give (3)
267 open my heart and let me prepare love with thy children (3)
362 prepare in the desert a highway ... for our God (1,4)
366 for his marriage feast prepare (1)
392 let every heart prepare him room (1)
406 prepare across the earth the King's highway (2)
445 he lives, my mansion to prepare (3)
454 there thou dost our place prepare (3)

prepared
86 thou hast prepared the feast of heavenly love (2)
115 the heaven prepared for me (1)
253 a spirit still prepared, and armed with jealous care (3)
348 living stones prepared for the temple near thy throne (4)
474 rise, my soul, and haste away to seats prepared above (1)

prepares
440 God has promised, Christ prepares it (2)

presence
12 art within, a qickening flame, a presence round about (2)
25 the joy that from thy presence springs (1)
25 devils at thy presence flee (4)
68 my table thou hast furnished in presence of my foes (4)
82 sweeter far thy face to see and in thy presence rest (1)
115 with his glorious presence here his life in us revealed (2)
122 he cannot turn away the presence of his Son (4)
129 O thou, in whose presence my soul takes delight (T,1)
152 in all my works thy presence find (2)
154 as in thy presence humbly I bow (2)
173 O young and fearless prophet, we need thy presence here (5)
219 thy presence fills my solitude (3)
256 waking or sleeping, thy presence my light (1)
259 all fear before thy presence flies (2)
276 Lord, we thy presence seek; may ours the blessing be (4)
288 all in Jesus' presence reign through ages without end (2)
289 I need thy presence every passing hour (3)
296 beneath the pine or palm, one unseen Presence she adores (2)
310 Jesus, we look to thee, thy promised presence claim (T,1)
317 with godly fear, we seek thy presence (2)
324 veil their faces to the presence (4)
349 vouchsafe thy presence now (1)
350 may we discern thy presence here (3)
363 let us thy inner presence feel (3)
383 and offered there, in his presence, their gold and myrrh (5)
409 and still he is nigh, his presence we have (2)
423 and in his blissful presence eternally rejoice (3)
489 may we feel thy presence near (3)
522 there, forever purified, in thy presence to abide (4)
526 who may abide thy presence (1)
534 may the shadow of thy presence around our camp be spread (2)

present
4 an ever present help and stay (3)
36 thy present life through all doth flow (1)

 37   everwhere that man can be, thou, God, art present there (3)
106   ever present, truest friend ... near thine aid to lend (2)
139   save us, a present Savior thou (3)
150   to serve the present age, my calling to fulfill (2)
157   warm, sweet, tender, even yet a present help is he (3)
231   set free from present sorrow we cheerfully can say (2)
310   present we know thou art, but O thyself reveal (4)
424   our praise and anthems before thee we present (2)
463   ever present help in need (1)
477   come with thy timeless judgment...match our present hour (1)
518   be present at our table, Lord (T,1)
548   standing in the living present (1)

presenting
510   to thee presenting, through thy Son, whate'er we have (3)

presents
249   his own hand presents the prize to thine aspiring eye (3)

preserve
 84   from sordid waves of worldly sea preserve us, Lord (2)
216   he shall with all-protecting care preserve thee (3)
216   preserve thee from the fowler's snare (3)
315   preserve the life thyself hast given (1)
521   his the loving purpose solely to preserve them (4)
521   to preserve them pure and holy (4)

preserves
 56   God preserves the souls of those who on his truth depend (5)

preservest
 52   life, while thou preservest life, a sacrifice shall be (4)

press
 53   why should this anxious load press down your weary mind (3)
157   we touch him in life's throng and press (4)
249   and press with vigor on (1)
251   life with trials hard may press me (3)
474   press onward to the prize (3)

pressed
142   though pressed by every foe (1)
229   peace, perfect peace, by thronging duties pressed (2)

presses
297   and to one hope she presses, with every grace endued (2)

pressing
246   hosts of sin . pressing hard to draw thee from the skies (1)
430   pressing onward as we can ..to this our hearts must tend (4)

pretended
412   that man to judge thee hath in hate pretended (1)

prevail
 42   sin and death shall not prevail (2)
 43   soon as the evening shades prevail (2)

216 when fearful plagues around prevail (3)
221 by the living Word of God I shall prevail (2)
245 if blessings or sorrows prevail (3)
305 gates of hell can never gainst that Church prevail (3)
464 more & more it spreads and grows ever mighty to prevail (2)

prevailing
  20 our helper he amid the flood of mortal ills prevailing (1)
371 o'er fear and doubt, o'er black despair prevailing (1)

prevails
459 to thee we owe the peace that still prevails (3)

prey
444 death cannot keep his prey ... He tore the bars away (3)

price
120 in my hand no price I bring; simply to thy cross I cling (2)
414 there was no other good enough to pay the price of sin (4)

priceless
220 Jesus, priceless treasure, source of purest pleasure (T,1)
220 Jesus, priceless treasure (T,1,3)
548 for the priceless gift of freedom (2)

pride
  86 our shepherd and our pride, our staff and song (3)
160 nor let thy foolish pride rebel (3)
173 amid our pride and glory to see thy face appear (5)
200 from ease & plenty save us; from pride of place absolve (4)
272 and spite of fears, pride ruled my will (2)
279 help me the first approach to feel of pride (1)
279 first approach to feel of pride or wrong desire (1)
280 help me the first approach to feel of pride or...desire (1)
280 of pride or wrong desire (1)
281 from all the filth of self and pride (3)
309 free from anger and from pride (5)
355 nation's pride o'erthrown went down to dust beside thee (2)
355 our pride is dust; our vaunt is stilled (4)
408 cast out our pride & shame that hinder to enthrone thee (3)
422 pomp .. show, nor lofty pride, nor boast above the least (1)
435 and pour contempt on all my pride (1)
470 bend our pride to thy control (3)
480 boundless as ocean's tide rolling in fullest pride (4)
484 take not thy thunder from us, but take away our pride (1)
547 land where my fathers died, land of the pilgrims' pride (1)

priest
  81 Jesus ... my prophet, priest, and king (3)
  86 thou art the great high priest (2)
100 Jesus, our great high priest, hath full atonement made (2)
484 tie in a living tether the prince and priest and thrall (3)

prince
  20 the Prince of Darkness grim, we tremble not for him (3)
303 the Prince is ever in them; the day-light is serene (2)
309 show thyself the Prince of Peace (1)

358   lo, the Prince of Peace, lo, the Son of God is come (3)
361   his name shall be the Prince of Peace forevermore adored (3)
387   hail the heaven-born Prince of Peace (3)
406   upon the highway of the Prince of Peace (3)
408   heal its ancient wrong, come, Prince of Peace, and reign (3)
420   the bleeding Prince of life and peace (3)
435   cross on which the Prince of Glory died (1)
450   no more we doubt thee, glorious Prince of life (3)
459   O holy Jesus, Prince of Peace and Savior (3)
484   tie in a living tether the prince and priest and thrall (3)

princedoms
    19   cry out, dominions, princedoms, powers ... alleluia (1)

principle
    279   I want a principle within of watchful, godly fear (T,1)
    280   I want a principle within of watchful, godly fear (T,1)

prints
    99   in his feet and hands are wound-prints, and his side (2)

prison
    243   who, thrust in prison or cast to flame (1)
    446   Christ hath burst his prison (2)

prisoner
    1   He sets the prisoner free (4)
    9   grants the prisoner sweet release (3)
    472   the prisoner leaps to loose his chains (4)

privilege
    261   what a privilege to carry everything to God in prayer (1)

prize
    82   Jesus, our only joy be thou, as thou our prize wilt be (5)
    239   while others fought to win the prize (2)
    240   Christ is the path, and Christ the prize (2)
    249   his own hand presents the prize to thine aspiring eye (3)
    294   beyond my highest joy I prize her heavenly ways (4)
    301   who have obtained the prize (1)
    474   press onward to the prize (3)
    516   parents love the sacred Word and all its wisdom prize (3)

proceeding
    257   Light of light, from God proceeding (3)
    402   westward leading, still proceeding (R)

proceeds
    15   from whom all good proceeds ... earth and heaven adore (1)
    463   Holy Ghost, who from both fore'er proceeds (3)

proclaim
    1   my gracious Master and my God, assist me to proclaim (2)
    4   all ye who own his power proclaim aloud (5)
    4   proclaim aloud the wondrous story! (5)
    14   the great salvation loud proclaim (3)
    17   and there proclaim, my God, how great thou art (4)

33   day unto day utter speech ... night to night proclaim (3)
39   his saving grace proclaim (1,3)
42   hosts on high, his power proclaim (2)
43   their great Original proclaim (1)
44   thy glory, Lord, proclaim (5)
44   mighty works and wondrous grace thy glory ... proclaim (5)
65   bless the Father ... forget not ... mercies to proclaim (1)
81   till then I would thy love proclaim (5)
81   proclaim with every fleeting breath (5)
98   here, to our waiting hearts, proclaim the sweetness (3)
100 redemption in his blood throughout the world proclaim (3)
196 the God of all-redeeming grace my God I will proclaim (4)
281 that I thy mercy may proclaim (2)
288 with saints enthroned on high thou...thy Lord proclaim (1)
299 proclaim to every people, tongue, and nation (3)
339 thy universal grace proclaim, thine all-redeeming love (4)
341 thee I shall constantly proclaim (4)
341 his only righteousness I show, his saving grace proclaim (5)
362 proclaim to a desolate people the coming of their King (2)
381 O morning stars, together proclaim the holy birth (2)
382 who sang creation's story now proclaim Messiah's birth (1)
387 with the angelic host proclaim (1)
409 ye servants of God, your Master proclaim (T,1)
409 the praises of Jesus the angels proclaim (3)
411 proclaim the good Physician's mind (3)
472 and infant voices shall proclaim their early blessings (3)
475 still wilt not hear thine inner God proclaim (1)

proclaimed
16   then be his love in Christ proclaimed (4)
36   the indwelling God, proclaimed of old (4)

proclaimeth
405 gold the King of kings proclaimeth (4)

proclaiming
460 each from age to age proclaiming God the one (1)

proclaims
75   the rending tomb proclaims thy conquering arm (3)

profanation
484 from sale and profanation of honor and the sword (2)

profaned
94   oft profaned his hallowed name (2)

proffer
2   for thine acceptance proffer all unworthily (4)

profit
242 ere her cause bring fame and profit (2)
458 their profit & their joy to know the mystery of his love (5)

profound
505 brings the night its peace profound (1)

prolong
326   here let me feast, and feasting, still prolong the hour (2)
326   prolong the hour of fellowship with thee (2)
374   why your joyous strain prolong (2)
547   let rocks their silence break, the sound prolong (3)

promise
9   none shall find his promise vain (2)
42   never shall his promise fail (2)
119   because thy promise I believe ... I come (5)
141   God will fulfill in every part each promise he has made (1)
208   just to rest upon his promise (1)
234   feel the promise is not vain that morn shall tearless be (3)
305   we have Christ's own promise, and that cannot fail (3)
358   what its signs of promise are (1)
406   to see the promise of the day fulfilled (3)
464   lo! the promise of a shower drops already from above (4)
507   promise, in this sacred hour, for God to live and die (2)

promised
47   lead us by faith to hope's true promised land (2)
92   the Lord has promised good to me (4)
121   thou hast promised to receive us (3)
164   O Jesus, I hasus, thou hast promised to all who follow thee (4)
164   Jesus, I have promised to serve thee to the end (4)
205   perfect rest to me is promised in my Father's home above (3)
281   enter ... promised rest ... Canaan of thy perfect love (5)
284   let me thy loving servant be ... taste thy promised rest (2)
310   Jesus, we look to thee, thy promised presence claim (T,1)
358   traveler, yes; it brings the day, promised day of Israel (1)
440   God has promised, Christ prepares it (2)
533   following ... incarnate God ... gained the promised rest (2)

promises
196   all his promises embrace, and to his glory live (2)
221   standing on the promises (T,1,2,3,4,R)
221   standing on the promises of Christ my King (1)
221   standing on the promises of God (1,2,3,4,R)
221   standing on the promises of God my Savior (R)
221   standing on the promises that cannot fail (2)
221   standing on the promises of Christ the Lord (3)
221   standing on the promises I cannot fail (4)
265   and thy rich promises in me fulfill (4)

prompt
162   at thy bidding may I move, prompt to serve & follow thee (2)

prone
93   prone to wander, Lord, I feel it (3)
93   prone to leave the God I love (3)
173   thoughts & actions less prone to please the crowd (1)
225   where I may lay me prone, and bare my soul in loneliness (3)

pronounced
37   and then pronounced them good (2)

proofs
83 from his bounty I receive such proofs of love divine (4)

prophet
81 Jesus ... my prophet, priest, and king (3)
138 I ask no dream, no prophet ecstasies (2)
173 O young and fearless prophet of ancient Galilee (T,1)
173 O young and fearless prophet, we need thy presence here (5)
390 lo! the days are hastening on, by prophet seen of old (3)

prophet's
30 in prophet's word he spoke of old; he speaketh still (2)

prophetic
131 come, Holy Ghost...source of the old prophetic fire (1)
131 source of... old prophetic fire, fountain of life & love (1)
296 truth is her prophetic gift, the soul, her sacred page (3)

prophets
8 prophets swell the glad refrain (3)
19 ye patriarchs and prophets blest (3)
99 saints, apostles, prophets, martyrs answer, Yes (7)
131 come, Holy Ghost, for moved by thee the prophets wrote (2)
131 moved by thee, the prophets wrote and spoke (2)
189 glorious day by prophets long foretold (1)
370 poets, prophets, scholars, saints (2)
371 speaking to saints, to prophets, kings, and sages (2)
440 prophets psalmists seers . sages . await . glory given (3)
460 God hath spoken by his prophets (T,1)
476 O send us forth, thy prophets true (1)
548 for our prophets and apostles, loyal to the living Word (3)

prosper
55 Lord, who doth prosper thy work and defend thee (3)
214 they gaily bloom and prosper cheerfully (2)
242 though the cause of evil prosper . truth alone is strong (4)
258 pray that he may prosper ever each endeavor (3)

prosperity
551 our cities with prosperity ... fields with plenteousness (2)

prosperous
242 and 'tis prosperous to be just (2)

prostrate
71 let angels prostrate fall (1)
87 falling prostrate at his feet (4)

protect
538 from rock and tempest, fire and foe protect them (4)
538 protect them wheresoe'er they go (4)
541 O God, protect the men who fly through lonely ways (2)
547 protect us by thy might, Great God, our King (4)

protected
54 thy providence protected them who thy great name adored (3)

protecting
46   the cloud of thy protecting love (1)
84   draw thy protecting net around the catch of... apostles (2)
216   he shall with all-protecting care preserve thee (3)

protects
370   praise him...for the Spirit which protects us (3)

proud
469   building proud towers which shall not reach to heaven (3)
500   thy throne shall never, like earth's proud empires, pass (4)

prove
63   the hour that darkest seemeth will his... goodness prove (3)
63   will his changeless goodness prove (3)
85   living deeds that prove how sweet to serve all others (3)
98   here may we prove the power of prayer (4)
114   we by his Spirit prove and know the things of God (4)
130   the length,and breadth, and height to prove (1)
131   let us thine influence prove (1)
144   what though the world deceitful prove (2)
146   believing where we cannot prove (1)
152   and prove thy good and perfect will (2)
178   thy friends unfaithful prove (2)
213   search, prove my heart, it yearns for thee (1)
223   but we never can prove the delights of his love until (3)
223   never can prove ... until all on the altar we lay (3)
240   trust ... trusting soul shall prove Christ is its life (3)
281   thy word may to the utmost prove (5)
285   I thirst, I faint, I die to prove ... love (1)
301   gift which he on one bestows, we all delight to prove (2)
310   thy name salvation is, which here we come to prove (2)
313   till all thy life we gain, and all thy fulness prove (2)
339   O let them spread thy name, their mission fully prove (4)
351   in larger worlds more fully prove the wonders of... love (4)
351   prove the wonders of redeeming love (4)
392   makes the nations prove the glories of his righeeousness (4)
411   and prove the Savior friend (3)
471   let all earth's sons thy mercy prove (1)
489   thus may all our sabbaths prove till we join ... above (4)
499   new ... the love our wakening and uprising prove (1)
528   unmindful of his favors prove (3)
549   then let us prove our heavenly birth in all we do & know (5)

proved
208   how I've proved him o'er and o'er (R)
543   O beautiful for heroes proved in liberating strife (3)

provide
57   for thee he will provide (4)
175   strength for thy labor the Lord will provide (4)
207   all you may need he will provide (3)
209   leave to thy God to order and provide (1)
240   His boundless mercy will provide (2)
522   God, our Maker, doth provide ...our wants to be supplied (1)
539   daily manna still provide you (2)

provided
  295 the swallow also for herself provided hath a nest (3)
  498 with so blest a friend provided, we upon our way ... go (2)
  512 the seed by him provided is sown o'er hill and plain (1)

providence
   54 thy providence protected them who thy great name adored (3)
  215 behind a frowning providence he hides a smiling face (4)
  219 thy providence turns all to good (3)
  510 providence hath brought us through another various year (2)

providential
   46 nor miss our providential way (2)

provision
  515 what large provision thou hast made (3)

provoke
   24 today attend his voice, nor dare provoke his rod (4)

pruning
  408 to plow-share beat the sword, to pruning-hook the spear (2)

psalm
  199 each loving life a psalm of gratitude (3)
  296 adores with silence, or with psalm (2)
  550 with prayer and psalm they worshiped thee (1)

psalmists
  440 prophets psalmists seers . sages . await . glory given (3)

psalms
   10 church with psalms must shout, no door can keep them out (2)
  233 the psalms of ancient days (3)

psaltery
   15 celebrate the eternal God with harp and psaltery (2)

publicans
  528 harlots and publicans and thieves (4)

publish
   51 publish with our latest breath thy love & guardian care (4)
  114 and publish to the sons of men the signs infallible (2)
  299 publish glad tidings, tidings of peace (R)
  409 and publish abroad his wonderful name (1)

publishes
   43 publishes to every land the work of an almighty hand (1)

pulse
  187 take my hands ... let them move ... impulse of thy love (1)
  198 pulse of one fraternity (3)
  198 in every heart and brain shall throb the pulse of one (3)
  316 while a breath, a pulse remains, will I remember thee (3)

pulses
  138 wean it from earth, through all its pulses move (1)
  235 breathe through the pulses of desire thy coolness (5)

purchase
224 heir of salvation, purchase of God (1)

purchased
166 and purchased my pardon on Calvary's tree (2)

pure
27 great Father of glory, pure Father of light (4)
33 o'er white expanses sparkling pure (2)
35 offering up on every shore her pure sacrifice of love (5)
60 thou flowing water, pure and clear (3)
67 what transport of delight from thy pure chalice floweth (5)
103 hope of the penitent, fadeless and pure (2)
103 flowing forth from the throne of God, pure from above (3)
120 save from wrath and make me pure (1)
125 make and keep me pure within (4)
133 until my heart is pure, until with thee I will one will (2)
135 kindle every high desire; perish self in thy pure fire (2)
143 pure, warm, and changeless be, a living fire (2)
156 I would be pure, for there are those who care (1)
159 pure delight . single hour ... before thy throne I spend (3)
172 the pure celestial fire to impart (1)
233 rejoice, ye pure in heart (T,1)
253 a pure desire that all may learn and glorify thy grace (4)
273 with thy spirit recreate me, pure and strong and true (1)
273 like the springs and running waters make me crystal pure (2)
273 keep me ever, by thy spirit, pure and strong and true (5)
276 blest are the pure in heart for they shall see ... God (T,1)
276 for his dwelling & his throne selects the pure in heart (3)
276 O give the pure and lowly heart, a temple meet for thee (4)
282 perfect & right & pure & good, a copy, Lord, of thine (4)
283 pure, unbounded love thou art (1)
283 finish ...thy new creation, pure and spotless let us be (4)
284 and make me pure within (1)
344 in knowledge pure their mind renew (2)
345 and pure devotion rise (4)
365 thy laws are pure, thy judgments right (5)
393 Son of God, love's pure light (3)
397 so may we with holy joy, pure and free from sins' alloy (3)
411 bless ... their works of pure unselfishness (5)
430 through thy cross made pure and white (5)
437 our hearts be pure from evil, that we may see aright (2)
488 where Gospel light is glowing with pure & radiant beams (3)
495 when the morning wakens, then may I arise pure and fresh (6)
495 pure and fresh and sinless in thy holy eyes (6)
502 like infant's slumbers pure and light (5)
506 O Spirit, pure and holy, possess these hearts so lowly (5)
515 may the hands be pure from stain with which...we gain (4)
517 grant us, then, pure hearts and patient (3)
521 to preserve them pure and holy (4)
522 grant that we wholesome grain and pure may be (2)
529 pure, universal love thou art (4)

purer
79 Jesus is purer, who makes the woeful heart to sing (2)
79 Jesus shines purer, than all the angels heaven can boast (3)
235 in purer lives thy service find (1)
268 purer light shall mark .. road that leads me to the Lamb (6)

purest
   209 sorrow forgot, love's purest joys restored (3)
   220 Jesus, priceless treasure, source of purest pleasure (T,1)
   220 whate'er we must bear still in thee lies purest pleasure (3)
   301 grace through every vessel flows in purest streams (2)
   301 in purest streams of love (2)
   372 O make thy Church, dear Savior, a lamp of purest gold (4)

purge
   200 purge us of low desire; lift us to high resolve (4)
   281 purge me from every evil blot (3)
   284 purge away my sin; from earth-born passions set me free (1)
   461 come as the fire, and purge our hearts (2)
   461 purge our hearts like sacrificial flame (2)
   522 from his field shall in that day all offenses purge away (3)
   546 with thy living fire of judgment purge this land (1)
   546 purge this land of bitter things (1)

purged
   438 Word of grace hath purged away the old and wicked leaven (4)
   483 when he had purged our stains, he took his seat above (2)

purified
   278 no longer ... my heart shall mourn ... purified by grace (3)
   522 there, forever purified, in thy presence to abide (4)

purify
    75 thou only canst inform the mind and purify the heart (2)

purity
    26 perfect in power, in love, and purity (3)

purple
   264 still, still with thee, when purple morning breaketh (T,1)
   543 for purple mountain majesties above the fruited plain (1)

purpose
    41 thou whose purpose moves before us toward the goal (4)
    74 wherefore, by God's eternal purpose thou art exalted (4)
   171 give us a purpose true (3)
   173 we marvel at the purpose that held thee to thy course (2)
   197 thy purpose for thy world we share (4)
   347 through mortal motive, scheme .. plan thy... purpose ran (2)
   347 thy wise eternal purpose ran (2)
   479 consecrating to thy purpose every gift thou dost impart (1)
   521 his the loving purpose solely to preserve them (4)

pursue
    70 through every period of my life thy goodness I'll pursue (4)
   152 my daily labor to pursue (1)
   186 thy bright example I pursue, to thee in all things rise (4)
   231 in holy contemplation we sweetly then pursue the theme (2)
   258 when thou evil wouldst pursue (3)
   425 O Savior meek, pursue thy road with palms (1)

pursued
   527 for me, who him to death pursued (1)

pursuing
    84   thou man-pursuing Fisherman, who harmest not but savest (2)

put
    65   he hath put away our sin (3)
    75   who put their trust in thee... death nor hell shall harm (3)
    94   put him to an open shame (2)
   248   put on the gospel armor, each piece put on with prayer (3)
   250   soldiers of Christ, arise and put your armor on (T,1)
   354   and death's dark shadows put to flight (4)
   539   put his arms unfailing round you (3)

qickening
    12   art within, a qickening flame, a presence round about (2)

quake
   235   speak through the earth-quake, wind and fire (5)
   308   though earth-quake shocks are threatening her (3)
   393   shepherds quake at the sight (2)

quaking
   220   though the earth be shaking, every heart be quaking (2)

quarrels
   354   bid envy, strife, and quarrels cease (3)

queen
   446   the queen of seasons, bright with the day of splendor (3)

quench
   279   catch .. wandering of my will .. quench .. kindling fire (1)
   280   and quench the kindling fire (1)

quenched
   117   my thirst was quenched, my soul revived (2)

quest
   214   obey the laws of God in their determined quest (1)
   214   their determined quest to follow in the saints' pathway (1)

questing
   371   questing hearts that long for peace and healing see (3)

quick
   191   men alert and quick his lofty precepts to translate (2)
   253   I want a godly fear, a quick discerning eye (3)
   279   quick as the apple of an eye, O God, my conscience make (3)
   280   quick as the apple of an eye, O God, my conscience make (3)
   441   quick from the dead my risen Lord is seen (3)

quickened
   479   dawns upon our quickened sight (3)

quickening
    36   thy life is in the quickening air (2)
    64   sun of our life, thy quickening ray sheds on our path (2)

134   with all thy quickening powers kindle a flame (1,5)
219   around me flows thy quickening life (3)
310   O might thy quickening voice the death of sin remove (5)
459   thine is the quickening power that gives increase (4)
527   thine eye diffused a quickening ray (3)

quickly
110   quickly arise and away (4)
111   come quickly in ... nor ever hence remove (4)
111   come quickly in, thou heavenly guest (4)
130   come quickly ... my Lord, & take possession of thine own (4)
130   come quickly from above (5)
173   while we betray so quickly and leave thee there alone (2)
265   come quickly and abide or life is vain (3)
282   come quickly from above (5)
353   thy people pray, come quickly, King of kings (5)
447   the three sad days have quickly sped (3)
522   even so,Lord, quickly come, bring thy final harvest home (4)

quiet
 68   he leadeth me the quiet waters by (1)
147   if on a quiet sea, toward heaven we calmly sail (T,1)
197   through quiet work in shop and home (1)
225   make in my heart a quiet place ... come & dwell therein (1)
321   thy supper, Lord, is spread in every quiet upper room (1)
333   of patient hope and quiet, brave endurance (2)
358   let thy wandering cease; hie thee to thy quiet home (3)
477   the quiet of a steadfast faith, calm of a call obeyed (2)

quietness
225   a little shrine of quietness, all sacred to itself (2)
235   drop thy still dews of quietness (4)

quivering
270   the murmuring wind, the quivering leaf ... tell us (3)
270   quivering leaf shall softly tell us thou art near (3)

race
 35   for thyself, best Gift Divine! to our race ... given (6)
 35   for thyself, best Gift ... to our race so freely given (6)
 39   the race of men confess the beauty of his holiness (3)
 66   saints triumphant ... gathered in from every race (4)
 71   chosen seed of Israel's race, ye ransomed from the fall (2)
122   his blood atoned for all our race (2)
136   till every age and race and clime shall blend (3)
171   O Master Workman of the race, thou man of Galilee (T,1)
173   knows not race nor station as boundaries of the mind (4)
192   join hands ... brothers of the faith whate'er your race (3)
198   a loftier race than e'er the world hath known shall rise (1)
204   where sound the cries of race and clan (1)
249   a heavenly race demands thy zeal and an immortal crown (1)
249   blest Savior, introduced by thee have I my race begun (4)
288   the battle's fought, the race is won (1)
296   one holy Church of God appears through every age & race (T)
351   from hence send forth a race of men of flaming heart (3)
351   race of men of flaming heart and stalwart mind (3)
365   when thy truth began its race, it touched ... every land (3)

371 to every land, to every race and clan (4)
395 ask the saved of all the race who have found his favor (1)
465 incarnate Deity, let ... ransomed race render in thanks (2)
476 no alien race, no foreign shore (1)
486 those who give up life's bounty to serve a race to be (2)
548 save the people from the clash of race and creed (4)

races
408 in Christ all races meet, their ancient feuds forgetting (2)
469 races and peoples, lo, we stand divided (2)

radiance
29 on us thy glance let fall in royal radiance (2)
203 and marveled at the radiance of thy face (2)
372 praise thee for the radiance ... from the hallowed page (1)
413 thy guiding radiance above us shall be a beacon to God (R)
416 from the cross the radiance streaming adds more luster (3)

radiancy
303 what radiancy of glory, what light beyond compare (1)
401 fill me, Radiancy divine; scatter all my unbelief (3)

radiant
7 see the morning sun ascending radiant in the eastern sky (T)
33 the radiant morns unfold (2)
43 no real voice nor sound amid the radiant orbs be found (3)
83 his head with radiant glories crowned (1)
85 thru thy life so radiant, earth's darkness turns to day (1)
189 human hatreds flee before the radiant eastern skies (1)
393 radiant beams from thy holy face (3)
488 where Gospel light is glowing with pure & radiant beams (3)

rage
20 his rage we can endure, for lo, his doom is sure (3)
142 faith that shines more bright & clear when tempests rage (3)
238 how the powers of darkness rage thy steps around (1)
353 left .. lonesome place of death, despite .. rage of foes (3)

raging
106 when the storms are raging sore ... whisper softly (2)
244 when the storms of life are raging, stand by me (T,1)
538 waters heard and hushed their raging at thy word (2)

raiment
450 angels in bright raiment rolled the stone away (1)

rain
97 he sends the sunshine and the rain (2)
97 sunshine and rain, harvest of grain, He's my friend (2)

231 a season of clear shining to cheer it after rain (1)
234 I trace the rainbow through the rain (3)
473 and sweetly distills in the dew and the rain (4)
513 the breezes and the sunshine, and soft, refreshing rain (1)
514 take our ... hopes and fears of sun and rain (2)

rainbow
    11   rainbow arch, his covenant sign (2)
    64   our rainbow arch thy mercy's sign (3)
   234   I trace the rainbow through the rain (3)

rains
   380   the star rains its fire while the beautiful sing (1,2)
   515   suns glow, rains fall, by power divine (2)

raise
    11   nations, come, your voices raise to the Lord in hymns (1)
    14   in cheerful sounds all voices raise (4)
    19   all saints triumphant, raise the song (3)
    19   raise the glad strain, alleluia! (1)
    22   high as the heavens our voices raise (3)
    23   raise to Christ our joyful strain (1)
    35   Lord of all, to thee we raise this our hymn of grateful (R)
    39   let all on earth their voices raise (T,1)
    45   the birds their carols raise (2)
    58   we raise it high, we send it on, the song (3)
    93   here I raise mine Ebenezer, hither to thy help I'm come (2)
   125   raise the fallen, cheer the faint (3)
   177   some song to raise, or prayer, something for thee (2)
   185   this be the parting cry my heart shall raise (4)
   188   raise my low self above, won by thy deathless love (1)
   213   and raise my head, and cheer my heart (3)
   233   raise high your free, exulting song (2)
   236   Savior, again to thy dear name we raise (T,1)
   263   out of my stony griefs Bethel I'll raise (4)
   325   rich blood that Jesus shed to raise our souls to heaven (2)
   343   with them loud chorus raise (2)
   350   in faith we here an altar raise (1)
   350   altar raise to thy great glory, God of praise (1)
   352   be in each song of praise which here thy people raise (2)
   360   by thine all-sufficient merit raise us ((2)
   360   raise us to thy glorious throne (2)
   374   while our hearts in love we raise (4)
   387   born to raise the sons of earth (3)
   424   to thee, now high exalted, our melody we raise (3)
   437   and, hearing, may raise the victory strain (2)
   439   raise your joys and triumphs high, Alleluia (1)
   446   raise the strain of triumphant gladness (1)
   446   come, ye faithful, raise the strain (T,1)
   448   come, ye faithful, raise the strain (T,1) (see 446)
   451   on this most holy day of days, our hearts ... we raise (5)
   451   our hearts and voices, Lord, we raise to thee (5)
   451   voices, Lord, we raise to thee, in jubilee and praise (5)
   487   our faith from seed to flower raise on this thy holy day (2)
   491   the toils of day are over; we raise our hymn to thee (3)
   509   thy goodness all our hopes shall raise (4)
   522   raise the song of harvest home (1)
   522   raise the glorious harvest home (4)
   524   to thee, O Lord, our hearts we raise (T,1)
   524   our hearts we raise in hymns of adoration (1)
   528   how shall I equal triumphs raise (1)

raised
345 accept the walls that human hands have raised ...to thee (1)
345 hands have raised, O God, to thee (1)

raises
4 my voice unwearied raises (4)
257 hear the cry thy people raises (3)

raiseth
263 e'en though it be a cross that raiseth me (1)

raising
446 Alleluia   yet again to the Spirit raising (5)

ran
70 with heedless steps I ran (3)
347 through mortal motive, scheme .. plan thy... purpose ran (2)
347 thy wise eternal purpose ran (2)

rang
377 the hostel rang with song and shout (2)
404 lo! above the earth rang out the angel chorus (2)
423 through pillared court and temple the lovely anthem rang (1)

range
12 beyond the range of sun and star, and yet beside us here (1)

rank
324 rank on rank the host of heaven spreads its vanguard (3)

ransom
127 thou hast for all a ransom paid (4)
354 o come, o come, Emmanuel, and ransom captive Israel (T,1)

ransom's
428 'Tis done! the precious ransom's paid! (3)

ransomed
16 with all our ransomed powers (4)
66 ransomed, healed, restored, forgiven (1)
67 my ransomed soul he leadeth (2)
71 chosen seed of Israel's race, ye ransomed from the fall (2)
100 return, ye ransomed sinners, home (R)
112 ransomed sinners, why will you slight his grace, and die (2)
143 O bear me safe above, a ransomed soul (4)
177 and when thy face I see, my ransomed soul shall be (4)
182 thy ransomed servant, I restore to thee thine own (2)
364 cause of endless exultation to his ransomed worshipers (3)
397 bring our ransomed souls at last where they need no star (4)
421 till all the ransomed Church of God be saved (3)
465 incarnate Deity, let ... ransomed race render in thanks (2)
465 ransomed race render in thanks their lives to thee (2)

rapt
41 rapt in reverence we adore thee (1)

rapture
   6   days of wonder ... beauty ... rapture, filled with light (1)
 224   visions of rapture now burst on my sight (2)
 301   what height of rapture shall we know when...we meet (5)
 335   souls that must forever live in rapture or in woe (3)
 364   with what rapture gaze we on those glorious scars (3)
 547   my heart with rapture thrills, like that above (2)

raptured
 291   filled with delight my raptured soul lives (3)
 433   till my raptured soul shall find rest beyond the river (R)

raptures
 128   and tell its raptures all abroad (1)

rapturous
  23   bound every heart with rapturous joy (3)
 227   O the rapturous height of that holy delight (5)
 291   O... transporting rapturous scene that rises to my sight (1)

rare
 397   as they offered gifts most rare at... manger rude & bare (3)
 405   Eastern sages at his cradle make oblations rich and rare (3)

rate
 134   and shall we then forever live at this poor dying rate (4)

raveled
 462   lifting the raveled mists of night (2)

ravens
 231   and he who feeds the ravens will give his children bread (3)

ray
  64   sun of our life, thy quickening ray sheds on our path (2)
 139   unseen by reason's glimmering ray (5)
 170   in hope that sends a shining ray far down the future's (4)
 234   my heart restores its borrowed ray (2)
 259   O Love, how cheering is thy ray (2)
 358   watchman, doth its beauteous ray (1)
 358   doth its beauteous ray aught of joy or hope foretell (1)
 527   thine eye diffused a quickening ray (3)

rays
  38   earth and heaven reflect thy rays (2)
 437   the Lord in rays eternal of resurrection light (2)

reach
  15   all the reach of heavenly art (2)
  96   thou didst reach forth thy hand and mine enfold (2)
 134   our souls, how heavily they go to reach eternal joys (2)
 136   prefected by thee, we reach creation's glorious goal (4)
 159   there are heights of joy that I may not reach till (4)
 184   if it would reach a monarch's throne (4)
 195   wing my words, that they may reach the hidden depths (3)
 203   they reach thy throne, encompass land and sea (1)
 206   no farthest reach where thou art not (2)

220   foes who would molest me cannot reach me here (2)
252   prayer .. sublimest strains .. reach the Majesty on high (3)
256   may I reach heaven's joys, O bright heaven's Sun (4)
259   no thought can reach, no tongue declare (1)
285   cannot reach the mystery ... length .. breadth .. height (2)
291   no chilling winds or poisonous breath can reach (2)
291   can reach that healthful shore (2)
291   when I shall reach that happy place ... be forever blest (3)
433   till I reach the golden strand just beyond the river (4)
469   building proud towers which shall not reach to heaven (3)
488   we reach the rest remaining to spirits of the blest (4)

reached
105   the voice of God hath reached my heart (5)

reaches
130   grace ... it reaches all mankind (2)

read
365   but when our eyes behold thy Word, we read thy name (1)
365   we read thy name in fairer lines (1)
368   guide & chart, wherein we read of realms beyond the sky (2)
462   to read forgiveness in thine eyes (3)
529   look on thy hands, and read it there (2)
545   I can read his righteous sentence by the dim ... lamps (2)

ready
102   all things in Christ are ready now (2)
104   Jesus ready stands to save you (1)
172   ready for all thy perfect will (4)
258   ready burning be the incense of thy powers (2)
267   ready, my God thy will to see (R)
267   silently now I wait for thee, ready my God (R)
274   make me ready when thy voice is truly heard (4)
325   all things are ready, come away (4)

real
43   no real voice nor sound amid the radiant orbs be found (3)
332   sure and real is the grace, the manner be unknown (4)

realizing
139   faith lends its realizing light (6)

realm
435   were the whole realm of nature mine (4)
535   thee in thy glorious realm they praise (3)

realms
205   my spirit ... wings its flight to realms of day (3)
324   Light of light descendeth from the realms of endless day (3)
368   guide & chart, wherein we read of realms beyond the sky (2)
382   angels, from the realms of glory (T,1)
472   people and realms of every tongue dwell (3)

reaping
514   take our plowing, seeding, reaping (2)

reared
  352   this temple, reared to thee, O may it ever be filled (1)

reason
  149   that is just the reason I tell it now to thee (2)
  412   alas, my treason, Jesus, hath undone thee (2)

reason's
  43   in reason's ear they all rejoice and utter forth (3)
  139   unseen by reason's glimmering ray (5)

reassure
  164   O speak to reassure me, to hasten or control (3)

reawakened
  279   O may the least omission pain my reawakened soul (4)
  280   O may the least omission pain my reawakened soul (4)

rebel
  32   rebel, ye waves, and o'er the land ... roar (2)
  138   to check the rising doubt,the rebel sigh (4)
  160   nor let thy foolish pride rebel (3)
  227   suffered and died to redeem a poor rebel like me (4)

rebels
  420   crucified for me and you to bring us rebels near to God (2)

recall
  237   when thou seest me waver, with a look recall (1)

receive
  1   new life the dead receive (5)
  76   humbled for a season, to receive a name (3)
  83   from his bounty I receive such proofs of love divine (4)
  87   when his loving arms receive us (3)
  99   if I ask him to receive me, will he say me nay (6)
  102   my message as from God receive (4)
  105   he still is waiting to receive (3)
  112   will you not his grace receive ... still refuse to live (3)
  114   we...his unknown peace receive & feel his blood applied (3)
  119   just as I am thou wilt receive (5)
  121   thou hast promised to receive us (3)
  125   safe into the haven guide; O receive my soul at last (1)
  130   assert thy claim, receive thy right (5)
  140   O let me now receive that gift! my soul without it dies (4)
  175   waiting the penitent child to receive (2)
  178   far more for others' sins than... wrongs that we receive (3)
  181   may we thy bounties thus as stewards true receive (2)
  186   Son of the carpenter, receive this humble work of mine (2)
  193   O may we all the loving mind that was in thee receive (5)
  196   sacred cup of saving grace I will with thanks receive (2)
  214   therefore the evil shall receive but grief (3)
  283   come, Almighty to deliver, let us all thy life receive (3)
  318   as thy guest in heaven receive me (3)
  332   let the wisest mortal show how we the grace receive (2)
  335   let them from the mouth of God ... solemn charge receive (1)

346   sovereign God, receive . gift thy willing servants offer (3)
367   thirsty souls receive supplies .. sweet refreshment find (2)
381   where meek souls will receive him... dear Christ enters (3)
392   let earth receive her King (1)
428   receive my soul, he cries (3)
454   Christ is worthy to receive (4)
465   glory, power, and praise receive for thy creating love (1)
515   may grateful hearts thy gifts receive (4)
519   freely we these gifts receive (1)
528   sinners alone his grace receive (4)
530   join us, in one spirit ... let us still receive of thine (2)

received
28   or earth received her frame (3)
122   five bleeding wounds he bears, received on Calvary (3)
227   when my heart first believed, what a joy I received (2)
372   Church from thee, her Master, received the gift divine (2)
456   and have the bright immensities received our risen Lord (T)

receives
137   inspire the living faith, which whosoe'er receives (4)
139   into himself he all receives, pardon and holiness (4)

recite
473   thy bountiful care, what tongue can recite (4)

reckon
336   gladly reckon all things loss so we may Jesus gain (5)

reclaimed
292   new-born souls, whose days, reclaimed from error's ways (4)

reclining
90   there in a manger on the hay reclining (1)
400   angels adore him in slumber reclining (2)

reclothe
235   reclothe us in our rightful mind (1)

recoil
204   thy heart has never known recoil (3)

reconciled
122   my God is reconciled; his pardoning voice I hear (4)
387   God and sinners reconciled (1)
489   show thy reconciled face (2)

reconciling
309   by thy reconciling love every stumbling block remove (2)

record
420   believe the record true (2)
465   let all the sons of men record and dwell upon thy love (4)

recreate
273   with thy spirit recreate me, pure and strong and true (1)

red
- 203 o'er hill and dale in saffron flame and red (4)
- 234 from the ground there blossoms red life (4)
- 419 his blood-red banner streams afar (1)
- 446 led them with unmoistened foot through... Red Sea waters (1)

reddening
- 490 rise to greet the sun, reddening the sky (T,1)

redeem
- 78 redeem us for eternal day from every power of darkness (3)
- 78 redeem us...when thou judgest all the sons of men (3)
- 227 suffered and died to redeem a poor rebel like me (4)
- 227 who hath died my poor soul to redeem (6)
- 296 redeem the evil time (4)
- 443 didst once, upon the cross ... suffer to redeem our loss (1)
- 443 endured the cross & grave ... sinners to redeem and save (2)
- 464 Jesus mighty to redeem, he alone the work hath wrought (3)

redeemed
- 18 life redeemed from death and sin (3)
- 203 but in the eyes of men, redeemed and free, a splendor (4)
- 288 redeemed from earth and pain, Ah! when shall we ascend (2)
- 292 redeemed at countless cost, from dark despair (2)
- 302 greet the blood redeemed hands on the eternal shore (5)
- 430 till amid the hosts of light, we in thee redeemed (5)
- 430 we in thee redeemed, complete (5)
- 482 mighty host, by thee redeemed, is marching in thy train (1)
- 511 a world redeemed by Christ-like love (2)
- 523 for souls redeemed, for sins forgiven (4)
- 528 a slave redeemed from death and sin (1)

Redeemer
- 166 my gracious Redeemer, my Savior art thou (1)
- 227 'twas a heaven below my Redeemer to know (3)
- 294 the Church our blest Redeemer saved (1)
- 335 may they in Jesus ...they preach, their own Redeemer see (4)
- 363 Redeemer, come, with us abide (3)
- 400 guide where our infant Redeemer is laid (1,5)
- 423 for Christ is our Redeemer, the Lord of heaven our King (3)
- 424 all glory, laud, and honor, to thee, Redeemer, King (T,1)
- 445 I know that my Redeemer lives (T,1,4)
- 455 all hail, Redeemer, hail! for thou hast died for me (4)
- 473 our Maker, Defender, Redeemer, and Friend (5)
- 482 O Christ, Redeemer, Brother, Friend, ride on, ride on (4)
- 517 thee, the world's Redeemer bore (2)

Redeemer's
- 1 my great Redeemer's praise (1)
- 14 let the Redeemer's name be sung (1)
- 282 my great Redeemer's throne (2)
- 434 your Redeemer's conflict see (1)
- 461 let our whole soul an offering be to our Redeemer's name (2)
- 489 pray ... through the dear Redeemer's name (2)

redeeming
- 93 mount of thy redeeming love (1)
- 122 his all-redeeming love, his precious blood, to plead (2)

165 triumph in redeeming grace (1)
196 the God of all-redeeming grace my God I will proclaim (4)
285 the greatness of redeeming love (1)
301 all praise to our redeeming Lord (T,1)
336 then let us make our boast of his redeeming power (4)
339 thy universal grace proclaim, thine all-redeeming love (4)
342 redeeming soul and body by water and the Word (2)
351 prove the wonders of redeeming love (4)
393 with the dawn of redeeming grace (3)
414 trust in his redeeming blood, and try his works to do (5)
417 the wonders of redeeming love and my unworthiness (2)
421 redeeming love has been my theme, & shall be till I die (4)
429 the great redeeming work is done (1)
439 love's redeeming work is done, Alleluia (3)
462 Spirit redeeming, give us grace when crucified (3)
465 render ... their lives to thee for thy redeeming grace (2)
480 didst come to bring on thy redeeming wing (2)

redeems
65 who redeems thee from destruction (2)

redemption
100 redemption in his blood throughout the world proclaim (3)
299 tidings of Jesus, redemption and release (R)

redress
468 this wicked earth redress (2)

reechoes
129 reechoes the praise of the Lord (5)

reed
290 the bruised reed he will not break, but strengthen (2)

refine
48 thy dross to consume, and thy gold to refine (4)
543 America! America! may God thy gold refine (3)

refining
278 refining fire, go through my heart; illuminate my soul (2)

reflect
38 earth and heaven reflect thy rays (2)

refrain
8 prophets swell the glad refrain (3)
185 sweet are thy messengers, sweet their refrain (3)

refresh
81 may the music of thy name refresh my soul in death (5)
165 O refresh us ... traveling through this wilderness (1)
552 refresh thy people on their toilsome way (4)

refreshing
255 so longs my soul, O God, for thee & thy refreshing grace (1)
268 where is the soul-refreshing view of Jesus and his word (2)
488 living water flowing with soul-refreshing streams (3)
513 the breezes and the sunshine, and soft, refreshing rain (1)

refreshment
   53   sweet refreshment find (3)
 367   thirsty souls receive supplies .. sweet refreshment find (2)

refuge
   47   Lord ... our refuge be (3)
   48   to you who for refuge to Jesus have fled (1)
   89   my help and refuge from my foes (1)
 125   other refuge have I none; hangs my helpless soul on thee (2)
 216   He is my refuge and my stay (2)
 216   I of the Lord my God will say, "He is my refuge ... (2)
 261   precious Savior, still our refuge (3)
 521   nesting bird nor star in heaven such a refuge ... given (1)
 551   be thou her refuge and her trust, her everlasting friend (4)

refuse
    5   let those refuse to sing who never knew our God (2)
 112   will you not his grace receive ... still refuse to live (3)
 186   thou didst not, Lord, refuse (1)
 258   Our God's bounteous gifts abuse not, Light refuse not (4)
 355   shall we again refuse thee (3)
 462   when weary feet refuse to climb, give us thy vision (5)
 528   refuse his righteousness to impart (3)
 528   refuse ... to impart by hiding it within my heart (3)

regard
   44   oh, what is man, in thy regard to hold so large a place (3)
   44   when I regard the wondrous heavens,thy handiwork on high (2)
 253   I want a true regard, a single steady aim (4)

regardest
    2   can it be that thou regardest songs of sinful man? (2)

reign
    3   come, and reign over us, Ancient of Days! (1)
    8   infinite thy vast domain, everlasting is thy reign (1)
   11   through his far domain, love is king where he doth reign (2)
   23   who reigns, and shall forever reign (1,4)
 135   King within my conscience reign (4)
 179   take thy great power and reign there alone (3)
 184   deathless it shall reign (2)
 239   sure I must fight, if I would reign (4)
 425   then take, O God, thy power, and reign (4)
 429   the reign of sin and death is o'er (3)
 438   the reign of death was ended (2)
 444   and he lives forever with his saints to reign (R)
 455   his reign shall know no endd (3)
 457   Lord our King, who reigns for us...shall forever reign (2)
 458   they reign with him above (5)
 471   in every heart reign thou alone (2)
 472   Jesus shall reign (T,1)
 476   help us to spread thy gracious reign till greed .. cease (2)
 481   holy city ... where Christ, the Lamb, doth reign (1)
 482   and thou in love shalt reign (1)
 516   unite ... in love to thee, and love to all will reign (4)
 531   ah, tear it thence and reign alone (2)
 531   reign alone, the Lord of every motion there (2)

reigned
116   long has evil reigned within (2)

reignest
544   show forth thy pity on high where thou reignest (1)

reigneth
55   Lord, who o'er all things so wondrously reigneth (2)
318   high o'er all the heavens he reigneth (1)
410   message ... that the Lord who reigneth above (3)

reigning
38   father love is reigning o'er us (4)

reigns
4   sing praise to God who reigns above (T,1)
15   praise the Lord who reigns above (T,1)
23   who reigns, and shall forever reign (1,4)
23   worship and thanks to him belong who reigns (4)
31   the Lord Jehovah reigns, his throne is built on high (T,1)
39   and reigns in glory there (2)
45   let the heavens ring! God reigns: let the earth be glad (3)
49   the Son, and him who reigns with them in highest heaven (3)
282   where Jesus reigns alone (2)
291   there God the Son forever reigns and scatters night away (2)
392   joy to the world! the Savior reigns (2)
403   his spirit only can bestow, who reigns in light above (1)
438   stripped of power, no more he reigns (2)
457   Lord our King, who reigns for us...shall forever reign (2)
472   blessings abound where'er he reigns (4)
483   Jesus, the Savior, reigns, the God of truth and love (2)

rejected
412   by foes derided, by thine own rejected, O most afflicted (1)

rejection
331   in thy trial and rejection ...thy sufferings on the tree (2)

rejoice
1   mournful, broken hearts rejoice; the humble poor believe (5)
21   come ye before him and rejoice (1)
38   call us to rejoice in thee (2)
42   sun and moon, rejoice before him (1)
43   in reason's ear they all rejoice and utter forth (3)
54   in God our shield we will rejoice & ever bless thy name (5)
60   thou rising morn, in praise rejoice (2)
77   let all, with heart and voice, before his throne rejoice (1)
106   weary souls fore'er rejoice (1)
110   they who believe on his name shall rejoice (4)
111   in sure and certain hope rejoice (3)
111   rejoice that thou wilt enter in (3)
128   well may this glowing heart rejoice (1)
129   thy foes will rejoice when my sorrows they see (3)
129   he looks! and ten thousands of angels rejoice (5)
162   thus may I rejoice to show that I feel the love I owe (4)
231   for while in him confiding, I cannot but rejoice (4)
233   rejoice, give thanks and sing (1)

233   rejoice, ye pure in heart (T,1)
233   rejoice, rejoice, rejoice, give thanks and sing (R)
252   angels in their songs rejoice and cry,"Behold he prays" (4)
262   here...my God, vouchsafe to stay & bid my heart rejoice (3)
310   bid our inmost souls rejoice in hope of perfect love (5)
366   we rejoice, and sing to thee our hymn of joy eternally (3)
380   we rejoice in the light, and we echo the song (4)
391   good Christian men, rejoice (T,1,2,3)
423   and in his blissful presence eternally rejoice (3)
449   let all mankind rejoice and say: Alleluia (2)
449   good Christian men, rejoice and sing (T,1)
483   rejoice, the Lord is King, your Lord and King adore (T,1)
483   rejoice, give thanks, and sing, and triumph evermore (1)
483   rejoice, again I say, rejoice (R)
483   rejoice in glorious hope! Our Lord the judge shall come (4)

rejoiced
378   the shepherds at those tidings rejoiced much in mind (4)
421   the dying thief rejoiced to see that fountain in his day (2)

rejoices
 49   wondrous things hath done, in whom his world rejoices (1)
366   at the thrilling cry rejoices (1)
379   all my hear this night rejoices (T,1)
440   Life eternal! heaven rejoices (3)

rejoicest
  2   we know that thou rejoicest o'er each work of thine (3)

rejoicing
 67   and home, rejoicing, brought me (3)
179   song of our spirits, rejoicing and free (R)
396   thus rejoicing, free from sorrow (2)
430   here we learn to serve and give, &, rejoicing, self deny (3)

release
  9   grants the prisoner sweet release (3)
106   waiting still for sweet release (3)
299   tidings of Jesus, redemption and release (R)
355   from old unfaith our souls release (3)
360   from our fears and sins release us (1)
454   thou didst suffer to release us (1)

released
281   O that I now, from sin released (5)

relent
155   there's no discouragement shall make him once relent (1)

reliance
211   place on the Lord reliance; my soul, with courage wait (2)

relief
 83   he flew to my relief (2)
145   let me at thy throne of mercy find a sweet relief (2)
275   my soul has often found relief (1)
489   bring relief for all complaints (4)

relieve
   119   wilt welcome, pardon, cleanse, relieve (5)
   121   thou hast mercy to relieve us (3)

relieved
    92   and grace my fears relieved (2)

religion
   552   thy true religion in our hearts increase (3)

rely
     9   happy the man whose hopes rely on Israel's God (2)
   150   help me to watch and pray and on thyself rely (4)

relying
   237   on thy truth relying, through that mortal strife (4)

remain
    50   that shadows fall on brightest hours, that thorns remain (3)
   209   in every change he faithful will remain (1)
   305   but the Church of Jesus constant will remain (3)
   332   these the virtues did convey, yet still remain the same (2)

remained
   438   the victory remained with life (2)

remainest
   468   thou in thy everlasting seat remainest God alone (3)

remaining
   488   we reach the rest remaining to spirits of the blest (4)

remains
   281   whose word, when heaven and earth shall pass, remains (1)
   281   remains and stands forever sure (1)
   316   while a breath, a pulse remains, will I remember thee (3)
   438   an empty form alone remains (2)

remember
    65   unto those who still remember his commandments, and obey (5
   272   remember not past years (2)
   316   this will I do, my dying Lord, I will remember thee (1)
   316   thy testamental cup I take, and thus remember thee (2)
   316   remember thee, and all thy pains, and all thy love to me (3)
   316   while a breath, a pulse remains, will I remember thee (3)
   316   when thou shalt in thy kingdom come ... Lord remember me (4
   317   spread with reverence this holy feast ... remember thee (1)
   328   how happy are thy servants, Lord, who thus remember thee (T
   331   in thy glorious resurrection ... we, Lord, remember thee (2)
   413   are ye able to remember, when a thief lifts up his eyes (2)

rememberest
   526   if thou rememberest each misdeed (1)

remembrance
   237   bring to my remembrance sad Gethsemane (2)
   331   taste it, kindly given, in remembrance, Lord, of thee (1)

remnant
227   now my remnant of days would I speak of his praise (6)

remold
413   remold them, make us, like thee, divine (R)

remotest
100   let all the nations know, to earth's remotest bound (1)
407   send God's love to earth's remotest part (1)

remove
103   earth has no sorrow but heaven can remove (3)
111   come quickly in ... nor ever hence remove (4)
143   blest Savior, then, in love, fear and distrust remove (4)
144   and earthly friends and hopes remove (2)
279   the burden of my soul remove, the hardness from my heart (4)
280   burden from my soul remove, the hardness from my heart (4)
293   and all fear of want remove (2)
309   by thy reconciling love every stumbling block remove (2)
309   let us then with joy remove to the family above (6)
310   O might thy quickening voice the death of sin remove (5)
326   the bread and wine remove: but thou art here (4)
338   our bodies may far off remove, we still are one in heart (1)
344   error and ignorance remove (2)
356   remove the veil of ancient words (2)
359   the tide of time shall never his covenant remove (4)
474   time shall soon this earth remove (1)
526   our works could ne'er our guilt remove (2)
550   till these eternal hills remove (4)

removed
431   from all removed, the Savior wrestles lone with fears (2)

rend
428   temple's veil in sunder breaks ... solid marbles rend (2)

render
  2   best that thou hast given, earth and heaven render thee (5)
 27   all praise we would render: O help us to see (4)
161   we render back the love thy mercy gave us (4)
184   force me to render up my sword and I shall conqueror be (1)
196   render to my God for all his mercy's store (1)
196   what shall I render to my God (T,1)
258   see thou render all thy feeble strength can pay (1)
318   there with joy thy praises render unto him (1)
398   and helpest them to render light back to thee again (2)
446   with the royal feast of feasts, comes its joy to render (3)
465   incarnate Deity, let ... ransomed race render in thanks (2)
465   render ... their lives to thee for thy redeeming grace (2)

rendered
530   love ... rendered all distinctions void (5)

rending
 75   the rending tomb proclaims thy conquering arm (3)
138   no sudden rending of the veil of clay (2)

renew
70 after death, in distant worlds, the glorious theme renew (4)
98 thy former mercies here renew (3)
180 Lord, I my vows to thee renew (2)
188 in thee my strength renew; give me my work to do (2)
246 renew it boldly every day, and help divine implore (2)
253 on thee, almighty to create, almighty to renew (1)
344 in knowledge pure their mind renew (2)
365 Lord, cleanse my sins, my soul renew (6)

renewed
58 the strength those weaklings that renewed (2)
128 that vow renewed shall daily hear (5)
282 a heart in every thought renewed and full of love divine (4)
365 thy noblest wonders here we view in souls renewed (6)
365 noblest wonders ... in souls renewed, and sins forgiven (6)

renewing
465 bless thine heart-renewing power (3)

renews
442 so, as he renews the earth, artist without rival (2)

renouncing
253 I want a sober mind, a self-renouncing will (2)

renown
517 may we keep our holy calling stainless in... fair renown (5)

rent
161 speak to our fearful hearts by conflict rent (1)
429 the veil is rent in Christ alone (2)

repair
91 alike at work and prayer to Jesus I repair (1)

repay
105 and basely his kind care repay (2)
223 but our toil he doth richly repay (2)
415 drops of grief can ne'er repay the debt of love I owe (5)

repeat
149 'tis pleasant to repeat (3)
172 my acts of faith and love repeat (4)
227 the story repeat, and the lover of sinners adore (3)
392 repeat the sounding joy (2)
392 while fields and floods, rocks, hills and plains repeat (2)
472 and earth repeat the loud amen (5)

repeating
370 each his word from God repeating (2)

repeats
43 nightly, to the listening earth repeats the story (2)
43 repeats the story of her birth (2)
321 every act of brotherhood repeats thy feast again (2)

repent
  94 now incline me to repent; let me now my sins lament (3)

repentance
  104 true belief and true repentance (2)

repine
  217 nor ever murmur nor repine; content whatever lot I see (3)

reply
  374 and the mountains in reply echoing their joyous strains (1)
  424 and mortal men and all things created make reply (2)
  439 sing, ye heavens, and earth reply, Alleluia (1)

repose
  48 the soul that on Jesus still leans for repose (5)
  89 thou hidden source of calm repose (T,1)
  264 sweet the repose beneath thy wings o'ershading (4)
  293 what can shake thy sure repose (1)
  493 O may my soul on thee repose and with sweet sleep (4)
  495 Jesus, give the weary calm and sweet repose (2)
  496 ere repose our spirits seal (1)
  531 and inly sigh for thy repose (1)
  531 my heart ... be free, when it hath found repose in thee (2)

reproach
  228 its shame and reproach gladly bear (4)
  292 with us the work to share, with us reproach to dare (3)

reprove
  279, 280 that moment, Lord, reprove (2)

require
  285 thy only love do I require (4)

requireth
  104 all the fitness he requireth is to feel your need of him (3)

requited
  318 never to my hurt invited, be thy love with love requited (3)

rescue
  56 when in distress to him I called, he to my rescue came (2)
  93 to rescue me from danger, interposed his precious blood (2)
  148 some poor fainting, struggling seaman you may rescue (R)
  148 you may rescue, you may save (R)
  175 rescue the perishing, duty demands it (4)
  175 rescue the perishing, care for the dying (T,1,R)

rescued
  463 by whose cross & death are we rescued from sin's misery (2)

rescues
  66 rescues us from all our foes (3)

reserve
  169 with no reserve and no delay, with all my heart, I come (2)

reserved
94 depth of mercy! can there be mercy still reserved for me (1)

residing
382 God with men is now residing (2)

residue
182 myself, my residue of days, I consecrate to thee (1)
510 residue of days or hours thine, wholly thine, shall be (5)

resign
118 to thee I all resign; thine is the work & only thine (3)
166 for thee all the follies of sin I resign (1)
167 into thy hand of love I would my all resign (1)
184 it must its crown resign (4)
337 in humble hope their charge resign (5)

resignation
470 save us from weak resignation to the evils we deplore (5)

resigned
282 a heart resigned, submissive, meek (2)

resolve
200 purge us of low desire; lift us to high resolve (4)

resolved
152 thee, only thee, resolved to know in all I think (1)

resolves
31 and where his love resolves to bless (2)

resort
129 where dost thou, dear Shepherd, resort with thy sheep (2)

resounding
504 thine is the glory, gleaming and resounding (3)
504 glory, gleaming and resounding through all creation (3)

respond
19 respond, ye souls in endless rest (3)

responsive
189 our hearts responsive ring (3)

rest
2 angel harps forever ringing, rest not day nor night (1)
19 respond, ye souls in endless rest (3)
38 ocean depth of happy rest (3)
45 I rest me in the thought of rocks and trees (1)
81 'tis manna to the hungry soul and to the weary, rest (2)
82 sweeter far thy face to see and in thy presence rest (1)
89 my rest in toil, my ease in pain (3)
95 while I rest upon thy word come ... bless me now, O Lord (2)
95 turn me not away unblest; calm my anguish into rest (3)
100 ye weary spirits, rest; ye mournful souls, be glad (2)
101 he will surely give you rest, by trusting in his word (1)

101 Jesus is the truth, the way that leads you into rest (3)
102 ye restless wanderers after rest (3)
110 Jesus is calling the weary to rest (2)
115 by faith I see the land of rest, the saints' delight (1)
117 come unto me and rest (1)
128 now rest, my long-divided heart (4)
128 fixed on this blissful center, rest (4)
132 rest upon this congregation ...the fulness of thy grace (2)
141 I rest, heart, mind, and soul the captive of thy grace (4)
147 but should the surges rise and rest delay to come (2)
149 hungering and thirsting to hear it like the rest (4)
159 till I rest in peace with thee (4)
185 once earthly joy I craved, sought peace and rest (2)
195 thy rest, thy joy, thy glory share (5)
205 perfect rest to me is promised in my Father's home above (3)
208 just from Jesus simply taking life & rest & joy & peace (3)
208 just to rest upon his promise (1)
220 in thine arm I rest me (2)
222 I rest on his unchanging grace (2)
224 perfect submission, all is at rest (3)
229 to do the will of Jesus: this is rest (2)
234 I rest my weary soul in thee (1)
235 O sabbath rest by Galilee! O calm of hills above (3)
247 'twixt me and the peacful rest (3)
251 heaven will bring me sweeter rest (3)
262 labor is rest .. pain is sweet if thou, my God, art here (2)
263 darkness be over me, my rest a stone (2)
268 return, O holy Dove, return, sweet messenger of rest (4)
269 lead us, O Father, to thy heavenly rest (4)
281 enter ... promised rest ... Canaan of thy perfect love (5)
283 let us all in thee inherit, let us find that second rest (2)
284 let me thy loving servant be ... taste thy promised rest (2)
291 I shall see my Father's face, and in his bosom rest (3)
295 behold, the sparrow findeth out a house wherein to rest (3)
297 the great Church victorious shall be the Church at rest (3)
297 and mystic sweet communion with those whose rest is won (4)
303 Jesus, in mercy bring us to that dear land of rest (4)
304 with love and longing turn to find their rest in thee (1)
304 hearts with love & longing ... find their rest in thee (1)
334 with the Holy Spirit's favor, rest upon them from above (1)
348 may thy spirit here give rest (2)
348 rest to the heart by sin oppressed (2)
350 here let the weary one find rest (4)
360 let us find our rest in thee (1)
362 and give to the weary rest (3)
365 nor ... spreading Gospel rest till through the world (4)
378 God rest you merry, Gentlemen, let nothing you dismay (T,1)
383 o'er Bethlehem it took its rest (4)
385 child ... who, laid to rest, on Mary's lap is sleeping (1)
417 a home within the wilderness, a rest upon the way (1)
433 till my raptured soul shall find rest beyond the river (R)
472 the weary find eternal rest (4)
474 forward tends to his abode, to rest in his embrace (2)
476 in whom all hearts find rest (2)
481 O shame to us who rest content while lust and greed (3)
488 O day of rest and gladness (T,1)
488 new graces ever gaining from this our day of rest (4)

488   we reach the rest remaining to spirits of the blest (4)
489   day of all thee week the best, emblem of eternal rest (1)
489   may we rest this day in thee (2)
497   who the day for toil hast given, for rest the night (1)
499   O Lord, in thy dear love fit us for perfect rest above (4)
500   thy praise shall hallow now our rest (1)
501   and none, O Lord, have perfect rest (4)
502   be my last thought, how sweet to rest (2)
502   rest forever on my Savior's breast (2)
503   heaven is touching earth with rest (1)
509   in scenes exalted or depressed thou art our joy ... rest (4)
516   and one their heavenly rest (1)
526   I rest upon his faithful word to them of contrite spirit (3)
531   my heart is pained, nor can it be at rest (1)
531   nor can it be at rest till it finds rest in thee (1)
532   in peace their sacred ashes rest (6)
533   following ... incarnate God ... gained the promised rest (2)
536   for all the saints, who from their labors rest (T,1)
537   for all the saints, who from their labors rest (T,1)
549   and met within thy holy place to rest awhile with thee (1)

resting
27   unresting, unhasting, and silent as light (2)
88   and I shall fancy his blessing resting on me (2)
117   I found in him a resting place, and he has made me glad (1)
141   Lord Jesus, make me whole; grant me no resting place (4)
221   resting in my Savior as my all-in-all (4)
506   long our day of testing, now comes the hour of resting (3)

restless
102   ye restless wanderers after rest (3)
107   tumult of our life's wild, restless sea (1)
202   tasks he gives are those he gave beside the restless sea (2)
204   among these restless throngs abide (5)
255   why restless, why cast down, my soul (4)
292   the wayward and the lost, by restless passions tossed (2)
329   our restless spirits yearn for thee (4)
538   whose arm hath bound the restless wave (1)

restlessness
219   calmness bends serene above, my restlessness to still (3)

restore
58   grace ... doth vanquish, doth restore us (2)
68   my soul he doth restore again (2)
129   restore, my dear Savior, the light of thy face (4)
175   feelings lie buried that grace can restore (3)
182   thy ransomed servant, I restore to thee thine own (2)
356   restore to us thy truth, O God, & make its meaning sure (2)
427   but thou dost light and life restore (3)

restored
66   ransomed, healed, restored, forgiven (1)
209   sorrow forgot, love's purest joys restored (3)
283   let us see thy great salvation perfectly restored (4)
301   bids us, each to each restored, together seek his face (1)
314   by thy gift of peace restored (2)

449   the life laid down, the life restored (4)
499   through sleep and darkness safely brought, restored (1)
499   restored to life and power and thought (1)

restores
199   the holier worship which he deigns to bless restores (2)
199   restores the lost, and binds the spirit broken (2)
234   my heart restores its borrowed ray (2)

restrain
495   those who plan some evil, from their sins restrain (4)

rests
202   brotherhood still rests in him, the brother of us all (2)
206   rests the unfolding of the years (3)
206   in thy strong hand eternally rests the ... years (3)
361   on his shoulder ever rests all power on earth and heaven (2)
500   and rests not now by day or night (2)

resume
490   with the gracious light I my toil resume (1)

resurrection
 62   our whole lives one resurrection ... life of life above (4)
115   we feel the resurrection near (2)
331   in thy glorious resurrection ... we, Lord, remember thee (2)
427   thy cross may bring us to thy joy and resurrection power (4)
437   the day of resurrection, earth, tell it out abroad (T,1)
437   the Lord in rays eternal of resurrection light (2)
440   sing the resurrection song (1)
442   brothers, praise him, for he brings all to resurrection (3)
446   welcomes in unwearied strains Jesus' resurrection (3)

retain
298   what they gain from thee forever ... blessed to retain (3)

retire
235   let sense be dumb, let flesh retire (5)

retreat
232   there is a calm, a sure retreat (1)
350   the guilty soul a sure retreat (4)
545   trumpet that shall never call retreat (3)

retrieve
112   God, who did your souls retrieve (2)

return
100   return, ye ransomed sinners, home (R)
172   and trembling to its source return ((2)
268   return, O holy Dove, return, sweet messenger of rest (4)
275   oft escaped the tempter's snare by thy return ... prayer (1)
275   anxious spirits burn with strong desires for thy return (2)
283   suddenly return and never, nevermore thy temples leave (3)
401   joyless the day's return till thy mercy's beams I see (2)
474   soon our Savior will return, triumphant in the skies (3)

returned
452   all good gifts returned with her returning King (2)
453   from the fight returned victorious (1)

returneth
237   when my dust returneth to the dust again (4)

returning
252   sinner's voice, returning from his ways (4)
258   gladly hail the sun returning (2)
452   all good gifts returned with her returning King (2)
497   when the constant sun returning unseals our eyes (2)
499   new mercies, each returning day, hover around us (2)

reveal
137   Spirit of faith, come down, reveal the things of God (T,1)
262   thyself reveal, while here o'er earth we rove (1)
310   present we know thou art, but O thyself reveal (4)
342   and let our daily living reveal thee everywhere (1)
356   show us the way the Master trod; reveal his saving power (1)
363   thy grace and love in us reveal (3)
476   whose life and death reveal thy face (5)
520   shine, Light Divine, reveal thy face (3)
520   reveal thy face where darkness else might be (3)

revealed
90   shining revealed through every task most lowly (2)
115   with his glorious presence here his life in us revealed (2)
371   thou hast revealed thy will to mortal men (2)
476   O God of beauty, oft revealed in dreams of human art (4)
549   worlds of science and of art, revealed and ruled by thee (4)

revealing
90   divine and human, in his deep revealing of God and man (4)
342   revealing in our witness the master teacher's art (3)
371   undimmed by time, the Word is still revealing (3)
371   revealing to sinful men thy justice and thy grace (3)
460   Man, revealing God to man (2)
479   till thy love's revealing light ... dawns (3)

reveals
365   but the blest volume thou hast writ reveals thy justice (2)
365   volume thou hast writ reveals thy justice and thy grace (2)
532   praise the Lord who now as then reveals in man his glory (1)

revile
178   thy foes might hate, despise, revile (2)

reviled
434   beaten, bound, reviled, arraigned (2)

revival
442   in his grace of glad new birth we must seek revival (2)

revived
117   my thirst was quenched, my soul revived (2)

revives
124 revives my fainting heart, healing all it hidden smart (2)
212 but then the Holy Spirit revives my soul again (1)

reviving
442 day is fast reviving (1)

revolt
94 now my foul revolt deplore (3)

revolving
492 live this short, revolving day as if it were our last (4)

reward
124 what the high reward I win, whose the name I glory in (1)
253 unmoved by threatening or reward (4)

rich
58 rich with the same eternal grace (4)
101 Jesus shed his precious blood rich blessings to bestow (2)
143 may thy rich grace impart strength to my fainting heart (2)
251 how rich is my condition: God & heaven are still my own (1)
265 and thy rich promises in me fulfill (4)
321 when life anew pours out its wine with rich sufficiency (3)
325 rich blood that Jesus shed to raise our souls to heaven (2)
343 O grant its rich and swelling notes may lift our souls (3)
399 rich in blessing, rule and might o'er all possessing (1)
405 Eastern sages at his cradle make oblations rich and rare (3)
435 or thorns compose so rich a crown (3)
453 rich the trophies Jesus brings (2)
470 rich in things and poor in soul (3)
490 always serving thee, sharing thy rich truth (2)
532 rich in art, made richer still the brotherhood of duty (4)

richer
234 in thine ocean depths its flow may richer, fuller be (1)
400 richer by far is the heart's adoration (4)
532 rich in art, made richer still the brotherhood of duty (4)

riches
119 poor, wretched, blind; sight, riches, healing of... mind (4)
256 riches I heed not, nor man's empty praise (3)
285 its riches are unsearchable (2)
341 that the world might taste & see the riches of his grace (3)

richest
132 bringing down the richest treasure man can wish (1)
132 richest treasure man can wish or God can send (1)
344 good desired and wanted most ...thy richest grace supply (1)
435 my richest gain I count but loss (1)

richly
223 but our toil he doth richly repay (2)

richness
546 feed ... with the richness of thy Word (2)

rid
119   and waiting not to rid my soul of one dark blot (2)

ride
422   so lowly doth the Savior ride a paltry borrowed beast (T,1)
422   ride on, O King, ride on your way (4)
425   ride on, ride on in majesty (T,1,2,3,4)
425   in lowly pomp ride on to die (2,4)
482   O thou eternal Christ of God, ride on (T,1)
482   O Holy Savior of mankind, ride on (2)
482   O thou whose dreams enthrall the heart, ride on (3)
482   ride on till tyranny and greed are evermore undone (3)
482   O Christ, Redeemer, Brother, Friend, ride on, ride on (4)

rides
215   and rides upon the storm (1)

right
4   lo! all is just and all is right (2)
11   tell ye forth his might, Lord of life ... truth & right (3)
20   were not the right man on our side (2)
50   so many glorious things are here, noble and right (1)
54   thy right hand thy powerful arm ... succor they implored (3)
74   didst yield the glory that of right was thine (1)
97   following him I know I'm right (3)
124   who will place me on his right (3)
130   assert thy claim, receive thy right (5)
135   Holy Spirit, Right divine (4)
155   he will make good his right to be a pilgrim (2)
169   I would work ever for the right (3)
190   to serve right gloriously the God who gave all worlds (3)
211   what terror can confound me, with God at my right hand (1)
240   Christ is thy strength, and Christ thy right (1)
269   lead us, O Father, in the paths of right (3)
277   I want the witness, Lord, that all I do is right (3)
279   if to the right or left I stray (2)
280   if to the right or left I stray (2)
282   perfect & right & pure & good, a copy, Lord, of thine (4)
337   Savior, like stars in thy right hand thy servants ... be (2)
362   and he will right the wrong (3)
365   thy laws are pure, thy judgments right (5)
383   right over the place where Jesus lay (4)
409   then let us adore and give him his right (4)
410   that shall turn their hearts to the right (1)
438   but now at God's right hand he stands (1)
438   let us joyful be and sing to God right thankfully (1)
457   enthroned at God's right hand he sits (2)
458   highest place ... heaven affords belongs to him by right (2)
468   thou art he who shall by right the nations all possess (2)
532   who helped the right, and fought the wrong (2)

righteous
48   upheld by my righteous, omnipotent hand (2)
104   not the righteous; sinners Jesus came to call (4)
214   the righteous ones shall be forever blest (T,1)
361   his righteous government and power shall over all extend (4)
460   God the one, the righteous Lord (1)

528   no need of him the righteous have (4)
544   God the all-righteous One! man hath defied thee (3)
545   I can read his righteous sentence by the dim ... lamps (2)

righteousness
65   to their children's children ...his righteousness extend (4)
68   me to walk doth make within the paths of righteousness (2)
127   Jesus, thy blood and righteousness my beauty are (T,1)
136   fill it...with righteousness and peace (1)
168   I'd sing his glorious righteousness (1)
169   be for truth and righteousness and thee (4)
214   but righteousness inspires those who have sought (4)
222   nothing less than Jesus' blood and righteousness (1)
222   dressed in his righteousness alone (4)
337   and clothe them with thy righteousness (1)
341   his only righteousness I show, his saving grace proclaim (5)
359   righteousness, in fountains, from hill to valley flow (3)
365   great Son of Righteousness, arise (5)
387   hail the Sun of Righteousness (3)
392   makes the nations prove the glories of his righteousness (4)
401   Sun of Righteousness, arise (1)
457   dead to sin, his members live the life of righteousness (3)
468   before him righteousness shall go, his royal harbinger (1)
476   O God of righteousness & grace, seen in Christ, thy Son (5)
527   clothed in righteousness divine (4)
528   refuse his righteousness to impart (3)

rightful
235   reclothe us in our rightful mind (1)
526   if each should have its rightful meed (1)

rightly
199   to worship rightly is to love each other (1)

rills
547   I love thy rocks and rills, thy woods and templed hills (2)

ring
45   let the heavens ring! God reigns: let the earth be glad (3)
91   let all the earth around ring joyous with the sound (3)
189   to this clear call of brotherhood our hearts ... ring (3)
189   our hearts responsive ring (3)
221   through eternal ages let his praises ring (1)
357   every voice in conceret ring evermore and evermore (2)
377   our sweetest carols gayly ring to welcome Christ (3)
424   to whom the lips of children made sweet hosannas ring (1)
482   men at last ... ring the bells of brotherhood & peace (3)
547   from every mountain side let freedom ring (1)
547   and ring from all the trees sweet freedom's song (3)

ringing
2   angel harps forever ringing, rest not day nor night (1)
153   heaven's trumpets ringing clear (2)
379   till the air, everywhere, now with joy is ringing (1)
395   all the hills were ringing (2)
524   the hills with joy are ringing (1)

rings
  45   round me rings the music of the spheres (1)
  453 while the vault of heaven rings (2)

ripe
  34   the ripe fruits in the garden: He made them everyone (3)

ripen
  523 when harvests ripen, thou art there, who givest all (2)

ripened
  514 ripened in this fruit and grain (2)

rise
  14   till suns shall rise and set no more (2)
  26   early in the morning our song shall rise to thee (1)
  37   that made the mountains rise (1)
  62   to him let each affection daily rise and round him move (4)
  98   to teach our faint desires to rise (4)
  117 look unto me, thy morn shall rise ... thy day be bright (3)
  120 when I rise to worlds unknown (3)
  125 rise to all eternity (4)
  134 in vain we strive to rise (3)
  136 we rise with him to life which soars beyond the grave (4)
  147 but should the surges rise and rest delay to come (2)
  159 but I long to rise in the arms of faith (1)
  174 rise up, O men of God! Have done with lesser things (T,1)
  174 rise up, O men of God! the Church for you doth wait (3)
  174 rise up, and make her great (3)
  174 as brothers of the Son of man, rise up, O men of God (4)
  174 rise up, o men of God, his kingdom tarries long (2)
  180 joyful rise to pay thy morning sacrifice (1)
  186 thy bright example I pursue, to thee in all things rise (4)
  198 a loftier race than e'er the world hath known shall rise (1)
  235 let us, like them, without a word rise up & follow thee (2)
  239 when that illustrious day shall rise (6)
  248 courage rise with danger & strength to strength oppose (2)
  264 shall rise the glorious thought, I am with thee (5)
  264 O in that hour, fairer than daylight dawning shall rise (5)
  302 on the eagle wings of love to joys celestial rise (1)
  304 its heavenly walls unseen around us rise (1)
  304 deep in loving human hearts its broad foundations rise (1)
  305 crowns and thrones may perish, kingdoms rise and wane (3)
  326 too soon we rise: the symbols disappear (4)
  332 how can heavenly spirits rise by earthly matter fed (3)
  345 and pure devotion rise (4)
  348 let thy church rise, strong and fair (1)
  352 let every anthem rise like incense to the skies (2)
  367 springs of consolation rise to cheer the fainting mind (2)
  387 joyful, all ye nations rise (1)
  398 rise in... new creation which springs from love and thee (3)
  434 Savior, teach us so to rise (4)
  439 death in vain forbids him rise, Alleluia (3)
  439 made like him, like him we rise, Alleluia (4)
  452 'tis thine own third morning, rise, O buried Lord (3)
  457 come, let us rise with Christ our Head (T,1)
  460 through the rise and fall of nations (3)

468 rise, God, judge thou the earth in might (2)
472 his name like sweet perfume shall rise (2)
472 rise with every morning sacrifice (2)
472 let every creature rise and bring his grateful honors (5)
474 rise, my soul, and stretch thy wings (T,1)
474 rise from transitory things toward heaven (1)
474 rise ... toward heaven, thy native place (1)
474 rise, my soul, and haste away to seats prepared above (1)
475 age after age their tragic empires rise (2)
485 rise like incense, each to thee, in noble thought & deed (1)
490 rise to greet the sun, reddening the sky (T,1)
493 teach me to die, that so I may rise glorious (3)
493 rise glorious at the Judgment Day (3)
497 may we, born anew like morning, to labor rise (2)
503 Lord of angels, on our eyes let eternal morning rise (4)
505 hope and faith and love rise glorious (4)
516 happy the home where ... praise is wont to rise (3)
533 give me the wings of faith to rise within the veil (T,1)
533 rise within the veil and see the saints above (1)
538 thus evermore shall rise to thee glad hymns of praise (4)

risen
62 Christ, the risen Christ, victorious (3)
366 her Star is risen; her Light is come (2)
387 risen with healing in his wings (3)
437 Christ the Lord hath risen, our joy that hath no endd (3)
439 Christ the Lord is risen today, Alleluia! (T,1)
441 quick from the dead my risen Lord is seen (3)
441 forth he came at Easter, like the risen grain (3)
443 Jesus Christ is risen today (T,1)
446 and from three days' sleep in death as a sun hath risen (2)
447 all glory to our risen Head! Alleluia (3)
449 the Lord of life is risen for aye (2)
449 thy name we bless, O risen Lord (4)
450 thine is the glory, risen, conquering Son (T,1,R)
450 Lo! Jesus meets thee, risen from the tomb (2)
456 and have the bright immensities received our risen Lord (T)

rises
231 it is the Lord, who rises with healing in his wings (1)
291 O... transporting rapturous scene that rises to my sight (1)
366 she wakes, she rises from her gloom (2)
447 He rises glorious from the dead (3)

riseth
441 now the green blade riseth from the buried grain (T,1)
481 already in the mind of God that city riseth fair (5)

rising
18 deeds and words and death and rising tell the grace (2)
18 death and rising tell the grace in heaven's plan (2)
28 before the rising sun (4)
60 thou rising morn, in praise rejoice (2)
70 when all thy mercies, O my God, my rising soul surveys (T,1)
95 O thou loving, blessed One, rising o'er me like the sun (4)
138 to check the rising doubt,the rebel sigh (4)
213 when rising floods my soul o'erflow (3)

330   when I fall on my knees with my face to the rising sun (R)
353   brighter than the rising morn when he, victorious, rose (3)

rite
321   beneath the forms of outward rite (T,1)
526   I rest upon his faithful word to them of contrite spirit (3)

rival
259   and reign without a rival there (1)
442   so, as he renews the earth, artist without rival (2)

river
  34   the purple-headed mountain, the river running by (2)
293   who can faint while such a river ... thirst assuage (2)
293   such a river ever will their thirst assuage (2)
433   till my raptured soul shall find rest beyond the river (R)
433   till I reach the golden strand just beyond the river (4)
459   from thee have flowed, as from a mighty river ... faith (4)
524   where flows the crystal river (3)

rivers
  48   the rivers of woe shall not thee overflow (3)
291   sweet fields arrayed in living green & rivers of delight (1)
474   rivers to the ocean run, nor stay in all their course (2)

road
219   I sink beside the road (2)
268   a light to shine upon the road that leads me to the Lamb (1)
268   purer light shall mark .. road that leads me to the Lamb (6)
406   build ye the road, and falter not, nor stay (2)
406   Lord, give us faith and strength the road to build (3)
425   O Savior meek, pursue thy road with palms (1)
425   road with palms and scattered garments strowed (1)
482   be the road uphill or down, unbroken or well trod (2)

roam
110   why from the sunshine of love wilt thou roam (1)
110   roam farther and farther away (1)

roar
  11   storm and flood and ocean's roar (3)
  32   rebel, ye waves, and o'er the land ... roar (2)
  32   waves ... with threatening aspect roar (2)
148   loud the angry billows roar (2)
230   the storm may roar without me, my heart may low be laid (1)
247   when at last I near the shore ... fearful breakers roar (3)

robe
355   robe of sorrow round thee (1)
473   whose robe is the light, whose canopy space (2)

robed
  8   and the white robed martyrs follow (3)
  79   robed in the blooming garb of spring: Jesus is fairer (2)
364   every eye shall now behold him robed in dreadful majesty (2)
426   robed in mortal flesh is dying crucified by sin for me (2)

robes
239   robes of victory through the skies (6)
239   and all thy armies shine in robes of victory (6)
524   bright robes of gold the fields adorn (1)

robest
398   thou robest in thy splendor the simplest ways of men (2)

rock
22   firm as a rock thy truth must stand (4)
58   their rock is our salvation (1)
120   Rock of Ages, cleft for me, let me hide myself in thee (T,1)
120   Rock of Ages, cleft for me, let me hide myself in thee (3)
195   that I may stand firm on the rock, and strong in thee (2)
205   gushing from the rock before me...a spring of joy I see (2)
210   who trust in God's unchanging love builds on the rock (1)
210   builds on the rock that naught can move (1)
222   on Christ, the solid rock, I stand (R)
245   O then to the Rock let me fly ... Rock ... higher than I (R)
245   O near to the Rock let me keep (3)
247   hiding rock and treacherous shoal (1)
274   in the shadow of the rock (2)
293   on the Rock of Ages founded (1)
417   the shadow of a mighty rock within a weary land (1)
536   thou wast their rock, their fortress, and their might (2)
538   from rock and tempest, fire and foe protect them (4)

Rock's
245   the Rock's blessed shadow, how sweet (2)

rocked
346   the rolling ocean, rocked with storms, sleeps (2)

rocks
45   I rest me in the thought of rocks and trees (1)
273   like .. rocks of towering grandeur make me strong & sure (2)
372   mid mists & rocks & quick-sands, still guides ...to thee (3)
392   while fields and floods, rocks, hills and plains repeat (2)
547   I love thy rocks and rills, thy woods and templed hills (2)
547   let rocks their silence break, the sound prolong (3)

rod
24   today attend his voice, nor dare provoke his rod (4)
67   thy rod and staff my comfort still (4)
68   thy rod and staff me comfort still (3)
142   will not murmur nor complain beneath the chastening rod (2)
534   kept ... people by the strength of thy staff and rod (1)

rode
423   the Lord of men and angels rode on in lowly state (2)

roll
30   his love shall be our strength and stay, while ages roll (3)
43   confirm the tidings as they roll (2)
125   while the nearer waters roll (1)
143   when death's cold, sullen stream shall o'er me roll (4)
247   unkown waves before me roll (1)

288   long as eternal ages roll, thou seest thy Savior's face (2)
291   though Jordan waves may roll, I'll fearless launch away (3)
478   not with swords loud clashing nor roll of stirring drums (2)

rolled
450   angels in bright raiment rolled the stone away (1)

rolling
17   I see the stars, I hear the rolling thunder (1)
22   when rolling years shall cease to move (4)
28   time, like an ever rolling stream (5)
32   the rolling sun stands still (1)
346   the rolling ocean, rocked with storms, sleeps (2)
365   the rolling sun, the changing light ...thy power confess (2)
371   from days of old, through swiftly rolling ages (2)
480   boundless as ocean's tide rolling in fullest pride (4)

rolls
243   march on.. soul w. strength ... strong the battle rolls (3)
500   unsleeping while earth rolls onward into light (2)
549   around us rolls the ceaseless tide of business (2)

room
321   upper room where fainting souls are fed (1)
321   thy supper, Lord, is spread in every quiet upper room (1)
355   awful love, which found no room in life where sin denied (2)
377   no room inside the hostel there for Joseph (1)
377   no room ... for Joseph or Madonna fair (1)
392   let every heart prepare him room (1)
528   his bleeding heart shall make you room (5)

rooms
218   Christ leads me through no darker rooms than he went (3)

Root
399   Root of Jesse, David's Son, my Lord and Master (1)

rooted
278   then shall my feet no longer rove rooted .. fixed in God (1)

rose
33   the hand that shaped the rose hath wrought the crystal (1)
33   thyself the vision passing by in crystal and in rose (3)
353   brighter than the rising morn when he, victorious, rose (3)
451   o'er death today rose triumphing, Alleluia (1)
455   rose victorious in the strife for those he came to save (2)
455   his glories now we sing who died, and rose on high (2)
488   for our salvation Christ rose from depths of earth (2)
527   I rose, went forth, and followed thee (3)

rough
245   and rough seems the path to the goal (1)
269   however rough and steep the path may be (4)

round
2   angel voices, ever singing round thy throne of light (T,1)
7   round thy throne, thy name confessing, (4)

12	art within, a qickening flame, a presence round about (2)
33	love deepens round the hearth (2)
43	all the stars that round her burn ... confirm (2)
43	solemn silence ... move round the dark terrestrial ball (3)
45	round me rings the music of the spheres (1)
50	so many gentle thoughts and deeds circling us round (2)
62	to him let each affection daily rise and round him move (4)
87	if temptations round you gather, breathe that holy name (2)
88	first let me hear how the children stood round his knee (2)
90	with all the listening people gathered round (3)
155	who so beset him round with dismal stories (2)
163	and round my heart still closely twine those ties (1)
229	peace, perfect peace, with sorrows surging round (3)
230	but God is round about me, and can I be dismayed (1)
287	every round goes higher ... soldiers of the cross (2)
293	round each habitation hovering, see the cloud and fire (3)
301	when round his throne we meet (5)
332	angels round our altars bow to search it out in vain (3)
343	Lord, while the music round us floats (3)
345	round these hallowed walls the storm of... passion dies (4)
355	robe of sorrow round thee (1)
365	sun, moon ... stars convey thy praise round the... earth (3)
365	convey thy praise round the whole earth and never stand (3)
366	choir immortal of angels round thy dazzling throne (3)
393	round yon virgin mother and child (1)
408	whole round world complete, from sunrise to its setting (2)
416	light of sacred story gathers round its head sublime (1,5)
437	Let the round world keep triumph, & all that is therein (3)
455	round his pierced feet fair flowers of paradise extend (3)
466	and clothe me round the while my path illuming (2)
470	lo! the hosts of evil round us scorn thy Christ (2)
473	and round it hath cast, like a mantle, the sea (3)
487	we gather round thy throne on this thy holy day (1)
495	spread their white wings above me, watching round my bed (5)
498	praise for mercies daily twining round us golden cords (1)
498	twining round us golden cords of love (1)
499	the trvial round, the common task will furnish all (3)
539	put his arms unfailing round you (3)

rove

63	his mercy brightens all the path in which we rove (1)
129	or alone in this wilderness rove (2)
262	thyself reveal, while here o'er earth we rove (1)
278	then shall my feet no longer rove rooted .. fixed in God (1)

royal

29	on us thy glance let fall in royal radiance (2)
71	bring forth the royal diadem and crown him Lord of all (1)
179	under the standard exalted and royal (1)
187	my heart ... it shall be thy royal throne (3)
248	lift high the royal banner, it must not suffer loss (1)
305	Christ, the royal Master, leads against the foe (1)
326	here drink with thee the royal wine of heaven (3)
402	star with royal beauty bright (R)
424	thou art the King of Israel, thou David's royal Son (1)
446	with the royal feast of feasts, comes its joy to render (3)
458	a royal diadem adorns the mighty victor's brow (1)
468	before him righteousness shall go, his royal harbinger (1)

royalty
422 his royalty is holiness, and love is in his face (2)

rudder
84 to periled sailor, rudder (1)

rude
397 as they offered gifts most rare at... manger rude & bare (3)
459 stilling the rude wills of men's wild behavior (3)
485 man's rude work deface no more the paradise of God (2)
538 who didst brood upon the waters dark and rude (3)

rugged
228 in the old rugged cross, stained with blood so divine (3)
228 so I'll cherish the old rugged cross (R)
228 on a hill far away stood an old rugged cross (T,1)
228 O that old rugged cross, so despised by the world (2)
228 I will cling to the old rugged cross (R)
228 to the old rugged cross I will ever be true (4)

ruined
41 soaring spire and ruined city, these our hopes ... show (3)
41 spire and ruined city, these our hopes and failures show (3)

rule
3 thou who almighty art, now rule in every heart (3)
37 I sing the wisdom that ordained the sun to rule the day (1)
46 our strength, thy grace; our rule, thy word (1)
243 gainst lies & lusts & wrongs let courage rule our souls (3)
359 to take away transgression, and rule in equity (1)
360 by thine own eternal spirit rule in all our hearts alone (2)
399 rich in blessing, rule and might o'er all possessing (1)
405 out of thee the Lord from heaven came to rule his Israel (1)
485 just rule ... fill ... earth with health & light & peace (2)
548 for the open door to manhood in the land the people rule (2)

ruled
209 the waves and winds still know his voice who ruled them (2)
209 his voice who ruled them while he dwelt below (2)
272 and spite of fears, pride ruled my will (2)
549 worlds of science and of art, revealed and ruled by thee (4)

ruler
45 God is the ruler yet (3)
79 fairest Lord Jesus, ruler of all nature (T,1)
256 still be my Vision, O Ruler of all (4)
469 Father eternal, ruler of creation (T,1)
552 be thou our ruler, guardian, guide and stay (2)

rulers
484 our earthly rulers falter, our people drift and die (1)

rules
392 he rules the world with truth and grace (4)
409 his kingdom is glorious and rules over all (1)
483 His kingdom cannot fail, he rules o'er earth and heaven (3)

rulest
  27 nor wanting, nor wasting, thou rulest in might (2)
  244 thou who rulest wind and water, stand by me (1)

ruleth
  409 God ruleth on high, almighty to save (2)

run
  80 and like thee, all my journey run (4)
  152 run my course with even joy (4)
  180 thy daily stage of duty run (1)
  240 run the straight race through God's good grace (2)
  266 and run not before him, whatever betide (3)
  298 One in might, and One in glory, while unending ages run (4)
  365 till through the world thy truth has run (4)
  464 now the Word doth swiftly run (2)
  472 where'er the sun does his successive journeys run (1)
  474 rivers to the ocean run, nor stay in all their course (2)

running
  34 the purple-headed mountain, the river running by (2)
  273 like the springs and running waters make me crystal pure (2)

rushes
  266 take time to be holy, the world rushes on (2)

rushing
  60 thou rushing wind that art so strong (2)

rustling
  45 in the rustling grass I hear him pass (2)

Sabaoth
  20 Lord Sabaoth, his name, from age to age the same (2)

sabbath
  235 O sabbath rest by Galilee! O calm of hills above (3)

sabbaths
  489 thus may all our sabbaths prove till we join ... above (4)

sacred
  3 come, holy Comforter, thy sacred witness bear (3)
  8 Lo! the apostolic train joins thy sacred name to hallow (3)
  22 ye nations, bow with sacred joy (1)
  71 O that with yonder sacred throng we at his feet may fall (5)
  128 while to that sacred shrine I move (2)
  131 unseal the sacred book (2)
  134 kindle a flame of sacred love in ... cold hearts of ours (1)
  172 kindle a flame of sacred love on ... altar of my heart (1)
  196 sacred cup of saving grace I will with thanks receive (2)
  225 a little shrine of quietness, all sacred to itself (2)
  296 truth is her prophetic gift, the soul, her sacred page (3)
  319 in memory of the Savior's love, we keep the sacred feast (T)
  344 the sacred discipline be given (1)
  350 here let thy sacred fire of old descend (2)
  367 teach me to love thy sacred Word ... find my Savior (4)

369   beyond the sacred page I seek thee, Lord (1)
372   it is the sacred casket where gems of truth are stored (2)
375   worship we our Jesus, but where-with for sacred sign (2)
405   sacred gifts of mystic meaning (4)
415   would he devote that sacred head for sinners such as I (1)
416   light of sacred story gathers round its head sublime (1,5)
418   O sacred head, now wounded (T,1)
418   O sacred Head ... with grief and shame weighed down (1)
428   see ... he bows his sacred head ... bows his head & dies (3)
465   adore thy sacred energy (3)
507   promise, in this sacred hour, for God to live and die (2)
516   parents love the sacred Word and all its wisdom prize (3)
520   steadfast faith & earnest prayer keep sacred vows secure (4)
532   in peace their sacred ashes rest (6)
551   unite us in the sacred love of knowledge, truth & thee (3)

sacredness
197   the sacredness of common things (1)

sacrifice
35   offering up on every shore her pure sacrifice of love (5)
52   life, while thou preservest life, a sacrifice shall be (4)
113   by thy cross and dying cries, by thy one great sacrifice (2)
122   the bleeding sacrifice in my behalf appears (1)
172   and make my sacrifice complete (4)
180   joyful rise to pay thy morning sacrifice (1)
186   all I think or speak or do is one great sacrifice (4)
196   offer the sacrifice of praise, and call upon his name (4)
352   a joyful sacrifice to thy blest name (2)
402   glorious now behold him arise ... God and sacrifice (5)
402   King and God and sacrifice (5)
425   to see the approaching sacrifice (3)
427   alone thou goest forth, O Lord, in sacrifice to die (T,1)
429   accomplished is the sacrifice (1)
434   God's own sacrifice complete (3)
435   all the vain things that charm me most, I sacrifice them (2)
435   I sacrifice them to his blood (2)
472   rise with every morning sacrifice (2)
510   all our consecrated powers a sacrifice to thee (5)
517   grant us then a deeper insight & new powers of sacrifice (4)
524   bring sacrifice of praise ... shouts of exultation (1)

sacrificial
461   purge our hearts like sacrificial flame (2)

sad
97   when I am sad, to him I go, no other one can cheer me so (1)
97   when I am sad, he makes me glad, He's my friend (1)
117   I came to Jesus as I was, weary and worn and sad (1)
218   if short, yet why should I be sad to soar to endless day (2)
237   bring to my remembrance sad Gethsemane (2)
390   above its sad & lowly plains they bend on hovering wing (2)
425   look down with sad and wondering eyes to see (3)
447   the three sad days have quickly sped (3)
492   how beauteous nature now! How dark and sad before (3)
501   for some are sick, and some are sad (3)

saddest
124 defeats my fiercest foes ... consoles my saddest woes (2)

sadness
  38 melt the clouds of sin and sadness (1)
132 Holy Ghost, dispel our sadness (T,1)
318 leave the gloomy haunts of sadness (1)
399 here in sadness eye and heart long for thy gladness (2)
446 God hath brought his Israel into joy from sadness (1)
488 O balm of care and sadness, most beautiful, most bright (1)
506 may weariness and sadness be lulled to peace & gladness (3)

safe
  57 from evil he will keep thee safe (4)
  58 safe in the same dear dwelling place (4)
  70 thine arm, unseen, conveyed me safe (3)
  92 'tis grace hath brought me safe thus far (3)
125 safe into the haven guide; O receive my soul at last (1)
143 O bear me safe above, a ransomed soul (4)
144 how safe, how calm, how satisfied the soul that clings (4)
144 how safe ... the soul that clings to thee (4)
209 all safe and blessed we shall meet at last (3)
229 in Jesus' keeping we are safe, and they (4)
230 and safe is such confiding, for nothing changes here (1)
271 land me safe on Canaan's side (3)
295 even thine own altars, where she safe ... may bring (4)
295 she safe her young ones forth may bring (4)
450 bring us safe through Jordan to thy home above (3)
496 we are safe, if thou art nigh (2)
517 little feet our steps may follow in a safe & narrow way (3)

safely
  57 watchful and unslumbering care his own he safely keeps (2)
  93 I hope, by thy good pleasure, safely to arrive at home (2)
216 with Almighty God abide and in his shadow safely hide (1)
258 for the night is safely ended (2)
269 only with thee we journey safely on (3)
445 He lives, to bring me safely there (3)
489 safely through another week (T,1)
490 Father, I implore, safely keep this child (2)
498 sure of being safely guided, guarded well from every foe (2)
499 through sleep and darkness safely brought, restored (1)
521 safely in his bosom gather (1)
522 all is safely gathered in ere the winter storms begin (1)

safety
216 to him for safety I will flee (2)

saffron
203 o'er hill and dale in saffron flame and red (4)

sages
371 speaking to saints, to prophets, kings, and sages (2)
382 sages, leave your contemplations (3)
405 Eastern sages at his cradle make oblations rich and rare (3)
440 prophets psalmists seers . sages . await . glory given (3)

said
48 what more can he say than to you he hath said (1)
157 through him the first fond prayers are said (5)
160 take up thy cross,the Savior said (T,1)
394 fear not, said he, for mighty dread had seized (2)
413 are ye able, said the Master, to be crucified with me (1)
515 and daily must the prayer be said (1)

sail
60 ye clouds that sail in heaven along, O praise him (2)
147 if on a quiet sea, toward heaven we calmly sail (T,1)

sailed
239 and sailed through bloody seas (2)

sailor
84 to periled sailor, rudder (1)

sailors
495 guard the sailors tossing on the deep, blue sea (3)

saint
337 to warn the sinner, cheer the saint (4)

sainted
314 our sainted ones in glory seated at our Father's board (3)

saintly
534 O keep us in the pathway their saintly feet have trod (2)

saints
19 all saints triumphant, raise the song (3)
23 saints on earth, with saints above ... voices ... employ (3)
26 holy, holy, holy! all the saints adore thee (2)
42 God hath made his saints victorious (2)
48 how firm a foundation, ye saints of the Lord (T,1)
53 beneath his watchful eye his saints securely dwell (2)
56 fear him, ye saints, and ... have nothing else to fear (4)
58 seek thee as thy saints ... sought in every generation (1)
58 ye saints to come, take up the strain (4)
66 saints triumphant, bow before him (4)
66 saints triumphant ... gathered in from every race (4)
99 saints, apostles, prophets, martyrs answer, Yes (7)
115 by faith I see the land of rest...saints' delight (1)
131 sound with...thy saints below, the depth of love divine (4)
183 how happy are the saints above (2)
196 praise him, ye saints, the God of love (5)
214 determined quest to follow in the saints' pathway (1)
215 ye fearful saints, fresh courage take (3)
239 thy saints in all this glorious war shall conquer (5)
288 with saints enthroned on high thou...thy Lord proclaim (1)
302 saints on earth unite to sing with those to glory gone (2)
305 brothers, we are treading where the saints have trod (2)
364 thousand saints attending swell the triumph of his train (1)
370 poets, prophets, scholars, saints (2)
371 speaking to saints, to prophets, kings, and sages (2)
382 saints, before the altar bending (4)

saith

sake

sale

salvation

288   and still to God salvation cry, salvation to the Lamb (1)
297   her charter of salvation, one Lord, one faith, one birth (2)
310   thy name salvation is, which here we come to prove (2)
355   to finish thy salvation (4)
385   the King of kings salvation brings (3)
404   and God sent us salvation that blessed Christmas morn (3)
408   its captain of salvation (1)
409   ascribing salvation to Jesus, our King (2)
409   Salvation to God, who sits on the throne (3)
412   death of anguish and thy bitter passion for my salvation (4)
454   thou didst free salvation bring (1)
463   who descended from his throne and for us salvation won (2)
468   surely to such as do him fear salvation is at hand (2)
470   let the search for thy salvation be our glory evermore (5)
488   for our salvation Christ rose from depths of earth (2)
504   send us thy salvation (3)

salvation's
188   cleanse it from guilt & wrong; teach it salvation's song (3)
293   with salvation's walls surrounded (1)

same
20   Lord Sabaoth, his name, from age to age the same (2)
28   to endless years the same (3)
58   the same sweet theme endeavor (4)
58   safe in the same dear dwelling place (4)
58   rich with the same eternal grace (4)
58   bless the same boundless giver (4)
66   praise him, still the same forever (2)
139   today as yesterday the same (1)
231   yet God the same abiding, his praise shall tune my voice (4)
308   Church is praying yet, a thousand years the same (1)
332   these the virtues did convey, yet still remain the same (2)
338   partakers of the Savior's grace ... same in mind & heart (4)
342   from age to age the same (2)
378   and unto certain shepherds brought tidings of the same (3)
383   and by the light of that same star three wise men came (3)
445   He lives, my Savior, still the same (4)
508   come, let us use the grace divine (T,1) (same as 507)
533   the long cloud of witnesses show the same path to heaven (2)

sanctified
416   bane and blessing, pain and pleasure ... are sanctified (4)
416   by the cross are sanctified (4)

sanctify
48   and sanctify to thee thy deepest distress (3)
109   Jesus, only Savior, sanctify forever (3)
228   to pardon and sanctify me (3)
278   scatter .. life through every part .. sanctify the whole (2)

sanctifying
29   the Spirit's sanctifying beam (2)
29   sanctifying beam upon our earthly senses stream (2)

sand
222   all other ground is sinking sand (R)

sands
127   Lord, I believe were sinners more than sands (4)
127   sinners more than sands upon the ocean shore (4)
372   mid mists & rocks & quick-sands, still guides ...to thee (3)

sang
331   in thy holy incarnation, when the angels sang thy birth (2)
382   who sang creation's story now proclaim Messiah's birth (1)
395   angels sang about his birth; wisemen sought & found him (2)
423   Hosanna, loud hosanna the little children sang (T,1)
423   children sang their praises, the simplest and the best (1)
424   to thee, before thy passion they sang .. hymns of praise (3)

sank
96   I walked and sank not on the storm-vexed sea (2)

sat
361   the people that in darkness sat (T,1)
451   who sat and spake unto the three (3)

Satan
373   the power of Satan breaking, our peace eternal making (1)
429   Satan hath lost his mortal power (3)

Satan's
89   my light in Satan's darkest hour (4)
378   save us all from Satan's power when we were gone astray (1)

satisfied
144   safe ... calm ... satisfied the soul that clings to thee (4)

satisfies
149   it satisfies my longings as nothing else can do (1)
490   glad for cotton coat, plain food satisfies (3)

save
23   he bled to save us from eternal death (2)
54   not their number nor ... strength ...their country save (2)
64   all, save the clouds of sin, are thine (3)
101   he will save you, he will save you, he will save you now (R)
104   Jesus ready stands to save you (1)
113   by thy power the lost to save (3)
116   humbly at thy cross I bow, save me, Jesus, save me now (4)
120   save from wrath and make me pure (1)
120   thou must save, and thou alone (2)
124   faith in him who died to save (4)
136   so ... we know ... power of him who came mankind to save (4)
139   by faith we know thee strong to save (3)
139   save us, a present Savior thou (3)
145   heal my wounded, broken spirit, save me by thy grace (3)
148   you may rescue, you may save (R)
150   a never-dying soul to save, and fit it for the sky (1)
160   cross endured to save thy soul from death and hell (3)
161   save us, thy people, from consuming passion (1)
161   by thy cross didst save us from death and dark despair (4)
161   didst save us...from sin and guilt (4)
163   he bled, he died to save me (2)

175   tell them of Jesus the mighty to save (1)
175   Jesus is merciful, Jesus will save (R)
200   from ease & plenty save us; from pride of place absolve (4)
256   naught be all else to me, save that thou art (1)
259   be thou my guide, and save me, who for me hast died (3)
299   tell how he stooped to save his lost creation (3)
307   save it from evil, guard it still (3)
378   save us all from Satan's power when we were gone astray (1)
391   Jesus Christ was born to save (3)
391   Christ was born to save (3)
409   God ruleth on high, almighty to save (2)
410   hath sent us his Son to save us (3)
414   where the dear Lord was crucified .. died to save us all (1)
419   who saw his Master in the sky, and called on him to save (2)
421   in a nobler, sweeter song, I'll sing thy power to save (5)
435   forbid it, Lord, that I should boast, save in the death (2)
435   boast, save in the death of Christ, my God (2)
439   once he died, our souls to save, Alleluia (2)
443   endured the cross & grave ... sinners to redeem and save (2)
455   rose victorious in the strife for those he came to save (2)
470   save us from weak resignation to the evils we deplore (5)
479   use the love thy spirit kindles still to save (2)
479   to save and make men whole (2)
484   bind all our lives together, smite us and save us all (3)
487   save us and cleanse our hearts (2)
491   Lover of men, O hear our call, and guard and save us (4)
491   guard and save us from them all (4)
496   thou canst save, and thou canst heal (1)
528   he came the lost to seek and save (4)
531   O Love, thy sovereign aid impart to save me (3)
531   to save me from low-thoughted care (3)
538   eternal Father, strong to save (T,1)
548   God of justice, save the people (4)
548   save the people from the clash of race and creed (4)

saved
 92   that saved a wretch like me (1)
100   and, saved from earth, appear before your Savior's face (4)
111   yield to be saved from sin (3)
294   saved with his own precious blood (1)
294   the Church our blest Redeemer saved (1)
395   ask the saved of all the race who have found his favor (1)
414   might go at last to heaven saved by his precious blood (3)
421   till all the ransomed Church of God be saved (3)
421   be saved to sin no more (3)
487   through grace alone are we saved (3)
535   and saved by grace alone (1)
544   praise him who saved them from peril and sword (4)

saves
  9   he saves the oppressed, he feeds the poor (2)
 71   hail him who saves you by his grace (2)
 83   he saves me from the grave (3)
137   saves whoe'er on Jesus call, and perfects them in love (4)
336   saves us to the uttermost till we can sin no more (4)

savest
84 thou man-pursuing Fisherman, who harmest not but savest (2)
329 thou savest those that on thee call (2)

saving
39 his saving grace proclaim (1,3)
39 hour, when earth shall feel his saving power (3)
98 the sweetness of thy saving name (3)
137 the grace which all may find, the saving power, impart (3)
196 sacred cup of saving grace I will with thanks receive (2)
341 his only righteousness I show, his saving grace proclaim (5)
351 make known to them thy saving grace (2)
355 upon a cross ... bound thee & mocked thy saving kingship (1)
356 show us the way the Master trod; reveal his saving power (1)
452 tread the path of darkness, saving strength to show (3)
471 let all thy saving grace adore (1)
541 uphold them with thy saving grace (2)

Savior
1 ye blind, behold your Savior come (6)
17 then sings my soul, my Savior God to thee (R)
69 mercy with the Savior...healing in his blood (1)
78 O Christ, thou Savior of us all ... hear us when we call (1)
81 Jesus, my Savior, shepherd, friend (3)
82 sweeter sound than thy blest name, O Savior of mankind (2)
94 there for me the Savior stands (4)
94 Savior stands, holding forth his wounded hands (4)
95 Light and life art thou within: Savior ...from every sin (4)
96 it was not I that found, O Savior true (1)
107 by thy mercies, Savior, may we hear thy call (5)
108 dear Savior, enter, enter, and leave us nevermore (3)
109 Jesus, only Savior, sanctify forever (3)
111 our common Savior praise (1)
112 God, your Savior, asks you why (2)
113 Savior,look with pitying eye; Savior, help me, or I die (R)
114 can my gracious Savior show my name inscribed in heaven (1)
121 Savior, like a shepherd lead us (T,1)
121 blessed Lord & only Savior, with thy love our bosom fill (4)
125 hide me, O my Savior hide (1)
128 fixed my choice on thee, my Savior and my God (1)
129 restore, my dear Savior, the light of thy face (4)
139 save us, a present Savior thou (3)
143 Savior divine! now hear me while I pray (1)
143 blest Savior, then, in love, fear and distrust remove (4)
144 O Holy Savior, friend unseen (T,1)
145 pass me not, O gentle Savior, hear my humble cry (T,1)
145 Savior, Savior, hear my humble cry (R)
154 touch me and heal me, Savior divine (3)
160 take up thy cross,the Savior said (T,1)
162 Savior, teach me, day by day, thine own lesson to obey (T,1)
166 my gracious Redeemer, my Savior art thou (1)
168 could I sound the glories forth which in my Savior shine (1)
168 then with my Savior, brother, friend (3)
175 tell the poor wanderer a Savior has died (4)
176 along my pilgrim journey, Savior, let we walk with thee (1)
177 Savior, thy dying love thou gavest me (T,1)
179 true-hearted, whole-hearted, Savior all-glorious (3)

205 all the way my Savior leads me (T,1,2,3)
208 precious Jesus, Savior, friend (4)
213 Savior, where'er thy steps I see (4)
221 standing on the promises of God my Savior (R)
221 resting in my Savior as my all-in-all (4)
224 this is my story, this is my song, praising my Savior (R)
224 praising my Savior all the day long (R)
224 I in my Savior am happy and blest (3)
226 Savior, more than life to me (T,1)
227 O how happy are they who the Savior obey (T,1)
227 by my Savior possessed, I was perfectly blest (5)
230 my Savior has my treasure, and he will walk with me (3)
236 Savior, again to thy dear name we raise (T,1)
247 Jesus, Savior, pilot me over life's tempestuous sea (T,1)
247 wondrous sovereign of the sea, Jesus Savior, pilot me (2)
247 Jesus, Savior, Pilot me (T,1,2)
249 blest Savior, introduced by thee have I my race begun (4)
251 they have left my Savior, too (2)
255 praise of him who is thy God, thy Savior, and thy King (4)
261 precious Savior, still our refuge (3)
265 O bless me now, my Savior, I come to thee (R)
275 I hasten to the place where God my Savior shows his face (2)
311 be her Savior, Lord, and guide (1)
311 telling of a Savior dear (2)
313 Savior, abide with us, and spread thy table in our heart (1)
334 may the grace of Christ our Savior (T,1)
337 Savior, like stars in thy right hand thy servants ... be (2)
340 with thine own pity, Savior (T,1)
363 the Savior of the world is here (1)
364 Savior, take the power and glory (4)
367 teach me to love thy sacred Word ... find my Savior (4)
372 O make thy Church, dear Savior, a lamp of purest gold (4)
378 for Jesus Christ our Savior was born upon this day (1)
380 and we greet in his cradle our Savior and King (4)
392 joy to the world! the Savior reigns (2)
393 Christ the Savior is born (4)
393 Christ the Savior is born (2)
394 the Savior, who is Christ the Lord (3)
395 such a babe in such a place, can he be the Savior (1)
400 Maker and Monarch and Savior of all (2)
410 we've a Savior to show to the nations (4)
410 Savior ... who the path of sorrow hath trod (4)
411 and prove the Savior friend (3)
415 alas! and did my Savior bleed (T,1)
420 come, sinners, see your Savior die (3)
422 so lowly doth the Savior ride a paltry borrowed beast (T,1)
425 O Savior meek, pursue thy road with palms (1)
428 behold the Savior of mankind nailed to the shameful tree (T)
431 in the garden now the suffering Savior prays alone (1)
431 from all removed, the Savior wrestles lone with fears (2)
434 Savior, teach us so to rise (4)
444 Jesus my Savior ... Jesus my Lord (1,2,3)
445 He lives, my Savior, still the same (4)
453 crown the Savior, angels, crown him (2)
453 crown the Savior King of kings (2)
454 hail ... universal Savior who hast borne our sin & shame (1)
459 O holy Jesus, Prince of Peace and Savior (3)

464 sons of God your Savior praise (3)
474 soon our Savior will return, triumphant in the skies (3)
482 O Holy Savior of mankind, ride on (2)
483 Jesus, the Savior, reigns, the God of truth and love (2)
496 Savior, breathe an evening blessing (T,1)
501 O Savior Christ, our woes dispel (3)
501 O Savior Christ, thou too art man (5)
502 sun of my soul, thou Savior dear (T,1)

Savior's
14 shout for joy and Savior's name (3)
83 majestic sweetness sits enthroned upon the Savior's brow (T)
100 and, saved from earth, appear before your Savior's face (4)
134 come, shed abroad a Savior's love, and... kindle ours (5)
288 long as eternal ages roll, thou seest thy Savior's face (2)
299 with none to tell them of the Savior's dying (2)
300 sing our Savior's worthy praise (1)
319 in memory of the Savior's love, we keep the sacred feast (T)
335 might fill an angel's heart and filled a Savior's hands (2)
338 partakers of the Savior's grace ... same in mind & heart (4)
371 see thy compassion in the Savior's face (3)
404 angel chorus that hailed our Savior's birth (2)
431 that sweetly soothe that Savior's woe (4)
453 mocking thus the Savior's claim (3)
502 rest forever on my Savior's breast (2)
506 Savior's cross is winning forgiveness for the sinning (4)
527 I ... gain an interest in the Savior's blood (1)

saw
83 he saw me plunged in deep distress (2)
268 where is... blessedness I knew when first I saw the Lord (2)
383 they looked up and saw a star shining in the east (2)
395 shepherds saw .. wondrous sight, heard .. angels singing (2)
396 saw the glory, heard the story, tidings of a Gospel true (2)
419 who saw his Master in the sky, and called on him to save (2)
421 by faith, I saw the stream thy flowing wounds supply (4)
464 saw ye not the cloud arise, little as a human hand (4)

say
48 what more can he say than to you he hath said (1)
91 the night becomes as day when from the heart we say (2)
99 if I ask him to receive me, will he say me nay (6)
117 I heard the voice of Jesus say (T,1,2,3)
118 what shall I say thy grace to move (4)
129 say, why in the valley of death should I weep (2)
137 no man can truly say that Jesus is the Lord unless (2)
155 then fancies flee away! I'll fear not what men say (3)
167 help me still to say, "My Lord, thy will be done" (1)
180 all I design or do or say (3)
212 just tell the love of Jesus, and say he died for all (2)
216 I of the Lord my God will say, "He is my refuge..." (2)
231 set free from present sorrow we cheerfully can say (2)
247 hear thee say to me, "Fear not, I will pilot thee" (3)
274 what hast thou to say to me (1)
332 who shall say how bread & wine God into man conveys (1)
383 the first Noel, the angel did say (T,1)
391 give ye heed to what we say: "Jesus Christ is born today (1)
400 say, shall we yield to him, in costly devotion (3)

420 and say, was ever grief like his (3)
439 sons of men and angels say, Alleluia (1)
449 let all mankind rejoice and say: Alleluia (2)
452 welcome, happy morning age to age shall say (T,1,4)
483 rejoice, again I say, rejoice (R)
517 that in all we do or say little ones our deeds may copy (3)
531 speak to my inmost soul and say, "I am thy love (4)
531 say "I am thy Love, thy God, thy all!" (4)

sayest
247 when thou sayest to them, "Be still" (2)

saying
103 here speaks the Comforter, tenderly saying (2)
107 saying, Christian, follow me (1)
107 saying, Christian, love me more (3)

says
223 what he says we will do, where he sends we will go (4)

scaffold
242 though her portion be the scaffold (4)
242 yet that scaffold sways the future (4)

scan
2 thou who art beyond the farthest mortal eye can scan (2)
215 blind unbelief is sure to err and scan his work in vain (5)
501 thy kind but searching glance can scan the very wounds (5)

scarce
17 sent him to die, I scarce can take it in (3)

scarcely
549 scarcely can we turn aside for one brief hour of prayer (2)

scarred
108 O Jesus, thou art knocking, and lo, that hand is scarred (2)

scars
364 with what rapture gaze we on those glorious scars (3)

scatter
278 scatter .. life through every part .. sanctify the whole (2)
401 fill me, Radiancy divine; scatter all my unbelief (3)
513 plow the fields and scatter the good seed on the land (1)

scattered
201 O thou who art the Shepherd of all the scattered sheep (T,1)
307 as grain, once scattered on the hillsides (4)
425 road with palms and scattered garments strowed (1)

scatters
291 there God the Son forever reigns and scatters night away (2)
341 Jesus! the name...scatters all their guilty fear (2)
341 It scatters...It turns their hell to heaven (2)
450 lovingly he greets thee, scatters fear and gloom (2)

scene
  144   help me, throughout life's changing scene, by faith (1)
  167   each changing future scene I gladly trust with thee (3)
  232   there is a scene where spirits blend (3)
  272   I do not ask to see the distant scene (1)
  291   O... transporting rapturous scene that rises to my sight (1)

scenes
   56   through all the changing scenes of life (T,1)
   88   scenes by the wayside, tales of the sea (1)
  149   when in scenes of glory I sing the new, new song (4)
  217   sometimes mid scenes of deepest gloom (2)
  433   near the cross .. Lamb of God bring its scenes before me (3)
  509   in scenes exalted or depressed thou art our joy ... rest (4)

scepter
    8   all on earth thy scepter claim (1)
  422   his scepter is his kindliness, his grandeur is his grace (2)
  455   crown him the Lord of peace, whose power a scepter sways (3)
  455   scepter sways from pole to pole, that wars may cease (3)

scheme
  347   through mortal motive, scheme .. plan thy... purpose ran (2)

scholars
  370   poets, prophets, scholars, saints (2)

school
  548   for the home, the church, the school (2)

science
  346   and science walks with humble feet (4)
  346   science walks ... to seek the God that faith hath found (4)
  476   O God of truth, whom science seeks (3)
  485   from thee all skill and science flow (T,1)
  549   worlds of science and of art, revealed and ruled by thee (4)

scoffs
   80   who like thee so humbly bore the scorn ... scoffs of men (3)

scorn
   80   who like thee so humbly bore the scorn ... scoffs of men (3)
  197   by loyal scorn of second best (3)
  312   nor scorn their humble name (2)
  378   the which his mother Mary did nothing take in scorn (2)
  418   how pale thou art with anguish, with sore abuse & scorn (1)
  470   lo! the hosts of evil round us scorn thy Christ (2)
  470   scorn thy Christ, assail his ways (2)
  484   the walls of gold entomb us, the swords of scorn divide (1)

scorned
  423   scorned ... little children should on his bidding wait (2)

scornfully
  418   now scornfully surrounded with thorns, thine only crown (1)

scorning
   90   let us arise, all meaner service scorning (5)

scourge
  482 we bear with thee the scourge and cross (2)

scrolls
  370 many diverse scrolls completing (2)

sea
   26 all thy works ... praise thy name in earth & sky & sea (4)
   26 casting down their golden crowns around the glassy sea (2)
   30 deep writ upon the human heart, on sea or land (2)
   36 God of earth, the sky, the sea (T,1)
   38 flashing sea, chanting bird and flowing fountain (2)
   41 master over sea and land (3)
   69 wideness in God's mercy like the wideness of the sea (1)
   84 from sordid waves of worldly sea preserve us, Lord (2)
   88 scenes by the wayside, tales of the sea (1)
   96 I walked and sank not on the storm-vexed sea (2)
  107 tumult of our life's wild, restless sea (1)
  147 if on a quiet sea, toward heaven we calmly sail (T,1)
  157 forever shared, forever whole, a never-ebbing sea (1)
  159 till I cross the narrow sea (4)
  176 bear me o'er life's fitful sea (3)
  195 wrestlers with the troubled sea (2)
  198 on earth and fire and sea and air (2)
  202 tasks he gives are those he gave beside the restless sea (2)
  203 they reach thy throne, encompass land and sea (1)
  215 he plants his footsteps in the sea (1)
  217 by waters still, o'er troubled sea ... hand ... leadeth (2)
  235 simple trust like theirs who heard beside the Syrian sea (2)
  244 when the world is tossing me like ship upon the sea (1)
  247 Jesus, Savior, pilot me over life's tempestuous sea (T,1)
  247 wondrous sovereign of the sea, Jesus Savior, pilot me (2)
  260 thy power flows in like flood tides from the sea (4)
  290 and so beside the silent sea I wait the muffled oar (4)
  343 stormy sea sings praise to God ... thunder & the shower (1)
  345 temple stands, built over earth and sea (1)
  369 as thou didst break the loaves beside the sea (1)
  372 it is the chart and compass that o'er life's surging sea (3)
  446 led them with unmoistened foot through... Red Sea waters (1)
  473 and round it hath cast, like a mantle, the sea (3)
  486 though earth and sea and heaven unite thy praise to sing (1)
  495 guard the sailors tossing on the deep, blue sea (3)
  505 now, on land and sea descending (T,1)
  523 O Lord of heaven and earth and sea (T,1)
  538 hear us when we cry to thee for those in peril on... sea (R)
  538 glad hymns of praise from land and sea (4)
  543 crown thy good with brotherhood ... sea to shining sea (1,4)
  545 in . beauty of the lilies Christ was born across the sea (4)
  548 mighty empire, stretching far o'er land and sea (1)
  549 thine ... the wealth of land and sea (4)
  550 our exiled fathers crossed the sea (1)

seal
   93 here's my heart, O take and seal it (3)
   93 seal it for thy courts above (3)
  131 unseal the sacred book (2)
  172 till death thy endless mercies seal (4)

444 vainly they watch his bed ... vainly they seal the dead (2)
446 nor the watchers, nor the seal hold thee as a mortal (4)
496 ere repose our spirits seal (1)
509 when death shall interrupt our songs and seal in silence (5)
509 seal in silence mortal tongues (5)

sealed
33 sent the hoary frost of heaven,the flowing waters sealed (1)
402 sealed in a stone-cold tomb (4)

seals
31 his truth confirms and seals the grace (2)
128 O happy bond, that seals my vows to him (2)

seaman
148 some poor fainting, struggling seaman you may rescue (R)
148 some poor seaman, tempest-tossed (3)

seamless
157 the healing of his seamless dress is by our beds of pain (4)

search
154 search me and try me, Master, today (2)
157 in vain we search the lowest deeps (2)
213 search, prove my heart, it yearns for thee (1)
332 angels round our altars bow to search it out in vain (3)
470 let the search for thy salvation be our glory evermore (5)

searching
12 or searching find thee out (2)
213 O thou, to whose all-searching sight (T,1)
501 thy kind but searching glance can scan the very wounds (5)

seas
9 he made the sky and earth and seas, with all their train (2)
24 formed the deeps unknown ... gave the seas their bound (2)
37 spread the flowing seas abroad and built the lofty skies (1)
40 deep seas obey thy voice (1)
45 of skies and seas; his hand the wonders wrought (1)
239 and sailed through bloody seas (2)
406 through jungles, sluggish seas, and mountain pass (2)
459 through seas dry-shod, through weary wastes bewildering (2)

season
76 humbled for a season, to receive a name (3)
231 a season of clear shining to cheer it after rain (1)
474 yet a season, and you know happy entrance will be given (3)

seasons
33 all beautiful the march of days as seasons come and go (T,1)
275 in seasons of distress and grief (1)
446 the queen of seasons, bright with the day of splendor (3)

seat
98 there they behold thy mercy seat (1)
103 come to the mercy seat, fervently kneel (1)
127 blood, which at the mercy seat of God...doth...plead (3)

177　at thy blest mercy seat, pleading for me (2)
232　'tis found beneath the mercy seat (1)
232　it is the blood-bought mercy seat (2)
232　they meet around one common mercy seat (3)
232　and glory crowns the mercy seat (4)
345　in worship bend before thy mercy seat (2)
397　so may we with willing feet ever seek thy mercy seat (2)
453　in the seat of power enthrone him (2)
468　thou in thy everlasting seat remainest God alone (3)
483　when he had purged our stains, he took his seat above (2)
545　sifting out the hearts of men before his judgment seat (3)

seated
314　our sainted ones in glory seated at our Father's board (3)
394　all seated on the ground (1)
454　seated at thy Father's side (3)

seats
474　rise, my soul, and haste away to seats prepared above (1)

second
197　by loyal scorn of second best (3)
283　let us all in thee inherit, let us find that second rest (2)
387　born to give them second birth (3)

secret
170　tell me thy secret (1)
203　we've sought and found thee in the secret place (2)
216　within the secret place of　God (1)
260　thou hearest...the secret thought, the hidden plan (2)
260　secret thought...hidden plan, wrought...or unexpressed (2)
266　spend much time in secret with Jesus alone (2)
276　secret of the Lord is theirs ... soul is Christ's abode (1)
351　and secret of thy heavenly peace (2)
494　pardon each infirmity, open fault, and secret sin (2)

sects
530　names and sects and parties fall: thou, O Christ art all (5)

secure
9　his truth forever stands secure (2)
28　still may we dwell secure (2)
89　secure I am if thou art mine (1)
140　what pain ... labor to secure my soul from endless death (2)
400　vainly with gifts would his favor secure (4)
477　bring justice to our land, that all may dwell secure (3)
520　steadfast faith & earnest prayer keep sacred vows secure (4)

securely
53　beneath his watchful eye his saints securely dwell (2)
539　with his sheep securely fold you (1)
539　neath his wings securely hide you (2)

secures
92　his word my hope secures (4)

see

3	thy sovereign majesty may we in glory see (4)
7	see the morning sun ascending radiant in the eastern sky (T)
17	I see the stars, I hear the rolling thunder (1)
26	though the eye of sinful man thy glory may not see (3)
27	all praise we would render: O help us to see (4)
34	he gave us eyes to see them, and lips that we might tell (4)
41	when we see thy lights of heaven ...thy power displayed (2)
47	in all the past ... thy hand we see (1)
47	through all our hopes and fears, thy hand we see (1)
81	when I see thee as thou art, I'll praise thee as I ought (4)
82	sweeter far thy face to see and in thy presence rest (1)
85	that men in thee may see what God is like (2)
90	we would see Jesus (T,1,2,3,4,5)
90	we would see Jesus on the mountain teaching (3)
90	we would see Jesus in his work of healing (4)
90	we would see Jesus in the early morning (5)
92	was blind, but now I see (1)
103	here see the bread of life; see waters flowing (3)
109	let me more of their beauty see (1)
115	by faith I see the land of rest, the saints' delight (1)
129	thy foes will rejoice when my sorrows they see (3)
137	'tis thine the blood to apply and give us eyes to see (1)
138	I see thy cross; there teach my heart to cling (3)
154	fill with thy spirit till all shall see Christ ...in me (4)
162	singing, till thy face I see, of his love (4)
164	I see the sights that dazzle, the tempting sounds I hear (2)
168	and I shall see his face (3)
171	who with the eyes of early youth eternal things did see (1)
171	see, like thee, our noblest work our Father's work to do (2)
173	amid our pride and glory to see thy face appear (5)
177	that each departing day henceforth may see (3)
177	and when thy face I see, my ransomed souls shall be
178	one with thyself, may every eye in us, thy brethren see (4)
186	end of my every action thou, in all things thee I see (3)
190	see how the giant sun soars up (2)
195	until thy blessed face I see (5)
200	I see my people falling in darkness and despair (2)
204	yet long these multitudes to see ... thy face (4)
205	gushing from the rock before me...a spring of joy I see (2)
213	Savior, where'er thy steps I see (4)
217	nor ever murmur nor repine; content whatever lot I see (3)
218	when grace hath made me meet thy blessed face to see (4)
227	O that all his salvation might see (4)
228	a wondrous beauty I see (3)
237	grant that I may never fail thy hand to see (3)
238	Christian, dost thou see them on the holy ground (T,1)
239	they see the triumph from afar (5)
240	only believe, and thou shalt see that Christ is all (4)
254	I see all that I would, but fail to be (1)
254	dear Master, in whose life I see (T,1)
258	see thou render all thy feeble strength can pay (1)
259	O Jesus, nothing may I see ... desire, or seek but thee (2)
262	let this my every hour employ, till I thy glory see (5)
266	thy friends in thy conduct his likeness shall see (2)
267	ready, my God thy will to see (R)
267	open my eyes that I may see (T,1)

267	that I may see glimpses of truth thou hast for me (1)
272	I do not ask to see the distant scene (1)
272	I loved to choose and see my path (2)
276	blest are the pure in heart for they shall see ... God (T,1)
278	I only for his glory burn, and always see his face (3)
281	that all mankind thy truth may see (2)
283	let us see thy great salvation perfectly restored (4)
284	when this life is past, I may the eternal brightness see (5)
285	first-born sons of light desire in vain its depths...see (2)
289	change and decay in all around I see (2)
291	I shall see my Father's face, and in his bosom rest (3)
293	see, the streams of living waters (2)
293	round each habitation hovering, see the cloud and fire (3)
295	thirsty soul longs ardently ... faints thy courts to see (2)
300	there... endless home shall be... Lord we soon shall see (4)
300	they are happy now ... we soon their happiness shall see (2)
305	forward into battle, see his banners go (1)
312	see Israel's Gentle Shepherd stand (T,1)
326	here, O My Lord, I see thee face to face (T,1)
327	here, O my Lord, I see thee face to face (T,1)
329	glad, when thy gracious smile we see (4)
335	may they in Jesus ...they preach, their own Redeemer see (4)
336	and are we yet alive and see each other's face (T,1)
340	see the thronged and darkening way (1)
341	that the world might taste & see the riches of his grace (3)
344	truth and love let all men see (3)
353	and we his face shall see (4)
357	that future years shall see, evermore and evermore (1)
358	traveler, o'er yon mountain's height see (1)
358	see that glory-beaming star (1)
358	ages are its own; see, it bursts o'er all the earth (2)
364	deeply wailing, shall the true Messiah see (2)
365	nations ...that see the light or feel the sun (4)
366	we follow till the halls we see where ... sup with thee (2)
366	halls we see where thou hast bid us sup with thee (2)
367	still new beauties may I see, and still increasing light (3)
371	questing hearts that long for peace and healing see (3)
371	see thy compassion in the Savior's face (3)
372	till, clouds & darkness ended ... see thee face to face (4)
374	come to Bethlehem & see him whose birth the angels sing (2)
374	see him in a manger laid whom .. choirs of angels praise (4)
381	O little town of Bethlehem, how still we see thee lie (T,1)
387	veiled in flesh the God-head see (2)
401	joyless the day's return till thy mercy's beams I see (2)
405	see them give, in deep devotion, gold and frankincense (3)
406	to see the promise of the day fulfilled (3)
417	upon that cross of Jesus mine eye at times can see (2)
420	come, sinners, see your Savior die (3)
421	the dying thief rejoiced to see that fountain in his day (2)
422	the day of peace we long to see (4)
425	look down with sad and wondering eyes to see (3)
425	to see the approaching sacrifice (3)
428	see ... he bows his sacred head ... bows his head & dies (3)
430	here, O Christ, our sins we see (2)
434	your Redeemer's conflict see (1)
434	see him at the judgment hall (2)
434	see him meekly bearing all (2)

435 see, from his head, his hands, his feet, sorrow and love (3)
437 our hearts be pure from evil, that we may see aright (2)
440 see that glowing firmament (4)
448 come, ye faithful, raise the strain (T,1) (see 446)
451 an angel clad in white they see (3)
453 see the Man of Sorrows now (1)
462 eyes that see, beyond the dark, the dawn and thee (5)
464 see how great a flame aspires (T,1)
498 every day will be the brighter when ... thy face we see (3)
498 when thy gracious face we see (3)
501 what if thy form we cannot see (2)
510 while on in Jesus' steps we go to see thy face above (4)
529 Traveler unkown, whom still I hold, but cannot see (1)
531 I see from far thy beauteous light (1)
533 rise within the veil and see the saints above (1)

seed
71 chosen seed of Israel's race, ye ransomed from the fall (2)
487 our faith from seed to flower raise on this thy holy day (2)
512 the seed by him provided is sown o'er hill and plain (1)
513 plow the fields and scatter the good seed on the land (1)
515 the life of earth and seed is thine (2)

seeding
514 take our plowing, seeding, reaping (2)

seeds
348 seeds of truth be sown where we lay this cornerstone (2)

seeing
85 and seeing think God's thoughts after thee (2)
469 O give us brother love for better seeing (4)
469 better seeing thy Word made flesh, and in a manger laid (4)

seek
20 still our ancient foe doth seek to work us woe (1)
41 yet thy love doth seek him still (2)
46 guide of all who seek the land above (1)
58 seek thee as thy saints ... sought in every generation (1)
75 he who would the Father seek, must seek him...by thee (1)
75 must seek him, Lord, by thee (1)
82 how good to those who seek (3)
96 he moved my soul to seek him, seeking me (1)
98 where'er they seek thee thou art found (1)
115 I seek my place in heaven (1)
121 early let us seek thy favor, early let us do thy will (4)
121 seek us when we go astray (2)
138 O let me seek thee, and O let me find (3)
145 trusting only in thy merit would I seek thy face (3)
185 now thee alone I seek, give what is best (2)
189 one common faith unites us all, we seek one common goal (3)
193 with confidence we seek thy face (1)
195 as thou hast sought, so let me seek ... erring children (1)
201 create in us a yearning for those whom thou dost seek (1)
201 nor seek our own salvation apart from others' need (2)
201 help us to seek thy kingdom that cometh from above (3)
240 lift up thine eyes, and seek his face (2)

257   now to seek and love and fear thee (1)
259   O Jesus, nothing may I see ... desire, or seek but thee (2)
260   more than our minds seek thee (4)
260   no more we seek thee from afar, nor ask thee for a sign (4)
262   thou callest me to seek thy face,'tis all I wish to seek (4)
266   forgetting in nothing His blessing to seek (1)
275   since he bids me seek his face (3)
276   Lord, we thy presence seek; may ours the blessing be (4)
301   bids us, each to each restored, together seek his face (1)
311   seek the lost until she find (3)
317   with godly fear, we seek thy presence (2)
329   to them that seek thee, thou art good (2)
340   who wander far shall seek and find and serve thee well (3)
346   science walks ... to seek the God that faith hath found (4)
355   to seek the kingdom of thy peace (3)
369   beyond the sacred page I seek thee, Lord (1)
382   seek the great Desire of nations (3)
383   to seek for a king was their intent (3)
397   so may we with willing feet ever seek thy mercy seat (2)
442   in his grace of glad new birth we must seek revival (2)
451   the faithful women went their way to seek the tomb (2)
451   to seek the tomb where Jesus lay, Alleluia (2)
457   seek the things above (1)
462   give us grace when crucified to seek thy face (3)
466   come down, O Love divine, seek thou this soul of mine (T,1)
487   thy blessing, Lord, we seek on this thy holy day (3)
489   let us now a blessing seek, waiting in his courts today (1)
503   gather us who seek thy face to the fold of thy embrace (2)
517   that we may bear it meetly ... seek thine aid the more (2)
528   he came the lost to seek and save (4)

seekest
234   O Joy that seekest me through pain (3)
260   thou seekest us in love and truth (4)

seeking
41   'tis thy will our hearts are seeking (4)
96   he moved my soul to seek him, seeking me (1)

seeks
474   fire ascending seeks the sun (2)
476   O God of truth, whom science seeks (3)

seem
144   though oft I seem to tread alone life's dreary waste (3)
149   for those who know it best seem hungering (4)
199   so shall the wide earth seem our Father's temple (3)
430   here earth's precious things seem dross (1)

seemest
146   thou seemest human and divine (3)

seemeth
63   the hour that darkest seemeth will his... goodness prove (3)

seemly
21   for it is seemly so to do (3)

seems
45 ne'er forget that though the wrong seems oft so strong (3)
149 what seems, each time I tell it, more wonderfully sweet (3)
149 more wonderful it seems than all the golden fancies (2)
245 O sometimes how long seems the day (2)
245 and rough seems the path to the goal (1)
358 for the morning seems to dawn (3)
389 he lays aside his majesty and seems as nothing worth (2)

seen
55 hast thou not seen how thy desires ... hath been granted (2)
114 what we have felt and seen with confidence we tell (2)
139 and God is seen by mortal eye (6)
146 whom we, that have not seen thy face (1)
167 My Jesus, as thou wilt! Though seen through many a tear (2)
178 patient love was seen in all thy life and death of woe (1)
203 we've seen thy glory like a mantle spread o'er hill and (4)
230 green pastures are before me, which yet I have not seen (3)
290 thou, O Lord, by whom are seen thy creatures as they be (3)
336 what troubles have see seen, what mighty conflicts past (2)
361 a glorious light have seen (1)
366 nor eye hath seen, nor ear hath yet attained to hear (3)
382 ye have seen his natal star (3)
390 lo! the days are hastening on, by prophet seen of old (3)
405 seen in fleshly form on earth (2)
429 the living way to heaven is seen (2)
441 quick from the dead my risen Lord is seen (3)
451 how blest are they who have not seen (4)
476 O God of righteousness & grace, seen in Christ, thy Son (5)
481 O holy city, seen of John (T,1)
545 mine eyes have seen the glory of the coming of the Lord (T)
545 I have seen him in the watchfires of a hundred ... camps (2)

seers
440 prophets psalmists seers...sages...await...glory given (3)
442 praise him, seers, heroes, kings, Heralds of perfection (3)

sees
253 and sees the tempter fly (3)
543 O beautiful for patriot dream that sees beyond the years (4)

seest
237 when thou seest me waver, with a look recall (1)
288 long as eternal ages roll, thou seest thy Savior's face (2)

seize
481 yea, bids us seize the whole of life and build its glory (5)

seized
394 fear not, said he, for mighty dread had seized (2)
394 mighty dread had seized their troubled mind (2)

selects
276 for his dwelling & his throne selects the pure in heart (3)

self
135 kindle every high desire; perish self in thy pure fire (2)
163 not alone the gift of life, but his own self he gave me (2)

188 raise my low self above, won by thy deathless love (1)
208 just from sin and self to cease (3)
225 of self and sin swept bare (4)
257 glorious Lord, thy self impart (3)
281 from all the filth of self and pride (3)
321 Master ... symbols shared thine own dear self impart (4)
324 he will give to all...faithful ...self for heavenly food (2)
417 my sinful self my only shame, my glory all the cross (3)
430 here we learn to serve and give, &, rejoicing, self deny (3)
497 let not ease and self enthrall us (2)
543 who more than self their country loved (3)

selfish
194 of selfish greed and fruitless gain (2)
204 above the noise of selfish strife (1)
470 shame our wanton, selfish gladness (3)

semblance
237 or, in darker semblance, cross-crowned Calvary (2)

send
58 we raise it high, we send it on, the song (3)
58 we send it on, the song that never endeth (3)
95 now, O Lord, this very hour, send thy grace (2)
95 send thy grace and show thy power (2)
132 richest treasure man can wish or God can send (1)
148 send a gleam across the wave (R)
171 O Thou who dost the vision send and givest each his task (3)
191 God send us men (T,1,2,3,4)
200 whom shall I send to shatter the fetters which they bear (2)
200 whom shall I send to succor my people in their need (1)
200 whom shall I send to loosen the bonds of shame and greed (1)
200 send us upon thine errand, let us thy servants be (3)
233 send forth the hymns our fathers loved (3)
237 should thy mercy send me sorrow, toil, and woe (3)
303 send hope before to grasp it, till hope be lost in sight (3)
314 world where thou... send us let thy kingdom come, O Lord (4)
339 convert, and send forth more into thy Church abroad (3)
340 o'er all the world thy spirit send (4)
350 here thine angelic spirits send their solemn praise (5)
351 from hence send forth a race of men of flaming heart (3)
407 the heart that bled and broke to send God's love (1)
407 send God's love to earth's remotest part (1)
476 O send us forth, thy prophets true (1)
476 send us forth ... to make all lands thine own ((1)
497 slumber sweet thy mercy send us (1)
504 send us thy salvation (3)

sendest
201 these, Father, are thy children thou sendest us to find (2)
263 all that thou sendest me, in mercy given (3)
267 voices of truth thou sendest clear (2)

sendeth
512 God sendeth from his abundant store the waters (1)
512 to bless the earth, God sendeth (T,1)

sending
371   to all the world the message thou art sending (4)
504   banish our weakness, health and wholeness sending (2)

sends
    9   he sends the laboring conscience peace (3)
   97   he sends the sunshine and the rain (2)
   97   he sends the harvest's golden grain (2)
  170   in hope that sends a shining ray far down the future's (4)
  223   what he says we will do, where he sends we will go (4)
  506   sharing ... the love that sends the showers (2)
  513   He sends the snow in winter (1)
  513   He sends ... the warmth to swell the grain (1)

sense
   35   for the mystic harmony linking sense to sound and sight (3)
  139   the things unknown to feeble sense (5)
  147   when the joys of sense depart, to live by faith alone (4)
  215   judge not the Lord by feeble sense (4)
  232   where sin and sense molest no more (4)
  235   let sense be dumb, let flesh retire (5)
  257   our knowledge, sense and sight lie in deepest darkness (2)

senses
   29   sanctifying beam upon our earthly senses stream (2)

sensibility
  279   a sensibility of sin, a pain to feel it near (1)
  280   a sensibility of sin, a pain to feel it near (1)

sensual
  301   a peace to sensual minds unknown, a joy unspeakable (4)

sent
   17   sent him to die, I scarce can take it in (3)
   33   sent the hoary frost of heaven,the flowing waters sealed (1)
  102   sent by my Lord, on you I call (2)
  210   and all deserving love hath sent (2)
  404   and God sent us salvation that blessed Christmas morn (3)
  410   hath sent us his Son to save us (3)
  440   know ... Jesus Christ whom thou hast sent (4)
  488   on thee our Lord victorious the Spirit sent from heaven (2)
  513   all good gifts around us are sent from heaven above (R)
  518   the bread of life sent down from heaven (3)

sentence
  545   I can read his righteous sentence by the dim ... lamps (2)

sepulcher
  405   myrrh his sepulcher foreshows (4)

seraph
  324   at his feet the six-winged seraph (4)
  394   spake the seraph and forthwith appeared a shining throng (5)
  527   in vain the first-born seraph tries to sound the depths (2)
  527   seraph tries to sound the depths of love divine (2)

seraphim
- 8   cherubim and seraphim, in unceasing chorus praising (2)
- 19   higher than ... cherubim more glorious than ... seraphim (2)
- 26   cherubim and seraphim falling down before thee (2)
- 376   Cherubim and seraphim thronged the air (3)

seraphs
- 19   bright seraphs, cherubim and thrones (1)

serene
- 202   we follow where the Master leads, serene and unafraid (1)
- 219   calmness bends serene above, my restlessness to still (3)
- 268   calm and serene my frame (6)
- 303   the Prince is ever in them; the day-light is serene (2)

sermon
- 487   bless the sermon in this place (4)

servant
- 74   who wast a servant that we might be free (3)
- 150   O, thy servant, Lord, prepare, a strict account to give (3)
- 164   that where thou art in glory there shall thy servant be (4)
- 182   thy ransomed servant, I restore to thee thine own (2)
- 186   servant of all, to toil for man (T,1)
- 238   well I know thy trouble, O my servant true (4)
- 274   Master, speak! thy servant heareth (T,1)
- 284   let me thy loving servant be ... taste thy promised rest (2)
- 288   servant   of God, well done! thy glorious warfare's past (T)

servant's
- 389   takes ...a servant's form who made the heaven and earth (2)
- 502   to hide thee from thy servant's eyes (1)

servants
- 52   how are thy servants blest, O Lord (T,1)
- 200   send us upon thine errand, let us thy servants be (3)
- 298   here vouchsafe to all thy servants what they ask of thee (3)
- 302   all the servants of our King, in earth & heaven are one (2)
- 328   how happy are thy servants, Lord, who thus remember thee (T)
- 337   Lord, thine ordained servants bless (1)
- 337   Savior, like stars in thy right hand thy servants ... be (2)
- 337   thy servants in the churches be (2)
- 339   Lord of the harvest, hear the needy servants' cry (T,1)
- 346   sovereign God, receive...gift thy willing servants offer (3)
- 409   ye servants of God, your Master proclaim (T,1)
- 411   where'er thy servants be (5)
- 447   from death's dread sting thy servants free (4)
- 479   we, thy servants, bring the worship not of voice alone (1)
- 483   and take his servants up to their eternal home (4)

serve
- 21   Him serve with mirth, his praise forth tell (1)
- 85   living deeds that prove how sweet to serve all others (3)
- 85   how sweet to serve all others, when we all others love (3)
- 107   serve and love thee best of all (5)
- 150   to serve the present age, my calling to fulfill (2)
- 162   at thy bidding may I move, prompt to serve & follow thee (2)

164 O Jesus, I have promised to serve thee to the end (T,1)
164 Jesus, I have promised to serve thee to the end (4)
169 I would serve thee with all my might ... to thee I come (3)
173 thy life is still a summons to serve humanity (1)
174 to serve the King of kings (1)
174 give heart and mind and soul and strength to serve (1)
182 and from this moment, live or die to serve my God alone (2)
184 my power is faint and low till I have learned to serve (3)
189 one claim unites all men in God to serve each human need (2)
190 to serve right gloriously the God who gave all worlds (3)
218 to love and serve thee is my share (1)
248 ye that are men now serve him against unnumbered foes (2)
283 serve thee as thy hosts above (3)
287 if you love him, why not serve him... soldiers ... cross (4)
340 who wander far shall seek and find and serve thee well (3)
399 thou hast won my heart to serve thee solely (1)
430 here we learn to serve and give, &, rejoicing, self deny (3)
486 those who give up life's bounty to serve a race to be (2)
493 sleep that may me more vigorous make to serve my God (4)
493 to serve my God when I awake (4)
498 give us strength to serve and wait till the glory breaks (3)
501 they who fain would serve thee best are conscious most (4)
542 let Christ be lifted up till all men serve him (3)

serves
192 who serves my Father as a son is surely kin to me (3)

service
 56 make you his service your delight (4)
 90 God and man in loving service met (4)
 90 let us arise, all meaner service scorning (5)
159 consecrate me now to thy service, Lord (2)
170 in lowly paths of service free (1)
189 our service strong and true (2)
192 his service is the golden cord close binding all mankind (2)
203 thy paths of service lead to blazoned heights (1)
235 in purer lives thy service find (1)
266 thou soon shall be fitted for service above (4)
314 in thy service, Lord, defend us (4)
349 in grateful service ... now their strong foundation lay (2)
479 Lord, whose love through humble service (T,1)
479 called from worship unto service, forth ... we go (4)

serving
203 beheld thee fairer yet while serving thee (2)
203 our hearts enthralled while serving thee (3)
203 a splendor greater yet while serving thee (4)
470 grant us courage serving thee whom we adore (5)
490 always serving thee, sharing thy rich truth (2)

set
  8 morn to set of sun, through the church the song goes on (3)
 14 till suns shall rise and set no more (2)
 40 thy hands have set the heavens with stars (1)
 90 at eventide before the sun was set (4)
173 thy steadfast face set forward where love and duty shone (2)
183 consecrated cross I'll bear till death shall set me free (3)

190 so let the love of Jesus come and set my soul ablaze (2)
213 O burst these bonds and set it free (1)
231 set free from present sorrow we cheerfully can say (2)
267 wonderful key that shall unclasp and set me free (1)
282 a heart from sin set free (1)
283 set our hearts at liberty (2)
284 purge away my sin; from earth-born passions set me free (1)
304 thy bounds are known to God alone,for they are set above (2)
359 he comes to break oppression, to set the captive free (1)
360 born to set thy people free (1)
363 heart ... make it a temple, set apart (2)
363 set apart ... from earthly use for heaven's employ (2)
364 those who set at naught and sold him (2)
398 thy light, so glad & golden, shall set on earth no more (1)
407 mighty God, set us aflame to show the glory of thy name (3)
429 and all may live from sin set free (3)
442 and set the meadows dancing (1)
470 set out feet on lofty places (4)
470 in the fight to set men free (4)
477 let .. be light again .. set thy judgments in .. earth (5)
486 through lands from sin set free ... God shall march (4)
489 from our worldly cares set free (2)
499 if on our daily course our mind be set to hallow (3)
499 mind be set to hallow all we find (3)
501 at even, ere the sun was set (T,1)
549 from daily tasks set free (1)

sets
1 He sets the prisoner free (4)
52 thy mercy sets us free (2)
464 sets the kingdoms on a blaze (1)
503 wait and worship while the night sets her evening lamps (1)

setting
408 whole round world complete, from sunrise to its setting (2)

settled
148 dark the night of sin has settled (2)

seven
467 who dost thy seven-fold gifts impart (1)

sever
163 those ties which naught can sever (1)
163 from him who loves me now so well, what power...sever (3)
163 what power my soul can sever (3)
521 neither life nor death shall ever from the Lord...sever (3)
521 nor...ever from the Lord his children sever (3)

shackles
199 then shall all shackles fall (4)

shade
4 by morning glow or evening shade his watchful eye ne'er (2)
57 thy shelter and thy shade (3)
492 sun itself is but thy shade, yet cheers both earth & sky (1)
492 mists of error & of vice which shade the universe (2)

shades
43 soon as the evening shades prevail (2)
299 one soul should perish lost in shades of night (1)
361 shined on them who long in shades of death have been (1)
401 triumph o'er the shades of night (1)

shadow
28 under the shadow of thy throne (2)
46 beneath thy shadow we abide (1)
125 cover my defenseless head with the shadow of thy wing (2)
216 with Almighty God abide and in his shadow safely hide (1)
242 behind the dim unknown, standeth God within the shadow (4)
245 the Rock's blessed shadow, how sweet (2)
274 in the shadow of the rock (2)
417 the shadow of a mighty rock within a weary land (1)
417 I take, O cross, thy shadow for my abiding place (3)
433 help me walk from day to day with its shadow o'er me (3)
534 may the shadow of thy presence around our camp be spread (2)

shadowed
204 on shadowed thresholds dark with fears (2)

shadows
50 that shadows fall on brightest hours, that thorns remain (3)
139 the clouds disperse, the shadows fly (6)
176 lead me through the vale of shadows (3)
245 O sometimes the shadows are deep (T,1)
264 when the bird waketh, and the shadows flee (1)
264 alone with thee amid the mystic shadows (2)
264 when the soul waketh, and life's shadows flee (5)
269 involved in shadows of a darksome night (3)
289 heaven's morning breaks, and earth's vain shadows flee (5)
354 and death's dark shadows put to flight (4)
407 in lands, where shadows hide the light (3)
413 are ye able when . shadows close around you with the sod (3)
495 shadows of the evening steal across the sky (1)
503 while the deepening shadows fall (3)
503 and shadows end (4)
529 the morning breaks, the shadows flee (4)

shadowy
245 or walking the shadowy vale (3)

shaft
216 no deadly shaft by day shall harm (5)

shake
48 that soul, though all hell should endeavor to shake (5)
122 arise, my soul, arise; shake off thy guilty fears (T,1)
180 shake off dull sloth (1)
209 thy hope, thy confidence let nothing shake (2)
293 what can shake thy sure repose (1)
428 hark, how he groans, while nature shakes (2)

shakes
428 hark, how he groans, while nature shakes (2)
464 shakes the trembling gates of hell (2)

shaking
220   though the earth be shaking, every heart be quaking (2)

shall
2   honor, glory, might, and merit thine shall ever be (5)
9   days of praise shall ne'er be past while life ... last (1,4)
9   praise shall employ my nobler powers (1,4)
9   none shall find his promise vain (2)
14   thy praise shall sound from shore to shore (2)
14   till suns shall rise and set no more (2)
17   when Christ shall come with shout of acclamation (4)
17   and take me home, what joy shall fill my heart! (4)
17   then I shall bow in humble adoration (4)
20   one little word shall fell him (3)
21   his truth ... shall from age to age endure (4)
22   earth, with her ten thousand tongues, shall fill (3)
22   shall fill thy courts with sounding praise (3)
22   when rolling years shall cease to move (4)
23   who reigns, and shall forever reign (1,4)
26   early in the morning our song shall rise to thee (1)
30   established is his law, and changeless it shall stand (2)
30   his love shall be our strength and stay, while ages roll (3)
31   strong is his arm, and shall fulfill his great decrees (3)
32   without his high behest ye shall not ... disturb (3)
32   shall not, in the mountain pine, disturb a sparrows nest (3)
39   hour, when earth shall feel his saving power (3)
42   sin and death shall not prevail (2)
42   laws which never shall be broken (1)
42   never shall his promise fail (2)
46   we shall not in the desert stray (2)
46   we shall not full direction need (2)
48   when through fiery trials thy pathways shall lie (4)
48   the rivers of woe shall not thee overflow (3)
48   my grace, all-sufficient, shall be thy supply (4)
48   the flame shall not hurt thee, I only design (4)
49   for thus it was, is now, and shall be evermore (3)
51   God shall lift up thy head (1)
51   so shall this night soon endd in joyous day (2)
51   so shall thou, wondering, own his way (3)
52   life, while thou preservest life, a sacrifice shall be (4)
52   death ... shall join our souls to thee (4)
52   death, when death shall be our lot (4)
53   hand which bears all nature up shall guard his children (2)
53   that hand .... shall guard his children well (2)
56   praises of my God shall still my heart and tongue employ (1,
56   your wants shall be his care (4)
56   to them and their posterity his blessing shall descend (5)
57   O whence shall come my aid (1)
61   for his mercies shall endure, ever faithful, ever sure (R)
68   goodness and mercy all my life shall surely follow me (5)
68   in God's house forevermore my dwelling place shall be (5)
74   given the name to which all knees shall bow (4)
75   who put their trust in thee... death nor hell shall harm (3)
76   at the name of Jesus every knee shall bow (T,1)
77   his love shall never end: Alleluia! Amen! (2)
77   life shall not end the strain; Alleluia! Amen! (3)
78   all hearts must bow; all things celestial thee shall own (2)

88   and I shall fancy his blessing resting on me (2)
92   yea, when this flesh and heart shall fail (5)
92   and mortal life shall cease (5)
92   I shall possess, within the veil ... life of joy & peace (5)
97   I'll trust him when life's fleeting days shall end (4)
105 God calling yet! shall I not hear (T,1)
105 earth's pleasures shall I still hold dear (1)
105 shall life's swift passing years all fly (1)
105 shall I give no heed, but still in bondage live (4)
105 shall I not rise? Can I his loving voice despise (2)
105 shall he knock, and I my heart the closer lock (3)
105 and shall I dare his spirit grieve (3)
106 when our days of toil shall cease (3)
110 they who believe on his name shall rejoice (4)
116 I shall full salvation find (1)
117 look unto me, thy morn shall rise ... thy day be bright (3)
118 what shall I say thy grace to move (4)
120 when my eyes shall close in death (3)
127 bold shall I stand in thy great day (2)
127 for who aught to my charge shall lay (2)
127 with joy shall I lift up my head (1)
128 that vow renewed shall daily hear (5)
130 what shall I do my God to love (T,1)
131 God, through himself, we then shall know (4)
133 so shall I never die (4)
134 and shall we then forever live at this poor dying rate (4)
135 be my Lord, and I shall be firmly bound, forever free (4)
136 till Christ shall dwell in human hearts (1)
136 till every age and race and clime shall blend (3)
136 shall blend their creeds in one (3)
136 and earth shall win true holiness (4)
140 if thou withdraw thyself from me, ah! whither shall I go (1)
140 O speak, and I shall live (3)
143 when death's cold, sullen stream shall o'er me roll (4)
147 soon shall our doubts and fears all yield to thy control (3)
147 thy tender mercies shall illume the midnight of the soul (3)
150 assured, if I my trust betray, I shall forever die (4)
151 mankind shall then be truly free (2)
154 fill with thy spirit till all shall see Christ ...in me (4)
155 there's no discouragement shall make him once relent (1)
155 no foes shall stay his might, though he with giants fight (2
155 we know we at the end shall life inherit (3)
160 his strength shall bear thy spirit up (2)
163 shall life or death, or earth or hell (3)
164 I shall not fear the battle if thou art by my side (1)
164 that where thou art in glory there shall thy servant be (4)
167 My Jesus as thou wilt! All shall be well for me (3)
168 and I shall see his face (3)
173 justice conquers violence and wars at last shall cease (3)
176 nor for fame my prayer shall be (2)
177 and when thy face I see, my ransomed souls shall be (4)
183 consecrated cross I'll bear till death shall set me free (3)
184 make me a captive, Lord,and then I shall be free (T,1)
184 force me to render up my sword and I shall conqueror be (1)
184 deathless it shall reign (2)
185 this all my prayer shall be: more love O Christ, to thee (2)
185 then shall my latest breath whisper thy praise (4)

185   this be the parting cry my heart shall raise (4)
185   this still its prayer shall be: more love, O Christ (4)
187   take my will & make it thine; it shall be no longer mine (3)
187   my heart ... it shall be thy royal throne (3)
192   in him shall true hearts everywhere ... communion find (2)
196   what shall I render to my God (T,1)
198   these things shall be (T,1)
198   a loftier race than e'er the world hath known shall rise (1)
198   they shall be gentle, brave, and strong (2)
198   inarmed shall live as comrades free (3)
198   nation with nation, land with land, inarmed shall live (3)
198   in every heart and brain shall throb the pulse of one (3)
198   new arts shall bloom of loftier mold (4)
198   every life shall be a song when all... earth is paradise (4)
199   then shall all shackles fall (4)
199   so shall the wide earth seem our Father's temple (3)
199   wild war music o'er the earth shall cease (5)
199   love shall tread out the baleful fire of anger (5)
200   who shall I send to shatter the fetters which they bear (2)
200   whom shall I send to succor my people in their need (1)
200   whom shall I send to loosen the bonds of shame and greed (1)
204   till sons of men shall learn thy love (6)
204   glorious from thy heaven above shall come the city (6)
204   shall come the city of our   God (6)
209   all now mysterious shall be bright at last (2)
209   hour ... when we shall be forever with the Lord (3)
209   all safe and blessed we shall meet at last (3)
211   his might thy heart shall strengthen (2)
211   mercy thy days shall lengthen (2)
214   therefore the evil shall receive but grief (3)
214   the righteous ones shall be forever blest (T,1)
214   their evil acts shall surely come to naught (4)
214   when God shall judge, their lot be woe (3)
214   past deeds shall come and them ensnare (4)
215   and shall break in blessings on your head (3)
216   no evil shall upon thee come (6)
216   my God, in him my trust shall be (2)
216   he shall with all-protecting care preserve thee (3)
216   no fatal stroke shall thee assail (3)
216   his outspread pinions shall thee hide (4)
216   his faithfulness shall ever be a shield and buckler (4)
216   no nightly terrors shall alarm (5)
216   no deadly shaft by day shall harm (5)
218   enough that Christ knows all, and I shall be with him (5)
221   by the living Word of God I shall prevail (2)
222   when he shall come with trumpet sound (2)
230   in heavenly love abiding no change my heart shall fear (T,1)
230   wherever he may guide me, no want shall turn me back (2)
231   yet God the same abiding, his praise shall tune my voice (4)
234   feel the promise is not vain that morn shall tearless be (3)
234   life that shall endless be (4)
236   with thee began, with thee shall endd the day (2)
236   then, when thy voice shall bid our conflict cease (4)
238   but that toil shall make thee some day all mine own (4)
238   peace shall follow battle; night shall end in day (3)
238   and the end of sorrow shall be near my throne (4)
239   shall I fear to own his cause .. blush to speak his name (1)

239   thy saints in all this glorious war shall conquer (5)
239   shall conquer though they die (5)
239   when that illustrious day shall rise (6)
239   the glory shall be thine (6)
240   lay hold on life ..it shall be thy joy & crown eternally (1)
240   trust ... trusting soul shall prove Christ is its life (3)
243   not long the conflict, soon the holy war shall cease (4)
248   from victory unto victory his army shall he lead (1)
248   to him that overcometh a crown of life shall be (4)
248   he with the King of glory shall reign eternally (4)
251   God's own hand shall guide thee there (4)
251   soon shall close thy earthly mission (4)
251   swift shall pass thy pilgrim days (4)
251   hope shall change to glad fruition (4)
255   O when shall I behold thy face, thou Majesty divine (2)
259   and when the storms of life shall cease (3)
262   my bounding heart shall own thy sway & echo to thy voice (3)
263   still all my song shall be, nearer, my God, to thee (1)
263   still all my song shall be, nearer, my God, to thee (5)
264   so shall it be the last, in that bright morning (5)
264   shall rise the glorious thought, I am with thee (5)
264   O in that hour, fairer than daylight dawning shall rise (5)
266   thy friends in thy conduct his likeness shall see (2)
266   thou soon shall be fitted for service above (4)
267   wonderful key that shall unclasp and set me free (1)
268   so shall my walk be close with God (6)
268   purer light shall mark .. road that leads me to the Lamb (6)
270   quivering leaf shall softly tell us thou art near (3)
275   thy wings shall my petition bear to him (3)
276   blest are the pure in heart for they shall see ... God (T,1)
277   hasten the joyful day which shall my sins consume (2)
277   old things shall be done away ... all things new become (2)
278   then shall my feet no longer rove rooted .. fixed in God (1)
278   no longer ... my heart shall mourn ... purified by grace (3)
281   which shall from age to age endure (1)
281   whose word, when heaven and earth shall pass, remains (1)
285   when shall I find my willing heart all taken up by thee (1)
288   redeemed from earth and pain, Ah! when shall we ascend (2)
291   when I shall reach that happy place ... be forever blest (3)
291   I shall see my Father's face, and in his bosom rest (3)
294   for her my tears shall fall, for her my prayers ascend (3)
294   till cares and toils shall end (3)
294   sure as thy truth shall last (5)
297   the great Church victorious shall be the Church at rest (3)
300   there... endless home shall be... Lord we soon shall see (4)
300   they are happy now ... we soon their happiness shall see (2)
301   what height of rapture shall we know when...we meet (5)
303   exult, O dust and ashes; the Lord shall be thy part (3)
306   we shall still be joined in heart and hope to meet again (4)
308   a mountain that shall fill the earth (4)
332   who shall say how bread and wine God into man conveys (1)
337   when the chief Shepherd shall appear (5)
340   who wander far shall seek and find and serve thee well (3)
341   thee I shall constantly proclaim (4)
346   let those learn, who here shall meet (4)
352   filled with thy majesty, till time shall end (1)
352   till we our God and King shall praise in heaven (4)

353   the King shall come (T,1)
353   and we his face shall see (4)
353   the King shall come when morning dawns (5)
354   rejoice! rejoice! Emmanuel shall come to thee, O Israel (R)
355   shall we again refuse thee (3)
357   that future years shall see, evermore and evermore (1)
359   he shall come down like showers upon the fruitful earth (3)
359   before him on the mountains shall peace, the herald, go (3)
359   to him shall prayer unceasing and daily vows ascend (4)
359   the tide of time shall never his covenant remove (4)
359   his name shall stand forever; that name to us is love (4)
361   his name shall be the Prince of Peace forevermore adored (3)
361   his righteous government and power shall over all extend (4)
361   his reign shall have no end (4)
362   valleys shall be exalted, the lofty hills brought low (1,4)
362   power and pomp of nations shall pass like a dream away (2)
362   he shall feed his flock like a shepherd (3)
364   every eye shall now behold him robed in dreadful majesty (2)
364   deeply wailing, shall the true Messiah see (2)
369   then shall all bondage cease, all fetters fall (2)
369   and I shall find my peace, my all-in-all (2)
373   this child ... our confidence and joy shall be (1)
375   love shall be our token; love be yours and love be mine (3)
376   heaven and earth shall flee away when he comes to reign (2)
382   suddenly the Lord, descending, in... temple shall appear (4)
390   shall come the time foretold (3)
390   peace shall over ... earth its ancient splendors fling (3)
390   when with the ever circling years shall come the time (3)
394   and this shall be the sign (3)
394   the heavenly babe you there shall find (4)
398   never shall darkness veil thee again from human eyes (1)
398   thy light, so glad & golden, shall set on earth no more (1)
400   say, shall we yield him, in costly devotion (3)
403   thine shall be a path, though thorny, bright (4)
403   for God, by grace, shall dwell in thee (4)
406   when war shall be no more and strife shall cease (3)
409   the great congregation his triumph shall sing (2)
410   that shall turn their hearts to the right (1)
410   for the darkness shall turn to dawning (R)
410   and Christ's great kingdom shall come on earth (R)
410   song ... that shall lift their hearts to the Lord (2)
410   song that shall conquer evil & shatter the spear & sword (2)
413   thy guiding radiance above us shall be a beacon to God (R)
416   never shall the cross forsake me (2)
418   language shall I borrow to thank thee, dearest friend (3)
421   dear dying Lamb, thy precious blood shall never lose (3)
421   thy precious blood shall never lose its power (3)
421   redeeming love has been my theme, & shall be till I die (4)
433   till my raptured soul shall find rest beyond the river (R)
440   soon the storms of time shall cease (1)
440   joy unknown, ... saints shall stand before the throne (4)
445   He lives, and I shall conquer death (3)
451   for they eternal life shall win, Alleluia (4)
452   welcome, happy morning age to age shall say (T,1,4)
453   every knee to him shall bow (1)
455   his reign shall know no end (3)
455   thy praise and glory shall not fail throughout eternity (4)

457 Lord our King, who reigns for us...shall forever reign (2)
466 shall far outpass the power of human telling (3)
468 before him righteousness shall go, his royal harbinger (1)
468 truth from the earth, like to a flower, shall bud (1)
468 truth ... shall bud and blossom then (1)
468 glory shall ere long appear to dwell within our land (2)
468 thou art he who shall by right the nations all possess (2)
468 the nations all whom thou hast made shall come (3)
468 all shall frame to bow them low before thee, Lord (3)
469 building proud towers which shall not reach to heaven (3)
469 how shall we love thee, holy, hidden Being (4)
471 not heaven's hosts shall swifter move than we on earth (4)
472 Jesus shall reign (T,1)
472 till moons shall wax and wane no more (1)
472 to him shall endless prayer be made (2)
472 his name like sweet perfume shall rise (2)
472 and infant voices shall proclaim their early blessings (3)
474 time shall soon this earth remove (1)
475 earth shall be fair, and all her people one (3)
475 nor till that hour shall God's whole will be done (3)
476 till greed and hate shall cease (2)
478 and holiness shall whisper the sweet amen of peace (2)
481 within whose four-square walls shall come no night (1)
481 the tears are wiped from eyes that shall not weep again (1)
483 rejoice in glorious hope! Our Lord the judge shall come (4)
485 when ever blue the sky shall gleam ... green the sod (2)
486 till through world made noble ... God shall march (4)
486 through lands from sin set free ... God shall march (4)
486 the armies of the living God shall march to victory (4)
487 as we go, lead us, Lord; we shall be thine evermore (4)
492 be glory, as it was, is now, and shall forever be (5)
494 soon from us the light of day shall forever pass away (3)
500 thy praise shall hallow now our rest (1)
500 so be it, Lord; thy throne shall never ... pass away (4)
500 thy throne shall never, like earth's proud empires, pass (4)
509 thy goodness all our hopes shall raise (4)
509 when death shall interrupt our songs and seal in silence (5)
509 in better worlds our souls shall boast (5)
510 residue of days or hours thine, wholly thine, shall be (5)
520 love like thine, that none shall ever stray (1)
521 neither life nor death shall ever from the Lord .. sever (3)
522 then the full corn shall appear (2)
522 God shall come, and shall take his harvest home (3)
522 from his field shall in that day all offenses purge away (3)
522 for the Lord our God shall come (3)
523 how shall we show our love to thee, who givest all (1)
528 where shall my wondering soul begin (T,1)
528 how shall I all to heaven aspire (1)
528 how shall I equal triumphs raise (1)
528 O how shall I the goodness tell, Father (2)
528 shall I slight my Father's love, or basely fear (3)
528 shall I, the hallowed cross to shun (3)
528 his bleeding heart shall make you room (5)
528 his open side shall take you in (5)
531 then shall my heart from earth be free (2)
538 thus evermore shall rise to thee glad hymns of praise (4)
544 falsehood and wrong shall not tarry beside thee (3)

544 so shall thy people, with thankful devotion praise him (4)
545 trumpet that shall never call retreat (3)
545 so the world shall be his footstool (5)
549 work shall be prayer, if all be wrought as thou wouldst (6)
550 thy blessing came, and still its power shall onward (2)
550 here thy name, O God of love ... children shall adore (4)
550 their children's children shall adore (4)

shalt
26 which wert, and art, and evermore shalt be (2)
110 bring him thy burden and thou shalt be blest (2)
210 though undeserving; thou yet shalt find it true for thee (3)
216 beneath his wings shalt thou confide (4)
240 only believe, and thou shalt see that Christ is all (4)
251 thou, from hence, my all shalt be (1)
251 while thou shalt smile upon me (2)
255 hope still, and thou shalt sing the praise of him (4)
258 thou with him shalt dwell, beholding Light enfolding (4)
266 by looking to Jesus, like him thou shalt be (2)
303 His only, his forever thou shalt be, and thou art (3)
310 thou in the midst of us shalt be, assembled in thy name (1)
316 when thou shalt in thy kingdom come ... Lord remember me (4
403 thou shalt find thy heart made truly his (2)
403 so shalt thou know that fellowship of love (1)
403 thou shalt own thy darkness passed away (3)
482 and thou in love shalt reign (1)
529 speak, or thou never hence shalt move (3)

shame
89 from sin ... grief & shame, I hide me, Jesus in thy name (1)
89 in shame my glory and my crown (3)
94 put him to an open shame (2)
108 shame on us, Christian brethren, his name & sign who bear (1)
108 O shame, thrice shame upon us, to keep his standing there (1)
108 O Lord, with shame and sorrow we open now the door (3)
127 from sin and fear, from guilt and shame (2)
160 take up thy cross, nor heed the shame (3)
200 whom shall I send to loosen the bonds of shame and greed (1)
228 the emblem of suffering and shame (1)
228 its shame and reproach gladly bear (4)
236 guard thou the lips from sin, the hearts from shame (2)
254 shine to shame and guide this life of mine (1)
408 cast out our pride & shame that hinder to enthrone thee (3)
417 my sinful self my only shame, my glory all the cross (3)
418 O sacred Head ... with grief and shame weighed down (1)
422 to heal the people of their shame, and nobleness instill (3)
427 till through our pity and our shame love answers (2)
434 shun not suffering, shame, or loss (2)
454 hail ... universal Savior who hast borne our sin & shame (1)
458 to them the cross with all its shame (4)
458 though shame and death to him (6)
470 shame our wanton, selfish gladness (3)
481 O shame to us who rest content while lust and greed (3)
486 conquer for thy sake despair and doubt and shame (4)
489 take away our sin and shame (2)
501 the very wounds that shame would hide (5)

shamed
219 shamed by its failures or its fears, I sink (2)

shameful
83 he bore the shameful cross ... carried all my grief (2)
428 behold the Savior of mankind nailed to the shameful tree (T)

shaped
33 the hand that shaped the rose hath wrought the crystal (1)

shapest
171 shapest man to God's own law, thyself the fair design (2)

share
153 slaves are we whene'er we share that devotion anywhere (3)
195 thy rest, thy joy, thy glory share (5)
197 thy purpose for thy world we share (4)
223 not a burden we bear, not a sorrow we share (2)
228 where his glory forever I'll share (4)
235 where Jesus knelt to share with thee the silence (3)
242 when we share her wretched crust (2)
261 who will all our sorrows share (2)
267 love with thy children thus to share (3)
270 O Love Divine, that stooped to share (T,1)
270 stooped to share our sharpest pang, our bitterest tear (1)
275 the joys I feel, the bliss I share (2)
284 and share thy joy at last (5)
292 with us the work to share, with us reproach to dare (3)
306 we share each other's woes, our mutual burdens bear (3)
328 who thy mysterious supper share, here at thy table fed (2)
427 that, as we share this hour, thy cross may bring ... joy (4)
456 where his loving people meet to share the gift divine (2)
469 sharing not our griefs, no joy can share (2)
479 thine abundant life to share (3)
530 hear us, who thy nature share, who thy mystic body are (1)
530 kindly for each other care; every member feel its share (4)
531 that strives with thee my heart to share (2)

shared
157 forever shared, forever whole, a never-ebbing sea (1)
321 Master ... symbols shared thine own dear self impart (4)

shares
440 every humble spirit shares it (2)

sharing
469 sharing not our griefs, no joy can share (2)
490 always serving thee, sharing thy rich truth (2)
506 beneath thy mighty caring the birds & beasts are sharing (2)
506 sharing ... the love that sends the showers (2)
506 sharing ... the hand that gives the flowers (2)

sharpest
270 stooped to share our sharpest pang, our bitterest tear (1)

shatter
200 who shall I send to shatter the fetters which they bear (2)
410 song that shall conquer evil & shatter the spear & sword (2)

shed

7	for his lovingkindness ever shed upon our earthly way (3)
101	Jesus shed his precious blood rich blessings to bestow (2)
119	but that thy blood was shed for me (1)
127	for me, e'en for my soul, was shed (3)
129	and smile at the tears I have shed (3)
134	come, shed abroad a Savior's love, and... kindle ours (5)
278	Jesus, thine all-victorious love shed in my heart abroad (T)
282	heart that always feels thy blood so freely shed for me (1)
285	O that it now were shed abroad in this poor stony heart (3)
298	and thy fullest benediction shed within its walls alway (2)
319	the cup in token of his blood that was for sinners shed (3)
320	wine of the soul in mercy shed (1)
320	look on the tears by sinners shed (2)
325	rich blood that Jesus shed to raise our souls to heaven (2)
329	shed o'er the world thy holy light (5)
370	light of knowledge, ever burning, shed on us (3)
370	light of knowledge ... shed on us thy deathless learning (3)
426	where the blood of Christ was shed (1,4)
433	the bright and morning star shed its beams around me (2)
543	America! America! God shed his grace on thee (1)
543	America! America! God shed his grace on thee (4)

shedding

370	shedding light that none can measure (1)

sheds

64	sun of our life, thy quickening ray sheds on our path (2)
64	sheds on our path the glow of day (2)
223	what a glory he sheds on our way (1)
232	place where Jesus sheds the oil of gladness on our heads (2)
456	as altar candle sheds its light as surely as a star (2)
480	where the Gospel's day sheds not its glorious day (1)

sheen

303	the pastures of the blessed are decked in glorious sheen (2)

sheep

21	and for his sheep he doth us take (2)
22	when like wandering sheep we strayed (2)
129	where dost thou, dear Shepherd, resort with thy sheep (2)
201	O thou who art the Shepherd of all the scattered sheep (T,1)
337	nourish the lambs and feed thy sheep (4)
383	in fields where they lay keeping their sheep (1)
412	lo, the Good Shepherd for the sheep is offered (3)
539	with his sheep securely fold you (1)

shelter

28	our shelter from the stormy blast (1)
57	thy shelter and thy shade (3)
225	a little shelter from life's stress (3)

shepherd

67	the King of love my Shepherd is (T,1)
67	Shepherd ... whose goodness faileth never (1)
67	Good Shepherd, may I sing thy praise within thy house (6)

```
   43   forever singing as they shine (3)
   74   that in our darkened hearts thy grace might shine (1)
   80   marks divine, that in thy meekness used to shine (1)
   85   in whom God's glory dwelleth,in whom man's virtues shine (1)
  118   fallen, till in me thine image shine (2)
  131   if thou within us shine (4)
  168   could I sound the glories forth which in my Savior shine (1)
  188   ever, O Christ, through mine let thy life shine (1)
  239   and all thy armies shine in robes of victory (6)
  254   let thy clear light forever shine (1)
  254   shine to shame and guide this life of mine (1)
  268   a light to shine upon the road that leads me to the Lamb (1)
  289   shine through the gloom and point me to the skies (5)
  372   still that light she lifteth o'er all the earth to shine (2)
  399   O deep within my heart now shine (2)
  428   and in full glory shine (4)
  456   there heavenly splendors shine (2)
  466   and let thy glorious light shine ever on my sight (2)
  505   soon as dies the sunset glory, stars of heaven shine (2)
  505   stars of heaven shine out above (2)
  536   we feebly struggle, they in glory shine (4)
```

shined
```
  361   the light has shined on them (1)
  361   shined on them who long in shades of death have been (1)
```

shines
```
   31   through all his mighty works amazing wisdom shines (3)
   37   moon shines full at his command, and all the stars obey (1)
   45   he shines in all that's fair (2)
   47   with thee to bless, the darkness shines as light (2)
   79   and all the twinkling starry host: Jesus shines brighter (3)
   79   Jesus shines purer, than all the angels heaven can boast (3)
  142   faith that shines more bright & clear when tempests rage (3)
  291   o'er ... wide-extended plains shines one eternal day (2)
  365   in every star thy wisdom shines (1)
  367   Father of mercies, in thy Word what endless glory shines (T)
  371   Word ... shines through the darkness of our earthly way (1)
  372   a lantern to our footsteps shines on from age to age (1)
  382   yonder shines the infant light (2)
  473   it breathes in the air, it shines in the light (4)
```

shineth
```
   63   everywhere his glory shineth (4)
  213   the darkness shineth as the light (1)
  372   it shineth like a beacon above the darkling world (3)
  381   yet in thy dark streets shineth the everlasting light (1)
  481   where the sun that shineth is God's grace for human good (4)
```
shining
```
   39   he made the shining worlds on high (2)
   43   spangled heavens, a shining frame (1)
   90   lo! his star is shining above the stable (1)
   90   shining revealed through every task most lowly (2)
  170   in hope that sends a shining ray far down the future's (4)
  231   a season of clear shining to cheer it after rain (1)
  366   of one pearl each shining portal (3)
  383   they looked up and saw a star shining in the east (2)
```

394   spake the seraph and forthwith appeared a shining throng (5)
400   cold on his cradle the dew-drops are shining (2)
401   more & more thyself display, shining to the perfect day (3)
498   ppraise for light so brightly shining on our steps (1)
498   shining on our steps from heaven above (1)
505   shining in the spirit's skies (4)
506   but mid the light declining the evening star is shining (1)
543   crown thy good with brotherhood ... sea to shining sea (1,4)
552   band of shining worlds in splendor through the skies (1)

ship
244   when the world is tossing me like ship upon the sea (1)

shoal
247   hiding rock and treacherous shoal (1)

shocks
308   though earth-quake shocks are threatening her (3)

shod
    through seas dry-shod, through weary wastes bewildering (2)

shone
173   thy steadfast face set forward where love and duty shone (2)
178   what grace, O Lord, and beauty shone (T,1)
394   the angel of the Lord came down, and glory shone around (1)
395   heaven's star shone brightly forth, glory all around him (2)
403   that light hath on thee shone in which is perfect day (3)
404   behold throughout the heavens there shone a holy light (1)
431   the star is dimmed that lately shone (1)

shop
197   through quiet work in shop and home (1)
481   lust and greed for gain in street and shop and tenement (3)
511   farm .. market, shop .. home, of mind and heart and hand (1)

shore
 11   breakers crashing on the shore (3)
 14   thy praise shall sound from shore to shore (2)
 32   and chains you to the shore (2)
 35   offering up on every shore her pure sacrifice of love (5)
 77   on heaven's blissful shore his goodness we'll adore (3)
127   sinners more than sands upon the ocean shore (4)
148   to us he gives the keeping of the lights along the shore (1)
148   longing for the lights along the shore (2)
247   when at last I near the shore ... fearful breakers roar (3)
290   no harm from him can come to me on ocean or on shore (4)
291   can reach that healthful shore (2)
302   greet the blood redeemed hands on the eternal shore (5)
398   long, alas, witholden, now spread from shore to shore (1)
472   his kingdom spread from shore to shore (1)
476   no alien race, no foreign shore (1)
476   who lightest every earnest mind of every clime and shore (3)

shores
296   from oldest time, on farthest shores ... she adores (2)
551   O guard our shores from every foe (2)

short
28   short as the watch that ends the night (4)
218   if short, yet why should I be sad to soar to endless day (2)
492   live this short, revolving day as if it were our last (4)

shortly
464   the Lord will shortly pour all the spirit of his love (4)

should
20   though this world, with devils filled should threaten (3)
25   tents of ease nor thrones of power should tempt my feet (2)
25   nor ... should tempt my feet to leave thy door (2)
45   why should my heart be sad? The Lord is King (3)
48   that soul, though all hell should endeavor to shake (5)
53   why should this anxious load press down your weary mind (3)
69   if our love were but more simple, we should take him at (2)
69   we should take him at his word (2)
76   'tis the Father's pleasure we should call him Lord (1)
118   I own it cannot be that I should fit myself for thee (3)
129   say, why in the valley of death should I weep (2)
129   O why should I wander, an alien from thee (3)
147   but should the surges rise and rest delay to come (2)
177   nor should I aught with-hold, dear Lord, from thee (1)
218   if short, yet why should I be sad to soar to endless day (2)
231   their wonted fruit should bear (4)
231   though vine nor fig tree neither ... fruit should bear (4)
231   all the field should wither .. flocks nor herds be there (4)
237   should thy mercy send me sorrow, toil, and woe (3)
237   or should pain attend me on my path below (3)
299   one soul should perish lost in shades of night (1)
418   O make me thine forever, and should I fainting be (3)
423   scorned ... little children should on his bidding wait (2)
435   forbid it, Lord, that I should boast, save in the death (2)
526   if each should have its rightful meed (1)
527   and can it be that I should gain (T,1)

shoulder
67   on his shoulder gently laid (3)
361   on his shoulder ever rests all power on earth and heaven (2)

shouldst
41   what is man that thou shouldst love him (2)
272   nor prayed that thou shouldst lead me on (2)
527   how can it be that thou, my Lord, shouldst die for me (1)

shout
10   church with psalms must shout, no door can keep them out (2
14   shout for joy and Savior's name (3)
17   when Christ shall come with shout of acclamation (4)
86   hither our children bring to shout thy praise (1)
190   shout with their shout of praise (2)
221   glory in the highest, I will shout and sing (1)
377   the hostel rang with song and shout (2)
380   Ay! we shout to the lovely evangel they bring (4)
551   let our hills and valleys shout the songs of liberty (3)

shouts
447 let shouts of holy joy outburst: Alleluia (2)
524 bring sacrifice of praise ... shouts of exultation (1)

show
15 praise the holy God of love, and all his greatness show (1)
39 his wonders to the nations show (1)
41 soaring spire and ruined city, these our hopes ... show (3)
41 spire and ruined city, these our hopes and failures show (3)
60 let them his glory also show (4)
82 ah, this nor tongue nor pen can show (4)
95 send thy grace and show thy power (2)
114 can my gracious Savior show my name inscribed in heaven (1)
137 Spirit of faith, descend and show the virtue of his name (3)
162 thus may I rejoice to show that I feel the love I owe (4)
171 show us thy will, we ask (3)
195 thy love to tell, thy praise to show (4)
201 help us by deeds of mercy to show that thou art kind (2)
201 in thy great salvation, show forth thy boundless love (3)
251 show thy face, and all is bright (2)
309 show thyself the Prince of Peace (1)
309 show how true believers live (4)
309 on the wings of angels fly; show how true believers die (6)
332 let the wisest mortal show how we the grace receive (2)
338 still in Jesus' footsteps tread & show his praise below (2)
341 his only righteousness I show, his saving grace proclaim (5)
354 to us the path of knowledge show (2)
356 show us the way the Master trod; reveal his saving power (1)
407 show us anew in Calvary the wondrous power (1)
407 mighty God, set us aflame to show the glory of thy name (3)
410 and show us that God is love (3)
410 we've a Savior to show to the nations (4)
422 pomp .. show, nor lofty pride, nor boast above the least (1)
452 tread the path of darkness, saving strength to show (3)
479 to.. child .. youth .. aged love in living deeds to show (4)
489 show thy reconciled face (2)
510 our lips & lives ... gladly show the wonders of thy love (4)
523 how shall we show our love to thee, who givest all (1)
533 the long cloud of witnesses show the same path to heaven (2)
544 show forth thy pity on high where thou reignest (1)

showed
370 told the story of the Word, and showed his glory (2)
528 how ... goodness tell ... which thou to me hast showed (2)

shower
132 as a gracious shower descend (1)
132 on our souls thy graces shower (2)
343 stormy sea sings praise to God ... thunder & the shower (1)
464 lo! the promise of a shower drops already from above (4)
471 abroad thy healing influence shower (3)
506 sharing ... the love that sends the showers (2)
512 with the gentle showers doth bless the springing grain (1)

showers
359 he shall come down like showers upon the fruitful earth (3)
506 sharing ... the love that sends the showers (2)
512 with the gentle showers doth bless the springing grain (1)

showeth
521   unto them his grace he showeth (3)

showing
161   showing to wandering souls the path of light (3)
293   showing that the Lord is near (3)

shown
171   boyhood faith that shown thy whole life through (1)
188   through me thy truth be shown, thy love made known (2)
344   thy wisdom in their lives be shown (4)
498   Jesus, for thy love most tender on the cross ... shown (2)
498   on the cross for sinners shown (2)

shows
223   for the favor he shows, and the joy he bestowes (3)
275   I hasten to the place where God my Savior shows his face (2)
405   myrrh his sepulcher foreshows (4)
509   the opening year thy mercy shows (1)

shrine
128   while to that sacred shrine I move (2)
225   a little shrine of quietness, all sacred to itself (2)
542   here are my hopes, my dreams, my holy shrine (1)

shrink
142   O for a faith that will not shrink (T,1)
373   ye shepherds, shrink not with affright (1)

shrouded
257   lie in deepest darkness shrouded (2)

shun
251   foes may hate, and friends may shun me (2)
270   no path we shun, no darkness dread (2)
434   shun not suffering, shame, or loss (2)
528   shall I, the hallowed cross to shun (3)

shut
415   well might .. sun in darkness hide...shut his glories in (3)

sick
104   come ... weak and wounded, sick and sore   (1)
118   pity and heal my sin-sick soul (2)
125   heal the sick, and lead the blind (3)
212   there is a balm in Gilead, to heal the sinsick soul (R)
292   sinsick and sorrow-worn, whom Christ doth heal (1)
479   as, O Lord, thy deep compassion healed the sick (2)
479   healed the sick and freed the soul (2)
480   health to the sick in mind, sight to the inly blind (2)
501   the sick, O Lord, around thee lay (1)
501   for some are sick, and some are sad (3)
502   watch by the sick; enrich the poor with blessings (5)

sickness
291   sickness and sorrow, pain and death are felt ... no more (2)

side
20 were not the right man on our side (2)
59 thou, Lord, wast at our side, all glory be thine (2)
99 in his feet and hands are wound-prints, and his side (2)
106 ever near the Christian's side (1)
120 from thy wounded side which flowed (1)
159 nearer, blessed Lord, to thy precious, bleeding side (R)
164 I shall not fear the battle if thou art by my side (1)
209 be still my soul; the Lord is on thy side (1)
223 or we'll walk by his side in the way (4)
226 let thy precious blood applied keep me ... near thy side (1)
242 for the good or evil side (1)
242 then to side with truth is noble (2)
271 land me safe on Canaan's side (3)
420 pardon for all flows from his side (2)
454 seated at thy Father's side (3)
455 crown him the Lord of love; behold his hands and side (4)
528 his open side shall take you in (5)
547 from every mountain side let freedom ring (1)

sideth
20 through him who with us sideth (4)

sifting
545 sifting out the hearts of men before his judgment seat (3)

sigh
138 to check the rising doubt,the rebel sigh (4)
252 prayer is the burden of a sigh, the falling of a tear (2)
255 I sigh to think of happier days, when thou...wast nigh (3)
531 and inly sigh for thy repose (1)

sighed
116 long my heart has sighed for thee (2)

sighing
359 give them songs for sighing ... darkness turn to light (2)
402 sorrowing, sighing, bleeding, dying (4)

sighs
51 God hears thy sighs and counts thy tears (1)

sight
9 the Lord pours eyesight on the blind (3)
27 thine angels adore thee, all veiling their sight (4)
28 a thousand ages in thy sight are like an evening gone (4)
31 no mortal eye can bear the sight (1)
35 for the mystic harmony linking sense to sound and sight (3)
47 faith's fair vision changes into sight (2)
67 thou spreadst a table in my sight (5)
76 at his voice creation sprang at once to sight (2)
115 a country far from mortal sight (1)
119 poor, wretched, blind; sight, riches, healing of... mind (4)
135 wake my spirit, clear my sight (1)
139 the invisible appears in sight (6)
150 arm me with jealous care, as in thy sight to live (3)
206 with worlds on worlds beyond our sight (4)

213　O thou, to whose all-searching sight (T,1)
224　visions of rapture now burst on my sight (2)
230　His wisdom ever waketh, his sight is never dim (2)
251　faith to sight and, prayer to praise (4)
257　our knowledge, sense and sight lie in deepest darkness (2)
277　according to thy mind & Word, well-pleasing in thy sight (3)
291　O... transporting rapturous scene that rises to my sight (1)
300　lift your eyes ... sons of light Zion's city is in sight (4)
303　send hope before to grasp it, till hope be lost in sight (3)
359　souls, condemned and dying, are precious in his sight (2)
377　the beasts a wondrous sight behold (2)
393　shepherds quake at the sight (2)
395　shepherds saw .. wondrous sight, heard .. angels singing (2)
453　look, ye saints! the sight is glorious (T,1)
453　O what joy the sight affords (4)
456　the heaven that hides him from our sight knows (2)
466　and let thy glorious light shine ever on my sight (2)
467　enable with perpetual light the dullness of... sight (2)
467　dullness of our blinded sight (2)
479　dawns upon our quickened sight (3)
480　thou who didst come to bring ... healing and sight (2)
480　health to the sick in mind, sight to the inly blind (2)
491　O Jesus, keep us in thy sight (1,3)
494　softly now the light of day fades upon our sight away (T,1)
503　when forever from our sight pass the stars, the day (4)

sights
164　I see the sights that dazzle, the tempting sounds I hear (2)

sign
　11　rainbow arch, his covenant sign (2)
　64　our rainbow arch thy mercy's sign (3)
108　shame on us,Christian brethren, his name & sign who bear (1)
157　O Lord and Master of us all; whate'er our name or sign (6)
161　who by this sign didst conquer grief and pain (5)
260　no more we seek thee from afar, nor ask thee for a sign (4)
374　love to God and all men, love for plea and gift and sign (3)
375　worship we our Jesus, but where-with for sacred sign (2)
375　love was born at Christmas; star & angels gave the sign (1)
394　and this shall be the sign (3)

signs
114　and publish to the sons of men the signs infallible (2)
358　what its signs of promise are (1)

silence
　43　solemn silence ... move round the dark terrestrial ball (3)
179　peal our the watchword! silence it never! (R)
235　silence of eternity, interpreted by love (3)
235　where Jesus knelt to share with thee the silence (3)
296　adores with silence, or with psalm (2)
324　let all mortal flesh keep silence (T,1)
346　mountains lift their solemn forms to watch in silence (2)
346　mountains ... watch in silence o'er the land (2)
509　when death shall interrupt our songs and seal in silence (5)
509　seal in silence mortal tongues (5)
547　let rocks their silence break, the sound prolong (3)

silent
27 unresting, unhasting, and silent as light (2)
33 laid a silent loveliness on hill and wood and field (1)
200 no field or mart is silent, no city street is dumb (2)
290 and so beside the silent sea I wait the muffled oar (4)
357 let no tongue on earth be silent (2)
381 above thy deep & dreamless sleep the silent stars go by (1)
385 for sinners here the silent Word is pleading (2)
393 silent night, holy night (T,1,2,3,4)
404 while shepherds kept their watching o'er silent flocks (1)
404 o'er silent flocks by night (1)
421 when this poor lisping, stammering tongue lies silent (5)
421 tongue lies silent in the grave (5)
462 in the gray valley let us hear thy silent voice (4)
462 let us hear thy silent voice: "Lo, I am near" (4)
486 silent courage pleads to heaven more eloquent than song (3)
500 the voice of prayer is never silent (3)
506 the day is slowly wending toward its silent ending (T,1)
532 in silent love be cherished (5)

silently
267 silently now I wait for thee, ready my God (R)
381 how silently, how silently the wondrous gift is given (3)

silver
60 thou silver moon with softer gleam (1)
187 take my silver and my gold (2)
488 to holy convocations the silver trumpet calls (3)

simple
69 if our love were but more simple, we should take him at (2)
90 preaching the blessedness which simple trust has found (3)
208 in simple faith to plunge me neath the healing ... flood (2)
235 simple trust like theirs who heard beside the Syrian sea (2)
365 thy Gospel makes the simple wise (5)
368 simple, child-like hearts (4)
548 keep her faith in simple manhood (4)

simplest
252 prayer is the simplest form of speech (3)
398 thou robest in thy splendor the simplest ways of men (2)
423 children sang their praises, the simplest and the best (1)

simplicity
84 praise in all simplicity the guiding Christ,our shepherd (1)

simply
120 in my hand no price I bring; simply to thy cross I cling (2)
208 just from Jesus simply taking life & rest & joy & peace (3)

sin
1 He breaks the power of canceled sin (4)
17 he bled and died to take away my sin (3)
18 life redeemed from death and sin (3)
25 guards our way from all the assaults of hell and sin (3)
29 to banish sin from our delight (3)
38 melt the clouds of sin and sadness (1)

381 cast out our sin, and enter in, be born in us today (4)
401 pierce the gloom of sin and grief (3)
414 there was no other good enough to pay the price of sin (4)
415 God, the mighty maker, died for man the creature's sin (3)
421 be saved to sin no more (3)
425 triumphs now begin o'er captive death and conqered sin (2)
426 robed in mortal flesh is dying crucified by sin for me (2)
429 the reign of sin and death is o'er (3)
429 and all may live from sin set free (3)
430 sin, which laid the cross on thee (2)
438 the night of sin is ended! Alleluia! (3)
454 hail ... universal Savior who hast borne our sin & shame (1)
454 every sin may be forgiven through .. virtue of thy blood (2)
457 dead to sin, his members live the life of righteousness (3)
486 through lands from sin set free ... God shall march (4)
489 take away our sin and shame (2)
492 O let thine orient beams the night of sin disperse (2)
494 pardon each infirmity, open fault, and secret sin (2)
494 from sin & sorrow free, take us Lord, to dwell with thee (3)
496 sin and want we come confessing (1)
501 for none are wholly free from sin (4)
502 let him no more lie down in sin (4)
522 gather thou thy people in, free from sorrow ... from sin (4)
527 long my imprisoned spirit lay fast bound in sin (3)
527 fast bound in sin and nature's night (3)
528 a slave redeemed from death and sin (1)
528 groaning beneath your load of sin (5)
529 I need not tell thee who I am, my sin and misery declare (2)

sin's
85 God's light to earth thou bringest to drive sin's night (1)
85 drive sin's night away (1)
398 till every tongue and nation, from sin's dominion free (3)
463 by whose cross & death are we rescued from sin's misery (2)
464 sin's strongholds it now o'erthrows (2)
478 lead on, O King eternal, till sin's fierce war ... cease (2)

since
144 since on thine arm thou bidst me lean (1)
155 since, Lord, thou dost defend us with thy spirit (3)
167 since thou on earth has wept and sorrowed oft alone (2)
217 since God through Jordan leadeth me (4)
272 faces...which I have loved long since and lost awhile (3)
275 since he bids me seek his face (3)
336 fightings without . fears within since we assembled last (2)
412 therefore, kind Jesus, since I cannot pay thee (5)
459 blessed ... with light and life since Eden's dawning day (1)
515 since every day by thee we live, may grateful hearts (4)
517 since the day the blessed mother thee ... bore (2)

sincere
197 to fuller life, through work sincere (2)
252 prayer is the soul's sincere desire (T,1)

sinful
2 can it be that thou regardest songs of sinful man? (2)
26 though the eye of sinful man thy glory may not see (3)
121 poor and sinful though we be (3)

281 cleanse me from every sinful thought (3)
356 unite us in thy will, O Lord, and end all sinful strife (2)
371 revealing to sinful men thy justice and thy grace (3)
417 my sinful self my only shame, my glory all the cross (3)

sing

1 o for a thousand tongues to sing (T,1)
3 help us thy name to sing, help us to praise! (1)
4 sing praise to God who reigns above (T,1)
4 all my toilsome way along I sing aloud thy praises (4)
5 let those refuse to sing who never knew our God (2)
6 blessings ... bounty ... joyful songs to thee we sing (2)
10 let all the world in every corner sing (T,1,2)
10 sing: my God and King! (1,2)
14 in songs of praise divinely sing (3)
15 him, in whom they move and live, let every creature sing (3)
17 and hear the birds sing sweetly in the trees (2)
19 O friends, in gladness let us sing (4)
21 sing to the Lord with cheerful voice (1)
24 come, sound his praise abroad, and hymns of glory sing (T,1)
37 I sing the almighty power of God (T,1)
37 I sing the wisdom that ordained the sun to rule the day (1)
37 I sing the goodness of the Lord (2)
38 stars and angels sing around thee (2)
39 sing the great Jehovah's praise and bless his holy name (1)
58 the Spirit who in them did sing to us his music lendeth (3)
59 sing praises to his name: he forgets not his own (1)
60 lift up your voice and with us sing Alleluia! Alleluia! (1)
60 O sing ye! Alleluia! (5)
66 evermore his praises sing, Alleluia! Alleluia! (1)
67 Good Shepherd, may I sing thy praise within thy house (6)
67 sing thy praise within thy house forever (6)
77 come, Christians, join to sing Alleluia! Amen! (T,1)
79 Jesus is purer, who makes the woeful heart to sing (2)
82 nor voice can sing, nor heart can frame (2)
86 Christ our triumphant King, we come thy name to sing (1)
86 and joyful sing (4)
88 one of his heralds, yes, I would sing loudest hosannas (3)
90 while the angels sing (1)
93 tune my heart to sing thy grace (1)
109 sing them over again to me (T,1)
149 when in scenes of glory I sing the new, new song (4)
166 I'll sing with the glittering crown on my brow (3)
167 and sing, in life or death, "My Lord, thy will be done" (1)
168 I'd sing his glorious righteousness (1)
168 I'd sing the characters he bears (2)
185 when they can sing with me, more love, O Christ, to thee (3)
187 take my voice ... let me sing always, only, for my King (2)
196 we sing the songs of heaven (5)
210 sing, pray, and keep his ways unswerving (3)
221 glory in the highest, I will shout and sing (1)
233 rejoice, give thanks and sing (1)
233 rejoice, rejoice, rejoice, give thanks and sing (R)
255 hope still, and thou shalt sing the praise of him (4)
284 that I may sing above to Father, Spirit, and to thee (6)
300 as we journey let us sing (1)
300 sing our Savior's worthy praise (1)
302 saints on earth unite to sing with those to glory gone (2)

305   this through countless ages men and angels sing (4)
319   in faith and memory thus we sing the wonders of his love (4)
352   glad songs to thee I sing; glad hearts to thee we bring (4)
357   angel hosts, his praises sing (2)
362   get thee up to the heights and sing (2)
366   men and angels sing before thee (3)
366   we rejoice, and sing to thee our hymn of joy eternally (3)
374   come to Bethlehem & see him whose birth the angels sing (2)
377   to you we sing this glad Noel (3)
378   now to the Lord sing praises, all you within this place (5)
380   the star rains its fire while the beautiful sing (1,2)
380   every hearth is aflame, and the beautiful sing (3)
381   praises sing to God the King, and peace to men on earth (2)
385   King, whom shepherds guard and angels sing (R)
386   sing, choirs of angels, sing in exultation (2)
386   O sing, all ye citizens of heaven above (2)
387   hark! the herald angels sing (T,1)
388   hark, the herald angels sing (T,1,R)
390   world in solemn stillness lay to hear the angels sing (1)
390   and ever o'er its Babel sounds the blessed angels sing (2)
390   whole world give back the song which now the angels sing (3)
392   and heaven and nature sing (1)
393   heavenly hosts sing Alleluia (2)
393   with the angels let us sing Alleluia to our King (4)
409   the great congregation his triumph shall sing (2)
421   in a nobler, sweeter song, I'll sing thy power to save (5)
423   Hosanna in the highest that ancient song we sing (3)
438   let us joyful be and sing to God right thankfully (1)
439   sing, ye heavens, and earth reply, Alleluia (1)
440   sing with all the sons of glory (T,1)
440   sing the resurrection song (1)
443   hymns of praise then let us sing (2)
443   sing we to our God above ... praise eternal as his love (3)
447   that we may live and sing to thee: Alleluia (4)
449   and sing with hearts uplifted high: Alleluia (3)
449   and sing today with one accord the life laid down (4)
449   good Christian men, rejoice and sing (T,1)
450   let his church with gladness hymns of triumph sing (2)
451   O sons and daughters, let us sing (T,1)
454   help to sing of Jesus' merits (4)
455   awake, my soul, and sing of him who died for thee (1)
455   his glories now we sing who died, and rose on high (2)
473   O gratefully sing his power and his love (1)
473   O tell of his might, O sing of his grace (2)
482   we hail thine august majesty and loud hosanna sing (4)
483   rejoice, give thanks, and sing, and triumph evermore (1)
486   though earth and sea and heaven unite thy praise to sing (1)
488   sing holy, holy, holy, to the great God Triune (1)
509   Great God, we sing that mighty hand (T,1)
510   sing to the Great Jehovah's praise (T,1)
528   or sing my great deliverer's praise (1)
535   they sing the Lamb in hymns above and we in hymns below (2)
547   sweet land of liberty, of thee I sing (1)
547   our fathers' God, to thee, Author of liberty ... we sing (4)

singers
532   praise we ... the singers sweetly gifted (3)

singing
2   angel voices, ever singing round thy throne of light (T,1)
7   singing with the whole creation (2)
8   angel choirs above are singing (2)
38   ever singing, march we onward   (4)
43   forever singing as they shine (3)
77   singing forever more Alleluia! Amen! (3)
162   singing, till thy face I see, of his love (4)
162   singing ... of his love who first loved me (4)
366   Zion hears the watchmen singing (2)
374   sweetly singing o'er the plains (1)
379   Christ is born   their choirs are singing (1)
395   shepherds saw .. wondrous sight, heard .. angels singing (2)
504   singing, we offer prayer and meditation (1)
512   all nature joins in singing a joyful song of praise (2)
524   valleys stand so thick with corn ... they are singing (1)
536   singing to Father, Son, and Holy Ghost, Alleluia (6)
544   singing in chorus from ocean to ocean (4)

single
159   O the pure delight of a single hour (3)
159   delight of a single hour...I spend before thy throne (3)
253   I want a true regard, a single steady aim (4)
484   lift up a living nation, a single sword to thee (3)

sings
6   blessings ... bounty ... joyful songs to thee we sing (2)
17   then sings my soul, my Savior God to thee (R)
25   great God, attend, while Zion sings (T,1)
34   each little bird that sings (1)
45   and to my listening ears all nature sings (1)
231   sometimes a light surprises the Christian while he sings (T)
343   stormy sea sings praise to God ... thunder & the shower (1)

sink
130   and sink me to perfection's height (5)
184   I sink in life's alarms when by myself I stand (1)
219   shamed by its failures or its fears, I sink (2)
219   I sink beside the road (2)
303   beneath the contemplation sink heart and voice oppressed (1)

sinking
222   all other ground is sinking sand (R)

sinks
213   when sinks my heart in waves of woe (3)
264   when sinks the soul, subdued by toil, to slumber (4)

sinless
491   call on thee that sinless the hours of dark may be (2)
495   pure and fresh and sinless in thy holy eyes (6)

sinned
23   when his creatures sinned, he bled (2)

sinner
69   welcome for the sinner and more graces for the good (1)
102   come, all the world! come, sinner, thou! (2)
109   sinner, list to the loving call (2)
114   how can a sinner know his sins on earth forgiven? (T,1)
122   nor let that ramsomed sinner die (3)
137   who did for every sinner die hath surely died for me (1)
287   sinner, do you love my Jesus ... soldiers of the cross (3)
337   to warn the sinner, cheer the saint (4)
350   the sinner pardon at thy feet (4)
457   worthy to be exalted thus, the Lamb for sinner slain (2)

sinner's
1   music in the sinner's ears ... life and health and peace (3)
111   stands knocking at the door of every sinner's heart (2)
118   Jesus, the sinner's friend, to thee (T,1,5)
252   prayer is the contrite sinner's voice (4)
252   sinner's voice, returning from his ways (4)
418   what ...my Lord, hast suffered was all for sinner's gain (2)

sinners
58   the grace those sinners that subdued (2)
71   sinners, whose love can ne'er forget the wormwood and (3)
76   from the lips of sinners unto whom he came (3)
94   me, the chief of sinners, spare (1)
100   return, ye ransomed sinners, home (R)
102   come, sinners, to the gospel feast (T,1)
104   come, ye sinners, poor and needy (T,1)
104   not the righteous; sinners Jesus came to call (4)
112   sinners, turn, why will you die (T,1,2,3)
112   ransomed sinners, why will you slight his grace, and die (2)
112   long-sought sinners, why will you grieve ... God and die (3)
127   forever doth for sinners plead (3)
127   Lord, I believe were sinners more than sands (4)
127   sinners more than sands upon the ocean shore (4)
227   the story repeat, and the lover of sinners adore (3)
228   for a world of lost sinners was slain (1)
319   the cup in token of his blood that was for sinners shed (3)
320   look on the tears by sinners shed (2)
341   Jesus ... name to sinners dear ... name to sinners given (2)
364   once for favored sinners slain (1)
385   for sinners here the silent Word is pleading (2)
387   God and sinners reconciled (1)
415   would he devote that sacred head for sinners such as I (1)
420   come, sinners, see your Savior die (3)
421   sinners, plunged beneath that flood (1)
443   endured the cross & grave ... sinners to redeem and save (2)
453   sinners in derision crowned him (3)
454   there for sinners thou art pleading (3)
489   may thy Gospel's joyful sound conquer sinners, comfort (4)
489   conquer sinners, comfort saints (4)
498   on the cross for sinners shown (2)
528   sinners alone his grace receive (4)

sinning
283   take away our bent to sinning (2)
506   Savior's cross is winning forgiveness for the sinning (4)

sins
94   now incline me to repent; let me now my sins lament (3)
110   come with thy sins; at his feet lowly bow (3)
114   how can a sinner know his sins on earth forgiven? (T,1)
115   happy ... who knows his sins forgiven (1)
178   far more for others' sins than... wrongs that we receive (3)
180   disperse my sins as morning dew (2)
196   who hath my sins forgiven (5)
261   all our sins and griefs to bear (1)
268   I hate the sins that ... drove thee from my breast (4)
268   I hate the sins that made thee mourn (4)
269   sins that...drove thee from my breast (4)
277   hasten the joyful day which shall my sins consume (2)
320   and in whose death our sins are dead (1)
360   from our fears and sins release us (1)
365   noblest wonders ... in souls renewed, and sins forgiven (6)
365   Lord, cleanse my sins, my soul renew (6)
392   no more let sins and sorrows grow (3)
420   Father's coeternal Son bore all my sins upon the tree (1)
421   there may I, though vile as he, wash all my sins away (2)
427   our sins, not thine, thou bearest, Lord (2)
429   cut off for sins, but not his own (1)
430   here, O Christ, our sins we see (2)
446   all the winter of our sins, long and dark, is flying (2)
454   all our sins on thee were laid (2)
495   those who plan some evil, from their sins restrain (4)
499   new perils past, new sins forgiven (2)
523   for souls redeemed, for sins forgiven (4)
526   I lay my sins before thee (1)
528   know ... feel my sins forgiven (2)

sins'
397   so may we with holy joy, pure and free from sins' alloy (3)

sinsick
212   there is a balm in Gilead, to heal the sinsick soul (R)
292   sinsick and sorrow-worn, whom Christ doth heal (1)

sister
35   for the joy of human love, brother, sister, parent,child (4)

sit
223   then in fellowship sweet we will sit at his feet (4)

sits
83   majestic sweetness sits enthroned upon the Savior's brow (T)
409   Salvation to God, who sits on the throne (3)
457   enthroned at God's right hand he sits (2)

sittest
459   Ancient of Days, who sittest throned in glory (T,1)

six
324   at his feet the six-winged seraph (4)

skies
11   skies with crimson clouds aflame (2)
14   from all the dwell below the skies (T,1)
32   and sweeps the howling skies (4)
35   for the glory of the skies (1)
37   spread the flowing seas abroad and built the lofty skies (1)
45   of skies and seas; his hand the wonders wrought (1)
91   when morning gilds the skies, my heart awaking cries (T,1)
138 no angel visitant, no opening skies (2)
189 human hatreds flee before the radiant eastern skies (1)
198 and mightier music thrill the skies (4)
230 bright skies will soon be o'er me, where darkest clouds (3)
239 must I be carried to the skies on flowery beds of ease (2)
239 robes of victory through the skies (6)
246 hosts of sin...pressing hard to draw thee from the skies (1)
289 shine through the gloom and point me to the skies (5)
352 let every anthem rise like incense to the skies (2)
377 in Bethlehem neath starlit skies (T,1)
387 join the triumph of the skies (1)
390 still through the cloven skies they come (2)
398 flooding the eastern skies (1)
401 Christ, whose glory fills the skies (T,1)
402 Alleluia, Alleluia! sounds through the earth and skies (5)
439 ours the cross, the grave, the skies, Alleluia (4)
442 He who skies & meadows paints fashioned all your virtue (3)
464 now it spreads along the skies (4)
474 soon our Savior will return, triumphant in the skies (3)
505 shining in the spirit's skies (4)
542 my country's skies are bluer than the ocean (2)
542 and skies are everywhere as blue as mine (2)
543 O beautiful for spacious skies, for amber waves of grain (T)
552 band of shining worlds in splendor through the skies (1)

skill
215 deep in unfathomable mines of never-failing skill (2)
343 Great God, to thee we consecrate our voices & our skill (3)
485 from thee all skill and science flow (T,1)
532 praise we the peaceful men of skill (4)
532 peaceful men of skill who builded homes of beauty (4)

sky
7   see the morning sun ascending radiant in the eastern sky (T)
9   he made the sky and earth and seas, with all their train (2)
26   all thy works ... praise thy name in earth & sky & sea (4)
34   the sunset, and the morning that brightens up the sky (2)
36   God of earth, the sky, the sea (T,1)
37   if I survey the ground I tread, or gaze upon the sky (2)
39   he framed the globe; he built the sky (2)
40   maker of earth and sky (1)
43   with all the blue ethereal sky (1)
77   let praises fill the sky;   Alleluia! Amen! (2)
90   while birds and flowers and sky above are preaching (3)
150 a never-dying soul to save, and fit it for the sky (1)
190 awake, awake to love and work, the lark is in the sky (T,1)
263 or if, on joyful wing cleaving the sky (5)
341 Jesus! the name high over all, in hell or earth or sky (T,1)

353   crowned with glory like the sun . lights the morning sky (2)
368   guide & chart, wherein we read of realms beyond the sky (2)
372   O Truth unchanged, unchanging, O Light of our dark sky (1)
380   there's a song in the air, there's a star in the sky (T,1)
384   I love thee, Lord Jesus, look down from the sky (2)
384   the stars in the sky looked down where he lay (1)
419   who saw his Master in the sky, and called on him to save (2)
425   the winged squadrons of the sky look down (3)
437   from death to life eternal, from earth unto the sky (1)
475   now, even now, once more from earth to sky peals forth (3)
485   when ever blue the sky shall gleam ... green the sod (2)
486   their unconsidered lives go up like incense to the sky (2)
490   rise to greet the sun, reddening the sky (T,1)
492   sun itself is but thy shade, yet cheers both earth & sky (1)
495   shadows of the evening steal across the sky (1)
503   evening lamps alight through all the sky (1)
541   men who fly through the great spaces of the sky (1)
541   men who fly through lonely ways beneath the sky (2)

sky's
490   my heart's freed from ill, fair blue sky's above (3)

slain
228   for a world of lost sinners was slain (1)
364   once for favored sinners slain (1)
441   in the grave they laid him, Love whom men had slain (2)
457   worthy to be exalted thus, the Lamb for sinner slain (2)

slave
528   a slave redeemed from death and sin (1)
545   and the soul of wrong his slave (5)

slaves
153   slaves are we whene'er we share that devotion anywhere (3)

sleep
11   waterfalls that never sleep (3)
381   above thy deep & dreamless sleep the silent stars go by (1)
381   while mortals sleep, the angels keep their watch (2)
393   holy infant so tender and mild sleep in heavenly peace (1)
446   and from three days' sleep in death as a sun hath risen (2)
475   would man but wake from out his haunted sleep (2)
484   from sleep and from damnation, deliver us, good Lord (2)
493   I, ere I sleep, at peace may be (2)
493   O may my soul on thee repose and with sweet sleep (4)
493   with sweet sleep my eyelids close (4)
493   sleep that may me more vigorous make to serve my God (4)
499   through sleep and darkness safely brought, restored (1)
502   when the soft dews of kindly sleep (2)
502   be every mourner's sleep tonight like infant's slumbers (5)
506   O Father, while we sleep, thy children keep (R)
538   and calm amid the storm didst sleep (2)

sleepeth
4   his watchful eye ne'er sleepeth (2)

sleeping
   256   waking or sleeping, thy presence my light (1)
   385   child ... who, laid to rest, on Mary's lap is sleeping (1)
   396   flocks were sleeping (2)

sleepless
   324   Cherubim, with sleepless eye, veil their faces (4)

sleeps
    57   thy guardian never sleeps (2)
   346   ocean ... sleeps in the hollow of his hand (2)
   346   the rolling ocean, rocked with storms, sleeps (2)
   441   laid in the earth like grain that sleeps unseen (2)

slight
   112   ransomed sinners, why will you slight his grace, and die (2)
   528   shall I slight my Father's love, or basely fear (3)

slighted
   544   earth hath forsaken meekness & mercy . slighted thy word (2)

slighting
   175   though they are slighting him, still he is waiting (2)

slippery
    70   when in the slippery paths of youth (3)

slopes
   203   blazoned heights and slopes of need (1)

sloth
   180   shake off dull sloth (1)

slow
    66   slow to chide and swift to bless (2)
   170   help me the slow of heart to move (2)
   468   the Lord will come and not be slow (T,1)

slowly
   506   the day is slowly wending toward its silent ending (T,1)

sluggish
   406   through jungles, sluggish seas, and mountain pass (2)

slum
   200   I hear my people crying in cot and mine and slum (2)

slumber
   105   and still my soul in slumber lie (1)
   264   when sinks the soul, subdued by toil, to slumber (4)
   400   angels adore him in slumber reclining (2)
   497   slumber sweet thy mercy send us (1)

slumbers
   502   be every mourner's sleep tonight like infant's slumbers (5)
   502   like infant's slumbers pure and light (5)

small
27   to all, life thou givest, to both great and small (3)
34   all creatures great and small (R)
218   my knowledge of that life is small (5)
235   O still, small voice of calm (5)
335   not a cause of small import the pastor's care demands (2)
379   here let all, great and small kneel in awe and wonder (3)
435   that were an offering far too small (4)
464   when he first the work begun, small & feeble was his day (2)

smart
124   revives my fainting heart, healing all it hidden smart (2)

smile
64   our midnight is thy smile withdrawn (3)
89   my smile beneath the tyrant's frown (3)
129   and smile at the tears I have shed (3)
199   each smile a hymn, each kindly deed a prayer (1)
251   while thou shalt smile upon me (2)
270   we smile at pain when thou art near (1)
272   and with the morn those angel faces smile (3)
293   thou mayest smile at all thy foes (1)
329   glad, when thy gracious smile we see (4)

smiling
215   behind a frowning providence he hides a smiling face (4)

smite
238   Christian, up and smite them, counting gain but loss (1)
484   bind all our lives together, smite us and save us all (3)
539   smite death's threatening wave before you (4)

snare
87   take the name of Jesus ever as a shield from every snare (2)
216   preserve thee from the fowler's snare (3)
275   oft escaped the tempter's snare by thy return ... prayer (1)

snares
92   through many dangers, toils ... snares I... already come (3)

snatch
175   snatch them in pity from sin and the grave (1)

snow
33   the crystal of the snow (1)
101   crimson flood that washes white as snow (2)
154   whiter than snow,Lord, wash me just now (2)
376   snow had fallen, snow on snow (1)
513   sends the snow in winter ... warmth to swell the grain (1)

soar
218   if short, yet why should I be sad to soar to endless day (2)
232   ah! there on eagle wings we soar (4)
439   soar we now where Christ has led, Alleluia (4)

soaring
27   thy justice like mountains high soaring above (2)
41   soaring spire and ruined city, these our hopes ... show (3)

soars
136   we rise with him to life which soars beyond the grave (4)
190   see how the giant sun soars up (2)

sobbing
481   there swells the sobbing human plaint (2)
481   sobbing human plaint that bids thy walls arise (2)

sober
253   I want a sober mind, a self-renouncing will (2)

sod
413   are ye able when . shadows close around you with the sod (3)
485   when ever blue the sky shall gleam ... green the sod (2)

soft
15   timbrels soft and cymbals loud in his high praise agree (2)
379   hark! a voice from yonder manger, soft and sweet (2)
502   when the soft dews of kindly sleep (2)
513   the breezes and the sunshine, and soft, refreshing rain (1)

softened
64   star of our hope, thy softened light cheers (2)

softer
60   thou silver moon with softer gleam (1)

softly
106   when the storms are raging sore ... whisper softly (2)
106   while they hear that sweetest voice whispering softly (1)
106   hearts grow faint, and hopes give o'er, whisper softly (2)
106   pleading nought but Jesus' blood, whisper softly (3)
270   quivering leaf shall softly tell us thou art near (3)
494   softly now the light of day fades upon our sight away (T,1)

soiled
467   anoint and cheer our soiled face with...thy grace (3)

solace
13   filled with solace, light and grace! (1)
203   abound with love and solace for the day (3)
261   thou wilt find a solace there (3)
546   solace .. its wide dominion .. the healing of thy wings (1)

sold
364   those who set at naught and sold him (2)

soldier
239   am I a soldier of the cross, a follower of the Lamb (T,1)

soldiers
248   ye soldiers of the cross (1)
250   soldiers of Christ, arise and put your armor on (T,1)
250   still let the Spirit cry, in all his soldiers, "Come" (3)
287   if you love him, why not serve him... soldiers ... cross (4)
287   every round goes higher ... soldiers of the cross (2)
287   climbing Jacob's ladder ... soldiers of the cross (T,1)

287   sinner, do you love my Jesus ... soldiers of the cross (3)
287   we are climbing higher, higher ... soldiers of the cross (5)
536   O may thy soldiers, faithful, true, and bold (3)

sole
180   in thy sole glory may unite (3)

solely
257   drawn from earth to love thee solely (1)
399   thou hast won my heart to serve thee solely (1)
521   his the loving purpose solely to preserve them (4)

solemn
33   the solemn splendors of the night (2)
43   solemn silence ... move round the dark terrestrial ball (3)
100   blow ye trumpet, blow! The gladly solemn sound (T,1)
128   high heavens, that heard the solemn vow (5)
259   O Jesus, in that solemn hour, in death as life (3)
264   the solemn hush of nature newly born (2)
264   a fresh and solemn splendor still is given (3)
294   her sweet communion, solemn vows (4)
308   we hear within the solemn voice of her unending song (2)
335   let them from the mouth of God ... solemn charge receive (1)
346   mountains lift their solemn forms to watch in silence (2)
350   here thine angelic spirits send their solemn praise (5)
350   their solemn praise with ours to blend (5)
390   world in solemn stillness lay to hear the angels sing (1)
501   hear, in this solemn evening hour (6)
507   never will throw off his fear who hears our solemn vow (4)

solid
24   watery worlds are all his own, and all the solid ground (2)
84   give milk . bread or solid food as fits my understanding (3)
222   on Christ, the solid rock, I stand (R)
428   temple's veil in sunder breaks ... solid marbles rend (2)

solitude
219   thy presence fills my solitude (3)
434   all is solitude and gloom; who hath taken him away (4)

solitudes
541   aloft in solitudes of space (2)

solve
123   Joseph's tomb could solve death's mystery (3)
123   I know not how that Joseph's tomb could solve death's (3)

some
50   that in the darkest spot of earth some love is found (2)
93   teach me some melodious sonnet (1)
148   some poor fainting, struggling seaman you may rescue (R)
148   some poor seaman, tempest-tossed (3)
149   some have never heard the message of salvation (3)
170   by some clear, winning word of love (2)
177   some offering bring thee now, something for thee (1)
177   some song to raise, or prayer, something for thee (2)
177   some work of love begun, some deed of kindness done (3)

177 some wanderer sought and won, something for thee (3)
191 men whose aim 'twill be not to defend some ancient creed (1)
203 but often in some far-off Galilee beheld thee fairer (2)
228 and exchange it some day for a crown (R)
228 then he'll call me some day to my home far away (4)
238 but that toil shall make thee some day all mine own (4)
242 some great cause, God's new Messiah (1)
464 kindled in some hearts it is (1)
495 those who plan some evil, from their sins restrain (4)
501 for some are sick, and some are sad (3)
501 and some have never loved thee well (3)
501 and some have lost the love they had (3)
502 if some poor wandering child of thine have spurned (4)

something
177 some offering bring thee now, something for thee (1)
177 some song to raise, or prayer, something for thee (2)
177 some wanderer sought and won, something for thee (3)
177 through all eternity, something for thee (4)

sometimes
212 sometimes I feel discouraged and think my work's in vain (1)
217 sometimes mid scenes of deepest gloom (2)
217 sometimes where Eden's bowers bloom (2)
231 sometimes a light surprises the Christian while he sings (T)
245 O sometimes the shadows are deep (T,1)
245 sorrows, sometimes how they sweep like tempests (1)
245 O sometimes how long seems the day (2)
245 and sometimes how weary my feet (2)
436 Oh! sometimes it causes me to tremble, tremble, tremble (R)

son
2 Father, Son, and Holy Spirit, blessed Trinity (5)
8 holy Father, holy Son, holy Spirit: three we name thee (4)
17 and when I think that God, his Son not sparing (3)
19 God ... Father, ... Son, ... Spirit, Three in One (4)
44 what the son of man, that thou dost visit him in grace (3)
49 the Son, and him who reigns with them in highest heaven (3)
60 praise, praise the Father, praise the Son (7)
78 to God the Father ... Son ... Spirit ... Three in One (4)
79 O thou of God and man the son, thee will I cherish (1)
80 pathway, trod in wondrous love, O Son of God (1)
80 thou Son of man, thou Light of light (2)
85 O Son of God incarnate, O Son of man divine (T,1)
90 Mary's son most holy, Light of the village life (2)
122 he cannot turn away the presence of his Son (4)
140 what did thine only Son endure before I drew my breath (2)
146 strong Son of God, immortal love (T,1)
174 as brothers of the Son of man, rise up, O men of God (4)
180 praise Father, Son, and Holy Ghost (4)
186 Son of the carpenter, receive this humble work of mine (2)
192 who serves my Father as a son is surely kin to me (3)
197 O Son of Man, who madest known (T,1)
204 we hear thy voice, O Son of man (1)
250 God supplies through his eternal Son (1)
256 thou my great Father, and I thy true son (2)
265 Most Holy One ... thou blessed Son (5)
265 O make me thine indeed, thou blessed Son (5)

26   early in the morning our song shall rise to thee (1)
32   and bid the choral song ascend to celebrate our God (5)
38   in the triumph song of life (4)
53   I'll drop my burden at his feet, and bear a song away (4)
58   their song to us descendeth (3)
58   his song in them, in us, is one (3)
58   we raise it high, we send it on, the song (3)
58   we send it on, the song that never endeth (3)
58   unbroken be the golden chain, keep on the song forever (4)
71   we'll join the everlasting song (5)
86   our shepherd and our pride, our staff and song (3)
86   unite to swell the song to Christ our King (4)
91   be this the eternal song through all the ages long (4)
129   my comfort by day and my song in the night (1)
149   when in scenes of glory I sing the new, new song (4)
177   some song to raise, or prayer, something for thee (2)
179   song of our spirits, rejoicing and free (R)
188   cleanse it from guilt & wrong; teach it salvation's song (3)
198   every life shall be a song when all... earth is paradise (4)
205   my song through endless ages: Jesus led me all the way (3)
224   this is my story, this is my song, praising my Savior (R)
227   Jesus all the day long was my joy and my song (4)
233   raise high your free, exulting song (2)
248   this day the noise of battle ... next, the victor's song (4)
263   still all my song shall be, nearer, my God, to thee (1)
263   still all my song shall be, nearer, my God, to thee (5)
292   the world to Christ we bring, with joyful song (4)
303   they stand, those halls of Zion, all jubilant with song (2)
305   blend with ours your voices in the triumph song (4)
308   we hear within the solemn voice of her unending song (2)
326   this is the hour of banquet and of song (2)
343   there is a voice in every star, in every breeze a song (1)
352   be in each song of praise which here thy people raise (2)
374   gladsome tidings be which inspire your heavenly song (2)
377   the hostel rang with song and shout (2)
380   there's a song in the air, there's a star in the sky (T,1)
380   and that song from afar has swept over the world (3)
380   we rejoice in the light, and we echo the song (4)
390   that glorious song of old (1)
390   whole world give back the song which now the angels sing (3)
394   angels praising God on high .. thus addressed their song (5)
410   we've a song to be sung to the nations (2)
410   song ... that shall lift their hearts to the Lord (2)
410   song that shall conquer evil & shatter the spear & sword (2)
421   in a nobler, sweeter song, I'll sing thy power to save (5)
423   Hosanna in the highest that ancient song we sing (3)
431   from heavenly plains is borne the song that angels know (4)
437   now let the heavens be joyful! Let earth her song begin (3)
440   sing the resurrection song (1)
447   the song of triumph has begun: Alleluia (1)
449   bring flowers of song to strew his way (2)
467   through ... ages all along this may be our endless song (4)
472   dwell on his love with sweetest song (3)
478   and now, O King eternal, we lift our battle song (1)
486   silent courage pleads to heaven more eloquent than song (3)
512   all nature joins in singing a joyful song of praise (2)
522   raise the song of harvest home (1)

524	thrice blessed ... harvest song ... never hath an ending (3)
536	steals on the ear the distant triumph song (5)
542	this is my song, O God of all the nations (T,1)
542	a song of peace for lands afar and mine (1)
542	O hear my song, thou God of all the nations (2)
542	a song of peace for their land and for mine (2)
547	and ring from all the trees sweet freedom's song (3)
550	thou heard'st well pleased, the song, the prayer (2)

songs

2	can it be that thou regardest songs of sinful man? (2)
5	then let our songs abound and every tear be dry (4)
6	blessings ... bounty ... joyful songs to thee we sing (2)
6	songs of glory, songs of triumph to our God and King (2)
14	in songs of praise divinely sing (3)
22	we'll crowd thy gates with thankful songs (3)
87	his songs our tongues employ (3)
93	streams of mercy never ceasing call for songs (1)
93	call for songs of loudest praise (1)
134	in vain we tune our formal songs (3)
168	in Loftiest songs of sweetest praise (2)
196	we sing the songs of heaven (5)
252	angels in their songs rejoice and cry, "Behold he prays" (4)
271	songs of praises I will ever give to thee (3)
352	glad songs to thee we sing; glad hearts to thee we bring (4)
359	give them songs for sighing ... darkness turn to light (2)
392	let men their songs employ (2)
438	loud songs of Alleluia! Alleluia! (1)
449	praise we in songs of victory that love, that life (3)
472	angels descend with songs again (5)
509	when death shall interrupt our songs and seal in silence (5)
510	inspires our choicest songs (1)
551	let our hills and valleys shout the songs of liberty (3)
552	our grateful songs before thy throne arise (1)

sonnet

93	teach me some melodious sonnet (1)

sons

28	bears all its sons away (5)
41	Spirit in our spirit speaking, make us sons of God (4)
78	redeem us...when thou judgest all the sons of men (3)
114	and publish to the sons of men the signs infallible (2)
204	till sons of men shall learn thy love (6)
243	the sons of fathers we by whom our faith is taught (2)
285	first-born sons of light desire in vain its depths...see (2)
293	well supply thy sons and daughters (2)
299	give of thy sons to bear the message glorious (4)
300	lift your eyes ... sons of light Zion's city is in sight (4)
351	be pleased to guide, each lengthening year, thy sons (2)
351	thy sons, O God, who gather here (2)
387	born to raise the sons of earth (3)
400	brightest and best of the sons of the morning (T,1)
439	sons of men and angels say, Alleluia (1)
440	sing with all the sons of glory (T,1)
446	Jacob's sons and daughters (1)
451	O sons and daughters, let us sing (T,1)

464 sons of God your Savior praise (3)
465 let all the sons of men record and dwell upon thy love (4)
471 let all earth's sons thy mercy prove (1)
472 and all the sons of want are blest (4)
517 sons and daughters look on life with eager eyes (4)
517 when our growing sons and daughters look on life (4)

soon
43 soon as the evening shades prevail (2)
51 so shall this night soon endd in joyous day (2)
147 soon shall our doubts and fears all yield to thy control (3)
230 bright skies will soon be o'er me, where darkest clouds (3)
243 not long the conflict, soon the holy war shall cease (4)
251 soon shall close thy earthly mission (4)
266 thou soon shall be fitted for service above (4)
277 soon or later then translate to my eternal bliss (4)
300 there... endless home shall be... Lord we soon shall see (4)
300 they are happy now ... we soon their happiness shall see (2)
326 too soon we rise: the symbols disappear (4)
428 but soon he'll break death's envious chain (4)
440 soon the storms of time shall cease (1)
474 time shall soon this earth remove (1)
474 soon our Savior will return, triumphant in the skies (3)
494 soon from us the light of day shall forever pass away (3)
505 soon as dies the sunset glory, stars of heaven shine (2)

soothe
431 unheard by mortals are the strains that sweetly soothe (4)
431 that sweetly soothe that Savior's woe (4)

soothes
81 it soothes his sorrows, heals his wounds (1)

sordid
84 from sordid waves of worldly sea preserve us, Lord (2)
237 or its sordid treasures spread to work me harm (2)

sore
97 my friend in trials sore (2)
99 art thou sore distressed (1)
104 come ... weak and wounded, sick and sore   (1)
106 when the storms are raging sore ... whisper softly (2)
418 how pale thou art with anguish, with sore abuse & scorn (1)
481 from women struggling sore for bread (2)

sorrow
60 ye who long pain and sorrow bear, praise God (5)
87 child of sorrow and of woe (1)
99 many a sorrow, many a labor, many a tear (4)
99 sorrow vanquished, labor ended, Jordan passed (5)
103 earth has no sorrow that heaven cannot cure (2)
103 earth has no sorrow that heaven cannot heal (1)
103 earth has no sorrow but heaven can remove (3)
108 O Lord, with shame and sorrow we open now the door (3)
136 and sin and sorrow cease (1)
167 through sorrow or through joy, conduct me as thine own (1)
185 let sorrow do its work, come grief or pain (3)

209   sorrow forgot, love's purest joys restored (3)
219   thought of thee is mightier than sin & pain & sorrow are (1)
223   not a burden we bear, not a sorrow we share (2)
231   set free from present sorrow we cheerfully can say (2)
236   our balm in sorrow, and our stay in strife (4)
237   should thy mercy send me sorrow, toil, and woe (3)
238   and the endd of sorrow shall be near my throne (4)
259   care, anguish, sorrow, melt away (2)
266   in joy or in sorrow, still follow the Lord (3)
269   through joy or sorrow, as thou deemest best (4)
270   and sorrow crown each lingering year (2)
277   bring the glorious liberty from sorrow, fear and sin (1)
281   from doubt and fear and sorrow free (4)
291   sickness and sorrow, pain and death are felt ... no more (2)
320   look on the heart by sorrow broken (2)
333   grant them the joy which brightens earthly sorrow (3)
355   robe of sorrow round thee (1)
396   thus rejoicing, free from sorrow (2)
410   Savior ... who the path of sorrow hath trod (4)
412   for me ... thy mortal sorrow, and thy life's oblation (4)
418   for this thy dying sorrow, thy pity without end (3)
426   cross of Jesus, cross of sorrow (T,1,4)
427   is this thy sorrow naught to us who pass unheeding by (1)
427   make us thy sorrow feel (2)
435   see, from his head, his hands, his feet, sorrow and love (3)
435   sorrow and love flow mingled down (3)
435   did e'er such love and sorrow meet (3)
440   death and sorrow, earth's dark story (1)
440   death and sorrow ... to the former days belong (1)
494   from sin & sorrow free, take us Lord, to dwell with thee (3)
522   unto joy or sorrow grown (2)
522   gather thou thy people in, free from sorrow ... from sin (4)

sorrow's
203   we've felt thy touch in sorrow's darkened way (3)
204   from famished souls, from sorrow's stress (3)

sorrowed
167   since thou on earth has wept and sorrowed oft alone (2)

sorrowing
183   who once went sorrowing here (2)
402   sorrowing, sighing, bleeding, dying (4)

sorrows
1   name ... that bids our sorrows cease (3)
81   it soothes his sorrows, heals his wounds (1)
107   in our joys and in our sorrows   (4)
129   thy foes will rejoice when my sorrows they see (3)
143   wipe sorrows tears away (3)
229   peace, perfect peace, with sorrows surging round (3)
245   sorrows, sometimes how they sweep like tempests (1)
245   if blessings or sorrows prevail (3)
261   who will all our sorrows share (2)
269   and doubts appall, and sorrows still increase (1)
392   no more let sins and sorrows grow (3)
431   for others' guilt the Man of Sorrows weeps in blood (3)

452 speak his sorrows ended; hail his triumph now (2)
453 see the Man of Sorrows now (1)
462 let us find thy hand when sorrows leave us blind (4)
474 all our sorrows left below .. earth exchanged for heaven (3)
521 and their sorrows all he knoweth (3)

sought
58 seek thee as thy saints ... sought in every generation (1)
62 through that precious love he sought us (2)
67 but yet in love he sought me (3)
74 by thee the outcast and the poor were sought (2)
93 Jesus sought me when a stranger (2)
96 I sought the Lord, and afterward I knew (T,1)
112 long-sought sinners, why will you grieve ... God and die (3)
177 some wanderer sought and won, something for thee (3)
185 once earthly joy I craved, sought peace and rest (2)
195 as thou hast sought, so let me seek ... erring children (1)
203 we've sought and found thee in the secret place (2)
214 but righteousness inspires those who have sought (4)
214 sought to gain fulfillment of their prayer (4)
251 all I've sought or hoped or known (1)
297 from heaven he came and sought her to be his holy bride (1)
395 angels sang about his birth; wisemen sought & found him (2)
549 these .. not the only walls wherein thou mayst be sought (3)

soul
4 with healing balm my soul he fills (1)
4 both soul and body bear your part (4)
13 where my soul in joyful duty waits (1)
16 with heart and soul and voice (1)
17 then sings my soul, my Savior God to thee (R)
30 he hath eternal life implanted in the soul (3)
48 the soul that on Jesus still leans for repose (5)
48 that soul, though all hell should endeavor to shake (5)
55 O my soul, praise him, for he is thy health & salvation (1)
64 center and soul of every sphere (1)
65 O my soul, bless God the Father (T,1)
65 bless the Father, o my soul (6)
66 praise, my soul, the King of heaven (T,1)
67 my ransomed soul he leadeth (2)
68 my soul he doth restore again (2)
70 when all thy mercies, O my God, my rising soul surveys (T,1)
70 unnumbered comforts to my soul thy tender care bestowed (2)
80 wondrous Lord, my soul would be ... conformed to thee (4)
80 my soul would be still more and more conformed to thee (4)
81 'tis manna to the hungry soul and to the weary, rest (2)
81 may the music of thy name refresh my soul in death (5)
89 thy mighty name salvation ... keeps my happy soul above (2)
96 he moved my soul to seek him, seeking me (1)
96 for thou wert long beforehand with my soul (3)
101 come, every soul by sin oppressed (T,1)
102 let every soul be Jesus' guest (1)
105 and still my soul in slumber lie (1)
116 soul and body thine to be wholly thine forevermore (3)
117 my thirst was quenched, my soul revived (2)
118 pity and heal my sin-sick soul (2)
119 and waiting not to rid my soul of one dark blot (2)

122 arise, my soul, arise; shake off thy guilty fears (T,1)
125 Jesus, lover of my soul,let me to thy bosom fly (T,1)
125 safe into the haven guide; O receive my soul at last (1)
125 other refuge have I none; hangs my helpless soul on thee (2)
126 Jesus, love of my soul,let me to thy bosom fly (T,1)
127 for me, e'en for my soul, was shed (3)
129 O thou, in whose presence my soul takes delight (T,1)
135 Holy Spirit, Truth divine, dawn upon this soul of mine (T,1)
138 but take the dimness of my soul away (2)
138 all, all thine own, soul, heart and strength and mind (3)
138 teach me the struggles of the soul to bear (4)
140 what pain ... labor to secure my soul from endless death (2)
140 O let me now receive that gift! my soul without it dies (4)
141 have faith in God, my soul, His cross forever stands (3)
141 I rest, heart, mind, and soul the captive of thy grace (4)
143 O bear me safe above, a ransomed soul (4)
144 safe ... calm ... satisfied the soul that clings to thee (4)
146 that mind and soul, according well, may make one music (5)
147 thy tender mercies shall illume the midnight of the soul (3)
150 a never-dying soul to save, and fit it for the sky (1)
159 Let my soul look up with a steadfast hope (2)
160 cross endured to save thy soul from death and hell (3)
163 what power my soul can sever (3)
164 O speak, and make me listen, thou guardian of my soul (3)
164 but, Jesus, draw thou nearer, & shield my soul from sin (2)
173 that learns to value beauty, in heart or brain or soul (4)
174 give heart and mind and soul and strength to serve (1)
177 in love my soul would bow, my heart fulfill its vow (1)
177 when thy face I see, my ransomed soul shall be (4)
180 awake, my soul, and with the sun (T,1)
188 draw thou my soul, O Christ, closer to thine (T,1)
188 lead forth my soul, O Christ, one with thine own (2)
189 one tender comfort broods upon the struggling human soul (3)
190 so let the love of Jesus come and set my soul ablaze (2)
205 my weary steps may falter, and my soul athirst may be (2)
209 be still my soul (T,1,2,3)
209 be still my soul; the Lord is on thy side (1)
209 be still my soul: thy best, thy heavenly friend (1)
210 God never yet forsook at need the soul that trusted him (3)
210 the soul that trusted him indeed (3)
211 place on the Lord reliance; my soul, with courage wait (2)
212 there is a balm in Gilead, to heal the sinsick soul (R)
212 but then the Holy Spirit revives my soul again (1)
213 when rising floods my soul o'erflow (3)
222 when all around my soul gives way, he... is all my hope (3)
225 where I may lay me prone, and bare my soul in loneliness (3)
225 where thou ... all my soul possess and I may find myself (2)
226 till my soul is lost in love (3)
227 sweet comfort and peace of a soul in its earliest love (1)
227 who hath died my poor soul to redeem (6)
231 when comforts are declining, he grants the soul again (1)
234 I rest my weary soul in thee (1)
240 trust ... trusting soul shall prove Christ is its life (3)
243 march on, o soul, with strength (T,1)
243 march on.. soul w. strength ... strong the battle rolls (3)
243 march on, O soul, march on, with strength (4)
245 like tempests over the soul (1)
246 my soul, be on thy guard, ten thousand foes arise (T,1)

246   fight on, my soul, till death...bring thee to thy God (4)
249   awake, my soul, stretch every nerve (T,1)
253   a soul inured to pain, to hardship, grief and loss (2)
255   so longs my soul, O God, for thee & thy refreshing grace (1)
255   for thee my God .. living God, my thirsty soul doth pine (2)
255   why restless, why cast down, my soul (4)
258   come, my soul, thou must be waking (T ,1)
264   when sinks the soul, subdued by toil, to slumber (4)
264   when the soul waketh, and life's shadows flee (5)
266   take time to be holy, be calm in thy soul (4)
275   my soul has often found relief (1)
275   truth and faithfulness engage the waiting soul to bless (3)
276   secret of the Lord is theirs ... soul is Christ's abode (1)
276   still to the lowly soul he doth himself impart (3)
278   refining fire, go through my heart; illuminate my soul (2)
278   my steadfast soul, from falling free ... no longer move (4)
279   awake my soul when sin is nigh, and keep it still awake (3)
279   the burden of my soul remove, the hardness from my heart (4)
279   O may the least omissions pain my reawakened soul (4)
280   burden from my soul remove, the hardness from my heart (4)
280   O may the least omission pain my reawakened soul (4)
280   awake my soul when sin is nigh and keep it still awake (3)
291   filled with delight my raptured soul lives (3)
295   thirsty soul longs ardently ... faints thy courts to see (2)
296   truth is her prophetic gift, the soul, her sacred page (3)
299   one soul should perish lost in shades of night (1)
299   pour out thy soul for them in prayer victorious (4)
318   deck thyself, my soul, with gladness (T,1)
318   light, who dost my soul enlighten (2)
320   wine of the soul in mercy shed (1)
342   redeeming soul and body by water and the Word (2)
350   the guilty soul a sure retreat (4)
365   Lord, cleanse my sins, my soul renew (6)
391   with heart and soul and voice (1,2,3)
401   visit, then, this soul of mine (3)
413   that his pardoned soul is worthy of a place in paradise (2)
413   believe that spirit triumphs .. commend .. soul to God (3)
428   receive my soul, he cries (3)
432   what wondrous love is this, O my soul (T,1,2)
432   bear the dreadful curse for my soul (1)
432   lay aside his crown for my soul (2)
433   till my raptured soul shall find rest beyond the river (R)
433   near the cross, a trembling soul, love & mercy found me (2)
434   love to man his soul sustained (2)
435   love so amazing, so divine, demands my soul, my life (4)
435   Love so amazing ... demands my soul, my life, my all (4)
445   He lives, my hungry soul to feed (2)
455   awake, my soul, and sing of him who died for thee (1)
461   let our whole soul an offering be to our Redeemer's name (2)
466   come down, O Love divine, seek thou this soul of mine (T,1)
466   so the yearning strong, with which the soul will long (3)
470   rich in things and poor in soul (3)
474   rise, my soul, and stretch thy wings (T,1)
474   rise, my soul, and haste away to seats prepared above (1)
474   so a soul that's born of God longs to view his... face (2)
479   healed the sick and freed the soul (2)
487   heart and soul consecrate on this thy holy day (4)

493 O may my soul on thee repose and with sweet sleep (4)
502 sun of my soul, thou Savior dear (T,1)
528 where shall my wondering soul begin (T,1)
531 speak to my...soul & say, "I am thy love...God...all" (4)
543 confirm thy soul in self-control, thy liberty in law (2)
545 O be swift, my soul, to answer him; be jubilant, my feet (3)
545 and the soul of wrong his slave (5)

soul's
79 thee will I honor, thou, my soul's glory, joy and crown (1)
252 prayer is the soul's sincere desire (T,1)

souls
19 respond, ye souls in endless rest (3)
23 our souls are his immortal breath (2)
52 death ... shall join our souls to thee (4)
56 God preserves the souls of those who on his truth depend (5)
87 name of Jesus! How it thrills our souls with joy (3)
100 ye weary spirits, rest; ye mournful souls, be glad (2)
102 come, all ye souls by sin oppressed (3)
106 weary souls fore'er rejoice (1)
112 God, who did your souls retrieve (2)
132 on our souls thy graces shower (2)
134 our souls, how heavily they go to reach eternal joys (2)
161 bringing to hungry souls the bread of life (2)
161 showing to wandering souls the path of light (3)
192 all Christly souls are one in him (4)
198 with flame of freedom in their souls (1)
204 from famished souls, from sorrow's stress (3)
232 and heaven comes down our souls to greet (4)
235 take from our souls the strain and stress (4)
243 gainst lies & lusts & wrongs let courage rule our souls (3)
257 let our hearts and souls be stirred (1)
292 new-born souls, whose days, reclaimed from error's ways (4)
310 bid our inmost souls rejoice in hope of perfect love (5)
312 for 'twas to bless such souls as these the Lord...came (2)
315 our needy souls sustain with fresh supplies of love (2)
319 bread of life with which our souls are fed (3)
320 the token that by thy grace our souls are fed (2)
321 upper room where fainting souls are fed (1)
325 rich blood that Jesus shed to raise our souls to heaven (2)
325 millions of souls, in glory now ... fed and feasted here (3)
328 so dear the tie where souls agree in Jesus' dying love (4)
329 and thirst our souls from thee to fill (3)
331 cheers our famished souls with food (1)
335 they watch for souls (3)
335 souls for whom the Lord did heavenly bliss forego (3)
335 souls that must forever live in rapture or in woe (3)
335 watch thou daily o'er their souls (4)
337 and love the souls whom thou dost love (3)
343 O grant its rich and swelling notes may lift our souls (3)
343 lift our souls on high (3)
350 when in faith our souls draw near (3)
355 from old unfaith our souls release (3)
359 souls, condemned and dying, are precious in his sight (2)
365 thy noblest wonders here we view in souls renewed (6)

365 noblest wonders ... in souls renewed, and sins forgiven (6)
367 thirsty souls receive supplies .. sweet refreshment find (2)
368 bread of our souls whereon we feed (2)
381 where meek souls will receive him... dear Christ enters (3)
397 bring our ransomed souls at last where they need no star (4)
407 thy witness in the souls of men (3)
438 Christ alone our souls will feed (4)
439 once he died, our souls to save, Alleluia (2)
446 'tis the spring of souls today (2)
462 make us souls that understand (2)
467 come, Holy Ghost, our souls inspire (T,1)
476 O God of truth, whom ... reverent souls adore (3)
481 how its splendor challenges the souls that greatly dare (5)
509 in better worlds our souls shall boast (5)
518 let manna to our souls be given (3)
523 for souls redeemed, for sins forgiven (4)
524 by thee the souls of men are fed with gifts of grace (2)
524 souls of men are fed with gifts of grace supernal (2)
532 whose music like a mighty wind the souls of men uplifted (3)
535 happy the souls to Jesus joined (T,1)
548 souls that passed and left no name (3)

souls'
491 be thou our souls' perserver, O God, for thou dost know (4)

sound
14 thy praise shall sound from shore to shore (2)
24 come, sound his praise abroad, and hymns of glory sing (T,1)
35 for the mystic harmony linking sense to sound and sight (3)
43 no real voice nor sound amid the radiant orbs be found (3)
55 let the amen sound from his people again (4)
82 nor can the memory find a sweeter sound than thy... name (2)
82 sweeter sound than thy blest name, O Savior of mankind (2)
86 so now, and till we die sound we thy praises high (4)
91 let all the earth around ring joyous with the sound (3)
92 amazing grace! how sweet the sound (T,1)
100 blow ye trumpet, blow! The gladly solemn sound (T,1)
131 sound with...thy saints below, the depth of love divine (4)
165 thanks we give & adoration for thy Gospel's joyful sound (2)
168 could I sound the glories forth which in my Savior shine (1)
204 where sound the cries of race and clan (1)
222 when he shall come with trumpet sound (4)
343 instruments of loftier sound assist his feeble praise (2)
489 may thy Gospel's joyful sound conquer sinners, comfort (4)
527 in vain the first-born seraph tries to sound the depths (2)
527 seraph tries to sound the depths of love divine (2)
547 let rocks their silence break, the sound prolong (3)

sounded
545 he has sounded forth the trumpet (3)

soundeth
107 day by day his sweet voice soundeth (1)

sounding
22 shall fill thy courts with sounding praise (3)
392 repeat the sounding joy (2)

sounds
- 14   in cheerful sounds all voices raise (4)
- 33   clearer sounds the angel hymn, "Good will to men" (2)
- 81   how sweet the name of Jesus sounds in a believer's ear (T,1)
- 164   I see the sights that dazzle, the tempting sounds I hear (2)
- 390   and ever o'er its Babel sounds the blessed angels sing (2)
- 402   Alleluia, Alleluia! sounds through the earth and skies (5)

source
- 89   thou hidden source of calm repose (T,1)
- 131   source of... old prophetic fire, fountain of life & love (1)
- 132   come, thou source of joy and gladness, breathe thy life (1)
- 172   and trembling to its source return ((2)
- 220   Jesus, priceless treasure, source of purest pleasure (T,1)
- 352   source of all strength thou art; thy gospel bless (3)
- 357   He is Alpha and Omega, He the source, the ending he (1)
- 474   both speed them to their source (2)
- 511   God ... the source of bounteous yield (1)

south
- 192   in him no south or north (1)
- 192   in him meet south and north (4)

sovereign
- 3   thy sovereign majesty may we in glory see (4)
- 22   He sovereign power, without our aid made us of clay (2)
- 23   His sovereign power our bodies made (2)
- 24   Jehovah is the sovereign God, the universal King (1)
- 25   O God, our King, whose sovereign sway (4)
- 31   his great decrees and sovereign will (3)
- 31   and will this sovereign King of glory condescend (4)
- 51   leave to his sovereign sway to choose and to command (3)
- 130   thy sovereign grace to all extends (2)
- 130   and depth of sovereign grace (1)
- 215   and works his sovereign will (2)
- 247   wondrous sovereign of the sea, Jesus Savior, pilot me (2)
- 346   sovereign God, receive . gift thy willing servants offer (3)
- 351   eternal God and sovereign Lord (T,1)
- 399   O Sovereign meek and lowly! (1)
- 415   and did my Sovereign die (1)
- 477   bring to our world of strife thy sovereign word of peace (4)
- 531   O Love, thy sovereign aid impart to save me (3)

sovereignty
- 203   neath the burdens there, thy sovereignty has held (3)

sown
- 348   seeds of truth be sown where we lay this cornerstone (2)
- 512   the seed by him provided is sown o'er hill and plain (1)
- 522   wheat and tares together sown (2)

space
- 206   though there be dark, unchartered space (4)
- 456   the Lord of interstellar space and conqueror of time (1)
- 473   whose robe is the light, whose canopy space (2)
- 541   aloft in solitudes of space (2)
- 549   behold us, Lord, a little space (T,1)

spaces
541   men who fly through the great spaces of the sky (1)

spacious
43   the spacious firmament on high (T,1)
543   O beautiful for spacious skies, for amber waves of grain (T)

spake
200   as once he spake in Zion, so now he speaks again (1)
394   spake the seraph and forthwith appeared a shining throng (5)
451   who sat and spake unto the three (3)
464   worthy ... work of him...who spake a world from naught (3)

spangled
43   spangled heavens, a shining frame (1)

spare
94   me, the chief of sinners, spare (1)

spares
66   father-like he tends and spares us (3)
521   from all evil things he spares them (2)

sparing
17   and when I think that God, his Son not sparing (3)

spark
464   kindled by a spark of grace (1)

sparkling
33   o'er white expanses sparkling pure (2)

sparrow
295   behold, the sparrow findeth out a house wherein to rest (3)

sparrows
32   shall not, in the mountain pine, disturb a sparrows nest (3)

speak
5   children of the heavenly King may speak ... joys abroad (2)
137   testify to all mankind, and speak in every heart (3)
140   O speak, and I shall live (3)
152   only thee...to know in all I think or speak or do (1)
161   speak to our fearful hearts by conflict rent (1)
164   O speak to reassure me, to hasten or control (3)
164   O speak, and make me listen, thou guardian of my soul (3)
168   O could I speak the matchless worth (T,1)
172   work and speak and think for thee (3)
186   all I think or speak or do is one great sacrifice (4)
195   that I may speak in living echoes of thy tone (1)
195   Lord, speak to me (T,1)
200   speak, and, behold! we answer; command, and we obey (4)
227   now my remnant of days would I speak of his praise (6)
235   speak through the earth-quake, wind and fire (5)
238   Christian, dost thou hear them, how they speak thee fair (3)
239   shall I fear to own his cause .. blush to speak his name (1)
262   speak to our hearts . let us feel . kindling of thy love (1)

262   to hear the whispers of thy grace & hear thee inly speak (4)
266   take time to be holy, speak oft with thy Lord (T,1)
274   speak, that I may follow faster (2)
274   Master speak ...thou knowest ..the yearning of my heart (3)
274   Master, speak! O, speak to me (4)
274   speak to me by name, O Master, let me know it is to me (2)
282   where only Christ is heard to speak (2)
339   let them speak thy Word of power (3)
340   teach thou our lips of thee to speak (3)
343   we bid the pealing organ wait to speak alone thy will (3)
352   speak, O eternal Lord, out of thy living Word (3)
452   speak his sorrows ended; hail his triumph now (2)
529   speak to my heart, in blessing speak (3)
529   speak, or thou never hence shalt move (3)
531   speak to my...soul & say, "I am thy love...God...all" (4)

speakest
85   in human form thou speakest to men the Father's mind (2)

speaketh
30   in prophet's word he spoke of old; he speaketh still (2)
460   God yet speaketh by his Spirit (3)
460   speaketh to the hearts of men (3)

speaking
18   God is speaking; praise him for his open Word (3)
41   Spirit in our spirit speaking, make us sons of God (4)
62   language, glad and golden, speaking to us day and night (1)
164   O let me hear thee speaking in accents clear and still (3)
371   speaking to saints, to prophets, kings, and sages (2)

speaks
1   He speaks, and listening to his voice (5)
32   he speaks, and in his heavenly height (1)
45   he speaks to me everywhere (2)
103   here speaks the Comforter, tenderly saying (2)
116   Jesus sweetly speaks to me (2)
136   when love speaks loud and clear (3)
200   as once he spake in Zion, so now he speaks again (1)

spear
408   to plow-share beat the sword, to pruning-hook the spear (2)
410   song that shall conquer evil & shatter the spear & sword (2)

sped
47   our heart's true home when all our years have sped (3)
397   as with joyous steps they sped to that lowly manger bed (2)
447   the three sad days have quickly sped (3)

speech
33   day unto day utter speech ... night to night proclaim (3)
252   prayer is the simplest form of speech (3)
252   speech that infant lips can try (3)
260   thou dost not wait till human speech...implore (1)
260   till human speech thy gifts divine implore (1)
476   in speech that flows to melody, in holiness of heart (4)

speeches
    484   from all the easy speeches that comfort cruel men (2)

speed
    296   O living Church, thine errand speed (4)
    299   give of thy wealth to speed them on their way (4)
    474   both speed them to their source (2)
    480   speed forth thy flight (3)

speedy
    359   he comes with succor speedy to those who suffer wrong (2)

spend
    25   to spend one day with thee on earth exceeds a thousand (1)
    159   pure delight . single hour ... before thy throne I spend (3)
    168   a blest eternity I'll spend triumphant in his grace (3)
    190   to spend thyself nor count the cost (3)
    266   spend much time in secret with Jesus alone (2)

spent
    161   who by our own false hopes and aims are spent (1)

sphere
    64   center and soul of every sphere (1)

spheres
    45   round me rings the music of the spheres (1)

spill
    198   to spill no drop of blood (2)

spire
    41   soaring spire and ruined city, these our hopes ... show (3)
    41   spire and ruined city, these our hopes and failures show (3)

spirit
    2   Father, Son, and Holy Spirit, blessed Trinity (5)
    3   Spirit of holiness, on us descend! (2)
    3   ne'er from us depart, Spirit of power! (3)
    8   holy Father, holy, Son, holy Spirit: three we name thee (4)
    19   God ... Father, ... Son, ... Spirit, Three in One (4)
    20   the Spirit and the gifts are ours through Him (4)
    30   his spirit floweth free, high surging where it will (2)
    36   thee in man's spirit we behold (4)
    36   man's spirit ... thine image and thyself are there (4)
    41   Spirit in our spirit speaking, make us sons of God (4)
    46   by thine unerring spirit led (2)
    58   the Spirit who in them did sing to us his music lendeth (3)
    60   praise the Spirit, Three in One (7)
    78   to God the Father ... Son ... Spirit ... Three in One (4)
    81   it makes the wounded spirit whole (2)
    105   and shall I dare his spirit grieve (3)
    106   Holy Spirit, faithful guide (T,1)
    112   God, the Spirit, asks you why (3)
    114   we by his Spirit prove and know the things of God (4)
    132   O hear our supplication, Blessed Spirit, God of peace (2)
    134   come, Holy Spirit, heavenly Dove (T,1,5)

135 Holy Spirit, Truth divine, dawn upon this soul of mine (T,1)
135 Holy Spirit, Love divine, glow within this heart of mine (2)
135 Holy Spirit, Power divine (3)
135 wake my spirit, clear my sight (1)
135 Holy Spirit, Right divine (4)
136 O Spirit of the living God, thou light and fire divine (T,1)
137 Spirit of faith, come down, reveal the things of God (T,1)
137 Spirit of faith, descend and show the virtue of his name (3)
138 Spirit of God, descend upon my heart (T,1)
139 whose Spirit breathes the active flame (1)
140 and here I will unwearied lie, till thou thy Spirit give (3)
145 heal my wounded, broken spirit, save me by thy grace (3)
154 fill with thy spirit till all shall see Christ ...in me (4)
155 since, Lord, thou dost defend us with thy spirit (3)
160 cross; let not its weight fill thy weak spirit with alarm (2
160 his strength shall bear thy spirit up (2)
161 still let thy spirit unto us be given (2)
180 and with thyself my spirit fill (2)
199 restores the lost, and binds the spirit broken (2)
201 create in us thy spirit; give us a love like thine (3)
205 when my spirit, clothed immortal, wings its flight (3)
205 my spirit ... wings its flight to realms of day (3)
212 but then the Holy Spirit revives my soul again (1)
224 born of his spirit, washed in his blood (1)
250 still let the Spirit cry, in all his soldiers, "Come" (3)
253 a spirit still prepared, and armed with jealous care (3)
257 till thy spirit breaks our night with the beams of truth (2)
266 thus led by his spirit to fountains of love (4)
267 open my eyes, illumine me, Spirit divine (R)
273 with thy spirit recreate me, pure and strong and true (1)
273 keep me ever, by thy spirit, pure and strong and true (5)
277 O come, and dwell with me, spirit of power within (T,1)
281 and let my spirit cleave to thee (4)
283 O breathe thy loving spirit into every troubled breast (2)
284 that I may sing above to Father, Spirit, and to thee (6)
298 laud and honor to the Father ...to the Son ...the Spirit (4)
303 who art, with God the Father and Spirit, ever blest (4)
337 pour out thy spirit from on high (T,1)
338 joined in one spirit to our Head (2)
340 o'er all the world thy spirit send (4)
342 baptizing in the name of Father, Son, and Spirit (2)
344 and ever by thy Spirit guide (4)
345 let the comforter and friend, thy Holy Spirit, meet (2)
348 may thy spirit here give rest (2)
349 to God the Father, God the Son, and Spirit we adore (4)
356 may one Lord .. faith .. Word, one Spirit lead us still (4)
360 by thine own eternal spirit rule in all our hearts alone (2)
369 my spirit pants for thee, O living word (1)
370 praise him...for the Spirit which protects us (3)
403 his spirit only can bestow, who reigns in light above (1)
405 unto thee, with God the Father and the Spirit, glory be (5)
413 believe that spirit triumphs .. commend .. soul to God (3)
419 a glorious band, the chosen few on whom the Spirit came (3)
440 every humble spirit shares it (2)
446 Alleluia yet again to the Spirit raising (5)
457 by the almighty Spirit led and filled with faith & love (1)
460 God yet speaketh by his Spirit (3)

350　here thine angelic spirits send their solemn praise (5)
354　come and cheer our spirits by thine advent here (4)
413　Lord, we are able, our spirits are thine (R)
413　heroic spirits answer now, as then, in Galilee (4)
454　help, ye bright angelic spirits (4)
488　we reach the rest remaining to spirits of the blest (4)
496　ere repose our spirits seal (1)

spirits'
260　our spirit's unseen friend, high heaven's Lord (1)

spite
151　living still, in spite of dungeon, fire and sword (1)
272　and spite of fears, pride ruled my will (2)
353　left .. lonesome place of death, despite .. rage of foes (3)

splendor
27　'tis only the splendor of light hideth thee (4)
29　o splendor of God's glory bright (T,1)
41　thou who wrought creation's splendor (1)
50　so full of splendor and of joy, beauty and light (1)
173　create in us... splendor that dawns when hearts are kind (4)
203　but in the eyes of men, redeemed and free, a splendor (4)
203　a splendor greater yet while serving thee (4)
258　come to him who made this splendor (1)
264　a fresh and solemn splendor still is given (3)
318　come into the daylight's splendor (1)
398　thou robest in thy splendor the simplest ways of men (2)
446　the queen of seasons, bright with the day of splendor (3)
473　pavilioned in splendor, and girded with praise (1)
481　how its splendor challenges the souls that greatly dare (5)
546　Judge eternal, throned in splendor (T,1)
552　band of shining worlds in splendor through the skies (1)

splendors
33　the solemn splendors of the night (2)
33　splendors ... burn brighter through the cold (2)
390　peace shall over ... earth its ancient splendors fling (3)
456　there heavenly splendors shine (2)

spoke
30　in prophet's word he spoke of old; he speaketh still (2)
131　moved by thee, the prophets wrote and spoke (2)

spoken
18　thanks to God whose Word was spoken (T,1)
18　Word was spoken in the deed that made the earth (1)
18　God has spoken; praise him for his open Word (1,2)
42　praise the Lord! for he hath spoken (1)
199　for he whom Jesus loved hath truly spoken (2)
293　glorious things of thee are spoken (T,1,3)
314　for the words, which thou hast spoken (1)
320　by whom the words of life were spoken (1)
460　God hath spoken by his prophets (T,1)
460　God hath ... spoken his unchanging Word (1)
460　God hath spoken by Christ Jesus (2)
460　spoken by ... Word incarnate, God of God, ere time began (2)

spot
  50   that in the darkest spot of earth some love is found (2)
 119   to thee whose blood can cleanse each spot (2)
 358   will its beams alone gild the spot that gave them birth (2)

spotless
  76   faithfully he bore it spotless to the last (3)
 193   and spotless here below (3)
 193   this is the bond of perfectness, thy spotless charity (6)
 220   thine I am, O spotless Lamb (1)
 283   finish ...thy new creation, pure and spotless let us be (4)
 344   give .. wisdom from above, spotless .. peaceable & kind (2)

sprang
  76   at his voice creation sprang at once to sight (2)

spread
   1   spread thro' all the earth abroad the honors of thy name (2)
  37   spread the flowing seas abroad and built the lofty skies (1)
  40   thy fingers spread the mountains and plains (1)
  43   spread the truth from pole to pole (2)
  44   thy glory thou hast spread afar in all the starry frame (1)
  58   the heavenly shield around them spread (2)
  71   go spread your trophies at his feet (3)
 132   spread thy light from the height which knows no measure (1)
 143   while life's dark maze I tread & griefs around me spread (3)
 203   we've seen thy glory like a mantle spread o'er hill and (4)
 237   or its sordid treasures spread to work me harm (2)
 309   come, and spread thy banner here (2)
 313   Savior, abide with us, and spread thy table in our heart (1)
 315   author of life divine, who hast a table spread (T,1)
 317   spread with reverence this holy feast ... remember thee (1)
 321   thy supper, Lord, is spread in every quiet upper room (1)
 326   this is the heavenly table spread for me (2)
 339   O let them spread thy name, their mission fully prove (4)
 398   long, alas, witholden, now spread from shore to shore (1)
 453   spread abroad the victor's fame (3)
 461   come as the dove & spread thy wings ... of peaceful love (3)
 472   his kingdom spread from shore to shore (1)
 476   help us to spread thy gracious reign till greed .. cease (2)
 495   through the long night watches may thine angels spread (5)
 495   spread their white wings above me, watching round my bed (5)
 498   spread thy love's broad banner o'er us (3)
 515   how wide the bounteous love is spread (3)
 524   where golden fields spread fair and broad (3)
 534   may the shadow of thy presence around our camp be spread (2)

spreading
 231   beneath the spreading heavens no creature but is fed (3)
 365   nor ... spreading Gospel rest till through the world (4)
 370   bringing freedom, spreading truth (1)

spreads
 324   rank on rank the host of heaven spreads its vanguard (3)
 324   spreads its vanguard on the way (3)
 325   the King of heaven his table spreads (T,1)
 331   Jesus spreads his banner o'er us (T,1)

331 banquet spreads before us of his mystic flesh and blood (1)
464 more & more it spreads and grows ever mighty to prevail (2)
464 now it spreads along the skies (4)
528 he spreads his arms to embrace you all (4)

spreadst
67 thou spreadst a table in my sight (5)

spring
29 o Light of light, light's living spring (1)
38 well-spring of the joy of living (3)
79 robed in...blooming garb of spring: Jesus is fairer (2)
125 spring thou up within my heart (4)
145 thou the spring of all my comfort, more than life for me (4)
178 gentleness and grace...spring from union,Lord, with thee (4)
184 it has no spring of action sure, it varies with the wind (2)
205 gushing from the rock before me...a spring of joy I see (2)
312 joyful that we ourselves are thine ... offspring (3)
354 O come, thou Day-spring (4)
359 love, joy and hope, like flowers, spring in his path (3)
359 spring in his path to birth (3)
387 offspring of the virgin's womb (2)
401 Day-spring from on high, be near (1)
442 spring has now unwrapped the flowers (T,1)
446 'tis the spring of souls today (2)
452 earth with joy confesses, clothing her for spring (2)
550 and spring adorns the earth no more (4)

springeth
441 love is come again like wheat that springeth green (R)

springing
293 streams of living waters, springing from eternal love (2)
366 all her heart with joy is springing (2)
512 with the gentle showers doth bless the springing grain (1)

springs
25 the joy that from thy presence springs (1)
180 guard my first springs of thought and will (2)
219 let me ... think of thee ... new heart springs up in me (2)
273 like the springs and running waters make me crystal pure (2)
367 springs of consolation rise to cheer the fainting mind (2)
398 rise in... new creation which springs from love and thee (3)

sprinkles
122 and sprinkles now the throne of grace (2)

spurned
502 if some poor wandering child of thine have spurned (4)
502 spurned today the voice divine (4)

squadrons
425 the winged squadrons of the sky look down (3)

square
481 within whose four-square walls shall come no night (1)

squared
  348 by wise master builders squared, here be living stones (4)

stable
   90 lo! his star is shining above the stable (1)
  376 in the bleak midwinter a stable place sufficed (2)
  377 but ah! within that stable old the beasts ... behold (2)

stablished
   30 established is his law, and changeless it shall stand (2)
  473 hath stablished it fast by a changeless decree (3)

staff
   67 thy rod and staff my comfort still (4)
   68 thy rod and staff me comfort still (3)
   86 our shepherd and our pride, our staff and song (3)
  534 kept ... people by the strength of thy staff and rod (1)

stage
  180 thy daily stage of duty run (1)

stain
  515 may the hands be pure from stain with which...we gain (4)

stained
  228 in the old rugged cross, stained with blood so divine (3)
  317 thy holy face is stained with bitter tears (2)
  434 love to man his soul sustained (2)

stainless
  517 may we keep our holy calling stainless in... fair renown (5)

stains
  269 while passion stains, and folly dims our youth (2)
  421 lose all their guilty stains (1)
  483 when he had purged our stains, he took his seat above (2)

stall
  396 infant holy, infant lowly, for his bed a cattle stall (T,1)
  400 low lies his head with the beasts of the stall (2)

stalwart
  189 our loyal love, our stalwart faith (2)
  351 race of men of flaming heart and stalwart mind (3)

stammering
  421 when this poor lisping, stammering tongue lies silent (5)

stand
   16 stand up and bless his glorious name (5)
   16 stand up and bless the Lord, ye people of his choice (T,1)
   16 stand up and bless the Lord your God (1)
   16 stand up and bless the Lord; the Lord your God adore (5)
   22 firm as a rock thy truth must stand (4)
   30 established is his law, and changeless it shall stand (2)
   31 his wrath and justice stand to guard his holy law (2)
   48 I'll strengthen thee,help thee, and cause thee to stand (2)

127   bold shall I stand in thy great day (2)
173   stand with humble courage for truth with hearts uncowed (1)
184   I sink in life's alarms when by myself I stand (1)
195   that I may stand firm on the rock, and strong in thee (2)
206   give us courage now to stand (1)
211   though hosts encamp around me, firm in the fight I stand (1)
219   held in thy law, I stand (4)
222   on Christ, the solid rock, I stand (R)
222   faultless to stand before the throne (4)
236   we stand to bless thee ere our worship cease (1)
243   in keenest strife, Lord, may we stand (3)
244   when the storms of life are raging, stand by me (T,1)
244   thou who rulest wind and water, stand by me (1)
244   in the midst of tribulation, stand by me (2)
244   in the midst of faults and failures, stand by me (3)
244   thou who knowest all about me, stand by me (3)
244   when I'm growing old and feeble, stand by me (4)
244   O thou Lily of the Valley, stand by me (4)
244   thou who never lost a battle, stand by me (2)
248   stand up, stand up for Jesus (T,1,2,3,4)
248   stand in his strength alone (3)
250   o'ercome through Christ alone, and stand entire at last (2)
250   stand ...in his great might ... all his strength endued (2)
291   on Jordan's stormy banks I stand (T,1)
294   I love thy Church, O God! Her walls before thee stand (2)
300   fear not, brethren; joyful stand (3)
300   joyful stand on the borders of our land (3)
303   they stand, those halls of Zion, all jubilant with song (2)
312   shepherd stand with all engaging charms (1)
312   see Israel's Gentle Shepherd stand (T,1)
324   and with fear and trembling stand (1)
337   within thy temple when they stand to teach the truth (2)
340   thou bidst us go with thee to stand against hell's (2)
340   stand against hell's marshalled powers (2)
359   his name shall stand forever; that name to us is love (4)
365   convey thy praise round the whole earth and never stand (3)
417   beneath the cross of Jesus I fain would take my stand (T,1)
440   joy unknown, ... saints shall stand before the throne (4)
446   but today amidst the twelve thou didst stand, bestowing (4)
469   races and peoples, lo, we stand divided (2)
486   who, when fears beset them, stand fast and fight and die (2)
504   active and watchful, stand we all before thee (1)
509   mighty hand by which supported still we stand (1)
524   valleys stand so thick with corn ... they are singing (1)

standard
179   under the standard exalted and royal (1)
233   still lift your standard high ... march in firm array (5)

standeth
242   behind the dim unknown, standeth God within the shadow (4)
544   yet to eternity standeth thy Word (3)

standing
108   O Jesus, thou art standing outside the fast-closed door (T)
108   O shame,thrice shame upon us, to keep his standing there (1)
221   standing on the promises (T,1,2,3,4,R)

221 standing on the promises of Christ my King (1)
221 standing on the promises of God (1,2,3,4,R)
221 standing on the promises of God my Savior (R)
221 standing on the promises that cannot fail (2)
221 standing on the promises of Christ the Lord (3)
221 standing on the promises I cannot fail (4)
253 forever standing on its guard and watching unto prayer (3)
460 one sure faith yet standing fast (3)
548 standing in the living present (1)

stands
9 his truth forever stands secure (2)
32 the rolling sun stands still (1)
53 his goodness stands approved, unchanged from day to day (4)
94 there for me the Savior stands (4)
94 Savior stands, holding forth his wounded hands (4)
104 Jesus ready stands to save you (1)
111 stands knocking at the door of every sinner's heart (2)
122 before the throne my surety stands (1)
141 have faith in God, my soul, His cross forever stands (3)
184 it only stands unbent amid the clashing strife (4)
242 while the coward stands aside (2)
281 remains and stands forever sure (1)
308 unshaken as eternal hills, immovable she stands (4)
345 thou, whose unmeasured temple stands (T,1)
345 temple stands, built over earth and sea (1)
362 he stands in the midst of nations (3)
438 but now at God's right hand he stands (1)
456 there stands he with unhurrying feet (2)
500 thy kingdom stands, and grows forever, till all ... own (4)

star
12 beyond the range of sun and star, and yet beside us here (1)
64 thy glory flames from sun and star (1)
64 star of our hope, thy softened light cheers (2)
90 lo! his star is shining above the stable (1)
117 I looked to Jesus, and I found in him my star, my sun (3)
167 let not my star of hope grow dim or disappear (2)
343 there is a voice in every star, in every breeze a song (1)
358 see that glory-beaming star (1)
358 higher yet that star ascends (2)
365 in every star thy wisdom shines (1)
366 her Star is risen; her Light is come (2)
375 love was born at Christmas; star & angels gave the sign (1)
379 hail the star, that from far bright with hope is burning (3)
380 there's a song in the air, there's a star in the sky (T,1)
380 the star rains its fire while the beautiful sing (1,2)
380 in the light of that star lie the ages impearled (3)
382 ye have seen his natal star (3)
383 they looked up and saw a star shining in the east (2)
383 and by the light of that same star three wise men came (3)
383 and to follow the star wherever it went (3)
383 this star drew nigh to the northwest (4)
393 wondrous star, lend thy light (4)
395 heaven's star shone brightly forth, glory all around him (2)
397 as with gladness men of old did the guiding star behold (T)
397 bring our ransomed souls at last where they need no star (4)

397	need no star to guide, where no clouds thy glory hide (4)
399	O morning star, how fair and bright (T,1)
400	Star of the East, the horizon adorning (1,5)
401	Day-star, in my heart appear (1)
402	following yonder star (1)
402	O star of wonder, star of night (R)
402	star with royal beauty bright (R)
405	fairer than the sun at morning was the star (2)
405	the star that told his birth (2)
408	the Day-star clear and bright of every man and nation (1)
431	the star is dimmed that lately shone (1)
433	the bright and morning star shed its beams around me (2)
456	as altar candle sheds its light as surely as a star (2)
476	whose power upholds both flower and flaming star (1)
492	we lift our hearts to thee, O Day-star from on high (T,1)
506	but mid the light declining the evening star is shining (1)
513	he paints the wayside flower, he lights the evening star (2)
521	nesting bird nor star in heaven such a refuge ... given (1)

starlit
377	in Bethlehem neath starlit skies (T,1)

starry
44	thy glory thou hast spread afar in all the starry frame (1)
79	and all the twinkling starry host: Jesus shines brighter (3)
552	almighty hand leads forth in beauty all the starry band (1)

stars
11	countless stars by night that shine (2)
17	I see the stars, I hear the rolling thunder (1)
35	sun and moon, and stars of light (2)
37	moon shines full at his command, and all the stars obey (1)
38	stars and angels sing around thee (2)
38	mortals join the happy chorus, which the... stars began (4)
38	chorus, which the morning stars began (4)
40	thy hands have set the heavens with stars (1)
41	bringing suns and stars to birth (1)
41	moon and stars, thy power displayed (2)
42	praise him, all ye stars of light (1)
43	all the stars that round her burn ... confirm (2)
44	the moon and stars ordained by thee (2)
76	thrones and dominations, stars upon their way (2)
78	creator of the stars of night (T,1)
263	sun, moon, and stars forgot, upward I fly (5)
337	Savior, like stars in thy right hand thy servants ... be (2)
365	sun, moon ... stars convey thy praise round the... earth (3)
381	above thy deep & dreamless sleep the silent stars go by (1)
381	O morning stars, together proclaim the holy birth (2)
384	the stars in the sky looked down where he lay (1)
474	sun and moon and stars decay (1)
486	O God, before whose altar the stars like tapers burn (T,1)
503	through the glory and the grace of the stars (3)
503	through ... stars that veil thy face our hearts ascend (3)
503	when forever from our sight pass the stars, the day (4)
503	pass the stars, the day, the night (4)
505	soon as dies the sunset glory, stars of heaven shine (2)
505	stars of heaven shine out above (2)
505	as the darkness deepens o'er us, lo! eternal stars arise (4)

state
147   teach us, in every state,to make thy will our own (4)
191   the patriots nations need ... the bulwarks of the state (4)
191   laws and habits of the state (2)
277   I ask no higher state, indulge me but in this (4)
423   the Lord of men and angels rode on in lowly state (2)

statesmen's
370   statesmen's, teacher's, hero's treasure (1)

station
7   so may we, in lowly station join the choristers above (2)
173   knows not race nor station as boundaries of the mind (4)
275   gladly take my station there and wait for thee (2)
453   Jesus takes the highest station (4)

stay
4   an ever present help and stay (3)
30   his love shall be our strength and stay, while ages roll (3)
105   I cannot stay; my heart I yield without delay (5)
115   what a blessed hope is ours while here on earth we stay (2)
155   no foes shall stay his might, though he with giants fight (2
170   teach me the wayward feet to stay (2)
216   He is my refuge and my stay (2)
222   he then is all my hope and stay (3)
236   our balm in sorrow, and our stay in strife (4)
262   here...my God, vouchsafe to stay & bid my heart rejoice (3)
265   stay thou near by (2)
289   who, like thyself, my guide and stay can be (3)
329   O Jesus, ever with us stay (3)
342   we at thy feet would stay (3)
383   and there it did both stop and stay (4)
384   and stay by my cradle till morning is nigh (2)
384   be near me, Lord Jesus, I ask thee to stay close by me (3)
406   build ye the road, and falter not, nor stay (2)
474   rivers to the ocean run, nor stay in all their course (2)
529   with thee all night I mean to stay (1)
552   be thou our ruler, guardian, guide and stay (2)

stayed
125   my trust on thee is stayed ... help from thee I bring (2)

steadfast
51   let us in life, in death, thy steadfast truth declare (4)
65   unto such as keep his covenant ... steadfast in his way (5)
159   Let my soul look up with a steadfast hope (2)
173   thy steadfast face set forward where love and duty shone (2)
191   of steadfast will, patient, courageous, strong and true (3)
278   my steadfast soul, from falling free ... no longer move (4)
333   assurance of tender charity and steadfast faith (2)
477   the quiet of a steadfast faith, calm of a call obeyed (2)
520   steadfast faith & earnest prayer keep sacred vows secure (4)

steady
253   I want a true regard, a single steady aim (4)
274   with obedience glad & steady still to follow every word (4)
355   new thorns to pierce that steady brow (1)

steal
495   shadows of the evening steal across the sky (1)

steals
398   Light of the world, thy beauty steals into every heart (2)
536   steals on the ear the distant triumph song (5)

steep
201   who lovest all thy lost ones on every mountain steep (1)
245   or climbing the mountain way steep (3)
269   however rough and steep the path may be (4)
419   they climbed the steep ascent of heaven through peril (3)
502   my wearied eyelids gently steep (2)

steeps
157   we may not climb the heavenly steeps (2)

stem
239   must I not stem the flood (3)

step
272   one step enough for me (1)
274   with a step more firm and free (2)

steps
58   the fire divine their steps that led ... before us (2)
70   with heedless steps I ran (3)
162   teach me thus thy steps to trace (3)
178   around thy steps below (1)
199   follow with reverent steps the great example of him (3)
205   my weary steps may falter, and my soul athirst may be (2)
213   Savior, where'er thy steps I see (4)
238   how the powers of darkness rage thy steps around (1)
249   forget the steps already trod and onward urge thy way (2)
263   there let the way appear, steps unto heaven (3)
371   guiding our steps to thine eternal day (1)
397   as with joyous steps they sped to that lowly manger bed (2)
498   praise for light so brightly shining on our steps (1)
498   shining on our steps from heaven above (1)
510   while on in Jesus' steps we go to see thy face above (4)
517   little feet our steps may follow in a safe & narrow way (3)

stern
543   pilgrim feet, whose stern, impassioned stress (2)

stewards
181   may we thy bounties thus as stewards true receive (2)

still
20   the body they may kill: God's truth abideth still (4)
20   still our ancient foe doth seek to work us woe (1)
28   still may we dwell secure (2)
30   who was, and is, and is to be, and still the same! (1,3)
30   in prophet's word he spoke of old; he speaketh still (2)
32   the rolling sun stands still (1)
41   yet thy love doth seek him still (2)
48   for I am thy God, and will still give thee aid (2)

48 the soul that on Jesus still leans for repose (5)
49 with countless gifts of love, and still is ours today (1)
54 as ... God our fathers owned, so thou art still our King (4)
56 praises of my God shall still my heart and tongue employ (1)
58 the fire divine ... still goeth bright before us (2)
58 heavenly shield...still high holden o'er us (2)
59 and pray that thou still our defender wilt be (3)
65 unto those who still remember his commandments, and obey (5)
66 praise him, still the same forever (2)
67 thy rod and staff my comfort still (4)
68 thy rod and staff me comfort still (3)
79 fair are the meadows, fairer still the woodlands (2)
79 fair is the sunshine, fairer still the moonlight (3)
80 my soul would be still more and more conformed to thee (4)
90 still as of old he calleth, "Follow me" (5)
94 depth of mercy! can there be mercy still reserved for me (1)
94 God is love! I know,I feel, Jesus weeps & loves me still (4)
99 if I still hold closely to him, what hath he at last (5)
105 and still my soul in slumber lie (1)
105 earth's pleasures shall I still hold dear (1)
105 he calls me still; can I delay (3)
105 shall I give no heed, but still in bondage live (4)
105 he calls me still; my heart, awake (4)
105 he still is waiting to receive (3)
106 waiting still for sweet release (3)
107 still he calls, in cares and pleasures (4)
112 will you not his grace receive ... still refuse to live (3)
121 blessed Jesus! Thou hast loved us, love us still (4)
125 while the tempest still is high (1)
125 leave ... leave me not alone, still support & comfort me (2)
144 with patient uncomplaining love, still ... cling to thee (2)
144 thy voice of love, in gentlest tone, still whispers (3)
144 thy voice ... still whispers, "Cling to me" (3)
151 living still, in spite of dungeon, fire and sword (1)
152 still to things eternal look (3)
153 keeping free our spirits still (4)
154 while I am waiting, yielded and still (1)
157 faith has still its Olivet, and love its Galilee (3)
161 still let thy spirit unto us be given (2)
163 and round my heart still closely twine those ties (1)
164 O let me hear thee speaking in accents clear and still (3)
167 help me still to say, "My Lord, thy will be done" (1)
170 still with thee in closer, dearer company (2)
172 still let me guard the holy fire (3)
172 and still stir up thy gift in me (3)
173 thy life is still a summons to serve humanity (1)
175 though they are slighting him, still he is waiting (2)
178 unwearied ... forgiveness still, thy heart ... only love (2)
185 this still its prayer shall be: more love, O Christ (4)
186 my heart is still with thee (5)
193 let us, still we pray, possess the mind that was in thee (6)
202 centuries still we hear the Master's winsome call (2)
202 brotherhood still rests in him, the brother of us all (2)
204 the cup of water given for thee still holds ...thy grace (4)
206 still may we trust thy love and grace (4)
209 be still my soul: thy best, thy heavenly friend (1)
209 be still my soul; the Lord is on thy side (1)

209   be still my soul (T,1,2,3)
209   the waves and winds still know his voice who ruled them (2)
210   only be still, and wait his leisure in cheerful hope (2)
213   O let thy hand support me still (4)
217   still 'tis God's hand that leadeth me (1)
217   still 'tis his hand that leadeth me (2)
217   by waters still, o'er troubled sea ... hand ... leadeth (2)
219   calmness bends serene above, my restlessness to still (3)
220   though the storms may gather, still have peace within (3)
220   who love the Father ... still have peace (3)
220   whate'er we must bear still in thee lies purest pleasure (3)
223   while we do his good will he abides with us still (1)
223   abides with us still & with all who will trust and obey (1)
233   yes, on through life's long path still chanting as ye go (4)
233   still lift your standard high ... march in firm array (5)
235   drop thy still dews of quietness (4)
235   O still, small voice of calm (5)
242   they must upward still & onward who would keep ... truth (3)
243   still made their glory in thy name (1)
250   still let the Spirit cry, in all his soldiers, "Come" (3)
251   how rich is my condition: God & heaven are still my own (1)
253   a spirit still prepared, and armed with jealous care (3)
255   hope still, and thou shalt sing the praise of him (4)
256   still be my Vision, O Ruler of all (4)
260   to hear thy voice we need but love ... listen & be still (3)
261   precious Savior, still our refuge (3)
263   still all my song shall be, nearer, my God, to thee (1)
263   still all my song shall be, nearer, my God, to thee (5)
264   still, still with thee, when purple morning breaketh (T,1)
264   still, still with thee! as to each new-born morning (3)
264   a fresh and solemn splendor still is given (3)
264   but sweeter still, to wake and find thee there (4)
266   in joy or in sorrow, still follow the Lord (3)
266   and, looking to Jesus, still trust in his Word (3)
268   How sweet their memories still (3)
269   and doubts appall, and sorrows still increase (1)
270   our hearts still whispering, "Thou art near" (2)
271   strong deliverer, be thou still my strength and shield (2)
272   sure it still will lead me on o'er moor and fen (3)
274   with obedience glad & steady still to follow every word (4)
276   still to the lowly soul he doth himself impart (3)
279   awake my soul when sin is nigh, and keep it still awake (3)
280   awake my soul when sin is nigh and keep it still awake (3)
288   and still to God salvation cry, salvation to the Lamb (1)
289   I triumph still, if thou abide with me (4)
299   behold how many thousands still are lying bound (2)
300   only thou our leader be, and we still will follow thee (4)
306   we shall still be joined in heart and hope to meet again (4)
307   save it from evil, guard it still (3)
317   our human pain still bearest thou with us (2)
325   millions more, still on the way, around the board appear (3)
326   here let me feast, and feasting, still prolong the hour (2)
326   thou art here, nearer than ever, still my shield and sun (4)
329   and long to feast upon thee still (3)
332   these the virtues did convey, yet still remain the same (2)
336   still he doth his help afford, and hides our life above (3)
338   our bodies may far off remove, we still are one in heart (1)

338 still in Jesus' footsteps tread & show his praise below (2)
355 still our wrongs may weave thee now new thorns (1)
356 may one Lord .. faith .. Word, one Spirit lead us still (4)
359 his kingdom still increasing, a kingdom without end (4)
364 dear tokens of his passion still his dazzling body bears (3)
367 still new beauties may I see, and still increasing light (3)
370 inspired those whose wisdom still directs us (3)
371 undimmed by time, the Word is still revealing (3)
372 mid mists & rocks & quick-sands, still guides ...to thee (3)
372 still guides, O Christ, to thee (3)
372 still that light she lifteth o'er all the earth to shine (2)
381 O little town of Bethlehem, how still we see thee lie (T,1)
390 still through the cloven skies they come (2)
390 still ... heavenly music floats o'er all the weary world (2)
395 he is still the undefiled, but no more a stranger (3)
402 westward leading, still proceeding (R)
409 and still he is nigh, his presence we have (2)
411 for still his love works wondrous charms (4)
413 are ye able? Still the Master whispers down eternity (4)
422 to heal the people of their shame, and nobleness instill (3)
445 He lives, my Savior, still the same (4)
459 to thee we owe the peace that still prevails (3)
459 pray we that thou wilt hear us, still imploring (5)
459 still imploring thy love and favor, kept to us always (5)
469 nation by nation still goes unforgiven (3)
475 still wilt not hear thine inner God proclaim (1)
479 still the children wander homeless (2)
479 still the hungry cry for bread (2)
479 still the captives long for freedom (2)
479 still in grief men mourn their dead (2)
479 use the love thy spirit kindles still to save (2)
501 thy touch has still its ancient power (6)
505 telling still the ancient story (2)
509 mighty hand by which supported still we stand (1)
509 by day, by night, at home, abroad, still we are guarded (2)
517 children thou hast given still may be our joy and crown (5)
529 Traveler unkown, whom still I hold, but cannot see (1)
530 join us, in one spirit ... let us still receive of thine (2)
530 still for more on thee we call ...who fillest all in all (2)
532 rich in art, made richer still the brotherhood of duty (4)
539 daily manna still provide you (2)
550 thy blessing came, and still its power shall onward (2)

stilled
355 our pride is dust; our vaunt is stilled (4)

stilling
459 stilling the rude wills of men's wild behavior (3)

stillness
390 world in solemn stillness lay to hear the angels sing (1)

stills
4 every faithless murmur stills (1)
247 as a mother stills her child thou canst hush (2)
247 as...stills her child thou canst hush the ocean wild (2)

sting
289   where is death's sting, where, grave, thy victory (4)
438   his sting is lost forever! Alleluia! (2)
439   where, O death, is now thy sting, Alleluia (2)
447   from death's dread sting thy servants free (4)
450   for her Lord now liveth; death hath lost its sting (2)

stir
172   and still stir up thy gift in me (3)

stirred
257   let our hearts and souls be stirred (1)

stirring
478   not with swords loud clashing nor roll of stirring drums (2)
479   stirring us to tireless striving (3)
511   the Church of Christ is stirring us to make the dream (2)

stirs
124   that delights and stirs me so (1)
124   this is that great thing I know ... delights & stirs me (4)

stone
263   darkness be over me, my rest a stone (2)
348   on this stone now laid with prayer (T,1)
349   as here with joy this stone we lay (1)
355   till not a stone was left on stone (2)
376   earth stood hard as iron, water like a stone (1)
450   angels in bright raiment rolled the stone away (1)

stones
348   by wise master builders squared, here be living stones (4)
348   living stones prepared for the temple near thy throne (4)

stony
263   out of my stony griefs Bethel I'll raise (4)
285   O that it now were shed abroad in this poor stony heart (3)

stood
21   his truth at all times firmly stood (4)
28   before the hills in order stood (3)
88   first let me hear how the children stood round his knee (2)
228   on a hill far away stood an old rugged cross (T,1)
243   who gainst enthroned wrong stood confident and bold (1)
324   of old on earth he stood, Lord of lords in human vesture (2)
329   thy truth unchanged hath ever stood (2)
376   earth stood hard as iron, water like a stone (1)
481   city that hath stood too long a dream (4)

stoop
117   thirsty one, stoop down and drink and live (2)
138   stoop to my weakness, might as thou art (1)

stooped
270   O Love Divine, that stooped to share (T,1)
270   stooped to share our sharpest pang, our bitterest tear (1)
299   tell how he stooped to save his lost creation (3)

stop
383 and there it did both stop and stay (4)

store
  50 I thank thee,Lord, that thou hast kept the best in store (4)
107 the vain world's golden store (3)
116 friends and time and earthly store (3)
187 my love ... I pour at thy feet its treasure-store (3)
196 render to my God for all his mercy's store (1)
344 store with thoughts divinely true (2)
473 the earth with its store of wonders untold (3)
502 blessings from thy boundless store (5)
512 God sendeth from his abundant store the waters (1)
522 but the fruitful ears to store in his garner evermore (3)

stored
351 when time in lowly dust has laid these stored walls (4)
372 it is the sacred casket where gems of truth are stored (2)
545 where the grapes of wrath are stored (1)

storied
351 these storied walls our hands have made (4)

stories
  88 tell me the stories of Jesus I love to hear (T,1)
  88 stories of Jesus, tell them to me (1)
155 who so beset him round with dismal stories (2)

storm
  11 storm and flood and ocean's roar (3)
  36 when lightnings flash and storm winds blow (2)
125 till the storm of life is past (1)
147 blest be the tempest, kind the storm (2)
147 kind the storm which drives us nearer home (2)
215 and rides upon the storm (1)
230 the storm may roar without me, my heart may low be laid (1)
345 storm of earth-born passion dies (4)
345 round these hallowed walls the storm of... passion dies (4)
378 left their flocks a feeding in tempest, storm, and wind (4)
473 and dark is his path on the wings of the storm (2)
538 and calm amid the storm didst sleep (2)

storms
  51 through waves and clouds and storms (2)
106 when the storms are raging sore ... whisper softly (2)
164 above the storms of passion, the murmurs of self-will (3)
220 sin and hell ... with their heaviest storms assail us (2)
220 though the storms may gather, still have peace within (3)
221 when the howling storms of doubt and fear assail (2)
244 when the storms of life are raging, stand by me (T,1)
259 and when the storms of life shall cease (3)
346 the rolling ocean, rocked with storms, sleeps (2)
440 soon the storms of time shall cease (1)
522 all is safely gathered in ere the winter storms begin (1)
541 be with them traversing the air in darkening storms (1)
541 in darkening storms or sunshine fair (1)

stormy

28	our shelter from the stormy blast (1)
199	stormy clangor of wild war music o'er the earth (5)
222	in every high and stormy gale, my anchor holds (2)
232	from every stormy wind that blows (T,1)
291	on Jordan's stormy banks I stand (T,1)
343	stormy sea sings praise to God ... thunder & the shower (1)
459	and calming passion's fierce and stormy gales (3)

story

43	nightly, to the listening earth repeats the story (2)
43	repeats the story of her birth (2)
62	their great story, God is love, and God is light (1)
62	let all our future days tell this story (2)
62	their glad story, God is life, and God is love (4)
149	I love to tell the story (T,1,2,3,4,R)
149	to tell the old, old story of Jesus and his love (R)
149	'twill be the old, old story that I have loved so long (4)
224	this is my story, this is my song, praising my Savior (R)
227	the story repeat, and the lover of sinners adore (3)
370	till they came, who told the story of the Word (2)
370	told the story of the Word, and showed his glory (2)
382	who sang creation's story now proclaim Messiah's birth (1)
395	Son of God, of humble birth, beautiful the story (3)
396	saw the glory, heard the story, tidings of a Gospel true (2)
410	we've a story to tell to the nations (T,1)
410	a story of truth and mercy, a story of peace and light (1)
416	light of sacred story gathers round its head sublime (1,5)
440	death and sorrow, earth's dark story (1)
459	thy love has blessed the wide world's wondrous story (1)
470	crown thine ancient Church's story (1)
505	telling still the ancient story (2)
532	the fathers named in story (1)

straight

167	straight to my home above I travel calmly on (3)
240	run the straight race through God's good grace (2)
362	make straight all the crooked places (1,4)
406	make straight, make straight the highway of the King (1)

straightness

273	like .. straightness of the pine trees let me upright be (3)

straightway

378	went to Bethlehem straightway, the blessed babe to find (4)

strain

19	raise the glad strain, alleluia! (1)
23	raise to Christ our joyful strain (1)
23	ascend for him our cheerful strain (4)
58	ye saints to come, take up the strain (4)
77	life shall not end the strain; Alleluia! Amen! (3)
170	help me bear the strain of toil, the fret of care (1)
202	we bear the strain of earthly care ... bear it not alone (T)
235	take from our souls the strain and stress (4)
374	why your joyous strain prolong (2)
437	and, hearing, may raise the victory strain (2)

446   raise the strain of triumphant gladness (1)
446   come, ye faithful, raise the strain (T,1)
448   come, ye faithful, raise the strain (T,1) (see 446)

strains
14   to every land the strains belong (4)
189   for what are sundering strains of blood (2)
252   prayer .. sublimest strains .. reach the Majesty on high (3)
284   the strains of praise and love (6)
343   sweet music fills the world abroad with strains of love (1)
343   strains of love and power (1)
374   and the mountains in reply echoing their joyous strains (1)
431   unheard by mortals are the strains that sweetly soothe (4)
446   welcomes in unwearied strains Jesus' resurrection (3)
500   nor die the strains of praise away (3)
524   strains of ... holy throng with ours today are blending (3)

strand
433   till I reach the golden strand just beyond the river (4)
550   and when they trod the wintry strand (1)

strange
41   mixture strange of good and ill (2)
527   who can explore his strange design (2)

stranger
9   he helps the stranger in distress (3)
93   Jesus sought me when a stranger (2)
395   there he lay, the undefiled, to the world a stranger (1)
395   he is still the undefiled, but no more a stranger (3)
438   It was a stranger and dreadful strife (2)

stray
46   we shall not in the desert stray (2)
143   nor let me ever stray from thee aside (3)
213   if in this darksome wild I stray (2)
226   trusting thee I cannot stray .. can never .. lose my way (2)
279   if to the right or left I stray (2)
279   from thee that I no more may stray (3)
280   from thee that I no more may stray (3)
280   if to the right or left I stray (2)
368   Lamp ... whereby we trace our path when wont to stray (1)
520   love like thine, that none shall ever stray (1)

strayed
22   when like wandering sheep we strayed (2)
67   perverse and foolish oft I strayed (3)

straying
103   joy of the desolate, light of the straying (2)

stream
28   time, like an ever rolling stream (5)
29   sanctifying beam upon our earthly senses stream (2)
117   I came to Jesus, and I drank of that life-giving stream (2)
143   when death's cold, sullen stream shall o'er me roll (4)
214   like trees beside a flowing stream (2)

271   whence the healing stream doth flow (2)
302   though now divided by...the narrow stream of death (3)
368   stream from the fount of heavenly grace (1)
393   glories stream from heaven afar (2)
421   by faith, I saw the stream thy flowing wounds supply (4)
433   there a precious fountain, free to all, a healing stream (1)
433   healing stream flows from calvary's mountain (1)

streameth
63   through the gloom his brightness streameth (3)

streaming
416   from the cross the radiance streaming adds more luster (3)

streams
67   where streams of living water flow (2)
93   streams of mercy never ceasing call for songs (1)
125   let the healing streams abound (4)
255   as pants the hart for cooling streams (T,1)
293   see, the streams of living waters (2)
293   streams of living waters, springing from eternal love (2)
301   grace through every vessel flows in purest streams (2)
301   in purest streams of love (2)
419   his blood-red banner streams afar (1)
473   it streams from the hills, it descends to the plain (4)
488   living water flowing with soul-refreshing streams (3)
536   through gates of pearl streams in the countless host (6)

street
200   no field or mart is silent, no city street is dumb (2)
481   lust and greed for gain in street and shop and tenement (3)

streets
204   O tread the city's streets again (5)
381   yet in thy dark streets shineth the everlasting light (1)

strength
16   God is our strength and song, and his salvation ours (4)
20   did we in our own strength confide (2)
30   his love shall be our strength and stay, while ages roll (3)
46   our strength, thy grace; our rule, thy word (1)
54   not their number nor ... strength ...their country save (2)
58   the strength those weaklings that renewed (2)
97   my life .. joy .. all; he is my strength ... day to day (1)
138   all, all thine own, soul, heart and strength and mind (3)
143   may thy rich grace impart strength to my fainting heart (2)
155   do but themselves confound, His strength the more is (2)
160   his strength shall bear thy spirit up (2)
163   my heart, my strength, my life, my all are his (2)
171   with the task sufficient strength (3)
174   give heart and mind and soul and strength to serve (1)
174   Church ... her strength unequal to her task (3)
175   strength for thy labor the Lord will provide (4)
179   strong in thy strength we will battle for thee (1)
182   Lord, in the strength of grace (T,1)
188   in thee my strength renew; give me my work to do (2)
200   our strength is dust and ashes, our years a passing hour (3)

210	he'll give thee strength, whate'er betide thee (1)
238	in the strength that cometh by the holy cross (1)
240	Christ is thy strength, and Christ thy right (1)
243	march on, o soul, with strength (T,1)
243	march on.. soul w. strength ... strong the battle rolls (3)
243	march on, O soul, march on, with strength (4)
244	when the hosts of sin assail ... strength begins to fail (2)
248	courage rise with danger & strength to strength oppose (2)
248	stand in his strength alone (3)
250	who ... strength of Jesus trusts is more than conqueror (1)
250	strong in the strength which God supplies (1)
250	from strength to strength go on (3)
250	stand ...in his great might ... all his strength endued (2)
253	Jesus, my strength, my hope, on thee I cast my care (T,1)
258	see thou render all thy feeble strength can pay (1)
271	strong deliverer, be thou still my strength and shield (2)
295	blest is the man whose strength thou art (5)
352	source of all strength thou art; thy gospel bless (3)
360	Israel's strength and consolation (1)
370	book of books, our people's strength (T,1)
399	fill me with joy and strength to be thy member (2)
406	Lord, give us faith and strength the road to build (3)
452	tread the path of darkness, saving strength to show (3)
481	give us, O God, the strength to build the city (4)
498	give us strength to serve and wait till the glory breaks (3)
534	kept ... people by the strength of thy staff and rod (1)

strengthen

48	I'll strengthen thee,help thee, and cause thee to stand (2)
98	prayer to strengthen faith and sweeten care (4)
195	O strengthen me (2)
211	his might thy heart shall strengthen (2)
290	the bruised reed he will not break, but strengthen (2)
290	strengthen and sustain (2)

strengthened

243	upheld and strengthened by thy hand (3)
315	strengthened by thy grace behold without a veil thy face (2)
345	who mourn ...they who fear, be strengthened as they pray (3)

stress

204	from famished souls, from sorrow's stress (3)
225	a little shelter from life's stress (3)
235	take from our souls the strain and stress (4)
543	pilgrim feet, whose stern, impassioned stress (2)

stretch

140	Father, I stretch my hands to thee (T,1)
195	I may stretch out a loving hand to wrestlers (2)
249	awake, my soul, stretch every nerve (T,1)
474	rise, my soul, and stretch thy wings (T,1)

stretching

548	mighty empire, stretching far o'er land and sea (1)

strew
449 bring flowers of song to strew his way (2)

stricken
417 from my stricken heart with tears two wonders I confess (2)

strict
150 O, thy servant, Lord, prepare, a strict account to give (3)
337 by day and night strict guard to keep (4)

strife
38   victors in the midst of strife (4)
151 we will love both friend and foe in all our strife (3)
161 to heal earth's wounds and endd her bitter strife (2)
184 it only stands unbent amid the clashing strife (4)
194 look down on all earth's sin and strife (3)
204 above the noise of selfish strife (1)
236 our balm in sorrow, and our stay in strife (4)
237 on thy truth relying, through that mortal strife (4)
237 when my last hour cometh, fraught with strife and pain (4)
242 in the strife of truth with falsehood (1)
243 in keenest strife, Lord, may we stand (3)
248 the strife will not be long (4)
284 amid the battle's strife (3)
309 bid our strife forever cease (1)
333 grant them the peace which calms all earthly strife (3)
354 bid envy, strife, and quarrels cease (3)
356 unite us in thy will, O Lord, and end all sinful strife (2)
406 when war shall be no more and strife shall cease (3)
438 It was a stranger and dreadful strife (2)
447 the strife is o'er the battle done (T,1)
450 life is naught without thee; aid us in our strife (3)
455 rose victorious in the strife for those he came to save (2)
477 bring to our world of strife thy sovereign word of peace (4)
486 those oppressed or lonely ... long at strife with pain (3)
536 and when the strife is fierce, the warfare long (5)
543 O beautiful for heroes proved in liberating strife (3)
548 from the strife of class & faction make our nation free (4)

string
15   praise him every tuneful string: (2)

stripes
47   Lord, by the stripes which wounded thee (4)
447 Lord, by the stripes that wounded thee (4)

stripped
438 stripped of power, no more he reigns (2)

strive
134 in vain we strive to rise (3)
135 by thee may I strongly live, bravely bear & nobly strive (3)
151 we will strive to win all nations unto thee (2)
303 strive, man, to win that glory, toil ..to gain .. light (3)

strives
531 is there a thing beneath the sun that strives with thee (2)
531 that strives with thee my heart to share (2)

striving
- 20   our striving would be losing (2)
- 238   striving, tempting, luring, goading into sin (2)
- 442   life in all.. growing powers toward .. light is striving (1)
- 479   stirring us to tireless striving (3)

strivings
- 235   till all our strivings cease (4)

stroke
- 216   no fatal stroke shall thee assail (3)

strong
- 19   ye holy twelve, ye martyrs strong (3)
- 31   strong is his arm, and shall fulfill his great decrees (3)
- 45   ne'er forget that though the wrong seems oft so strong (3)
- 47   when we are strong, Lord, leave us not alone (3)
- 51   how wise, how strong his hand (3)
- 60   thou rushing wind that art so strong (2)
- 86   lead us to where thou hast trod, our faith make strong (3)
- 139   by faith we know thee strong to save (3)
- 139   with strong commanding evidence their... origin display (5)
- 146   strong Son of God, immortal love (T,1)
- 156   I would be strong, for there is much to suffer (1)
- 162   strong to follow in thy grace (3)
- 169   just as I am, young, strong and free (4)
- 170   in work that keeps faith sweet and strong (3)
- 179   strong in thy strength we will battle for thee (1)
- 184   imprison me within thine arms ... strong ... be my hand (1)
- 189   our service strong and true (2)
- 191   of steadfast will, patient, courageous, strong and true (3)
- 194   of tarnished honor, falsely strong (2)
- 195   that I may stand firm on the rock, and strong in thee (2)
- 198   they shall be gentle, brave, and strong (2)
- 206   in thy strong hand eternally rests the ... years (3)
- 211   God is my strong salvation; what foe have I to fear (T,1)
- 219   I feel thy strong and tender love, and all is well again (1)
- 221   bound to him eternally by love's strong cord (3)
- 233   with voice as full and strong as ocean's surging praise (3)
- 233   strong men and maidens fair (2)
- 242   though the cause of evil prosper . truth alone is strong (4)
- 243   like those strong men of old (1)
- 243   march on.. soul w. strength ... strong the battle rolls (3)
- 250   strong in the Lord of hosts, and in his mighty power (1)
- 250   strong in the strength which God supplies (1)
- 271   strong deliverer, be thou still my strength and shield (2)
- 273   with thy spirit recreate me, pure and strong and true (1)
- 273   like .. rocks of towering grandeur make me strong & sure (2)
- 273   keep me ever, by thy spirit, pure and strong and true (5)
- 275   anxious spirits burn with strong desires for thy return (2)
- 308   we mark her goodly battlements & her foundations strong (2)
- 346   the Lord our God alone is strong (T,1)
- 348   let thy church rise, strong and fair (1)
- 349   in grateful service ... now their strong foundation lay (2)
- 359   to help the poor and needy, and bid the weak be strong (2)
- 362   word of our God endureth ... arm of the Lord is strong (3)

366 the strong in grace, in truth victorious (2)
411 bind strong the bond of brotherhood of those who fight (1)
428 and earth's strong pillars bend (2)
438 Christ Jesus lay in death's strong bands (T,1)
466 so the yearning strong, with which the soul will long (3)
468 and wonders great by thy strong hand are done (3)
478 through days of preparation thy grace has made us strong (1)
490 warrior-like and strong, comely as a groom (1)
497 strong through thee whate'er befall us, O God most wise (2)
532 praise we the wise and brave and strong (2)
532 wise and brave and strong who graced their generation (2)
536 and hearts are brave again, and arms are strong (5)
538 eternal Father, strong to save (T,1)
548 strong as when her life began (4)
552 be thy strong arm our ever sure defense (3)

stronger
285 stronger his love than death or hell (2)

strongholds
464 sin's strongholds it now o'erthrows (2)

strongly
122 they pour effectual prayers; they strongly plead for me (3)
135 by thee may I strongly live, bravely bear & nobly strive (3)

strove
112 He, who all your lives hath strove (3)

strowed
425 road with palms and scattered garments strowed (1)

struggle
536 we feebly struggle, they in glory shine (4)

struggles
138 teach me the struggles of the souls to bear (4)

struggling
148 some poor fainting, struggling seaman you may rescue (R)
189 one tender comfort broods upon the struggling...soul (3)
481 from women struggling sore for bread (2)

stumble
269 blindly we stumble when we walk alone (3)

stumbling
309 by thy reconciling love every stumbling block remove (2)

sturdy
413 yea, the sturdy dreamers answered (1)

subdue
29 with love all envy to subdue (4)
76 there let him subdue all that is not holy (4)
76 there let him subdue...all that is not true (4)

subdued
  58 the grace those sinners that subdued (2)
 264 when sinks the soul, subdued by toil, to slumber (4)

subdues
  31 subdues the powers of hell, confounds their dark designs (3)

sublime
  32 his voice sublime is heard afar (4)
 296 fulfill thy task sublime (4)
 416 light of sacred story gathers round its head sublime (1,5)
 456 trace through corridors sublime (1)

sublimest
 252 prayer .. sublimest strains .. reach the Majesty on high (3)

submission
 224 perfect submission, perfect delight (2)
 224 perfect submission, all is at rest (3)

submissive
 282 a heart resigned, submissive, meek (2)

submits
 457 every vanquished foe submits to his victorious cross (2)

subside
 271 when I tread the verge of Jordan, bid ... fears subside (3)
 271 bid my anxious fears subside (3)

subsisting
 139 future and past subsisting now (3)

subtle
 113 by thy conflict in... hour of the subtle tempter's power (1)

success
   3 come, and thy people bless, and give thy Word success (2)
 543 till all success be nobleness and every gain divine (3)

successive
 472 where'er the sun does his successive journeys run (1)

succor
  54 thy right hand thy powerful arm ... succor they implored (3)
 200 whom shall I send to succor my people in their need (1)
 359 he comes with succor speedy to those who suffer wrong (2)

such
  65 unto such as keep his covenant ... steadfast in his way (5)
  83 from his bounty I receive such proofs of love divine (4)
  97 beautiful life with such a friend (4)
  98 such ever bring thee where they come (2)
 142 Lord, give me such a faith as this (4)
 163 I've found a Friend, O such a Friend (T,1,2,3)
 230 and safe is such confiding, for nothing changes here (1)

293 who can faint while such a river ...their thirst assuage (2)
312 for 'twas to bless such souls as these the Lord...came (2)
325 not paradise, with all its joys ... such delight afford (1)
385 why lies he in such mean estate (2)
395 such a babe in such a place, can he be the Savior (1)
415 would he devote that sacred head for sinners such as I (1)
435 did e'er such love and sorrow meet (3)
468 surely to such as do him fear salvation is at hand (2)
521 nesting bird nor star in heaven such a refuge ... given (1)

sudden
138 no sudden rending of the veil of clay (2)

suddenly
283 suddenly return and never, nevermore thy temples leave (3)
382 suddenly the Lord, descending, in... temple shall appear (4)

suffer
102 nor suffer him to die in vain (4)
156 I would be strong, for there is much to suffer (1)
176 gladly will I toil & suffer, only let me walk with thee (2)
210 if thou but suffer God to guide thee (T,1)
220 I will suffer naught to hide thee (1)
237 nor for fear or favor suffer me to fall (1)
248 lift high the royal banner, it must not suffer loss (1)
270 content to suffer while we know ... thou art near (4)
359 he comes with succor speedy to those who suffer wrong (2)
426 perfect man on thee did suffer (1,4)
443 didst once, upon the cross ... suffer to redeem our loss (1)
454 thou didst suffer to release us (1)
458 they suffer with their Lord below (5)

suffered
227 "He hath loved me," I cried, "He hath suffered and died (4)
227 suffered and died to redeem a poor rebel like me (4)
228 for 'twas on that old cross Jesus suffered and died (3)
414 we believe it was for us he hung and suffered there (2)
417 the very dying form of One who suffered there for me (2)
418 what ...my Lord, hast suffered was all for sinner's gain (2)

sufferer
495 comfort every sufferer watching late in pain (4)

suffering
228 the emblem of suffering and shame (1)
259 in suffering be thy love my peace (3)
431 in the garden now the suffering Savior prays alone (1)
434 shun not suffering, shame, or loss (2)

sufferings
331 in thy trial and rejection ...thy sufferings on the tree (2)
426 very God himself is bearing all the sufferings of time (3)

sufficed
376 in the bleak midwinter a stable place sufficed (2)
376 sufficed the Lord God Almighty, Jesus Christ (2)

sufficiency
321   when life anew pours out its wine with rich sufficiency (3)

sufficient
  28   sufficient is thine arm alone (2)
  48   my grace, all-sufficient, shall be thy supply (4)
  89   thou all sufficient love divine (1)
171   with the task sufficient strength (3)
360   by thine all-sufficient merit raise us ((2)

suggest
180   direct, control, suggest this day (3)

sullen
143   when death's cold, sullen stream shall o'er me roll (4)

summer
  34   the cold wind in the winter, the pleasant summer sun (3)

summons
173   thy life is still a summons to serve humanity (1)
200   the voice of God is calling its summons unto men (T,1)
200   we heed, O Lord, thy summons, and answer: here are we (3)
511   a world in need now summons us to labor,love and give (2)

sun
   7   see the morning sun ascending radiant in the eastern sky (T)
   8   morn to set of sun, through the church the song goes on (3)
  12   beyond the range of sun and star, and yet beside us here (1)
  25   God is our sun, he makes our day (3)
  28   before the rising sun (4)
  29   o thou true Sun, on us thy glance let fall (2)
  32   the rolling sun stands still (1)
  34   the cold wind in the winter, the pleasant summer sun (3)
  35   sun and moon, and stars of light (2)
  37   I sing the wisdom that ordained the sun to rule the day (1)
  38   opening to the sun above (1)
  42   sun and moon, rejoice before him (1)
  43   the unwearied sun, from day to day (1)
  57   neath sun or m'oon, by day or night ... not be afraid (3)
  60   thou burning sun with golden beam (1)
  64   thy glory flames from sun and star (1)
  64   sun of our life, thy quickening ray sheds on our path (2)
  90   at eventide before the sun was set (4)
  95   O thou loving, blessed One, rising o'er me like the sun (4)
117   I looked to Jesus, and I found in him my star, my sun (3)
180   awake, my soul, and with the sun (T,1)
190   see how the giant sun soars up (2)
256   may I reach heaven's joys, O bright heaven's Sun (4)
258   gladly hail the sun returning (2)
263   though like a wanderer, the sun gone down (2)
263   sun, moon, and stars forgot, upward I fly (5)
318   sun, who all my life dost brighten (2)
326   thou art here, nearer than ever, still my shield and sun (4)
330   when I fall on my knees with my face to the rising sun (R)
353   crowned with glory like the sun...lights the morning sky (2)
365   the rolling sun, the changing light ...thy power confess (2)

365   sun, moon ... stars convey thy praise round the... earth (3)
365   nations ...that see the light or feel the sun (4)
387   hail the Sun of Righteousness (3)
401   Sun of Righteousness, arise (1)
405   fairer than the sun at morning was the star (2)
415   well might the sun in darkness hide (3)
415   sun in darkness hide and shut his glories in (3)
416   when the sun of bliss is beaming light and love (3)
438   Christ is...the Sun that warms and lights us (3)
446   and from three days' sleep in death as a sun hath risen (2)
472   where'er the sun does his successive journeys run (1)
474   sun and moon and stars decay (1)
474   fire ascending seeks the sun (2)
481   where the sun that shineth is God's grace for human good (4)
490   rise to greet the sun, reddening the sky (T,1)
492   sun itself is but thy shade, yet cheers both earth & sky (1)
497   when the constant sun returning unseals our eyes (2)
501   at even, ere the sun was set (T,1)
502   sun of my soul, thou Savior dear (T,1)
514   take our plowing...reaping, hopes and fears of sun (2)
514   seeding, reaping, hopes and fears of sun and rain (2)
531   is there a thing beneath the sun that strives with thee (2)

sunder
306   when we asunder part, it gives us inward pain (4)
428   temple's veil in sunder breaks ... solid marbles rend (2)

sundered
232   though sundered far, by faith they meet (3)

sundering
189   for what are sundering strains of blood (2)

sung
14   let the Redeemer's name be sung (1)
14   sung through every land by every tongue (1)
93   sung by flaming tongues above (1)
410   we've a song to be sung to the nations (2)

sunlight
273   like thy dancing waves in sunlight make me glad and free (3)
542   and sunlight beams on clover-leaf and pine (2)
542   but other lands have sunlight too, and clover (2)

sunrise
408   whole round world complete, from sunrise to its setting (2)

suns
14   till suns shall rise and set no more (2)
41   bringing suns and stars to birth (1)
456   do flaming suns his footsteps trace (1)
515   suns glow, rains fall, by power divine (2)

sunset
34   the sunset, and the morning that brightens up the sky (2)
505   soon as dies the sunset glory, stars of heaven shine (2)

sunshine
69   lives would be all sunshine in the sweetness of our Lord (2)
79   fair is the sunshine, fairer still the moonlight (3)
97   he sends the sunshine and the rain (2)
97   sunshine and rain, harvest of grain, He's my friend (2)
110 why from the sunshine of love wilt thou roam (1)
289 through cloud and sunshine, Lord, abide with me (3)
417 I ask no other sunshine than the sunshine of his face (3)
438 his grace ... doth impart eternal sunshine to the heart (3)
513 the breezes and the sunshine, and soft, refreshing rain (1)
523 the golden sunshine, vernal air, sweet flowers and fruit (2)
541 in darkening storms or sunshine fair (1)

sunshine's
36   thy love is in the sunshine's glow (2)
234 in thy sunshine's blaze its day may brighter, fairer be (2)

sunward
38   joyful music leads us sunward (4)

sup
111 sup with us, and let the feast be everlasting love (4)
313 there sup with us in love divine; thy body and thy blood (2)
366 we follow till the halls we see where ... sup with thee (2)
366 halls we see where thou hast bid us sup with thee (2)

supernal
19   supernal anthems echoing, alleluia, alleluia! (3)
524 souls of men are fed with gifts of grace supernal (2)

superstition's
407 the futile cries of superstition's cruel creed (2)

supper
321 thy supper, Lord, is spread in every quiet upper room (1)
328 who thy mysterious supper share, here at thy table fed (2)

supplication
132 O hear our supplication, Blessed Spirit, God of peace (2)

supplied
522 God, our Maker, doth provide ...our wants to be supplied (1)

supplies
61   his full hand supplies their need (3)
250 God supplies through his eternal Son (1)
250 strong in the strength which God supplies (1)
315 our needy souls sustain with fresh supplies of love (2)
332 drink herewith divine supplies and eat immortal bread (3)
367 thirsty souls receive supplies... sweet refreshment find (2)
490 all my countless needs thy kind hand supplies (3)

supply
48   my grace, all-sufficient, shall be thy supply (4)
89   in want my plentiful supply (4)
293 well supply thy sons and daughters (2)
337 graces and gifts to each supply (1)

339   answer ... faith's effectual prayer ... our needs supply (1)
344   good desired and wanted most ...thy richest grace supply (1)
421   by faith, I saw the stream thy flowing wounds supply (4)

support
125   leave ... leave me not alone, still support & comfort me (2)
213   O let thy hand support me still (4)
222   his oath, his covenant, his blood support me (3)
222   support me in the whelming flood (3)

supported
239   I'll bear the toil, endure the pain, supported (4)
239   supported by thy word (4)
509   mighty hand by which supported still we stand (1)

supports
9   the Lord supports the fainting mind (3)

supreme
214   and in their time bear fruit supreme (2)

sure
20   his rage we can endure, for lo, his doom is sure (3)
21   his mercy is forever sure (4)
28   and our defense is sure (2)
52   how sure is their defense (1)
61   for his mercies shall endure, ever faithful, ever sure (R)
99   finding, following, keeping, struggling...sure to bless (7)
111   in sure and certain hope rejoice (3)
184   it has no spring of action sure, it varies with the wind (2)
215   blind unbelief is sure to err and scan his work in vain (5)
232   there is a calm, a sure retreat (1)
239   sure I must fight, if I would reign (4)
272   sure it still will lead me on o'er moor and fen (3)
273   like .. rocks of towering grandeur make me strong & sure (2)
281   remains and stands forever sure (1)
293   what can shake thy sure repose (1)
294   sure as thy truth shall last (5)
298   Christ is made the sure foundation (T,1)
332   sure and real is the grace, the manner be unknown (4)
350   the guilty soul a sure retreat (4)
356   restore to us thy truth, O God, & make its meaning sure (2)
460   one sure faith yet standing fast (3)
498   sure of being safely guided, guarded well from every foe (2)
552   be thy strong arm our ever sure defense (3)

surely
55   surely his goodness and mercy here daily attend thee (3)
68   goodness and mercy all my life shall surely follow me (5)
101   he will surely give you rest, by trusting in his word (1)
137   who did for every sinner die hath surely died for me (1)
140   surely thou canst not let me die (3)
154   power, all power, surely is thine (3)
192   who serves my Father as a son is surely kin to me (3)
214   their evil acts shall surely come to naught (4)
379   all you need I will surely give you (2)

456 as altar candle sheds its light as surely as a star (2)
468 surely to such as do him fear salvation is at hand (2)

surety
99 yea, a crown, in very surety, but of thorns (3)
122 before the throne my surety stands (1)

surges
147 but should the surges rise and rest delay to come (2)

surging
30 his spirit floweth free, high surging where it will (2)
229 peace, perfect peace, with sorrows surging round (3)
233 with voice as full and strong as ocean's surging praise (3)
372 it is the chart and compass that o'er life's surging sea (3)
407 we hear the throb of surging life, the clank of chains (2)

surprise
290 I know not what the future hath of marvel or surprise (T,1)

surprises
231 sometimes a light surprises the Christian while he sings (T)

surrender
498 we would praise thee and surrender all our hearts (2)
498 surrender all our hearts to be thine own (2)

surrendered
179 freely surrendered and wholly thine own (3)

surround
5 while ye surround his throne (1)
38 all thy works with joy surround thee (2)
343 like them, let man the throne surround (2)
496 angel guards from thee surround us (2)

surrounded
293 with salvation's walls surrounded (1)
418 now scornfully surrounded with thorns, thine only crown (1)
469 in wrath and fear, by jealousies surrounded (3)

survey
37 if I survey the ground I tread, or gaze upon the sky (2)
249 a cloud of witnesses around holds thee in full survey (2)
435 when I survey the wondrous cross (T,1)

surveys
70 when all thy mercies, O my God, my rising soul surveys (T,1)

sustain
253 bold to take up, firm to sustain the consecrated cross (2)
290 strenthen and sustain (2)
315 our needy souls sustain with fresh supplies of love (2)
376 our God, heaven cannot hold him, nor earth sustain (2)

sustained
434 love to man his soul sustained (2)

sustaineth
55 shieldeth thee under his wings ... so gently sustaineth (2)

swallow
295 the swallow also for herself provided hath a nest (3)

swallowed
429 'tis swallowed up in victory (3)

swathing
394 all meanly wrapped in swathing bands & in a manger laid (4)

sway
25 O God, our King, whose sovereign sway (4)
51 leave to his sovereign sway to choose and to command (3)
154 hold o'er my being absolute sway (4)
157 we own thy sway, we hear thy call (6)
262 my bounding heart shall own thy sway & echo to thy voice (3
408 new life, new hope awakes where-e'er men own his sway (1)
471 till all thy foes confess thy sway (2)
500 till all thy creatures own thy sway (4)

sways
242 yet that scaffold sways the future (4)
455 crown him the Lord of peace, whose power a scepter sways (
455 scepter sways from pole to pole, that wars may cease (3)

sweep
245 sorrows, sometimes how they sweep like tempests (1)

sweeps
32 and sweeps the howling skies (4)

sweet
5 join in a song with sweet accord (1)
8 fill .. heavens with sweet accord: holy, holy, holy Lord (2)
9 grants the prisoner sweet release (3)
11 with sweet music fill the air (1)
53 sweet refreshment find (3)
58 the same sweet theme endeavor (4)
81 how sweet the name of Jesus sounds in a believer's ear (T,1)
85 living deeds that prove how sweet to serve all others (3)
85 how sweet to serve all others, when we all others love (3)
91 powers of darkness fear, when this sweet chant they hear (2)
92 amazing grace! how sweet the sound (T,1)
106 waiting still for sweet release (3)
107 day by day his sweet voice soundeth (1)
129 and let the sweet tokens of pardoning grace bring joy (4)
145 let me at thy throne of mercy find a sweet relief (2)
149 what seems, each time I tell it, more wonderfully sweet (3)
157 warm, sweet, tender, even yet a present help is he (3)
170 in work that keeps faith sweet and strong (4)
185 sweet are thy messengers, sweet their refrain (3)
204 the sweet compassion of thy face (4)
208 'tis so sweet to trust in Jesus (T,1)
208 O how sweet to trust in Jesus (2)
208 yes, 'tis sweet to trust in Jesus (3)

218	if thy work on earth be sweet, what will thy glory be (4)
223	then in fellowship sweet we will sit at his feet (4)
227	sweet comfort and peace of a soul in its earliest love (1)
227	tongue can never express the sweet comfort and peace (1)
227	that sweet comfort was mine (2)
232	a place than all beside more sweet (2)
245	the Rock's blessed shadow, how sweet (2)
257	by thy teachings sweet and holy (1)
262	labor is rest .. pain is sweet if thou, my God, art here (2)
264	dawns the sweet consciousness, I am with thee (1)
264	sweet the repose beneath thy wings o'ershading (4)
268	How sweet their memories still (3)
268	return, O holy Dove, return, sweet messenger of rest (4)
275	sweet hour of prayer (T,1,2,3)
285	O love divine, how sweet thou art (T,1)
291	sweet fields arrayed in living green & rivers of delight (1)
294	her sweet communion, solemn vows (4)
297	and mystic sweet communion with those whose rest is won (4)
301	if our fellowship below in Jesus be so sweet (5)
303	O sweet and blessed country, the home of God's elect (4)
303	O sweet and blessed country that eager hearts expect (4)
326	giving sweet foretaste of the festal joy (5)
328	tongue can tell our sweet accord ... perfect harmony (1)
334	possess in sweet communion, joys ... earth cannot afford (2)
343	sweet music fills the world abroad with strains of love (1)
350	like incense sweet to thee ascend (2)
367	thirsty souls receive supplies... sweet refreshment find (2)
379	hark! a voice from yonder manger, soft and sweet (2)
380	for the virgin's sweet boy is the Lord of the earth (2)
384	the little Lord Jesus laid down his sweet head (1)
385	whom angels greet with anthems sweet (1)
424	to whom the lips of children made sweet hosannas ring (1)
430	here earth's bitter things grow sweet (1)
455	flowers of paradise extend their fragrance ever sweet (3)
472	his name like sweet perfume shall rise (2)
478	and holiness shall whisper the sweet amen of peace (2)
493	O may my soul on thee repose and with sweet sleep (4)
493	with sweet sleep my eyelids close (4)
495	Jesus, give the weary calm and sweet repose (2)
497	slumber sweet thy mercy send us (1)
502	be my last thought, how sweet to rest (2)
516	happy the home where Jesus' name is sweet to every ear (2)
523	the golden sunshine, vernal air, sweet flowers and fruit (2)
523	sweet flowers and fruit thy love declare (2)
547	my country, 'tis of thee, sweet land of liberty (T,1)
547	sweet land of liberty, of thee I sing (1)
547	and ring from all the trees sweet freedom's song (3)

sweeten
98	prayer to strengthen faith and sweeten care (4)

sweeter
82	sweeter far thy face to see and in thy presence rest (1)
82	nor can the memory find a sweeter sound than thy... name (2)
82	sweeter sound than thy blest name, O Savior of mankind (2)
251	heaven will bring me sweeter rest (3)
264	but sweeter still, to wake and find thee there (4)
421	in a nobler, sweeter song, I'll sing thy power to save (5)

sweetest
- 106   while they hear that sweetest voice (1)
- 106   while they hear that sweetest voice whispering softly (1)
- 168   in Loftiest songs of sweetest praise (2)
- 222   I dare not trust the sweetest frame (1)
- 318   joy, the sweetest man e'er knoweth (2)
- 377   our sweetest carols gayly ring to welcome Christ (3)
- 379   as I hear, far and near, sweetest angels voices (1)
- 454   bring your sweetest, noblest lays (4)
- 472   dwell on his love with sweetest song (3)

sweetly
- 17   and hear the birds sing sweetly in the trees (2)
- 109   sweetly echo the gospel call (3)
- 116   Jesus sweetly speaks to me (2)
- 231   in holy contemplation we sweetly then pursue the theme (2)
- 374   sweetly singing o'er the plains (1)
- 431   unheard by mortals are the strains that sweetly soothe (4)
- 431   that sweetly soothe that Savior's woe (4)
- 473   and sweetly distills in the dew and the rain (4)
- 530   sweetly may we all agree, touched with loving sympathy (4)
- 532   praise we ... the singers sweetly gifted (3)

sweetness
- 69   lives would be all sunshine in the sweetness of our Lord (2)
- 82   thought of thee with sweetness fills the breast (1)
- 83   majestic sweetness sits enthroned upon the Savior's brow (T)
- 98   here, to our waiting hearts, proclaim the sweetness (3)
- 98   the sweetness of thy saving name (3)

swell
- 8   prophets swell the glad refrain (3)
- 86   unite to swell the song to Christ our King (4)
- 364   thousand saints attending swell the triumph of his train (1)
- 513   sends the snow in winter ... warmth to swell the grain (1)
- 547   let music swell the breeze (3)

swelling
- 232   from every swelling tide of woes (1)
- 343   O grant its rich and swelling notes may lift our souls (3)

swells
- 481   there swells the sobbing human plaint (2)

swept
- 225   of self and sin swept bare (4)
- 380   and that song from afar has swept over the world (3)

swift
- 66   slow to chide and swift to bless (2)
- 105   shall life's swift passing years all fly (1)
- 187   take my feet ... let them be swift & beautiful for thee (1)
- 251   swift shall pass thy pilgrim days (4)
- 289   swift to its close ebbs out life's little day (2)
- 296   feet on mercy's errands swift do make her pilgrimage (3)
- 406   pass on and carry swift the news ye bring (1)
- 545   lightning of his terrible swift sword (1)
- 545   O be swift, my soul, to answer him; be jubilant, my feet (3)

swifter
  471   not heaven's hosts shall swifter move than we on earth (4)
  471   not ... swifter ... than we on earth, to do thy will (4)

swiftly
  371   from days of old, through swiftly rolling ages (2)
  464   now the Word doth swiftly run (2)

sword
    3   come, thou incarnate Word, gird on thy mighty sword (2)
   54   not their courage nor their sword ... salvation gave (2)
  151   living still, in spite of dungeon, fire and sword (1)
  184   force me to render up my sword and I shall conqueror be (1)
  221   overcoming daily with the Spirit's sword (3)
  408   to plow-share beat the sword, to pruning-hook the spear (2)
  410   song that shall conquer evil & shatter the spear & sword (2)
  456   and point Orion's sword (1)
  484   from sale and profanation of honor and the sword (2)
  484   lift up a living nation, a single sword to thee (3)
  544   thunder thy clarion, the lightning thy sword (1)
  544   praise him who saved them from peril and sword (4)
  545   he hath loosed the fateful lightning of his ... sword (1)
  545   lightning of his terrible swift sword (1)
  546   cleave our darkness with thy sword (2)
  548   not for conquests of the sword (2)

swords
  478   not with swords loud clashing nor roll of stirring drums (2)
  484   the walls of gold entomb us, the swords of scorn divide (1)

symbols
  321   Master ... symbols shared thine own dear self impart (4)
  326   too soon we rise: the symbols disappear (4)

sympathizing
  306   and often for each other flows the sympathizing tear (3)

sympathy
  530   sweetly may we all agree, touched with loving sympathy (4)

Syrian
  235   simple trust like theirs who heard beside the Syrian sea (2)

systems
  146   our little systems have their day (4)

tabernacles
  295   the tabernacles of thy grace how pleasant, Lord, they be (1)

table
   67   thou spreadst a table in my sight (5)
   68   my table thou hast furnished in presence of my foes (4)
  313   Savior, abide with us, and spread thy table in our heart (1)
  315   author of life divine, who hast a table spread (T,1)
  325   the King of heaven his table spreads (T,1)
  326   this is the heavenly table spread for me (2)
  328   who thy mysterious supper share, here at thy table fed (2)

take

17	and take me home, what joy shall fill my heart! (4)
17	sent him to die, I scarce can take it in (3)
17	he bled and died to take away my sin (3)
21	and for his sheep he doth us take (2)
52	in the confidence of prayer our hearts take hold on thee (2)
58	ye saints to come, take up the strain (4)
60	ye men of tender heart, forgiving others, take your part (5)
69	if our love were but more simple, we should take him at (2)
69	we should take him at his word (2)
87	take the name of Jesus with you (T,1)
87	take it, then, where'er you go (1)
87	take the name of Jesus ever as a shield from every snare (2)
93	here's my heart, O take and seal it (3)
95	take my guilt and grief away (1)
98	and, going, take thee to their home (2)
118	open thine arms, and take me in (1,5)
125	freely let me take of thee (4)
130	come quickly ... my Lord, & take possession of thine own (4)
137	thou take the veil away and breathe the living Word (2)
138	but take the dimness of my soul away (2)
143	take all my guilt away (1)
160	take up thy cross (1,2,3,4)
160	take up thy cross, nor heed the shame (3)
160	take up thy cross,the Savior said (T,1)
160	take up thy cross and follow Christ (4)
161	take thou our lives, and use them as thou wilt (4)
179	take thy great power and reign there alone (3)
187	take my life, and let it be consecrated, Lord, to thee (T,1)
187	take my moments and my days (1)
187	take my feet ... let them be swift & beautiful for thee (1)
187	take my voice ... let me sing always, only, for my King (2)
187	take my lips ... let them be filled with messages from (2)
187	take my silver and my gold (2)
187	take my intellect ... use every power as thou ... choose (2)
187	take my will & make it thine; it shall be no longer mine (3)
187	take my heart, it is thine own (3)
187	take my love, my Lord (3)
187	take myself, and I will be ever, only, all for thee (3)
187	take my hands ... let them move ... impulse of thy love (1)
196	I'll take the gifts he hath bestowed, & ... ask for more (1)
200	take us, and make us holy; teach us thy will and way (4)
207	through every day, o'er all the way He will take care (R)
207	God will take care of you (1,2,3,4,R)
208	and to take him at his word (1)
210	heart content to take whate'er thy Father's pleasure (2)
215	ye fearful saints, fresh courage take (3)
235	take from our souls the strain and stress (4)
237	Jesus, take me, dying, to eternal life (4)
246	take thee, at thy parting breath, to his divine abode 4)
250	but take, to arm you for the fight, the panoply of God (2)
253	bold to take up, firm to sustain the consecrated cross (2)
261	we...never be discouraged, take it to the Lord in prayer (2)
261	take it to the Lord in prayer (2,3)
261	in his arms he'll take and shield thee (3)
266	take time to be holy, speak oft with thy Lord (T,1)
266	take time to be holy, the world rushes on (2)

266 take time to be holy, let him be thy guide (3)
266 take time to be holy, be calm in thy soul (4)
275 gladly take my station there and wait for thee (2)
283 take away our bent to sinning (2)
283 till in heaven we take our place (4)
310 we meet, the grace to take which thou hast freely given (3)
316 thy testamental cup I take, and thus remember thee (2)
319 by faith we take the bread of life (3)
336 let us take up the cross till we the crown obtain (5)
342 lo, I am with you alway. We take thy guiding hand (4)
359 to take away transgression, and rule in equity (1)
364 Savior, take the power and glory (4)
366 your lamps with gladness take; Alleluia! (1)
378 the which his mother Mary did nothing take in scorn (2)
417 beneath the cross of Jesus I fain would take my stand (T,1)
417 I take, O cross, thy shadow for my abiding place (3)
425 then take, O God, thy power, and reign (4)
471 take to thyself thy mighty power (1)
483 and take his servants up to their eternal home (4)
484 take not thy thunder from us, but take away our pride (1)
489 take away our sin and shame (2)
494 from sin & sorrow free, take us Lord, to dwell with thee (3)
502 ere through the world our way we take (6)
514 take the finest of our harvest, crops we grow (1)
514 God ... take the gratitude we give (1)
514 take our plowing, seeding, reaping (2)
514 take our ... hopes and fears of sun and rain (2)
514 in these crops of your creation, take, O God: (3)
522 God shall come, and shall take his harvest home (3)
528 his open side shall take you in (5)

taken
251 Jesus, I my cross have taken (T,1)
285 when shall I find my willing heart all taken up by thee (1)
434 all is solitude and gloom; who hath taken him away (4)

takes
43 the moon takes up the wondrous tale (2)
129 O thou, in whose presence my soul takes delight (T,1)
250 till Christ descends ... and takes the conquerors home (3)
358 darkness takes its flight; doubt & terror are withdrawn (3)
389 takes ...a servant's form who made the heaven and earth (2)
411 as in days of old he takes the wounded to his arms (4)
453 Jesus takes the highest station (4)

taketh
230 He knows the way he taketh, and I will walk with him (2)
521 though he giveth or he taketh, God ... ne'er forsaketh (4)

taking
208 just from Jesus simply taking life & rest & joy & peace (3)

tale
43 the moon takes up the wondrous tale (2)

tales
88 scenes by the wayside, tales of the sea (1)

talk
225 and talk with thee in prayer (4)
262 talk with us, Lord (T,1)

tapers
486 O God, before whose altar the stars like tapers burn (T,1)

tares
522 wheat and tares together sown (2)
522 give his angels charge at last ... fire .. tares to cast (3)

tarnished
194 of tarnished honor, falsely strong (2)

tarries
174 rise up, o men of God, his kingdom tarries long (2)

tarry
104 if you tarry till you're better, you will never come (4)
544 falsehood and wrong shall not tarry beside thee (3)

task
90 shining revealed through every task most lowly (2)
152 task thy wisdom ... assigned O let me cheerfully fulfill (2)
171 O Thou who dost the vision send and givest each his task (3)
171 with the task sufficient strength (3)
174 Church ... her strength unequal to her task (3)
202 our brother Christ ... makes our task his own (1)
217 when my task on earth is done (4)
296 fulfill thy task sublime (4)
342 the task looms large before us; we follow without fear (4)
497 gird us for the task that calls us (2)
499 the trvial round, the common task will furnish all (3)

tasks
197 the challenge of our tasks to face (3)
202 tasks he gives are those he gave beside the restless sea (2)
549 from daily tasks set free (1)

taste
115 we more than taste the heavenly powers (2)
142 whate'er may come, I'll taste ... the hallowed bliss (4)
183 now they taste unmingled love, and joy without a tear (2)
284 let me thy loving servant be ... taste thy promised rest (2)
326 here taste afresh the calm of sin forgiven (3)
329 we taste thee, O thou living bread (3)
331 taste it, kindly given, in remembrance, Lord, of thee (1)
332 let us taste the heavenly powers (4)
341 that the world might taste & see the riches of his grace (3)
489 here afford us, Lord, a taste of our everlasting feast (3)
531 to feel thy power, to hear thy voice, to taste thy love (4)
531 to taste thy love, be all my choice (4)

tastes
142 tastes even now the hallowed bliss of an eternal home (4)

tasting
  457   tasting the celestial powers, we banquet on his love (3)

taught
   92   'twas grace that taught my heart to fear (2)
  243   the sons of fathers we by whom our faith is taught (2)
  337   teach the truth as taught by thee (2)
  549   prayer, by thee inspired and taught ... with work be one (6)

teach
   38   teach us how to love each other (3)
   41   teach us more of human pity that we in thine image grow (3)
   93   teach me some melodious sonnet (1)
   98   to teach our faint desires to rise (4)
  109   words of life and beauty teach me faith and duty (1)
  136   teach us to utter living words of truth (3)
  138   teach me to feel that thou art always nigh (4)
  138   teach me the struggles of the soul to bear (4)
  138   teach me the patience of unanswered prayer (4)
  138   teach me to love thee as thine angels love (5)
  138   I see thy cross; there teach my heart to cling (3)
  147   teach us, in every state,to make thy will our own (4)
  162   Savior, teach me, day by day, thine own lesson to obey (T,1)
  162   teach me thus thy steps to trace (3)
  170   teach me thy patience (3)
  170   teach me the wayward feet to stay (2)
  188   cleanse it from guilt & wrong; teach it salvation's song (3)
  195   teach the precious things thou dost impart (3)
  195   O teach me, Lord, that I may teach (3)
  200   take us, and make us holy; teach us thy will and way (4)
  242   new occasions teach new duties (3)
  252   Lord, teach us how to pray (6)
  265   teach me thy will (4)
  337   within thy temple when they stand to teach the truth (2)
  337   teach the truth as taught by thee (2)
  340   teach thou our lips of thee to speak (3)
  367   teach me to love thy sacred Word ... find my Savior (4)
  372   teach thy wandering pilgrims by this their path to trace (4)
  434   Savior, teach us so to rise (4)
  467   teach us to know the Father, Son, and Thee (4)
  476   teach us to ban .. ugliness that blinds our eyes to thee (4)
  487   pray God to teach us here on this thy holy day (2)
  493   teach me to live, that I may dread the grave as little (3)
  493   teach me to die, that so I may rise glorious (3)
  520   may church and home combine to teach thy perfect way (1)

teacher's
  342   revealing in our witness the master teacher's art (3)
  370   statesmen's, teacher's, hero's treasure (1)

teaches
  484   from all ... terror teaches, from lies of tongue and pen (2)

teaching
   90   we would see Jesus on the mountain teaching (3)
  349   may benedictions here attend the teaching of thy word (3)
  368   to its heavenly teaching turn with ... childlike hearts (4)
  490   venerating age, humbly teaching youth (2)

teachings
257 by thy teachings sweet and holy (1)

tear
    5 then let our songs abound and every tear be dry (4)
  99 many a sorrow, many a labor, many a tear (4)
167 My Jesus, as thou wilt! Though seen through many a tear (2)
183 now they taste unmingled love, and joy without a tear (2)
252 prayer is the burden of a sigh, the falling of a tear (2)
268 help me to tear it from thy throne and worship only thee (5)
270 stooped to share our sharpest pang, our bitterest tear (1)
306 and often for each other flows the sympathizing tear (3)
531 ah, tear it thence and reign alone (2)

tearless
234 feel the promise is not vain that morn shall tearless be (3)

tears
  51 God hears thy sighs and counts thy tears (1)
108 thorns thy brow encircle, and tears thy face have marred (2)
113 by thy birth and by thy tears (T,1)
120 could my tears forever flow (2)
129 and smile at the tears I have shed (3)
143 wipe sorrows tears away (3)
204 we catch the vision of thy tears (2)
209 when change and tears are past (3)
289 ills have no weight, and tears no bitterness (4)
294 for her my tears shall fall, for her my prayers ascend (3)
317 thy holy face is stained with bitter tears (2)
320 look on the tears by sinners shed (2)
415 and melt mine eyes to tears (4)
417 from my stricken heart with tears two wonders I confess (2)
431 heeds not his Master's grief and tears (2)
481 the tears are wiped from eyes that shall not weep again (1)
543 thine alabaster cities gleam undimmned by human tears (4)

tell
    6 tell thy goodness ... thy mercies ... thy glorious might (1)
  11 tell ye forth his might, Lord of life ... truth & right (3)
  18 deeds and words and death and rising tell the grace (2)
  18 death and rising tell the grace in heaven's plan (2)
  21 Him serve with mirth, his praise forth tell (1)
  34 he gave us eyes to see them, and lips that we might tell (4)
  62 let all our future days tell this story (2)
  88 tell me the stories of Jesus I love to hear (T,1)
  88 things I would ask him to tell me if he were here (1)
  88 stories of Jesus, tell them to me (1)
103 here bring your wounded hearts, here tell your anguish (1)
114 what we have felt and seen with confidence we tell (2)
128 and tell its raptures all abroad (1)
149 I love to tell the story (T,1,2,3,4,R)
149 to tell the old, old story of Jesus and his love (R)
149 that is just the reason I tell it now to thee (2)
149 what seems, each time I tell it, more wonderfully sweet (3)
170 tell me thy secret (1)
175 tell them of Jesus the mighty to save (1)
175 tell the poor wanderer a Savior has died (4)

195 thy love to tell, thy praise to show (4)
212 just tell the love of Jesus, and say he died for all (2)
270 the murmuring wind, the quivering leaf ... tell us (3)
270 quivering leaf shall softly tell us thou art near (3)
299 mission ... to tell to all the world that God is Light (1)
299 with none to tell them of the Savior's dying (2)
299 tell how he stooped to save his lost creation (3)
328 tongue can tell our sweet accord ... perfect harmony (1)
340 of thy great love to tell (3)
358 watchman, tell us of the night (T,1,2,3)
381 we hear the Christmas angels the great glad tidings tell (4)
404 go, tell it on the mountain (T,R)
410 we've a story to tell to the nations (T,1)
414 may not know ... cannot tell, what pains he had to bear (2)
437 the day of resurrection, earth, tell it out abroad (T,1)
473 O tell of his might, O sing of his grace (2)
528 O how shall I the goodness tell, Father (2)
528 how ... goodness tell ... which thou to me hast showed (2)
529 I need not tell thee who I am, my sin and misery declare (2)
529 tell me thy name and tell me now (2)
529 and tell me if thy name be Love (3)

telling
311 telling of a Savior dear (2)
466 shall far outpass the power of human telling (3)
505 telling still the ancient story (2)

tempest
125 while the tempest still is high (1)
147 blest be the tempest, kind the storm (2)
378 left their flocks a feeding in tempest, storm, and wind (4)
538 from rock and tempest, fire and foe protect them (4)

tempests
37 clouds arise, and tempests blow by order from thy throne (3)
142 faith that shines more bright & clear when tempests rage (3)
245 sorrows, sometimes how they sweep like tempests (1)
245 like tempests over the soul (1)
308 and tempests are abroad (3)

tempestuous
247 Jesus, Savior, pilot me over life's tempestuous sea (T,1)

temple
13 to my heart O enter thou, let it be thy temple now (2)
55 all ye who hear,now to his temple draw near (1)
199 so shall the wide earth seem our Father's temple (3)
276 O give the pure and lowly heart, a temple meet for thee (4)
298 to this temple, where we call thee, come, O Lord (2)
337 within thy temple when they stand to teach the truth (2)
345 thou, whose unmeasured temple stands (T,1)
345 temple stands, built over earth and sea (1)
346 and let these halls thy temple be (3)
348 living stones prepared for the temple near thy throne (4)
349 of God's great temple thou (1)
352 this temple, reared to thee, O may it ever be filled (1)
363 heart ... make it a temple, set apart (2)

382   suddenly the Lord, descending, in... temple shall appear (4)
423   through pillared court and temple the lovely anthem rang (1)
522   come to God's own temple, come (1)

temple's
428   temple's veil in sunder breaks ... solid marbles rend (2)

templed
547   I love thy rocks and rills, thy woods and templed hills (2)

temples
283   suddenly return and never, nevermore thy temples leave (3)

tempt
25   tents of ease nor thrones of power should tempt my feet (2)
25   nor ... should tempt my feet to leave thy door (2)

temptation
211   in darkness and temptation, my light, my help is near (1)
331   in thy fasting and temptation ...thy labors on the earth (2)

temptation's
76   crown him as your captain in temptation's hour (4)

temptations
87   if temptations round you gather, breathe that holy name (2)
261   have we trials and temptations ... trouble anywhere (2)
265   temptations lose their power when thou art nigh (2)

tempted
501   thou hast been troubled, tempted, tried (5)

tempter
175   down in the human heart, crushed by the tempter (3)
253   and sees the tempter fly (3)

tempter's
113   by thy conflict in... hour of the subtle tempter's power (1)
275   oft escaped the tempter's snare by thy return ... prayer (1)
289   what but thy grace can foil the tempter's power (3)
434   ye that feel the tempter's power (1)

tempting
161   walk thou beside us lest the tempting by-ways lure us (3)
164   I see the sights that dazzle, the tempting sounds I hear (2)
238   striving, tempting, luring, goading into sin (2)

ten
22   earth, with her ten thousand tongues, shall fill (3)
129   he looks! and ten thousands of angels rejoice (5)
246   my soul, be on thy guard, ten thousand foes arise (T,1)

tend
181   to tend the lone and fatherless is angels' work below (3)
430   pressing onward as we can ..to this our hearts must tend (4)
521   God his own doth tend and nourish (2)

tended
258   God hath tended with his care thy helpless hours (2)

tender
  4   as with a mother's tender hand (3)
 60   ye men of tender heart, forgiving others, take your part (5)
 70   unnumbered comforts to my soul thy tender care bestowed (2)
121   much we need thy tender care (1)
147   thy tender mercies shall illume the midnight of the soul (3)
157   warm, sweet, tender, even yet a present help is he (3)
163   so kind and true and tender, so wise a counselor & guide (3)
189   one tender comfort broods upon the struggling human soul (3)
204   from tender childhood's helplessness (3)
205   can I doubt his tender mercy (1)
219   I feel thy strong and tender love, and all is well again (1)
226   may thy tender love to me bind me closer .. Lord to thee (R)
265   no tender voice like thine can peace afford (1)
279   grant me the filial awe I pray .. tender conscience give (3)
280   grant me the filial awe, I pray, the tender conscience (3)
280   the tender conscience give (3)
312   hark, how he calls the tender lambs (1)
333   assurance of tender charity and steadfast faith (2)
384   bless all the dear children in thy tender care (3)
393   holy infant so tender and mild sleep in heavenly peace (1)
473   thy mercies how tender, how firm to the end (5)
498   Jesus, for thy love most tender on the cross ... shown (2)

tenderest
495   with thy tenderest blessing may our eyelids close (2)

tenderly
103   here speaks the Comforter, tenderly saying (2)
110   Jesus is tenderly calling thee home (T,1)
110   calling today, Jesus is tenderly calling today (R)

tends
 66   father-like he tends and spares us (3)
474   forward tends to his abode, to rest in his embrace (2)

tenement
481   lust and greed for gain in street and shop and tenement (3)

tents
 25   tents of ease nor thrones of power should tempt my feet (2)
478   henceforth in fields of conquest thy tents ... our home (1)

terrestrial
 43   solemn silence ... move round the dark terrestrial ball (3)
 71   let every kindred, every tribe on this terrestrial ball (4)
 78   and things terrestrial, Lord alone (2)

terrible
545   lightning of his terrible swift sword (1)

terror
211   what terror can confound me, with God at my right hand (1)
358   darkness takes its flight; doubt & terror are withdrawn (3)
484   from all ... terror teaches, from lies of tongue and pen (2)

terrors
216   no nightly terrors shall alarm (5)
544   let not thy wrath in its terrors awaken (2)

test
157   we test our lives by thine (6)
197   by effort true to meet each test (3)
207   no matter what may be the test (4)

testamental
316   thy testamental cup I take, and thus remember thee (2)

testify
137   testify to all mankind, and speak in every heart (3)

testing
506   long our day of testing, now comes the hour of resting (3)

tether
484   tie in a living tether the prince and priest and thrall (3)

thank
49   now thank we all our God with heart and hands and voices (T)
50   my God, I thank thee,who hast made the earth so bright (T,1)
50   I thank thee, too, that thou hast made joy to abound (2)
50   I thank thee more that all our joy is touched with pain (3)
50   I thank thee,Lord, that thou hast kept the best in store (4)
84   thank we all the mighty Child through whom we know thee (3)
171   we thank thee for thy boyhood faith (1)
203   we thank thee, Lord (T,1)
307   Father, we thank thee who hast planted (T,1)
370   thank we those who toiled in thought (2)
418   language shall I borrow to thank thee, dearest friend (3)
500   we thank thee that thy Church, unsleeping (2)
513   then thank the Lord, O thank the Lord for all his love (R)
513   we thank thee...O Father, for all things bright & good (3)
518   we thank thee, Lord, for this our food (2,3)
525   we thank thee, O Lord (1,2,3)
525   for peace on earth, both far and near, we thank thee (1)

thankful
22   we'll crowd thy gates with thankful songs (3)
259   O knit my thankful heart to thee (1)
312   we bring them, Lord, in thankful hands (3)
513   and what thou most desirest, our humble, thankful hearts (3)
522   come, ye thankful people come (T,1)
544   so shall thy people, with thankful devotion praise him (4)

thankfully
438   let us joyful be and sing to God right thankfully (1)

thankfulness
415   dissolve my heart in thankfulness (4)
523   we owe thee thankfulness and praise, who givest all (3)

thankless
112   thankless creatures, why will you cross his love and die (1)

thanks
- 18   thanks to God whose word was spoken (T,1)
- 18   thanks to God whose Word incarnate (2)
- 18   thanks to God whose Word is answered (3)
- 20   no thanks to them, abideth (4)
- 23   worship and thanks to him belong (1)
- 23   worship and thanks to him belong who reigns (4)
- 49   all praise and thanks to God the Father now be given (3)
- 165   thanks we give & adoration for thy Gospel's joyful sound (2)
- 196   sacred cup of saving grace I will with thanks receive (2)
- 233   rejoice, give thanks and sing (1)
- 233   rejoice, rejoice, rejoice, give thanks and sing (R)
- 314   now we give thee thanks, O Lord (1)
- 336   glory and thanks to Jesus give for his almighty grace (1)
- 409   and thanks never ceasing, and infinite love (4)
- 465   incarnate Deity, let ... ransomed race render in thanks (2)
- 483   rejoice, give thanks, and sing, and triumph evermore (1)
- 491   the day is past and over; all thanks, O Lord, to thee (T,1)
- 548   but for conquests of the spirit give we thanks to thee (2)
- 548   give we thanks to thee, O Lord (2)
- 548   for all heroes of the spirit, give we thanks ... O Lord (3)

thanksgiving
- 357   hymn & chant & high thanksgiving & unwearied praises be (3)
- 548   Lord, we would with deep thanksgiving praise thee (1)

theme
- 58   the same sweet theme endeavor (4)
- 62   gladsome is the theme and glorious (3)
- 70   after death, in distant worlds, the glorious theme renew (4)
- 149   'twill be my theme in glory (R)
- 231   the theme of God's salvation, and find it ever new (2)
- 231   in holy contemplation we sweetly then pursue the theme (2)
- 421   redeeming love has been my theme, & shall be till I die (4)
- 458   his people's hope ... their everlasting theme (6)
- 458   his people's wealth their everlasting theme (6)

themes
- 14   your lofty themes, ye mortals, bring (3)

themselves
- 155   do but themselves confound, His strength the more is (2)
- 304   our hearts in love and worship turn to find themselves (2)
- 304   hearts ... turn to find themselves in thee (2)

thence
- 531   ah, tear it thence and reign alone (2)

therefore
- 214   therefore the evil shall receive but grief (3)
- 412   therefore, kind Jesus, since I cannot pay thee (5)

therein
- 225   make in my heart a quiet place...come ... dwell therein (1)
- 437   let the round world keep triumph, & all that is therein (3)

thick
469 through the thick darkness covering every nation (1)
524 valleys stand so thick with corn ... they are singing (1)
539 when life's perils thick confound you (3)

thief
413 are ye able to remember, when a thief lifts up his eyes (2)
421 the dying thief rejoiced to see that fountain in his day (2)

thieves
528 harlots and publicans and thieves (4)

thing
124 ask ye what great thing I know (T,1)
124 this is that great thing I know ... delights & stirs me (4)
531 is there a thing beneath the sun that strives with thee (2)

things
12 dearer than all things I know is child-like faith to me (4)
15 let all things praise the Lord (3)
34 all things bright and beautiful (T,R)
34 all things wise and wonderful: .. Lord God made them all (R)
34 how great is God Almighty, who has made all things well (4)
40 many and great, O God, are thy things (T,1)
49 wondrous things hath done, in whom his world rejoices (1)
50 so many glorious things are here, noble and right (1)
55 Lord, who o'er all things so wondrously reigneth (2)
60 let all things their creator bless (7)
61 all things living he doth feed (3)
78 all hearts must bow; all things celestial thee shall own (2)
78 and things terrestrial, Lord alone (2)
88 things I would ask him to tell me if he were here (1)
102 all things in Christ are ready now (2)
114 we by his Spirit prove and know the things of God (4)
114 things which freely of his love he hath on us bestowed (4)
137 Spirit of faith, come down, reveal the things of God (T,1)
139 the things unknown to feeble sense (5)
149 of unseen things above, of Jesus and his glory (1)
152 still to things eternal look (3)
171 who with the eyes of early youth eternal things did see (1)
174 rise up, O men of God! Have done with lesser things (T,1)
186 end of my every action thou, in all things thee I see (3)
186 thy bright example I pursue, to thee in all things rise (4)
193 up unto thee, our living Head let us in all things grow (3)
194 to brighter hopes and kindlier things (1)
195 teach the precious things thou dost impart (3)
197 the sacredness of common things (1)
198 these things shall be (T,1)
205 I know whate'er befall me, Jesus doeth all things well (1)
219 hand in all things I behold ... all things in thy hand (4)
250 having all things done, and all your conflicts passed (2)
253 give me on thee to wait till I can all things do (1)
254 help me, oppressed by things undone (2)
258 Light enfolding all things in unclouded day (4)
277 old things shall be done away ... all things new become (2)
285 let earth and heaven and all things go (4)
293 glorious things of thee are spoken (T,1,3)

325 all things are ready, come away (4)
326 here would I touch and handle things unseen (1)
336 gladly reckon all things loss so we may Jesus gain (5)
347 all things are thine (T,1)
354 and order all things far and nigh (2)
357 of the things that are, that have been (1)
397 and, when earthly things are past (4)
424 and mortal men and all things created make reply (2)
430 here earth's precious things seem dross (1)
430 here earth's bitter things grow sweet (1)
435 all the vain things that charm me most, I sacrifice them (2)
437 all things seen and unseen their notes in gladness blend (3)
457 seek the things above (1)
470 rich in things and poor in soul (3)
474 rise from transitory things toward heaven (1)
504 Monarch of all things, fit us for thy mansions (2)
513 he only is the Maker of all things near and far (2)
513 we thank thee...O Father, for all things bright & good (3)
521 from all evil things he spares them (2)
525 for life and health, those common things (2)
525 common things which every day and hour brings (2)
546 purge this land of bitter things (1)
548 praise thee most for things unseen (1)

think
  17 and when I think that God, his Son not sparing (3)
  85 and seeing think God's thoughts after thee (2)
 152 thee, only thee, resolved to know in all I think (1)
 152 only thee...to know in all I think or speak or do (1)
 160 nor think till death to lay it down (4)
 172 work and speak and think for thee (3)
 186 all I think or speak or do is one great sacrifice (4)
 212 sometimes I feel discouraged and think my work's in vain (1)
 219 let me ... think of thee ... new heart springs up in me (2)
 246 ne'er think the victory won, nor lay thine armor down (3)
 255 I sigh to think of happier days, when thou...wast nigh (3)
 284 Lord Jesus, think on me (T,1,2,3,4,5,6)
 412 think on thy pity ... love unswerving, not my deserving (5)

thinking
 441 thinking that never he would wake again (2)
 514 all our thinking, planning, waiting (2)

thinks
 146 he thinks he was not made to die (2)

third
 452 'tis thine own third morning, rise, O buried Lord (3)

thirst
 117 my thirst was quenched, my soul revived (2)
 205 my weary steps may falter, and my soul athirst may be (2)
 285 I thirst, I faint, I die to prove ... love (1)
 293 who can faint while such a river ...their thirst assuage (2)
 329 and thirst our souls from thee to fill (3)

thirsting

149   hungering and thirsting to hear it like the rest (4)
220   till it well-nigh fainted, thirsting after thee (1)

thirsty

117   thirsty one, stoop down and drink and live (2)
255   for thee my God .. living God, my thirsty soul doth pine (2)
295   thirsty soul longs ardently ... faints thy courts to see (2)
367   thirsty souls receive supplies .. sweet refreshment find (2)
464   hangs o'er all the thirsty land (4)

thither

10   the heavens are not too high, his praise may thither fly (1)

thorns

50   that shadows fall on brightest hours, that thorns remain (3)
99   yea, a crown, in very surety, but of thorns (3)
108   thorns thy brow encircle, and tears thy face have marred (2)
144   life's dreary waste with thorns o'er-grown (3)
166   I love thee for wearing the thorns on thy brow (2)
355   mocked ... by thorns with which they crowned thee (1)
355   still our wrongs may weave thee now new thorns (1)
355   new thorns to pierce that steady brow (1)
392   nor thorns infest the ground (3)
418   now scornfully surrounded with thorns, thine only crown (1)
435   or thorns compose so rich a crown (3)
458   the head that once was crowned with thorns (T,1)

thorny

209   through thorny ways leads to a joyful end (1)
403   thine shall be a path, though thorny, bright (4)

thoroughfare

543   a thoroughfare for freedom beat across the wilderness (2)

thought

9   while life, and thought, and being last (1,4)
30   first ... last: beyond all thought His timeless years! (1)
45   I rest me in the thought of rocks and trees (1)
74   thou camest to us in lowliness of thought (2)
81   and cold my warmest thought (4)
82   Jesus, the very thought of thee (T,1)
82   thought of thee with sweetness fills the breast (1)
85   O Mind of God incarnate, O Thought in flesh enshrined (2)
85   God's thought to earth thou bringest (2)
180   guard my first springs of thought and will (2)
191   live out the laws of Christ in ... thought & word & deed (1)
195   o'erflow in kindling thought and glowing word (4)
195   until my very heart o'erflow in kindling thought (4)
206   thou art the thought beyond all thought (2)
217   He leadeth me: O blessed thought (T,1)
219   thought of thee is mightier than sin & pain & sorrow are (1)
256   thou my best thought, by day or by night (1)
259   no thought can reach, no tongue declare (1)
260   secret thought .. hidden plan, wrought ..or unexpressed (2)
260   our highest thought thy will (3)
264   shall rise the glorious thought, I am with thee (5)

266   each thought and each motive beneath his control (4)
279   give me to feel an idle thought as actual wickedness (2)
280   give me to feel an idle thought as actual wickedness (2)
281   cleanse me from every sinful thought (3)
282   a heart in every thought renewed and full of love divine (4)
309   lowly, meek, in thought & word, altogether like our Lord (3)
333   O perfect Love, all human thought transcending (T,1)
347   thy will was in the builder's thought (2)
370   thank we those who toiled in thought (2)
485   rise like incense, each to thee, in noble thought & deed (1)
499   restored to life and power and thought (1)
502   be my last thought, how sweet to rest (2)
525   which all our better thought inspires (3)

thoughted
531   to save me from low-thoughted care (3)

thoughts
35   for all gentle thoughts and mild (4)
50   so many gentle thoughts and deeds circling us round (2)
85   and seeing think God's thoughts after thee (2)
173   thoughts & actions less prone to please the crowd (1)
220   hence, all thoughts of sadness! (3)
263   then, with my waking thoughts bright with thy praise (4)
273   like the arching of the heavens lift my thoughts above (4)
344   store with thoughts divinely true (2)
499   new thoughts of God, new hopes of heaven (2)
506   all evil thoughts expelling, now make in us thy dwelling (5)

thousand
1   o for a thousand tongues to sing (T,1)
22   earth, with her ten thousand tongues, shall fill (3)
25   to spend one day with thee on earth exceeds a thousand (1)
25   one day with thee ... exceeds a thousand days of mirth (1)
28   a thousand ages in thy sight are like an evening gone (4)
83   had I a thousand hearts to give, Lord ... all be thine (4)
246   my soul, be on thy guard, ten thousand foes arise (T,1)
308   Church is praying yet, a thousand years the same (1)
364   thousand saints attending swell the triumph of his train (1)

thousands
2   thousands only live to bless thee (1)
129   he looks! and ten thousands of angels rejoice (5)
299   behold how many thousands still are lying bound (2)
346   accept the prayers that thousands lift (3)

thrall
484   tie in a living tether the prince and priest and thrall (3)

threaten
20   world ... threaten to undo us (3)
20   though this world, with devils filled should threaten (3)

threatening
32   waves ... with threatening aspect roar (2)
253   unmoved by threatening or reward (4)
308   though earth-quake shocks are threatening her (3)
539   smite death's threatening wave before you (4)

three
3	to thee, great One in Three eternal praises be (4)
8	holy Father, holy Son, holy Spirit: three we name thee (4)
19	God ... Father, ... Son, ... Spirit, Three in One (4)
26	God in three persons, blessed Trinity! (1,4)
60	praise the Spirit, Three in One (7)
78	to God the Father ... Son ... Spirit ... Three in One (4)
297	yet she on earth hath union with God the Three in One (4)
298	ever Three and ever One (4)
352	to the great One in Three (4)
377	three wise men bearing gifts of gold (2)
383	and by the light of that same star three wise men came (3)
383	three wise men came from country far (3)
383	then entered in those wise men three (5)
402	we three kings of Orient are (T,1)
441	he that for three days in the grave had lain (3)
446	and from three days' sleep in death as a sun hath risen (2)
447	the three sad days have quickly sped (3)
451	who sat and spake unto the three (3)
480	holy and blessed Three, Glorious Trinity, (4)
488	Church her voice upraises to thee, blest Three in One (4)
492	to God the Father, Son, and Spirit, One in Three (5)

threshold
108	in lowly patience waiting to pass the threshold o'er (1)

thresholds
204	on shadowed thresholds dark with fears (2)

thrice
108	O shame,thrice shame upon us, to keep his standing there (1)
524	thrice blessed ... harvest song ... never hath an ending (3)

thrill
198	and mightier music thrill the skies (4)

thrilling
366	at the thrilling cry rejoices (1)

thrills
87	name of Jesus! How it thrills our souls with joy (3)
547	my heart with rapture thrills, like that above (2)

throb
198	in every heart and brain shall throb the pulse of one (3)
407	we hear the throb of surging life, the clank of chains (2)

throbbing
33	life mounts in every throbbing vein (2)

throne
2	angel voices, ever singing round thy throne of light (T,1)
4	cast each false idol from his throne (5)
5	while ye surround his throne (1)
7	round thy throne, thy name confessing, (4)
22	before Jehovah's awful throne (T,1)
24	come, worship at his throne ... bow before the Lord (3)

28   under the shadow of thy throne (2)
31   the Lord Jehovah reigns, his throne is built on high (T,1)
37   clouds arise, and tempests blow by order from thy throne (3)
53   haste to your heavenly Father's throne (3)
64   before ... blazing throne we ask no luster of our own (4)
77   let all, with heart and voice, before his throne rejoice (1)
103 flowing forth from the throne of God, pure from above (3)
113 by thy high, majestic throne (3)
120 and behold thee on thy throne (3)
122 before the throne my surety stands (1)
122 and sprinkles now the throne of grace (2)
130 my longing heart vouchsafe to make thine ... throne (4)
130 thine everlasting throne (4)
145 let me at thy throne of mercy find a sweet relief (2)
159 pure delight . single hour ... before thy throne I spend (3)
168 the forms of love he wears, exalted on his throne (2)
184 if it would reach a monarch's throne (4)
187 my heart ... it shall be thy royal throne (3)
203 they reach thy throne, encompass land and sea (1)
222 faultless to stand before the throne (4)
229 Jesus we know, and he is on the throne (5)
238 and the endd of sorrow shall be near my throne (4)
242 and upon the throne be wrong (4)
268 help me to tear it from thy throne and worship only thee (5)
275 and bids me at my Father's throne (1)
276 the Lord, who left the throne our life & peace to bring (2)
276 for his dwelling & his throne selects the pure in heart (3)
282 my great Redeemer's throne (2)
301 when round his throne we meet (5)
306 before our Father's throne we pour our ardent prayers (2)
333 lowly we kneel in prayer before thy throne (1)
340 their praises at thy throne (4)
343 like them, let man the throne surround (2)
348 living stones prepared for the temple near thy throne (4)
360 raise us to thy glorious throne (2)
364 yea, Amen! let all adore thee high on thy eternal throne (4)
366 choir immortal of angels round thy dazzling throne (3)
389 let all together praise our God upon his lofty throne (T,1)
409 Salvation to God, who sits on the throne (3)
440 joy unknown, ... saints shall stand before the throne (4)
455 crown him with many crowns, the Lamb upon his throne (T,1)
460 God is King, his throne eternal (1)
463 who descended from his throne and for us salvation won (2)
487 we gather round thy throne on this thy holy day (1)
500 so be it, Lord; thy throne shall never ... pass away (4)
500 thy throne shall never, like earth's proud empires, pass (4)
527 bold I approach the eternal throne, and claim the crown (4)
535 and bow before thy throne (3)
552 our grateful songs before thy throne arise (1)

throned
408 Christ is throned as Lord, men ... forsake their fear (2)
426 here the King of all the ages throned in light (2)
426 throned in light ere worlds could be (2)
459 Ancient of Days, who sittest throned in glory (T,1)
517 throned upon a mother's knee (1)
546 Judge eternal, throned in splendor (T,1)

thrones
      19   bright seraphs, cherubim and thrones (1)
      25   tents of ease nor thrones of power should tempt my feet (2)
      76   thrones and dominations, stars upon their way (2)
     305   crowns and thrones may perish, kingdoms rise and wane (3)

throng
      71   O that with yonder sacred throng we at his feet may fall (5)
      86   let all the holy throng, who to thy Church belong (4)
     157   we touch him in life's throng and press (4)
     303   and bright with many an angel, and all the martyr throng (2)
     305   onward, then, ye people, join our happy throng (4)
     380   comes down through the night from the heavenly throng (4)
     394   spake the seraph and forthwith appeared a shining throng (5)
     524   strains of ... holy throng with ours today are blending (3)

thronged
     340   see the thronged and darkening way (1)
     376   Cherubim and seraphin thronged the air (3)

thronging
     229   peace, perfect peace, by thronging duties pressed (2)

throngs
     204   among these restless throngs abide (5)

through
       4   through all grief distressing (3)
       8   morn to set of sun, through the church the song goes on (3)
      11   through his far domain, love is king where he doth reign (2)
      14   sung through every land by every tongue (1)
      17   when through the woods and forest glades I wander (2)
      20   God hath willed His truth to triumph through us (3)
      20   the Spirit and the gifts are ours through Him (4)
      20   through him who with us sideth (4)
      31   through all his mighty works amazing wisdom shines (3)
      33   splendors ... burn brighter through the cold (2)
      36   thy present life through all doth flow (1)
      47   through all the circling years, we trust in thee (1)
      47   through all our hopes and fears, thy hand we see (1)
      47   through paths unknown we follow thee (3)
      48   when through fiery trials thy pathways shall lie (4)
      48   when through the deep waters I call thee to go (3)
      51   through waves and clouds and storms (2)
      56   through all the changing scenes of life (T,1)
      62   through that precious love he sought us (2)
      63   through the gloom his brightness streameth (3)
      67   so through all the length of days (6)
      70   through every period of my life thy goodness I'll pursue (4)
      80   who like thee ... go so patient through a world of woe (2)
      82   Jesus, be thou our glory now and through eternity (5)
      84   thank we all the mighty Child through whom we know thee (3)
      84   Child through whom we know thee, God of peace (3)
      86   guiding in love and truth through devious ways (1)
      90   shining revealed through every task most lowly (2)
      91   be this the eternal song through all the ages long (4)
      92   through many dangers, toils ... snares I... already come (3)

127 fully absolved through these I am (2)
131 God, through himself, we then shall know (4)
138 wean it from earth, through all its pulses move (1)
151 through the truth that comes from God (2)
157 through him the first fond prayers are said (5)
165 O refresh us ... traveling through this wilderness (1)
167 through sorrow or through joy, conduct me as thine own (1)
167 My Jesus, as thou wilt! Though seen through many a tear (2)
171 boyhood faith that shown thy whole life through (1)
176 lead me through the vale of shadows (3)
177 in joy, in grief, through life, dear Lord, for thee (4)
177 through all eternity, something for thee (4)
186 careless through outward cares I go (5)
188 joyful to follow thee through paths unknown (2)
188 through me thy truth be shown, thy love made known (2)
188 ever, O Christ, through mine let thy life shine (1)
197 to fuller life, through work sincere (2)
197 through quiet work in shop and home (1)
202 through din of market, whirl of wheels (1)
205 my song through endless ages: Jesus led me all the way (3)
205 who through life has been my guide (1)
206 by whose hand through years long past our lives were led (1)
207 through every day, o'er all the way He will take care (R)
207 through days of toil when heart doth fail (2)
209 through thorny ways leads to a joyful end (1)
210 and hope in him through all thy ways (1)
210 and bear thee through the evil days (1)
217 since God through Jordan leadeth me (4)
218 Christ leads me through no darker rooms than he went (3)
218 than he went through before (3)
221 through eternal ages let his praises ring (1)
226 through .. changing world below lead me gently ..as I go (2)
231 it can bring with it nothing but he will bear us through (3)
233 yes, on through life's long path still chanting as ye go (4)
233 as warriors through the darkness toil (5)
234 O Joy that seekest me through pain (3)
234 I trace the rainbow through the rain (3)
235 speak through the earth-quake, wind and fire (5)
235 breathe through the pulses of desire thy coolness (5)
236 grant us thy peace, Lord, through the coming night (3)
237 on thy truth relying, through that mortal strife (4)
239 robes of victory through the skies (6)
239 and sailed through bloody seas (2)
240 run the straight race through God's good grace (2)
250 God supplies through his eternal Son (1)
250 o'ercome through Christ alone, and stand entire at last (2)
260 through open gates thy power flows in (4)
269 lead us through Christ, the true and living Way (1)
269 through joy or sorrow, as thou deemest best (4)
271 Pilgrim through this barren land (1)
278 refining fire, go through my heart; illuminate my soul (2)
278 scatter .. life through every part .. sanctify the whole (2)
284 through darkness & perplexity point ...the heavenly way (4)
288 all in Jesus' presence reign through ages without end (2)
289 shine through the gloom and point me to the skies (5)
289 through cloud and sunshine, Lord, abide with me (3)
296 one holy Church of God appears through every age & race (T)

301	grace through every vessel flows in purest streams (2)
305	this through countless ages men and angels sing (4)
318	through the gifts thou here dost give me (3)
332	explains the wondrous way how through these virtues came (2)
346	through ages long his wisdom and his power display (1)
347	through mortal motive, scheme .. plan thy... purpose ran (2)
365	nor ... spreading Gospel rest till through the world (4)
365	till through the world thy truth has run (4)
371	Word ... shines through the darkness of our earthly way (1)
371	from days of old, through swiftly rolling ages (2)
380	comes down through the night from the heavenly throng (4)
390	still through the cloven skies they come (2)
402	Alleluia, Alleluia! sounds through the earth and skies (5)
406	through desert ways, dark fen, and deep morass (2)
406	through jungles, sluggish seas, and mountain pass (2)
416	joys that through all time abide (4)
419	they climbed the steep ascent of heaven through peril (3)
419	through peril, toil, and pain (3)
423	through pillared court and temple the lovely anthem rang (1)
427	till through our pity and our shame love answers (2)
430	through thy cross made pure and white (5)
442	through each wonder of fair days God himself expresses (2)
450	make us more than conquerors through thy deathless love (3)
450	bring us safe through Jordan to thy home above (3)
454	life is given through thy name (1)
454	every sin may be forgiven through .. virtue of thy blood (2)
455	and hail him as thy matchless King through all eternity (1)
456	trace through corridors sublime (1)
459	through seas dry-shod, through weary wastes bewildering (2)
460	through the rise and fall of nations (3)
467	through ... ages all along this may be our endless song (4)
469	through the thick darkness covering every nation (1)
478	through days of preparation thy grace has made us strong (1)
479	Lord, whose love through humble service (T,1)
480	through the world far and wide, let there be light (4)
486	till through world made noble ... God shall march (4)
486	through lands from sin set free ... God shall march (4)
487	through grace alone are we saved (3)
488	on thee the high and lowly, through ages joined in tune (1)
489	safely through another week (T,1)
489	pray ... through the dear Redeemer's name (2)
491	guard us through the coming night (1,2,3)
491	how many are the perils through which we have to go (4)
495	through the long night watches may thine angels spread (5)
497	strong through thee whate'er befall us, O God most wise (2)
498	thy glory breaks before us through the city's open gate (3)
499	through sleep and darkness safely brought, restored (1)
500	through all the world her watch is keeping (2)
502	ere through the world our way we take (6)
503	evening lamps alight through all the sky (1)
503	through the glory and the grace of the stars (3)
503	through ... stars that veil thy face our hearts ascend (3)
504	glory, gleaming and resounding through all creation (3)
507	give up ourselves, through Jesus' power (2)
509	adored through all our changing days (4)
510	providence hath brought us through another various year (2)
510	to thee presenting, through thy Son, whate'er we have (3)

526 thou grantest pardon through thy love (2)
527 claim the crown, through Christ my own (4)
536 through gates of pearl streams in the countless host (6)
541 men who fly through the great spaces of the sky (1)
541 O God, protect the men who fly through lonely ways (2)
541 men who fly through lonely ways beneath the sky (2)
546 cleanse the body of this nation through the glory (2)
546 cleanse the body ... through the glory of the Lord (2)
550 through all ages bear the memory of that holy hour (2)
552 band of shining worlds in splendor through the skies (1)

throughout
17 thy power throughout the universe displayed (1)
65 all throughout his vast dominion bless the Father (6)
100 redemption in his blood throughout the world proclaim (3)
130 throughout the world its breadth is known (3)
144 help me, throughout life's changing scene, by faith (1)
192 fellowship of love throughout the whole wide earth (1)
192 one in him throughout the whole wide earth (4)
236 grant us thy peace throughout our earthly life (4)
404 behold throughout the heavens there shone a holy light (1)
455 thy praise and glory shall not fail throughout eternity (4)

throw
311 may she holy triumphs win, overthrow the hosts of sin (4)
507 never will throw off his fear who hears our solemn vow (4)

thrust
202 and thrust of driving trade (1)
243 who, thrust in prison or cast to flame (1)

thunder
17 I see the stars, I hear the rolling thunder (1)
343 stormy sea sings praise to God ... thunder & the shower (1)
484 take not thy thunder from us, but take away our pride (1)
544 thunder thy clarion, the lightning thy sword (1)

thunderclouds
473 his chariots of wrath the deep thunderclouds form (2)

thunders
31 the thunders of his hand keep the wide world in awe (2)
440 when, amidst earth's closing thunders (4)

thwart
258 but that he may ever thwart thee and convert thee (3)

tide
232 from every swelling tide of woes (1)
359 the tide of time shall never his covenant remove (4)
378 this holy tide of Christmas all other doth deface (4)
480 boundless as ocean's tide rolling in fullest pride (4)
549 around us rolls the ceaseless tide of business (2)
549 ceaseless tide of business, toil, and care (2)

tides
260 thy power flows in like flood tides from the sea (4)

tidings
- 43 all the planets in their turn confirm the tidings (2)
- 43 confirm the tidings as they roll (2)
- 299 publish glad tidings, tidings of peace (R)
- 299 tidings of Jesus, redemption and release (R)
- 362 O Zion, that bringest good tidings, get thee up (2)
- 374 gladsome tidings be which inspire your heavenly song (2)
- 378 O tidings of comfort and joy, comfort and joy (R)
- 378 and unto certain shepherds brought tidings of the same (3)
- 378 the shepherds at those tidings rejoiced much in mind (4)
- 381 we hear the Christmas angels the great glad tidings tell (4)
- 394 glad tidings of great joy I bring to you and all mankind (2)
- 396 saw the glory, heard the story, tidings of a Gospel true (2)
- 406 immortal tidings in your mortal hands (1)

tie
- 306 blest be the tie that binds our hearts in Christian love (T)
- 314 may the Church that waiteth for thee keep love's tie (3)
- 314 keep love's tie unbroken, Lord (3)
- 328 so dear the tie where souls agree in Jesus' dying love (4)
- 484 tie in a living tether the prince and priest and thrall (3)

ties
- 163 those ties which naught can sever (1)

till
- 14 till suns shall rise and set no more (2)
- 64 till all thy living altars claim one holy light (5)
- 81 till then I would thy love proclaim (5)
- 86 so now, and till we die sound we thy praises high (4)
- 99 not till earth and not till heaven pass away (6)
- 104 if you tarry till you're better, you will never come (4)
- 117 till traveling days are done (3)
- 118 fallen, till in me thine image shine (2)
- 118 and lost, I am, till thou art mine (2)
- 125 till the storm of life is past (1)
- 128 till in life's latest hour I bow (5)
- 133 till I am wholly thine (3)
- 136 till Christ shall dwell in human hearts (1)
- 136 till every age and race and clime shall blend (3)
- 140 and here I will unwearied lie, till thou thy Spirit give (3)
- 151 we will be true to thee till death (R)
- 154 fill with thy spirit till all shall see Christ ...in me (4)
- 159 there are depths of love that I cannot know till (4)
- 159 till I cross the narrow sea (4)
- 159 there are heights of joy that I may not reach till (4)
- 159 till I rest in peace with thee (4)
- 160 nor think till death to lay it down (4)
- 162 singing, till thy face I see, of his love (4)
- 172 till death thy endless mercies seal (4)
- 183 consecrated cross I'll bear till death shall set me free (3)
- 184 it cannot freely move till thou hast wrought its chain (2)
- 184 my power is faint and low till I have learned to serve (3)
- 184 my will is not my own till thou hast made it thine (4)
- 188 till earth, as heaven, fulfill God's holy will (3)
- 193 till thou hast made us free indeed (3)
- 196 till, gathered to the Church above (5)

204 till sons of men shall learn thy love (6)
220 till it well-nigh fainted, thirsting after thee (1)
226 till this fleeting, fleeting life is o'er (3)
226 till my soul is lost in love (3)
228 till my trophies at last I lay down (R)
233 toil till dawns the golden day (5)
235 till all our strivings cease (4)
246 work of faith will not be done till thou obtain .. crown (3)
246 fight on, my soul, till death...bring thee to thy God (4)
248 till every foe is vanquished, and Christ is Lord indeed (1)
250 till Christ the Lord descends from high (3)
250 till Christ descends ... and takes the conquerors home (3)
253 give me on thee to wait till I can all things do (1)
257 till thy spirit breaks our night with the beams of truth (2)
260 dost not wait till human speech thy gifts ... implore (1)
260 and toil, till all are thine (4)
262 let this my every hour employ, till I thy glory see (5)
271 bread of heaven, feed me till I want no more (1)
272 o'er crag and torrent, till the night is gone (3)
283 till we cast our crowns before thee (4)
283 till in heaven we take our place (4)
294 till cares and toils shall end (3)
303 send hope before to grasp it, till hope be lost in sight (3)
313 till all thy life we gain, and all thy fulness prove (2)
336 saves us to the uttermost till we can sin no more (4)
336 let us take up the cross till we the crown obtain (5)
340 till earth and heaven together blend their praises (4)
344 till all our earth is filled with God (4)
352 filled with thy majesty, till time shall end (1)
352 till we our God and King shall praise in heaven (4)
355 till not a stone was left on stone (2)
365 nor ... spreading Gospel rest till through the world (4)
365 till through the world thy truth has run (4)
365 till Christ has all the nations blest (4)
366 we follow till the halls we see where ... sup with thee (2)
370 till they came, who told the story of the Word (2)
372 till, clouds & darkness ended ... see thee face to face (4)
379 till the air, everywhere, now with joy is ringing (1)
384 and stay by my cradle till morning is nigh (2)
396 shepherds keeping vigil till the morning new (2)
398 till everything that's human be filled with the divine (3)
398 till every tongue and nation, from sin's dominion free (3)
401 joyless the day's return till thy mercy's beams I see (2)
421 till all the ransomed Church of God be saved (3)
421 redeeming love has been my theme, & shall be till I die (4)
427 till through our pity and our shame love answers (2)
430 till amid the hosts of light, we in thee redeemed (5)
433 till my raptured soul shall find rest beyond the river (R)
433 till I reach the golden strand just beyond the river (4)
454 for saints ... interceding till in glory they appear (3)
466 O let it freely burn, till earthly passions turn to dust (2)
466 for none can guess its grace, till he become the place (3)
471 till all thy foes confess thy sway (3)
472 till moons shall wax and wane no more (1)
475 nor till that hour shall God's whole will be done (3)
476 help us to spread thy gracious reign till greed .. cease (2)
476 till greed and hate shall cease (2)

476   till ... know the loveliness of lives made fair and free (4)
478   lead on, O King eternal, till sin's fierce war ... cease (2)
479   till thy love's revealing light ... dawns (3)
482   ride on till tyranny and greed are evermore undone (3)
486   till through world made noble ... God shall march (4)
489   thus may all our sabbaths prove till we join ... above (4)
489   till we join the Church above (4)
498   give us strength to serve and wait till the glory breaks (3)
500   thy kingdom stands, and grows forever, till all ... own (4)
500   till all thy creatures own thy sway (4)
502   abide with me from morn till eve (3)
509   that mercy crowns it till it close (1)
529   and wrestle till the break of day (1)
531   nor can it be at rest till it finds rest in thee (1)
539   God be with you till me meet again (T,R)
540   God be with you till we meet again (T,R)
542   let Christ be lifted up till all men serve him (3)
543   till all success be nobleness and every gain divine (3)
548   till it find its full fruition in the brotherhood of man (4)
550   till these eternal hills remove (4)

timbrels
15   timbrels soft and cymbals loud in his high praise agree (2)

time
28   time, like an ever rolling stream (5)
51   he gently clears thy way; wait thou his time (2)
102   this is the time; no more delay (5)
116   friends and time and earthly store (3)
149   what seems, each time I tell it, more wonderfully sweet (3)
214   and in their time bear fruit supreme (2)
242   time makes ancient good uncouth (3)
262   with thee conversing, we forget all time & toil and care (2)
266   take time to be holy, speak oft with thy Lord (T,1)
266   take time to be holy, the world rushes on (2)
266   spend much time in secret with Jesus alone (2)
266   take time to be holy, let him be thy guide (3)
266   take time to be holy, be calm in thy soul (4)
296   redeem the evil time (4)
296   from oldest time, on farthest shores ... she adores (2)
338   joy .. grief .. time .. place .. life nor death can part (4)
351   when time in lowly dust has laid these stored walls (4)
352   filled with thy majesty, till time shall end (1)
359   hail in the time appointed, his reign on earth begun (1)
359   the tide of time shall never his covenant remove (4)
371   undimmed by time, the Word is still revealing (3)
387   late in time behold him come (2)
390   shall come the time foretold (3)
390   when with the ever circling years shall come the time (3)
416   towering o'er the wrecks of time (1,5)
416   joys that through all time abide (4)
426   very God himself is bearing all the sufferings of time (3)
434   there adoring at this feet mark the miracle of time (3)
440   soon the storms of time shall cease (1)
445   He lives, to help in time of need (2)
456   the Lord of interstellar space and conqueror of time (1)
460   spoken by ... Word incarnate, God of God, ere time began (2)

462 Spirit of love, at evening time when weary (5)
474 time shall soon this earth remove (1)
476 no time, no near nor far (1)
512 waters of the spring-time, enriching it once more (1)
513 seed-time & the harvest, our life, our health, our food (3)
544 give to us peace in our time, O Lord (1,2,3)

timeless
30 first ... last: beyond all thought His timeless years! (1)
477 come with thy timeless judgment . match our present hour (1)

timely
213 Jesus, thy timely aid impart (3)

times
21 his truth at all times firmly stood (4)
47 God of the past, our times are in thy hand (2)
417 upon that cross of Jesus mine eye at times can see (2)

tiny
34 he made their tiny wings (1)

tireless
479 stirring us to tireless striving (3)

tires
525 for love of thine, which never tires (3)

title
453 own his title, praise his name (3)

today
2 here, great God, today we offer of thine own to thee (4)
24 today attend his voice, nor dare provoke his rod (4)
49 with countless gifts of love, and still is ours today (1)
110 calling today, calling today (1,2)
110 calling today, Jesus is tenderly calling today (R)
110 waiting today, waiting today (3)
110 hear him today, hear him today (4)
139 today as yesterday the same (1)
139 faith like its finisher and Lord today as yesterday (1)
154 search me and try me, Master, today (2)
298 come, O Lord of hosts, today (2)
347 hence with grateful hearts today (1)
381 cast out our sin, and enter in, be born in us today (4)
389 for he uncloses heaven today and gives to us his Son (1)
391 give ye heed to what we say: Jesus Christ is born today (1)
391 Christ is born today (1)
439 Christ the Lord is risen today, Alleluia! (T,1)
443 Jesus Christ is risen today (T,1)
446 'tis the spring of souls today (2)
446 but today amidst the twelve thou didst stand, bestowing (4)
449 and sing today with one accord the life laid down (4)
451 o'er death today rose triumphing, Alleluia (1)
452 hell today is vanquished, heaven is won today (1,4)
462 today with thee in paradise (3)
487 look into our hearts & minds today ... this thy holy day (1)

488   today on weary nations the heavenly manna falls (3)
489   let us now a blessing seek, waiting in his courts today (1)
502   spurned today the voice divine (4)
511   so we today first fruits would bring (1)
524   strains of ... holy throng with ours today are blending (3)

together
59   we gather together to ask the Lord's blessing (T,1)
189   here together, brother men, we pledge the Lord anew (2)
301   bids us, each to each restored, together seek his face (1)
309   lowly, meek, in thought & word, altogether like our Lord (3)
330   let us break bread together on our knees (T,1)
330   Let us drink wine together on our knees (2)
330   let us praise God together on our knees (3)
340   till earth and heaven together blend their praises (4)
381   O morning stars, together proclaim the holy birth (2)
389   let all together praise our God upon his lofty throne (T,1)
484   bind all our lives together, smite us and save us all (3)
522   wheat and tares together sown (2)

toil
89   my rest in toil, my ease in pain (3)
106   when our days of toil shall cease (3)
107   turned from home and toil and kindred (2)
107   days of toil and hours of ease (4)
170   help me bear the strain of toil, the fret of care (1)
176   gladly will I toil & suffer, only let me walk with thee (2)
186   servant of all, to toil for man (T,1)
204   from woman's grief, man's burdened toil (3)
207   through days of toil when heart doth fail (2)
223   but our toil he doth richly repay (2)
233   toil till dawns the golden day (5)
233   as warriors through the darkness toil (5)
237   should thy mercy send me sorrow, toil, and woe (3)
238   but that toil shall make thee some day all mine own (4)
239   I'll bear the toil, endure the pain, supported (4)
260   content to pray, in life and love, and toil (4)
260   and toil, till all are thine (4)
262   with thee conversing, we forget all time & toil and care (2)
264   when sinks the soul, subdued by toil, to slumber (4)
297   mid toil and tribulation, and tumult of her war (3)
303   strive, man, to win that glory, toil ..to gain .. light (3)
419   through peril, toil, and pain (3)
490   with the gracious light I my toil resume (1)
497   who the day for toil hast given, for rest the night (1)
515   thou art in all; not e'en the powers by which we toil (2)
515   not e'en the power by which we toil for bread are ours (2)
549   ceaseless tide of business, toil, and care (2)

toiled
370   thank we those who toiled in thought (2)

toiling
242   toiling up new Calvaries ever (3)
245   but toiling in life's dusty way (2)

toils
     92   through many dangers, toils ... snares I... already come (3)
    294   to her my cares and toils be given (3)
    294   till cares and toils shall endd (3)
    491   the toils of day are over; we raise our hymn to thee (3)

toilsome
      4   all my toilsome way along I sing aloud thy praises (4)
    552   refresh thy people on their toilsome way (4)

token
    319   the cup in token of his blood that was for sinners shed (3)
    320   be thy feast to us the token (2)
    320   the token that by thy grace our souls are fed (2)
    375   love shall be our token; love be yours and love be mine (3)

tokens
    129   and let the sweet tokens of pardoning grace bring joy (4)
    364   dear tokens of his passion still his dazzling body bears (3)

told
     54   O Lord, our fathers oft have told in our attentive ears (T,1)
    159   I have heard thy voice, and it told thy love to me (1)
    370   till they came, who told the story of the Word (2)
    370   told the story of the Word, and showed his glory (2)
    405   the star that told his birth (2)
    473   the earth with its store of wonders untold (3)

tomb
     75   the rending tomb proclaims thy conquering arm (3)
    123   Joseph's tomb could solve death's mystery (3)
    123   I know not how that Joseph's tomb could solve death's (3)
    402   sealed in a stone-cold tomb (4)
    434   early hasten to the tomb (4)
    434   tomb where they laid his breathless clay (4)
    436   were you there when they laid him in the tomb (3)
    450   Lo! Jesus meets thee, risen from the tomb (2)
    451   the faithful women went their way to seek the tomb (2)
    451   to seek the tomb where Jesus lay, Alleluia (2)

tomb's
    446   neither might the gates of death ... tomb's dark portal (4)
    446   who, triumphant, burst the bars of the tomb's dark portal (5)

tomorrow
    231   let the unknown tomorrow bring with it what it may (2)

tone
    144   thy voice of love, in gentlest tone, still whispers (3)
    195   that I may speak in living echoes of thy tone (1)
    366   with harp and cymbal's clearest tone (3)

tongue
     14   sung through every land by every tongue (1)
     56   praises of my God shall still my heart and tongue employ (1)
     74   let every tongue confess ... one accord ... Jesus Christ (5)
     76   every tongue confess him King of glory now (1)

82   ah, this nor tongue nor pen can show (4)
227   tongue can never express the sweet comfort and peace (1)
259   no thought can reach, no tongue declare (1)
299   proclaim to every people, tongue, and nation (3)
328   tongue can tell our sweet accord ... perfect harmony (1)
357   let no tongue on earth be silent (2)
398   till every tongue and nation, from sin's dominion free (3)
419   like him... pardon on his tongue in midst of mortal pain (2)
421   when this poor lisping, stammering tongue lies silent (5)
421   tongue lies silent in the grave (5)
472   people and realms of every tongue dwell (3)
473   thy bountiful care, what tongue can recite (4)
484   from all ... terror teaches, from lies of tongue and pen (2)

tongues
1   your loosened tongues employ (6)
1   o for a thousand tongues to sing (T,1)
22   earth, with her ten thousand tongues, shall fill (3)
87   his songs our tongues employ (3)
93   sung by flaming tongues above (1)
134   hosannas languish on our tongues and our devotion dies (3)
371   myriad tongues, in one great anthem blending (4)
371   tongues ... acclaim with joy thy wondrous gift to man (4)
469   envious of heart, blind-eyed, with tongues confounded (3)
509   seal in silence mortal tongues (5)
547   let mortal tongues awake; let all that breathe partake (3)

tonight
381   hopes and fears of all the years are met in thee tonight (1)
502   be every mourner's sleep tonight like infant's slumbers (5)

took
96   'twas not so much that I on thee took hold (2)
383   o'er Bethlehem it took its rest (4)
480   chaos and darkness heard and took their flight (1)
483   when he had purged our stains, he took his seat above (2)

top
173   while ever on the hill-top before thee loomed the cross (2)

torch
234   I yield my flickering torch to thee (2)

tore
444   death cannot keep his prey ... He tore the bars away (3)

torrent
272   o'er crag and torrent, till the night is gone (3)

tossed
119   though tossed about with many a conflict, many a doubt (3)
148   some poor seaman, tempest-tossed (3)
292   the wayward and the lost, by restless passions tossed (2)

tossing
244   when the world is tossing me like ship upon the sea (1)
495   guard the sailors tossing on the deep, blue sea (3)

touch

16 to touch our lips, our minds inspire (3)
154 touch me and heal me, Savior divine (3)
157 we touch him in life's throng and press (4)
203 we've felt thy touch in sorrow's darkened way (3)
326 here would I touch and handle things unseen (1)
390 angels bending near ... earth to touch ... harps of gold (1)
441 thy touch can call us back to life again (4)
462 touch thou our dust with spirit-hand (2)
501 thy touch has still its ancient power (6)
505 at his touch our burdens fall (3)

touched

50 I thank thee more that all our joy is touched with pain (3)
175 touched by a loving heart, wakened by kindness (3)
193 touched by the lodestone of thy love (3)
365 when thy truth began its race, it touched ... every land (3)
365 thy truth ... touched and glanced on every land (3)
530 sweetly may we all agree, touched with loving sympathy (4)

touchest

273 God, who touchest earth with beauty (T,1)
273 God, who touchest earth with beauty, make my heart anew (5)

touching

503 heaven is touching earth with rest (1)

toward

41 thou whose purpose moves before us toward the goal (4)
41 toward the goal that thou hast planned (4)
147 if on a quiet sea, toward heaven we calmly sail (T,1)
193 ever toward each other move, and ever move toward thee (4)
399 toward thee longing doth possess me; turn and bless me (2)
442 life in all.. growing powers toward .. light is striving (1)
474 rise from transitory things toward heaven (1)
474 rise ... toward heaven, thy native place (1)
506 the day is slowly wending toward its silent ending (T,1)

tower

171 build us a tower of Christ-like height (2)

towering

11 towering mountain, canyon deep (3)
273 like .. rocks of towering grandeur make me strong & sure (2)
416 towering o'er the wrecks of time (1,5)

towers

469 building proud towers which shall not reach to heaven (3)

town

381 O little town of Bethlehem, how still we see thee lie (T,1)
394 to you in David's town, this day is born of David's line (3)

toys

134 fond of these earthly toys (2)

trace
162 teach me thus thy steps to trace (3)
234 I trace the rainbow through the rain (3)
368 Lamp ... whereby we trace our path when wont to stray (1)
372 teach thy wandering pilgrims by this their path to trace (4)
456 do flaming suns his footsteps trace (1)
456 trace through corridors sublime (1)
474 thy better portion trace (1)

track
242 Christ, thy bleeding feet we track (3)

trade
202 and thrust of driving trade (1)

traffic
225 mid all the traffic of the ways (T,1)

tragic
475 age after age their tragic empires rise (2)

trail
486 whose bones lie white along the trail (2)
486 trail which leads the world to thee (2)

train
8 Lo! the apostolic train joins thy sacred name to hallow (3)
9 he made the sky and earth and seas, with all their train (2)
315 and feed and train us up for heaven (1)
344 discipline ... to train and bring them up for heaven (1)
364 thousand saints attending swell the triumph of his train (1)
419 who follows in his train (1,2)
419 patient bears his cross below ... follows in his train (1)
419 O God, to us may grace be given to follow in their train (3)
482 mighty host, by thee redeemed, is marching in thy train (1)

tramples
253 tramples down and casts behind the baits of pleasing ill (2)

trampling
545 he is trampling out the vintage where the grapes (1)

transaction's
128 'tis done: the great transaction's done (3)

transcending
333 O perfect Love, all human thought transcending (T,1)

transfigures
545 with a glory in his bosom that transfigures you and me (4)

transgression
359 to take away transgression, and rule in equity (1)
418 mine was the transgression, but thine the deadly pain (2)

transgressions
65 who forgiveth thy transgressions (2)

transient
143 when ends life's transient dream (4)

transitory
474 rise from transitory things toward heaven (1)

translate
191 men alert and quick his lofty precepts to translate (2)
277 soon or later then translate to my eternal bliss (4)

transmits
332 how the wine transmits his blood (1)

transport
67 what transport of delight from thy pure chalice floweth (5)

transported
70 transported with the view, I'm lost in wonder, love, and (1)

transporting
291 O... transporting rapturous scene that rises to my sight (1)

travailed
408 the world has waited long, has travailed long in pain (3)

travel
167 straight to my home above I travel calmly on (3)

traveler
358 traveler, o'er yon mountain's height see (1)
358 traveler, yes; it brings the day, promised day of Israel (1)
358 watchman ... traveler (1,2,3)
529 come, O thou traveler unknown (T,1)
529 Traveler unkown, whom still I hold, but cannot see (1)

traveler's
368 brook by the traveler's way (1)

traveling
117 till traveling days are done (3)
165 O refresh us ... traveling through this wilderness (1)
300 we are traveling home to God in the way our fathers trod (2)

traverse
402 bearing gifts we traverse afar (1)

traversing
541 be with them traversing the air in darkening storms (1)

treacherous
247 hiding rock and treacherous shoal (1)

tread
37 if I survey the ground I tread, or gaze upon the sky (2)
143 while life's dark maze I tread & griefs around me spread (3)
144 though oft I seem to tread alone life's dreary waste (3)
174 tread where his feet have trod (4)

199   love shall tread out the baleful fire of anger (5)
204   O tread the city's streets again (5)
205   cheers each winding path I tread (2)
250   tread all the powers of darkness down (3)
270   though long the weary way we tread (2)
271   when I tread the verge of Jordan, bid ... fears subside (3)
338   still in Jesus' footsteps tread & show his praise below (2)
452   tread the path of darkness, saving strength to show (3)

treading
305   brothers, we are treading where the saints have trod (2)

treason
412   alas, my treason, Jesus, hath undone thee (2)

treasure
132   bringing down the richest treasure man can wish (1)
132   richest treasure man can wish or God can send (1)
220   Jesus, priceless treasure, source of purest pleasure (T,1)
220   Jesus, priceless treasure (T,1,3)
227   and have laid up their treasure above (1)
230   my Savior has my treasure, and he will walk with me (3)
256   High King of heaven, my treasure thou art (3)
318   let me measure, Lord, how vast and deep its treasure (3)
370   statesmen's, teacher's, hero's treasure (1)

treasures
84   the world knows not nor treasures (3)
215   he treasures up his bright designs (2)
237   or its sordid treasures spread to work me harm (2)
397   all our costliest treasures bring, Christ to thee (3)
397   treasures bring, Christ, to thee, our heavenly King (3)

treat
108   I died for you, my children, and will ye treat me so (3)
232   there is a calm, a sure retreat (1)
350   the guilty soul a sure retreat (4)
545   trumpet that shall never call retreat (3)

tree
27   we blossom and flourish as leaves on the tree (3)
35   hill and vale, and tree and flower (2)
88   waving a branch of a palm tree high in my hand (3)
166   purchased my pardon on Calvary's tree (2)
199   in its ashes plant the tree of peace (5)
231   though vine nor fig tree neither...fruit should bear (4)
331   in thy trial & rejection...thy sufferings on the tree (2)
364   pierced and nailed him to the tree (2)
415   for crimes that I have done he groaned upon the tree (2)
420   Father's coeternal Son bore all my sins upon the tree (1)
428   behold the Savior of mankind nailed to the shameful tree (T)
436   were you there when they nailed him to the tree (2)

trees
17   and hear the birds sing sweetly in the trees (2)
45   I rest me in the thought of rocks and trees (1)
214   like trees beside a flowing stream (2)

273 like .. straightness of the pine trees let me upright be (3)
547 and ring from all the trees sweet freedom's song (3)

tremble
20 the Prince of Darkness grim, we tremble not for him (3)
142 that will not tremble on the brink of any earthly woe (1)
238 Christian, never tremble, never be downcast (2)
436 Oh! sometimes it causes me to tremble, tremble, tremble (R)

trembled
404 the shepherds feared and trembled (2)

trembles
252 the motion of a hidden fire that trembles in the breast (1)

trembling
172 and trembling to its source return ((2)
206 forgive ... our wild alarms, our trembling fears (3)
270 and trembling faith is changed to fear (3)
283 visit us with thy salvation; enter every trembling heart (1)
324 and with fear and trembling stand (1)
433 near the cross, a trembling soul, love & mercy found me (2)
464 shakes the trembling gates of hell (2)

trial
43 solemn silence ... move round the dark terrestrial ball (3)
56 O make but trial of his love; experience will decide (3)
71 let every kindred, every tribe on this terrestrial ball (4)
78 and things terrestrial, Lord alone (2)
205 gives me grace for every trial (2)
237 in the hour of trial, Jesus, plead for me (T,1)
331 in thy trial and rejection ...thy sufferings on the tree (2)

trials
48 when through fiery trials thy pathways shall lie (4)
97 my friend in trials sore (2)
251 life with trials hard may press me (3)
261 have we trials and temptations ... trouble anywhere (2)
463 who upholds and comforts us in all trials, fears & needs (3)

tribe
71 let every kindred, every tribe on this terrestrial ball (4)

tribes
343 To God the tribes of ocean cry, and birds upon the wing (2)
425 hark! all the tribes hosanna cry (1)

tribulation
59 let thy congregation escape tribulation (3)
244 in the midst of tribulation, stand by me (2)
297 mid toil and tribulation, and tumult of her war (3)

tribute
66 to his feet thy tribute bring (1)
343 to God the powers that dwell on high ... tribute bring (2)
343 their tuneful tribute bring (2)

tried
   18   his the fires that tried her worth (1)
   144 though faith and hope may long be tried (4)
   311 while on earth her faith is tried (1)
   501 thou hast been troubled, tempted, tried (5)

tries
   273 turn my dreams to noble action, ministries of love (4)
   527 in vain the first-born seraph tries to sound the depths (2)
   527 seraph tries to sound the depths of love divine (2)

trim
   148 trim your feeble lamp, my brother! (3)

Trinity
   2   Father, Son, and Holy Spirit, blessed Trinity (5)
   463 blest and Holy Trinity, praise forever be to thee (3)
   480 holy and blessed Three, Glorious Trinity, (4)
   480 Glorious Trinity, Grace, Love and Might (4)
   504 all holy Father, Son, and equal Spirit, Trinity blessed (3)
   538 O Trinity of love and power, our brethren shield (4)

triple
   488 thus on thee most glorious a triple light was given (2)

triumph
   6   songs of glory, songs of triumph to our God and King (2)
   20   God hath willed His truth to triumph through us (3)
   38   in the triumph song of life (4)
   83   he makes me triumph over death (3)
   113 by thy triumph o'er the grave (3)
   165 let us each, thy love possessing, triumph (1)
   165 triumph in redeeming grace (1)
   239 they see the triumph from afar (5)
   289 I triumph still, if thou abide with me (4)
   305 blend with ours your voices in the triumph song (4)
   364 thousand saints attending swell the triumph of his train (1)
   387 join the triumph of the skies (1)
   401 triumph o'er the shades of night (1)
   409 the great congregation his triumph shall sing (2)
   437 Let the round world keep triumph, & all that is therein (3)
   444 with a mighty triumph o'er his foes (R)
   447 the song of triumph has begun: Alleluia (1)
   449 now is the triumph of our King (1)
   450 let his church with gladness hymns of triumph sing (2)
   452 speak his sorrows ended; hail his triumph now (2)
   482 establish thou forevermore the triumph now begun (1)
   483 rejoice, give thanks, and sing, and triumph evermore (1)
   533 ascribe ... their triumph to his death (1)
   536 steals on the ear the distant triumph song (5)

triumphant
   19   all saints triumphant, raise the song (3)
   59   we all do extol thee, thou leader triumphant (3)
   66   saints triumphant, bow before him (4)
   66   saints triumphant ... gathered in from every race (4)
   86   Christ our triumphant King, we come thy name to sing (1)

168   a blest eternity I'll spend triumphant in his grace (3)
353   when morning dawns and light triumphant breaks (1)
386   O come, all ye faithful, joyful and triumphant (T,1)
419   who best can drink his cup of woe, triumphant over pain (1)
443   our triumphant holy day (1)
446   raise the strain of triumphant gladness (1)
446   who,triumphant, burst the bars of the tomb's dark portal (5)
453   hark, those loud triumphant chords (4)
457   and only wish the joy to know of our triumphant friend (1)
474   soon our Savior will return, triumphant in the skies (3)
535   Church triumphant in thy love, their mighty joys we know (2)

triumphed
124   him who triumphed o'er the grave (4)
455   crown him the Lord of life, who triumphed o'er the grave (2)

triumphing
451   o'er death today rose triumphing, Alleluia (1)

triumphs
1   glories of my God and King, the triumphs of his grace (1)
170   in trust that triumphs over wrong (3)
311   may she holy triumphs win, overthrow the hosts of sin (4)
355   O love that triumphs over loss we bring our hearts (4)
413   believe that spirit triumphs .. commend .. soul to God (3)
425   O Christ, thy triumphs now begin o'er captive death (2)
425   triumphs now begin o'er captive death and conqered sin (2)
439   raise your joys and triumphs high, Alleluia (1)
471   the triumphs of thy love display (2)
528   how shall I equal triumphs raise (1)

Triune
459   O Triune God, with heart and voice adoring (5)
465   Eternal, Triune Lord, let all the hosts above (4)
488   sing holy, holy, holy, to the great God Triune (1)

trivial
499   trivial round, the common task will furnish all (3)

trod
60   Christ our Lord the way hath trod (6)
80   pathway, trod in wondrous love, O Son of God (1)
86   lead us to where thou hast trod, our faith make strong (3)
174   tread where his feet have trod (4)
204   and follow where thy feet have trod (6)
249   forget the steps already trod and onward urge thy way (2)
252   the path of prayer thyself hast trod (6)
300   we are traveling home to God in the way our fathers trod (2)
305   brothers, we are treading where the saints have trod (2)
356   show us the way the Master trod; reveal his saving power (1)
368   without thee how could earth be trod (3)
410   Savior ... who the path of sorrow hath trod (4)
482   be the road uphill or down, unbroken or well trod (2)
533   they marked the footsteps that he trod (2)
534   journey which faithless feet ne'er trod (1)
534   O keep us in the pathway their saintly feet have trod (2)
550   and when they trod the wintry strand (1)
550   where their pilgrim feet have trod ... God ... guards (3)

trophies
   71   go spread your trophies at his feet (3)
  228   till my trophies at last I lay down (R)
  453   rich the trophies Jesus brings (2)

trouble
   56   in trouble and in joy (1)
  238   well I know thy trouble, O my servant true (4)
  251   man may trouble and distress me (3)
  261   have we trials and temptations ... trouble anywhere (2)

troubled
   81   and calms the troubled breast (2)
  195   wrestlers with the troubled sea (2)
  217   by waters still, o'er troubled sea ... hand ... leadeth (2)
  250   the troubled heart thy comfort blest (4)
  283   O breathe thy loving spirit into every troubled breast (2)
  394   mighty dread had seized their troubled mind (2)
  477   bring to our troubled minds, uncertain and afraid (2)
  501   thou hast been troubled, tempted, tried (5)

troubles
   28   be ...our guard while troubles last and our eternal home (6)
   48   for I will be with thee thy troubles to bless (3)
  336   what troubles have we seen, what mighty conflicts past (2)

true
   27   in all life thou livest, the true life of all (3)
   29   o thou true Sun, on us thy glance let fall (2)
   47   lead us by faith to hope's true promised land (2)
   47   our heart's true home when all our years have sped (3)
   75   thy Word alone true wisdom can impart (2)
   76   there let him subdue ... all that is not true (4)
   96   it was not I that found, O Savior true (1)
   97   true to him I'll be (3)
   97   how could I this friend deny, when he's so true to me (3)
  104   true belief and true repentance (2)
  136   and earth shall win true holiness (4)
  149   because I know 'tis true (1)
  151   we will be true to thee till death (R)
  156   I would be true,for there are those who trust me (T,1)
  163   so kind and true and tender, so wise a counselor & guide (3)
  171   give us a purpose true (3)
  179   true hearted, whole hearted, fullest allegiance (2)
  181   may we thy bounties thus as stewards true receive (2)
  189   our service strong and true (2)
  191   of steadfast will, patient, courageous, strong and true (3)
  192   in him shall true hearts everywhere ... communion find (2)
  197   O Workman true, may we fulfill in daily life (2)
  197   by effort true to meet each test (3)
  210   though undeserving; thou yet shalt find it true for thee (3)
  228   to the old rugged cross I will ever be true (4)
  238   well I know thy trouble, O my servant true (4)
  253   I want a true regard, a single steady aim (4)
  256   be thou my Wisdom, and thou my true Word (2)
  256   thou my great Father, and I thy true son (2)
  258   when thine aim is good and true (3)

269 lead us through Christ, the true and living Way (1)
273 with thy spirit recreate me, pure and strong and true (1)
273 keep me ever, by thy spirit, pure and strong and true (5)
282 believing, true, and clean (3)
301 Christ, the true, the only light (1)
309 show how true believers live (4)
309 on the wings of angels fly; show how true believers die (6)
321 the blessed cup is only passed true memory of thee (3)
344 store with thoughts divinely true (2)
346 true wisdom is with reverence crowned (4)
364 deeply wailing, shall the true Messiah see (2)
368 true manna from on high (2)
372 to bear before the nations thy true light as of old (4)
378 with true love and brotherhood each other now embrace (4)
396 saw the glory, heard the story, tidings of a Gospel true (2)
401 Christ, the true, the only light (1)
408 Christ is the world's true light (T,1)
420 believe the record true (2)
438 then let us feast this Easter Day on the true bread (4)
438 feast this Easter Day on the true bread of heaven (4)
446 comes to glad Jerusalem who with true affection (3)
452 Him, their true creator, all his works adore (1,4)
452 come then, true and faithful, now fulfill thy word (3)
463 we believe in one true God (T,1)
476 O send us forth, thy prophets true (1)
476 until true wisdom from above . make life's pathway clear (3)
511 to make the dream come true (2)
520 hallowed dwelling where true joy and peace endure (4)
536 thou, in the darkness drear, their one true light (2)
536 O may thy soldiers, faithful, true, and bold (3)
542 with hopes and dreams as true and high as mine (1)
552 thy true religion in our hearts increase (3)

truehearted
179 truehearted, wholehearted, faithful and loyal (T,1)

truest
106 ever present, truest friend ... near thine aid to lend (2)
220 truest friend to me, long my heart hath panted (1)
274 knowest all its truest need (3)

truly
136 descend upon thy Church once more & make it truly thine (1)
137 no man can truly say that Jesus is the Lord unless (2)
151 mankind shall then be truly free (2)
199 for he whom Jesus loved hath truly spoken (2)
274 make me ready when thy voice is truly heard (4)
339 the harvest truly, Lord, is great; the laborers are few (2)
403 thou shalt find thy heart made truly his (2)

trumpet
100 blow ye trumpet, blow! The gladly solemn sound (T,1)
100 the gospel trumpet hear, the news of heavenly grace (4)
222 when he shall come with trumpet sound (4)
248 the trumpet call obey (2)
488 to holy convocations the silver trumpet calls (3)
545 he has sounded forth the trumpet (3)
545 trumpet that shall never call retreat (3)

trumpets
  153 give us courage, let us hear heaven's trumpets ringing (2)
  153 heaven's trumpets ringing clear (2)

trust
  47   God of our life ... we trust in thee (T,1)
  47   through all the circling years, we trust in thee (1)
  53   trust his constant care (1)
  75   who put their trust in thee... death nor hell shall harm (3)
  90   preaching the blessedness which simple trust has found (3)
  97   I'll trust him when life's fleeting days shall end (4)
  97   I want no better friend; I trust him now (4)
  101 only trust him, only trust him, only trust him now (R)
  125 my trust on thee is stayed ... help from thee I bring (2)
  141 have faith in God, my heart, trust and be unafraid (T,1)
  150 assured, if I my trust betray, I shall forever die (4)
  156 I would be true,for there are those who trust me (T,1)
  167 each changing future scene I gladly trust with thee (3)
  170 in trust that triumphs over wrong (3)
  181 all...we have is thine alone, a trust, O Lord, from thee (1)
  206 forgive our wavering trust in thee (3)
  206 still may we trust thy love and grace (4)
  208 'tis so sweet to trust in Jesus (T,1)
  208 Jesus, Jesus, how I trust him (R)
  208 Jesus, precious Jesus! O for grace to trust him more (R)
  208 O how sweet to trust in Jesus (2)
  208 just to trust his cleansing blood (2)
  208 yes, 'tis sweet to trust in Jesus (3)
  208 I'm so glad I learned to trust thee, precious Jesus (4)
  210 who trust in God's unchanging love builds on the rock (1)
  210 so do thine own part faithfully, and trust his word (3)
  215 but trust him for his grace (4)
  216 my God, in him my trust shall be (2)
  216 because thy trust is God alone (6)
  222 I dare not trust the sweetest frame (1)
  223 abides with us still & with all who will trust and obey (1)
  223 trust and obey, for there's no other way to be happy (R)
  223 no other way to be happy in Jesus, but to trust and obey (R)
  223 not a frown ... cross, but is blest if we trust and obey (2)
  223 joy he bestows are for them who will trust and obey (3)
  223 never fear, only trust and obey (4)
  235 simple trust like theirs who heard beside the Syrian sea (2)
  240 trust and...prove Christ is its life and...its love (3)
  240 trust and thy trusting soul shall prove Christ (3)
  248 arm of flesh will fail you, ye dare not trust your own (3)
  266 and, looking to Jesus, still trust in his Word (3)
  275 believe his Word and trust his grace (3)
  317 he drank the cup on Golgatha. His grace we trust (1)
  333 with child-like trust that fears nor pain nor death (2)
  351 and dare to trust the living God (3)
  414 trust in his redeeming blood, and try his works to do (5)
  473 in Thee do we trust, nor find Thee to fail (5)
  509 our helper, God, in whom we trust, in better worlds (5)
  517 hope to trust them, faith to guide them (4)
  526 he is merciful and just, here is my comfort and my trust (3)
  551 be thou her refuge and her trust, her everlasting friend (4)

trusted
- 210   God never yet forsook at need the soul that trusted him (3)
- 210   the soul that trusted him indeed (3)
- 550   the God they trusted guards their graves (3)

trusting
- 101   he will surely give you rest, by trusting in his word (1)
- 116   I am trusting, Lord, in thee, blessed Lamb of Calvary (4)
- 145   trusting only in thy merit would I seek thy face (3)
- 226   trusting thee I cannot stray .. can never .. lose my way (2)
- 240   trust ... trusting soul shall prove Christ is its life (3)
- 433   near the cross I'll watch & wait, hoping, trusting ever (4)
- 490   may this day be blest, trusting Jesus' love (3)

trusts
- 25   blest is the man that trusts in thee (4)
- 250   who ... strength of Jesus trusts is more than conqueror (1)

truth
- 9   his truth forever stands secure (2)
- 11   tell ye forth his might, Lord of life ... truth & right (3)
- 14   eternal truth attends thy word (2)
- 20   God hath willed His truth to triumph through us (3)
- 20   the body they may kill: God's truth abideth still (4)
- 21   his truth at all times firmly stood (4)
- 21   his truth ... shall from age to age endure (4)
- 22   firm as a rock thy truth must stand (4)
- 31   his truth confirms and seals the grace (2)
- 43   spread the truth from pole to pole (2)
- 51   let us in life, in death, thy steadfast truth declare (4)
- 56   blest are they, and only they, who in his truth confide (3)
- 56   God preserves the souls of those who on his truth depend (5)
- 64   Lord ... whose light is truth, whose warmth is love (4)
- 64   grant us thy truth to make us free (5)
- 75   thou art the Truth (2)
- 75   thou art the Way, the Truth, the Life (4)
- 75   grant us that way to know, that truth to keep (4)
- 85   learn from thee their duty, the truth, the life, the way (4)
- 86   guiding in love and truth through devious ways (1)
- 90   the Christ of God, the life, the truth, the way (2)
- 101   Jesus is the truth, the way that leads you into rest (3)
- 125   thou art full of truth and grace (3)
- 131   unlock the truth, thyself the key (2)
- 135   Holy Spirit, Truth divine, dawn upon this soul of mine (T,1)
- 136   teach us to utter living words of truth (3)
- 136   truth which all may hear (3)
- 151   through the truth that comes from God (2)
- 165   ever faithful ... to the truth may we be found (2)
- 169   to be the best that I can be for truth ... and thee (4)
- 169   be for truth and righteousness and thee (4)
- 173   stand with humble courage for truth with hearts uncowed (1)
- 188   through me thy truth be shown, thy love made known (2)
- 191   men with hearts ablaze .. truth to love .. wrong to hate (4)
- 211   his truth be thine affiance, when faint and desolate (2)
- 237   on thy truth relying, through that mortal strife (4)
- 242   then to side with truth is noble (2)
- 242   though the cause of evil prosper . truth alone is strong (4)

242   in the strife of truth with falsehood (1)
242   they must upward still & onward who would keep ... truth (3)
242   who would keep abreast of truth (3)
252   O Thou by whom we come to God ... Life ... Truth ... Way (6)
257   till thy spirit breaks our night with the beams of truth (2)
257   beams of truth unclouded (2)
260   thou seekest us in love and truth (4)
267   that I may see glimpses of truth thou hast for me (1)
267   open my mouth, and let me bear gladly the warm truth (3)
267   let me bear gladly the warm truth everywhere (3)
267   open my eyes, that I may hear voices of truth (2)
267   voices of truth thou sendest clear (2)
269   lead us, O Father, in the paths of truth (2)
275   truth and faithfulness engage the waiting soul to bless (3)
279   Almighty God of truth and love, to me thy power impart (4)
280   Almighty God of truth and love, to me thy power impart (4)
281   God of all power and truth and grace (T,1)
281   that all mankind thy truth may see (2)
294   sure as thy truth shall last (5)
296   truth is her prophetic gift, the soul, her sacred page (3)
329   thy truth unchanged hath ever stood (2)
337   within thy temple when they stand to teach the truth (2)
337   teach the truth as taught by thee (2)
344   truth and love let all men see (3)
348   seeds of truth be sown where we lay this cornerstone (2)
351   who honor truth, nor fear the crowd (3)
352   do thou the truth impart unto each waiting heart (3)
356   restore to us thy truth, O God, & make its meaning sure (2)
358   blessedness and light, peace & truth its course portends (2)
365   when thy truth began its race, it touched ... every land (3)
365   thy truth ... touched and glanced on every land (3)
365   till through the world thy truth has run (4)
366   the strong in grace, in truth victorious (2)
369   bless thou the truth, dear Lord, to me, to me (2)
370   bringing freedom, spreading truth (1)
372   O Truth unchanged, unchanging, O Light of our dark sky (1)
372   it is the sacred casket where gems of truth are stored (2)
392   he rules the world with truth and grace (4)
399   thou beamest forth in truth and light (1)
410   a story of truth and mercy, a story of peace and light (1)
410   might come to the truth of God (4)
468   truth from the earth, like to a flower, shall bud (1)
468   truth ... shall bud and blossom then (1)
476   O God of truth, whom science seeks (3)
476   O God of truth, whom ... reverent souls adore (3)
480   Spirit of truth and love, life-giving, holy Dove (3)
483   Jesus, the Savior, reigns, the God of truth and love (2)
490   always serving thee, sharing thy rich truth (2)
545   his truth is marching on (1)
545   Glory! glory! Hallelujah ... His truth is marching on (R)
549   in truth and patience wrought (3)
550   laws, freedom, truth, and faith in God came (3)
551   unite us in the sacred love of knowledge, truth & thee (3)

try
154   search me and try me, Master, today (2)
252   speech that infant lips can try (3)
414   trust in his redeeming blood, and try his works to do (5)

trying
  148   trying now to make the harbor (3)

tumult
  107   Jesus calls us o'er the tumult (T,1)
  107   tumult of our life's wild, restless sea (1)
  297   mid toil and tribulation, and tumult of her war (3)
  380   there's a tumult of joy o'er the wonderful birth (2)
  538   and bid their angry tumult cease (3)

tumults
  469   by wars and tumults love is mocked, derided (2)

tune
   23   come, let us tune our loftiest song (T,1)
   93   tune my heart to sing thy grace (1)
  134   in vain we tune our formal songs (3)
  231   yet God the same abiding, his praise shall tune my voice (4)
  488   on thee the high and lowly, through ages joined in tune (1)

tuned
  255   when every heart was tuned to praise (3)

tuneful
   15   praise him every tuneful string: (2)
  343   their tuneful tribute bring (2)

turmoil
  460   'mid the world's despair and turmoil one firm anchor (1)

turmoils
  225   turmoils without, within (1)

turn
   29   to make ill-fortune turn to fair (4)
   37   where'er I turn my eye (2)
   43   all the planets in their turn confirm the tidings (2)
   95   turn me not away unblest; calm my anguish into rest (3)
  110   he will not turn thee away (2)
  112   sinners, turn, why will you die (T,1,2,3)
  121   blessed Jesus! We will early turn to thee (3)
  143   be thou my guide; bid darkness turn to day (3)
  230   wherever he may guide me, no want shall turn me back (2)
  236   turn thou for us its darkness into light (3)
  273   turn my dreams to noble action, ministries of love (4)
  304   with love and longing turn to find their rest in thee (1)
  304   our hearts in love and worship turn to find themselves (2)
  304   hearts ... turn to find themselves in thee (2)
  329   we turn unfilled to thee again (1)
  359   give them songs for sighing ... darkness turn to light (2)
  368   to its heavenly teaching turn with ... childlike hearts (4)
  399   toward thee longing doth possess me; turn and bless me (2)
  410   that shall turn their hearts to the right (1)
  410   for the darkness shall turn to dawning (R)
  434   turn not from his griefs away (1)
  466   O let it freely burn, till earthly passions turn to dust (2)
  466   passions turn to dust and ashes in its heat consuming (2)

475 turn back, O man, forswear thy foolish ways (T,1)
486 at whose inscrutable decree the planets wheel and turn (1)
486 face the darkness undismayed and turn their loss to gain (3)
549 scarcely can we turn aside for one brief hour of prayer (2)
122 he cannot turn away the presence of his Son (4)

turned
107 turned from home and toil and kindred (2)
408 freedom her bondage breaks, and night is turned to day (1)

turnest
219 and turnest my mourning into praise (4)

turning
41 from thy ways so often turning (2)

turns
85 thru thy life so radiant, earth's darkness turns to day (1)
219 thy providence turns all to good (3)
242 with the cross that turns not back (3)
270 when drooping pleasure turns to grief (3)
341 scatters all ... guilty fear .. turns .. hell to heaven (2)

twelve
19 ye holy twelve, ye martyrs strong (3)
419 twelve valiant saints, their hope they knew (3)
446 but today amidst the twelve thou didst stand, bestowing (4)

twine
163 and round my heart still closely twine those ties (1)

twining
498 praise for mercies daily twining round us golden cords (1)
498 twining round us golden cords of love (1)

twinkling
79 and all the twinkling starry host: Jesus shines brighter (3)

twixt
242 choice goes by forever twixt that darkness & that light (1)
247 'twixt me and the peaceful rest (3)
454 peace is made twixt man and God (2)

two
254 what I dream & what I do in my weak days are always two (2)
417 from my stricken heart with tears two wonders I confess (2)

tyranny
482 ride on till tyranny and greed are evermore undone (3)

tyrant's
89 my smile beneath the tyrant's frown (3)
422 thus the great Messiah came to break the tyrant's will (3)

ugliness
476 teach us to ban .. ugliness that blinds our eyes to thee (4)

unaccompanied
401 dark and cheerless is the morn unaccompanied by thee (2)

unafraid
141 have faith in God, my heart, trust and be unafraid (T,1)
202 we follow where the Master leads, serene and unafraid (1)

unanswered
138 teach me the patience of unanswered prayer (4)

unbelief
145 kneeling there in deep contrition, help my unbelief (2)
214 not like that go the men of unbelief (3)
214 men of unbelief ... are like chaff the wind doth blow (3)
215 blind unbelief is sure to err and scan his work in vain (5)
401 fill me, Radiancy divine; scatter all my unbelief (3)

unbent
184 it only stands unbent amid the clashing strife (4)

unblest
95 turn me not away unblest; calm my anguish into rest (3)

unbounded
283 pure, unbounded love thou art (1)
318 whose grace unbounded hath this wondrous banquet founded (1)

unbroken
38 center of unbroken praise (2)
58 unbroken be the golden chain, keep on the song forever (4)
314 keep love's tie unbroken, Lord (3)
482 be the road uphill or down, unbroken or well trod (2)

unceasing
8 cherubim and seraphim, in unceasing chorus praising (2)
359 to him shall prayer unceasing and daily vows ascend (4)

uncertain
477 bring to our troubled minds, uncertain and afraid (2)

unchanged
53 his goodness stands approved, unchanged from day to day (4)
296 unchanged by changing place (91)
329 thy truth unchanged hath ever stood (2)
372 O Truth unchanged, unchanging, O Light of our dark sky (1)

unchanging
210 who trust in God's unchanging love builds on the rock (1)
222 I rest on his unchanging grace (2)
372 O Truth unchanged, unchanging, O Light of our dark sky (1)
460 God hath ... spoken his unchanging Word (1)
460 God abides, his Word unchanging (3)

unchartered
206 though there be dark, unchartered space (4)

uncheered
269 and age comes on, uncheered by faith or hope (2)

unclasp
267 wonderful key that shall unclasp and set me free (1)

uncloses
389 for he uncloses heaven today and gives to us his Son (1)

unclouded
257 beams of truth unclouded (2)
258 Light enfolding all things in unclouded day (4)

uncomplaining
144 with patient uncomplaining love, still ... cling to thee (2)

unconfimed
130 immense and unconfimed; from age to age it never ends (2)

unconsidered
486 their unconsidered lives go up like incense to the sky (2)

uncouth
242 time makes ancient good uncouth (3)

uncowed
173 stand with humble courage for truth with hearts uncowed (1)

unction
67 thy unction grace bestoweth (5)
132 author of the new creation, come with unction (2)
132 come with unction and with power (2)
467 thy blessed unction from above is comfort, life & fire (2)

undaunted
475 peals forth in joy man's old undaunted cry (3)

undefiled
395 there he lay, the undefiled, to the world a stranger (1)
395 he is still the undefiled, but no more a stranger (3)

under
28 under the shadow of thy throne (2)
55 shieldeth thee under his wings ... so gently sustaineth (2)
65 ever under his control (6)
179 under the standard exalted and royal (1)

undergo
452 thou, of life the author, death didst undergo (3)

underlies
290 assured alone that life and death God's mercy underlies (1)

understand
136 the language all men understand (3)
244 when I've done the best I can &... friends misunderstand (3)
462 make us souls that understand (2)

understanding
84 give milk . bread or solid food as fits my understanding (3)

undertake
209 God doth undertake to guide ... future as ... the past (2)

undeserving
210 though undeserving; thou yet shalt find it true for thee (3)

undimmed
371 undimmed by time, the Word is still revealing (3)
543 thine alabaster cities gleam undimmed by human tears (4)

undismayed
51 give to the winds thy fears; hope and be undismayed (T,1)
300 Jesus Christ, our Father's Son, bids us undismayed go on (3)
486 face the darkness undismayed and turn their loss to gain (3)

undivided
8 though in essence only One; undivided God we claim thee (4)
328 many, and yet but one are we, one undivided bread (2)

undo
20 world ... threaten to undo us (3)

undone
118 to thee, lost and undone, for aid I flee (1,5)
254 help me, oppressed by things undone (2)
311 judge her not for work undone (4)
412 alas, my treason, Jesus, hath undone thee (2)
482 ride on till tyranny and greed are evermore undone (3)

undying
446 from his light, to whom we give laud and praise undying (2)

unending
298 One in might, and One in glory, while unending ages run (4)
308 we hear within the solemn voice of her unending song (2)
317 Immanuel, heaven's joy unending (3)

unequal
174 Church ... her strength unequal to her task (3)

unerring
46 by thine unerring spirit led (2)
509 by his unerring counsel led (2)

unexpressed
260 secret thought .. hidden plan, wrought ..or unexpressed (2)

unfailing
371 O God of light, thy Word, a lamp unfailing (T,1)
539 put his arms unfailing round you (3)

unfaith
355 from old unfaith our souls release (3)

unfaithful
178 thy friends unfaithful prove (2)

unfathomable
215 deep in unfathomable mines of never-failing skill (2)
332 O the depth of love divine, the unfathomable grace (T,1)

unfathomed
33 thou from whose unfathomed law the year in beauty flows (3)
531 whose height, whose depth unfathomed no man knows (1)

unfilled
329 we turn unfilled to thee again (1)

unflinching
173 O help us walk unflinching in paths that lead to peace (3)

unfold
33 the radiant morns unfold (2)
38 hearts unfold like flowers before thee (1)
389 this day again those gates unfold (4)

unfoldest
60 dear mother earth, who day by day unfoldest blessings (4)
60 unfoldest blessings on our way, O praise him (4)

unfolding
206 rests the unfolding of the years (3)

unforgiven
469 nation by nation still goes unforgiven (3)

unfurled
184 flag can only be unfurled when thou shall breathe (3)
184 unfurled when thou shalt breathe from heaven (3)
372 it floateth like a banner before God's host unfurled (3)
390 with peaceful wings unfurled (2)

unhasting
27 unresting, unhasting, and silent as light (2)

unheard
274 though least and lowest, let me not unheard depart (3)
431 unheard by mortals are the strains that sweetly soothe (4)

unheeding
427 is this thy sorrow naught to us who pass unheeding by (1)

unhelped
269 unhelped by thee, in error's maze we grope (2)

unhurrying
456 there stands he with unhurrying feet (2)

union
178 gentleness and grace...spring from union, Lord, with thee (4)
297 yet she on earth hath union with God the Three in One (4)
334 may they abide in union with each other and the Lord (2)

unite
   86   unite to swell the song to Christ our King (4)
  173   who would unite the nations in brotherhood for all (3)
  180   in thy sole glory may unite (3)
  302   saints on earth unite to sing with those to glory gone (2)
  307   unite it, cleansed and conformed into thy will (3)
  309   each to each unite, endear (2)
  344   unite the pair . long disjoined, knowledge & vital piety (3)
  356   unite us in thy will, O Lord, and endd all sinful strife (2)
  486   though earth and sea and heaven unite thy praise to sing (1)
  516   unite our hearts in love to thee (4)
  516   unite ... in love to thee, and love to all will reign (4)
  551   unite us in the sacred love of knowledge, truth & thee (3)

united
  193   Jesus, united by grace, and each to each endeared (T,1)
  408   One Lord, in one great name united us all who own thee (3)
  504   bring us to heaven, where thy saints united joy (2)
  504   saints united joy without ending (2)
  533   with united breath, ascribe their conquest to the Lamb (1)
  542   and hearts united learn to live as one (3)

unites
  189   one common faith unites us all, we seek one common goal (3)
  189   one claim unites all men in God to serve each human need (2)

uniting
  338   blest be the dear uniting love that will not let us part (T)

universal
   24   Jehovah is the sovereign God, the universal King (1)
  339   thy universal grace proclaim, thine all-redeeming love (4)
  454   hail ... universal Savior who hast borne our sin & shame (1)
  529   pure, universal love thou art (4)

universe
   17   thy power throughout the universe displayed (1)
  492   the mists of error and of vice which shade the universe (2)
  503   Lord of life, beneath the dome of the universe thy home (2)

unknown
   24   formed the deeps unknown ... gave the seas their bound (2)
   47   through paths unknown we follow thee (3)
  114   we...his unknown peace receive & feel his blood applied (3)
  119   thy love unknown hath broken every barrier down (6)
  120   when I rise to worlds unknown (3)
  139   the things unknown to feeble sense (5)
  188   joyful to follow thee through paths unknown (2)
  229   peace, perfect peace, our future all unknown (5)
  231   let the unknown tomorrow bring with it what it may (2)
  242   behind the dim unknown, standeth God within the shadow (4)
  247   unknown waves before me roll (1)
  301   a peace to sensual minds unknown, a joy unspeakable (4)
  332   sure and real is the grace, the manner be unknown (4)
  333   and to life's day the glorious unknown morrow (3)
  440   joy unknown, ... saints shall stand before the throne (4)
  476   no child unsought, unknown (1)
  509   the future, all to us unknown (3)

529 come, O thou traveler unknown (T,1)
529 Traveler unknown, whom still I hold, but cannot see (1)

unless
137 no man can truly say that Jesus is the Lord unless (2)

unlock
131 unlock the truth, thyself the key (2)
414 he only could unlock the gate of heaven and let us in (4)

unmeasured
18 here we drink of joy unmeasured (3)
345 thou, whose unmeasured temple stands (T,1)

unmindful
528 unmindful of his favors prove (3)

unmingled
183 now they taste unmingled love, and joy without a tear (2)

unmixed
251 not in joy to charm me were that joy unmixed with thee (3)

unmoistened
446 led them with unmoistened foot through... Red Sea waters (1)

unmoved
253 unmoved by threatening or reward (4)

unnumbered
70 unnumbered comforts to my soul thy tender care bestowed (2)
248 ye that are men now serve him against unnumbered foes (2)

unresting
27 unresting, unhasting, and silent as light (2)

unrighteousness
125 just and holy is thy name; I am all unrighteousness (3)

unseal
131 unseal the sacred book (2)

unseals
497 when the constant sun returning unseals our eyes (2)

unsearchable
285 its riches are unsearchable (2)

unseen
70 thine arm, unseen, conveyed me safe (3)
84 thou givest us that good unseen the world knows not (3)
139 unseen by reason's glimmering ray (5)
144 O Holy Savior, friend unseen (T,1)
149 of unseen things above, of Jesus and his glory (1)
260 our spirits' unseen friend, high heaven's Lord (1)
296 beneath the pine or palm, one unseen Presence she adores (2)
304 its heavenly walls unseen around us rise (1)

326 here would I touch and handle things unseen (1)
347 thy hand unseen amidst us wrought (2)
437 all things seen & unseen their notes in gladness blend (3)
441 laid in the earth like grain that sleeps unseen (2)
548 praise thee most for things unseen (1)

unshaken
308 unshaken as eternal hills, immovable she stands (4)

unsleeping
500 we thank thee that thy Church, unsleeping (2)
500 unsleeping while earth rolls onward into light (2)

unslumbering
57 watchful and unslumbering care his own he safely keeps (2)

unsought
219 thou leadest me by unsought ways (4)
476 no child unsought, unknown (1)

unspeakable
89 in grief my joy unspeakable (4)
137 cry, with joy unspeakable, "...my Lord, my God" (2)
301 a peace to sensual minds unknown, a joy unspeakable (4)

unswerving
210 sing, pray,and keep his ways unswerving (3)
412 think on thy pity ... love unswerving, not my deserving (5)

untamed
84 to untamed colt, the bridle, (1)

untired
213 dauntless, untired, I follow thee (4)

untold
473 the earth with its store of wonders untold (3)

untried
290 if my heart and flesh are weak to bear an untried pain (2)

untrod
362 a call from the ways untrod (1,4)

untrue
251 thou art not, like man, untrue (2)

unuttered
252 prayer ... unuttered or expressed (1)

unwasted
296 unwasted by the lapse of years (1)

unwearied
4 my voice unwearied raises (4)
43 the unwearied sun, from day to day (1)
140 and here I will unwearied lie, till thou thy Spirit give (3)

178   unwearied ... forgiveness still, thy heart ... only love (2)
357   hymn & chant & high thanksgiving & unwearied praises be (3)
446   welcomes in unwearied strains Jesus' resurrection (3)

unwon
311   judge her not for fields unwon (4)

unworthily
2   for thine acceptance proffer all unworthily (4)

unworthiness
417   the wonders of redeeming love and my unworthiness (2)

unworthy
520   let all unworthy aims depart, imbue us with thy grace (2)

unwrapped
442   spring has now unwrapped the flowers (T,1)

upheld
48   upheld by my righteous, omnipotent hand (2)
243   upheld and strengthened by thy hand (3)

uphill
482   be the road uphill or down, unbroken or well trod (2)

uphold
539   by his counsels guide, uphold you (1)
541   uphold them with thy saving grace (2)

upholden
62   God is love, by him upholden (T,1)
62   by him upholden hang the glorious orbs of light (1)

upholds
463   who upholds and comforts us in all trials, fears & needs (3)
476   Eternal God, whose power upholds (T,1)
476   whose power upholds both flower and flaming star (1)

uplifted
449   and sing with hearts uplifted high: Alleluia (3)
532   whose music like a mighty wind the souls of men uplifted (3)

uplifts
32   the Lord uplifts his awful hand and chains you (2)

upper
321   upper room where fainting souls are fed (1)

upraises
488   Church her voice upraises to thee, blest Three in One (4)

upright
273   like .. straightness of the pine trees let me upright be (3)

uprising
499   new ... the love our wakening and uprising prove (1)

upward
242 they must upward still & onward who would keep ... truth (3)
252 the upward glancing of an eye, when none but God is near (2)
263 sun, moon, and stars forgot, upward I fly (5)

urge
249 forget the steps already trod and onward urge thy way (2)

use
121 for our use thy folds prepare (1)
161 take thou our lives, and use them as thou wilt (4)
187 take my intellect ... use every power as thou ... choose (2)
195 O use me, Lord, use even me, just as thou wilt and when (5)
200 but thou canst use our weakness to magnify thy power (3)
363 set apart ... from earthly use for heaven's employ (2)
479 use the love thy spirit kindles still to save (2)
507 come, let us use the grace divine (T,1)
508 come, let us use the grace divine (T,1) (same as 507)

used
80 marks divine, that in thy meekness used to shine (1)

usher
373 and usher in the morning (1)
422 while men of low degree exalt and usher in the day (4)

utmost
206 thou art...the gift beyond our utmost prayer (2)
281 thy word may to the utmost prove (5)

utter
33 day unto day utter speech ... night to night proclaim (3)
43 in reason's ear they all rejoice and utter forth (3)
43 utter forth a glorious voice (3)
95 mercy now, O Lord, I plead in this hour of utter need (3)
136 teach us to utter living words of truth (3)

uttermost
336 saves us to the uttermost till we can sin no more (4)

vain
9 none shall find his promise vain (2)
86 while in our mortal pain none calls on thee in vain (2)
102 nor suffer him to die in vain (4)
105 vain world, farewell, from thee I part (5)
107 Jesus calls us from the worship of the vain (3)
107 the vain world's golden store (3)
134 in vain we tune our formal songs (3)
134 in vain we strive to rise (3)
157 in vain we search the lowest deeps (2)
212 sometimes I feel discouraged and think my work's in vain (1)
215 blind unbelief is sure to err and scan his work in vain (5)
219 I look to thee in every need and never look in vain (T,1)
234 feel the promise is not vain that morn shall tearless be (3)
237 with forbidden pleasures would this vain world charm (2)
265 come quickly and abide or life is vain (3)
285 first-born sons of light desire in vain its depths...see (2)

289 heaven's morning breaks, and earth's vain shadows flee (5)
332 angels round our altars bow to search it out in vain (3)
435 all the vain things that charm me most, I sacrifice them (2)
439 death in vain forbids him rise, Alleluia (3)
481 cry Christ hath died in vain (3)
527 in vain the first-born seraph tries to sound the depths (2)

vainly
400 vainly we offer each ample oblation (4)
400 vainly with gifts would his favor secure (4)
444 vainly they watch his bed ... vainly they seal the dead (2)

vale
35 hill and vale, and tree and flower (2)
38 field and forest, vale and mountain, flowery meadow (2)
67 in death's dark vale I fear no ill (4)
68 yea, though I walk in death's dark vale (3)
176 lead me through the vale of shadows (3)
245 or walking the shadowy vale (3)

vales
512 with corn the vales are covered (2)

valiant
155 he who would valiant be 'gainst all disaster (T,1)
179 valiant endeavor and loving obedience (2)
419 twelve valiant saints, their hope they knew (3)

valley
129 say, why in the valley of death should I weep (2)
244 O thou Lily of the Valley, stand by me (4)
359 righteousness, in fountains, from hill to valley flow (3)
462 in the gray valley let us hear thy silent voice (4)

valleys
362 valleys shall be exalted, the lofty hills brought low (1,4)
524 valleys stand so thick with corn ... they are singing (1)
551 let our hills and valleys shout the songs of liberty (3)

value
173 that learns to value beauty, in heart or brain or soul (4)

vanguard
324 rank on rank the host of heaven spreads its vanguard (3)
324 spreads its vanguard on the way (3)

vanish
324 powers of hell may vanish as the darkness clears away (3)

vanquish
58 grace ... doth vanquish, doth restore us (2)

vanquished
99 sorrow vanquished, labor ended, Jordan passed (5)
248 till every foe is vanquished, and Christ is Lord indeed (1)
452 hell today is vanquished, heaven is won today (1,4)
457 every vanquished foe submits to his victorious cross (2)

varies
184 it has no spring of action sure, it varies with the wind (2)

various
501 we, oppressed with various ills, draw near (2)
510 providence hath brought us through another various year (2)

vast
8 infinite thy vast domain, everlasting is thy reign (1)
22 vast as eternity thy love (4)
65 all throughout his vast dominion bless the Father (6)
318 let me measure, Lord, how vast and deep its treasure (3)
428 vast the love that him inclined to bleed & die for thee (1)

vault
453 while the vault of heaven rings (2)

vaunt
355 our pride is dust; our vaunt is stilled (4)

veil
47 with each new day, when morning lifts the veil (1)
92 I shall possess, within the veil ... life of joy & peace (5)
137 thou take the veil away and breathe the living Word (2)
138 no sudden rending of the veil of clay (2)
222 my anchor holds within the veil (2)
315 strengthened by thy grace behold without a veil thy face (2)
324 Cherubim, with sleepless eye, veil their faces (4)
324 veil their faces to the presence (4)
356 remove the veil of ancient words (2)
398 never shall darkness veil thee again from human eyes (1)
428 temple's veil in sunder breaks ... solid marbles rend (2)
429 the veil is rent in Christ alone (2)
503 through ... stars that veil thy face our hearts ascend (3)
533 give me the wings of faith to rise within the veil (T,1)
533 rise within the veil and see the saints above (1)

veiled
387 veiled in flesh the God-head see (2)

veiling
27 thine angels adore thee, all veiling their sight (4)

veils
222 when darkness veils his lovely face (2)

vein
33 life mounts in every throbbing vein (2)

veins
421 drawn from Emmanuel's veins (1)

venerating
490 venerating age, humbly teaching youth (2)

verdant
67 where the verdant pastures grow (2)

verge
271   when I tread the verge of Jordan, bid ... fears subside (3)

vernal
523   the golden sunshine, vernal air, sweet flowers and fruit (2)

very
82   Jesus, the very thought of thee (T,1)
95   now, O Lord, this very hour, send thy grace (2)
99   yea, a crown, in very surety, but of thorns (3)
195   until my very heart o'erflow in kindling thought (4)
238   thou art very weary; I was weary too (4)
295   my very heart and flesh cry out, O Loving God, for thee (2)
417   the very dying form of One who suffered there for me (2)
426   very God himself is bearing all the sufferings of time (3)
501   thy kind but searching glance can scan the very wounds (5)
501   the very wounds that shame would hide (5)

vesper
505   let our vesper hymn be blending ... holy calm around (1)

vessel
301   grace through every vessel flows in purest streams (2)

vesture
324   of old on earth he stood, Lord of lords in human vesture (2)

vexed
96   I walked and sank not on the storm-vexed sea (2)

vibrate
175   chords that were broken will vibrate once more (3)

vice
492   the mists of error and of vice which shade the universe (2)

victor
423   victor palm branch waving, and chanting clear and loud (2)
444   he arose a victor from the dark domain (R)

victor's
243   look up! the victor's crown at length! (4)
248   this day the noise of battle ... next, the victor's song (4)
453   crowns become the victor's brow (1)
453   spread abroad the victor's fame (3)
458   a royal diadem adorns the mighty victor's brow (1)
536   and win with them the victor's crown of gold (3)

victorious
3   Father all glorious, o'er all victorious (1)
27   almighty, victorious, thy great name we praise (1)
42   God hath made his saints victorious (2)
62   Christ, the risen Christ, victorious (3)
76   brought it back victorious when from death he passed (3)
161   O Christ, o'er death victorious (5)
179   over our wills and affections victorious (3)
278   Jesus, thine all-victorious love shed in my heart abroad (T)

297 the great Church victorious shall be the Church at rest (3)
299 pour out thy soul for them in prayer victorious (4)
353 brighter than the rising morn when he, victorious, rose (3)
366 the strong in grace, in truth victorious (2)
399 thou art holy, fair and glorious, all victorious (1)
409 that name all-victorious of Jesus extol (1)
453 from the fight returned victorious (1)
455 rose victorious in the strife for those he came to save (2)
457 every vanquished foe submits to his victorious cross (2)
488 on thee our Lord victorious the Spirit sent from heaven (2)

victors
  38 victors in the midst of strife (4)

victory
  239 robes of victory through the skies (6)
  239 and all thy armies shine in robes of victory (6)
  246 ne'er think the victory won, nor lay thine armor down (3)
  248 from victory unto victory his army shall he lead (1)
  249 crowned with victory at thy feet I'll lay .. honors down (4)
  256 High King of heaven, my victory won (4)
  289 where is death's sting, where, grave, thy victory (4)
  357 honor, glory, & dominion, and eternal victory, evermore (3)
  429 'tis swallowed up in victory (3)
  437 our Christ hath brought us over with hymns of victory (1)
  437 and, hearing, may raise the victory strain (2)
  438 the victory remained with life (2)
  439 where's thy victory, boasting grave? Alleluia (2)
  447 the victory of life is won (1)
  449 praise we in songs of victory that love, that life (3)
  450 endless is the victory thou o'er death hast won (1,R)
  486 the armies of the living God shall march to victory (4)
  487 give joy of thy victory on this thy holy day (3)
  533 I ask them whence their victory came (1)

victory's
  217 when by thy grace the victory's won (4)

view
  70 transported with the view, I'm lost in wonder, love, and (1)
  171 that we the land may view (2)
  268 where is the soul-refreshing view of Jesus and his word (2)
  339 on thee we humble wait, our wants are in thy view (2)
  365 thy noblest wonders here we view in souls renewed (6)
  394 to human view displayed (4)
  474 so a soul that's born of God longs to view his... face (2)
  474 longs to view his glorious face (2)
  492 with joy we view the pleasing change (3)

vigil
  396 shepherds keeping vigil till the morning new (2)

vigor
  249 and press with vigor on (1)

vigorous
  493 sleep that may me more vigorous make to serve my God (4)

vile
239   is this vile world a friend to grace to help me...to God (3)
421   there may I, though vile as he, wash all my sins away (2)

village
90   Mary's son most holy, Light of the village life (2)
90   Light of the village life from day to day (2)

vine
231   though vine nor fig tree neither ... fruit should bear (4)

vintage
545   he is trampling out the vintage where the grapes (1)

violence
173   justice conquers violence and wars at last shall cease (3)
213   no foes, no violence I fear (2)

virgin
393   round yon virgin mother and child (1)

virgin's
380   for the virgin's sweet boy is the Lord of the earth (2)
387   offspring of the virgin's womb (2)

virgins
366   come forth, ye virgins, night is past (1)

virtue
137   Spirit of faith, descend and show the virtue of his name (3)
242   the multitude make virtue of the faith they had denied (2)
442   He who skies & meadows paints fashioned all your virtue (3)
454   every sin may be forgiven through .. virtue of thy blood (2)

virtues
19   cry out ... virtues, arch-angels, angels' choirs (1)
85   in whom God's glory dwelleth,in whom man's virtues shine (1)
332   explains the wondrous way how through these virtues came (2)
332   these the virtues did convey, yet still remain the same (2)

virtuous
151   by kindly words and virtuous life (3)

visage
418   how does that visage languish .. once was bright as morn (1)

visible
455   those wounds, yet visible above, in beauty glorified (4)

vision
33   thyself the vision passing by in crystal and in rose (3)
47   faith's fair vision changes into sight (2)
171   O Thou who dost the vision send and givest each his task (3)
191   with vision clear and mind equipped His will to learn (3)
204   we catch the vision of thy tears (2)
256   be thou my vision, O Lord of my heart (T,1)
256   Heart of my own heart, whatever befall ... be my vision (4)

256 still be my Vision, O Ruler of all (4)
297 with the vision glorious, her longing eyes are blest (3)
350 grant the vision inly given of this thy house (5)
462 when weary feet refuse to climb, give us thy vision (5)
479 as we worship, grant us vision (3)

visions
194 visions of a larger good & holier dreams of brotherhood (1)
224 visions of rapture now burst on my sight (2)
382 brighter visions beam afar (3)
495 grant to little children visions bright of thee (3)

visit
44 what the son of man, that thou dost visit him in grace (3)
283 visit us with thy salvation; enter every trembling heart (1)
401 visit, then, this soul of mine (3)
466 and visit it with thine own ardor glowing (1)

visitant
138 no angel visitant, no opening skies (2)

vital
252 prayer is the Christian's vital breath (5)
344 unite the pair . long disjoined, knowledge & vital piety (3)

vocation
342 until each life's vocation accents thy holy way (3)

voice
1 He speaks, and listening to his voice (5)
4 my voice unwearied raises (4)
9 when my voice is lost in death (1,4)
16 with heart and soul and voice (1)
18 his the voice that called a nation (1)
18 Word is answered by the Spirit's voice within (3)
21 sing to the Lord with cheerful voice (1)
24 today attend his voice, nor dare provoke his rod (4)
32 his voice sublime is heard afar (4)
40 deep seas obey thy voice (1)
42 worlds his mighty voice obeyed (1)
43 no real voice nor sound amid the radiant orbs be found (3)
43 utter forth a glorious voice (3)
60 lift up your voice and with us sing Alleluia! Alleluia! (1)
60 ye lights of evening, find a voice (2)
76 at his voice creation sprang at once to sight (2)
77 let all, with heart and voice, before his throne rejoice (1)
82 nor voice can sing, nor heart can frame (2)
105 shall I not rise? Can I his loving voice despise (2)
105 the voice of God hath reached my heart (5)
106 while they hear that sweetest voice (1)
106 while they hear that sweetest voice whispering softly (1)
107 day by day his sweet voice soundeth (1)
110 Jesus is pleading; O list to his voice (4)
111 thro' grace we harken to thy voice (3)
117 I heard the voice of Jesus say (T,1,2,3)
122 my God is reconciled; his pardoning voice I hear (4)
128 charmed to confess the voice divine (3)

129   he speaks! and eternity, filled with his voice (5)
144   thy voice of love, in gentlest tone, still whispers (3)
144   thy voice ... still whispers, "Cling to me" (3)
159   I have heard thy voice, and it told thy love to me (1)
159   I am thine, O Lord, I have heard thy voice (T,1)
187   take my voice ... let me sing always, only, for my King (2)
190   come, let thy voice be one with theirs (2)
200   the voice of God is calling its summons unto men (T,1)
204   we hear thy voice, O Son of man (1)
209   the waves and winds still know his voice who ruled them (2)
209   his voice who ruled them while he dwelt below (2)
231   yet God the same abiding, his praise shall tune my voice (4)
233   with voice as full and strong as ocean's surging praise (3)
235   O still, small voice of calm (5)
236   then, when thy voice shall bid our conflict cease (4)
249   God's all-animating voice that calls thee from on high (3)
252   prayer is the contrite sinner's voice (4)
252   sinner's voice, returning from his ways (4)
258   but his Spirit's voice obey (4)
260   to hear thy voice we need but love ... listen & be still (3)
262   my bounding heart shall own thy sway & echo to thy voice (3
265   no tender voice like thine can peace afford (1)
274   longing for thy voice that cheereth (1)
274   make me ready when thy voice is truly heard (4)
303   beneath the contemplation sink heart and voice oppressed (1)
308   we hear within the solemn voice of her unending song (2)
310   O might thy quickening voice the death of sin remove (5)
311   may her voice be ever clear, warning of a judgment near (2)
324   as with ceaseless voice they cry, Alleluia (4)
343   there is a voice in every star, in every breeze a song (1)
357   every voice in conceret ring evermore and evermore (2)
362   there's a voice in the wilderness crying (T,1,4)
379   hark! a voice from yonder manger, soft and sweet (2)
391   with heart and soul and voice (1,2,3)
423   O may we ever praise him with heart and life and voice (3)
459   O Triune God, with heart and voice adoring (5)
462   in the gray valley let us hear thy silent voice (4)
479   we, thy servants, bring the worship not of voice alone (1)
479   not of voice alone, but heart (1)
483   lift up your heart, lift up your voice (R)
488   Church her voice upraises to thee, blest Three in One (4)
500   the voice of prayer is never silent (3)
502   spurned today the voice divine (4)
531   to feel thy power, to hear thy voice, to taste thy love (4)
538   O Christ, whose voice the waters heard (2)

voices
2   angel voices, ever singing round thy throne of light (T,1)
2   thou ... ears and hands and voices for thy praise design (3)
2   heart and minds ... hands and voices ... choicest melody (4)
7   hear the angel voices blending ... praise to God on high (1)
11   voices raise to the Lord in hymns of praise (1)
11   nations, come, your voices raise to the Lord in hymns (1)
14   in cheerful sounds all voices raise (4)
22   high as the heavens our voices raise (3)
23   saints on earth, with saints above ... voices ... employ (3)
23   your voices in his praise employ (3)

39   let all on earth their voices raise (T,1)
49   now thank we all our God with heart and hands and voices (T)
111 to him with joyful voices give the glory of his grace (1)
267 open my eyes, that I may hear voices of truth (2)
267 voices of truth thou sendest clear (2)
305 blend with ours your voices in the triumph song (4)
343 Great God, to thee we consecrate our voices & our skill (3)
366 midnight hears the welcome voices (1)
379 as I hear, far and near, sweetest angels voices (1)
440 join, O man, the deathless voices (3)
451 our hearts and voices, Lord, we raise to thee (5)
451 voices, Lord, we raise to thee, in jubilee and praise (5)
459 to thee all knees are bent, all voices pray (1)
472 and infant voices shall proclaim their early blessings (3)

voicing
396 praises voicing greet the morrow (2)

void
268 they have left an aching void the world can never fill (3)
530 love ... rendered all distinctions void (5)

volume
365 but the blest volume thou hast writ reveals thy justice (2)
365 volume thou hast writ reveals thy justice and thy grace (2)

vouchsafe
130 my longing heart vouchsafe to make thine ... throne (4)
262 here...my God, vouchsafe to stay & bid my heart rejoice (3)
298 here vouchsafe to all thy servants what they ask of thee (3)
349 vouchsafe thy presence now (1)
418 look on me with thy favor, vouchsafe to me thy grace (2)

vow
128 high heavens, that heard the solemn vow (5)
128 that vow renewed shall daily hear (5)
177 in love my soul would bow, my heart fulfill its vow (1)
507 never will throw off his fear who hears our solemn vow (4)

vows
128 O happy bond, that seals my vows to him (2)
169 my life to give, my vows to pay (2)
180 Lord, I my vows to thee renew (2)
196 my vows I will to his great name before his people pay (3)
294 her sweet communion, solemn vows (4)
359 to him shall prayer unceasing and daily vows ascend (4)
510 we all, with vows and anthems new, before our God appear (2)
520 steadfast faith & earnest prayer keep sacred vows secure (4)

wading
106 wading deep the dismal flood (3)

wage
411 battle with the body's ills and wage the holy war (2)

wailing
364 deeply wailing, shall the true Messiah see (2)

wait
32	ye monarchs, wait his nod (5)
51	he gently clears thy way; wait thou his time (2)
105	I wait, but he does not forsake (4)
108	O love that passeth knowledge, so patiently to wait (2)
129	and myriads wait for his word (5)
174	rise up, O men of God! the Church for you doth wait (3)
206	and wait thy word, let there be light (4)
210	only be still, and wait his leisure in cheerful hope (2)
211	place on the Lord reliance; my soul, with courage wait (2)
236	then, lowly kneeling, wait thy word of peace (1)
253	give me on thee to wait till I can all things do (1)
260	dost not wait till human speech thy gifts ... implore (1)
267	silently now I wait for thee, ready my God (R)
275	gladly take my station there and wait for thee (2)
275	I'll cast on him my every care and wait for thee (3)
290	and so beside the silent sea I wait the muffled oar (4)
339	on thee we humble wait, our wants are in thy view (2)
343	we bid the pealing organ wait to speak alone thy will (3)
355	we wait thy revelation (4)
423	scorned ... little children should on his bidding wait (2)
433	near the cross I'll watch & wait, hoping, trusting ever (4)
498	give us strength to serve and wait till the glory breaks (3)
503	wait and worship while the night sets her evening lamps (1)
505	while we kneel confessing, we humbly wait thy blessing (4)
526	his help I wait with patience (3)

waited
408	the world has waited long, has travailed long in pain (3)

waiteth
314	may the Church that waiteth for thee keep love's tie (3)

waiting
60	death, waiting to hush our latest breath (6)
98	here, to our waiting hearts, proclaim the sweetness (3)
105	he still is waiting to receive (3)
106	waiting still for sweet release (3)
108	in lowly patience waiting to pass the threshold o'er (1)
110	Jesus is waiting, O come to him now (3)
110	waiting today, waiting today (3)
119	and waiting not to rid my soul of one dark blot (2)
154	while I am waiting, yielded and still (1)
175	though they are slighting him, still he is waiting (2)
175	waiting the penitent child to receive (2)
224	watching and waiting, looking above (3)
274	waiting for thy gracious word (1)
275	truth and faithfulness engage the waiting soul to bless (3)
352	do thou the truth impart unto each waiting heart (3)
407	the world is waiting for thy Word (2)
444	waiting the coming day (1)
489	let us now a blessing seek, waiting in his courts today (1)
514	all our thinking, planning, waiting (2)

waits
13	where my soul in joyful duty waits (1)
13	waits for him who answers prayer (1)

297   she waits the consumation of peace forevermore (3)
363   behold the King of glory waits (1)
440   there on high our welcome waits (2)
531   my heart that lowly waits thy call (4)

wake
135   wake my spirit, clear my sight (1)
264   but sweeter still, to wake and find thee there (4)
366   wake, awake, for night is flying (T,1)
441   thinking that never he would wake again (2)
475   would man but wake from out his haunted sleep (2)
502   come near and bless us when we wake (6)

wakened
175   touched by a loving heart, wakened by kindness (3)

wakening
499   new ... the love our wakening and uprising prove (1)

wakens
495   when the morning wakens, then may I arise pure and fresh (6)

wakes
63   bliss he wakes and woe he lightens (1)
366   she wakes, she rises from her gloom (2)
476   O God of love, whose spirit wakes in every human breast (2)

waketh
230   His wisdom ever waketh, his sight is never dim (2)
264   when the bird waketh, and the shadows flee (1)
264   when the soul waketh, and life's shadows flee (5)

waking
256   waking or sleeping, thy presence my light (1)
258   come, my soul, thou must be waking (T ,1)
263   then, with my waking thoughts bright with thy praise (4)
407   O Master of the waking world (T,1)

walk
68   me to walk doth make within the paths of righteousness (2)
68   yea, though I walk in death's dark vale (3)
96   I find, I walk, I love, but oh, the whole of love (3)
117   and in that light of life I'll walk (3)
152   and closely walk with thee to heaven (4)
161   walk thou beside us lest the tempting by-ways lure us (3)
170   O Master, let me walk with thee (T,1)
173   O help us walk unflinching in paths that lead to peace (3)
176   along my pilgrim journey, Savior, let we walk with thee (1)
176   gladly will I toil & suffer, only let me walk with thee (2)
223   when we walk with the Lord in the light of his Word (T,1)
223   or we'll walk by his side in the way (4)
230   He knows the way he taketh, and I will walk with him (2)
230   my Savior has my treasure, and he will walk with me (3)
268   O for a closer walk with God (T,1)
268   so shall my walk be close with God (6)
269   blindly we stumble when we walk alone (3)
338   O may we ever walk in him, and nothing know beside (3)

403 walk in the light! (T,1,2,3,4)
433 help me walk from day to day with its shadow o'er me (3)
496 though destruction walk around us (2)

walked
96 I walked and sank not on the storm-vexed sea (2)

walkedst
538 who walkedst on the foaming deep (2)

walking
245 or walking the shadowy vale (3)
535 walking in all his ways, they find their heaven on earth (9)

walks
202 beside us walks our brother Christ (1)
203 he who journeys in them walks with thee (1)
216 nor pestilence that walks by night (5)
346 and science walks with humble feet (4)
346 science walks ... to seek the God that faith hath found (4)

wall
414 there is a green hill far away, beyond the city wall (T,1)
429 middle wall is broken down and all mankind may enter in (2)

walls
98 thou, within no walls confined (2)
293 with salvation's walls surrounded (1)
294 I love thy Church, O God! Her walls before thee stand (2)
298 and thy fullest benediction shed within its walls alway (2)
304 its heavenly walls unseen around us rise (1)
345 accept the walls that human hands have raised ...to thee (1)
345 round these hallowed walls the storm of... passion dies (4)
347 O Father, deign these walls to bless (3)
349 these walls for thine own sake ... be pleased to bless (2)
351 when time in lowly dust has laid these stored walls (4)
351 these storied walls our hands have made (4)
481 within whose four-square walls shall come no night (1)
481 sobbing human plaint that bids thy walls arise (2)
484 the walls of gold entomb us, the swords of scorn divide (1)
549 these .. not the only walls wherein thou mayst be sought (3)

wander
17 when through the woods and forest glades I wander (2)
93 prone to wander, Lord, I feel it (3)
129 O why should I wander, an alien from thee (3)
164 no wander from the pathway if thou wilt be my guide (1)
340 who wander far shall seek and find and serve thee well (3)
479 still the children wander homeless (2)

wanderer
106 wanderer, come, Follow me, I'll guide thee home (R)
175 tell the poor wanderer a Savior has died (4)
177 some wanderer sought and won, something for thee (3)
263 though like a wanderer, the sun gone down (2)

wanderers
102 ye restless wanderers after rest (3)

wandering
  22 when like wandering sheep we strayed (2)
  62 wandering from his holy ways (2)
  93 wandering from the fold of God (2)
  93 let thy goodness, like a fetter, bind my wandering heart (3)
  93 let thy goodness ... bind my wandering heart to thee (3)
 161 showing to wandering souls the path of light (3)
 279 catch .. wandering of my will .. quench .. kindling fire (1)
 280 to catch the wandering of my will (1)
 358 let thy wandering cease; hie thee to thy quiet home (3)
 372 teach thy wandering pilgrims by this their path to trace (4)
 502 if some poor wandering child of thine have spurned (4)

wane
 305 crowns and thrones may perish, kingdoms rise and wane (3)
 472 till moons shall wax and wane no more (1)

waneth
  63 man decays and ages move; but his mercy waneth never (2)

want
  68 the Lord's my Shepherd, I'll not want (T,1)
  89 in want my plentiful supply (4)
  97 I want no better friend; I trust him now (4)
 125 thou, O Christ, art all I want (3)
 230 wherever he may guide me, no want shall turn me back (2)
 253 I want a sober mind, a self-renouncing will (2)
 253 I want a godly fear, a quick discerning eye (3)
 253 I want a true regard, a single steady aim (4)
 271 bread of heaven, feed me till I want no more (1)
 277 I want the witness, Lord, that all I do is right (3)
 279 I want a principle within of watchful, godly fear (T,1)
 280 I want a principle within of watchful, godly fear (T,1)
 286 Lord I want to be like Jesus in my heart (4)
 286 Lord, I want to be more loving in my heart (2)
 286 Lord, I want to be a Christian in my heart (T,1)
 286 Lord, I want to be more holy in my heart (3)
 293 and all fear of want remove (2)
 472 and all the sons of want are blest (4)
 487 Jesus, we want to meet on this thy holy day (T,1)
 496 sin and want we come confessing (1)
 515 wide as the want of daily bread (3)

wanted
 344 good desired and wanted most ...thy richest grace supply (1)

wanting
  27 nor wanting, nor wasting, thou rulest in might (2)
 248 where duty calls or danger, be never wanting there (3)

wanton
 470 shame our wanton, selfish gladness (3)

wants
  56 your wants shall be his care (4)
  75 make all my wants and wishes known (1)
 184 it wants the needed fire to glow ... the breeze to nerve (3)

210 nor doubt our inmost wants are known to him (2)
275 make all my wants and wishes known (1)
339 on thee we humble wait, our wants are in thy view (2)
505 now, our wants and burdens leaving to his care (3)
522 God, our Maker, doth provide ...our wants to be supplied (1)

war
89 in war my peace, in loss my gain (3)
199 wild war music o'er the earth shall cease (5)
199 stormy clangor of wild war music o'er the earth (5)
239 thy saints in all this glorious war shall conquer (5)
243 not long the conflict, soon the holy war shall cease (4)
297 mid toil and tribulation, and tumult of her war (3)
305 onward, Christian soldiers! marching as to war (T,1,R)
355 in the night of hate and war we perish as we lose thee (3)
406 when war shall be no more and strife shall cease (3)
411 battle with the body's ills and wage the holy war (2)
419 the Son of God goes forth to war (T,1)
419 the Son of God goes forth to war, a kingly crown to gain (1)
477 that war may haunt .. earth no more and desolation cease (4)
478 lead on, O King eternal, till sin's fierce war ... cease (2)

war's
552 from war's alarms, from deadly pestilence (3)

ward
314 in our hearts keep watch and ward (4)

warfare
243 faith's warfare ended, won the home of endless peace (4)
536 and when the strife is fierce, the warfare long (5)

warfare's
288 servant of God, well done! thy glorious warfare's past (T)

warm
143 pure, warm, and changeless be, a living fire (2)
157 warm, sweet, tender, even yet a present help is he (3)
267 open my mouth, and let me bear gladly the warm truth (3)
267 let me bear gladly the warm truth everywhere (3)
345 may faith grow firm, and love grow warm (4)
401 inward light impart, cheer my eyes and warm my heart (2)

warmest
81 and cold my warmest thought (4)

warms
438 Christ is...the Sun that warms and lights us (3)
525 and warms our lives with heavenly fires (3)

warmth
60 thou givest man both warmth and light (3)
64 Lord ... whose light is truth, whose warmth is love (4)
513 sends the snow in winter ... warmth to swell the grain (1)

warn
337 to warn the sinner, cheer the saint (4)

warning
311   may her voice be ever clear, warning of a judgment near (2)
373   but hear the angel's warning (1)

warring
470   cure thy children's warring madness (3)

warrior
490   warrior-like and strong, comely as a groom (1)

warriors
233   as warriors through the darkness toil (5)
243   heroic warriors, ne'er from Christ ... enticed (2)

wars
173   justice conquers violence and wars at last shall cease (3)
455   scepter sways from pole to pole, that wars may cease (3)
469   by wars and tumults love is mocked, derided (2)

wash
154   whiter than snow,Lord, wash me just now (2)
421   there may I, though vile as he, wash all my sins away (2)

washed
224   born of his spirit, washed in his blood (1)

washes
101   crimson flood that washes white as snow (2)

waste
144   though oft I seem to tread alone life's dreary waste (3)
144   life's dreary waste with thorns o'er-grown (3)
216   nor plagues that waste in noonday light (5)

wastes
459   through seas dry-shod, through weary wastes bewildering (2)

wasting
27   nor wanting, nor wasting, thou rulest in might (2)

watch
28   short as the watch that ends the night (4)
150   help me to watch and pray and on thyself rely (4)
152   and every moment watch and pray (3)
238   gird thee for the battle; watch and pray and fast (2)
242   keeping watch above his own (4)
246   O watch and fight and pray; the battle ne'er give o'er (2)
307   watch o'er thy Church, O Lord, in mercy (3)
314   in our hearts keep watch and ward (4)
335   they watch for souls (3)
335   watch thou daily o'er their souls (4)
335   that they may watch for thee (4)
337   to watch and pray, and never faint (4)
346   mountains lift their solemn forms to watch in silence (2)
346   mountains ... watch in silence o'er the land (2)
381   while mortals sleep, the angels keep their watch (2)
381   angels keep their watch of wondering love (2)

385   while shepherds watch are keeping (1)
433   near the cross I'll watch & wait, hoping, trusting ever (4)
434   watch with him one bitter hour (1)
444   vainly they watch his bed ... vainly they seal the dead (2)
500   through all the world her watch is keeping (2)
502   watch by the sick; enrich the poor with blessings (5)

watched
394   while shepherds watched their flocks by night (T,1)

watchers
19   ye watchers and ye holy ones (T,1)
446   nor the watchers, nor the seal hold thee as a mortal (4)

watches
64   cheers the long watches of the night (2)
97   he watches o'er me day and night (3)
495   through the long night watches may thine angels spread (5)

watchest
496   thou art he... never weary, watchest where thy people be (3)

watchfires
545   I have seen him in the watchfires of a hundred ... camps (2)
545   watchfires of a hundred circling camps (2)

watchful
4   by morning glow or evening shade his watchful eye ne'er (2)
4   his watchful eye ne'er sleepeth (2)
53   beneath his watchful eye his saints securely dwell (2)
57   watchful and unslumbering care his own he safely keeps (2)
279   I want a principle within of watchful, godly fear (T,1)
280   I want a principle within of watchful, godly fear (T,1)
504   active and watchful, stand we all before thee (1)

watching
148   eager eyes are watching, longing for the lights (2)
224   watching and waiting, looking above (3)
253   forever standing on its guard and watching unto prayer (3)
382   watching o'er your flocks by night (2)
382   watching long in hope and fear (4)
404   while shepherds kept their watching o'er silent flocks (1)
495   spread their white wings above me, watching round my bed (
495   comfort every sufferer watching late in pain (4)
514   all our labor ... watching, all our calendar of care (3)

watchman
358   watchman, tell us of the night (T,1,2,3)
358   watchman, doth its beauteous ray (1)
358   watchman ... traveler (1,2,3)

watchmen
335   let Zion's watchmen all awake (T,1)
366   the watchmen on the heights are crying (1)
366   Zion hears the watchmen singing (2)

watchword
252   his watchword at the gates of death (5)

water
  60   thou flowing water, pure and clear (3)
  67   where streams of living water flow (2)
117   behold, I freely give the living water (2)
120   let the water and the blood (1)
204   the cup of water given for thee still holds ...thy grace (4)
244   thou who rulest wind and water, stand by me (1)
297   she is his new creation by water and the word (1)
342   redeeming soul and body by water and the Word (2)
376   earth stood hard as iron, water like a stone (1)
488   living water flowing with soul-refreshing streams (3)

watered
513   but it is fed and watered by God's almighty hand (1)

waterfalls
  11   waterfalls that never sleep (3)

waters
  33   sent the hoary frost of heaven,the flowing waters sealed (1)
  40   lo, at thy word the waters were formed (1)
  48   when through the deep waters I call thee to go (3)
  68   he leadeth me the quiet waters by (1)
103   here see the bread of life; see waters flowing (3)
125   while the nearer waters roll (1)
217   by waters still, o'er troubled sea ... hand ... leadeth (2)
273   like the springs and running waters make me crystal pure (2)
293   see, the streams of living waters (2)
293   streams of living waters, springing from eternal love (2)
446   led them with unmoistened foot through... Red Sea waters (1)
512   God sendeth from his abundant store the waters (1)
512   waters of the spring-time, enriching it once more (1)
538   O Christ, whose voice the waters heard (2)
538   waters heard and hushed their raging at thy word (2)
538   O Holy Spirit, who didst brood upon the waters (3)
538   who didst brood upon the waters dark and rude (3)

waters'
480   move o'er the waters' face, bearing the lamp of grace (3)

watery
  24   watery worlds are all his own, and all the solid ground (2)

wave
148   send a gleam across the wave (R)
217   e'en death's cold wave I will not flee (4)
233   your glorious banner wave on high (1)
538   whose arm hath bound the restless wave (1)
539   smite death's threatening wave before you (4)
545   he is coming like the glory of the morning on the wave (5)

waver
237   when thou seest me waver, with a look recall (1)

wavering

206   forgive our wavering trust in thee (3)

waves

32   rebel, ye waves, and o'er the land...roar (2)
32   waves...with threatening aspect roar (2)
51   through waves and clouds and storms (2)
84   from sordid waves of worldly sea perserve us, Lord (2)
209   waves & winds still know his voice who ruled them (2)
213   when sinks my heart in waves of woe (3)
247   unknown waves before me roll (1)
247   boisterous waves obey thy will (2)
273   like thy dancing waves in sunlight make me glad & free (3)
291   though Jordan waves may roll, I'll fearless launch away (3)
513   winds and waves obey him, by him the birds are fed (2)
543   O beautiful for spacious skies, for amber waves of grain (T)
550   faith in God came with those exiles o'er the waves (3)

waving

88   waving a branch of a palm tree high in my hand (3)
423   victor palm branch waving, & chanting clear & loud (2)

wax

472   till moons shall wax and wane no more (1)

way

4   all my toilsome way along I sing aloud thy praises (4)
7   for his lovingkindness ever shed upon our earthly way (3)
12   that makes the darkest way I go an open path to thee (4)
25   guards our way from all the assaults of hell and sin (3)
25   God is our shield, he guards our way (3)
46   nor miss our providential way (2)
49   who, from our mother's arms hath blessed us on our way (1)
51   he gently clears thy way; wait thou his time (2)
51   so shall thou, wondering, own his way (3)
60   unfoldest blessings on our way, O praise him (4)
60   Christ our Lord the way hath trod (6)
65   unto such as keep his covenant ... steadfast in his way (5)
75   thou art the way: to thee alone (T,1)
75   thou art the Way, the Truth, the Life (4)
75   grant us that way to know, that truth to keep (4)
76   thrones and dominations, stars upon their way (2)
85   learn from thee their duty, the truth, the life, the way (4)
90   the Christ of God, the life, the truth, the way (2)
101   Jesus is the truth, the way that leads you into rest (3)
121   be the guardian of our way (2)
154   have thine own way, Lord, have thine own way (T,1,2,3,4)
170   and guide them in the homeward way (2)
170   far down the future's broadening way (4)
173   again to lead us forward along God's holy way (5)
175   back to the narrow way patiently win them (4)
200   take us, and make us holy; teach us thy will and way (4)
203   we've felt thy touch in sorrow's darkened way (3)
205   all the way my Savior leads me (T,1,2,3)
205   my song through endless ages: Jesus led me all the way (3)
207   through every day, o'er all the way He will take care (R)
213   be thou my light, be thou my way (2)

215 God moves in a mysterious way his wonders to perform (T,1)
222 when all around my soul gives way, he... is all my hope (3)
223 what a glory he sheds on our way (1)
223 trust and obey, for there's no other way to be happy (R)
223 no other way to be happy in Jesus, but to trust and obey (R)
223 or we'll walk by his side in the way (4)
226 trusting thee I cannot stray .. can never .. lose my way (2)
230 He knows the way he taketh, and I will walk with him (2)
234 O Light that followest all my way (2)
236 grant us thy peace upon our homeward way (2)
240 life with its way before us lies (2)
245 but toiling in life's dusty way (2)
245 or climbing the mountain way steep (3)
249 forget the steps already trod and onward urge thy way (2)
252 O Thou by whom we come to God ... Life ... Truth ... Way (6)
263 there let the way appear, steps unto heaven (3)
269 lead us through Christ, the true and living Way (1)
270 though long the weary way we tread (2)
284 through darkness & perplexity point ...the heavenly way (4)
299 give of thy wealth to speed them on their way (4)
300 we are traveling home to God in the way our fathers trod (2)
324 spreads its vanguard on the way (3)
325 millions more, still on the way, around the board appear (3)
332 explains the wondrous way how through these virtues came (2)
340 see the thronged and darkening way (1)
342 until each life's vocation accents thy holy way (3)
345 may they who err be guided here to find the better way (3)
356 show us the way the Master trod; reveal his saving power (1)
368 brook by the traveler's way (1)
371 Word ... shines through the darkness of our earthly way (1)
397 Holy Jesus, every day keep us in the narrow way (4)
416 light and love upon my way (3)
417 a home within the wilderness, a rest upon the way (1)
422 ride on, O King, ride on your way (4)
429 the living way to heaven is seen (2)
449 bring flowers of song to strew his way (2)
451 the faithful women went their way to seek the tomb (2)
464 now it wins its widening way (2)
489 God has brought us on our way (1)
498 with so blest a friend provided, we upon our way ... go (2)
502 ere through the world our way we take (6)
517 little feet our steps may follow in a safe & narrow way (3)
520 may church and home combine to teach thy perfect way (1)
552 refresh thy people on their toilsome way (4)
552 thy Word our law, thy paths our chosen way (2)

ways
41 marveling at thy mystic ways (1)
41 from thy ways so often turning (2)
62 wandering from his holy ways (2)
85 in thee love's ways we find (3)
86 guiding in love and truth through devious ways (1)
161 walk thou beside us lest the tempting by-ways lure us (3)
204 where cross the crowded ways of life (T,1)
209 through thorny ways leads to a joyful endd (1)
210 and hope in him through all thy ways (1)
210 sing, pray,and keep his ways unswerving (3)

219   thou leadest me by unsought ways (4)
225   mid all the traffic of the ways (T,1)
235   forgive our foolish ways (1)
252   sinner's voice, returning from his ways (4)
292   new-born souls, whose days, reclaimed from error's ways (4)
294   beyond my highest joy I prize her heavenly ways (4)
295   in whose heart are thy ways (5)
300   glorious in his works and ways (1)
332   only meet us in thy ways and perfect us in one (4)
342   inspire our ways of learning ... earnest, fervent prayer (1)
354   and cause us in her ways to go (2)
362   a call from the ways untrod (1,4)
398   thou robest in thy splendor the simplest ways of men (2)
406   through desert ways, dark fen, and deep morass (2)
442   beauty follows all his ways, as the world he blesses (2)
470   scorn thy Christ, assail his ways (2)
475   turn back, O man, forswear thy foolish ways (T,1)
481   city ... whose laws are love, whose ways are brotherhood (4)
535   walking in all his ways, they find their heaven on earth (9)
541   O God, protect the men who fly through lonely ways (2)
541   men who fly through lonely ways beneath the sky (2)

wayside
  88   scenes by the wayside, tales of the sea (1)
513   he paints the wayside flower, he lights the evening star (2)

wayward
170   teach me the wayward feet to stay (2)
292   the wayward and the lost, by restless passions tossed (2)

weak
  81   weak is the effort of my heart (4)
104   come ... weak and wounded, sick and sore (1)
116   I am poor and weak and blind (1)
160   cross; let not its weight fill thy weak spirit with alarm (2
184   my heart is weak and poor until it master find (2)
201   the hopeless and the burdened, the crippled and the weak (1)
254   what I dream & what I do in my weak days are always two (2)
261   are we weak & heavy laden, cumbered with a load of care (3)
266   make friends of God's children, help those who are weak (1)
271   I am weak, but thou art mighty (1)
290   if my heart and flesh are weak to bear an untried pain (2)
325   nor weak excuses frame (4)
359   to help the poor and needy, and bid the weak be strong (2)
373   this child, now weak in infancy (1)
470   save us from weak resignation to the evils we deplore (5)
529   yield to me now, for I am weak (3)
529   weak, but confident in self-despair (3)

weaklings
  58   the strength those weaklings that renewed (2)

weakness
  89   in weakness my almighty power (4)
138   stoop to my weakness, might as thou art (1)
156   I would be humble, for I know my weakness (2)
200   but thou canst use our weakness to magnify thy power (3)

259   in weakness be thy love my power (3)
261   Jesus knows our every weakness (2)
486   man in his weakness yet may give a worthier offering (1)
504   banish our weakness, health and wholeness sending (2)

wealth
   299   give of thy wealth to speed them on their way (4)
   458   his people's wealth their everlasting theme (6)
   511   the wealth of this good land (1)
   549   thine ... the wealth of land and sea (4)

wean
   138   wean it from earth, through all its pulses move (1)

wear
   160   may hope to wear the glorious crown (4)
   183   go home my crown to wear, for there's a crown for me (3)
   519   health and food and clothes to wear (1)

wearied
   502   my wearied eyelids gently steep (2)

weariness
   326   and all my weariness upon thee lean (1)
   506   may weariness and sadness be lulled to peace & gladness (3)

wearing
   166   I love thee for wearing the thorns on thy brow (2)

wears
   168   the forms of love he wears, exalted on his throne (2)

weary
   53   why should this anxious load press down your weary mind (3)
   81   'tis manna to the hungry soul and to the weary, rest (2)
   99   art thou weary, art thou languid (T,1)
   100   ye weary spirits, rest; ye mournful souls, be glad (2)
   104   come,ye weary, heavy laden bruised & mangled by the fall (4)
   106   weary souls fore'er rejoice (1)
   110   Jesus is calling the weary to rest (2)
   117   weary one, lay down, thy head upon my breast (1)
   117   I came to Jesus as I was, weary and worn and sad (1)
   118   weary of earth, myself, and sin (1,5)
   140   Author of faith! to thee I lift my weary, longing eyes (4)
   154   wounded and weary, help me, I pray (3)
   194   thy world is weary of its pain (2)
   205   my weary steps may falter, and my soul athirst may be (2)
   207   lean, weary one, upon his breast (4)
   234   I rest my weary soul in thee (1)
   238   thou art very weary; I was weary too (4)
   245   and sometimes how weary my feet (2)
   270   though long the weary way we tread (2)
   350   here let the weary one find rest (4)
   362   and give to the weary rest (3)
   390   still ... heavenly music floats o'er all the weary world (2)
   417   the shadow of a mighty rock within a weary land (1)
   459   through seas dry-shod, through weary wastes bewildering (2)

462 Spirit of love, at evening time when weary (5)
462 when weary feet refuse to climb, give us thy vision (5)
472 the weary find eternal rest (4)
488 today on weary nations the heavenly manna falls (3)
495 Jesus, give the weary calm and sweet repose (2)
496 thou art he... never weary, watchest where thy people be (3)

weave
355 still our wrongs may weave thee now new thorns (1)

week
489 safely through another week (T,1)
489 day of all thee week the best, emblem of eternal rest (1)

weep
94 weep, believe, and sin no more (3)
129 say, why in the valley of death should I weep (2)
167 if I must weep with thee, "My lord, thy will be done" (2)
175 weep o'er the erring one, lift up the fallen (1)
279 let me weep my life away for having grieved thy love (2)
280 let me weep my life away for having grieved thy love (2)
475 built while they dream, and in that dreaming weep (2)
481 the tears are wiped from eyes that shall not weep again (1)

weeps
32 and sweeps the howling skies (4)
94 God is love! I know,I feel, Jesus weeps & loves me still (4)
431 for others' guilt the Man of Sorrows weeps in blood (3)

weighed
418 O sacred Head ... with grief and shame weighed down (1)

weight
160 cross; let not its weight fill thy weak spirit with alarm (2
289 ills have no weight, and tears no bitterness (4)
479 whose love ... bore the weight of human need (1)

welcome
62 welcome story! love lives on, and death is dead (3)
69 welcome for the sinner and more graces for the good (1)
102 in Christ a hearty welcome find (3)
104 ye needy, come...welcome; God's free bounty glorify (2)
119 wilt welcome, pardon, cleanse, relieve (5)
319 every humble, contrite heart is made a welcome guest (1)
342 we welcome thy command (4)
366 midnight hears the welcome voices (1)
377 our sweetest carols gayly ring to welcome Christ (3)
377 welcome Christ, the infant King (3)
440 there on high our welcome waits (2)
452 welcome, happy morning age to age shall say (T,1,4)

welcomes
446 welcomes in unwearied strains Jesus' resurrection (3)

well
34 how great is God Almighty, who has made all things well (4)
53 that hand .... shall guard his children well (2)

66   well our feeble frame he knows (3)
128   well may this glowing heart rejoice (1)
146   that mind and soul, according well, may make one music (5)
163   from him who loves me now so well, what power ... sever (3)
167   My Jesus as thou wilt! All shall be well for me (3)
168   well, the delightful day will come (3)
205   I know whate'er befall me, Jesus doeth all things well (1)
219   I feel thy strong and tender love, and all is well again (1)
238   well I know thy trouble, O my servant true (4)
288   servant of God, well done! thy glorious warfare's past (T)
293   well supply thy sons and daughters (2)
340   who wander far shall seek and find and serve thee well (3)
377   and so, good friends, we wish you well (3)
415   well might... sun in darkness hide...shut his glories in (3)
482   be the road uphill or down, unbroken or well trod (2)
498   sure of being safely guided, guarded well from every foe (2)
501   and some have never loved thee well (3)
507   if thou art well pleased to hear, come down (4)
550   thou heard'st well pleased, the song, the prayer (2)

wending
506   the day is slowly wending toward its silent ending (T,1)

went
183   who once went sorrowing here (2)
218   Christ leads me through no darker rooms than he went (3)
218   than he went through before (3)
302   by faith we join our hands with those that went before (5)
308   kings and empires ... of old that went and came (1)
355   nation's pride o'erthrown went down to dust beside thee (2)
378   went to Bethlehem straightway, the blessed babe to find (4)
383   and to follow the star wherever it went (3)
424   the people of the Hebrews with palms before thee went (2)
451   the faithful women went their way to seek the tomb (2)
501   O with what joy they went away (1)
527   I rose, went forth, and followed thee (3)

wept
167   since thou on earth has wept and sorrowed oft alone (2)

west
65   far as east from west is distant (3)
192   in Christ there is no east or west (T,1)
192   in Christ now meet both east and west (4)
503   day is dying in the west (T,1)

westward
402   westward leading, still proceeding (R)

wet
190   the fields are wet with diamond dew (1)

whate'er
29   to guide whate'er we nobly do (4)
139   whate'er we hope, by faith we have (3)
142   whate'er may come, I'll taste ... the hallowed bliss (4)
152   whate'er thy bounteous grace hath given (4)

152   for thee delightfully employ whate'er ... hath given (4)
157   O Lord and Master of us all; whate'er our name or sign (6)
181   we give thee but thine own, whate'er the gift may be (T,1)
181   whate'er for thine we do, O Lord, we do it unto thee (4)
192   join hands ... brothers of the faith whate'er your race (3)
205   I know whate'er befall me, Jesus doeth all things well (1)
207   be not dismayed whate'er betide (T,1)
210   he'll give thee strength, whate'er betide thee (1)
210   heart content to take whate'er thy Father's pleasure (2)
217   whate'er I do, where'er I be (1)
220   whate'er we must bear still in thee lies purest pleasure (3)
268   the dearest idol I have known, whate'er that idol be ((5)
497   strong through thee whate'er befall us, O God most wise (2)
510   to thee presenting, through thy Son, whate'er we have (3)
526   thy grace hath wrought whate'er in him is worthy (2)

whatever
217   nor ever murmur nor repine; content whatever lot I see (3)
256   Heart of my own heart, whatever befall ... be my vision (4)
266   and run not before him, whatever betide (3)

wheat
441   wheat that in dark earth many days has lain (1)
441   love is come again like wheat that springeth green (R)
522   wheat and tares together sown (2)

wheel
486   at whose inscrutable decree the planets wheel and turn (1)

wheels
202   through din of market, whirl of wheels (1)

whelming
222   support me in the whelming flood (3)

when
9   when my voice is lost in death (1,4)
17   when Christ shall come with shout of acclamation (4)
17   O Lord my God, when I in awesome wonder (1)
17   when through the woods and forest glades I wander (2)
17   when I look down from lofty mountain grandeur (2)
17   and when I think that God, his Son not sparing (3)
22   when like wandering sheep we strayed (2)
22   when rolling years shall cease to move (4)
23   when his creatures sinned, he bled (2)
36   and when the morning breaks in power, we hear thy word (3)
36   when lightnings flash and storm winds blow (2)
39   hour, when earth shall feel his saving power (3)
41   when we see thy lights of heaven ...thy power displayed (2)
44   when I regard the wondrous heavens,thy handiwork on high (2)
47   when we are strong, Lord, leave us not alone (3)
47   with each new day, when morning lifts the veil (1)
\ 47   our heart's true home when all our years have sped (3)
48   when through fiery trials thy pathways shall lie (4)
48   when through the deep waters I call thee to go (3)
49   and keep us in his grace, and guide us when perplexed (2)
52   death, when death shall be our lot (4)

56   when in distress to him I called, he to my rescue came (2)
70   when all thy mercies, O my God, my rising soul surveys (T,1)
70   when in the slippery paths of youth (3)
76   brought it back victorious when from death he passed (3)
78   O Christ, thou Savior of us all ... hear us when we call (1)
78   we pray thee, hear us when we call (1)
78   redeem us...when thou judgest all the sons of men (3)
81   when I see thee as thou art, I'll praise thee as I ought (4)
85   how sweet to serve all others, when we all others love (3)
87   when his loving arms receive us (3)
87   when our journey is complete (4)
91   when morning gilds the skies, my heart awaking cries (T,1)
91   the night becomes as day when from the heart we say (2)
91   powers of darkness fear, when this sweet chant they hear (2)
92   yea, when this flesh and heart shall fail (5)
93   Jesus sought me when a stranger (2)
97   when I am sad, to him I go, no other one can cheer me so (1)
97   when I am sad, he makes me glad, He's my friend (1)
97   how could I this friend deny, when he's so true to me (3)
97   I'll trust him when life's fleeting days shall endd (4)
106 when the storms are raging sore ... whisper softly (2)
106 when our days of toil shall cease (3)
120 when my eyes shall close in death (3)
120 when I rise to worlds unknown (3)
121 blessed Jesus! Hear, O hear us, when we pray (2)
121 seek us when we go astray (2)
129 thy foes will rejoice when my sorrows they see (3)
136 when love speaks loud and clear (3)
142 when in danger knows no fear, in darkness feels no doubt (3)
142 faith that shines more bright & clear when tempests rage (3)
143 when ends life's transient dream (4)
143 when death's cold, sullen stream shall o'er me roll (4)
147 when the joys of sense depart, to live by faith alone (4)
149 when in scenes of glory I sing the new, new song (4)
159 when I kneel in prayer, and with thee, my God (3)
168 when my dear Lord will bring me home (3)
173 create in us... splendor that dawns when hearts are kind (4)
177 and when thy face I see, my ransomed souls shall be
184 I sink in life's alarms when by myself I stand (1)
184 flag can ...be unfurled when thou... breathe from heaven (3)
185 when they can sing with me, more love, O Christ, to thee (3)
195 O use me, Lord, use even me, just as thou wilt and when (5)
195 just as thou wilt, and when, and where (5)
198 every life shall be a song when all... earth is paradise (4)
205 when my spirit, clothed immortal, wings its flight (3)
207 when dangers fierce your path assail (2)
207 through days of toil when heart doth fail (2)
209 when change and tears are past (3)
209 when disappointment, grief, and fear are gone (3)
209 hour ... when we shall be forever with the Lord (3)
211 his truth be thine affiance, when faint and desolate (2)
213 when rising floods my soul o'erflow (3)
213 when sinks my heart in waves of woe (3)
214 when God shall judge, their lot be woe (3)
216 when fearful plagues around prevail (3)
217 when by thy grace the victory's won (4)
217 when my task on earth is done (4)

321   when life anew pours out its wine with rich sufficiency (3)
328   then only can it closer be, when all are joined above (4)
329   glad, when thy gracious smile we see (4)
329   blest, when our faith can hold thee fast (4)
330   when I fall on my knees with my face to the rising sun (R)
331   in thy holy incarnation, when the angels sang thy birth (2)
337   within thy temple when they stand to teach the truth (2)
337   when their work is finished here (5)
337   when the chief Shepherd shall appear (5)
350   may our prayers, when here we bend ...to thee ascend (2)
350   when in faith our souls draw near (3)
351   when time in lowly dust has laid these stored walls (4)
353   when morning dawns and light triumphant breaks (1)
353   when beauty gilds the eastern hills (1)
353   brighter than the rising morn when he, victorious, rose (3)
353   when Christ our King in beauty comes (4)
353   the King shall come when morning dawns (5)
355   Lord Christ, when first thou cam'st to men (T,1)
365   but when our eyes behold thy Word, we read thy name (1)
365   when thy truth began its race, it touched ... every land (3)
368   Lamp ... whereby we trace our path when wont to stray (1)
376   heaven and earth shall flee away when he comes to reign (2)
378   save us all from Satan's power when we were gone astray (1)
390   when with the ever circling years shall come the time (3)
397   and, when earthly things are past (4)
406   when war shall be no more and strife shall cease (3)
413   are ye able to remember, when a thief lifts up his eyes (2)
413   are ye able when . shadows close around you with the sod (3)
416   when the woes of life o'ertake me (2)
416   when the sun of bliss is beaming light and love (3)
421   when this poor lisping, stammering tongue lies silent (5)
435   when I survey the wondrous cross (T,1)
436   were you there when they crucified my Lord (1)
436   were you there when they nailed him to the tree (2)
436   were you there when they laid him in the tomb (3)
438   when life and death contended (2)
440   when, amidst earth's closing thunders (4)
441   when our hearts are wintry, grieving, or in pain (4)
462   Spirit redeeming, give us grace when crucified (3)
462   give us grace when crucified to seek thy face (3)
462   let us find thy hand when sorrows leave us blind (4)
462   Spirit of love, at evening time when weary (5)
462   when weary feet refuse to climb, give us thy vision (5)
464   when he first the work begun, small & feeble was his day (2)
483   when he had purged our stains, he took his seat above (2)
485   hasten, Lord ... perfect day when pain & death ... cease (2)
485   when ever blue the sky shall gleam ... green the sod (2)
486   who, when fears beset them, stand fast and fight and die (2)
493   to serve my God when I awake (4)
495   when the morning wakens, then may I arise pure and fresh (6)
497   when the constant sun returning unseals our eyes (2)
498   every day will be the brighter when ... thy face we see (3)
498   when thy gracious face we see (3)
498   every burden will be lighter when ... it comes from thee (3)
498   when we know it comes from thee (3)
502   when the soft dews of kindly sleep (2)
502   abide with me when night is nigh (3)

502   come near and bless us when we wake (6)
503   when forever from our sight pass the stars, the day (4)
509   when death shall interrupt our songs and seal in silence (5)
516   when one their wish, and one their prayer (1)
516   happy the home when God is there (T,1)
517   when all the work is over and we lay the burden down (5)
517   when our growing sons and daughters look on life (4)
523   when harvests ripen, thou art there, who givest all (2)
531   my heart ... be free, when it hath found repose in thee (2)
536   and when the strife is fierce, the warfare long (5)
538   hear us when we cry to thee for those in peril on... sea (R)
539   when life's perils thick confound you (3)
548   strong as when her life began (4)
550   and when they trod the wintry strand (1)

whence
57   O whence shall come my aid (1)
271   whence the healing stream doth flow (2)
318   fount, whence all my being floweth (2)
533   I ask them whence their victory came (1)

whene'er
151   O how our hearts beat high with joy whene'er we hear (1)
151   whene'er we hear that glorious word (1)
153   slaves are we whene'er we share that devotion anywhere (3)

where'er
37   where'er I turn my eye (2)
87   take it, then, where'er you go (1)
98   Jesus, where'er thy people meet (T,1)
98   where'er they seek thee thou art found (1)
103   come, ye disconsolate, where'er ye languish (T,1)
213   Savior, where'er thy steps I see (4)
217   whate'er I do, where'er I be (1)
259   where'er thy healing beams arise (2)
329   where'er our changeful lot is cast (4)
411   where'er they heal the maimed and blind (3)
411   where'er they heal ... let love of Christ attend (3)
411   where'er thy servants be (5)
472   where'er the sun does his successive journeys run (1)
472   blessings abound where'er he reigns (4)
478   gladness breaks like morning where'er thy face appears (3)

whereby
368   Lamp ... whereby we trace our path when wont to stray (1)

wherefore
74   wherefore, by God's eternal purpose thou art exalted (4)

wherein
295   behold, the sparrow findeth out a house wherein to rest (3)
368   guide & chart, wherein we read of realms beyond the sky (2)
466   the place wherein the Holy Spirit makes his dwelling (3)
549   these .. not the only walls wherein thou mayst be sought (3)

whereon
368   bread of our souls whereon we feed (2)

wheresoe'er
538 protect them wheresoe'er they go (4)

wherever
230 wherever he may guide me, no want shall turn me back (2)
383 and to follow the star wherever it went (3)

whether
218 Lord, it belongs not to my care whether I die or live (T,1)
227 whether many or few, all my years are his due (6)

whirl
202 through din of market, whirl of wheels (1)

whirlwind
32 he yokes the whirlwind to his car (4)

whisper
106 when the storms are raging sore ... whisper softly (2)
106 hearts grow faint, and hopes give o'er, whisper softly (2)
106 pleading nought but Jesus' blood, whisper softly (3)
185 then shall my latest breath whisper thy praise (4)
478 and holiness shall whisper the sweet amen of peace (2)
529 I hear thy whisper in my heart (4)

whispering
106 while they hear that sweetest voice whispering softly (1)
270 our hearts still whispering, "Thou art near" (2)

whispers
144 thy voice of love, in gentlest tone, still whispers (3)
144 thy voice ... still whispers, "Cling to me" (3)
157 last low whispers of our dead are burdened with his name (5)
224 echoes of mercy, whispers of love (2)
229 the blood of Jesus whispers peace within (1)
262 to hear the whispers of thy grace & hear thee inly speak (4)
413 are ye able? Still the Master whispers down eternity (4)

whit
116 I am every whit made whole; glory, glory to the Lamb! (5)

white
8 and the white robed martyrs follow (3)
33 o'er white expanses sparkling pure (2)
45 morning light ... lily white declare ... maker's praise (2)
101 crimson flood that washes white as snow (2)
430 through thy cross made pure and white (5)
451 an angel clad in white they see (3)
486 whose bones lie white along the trail (2)
495 spread their white wings above me, watching round my bed (5)

whiter
154 whiter than snow,Lord, wash me just now (2)

whither
140 if thou withdraw thyself from me, ah! whither shall I go (1)

whole

7	singing with the whole creation (2)
62	our whole lives one resurrection ... life of life above (4)
81	it makes the wounded spirit whole (2)
96	I find, I walk, I love, but oh, the whole of love (3)
96	the whole of love is but my answer, Lord, to thee (3)
116	I am every whit made whole; glory, glory to the Lamb (5)
118	'tis thou alone canst make me whole (2)
136	holiness which makes thy children whole (4)
141	Lord Jesus, make me whole; grant me no resting place (4)
157	forever shared, forever whole, a never-ebbing sea (1)
157	and we are whole again (4)
171	boyhood faith that shown thy whole life through (1)
173	longs to bind God's children into one perfect whole (4)
179	true hearted, whole hearted, fullest allegiance (2)
192	fellowship of love throughout the whole wide earth (1)
192	one in him throughout the whole wide earth (4)
212	there is a balm in Gilead, to make the wounded whole (T,R)
278	scatter .. life through every part .. sanctify the whole (2)
279	drive me to... grace again which makes the wounded whole (4)
280	drive me to...grace again, which makes the wounded whole (4)
354	fill the whole world with heaven's peace (3)
365	convey thy praise round the whole earth and never stand (3)
390	whole world give back the song which now the angels sing (3)
408	whole round world complete, from sunrise to its setting (2)
435	were the whole realm of nature mine (4)
461	let our whole soul an offering be to our Redeemer's name (2)
475	nor till that hour shall God's whole will be done (3)
479	to save and make men whole (2)
481	yea, bids us seize the whole of life and build its glory (5)
487	Holy Spirit, make us whole (4)

wholehearted

179	truehearted, wholehearted, faithful and loyal (T,1)

wholeness

504	banish our weakness, health and wholeness sending (2)

wholesome

522	Lord of harvest, grant that we wholesome grain ... be (2)
522	grant that we wholesome grain and pure may be (2)

wholly

116	soul and body thine to be wholly thine forevermore (3)
133	till I am wholly thine (3)
143	O let me from this day be wholly thine (1)
179	freely surrendered and wholly thine own (3)
222	but wholly lean on Jesus' name (1)
259	thine wholly, thine alone, I'd live (1)
344	thine, wholly thine, to die and live (3)
501	for none are wholly free from sin (4)
510	residue of days or hours thine, wholly thine, shall be (5)

whosoe'er

137	inspire the living faith, which whosoe'er receives (4)

why

wicked

wickedness

wide

widely

wideness

widening

widow
```
 9  widow and the fatherless (3)
199  and feeds the widow and the fatherless (2)
```

wild
```
107  tumult of our life's wild, restless sea (1)
199  wild war music o'er the earth shall cease (5)
199  stormy clangor of wild war music o'er the earth (5)
206  forgive ... our wild alarms, our trembling fears (3)
213  if in this darksome wild I stray (2)
247  mother stills ... child ... canst hush ... ocean wild (1)
459  stilling the rude wills of men's wild behavior (3)
538  and give, for wild confusion, peace (3)
```

wilderness
```
129  or alone in this wilderness rove (2)
165  O refresh us ... traveling through this wilderness (1)
362  there's a voice in the wilderness crying (T,1,4)
417  a home within the wilderness, a rest upon the way (1)
512  the wilderness is fruitful, and joyful are the hills (2)
543  a thoroughfare for freedom beat across the wilderness (2)
```

will
```
 20  we will not fear (3)
 30  his spirit floweth free, high surging where it will (2)
 31  his great decrees and sovereign will (3)
 31  and will this sovereign King of glory condescend (4)
 31  and will he write his name, my Father and my friend? (4)
 32  the winds obey his will (1)
 41  'tis thy will our hearts are seeking (4)
 48  for I am thy God, and will still give thee aid (2)
 48  for I will be with thee thy troubles to bless (3)
 48  I will not, I will not desert to his foes (5)
 54  in God our shield we will rejoice & ever bless thy name (5)
 56  O make but trial of his love; experience will decide (3)
 56  experience will decide how blest are they (3)
 56  fear him...and you will then have nothing else to fear (3)
 57  he will not let thy foot be moved (2)
 57  from evil he will keep thee safe (4)
 57  for thee he will provide (4)
 57  thy going out, thy coming in, forever he will guide (4)
 59  he chastens and hastens his will to make known (1)
 63  the hour that darkest seemeth will his... goodness prove (3)
 63  will his changeless goodness prove (3)
 68  yet will I fear no ill for thou art with me (3)
 76  let his will enfold you in its light and power (4)
 79  O thou of God and man the son, thee will I cherish (1)
 79  thee will I honor, thou, my soul's glory, joy and crown (1)
 85  O Will of God incarnate, so human, so divine (4)
 85  God's will to earth thou bringest that all ... may learn (4)
 87  it will joy and comfort give you (1)
 92  and grace will lead me home (3)
 92  he will my shield and portion be as long as life endures (4)
 99  if I ask him to receive me, will he say me nay (6)
101  he will surely give you rest, by trusting in his word (1)
101  he will save you, he will save you, he will save you now (R)
```

104 if you tarry till you're better, you will never come (4)
108 I died for you, my children, and will ye treat me so (3)
110 he will not turn thee away (2)
112 sinners, turn, why will you die (T,1,2,3)
112 thankless creatures, why will you cross his love and die (1)
112 will you let him die in vain? Crucify your Lord again? (2)
112 ransomed sinners, why will you slight his grace, and die (2)
112 long-sought sinners, why will you grieve ... God and die (3)
112 will you not his grace receive ... still refuse to live (3)
116 I will cleanse you from all sin (2)
121 blessed Jesus! We will early turn to thee (3)
121 early let us seek thy favor, early let us do thy will (4)
124 who is life in life to me ... the death of death will be (3)
124 who will place me on his right (3)
129 thy foes will rejoice when my sorrows they see (3)
133 will one will, to do and to endure (2)
133 until my heart is pure, until with thee I will one will (2)
135 fill and nerve this will of mine (3)
136 earth ... form one brotherhood by whom thy will is done (3)
140 and here I will unwearied lie, till thou thy Spirit give (3)
141 God will fulfill in every part each promise he has made (1)
142 O for a faith that will not shrink (T,1)
142 that will not tremble on the brink of any earthly woe (1)
142 will not murmur nor complain beneath the chastening rod (2)
142 in the hour of grief or pain will lean upon its God (2)
147 teach us, in every state,to make thy will our own (4)
149 'twill be my theme in glory (R)
149 'twill be the old, old story that I have loved so long (4)
150 O may it all my powers engage to do my Master's will (2)
151 we will be true to thee till death (R)
151 we will strive to win all nations unto thee (2)
151 we will love both friend and foe in all our strife (3)
152 and prove thy good and perfect will (2)
153 offering lives if it's thy will (4)
154 mold me and make me after thy will (1)
155 he will make good his right to be a pilgrim (2)
159 and my will be lost in thine (2)
164 above the storms of passion, the murmurs of self-will (3)
167 my Jesus, as thou wilt! O may thy will be mine (T,1)
167 if I must weep with thee, "My Lord, thy will be done" (2)
168 when my dear Lord will bring me home (3)
168 well, the delightful day will come (3)
171 show us thy will, we ask (3)
172 ready for all thy perfect will (4)
175 Jesus is merciful, Jesus will save (R)
175 he will forgive if they only believe (2)
175 chords that were broken will vibrate once more (3)
175 strength for thy labor the Lord will provide (4)
176 gladly will I toil & suffer, only let me walk with thee (2)
179 King of our lives, by thy grace we will be (1)
179 King of our lives, by thy grace we will be (R)
179 strong in thy strength we will battle for thee (1)
180 guard my first springs of thought and will (2)
184 my will is not my own till thou hast made it thine (4)
187 take my will & make it thine; it shall be no longer mine (3)
187 take myself, and I will be ever, only, all for thee (3)

188	breathe into every wish thy will divine (1)
188	till earth, as heaven fulfill God's holy will (3)
191	men whose aim 'twill be not to defend some ancient creed (1)
191	of steadfast will, patient, courageous, strong and true (3)
191	His will to learn, his work to do (3)
191	with vision clear and mind equipped His will to learn (3)
196	sacred cup of saving grace I will with thanks receive (2)
196	my vows I will to his great name before his people pay (3)
196	the God of all-redeeming grace my God I will proclaim (4)
197	fulfill in daily life thy Father's will (2)
200	take us, and make us holy; teach us thy will and way (4)
207	nothing you ask will be denied (3)
207	through every day, o'er all the way He will take care (R)
207	God will take care of you (1,2,3,4,R)
207	all you may need he will provide (3)
209	in every change he faithful will remain (1)
211	the Lord will give thee peace (2)
215	and works his sovereign will (2)
215	God is his own interpreter, and he will make it plain (5)
216	I of the Lord my God will say, "He is my refuge ... (2)
216	to him for safety I will flee (2)
217	e'en death's cold wave I will not flee (4)
218	if life belong, I will be glad that I may long obey (2)
218	if thy work on earth be sweet, what will thy glory be (4)
219	to nerve my faltering will (3)
220	I will suffer naught to hide thee (1)
220	I will ... ask for naught beside thee (1)
220	Jesus will not fail us (2)
221	glory in the highest, I will shout and sing (1)
223	while we do his good will he abides with us still (1)
223	abides with us still & with all who will trust and obey (1)
223	then in fellowship sweet we will sit at his feet (4)
223	what he says we will do, where he sends we will go (4)
223	joy he bestows are for them who will trust and obey (3)
228	I will cling to the old rugged cross (R)
228	to the old rugged cross I will ever be true (4)
229	to do the will of Jesus: this is rest (3)
230	He knows the way he taketh, and I will walk with him (2)
230	my Savior has my treasure, and he will walk with me (3)
230	bright skies will soon be o'er me, where darkest clouds (3)
231	who gives the lilies clothing will clothe his people,too (3)
231	it can bring with it nothing but he will bear us through (3)
231	and he who feeds the ravens will give his children bread (3)
240	His boundless mercy will provide (2)
246	work of faith will not be done till thou obtain .. crown (3)
247	boisterious waves obey thy will (2)
248	arm of flesh will fail you, ye dare not trust your own (3)
248	the strife will not be long (4)
251	'twill but drive me to thy breast (3)
251	heaven will bring me sweeter rest (3)
253	I want a sober mind, a self-renouncing will (2)
260	our highest thought thy will (3)
260	we would not bend thy will to ours (3)
261	who will all our sorrows share (2)
265	teach me thy will (4)
267	ready, my God thy will to see (R)

267 everything false will disappear (2)
271 songs of praises I will ever give to thee (3)
272 and spite of fears, pride ruled my will (2)
272 sure it still will lead me on o'er moor and fen (3)
279 catch .. wandering of my will .. quench .. kindling fire (1)
280 to catch the wandering of my will (1)
290 the bruised reed he will not break, but strengthen (2)
300 only thou our leader be, and we still will follow thee (4)
305 but the Church of Jesus constant will remain (3)
307 unite it, cleansed and conformed into thy will (3)
316 this will I do, my dying Lord, I will remember thee (1)
316 while a breath, a pulse remains, will I remember thee (3)
324 he will give to all.. faithful .. self for heavenly food (2)
338 blest be the dear uniting love that will not let us part (T)
343 we bid the pealing organ wait to speak alone thy will (3)
347 thy will was in the builder's thought (2)
356 unite us in thy will, O Lord, and end all sinful strife (2)
356 one great Church go forth in might to work God's .. will (4)
356 work God's perfect will (4)
358 will its beams alone gild the spot that gave them birth (2)
362 and he will right the wrong (3)
368 will of his glorious Son (3)
371 thou hast revealed thy will to mortal men (2)
379 all you need I will surely give you (2)
381 where meek souls will receive him... dear Christ enters (3)
390 peace on the earth, good will to me (1)
394 good will ... from heaven to men begin and never cease (6)
411 O God, whose will is life and good (T,1)
411 will is life and good for all of mortal breath (1)
412 I do adore thee, and will ever pray thee (5)
422 thus the great Messiah came to break the tyrant's will (3)
438 Christ alone our souls will feed (4)
464 the Lord will shortly pour all the spirit of his love (4)
466 so the yearning strong, with which the soul will long (3)
468 the Lord will come and not be slow (T,1)
469 thy kingdom come, O Lord, thy will be done (1,2,3,4)
471 not ... swifter ... than we on earth, to do thy will (4)
474 soon our Savior will return, triumphant in the skies (3)
474 yet a season, and you know happy entrance will be given (3)
475 nor till that hour shall God's whole will be done (3)
476 by whom thy will was done (5)
479 hope and health, good will and comfort (4)
482 if so thy will is done (2)
498 every day will be the brighter when ... thy face we see (3)
498 every burden will be lighter when ... it comes from thee (3)
499 the trivial round, the common task will furnish all (3)
507 never will throw off his fear who hears our solemn vow (4)
516 unite ... in love to thee, and love to all will reign (4)
530 placed according to thy will let us all our work fulfill (3)
531 chase this self-will from all my heart (3)
542 thy kingdom come; on earth thy will be done (3)
542 myself I give thee; let thy will be done (3)

willed
20 God hath willed His truth to triumph through us (3)

willing
104 he is able, he is willing; doubt no more (1)

285	when shall I find my willing heart all taken up by thee (1)
299	he who made all nations is not willing one ... perish (1)
346	sovereign God, receive...gift thy willing servants offer (3)

| 397 | so may we with willing feet ever seek thy mercy seat (2) |
| 457 | to him our willing hearts we give (3) |

wills

85	free wills ... thou givest, that we may make them thine (4)
146	our wills are ours, we know not how (3)
146	our wills are ours, to make them thine (3)
179	over our wills and affections victorious (3)
260	but blend our wills to thine (3)
411	empower the hands and hearts and wills of friends (2)
459	stilling the rude wills of men's wild behavior (3)
469	his conquering cross no kingdom wills to bear (2)

wilt

2	can we feel that thou art near us and wilt hear us? (2)
59	and pray that thou still our defender wilt be (3)
82	Jesus, our only joy be thou, as thou our prize wilt be (5)
110	why from the sunshine of love wilt thou roam (1)
111	rejoice that thou wilt enter in (3)
119	just as I am thou wilt receive (5)
119	wilt welcome, pardon, cleanse, relieve (5)
146	thou wilt not leave us in the dust (2)
161	take thou our lives, and use them as thou wilt (4)
164	no wander from the pathway if thou wilt be my guide (1)
195	O use me, Lord, use even me, just as thou wilt and when (5)
195	just as thou wilt, and when, and where (5)
208	I know ... thou art with me, wilt be with me to the endd (4)
234	O Love that wilt not let me go (T,1)
261	thou wilt find a solace there (3)
459	pray we that thou wilt hear us, still imploring (5)
475	still wilt not hear thine inner God proclaim (1)

win

20	he must win the battle (2)
75	that life to win, whose joys eternal flow (4)
124	what the high reward I win, whose the name I glory in (1)
136	and earth shall win true holiness (4)
151	we will strive to win all nations unto thee (2)
175	back to the narrow way patiently win them (4)
239	while others fought to win the prize (2)
250	and win the well-fought day (3)
257	thou alone to God canst win us (2)
299	or of the life he died for them to win (2)
303	strive, man, to win that glory, toil ..to gain .. light (3)
311	may she holy triumphs win, overthrow the hosts of sin (4)
340	we go to win the lost to thee; O Help us, Lord, we pray (1)
451	for they eternal life shall win, Alleluia (4)
536	and win with them the victor's crown of gold (3)

wind

32	he yokes the whirlwind to his car (4)
34	the cold wind in the winter, the pleasant summer sun (3)
60	thou rushing wind that art so strong (2)
136	blow, wind of God, with wisdom blow (2)

184 it has no spring of action sure, it varies with the wind (2)
214 men of unbelief ... are like chaff the wind doth blow (3)
232 from every stormy wind that blows (T,1)
235 speak through the earth-quake, wind and fire (5)
244 thou who rulest wind and water, stand by me (1)
270 the murmuring wind, the quivering leaf ... tell us (3)
376 in the bleak midwinter, frosty wind made moan (T,1)
378 left their flocks a feeding in tempest, storm, and wind (4)
532 whose music like a mighty wind the souls of men uplifted (3)

winding
205 cheers each winding path I tread (2)

winds
32 the winds obey his will (1)
32 ye winds of night, your force combine (3)
36 when lightnings flash and storm winds blow (2)
51 give to the winds thy fears; hope and be undismayed (T,1)
209 the waves and winds still know his voice who ruled them (2)
291 no chilling winds or poisonous breath can reach (2)
513 the winds and waves obey him, by him the birds are fed (2)

wine
163 and round my heart still closely twine those ties (1)
313 that living bread ... heavenly wine be our immortal food (2)
314 for the wine, which thou hast poured (91)
315 furnished with mystic wine and everlasting bread (1)
320 wine of the soul in mercy shed (1)
321 when life anew pours out its wine with rich sufficiency (3)
326 here drink with thee the royal wine of heaven (3)
326 the bread and wine remove: but thou art here (4)
330 Let us drink wine together on our knees (2)
331 wine of gladness, flowing free (1)
332 who shall say how bread and wine God into man conveys (1)
332 how the wine transmits his blood (1)

wing
16 and wing to heaven our thought! (3)
84 to bird in flight, controlling wing (1)
125 cover my defenseless head with the shadow of thy wing (2)
195 wing my words, that they may reach the hidden depths (3)
263 or if, on joyful wing cleaving the sky (5)
343 To God the tribes of ocean cry, and birds upon the wing (2)
382 wing your flight o'er all the earth (1)
390 above its sad & lowly plains they bend on hovering wing (2)
480 didst come to bring on thy redeeming wing (2)

winged
136 burn, winged fire! inspire our lips with flaming love (2)
251 armed by faith and winged by prayer (4)
324 at his feet the six-winged seraph (4)
425 the winged squadrons of the sky look down (3)

wings
34 he made their tiny wings (1)
55 shieldeth thee under his wings ... so gently sustaineth (2)
131 expand thy wings, celestial Dove (3)

205   when my spirit, clothed immortal, wings its flight (3)
205   my spirit ... wings its flight to realms of day (3)
207   beneath his wings of love abide (1)
216   beneath his wings shalt thou confide (4)
231   it is the Lord, who rises with healing in his wings (1)
232   ah! there on eagle wings we soar (4)
264   sweet the repose beneath thy wings o'ershading (4)
275   thy wings shall my petition bear to him (3)
302   on the eagle wings of love to joys celestial rise (1)
309   on the wings of angels fly; show how true believers die (6)
387   risen with healing in his wings (3)
390   with peaceful wings unfurled (2)
461   come as the dove & spread thy wings ... of peaceful love (3)
473   and dark is his path on the wings of the storm (2)
474   rise, my soul, and stretch thy wings (T,1)
493   keep me, King of kings, beneath thine own almighty wings (1)
495   spread their white wings above me, watching round my bed (5)
533   give me the wings of faith to rise within the veil (T,1)
539   neath his wings securely hide you (2)
546   solace .. its wide dominion .. the healing of thy wings (1)

winning
59   so from the beginning the fight we were winning (2)
170   by some clear, winning word of love (2)
506   Savior's cross is winning forgiveness for the sinning (4)

wins
464   now it wins its widening way (2)

winsome
202   centuries still we hear the Master's winsome call (2)

winter
34   the cold wind in the winter, the pleasant summer sun (3)
446   all the winter of our sins, long and dark, is flying (2)
513   sends the snow in winter ... warmth to swell the grain (1)
522   all is safely gathered in ere the winter storms begin (1)

winter's
383   on a cold winter's night that was so deep (1)

wintry
441   when our hearts are wintry, grieving, or in pain (4)
550   and when they trod the wintry strand (1)

wipe
143   wipe sorrows tears away (3)

wiped
481   the tears are wiped from eyes that shall not weep again (1)

wisdom
7   wisdom, honor, power, blessing ... we cry (4)
31   through all his mighty works amazing wisdom shines (3)
37   I sing the wisdom that ordained the sun to rule the day (1)
44   on man thy wisdom ... bestowed a power well-nigh divine (4)
52   eternal wisdom is their guide, their help omnipotence (1)
63   God is wisdom, God is love (R)

377   and so, good friends, we wish you well (3)
457   and only wish the joy to know of our triumphant friend (1)
516   when one their wish, and one their prayer (1)

wishes
275   make all my wants and wishes known (1)

wishful
291   cast a wishful eye to Canaan's fair and happy land (1)

withdraw
140   if thou withdraw thyself from me, ah! whither shall I go (1)

withdrawn
 64   our midnight is thy smile withdrawn (3)
358   darkness takes its flight; doubt & terror are withdrawn (3)

wither
 27   and wither and perish, but naught changeth thee (3)
231   all the field should wither... flocks nor herds be there (4)

withhold
187   not a mite would I withhold (2)

within
  4   within the kingdom of his might (2)
 12   art within, a qickening flame, a presence round about (2)
 18   Word is answered by the Spirit's voice within (3)
 25   guards ... from foes without and foes within (3)
 25   might I enjoy the meanest place within thy house (2)
 65   all within me bless his name (1)
 67   Good Shepherd, may I sing thy praise within thy house (6)
 67   sing thy praise within thy house forever (6)
 68   me to walk doth make within the paths of righteousness (2)
 92   I shall possess, within the veil ... life of joy & peace (5)
 95   Light & life thou art within: Savior...from every sin (4)
 98   thou, within no walls confined (2)
116   long has evil reigned within (2)
119   fightings and fears within, without (3)
125   make and keep me pure within (4)
125   spring thou up within my heart (4)
131   if thou within us shine (4)
135   Holy Spirit, Love divine, glow within this heart of mine (2)
135   King within my conscience reign (4)
164   my foes are ever near me, around me and within (2)
184   imprison me within thine arms ... strong ... be my hand (1)
216   within the secret place of   God (1)
220   though the storms may gather, still have peace within (3)
222   my anchor holds within the veil (2)
225   turmoils without, within (1)
229   the blood of Jesus whispers peace within (1)
238   Christian, dost thou feel them, how they work within (2)
242   behind the dim unknown, standeth God within the shadow (4)
257   thou must work all good within us (2)
277   O come, and dwell with me, spirit of power within (T,1)
279   I want a principle within of watchful, godly fear (T,1)
280   I want a principle within of watchful, godly fear (T,1)
282   life nor death can part from him that dwells within (3)

284 and make me pure within (1)
298 and thy fullest benediction shed within its walls alway (2)
307 planted thy holy name within our hearts (1)
308 we hear within the solemn voice of her unending song (2)
336 fightings without...fears within since we assembled last (2)
337 within thy temple when they stand to teach the truth (2)
377 a babe within a manger lies (1)
377 but ah! within that stable old the beasts ... behold (2)
378 and laid within a manger upon this blessed morn (2)
378 now to the Lord sing praises, all you within this place (5)
399 O deep within my heart now shine (2)
417 the shadow of a mighty rock within a weary land (1)
417 _a home within the wilderness, a rest upon the way (1)
466 O Comforter, draw near, within my heart appear (1)
468 glory shall ere long appear to dwell within our land (2)
481 within whose four-square walls shall come no night (1)
494 eye naught escapes without, within (2)
501 conscious most of wrong within (4)
520 within... home let every heart become thy dwelling place (2)
528 refuse ... to impart by hiding it within my heart (3)
533 give me the wings of faith to rise within the veil (T,1)
533 rise within the veil and see the saints above (1)
549 and met within thy holy place to rest awhile with thee (1)

witholden
398 long, alas, witholden, now spread from shore to shore (1)

without
21 without our aid he did us make (2)
22 He sovereign power, without our aid made us of clay (2)
25 guards ... from foes without and foes within (3)
32 without his high behest ye shall not ... disturb (3)
65 as it was without beginning so it lasts without an endd (4)
97 without him I would fall (1)
101 believe in him without delay, and you are fully blest (3)
104 without money, come to Jesus Christ and buy (2)
105 I cannot stay; my heart I yield without delay (5)
119 just as I am, without one plea (T,1)
119 fightings and fears within, without (3)
140 O let me now receive that gift! my soul without it dies (4)
183 now they taste unmingled love, and joy without a tear (2)
225 turmoils without, within (1)
230 the storm may roar without me, my heart may low be laid (1)
235 let us, like them, without a word rise up & follow thee (2)
259 and reign without a rival there (1)
269 without thy guiding hand we go astray (1)
283 pray and praise thee without ceasing (3)
288 all in Jesus' presence reign through ages without endd (2)
315 strengthened by thy grace behold without a veil thy face (2)
336 fightings without...fears within since we assembled last (2)
342 the task looms large before us; we follow without fear (4)
359 his kingdom still increasing, a kingdom without end (4)
368 without thee how could earth be trod (3)
377 yet none there were who looked without (2)
418 for this thy dying sorrow, thy pity without end (3)
442 so, as he renews the earth, artist without rival (2)
450 life is naught without thee; aid us in our strife (3)

454   loudest praises, without ceasing (4)
494   eye naught escapes without, within (2)
502   for without thee I cannot live (3)
502   for without thee I dare not die (3)
504   saints united joy without ending (2)

witness
3   come, holy Comforter, thy sacred witness bear (3)
137   make to us the God-head known, & witness with the blood (1)
137   the witness in himself he hath, and consciously believes (4)
277   I want the witness, Lord, that all I do is right (3)
342   revealing in our witness the master teacher's art (3)
407   thy witness in the souls of men (3)

witnesses
249   a cloud of witnesses around holds thee in full survey (2)
533   the long cloud of witnesses show the same path to heaven (2)

woe
20   still our ancient foe doth seek to work us woe (1)
48   the rivers of woe shall not thee overflow (3)
63   bliss he wakes and woe he lightens (1)
80   who like thee ... go so patient through a world of woe (2)
87   child of sorrow and of woe (1)
142   that will not tremble on the brink of any earthly woe (1)
178   patient love was seen in all thy life and death of woe (1)
181   to comfort and to bless, to find a balm for woe (3)
213   when sinks my heart in waves of woe (3)
214   when God shall judge, their lot be woe (3)
233   in gladness and in woe (4)
237   should thy mercy send me sorrow, toil, and woe (3)
270   on thee we fling our burdening woe (4)
284   with care and woe oppressed (2)
335   souls that must forever live in rapture or in woe (3)
379   voice...doth entreat: Flee from woe and danger (2)
419   who best can drink his cup of woe, triumphant over pain (1)
431   that sweetly soothe that Savior's woe (4)

woeful
79   Jesus is purer, who makes the woeful heart to sing (2)

woes
124   defeats my fiercest foes ... consoles my saddest woes (2)
232   from every swelling tide of woes (1)
263   so by my woes to be nearer, my God, to thee (4)
306   we share each other's woes, our mutual burdens bear (3)
416   when the woes of life o'ertake me (2)
501   O Savior Christ, our woes dispel (3)

woke
527   I woke, the dungeon flamed with light (3)

woman's
204   from woman's grief, man's burdened toil (3)

womb
387   offspring of the virgin's womb (2)

women
451 the faithful women went their way to seek the tomb (2)
481 from women struggling sore for bread (2)
517 thou... crowned us with an honor women never knew before (2)

won
177 some wanderer sought and won, something for thee (3)
188 raise my low self above, won by thy deathless love (1)
217 when by thy grace the victory's won (4)
243 faith's warfare ended, won the home of endless peace (4)
246 ne'er think the victory won, nor lay thine armor down (3)
256 High King of heaven, my victory won (4)
288 the battle's fought, the race is won (1)
297 and mystic sweet communion with those whose rest is won (4)
368 with thee how could ... heaven itself be won (3)
399 thou hast won my heart to serve thee solely (1)
439 fought the fight, the battle won, Alleluia (3)
447 the victory of life is won (1)
450 endless is the victory thou o'er death hast won (1,R)
452 hell today is vanquished, heaven is won today (1,4)
463 who descended from his throne and for us salvation won (2)
482 until in every land and clime thine ends of love are won (4)

wonder
6 days of wonder ... beauty ... rapture, filled with light (1)
17 O Lord my God, when I in awesome wonder (1)
33 in ever-changing words of light, the wonder of thy name (3)
41 o how glorious, full of wonder (T,1)
41 full of wonder is thy name o'er all the earth (1)
70 transported with the view, I'm lost in wonder, love, and (1)
70 lost in wonder, love, and praise (1)
283 lost in wonder, love and praise (4)
332 thine to bless, 'tis only ours to wonder and adore (4)
379 here let all, great and small kneel in awe and wonder (3)
402 O star of wonder, star of night (R)
442 through each wonder of fair days God himself expresses (2)

wonderful
34 all things wise and wonderful...Lord God made them all (R)
109 wonderful words of life (1,2,3)
109 beautiful words, wonderful words,wonderful words of life (R)
109 Christ,the blessed one, give to all wonderful words of (2)
149 more wonderful it seems than all the golden fancies (2)
267 wonderful key that shall unclasp and set me free (1)
267 place in my hands the wonderful key (1)
361 the Wonderful, the Counselor, the great and mighty Lord (3)
380 there's a tumult of joy o'er the wonderful birth (2)
389 behold the wonderful exchange our Lord with us doth make (3)
409 and publish abroad his wonderful name (1)

wonderfully
69 the heart of the Eternal is most wonderfully kind (2)
149 what seems, each time I tell it, more wonderfully sweet (3)

wondering
51 so shall thou, wondering, own his way (3)
106 wondering if our names were there (3)

381   angels keep their watch of wondering love (2)
425   look down with sad and wondering eyes to see (3)
528   where shall my wondering soul begin (T,1)

wonders
  37   Lord, how thy wonders are displayed (2)
  39   his wonders to the nations show (1)
  41   hast given man dominion o'er the wonders of thy hand (3)
  45   of skies and seas; his hand the wonders wrought (1)
  54   thy wonders in their days performed (1)
215   God moves in a mysterious way his wonders to perform (T,1)
319   in faith and memory thus we sing the wonders of his love (4)
351   in larger worlds more fully prove the wonders of... love (4)
351   prove the wonders of redeeming love (4)
365   thy noblest wonders here we view in souls renewed (6)
365   noblest wonders ... in souls renewed, and sins forgiven (6)
392   and wonders of his love (4)
417   from my stricken heart with tears two wonders I confess (2)
417   the wonders of redeeming love and my unworthiness (2)
440   life eternal! O what wonders crowd on faith (4)
468   and wonders great by thy strong hand are done (3)
473   the earth with its store of wonders untold (3)
510   our lips & lives ... gladly show the wonders of thy love (4)

wondrous
   4   proclaim aloud the wondrous story! (5)
  41   o how wondrous, o how glorious is thy name in every land (4)
  43   the moon takes up the wondrous tale (2)
  44   when I regard the wondrous heavens,thy handiwork on high (2)
  44   mighty works and wondrous grace thy glory ... proclaim (5)
  49   wondrous things hath done, in whom his world rejoices (1)
  80   pathway, trod in wondrous love, O Son of God (1)
  80   wondrous Lord, my soul would be ... conformed to thee (4)
168   and magnify the wondrous grace which made salvation mine (1
177   help me the cross to bear, thy wondrous love declare (2)
228   has a wondrous attraction for me (2)
228   a wondrous beauty I see (3)
233   God's wondrous praise declare (2)
247   wondrous sovereign of the sea, Jesus Savior, pilot me (2)
318   whose grace unbounded hath this wondrous banquet founded (1
332   explains the wondrous way how through these virtues came (2)
346   his wondrous works ... his wisdom and his power display (1)
371   tongues ... acclaim with joy thy wondrous gift to man (4)
377   the beasts a wondrous sight behold (2)
381   how silently, how silently the wondrous gift is given (3)
393   wondrous star, lend thy light (4)
395   shepherds saw .. wondrous sight, heard .. angels singing (2)
407   show us anew in Calvary the wondrous power (1)
407   wondrous power that makes men free (1)
411   for still his love works wondrous charms (4)
432   what wondrous love is this, O my soul (T,1,2)
435   when I survey the wondrous cross (T,1)
459   thy love has blessed the wide world's wondrous story (1)

wondrously
  55   Lord, who o'er all things so wondrously reigneth (2)

wont
  368 Lamp ... whereby we trace our path when wont to stray (1)
  516 happy the   home where ... praise is wont to rise (3)

wonted
  231 their wonted fruit should bear (4)
  298 with thy wonted loving-kindness hear thy people (2)

wood
  33   laid a silent loveliness on hill and wood and field (1)

woodlands
  79   fair are the meadows, fairer still the woodlands (2)

woods
  17   when through the woods and forest glades I wander (2)
  547 I love thy rocks and rills, thy woods and templed hills (2)

wooed
  112 wooed you to embrace his love (3)

wooing
  109 all so freely given, wooing us to heaven (2)

word
  3   come, and thy people bless, and give thy Word success (2)
  3   come, thou incarnate Word, gird on thy mighty sword (2)
  14   eternal truth attends thy word (2)
  18   Word incarnate glorified the flesh of man (2)
  18   God is speaking; praise him for his open Word (3)
  18   thanks to God whose word was spoken (T,1)
  18   Word was spoken in the deed that made the earth (1)
  18   God has spoken; praise him for his open Word (1,2)
  18   thanks to God whose Word incarnate (2)
  18   Word is answered by the Spirit's voice within (3)
  18   thanks to God whose Word is answered (3)
  19   thou bearer of the eternal Word (2)
  20   one little word shall fell him (3)
  20   that word above all earthly powers ... abideth (4)
  24   we are his works ... formed us by his Word (3)
  30   in prophet's word he spoke of old; he speaketh still (2)
  31   I love his name, I love his word (4)
  36   and when the morning breaks in power, we hear thy word (3)
  36   we hear thy word, "Let there be light" (3)
  37   He formed the creatures with his Word (2)
  40   lo, at thy word the waters were formed (1)
  46   our strength, thy grace; our rule, thy word (1)
  48   laid for your faith in his excellent Word (1)
  69   we should take him at his word (2)
  75   thy Word alone true wisdom can impart (2)
  76   who from the beginning was the mighty Word (1)
  86   Jesus, thou Christ of God, by thy perennial Word lead (3)
  92   his word my hope secures (4)
  95   while I rest upon thy word come ... bless me now, O Lord (2)
  101 he will surely give you rest, by trusting in his word (1)
  129 and myriads wait for his word (5)
  135 Word of God and inward light (1)

137   thou take the veil away and breathe the living Word (2)
139   Author of faith, eternal Word (T,1)
149   message of salvation from God's own holy Word (3)
151   whene'er we hear that glorious word (1)
170   by some clear, winning word of love (2)
181   and we believe thy word, though dim our faith may be (4)
191   live out the laws of Christ in ... thought & word & deed (1)
195   o'erflow in kindling thought and glowing word (4)
197   we pray in deed and word, thy kingdom come on earth (4)
206   and wait thy word, let there be light (4)
208   and to take him at his word (1)
210   so do thine own part faithfully, and trust his word (3)
221   by the living Word of God I shall prevail (2)
223   when we walk with the Lord in the light of his Word (T,1)
235   let us, like them, without a word rise up & follow thee (2)
236   then, lowly kneeling, wait thy word of peace (1)
239   supported by thy word (4)
256   be thou my Wisdom, and thou my true Word (2)
257   blessed Jesus, at thy word (T,1)
266   and, looking to Jesus, still trust in his Word (3)
266   abide with him always, and feed on his Word (1)
268   where is the soul-refreshing view of Jesus and his word (2)
274   waiting for thy gracious word (1)
274   with obedience glad & steady still to follow every word (4)
275   believe his Word and trust his grace (3)
277   according to thy mind & Word, well-pleasing in thy sight (3)
281   whose word, when heaven and earth shall pass, remains (1)
281   thy word may to the utmost prove (5)
293   he, whose word cannot be broken formed thee (1)
297   she is his new creation by water and the word (1)
309   lowly, meek, in thought & word, altogether like our Lord (3)
316   according to thy gracious word, in meek humility (T,1)
339   let them speak thy Word of power (3)
342   thee, our Father, in thy eternal Word (1)
342   redeeming soul and body by water and the Word (2)
349   may benedictions here attend the teaching of thy word (3)
352   speak, O eternal Lord, out of thy living Word (3)
356   O let thy Word be light anew to every nation's life (3)
356   may one Lord .. faith .. Word, one Spirit lead us still (4)
362   word of our God endureth ... arm of the Lord is strong (3)
365   but when our eyes behold thy Word, we read thy name (1)
365   and make thy Word my guide to heaven (6)
367   Father of mercies, in thy Word what endless glory shines (T)
367   teach me to love thy sacred Word ... find my Savior (4)
368   Word of the ever-living God (3)
369   my spirit pants for thee, O living word (1)
370   each his word from God repeating (2)
370   till they came, who told the story of the Word (2)
370   told the story of the Word, and showed his glory (2)
370   praise him for the Word made flesh (3)
371   O God of light, thy Word, a lamp unfailing (T,1)
371   Word ... shines through the darkness of our earthly way (1)
371   undimmed by time, the Word is still revealing (3)
372   O Word of God incarnate, O Wisdom from on high (T,1)
372   it is the heaven-drawn picture of thee, the living Word (2)
385   for sinners here the silent Word is pleading (2)
386   Word of the Father, now in flesh appearing (3)

407   the world is waiting for thy Word (2)
438   Word of grace hath purged away the old and wicked leaven (4)
452   come then, true and faithful, now fulfill thy word (3)
460   God hath ... spoken his unchanging Word (1)
460   spoken by ... Word incarnate, God of God, ere time began (2)
460   age-long Word expounding God's own message now as then (3)
460   God abides, his Word unchanging (3)
464   now the Word doth swiftly run (2)
464   he hath given the word of grace (3)
464   Jesus' word is glorified (3)
469   better seeing thy Word made flesh, and in a manger laid (4)
477   bring to our world of strife thy sovereign word of peace (4)
480   thou, whose almighty Word chaos and darkness heard (T,1)
501   no word from thee can fruitless fall (6)
516   parents love the sacred Word and all its wisdom prize (3)
526   I rest upon his faithful word to them of contrite spirit (3)
538   waters heard and hushed their raging at thy word (2)
544   earth hath forsaken meekness & mercy...slighted thy word (2)
544   yet to eternity standeth thy Word (3)
544   praise him who saved them from peril and sword (4)
545   he hath loosed the fateful lightning of his ... sword (1)
545   lightning of his terrible swift sword (1)
546   cleave our darkness with thy sword (2)
546   feed thy faint and hungry peoples with...thy Word (2)
546   feed ... with the richness of thy Word (2)
548   for our prophets and apostles, loyal to the living Word (3)
552   thy Word our law, thy paths our chosen way (2)

words

18   deeds and words and death and rising tell the grace (2)
33   in ever-changing words of light, the wonder of thy name (3)
88   words full of kindness, deeds full of grace (2)
109   wonderful words of life (1,2,3)
109   beautiful words, wonderful words,wonderful words of life (R)
109   words of life and beauty teach me faith and duty (1)
109   Christ,the blessed one, give to all wonderful words of (2)
136   teach us to utter living words of truth (3)
151   by kindly words and virtuous life (3)
195   wing my words, that they may reach the hidden depths (3)
217   O words with heavenly comfort fraught (1)
241   fight the good fight (T,1) (words identical to 240)
314   for the words, which thou hast spoken (1)
320   by whom the words of life were spoken (1)
356   remove the veil of ancient words (2)
356   ancient words, their message long obscure (2)
507   no more our God forsake, or cast his words behind (3)

work

2   we know that thou rejoicest o'er each work of thine (3)
20   still our ancient foe doth seek to work us woe (1)
43   publishes to every land the work of an almighty hand (1)
44   when I regard the wondrous heavens,thy handiwork on high (2)
55   Lord, who doth prosper thy work and defend thee (3)
90   we would see Jesus in his work of healing (4)
91   alike at work and prayer to Jesus I repair (1)
112   fatal cause demands, asks the work of his own hands (1)
118   to thee I all resign; thine is the work and only thine (3)

139   increase in us the kindled fire...work of faith fulfill (2)
169   I would work ever for the right (3)
170   in work that keeps faith sweet and strong (3)
171   did ye not know it is my work My Father's work to do (1)
171   see, like thee, our noblest work our Father's work to do (2)
171   that it may be our highest joy, our Father's work to do (3)
172   Jesus, confirm my heart's desire to work ... for thee (3)
172   work and speak and think for thee (3)
177   some work of love begun, some deed of kindness done (3)
181   to tend the lone and fatherless is angels' work below (3)
185   let sorrow do its work, come grief or pain (3)
186   Son of the carpenter, receive this humble work of mine (2)
188   in thee my strength renew; give me my work to do (2)
190   awake, awake to love and work, the lark is in the sky (T,1)
191   His will to learn, his work to do (3)
197   to fuller life, through work sincere (2)
197   through quiet work in shop and home (1)
197   in work that gives effect to prayer (4)
199   him whose holy work was doing good (3)
215   blind unbelief is sure to err and scan his work in vain (5)
218   if thy work on earth be sweet, what will thy glory be (4)
219   discouraged in... work of life, disheartened by its load (2)
237   or its sordid treasures spread to work me harm (2)
238   Christian, dost thou feel them, how they work within (2)
246   work of faith will not be done till thou obtain .. crown (3)
257   thou must work all good within us (2)
260   our dreams, our aims, our work, our lives are prayers (1)
292   with us the work to share, with us reproach to dare (3)
311   judge her not for work undone (4)
337   when their work is finished here (5)
356   one great Church go forth in might to work God's .. will (4)
356   work God's perfect will (4)
429   the great redeeming work is done (1)
439   love's redeeming work is done, Alleluia (3)
464   when he first the work begun, small & feeble was his day (2)
464   Jesus mighty to redeem, he alone the work hath wrought (3)
464   worthy ... work of him...who spake a world from naught (3)
470   free our hearts to work and praise (2)
471   in us the work of faith fulfill (4)
479   on the cross, forsaken, work thy mercy's perfect deed (1)
485   man's rude work deface no more the paradise of God (2)
502   now, Lord, the gracious work begin (4)
517   when all the work is over and we lay the burden down (5)
530   placed according to thy will let us all our work fulfill (3)
549   on homeliest work thy blessing falls (3)
549   work shall be prayer, if all be wrought as thou wouldst (6)
549   prayer, by thee inspired and taught ... with work be one (6)

work's
212   sometimes I feel discouraged and think my work's in vain (1)

workers
339   as workers with their God (3)

Workman
171   O Master Workman of the race, thou man of Galilee (T,1)
197   O Workman true, may we fulfill in daily life (2)

197   thou Master Workman, grant us grace (3)

works
24   we are his works ... formed us by his Word (3)
26   all thy works ... praise thy name in earth & sky & sea (4)
31   through all his mighty works amazing wisdom shines (3)
38   all thy works with joy surround thee (2)
44   mighty works and wondrous grace thy glory ... proclaim (5)
152   in all my works thy presence find (2)
215   and works his sovereign will (2)
300   glorious in his works and ways (1)
311   bless her works in thee begun (4)
343   nature's works ... to whom they all belong (1)
343   all nature's works his praise declare (T,1)
346   his wondrous works ... his wisdom and his power display (1)
362   the works of men decay (2)
411   for still his love works wondrous charms (4)
411   O Father, look from heaven and bless ... their works (5)
411   bless ... their works of pure unselfishness (5)
414   trust in his redeeming blood, and try his works to do (5)
452   Him, their true creator, all his works adore (1,4)
526   our works could ne'er our guilt remove (2)

world
10   let all the world in every corner sing (T,1,2)
14   fill the world with loudest praise (4)
20   world ... threaten to undo us (3)
20   though this world, with devils filled should threaten (3)
22   wide as the world is thy command (4)
31   the thunders of his hand keep the wide world in awe (2)
45   this is my Father's world (T,1,2,3)
49   wondrous things hath done, in whom his world rejoices (1)
49   and free us from all ills in this world and the next (2)
61   he, with all-commanding might, filled the new-made world (2)
61   filled the new-made world with light (2)
80   who like thee ... go so patient through a world of woe (2)
84   thou givest us that good unseen the world knows not (3)
84   the world knows not nor treasures (3)
97   Jesus is all the world to me (T,1,2,3,4)
100   redemption in his blood throughout the world proclaim (3)
105   vain world, farewell, from thee I part (5)
123   know not how that Calvary's cross a world ... could free (2)
123   Calvary's cross a world from sin could free (2)
130   throughout the world its breadth is known (3)
137   O that the world might know the all-atoning Lamb (3)
144   what though the world deceitful prove (2)
160   the world forsake, and humbly follow after me (1)
161   hope of the world T,1,2,3,4,5)
164   O let me feel thee near me, the world is ever near (2)
183   must ... all the world go free (1)
184   it cannot drive the world until itself be driven (3)
188   lift thou thy world, O Christ, closer to thee (3)
194   thy world is weary of its pain (2)
197   thy purpose for thy world we share (4)
198   a loftier race than e'er the world hath known shall rise (1)
226   lost in love, in a brighter, brighter world above (3)
226   through .. changing world below lead me gently ..as I go (2)

228   for a world of lost sinners was slain (1)
228   O that old rugged cross, so despised by the world (2)
229   peace, perfect peace, in this dark world of sin (T,1)
237   with forbidden pleasures would this vain world charm (2)
239   is this vile world a friend to grace to help me...to God (3)
244   when the world is tossing me like ship upon the sea (1)
251   let the world despise and leave me (2)
266   take time to be holy, the world rushes on (2)
268   they have left an aching void the world can never fill (3)
275   that calls me from a world of care (1)
278   Christ is all the world to me, and all my heart is love (4)
292   the world to Christ we bring, with loving zeal (1)
292   Christ for the world we sing! (T,1,2,3,4)
292   the world to Christ we bring, with fervent prayer (2)
292   the world to Christ we bring, with one accord (3)
292   the world to Christ we bring, with joyful song (4)
299   mission ... to tell to all the world that God is Light (1)
308   not like kingdoms of the world thy holy Church, O God (3)
314   world where thou... send us let thy kingdom come, O Lord (4)
320, 322, 323   bread of the world in mercy broken (T,1)
329   shed o'er the world thy holy light (5)
340   o'er all the world thy spirit send (4)
341   that the world might taste & see the riches of his grace (3)
341   bold to confess thy glorious name before a world of foes (4)
343   sweet music fills the world abroad with strains of love (1)
354   fill the whole world with heaven's peace (3)
363   the Savior of the world is here (1)
365   nor ... spreading Gospel rest till through the world (4)
365   till through the world thy truth has run (4)
365   bless the dark world with heavenly light (5)
371   to all the world the message thou art sending (4)
372   it shineth like a beacon above the darkling world (3)
380   and that song from afar has swept over the world (3)
381   no ear may hear his coming, but in this world of sin (3)
390   world in solemn stillness lay to hear the angels sing (1)
390   still ... heavenly music floats o'er all the weary world (2)
390   whole world give back the song which now the angels sing (3
392   joy to the world, the Lord is come (T,1)
392   he rules the world with truth and grace (4)
395   there he lay, the undefiled, to the world a stranger (1)
398   light of the world, we hail thee (T,1)
398   Light of the world, thy beauty steals into every heart (2)
398   Light of the world, Illumine ... darkened earth of thine (3)
405   to the world its God announcing (2)
407   O Master of the waking world (T,1)
407   the world is waiting for thy Word (2)
408   whole round world complete, from sunrise to its setting (2)
408   the world has waited long, has travailed long in pain (3)
417   content to let the world go by, to know no gain nor loss (3)
437   Let the round world keep triumph, & all that is therein (3)
442   all the world with beauty fills (1)
442   beauty follows all his ways, as the world he blesses (2)
449   to all the world glad news we bring (1)
461   Spirit divine ... make this world thy home (4)
464   worthy ... work of him...who spake a world from naught (3)
469   if we love not the world which thou hast made (4)
477   bring to our world of strife thy sovereign word of peace (4)

480 through the world far and wide, let there be light (4)
486 trail which leads the world to thee (2)
486 till through world made noble ... God shall march (4)
493 that with the world, myself, and thee...at peace may be (2)
500 through all the world her watch is keeping (2)
502 ere through the world our way we take (6)
511 a world in need now summons us to labor,love and give (2)
511 a world redeemed by Christ-like love (2)
522 all the world is God's own field (2)
536 who thee by faith before the world confessed (1)
545 so the world shall be his footstool (5)

world's
 107 the vain world's golden store (3)
 117 I am this dark world's light (3)
 356 break forth ... upon the world's dark hour (1)
 408 Christ is the world's true light (T,1)
 410 that all of the world's great peoples might come (4)
 459 thy love has blessed the wide world's wondrous story (1)
 460 'mid the world's despair and turmoil one firm anchor (1)
 517 thee, the world's Redeemer bore (2)

worldly
 84 from sordid waves of worldly sea preserve us, Lord (2)
 176 not for ease or worldly pleasure (2)
 489 from our worldly cares set free (2)

worlds
 5 marching ... to fairer worlds on high (4)
 11 join the angel song, all the worlds to him belong (1)
 17 consider all the worlds thy hands have made (1)
 24 watery worlds are all his own, and all the solid ground (2)
 39 he made the shining worlds on high (2)
 42 worlds his mighty voice obeyed (1)
 70 after death, in distant worlds, the glorious theme renew (4)
 120 when I rise to worlds unknown (3)
 127 midst flaming worlds, in these arrayed (1)
 190 all worlds that are, and all that are to be (3)
 190 worlds awake to cry their blessings on the Lord of life (1)
 190 to serve right gloriously the God who gave all worlds (3)
 206 with worlds on worlds beyond our sight (4)
 351 in larger worlds more fully prove the wonders of... love (4)
 357 ere the worlds began to be (1)
 426 throned in light ere worlds could be (2)
 509 our helper, God, in whom we trust, in better worlds (5)
 509 in better worlds our souls shall boast (5)
 549 worlds of science and of art, revealed and ruled by thee (4)
 552 band of shining worlds in splendor through the skies (1)

wormwood
 71 sinners, whose love can ne'er forget the wormwood and (3)
 71 ne'er forget the wormwood and the gall (3)

worn
 117 I came to Jesus as I was, weary and worn and sad (1)
 292 sinsick and sorrow-worn, whom Christ doth heal (1)

worship
23   worship and thanks to him belong (1)
23   worship and thanks to him belong who reigns (4)
24   come, worship at this throne; come, bow before the Lord (3)
60   worship him in humbleness, O praise him! Alleluia! (7)
107   Jesus calls us from the worship of the vain (3)
199   to worship rightly is to love each other (1)
199   the holier worship which he deigns to bless restores (2)
236   we stand to bless thee ere our worship cease (1)
268   help me to tear it from thy throne and worship only thee (5)
304   our hearts in love and worship turn to find themselves (2)
345   meet with those who here in worship bend (2)
345   in worship bend before thy mercy seat (2)
375   worship we the God-head, Love incarnate, Love divine (2)
375   worship we our Jesus, but where-with for sacred sign (2)
382   come and worship, worship Christ, the new-born King (R)
402   worship him, God on high (3)
409   fall down on their faces and worship the Lamb (3)
454   worship, honor, power, and blessing Christ is worthy (4)
473   O worship the King, all glorious above (T,1)
479   we, thy servants, bring the worship not of voice alone (1)
479   as we worship, grant us vision (3)
479   called from worship unto service, forth ... we go (4)
503   wait and worship while the night sets her evening lamps (1)

worshiped
376   but his mother only, in her maiden bliss, worshiped (3)
376   worshiped the beloved with a kiss (3)
405   Jesus, whom the Gentiles worshiped at thy glad epiphany (5)
550   with prayer and psalm they worshiped thee (1)

worshipers
364   cause of endless exultation to his ransomed worshipers (3)

worst
111   worst need keep him out no more or force him to depart (2)
447   the powers of death have done their worst (2)

worth
18   his the fires that tried her worth (1)
168   O could I speak the matchless worth (T,1)
186   worth to my meanest labor give by joining it to thine (2)
389   he lays aside his majesty and seems as nothing worth (2)

worthier
486   man in his weakness yet may give a worthier offering (1)

worthy
153   God of love ... God of power make us worthy of this hour (4)
300   sing our Savior's worthy praise (1)
413   that his pardoned soul is worthy of a place in paradise (2)
454   worship, honor, power, and blessing Christ is worthy (4)
454   Christ is worthy to receive (4)
457   worthy to be exalted thus, the Lamb for sinner slain (2)
464   worthy ... work of him...who spake a world from naught (3)
526   thy grace hath wrought whate'er in him is worthy (2)

wound
    99   in his feet and hands are wound-prints (2)

wounded
    47   Lord, by the stripes which wounded thee (4)
    81   it makes the wounded spirit whole (2)
    94   Savior stands, holding forth his wounded hands (4)
    103 here bring your wounded hearts, here tell your anguish (1)
    104 come ... weak and wounded, sick and sore   (1)
    120 from thy wounded side which flowed (1)
    145 heal my wounded, broken spirit, save me by thy grace (3)
    154 wounded and weary, help me, I pray (3)
    212 there is a balm in Gilead, to make the wounded whole (T,R)
    279 drive me to... grace again which makes the wounded whole (4)
    280 drive me to...grace again, which makes the wounded whole (4)
    355 O wounded hands of Jesus, build in us thy new creation (4)
    411 as in days of old he takes the wounded to his arms (4)
    418 O sacred head, now wounded (T,1)
    447 Lord, by the stripes that wounded thee (4)

wounds
    81   it soothes his sorrows, heals his wounds (1)
    122 five bleeding wounds he bears, received on Calvary (3)
    161 to heal earth's wounds and endd her bitter strife (2)
    421 by faith, I saw the stream thy flowing wounds supply (4)
    455 those wounds, yet visible above, in beauty glorified (4)
    501 thy kind but searching glance can scan the very wounds (5)
    501 the very wounds that shame would hide (5)

wrapped
    394 all meanly wrapped in swathing bands & in a manger laid (4)

wrath
    31   his wrath and justice stand to guard his holy law (2)
    94   can my God his wrath forbear (1)
    120 save from wrath and make me pure (1)
    469 in wrath and fear, by jealousies surrounded (3)
    473 his chariots of wrath the deep thunderclouds form (2)
    528 I, a child of wrath & hell ... be called a child of God (2)
    544 let not thy wrath in its terrors awaken (2)
    545 where the grapes of wrath are stored (1)

wrecks
    416 towering o'er the wrecks of time (1,5)

wrestle
    250 wrestle and fight and pray (3)
    529 and wrestle till the break of day (1)

wrestlers
    195 I may stretch out a loving hand to wrestlers (2)
    195 wrestlers with the troubled sea (2)

wrestles
    431 from all removed, the Savior wrestles lone with fears (2)

wretch
    92   that saved a wretch like me (1)

wretched
  119 poor, wretched, blind; sight, riches, healing of... mind (4)
  242 when we share her wretched crust (2)

wretchedness
  204 in haunts of wretchedness and need (2)

wring
  481 wring gold from human pain (3)

writ
  30   deep writ upon the human heart, on sea or land (2)
  365 but the blest volume thou hast writ reveals thy justice (2)
  365 volume thou hast writ reveals thy justice and thy grace (2)

write
  31   and will he write his name, my Father and my friend? (4)
  282 write thy new name upon my heart (5)

written
  122 my name is written on his hands (1)

wrong
  45   ne'er forget that though the wrong seems oft so strong (3)
  170 in trust that triumphs over wrong (3)
  174 bring ... day of brotherhood ... end the night of wrong (2)
  188 cleanse it from guilt & wrong; teach it salvation's song (3)
  191 men with hearts ablaze .. truth to love .. wrong to hate (4)
  194 and all its ancient deeds of wrong (2)
  242 and upon the throne be wrong (4)
  243 who gainst enthroned wrong stood confident and bold (1)
  279 first approach to feel of pride or wrong desire (1)
  280 of pride or wrong desire (1)
  359 he comes with succor speedy to those who suffer wrong (2)
  362 and he will right the wrong (3)
  408 heal its ancient wrong, come, Prince of Peace, and reign (3)
  419 he prayed for them that did the wrong (2)
  486 who with love and meekness outlast the years of wrong (3)
  501 conscious most of wrong within (4)
  532 who helped the right, and fought the wrong (2)
  544 falsehood and wrong shall not tarry beside thee (3)
  545 and the soul of wrong his slave (5)

wrongs
  29   and give us grace our wrongs to bear (4)
  178 far more for others' sins than... wrongs that we receive (3)
  243 gainst lies & lusts & wrongs let courage rule our souls (3)
  355 still our wrongs may weave thee now new thorns (1)

wrote
  131 come, Holy Ghost, for moved by thee the prophets wrote (2)
  131 moved by thee, the prophets wrote and spoke (2)
  371 sages, who wrote the message with immortal pen (2)

wrought
  33   the hand that shaped the rose hath wrought the crystal (1)
  41   thou who wrought creation's splendor (1)
  45   of skies and seas; his hand the wonders wrought (1)

74	by thy death was God's salvation wrought (2)
184	it cannot freely move till thou hast wrought its chain (2)
260	secret thought .. hidden plan, wrought ..or unexpressed (2)
347	thy hand unseen amidst us wrought (2)
463	by whose mighty power alone all is made & wrought & done (1)
464	Jesus mighty to redeem, he alone the work hath wrought (3)
526	thy grace hath wrought whate'er in him is worthy (2)
526	but must confess thy grace hath wrought (2)
549	in truth and patience wrought (3)
549	work shall be prayer, if all be wrought as thou wouldst (6)

yea

2	can we feel that thou art near ... hear ...? yea, we can (2)
68	yea, though I walk in death's dark vale (3)
92	yea, when this flesh and heart shall fail (5)
99	yea, a crown, in very surety, but of thorns (3)
119	yea, all I need, in thee to find (4)
119	now, to be thine, yea, thine alone...I come (6)
364	yea, Amen! let all adore thee high on thy eternal throne (4)
386	yea, Lord, we greet thee, born this happy morning (3)
413	yea, the sturdy dreamers answered (1)
413	yea ... to the death we follow thee (1)
481	yea, bids us seize the whole of life and build its glory (5)
526	yea, e'en the best life faileth (2)

year

33	thou from whose unfathomed law the year in beauty flows (3)
100	the year of jubilee is come! (R)
270	and sorrow crown each lingering year (2)
351	be pleased to guide, each lengthening year, thy sons (2)
509	the opening year thy mercy shows (1)
510	providence hath brought us through another various year (2)
510	bring the grand sabbatic year, the jubilee of heaven (6)
512	the year with good he crownest ... earth his mercy fills (2)
525	for all the blessings of the year (T,1)

yearn

329	our restless spirits yearn for thee (4)

yearning

41	child of earth, yet full of yearning (2)
50	a yearning for a deeper peace not known before (4)
201	create in us a yearning for those whom thou dost seek (1)
274	Master speak ...thou knowest ..the yearning of my heart (3)
379	love him, who with love is yearning (3)
466	so the yearning strong, with which the soul will long (3)

yearns

213	search, prove my heart, it yearns for thee (1)

years

22	when rolling years shall cease to move (4)
28	our hope for years to come (1,6)
28	to endless years the same (3)
47	through all the circling years, we trust in thee (1)
47	God of the coming years ... we follow thee (3)
47	our heart's true home when all our years have sped (3)
54	in more ancient years (1)

105   shall life's swift passing years all fly (1)
190   Great Lord of years and days (2)
200   our strength is dust and ashes, our years a passing hour (3)
206   by whose hand through years long past our lives were led (1)
206   rests the unfolding of the years (3)
206   in thy strong hand eternally rests the ... years (3)
227   whether many or few, all my years are his due (6)
272   remember not past years (2)
296   unwasted by the lapse of years (1)
308   Church is praying yet, a thousand years the same (1)
357   that future years shall see, evermore and evermore (1)
381   hopes and fears of all the years are met in thee tonight (1)
390   when with the ever circling years shall come the time (3)
456   where light-years frame the Pleiadades (1)
486   who with love and meekness outlast the years of wrong (3)
543   O beautiful for patriot dream that sees beyond the years (4)

yes
88   one of his heralds, yes, I would sing loudest hosannas (3)
99   saints, apostles, prophets, martyrs answer, Yes (7)
208   yes, 'tis sweet to trust in Jesus (3)
233   yes, on through life's long path still chanting as ye go (4)
358   traveler, yes; it brings the day, promised day of Israel (1)

yesterday
139   today as yesterday the same (1)
139   faith like its finisher and Lord today as yesterday (1)

yet
12   beyond the range of sun and star, and yet beside us here (1)
41   child of earth, yet full of yearning (2)
41   yet thy love doth seek him still (2)
45   God is the ruler yet (3)
50   we have enough, yet not too much, to long for more (4)
64   yet to each loving heart how near (1)
66   Alleluia! Alleluia! widely yet his mercy flows (3)
67   but yet in love he sought me (3)
68   yet will I fear no ill for thou art with me (3)
77   praise yet the Lord again; Alleluia! Amen! (3)
80   so meek, so lowly, yet so high, so glorious in humility (3)
157   warm, sweet, tender, even yet a present help is he (3)
203   beheld thee fairer yet while serving thee (2)
203   a splendor greater yet while serving thee (4)
204   yet long these multitudes to see ... thy face (4)
210   God never yet forsook at need the soul that trusted him (3)
210   though undeserving; thou yet shalt find it true for thee (3)
218   if short, yet why should I be sad to soar to endless day (2)
230   green pastures are before me, which yet I have not seen (3)
231   yet God the same abiding, his praise shall tune my voice (4)
242   yet that scaffold sways the future (4)
263   yet in my dreams I'd be nearer, my God, to thee (2)
297   elect from every nation, yet one o'er all the earth (2)
297   yet she on earth hath union with God the Three in One (4)
308   but, Lord, thy Church is praying yet (1)
308   Church is praying yet, a thousand years the same (1)
318   yet to dwell with thee he deigneth (1)
324   King of kings, yet born of Mary (2)
326   yet, passing, points to the glad feast above (5)

328 many, and yet but one are we, one undivided bread (2)
332 these the virtues did convey, yet still remain the same (2)
336 and are we yet alive and see each other's face (T,1)
336 yet out of all the Lord hath brought us by his love (3)
358 higher yet that star ascends (2)
360 born thy people to deliver, born a child and yet a King (2)
366 nor eye hath seen, nor ear hath yet attained to hear (3)
366 nor ear hath yet attained to hear what there is ours (3)
376 yet what can I give him: give my heart (4)
377 yet none there were who looked without (2)
381 yet in thy dark streets shineth the everlasting light (1)
440 O what glory, far exceeding all... eye has yet perceived (2)
446 Alleluia yet again to the Spirit raising (5)
451 and yet whose faith hath constant been (4)
455 those wounds, yet visible above, in beauty glorified (4)
460 God yet speaketh by his Spirit (3)
460 one sure faith yet standing fast (3)
474 yet a season, and you know happy entrance will be given (3)
475 yet thou, her child, whose head is crowned with flame (1)
486 man in his weakness yet may give a worthier offering (1)
492 sun itself is but thy shade, yet cheers both earth & sky (1)
536 yet all are one in thee, for all are thine (4)
544 yet to eternity standeth thy Word (3)

yield
74 didst yield the glory that of right was thine (1)
105 I cannot stay; my heart I yield without delay (5)
111 yield to be saved from sin (3)
147 soon shall our doubts and fears all yield to thy control (3)
234 I yield my flickering torch to thee (2)
294 Zion ... be given the brightest glories earth can yield (5)
312 and yield them up to thee (3)
400 say, shall we yield him, in costly devotion (3)
511 God ... the source of bounteous yield (1)
522 fruit unto his praise to yield (2)
529 yield to me now, for I am weak (3)

yielded
154 while I am waiting, yielded and still (1)

yielding
179 yielding henceforth to our glorious King (2)

yoke
152 give me to bear thy easy yoke (3)
446 loosed from Pharaoh's bitter yoke (1)

yokes
32 he yokes the whirlwind to his car (4)

yon
358 traveler, o'er yon mountain's height see (1)
393 round yon virgin mother and child (1)

yonder
71 O that with yonder sacred throng we at his feet may fall (5)
379 hark! a voice from yonder manger, soft and sweet (2)
379 come, then, let us hasten yonder (3)

382   yonder shines the infant light (2)
402   following yonder star (1)

young
  169   Friend of the young, who lovest me (1)
  169   just as I am, young, strong and free (4)
  173   O young and fearless prophet of ancient Galilee (T,1)
  173   O young and fearless prophet, we need thy presence here (5)
  295   her young ones forth may bring (4)

youth
   70   when in the slippery paths of youth (3)
   86   shepherd of eager youth (T,1)
  171   who with the eyes of early youth eternal things did see (1)
  233   bright youth and snow-crowned age (2)
  233   from youth to age, by night and day (4)
  269   while passion stains, and folly dims our youth (2)
  479   forth in thy dear name we go to the child, the youth (4)
  479   to.. child .. youth .. aged love in living deeds to show (4)
  490   venerating age, humbly teaching youth (2)

zeal
  120   could my zeal no languor know (2)
  136   inspire our lips with flaming love and zeal to preach (2)
  143   my zeal inspire (2)
  249   a heavenly race demands thy zeal and an immortal crown (1)
  292   the world to Christ we bring, with loving zeal (1)
  337   wisdom and zeal and faith impart (3)
  533   his zeal inspired their breast (2)

Zion
   13   Zion, let me enter there (1)
   25   great God, attend, while Zion sings (T,1)
  200   as once he spake in Zion, so now he speaks again (1)
  293   Zion, city of our God (1,3)
  294   Zion ... be given the brightest glories earth can yield (5)
  299   O Zion, haste, thy mission high fulfilling (T,1)
  299   O Zion, haste to bring the brighter day (4)
  303   they stand, those halls of Zion, all jubilant with song (2)
  362   O Zion, that bringest good tidings, get thee up (2)
  366   Zion hears the watchmen singing (2)

Zion's
  298   Holy Zion's help forever and her confidence alone (1)
  300   lift your eyes ... sons of light Zion's city is in sight (4)
  335   let Zion's watchmen all awake (T,1)

WRITE-IN TABLE COMPARING METHODIST WITH OTHER HYMNALS

_____	1	_____	61	_____	121	_____	181	_____	241
_____	2	_____	62	_____	122	_____	182	_____	242
_____	3	_____	63	_____	123	_____	183	_____	243
_____	4	_____	64	_____	124	_____	184	_____	244
_____	5	_____	65	_____	125	_____	185	_____	245
_____	6	_____	66	_____	126	_____	186	_____	246
_____	7	_____	67	_____	127	_____	187	_____	247
_____	8	_____	68	_____	128	_____	188	_____	248
_____	9	_____	69	_____	129	_____	189	_____	249
_____	10	_____	70	_____	130	_____	190	_____	250
_____	11	_____	71	_____	131	_____	191	_____	251
_____	12	_____	72	_____	132	_____	192	_____	252
_____	13	_____	73	_____	133	_____	193	_____	253
_____	14	_____	74	_____	134	_____	194	_____	254
_____	15	_____	75	_____	135	_____	195	_____	255
_____	16	_____	76	_____	136	_____	196	_____	256
_____	17	_____	77	_____	137	_____	197	_____	257
_____	18	_____	78	_____	138	_____	198	_____	258
_____	19	_____	79	_____	139	_____	199	_____	259
_____	20	_____	80	_____	140	_____	200	_____	260
_____	21	_____	81	_____	141	_____	201	_____	261
_____	22	_____	82	_____	142	_____	202	_____	262
_____	23	_____	83	_____	143	_____	203	_____	263
_____	24	_____	84	_____	144	_____	204	_____	264
_____	25	_____	85	_____	145	_____	205	_____	265
_____	26	_____	86	_____	146	_____	206	_____	266
_____	27	_____	87	_____	147	_____	207	_____	267
_____	28	_____	88	_____	148	_____	208	_____	268
_____	29	_____	89	_____	149	_____	209	_____	269
_____	30	_____	90	_____	150	_____	210	_____	270
_____	31	_____	91	_____	151	_____	211	_____	271
_____	32	_____	92	_____	152	_____	212	_____	272
_____	33	_____	93	_____	153	_____	213	_____	273
_____	34	_____	94	_____	154	_____	214	_____	274
_____	35	_____	95	_____	155	_____	215	_____	275
_____	36	_____	96	_____	156	_____	216	_____	276
_____	37	_____	97	_____	157	_____	217	_____	277
_____	38	_____	98	_____	158	_____	218	_____	278
_____	39	_____	99	_____	159	_____	219	_____	279
_____	40	_____	100	_____	160	_____	220	_____	280
_____	41	_____	101	_____	161	_____	221	_____	281
_____	42	_____	102	_____	162	_____	222	_____	282
_____	43	_____	103	_____	163	_____	223	_____	283
_____	44	_____	104	_____	164	_____	224	_____	284
_____	45	_____	105	_____	165	_____	225	_____	285
_____	46	_____	106	_____	166	_____	226	_____	286
_____	47	_____	107	_____	167	_____	227	_____	287
_____	48	_____	108	_____	168	_____	228	_____	288
_____	49	_____	109	_____	169	_____	229	_____	289
_____	50	_____	110	_____	170	_____	230	_____	290
_____	51	_____	111	_____	171	_____	231	_____	291
_____	52	_____	112	_____	172	_____	232	_____	292
_____	53	_____	113	_____	173	_____	233	_____	293
_____	54	_____	114	_____	174	_____	234	_____	294
_____	55	_____	115	_____	175	_____	235	_____	295
_____	56	_____	116	_____	176	_____	236	_____	296
_____	57	_____	117	_____	177	_____	237	_____	297
_____	58	_____	118	_____	178	_____	238	_____	298
_____	59	_____	119	_____	179	_____	239	_____	299
_____	60	_____	120	_____	180	_____	240	_____	300

WRITE-IN TABLE COMPARING METHODIST WITH OTHER HYMNALS

_____ 301	_____ 361	_____ 421	_____ 481	_____ 541
_____ 302	_____ 362	_____ 422	_____ 482	_____ 542
_____ 303	_____ 363	_____ 423	_____ 483	_____ 543
_____ 304	_____ 364	_____ 424	_____ 484	_____ 544
_____ 305	_____ 365	_____ 425	_____ 485	_____ 545
_____ 306	_____ 366	_____ 426	_____ 486	_____ 546
_____ 307	_____ 367	_____ 427	_____ 487	_____ 547
_____ 308	_____ 368	_____ 428	_____ 488	_____ 548
_____ 309	_____ 369	_____ 429	_____ 489	_____ 549
_____ 310	_____ 370	_____ 430	_____ 490	_____ 550
_____ 311	_____ 371	_____ 431	_____ 491	_____ 551
_____ 312	_____ 372	_____ 432	_____ 492	_____ 552
_____ 313	_____ 373	_____ 433	_____ 493	
_____ 314	_____ 374	_____ 434	_____ 494	
_____ 315	_____ 375	_____ 435	_____ 495	
_____ 316	_____ 376	_____ 436	_____ 496	
_____ 317	_____ 377	_____ 437	_____ 497	
_____ 318	_____ 378	_____ 438	_____ 498	
_____ 319	_____ 379	_____ 439	_____ 499	
_____ 320	_____ 380	_____ 440	_____ 500	
_____ 321	_____ 381	_____ 441	_____ 501	
_____ 322	_____ 382	_____ 442	_____ 502	
_____ 323	_____ 383	_____ 443	_____ 503	
_____ 324	_____ 384	_____ 444	_____ 504	
_____ 325	_____ 385	_____ 445	_____ 505	
_____ 326	_____ 386	_____ 446	_____ 506	
_____ 327	_____ 387	_____ 447	_____ 507	
_____ 328	_____ 388	_____ 448	_____ 508	
_____ 329	_____ 389	_____ 449	_____ 509	
_____ 330	_____ 390	_____ 450	_____ 510	
_____ 331	_____ 391	_____ 451	_____ 511	
_____ 332	_____ 392	_____ 452	_____ 512	
_____ 333	_____ 393	_____ 453	_____ 513	
_____ 334	_____ 394	_____ 454	_____ 514	
_____ 335	_____ 395	_____ 455	_____ 515	
_____ 336	_____ 396	_____ 456	_____ 516	
_____ 337	_____ 397	_____ 457	_____ 517	
_____ 338	_____ 398	_____ 458	_____ 518	
_____ 339	_____ 399	_____ 459	_____ 519	
_____ 340	_____ 400	_____ 460	_____ 520	
_____ 341	_____ 401	_____ 461	_____ 521	
_____ 342	_____ 402	_____ 462	_____ 522	
_____ 343	_____ 403	_____ 463	_____ 523	
_____ 344	_____ 404	_____ 464	_____ 524	
_____ 345	_____ 405	_____ 465	_____ 525	
_____ 346	_____ 406	_____ 466	_____ 526	
_____ 347	_____ 407	_____ 467	_____ 527	
_____ 348	_____ 408	_____ 468	_____ 528	
_____ 349	_____ 409	_____ 469	_____ 529	
_____ 350	_____ 410	_____ 470	_____ 530	
_____ 351	_____ 411	_____ 471	_____ 531	
_____ 352	_____ 412	_____ 472	_____ 532	
_____ 353	_____ 413	_____ 473	_____ 533	
_____ 354	_____ 414	_____ 474	_____ 534	
_____ 355	_____ 415	_____ 475	_____ 535	
_____ 356	_____ 416	_____ 476	_____ 536	
_____ 357	_____ 417	_____ 477	_____ 537	
_____ 358	_____ 418	_____ 478	_____ 538	
_____ 359	_____ 419	_____ 479	_____ 539	
_____ 360	_____ 420	_____ 480	_____ 540	

3254